The Oxford History of Classical Reception in English Literat

GENERAL

DAVID H

AND

CHARLES MAR DALE

Patrick Cheney is Edwin Erle Sparks Professor of English and Comparative Literature at Pennsylvania State University. He has been a Visiting Research Fellow at Merton College, University of Oxford, and a recipient of the Faculty Scholar Medal at Pennsylvania State University for research in the humanities. He is General Editor of the *Oxford History of Poetry in English,* and a Visiting Fellow of All Souls College, Oxford. His publications have focused on the reception of classical ideas of authorship.

Philip Hardie is a Senior Research Fellow of Trinity College, Cambridge, and Honorary Professor of Latin at the University of Cambridge. He is a Fellow of the British Academy and was Corpus Christi Professor of the Latin Language and Literature at the University of Oxford (2002–6). He holds an honorary doctorate from the University of Thessaloniki, and was the recipient of the Premio Internazionale Virgilio (Mantova) in 2012. He has published extensively both on ancient Latin literature and on its reception.

The Oxford History of Classical Reception in English Literature

The Oxford History of Classical Reception (*OHCREL*) is designed to offer a comprehensive investigation of the numerous and diverse ways in which literary texts of the classical world stimulated responses and refashioning by English writers. Covering the full range of English literature from the early Middle Ages to the present day, *OHCREL* both synthesizes existing scholarship and presents cutting-edge new research, employing an international team of expert contributors for each of the five volumes.

1. 800–1558
2. 1558–1660
3. 1660–1790
4. 1780–1880
5. AFTER 1880

The Oxford History of Classical Reception in English Literature

Volume 2 (1558–1660)

EDITED BY

PATRICK CHENEY

AND

PHILIP HARDIE

OXFORD
UNIVERSITY PRESS

OXFORD
UNIVERSITY PRESS

Great Clarendon Street, Oxford, OX2 6DP,
United Kingdom

Oxford University Press is a department of the University of Oxford.
It furthers the University's objective of excellence in research, scholarship,
and education by publishing worldwide. Oxford is a registered trade mark of
Oxford University Press in the UK and in certain other countries

First published 2015
First published in paperback 2020

Published in the United States of America by Oxford University Press
198 Madison Avenue, New York, NY 10016, United States of America

British Library Cataloguing in Publication Data
Data available

Library of Congress Cataloging in Publication Data
Data available

ISBN 978–0–19–954755–5 (Hbk.)
ISBN 978–0–19–885916–1 (Pbk.)

Contents

List of Contributors ix
Preface xi

1. Introduction 1
PATRICK CHENEY AND PHILIP HARDIE

I. Institutions and Contexts

2. The Classics in Humanism, Education, and Scholarship 29
PETER MACK

3. The Availability of the Classics: Readers, Writers, Translation, Performance 57
STUART GILLESPIE

4. Classical Rhetoric in English 75
PETER MACK

5. The Classics in Literary Criticism 87
GAVIN ALEXANDER

6. Classicism and Christianity 103
MARK VESSEY

7. Women Writers and the Classics 129
JANE STEVENSON

8. Cultural Contexts 147
a. Politics and Nationalism 147
CURTIS PERRY

b. Sexuality and Desire 159
CORA FOX

c. Literary Careers 172
PATRICK CHENEY

d. Fame and Immortality 187
PHILIP HARDIE

II. Genre

9. Pastoral and Georgic — 201
HELEN COOPER

10. Epic Poetry — 225
PHILIP HARDIE

11. Elizabethan Minor Epic — 253
LYNN ENTERLINE

12. The Epistolary Tradition — 273
WILLIAM FITZGERALD

13. Prose Romance — 291
HELEN MOORE

14. Elegy, Hymn, Epithalamium, Ode: Some Renaissance Reinterpretations — 311
ROLAND GREENE

15. Complaint, Epigram, and Satire — 345
SUSANNA BRAUND

16. Tragedy — 373
GORDON BRADEN

17. Comedy — 395
BRUCE R. SMITH

18. Tragicomedy — 419
TANYA POLLARD

19. Historiography and Biography — 433
BART VAN ES

20. Discursive and Speculative Writing — 461
REID BARBOUR AND CLAIRE PRESTON

III. Authors

21. Homer — 487
JESSICA WOLFE

22. Plato — 503
ELIZABETH JANE BELLAMY

23. Virgil and Ovid — 517
MAGGIE KILGOUR

24. Horace — 539
VICTORIA MOUL (with a contribution by Charles Martindale)

25. Spenser — 557
RICHARD A. MCCABE

26. Marlowe — 579
CHARLES MARTINDALE

27. Shakespeare — 599
COLIN BURROW

28. Jonson — 621
SEAN KEILEN

29. Early Milton — 641
THOMAS H. LUXON

Classical Reception in English Literature, 1558–1660: An Annotated Bibliography — 657
CRAIG KALLENDORF

Index — 743

List of Contributors

Gavin Alexander
University of Cambridge

Reid Barbour
University of North Carolina

Elizabeth Jane Bellamy
University of New Hampshire

Gordon Braden
University of Virginia

Susanna Braund
University of British Columbia

Colin Burrow
All Souls College, Oxford

Patrick Cheney
Penn State University

Helen Cooper
Magdalene College, Cambridge

Lynn Enterline
Vanderbilt University

William Fitzgerald
King's College London

Cora Fox
Arizona State University

Stuart Gillespie
Glasgow University

Roland Greene
Stanford University

Philip Hardie
Trinity College, Cambridge

Craig Kallendorf
Texas A&M University

Sean Keilen
University of California at Santa Cruz

Maggie Kilgour
McGill University

Thomas H. Luxon
Dartmouth College

Richard A. McCabe
Merton College, Oxford

Peter Mack
University of Warwick

Charles Martindale
University of York

Helen Moore
Corpus Christi College, Oxford

Victoria Moul
University College London

Curtis Perry
University of Illinois at Urbana-Champaign

Tanya Pollard
Brooklyn College

Claire Preston
Queen Mary University of London

Bruce R. Smith
University of Southern California

Jane Stevenson
Campion Hall, Oxford

Bart van Es
St Catherine's College, Oxford

Mark Vessey
University of British Columbia

Jessica Wolfe
University of North Carolina

Preface

The present volume is one of five that will make up *The Oxford History of Classical Reception in English Literature* (henceforth *OHCREL*). Each volume of *OHCREL* has its own editor or team of editors, who determine, within agreed overall guidelines, the appropriate shape and emphasis for the particular period covered by their volume. *OHCREL* charts English writers' engagement and dialogue with ancient Greek and Roman literature from the early Middle Ages to the present day. *OHCREL* is, we hope, sufficiently comprehensive in scope to be legitimately described as a *History*, rather than a series of discrete critical essays. It should thus prove a valuable reference resource for students in the field. But *OHCREL* is intended to be attractive and accessible to a wide range of readers, so discursive interest is given priority over encyclopedic inclusiveness. Some potentially important aspects of the subject will thus receive only brief and passing discussion. *OHCREL*'s main target audience is the serious student of classical and English literature, from (roughly) second-year undergraduate level upwards, but it is hoped that its methods and approach will be such as to appeal to a wide range of readers from a variety of disciplines and backgrounds, within and outside the university.

The title of *OHCREL* includes three potentially contentious terms that need immediate clarification: 'Literature', 'English', and 'Reception'. The main business of *OHCREL* is the close and sophisticated critical engagement with the complex interaction between classical and English literary texts from the early Middle Ages to the present. A comprehensive, totalizing, history of the impact of classical upon English culture would have to be undertaken on a scale far larger than that of *OHCREL*, and would, in any case, run the risk of lacking all coherent focus, purpose, and integrity. The editors of and contributors to *OHCREL* believe, moreover, that legitimate (albeit sometimes 'fuzzy' and always debatable) distinctions can be made—and are, in practice, regularly made—between 'literary history' and cultural history more generally, without that involving any inert acceptance of an unscrutinized literary 'canon', or merely conventional assumptions about what constitutes 'the literary'. Our main emphasis will fall on literary texts of high quality and maximum historical importance. We are aware that neither of these categories is a fixed and agreed entity. But we do not believe that either can be occluded, ignored, or simply subsumed within other intellectual categories. *OHCREL* positively encourages and incorporates debate about questions of 'literary quality' and 'historical importance', rather than assume them as reified 'givens'.

OHCREL conceives of 'reception' as a complex dialogic exchange between two bodies of writing, rather than a one-way 'transmission' of fixed and known entities. Attention is certainly given to matters traditionally encompassed under such terms as 'influence', 'echo', and 'allusion', but *OHCREL* also explores the ways in which classical texts have been remade and refashioned by English writers in ways that might cast (now, as well as then) as much light on the originals as on their English 'derivatives'. *OHCREL* certainly does not assume that 'reception' simply charts the afterlife of a fixed and closed canon. Nor does it assume that past readings of classical texts can always be confidently dismissed from the vantage point (whether critical or ideological) of the present. *OHCREL* conceives of reception as a dynamic activity in which meaning is constantly generated and regenerated, rather than simply received. Contributors have been encouraged to think actively about the issues and processes involved in the activity of reception, rather than to take over any existing model inertly.

The title of *OHCREL* is, we think, neater and more memorable than more strictly accurate, but clumsier, alternatives (for example, *The Oxford History of Classical Reception in Literatures in English*). But substantial coverage will, of course, be given in the last two volumes to non-English literature in the English language, including American, Irish, and Caribbean material. The first volume will encompass writing in English from before the Norman Conquest. Literature in Gaelic, Irish, or Scots, however, does not come within its main remit. Nor, in the project more generally, does neo-Latin literature. Nor do (in later volumes) such non-literary cultural productions as comic books or films. Nor do translations of non-classical foreign works *into* English, such as *Quo Vadis*? Nor (for the reasons given above) do such phenomena as the incorporation of classical architecture in English landscape gardens, the broader influence of Roman republicanism on English political thought, or the collection of classical antiquities on the Grand Tour. We stress, however, 'within its main remit'. Such matters are, of course, discussed by contributors *en passant*, if they bear on the main subject of their chapter. The same applies to theatrical performances. No hard-and-fast distinction, of course, can be made between drama-on-the-page and drama-in-performance. Nevertheless, *OHCREL* will be specifically *literary* in its focus, and viable (albeit 'fuzzy') distinctions can, we think, be made between accounts that stress the textual, rather than performance, elements in plays. Attention is certainly given to the circumstances in which classical literature was read (commentaries, textbooks, *florilegia*, mythographies, and so on), but, again, these do not form the main focus of *OHCREL*.

A detailed rationale for the organization of the present volume is laid out in the first part of the 'Introduction' (Chapter 1), which then goes on to offer reflections on two areas of central importance for classical reception in the English Renaissance: ideas of authorship, and imitation and intertextuality.

Each chapter is accompanied by endnotes that document and reference the discussion within the chapter itself. The Bibliography is intended to provide guidance on further reading on the subject as a whole: as well as collecting many of the items referred to by particular contributors to the volume itself, it provides pointers towards discussions of matters touched on only briefly, or not at all, in the volume.

Since the envisaged audience of *OHCREL* includes readers from a variety of disciplines (including those unused to the presentational conventions adopted in earlier English texts), a policy rather different from the norm has been adopted with regard to quotations. All quotations in the volume, with the exception of those from Edmund Spenser, have been presented in modernized spelling and punctuation, though references have been supplied (for the reader's convenience) to the standard library editions, most of which are in 'old spelling' form. The modernization of titles has been left to the discretion of individual contributors.

Quotations from classical authors generally use the Loeb texts and translations, sometimes modified in detail. For readers' convenience, all Greek words quoted in the text are transliterated. The editions of English authors used are cited in the endnotes on their first occurrence in each chapter, with the exception of the most frequently quoted authors, for which the following editions are used:

Jonson, *Works*: *The Works of Ben Jonson*, ed. C. H. Herford and Percy and Evelyn Simpson, 11 vols (Oxford, 1963–7)[1]

Milton, *Poems*: *The Poems of John Milton*, ed. John Carey and Alastair Fowler (Harlow, 1968)

Milton, *Prose Works*: *Complete Prose Works of John Milton*, ed. Don M. Wolfe, 8 vols (New Haven, 1953–82)

Shakespeare: *The Riverside Shakespeare*, ed. G. Blakemore Evans, 2nd edn (Boston, 1997)

Spenser, *Faerie Queene*: *Spenser. The Faerie Queene*, ed. A. C. Hamilton (London and New York, 1977)

Spenser, *Shorter Poems*: *Edmund Spenser. The Shorter Poems*, ed. Richard A. McCabe (Harmondsworth, 1999)

London is the place of publication where no place of publication is given in the bibliographical details.

At Penn State, we would like to thank Katharine Cleland early on, and more recently Paul Zajac, for serving as loyal research assistants on the volume. They performed stellar work on a long and complex project, and we are grateful for the help they gave us. We would also like to thank Robin Schulze, former Head of the English Department at Penn State, and Mark Morrisson, the current Head, as well as Susan Welch, Dean of the College of Liberal Arts, for assistance along the way. Finally, we would like to thank the contributors for their excellent work on behalf of *OHCREL*, Volume 2.

[1] Those chapters that deal substantially with Ben Jonson were submitted in their final form before the appearance of the 2012 Cambridge edition of the *Works*, and it has unfortunately not been practical to convert references to this edition.

In June 2008 a conference was held in Cambridge, gathering the greater part of the contributors for a workshop as the volume began to take shape; we are grateful to the Cambridge University Centre for Research in the Arts, Social Sciences and Humanities for hosting the occasion and for financial support; and, for further financial support, to the British Academy, the Classics Faculty, University of Cambridge, and the Sackler Conference Fund, Trinity College, Cambridge.

CHAPTER 1

Introduction

PATRICK CHENEY AND PHILIP HARDIE

Volume 2 of *The Oxford History of Classical Reception in English Literature* (*OHCREL*) focuses on the dates 1558–1660, because this time span helps define the English 'Renaissance' as literary history's inaugural 'rebirth' of classicism. The dates mark a historical period that begins with the coronation of Queen Elizabeth I in 1558 and ends with the return of Charles II as king of England in 1660. The link between political and literary history is more than a convenience, however, because of the remarkable surge of literary authors who, at this time, *recover the classics* largely within the crucible of monarchical court politics.

Nonetheless, the dates 1558–1660 are in large part arbitrary, and indeed literary historians often give different dates for the Renaissance. The most common dates run from 1485, the coronation of Henry VII uniting the Houses of York and Lancaster after the War of the Roses had devastated England for a hundred years, and 1674, the publication of Milton's final version of *Paradise Lost*, an epic poem modelled on Homer and Virgil that, for many, crowns the English Renaissance. Scholars often prefer these dates because they provide a more accurate historical context for gauging how a major author like Milton produced his epic art—aided, of course, by those who preceded him, from Skelton, Wyatt, and Surrey early in the sixteenth century, to Spenser, Sidney, and Shakespeare in the Elizabethan era, to Donne, Jonson, and Marvell in the Jacobean, Caroline, and Interregnum eras. The editorial decision to include the first half of the sixteenth century in volume 1 of *OHCREL* mirrors a recent professional movement aiming to bridge the 'medieval' and 'Renaissance' periods, allowing the medieval to gain a greater inroad into the 'modern'—a topic to which we will return. The decision itself is not without consequences, because it bifurcates the sixteenth century, when in fact authors such as Spenser and Sidney self-consciously present themselves as carrying on the work of Skelton and Surrey, to cite just a few examples. Necessarily, chapters in the present volume will occasionally discuss material appropriate to volume 1, just as they will occasionally venture into 'the long eighteenth century' covered in volume 3.

We have divided the volume into three major parts. The first part, 'Institutions and Contexts', consists of this introduction and ten chapters, and aims to lay the historical foundation. The second part, 'Genre', consists of twelve chapters, and addresses the central literary forms, emphasizing how English authors rework classical forms. Genre, this part of the volume aims to makes clear, is a major framework for the recovery of classicism by English authors. The third part, 'Authors', consists of nine chapters, four on classical authors whose presence was central for the period, and five on English authors who are especially important to a critical narrative of classical reception.

In keeping with the General Editors' design, our history is a 'literary history', but we interpret the link between the two concepts differently from many literary historians. Where most see their task as that of unearthing the social, political, and economic networks from which literary texts emerge, we reverse the procedure. For we take the word 'literary' to heart, and aim to historicize it; the effect is to unearth a bedrock process of literariness grounded historically in authorship, genre, and imitation. We view the historical figures we bring front and centre—Homer, Plato, Virgil, Ovid, Horace; Spenser, Marlowe, Shakespeare, Jonson, Milton—as *authors*. We see them writing in *genres*—for example, epic, prose dialogue, georgic, elegy, ode, hymn, minor epic, tragedy, comedy, pastoral. And we focus on how authors use genre as the framework within which to *imitate* the classics. For us, imitation includes a host of interconnections between antiquity and the Renaissance. For instance, English authors imitate classical authors' literary careers (the way Spenser does Virgil and Ovid); they also imitate genre-based *ideas*, since each genre tends to have an organizing idea at its centre, which authors can then vary endlessly (for instance, after Virgil, epic focuses on the idea of nationalism); and finally—perhaps most profoundly—English authors imitate classical *language* (key words, phrases, passages). The imitation of Greek and especially Latin into English becomes a hallmark of the era.

We share the General Editors' commitment to the methodology of 'reception' as a 'dialogue' between 'past and present', a 'two-way process of understanding, backwards and forwards, which illuminates antiquity as much as modernity': 'Milton's reception of Virgil is thus potentially of as much significance for Virgilians as for Miltonists, as much a part of Classics as it is of English literature.'[1] Nonetheless, whereas this reception model 'switch[es] the focus from producers to receivers',[2] we have designed our volume in terms of the producers. Instead of 'readers', we highlight 'authors' (who of course are themselves readers). We do so because the particular moment in which our volume appears invites us to participate in a specific professional conversation. As the General Editors point out, a turn to reception has characterized literary studies since the 1980s, and was especially prominent toward the end of the twentieth century. In contrast, 'authorship studies' is currently one of the most vibrant areas of research and debate.

In particular, a backlash has set in against the 1960s work of Roland Barthes on 'the death of the author' and Michel Foucault on 'the author function'.[3] These mid-twentieth-century theories powerfully contested the model of writing that prevailed at the time: an author-based model that privileges the autonomy of the creator of literary works, at the expense of both the 'intertextual' nature of all language and the cultural institutions and practices that produce those works. For Barthes, writing is intertextual, in that by its very nature it consists of tissues of other bits of writing.

Barthes was working from Julia Kristeva's text-based model of 'intertextuality', which denies authority to the creator of a work and instead inspects the network of texts that make it up.[4] As a methodology, intertextuality helps advance 'the death of the author', because it no longer tries to gauge the author's 'intention'; and any utterance encodes countless, anonymous tissues of other discourse. In making intertextuality the death knell of the Western author, Barthes inaugurated the most potent—and infamous—methodology of the late twentieth century, and it remains alive well into the early twenty-first.

Barthes's work aligned with that of Foucault on the 'author function', which similarly denies authority to an author, and instead locates production in the pressures of institutions and thus 'power'. Foucault's project had a tremendous influence on Renaissance studies, shifting interest from the meaning of the author to the subject of power. The individual was imagined as subjected to cultural pressures in the production of language. In none of this, we hasten to add, is there much interest in classicism. In fact, we might say, imitation was usurped by ideology; classicism, by constructionism.

Following on from Foucault, Barthes, Kristeva, and others, it became fashionable in Renaissance studies during the 1980s and 1990s to engage in 'New Historicism' (in America) and 'Cultural Materialism' (in Britain): to do research on institutions, not authors; on social and political power rather than individual creativity. Yet out of this crucible, paradoxically, authorship studies emerged, as an intoxicating new principle supplanted 'individuation': 'collaboration'.[5] Critics began to emphasize the way an author became implicated in a whole range of cultural agents in the production of texts: from scribes, publishers, printers, and compositors to businessmen, monarchs, and powerful courtiers. The fallout is still with us.[6]

Starting in the 1990s, however, several leading Renaissance critics began to resist the extreme, authoritarian pull especially of Foucault. The most important statement comes from Louis Montrose:

> Foucault's own anti-humanist project is to anatomize the subject's subjection to the disciplinary discourses of power. I find this aspect of Foucault's vision—his apparent occlusion of a space for human agency—to be extreme. In other words, my intellectual response is that his argument is unconvincing, and my visceral response is that it is intolerable.[7]

Richard Helgerson put this methodology succinctly: Shakespeare 'helped make the world that made him'.[8] While critics such as Helgerson and Montrose were trying to walk a fine line between individuation and collaboration, between the death of the author and the author working in 'reciprocal' relation with collaborators, in practice they tended to emphasize the 'history' in 'literary history'.[9] At the same time, other leading critics remained committed to the revisionist revolution. David Scott Kastan, for instance, has continued to adhere to a Barthesian- and Foucaldian-based methodology, primarily in his work on Shakespeare: 'Shakespeare had no obvious interest in the printed book. Performance was the only form of publication he sought for his plays.'[10]

Today, Shakespeare is the lightning rod for authorship studies, because of his standing as a world-class figure. In a 2003 book titled *Shakespeare as Literary Dramatist*, Lukas Erne challenged the idea that Shakespeare eschewed a literary authorship, arguing that he wrote his plays not merely for the stage but also for the page: 'The assumption of Shakespeare's indifference to the publication of his plays is a myth.'[11] The argument has proved controversial, and Kastan, for one, has not been persuaded; nor is he alone. As the current volume goes to press, a healthy debate continues over what has become known as 'The Return of the Author', with Erne's sequel, *Shakespeare and the Book Trade*, just recently published.[12] Most recent work on 'The Return of the Author' neglects English Renaissance classicism.

Curiously, while critics were denying the status of author to Shakespeare, others were publishing books, articles, and editions that established Shakespeare's reworking not simply of Plutarch but of Virgil and Ovid, Lucan and Homer (via Chapman's translations). For instance, around the time that Kastan was writing *Shakespeare and the Book*, arguing that only after the First Folio of 1623 did Shakespeare become an 'author', Heather James published *Shakespeare's Troy*, arguing that plays like *Troilus and Cressida* show an author fully engaged with classicism, especially Virgil and Ovid.[13] The two conversations have been carried out largely independently of each other; they pass in the night.

Shakespeare may seem a special case, but similar arguments denying the status of author to Marlowe have multiplied, as critics came to speak of a 'Marlowe effect': 'Marlowe' is an 'effect' because the texts of his that have come down to us stand at several removes from his creation, which is now irreparably lost.[14] For instance, after Marlowe died in 1593, *Doctor Faustus* would not be published until 1604, in what has come to be known as the A-text, while in 1616 a radically different text appeared, known as the B-text. Not only do we have two texts; we also have two authors, for scholars have determined that Marlowe wrote only some of the extant scenes. We have not even been able to determine whether Marlowe wrote the play early in his career (1588–9) or late (1592–3). Such *doubleness* has made it seem wise to deny the status of author to Christopher Marlowe: if anyone was 'socially constructed', it was the author(s) of *Doctor Faustus* (see Charles Martindale, Chapter 26, this volume).

While critics tend to declassify Marlowe and Shakespeare as authors, they agree that the modern notion of the author—the notion we hold today—begins to appear first in Spenser, and next in Jonson.[15] Critics such as Helgerson and Montrose have persuasively shaped Spenser studies, in particular, by studying his authorship within the context of monarchy, concentrating on his innovative 'self-presentation' and his 'reciprocal' model of authorship relating his work to Queen Elizabeth: Spenser uses the nascent medium of print to present himself as an author to and of the nation; and in turn the author is shaped by the national leader he addresses. 'The subject of Elizabeth' and the 'Spenserian subject' are bound up in each other.[16] By concentrating on the historical moment in which Spenserian authorship emerges—what Helgerson terms a 'synchronic' interest—such leading voices have shown correspondingly little interest in 'diachrony', in which authorship grows out of classical authors.

Volume 2 of *OHCREL* aims to suggest just how vital classical literary culture is to the invention of the English Renaissance, to English Renaissance studies, and thus to English Renaissance authorship. We would argue for a close symbiosis between the renowned literary achievement between 1558 and 1660 and the authorial project of imitating the classics. The English Renaissance can be closely associated with the recovery of antiquity in poetry, drama, and prose. We do not mean that other important agents were not on the scene; they were, including the influence of Christianity and Scripture (see Mark Vessey, Chapter 6, this volume). Yet the works that Spenser and his contemporaries produced in pastoral, epic, ode, epithalamium, hymn, comedy, tragedy, satire, epigram, complaint, and other genres were classical in origin, in frame, and in ideation. Spenser did not write *The Shepheardes Calender* because he wished to imitate the pastoralism of Scripture; he made the choice to publish his first work in the genre in imitation of Virgil, who inaugurated his career with the *Eclogues*. Spenser could do so because his 'syncretic' mindset reconciled Virgilian pastoral with the pastoral of Scripture, the Roman Tityrus with the Hebraic David. Much literary history of the time underwrote the reconciliation, including such books in the native (English) tradition as *The Kalender of Shepherds*, as well as the long tradition of pastoral itself, from the Greek Alexandrian inventor of the form, Theocritus, to the first Elizabethan to publish a set of eclogues, Barnabe Googe (1563). The list of 'influences' on Spenser includes those who wrote eclogues before him—the *Calender*'s glossator, 'E.K.', mentions Theocritus, Virgil, Moschus, Petrarch, Boccaccio, Sannazaro, and Marot, while we could add the Greek Bion and the Henrician Alexander Barclay—and those such as Ovid, Horace, and Chaucer, who did not write eclogues, but whom Spenser nonetheless assimilates to the form (see Helen Cooper, Chapter 9, this volume). However complex the context is for Spenser's writing of pastoral, the key point is that his decision originated in a classical author, and his name was Virgil.[17]

We believe that a volume on 'classical reception' in English 'Renaissance' literature can profitably participate in current authorship studies.[18] In the remaining two sections of this introduction, we will first situate our connection between *renaissance* and *authorship* in terms of the professional conversation on the 'period concept', from Jacob Burckhardt to Leonard Barkan; and, second, we will look further into the relation between imitation and intertextuality. In both sections, we try to rethink 'classical reception' by charting *the author of the renaissance* in terms of *the renaissance of the author*. In this project, English Renaissance authorship is neither strictly individuated nor collaborative but *intertextual*.

Indeed, in Renaissance studies today authors are very much alive; they have intentions; they present themselves; but in no way does this mean that we should limit interpretation to authorial agency. In fact, it is important to register the working of other agents. One of the most important, in the General Editors' reception model, is the classical author himself. Reception and authorship are not antithetical, but part of a larger hermeneutic linking 'past' with 'present'—and both with the 'future'—along a 'two-way' path that connects antiquity to modernity, modernity to antiquity. Readers are critical to this process; they conduct the research.[19]

We argue, then, that it is useful to define the English Renaissance in terms of classical authorship because the seminal literary achievement of this period was to invent an originary English authorship out of an engagement with the classical idea of the author (partly mediated, of course, by such medieval authors as Chaucer, Gower, and Lydgate, the native triumvirate to whom sixteenth-century writers so often pay tribute). According to this idea, a writer imitates literary forms written by preceding authors, and he or she puts together a structure of genres to invent a literary career, one that writes the nation along lines that are at once gendered and religious.

Renaissance Authorship

In imitating the classics, Renaissance authors participate in a cultural movement known as 'humanism', an educational programme begun in fourteenth- and fifteenth-century Italy that aimed to train boys in classical Latin and, to some extent, in Greek.[20] This movement relied in part on works lost since antiquity that the humanists painstakingly unearthed, then disseminated, translated, and integrated into the vernacular (see Peter Mack, Chapter 2, this volume). Petrarch is usually identified as the founding father of the European Renaissance for his leadership role in this project.[21] Petrarch self-consciously severed his own authorship from that of the 'medieval' past in order to mark himself as distinctly 'modern', his work 'novel'. Petrarch does not use the Italian or Latin word for *renaissance* (French 'rebirth'), but he understood himself to be engaged in a wide-scale attempt to give new life to antiquity.

Yet the term 'Renaissance' applied to this enterprise needed to wait until the mid-nineteenth century, when the French historian Jules Michelet used the term in his *History of France* (1855), followed more influentially by the Swiss historian Jacob Burckhardt in his landmark study *The Civilization of the Renaissance in Italy* (1860). For the next hundred years, and up to the close of the twentieth century, when Barkan published *Unearthing the Past: Archaeology and Aesthetics in the Making of Renaissance Culture* (1999), scholars attempted to define the 'Renaissance', to mark it off as a distinct epoch, separate from the Middle Ages and connected to modernity.[22]

Strikingly, however, many influential voices in this conversation today look away from antiquity when trying to locate the point of origin for the period concept. This helps account for much mainstream criticism since 1980—the publication date of Stephen Greenblatt's inaugural work of New Historicism, *Renaissance Self-Fashioning*.[23] In this climate, we might wish to account for a volume that defines the Renaissance in terms of classicism. One consequence, we believe, can be a fresh awareness of an intellectual project that reconciles imitation with ideology, authorship with politics, classicism with constructionism.

Nonetheless, a recent authoritative study of the period concept has a different goal—namely, to look into the history of scholarship behind the word 'Renaissance' that valorizes the 'modern' at the expense of the 'medieval'. In 2007, Margreta de Grazia published her latest instalment on periodization, 'The Modern Divide: From Either Side', which aims not to solve the problem it pinpoints, but, more modestly, 'to point it out': today we accept the nineteenth-century narrative of the Renaissance as originating in Europe roughly between 1400 and 1600 (the dates vary depending on the historian), but then we rely on the twentieth-century rejection of such 'teleology' by Foucault and others, for whom 'the progression of continuous history has been judged too partial to the dominant power'.[24] The effect, says de Grazia, is to create a 'divide' between 'medieval' and 'modern'.[25]

The nineteenth-century narratives de Grazia discusses are three in particular, and all are important here, not simply because they have been so influential but also because they tend to eschew classicism. First, Georg Wilhelm Friedrich Hegel located the break with the medieval and the advent of the modern in Martin Luther, the German monk who launched the Reformation in 1517 by nailing his *Ninety-Five Theses* to the cathedral door in Wittenberg. Luther rejects the 'medieval material fixation' on pilgrimage to the Holy Land as the mark of Christian salvation, and turns the eye of the faithful 'inward in what Hegel termed "that meditative introversion of the soul upon itself"', known as '*solafideism*, "the simple doctrine" that faith was all that mattered'.[26] Second, Burckhardt responded to Hegel by locating the birth of the modern not in Germany but in Italy, not in '1500' but in '1300', and not in Luther's 'strict inner conscience' but rather in 'raw unbridled will': that is to say, not in 'ideation' but in 'cultural and political event'.[27] Whereas Hegel saw the modern as a 'rebirth', Burckhardt saw it as 'a birth': '"the birth of man"—of man as individual as opposed to man as subject to the "general categories" of the Middle Ages (of race, people, party, family, or community)', issuing 'not from the retrieval of antiquity but rather from the lapsed civic and religious strictures of the independent city-states'.[28] Third, Karl Marx subordinated individuals to account for the birth of the modern through the 'prehistory of capitalist economic production', begun in 'the long sixteenth century', which forms 'the prelude of the revolution that laid the foundation of the capitalist mode of production'.[29]

Here is de Grazia's helpful summary:

> All three nineteenth-century historiographies—Hegel's theodicy, Burckhardt's cultural history, and Marx's economic prehistory—conferred upon the Renaissance the status of inaugural epoch of the modern. And all three lighted upon it in order to set the modern into motion in a particular direction: Hegel's Reformation leading to the emancipation of consciousness, Burckhardt's Renaissance reactivating the individual's dynamic creative energies, Marx's primitive accumulation culminating in equitable distribution of labor and resources. And all three had their trajectories push off against a lackluster past of Catholicism, medievalism, and feudalism, respectively.[30]

De Grazia's history helps account for why the present volume might come into being, allowing us to speak of the Renaissance as the intertextual network of authors who write within culture, in a model that links the past to the present and to the future, aware of achievement and limitation alike.

Here the General Editors make an invaluable point. 'The Renaissance was a myth': 'not in the sense that it was untrue, but in the sense that it was a story of resonance and power'.[31] Rather than saying only that 'the Renaissance was constructed', we can say that Renaissance authors participated in the construction. The binary is neither true nor necessary.

An example occurs in book 1, canto 6, of *The Faerie Queene*, where the arch-Protestant poet of Elizabethan England constructs a British Reformation myth of the Renaissance that readers are left to reconstruct. While narrating the quest of the Redcrosse Knight, Spenser turns to the fortunes of the beloved whom the hero of 'holiness' has abandoned, Una (a figure for the truth of the English Protestant Church). For the young knight believes that his lady is unchaste, since he thinks he sees her coupling with a lustful squire, when in fact he is the victim of a magically induced vision created by the hermit Archimago (a figure for the demonic magic of the Catholic priest). As the villain Sansloy ('without law') attempts to rape Una, suddenly some woodland satyrs arrive; they are so horrible in sight that they scare the paynim to flee. These satyrs then take Una home and worship her as the truth, until she can escape their idolatry through help from their human kinsman, Sir Satyrane.

Spenser's allegory is complex, but the satyrs' religious worship, led by 'old Sylvanus' (*Faerie Queene*, 1. 6. 16. 3), and conducted through rituals of dance, song, and musical instruments, deploys a classical myth (the satyr community) to critique early 'Roman' forms of idolatrous worship *as they get into the literary tradition*. One form is singled out, as the satyrs 'daunc[e]... round' Una:

> Shouting, and singing all a shepheards ryme,
> And with greene braunches strowing all the ground,
> Do worship her, as Queene, with olive girlond cround.
> (1. 6. 13. 7–9)

Thus, Spenser offsets his own English Virgilian epic (1. Proem. 1), serving the true religion from the false religions of classical and late-sixteenth-century Rome, localized in lowly pastoral. His Reformation allegory is a myth of the Renaissance, not simply because it deploys a classical topos, but more particularly because it presents that *topos* as itself a cultural agent, which the reader is to reconstruct through various signs planted in Faeryland (*Faerie Queene*, 6. Proem). In this way, Spenser's story of Una among the satyrs qualifies as a Protestant myth about classical Renaissance authorship.[32]

Spenser's story linking classicism to Christianity exemplifies one of the main critical models of periodization to emerge from the twentieth century: that of Douglas Bush, who saw the era as reconciling classical culture with Scripture: 'If the classical revival produced rich fruit and not mere wax flowers, one main reason was the strength of medieval and Christian traditions and beliefs.'[33] Bush did not invent the idea of this reconciliation, for Renaissance writers were themselves self-conscious about the attempt. In the fifteenth century, the scholar Marsilio Ficino made it his project to fuse Platonism with Christianity, known as Christian Neoplatonism. In Elizabethan England, Spenser is hard at the game of reconciliation, as many studies make clear (see Elizabeth Bellamy, Chapter 22, this volume). In the mid-seventeenth century, Milton is still pursuing his own reconciliation, between classical and Christian pastoral, as the title of *Lycidas* records (see Thomas Luxon, Chapter 29, this volume).[34]

Bush's Renaissance has played a role in the only recent book-length study of the period concept as a professional discourse, *The Idea of the Renaissance*, by William Kerrigan and Gordon Braden.[35] In their history, Bush opposes Burckhardt, who had secularized the Renaissance, set it in the fourteenth and fifteenth centuries, and confined it to Italy. Bush plants the concept north in England, and sees it flourishing in the sixteenth and seventeenth centuries. In contrast, Kerrigan and Braden aim to recuperate 'Burckhardt's Renaissance', because his narrative about the modern as the change from group identity to individual identity gets it right—gets it right, that is, for the late 1980s, when the 'subject' was all the rage.[36]

The attempt to identify 'subjectivity' as the heart of the Renaissance advances the Barthesian 'death of the author' and the Foucaldian 'author function', since subjectivity views the individual as constructed by history. Indeed, this is Greenblatt's model in *Renaissance Self-Fashioning*: Renaissance selves are fashioned by institutions of power. We can see a version of this model in Joel Fineman's *Shakespeare's Perjured Eye: The Modern Invention of Subjectivity*, under attack in Harold Bloom's *Shakespeare: The Invention of the Human*, which replaces subjectivity with an author-based Hegelian 'consciousness'.[37] In this group, only Fineman displays much interest in classicism. While Greenblatt rejects 'influence' as a critical methodology, Bloom writes his seminal work, *The Anxiety of Influence*, to centre literary relations in the English Romantic era, studying how Wordsworth, Coleridge, and others struggled in the dark shadow of Milton, Shakespeare, and Spenser.[38]

Yet one mid-twentieth-century model joins Bush in including classicism as part of its period concept. In *Renaissance and Renascences in Western Art*, Erwin Panofsky introduced an influential swerve. In de Grazia's words, 'it was not the return to antiquity that distinguished the period 1400–1600', since several previous eras had made that return ('the Carolingian renaissance in the ninth century, the Ottonian and Anglo-Saxon *renovatii* [*sic*] of around 1000, and the proto-Renaissance of the twelfth century'). Rather, the Renaissance could be born only once 'it had first died': 'At a certain point around 1400, antiquity was pronounced dead.'[39] As Panofsky himself put it: 'The Renaissance came to realize that Pan was dead... The classical past was looked upon, for the first time, as a totality cut off from the present': 'The Middle Ages had left antiquity unburied and alternately galvanized and exorcised its corpse. The Renaissance stood weeping at its grave and tried to resurrect its soul.'[40]

Recently, Barkan has resurrected this model but given it his own swerve, the late-fifteenth- and early sixteenth-century moment, when suddenly great artworks from the classical past were unearthed, such as the discovery in 1485 of a young girl's body perfectly preserved after fifteen hundred years of burial, or the discovery in 1506 of antiquity's great statue the *Laocoön*: 'Rome contained a whole population in marble... the authentic life of antiquity is emerging from the ground, demanding that the moderns hear its voice and respond with a voice of their own.'[41] In short, a history of criticism and scholarship of the Renaissance exhibits a series of fits and starts, continuities and discontinuities, offshoots and objections. The time appears ripe to revisit the topic.[42]

What, more particularly, did classical authorship look like? And how did it get into 'the Renaissance imagination'? To answer the first question, we may take the cue of Gordon Braden in his *Petrarchan Love and the Continental Renaissance*, which suggests that 'the master topos of post-classical European literature [is the] unprecedented union... of subjective vision and objective fact'.[43] Braden works from Ernst Robert Curtius, who says in *European Literature and the Latin Middle Ages*: 'The whole plentitude of his [Dante's] inner vision must be applied to the whole extent of the world, to all the depths and heights of the world above... A structure of language and thought is created... as inalterable as the cosmos... poetic production can be compared with that of the creator of the universe.'[44] Yet the *topos* traces to antiquity: to Homer and Hesiod, as well as to Plato, but most importantly for Dante and later writers such as Spenser and Milton, to Virgil, as Philip Hardie allows us to see in *Cosmos and Imperium*.[45] Indebted to Virgil and his own imitation of Latin and Greek predecessors, English Renaissance authorship, above all, represents the material artefact of the work in the shape of the cosmos in order to write the nation in the context of Christian eternity.[46]

The phrase 'Renaissance imagination' comes from Harry Berger, Jr, one of the most eloquent cartographers of the concept, in his *Second World and Green World: Studies in Renaissance Fiction-Making*. Berger's goal, shared by many critics of the later twentieth century, was to distinguish the Renaissance imagination from the medieval and the classical. According to Berger, Greeks such as Homer and Plato had represented the cosmos as an image of the human mind; the representation was thus a form of mental projection that made reality appear man-made. St Augustine took this *interior* model and saw it as the product of an *exterior* agent, God, who used the Word as the shaping hand of creation. Here, writes Berger, 'we are faced with the peculiar fact that at no time in our history did the human imagination so completely control the universe': 'The official or prevailing image of the world, from the time of the early church Fathers up through the fifteenth century, was a completely organized and esthetically integrated system of projections—an artistic triumph rarely exceeded in history, characteristic in every way of the mind's processes, its interpretations and forms of thought.'[47] The Renaissance era is ground-breaking, Berger writes, because it becomes *self-conscious* about this mental projection.[48]

History is indeed a story; its 'truth' lies in an awareness of its status as fiction-making. In the present volume, we are telling a story, and this section will conclude by addressing the *content* of English classical authorship: the epochal attempt to write authorship by relating 'subjective vision' to 'objective fact'. For Berger, 'the Renaissance imagination' distinguishes between three *types* of 'world'. The first is the material world created by God, which we call reality and inhabit as readers. The second world is the *heterocosm* ('other world'), which the poet creates as an artefact by imitating the first world of God. The third world is the 'green world' inside the heterocosm, a fictional environment of forests, fields, and gardens, which characters inside the story enter. English Renaissance authors tell fictions about places other than green worlds—most prominently, the court—but a poem like Andrew Marvell's 'The Garden' (featured by Berger) indicates how important the green world is to Renaissance fiction-making. In such terms, an author creates a work in the shape of the cosmos, and he or she centres it on a green world, in order to ask the key question that fiction can ask: is the 'world' a place of repose where we feel redeemed; or is it a darker place where we 'give up'? Shakespeare's comedies and romances, including *As You Like It* and *The Tempest*, follow Spenser in transferring responsibility for answering this question to the audience, compelling us, as Berger puts it, 'to transform the bounded moment of esthetic delight into a model or guide for action'.[49]

We do not have space to chart this model in any detail, but it might be useful to point to its presence in three major examples. First, in book 6, canto 10, of *The Faerie Queene* Spenser introduces a Virgilian model based on book 6 of the *Aeneid*, Aeneas' descent to the underworld to see a vision of Roman history. On Mt Acidale, Spenser's pastoral persona, Colin Clout, uses his pipe to conjure up a vision of the Three Graces, who dance in a circle around a Fourth Grace (Colin's beloved), and are themselves encircled by a dancing troupe of a 'hundred naked maidens' (*Faerie Queene*, 6. 10. 11. 8). In this configuration of three concentric circles, Spenser represents the poet using his artefact to construct a green world as part of the Ptolemaic universe.

Spenser understands the fragility of the poet's cosmic vision of grace, for the hero of book 6, the knight Calidore, causes the vision to vanish when he steps forward to 'know' it (6. 10. 17. 8). Second, in *The Tempest*, Act 5, scene 1, Shakespeare uses an Ovidian model when an author-figure, the magician Prospero, delivers his farewell to magic, based on a speech by the enchantress Medea in book 7 of the *Metamorphoses*. In Prospero's speech (*Tempest*, 5. 1. 33–57), which Jonathan Bate calls Shakespeare's 'most sustained Ovidian borrowing', the key word is 'make' (5. 1. 37, 39, 47), as Prospero reviews the way his art has shaped the cosmos, ''twixt the green sea and the azur'd vault, | Set warring war' (5. 1. 53–4).[50] And, finally, Chapman constructs a Homeric model in his translation of 'Achilles' Shield' from book 18 of the *Iliad*, when the poet finds embossed on the epic hero's martial weapon a panoramic scene of the universe, sky, sea, and land, animated by the various arts of the human. In all three examples, we glimpse a representation of the author's work in the shape of the universe. In all three, an English Renaissance author re-embroiders a passage from classical culture. All three, therefore, conduct a fiction-making authorship in terms of classical imitation.

The late-twentieth-century interest in distinguishing the Renaissance from the Middle Ages has given way early in the twenty-first century to a generation of medievalists who try to bring the two eras into conversation. Volume 1 of *OHCREL* will be the latest example, but it is preceded by volume 2 of The Oxford English Literary History, *Reform and Revolution . . . 1300–1547*, in which James Simpson sees the sixteenth century as an unfortunate interlude between the premier values of both the medieval and the modern: political liberty and artistic freedom. According to this narrative, the Renaissance, rather than being a time of triumph, is a time of political oppression and artistic failure.[51]

In 2010, Simpson and Brian Cummings consolidated this project in another monumental publication, from the Oxford Twenty-First Century Approaches to Literature series, titled *Cultural Reformations: Medieval and Renaissance in Literary History*, which argues the need to break down the 'standard boundaries' between the two periods and to stop seeing the Renaissance as 'the origin and final triumph of reformed religion'.[52] Curiously, the very next year Stephen Greenblatt published the Pulitzer Prize winning *The Swerve: How the World Became Modern*, which ignores Simpson's work and unabashedly resorts to a model of 'The Renaissance' as the recovery of antiquity: 'Greek and Roman classics, largely displaced from our curriculum, have in fact definitely shaped modern consciousness.'[53] Greenblatt's particular story is about the recovery of a single book, Lucretius' *De Rerum Natura* (*On the Nature of Things*), in 1417, by Poggio Bracciolini, and its dissemination through manuscript and print culture: 'In my view, and by no means mine alone, the culture in the wake of antiquity that best epitomized the Lucretian embrace of beauty and pleasure and propelled it forward as a legitimate and worthy human pursuit was that of the Renaissance.'[54] At present, these two radically different views of the Renaissance remain unreconciled.

Imitation and Intertextuality

In this section we take a closer look at the ways in which a focus on our authors' use of classical antiquity may be put to the service of a dynamic reception history of a kind that has a claim to be a necessary and integral part of any literary history of the period, and not to be detached from wider discussions of political and cultural contexts.

Renewed and closer engagement with Latin and Greek authors feeds through into a reconfiguration of the forms in which writers and readers of the Renaissance thought about and expressed their identities as political and social animals. Roman historical and poetic accounts of civil war shaped the ways in which the English thought about their own civil wars, both those that preceded the establishment of the Tudor dynasty, and those that brought the Stuart dynasty to an end. Cicero's *De Officiis*, 'Tully's Offices', provided 'virtually the whole framework for civic humanist discussions of the active life'.[55] Curtis Perry (Chapter 8a, this volume) shows how pervasively English thinking on the mutability and possibilities of political institutions was conducted through a reading of Roman historiography. Republican theory of the sixteenth and seventeenth centuries is inseparable from the Taciteanism of the time (van Es, Chapter 19, this volume). The myths of nationhood with which Tudor and Stuart monarchs fostered national solidarity were calqued in large part on Virgil's *Aeneid*, with upbeat reference to *Eclogue* 4's proclamation of the return of the Golden Age. The private citizen might take as a touchstone for his or her own desires and sexuality Latin love poetry, especially Ovid (see Cora Fox, Chapter 8b, this volume). The stage and the epyllion form (Lynn Enterline, Chapter 11, this volume) provided spaces in which the erotic fantasies of Ovid's *Metamorphoses* might be played out, freed to an extent from the constraints of the Christian denial of the flesh.

As we have seen, the Virgilian model for the poet as spokesperson for the nation and as supplier of charter myths was one embraced above all by Spenser, both in his debut appearance as a fully-fledged author in *The Shepheardes Calender*, and then in *The Faerie Queene*. The English Renaissance saw the development of various models of the literary career, following the precedents of, in particular, Virgil, Ovid, and Horace (Patrick Cheney, Chapter 8c, this volume). Ben Jonson plays a particularly important role in establishing the authority of the author, whose independent identity is stamped on the 1616 publication of his collected *Works*, aspiring to the monumentality of an edition of the *Opera* of one of the great classical authors. The most classicizing of all English authors of the period, Jonson cuts a literary self for his own age largely out of the cloth of the ancients, and in particular out of his reading of the authorial personality of Horace, an early modern self-fashioning through imitation of the ancients (for full discussion, see Sean Keilen, Chapter 28, this volume). The laureate career path, to use Richard Helgerson's terminology,[56] set its sights on a crown of lasting fame, whose imagery and ideology are predominantly classical, drawing in particular on well-known texts by Virgil, Horace, Ovid, and Statius (Philip Hardie, Chapter 8d, this volume). Helgerson's non-laureate career pattern of the 'amateur' is itself defined in opposition to, and so presupposes, the ideals of mid-sixteenth-century humanism. Furthermore, there were well-known ancient Roman models in Catullus and the love-elegists for a literary career that rebelled against the expectations of civic and personal duty (Roland Greene, Chapter 14, this volume). It has been argued that imitation of Ovid and Petrarch in *Astrophil and Stella* is integral to Philip Sidney's exploration of a lyric subjectivity that tends to undermine the ideology of Sidney's public roles.[57]

When Renaissance authors talk about imitation, they are well aware that their own practice in imitating the ancients is itself an imitation of the imitation of Greek texts by Roman writers. As Maggie Kilgour points out (Chapter 23, this volume), Roger Ascham, whose *The Scholemaster* contains one of the most substantial English Renaissance discussions of imitation, urged students to study how an ancient author transformed his source—for example, Virgil imitating Homer, or Cicero imitating Demosthenes—by leaving out some things, adding others, or changing the words and matter. Renaissance readers and writers were thus encouraged to reflect on how earlier and later texts relate to each other, with consequences for their own practice of imitation and allusion.

The early modern cultural historian may in turn reflect on how studies of the relationship between Greece and Rome in antiquity might offer starting points for thinking about the relationship of the English Renaissance (as a part of the wider European Renaissance) to Greco-Roman antiquity. Historians of Latin culture and literature, in particular, have developed powerful methods for understanding the ways in which Roman culture develops its Roman specificity in response to the adaptation of Greek culture.[58] The construction of a Roman cultural and literary identity is unthinkable without the 'Hellenization of Rome', and those aspects of their culture and society that the Romans think of as 'Roman' tend to be defined through a conscious contrast with Greek ways of doing things. At the level of detailed literary analysis, Latinists have shown how intertextuality between Latin and Greek literary texts is constitutive of the aims and character of Latin literature, paradigmatically in Virgil's creation of the Roman national epic, the *Aeneid*, through sustained and intricate dialogue with the Homeric epics and with the post-Homeric Greek literary tradition. The same is true across the gamut of literary kinds used by Roman writers, even in the case of satire, of which Quintilian famously said, 'satire is completely ours (i.e. Roman)'.

There are significant structural differences between the relationship of ancient Rome to Greece and the relationship of post-classical European culture to antiquity. Roman culture grew and developed in close contact with the Greek world (whose culture in the eastern empire indeed lasted longer than the Western, Latin, empire), whereas the successive 'renaissances' in Christian Europe, after the fall of the Western Roman Empire, look back to a classical culture whose pastness is increasingly recognized. While there is a continuity between the Christian culture of late antiquity and post-classical Europe, there is an ideological gulf between Christianity and pagan classical culture of a kind that never existed within the pre-Christian Greco-Roman world. Despite these differences, an awareness of how classicists in recent decades have approached the interaction between Greek and Roman may be useful for thinking about the dynamics of classical reception within Renaissance literature, in a complex process of appropriation, identification, and differentiation. Nor is the paganism of antiquity without its allures: the pagan classics offer a space in which the Christian of the Renaissance can enjoy a holiday from a sense of original sin and the need to discipline the flesh, as, *mutatis mutandis*, for an ancient Roman readership the world of Greek myth can offer a glamorous escape from everyday mundanity.[59]

The difference that is registered in the sheer sense of the pastness of classical antiquity leads to a Petrarchan sense of loss and frustration, together with an intense desire for contact and reunion. Although gunpowder and the printing press were regularly cited as examples of post-antique inventions that greatly extended the powers of mankind (for good or for evil),[60] and although the opening-up of the New World burst open the limits set to the ancient Mediterranean world by the Pillars of Hercules, the period covered by this volume does not see a determined attempt, at least in the literary sphere, to claim a superiority of the modern over the ancient and so to relegate classical literature to history. Samuel Daniel's assertion, in *A Defence of Ryme*, that 'all our understandings are not to be built by the square of Greece and Italy',[61] comes in the particular context of an argument against the necessity of following classical metrical models. But the quarrel of the ancients and moderns lies in the future, being usually regarded as one of the imports from France brought over with Charles II in 1660 (see Bruce Smith, Chapter 17, this volume).[62] When Jonson tells Shakespeare that

> I would...
> . . . . .
> when thy socks were on,
> Leave thee alone for the comparison
> Of all that insolent Greece or haughty Rome
> Sent forth, or since did from their ashes come,[63]

he is engaging in a kind of rivalrous comparison entirely contained *within* a culture of imitation; Jonson's similar comment on Bacon's having 'performed that in our tongue which may be compared either to insolent Greece or haughty Rome' (Jonson, 'On Bacon', *Discoveries*; *Works*, 8. 591) is itself an imitation of a challenge to the superiority of Greek rhetoric by Seneca the Elder, *Contr.* 1. praef. 6: 'all that Roman eloquence could put beside or above that of insolent Greece flourished about the time of Cicero.'

The radical unsettling and erosion of the classical system of genres, at least in verse, also lie in the future. One sign of the maturity of ancient Latin literature was the creation in the Augustan period of works in a range of genres that could stand comparison with their great Greek models, so establishing what was perceived as a canon of Latin works. An analogous ambition to create works in English that engage closely with classical models but at the same time assert an independence in their address to the audiences and concerns of their contemporary world is perceptible in many writers of the period.

But how, more specifically, do literary texts of the period relate to the texts of Greek and Latin antiquity? A good place to start is with Renaissance theories of imitation, a central part of the literary criticism of the time (see Gavin Alexander, Chapter 5, this volume).[64] Terence Cave puts his finger on the immediate relevance of these writings for the subject of this book when he notes that 'the problems which sixteenth-century theorists discuss under the heading of "imitation" reappear in literary historical method, as the study of sources, influences, or traditions'.[65] Unsurprisingly, Renaissance theorists themselves draw on ancient writers on the subject,[66] with key texts in Seneca, Quintilian, Macrobius, in a line that goes via Petrarch, to the early sixteenth-century European humanist scholars, with the hot spot of the debate over Ciceronianism, and so to Renaissance England. G. W. Pigman identifies three major classes of images and analogies relating to imitation: transformative, dissimulative, and eristic.[67] All three lay emphasis on the active creation of an authorial self, rather than a passive following in the footsteps of a great writer of the past. Seneca, in his eighty-fourth *Moral Epistle* on how to assimilate one's reading, supplies metaphors for imitation that were imitated again and again.[68] First, the image of the bee that collects materials from flowers to make into honey, homogeneous and of a single taste. The bee, gathering pollen from flowers, can also be an image for an anthologizing approach, producing a mosaic of textual fragments cunningly fitted together, a model of eclectic imitation. Secondly, the image of digestion, closely related to the honey-making image, by which a variety of foods is transformed into the flesh and blood of our own persons. Thirdly, filial similarity, in which personal individuality coexists with family resemblance, in contrast to the unproductive similarity of a portrait, or, in another common metaphor, to the unintelligent imitation of a monkey, imitation as aping. Another common figure for the relationship to a great writer of the past was metempsychosis, the conceit that the soul of a dead poet had been reborn in a living poet, a localized moment of renaissance.[69] In one of the foundational moments of Roman literature, Ennius claimed in the prologue to his epic on Roman history that he was the reincarnated Homer. Spenser claims to find the courage to strive with Chaucer in providing a continuation to the latter's unfinished 'The Squire's Tale', because

> through infusion sweete
> Of thine own spirit, which doth in me survive,
> I follow here the footing of thy feete.
>
> (*Faerie Queene*, 4. 2. 34.6–8)

Spenser is a rather exceptional case of an English Renaissance poet who places the reception of earlier English poetry at the heart of his imitative practice; in the most well-known instance of the figure, Frances Meres wrote that 'As the soul of Euphorbus was thought to live in Pythagoras: so the sweet witty soul of Ovid lives in mellifluous and honey-tongued Shakespeare', in a catalogue juxtaposing English writers with their classical equivalents that was itself transplanted wholesale from another Renaissance writer.[70]

Honey-making, digestion, father–son likeness, metempsychosis—all these images present imitation as a positive and dynamic process or relationship, through which the past is used to produce the materials of a living present, in contrast to the more static and inert metaphors concealed in 'influence' or 'tradition'. With regard to the study of allusion and intertextuality, there is a tension between 'dissimulative' Renaissance models of imitation that advocate so thorough an appropriation of the source texts that they are unrecognizable by the reader, and models that allow the source texts to remain visible through the changes exercised in the course of imitation, or that actively encourage the reader to compare source and imitation through an openly declared rivalry (emulation, *aemulatio*) between an author and his model.[71]

These author-based models of imitation need not limit the ways in which modern intertextualists read Renaissance texts. What is concealed, once revealed, may tell us important things about a text's relationship to classical antiquity, and, even if it could be shown in a particular case that an author intended to dissimulate a borrowing, authorial intention need not invalidate a reading that exploits a resemblance. Petrarch, who made a point about not repeating the exact words of classical authors in his own Latin poetry, tells how he was caught out by Giovanni Malpaghini when the latter pointed to an exact replication of a Virgilian phrase from *Aeneid* 6 in his *Bucolicum Carmen*. G. W. Pigman develops a subtle reading of the echo as a clever allusion that reaches further into the context of the Virgilian tag, but only as a warning against the pitfalls of building such an interpretation on a 'coincidental' parallel.[72] But one could turn this round by denying the author Petrarch complete control over the meanings of his uses of tradition, and so empowering the reader in his or her own pursuit of allusivity.

The insights preserved in the ancient and Renaissance writings on imitation can usefully be put together with the range of new approaches that have been developed in recent decades in the names of allusion and intertextuality. There have been significant interventions in Renaissance studies, although for the most part not in English Renaissance studies. Two landmarks in particular deserve mention. First, Terence Cave's *The Cornucopian Text: Problems of Writing in the French Renaissance*. Cave is concerned with questions of identity and difference; with the production of authentic discourse and the possibility of 'self-expression' through the reading and appropriation of classical texts by, among others, Erasmus and Montaigne; and with the tension between the meanings of *copia* as 'plenitude' and *copia* as 'copy'. The most influential study of Renaissance imitation has been Thomas Greene's *The*

Light in Troy: Imitation and Discovery in Renaissance Poetry, largely on Italian and French authors, but concluding with chapters on Wyatt and Ben Jonson.[73] Greene elaborates a fourfold typology of imitation, which may be arranged along a spectrum of continuity and discontinuity (or distance): (1) A 'sacramental' or 'reproductive' form of imitation, homage to sacred objects unassimilable into modernity. (2). 'Eclectic' or 'exploitative' imitation, in which the past is a storehouse of topoi for opportunistic use. (3) 'Heuristic' imitation, which both advertises its models, and then measures its distance from them, constructing a literary aetiology or genealogy. (4) 'Dialectical' imitation, which allows for an exchange of mutual criticism between the imitating and imitated texts. Greene's approach has affinities with the 'anxiety of influence' of his Yale colleague Harold Bloom. It runs the risk of being too *dirigiste* in assigning particular instances of imitation to one category or the other, but it has had the beneficial effect of bringing imitation studies in out of the cold.

Greene's *The Light in Troy* appeared just before the explosion of interest in allusion and intertextuality on the part of classical Latinists.[74] Some Renaissance English scholars have drawn productively on the work of Latinists in approaching allusion in their own texts, but there is surely scope for more interaction between classicists and Renaissance specialists. For example, Latinists have looked hard at the phenomenon of what is variously called 'double allusion' or 'window reference'[75] whereby an author alludes to text A, and at the same time to text B, to which text A already alludes. Independently, it would seem, Daniel Javitch discussed what he calls 'genealogical imitations' in *Orlando Furioso*, where Ariosto imitates, for example, a Virgilian passage and its prior imitation by Statius, or Boccaccio imitating Dante.[76] Javitch does cite Greene's *The Light in Troy*, but Greene uses the notion of genealogical imitation in a different sense. Stephen Hinds shows how Latin poets write literary history into their allusions;[77] Maggie Kilgour (Chapter 23, this volume) takes the example of John Weever's *Faunus and Melliflora* (1610), in which the character Faunus, the son of Picus, looks back to *Aeneid* 7 through *Metamorphoses* 14, and the satyrs who come to England with Trojan Brut are a figure for the immigration of satire as the next generation after Ovidian epyllion.

Latinists have directed attention to poetic and metapoetic markers of allusion in the text, 'Alexandrian footnotes' (phrases of the kind 'as the story goes'), and 'tropics of allusivity', or, in Alessandro Barchiesi's phrase, 'tropes of intertextuality', such things as Fate and fame, dreams, prophecy, images, echoes.[78] An example of this kind of analysis applied to a Renaissance text and its classical model is Colin Burrow's study of the language of imitation and imaging in Ovid and Spenser, *mimesis* in the sense of the visual artist's imitation of nature functioning as a figure for the literary artist's imitation of prior texts.[79]

Greene focuses on the degrees of distancing involved in imitative and allusive practice. Distance and nearness form a polarity that can usefully be extended in a number of directions. The distance between pagan antiquity and Christian culture could be exploited for polemical or contrastive effects, as in Richard McCabe's appeal (Chapter 25, this volume) to René Girard's 'mimésis de l'antagonisme', in a discussion of Spenser's Christianization of his classical epic models. This absolute confessional distance is relativized if one takes the longer view of the classical past that includes the Christian Greek and Latin writers of late antiquity, poets such as Prudentius and the biblical paraphrasts, and the church fathers, whose works were constantly enlisted in the religious debates that raged throughout the sixteenth and seventeenth centuries. Mark Vessey (Chapter 6, this volume) highlights the continuing influence of an Erasmian humanism that did not seek to segregate (pagan) classical and Christian 'good letters'.

The earlier part, at least, of our period was more distant from Greek classics than from Latin, for the simple reason that far fewer educated Englishmen read Greek than read Latin. But a widespread bilingualism in English and Latin worked to keep the Latin classics constantly at the forefront of the cultural consciousness of the elite, and that closeness to classical Latin texts was reinforced by the flourishing practice of new writing in Latin. English neo-Latin literature is not a central concern of *OHCREL*, but it is important to remember that some of the most important writers of the period, including Marvell, Milton, and Cowley, were bilingual in their output.[80] Milton's decision to write his great epic in English was a conscious act of distancing English poetry from the dominant classical language of the Renaissance.

For those contemporaries with less than fluent Latin and Greek, the distance between antiquity and the present day could be bridged by English translations of classical texts; Chapman's *Iliad* and *Odyssey* made Homer available to a far wider audience than the small number who could read Greek. Translations were themselves often an exercise in emulating the ancient authors, in order to show that the resources of the English language were equal to those of Greek and Latin. There is no sharp distinction between imitation and translation, as can easily be felt by moving along John Dryden's spectrum of translation to paraphrase to metaphrase.[81] Translations are a major part of the literary output of this period (and even more so of the period covered by volume 3), and play an important role in the development of English literature as a whole.[82]

At the same time, translation may distance readers from Greece and Rome, through the interposition of a textual layer between the present day and classical antiquity. Shakespeare imitates Ovid through the medium of Golding's translation of the *Metamorphoses*; but Shakespeare also remembered the Ovid that he had read in Latin at Stratford Grammar School, and doubtless he went back later to the Latin as well as to Golding.[83] The frequently mediated nature of the reception of classics in the Renaissance should never be forgotten. Virgil wrote perhaps 600 years after Homer, and in full awareness of the intervening traditions of interpretations and imitations of Homer. The millennium and a half that separates English Renaissance writers from, for example, the writers of Augustan Rome was not a period of continuous and consistent evolution of classical forms, but in many genres there is a multiplication of intermediaries between classical texts and their Renaissance descendants, in some cases detouring through other vernaculars. The 'double allusion' beloved of classical Latinists may be extended into longer chains of reference. *The Faerie Queene* draws directly on the epics of Virgil and Ovid, but also approaches the classical models more indirectly via *Orlando furioso* and *Gerusalemme liberata*. Pastoral is an especially densely layered genre. Maggie Kilgour (Chapter 23, this volume) shows how Marvell's 'Damon the Mower' places itself in a tradition of pastoral complaint that looks back through the Polyphemus of *Metamorphoses* 13, to Ovid's own models in Virgil's second *Eclogue*, and to Virgil's models in Theocritus' *Idylls*. A Renaissance pastoral poem like this is fully alert to the intertextual and literary–historical self-consciousness built into the classical genre of pastoral,[84] and extends it through allusion to earlier Renaissance examples of the genre, both vernacular and neo-Latin. Philip Sidney exploits tensions between Petrarch, and one of Petrarch's own models for his first-person love poetry, Ovid, in his sonnet sequence *Astrophil and Stella*.[85]

The question of distancing also arises with regard to the ways in which the Renaissance reads its classical texts: what kind of a distance does that set between Renaissance and modern ways of approaching the ancient world, and, related, what kind of a distance does that set between Renaissance readers and what we might now wish to reconstruct as ancient ways of reading and responding to texts? The allegorical and exemplary reading practices prevalent in our period are now largely out of fashion (which is not to say that many recent reading fashions are not allegorical, even if not acknowledged as such). Much of the medieval and Renaissance tradition of allegorization would now seem ahistorical, although the importance of ancient allegorical practices, in both reading and writing, in the centuries before the explosion of such in late antiquity is now being properly recognized. An exemplary approach to texts certainly was widespread in antiquity; that it is now out of fashion says more about modern tastes than about a concern for historical reconstruction.[86]

Modern studies of allusion tend to presuppose ideal readers who think of texts as wholes, and who hold in their minds the interrelations between parts of texts. Renaissance readers, it has been argued, were conditioned by their education and by the habit of excerpting choice flowers from texts for their commonplace books to fragment texts, and were so discouraged from taking a broader view of the unity and interconnections of a text.[87] But it is overly restrictive to suppose that such habituation, for such purposes, suppressed more holistic ways of reading. The fact that our reading of English Renaissance texts for an allusivity that presupposes a wider readerly embrace of model texts by authors of the time leads to productive results may tell us only about our own ability to make patterns, but there is a fair possibility that it corresponds to an authorial pattern-making, and one that contemporary readers might be expected to share. Jessica Wolfe notes (Chapter 21, this volume) George Chapman's protest about the practice of excerpting proverbs from Homer's epics: 'Homer... must not be read for a few lines with leaves turned over capriciously in dismembered fractions, but throughout—the whole drift, weight and height of his works set before the apprehensive eyes of his judge.'[88]

In the later part of our period, the distance from antiquity is lessened by neoclassical tendencies, as writers, partly guided by developments in literary criticism and literary scholarship, aimed at a more faithful reconstruction of classical forms. Jonson's neoclassicism is routinely contrasted with Shakespeare's freer and less scholastic imitation of classical models; Jonson is followed by, for example, Abraham Cowley's 'Pindaric Odes', which combine translations of Pindar with new poems in the manner of Pindar, and Cowley's unfinished biblical epic the *Davideis*, accompanied by Cowley's own scholarly notes on his own poem. This is the road that leads to *Paradise Lost*, from one point of view a *tour de force* of learned classicizing, from another a poem deeply embedded in the history and controversies of Milton's lifetime. But neoclassicism, aiming at the 'correct' imitation of ancient forms, could also drive a wedge between modernity and classical antiquity, confirming distance and encouraging the development of new and unclassical forms of literature.

In conclusion, we see a close authorial engagement with the genres, forms, and language of classical literature as being at the heart of the literary practice of the English Renaissance, and of fundamental importance for the functions of literature within the society of the period. The reception of classical antiquity is not an 'extra' in the study of English Renaissance literature, a perhaps regrettable product of the dominant educational system of the time, something that acted as a drag on modernity's discovery of itself. So, far from being an inert and backward-looking source of materials and forms that were transformed into something vital and innovative by a nascent modernity, the authorial imitation and reworking of classical texts were central to the literature of the English Renaissance.

Notes

1. David Hopkins and Charles Martindale, 'Introduction', in *The Oxford History of Classical Reception in English Literature*, vol. 3: *1660–1790* (Oxford, 2012), 5.
2. Martindale and Hopkins (eds), 'Introduction', 3.
3. Roland Barthes, 'The Death of the Author', in Vincent B. Leitch et al. (eds), *The Norton Anthology of Theory and Criticism* (New York, 2001), 1466–70; Michel Foucault, 'What Is an Author?', in *The Foucault Reader*, ed. Paul Rabinow (New York, 1984), 101–20. On Barthes and Foucault writing 'the two most influential essays on authorship in twentieth-century criticism', see Andrew Bennett, *The Author*, New Critical Idiom (New York, 2005), 5.
4. Julia Kristeva, 'Word, Dialogue, and Novel', in *The Kristeva Reader*, trans. Alice Jardine, Thomas Gora, and Leon S. Roudiez, ed. Toril Moi (New York, 1986), 33–61. On the importance of the concept, including in today's methodology, see Patrick Cheney, 'Intertextuality', in Roland Greene (ed.), *Princeton Encyclopedia of Poetry and Poetics*, 4th edn (Princeton, 2012), 716–18.
5. See David Scott Kastan, *Shakespeare and the Book* (Cambridge, 2001). On collaboration, see Wendy Wall, *The Imprint of Gender: Authorship and Publication in the*

English Renaissance (Cornell, 1993); Jeffrey Masten, *Textual Intercourse: Collaboration, Authorship, and Sexualities in Renaissance Drama* (Cambridge, 1997).

6. See, e.g. Robert Weimann, *Author's Pen and Actor's Voice: Playing and Writing in Shakespeare's Theatre*, ed. Helen Higbee and William West (Cambridge, 2000); Tiffany Stern, *Making Shakespeare: From Stage to Page* (2004).
7. Louis Montrose, 'Spenser's Domestic Domain: Poetry, Property, and the Early Modern Subject', in Margreta de Grazia, Maureen Quilligan, and Peter Stallybrass (eds), *Subject and Object in Renaissance Culture* (Cambridge, 1996), 92.
8. Richard Helgerson, *Forms of Nationhood: The Elizabethan Writing of England* (Chicago, 1992), 215.
9. See Michael D. Bristol, *Big-Time Shakespeare* (New York, 1996), whose model of authorship remains unmatched: 'Authorship need not be understood as a sovereign and proprietary relationship to specific utterances. It is perhaps more fully theorized in terms of dialogue and ethical sponsorship. The author is both debtor and trustee of meaning rather than sole proprietor; authorship is always ministerial rather than magisterial' (p. 58).
10. Kastan, *Shakespeare and the Book*, 6.
11. Lukas Erne, *Shakespeare as Literary Dramatist* (Cambridge, 2003), 26.
12. Lukas Erne, *Shakespeare and the Book Trade* (Cambridge, 2013). 'The Return of the Author' is the title of the Forum for *Shakespeare Studies*, 36 (2008), 19–131, ed. Patrick Cheney. In his essay in this Forum, Kastan continues his disagreement with Erne, whose essay also appears.
13. Heather James, *Shakespeare's Troy: Drama, Politics, and the Translation of Empire* (Cambridge 1997). Studies of classicism and Shakespeare are countless; see Colin Burrow, Chapter 27, this volume.
14. Leah Marcus, 'Textual Indeterminancy and Ideological Difference: The Case of *Dr Faustus*', *Renaissance Drama*, 20 (1989), 1–29; Thomas Healy, *Christopher Marlowe* (Plymouth, England, 1994).
15. Wendy Wall, 'Authorship and the Material Conditions of Writing', in Arthur F. Kinney (ed.), *Cambridge Companion to English Literature 1500–1600* (Cambridge, 2000), 64–89.
16. For Richard Helgerson's principle of self-presentation, see *Self-Crowned Laureates: Spenser, Jonson, Milton, and the Literary System* (Berkeley and Los Angeles, 1983). For Montrose's principle of reciprocity, see 'The Elizabethan Subject and the Spenserian Text', in Patricia Parker and David Quint (eds), *Literary Theory/Renaissance Texts* (Baltimore, 1986), 303–40.
17. Patrick Cheney, 'Spenser's Pastorals: *The Shepheardes Calender* and *Colin Clouts Come Home Againe*', in Andrew Hadfield (ed.), *The Cambridge Companion to Spenser* (Cambridge, 2001), 79–105.
18. By 'we', we mean the volume editors, not the contributors, who have written about their topic as they see fit.
19. See also Charles Martindale, *Redeeming the Text: Latin Poetry and the Hermeneutics of Reception* (Cambridge, 1993).
20. The schools taught boys to read the New Testament in Greek, and some, such as Westminster, emphasized classical Greek. Such authors as Sidney and Jonson were proficient in Greek.
21. See, e.g. Erwin Panofsky, *Renaissance and Renascences in Western Art* (1960; New York, 1961), 11–21.
22. Jules Michelet, *Histoire de France/Michelet: Présentée et Commentée par Claude Mettra*, 18 vols (Lausanne, 1965–7); Jacob Burckhardt, *The Civilization of the Renaissance in Italy*, 2 vols (New York, 1958); Leonard Barkan, *Unearthing the Past: Archaeology and Aesthetics in the Making of*

Renaissance Culture (New Haven, 1999). Needless to say, Barkan brings an unmatched sophistication to the 'aesthetics' of 'Renaissance Culture' (the book subtitle). As Panofsky points out, in 1550 Vasari spoke of '*la rinascita*', but applied the rebirth only to art (*Renaissance and Renascences*, 31).

23. Stephen Greenblatt, *Renaissance Self-Fashioning: More to Shakespeare* (Chicago, 1980).
24. Margreta de Grazia, 'The Modern Divide: From Either Side', *Journal of Medieval and Early Modern Studies*, 37 (2007), 461. De Grazia has been instrumental in turning attention away from Renaissance subjectivity to Renaissance objectivity; see her introduction to *Subject and Object*. See also Lisa Jardine, *Worldly Goods: A New History of the Renaissance* (New York, 1996).
25. De Grazia, 'The Modern Divide: From Either Side', 463.
26. De Grazia, 'The Modern Divide: From Either Side', 459.
27. De Grazia, 'The Modern Divide: From Either Side', 459–60.
28. De Grazia, 'The Modern Divide: From Either Side', 460–1. Burckhardt does devote part 3 of his study to 'The Revival of Antiquity', but 'one of the chief propositions of... his book' is that 'it was not the revival of antiquity alone, but its union with the genius of the Italian people, which achieved the conquests of the Western world' (*Civilization*, 1. 175). Later, he identifies the classical revival as one of four 'elements' making up the Renaissance in Italy, along with 'the popular character', 'chivalry', and 'the influence of religion and the Church' (1. 179). His generalized chapter on 'The Old Authors' has little to do with the specifics of imitation.
29. De Grazia, 'The Modern Divide: From Either Side', 461.
30. De Grazia, 'The Modern Divide: From Either Side', 461.
31. Hopkins and Martindale, 'Introduction', 9.
32. Cf. Hamilton's summary of interpretation on the satyrs episode: '**Satyres**... symbolize concupiscence... They are associated with the desolation of Palestine... and their presence here has been variously identified: historically, as ignorant Christians... the Jews... savage people responding to religion... the Gaelic population of Ireland... morally, as "nature without nurture"... or uncorrupted human nature' (ed., *Faerie Queene* (New York, 2001), 83).
33. Douglas Bush, *Prefaces to Renaissance Literature* (New York, 1965), 4.
34. A landmark study remains Paul Oskar Kristeller, *Renaissance Thought and its Sources*, ed. Michael Mooney (New York, 1979).
35. William Kerrigan and Gordon Braden, *The Idea of the Renaissance* (Baltimore, 1989).
36. While Burckhardt's individual and the poststructural subject differ, Kerrigan and Braden aim to connect the two.
37. Joel Fineman, *Shakespeare's Perjured Eye: The Modern Invention of Subjectivity* (Berkeley and Los Angeles, 1986); Harold Bloom, *Shakespeare: The Invention of the Human* (New York, 1998).
38. Harold Bloom, *The Anxiety of Influence: A Theory of Poetry*, 2nd edn (New York, 1997). Bloom's final book is *The Anatomy of Influence: Literature as a Way of Life* (New Haven, 2011). See Patrick Cheney, 'Influence', in Greene (ed.), *Princeton Encyclopedia of Poetry and Poetics*, 703–5.
39. De Grazia, 'The Modern Divide: From Either Side', 455–6.
40. Panofsky, *Renaissance and Renascences*, 113.
41. Barkan, *Unearthing the Past*, 63. For Barkan's earlier landmark study of Renaissance classicism, see *The Gods Made Flesh:*

Metamorphosis and the Pursuit of Paganism (New Haven, 1986).

42. On the death of the Renaissance during the mid-seventeenth century, see William J. Bouwsma, *The Waning of the Renaissance 1550–1640* (New Haven, 2000). In *The Oxford Dictionary of the Renaissance* (Oxford, 2003), Gordon Campbell selects the 'core period' dates of 1415 and 1618, 'the two Defenestrations of Prague' (p. vii). In its entry on 'Renaissance', this *Dictionary* defines the period this way: 'a model of cultural descent in which the culture of fifteenth- and sixteenth-century Europe is represented as a repudiation of medieval values in favour of the revival of the culture of ancient Greece and Rome' (p. 655). For a still valuable history of criticism on the Renaissance, see Wallace K. Ferguson, *The Renaissance in Historical Thought: Five Centuries of Interpretation* (1948; Toronto, 2006). For a more recent, and specified, overview, see Robin Sowerby, *The Classical Legacy in Renaissance Poetry* (Harlow, 1994), which is arranged by genres.
43. Gordon Braden, *Petrarchan Love and the Continental Renaissance* (New Haven, 1999), 60.
44. Ernst Robert Curtius, *European Literature and the Latin Middle Ages*, trans. Willard R. Trask (Princeton, 1953), 379, 400.
45. Philip Hardie, *Virgil's 'Aeneid': Cosmos and Imperium* (Oxford, 1986).
46. See Patrick Cheney, *Reading Sixteenth-Century Poetry* (Oxford, 2011), chs 3, 8.
47. Harry Berger, *Second World and Green World: Studies in Renaissance Fiction-Making*, ed. John Patrick Lynch (Berkeley and Los Angeles, 1988), 52.
48. Berger, *Second World and Green World*, 55.
49. Berger, *Second World and Green World*, 37.
50. Jonathan Bate, *Shakespeare and Ovid* (Oxford, 1993), 149.
51. Simpson, *Reform and Revolution*, vol. 2: *1300–1547*, Oxford English Literary History (Oxford, 2002).
52. Brian Cummings and James Simpson (eds), *Cultural Reformations: Medieval and Renaissance in Literary History* (Oxford, 2010), 5, 6.
53. Stephen Greenblatt, *The Swerve: How the World Became Modern* (New York, 2011), 8.
54. Greenblatt, *The Swerve*, 8.
55. Quentin Skinner, *Visions of Politics*, 3 vols (Cambridge, 2002), vol. 2: *Renaissance Virtues*, 218–19.
56. Helgerson, *Self-Crowned Laureates*.
57. Paul Allen Miller, 'Sidney, Petrarch, and Ovid, or Imitation as Subversion', *Engish Literary History*, 58 (1991), 499–522.
58. Erich S. Gruen, *Culture and National Identity in Republican Rome* (1993); Denis Feeney, *Literature and Religion at Rome: Cultures, Contexts, and Beliefs* (Cambridge, 1998), ch. 2; Andrew Wallace-Hadrill, *Rome's Cultural Revolution* (Cambridge, 2008).
59. See William Fitzgerald, *Catullan Provocations: Lyric Poetry and the Drama of Position* (Berkeley and Los Angeles, 1995), ch. 6.
60. Francis Bacon, *Novum Organum*, I. 129 (*The Oxford Francis Bacon*, 15 vols (Oxford, 1996–), II. 195): 'Printing, gunpowder and the compass . . . whence have followed innumerable changes, in so much that no empire, no sect, no star seems to have exerted greater power and influence in human affairs than these mechanical discoveries.'
61. Samuel Daniel, *The Complete Works*, ed. A. B. Grosart, 5 vols (1885–96), 4. 46.
62. See further, D. Hopkins, 'The French Connection', in *Oxford History of Classical Reception in English Literature*, vol. 3, 166–70.
63. Jonson, 'To the memory of my beloved, the author, Mr William Shakespeare', ll. 32–40; *Works*, 8. 391.

64. In general, see H. Gmelin, 'Das Prinzip der Imitation in den romanischen Literaturen der Renaissance', *Romanische Forschungen*, 46 (1932), 83–360; Harold O. White, *Plagiarism and Imitation during the English Renaissance* (Cambridge, MA, 1935); G. W. Pigman, 'Versions of Imitation in the Renaissance', *Renaissance Quarterly*, 33 (1980), 1–32; B. Vickers (ed.), *English Renaissance Literary Criticism* (Oxford, 1999), 22–39; Ann Moss, 'Literary Imitation in the Sixteenth Century: Writers and Readers, Latin and French', in Glynn P. Norton (ed.), *The Cambridge History of Literary Criticism*, vol. 3: *The Renaissance* (Cambridge, 1999), ch. 9; Gregory Machacek, 'Allusion', *PMLA* 122 (2007), 522–36. Colin Burrow's 2011 Blackwell Bristol Lectures on 'Imitation' (forthcoming) are a major contribution to the topic.
65. Terence Cave, *The Cornucopian Text* (Oxford, 1979), 76.
66. For a lucid account of ancient imitation-theory, see Donald A. Russell, '*De imitatione*', in D. West and T. Woodman (eds), *Creative Imitation and Latin Literature* (Cambridge, 1979), 1–16.
67. Pigman, 'Versions of Imitation', 4.
68. On Jonson's assimilation of the classical images for imitation, see Richard S. Peterson, *Imitation and Praise in the Poems of Ben Jonson* (New Haven, 1981), ch. 1.
69. See Stuart Gillespie, 'Literary Afterlives: Metempsychosis from Ennius to Jorge Luis Borges', in Philip Hardie and Helen Moore (eds), *Classical Literary Careers and their Reception* (Oxford, 2010), 209–25.
70. Frances Meres, *Palladis Tamia* (1598), cited in Vickers (ed.), *English Renaissance Literary Criticism*, 28.
71. On Renaissance emulation, see Vernon G. Dickson, '"A Pattern, Precedent, and Lively Warrant": Emulation, Rhetoric, and Cruel Propriety in *Titus Andronicus*', *Renaissance Quarterly*, 62 (2009), 376–409.
72. G. W. Pigman, 'Neo-Latin Imitation of the Latin Classics', in P. Godman and O. Murray (eds), *Latin Poetry and the Classical Tradition: Essays in Medieval and Renaissance Literature* (Oxford, 1990), 199–210.
73. Thomas M. Greene, *The Light in Troy: Imitation and Discovery in Renaissance Poetry* (New Haven, 1982). Other important discussions include John Hollander, *The Figure of Echo: A Mode of Allusion in Milton and After* (Berkeley and Los Angeles, 1981), and Peterson, *Imitation and Praise in the Poems of Ben Jonson*. Christopher Ricks, *Allusion to the Poets* (Oxford, 2002) starts chronologically with Dryden, but has much to interest the student of our period.
74. Landmarks include Gian Biagio Conte, *The Rhetoric of Imitation: Genre and Poetic Memory in Virgil and Other Latin Poets*, ed. C. Segal (Ithaca, NY, 1986); Joseph Farrell, *Vergil's Georgics and the Traditions of Ancient Epic* (Oxford, 1991); Stephen Hinds, *Allusion and Intertext: Dynamics of Appropriation in Roman Poetry* (Cambridge, 1998).
75. Richard F. Thomas, 'Virgil's *Georgics* and the Art of Reference', *Harvard Studies in Classical Philology*, 90 (1986), 171–98 (repr. in *Reading Virgil and his Texts: Studies in Intertextuality* (Ann Arbor, 1999), ch. 4); James C. McKeown, *Ovid Amores*, vol. 1: *Text and Prolegomena* (Liverpool, 1987), 37–45, 'Double Allusion'.
76. Daniel Javitch, 'The Imitation of Imitations in Orlando Furioso', *Renaissance Quarterly*, 38 (1985), 215–39.
77. Stephen Hinds, 'Diachrony: Literary History and its Narratives', in *Allusion and Intertext*, ch. 3.
78. Alessandro Barchiesi, 'Tropes of Intertextuality in Roman Epic', in *Speaking Volumes: Narrative and Intertext in Ovid and Other Latin Poets* (2001), 129–40.

79. Colin Burrow, '"Full of the Maker's Guile": Ovid on Imitating and the Imitation of Ovid', in Philip Hardie, Alessandro Barchiesi, and Stephen Hinds (eds), *Ovidian Transformations: Essays on Ovid's Metamorphoses and its Reception* (Cambridge, 1999), 271–87.
80. See Luke B. T. Houghton and Gesine Manuwald (eds), *Neo-Latin Poetry in the British Isles* (2012).
81. John Dryden, 'Preface to *Ovid's Epistles*', in John Dryden, *The Works*, gen. eds Edward Niles Hooker, H. T. Swedenberg, Jr, and Vinton A. Dearing, 20 vols (Berkeley and Los Angeles, 1956), I. 114–15.
82. See the manifesto for a literary history that takes full account of translations of the classics, by Stuart Gillespie, *English Translation and Classical Reception: Towards a New Literary History* (Malden, MA, 2011). Robin Sowerby (*The Augustan Art of Poetry: Augustan Translation of the Classics* (Oxford, 2006)) makes the case that translations of Latin poetry played a key role in the translation of a Roman Augustan aesthetic into a vernacular equivalent in seventeenth- and early eighteenth-century poetry. For much fuller discussion of translation in our period, see Gordon Braden, Robert Cummings, and Stuart Gillespie (eds), *The Oxford History of Literary Translation in English*, vol. 2: *1550–1660* (Oxford, 2010).
83. For a demonstration of this, see Bate, *Shakespeare and Ovid*, 8.
84. See T. K. Hubbard, *The Pipes of Pan: Intertextuality and Literary Filiation in the Pastoral Tradition from Theocritus to Milton* (Ann Arbor, 1998). Marlowe anticipates Marvell's exploitation of the layered intertextuality of pastoral in 'The Passionate Shepherd to his Love', as shown by Patrick Cheney, 'Career Rivalry and the Writing of Counter-Nationhood: Ovid, Spenser, and Philomela in Marlowe's "The Passionate Shepherd to his Love"', *English Literary History*, 115 (1998), 523–55.
85. Miller, 'Sidney, Petrarch, and Ovid'.
86. On allegory and epic, see Philip Hardie, Chapter 10, this volume. On exemplary Renaissance readings of epic, for models of virtuous conduct to imitate, see Craig Kallendorf, *In Praise of Aeneas: Virgil and Epideictic Rhetoric in the Early Italian Renaissance* (Hanover, NH, 1989); see also Jane Grogan, *Exemplary Spenser: Visual and Poetic Pedagogy in 'The Faerie Queene'* (Farnham, 2009). For a reading practice that extends beyond the exemplary to a political reading for action, see Lisa Jardine and Anthony Grafton, '"Studied for action": How Gabriel Harvey Read his Livy', *Past and Present*, 129 (1990), 231–46.
87. The case is made by Mary Thomas Crane, *Framing Authority: Sayings, Self, and Society in Sixteenth-Century England* (Princeton, 1993); for counter-arguments, see Raphael Lyne, *Ovid's Changing Worlds: English Metamorphoses 1567–1632* (Oxford, 2001), 36–8. See also Heather James, 'Shakespeare, the Classics, and the Forms of Authorship', *Shakespeare Studies*, 36 (2008), 80–9.
88. George Chapman, 'To the Most Honoured Earl, Earl Marshal', in *Achilles' Shield*, in *Chapman's Homer: The Iliad*, ed. Allardyce Nicoll (Princeton, 1998), 544.

PART I

Institutions and Contexts

CHAPTER 2

The Classics in Humanism, Education, and Scholarship

PETER MACK

This chapter is concerned with the ways in which English students obtained access to classical texts, learned how to read them, and began to imitate them. It will describe the classical texts taught at school and university. In school the imitation of classical texts would have taken place in Latin (and occasionally in Greek); in later life mainly in the vernacular, though some English writers continued to express themselves in Latin and (to a lesser extent) Greek throughout the seventeenth century. As the rest of this volume will show, the study of classical literature was an important basis for every kind of writing in this period.

English writers of the late sixteenth and early seventeenth centuries first met classical texts and were first taught how to read them through an educational system that was dominated by humanism. The humanists promoted the study of the legacy of the ancient world. Their activities included recovering old manuscripts and editing classical texts, improving the quality of Latin style and reintroducing the study of the Greek language, writing commentaries on classical texts and amassing knowledge about antiquity, imitating classical pastoral, epic, tragedy, and satire, at first in Latin and later in the vernacular languages, and applying classical rhetoric to modern conditions. Humanism, which originated in Padua in the later thirteenth century, eventually influenced most aspects of Renaissance and early modern culture, including Bible study, theology, philosophy, political thought, law, science, music, and the visual arts.[1] By 1558 the prestige and influence of the humanist movement within England was assured, but English writers continued to compose orations and treatises encouraging the study of classical texts.

I shall begin this chapter by discussing the roots of sixteenth-century English humanism and some of its literary expressions, then I shall look at the texts studied and the techniques of reading and writing taught, first in the grammar school and then in the universities, in the period 1558–1660. Finally I shall say a little about English classical scholarship and editing in the same period.

English Humanism

The previous volume in this series will include chapters on the fifteenth-century origins of English humanism, when scholars had to go to the Continent to learn Greek and acquire a humanist education, and about the growth of humanism in the Henrician period. In the early years of the sixteenth century Erasmus was in touch with several English scholars, was twice (1499–1500, 1509–14) personally in residence in England, and encouraged and assisted John Colet in the foundation of St Paul's School.[2] His inspiration remained central for English humanists in the Elizabethan period. The most important practical step taken in the early sixteenth century, which continued under Elizabeth, was the foundation or re-establishment of town grammar schools, whose statutes required a humanist programme of training.

Erasmus' *De Ratione Studii* is both a manifesto for humanist education and an outline of the subjects and authors to be studied and the methods by which texts should be taught.

> In principle, knowledge as a whole seems to be of two kinds, of things and of words. Knowledge of words comes earlier, but that of things is the more important. But some, the 'uninitiated' as the saying goes, while they hurry on to learn about things, neglect a concern for language and, striving after a false economy, incur a heavy loss. For, since things are learnt only by the sounds we attach to them, a person who is not skilled in the force of language is, of necessity, short-sighted, deluded, and unbalanced in his judgement of things as well.[3]

Erasmus argues, perhaps unrealistically, that the Greek and Latin languages should be studied together ('not only because almost everything worth learning is set forth in these two languages, but in addition because each is so cognate to the other that both can be more quickly assimilated when they are taken in conjunction'[4]). He wants the grammar to be dealt with quickly so that pupils can move on to reading texts.

> For a true ability to speak correctly is best fostered both by conversing and consorting with those who speak correctly and by the habitual reading of the best stylists.[5]

Among Greek writers he specifies Lucian, Demosthenes, Herodotus, Aristophanes, Homer, and Euripides; among the Romans, Terence (or Plautus), Virgil, Horace, Cicero, and Caesar (and perhaps Sallust as well). These writers are enough for learning the languages. For learning about things pupils will need to study Pliny, Macrobius, Athenaeus, Aulus Gellius, Plato, Aristotle, Homer, Ovid, and many other authors. Erasmus gives instructions for the notebooks in which pupils should store the treasures culled from their reading in order to reuse them, for the writing exercises that they should be set, and for the teachers' approach to reading texts with their pupils. After giving an introduction that discusses the reasons for reading the book, the author's life, the genre, the plot, and the metre, the teacher should examine the text in detail, pointing out grammatical stylistic, rhetorical, and ethical issues.

> He should carefully draw their attention to any purple passage, archaism, neologism, Graecism, any obscure or verbose expression, any abrupt or confused order, any etymology, derivation, or composition worth knowing, any point of orthography, figure of speech, or rhetorical passages, or embellishment or corruption. Next he should compare parallel passages in authors, bringing out differences and similarities—what has been imitated, what merely echoed, where the source is different... Finally he should turn to philosophy and skilfully bring out the moral implication of the poets' stories, or employ them as models.[6]

Erasmus' work serves as a model to the English for the characteristic Renaissance genre of the treatise on education, which aims to praise classical education, to set out a (sometimes Utopian) programme of study, and to suggest teaching techniques and exercises. The most famous English example of the genre is Roger Ascham's *The Scholemaster*, published posthumously and unfinished from his papers in 1570. Ascham's debt to Erasmus' *De Ratione Studii* is made obvious when he addresses the question of the relation between words and things with which Erasmus had begun his treatise.

> You know not, what hurt you do to learning, that care not for words, but for matter, and so make a divorce betwixt the tongue and the heart. For mark all ages: look upon the whole course of both the Greek and Latin tongue, and you shall surely find, that, when apt and good words began to be neglected, and properties of those two tongues to be confounded, than also began ill deeds to spring: strange matters to oppress good orders, new and fond opinions to strive with old and true doctrine, first in Philosophy: and after in Religion.[7]

Ascham's preface announces 'three special points' to which he has paid 'earnest respect' throughout the work: 'truth of religion, honesty in living, [and] right order in learning'.[8] He emphasizes a humane approach to teaching, seeking interest and enthusiasm rather than coercion and fear. He gives strong reasons for preferring that pupils should rather be 'allured to learning by gentleness and love, than compelled to learning by beating and fear'.[9]

Ascham directs that pupils should begin with the basic grammar, which they should learn rapidly so that they can move on to exercise their knowledge of the language by reading Cicero's simpler letters, collected by the Strasbourg humanist and schoolmaster Johann Sturm (1507–89). After the master and pupil have together construed the Latin text into English orally several times, the pupil must make his own written translation of the Latin. After checking the translation, the master should take away the Latin text and after about an hour ask the pupil to translate his own

English version back into Latin. The pupil's version can then be compared with Cicero's original in order to bring out ways of improving the pupil's Latin. For Ascham the rules of concord are best taught and reinforced through examples.

Using the same method of 'good understanding the matter, plain construing, diligent parsing, daily translating, cheerful admonishing, and heedful amending of faults, never leaving behind just praise for well doing', the master should turn next to a good portion of a comedy by Terence.[10] As well as their Latin texts, pupils should have three exercise books: one for their English translations of their Latin texts, a second for their Latin translations of their English, and a third to gather notable points about the texts they have read under six headings: literal (*proprium*), metaphorical, synonyms, distinctions between related terms, contraries, and phrases. This notation applied to the letters and later to some of Cicero's orations 'shall work such a right choice of words, so straight a framing of sentences, such a true judgement, both to write skilfully, and speak wittily, as wise men shall both praise and marvel at'.[11]

The next stage involves a gradual extension of the reading matter, continuing with daily translation but construing and parsing only where the pupils seem not to understand, to Cicero's *De Amicitia* and his long letter to his brother Quintus, to Terence and Plautus, and to Caesar's *Commentaries* and selected speeches from Livy's history. The teacher may translate into English some passages from Cicero that the pupil has not seen, in order for the pupils to turn it back into Latin.[12] Or the teacher may write an English letter or an English version of one of the *progymnasmata* exercises for the pupil to translate into Latin. Ascham commends the technique of double translation, which he later extends also to Greek, as the most effective way of teaching the classical languages. Following his mentor Sturm, he also gives great importance to imitation and in particular to studying the use that Roman authors made of Greek texts, noting what is retained, what omitted, what added, what reduced, what changed in order and what altered in words, sentence structure, or substance.[13] Throughout the work Ascham emphasizes the benefit of teaching the rules of language, argument, and expression through the study of examples.[14] Ascham takes a passionate interest in promoting the best ways of teaching children Latin and Greek. He believes that a really sound understanding of both languages and a reading of their best writers will contribute effectively to strong morality, wide learning, and the promulgation of true religion.

Ascham's *The Scholemaster* can be linked both to treatises on the behaviour and education of the elite, such as Castiglione's *The Courtier* (1528), translated into English by Sir Thomas Hoby in 1561 (and into Latin in 1571 by the Englishman Bartholomew Clerke),[15] and Sir Thomas Elyot's *The Book Named the Governor* (1531) and to more detailed treatises on the syllabus and methods of grammar-school teaching, such as John Brinsley's *Ludus Literarius* (1612) and Charles Hoole's *A New Discovery of the Old Art of Teaching Schoole* (1660), which I shall use in my discussion of grammar schools in the next section. John Milton's tractate *Of Education* (1644) rejects the organization and ordering of education in his day but shares many of the same presumptions. The aim of education is to acquire knowledge and love of God and to fit a man 'to perform justly, skilfully and magnanimously all the offices, both private and public, of peace and war'.[16] Education will necessarily begin with 'the languages of those people who have at any time been most industrious after wisdom'[17]—that is to say, primarily Latin and Greek. But the languages should be learned as quickly as possible so that the pupils can progress to matter (always learned, in humanist fashion from the study of classical texts): agriculture, Greek, arithmetic, geometry, astronomy, geography, physics, fortification, architecture, meteorology, plants, living creatures, anatomy, medicine. Then they will study poetry, ethics, scripture, Italian, politics, and history. Only at the end of the course will they learn about logic, rhetoric, and poetics, so that they can effectively communicate the knowledge they have.[18]

The Grammar School

The Elizabethan grammar-school syllabus had three main elements.[19] The first years are given over to learning how to read, write, and speak Latin. Pupils begin by learning the rules of Latin grammar, which they practise by learning and imitating elementary texts and dialogues, such as *Cato's Distichs*, the *Sententiae Pueriles*,[20] a Latin version of Aesop's *Fables*, dialogues by Erasmus and Castalio, and poems by Mancini and Mantuan.[21] Several of these elementary texts have a strong Christian orientation, and all the statutes of grammar schools refer to prayers and churchgoing as essential components of the programme. The later years are devoted to a fairly consistent course in Latin literature: Cicero's *Epistles*, Terence, Virgil's *Eclogues* and *Aeneid* (and sometimes the *Georgics* as well), Cicero's *De Amicitia*, *De Senectute*, and *De Officiis*, Caesar or Sallust, Ovid (usually *Tristia* and *Metamorphoses*), and Horace. In the third place, the syllabi and the educational theorists propose a series of writing exercises to be practised by the students. Composition of these forms of writing is supported by analysis and imitation of Latin authors and by three handbooks: a letter-writing manual, Aphthonius' *Progymnasmata*, and Erasmus' *De Copia*. While some of the statutes are probably too ambitious in the list of texts proposed for pupils' reading (perhaps because the documents were partly intended to reassure the wealthy people or corporations endowing a particular school that they would be getting value for money), it does seem that schools in or near London (such as Westminster, St Paul's, and Harrow) may have studied Greek and a wider range of texts, including Cicero's *Orations*, *Tusculan Disputations*, and/or *De Natura Deorum*, Livy, Isocrates, Demosthenes, and Hesiod.[22]

An example of the more ambitious type of syllabus from the seventeenth century is the 'Conjectured Curriculum of St Paul's School 1618–25', which D. L. Clark derived from a Trinity College Cambridge manuscript. The school is divided into eight classes. Pupils would know how to read and write before they entered the school aged about 7. Successful pupils would enter one of the universities at 15 or 16.

1. Latin Grammar. Read *Sententiae Pueriles* and Lily, *Carmen de Moribus*.
2. Latin Grammar. Read *Cato's Distichs* and Latin translation of Aesop.
3. Latin Grammar. Read Erasmus, *Colloquia* and portions of Terence, for colloquial Latin, and Ovid, *Tristia*, for poetry.
4. Latin Grammar. Read Ovid, *Heroides* and *Metamorphoses* (and perhaps other elegiac poets), and Caesar and perhaps Justin for history.
5. Begin Greek Grammar, and continue with some review of Latin Grammar. Read Sallust for history and Virgil, *Eclogues*.
6. Greek Grammar and the Greek New Testament. Begin Cicero (*Epistles* and *De Officiis*), continue Virgil (*Aeneid*), and perhaps take up Martial.
7. Greek Grammar. Read selection of Greek poets (including perhaps Hesiod, Theognis, Pindar and Theocritus), Cicero, *Orations* and Horace.
8. Hebrew Grammar and Psalms. Read Homer, Euripides, Isocrates (and perhaps Demosthenes), Persius and Juvenal.[23]

One might compare this list with the one that Hoole gives at the end of his work for the programme at Rotherham Grammar School before he began to teach there in 1636, which he tells us was 'the same that most Schoolmasters yet use', in 1659.[24] There are nine classes and the entry expectations are the same as at St Paul's.

1. Learn accidents of Latin Grammar by heart and begin learning the rules.
2. Repeat the accidents; learn the rules in *Propria quae Maribus* and read and exercise in *Sententiae Pueriles*.
3. Repetition of Latin Grammar and syntax; read *Cato's Distichs* and Latin translation of Aesop.
4. More repetitions of rules of syntax, grammatical figures, and prosody. Read Terence and Mantuan.
5. Latin Grammar and begin Greek Grammar. Begin Rhetoric with Butler, *Rhetorica*. Read Ovid, *Metamorphoses*, Cicero, *De Officiis*, and selections from Latin poetry in the anthology *Flores Poetarum*.
6. Greek Grammar and Greek New Testament, Virgil and Cicero's *Orations*. Translate from Greek into Latin.
7. Greek Grammar. Read Isocrates, Horace and Seneca's *Tragedies*.
8. Greek Grammar. Hesiod, Juvenal, Persius.
9. Begin Hebrew Grammar. Read Homer and 'some comical author'.

In comparison with the sixteenth-century syllabi, neither of these gives such a prominent place to Cicero's letters (though there are other reasons for thinking that the easier letters did continue to be used as elementary readers, as Sturm and Ascham insisted), both give far more emphasis to Greek and even begin Hebrew. It seems that, while Greek may have been wished for in the earlier statutes and actually taught only in the larger centres, as the pool of Greek teachers grew it was taught more frequently throughout the country, not least because it gave access to the original text of the New Testament. The course that Hoole himself taught from 1636 and argued for in his book was much more ambitious in terms of the number of authors to be studied. Hoole thought that it was very important to move students on as quickly as possible from the rote learning of the grammar rules to the appreciation of their practical use by the best authors.

1. Latin Grammar (Lily). Latin vocabulary (*Orbis Pictus*), *Sententiae Pueriles*. Lords' Prayer, Creed, and ten commandments in Latin and English.
2. Latin Grammar. Rules of *Propria quae Maribus*, Cato's *Distichs*, Corderius' *Dialogues*.
3. Latin syntax. Prosody. Latin New Testament and English Bible. Latin translation of Aesop, *Janua Linguarum*.[25] More dialogues (Erasmus, Castalio), Mantuan, Latin catechism.
4. Latin Grammar. Rules of rhetoric. Begin Greek Grammar. Latin New Testament. Terence. Cicero, *Epistles*, Ovid, *Tristia*, *Metamorphoses*. Double translation (into English and back to Latin).
5. Latin Grammar and Greek Grammar (Camden). *Elementa Rhetorices*. Aphthonius, Isocrates, Theognis, Justin's *History*, Caesar's *Commentaries*, Virgil, Aesop (in Greek), Themes.
6. Begin Hebrew Grammar (Buxtorf's *Epitome*). Revise Latin and Greek Grammar. Hesiod, Homer, Pindar, Lycophron, Horace, Juvenal, Persius, Lucan, Seneca's *Tragedies*, Lucian, Cicero's *Orations*, Pliny's *Panegyrics*, Quintilian's *Declamations*, Goodwin's *Antiquities*. Themes, orations and declamations in Latin and Greek. Verse composition.[26]

Hoole is most concerned to improve on his predecessors in trying to make his pupils always understand what they are doing and why they are doing it. He finds rote-learning backed up by threats wasteful and ineffective. Instead he wants to engage the interest and intelligence of his pupils—for example, by always giving them an overview of the material they need to learn and dividing it into groups so that they can understand the progress they are making. Like Brinsley, as we shall see, he thinks that pupils can be helped to understand the usefulness of particular expressions and the meaning of texts through systematic questioning and dialogue.

Hoole makes much more open use of English in his teaching than earlier theorists of the grammar school. Among the earliest readers he proposes in both classical languages are religious texts that the pupils will already know well in English. When he introduces pupils to Latin poetry he also sets them to read English poets, such as George Herbert, Quarles, and Sandys's translation of Ovid so that they can get a feeling for the effect of poetry through their native language.[27] He advises pupils to translate portions of Ovid's *Metamorphoses* into English prose, to ornament the English version with epithets, phrases, sayings, and proverbs and then translate their elaborated English version back into Latin prose in order to exercise their powers of amplification and come to grips with the differences between Latin prose and poetry.[28] Then they can try to turn the Latin prose back into English verse. As in other grammar schools, Hoole gave an important place to reading Scripture in English and to the pupils repeating on Monday different types of material garnered from the English sermon they had heard in church on Sunday.[29]

Hoole encourages the pupils to read a much wider range of authors than earlier schools had attempted, particularly in the sixth form. This is especially apparent in the lists of classical and subsidiary (this latter class includes both reference works and additional primary reading) books ('A note of School Authors, most proper for every Form of Scholars in a Grammar-School'), which he provides for all classes immediately after his preface.[30] He notices this as a possible criticism and responds to it with three arguments:

> 1. That I have to deal with children who are delighted and refreshed with variety of books, as well as of sports, and meats.
> 2. That a Schoolmaster's aim being to teach them Languages, and Oratory, and Poetry, as well as Grammar, he must necessarily employ them in many Books which tend thereunto.
> 3. That the classical Authors are the same with other Schools, and Subsidiaries may be provided at a common charge as I shall afterwards show.[31]

Hoole evidently sees one part of the criticism here as related to the number of books that a pupil would be expected to buy. His response suggests that the subsidiary books would be bought collectively by the class for common use. Other references indicate that, as was probably the case in other grammar schools, several of the books would be read only in part. For example, he tells us that for Homer two books taken either from the *Iliad* or the *Odyssey* should be sufficient.[32] His instructions for reading Virgil include taking the *Eclogues* in small sections at first, then whole poems at a time, but 'after they have passed the *Georgics* by the Master's help, he may leave them to read the *Aeneid* by themselves, having Cerda or Servius at hand to resolve them in places more difficult for them to construe'.[33]

The idea that pupils should taste a range of authors in order to put them in a position to read more thoroughly on their own is also evident in the instructions that he gives for the private teaching of 'young gentlemen' who need to make progress especially quickly. After a brief tour of the accidents and the rules of concord, the pupil moves on to the Latin New Testament, read with the help of the English Bible, Corderius' dialogues, the *Janua Latinae Linguae*, for sentences and vocabulary, Aesop's *Fables*, and Terence.[34]

> After he is once Master of his style, he will be pretty well able for any Latin book, of which I allow him to take his choice. Whether he will read Tully [Cicero], Pliny, Seneca, or Lipsius for Epistles; Justin, Sallust, Lucius Florus or Caesar for History; Virgil, Ovid,

> Lucan, or Horace for Poetry. And when I see he can read these understandingly, I judge him able to peruse any Latin author of himself, by the help of Cooper's Dictionary, and good commentators or Scholiasts.[35]

Hoole points out that all these authors are available in English, as well as Livy, Pliny's *Natural History*, and Tacitus. He suggests that these private pupils should use the English translation to help them with the Latin, though he still wants them to make translations of their own from time to time.[36] Hoole also seems very concerned that pupils should have a wide range of knowledge in mythology and ancient history in order to have a store of examples to use in their own compositions.

Hoole finds a place for rhetoric in his scheme. This chiefly involves learning the tropes and figures, first from a grammar book and later from a Ramist rhetoric.[37] He also mentions the importance of practising letter-writing, exercising the pupils using Aphthonius' *Progymnasmata* and, as we have seen, giving them exercises in amplification.[38] Unlike sixteenth-century statutes and teaching manuals, Hoole makes no reference to Erasmus' *De Copia*.

Like other seventeenth-century plans of study, Hoole's *New Discovery* finds an important place for Greek and seeks to begin the teaching of Hebrew. Hoole lays particular stress on Hebrew, pointing out that, while some defer Hebrew to the university, 'I may say it is rarely attained there by any that have not gotten (at least) the rudiments of it before hand, at a Grammar School'.[39] As we shall see, the universities in the seventeenth century seem to have expected that a good part of the study of Aristotle would be based on the Greek text (where the Latin Aristotle was more usual in the sixteenth century), which in turn depends on a good proportion of the pupils knowing Greek from school. Hoole even makes reference to the teaching of Arabic and other oriental tongues at Westminster school, though he does not himself attempt this.[40]

Teaching Latin Literature

Latin literature was taught for the instructional matter it contained, as a model of writing for imitation, and in order to improve pupils' ability to use Latin vocabulary and grammar. In the earlier classical texts, usually Cicero's letters and Terence, pupils were expected to analyse sentences word by word. With the later texts and with abler pupils, grammatical analysis focused on difficult passages. The reading of classical texts was also expected to provide subject matter, vocabulary, and models for Latin speaking and written composition. Terence was chosen for the purity of his use of Latin and for the applicability of many of his phrases to everyday situations, as well as for the delightful perceptiveness of his observation of character.[41] Cicero's letters exhibited the most admired Latin stylist writing an everyday form of composition ideal for the pupils' imitation.

The educational theorists agreed on the broad pattern for the teaching of classical texts. The teacher should begin by giving a general introduction to the author, the genre of writing, and the work to be studied. The text should be read in Latin and its meaning explained, either by Latin paraphrase or by translation.[42] The teacher should then discuss some of the following: difficult or unusual words, historical or cultural issues, questions of style, parallels with other texts. In his instructions for reading, which were included in Lily's *Brevissima Institutio*, Erasmus suggested that pupils should read texts four times: at first straight through to catch the general meaning; then word by word sorting out vocabulary and constructions; thirdly for rhetoric, picking out figures, elegant expressions, *sententiae*, proverbs, histories, fables, and comparisons; and finally ethically, noting exemplary stories and moral teaching.[43] Cardinal Wolsey's statutes for Ipswich grammar school outlined a very similar method of teaching classical Latin texts.[44]

Given that the volume of space required for some texts (such as Virgil's works or Ovid's *Metamorphoses*) leaves the commentator with space only for an introduction and marginal notes, Erasmus' and Wolsey's instructions are broadly consistent with the generality of Renaissance commentaries on classical texts. Most of the commentaries on longer texts include arguments, which provide a summary in advance to each section of a work. This is consistent with the educational theorists' requirement that the pupils should understand the context within which they are parsing, paraphrasing, and annotating difficulties. To some extent these sectional summaries counteract the tendency to fragmentation implicit in the emphasis on the analysis and recording of individual sentences.[45] In his chapter on construing extempore, to which he often cross-refers as his model of commentary, Brinsley outlines the manner in which his pupils should approach a text for which they have no commentary to hand.

> 2 Where they have no help but the bare author and that they must construe wholly of themselves, call upon them oft to labour to understand and keep in fresh memory the argument, matter and drift of the place which they are to construe…
>
> 3 To consider well of all the circumstances of each place, which are comprehended most of them in this plain verse:
>
> *Quis, quid, cui, causa, locus, quo tempore, prima sequela.*
>
> That is, who speaks in that place, what he speaks, to whom he speaks, upon what occasion he speakes, or to what end, where he spake, at what time it was, what went before in the sentences next, what followeth next after…[46]

Brinsley's instructions focus on understanding the author's vocabulary and constructions, but he believes that the best aid to construing is an awareness of the local and general context of a passage. Brinsley urges his pupils to explore local context in terms of speaker, audience, purpose, and occasion. He asks not for the technical rhetoric of a labelling of verbal patterns but for an approach to the text as embedded in the relation between speaker, audience, purpose, and occasion that is rhetorical in the broader sense. Hoole agrees with Brinsley on the importance of context in construing sentences and on the usefulness of his seven questions in establishing context.[47] In their reading of more advanced texts, such as Terence and Ovid's *Metamorphoses*, pupils are expected to collect useful words and phrases, to construe grammatically, to observe examples of tropes and figures, derivations and differences, and to make use of the narratives in their own compositions.[48] He suggests that Terence offers the teacher very good opportunities for discussing 'decorum of both things and words, and how fitting both they are for such persons to do or speak, as are there represented, and upon such occasions as they did and spoke them'.[49] He gives examples of comments on *Andria* that draw moral lessons from the play. The words of the speeches will provide them with material that they can enlarge upon in their own compositions. Finally he suggests that some of the scenes should be acted out by the pupils, to give them practice in pronunciation and gesture. 'This acting of a piece of a comedy, or a colloquy sometimes, will be an excellent means to prepare them to pronounce orations with a grace.'[50]

Composition Exercises

The principal forms of written Latin composition practised in the grammar school were letters and themes (essays on moral topics).[51] One or two syllabi specify declamation as a grammar-school exercise, but Brinsley finds it more suitable for universities or for the very best pupils.[52] According to Kempe, letter-writing was initially taught through varying phrases from some of the simpler letters from book 14 of Cicero's *Ad Familiares*.[53] Later, pupils would be instructed to write letters either within realistic schoolboy situations like those presented in the dialogues, or within situations arising from their reading of classical texts, where the words of their author would provide the main material. Thus the free space of the letter would be filled with matter extracted from reading. Imitation would be assisted by the study of a letter-writing manual. Several of the syllabuses specify textbooks that the pupils should read to assist in composition, most frequently Erasmus' *De Conscribendis Epistolis* for letters, Aphthonius' *Progymnasmata* for themes and other composition exercises, and Erasmus' *De Copia* for facility and style more generally. Since these three works were also several times printed in England in the sixteenth century, it is reasonable to assume that they were fairly widely used.

Aphthonius' *Progymnasmata* is a fourth-century Greek group of writing exercises that were usually presented to Renaissance schoolboys in a Latin translation by Rudolph Agricola, with commentary and additional examples chosen by Reinhard Lorichius.[54] The *Progymnasmata* provides a graded sequence of fourteen exercises in composition, beginning with the fable (which consists of a story with a moral attached) and building up to the proposal for a law (a set of arguments in favour of a new law and a refutation of objections).[55] The exercises make use of the early reading material (fables, moral sentences) and add different materials and forms (description, speech for a character) that can later be incorporated in larger compositions.

Aphthonius comes closest to the theme in the thesis, his penultimate exercise. The thesis is defined as an enquiry, investigating an issue through speech. It is divided into civil (concerning active life or city business) and contemplative (concerned with the mind). It consists of a preface, urging or praising a particular course of action, a narration of what is involved, arguments from the legitimate, the just, the useful, and the possible, a series of brief objections answered fully, and a conclusion.[56] The thesis builds on parts of the earlier exercise of the commonplace,[57] but adds the refutation of objections, thus moving in the direction of the full four-part oration. Like Aphthonius' other exercises, it serves as a preparation for topical invention.[58]

English writers treated the theme as an advanced exercise with a fixed structure. Christopher Johnson, the master at Winchester in the 1560s, taught the theme as a combination of *sententia*, developed commonplace, and proof.[59] Brinsley expected pupils to follow the structure of the classical oration (*exordium*, narration, arguments in favour, refutation of opposing arguments, and conclusion).[60] Hoole's instructions on writing themes focus on the need for the pupils to provide themselves with adequate material. He urges them to compile commonplace books from their reading, collecting short histories, fables, proverbs, emblems, laws, witty sentences, rhetorical embellishments, and descriptions. He suggests classical texts that will provide material under each of these headings. Once the subject of the theme has been announced, pupils should search their commonplace books according to the theme's key words. The teacher should ensure that each pupil has adequate collections of material and should then provide models for structure (which may be drawn from Aphthonius) and imitation. The pupils should be encouraged to compete in writing each section of the theme, first in English and then in Latin. His instructions suggest that he prefers themes to follow the structure of the classical oration.[61] Ralph Johnson, writing later in the seventeenth century, provided an equally firm and slightly different structure in which the refutation is dropped and the topics of the arguments in favour are specified (*exordium*, narration, cause, contrary, comparison, example, testimony, conclusion).[62] The third to seventh sections of this structure, derived from the topics of invention, draw on Aphthonius' exercises.

Universities

Oxford and Cambridge were of central importance to national life in the sixteenth and seventeenth centuries. A relatively high proportion of the male population (around 1.6 per cent in the later decades of the sixteenth century), including most of the elite, were educated there, sons of prosperous husbandmen and yeomen, burgesses from the towns, country gentlemen, professional men, and the lower ranks of the titled. McConica's analysis of Oxford matriculation records for the late sixteenth century suggests that almost half the entrants belonged to the gentry.[63] His study of the records of Corpus Christi College, Oxford, shows that university graduates went on to become priests, country gentlemen, school teachers, academics, royal servants, doctors, lawyers, and tradesmen.[64] Typically pupils matriculated aged 15 to 16 after completing their grammar-school studies. By 1600 around 44 per cent of matriculants went on to take the Bachelor of Arts degree, in principle four years after matriculation. Many of the others attended university for two or three years, without intending to take a degree; some of this group moved to London to study law at the Inns of Court. Of those who graduated, about 12 per cent went on to take higher degrees, almost all of them in theology.[65]

The monarchs and their counsellors took a personal interest in university affairs. Queen Elizabeth made three formal visitations to her universities, each of which lasted almost a week and required the transfer of the whole machinery of government to Oxford and Cambridge.[66] Under Charles I, William Laud, one of his most trusted advisors and later Archbishop of Canterbury, became Chancellor of the University of Oxford and reformed the statutes of the university. From 1642 to 1646 Charles resided in Oxford and ruled the kingdom from there. The Commonwealth authorities organized three visitations of the university.[67] The national authorities understood very well the importance of the universities in the education of the elite and the maintenance of any religious settlement.

Recent studies of Oxford in the sixteenth and seventeenth centuries by James McConica and Mordechai Feingold have changed our view of university teaching in the period. They have shown that within the colleges, under the supervision of individual tutors, students could pursue a wide range of different and more innovative types of study alongside the traditional requirements of the university statutes, which in the BA degree were principally for rhetoric and Aristotelian logic.[68]

Throughout the period the university statutes require extensive study of rhetoric and logic, together with some moral and natural philosophy. At Cambridge the first of the four years stipulated for the BA degree in the statutes of 1570 was devoted to rhetoric; the set texts were Quintilian, Hermogenes, or any of Cicero's rhetoric manuals or speeches. Rather surprisingly, the statutes specify that the texts should be explained in and translated into English.[69] Two years of the BA are devoted to dialectic. The professor of dialectic is instructed to lecture on Aristotle's *Sophistical Refutations* or Cicero's *Topica*.[70] The nine lecturers (four of them for dialectic) mentioned in the 1560 statutes of Trinity College, Cambridge, were required to teach, respectively: introduction to Greek; Greek literature; Latin (mostly Cicero); mathematics; an introduction to dialectic; Porphyry's *Isagoge* or Aristotle's *Categories* or *De Interpretatione*; *Prior Analytics*, *Posterior Analytics*, or Agricola's *De Inventione Dialectica*; Aristotle's *Topica*; an Aristotelian work on natural philosophy.[71] Some of the expression of this statute suggests that all these works were in fact taught as a cycle of Aristotelian logic, which seems more sensible than treating these texts as alternatives.

In the Oxford Statutes of 1564/5 the grammar course, which lasts for two of the sixteen terms (four per year) of the BA, required Linacre's *Rudiments*, Virgil, Horace, or Cicero's *Epistles*. The four terms for rhetoric were devoted to Aristotle's *Rhetoric* or Cicero's rhetorical works or orations. Five terms are devoted to dialectic, with lectures on Porphyry's *Isagoge* or any book of Aristotle's *Organon*.[72] Sixteenth-century Oxford college statutes stipulate lectures in Humanity (usually involving Latin poetry, history, and rhetoric), Greek, and rhetoric.[73] The Laudian statutes of 1636 provided for lecturers in Grammar (Prisican, Linacre, and selected Latin and Greek authors) and Rhetoric (Aristotle, Cicero, Quintilian, or Hermogenes), which students were expected to attend throughout their first year. The Lecturers in Dialectic (Porphyry's *Isagoge* and Aristotle's *Organon*) and Moral Philosophy (Aristotle's *Ethics*, *Politics*, and *Economics*) addressed the students of the second to fourth years. The lecturer in natural philosophy lectured on Aristotle's *Physics* or *Metaphysics*. The Regius Professor of Greek was to lecture on grammar, propriety of diction, Homer, Demosthenes, and Isocrates to students from the second year until the Master's degree (taken after seven years), while the Regius Professor of Hebrew lectured on grammar and the Bible to students from the fifth to the eighth year, unless they had declared for higher degrees in Medicine or Law. The Camden Professor of History addressed all students after the BA, taken in the fourth year, on Florus and other Roman historians. There were also lectures on Geometry, Astronomy, and Music. As well as attending the required lectures, pupils followed a course of study prescribed by their college tutor and took part in university and college disputations.[74]

The importance of rhetoric in the Elizabethan university is confirmed by the lists of books owned by students who died in residence. Cicero's *Orations* (60 entries in 173 relevant Cambridge lists) and his rhetorical works, especially the pseudo-Ciceronian *Rhetorica ad Herennium* (50 entries) occur very frequently on the lists. Quintilian's *Institutio Oratoria* (37 entries), Cicero's *De Oratore* (19), Aphthonius (18), and Aristotle's *Rhetoric* (28) are less frequent but still found quite often. There are also a reasonable number (16) of entries for Hermogenes.[75] Modern rhetorics listed include Erasmus' *Ecclesiastes* (27), *De Copia* (35), and *De Conscribendis Epistolis* (27), 13 entries for Melanchthon's rhetoric (probably *Elementa Rhetorices*, but one cannot be sure), and 9 for Talon. The great importance of dialectic is also clearly demonstrated with 89 listings of Aristotle's logic (including 34 sets of the complete works), 45 of Agricola's *De Inventione Dialectica*, 30 of dialectic texts by Melancthon, 18 of Caesarius's *Dialectica*, 17 by Ramus, and 12 by Seton, whose textbook was explicitly written to be taught at Cambridge.

English pupils would first read one of the classical textbooks of the whole of rhetoric, such as *Rhetorica ad Herennium* or Quintilian's *Institutio Oratoria*, at university rather than at grammar school. The teaching of rhetoric at the universities was closely connected to the study of classical literature. Those booklists that contain rhetoric texts almost always include a good deal of classical literature. Ralph Cholmondely's Oxford notebook collects quotations from Cicero's orations and philosophical works alongside notes on a lecture course on his *Partitiones Oratoriae*. Each section of the text is summarized as a main question, to which the commentary adds the opinions of classical and Renaissance authorities, including Quintilian, Agricola, Latomus, Strebaeus, and Talon. The commentary includes objections and replies intended to prepare students for disputations on rhetoric.[76] In his Oxford lectures on Aristotle's *Rhetoric* John Rainolds assumes that his audience already has a complete knowledge of classical rhetoric. He considers how much the underlying assumptions of rhetoric, as they are presented in the early chapters of Aristotle's *Rhetoric*, are consistent with a Christian outlook and useful in a modern context. Rainolds devotes a good deal of his commentary to attacking Aristotle's ethical assumptions. For Rainolds, the *honestum* must always be upheld, especially when it conflicts with the expedient. Rainolds finds that Aristotle's arguments are based on worldly appearance rather than on truth. By concentrating on philosophical questions that arise from Aristotle's text, Rainolds discusses rhetoric in a way that suits the exercise of disputation, but he also forces his audience to face the moral question within rhetoric, where the grammar school had taken a more instrumental approach to the effectiveness of proverbs in winning assent for arguments.[77]

Logic textbooks composed for English universities by Seton, Case, and Sanderson emphasize the connections between rhetoric and logic and the way in which the principles of logic can be used in everyday language and to generate texts useful in contemporary situations.[78] McConica shows that, while almost all students in Elizabethan Oxford followed a basis of studies in Latin literature, rhetoric, and dialectic, many of them read widely in history, mathematics, physics, ethics, theology, modern languages, and Greek.[79] The incomplete diary of the Carnsew brothers (Christ Church, 1570s) shows them practising letter-writing, constructing syllogisms, and studying Sturm, Sallust's *Jugurthine War*, *Rhetorica ad Herennium*, Foxe's sermons, Caesar's *Gallic War*, logic textbooks by Valerius, Caesarius, and Melanchthon, Cicero's *De Amicitia*, Aristotle's *Ethics*, Josephus' *Jewish History*, Agricola's *De Inventione Dialectica*, and textbooks of mathematics and astronomy.[80] Feingold argues that the undergraduate curriculum in seventeenth-century Oxford provided students with a grounding in the entire arts and sciences curriculum, partly as a consequence of improvements in the teaching of Greek in grammar schools.[81] Feingold shows that in moral philosophy Oxford tutors always taught Aristotle's *Ethics* and generally also recommended other classical authors such as Cicero, Plutarch, and Seneca, but differed in the modern handbooks they suggested as introductions and commentaries.[82] The Camden Professor of History was required to lecture on Florus' *Epitome*, an abridgement of Roman history up to the wars of Augustus, but generally supplemented that text with information derived from other classical historians and from more recent studies of ancient history.[83]

The central document for Cambridge BA teaching in the seventeenth century is Richard Holdsworth's *Directions for a Student in the Universitie*, which organizes and lists the books to be studied by an undergraduate in the four years of the BA degree.[84]

The student is directed to begin his course by reading and copying out the instructions so as to have a clear idea of what he is trying to achieve and what he needs to read each term (see Table 2.1).

Holdsworth's scheme begins with a strong focus on logic. The morning studies are devoted to the student's philosophical education: logic, ethics, and physics. In each case he begins with an overview of the whole subject, following this up with longer textbooks and then with exercises and disputations. The requirement for a set number of disputations in order to obtain a degree gives additional importance to logic within the syllabus. In the third and fourth years Holdsworth's pupils go back over logic, ethics, physics, and the *parva naturalia*, this time working from Aristotle's Greek text, with the help of commentaries. Holdsworth emphasizes the importance of this phase for both language and learning.

> The reading of Aristotle will not only conduce much to your study of controversy, being read with a commentator, but also help you in Greek, and indeed crown all your other learning, for he can hardly deserve the name of scholar, that is not in some measure acquainted with his works. Gather short memorial notes in Greek out of him, and observe all his terms.[85]

The student's progress through Aristotle's logical and physical works is supplemented with a study of Seneca's *Natural Questions* and Lucretius, read largely for their contribution to philosophical Latin style in preparation for the pupils' round of disputations for graduation and with a summary of theology, intended as preparation for the next stage of their studies.[86]

The student's afternoons are devoted to more literary studies, including a wide survey of Latin writers and a selection of the most important Greek writers. The study of Greek and Latin history, oratory and poetry, is essential, Holdsworth insists.

> Studies not less necessary than the first [i.e. the morning readings], if not more useful, especially Latin, and oratory, without which all other learning though never so eminent, is in a manner void and useless, without those you will be baffled in your disputes, disgraced and vilified in public examinations, laughed at in speeches and declamations. You will never dare to appear in any act of credit in the University, nor must you look for preferment by your learning only. The necessity of this study above the rest is the cause that it is to be continued through all the four years in the afternoons.[87]

Holdsworth gives the strongest possible endorsement of the importance of grammar, rhetoric, and the study of Latin literature in the seventeenth-century university. Laud's statutes had made a very similar point when they insisted on an examination for all students seeking the BA.

> The examination is not to be on philosophical subjects merely, to which limits the narrow learning of the last age was confined, but also matters of philology; and a principal object of inquiry with the examiners will be what facility the several persons have of expressing their thoughts in Latin; for it is our will that no persons shall

Table 2.1. Richard Holdsworth, *Directions for a Student in the Universitie*: books to be studied by an undergraduate in the four years of the BA degree

Term	Morning	Afternoon
Year 1 Term 1	Short System of Logic Larger textbook of Logic	These Directions Goodwin, *Roman Antiquities* Justinus, *Historia*
Year 1 Term 2	Logical Controversies Another Logic textbook	Cicero, *Epistles* Erasmus, *Colloquia* Terence, Cicero, *Epistles*
Year 1 Term 3	Logical Controversies and Disputations	Ross, *Mystagogus Poeticus* (a guide to mythology) Ovid, *Metamorphoses* Greek New Testament
Year 1 Term 4	Brief system of Ethics Longer system of Ethics	Terence Erasmus, *Colloquia* Theognis
Year 2 Term 1	Brief system of Physics Longer system of physics	Latin grammar and Valla, *Elegantiae* Greek grammar and Vigerius on idioms
Year 2 Term 2	Controversies in Logic, Ethics and Physics	Cicero, *De Senectute*, *De Amicitia*, *Tusculan Disputations*, *De Oratore* Aesop's *Fables* in Greek
Year 2 Term 3	Brief system of Metaphysics Longer system of Metaphysics	Florus Sallust Quintus Curtius
Year 2 Term 4	Controversies of all types	Virgil, *Eclogues*, *Georgics* Ovid, *Heroides*, Horace, Martial, Hesiod, Theocritus
Year 3 Term 1	Controversies of all types for the whole year Scaliger, *De Subtilitate*	Caussin, *Eloquentiae Sacrae et Humanae Parallela*
Year 3 Term 2	Aristotle, *Organon*, with the commentary of Brierwood	Cicero, *Orations*
Year 3 Term 3	Aristotle, *Physics*	Demosthenes, *Orations* Strada, *Prolusiones* Turner, *Orations* Quintilian, *Declamations*
Year 3 Term 4	Aristotle, *Ethics*	Juvenal, Persius, Claudian, Virgil, *Aeneid* Homer, *Iliad*
Year 4 Term 1	Seneca, *Natural Questions* Lucretius	Cluverius, *General History* Livy, Suetonius
Year 4 Term 2	Aristotle, *De anima* and *De Coelo* with commentary	Aulus Gellius, Macrobius, *Saturnalia*, Plautus
Year 4 Term 3	Aristotle, *Meteorologia* with commentary	Cicero, *Orations*, *De Officiis*, *De Finibus*
Year 4 Term 4	Wendelin, *Summa of Christian Theology*	Seneca, *Tragedies*, Lucan, Statius, Homer, *Iliad*, *Odyssey*

> be admitted to the bachelorship of arts but those who can with consistency and readiness... express their thoughts in Latin on matters of daily occurrence.[88]

The students begin their classics course with Goodwin's English exposition of Roman antiquities and Justinus' epitome of Pompeius Trogus' universal history in order to acquire a basic knowledge of Roman manners and customs and ancient history, which will help them understand all their classical texts, reducing the need for further commentary. The subsequent emphasis on Cicero's letters, Erasmus, and Terence is intended to gain purity in Latin style. Their reading is meant to be paired with composition exercises in the same genre.[89] The reading of Ovid should be prepared by the study of a compendium of classical mythology and of maps of Greece and the Roman Empire.[90]

Holdsworth emphasizes both the subject matter of the texts, which will provide material to enrich pupils' own compositions, and the benefits that their reading will provide for their Latin style and pronunciation. Where the first year of the literature course had concentrated on the most central authors and the first reading of Greek texts, with the New Testament, the second year provides a very wide diet of Latin literature and history, varied with a little Greek. The fourth term of the second year is given over to a range of poets (Virgil, Ovid, Horace, Martial, Hesiod, Theocritus), who must be read quickly (Holdsworth suggests a fortnight each) and selectively.[91] Holdsworth wants his pupils to be acquainted with a wide range of authors (and he allows that they will enlarge their reading once they have completed the bachelor's degree), but his most important criterion in selection is the help that particular authors will give his pupils in improving their style and in providing materials that they can reuse.

The first half of the second year is given over to rhetoric, for which Holdsworth recommends Nicolas Caussin's immense *Eloquentiae Sacrae et Humanae Parallela*, with its gathering of materials from a range of Greek rhetorical sources, rather than one of the classical rhetoric textbooks.[92] Holdsworth emphasizes the great value of rhetoric for writing, learning, and practical life and also, in true humanist vein, the close connection between logic and rhetoric, either of which he sees as inadequate without the other.

To obtain a degree students had to participate in disputations. A Renaissance disputation often began with a speech by one of the participants (the respondent). The other participant (the opponent) then made an argument against the respondent's view. The respondent repeated the substance of this argument and denied it. The opponent then made another argument that the respondent repeated and replied to, either agreeing or denying the argument (and perhaps giving a reason). The opponent aimed to force the respondent either to agree to the opponent's first argument or to contradict himself. The opponent would often make arguments that appeared irrelevant to the question at issue (but that could later be shown to be connected). The respondent needed to take careful account of the implications of either agreeing or disagreeing with a particular argument. The respondent often distinguished different senses of the words that the opponent put to him, agreeing with them in one implied sense but disagreeing in another. The whole exercise called for great mental and verbal agility on the part of the participants.[93] Disputations between eminent scholars were often staged as intellectual entertainments for important visitors to the university such as the queen and her court. The practice of disputation had a considerable impact on the way in which debates were conducted in the privy council and in parliament.[94]

Holdsworth gives his pupils some helpful advice on the way to prepare for disputations. Once they have mastered the outline of logic or physics, they should discover which questions are usually disputed, such as 'what is logic?' or 'is logic an art?' Then they should examine a range of textbooks and commentaries (he suggests Brierwood, Eustachius, the Coimbra, and Complutensian commentaries on the *Organon* and others) in order to discover the principal arguments that have been made on that question in order to understand the controversy.[95]

> This being done gather the sum and substance of it in your paper-book, as short and clear as you can, which you can do most easily and readily in this method. First set down the state of the question. Then give a reason or 2 why it is held so, and lastly choose 2 or 3 of the principal Arguments from the rest of their answers... This will be enough to make you able to give an account of it upon any occasion, and with a little warning dispute on it.[96]

These documents show very clearly that all students for the bachelor's degree would have studied a wide range of standard literary texts in Latin and Greek, including Virgil, Homer, Cicero, Ovid, Horace, and the New Testament, together with some rhetorical theory (principally Cicero, Quintilian, and Aristotle), and a good deal of logic (including most if not all of Aristotle's *Organon*). Most would also have studied some natural philosophy (based on Aristotle), ethics (Aristotle and Cicero), and history (for example, Florus, Sallust, Suetonius, and Livy). Students would also have read a range of other classical and modern texts depending on their and their tutors' individual interests.

Scholarship and Editing

Historians have generally regarded classical scholarship and editing in England as being largely derivative of, and inferior to, contemporary scholarship on the continent.[97] The best-equipped English scholars devoted themselves to biblical rather than classical scholarship. When Casaubon came to England in 1610, King James directed his interests towards theology.[98] But English scholars possessed very good linguistic skills and excellent access to classical texts. They could produce scholarship of a very high standard, even though they did not generally publish impressive large-scale works and editions. Brink points to the 'intellectual freshness and critical independence' of Thomas Gataker (1574–1654) in his *Adversaria Miscellanea* and praises the philological acumen of John Pearson (1613–86) in his notes on the text of Aeschylus.[99] Feingold draws attention to the high standard of classical scholarship shown by Patrick Young (1584–1652), the royal librarian, Henry Jacob the younger (1608–52), Edmund Chilmead (1610–54), and others. This basic level of scholarship was fundamental to the great achievements of English biblical and theological scholarship in the seventeenth century, notably the King James Translation and the Polyglot Bible.[100]

In the whole period 1558–1660 the great majority of classical and learned texts used in Britain were imported from the Continent, and it appears that continental books were easily and widely available in London.[101] G. J. Toomer cites the example of George Thomason writing to Cardinal Barberini in Rome and offering his help in securing books 'printed in other parts of the world, which I am many times master of. You may remember at your being here we are generally better furnished with books from all parts then is any parte of Christendom besides.'[102] English scholars enjoyed easy access to the most thorough and up-to-date continental commentaries, as we have seen in the references given by Hoole and Holdsworth.[103] There were many notable English private collections of classical texts. Both universities possessed large libraries and many cathedrals and parish churches possessed smaller collections.[104] Even though London lacked a large public library, scholars and general readers could find virtually any classical text they needed.

As a result of Henry Bynneman's patent from the 1570s onwards, the basic classical texts used in schools (such as Virgil, Terence, Horace, and various works of Cicero) began to be printed in England.[105] Initially these were copies of continental editions; later English scholars provided commentaries to the texts. As the list of printings in Table 2.2 demonstrates, the volume of editions of the classical texts used in grammar schools produced in England (usually in London, but sometimes in Oxford or Cambridge) grew considerably in the early decades of the seventeenth century.[106]

The commentaries produced by Englishmen generally reflect the preoccupations of grammar-school teaching. In John Bond's commentary on Horace, the main focus is on imparting basic linguistic knowledge, what a word means, how a construction works. Just like the much briefer Manutius observations that accompany early English editions of Virgil, Bond's aim is to give pupils the means to read Horace for themselves. He gives a few notes on the implications of the words and a few with rhetorical import, noting allegories and metaphors. Usually his glosses are in Latin, but just occasionally he gives an English gloss for clarification. In comparison with earlier school commentaries on Horace, Bond tends to shorten the headnotes, which usually gave a summary of the structure and the moral teaching of the poem. His preface indicates that his main aim is to give readers all the information that will enable them to read Horace for themselves.

> Here kind reader you will certainly find that I have not passed over any word, phrase or sentence which is hard to understand in this whole author without having explicated it,

Table 2.2. English Printings of Selected Classical Authors in Latin and Greek, 1550–1660, from STC and Wing

Authors	Titles and dates of printings
Aphthonius	*Progymnasmata*, 1572, 1575, 1580, 1583, 1594, 1596, 1605, 1611, 1616, 1623, 1631, 1635, 1636, 1650, 1655.
Aristotle	*Ethics*, Latin, 1581, 1590
	Posterior Analytics, Latin, 1594, 1631
	Physics, Latin, 1583
	Poetics, Latin, 1623
	Rhetoric, Greek/Latin, 1619, Hobbes's epitome, 1637
Caesar	1585, 1590, 1601, 1655
'Cato'	*Distichs*, etc, 1553, 1555, 1561, 1562, 1569-70, 1572, 1574, 1577, 1580, 1592, 1598, 1607, 1610, 1620, 1621, 1623, 1625, 1628, 1634, 1639, 1641, 1646, 1651, 1652 (2), 1659.
Cicero	*Philosophical Works* (includes *De Officiis*) 1573, 1574, with Manutius notes 1579, 1584
	De Officiis with annotations of Erasmus, Melanchthon, Latomus, 1587, 1590, 1593, 1594, 1595, 1598, 1604, 1606, 1611, 1614, 1616, 1621, 1623, 1626, 1628, 1629, 1630 (2), 1631, 1633, 1635 (2), 1638, 1639; 1648, 1651, 1660; Latin/English: 1558, 1568, 1574, 1583, 1596
	Tusculan Disputations, 1574, 1577, 1591, 1599, 1615, 1628, 1636
	Epistolae ad Familiares, 1571, 1574, 1575, 1577, 1579, 1581, 1584, 1585, 1590, 1591, 1595, 1602, 1607, 1618, 1625, 1630, 1631, 1634 (2), 1635, 1637, 1640, 1656.
	Orations, 3 vols, 1579–80, 1585; vol. 1, 1587, 1601, 1616; vol. 2, 1596, 1612, 1618, 1636; vol. 3, 1600, 1612
	De Oratore, 1573, 1589
	De Inventione/Rhetorica ad Herennium, 1574, 1579
Florus	1631, 1638 (2), 1650
Homer	*Iliad*, 1591, 1648
Horace	1574, 1578, 1585, 1592, 1602, 1604, 1607; editions with Bond's notes: 1606, 1608, 1611, 1614, 1620, 1630, 1637
Juvenal	Printed with Horace editions prior to Bond, then 1612, 1615, 1620, 1633, 1648, 1656, 1660
Livy	1589
Martial	1615, 1633, 1655
Minor Greek Poets	1635, 1651
Ovid	*Opera Omnia*, 1656
	Metamorphoses, 1570, 1572, 1576, 1582, 1584, 1585, 1589, 1601, 1602, 1612, 1617, 1620, 1628, 1630 (2), 1631, 1633, 1636, 1650, 1660; Farnaby edn, 1636
	Fasti, 1574, 1583, 1614
	Heroides, 1583 (2), 1594, 1602, 1631, 1635 (2), 1649, 1653, 1656, 1658
	Tristia, 1574, 1581, 1583, 1612, 1614, 1638, 1653, 1660
Persius	Printed with Juvenal, and 1614
Quintilian	1629, 1641
Sallust	1569, 1573 (2), 1601, 1615, 1639
Suetonius	No Latin edition before 1661
Tacitus	No Latin edition but 7 edns of English translations of individual works
Terence	1575, 1583, 1585, 1589, 1597, 1611, 1619, 1624, 1627, 1629, 1633 (2), 1635, 1636 (2), 1642, 1647, 1648, 1651, 1654, 1655, 1656
Virgil	1570, 1572, 1576, 1580, 1583, 1584, 1593, 1597, 1602, 1612, 1613, 1616, 1620, 1632, 1634, 1649, 1650(2), 1654, 1657, 1658, Farnaby edn 1634

> explained it or made it easy, as briefly as possible. I have briefly dealt with all regions, states, towns, villages, mountains, valleys, fields, seas, rivers, proper and family names, laws and customs of peoples, unusual forms of words and in short everything which is a little abstruse in Horace in such a way that anyone who is reasonably well-versed in Latin will very easily understand Horace himself.[107]

Thomas Farnaby's edition of Virgil is in many respects more like the continental editions previously used in English schools. He reprints the well-established Latin arguments that set out the structure of the individual poems of the *Eclogues* and the separate books of the longer poems. He explains unfamiliar words and Roman customs and expectations. He glosses proper names, gives Greek parallels, explains what is happening in the narrative and refers to views of other critics. Farnaby makes fewer comments on rhetoric and style.[108]

Bond's and Farnaby's editions are not advanced contributions to classical studies, but they do give an idea of the kind of linguistic, cultural, and rhetorical information that teachers thought that grammar-school students needed in order to understand Latin literature. They contribute to the elementary part of a broader education in reading Latin literature.

At the more advanced level of grammar teaching, R. Francklin published his *Orthotonia seu Tractatus de Tonis in Lingua Graecanica* (1629), which was printed three times up to 1660. Francklin sets out the rules for the inclusion of different types of accent in Greek, giving copious examples both of the general principles and of the exceptions to each rule. The work is thorough and detailed and set out with great clarity. It was probably as useful to students as the author's introduction and the commendatory letters from the Bishop of Lincoln and the Professor of Greek at Cambridge indicate.[109]

English classical scholarship of the early seventeenth century is now famous for two particular contributions: the edition of the works of St John Chrysostom, more complete than any previously published and based on a wide range of manuscripts, supervised by Henry Savile at Eton 1610–12, and the work of John Selden (1584–1654). Selden was primarily a lawyer and a parliamentarian but he produced a wealth of scholarly works, particularly on issues of legal history, English customs, and rabbinical law. His works display an immense knowledge of Latin, Greek, Hebrew, and some acquaintance with Arabic and other near Eastern languages. According to G. J. Toomer, his greatest contribution to classical scholarship was the edition of Arundel's inscriptions, *Marmora Arundelliana* (1628), completed in about a year with the assistance of Patrick Young and Richard Jones. Toomer singles out for praise the edition of the *Marmor Parium*, for which Selden provides transcriptions, a chronological apparatus, and a comparative table of events dated according to different chronologies. 'If we consider this as a whole we must judge it a stupendous achievement. Selden has correctly analysed and laid out the structure of a document of a kind completely unknown before, which is poorly preserved, and has illuminated many of its factual details by adducing other ancient sources.'[110] Toomer also comments on the vast knowledge of classical texts shown and the brilliant emendations to some of them proposed in Selden's *De Diis Syriis* (1617, 1629).[111]

Conclusion

Thanks to the success of early sixteenth-century humanists in reforming and endowing schools, there was a strong emphasis on Latin language and literature in English schools and universities between 1558 and 1660. The grammar-school syllabus made a central group of classical texts (Cicero's letters and *De Officiis*, Terence, Virgil, Horace, Ovid, and Sallust or Caesar) widely known. During the seventeenth century, Greek grammar, the Greek New Testament, Homer, Hesiod and Isocrates were commonly taught in the grammar schools. Virtually all the classical texts were available to English readers in up-to-date editions and with commentaries. English printing of classical texts increased. Rhetoric and logic had a considerable influence on the ways in which texts were taught and understood. University students undertook diverse and often wide-ranging schemes of reading, around a central core of rhetoric, Latin literature, logic, and Aristotle (increasingly studied in Greek in the seventeenth century). English scholars displayed a good range of essential skills and a good standard of knowledge, but, with a few exceptions, their achievements were greater in the field of biblical studies and theology than in classical studies.

Notes

1. On humanism, see R. Sabbadini, *Il metodo degli umanisti* (Florence, 1920); P. O. Kristeller, *Renaissance Thought and its Sources* (New York, 1979); A. Rabil, Jr (ed.), *Renaissance Humanism: Foundations, Forms and Legacy*, 3 vols (Philadelphia, 1988); J. Kraye (ed.), *The Cambridge Companion to Renaissance Humanism* (Cambridge, 1996); R. Witt, *In the Footsteps of the Ancients: The Origins of Humanism from Lovati to Bruni* (Leiden, 2000).
2. C. Augustijn, *Erasmus: His Life, Works and Influence* (Toronto, 1991), 31–3, 35–7.
3. Erasmus, *Opera omnia*, I-2, ed. J.-C. Margolin (Amsterdam, 1971), 113; trans. B. MacGregor, *Collected Works of Erasmus*, 24 (Toronto, 1978), 666.
4. Erasmus, *Opera omnia*, I-2. 114; trans. MacGregor, *Collected Works*, 667.
5. Erasmus, *Opera omnia*, I-2. 115; trans. MacGregor, *Collected Works*, 669.
6. Erasmus, *Opera omnia*, I-2. 137–8; trans. MacGregor, *Collected Works*, 683.
7. R. Ascham, *English Works*, ed. W. A. Wright (Cambridge, 1904) 265.
8. Ascham, *English Works*, 180.
9. Ascham, *English Works*, 197.
10. Ascham, *English Works*, 185.
11. Ascham, *English Works*, 187.
12. Ascham, *English Works*, 238–9.
13. Ascham, *English Works*, 267–8. Sturm, *De imitatione oratoria* (Strasbourg, 1574). Sturm's educational works are helpfully translated in L. W. Spitz and B. S. Tinsley,

Johann Sturm on Education (St Louis, 1995).

14. Ascham, *English Works*, 268–70, 278.
15. B. Clerke, *De Curiali Sive Aulico*. This Latin version was printed six times in England up to 1612, compared to four editions of Hoby's English translation. J. W. Binns, *Intellectual Culture in Elizabethan and Jacobean England* (Leeds, 1990), 258–64.
16. Milton, *On Education*, ed. O. M. Ainsworth (New Haven, 1928), 52, 55; *Prose Works*, 2. 366–7, 378–9.
17. Milton, *On Education*, 52; *Prose Works*, 2. 369.
18. Milton, *On Education*, 56–60; *Prose Works*, 2. 388–406.
19. Since I have written both on the grammar school and on the university in the Elizabethan period in P. Mack, *Elizabethan Rhetoric* (Cambridge, 2002), 11–75, I have tried to complement that treatment by giving more attention to post-1603 documents in this chapter. In some places in the next four sections I repeat what I said there.
20. A selection of short sentences intended to give pupils practice in Latin accidence, syntax, and expression composed by Leonhard Culmann (*c.*1500–61) and widely used in English schools.
21. Dominici Mancini (fl. 1478–91) wrote poems on the four cardinal virtues. Baptista Mantuan (1448–1516) composed eclogues.
22. T. W. Baldwin, *Shakspere's Small Latine and Lesse Greeke*, 2 vols (Urbana, IL, 1944), 1. 122–4, 310, 342–4, 345–51; Mack, *Elizabethan Rhetoric*, 12–14.
23. D. L. Clark, *John Milton at St Paul's School* (New York, 1948), 121.
24. C. Hoole, *A New Discovery of the Old Art of Teaching School* (1660), sigs N7^{r}–8^{v}.
25. This must be William Bathe's *Janua Linguarum*, first published in Salamanca in 1611 but later printed twelve times in England, rather than J. A. Comenius' work, which was printed in England both as *Gate of Tongues Unlocked and Opened* (1631) and as *Janua Linguarum Reserata* (1636), reprinted many times later. See STC 14466–14472.5; 15077.3–15082; Wing 5508A–5521.
26. Hoole, *New Discovery*, sigs A(2)5^{v}–B10^{v}, C4^{r}–5^{r}, D5^{r}, G11^{v}–12^{v}, H11^{v}–12^{r}, I6^{v}–8^{r}.
27. Hoole, *New Discovery*, sigs A(1)10^{v}, G8^{v}.
28. Hoole, *New Discovery*, sig. G10^{v}.
29. Hoole, *New Discovery*, sigs M3^{r}–5^{v}.
30. Hoole, *New Discovery*, sigs A(1)9^{r}–12^{v}.
31. Hoole, *New Discovery*, sig. I9^{r}.
32. Hoole, *New Discovery*, sig. I3^{v}.
33. Hoole, *New Discovery*, sig. H7^{v}. The Jesuit Juan Luis de la Cerda (1558–1643) wrote a lengthy and important commentary on Virgil.
34. Hoole, *New Discovery*, sigs F1^{r}–3^{r}.
35. Hoole, *New Discovery*, sig. F2^{v}.
36. Hoole, *New Discovery*, sig. F1^{v}.
37. Hoole, *New Discovery*, sigs F7^{v}–8^{v}.
38. Hoole, *New Discovery*, sigs G7^{v}, G10^{v}, H3^{v}.
39. Hoole, *New Discovery*, sig. I1^{v}.
40. Hoole, *New Discovery*, sig. I2v–3^{r}.
41. Erasmus, *De Ratione Studii*, in *Opera Omnia*, I-2. 115; Melanchthon, *Enarratio Comoediarum Terentii*, in *Opera Omnia*, ed. C. Bretschneider, *Corpus Reformatorum*, 28 vols (Brunswick, 1834–60), 19, cols 692, 694, 695.
42. John Brinsley's frequent remarks (e.g. *Ludus Literarius* (1612), pp. xxv–vii, 103–21) about the time that the master would save by providing pupils with a printed translation may suggest that translation in class was actually the norm, though it should not be forgotten that this advice also promoted the sale of his own works.
43. Lily, *Brevissima Institutio*, sig. H5^{r-v}. Erasmus, letter 56, in *Opus Epistolarum Erasmi*, ed. P. S. Allen, 1. 171–3; example of *epistola monitoria* in *De Conscribendis Epistolis*, ed. J. C. Margolin, in *Opera Omnia*, I-2. 496–8. This letter had also

formed part of *Familiarum Colloquiorum Formulae*: J. Chomarat, *Grammaire et Rhétorique chez Erasme* (Paris, 1981), 513–16.

44. T. Wolsey, in J. Colet, *Rudimenta Grammatices et Docendi Methodus... Per Thomam Cardinalem* (1529), STC 5542.3 (=25944), sig. A4[r–v], trans. in J. T. Philipps, *A Compendious Way of Teaching Antient and Modern Languages* (1750), 350–1, quoted by T. W. Baldwin, *Shakspere's Five-Act Structure* (Urbana, IL, 1947), 169.
45. A. Grafton and L. Jardine, *From Humanism to the Humanities* (1986), 9–28, 142–57, 181–200; M. T. Crane, *Framing Authority: Sayings, Self and Society in Sixteenth-Century England* (Princeton, 1993); W. Ong, 'Commonplace Rhapsody: Ravisius Textor, Zwinger and Shakespeare', in R. R. Bolgar (ed.), *Classical Influences on European Culture 1500–1700* (Cambridge, 1976), 91–126.
46. Brinsley, *Ludus Literarius*, 123–4. In Brinsley's text, 'quid' in line 7 is omitted, but the following paragraph makes it clear that it is required.
47. Hoole, *New Discovery*, sig. C12[r–v]. Hoole refers to Brinsley's page number here and repeats his error of omitting 'quid' from the Latin list, while including 'what is spoken' in the English explanation.
48. Hoole, *New Discovery*, sigs F10[v]–11[r], G10[r]–[v].
49. Hoole, *New Discovery*, sig. F11[r]–.
50. Hoole, *New Discovery*, sigs F11[v]–G1[r].
51. Baldwin, *Shakspere's Small Latine*, 1. 25, 343, 348–50. At Sandwich the fourth, fifth, and sixth classes were instructed to practise the exercises of Aphthonius: Baldwin, *Shakspere's Small Latine*, 1. 343.
52. Baldwin, *Shakspere's Small Latine*, 1. 349–50; Brinsley, *Ludus Literarius*, 185.
53. W. Kempe, *The Education of Children in Learning* (1588), facsimile reprint in *Four Tudor Books on Education*, ed. R. D. Pepper (Gainesville, FL, 1966), 229–30. Cf. Brinsley, *Ludus Literarius*, p. xiv.
54. Aphthonius, *Progymnasmata*, with the commentary of Lorichius (1575).
55. The full series is: fable, narrative, chreia (an elaboration of a saying or action), proverb, confutation, proof, commonplace, praise, vituperation, comparison, speech for a character (*ethopoeia*), description, thesis, proposal for a law. One of the subtypes of speech for a character is *prosopopeia*, speech for an imagined character, which appears in style manuals as a figure of thought, personification: Aphthonius, *Progymnasmata*, sigs Y8[v]–Z5[v].
56. Aphthonius, *Progymnasmata*, sigs Cc7[r]–Dd7[v].
57. The commonplace, defined as a speech that presents the good or bad that inhere in something ('Locus communis est oratio bona aut mala quae alicui insunt argumentans') consists of: introduction, contrary, exposition, comparison, sententia, digression, exclusion of pity, arguments from the legitimate, the just, the useful and the possible, and conclusion: Aphthonius, *Progymnasmata*, sigs M4[v]–7[v].
58. Aphthonius provides the pupil with a small number of subjects to insert in each particular form. In topical invention the student will have to select from material found through all the topics. See Peter Mack, Chapter 4, this volume.
59. Baldwin, *Shakspere's Small Latine*, 1. 334–6. Ian Michael (*The Teaching of English from the Sixteenth Century to 1870* (Cambridge, 1987), 268–78) has some valuable comments on the teaching of themes; also P. Mack, 'Rhetoric and the Essay', *Rhetoric Society Quarterly* 23/2 (Spring 1993), 41–9.
60. Brinsley, *Ludus Literarius*, 174–9.
61. Hoole, *New Discovery*, sig. H8[r]–10[v].
62. Ralph Johnson, *The Scholar's Guide* (1665; repr. Menston, 1971), 15–16.
63. J. K. McConica (ed.), *A History of the University of Oxford*, vol. 3, *The Collegiate University* (Oxford, 1986), 54–5, 722–3, 728;

L. Stone, 'The Size and Composition of the Oxford Student Body 1580–1909', in Stone (ed.), *The University in Society* (Princeton, 1974), 3–110 (esp. 103); Rosemary O'Day, *Education and Society 1500–1800* (1982), 86–90.

64. McConica (ed.), *Collegiate University*, 728.
65. McConica (ed.), *Collegiate University*, 685, 156.
66. J. G. Nichols (ed.), *The Progresses of Queen Elizabeth*, 3 vols (1823), 1. 149–89, 206–47; 3. 144–67; Penry Williams, 'Church State and University 1558–1603', in McConica (ed.), *Collegiate University*, 397–440; C. E. Mallet, *A History of the University of Oxford*, 3 vols (1924–7), 2. 231–2, 342–6; K. Fincham, 'Oxford and the Early Stuart Polity', in N. Tyacke (ed.), *The History of the University of Oxford*, vol. IV: *Seventeenth Century Oxford* (Oxford, 1997), 179–210.
67. Mallet, *History*, 2. 303–403.
68. McConica (ed.), *Collegiate University*, 1–68, 645–732; M. Feingold, *The Mathematicians' Apprenticeship: Science, Universities and Society in England 1560–1640* (Cambridge, 1984), and M. Feingold, 'The Humanities', in Tyacke (ed.), *The History of the University of Oxford*, vol. IV: *Seventeenth Century Oxford*, 211–448.
69. 'Praelector rhetorices Quintilianum, Hermogenem aut aliquem alium librum oratoriarum Ciceronis. Quos omnes libros vulgari lingua pro captu et intelligentia auditorum explicabit interpretabiturque' (*Documents Relating to the University and Colleges of Cambridge*, 3 vols (1852), 1. 457).
70. *Documents . . . Cambridge*, 1. 457–9.
71. J. B. Mullinger, *The University of Cambridge*, 3 vols (Cambridge, 1873–1911), 2. 595–7.
72. Strickland Gibson (ed.), *Statuta Antiqua Universitatis Oxoniensis* (Oxford, 1931), 389–90.
73. McConica (ed.), *Collegiate University*, 21, 46, 56, 337–8, 342.
74. Mallet, *History*, 2. 321–3.
75. The figure of 173 comes from the pre-1600 Cambridge lists, omitting the booksellers' entries. Elizabeth Leedham-Green, *Books in Cambridge Inventories*, 2 vols (Cambridge, 1986). The Oxford figures are proportionally comparable, but many of the Oxford lists have still to be published.
76. Bodleian Library MS Lat misc e.114, fos 2^{r}–49^{v}.
77. L. D. Green, *John Rainolds's Oxford Lectures on Aristotle's Rhetoric* (Newark, DE 1986), 240–5, 302–4, 348.
78. John Seton, *Dialectica*, with the notes of P. Carter (1572); John Case, *Summa Veterum Interpretum in Universam Dialecticam* (1584), $A4^{v}$, $B1^{r}$, $Kk1^{r-v}$; Robert Sanderson, *Logicae Artis Compendium*, ed. E. J. Ashworth (Bologna, 1985), 243–59, 317–28, Mack, *Elizabethan Rhetoric*, 56–7.
79. McConica (ed.), *Collegiate University*, 695–710.
80. PRO SP46.15 fols 212–20, McConica (ed.), *Collegiate University*, 695–9.
81. Feingold, 'The Humanities', 215–18, 256. He gives examples of booklists and programmes of study illustrating the wide range of classical authors studied at pp. 250–1, 258–60, 323.
82. Feingold, 'The Humanities', 321–5.
83. Feingold, 'The Humanities', 341, 345, 351–3.
84. H. F. Fletcher, *The Intellectual Development of John Milton*, 2 vols (Urbana, IL, 1956–61), 2. 623–55.
85. Fletcher, *Intellectual Development of Milton*, 2. 643.
86. Fletcher, *Intellectual Development of Milton*, 2. 645–6.
87. Fletcher, *Intellectual Development of Milton*, 2. 637.
88. Feingold, 'The Humanities', 215, quoting *Oxford University Statutes*, trans. G. R. M. Ward, 2 vols (1845–51), 1. 65–7.
89. Fletcher, *Intellectual Development of Milton*, 2. 638.

90. Fletcher, *Intellectual Development of Milton*, 2. 639.
91. Fletcher, *Intellectual Development of Milton*, 2. 642.
92. Fletcher, *Intellectual Development of Milton*, 2. 643.
93. Mack, *Elizabethan Rhetoric*, 58–66, 71–3.
94. Mack, *Elizabethan Rhetoric*, 176–252.
95. Fletcher, *Intellectual Development of Milton*, 2. 635–6.
96. Fletcher, *Intellectual Development of Milton*, 2. 636.
97. Binns, *Intellectual Culture in Elizabethan and Jacobean England*, 194; C. O. Brink, *English Classical Scholarship* (Cambridge, 1986), 13–14.
98. Feingold, 'The Humanities', 262–3, 266.
99. Brink, *English Classical Scholarship*, 14–17.
100. Feingold, 'The Humanities', 265–9; N. Barker, 'The Polyglot Bible', in J. Barnard and D. F. McKenzie (eds), *The Cambridge History of the Book in Britain*, vol. 4: *1557–1695* (Cambridge, 2002), 648–51.
101. J. Roberts, 'The Latin Trade', in Barnard and McKenzie (eds), *The Cambridge History of the Book in Britain*, vol. 4: *1557–1695*, 141–73.
102. G. J. Toomer, *John Selden: A Life in Scholarship*, 2 vols (Oxford, 2009), 47–8, citing PRO 31/9/94, 116–17.
103. Hoole, *New Discovery*, sig. H7^{v}, Fletcher, *Intellectual Development*, 2. 635–6. On Renaissance commentaries, see A. Buck and O. Herding (eds), *Der Kommentar in der Renaissance* (Boppard, 1975); A. Moss, *Ovid in Renaissance France* (London, 1982); A. Grafton, 'Renaissance Readers and Ancient Texts: Comments on some Commentaries', *Renaissance Quarterly*, 38 (1985), 615–49; O. Besomi and C. Caruso (eds), *Il commento ai testi* (Basle, 1992); P. Mack, 'Ramus Reading: The Commentaries', *Journal of the Warburg and Courtauld Institutes*, 61 (1998), 111–41; P. Mack, 'Melanchthon's Commentaries on Latin Literature', in G. Frank and K. Meerhoff (eds), *Melanchthon und Europa II* (Stuttgart, 2002), 29–52; M. Pade (ed.), *On Renaissance Commentaries* (Hildesheim, 2005).
104. E. Leedham-Green and D. McKitterick, 'Ownership: Private and Public Libraries', in Barnard and McKenzie (eds), *The Cambridge History of the Book in Britain*, vol. 4: *1557–1695*, 323–38.
105. Thanks to a letter of recommendation from Archbishop Parker in August 1569, Bynneman received a patent in classical school texts, some of which he published himself, while licensing others to other printers. Baldwin, *Shakespere's Small Latine*, 1. 494–531, *STC*, III, app. D, pp. 200–2.
106. The figures also suggest a decline after 1640, but this may also reflect the change in source from STC to Wing.
107. Horace, *Poemata, Scholiis... a Joanne Bond Illustrata* (1611), sigs A4^{v}–5^{r}.
108. Virgil, *Opera. Notis a Thomae Farnabii* (1634). On Farnaby, see R. W. Serjeantson, 'Thomas Farnaby (1575?–1647)', in E. Malone (ed.), *British Rhetoricians and Logicians, 1500–1600, First series*, Dictionary of Literary Biography vol. 236 (Columbia, SC, 2003) 108–16.
109. R.F., *Orthotonia*, 2nd edn (1633), STC 11327, sigs A2^{r}–B1^{v}, B7^{r}–C4^{r}.
110. Toomer, *Selden*, 366.
111. Toomer, *Selden*, 211–12, 256.

CHAPTER 3

The Availability of the Classics

Readers, Writers, Translation, Performance

STUART GILLESPIE

How classical literary works were experienced by the many early modern English authors who responded to them could be said to be the subject of the present volume as a whole, and these experiences were obviously, and happily, various. Yet these experiences also had many starting points and parameters in common, because over the period 1558–1660 in the English-speaking world readers and writers approached ancient works by common routes. The curriculum followed in the English grammar school, for example, guaranteed basic conversance with a number of Latin authors—authors whose prestige was on an altogether higher level than that of any English writer (Latin and much less comprehensively Greek were the only languages taught in most schools). These Latin authors were not the same ones who had enjoyed high status in the Middle Ages. Other new developments over this period, such as the arrival of fresh English translations of ancient authors, or the staging of ancient dramatic texts, are also of great significance for English writers, both reflecting and encouraging the adoption of ancient works for emulation in the present, as opposed to regarding them as inimitable paragons of the past. As Robert Miola puts it: 'Ancient texts in the Renaissance . . . surcharged with humanistic commentary in editions, adapted in Renaissance productions, translations, and plays, are . . . in an important sense contemporary, and, therefore, participants in the same circulation of energy and exchange.'[1] It is with some of these common aspects of the experience of classical works that this chapter is concerned, and the focus will sometimes be on what is known of the experience of particular English writers. But we shall also ask what their early modern experiences did to the ancient texts themselves.

Readers and Writers

With few exceptions, reading begins at school, and the new humanist approach that gradually took over European school education during the sixteenth century led to a period of almost 400 years' duration in which the same basic canon of classical authors underwrote school textbooks and teaching. In England, the curriculum Colet devised for St Paul's School in London was widely adopted and adapted for English grammar schools.[2] And all across Europe, children learned to read in Latin. In Protestant and Catholic countries alike, schools taught Roman rhetoric, moral philosophy, and history to future public servants and churchmen. 'By the end of the 1530s', writes Antony Grafton, 'intellectuals and gentlemen throughout Europe had turned to Rome as enthusiastically as the Romans themselves had once turned to Greece'. But, as Grafton also points out, unlike the Romans seeking communion with Greece, the latter-day Europeans had to recover the cultural ideals they sought from dead institutions, corrupt texts, and a mass of misinformation.[3]

Rome offered a high literature that could be imitated in vernaculars. School training inculcated this habit, and its products would typically pen Ovidian, Virgilian, and Senecan pastiches before composing vernacular epics or tragedies. Sixteenth- and seventeenth-century teachers did not merely tolerate English as an unavoidable evil, or an accidental by-product of Latin learning. It is because humanist teachers were concerned with the quality of the vernacular, even if English did not have its own place in school timetables, that, by teaching Latin and Greek rhetoric as transferable skills, the schools laid the foundations for writing in English from the Tudor era onwards. No school produced more English writers than Westminster, whose curriculum took the learned languages further than most, embracing Hebrew and Arabic, and in the later decades of the sixteenth century combining classical Greek and Latin models when Greek was disappearing from rival schools. Ben Jonson, taught there by William Camden the antiquary, was one beneficiary. Under the later headmastership of Richard Busby (from 1638), translation was evidently accorded a central role. Busby, the most celebrated schoolmaster of his age and something of a legend in his own lifetime, eventually earning the honour of burial in Westminster Abbey, himself compiled excellent Greek and Latin grammars (and an English one too). John Dryden, who attended Westminster School in the 1640s, saw his mature translations as not discontinuous with the exercises he carried out for Busby, recalling in the argument to his version of Persius' Third Satire (1693) that his first attempt on the poem, together with many another 'Thursday night's exercise' from his schooldays, was still in the hands of his 'learned master'. The Westminster curriculum in Dryden's time involved 'exercises in translating English into Latin, Greek into Latin, and Latin into Greek'.[4] The school was admittedly exceptional, and renowned for its classical language teaching; but it was also in itself a cultural powerhouse. Westminster-trained writers and translators of Dryden's and previous generations include William Cartwright, Abraham Cowley, George Herbert, Thomas Randolph, John Studley, and Richard Taverner.

Needless to say, the university-level study to which these men were then promoted deepened their acquaintance with classical literature. Classical authorities were heavily involved in their progress through, say, moral philosophy (Plutarch, Seneca), while their study of classical literature itself (Horace's *Sermones*, say) was an in-depth affair, following time-honoured methods (analysis in turn of 'grammar', 'rhetoric', 'logic'). As for what the key texts were, one well-known mid-seventeenth-century document outlining undergraduate life, the 'rules' of James Duport (later Master of Magdalene College, Cambridge), gives representative guidance, Duport advising students 'to read, among the ancient classical authors, the best, and of the best note as Homer, Aristotle, Virgil, Tully, Seneca, Plutarch, and the like'.[5] Duport, like Dryden, was educated at Westminster and Trinity College, Cambridge. Dryden himself recalled reading the notes on Plutarch in Charles de la Rue's edition in Trinity College library.[6] Dryden's extensive use of classical texts in his own later work (especially as a translator) has been traced in some detail,[7] and, for all his cavils at 'Dutch commentators', it is evident that he availed himself of the learning of the full range of editors and commentators (for editions, see further Peter Mack, Chapter 2, this volume). More unexpected, perhaps, is the mature Dryden's interest in French translations of classics: auction catalogues of the early 1680s show him purchasing French versions of Arrian, Caesar, Cornelius Nepos, Herodotus, Lucan, Lucian, Ovid, Polybius, and Thucydides.[8]

The composition of individual book collections and libraries tells us more about what ancient literature was read—and in what form—beyond the education system. Individuals have diverse tastes and priorities, but certain broad patterns are nevertheless clear. First it should be stressed that overwhelming Latinity is the norm for all private as for all institutional libraries of the early modern period. It could be said that Latin was simply the form in which the world's learning, secular as well as spiritual, was available for access. Furthermore, the importance of reading authors in their original language was an established precept of the age, promulgated in such guides for the middle classes as Henry Peacham's *Compleat Gentleman*, 1622. Peacham's attention to geography, cosmology, geometry, and the liberal arts are all echoed in the contents of the English Renaissance libraries from which records and/or primary materials survive, and again leads naturally to a preponderance of Latin works, though not necessarily to a preponderance of ancient works. The nobility was if anything still more strongly disposed to view Latin as the language of culture, and to look on the vernacular as unworthy. Sir Thomas Bodley called playbooks 'baggage-books' and refused to have them in his library; in general he scorned English-language publications as 'idle books and riff-raffs'.[9]

Hence editions of Latin authors of all kinds, supplemented by editions of non-Latin authors (ancient and modern) translated into Latin, made up the bulk of all Renaissance libraries. And these libraries, we should remember, were normally far more heavily biased towards theology and philosophy, even towards language, grammar, and rhetoric, than anything we should now think of as literature. Both things are true of the book collection belonging to John, Lord Lumley, one of the last of the Elizabethan nobles (*c.*1533–1609).[10] His wealth allowed him to become one of the great Elizabethan collector–patrons, and his library was one of the largest of the era. The 1609 catalogue lists almost 3,000 books, incorporating some inherited collections. Lumley's first wife, Jane (d.1577), was a translator of Euripides (for her work, see Jane Stevenson, Chapter 7, this volume); Lumley himself knew Latin and probably some Greek, French, and Italian. Only 12 per cent of his collection was in a vernacular language, with the other 88 per cent composed of Latin, Greek, and Hebrew books. Since all items in the last two languages were inherited, it is easy to see where his preferences lay. The Lumley library's subject matter embraced theology (36 per cent), history (22 per cent), and science, with good support in philosophy, music, politics, economics, and practical subjects.[11] Literature is there too, but with a heavy bias towards continental neo-Latin material.

We know that literary figures fortunate enough to have possessed sizeable book collections sometimes constitute exceptions to these patterns. Among Ben Jonson's surviving books, almost half the items are what he would have called poetry and poetics, and about half of these are texts of, translations of, or commentaries on Greek and Roman authors. There is only a handful of original works in English, whereas 'it is safe to assume . . . Jonson owned works by every single Greek and Latin poet of any importance whatsoever',[12] 'safe' because he owned so many anthologies. Anthologies and similar collections should not be overlooked as an affordable source of multiple classical texts for private use. Two in Jonson's possession between them covered virtually all extant Greek and Latin poetry respectively: *Poetae Graeci Veteres*, in two volumes with Latin translations (Geneva, 1614), and *Chorus Poetarum* (Lyons, 1616), a heavily Jesuit-censored edition, in Jonson's copy of which many expurgated passages have been reinserted in a minute version of his own hand.[13] Jonson also owned five volumes of *Lampas, Sive Fax Artium Liberalium* (1602–6), a large-scale anthology of Renaissance critical treatises on the ancients.

Jonson's friend Drummond of Hawthornden, the minor poet, had an unusually good command of languages and a special interest in continental verse, but his sizeable working library, collected in the first quarter of the seventeenth century, is also predictably heavy on literature in Latin, with over sixty Greek items too.[14] Of ancient playwrights, for instance, he owned texts of Seneca, Plautus, Terence, and Aristophanes, but no English translations of them are found in his catalogue. In some of these cases no published English version was, to be sure, available at this date. Nor could Drummond have bought a worthwhile English version of, say, Juvenal to match his Latin one. But he chose to rely on Latin texts rather than acquire the recent English Pliny (1601) or Suetonius (1606) translations. He had a Latin Thucydides but no Greek text; for Herodian, Homer, and Polybius, he owned both.

Drummond's library, like Jonson's, nevertheless does reflect some active interest in English translations. He read translations of modern European works much more extensively than translations of ancient authors,[15] but he owned the Marlowe–

Chapman *Hero and Leander* and May's Lucan (he naturally owned a Latin Lucan too). In 1611 he read one of the recent Savile–Grenewey English Tacitus translations (but his library contained a Latin–Italian text of the *Histories* as well). He would have been able to compare more than one translation of the *Aeneid*, since he owned those by Douglas and Stanyhurst, as well as Abraham Fraunce's *Eclogues* and *Georgics*. Similarly, Drummond's library contained both Golding's and Sandys's versions of the *Metamorphoses*.

Comparison between Ovid translations was not quite possible within the library of Robert Burton (the anatomist of melancholy), whose somewhat larger collection of books acquired from 1594 to 1640 contained Thomas Overbury's *Remedia Amoris*, Thomas Underdown's *Ibis*, and Francis Beaumont's retelling of the story of *Salmacis and Hermaphroditus*.[16] While other translations can be found in it (for example, the first edition of Hobbes's Thucydides), Burton's library, like all others of his time, is far richer in Latin than English-language texts. There is, as it happens, no Latin Ovid, but, taking the catalogue pages for the letters A–C, ancient authors printed in the Latin are Achilles Tatius, Apollonius Rhodius, Apuleius, Boethius, Caesar, Catullus, and Quintus Curtius. There are also Greek and/or Latin texts of Anacreon, Aristotle, and Ausonius. For a man whose main concerns lay with modern phenomena and current affairs, and 74 per cent of whose 1,738-book library consisted of items first published in his lifetime,[17] the showing of classical writers is not inconsiderable.

Where 'professional' writers are concerned, of course, the books they used for their trade may sometimes have been borrowed from the collection of a patron or associate. Because of the prohibitive cost of owning the works he used as sources, it is sometimes speculated that Shakespeare had access to Southampton's library. There is no evidence either way. Neither have most writers left behind any direct record of what their reading consisted of, but at least some of it can often be reconstructed inferentially from their works. So it is that a study of *Shakespeare's Books* is able to deal with his direct use as poet and playwright of some 200 authors, of which a sizeable minority are ancient.[18] It is often possible, too, to show that he used the English translations of the day—an especially innovative and stimulating day where ancient literature was concerned. Shakespeare's Plutarch will be mentioned below; for his classicism at large, see Colin Burrow, Chapter 27, this volume.

A look at one further private library, the records of which allow us to follow developments over time, as it is first built up and then moves through succeeding generations of owners, may be worthwhile. Sir Thomas Knyvett of Ashwellthorpe (b. *c.*1539), a Norfolk collector of the Elizabethan era, gathered a library of over 1,400 printed books and at least 70 manuscripts by the time of his death in 1618.[19] In a library intended to encompass most branches of knowledge, some 9 per cent of these books were in English, another 15 per cent in French, Italian, Spanish, or (a handful) Greek. Three-quarters were in Latin. What follows concentrates on the (minority) ancient authors. At first, in the 1560s, Knyvett naturally enough gathered standard works, many probably from the family library: an illustrated Virgil (Venice, 1522) with Servius' commentary; the Hervagius editions of Ovid (Basle, 1550) and Seneca (1557); the Froben edition of Juvenal and Persius (1551) with extensive commentaries; a Boethius of 1498. In the early 1570s he seems to have been establishing himself as a serious collector, acquiring such elaborate items as Beroaldus' Apuleius (Venice, 1516) and Porphyry's commentary on Ptolemy (Basle, 1559). In 1584 Knyvett was searching (unsuccessfully) for a copy of Hesiod's *Works and Days* in Greek. It took him until 1608 to purchase Horapollo's *Hieroglyphica* (Augsburg, 1595) and Thomas Cooper's *Thesaurus Linguae Romanae et Britannicae* (1584). Having developed a special interest in emblems, he found the means to afford Vaenius' *Emblemata* (Antwerp, 1607) accompanying the poems of Horace. The few vernacular translations of ancient authors in his library include the folio of Thomas Nicholls's Thucydides (1550) and Gavin Douglas's *Aeneid* (1553).

Knyvett's collection does much to enlighten us about Elizabethan libraries. The view of ancient literature (and the position it merits) that it reflects is that not of a scholar or an aristocrat, but of a man who read and collected for pleasure. This view is of its time. The collection's next owner, during the difficult decades of the mid-seventeenth century, was Knyvett's grandson (also Thomas, 1595–1658), under whom things took a significant new turn: few books in languages other than English are recorded as arriving. To his grandfather's thinly populated English poetry shelf he added Donne and Herbert. He also added Sandys's Ovid. The following generation's custodianship takes us closer to classical translation: at the start of his adult life Sir John Knyvett (d. 1673) had translated Juvenal,[20] while at its end he willed his copy of Ogilby's English Virgil (1660) to his son-in-law. It is to the translation of ancient authors that we now turn.

Translation

The subject of this section has been glimpsed in the previous one, and also connects with the next, on performance. Like a performance, a translation is only one possible way of representing a text, and, as translators realize, all translations will eventually be succeeded, and probably superseded, by others. In other words, translations, like performances, are of their time. Renaissance English translations use the idioms of the present, not the past, and they have a strong tendency to make ancient authors think in terms of contemporary English scenes and details. In this period translators can adopt aggressively up-to-date or distinctively vernacular language, and replace Greek or Roman with native English cultural practices of all kinds. Some of the characters in Golding's *Metamorphoses* speak with West Country accents, or display a knowledge of English fairy lore.

What follows concerns translation into English, though the translation of Greek texts into Latin is another dimension of how ancient works were becoming available, at least to some classes of reader.[21] That is a reminder of a basic limitation in early modern English translators of classical texts: Greek was to them a language far more remote than the Latin with which they had enjoyed easy familiarity since their schooldays. In translating Homer around 1600, for example, George Chapman would have been reliant on the literal Latin text facing the Greek in his edition. That is, although Chapman liked to pretend otherwise, the words evoked a Latin equivalent before they suggested any cognates or context in Greek. It would be anachronistic to imagine that translating Greek was ever in this period the routine task it was to become in later eras: education simply did not provide for the level of Greek training on offer in Victorian schools. Even those with comparatively good Greek were inclined to use Latin translations to check their understanding. Of the twenty-nine Greek texts found among Ben Jonson's extant library books, only two are unaccompanied by Latin versions.[22] The availability of good French texts of major works by an author such as Plato explains in large part why the anglophone world did not find translation of Plato a pressing need until after 1660.[23]

Up to a quarter of books printed in the Elizabethan era seem to have been translations, and a similar proportion probably applies for the first half of the seventeenth century.[24] In a recent 3,000-item listing of the more literary book-length English translations from all languages recorded as published in the period 1550–1660, some 40 per cent are translations of works originally in Latin. The market for translations from the Latin was sizeable, then. Ancient writings play their part in this statistic, but high numbers of contemporary works, especially on religious and topical subjects, make up the bulk.[25] In this sample, classical and patristic Greek originals account for about 8 per cent to Latin's 40 per cent, but, for the reasons just given, many of these works are Englished via intermediate Latin texts.[26]

What authors and texts were translated? To begin at the most familiar level of classical learning, school texts often included translations alongside selections from beginners' authors such as Aesop and Terence. These unpretentious aids to learning probably reached a wider readership than any other type of translation, with the exception of the Bible. The translations are often in 'grammatical' form—that is, with the English syntax conformed to the Latin for pedagogical purposes. One once-famous compilation by the schoolmaster Nicholas Udall first appeared in 1533: *Flours for Latine Spekynge Selected and Gathered oute of Terence, and the Same Translated into Englysshe*. Another was *The Distichs of Cato*, used in England with the annotations of Erasmus, presented as an aid to Latin language learning in 1540 by Richard Taverner in a bilingual text reprinted in 1553, 1555, and 1562, then supplanted in 1577 by an anonymous version 'newly englished to the comfort of all young scholars', itself reprinted in 1584. 'Cato', as it was called, has been singled out as '*par excellence* the first of schoolbooks, and the elementary moral treatise of the Middle Ages'. This collection of proverbial wisdom and moral precept (authorship unknown, but 3rd or 4th century AD) was edited, augmented, selected, and in time translated into a dozen European vernaculars, 'first as a means to assist in the understanding of the original, or in verse, emulating the Latin in a modern language'.[27] Such compilations, forgotten today, were in use on a massive scale (and their users, we might bear in mind, will have included almost every historically identifiable male in early modern England). First experiences of ancient Latin texts came not in the form of complete works of verse or prose, but from the excerpts in such collections of wit, wisdom, *sententiae*, 'dicta', in which the Latin was often accompanied by more or less literal English translations (other examples would be the proverbs of Publilius Syrus and the *Dicta Sapientum*).[28]

Classical translation was also a growth industry at a more exalted level, for there were many more motives to it than the pedagogical. The result was the arrival of an expanding corpus of English-language classics, sometimes read, it has long been established, by English writers. There was no programme, no state patronage (as for translation in seventeenth-century France), but national pride and the high ambitions entertained for the English language made for a sense of common purpose. Sixteenth-century translators embarked on the vernacularization of Ovid, extending to most of the corpus in published verse translations by 1572; of Horace's *Sermones* and *Ars Poetica*; of Martial and Ausonius; of Seneca's tragedies; of Homer; of Longus, Heliodorus, and Apuleius. The exemplary and informative works of classical historians received much attention: Sallust (translations printed from *c.*1520), Caesar (1530, 1565), Livy (1544, 1570), Thucydides (1550), Herodian (1556), Polybius (1568), Appian (1578), and Tacitus (1591, 1598). For the sixteenth century, literature or 'letters' could also include such authors as Proclus (1550), Euclid (1570), and Vegetius (1572), as well, of course, as moralists such as Epictetus (1567) and orators and rhetoricians such as Isocrates (1534, 1576, 1580) and Demosthenes (1570).[29]

We can glean from many of the prefaces and advertisements to such translations what kind of readership their authors expected, and these expectations varied. Sometimes translators had in mind the young, the unlearned, or the female reader, whereas at others they expect the close scrutiny of scholars. But the question to be asked in the present context is: what did translations offer English writers, at least after their schooling had been completed?[30] This is a far more specialized matter, the usual assumptions about which look distinctly questionable. It is sometimes supposed, for instance, that the principal role of translation in English literary history was to make available for new treatment the 'raw material' ancient texts contained—particularly the narrative materials of history, myth, and fable. In general this is a mistake: English translations were in most cases not required, let alone preferred, for these purposes. School knowledge of Livy served Shakespeare well in *The Rape of Lucrece*, while the fable of the body's members in *Coriolanus* draws on Livy's Latin and, it seems, retellings by Sidney, Erasmus, Camden, and others.[31] Notably, though, the 1600 translation of Livy's history by Philemon Holland is not a confirmed source for Shakespeare; in this case and many others, we look in vain for translations that are decisive in making material available, because the material was already available in other forms within the Latin-soaked culture of the early modern era. In any event, the Renaissance preference was for direct contact with the classics wherever possible. Of the three surviving English plays from the 1600s based on Livian history, respectively by Thomas Heywood (*The Rape of Lucrece*), Heywood with John Webster (*Appius and Virginia*), and John Marston (*Sophonisba*), all use Livy and/or other classical sources (Appian, Dionysius of Halicarnassus) directly. And, although all the playwrights would have been aware of contemporary retellings of the relevant narratives (such as William Painter's), and, given the dates of their work, of Holland's recent translation, they made little, or sometimes no, apparent use of either in preparing their scripts.[32]

It is sometimes supposed, alternatively, that the role of classical translation for English writers in the period was to make available fresh stylistic and formal models. It is true that effects used by translators to approximate Greek or Latin features can become a resource for English poets. Compound epithets ('wine-dark sea'), for instance, often tend to carry a whiff of the Homeric about them, creating a resonance in itself.[33] But it is not necessary to read a translation of Homer to find out what a compound epithet looks like. Some of the potential of blank verse can be worked out because Surrey's partial translation of Virgil shows that iambic pentameter can read more like Latin hexameters if it goes unrhymed.[34] But the role of translation is hardly direct here, and the blank verse writers of the late sixteenth century do not think of Virgil as their model (indeed, the major leap forward for blank verse comes with the inspired idea of using it in the non-Virgilian environment of the stage). Successful metrical innovations are much easier to find in translations from modern literatures (sonnets, *ottava rima*) than classical: indeed, classical translation was sometimes backward-looking in this respect, and the fourteeners of Chapman's Homer, or of the cumbrous complete Seneca of the 1580s, would have been disastrous models for the English verse of the future to follow. The experimental quantitative metres in which so much energy was invested by Thomas Campion and a number of his contemporaries in another type of response to the question of how to translate classical verse were largely a dead end.[35] And the extensive eighteenth-century tradition of the English ode was not launched by early translations of Pindar or Horace, but by the looser imitations of Cowley's *Pindarique Odes* (1656).

It would be wrong to dismiss altogether the claim that translations gave access to narrative material, or helped English writers to adopt and adapt classical forms and styles, but these vague propositions require much refinement and qualification. The classical translations read and used by English writers played a role more diffuse, more subtle, and, it should be underlined, one grounded upon what the translators brought—or added—to their originals. Translators who brought little (such as the authors of textbook trots) seem to have correspondingly little impact on writers. But some translators aimed to bring much. Some of the metaphors they use reveal that translation was seen not just as a stimulus, but, in other moods and contexts, as a form of partnership, or even of dominance (metaphors can include tropes of invasion, colonization, and conquest).[36] Translators who think this way do not see themselves as conduits, as passive intermediaries, but as actively contributing to or even taking charge of the work in question. And what counts for subsequent English writers is not that translators neutrally 'convey' something (often something long familiar and already available in various other forms), but that their particular performance, their unique re-enactment, seems to allow new prospects and possibilities to be glimpsed. This can happen at many levels. Ovid is represented as an English country gentleman (or as a Restoration rake), Theseus as a Tudor monarch, Achilles as a rebellious earl.[37] Some new piece of English phrasing, once it has been used by a translator, is found apt, and begins a new career among English poets—the word 'slippery' to describe the precarious security a courtier's life entails, say.[38]

Golding's Ovid gives us an example of a more thoroughgoing Renaissance Englishing of an ancient text. Golding's wish to enrich his native language was widely shared, but this is by no means normally a matter of creating new, Latinate English words. Again, it is more complicated than that: Golding, like others, preferred to stick to a clearly English idiom. Gordon Braden has shown how in this he went beyond contemporaries such as Thomas Phaer in his *Eneidos* (1558) or John Studely in his *Medea* (1566), in his command of 'quirky, vigorous little terms' such as 'gnorr', 'smudge', or 'chank', and in his readiness to unfold a Latin word into a string of English equivalents: 'hirtus' gives 'harsh and shirle', 'pugnes' becomes 'strive, struggle, wrest and writhe'.[39] And Madeleine Forey has summed up the general transformation of the Ovidian world that Golding effects:

> It is a world of raspberries, hips and haws rather than mountain strawberries, crabs rather than octopuses, lapwings rather than hoopoes. One encounters witches, pucks, elves and fairies not nymphs... Music is provided by pots and pans not clashing cymbals, viols not lyres, and shawms not flutes. The dead are placed in coffins not urns.[40]

It is a matter not of generating new vocabulary or exotic scenery, but of finding a possible English idiom. Whatever reservations we may have today about 'domestication', such a translation as Golding's Ovid constructs a bridge between English and Roman worlds, a route by which writerly use of the ancient text is facilitated.

Or we might consider Plutarch's *Parallel Lives* as an example of the impact of translation. The continental folio editions of the *Lives* in the sixteenth century (in Latin from an early date) were too expensive to be purchased by the ordinary cultivated reader. Instead, the numerous European vernacular versions were, to judge by the publishing record, easily the preferred form in which to acquire the book,[41] but, even so, the *Lives* were not standard reading for most of our era. They were not prescribed in Elyot's *Governor* (1531), nor in Ascham's *Scholemaster* (1570). The *Moralia*, much valued for their wise sayings, were available in convenient selections; the *Lives* not. And the arrival of the French scholar Jacques Amyot's celebrated version in 1559, then of Sir Thomas North's English one of 1579, did not do much to change this position: throughout this period, they too were available solely in expensive folios designed for libraries (whether those of wealthy individuals or of institutions). Thus, although knowledge of Plutarch's narratives was available from various secondary sources, it was not the case that translation unlocked Plutarchan biography for most English readers.

However, one English writer discovered Plutarch through North's translation, and what he discovered was, importantly, what North and his predecessor Amyot had done to Plutarch. Amyot had supplied high-quality scholarship, including many original emendations and interpretations. Amyot tended to expand and explain Plutarch, whom he characterized as writing 'doctement et gravement' rather than 'doucement et facilement'. North, translating from the French and not the Greek, could augment his work by turning Plutarch into a contemporary, deploying a rich Elizabethan idiom and a modern tone, his forceful and picturesque language sometimes replacing less colourful expression in the French. Shakespeare, who seems to have used neither French nor Greek nor Latin texts, approached North's volume with great interest and care, ranging among Plutarch's narratives for supplementary material on characters he was interested in, and combining what he found with knowledge from other sources. It is well known that Shakespeare's use of North goes very far beyond the acquisition of narrative material, at some points extending to taking over and versifying the actual words of the translation, at others to pondering the meaning of values such as 'constancy'. The chronology of Shakespeare's work from *Julius Caesar* onwards suggests, too, that his reading of North's Plutarch induced a fresh interest, after the non-Plutarchan *Titus Andronicus*, in the matter of Rome: that is, Shakespeare's so-called Roman plays might very well not have been written at all were it not for his discovery of this translation. Shakespeare's use of North extends well beyond the four 'Roman plays'. For example, Plutarch's presence has been discerned behind Shakespeare's English histories as a structural model (*Henry V* having 'the structure of a classic Plutarch life'), while Brutus and Portia's marriage leaves its mark on Lady Percy in *Henry IV*.[42] Even Hamlet and Macbeth have been seen as developments of a Shakespearean concern with interiority that began with Brutus in *Julius Caesar*.[43] In a word, it could be argued that North's Plutarch—North's performance of Plutarch—is somewhere close to the centre of Shakespeare's artistic life. Naturally enough, Shakespeare's versions of North—Shakespeare's Cleopatra or Shakespeare's Coriolanus—became the form in which 'Plutarch' was familiar to many of his contemporaries.

Performance

The landmark stage performance of an ancient work in the modern world took place in Rome in the mid-1480s, when students at Pomponius Laetus' academy acted out Seneca's *Hippolytus*—the first public performance of an ancient tragedy for over 1,000 years.[44] Partly inspired by this example, Cambridge colleges began to include performances of comedies by Terence as part of their Christmas festivities as early as 1510–11, while the Henrician court was entertained by the *Menaechmi* in 1526. Classical tragedy in performance in Britain is recorded no earlier than the mid-1540s, when Seneca's *Hippolytus* was staged at Westminster School, but it is probable that examples from preceding decades went unnoted. And, by the mid-sixteenth century, Plautus, Terence, and Seneca were beginning to offer an increasingly popular alternative to the diet of saints' plays and morality cycles that had persisted on the British stage since the Middle Ages. The academic settings of many of these early performances (in Latin and occasionally Greek) indicate the core purpose, for the precepts of Cicero and Quintilian on the education of Roman orators lay behind this acting-out of the very plays that the Roman forebears of Pomponius' students were supposed to have seen.

From these beginnings, the story could be rehearsed of the rediscovery in Britain of at least portions of the classical dramatic corpus through performance—'not through the books of humanist scholars, but on the stages of schools, colleges, inns of court, and royal court, and finally in the public theaters'.[45] But this story has already been told numerous times,[46] and need not, as such, be rehearsed again here. Nor need the particular refractions of ancient drama in the work of individual English dramatists be addressed here, since this is the subject of other chapters in the present volume. What follows deals, instead, with what might be called the infrastructure that performances of classical plays made available to the English stage, including the ways in which these performances constructed the ancient plays. For, just as ancient plays encouraged modern audiences to rethink how they looked at drama, the protagonists of Greek and Roman tragedy and comedy were forced to conform themselves to the staging traditions and moral assumptions of the Renaissance.

This last phenomenon can best be understood through the venues and occasions of performance. The ancient plays were for most of the sixteenth century staged in private rather than public theatres, within such contexts as (in England) Christmas celebrations, court festivals, academic entertainments, or elaborate Arthurian fantasy for the diversion of a monarch. This meant that their contexts tended to involve the affirmation of conservative social values, and the ancient plays were often obliged to fit in with what amounted to a programme of education in moral wisdom and virtuous action. In some cases performances were given directly under royal patronage, as at Westminster School, where Queen Elizabeth required that a Latin play (as well as an English one) be staged every year at Christmas.[47] But they were expected to yield this kind of moral enlightenment when staged in the Inns of Court, too, a notable meeting-point of humanist ideals and real-world priorities. Cicero's own testimony confirmed they could indeed supply it by explaining theatrical experience in rhetorical, moral, and political terms.[48]

As the sixteenth century continued, and as the stagings move from private performances in Latin or Greek to English adaptations in the public theatres, ancient drama took on a new complexion. The romantic contexts and chivalric devices of mid-century English (and European) stagings of comedies had blunted their satirical edge, but eventually satire overtook romance as a priority, and, in the age of Donne and Marston, Aristophanes came into his own. *Plutus*, the play freest of recondite contemporary allusions and obscure Greek idioms, became the late Renaissance favourite, translated into Latin and adapted into other languages.[49] For tragedy, meanwhile, Seneca, by every measure the most prominent ancient tragedian for the Renaissance, seemed readily accommodable to contemporary tastes: he was a moralist whose ethical dilemmas were posed by characters who played the sort of roles medieval drama had made familiar.[50] But, while on the private stage Phaedra or Medea tended to be presented as objects of the audience's moral judgement, the public theatre's classically based tragedy (Shakespeare's *Titus Andronicus*, first performed 1588/93, for example), tended to leave verdicts more open-ended.[51] In a parallel development, the Greek and Latin texts, at first treated respectfully for stage performance, were later cut and augmented, often to achieve a more romantic flavour,[52] then eventually adapted more freely still in their English incarnations, ranging in sophistication from the anonymous farce *Jack Juggler* (written mid-1560s?) to Shakespeare's *Comedy of Errors* (performed *c.*1594), both partly based on Plautus' *Amphitruo*. Significantly, in their transition to the public stage classical comedies were never performed under their own titles: they were seen as a coterie entertainment, and not thought likely to attract popular audiences. All the same, in reworked form their material did attract them, as these examples remind us. There are, too, some indications that knowledge of the Latin and Greek plays extended beyond coteries: what else is to be made of the first scene of Chapman's *The Gentleman Usher* (published 1606), in which Sarpego relives his performance of the title role in *Curculio*, puts on a 'parasite's dress', and quotes several lines of the Latin?[53]

If the assumptions of the early modern era had profound effects on performance of ancient plays, how were early modern conceptions of drama affected by the rediscovered works? Today an imaginative leap is required to realize just how radical are the implications of this question, and what was at stake in the revival of ancient tragedy, in particular, for performance purposes and not just for the study. For Seneca and other tragedians, while available to readers through the Middle Ages, had remained firmly on the page, partly because of offputting misconceptions about ancient theatrical practice (it was thought Seneca had been performed in dumb show while a single speaker declaimed all the lines). Thus the performance at Pomponius' academy came at the end of many centuries wholly ignorant of stage tragedy (whereas comedy had survived as a spectacle in various forms), and it was played in front of an audience whose idea of serious theatre consisted of dramatized Bible stories and other 'sacred drama'. The prologue composed for the printed version had to explain what tragedy was, and why anyone would wish to see such a play.[54] The use of the term 'tragedy' for specifically dramatic as opposed to merely narrative purposes was still consolidating itself in English when our period begins in 1558.

Similarly, it may be hard to grasp just how deeply the nature of English drama in its early modern forms was determined by the all-conquering priority of the rhetorical, and just how crucially the plays of the younger Seneca opened the way to this, at least for tragedy.[55] Thomas Nashe's famous jibe at the Elizabethan playwrights who scanned translations of Seneca for purple passages—'if you entreat him fair . . . he will yield you whole Hamlets, I should say handfuls of tragical speeches'[56]—suggests only one side: hardly less striking is their drive to embrace *sententiae*. All this will be a theme of a later chapter (Gordon Braden, Chapter 16, this volume), but under the present heading it might be stressed that 'rhetorical' is not in this context antithetical to 'dramatic'. Alexander Neville saw his 1563 *Oedipus* translation as a 'tragical and pompous show upon stage',[57] incorporating enhancements of onstage effects while never hesitating to amplify and elaborate moral points to which Seneca himself had apparently failed to give adequate weight.[58]

These are some of the fundamental possibilities opened up to the English stage by the revival of classical drama. Several other major formal items also come under this heading, of which we shall briefly consider the use of five-act structure, ghost scenes, and the revenge motive. Their wide importance dictates their mention here, even though we cannot really say whether it was direct reading or viewing of ancient plays, or more indirect routes of transmission, that drew their possibilities to the attention of English dramatists. Perhaps a better way of describing the connection is to say that English playwrights would have been unlikely to set as much store by these features were it not for classical precedent.

From his schooldays, it has been supposed, the sixteenth-century European dramatist felt the desire, in T. W. Baldwin's words, 'to imitate Terence, not merely in separate sections, but even in the writing of a whole play. When he thought of writing a play, he naturally thought of the one and only correct method, that which the teachers and commentators said was the way of Terence.'[59] This method was the 'five-act formula' into which the ancient grammarians had divided Terence's plays, set out in the Renaissance by Landino and explained by Willich in his 1550 commentary on *Andria*—Act 3 has the 'sequence of perturbations', Act 4 exhibits the 'desperate state of the matter', and so on.[60] Of course, this does not presuppose that English playwrights read Willich or Landino, and, in any case, Terence was not the only possible ancient model for such a structure. It has long been thought that for the public theatre it was Kyd, in his *Spanish Tragedy* (completed in or about 1587), who pioneered the five-act structure, and his immediate classical model in many other respects was Seneca. Whatever the details, however, it is more than a coincidence that five-act plays become standard on the British stage once knowledge of and about ancient drama becomes more widespread.

Kyd's *Spanish Tragedy* happens to supply the other generic classical features to be noted here: ghost scenes and revenge. Again, direct relationships with classical drama are not easy to prove in general terms. Seneca's role, promoted by earlier commentators, has been challenged by those who stress that ghosts are conspicuous in earlier English literature, and personifications of revenge are found in many medieval works.[61] But to argue that the Elizabethan stage ghost derives from *de casibus* tragedy[62] and not Seneca is to assume 'that these traditions are discrete in original formulation and exclusive in subsequent tradition',[63] when this is not the case: a complex interplay of ancient and modern backgrounds is almost inevitably the scenario involved. It is perhaps where individual Renaissance plays are at issue, however, and the use of several classical features together can be evidenced, that the connections become most convincing. *Richard III*, for Harold Brooks, uses Seneca's *Troades* for its chorus of women, Richard's wooing of Anne derives from *Hercules Furens* and *Hippolytus*, and their stichomythia, the gnomic sayings, and the forensic oratory evoke the same ancient author.[64] Shakespeare's play is, of course, also a tragedy of blood in which the bloodshed is (largely) offstage, and revenge, made a most prominent motive, is demanded by ghosts.

Notes

1. Robert S. Miola, *Shakespeare and Classical Comedy* (Oxford, 1994), 15–16.
2. T. W. Baldwin, *William Shakespere's Small Latin and Lesse Greeke*, 2 vols (Urbana, IL, 1944–50), is still a useful guide to this curriculum, but more briefly see Peter Mack, Chapter 2, this volume.
3. A. T. Grafton, 'The Renaissance', in Richard Jenkyns (ed.), *The Legacy of Rome: A New Appraisal* (Oxford, 1992), 97–123 (100).
4. James Anderson Winn, *John Dryden and his World* (New Haven, 1987), 45.
5. Duport's rules survive in two manuscripts, one of them printed (but with many inaccuracies) by G. M. Trevelyan, 'Undergraduate Life under the Protectorate', *Cambridge Review*, 22 May 1943, 328–30.
6. The accuracy of Dryden's memory on this point is, however, questioned by Paul Hammond, 'Dryden and Trinity', *Review of English Studies*, 141 (1985), 35–57 (52).
7. J. McG. Bottkol, 'Dryden's Latin Scholarship', *Modern Philology*, 40 (1942–3), 241–54.
8. T. A. Birrell, 'John Dryden's Purchases at Two Books Auctions, 1680 and 1682', *English Studies*, 42 (1961), 193–217 (196).
9. J. N. L. Myers et al., *The Bodleian Library in the Seventeenth Century* (Oxford, 1951), 12.
10. Sears Jayne and Francis R. Johnston (eds), *The Lumley Library: The Catalogue of 1609* (1956).
11. Percentages from David McPherson, *Ben Jonson's Library and Marginalia: An Annotated Catalogue* (= *Studies in Philology*, 71/5 (1974)), 10; but, because of the difficulties of classifying numerous items, the figures are no more than approximate.
12. McPherson, *Ben Jonson's Library*, 8.
13. McPherson, *Ben Jonson's Library*, 12.
14. Robert H. MacDonald (ed.), *The Library of Drummond of Hawthornden* (Edinburgh, 1971).
15. The list Drummond maintained of his reading in his post-college years 1604–16 is printed by MacDonald in an appendix (*Library*, 228–31).
16. Nicolas K. Kiessling, *The Library of Robert Burton* (Oxford, 1988).
17. Kiessling, *Library*, p. xxxi.
18. Stuart Gillespie, *Shakespeare's Books: A Dictionary of Shakespeare Sources* (2001).
19. Many of the books and almost all the manuscripts have been in Cambridge University Library since 1715. All infor-

mation here is based on D. J. McKitterick, *The Library of Sir Thomas Knyvett of Ashwellthorpe c.1539–1618* (Cambridge, 1978).

20. Stuart Gillespie, 'Two Seventeenth-Century Translations of Two Dark Roman Satires: John Knyvett's Juvenal 1 and J.H.'s *In Eutropium* 1', *Translation and Literature*, 21 (2012), 43–66.
21. For bibliography, see J. W. Binns, 'Latin Translations from Greek in Renaissance England, 1550–1640', *Humanistica Lovaniensia*, 27 (1978), 128–59.
22. McPherson, *Ben Jonson's Library*, 17–18.
23. A comparative table showing dates of translations of each major classical Latin writer into English, French, and other European languages to 1600 is given by R. R. Bolgar, *The Classical Heritage and its Beneficiaries* (Cambridge, 1954), 526–41. This is corrected and supplemented by Holger Nørgaard, 'Translations of the Classics into English before 1600', *Review of English Studies*, 9 (1958), 164–72.
24. An early attempt at enumeration was Julia G. Ebel, 'A Numerical Survey of Elizabethan Translations', *The Library*, 22 (1967), 105–27. More recently, and for upward revision of Ebel's 18% estimate as well as application of it to the seventeenth century, see Brenda M. Hosington, 'Commerce, Printing, and Patronage', in Gordon Braden, Robert Cummings, and Stuart Gillespie (eds), *The Oxford History of Literary Translation in English*, vol. 2: *1550–1660* (Oxford, 2010), 47–57 (47).
25. This helps explain why translations from the Latin are less prominent in general library collections (not strongly embracing such topics) than in the overall output of the printing trade.
26. Gordon Braden, 'An Overview', in Braden et al. (eds), *Oxford History of Literary Translation*, 2. 3–11 (9).
27. Henry Burrowes Lathrop, *Translations into English from Caxton to Chapman* (Madison, WI, 1933), 16. See also Peter Mack, Chapter 2, this volume.
28. For a list of school translations in use to 1600 or so, see J. P. Tuck, 'The Use of English in Latin Teaching in the Sixteenth Century', *Durham Research Review*, 1 (1950), 22–30.
29. Many of these items will receive attention at appropriate points in later chapters. For a checklist of English translations of ancient authors 1550–1700 arranged by ancient author, see Robert Cummings and Stuart Gillespie, 'Translations from Greek and Latin Classics 1550–1700: A Revised Bibliography', *Translation and Literature*, 18 (2009), 1–42.
30. The formal classical translations carried out by major writers themselves, often an important venue for formal and stylistic experiment, are treated at the appropriate points in ensuing chapters.
31. See further Baldwin, *Shakspere's Small Latin*, 2. 573; Kenneth Muir, 'Menenius' Fable', *Notes & Queries*, 198 (1953), 240–2; Kenneth Muir, *The Sources of Shakespeare's Plays* (1977), 238.
32. For a full exposition of the evidence from these plays, see Peter Culhane, 'Livy in Early Jacobean Drama', *Translation and Literature*, 14 (2005), 21–44.
33. See further Kenneth Haynes, *English Literature and Ancient Languages* (Oxford, 2003), for the claim that the adoption of compound adjectives has been one way for English poets to explore 'the alien value, desired or threatening, of Greece' (p. 105).
34. This point is made, and the development contextualized, by Robert Cummings, 'Translation and Literary Innovation', in Braden et al. (eds), *Oxford History of Literary Translation*, 2. 32–44 (42).
35. This episode is most fully treated in Derek Attridge, *Well-Weighed Syllables: Elizabethan Verse in Classical Metres* (Cambridge, 1974).

36. For attitudes to the practice of translation in the Tudor period, see Massimiliano Morini, *Tudor Translation in Theory and Practice* (Aldershot, 2006).
37. The first instalment of Chapman's Homer, *Seaven Bookes of the Iliades* (1598), was dedicated to the Earl of Essex. For the view that Chapman's identification of Achilles with Essex, whose rebellion took place in 1601, accounts for the changes in the 1608 *Homer... in Twelve Bookes*, see John Channing Briggs, 'Chapman's *Seaven Bookes of the Iliades*: Mirror for Essex', *Studies in English Literature 1500–1900*, 21 (1981), 59–73.
38. First so used in English verse by Wyatt to translate the word *lubrico* in his version of the Senecan chorus 'Stet quicumque volet' (from *Thyestes*). See further Stuart Gillespie, *English Translation and Classical Reception* (Malden, MA, 2011), 41–3.
39. Gordon Braden, *The Classics and English Renaissance Poetry: Three Case Studies* (New Haven, 1978), 16–17.
40. *Ovid's Metamorphoses*, trans. Arthur Golding, ed. Madeleine Forey (Baltimore, 2002), p. xxiii, with parenthetical references omitted.
41. For analysis of the publishing record, see Peter Burke, 'A Survey of the Popularity of Ancient Historians, 1450–1700', *History and Theory*, 5 (1966), 135–52 (138–9).
42. Judith Mossmann, '*Henry V* and Plutarch's Alexander', *Shakespeare Quarterly*, 45 (1994), 57–73.
43. Martin Mueller, 'Plutarch's "Life of Brutus" and the Play of its Repetitions in Shakespearean Drama', *Renaissance Drama*, 22 (1991), 47–93.
44. Pomponius would probably not have suspected that this was very likely the first time Seneca's stoical recasting of Euripides had *ever* been performed.
45. Bruce R. Smith, *Ancient Scripts and Modern Experience on the English Stage, 1500–1700* (Princeton, 1988), 5.
46. Major histories of European and English drama, such as, respectively, Creiznach's and F. P. Wilson's, are one source. Wilhelm Creiznach, *Geschichte Des Neueren Dramas*, 5 vols (Halle, 1893–1916); F. P. Wilson, *The English Drama, 1485–1585*, ed. G. K. Hunter (Oxford, 1969).
47. For more on the Westminster productions and other academic performances, see Bruce Smith, Chapter 17, this volume.
48. As is pointed out by Smith, *Ancient Scripts*, 119; for Cicero's approach to theatre, see pp. 14–25.
49. Smith, *Ancient Scripts*, 170. See also his discussion of Aristophanes' revival in Chapter 17, this volume.
50. For productions of Seneca in this period, see Bruce R. Smith, 'Toward the Rediscovery of Tragedy: Productions of Seneca's Plays on the English Renaissance Stage', *Renaissance Drama*, 9 (1978), 3–37. Howard B. Norland, 'Adapting to the Times: Expansion and Interpolation in the Elizabethan Translations of Seneca', *Classical and Modern Literature*, 16 (1996), 241–66, is a full account of the composite Newton translation paying special attention to the translators' emphases on emotional and ethical dimensions.
51. For a general discussion of the Senecanism of *Titus*, see Robert S. Miola, *Shakespeare and Classical Tragedy: The Influence of Seneca* (Oxford, 1992), 13–32.
52. Smith (*Ancient Scripts*, 157–9) analyses the example of the *Aulularia* given in Christ Church, Oxford, in 1564.
53. For Chapman's play, see Bruce Smith, Chapter 17, this volume.
54. See further Smith, 'Rediscovery of Tragedy', 3.
55. The Younger Seneca had yet to be distinguished in the sixteenth century from his father Seneca the Elder, the famous rhetorician, the merged identity strengthening the perceived relationship between drama and rhetoric in Senecan play texts.

56. Thomas Nashe, Preface to Greene's *Menaphon* (1589), in G. Gregory Smith (ed.), *Elizabethan Critical Essays*, 2 vols (Oxford, 1904), I. 307–20 (312).
57. Alexander Neville, *The Lamentable Tragedie of Oedipus* (1563), sig. A3[v].
58. On Neville's version of *Oedpius*, see further Smith, *Ancient Scripts*, 205–13.
59. T. W. Baldwin, *Shakspere's Five-Act Structure: Shakspere's Early Plays on the Background of Renaissance Theories of Five-Act Structure from 1470* (Urbana, 1947).
60. For the Renaissance commentary tradition on ancient drama, see, as well as Baldwin, *Five-Act Structure*, Marvin T. Herrick, *Comic Theory in the Sixteenth Century* (Urbana, 1950), Edwin W. Robbins, *Dramatic Characterization in Printed Comedies on Terence 1473–1600* (Urbana, 1951), and Joel Altman, *The Tudor Play of Mind* (Berkeley and Los Angeles, 1978).
61. The medieval precedents are stressed by Howard Baker, 'Ghosts and Guides: Kyd's "Spanish Tragedy" and the Medieval Tragedy', *Modern Philology*, 33 (1935), 27–35. G. K. Hunter continues the line of argument in 'Seneca and the Elizabethans', and 'Seneca and Elizabethan Tragedy', in C. D. N. Costa (ed.), *Seneca* (1974), 17–26, 166–204.
62. *De casibus* tragedies are stories named after Boccaccio's *De Casibus Virorum Illustrium* (*Examples of Famous Men*), a collection of moral tales of those who fell from the heights of happiness. Both Shakespeare and Marlowe present characters who show awareness of the *de casibus* tradition.
63. Miola, *Shakespeare and Classical Tragedy*, 4.
64. Harold F. Brooks, '"Richard III": Unhistorical Amplifications: The Women's Scenes and Seneca', *Modern Language Review*, 75 (1980), 721–37.

CHAPTER 4

Classical Rhetoric in English

PETER MACK

Classical rhetoric (an advanced training in the use of the resources of language for persuasion) had an immense influence on English literature and English expression more generally in the Renaissance.[1] It affected the way students were taught to interpret texts and it influenced their expression at every level, both in Latin and in the vernacular. The highest form of English oratory was sermon-writing, which in our period was profoundly influenced by the principles of classical rhetoric. The influence of rhetoric was largely exercised through the Latin medium of the English educational system. As we have seen in Chapter 2, the grammar-school syllabus was directed to teaching Latin reading, writing, and speaking, and to readings of classical literature and writing exercises that were profoundly influenced by rhetorical ideas. At the grammar school, rhetorical doctrines were mainly conveyed through sixteenth-century Latin texts such as letter-writing manuals, lists of the tropes and figures, and (especially in the sixteenth century) Erasmus' *De Copia*. One classical text that was used was Aphthonius' *Progymnasmata* (writing exercises) in the much augmented Latin translation by Agricola and Lorichius first published in 1542. Rhetoric occupied a much smaller part of the syllabus at university, but it was there that students were more likely to read and be taught classical manuals of rhetoric, including the anonymous *Rhetorica ad Herennium*, Cicero's *De Inventione*, *Partitiones Oratoriae*, and *De Oratore*, Quintilian's *Institutio Oratoria*, Aristotle's *Rhetoric*, and parts of the corpus attributed to Hermogenes.[2]

Classical rhetoric taught a disparate range of techniques concerned with (for example) the construction of arguments and narratives, self-presentation, memory, voice modulation, gesture, the construction of rhythmic sentences, and the manipulation of an audience's emotions. Grammar-school training focused on a smaller but still wide range of doctrines, which presented pupils with ways of analysing and learning from the classical authors they read, and which included: the collection and exploitation of moral axioms; the construction of narratives and their use in teaching; the content of letters, together with their organization and address to their audience; the topics of praise, honour, and advantage; amplification of a text; the collection and composition of commonplaces; and the tropes and figures of rhetoric.[3] Pupils would also have devoted considerable attention to the imitation of classical models. Grammar-school rhetorical teaching was as much about reading as about writing, since students were trained to read as fellow-practitioners, collecting material that they might reuse in their own writings and learning from the ways in which classical authors used devices described in rhetoric, such as metaphor or simile. University students would have covered the whole range of rhetorical doctrines, placing particular emphasis on argumentative techniques that would be useful to them in their disputations, including the topics of invention, the presentation of valid and effective arguments, making distinctions and definitions, the organization of an argumentative text, and dialectical reading (analysing to bring out the underlying argumentative structures).[4]

Literary scholarship has amply demonstrated the impact of rhetorical ideas and structures on English poets of the sixteenth and seventeenth centuries.[5] The delight that some writers take in elegant structures of repetition and substitution is evidently linked to an appreciation by writer and audience of the figures of rhetoric.

> RICHARD II. What must the king do now? Must he submit?
> The king shall do it. Must he be depos'd?
> The king shall be contented. Must he lose
> The name of king? A God's name, let it go.
> I'll give my jewels for a set of beads;
> My gorgeous palace for a hermitage;
> My gay apparel for an almsman's gown;
> My figur'd goblets for a dish of wood;
> My sceptre for a palmer's walking staff;
> My subjects for a pair of carved saints,
> And my large kingdom for a little grave,
> A little, little grave, an obscure grave,
> Or I'll be buried in the king's highway,
> Some way of common trade, where subjects' feet
> May hourly trample on their sovereign's head.
>
> (*Richard II*, 3. 3. 142–56)

The elaborate patterning of the phrases is both very powerful and quite evident, even before one points out the rhetorical questions in lines 1–4, the chiasmus in line 4, the anaphora with zeugma and isocolon in lines 5–11 and the intensification of the obscurity and humiliation of Richard's grave in lines 11–15.[6] Brian Vickers has provided examples of many of the figures of speech from *Richard III* alone.[7] Where it used to be thought that Shakespeare used figures of speech less as his career developed, Stefan Keller has recently shown that the figures are still intensively used in the major tragedies and the late plays.[8] Rhetorical ideas also played an important part in the way Shakespeare constructed arguments and rewrote passages from Plutarch.[9]

More workaday users of language, such as writers of letters, memoranda, parliamentary speeches, sermons, histories, and controversies, used rhetorical devices as much as poets did.[10]

Rhetoric provided readers with tools for anatomizing and interpreting texts. It gave writers a range of structures, arguments, approaches, and verbal techniques from which they could choose, according to rhetorical principles, those most likely to move or persuade their envisaged audience. For English literature between 1558 and 1660, doctrines derived from classical rhetoric provide a crucial, contemporary approach to analysis. It also stimulated a small but interesting genre of English writing, the English manuals of rhetoric, to which the next section of this chapter is devoted.

Rhetoric Manuals

Rhetoric manuals in English absorbed and adapted classical teaching. Classical manuals of rhetoric were not translated into English entire during this period, though the main material of Aristotle's *Rhetoric* was summarized in Thomas Hobbes's *A Briefe of the Art of Rhetorique* (1637, reprinted 1651) and the rules from Aphthonius' *Progymnasmata* were translated with new English examples in Richard Rainolde's *Foundacion of Rhetorike* (1563). There was no English translation in this period of any rhetorical textbook by Cicero, Quintilian, or Hermogenes. Rhetoric was a highly prestigious practical subject. Rather than being treated as classics that ought to be studied integrally in English and therefore required translation, ancient rhetoric textbooks were seen as sources of practical doctrine that needed to be presented in a way that would be most helpful to an English readership. In some cases the English author got access to this classical teaching through a Renaissance Latin or vernacular author; in others the Englishman combined teaching from continental Renaissance and classical authorities through direct consultation of the texts. None of the English writers makes much of an original contribution to rhetorical theory, though many of them compose new examples.

English manuals of rhetoric in this period fall into five main genres: textbooks of the whole of rhetoric; lists of the tropes and figures with explanations and examples; letter-writing manuals; preaching manuals; and versions of the Ramus/Talon rhetoric textbook, which combined a shortened list of tropes and figures with a discussion of delivery.[11] Standing outside these groups is John Bulwer's *Chironomia or The Art of Manuall Rhetorique* (1644, reprinted 1648), which collects and elaborates the instructions of classical rhetoric on the use of hand gestures. The most successful of the English-language rhetoric manuals in our period were three of the earliest ones, Thomas Wilson's *Arte of Rhetorique* (1553), with eight editions up to 1585, William Fulwood's epistolary manual and collection, *Enemie of Idlenesse* (1568), with ten editions up to 1621, and Angel Day's *English Secretorie* (1586), with nine editions up to 1635. In this chapter I shall first review each of these five genres and then discuss six texts in greater detail: the three listed in the previous sentence, John Hoskins's influential manuscript *Directions for Speech and Style* (*c.*1599), John Wilkins's *Ecclesiastes* (1646), which was printed eleven times up to 1693, and Obadiah Walker's *Some Instructions concerning the Art of Oratory* (1659, reprinted 1682).

In sixteenth- and seventeenth-century England manuals of the whole of rhetoric were more likely to be studied at university. This, or the greater popularity of the simplifying Ramist approach, may explain the fact that only three English manuals of the whole of rhetoric were printed in our period, the works by Walker and Wilson to be discussed later, and Thomas Hobbes's *A Briefe of the Art of Rhetorique*, printed anonymously in 1637. The work originates in a manuscript abbreviation of Theodore Goulston's Latin translation of Aristotle's *Rhetoric*, which Hobbes had used for teaching Latin–English translation and rhetoric to his pupil William Cavendish (1617–84), third Earl of Devonshire. Hobbes shortens Goulston's sentences and omits material that he considers too difficult (for example, Aristotle's distinction between rhetoric and dialectic (1.1), many of the examples, and the discussion of ethos, pathos, and logos (1.2)), but the work provides a useful short summary of Aristotle's principal teachings.[12]

Lists of the tropes and figures featured both in independent works, such as Richard Sherry's *Treatise of Schemes and Tropes* (1550), Henry Peacham's *Garden of Eloquence* (1577, revised 1593), and John Smith's *Mysterie of Rhetorique Unvail'd* (1657), and as part of longer and composite works, including the works by Wilson and Day listed above, the third book of George Puttenham's *Arte of English Poesie* (1589), and Thomas Blount's *Academie of Eloquence* (1653), which also included a commonplace book, formulae of short English expressions, and a collection of model letters, but which relied very heavily on Hoskins's *Directions* for its version of the tropes and figures. These works depended ultimately on the descriptions of the tropes and figures in *Rhetorica ad Herennium* IV and Quintilian's *Institutio oratoria* VIII and IX, but they also copied Mosellanus' *Tabulae de schematibus et tropis* (1516), Melanchthon's *Institutiones rhetoricae* (1521), Joannes Susenbrotus' *Epitome troporum ac schematum* (1540), and each other.[13] English writers used their knowledge of the tropes and figures both to interpret texts, including the Bible, and to enrich their writing style.

Letter-writing manuals included the two very popular books by Fulwood and Day mentioned above, and Abraham Fleming's *A Panoplie of Epistles* (1576). Works that give model letters without specific instructions for letter-writing include: the anonymous *Cupids Messanger* (1633), John Browne's *Marchant's Avizo* (1589, with five further editions), and Thomas Gainsford's *The Secretaries Study* (1616). Letter-writing manuals generally include: general advice on the style, length, address, and conclusions for letters, and a classification of letter-types with instructions for and examples of each type. The English manuals rely both on Renaissance Latin textbooks, especially Erasmus' *De Conscribendis Epistolis* (1522), and on vernacular treatises in French, particularly Pierre Fabri's *Le Grant et vray art de pleine rhétorique* (1521) and P. Durand's *Le Stile et maniere de composer, dicter et scrire toute sorte d'epistres* (1553).[14]

Sermon manuals involve compromises between classical principles of rhetoric and practices of sermon-giving, usually with a strong emphasis on exposition of a particular Bible text. Preaching manuals usually discuss the method of interpreting the Bible, the different types of sermon, the structure of the sermon, the emotions to be aroused in the congregation, and the preacher's approach to preparation and delivery.[15] The best-known English sermon manuals of the sixteenth century were translations from Latin originals, Niels Hemmingsen's *The Preacher* (1574, 1576) and Andreas Hyperius' *The Practis of Preaching* (printed twice in 1577).[16] William Perkins's *Prophetica* (1592), which had six Latin editions, was translated as *The Arte of Prophecying* (1607, reprinted 1631).[17] Many more English sermon manuals were produced in the seventeenth century, including William Ames's 'Of Making Sermons' (1639), a chapter of his *De Conscientia* (1630) translated into English as *Conscience* (1639, reprinted three times), Richard Baxter's *The Reformed Pastor* (1656, reprinted twice), Richard Bernard's *The Faithful Shepherd* (1607, reprinted 1609), John Brinsley's *The Preachers Charge* (1631, two printings), William Chappell's *The Preacher* (1656), Thomas Hall's *Rhetorica Sacra* (1654, reprinted 1655), John Prideaux's *Sacred Eloquence* (1659), and John Wilkins's *Ecclesiastes* (1646).[18] George Herbert depicts the preaching of his ideal parson in *A Priest to the Temple* (1652). His preacher wins over the audience with his earnestness, his careful observation, and his address to the particular needs of sections of his audience. The 'character of his sermon is holiness', achieved through choosing texts of devotion, 'dipping and seasoning all our words and sentences in our hearts', making many apostrophes to God, frequently wishing for and rejoicing in the good of his congregation, and urging the presence and majesty of God.[19]

Translations and adaptations of Ramus and Talon's shortened version of rhetoric, mainly consisting of four tropes and nineteen figures, included: John Barton's *The Art of Rhetorick Concisely and Compleatly Handled* (1634), Dudley Fenner's *The Artes of Logike and Rhethorike* (1584, reprinted twice), Abraham Fraunce's *Arcadian Rhetorike* (1588), Thomas Horne's bilingual *Rhetoricae Compendium Latino-Anglice* (1651), and Alexander Richardson, *The Logicians School-Master... Talaeus his Rhetorick* (1629, 1657).[20] Following Ramus' own preferences, English Ramists illustrate their relatively sparse syllabus of doctrines with many examples from Latin, English, and European literature.

English-Language Manuals and Classical Rhetoric

Analysis of six of the most successful English-language manuals will show how English authors adapted the classical teachings of rhetoric to their early modern vernacular readers and how the classical tradition of rhetoric prompted thinking about the resources of expression in English. Sir Thomas Wilson's *Arte of Rhetorique* teaches the whole traditional syllabus of rhetoric in six sections (introduction, invention, disposition, style, memory, and delivery).[21] Wilson's most significant adaptations of the traditional syllabus occur in his longest section, on invention, in which relatively short summaries of the principal doctrines are illustrated with often lengthy examples, including a translation of Erasmus' model letter persuading a young man to marry from *De Conscribendis Epistolis*.[22] The work opens with a praise of the power of eloquence in which material taken from Cicero's *De Inventione* and *De Oratore* is rewritten as a protestant explanation of the way in which God's 'appointed ministers' overcame the consequences of the fall.[23]

Wilson organizes his account of invention around the three genres of oratory (placing demonstrative oratory first), the seven parts of the oration (he reaches seven by treating proposition, division, confirmation, and confutation as separate parts), amplification and emotion, and humour. Near the beginning of his discussion of invention he emphasizes the importance of reflecting on context, subject matter, and audience.

> Not only is it necessary to know what manner of cause we have taken in hand, when we first enter upon any matter, but also it is wisdom to consider the time, the place, the man for whom we speak, the man against whom we speak, the matter whereof we speak, and the judges before whom we speak, the reasons that best serve to further our cause. (pp. 51–2)

Before attempting to apply the rules and strategies of rhetoric, the speaker needs to reflect on the nature of the case in which he is involved and the means that are most likely to bring success. Under demonstrative oratory Wilson teaches topics for confirmation (including honourable, possible, easy, difficult), the seven circumstances through which an event can be described or amplified (who, what, where, by what help, why, how, and when), a short list of topics of invention and some discussion of the cardinal virtues (pp. 60, 65–6, 71–6). Here Wilson seems to summarize a good deal of material from Cicero's treatises on rhetoric and *De Officiis*. On amplification, Wilson mainly works from Quintilian and from Erasmus' *Ecclesiastes*; on emotion, he relies on Rudolph Agricola's *De Inventione Dialectica*; and, on humour, he takes his doctrines from Cicero's *De Oratore*, adding many stories of his own or from the oral tradition. His account of the tropes relies mainly on modern adapters for classical teaching: Melanchthon, Sherry, and Susenbrotus; for the figures of thought he uses *De Oratore*, supplementing it with Erasmus' *De Copia* and Susenbrotus (pp. 203–13); for similitude, for example, *copie*, and fables he mainly follows *De copia* (pp. 213–22); his section on the figures of words is based mainly on Quintilian, Susenbrotus, and *Rhetorica ad Herennium* (pp. 224–32). Wilson makes classical and humanist teaching on all aspects of rhetoric and dialectic easily available to English readers without Latin.

The first book of William Fulwood's *The Enemie of Idlenesse* provides instructions for composing forty-five types of letter useful in everyday life, such as 'How to request a temporal benefit', 'How to write a letter of complaint for a misfortune', 'How to certify some news lately happened'. For each type Fulwood provides simple instructions, usually in four parts and a constructed example. The remaining three books give model letters of various kinds, some translated from well-known writers, others apparently fictitious. For the most part Fulwood follows P. Durand's *Le Stile et maniere de composer, dicter et escrire toute sorte d'epistres* very closely, with some omissions and some changes of order. Almost all Fulwood's model letters are translated from Durand. But Fulwood adds a great deal of didactic material, especially in the first book. His brief instructions for the topics to be included in each type of letter appear to be translated from Pierre Fabri's *Le Grant et vray art*. Fulwood follows Fabri in defining the letter as 'a declaration (by writing) of the minds of such as be absent, one of them to another, even as though they were present'.[24] At the same time Fulwood includes many letters that are in Durand but not in Fabri. It seems likely that Fulwood had both French books before him, but perhaps he had direct access to a common source of both. Fulwood provides a complete English-language manual of letter-writing, with many examples for imitation.

Angel Day's *The English Secretorie* (1586) offers a general introduction to letter-writing, followed by instructions for and examples of thirty-three types of letter and, in later editions, a treatise on the tropes and schemes and a guide to the secretary's conduct. Day defines the letter as 'the messenger or familiar speech of the absent, for that therein is discovered whatsoever the mind wisheth in such cases to have delivered'.[25] Letters are so varied because they correspond to human motivations and experiences (B1^{r}). Day is careful to combine observations on the nature of letters with a presentation of many of the principal doctrines of rhetoric. So, for example, he states very firmly that a letter should have five parts (and outlines the contents of the five traditional sections of the oration: Exordium, Narratio and proposition, Confirmation, Confutatio, and Conclusio) but then adds that all letters also have four particular elements (the salutation, the farewell, the subscription, and the outward direction) and provides advice on, and examples of, each (C2^{r}–D2^{r}). Day's discussion of demonstrative letters includes an account of the topics of praise of the person, the topics of virtue, and the arguments from necessity and usefulness (the latter two often found in the deliberative section of the rhetoric manual) (E3^{v}–F2^{r}). He opens his discussion of judicial epistles with a summary of the rhetorical doctrine of status (U3^{r}–4^{r}). But at the very beginning of the treatise he also emphasizes three principal points to be borne in mind in writing letters: aptness of words and sentences (which involves correctness and clarity), brevity of speech (saying everything that is required in order to be understood, but avoiding repetition and digression), and comeliness in deliverance (suiting the letter to the dignity of the recipient and the decorum of the subject matter) (B1^{v}–3^{r}). In deliberative letters Day places great emphasis on the role of praise, hope, and sympathy in persuasion and on the need to suit the letter to its recipient (G4^{v}).

For each type of letter Day provides at least one example with marginal notes that point out the topics of the letter and the figures of rhetoric employed. Much of the teaching of the book is conveyed through the examples. From time to time Day makes general observations on the lessons to be drawn from them (e.g. N4$^{r–v}$, O1^{v},

O4^{v}, P1^{r}). Day also provides advice on writing replies to several types of letter, giving examples (e.g. H3^{r}–4^{r}, M3^{r}–4^{r}, O1^{r-v}, P2^{r}–3^{v}). Day summarizes many of the key doctrines of classical rhetoric, adds pertinent observations on letter-writing (some of them borrowed from Erasmus), and composes appropriate English examples.

John Hoskins composed his *Directions for Speech and Style* around 1599 as instructions for a young gentleman studying at the Inns of Court as a guide to the best ways of speaking, writing letters, and conversing.[26] Hoskins proclaims eloquent speech as a testimony of the speaker's mind and the harmony of creation.

> The conceits of the mind are pictures of things and the tongue is interpreter of those pictures. The order of God's creatures in themselves is not only admirable and glorious, but eloquent; then he that could apprehend the consequences of things, in their truth, and utter his apprehensions as truly were a right orator. Therefore Cicero said as much when he said, *dicere recte nemo potest nisi qui prudenter intelligit* ('No one can speak correctly who does not understand wisely').[27]

Although Hoskins aims to teach eloquence in general, he mentions only two parts of rhetoric: invention and fashion, devoting the bulk of his treatise to a discussion of the tropes and figures.

> In writing of letters there is to be regarded the invention and the fashion. For the invention, that ariseth upon your business, whereof there can be no rules of more certainty or precepts of better direction given you than conjecture can lay down of all the several occasions of all particular men's lives and vocations... When you have invented... then are you to proceed to the ordering of it and the digestion of parts; which is sought out of circumstances. One is the understanding of the person to whom you write: the other is the coherence of the sentences. For man's capacity and delight, you are to weigh what will be apprehended first with great delight and attention, what next regarded and longed for especially, and what last will leave most satisfaction and, as it were, the sweetest memorial and brief of all that is past, in his understanding whom you write to. (p. 4)

For letter-writing at least, Hoskins lays aside the intricate rules of invention and the traditions of the five-part oration: invention is a matter of saying what you want to say; disposition requires that you suit your material to your audience. As Hudson points out, this resembles the approach of Justus Lipsius in his *Epistolica Institutio* (1591).[28] Fashion consists of four qualities of style: brevity, perspicuity, plainness, and respect to the person addressed.

Hoskins divides the thirty-six figures he describes into three classes, those used in varying, in amplification, and in illustration (or description) (p. 51). He takes the general definition of each figure from the rhetorical tradition (and sometimes directly from Quintilian or *Rhetorica ad Herennium*) but adds examples he has chosen from Sidney's *Arcadia* and commentary of his own on the use of the figure. He had provided his original pupil with a marked copy of Sidney's work with the figures noted in manuscript in the margin. Hoskins's text survives in manuscript copies and in the extracts from it that were copied in Ben Jonson's *Discoveries* (first printed in 1641), in Thomas Blount's *Academie of Eloquence* (1653), printed seven times up to 1683, and in John Smith's *Mysterie of Rhetorique Unvail'd* (1657), printed six times up to 1688. Hoskins's manuscript treatise written for the son of a friend thus enjoyed a much longer and wider circulation than any of the printed sixteenth-century rhetoric manuals.

John Wilkins's *Ecclesiastes or a Discourse concerning the Gift of Preaching as it Fals under the Rules of Art*, which was printed eleven times between 1646 and 1693, largely takes the form of a study guide, pointing the preacher towards a variety of commentaries on books of the Bible and studies of particular issues that might need to be discussed in a sermon. Wilkins defines the art of preaching as 'such an expertness and facility in the right handling and dividing the word of truth as may approve us to be workmen that need not be ashamed'.[29] This requires both spiritual ability, which must be obtained through prayer, and knowledge of the art, which consists of method, matter, and expression. Method is a regular frame in which the parts of the sermon are so linked that the preacher can devise and remember them and the audience understand and retain the teaching. This consists of three elements: explication of the text, confirmation of its teaching through arguments from the topics of invention and resolution of doubts, and application of the text, to instruct, reprove, console, or exhort the congregation (pp. 5–9). In addition to these three parts the sermon will have a preface, which aims to make the audience favourable, teachable and attentive, transitions, and a conclusion (p. 10). Wilkins provides some general rules for the interpretation of texts, and observations on proof and amplification (pp. 11–12, 18–25). The material for the sermon will be found partly through reading Scripture and partly through consulting the theological authorities listed. The expression of the sermon should be plain and natural, full and without tautology, sound and wholesome, and affectionate and cordial, 'as proceeding from the heart' (pp. 128–30).

Although Wilkins emphasizes the plainness and spirituality of the preacher, spurning the tropes, figures, and all rhetorical flourishes, nevertheless we can see how elements of the programme of classical rhetoric (such as the doctrine of the exordium and the topics of invention) retain a place in his conception of preaching.

Obadiah Walker's *Some Instructions concerning the Art of Oratory Collected for the Use of a Friend a Young Student* (1659) divides oratory into seven sections: invention, elocution, ornament, style, recitation (in which the student is advised to read compositions out to a friend to check the language against the judgement of both their ears (pp. 113–18)), pronunciation, and delivery (sig. A2^{r}–3^{v}).[30] Invention is primarily a matter of using a set of elementary questions (Who? Where? What? With whose help? Why? When?) and the topics of invention to devise one's own arguments, then of checking what other people have found, of ordering one's arguments, and of writing transitions between them, using some of the topics (such as cause, effect, similitude, contrary) or some of the figures (*gradatio*, questioning, and comparison) (pp. 2–15).

On disposition (which he treats as part of invention) Walker advises the student to write down all the arguments that come to mind, to critique them, and then to divide them into headings. Four of the headings should be chosen, and the student must work out the best logical order in which to present these four (pp. 15–18). Although this approach certainly uses familiar rhetorical techniques, the idea of letting the shape of the composition emerge from the materials found (rather than trying to set them out in a preordained structure, such as the four-part oration) is new and interesting.

Three of Walker's sections relate to style. Under elocution he discusses words to avoid and sentence construction, especially patterning of sentences, cadence, and rhythm (pp. 24–50). Ornament is devoted to some of the tropes and figures, selected and organized in a new way: epithets, metaphors, similes, contraries and dissimilarities, and amplification, which includes figures of repetition, multiplication, different types of enumeration and aetiology, specifying causes and effects (pp. 51–87). Style begins with variation, using some of the figures of thought (such as interrogation, doubt, correction, and concession) and includes clarity and the question of the different levels of style (pp. 87–113). In these sections material of classical origin is presented in new combinations and with firmly expressed purposes. As one reads the sections on style, it becomes clear from the explanations and examples that Walker assumes that the reader understands Latin. In fact it appears that *Some Instructions* is an English language text about how to write effective Latin prose.

The principal doctrines of rhetoric were available to readers in English throughout the period between 1550 and 1660. Manuals of the tropes and figures, letter-writing textbooks, and guides to sermon-writing were especially popular in English. But all these English textbooks were heavily reliant on classical and Renaissance Latin works. In this period rhetoric was regarded as a training of practical usefulness rather than as an aspect of classical culture, hence the absence of translations of rhetoric textbooks, or rather their replacement by English-language adaptations. But Latin remained the language of instruction in grammar school and university, so English rhetoric operated within a bilingual culture. We have seen that some of the English manuals assume that their readers have access to texts in Latin (or are even composing Latin works of their own). I have shown elsewhere that sixteenth-century English manuals include rhetorical figures that work only in an inflected language like Latin.[31] Some of our writers advise their readers to think about what they want to say to their audience and then express that message in the way that will be clearest and most accessible to that particular audience, but the general assumption of the textbook-writers is that their audience wishes to write elevated, educated English, which means Latinate English, in order to obtain a hearing from influential audiences. Classical rhetoric was useful to English readers because it taught many effective verbal strategies but also because the way of speaking it inculcated conveyed prestige and power.

Notes

1. I am grateful to Lawrence D. Green, Jerry Murphy, and Jennifer Richards for their invaluable help. Essential material on this topic is to be found in W. S. Howell, *Logic and Rhetoric in England 1500–1700* (Princeton, 1956); H. F. Plett, *English Renaissance Rhetoric and Poetics: A Systematic Bibliography* (Leiden, 1995); L. D. Green and J. J. Murphy (eds), *Renaissance Rhetoric Short-Title Catalogue 1460–1700* (Aldershot, 2006). On classical rhetoric more generally, see Jennifer Richards, *Rhetoric* (2007); H. Lausberg, *Handbook of Literary Rhetoric* (Leiden, 1998).
2. P. Mack, *Elizabethan Rhetoric* (Cambridge, 2002), 11–14, 24–32, 48–57.
3. Mack, *Elizabethan Rhetoric*, 32–46.
4. Mack, *Elizabethan Rhetoric*, 58–75.
5. M. Joseph, *Shakespeare's Use of the Arts of Language* (New York, 1947); B. Vickers, *Classical Rhetoric in English Poetry* (1970); Thomas O. Sloane and R. B. Waddington (eds), *The Rhetoric of Renaissance Poetry* (Berkeley and Los Angeles, 1974); B. Vickers, *In Defence of Rhetoric* (Oxford, 1988), 294–339, 375–434; N. Rhodes, *The Power of Eloquence and English Renaissance Literature* (Basingstoke, 1992); H. F. Plett, *Rhetoric and Renaissance Culture* (Berlin, 2004).
6. Rhetorical terms are defined in R. Lanham, *A Handlist of Rhetorical Terms* (Berkeley and Los Angeles, 1991).
7. B. Vickers, 'Shakespeare's Use of Rhetoric', in K. Muir and S. Schoenbaum (eds), *A New Companion to Shakespeare Studies* (Cambridge, 1971), 83–98.
8. Stefan Daniel Keller, *The Development of Shakespeare's Rhetoric* (Tübingen, 2009).
9. P. Mack, *Reading and Rhetoric in Montaigne and Shakespeare* (2010), 74–88.
10. Mack, *Elizabethan Rhetoric*, 103–294.
11. On Ramus and Talon, see P. Mack, *A History of Renaissance Rhetoric 1380–1620* (Oxford, 2011), 136–53 and bibliography cited there.
12. J. T. Harwood (ed.), *The Rhetorics of Thomas Hobbes and Bernard Lamy* (Carbondale, IL, 1986), 1–128.
13. Mack, *Elizabethan Rhetoric*, 84–102.
14. K. G. Hornbeak, 'The Complete Letter-Writer in English', *Smith College Studies in Modern Languages*, 15 (1934), 1–150; J. Robertson, *The Art of Letter Writing* (1942); Lynne Magnusson, *Shakespeare and Social Dialogue* (Cambridge, 1999); Mack, *History of Renaissance Rhetoric*, 228–9, 256, 284–91.
15. Mack, *History of Renaissance Rhetoric*, 257–78.
16. The English translation appears to be considerably developed from the Latin original. It would be worth investigating these changes in more detail.
17. Mack, *History of Renaissance Rhetoric*, 273–4.
18. Mary Morrissey, 'Scripture, Style and Persuasion in Seventeenth-Century English Theories of Preaching', *Journal of Ecclesiastical History*, 53 (2002), 686–706; Mack, *Elizabethan Rhetoric*, 253–92; A. Pettegree, *Reformation and the Culture of Persuasion* (Cambridge, 2005), 10–39. On early modern English sermons more generally, see A. Hunt, *The Art of Hearing* (Cambridge, 2010); M. Morrissey, *Politics and the Paul's Cross Sermons 1558–1642* (Oxford, 2011); H. Adlington, P. McCullough, and E. Rhatigan (eds), *The Oxford Handbook of the Early Modern Sermon* (Oxford, 2011).
19. George Herbert, *Works*, ed. F. E. Hutchinson (Oxford, 1941), 232–5.
20. Howell, *Logic and Rhetoric*, 247–82. On the place of rhetoric in Ramus's system, see P. Mack, 'Ramus and Ramism: Rhetoric and Dialectic', in S. J. Reid and

E. Wilson (eds), *Ramus, Pedagogy and the Liberal Arts* (Farnham, 2011), 7–23.

21. Thomas Wilson, *The Art of Rhetoric (1560)*, ed. P. Medine (University Park, PA, 1994), 15; further references, including those in the text, are to this edition; P. Medine, *Thomas Wilson* (Boston, 1986), 55–74; Howell, *Logic and Rhetoric*, 98–110.
22. Wilson, *Art of Rhetoric*, 79–100; Erasmus, *Opera Omnia* I-2, ed. J. C. Margolin (Amsterdam, 1971), 400–28.
23. Wilson, *Art of Rhetoric*, 41–3; Cicero, *De Inventione* I. 1–5, *De Oratore* I. 33.
24. W. Fulwood, *The Enimie of Idlenesse* (1582), sig. B1r. Cf. Fabri, *Cy ensuit le grant et vray art de pleine rhétorique* (Rouen, 1521; repr. Geneva, 1972), sig. N1r. The letter-writing manual occupies the third section of the book. The definition seems to be adapted from Cicero's definition in *Ad Familiares* 2.4.1. Mack, *History of Renaissance Rhetoric*, 228–30, 284–90.
25. A. Day, *The English Secretary (1599)*, facsimile ed. R. Evans (Gainesville, 1967), sig. B1r; further references, including those in the text, are to this edition.
26. John Hoskins, *Directions for Speech and Style*, ed. H. H. Hudson (Princeton, 1935), pp. xiv–xv, 2–3; further references, including those in the text, are to this edition.
27. Hoskins, *Directions*, 2, 54–6; Cicero, *Brutus* 6.23. Hudson points out that Hoskins's first two sentences resemble the views of Pierre de la Primaudaye, translated by T. Bowes as *The French Academie*, two parts (1586, 1594).
28. Mack, *History of Renaissance Rhetoric*, 254–6; Hoskins, *Directions*, 56–7.
29. John Wilkins, *Ecclesiastes or a Discourse concerning the Gift of Preaching as it Fals under the Rules of Art* (1651), 4. Further references, including those in the text, are to this edition.
30. Obadiah Walker, *Some Instructions concerning the Art of Oratory Collected for the Use of a Friend a Young Student* (1659); further references, including those in the text, are to this edition.
31. Mack, *Elizabethan Rhetoric*, 95–102.

CHAPTER 5

The Classics in Literary Criticism

GAVIN ALEXANDER

All of the key thoughts expressed by literary critics of the English Renaissance have a source in classical writings. A brief list (by no means comprehensive) of the more prominent commonplaces and contested ideas in classical and Renaissance literary criticism might look like this:[1]

- poetry (*poēsis*, making) may be broadly defined as fiction-making rather than versification;
- poetry is an art of *mimēsis* or imitation (though what it imitates is a key area of discord: nature, quasi-Platonic ideas, Aristotelian universals?);
- poetry has a moral function (it should make the reader better) and thus a social and political function; the good poet should, therefore, be a good person;
- nature is the source and standard of art: art should, in various ways, resemble nature;
- the reader's/audience's belief in the truth or at least the vivid truthlikeness of the poetic representation is a key aim;
- imagined speech and action should accord with rules of decorum;
- different rules of decorum, style, dramatic or narrative structure, mode of delivery, versification, and so forth, pertain to the different genres;
- different genres aim at different effects (aesthetic, moral, psychological, etc.) on their readers and audiences;
- poetry can be contrasted with philosophy and history in terms of its truth content and didactic function;
- both unity and variety are valued in style and in metrical or narrative form (they may, therefore, be in tension, or be seen as antithetical);
- both plot (logical, plausible, appropriate in scale) and character (believable, engaging of sympathy, instructive) are important components and may compete for precedence.

Because Renaissance thought about literature is so reliant on classical writings, the problem Donald Russell identifies with ancient criticism, that it 'is fundamentally not equal to the task of appraising classical literature',[2] would appear to be mirrored in the Renaissance. But the self-consciousness with which literary writers of the English Renaissance engaged theoretical questions in their poems, prose writings, and plays suggests that theory may yet have much light to shed on practice.

Poetics, Rhetoric, and Education

Whether it is Roger Ascham writing at the beginning of this volume's timeframe or John Milton writing towards its end, we see in early discussions of classical critics that poetics has a struggle to detach itself from rhetoric, and rhetoric not just as an art of language but as a system of education. Ascham and his Cambridge colleagues had, he reports, 'many pleasant talks together, in comparing the precepts of Aristotle and Horace *De Arte Poetica* with the examples of Euripides, Sophocles, and Seneca',[3] but he tells us this in a work called *The Scholemaster* (published posthumously in 1570), in which Ascham sets out his method of education in the Latin language founded on the imitation of classical models. He is momentarily interested, it is true, in the possibility of vernacular drama that is better 'able to abide the true touch of Aristotle's precepts and Euripides' examples', but he is digressing from his main subject, which is education. That Ascham works by relating precepts to examples is typical. We might say that English Renaissance literature is founded on the preference of example to precept, in imagining both how literary texts might teach their readers moral lessons ('So much more profitable and gracious is doctrine by example than by rule', says Spenser of his *Faerie Queene*[4]) and how new texts might be better written (Aeschylus, Sophocles, and Euripides are for Milton 'the best rule to all who endeavour to write tragedy'[5]). But Ascham's ultimate aim is not a better understanding of drama but rather the recommending of good examples 'in choice of words, in framing of sentences, in handling of arguments, and use of right form, figure, and number, proper and fit for every matter'.[6] Once Horace and Aristotle have helped Ascham determine which are the best plays, they can therefore be set aside, and so too can any consideration of those plays as plays: poetics is here in the service of rhetorical education.

That condition is as evident three-quarters of a century later when Milton writes *Of Education* (1644). Milton's schoolboys study logic

> until it be time to open her contracted palm into a graceful and ornate rhetoric taught out of the rule of Plato, Aristotle, Phalereus, Cicero, Hermogenes, Longinus. To which poetry would be made subsequent, or, indeed, rather precedent, as being less subtile and fine, but more simple, sensuous, and passionate; I mean not here the prosody of a verse, which they could not but have hit on before among the rudiments of grammar, but that sublime art which in Aristotle's *Poetics*, in Horace, and the Italian commentaries of Castelvetro, Tasso, Mazzoni, and others, teaches what the laws are of a true epic

poem, what of a dramatic, what of a lyric, what decorum is, which is the grand masterpiece to observe.[7]

Milton's authorities include those rhetorical critics whose writings on style had much to say about imaginative literature: the Demetrius (probably not Demetrius of Phaleron, though the identification was common) who wrote *On Style*, Hermogenes, author of *On Types*, and the shadowy 'Longinus' to whom was attributed the great treatise *On the Sublime*. And they include some major ancient and modern writers on poetics. But in both cases Milton's interest is not in teaching his students how to be poets, but in refining their education as orators: Aristotle, Horace, and the Italian critics help us to understand a type of rhetoric offered to the young because it is 'more simple, sensuous, and passionate'. Poetics was for children, then, and so was poetry. Aristophanes, in *Frogs*, might have represented poets as the teachers of adults, but the development of the ancient educational system meant that, by the time Plutarch wrote his essay on the cautions to be used in teaching the young to read poetry (*De Audiendis Poetis*), a work that had a great influence in the Renaissance, poetry, as well as its theory, was something taught to schoolboys.[8] Brian Vickers is right that such coherence as Renaissance poetics has comes from its overwhelmingly rhetorical (and therefore ethical) concerns,[9] but this rhetoricization of poetics was an achievement not of the sixteenth-century humanists but of the educationalists of the ancient world. Aristotle's ability to isolate poetics—to an extent—from rhetoric and ethics was exceptional.

Kinds of Source and Modes of Response

Poetics re-emerged in the sixteenth century, then, not by ignoring the various disciplines and practices that neighboured it, but by reassessing its relation to them. Milton's remarks direct us to the variety of sources involved: writings not only on poetry, but on philosophy, rhetoric, and grammar. Rhetoric has been discussed above by Peter Mack (Chapter 4) but a brief survey of the early reception and availability of the key classical works in those other fields is useful. Horace's *Ars Poetica* was the only major text that was in no sense rediscovered in the Renaissance. In Italy, editions of Horace accreted detailed commentaries amounting to 'compendiums of all knowledge about the poetic art, so that Horace's work was no longer a theory of poetry, but the theory of poetry, the summum of all useful ideas about the art',[10] and indeed an instrument for collating them. An increasing number of editions of Horace printed in England from 1574 onwards derived from this continental tradition, and coincided with the first translation of the *Ars* into English verse, by Thomas Drant (in *Horace his Arte of Poetrie, Pistles [sic], and Satyrs Englished*, 1567). A translation by Ben Jonson, printed in 1640, was a vast improvement; a partial translation (ll. 1–178) by Ascham's pupil Queen Elizabeth I also survives, in her hand and dated 1598.[11] William Webbe helped the Latinless to make sense of Horace by Englishing the 'canons' (a rule-by-rule digest of the *Ars* and the epistle to Augustus) from Fabricius' 1560 Horace edition, in his *A Discourse of English Poetrie* (1586).[12]

The discussions of versification, accent, and literary genre in the late-classical grammarians are another case where we find continuity between the medieval and Renaissance critical traditions. The *artes grammaticae* of Donatus, Diomedes, Priscian, and others remained influential and the tradition was continued in works such as George Buchanan's posthumously printed *De Prosodia* (1595) or Richard Lloyd's *Artis Poeticae* (1653). Editions of Terence included the traditional accompaniment of the essays on drama by Evanthius and Donatus.[13] The grammarians had clarified and codified the conflicting hints of earlier classical writers. Diomedes, for example, fleshed out the beguiling and brief thoughts of Plato and Aristotle on the three modes of poetry (narrative/diegetic, dramatic/mimetic, mixed).[14] The encounter with literary categories within the grammatical system predisposed Renaissance readers to infer greater method in the likes of Horace and to reconcile classical authorities with each other.

Plato's thoughts about *mimesis* in the *Republic* and his tongue-in-cheek account of inspiration in the *Ion*, along with other dialogues bearing on literary questions, were becoming widely known and cited through continental editions (and Latin translations). Aristotle's *Poetics* was the rising star of the sixteenth century in Italy after Latin translations were printed in 1498 and 1536 (a parallel text), and many more texts and commentaries followed, although only a single edition was printed in England in the period: Goulston's Latin translation of 1623. The *Poetics* was little used in England before Sidney, and early references to it, like Ascham's, are slight and passing.[15] Gabriel Harvey wishes in the margins of his copy of George Gascoigne's 'Certain Notes of Instruction' (1575), the first work of literary criticism in English, that Gascoigne had followed 'Horace's and Aristotle's *Ars Poetica*'.[16] No certain signs of first-hand engagement are shown by William Webbe's several mentions in *A Discourse of English Poetrie*; or Sir John Harington's garbled account in 1591 of '*peripeteia*, which I interpret an agnition of some unlooked-for fortune, either good or bad, and a sudden change thereof';[17] or Francis Meres's commonplacing in 1600, with no reference to Aristotle, of the idea that we can take pleasure from the representation of things we do not like to see in real life.[18] Hermogenes and Dionysius of Halicarnassus were being read, or talked about, by Ascham at least,[19] but precise uses are hard to trace. Longinus is often assumed to be unknown before Boileau's 1674 French translation *Traité du sublime ou du merveilleux dans le discours*, but this is far from true.[20] Continental editions were available from the 1550s, in Greek, then Italian, then Latin, and a developing interest in England led to Gerard Langbaine's Greek and Latin edition of 1636 (reprinted in 1638 and 1650), and saw John Hall produce an English translation in 1652. The term *sublime* would, after Boileau, free the reception of Longinus from its original, rhetorical framework. In Hall's translation, *sublime* and cognate terms figure occasionally, but his preferred term is *height*, pointing to a grandeur of rhetorical style rather than to an aesthetic of the sublime. The first vernacular engagement with Longinus is George Chapman's discussion of his comparison of the *Iliad* and the *Odyssey* (*On the Sublime*, 11) in the preface to Chapman's Homer of 1614.[21]

Two related habits of Renaissance thought prevent us from finding as often as we would wish an extended engagement with a classical thinker's ideas. One is the tradition of reading in order to extract commonplaces, and—the consequence—the writing of texts that have been built from such extractions. The other is what Weinberg identifies as a widespread 'unawareness of the art of considering and analyzing texts as complete and consistent philosophical documents'.[22] Of course, certain key ideas were already commonplaces in the ancient world: for example, Gorgias, as reported by Plutarch and thence by Harington and others, on how through the power of (literary) rhetoric 'he that is deceived is wiser than he that is not deceived, and he that doth deceive is honester than he that doth not deceive'.[23] But it seems to matter little what the context of the commonplace is, so long as its author has authority. So, if the topic is the *furor poeticus*, the whole of Plato's *Ion* has equal value with a brief, passing mention of poetic inspiration in the first of Cicero's *Tusculan Disputations*.[24]

This love of the quotable commonplace is only one reason for Horace's popularity, but his dominance can be overstated. The reading of Aristotle through a Horatian lens that has been observed in the Italian tradition[25] was certainly reflected in Britain—witness John Dryden's remark in 1668: 'Of that book which Aristotle has left us, *peri tes Poietikes*, Horace's *Art of Poetry* is an excellent comment.'[26] But it is also important to recognize that Horace himself was read (rightly) in the context of the rhetorical tradition that lay behind his formulations about style, arrangement, credibility, and decorum. His famous passage on moving an audience with convincing tears ('si vis me flere . . .', ll. 101–18) reflects ideas developed in greater detail by Cicero (*De Oratore* 2. 45. 189–47. 196) and Quintilian (*Institutio Oratoria* 6. 2. 26–36), taken forward in the Renaissance rhetorical tradition by Thomas Wilson,[27] migrating into moral philosophy[28] and art theory,[29] and scrutinized in literary practice in representations of dissemblers like Shakespeare's Iago or in the would-be persuasive tears of Renaissance sonneteers. When Sidney tells us that 'many of such writings as come under the banner of unresistible love, if I were a mistress, would never persuade me they were in love, so coldly they apply fiery speeches, as men that had rather read lovers' writings, and so caught up certain swelling phrases . . . than that in truth they feel those passions',[30] he owes relatively little to Horace. Horace wrote famously of the civilizing and educative influence of poetry (*Ars*, ll. 391–401), but when Renaissance writers treated these themes at greater length they found more material for rhetorical *inventio* in Strabo and in Cicero's speech in defence of Archias the poet, as well as in Isocrates' praise of rhetoric for *its* civilizing influence.[31]

The Scope of Vernacular Criticism

Vernacular criticism comes in various forms: the poem about poetry; the prose defence of poetry, or praise of it; the preface and the prologue; satire; the treatise; the set of notes. What is lacking before Davenant's *Discourse upon Gondibert* (1650) is a treatise on a single genre, of which there had been scores in Italy (heroic poem, tragicomedy, even madrigal). Not that good work on single genres is lacking. Michael Drayton wrote a series of brilliant, brief prefaces, gathered in his 1619 *Poems*—on the versification of his heroic poem *The Barons' Wars* as well as questions of genre; on pastoral; on odes—which are remarkable for their fluent summaries of commonplaces from classical poetics, and their demonstration of the relevance of a largely inherited theory to practice. Dudley North's short essay on clarity and obscurity in lyric poetry, written around 1610 though printed only in 1645, is another relatively rare example of developed criticism of contemporary literature in the terms of classical poetics.[32] It is the reference to modern practice that is often lacking. Modern critics wrote about literature in inherited terms and usually restricted themselves to the discussion of ancient literature. Readerly myopia and a necessary Renaissance historical amnesia helped: Webbe's 'I know no memorable work written by any poet in our English speech until twenty years past'[33] was a typical attitude. The usual mode was, therefore, not description but prescription, ignoring the disappointing present and imagining an ideal future. Critics also made only limited reference to each other, except in the controversial area of the theory of versification.

Questions of the morality of imaginative literature were pressing throughout the period, not least because of the polemical pressures applied by fun-hating puritans. The shape of the debate was familiar from the ancient philosophers and critics. Plato's imagined banning of poets from an imaginary republic had seen little reaction from Aristotle, from whom we may draw a conclusion really only implicit in the *Poetics*: poetry does good to the individual (if only of a therapeutic rather than a didactic kind) and thus to the state. But the rhetorical context of later writings on poetry ensured that its civic role was foregrounded. Horace, here in Jonson's translation, had offered a choice: 'Poets would either profit, or delight, | Or, mixing sweet and fit, teach life the right.'[34] But for most Renaissance critics—with their humanist (and rhetorical) commitment to civic utility—there was no either/or: delight was acceptable only as a means to a didactic end. Jonson built on the rhetorical tradition's idealization of the orator as a good man skilled in speaking and (in Cicero's view) a thorough philosopher, and followed the lead of Horace and Strabo, when he insisted: 'We do not require in [the poet] mere elocution, or an excellent faculty in verse, but the exact knowledge of all virtues and their contraries; with ability to render the one loved, the other hated, by his proper embattling them.'[35] This emphasis on morality created a problem, since existing literature was full of characters and actions that were far from exemplary, and so might be suspected of endangering morals rather than improving them. Plutarch's sensible voice ('Poetry…is an imitation of the manners and lives of men, who are not perfect, pure, and irreproachable, but involved in passions, false opinions, and ignorance'; we should learn 'to praise the technique and skill of the imitation, but to censure and abuse the habits and activities represented'[36]) may have done much to license such practice, but it had little impact on theory.

Lodge, writing in 1579, opted for the old defence of allegory,[37] which could wrench an edifying meaning from the most salacious tale. One of the period's great works—Spenser's *The Faerie Queene*—was to be written in the allegorical mode, and Spenser himself, following the theoretical and practical lead of the Italian epic poet Tasso,[38] offered an untroubled account of how poetry might say one thing on the surface and teach another beneath that shell.[39] But allegory—as a way of writing and of reading—was increasingly seen as an outmoded mode, which did not belong in the new Aristotelian (and Sidneian) poetics of verisimilar *mimesis*. Spenser was followed, less convincingly, by Harington, in the extensive prefatory 'Apology' to his 1591 translation of Ariosto's *Orlando furioso*, a case where the racy content is harder to explain away. Plutarch's attitude had been that complex allegoresis is an unnecessary readerly strategy if we allow that representations of bad deeds are meant to be warnings and not invitations,[40] and he was followed by Webbe, who argues over-optimistically that 'the wantonest poets of all, in their most lascivious works . . . sought rather . . . to withdraw men's minds . . . from such foul vices than to allure them to embrace such beastly follies as they detected'.[41] Sidney's position is less tolerant of the representation of immorality, and is essentially that stated by Plato in the *Republic*: 'Young people can't distinguish the allegorical from the non-allegorical, and what enters the mind at that age tends to become indelible and irremovable. Hence the prime need to make sure that what they first hear is devised as well as possible for the implanting of virtue.'[42] The Sidneian position won out, in theory at least, and among Sidney's heirs is William Davenant, who in 1650 criticized Spenser's romance impossibilities and allegorical proceeding with an economy that crystallized the misgivings that had been around for as long as *The Faerie Queene*: Spenser's subject matter should have been 'more natural and therefore . . . more useful'.[43]

Allegory sat well, as for some ancient writers, alongside a theory of inspiration.[44] Lodge, responding to the puritan Stephen Gosson's attack on poetry and plays, insists that 'poetry is a heavenly gift, a perfect gift',[45] but Horace's scorn for the poet who wants to be thought inspired (*Ars*, ll. 295–301) carried weight. When Michael Drayton, writing in 1627, praises Christopher Marlowe, inspiration has become historicized. It is something that Marlowe (on whom see Charles Martindale, Chapter 26, this volume) has acquired by immersing himself in the imitation and translation of classical poets:

> Neat Marlowe, bathèd in the Thespian springs,
> Had in him those brave translunary things
> That the first poets had; his raptures were
> All air and fire, which made his verses clear:
> For that fine madness still he did retain,
> Which rightly should possess a poet's brain.[46]

For Chapman, in 1598, 'Homer's Poems were writ from a free fury, an absolute and full soul, Virgil's out of a courtly, laborious, and altogether imitatory spirit':[47] the *furor poeticus* belongs to the early generations of the ancient poets. In 1650 Hobbes memorably followed Davenant's scorn of '*inspiration*, a dangerous word': 'I can imagine no cause... by which a man, enabled to speak wisely from the principles of nature and his own meditation, loves rather to be thought to speak by inspiration, like a Bagpipe.'[48]

English Poetics

The first critical work in English to offer anything like a complete poetics was George Puttenham's *The Arte of English Poesie* (1589). In the first of its three books Puttenham follows Horace and Scaliger (his *Poetices Libri Septem* of 1561 was the most influential of the continental treatises) with an idealized historical account of the birth and nature of the various genres. The genres were an awkward classical inheritance. Rosenmeyer observes a gulf in all the key sources—Horace, Quintilian, Diomedes—between the kinds habitually listed and the kinds being written,[49] and this is very much the case in Scaliger and Puttenham too: the taxonomy of genres describes no actual practice. But Puttenham's book 2, on 'proportion' or the theory of versification, is much better, mostly because in this field Puttenham is a self-confessed 'autodidaktos',[50] making up theory by observing practice. His third book is the most celebrated. Here he does a thorough job of translating the classical theory of rhetoric, and especially *elocutio*, into a system to be used by poets, governed, of course, by an Horatian–rhetorical decorum or (the usual English term) 'decency'.

Though published in 1589, three years after Philip Sidney's death, most of Puttenham's work dates from a decade or two earlier. Sidney's *The Defence of Poesy* (written *c.*1580; printed 1595), by far the most important critical work of the English tradition, is more up to date in every way. Here is Sidney's famous definition of poetry: 'Poesy, therefore, is an art of imitation, for so Aristotle termeth it in the word *mimēsis*, that is to say, a representing, counterfeiting, or figuring forth—to speak metaphorically, a speaking picture—with this end: to teach and delight.'[51] Marvin Herrick calls this 'a good Horatian view of the early passages in the *Poetics*',[52] but Horace is a slight presence for Sidney, with only two clear uses of the *Ars* compared to at least seven, detailed, references to the *Poetics*. In this respect Sidney coincides with Scaliger, a key source. To Horatian teaching and delighting Sidney adds the third function of rhetoric, only implicit in Horace and Scaliger, and it becomes his trump card. Poetry teaches, delights, and *moves*: 'to be moved to do that which we know, or to be moved with desire to know—*hoc opus, hic labor est.*'[53] We can see from the collocation of *mimesis* and the 'speaking picture' in that initial definition that Sidney has also been reading Plutarch:

> We shall keep our young student under control even better if, the moment we introduce him to works of poetry, we indicate that poetry is an art of imitation, a capacity

> analogous to painting. He should of course be given the familiar dictum that 'poetry is speaking painting and painting silent poetry'; but in addition to this, let us explain that when we see a picture . . . we feel pleasure and admiration not because it is beautiful but because it is *like*.[54]

And this attention to Plutarch makes more notable Sidney's deviation from him. Instead of Plutarch's pragmatism (praise the imitation not the action; exercise discrimination), Sidney theorizes a black-and-white poetics in which fictional characters are so clearly either good or bad that the reader will almost involuntarily wish to emulate the good and shun the bad. That is his rhetorical inheritance—the poet as orator, leading the reader where he chooses.

As a case study in intractably complex genealogies, we can look at Sidney's version of Aristotle's tragic effect (*Poetics* 1449^{b}), the emotions now being stirred to didactic rather than cathartic ends, and fear and pity becoming 'admiration and commiseration'.[55] Where does 'admiration' (or wonder) come from and why has it replaced fear? Wonder is found alongside pity and terror in Plato (*Ion* 535b–c), and in close proximity to them in Aristotle: required in tragedy, wonder has more scope in epic, where credibility is not challenged by direct representation (*Poetics* 1460^{a}; cf. 1452^{a}). Wonder is a fundamental aesthetic response for Plotinus, as for Minturno among the moderns.[56] Trissino brought pity, fear, and wonder together in his revision of Aristotle.[57] A number of Italian critics engaged in reconciling Horace and Aristotle had added wonder to their Horatian teach–delight or rhetorical teach–delight–move formulae.[58] But wonder was also seen as a key component of romance, and arose frequently in Renaissance debates about verisimilitude versus romance impossibilities (debates of course informed by Aristotle on likely impossibilities and unconvincing possibilities).[59] Sidney very deliberately inserts his 'admiration and commiseration' formula into his prose romance *Arcadia*, where it describes a moment of strong emotions within the fiction.[60] This might suggest that the influence of romance is crucial in promoting wonder above terror, were the episode in question not a moment of explicit tragedy within Sidney's story. It is more likely that for Sidney wonder was simply more decorous, and ultimately more constructive, than terror. Cunningham has investigated the question in relation to Shakespeare, whose Horatio asks Fortinbras at the end of *Hamlet* 'What is it you would see? | If aught of woe or wonder, cease your search' (5. 2. 362–3). It has been noted that in Goulston's Latin translation of the *Poetics* (1623), clarifications and interpolations give 'tragic "admiratio" an importance which is does not have in other seventeenth and eighteenth century versions of the *Poetics*'.[61] Corneille and Dryden subsequently isolate admiration and fear, and admiration and pity, respectively, responding to Goulston perhaps, or to a movement that included both Goulston and Sidney as well as Shakespeare.[62]

Sidney is interested by Aristotle's demonstration that poetry is more philosophical than history because it deals in the general, or universal, rather than the particular (*Poetics* 1451^{a-b}), and by the tragic unities of action, time, and place implicit in Aristotle

(*Poetics* 1449^b, 1451^a), evident in classical practice, and recently spelled out by Castelvetro.[63] Sidney's student William Scott follows his hero with an even closer reading of the *Poetics*,[64] and Jonson—now with access to the skilled exposition of Daniel Heinsius (1611)—develops this trend, and brings 'classical criticism in England another step closer to the true Aristotle'.[65] Sidney realizes in his theory of poetry what is only implicit in the *Poetics* but evident enough when one steps back from it—the involution of Aristotle's theory of poetry with his ethical and political thought: 'For, as Aristotle saith, it is not *gnōsis* but *praxis* must be the fruit.'[66] It is true, and characteristic of his day, that Sidney lacks a full understanding of Aristotelian/Horatian unity—he has sympathy for mixed genres and complex, episodic plots.[67] Indeed, it is not plot but character that is his primary concern, and in this he follows Scaliger over Aristotle. Poetry must offer 'notable images of virtues, vices, or what else',[68] and by that Sidney means exemplary characters. 'If the poet do his part aright, he will show you in Tantalus, Atreus, and such like, nothing that is not to be shunned, in Cyrus, Aeneas, Ulysses each thing to be followed, where the historian, bound to tell things as things were, cannot be liberal—without he will be poetical—of a perfect pattern,' Sidney says, making a point about the moral efficacy of poetic licence developed by Bacon and others.[69]

The other cornerstone of Sidney's theory is Plato's theory of ideas, in the modified Neoplatonic form developed by Cicero, Seneca, and Plotinus, among others: an artist creates a *mimesis* not of any particular thing in the world but of an *idea*.[70] So Sidney:

> any understanding knoweth the skill of each artificer standeth in that *idea* or fore-conceit of the work, and not in the work itself. And that the poet hath that *idea* is manifest by delivering them forth in such excellency as he had imagined them; which delivering forth also is not wholly imaginative ... but so far substantially it worketh, not only to make a Cyrus, which had been but a particular excellency as nature might have done, but to bestow a Cyrus upon the world to make many Cyruses, if they will learn aright why and how that maker made him.[71]

While ancient writers could imagine idealized characters, 'the whole idea of the writer as somehow creating a new world, rather than merely offering a partial image of the world of the senses, is in general alien to Greek and Roman thinking'.[72] But Sidney's poet, certainly following Scaliger and possibly misreading Macrobius' comparison of Virgil to God/Nature,[73] creates a 'second nature': 'Nature never set forth the earth in so rich tapestry as divers poets have done, neither with so pleasant rivers, fruitful trees, sweet-smelling flowers, nor whatsoever else may make the too-much-loved earth more lovely: her world is brazen, the poets only deliver a golden.'[74] This enables one of his more celebrated manœuvres—a Neoplatonic response to Plato's famous objections to fiction in the *Republic*. An artistic creator of verisimilar imaginary things represents not nature but the workings of nature, and so cannot be accused of peddling copies of copies of the ideas: 'for the poet, he nothing affirms, and therefore never lieth.'[75]

The Shape of Things to Come

Sidney's, we see, is a visual poetics, a point not lost on those such as William Scott and Franciscus Junius who studied classical and Italian art theory and related it to Horatian and Sidneian poetics. That emphasis, again, has a rhetorical ancestry, in the theory of *enargeia* or convincing description elaborated from the classical sources by Erasmus and all the Elizabethan rhetoricians. Jonson's attention to the visual in *Discoveries* is in this tradition,[76] and one of the most important early seventeenth-century critical works, Junius' *The Painting of the Ancients* (1638, after his Latin version of 1637), builds firmly on these foundations in providing a full collation of classical sources on art theory and on the visual analogy in poetics. Often ignored, Junius takes his commonplacing (and his urge to reconcile all classical voices with each other) so far that any theory is hard to make out, but he is of particular importance for giving us the first sustained response to Longinus in English: '"Art is then perfect," saith Dionysius Longinus, "when she seemeth to be Nature"'[77]—just one of many quotations.

For Jonson, following Aristotle more faithfully than had Sidney in his poetics of character, 'the fable and fiction is (as it were) the form and soul of any poetical work or poem'.[78] This theoretical commitment is evident not only in the prefaces and prologues of his plays, most notably the 'Induction' to *Every Man out of his Humour* (1600), where two on-stage critics run the Horatian rule over the play to come, but in their construction too. Jonson also claimed to have written some 'observations upon Horace his *Art of Poetry*, which, with the text translated, I intend shortly to publish',[79] in which he used Aristotle to illuminate Horace, but only the translation survived the fire that damaged his library in 1623.[80] Jonson's classicism was not blind: 'For to all the observations of the ancients, we have our own experience; which, if we will use and apply, we have better means to pronounce... Truth lies open to all; it is no man's several.'[81] These famous remarks (less original than they sound in their English dress, being a commonplacing of the early sixteenth-century Spanish humanist Juan Luis Vives) echo Samuel Daniel's in *A Defence of Rhyme* (1603):

> we should not so soon yield our consents captive to the authority of antiquity, unless we saw more reason; all our understandings are not to be built by the square of Greece and Italy. We are the children of nature as well as they; we are not so placed out of the way of judgement but that the same sun of discretion shineth upon us.[82]

Such relativism is unusual at this date, and a more rigid neoclassicism would soon become the dominant tone, though not before Davenant had attempted an interesting theoretical fusion of the dramatic and the epic in the *Discourse* (1650) on his heroic poem *Gondibert*.

When Thomas Carew bids a verse farewell to the late John Donne in 1633, he tells his hero that

the flame
Of thy brave soul ... shot such heat and light
As burnt our earth, and made our darkness bright.[83]

Or take Dudley North, writing in around 1610 about what would later be called metaphysical poetry: 'lines of a far-fetched and laboured fancy, with allusions and curiosity, and in similes of little more fruit or consequence than to ravish the reader into the writer's fine chameleon colours, and feed him with air, I approve not so much as height and force of spirit sententiously and weightily exhibited ... art is best expressed where it least appears.'[84] If these are not yet evidence of the influence of Longinus' *On the Sublime*, they are a clear sign that the intellectual climate was ready for it. But it was into a volatile England that Longinus was translated by John Hall in 1652. The theatres had remained closed since 1642 as the puritans took over the country, so that Nashe's casual analogy in 1589 about objectors to poetry, 'as in Plato's, so in Puritans' common wealth',[85] now seemed prophetic. Hall used the analogy of the Greek and Roman republican context of classical eloquence as justification for dedicating his Longinus to the parliamentarian Bulstrode Whitelocke.[86] His translation was perhaps the culmination of a phase of development nipped in the bud with the Restoration of monarchy in 1660.

But in certain respects puritanism enabled neoclassicism. Davenant was obliged to theorize, and produce, the first English opera because plays were banned. Attributed to Davenant is the anonymous *A Proposition for Advancement of Morality, by a New Way of Entertainment of the People* (1654), in which an academy for edifying musico-theatrical entertainments for the masses is proposed on classical grounds and with the panoply of classical commonplaces about the power of music and song wheeled out. In the *Discourse upon Gondibert* the royalist Davenant again divides art's audience, but here poetic teaching relies on a trickle-down effect: 'The common crowd, of whom we are hopeless, we desert, being rather to be corrected by laws, where precept is accompanied by punishment, than to be taught by poesy.'[87] The years of civil war and interregnum see the social dimension of poetics tested in relation to actual politics, and make pressing the search for a nationally useful Christian epic described and theorized by Milton, Cowley, and Davenant.[88] Only by combining classical rule and Christian content can the modern poet deliver what Davenant calls 'explicable virtue'.[89]

Notes

1. The following anthologies are useful for further study and are referred to wherever possible here: D. A. Russell and M. Winterbottom (eds), *Ancient Literary Criticism* (Oxford, 1972), supplemented by an appendix of further excerpts in D. A. Russell, *Criticism in Antiquity*, 2nd edn (1995); Allan H. Gilbert (ed.), *Literary Criticism: Plato to Dryden* (Detroit, MI, 1962), which has good coverage of the

Italian sources; Alex Preminger, O. B. Hardison, Jr, and Kevin Kerrane (eds), *Classical and Medieval Literary Criticism: Translations and Interpretations* (New York, 1974); G. Gregory Smith (ed.), *Elizabethan Critical Essays*, 2 vols (1904); Brian Vickers (ed.), *English Renaissance Literary Criticism* (Oxford, 1999); Gavin Alexander (ed.), *Sidney's 'The Defence of Poesy' and Selected Renaissance Literary Criticism* (2004); and J. E. Spingarn (ed.), *Critical Essays of the Seventeenth Century*, 3 vols (1908). Further reading can start with Glyn Norton (ed.), *The Cambridge History of Literary Criticism*, vol. 3: *The Renaissance* (Cambridge, 1999); Brian Vickers, 'Rhetoric and Poetics', in Charles B. Schmitt, Quentin Skinner, and Eckhard Kessler (eds), *The Cambridge History of Renaissance Philosophy* (Cambridge, 1988), 715–45; Clark Hulse, 'Tudor Aesthetics', in Arthur F. Kinney (ed.), *The Cambridge Companion to English Literature, 1500–1600* (Cambridge, 2000), 29–63; and the introductions to the anthologies edited by Vickers and Alexander.

2. Russell, *Criticism in Antiquity*, 6.
3. Vickers (ed.), *English Renaissance Literary Criticism*, 151–2.
4. Vickers (ed.), *English Renaissance Literary Criticism*, 299.
5. Preface to *Samson Agonistes* (1671), in Spingarn (ed.), *Critical Essays*, 1. 209.
6. Vickers (ed.), *English Renaissance Literary Criticism*, 152, 151.
7. Vickers (ed.), *English Renaissance Literary Criticism*, 605.
8. Cf. Russell, *Criticism in Antiquity*, 84–5.
9. Vickers (ed.), *English Renaissance Literary Criticism*, 10, 14, 53.
10. Bernard Weinberg (ed.), *A History of Literary Criticism in the Italian Renaissance*, 2 vols (Chicago, 1974), 1. 85.
11. In Janel Mueller and Joshua Scodel (eds), *Elizabeth I: Translations, 1592–98* (Chicago, 2009).
12. Smith (ed.), *Elizabethan Critical Essays*, 1. 290–301.
13. In Preminger et al. (eds), *Classical and Medieval Literary Criticism*, 299–309.
14. Plato: *Republic*, bk 3 (392–4); this and all further references to Plato are by the traditional Stephanus numbers. Aristotle: *Poetics* 1448*a*; all further references are to Becker numbers, as here. Diomedes: *Artis Grammaticae Libri III*, 3, in *Grammatici Latini*, ed. Heinrich Keil, 8 vols (Leipzig, 1855–80), 1. 482–3.
15. The supposed first reference is by John Cheke in 1542: see Marvin T. Herrick, *The Poetics of Aristotle in England* (New Haven, 1930), 16.
16. Vickers (ed.), *English Renaissance Literary Criticism*, 164 n. 10.
17. Vickers (ed.), *English Renaissance Literary Criticism*, 319.
18. Smith (ed.), *Elizabethan Critical Essays*, 2. 309 (*Poetics* 1448^{b}).
19. Vickers (ed.), *English Renaissance Literary Criticism*, 146–7, 153.
20. For Longinus' early reception in the English tradition, see William Ringler, 'An Early Reference to Longinus', *MLN* 53 (1938), 23–4 (an extensive quotation (in Latin) in an Oxford lecture on rhetoric by John Rainolds from 1573/4); T. J. B. Spencer, 'Longinus in English Criticism: Influences before Milton', *Review of English Studies*, 8 (1957), 137–43; and Patrick Cheney, '"The forms of things unknown": English Authorship and the Early Modern Sublime', in Guillemette Bolens and Lukas Erne (eds), *Medieval and Early Modern Authorship* (Tübingen, 2011), 137–60.
21. Vickers (ed.), *English Renaissance Literary Criticism*, 522.
22. Weinberg (ed.), *History*, 1. 64.
23. *Moralia*, 348d and 15d (Stephanus numbers); Vickers (ed.), *English Renaissance Literary Criticism*, 307.
24. *Tusculan Disputations*, 1. 26. 64, picked up, e.g. by Webbe (Smith (ed.), *Elizabethan*

Critical Essays, 1. 231) and Meres (Smith (ed.), *Elizabethan Critical Essays*, 2. 313).

25. See Marvin T. Herrick, *The Fusion of Horatian and Aristotelian Literary Criticism, 1531–1555* (Urbana, IL, 1946), and Weinberg (ed.), *History*, esp. ch. 4.
26. *An Essay of Dramatic Poesy*, in Gilbert (ed.), *Literary Criticism: Plato to Dryden*, 606.
27. Vickers (ed.), *English Renaissance Literary Criticism*, 118.
28. Thomas Wright, *The Passions of the Minde in Generall* (1604), sigs M6[v]–7[r].
29. Franciscus Junius, *The Painting of the Ancients* (1638), 299–300.
30. Alexander (ed.), *Sidney's 'The Defence of Poesy'*, 49.
31. Strabo: Russell and Winterbottom (eds), *Ancient Literary Criticism*, 300–5. Isocrates: *Nicocles* 6–9.
32. See Vickers (ed.), *English Renaissance Literary Criticism*, 504–11.
33. Smith (ed.), *Elizabethan Critical Essays*, 1. 239.
34. Alexander (ed.), *Sidney's 'The Defence of Poesy'*, 306 (*Ars Poetica* 333–4).
35. Vickers (ed.), *English Renaissance Literary Criticism*, 568. Cf. Russell and Winterbottom (eds), *Ancient Literary Criticism*, 302 (Strabo), 417–23 (Quintilian); Horace, *Ars Poetica* 309–16.
36. Russell and Winterbottom (eds), *Ancient Literary Criticism*, 527, 514.
37. Thomas Lodge, 'A Defence of Poetry' (1579), in Smith (ed.), *Elizabethan Critical Essays*, 1. 63–86.
38. Cf. Weinberg (ed.), *History*, 1. 206–7.
39. In the so-called Letter to Ralegh printed with *The Faerie Queene* in 1590: Vickers (ed.), *English Renaissance Literary Criticism*, 297–301.
40. Russell and Winterbottom (eds), *Ancient Literary Criticism*, 516–17.
41. Smith (ed.), *Elizabethan Critical Essays*, 1. 251.
42. *Republic* 378d–e, in Russell and Winterbottom (eds), *Ancient Literary Criticism*.
43. Spingarn (ed.), *Critical Essays*, 2. 6.
44. Cf. Russell, *Criticism in Antiquity*, 95–8.
45. Smith (ed.), *Elizabethan Critical Essays*, 1. 75.
46. Alexander (ed.), *Sidney's 'The Defence of Poesy'*, 294.
47. Smith (ed.), *Elizabethan Critical Essays*, 2. 298.
48. Spingarn (ed.), *Critical Essays*, 2. 25, 59.
49. Thomas G. Rosenmeyer, 'Ancient Literary Genres: A Mirage?', in Andrew Laird (ed.), *Oxford Readings in Ancient Literary Criticism* (Oxford, 2006), 434.
50. Alexander (ed.), *Sidney's 'The Defence of Poesy'*, 103.
51. Alexander (ed.), *Sidney's 'The Defence of Poesy'*, 10.
52. Herrick, *Fusion*, 24.
53. Alexander (ed.), *Sidney's 'The Defence of Poesy'*, 22.
54. Russell and Winterbottom (eds), *Ancient Literary Criticism*, 513.
55. Alexander (ed.), *Sidney's 'The Defence of Poesy'*, 27, 46.
56. See J. V. Cunningham, *Woe or Wonder: The Emotional Effect of Shakespearian Tragedy* (Denver, CO, 1951), 67, 82, and ch. 4 *passim*.
57. Weinberg (ed.), *History*, 2. 752.
58. e.g. Weinberg (ed.), *History*, 1. 138–9, 1. 149.
59. *Poetics* 1460[a]. On wonder in Renaissance poetics, cf. James Biester, *Lyric Wonder: Rhetoric and Wit in Renaissance English Poetry* (Ithaca, NY, 1997).
60. *The Countess of Pembroke's Arcadia (The New Arcadia)*, ed. Victor Skretkowicz (Oxford, 1987), 399: 'the rareness of the accident matching together the rarely matched together—pity with admiration.'
61. Mary Gallagher, 'Goulston's *Poetics* and Tragic "Admiratio"', *Revue de Littérature Comparée*, 39 (1965), 614–19 (619).
62. Gallagher, 'Goulston's *Poetics*', 614; cf. Herrick, *Aristotle*, 27–8.
63. See Weinberg (ed.), *History*, 1. 508–10.

64. William Scott, *The Model of Poesy*, ed. Gavin Alexander (Cambridge, 2013).
65. Herrick, *Aristotle*, 38.
66. Alexander (ed.), *Sidney's 'The Defence of Poesy'*, 22; and cf. 13 on *architektonikē*.
67. Cf. Herrick, *Aristotle*, 26.
68. Alexander (ed.), *Sidney's 'The Defence of Poesy'*, 12.
69. Alexander (ed.), *Sidney's 'The Defence of Poesy'*, 19. Bacon (1605): Vickers (ed.), *English Renaissance Literary Criticism*, 461–2. Cf. Davenant and Hobbes (Spingarn (ed.), *Critical Essays*, 2. 10–11, 2. 61–2).
70. See Alexander (ed.), *Sidney's 'The Defence of Poesy'*, 323–4; and cf. Weinberg (ed.), *History*, 1. 181, 420, for examples of Italian analogues.
71. Alexander (ed.), *Sidney's 'The Defence of Poesy'*, 9.
72. Russell, *Criticism in Antiquity*, 100.
73. Russell, *Criticism in Antiquity*, 197.
74. Alexander (ed.), *Sidney's 'The Defence of Poesy'*, 9.
75. Alexander (ed.), *Sidney's 'The Defence of Poesy'*, 34.
76. Vickers (ed.), *English Renaissance Literary Criticism*, 568–70.
77. Junius, *Painting*, 305; cf. Russell and Winterbottom (eds), *Ancient Literary Criticism*, 484.
78. Vickers (ed.), *English Renaissance Literary Criticism*, 581 and cf. *Poetics* 1450^{a}.
79. *Sejanus* (1605), in Spingarn (ed.), *Critical Essays*, 1. 10.
80. See 'An Execration upon Vulcan', ll. 89–91, in Ian Donaldson (ed.), *Ben Jonson* (Oxford, 1985).
81. Vickers (ed.), *English Renaissance Literary Criticism*, 559.
82. Alexander (ed.), *Sidney's 'The Defence of Poesy'*, 217.
83. Vickers (ed.), *English Renaissance Literary Criticism*, 555.
84. Vickers (ed.), *English Renaissance Literary Criticism*, 511.
85. Smith (ed.), *Elizabethan Critical Essays*, 1. 319.
86. *Peri hupsous, Or Dionysius Longinus of the Height of Eloquence* (1652), sigs A3^{r}–B5^{v}. See further David Norbrook, *Writing the English Republic: Poetry, Rhetoric and Politics, 1627–1660* (Cambridge, 1999), esp. 137–9, 215–16.
87. Spingarn (ed.), *Critical Essays*, 2. 14.
88. Milton: *The Reason of Church-government* (1641), in Vickers (ed.), *English Renaissance Literary Criticism*, 591–7. Cowley: preface to *Poems* (1656), in Spingarn (ed.), *Critical Essays*, 2. 86–90.
89. Spingarn (ed.), *Critical Essays*, 2. 9.

CHAPTER 6

Classicism and Christianity

MARK VESSEY

Classicism, Christianity, 'Renaissance' Literary History

> The message I bring is that you lost your way long ago, perhaps as long as five centuries ago. The handful of men among whom the movement originated of which you represent, I fear, the sad tail—those men were animated, at least at first, by the purpose of finding the True Word, by which they understood then, and I understand now, the redemptive word.
>
> That word cannot be found in the classics, whether you understand the classics to mean Homer and Sophocles or whether you understand them to mean Shakespeare and Dostoevsky.
>
> (J. M. Coetzee, *Eizabeth Costello*, 2003)

These words are spoken to a university graduating class in the humanities by Sister Bridget Costello, recipient of an honorary doctorate of letters, in J. M. Coetzee's *Elizabeth Costello*.[1] Coetzee's fiction is subtitled 'Eight Lessons' in some printings, and Sister Bridget's oration is one in a series of lectures that supply its main structure. The final chapter (before a postscript letter addressed to Francis Bacon, dated 'This 11 September, AD 1603') reprises Kafka's story 'Before the Law' in a register suggested by a famous lecture on that text by Jacques Derrida. Derrida was concerned with the historicity of 'literature' as a modern institution, one whose guardians ('critics, academics, literary theorists, writers, and philosophers') deferred in their turn to a higher and other law, evoked—in Derrida's reading—by the priest in *The Trial* as the 'Law' of those 'Scriptures' to which the story of 'Before the Law' would have been a preface.[2] Almost the last motion of *Elizabeth Costello* is the heroine's unspoken imprecation, 'A curse on literature!'

Sister Bridget is a Catholic missionary nun, but Coetzee has made her a classicist too. It is she who enlarges the book's horizons to take in the long history of Western ways with texts, including the kind or kinds of text that we have grown used to thinking of as 'literary'. Upon receiving an honorary degree in '*litterae humaniores*, humane letters or, more loosely, the humanities', she offers the graduating class an account of their vocation, beginning with the humanist movement of the fifteenth century, which produced the formula *studia humanitatis*, meaning 'humane studies, studies in man and the nature of man, as distinct from *studia divinitatis*, studies pertaining to the divine'. According to her, the 'living breath' of humane studies was originally 'textual scholarship', which she claims was invented for the purpose of biblical exegesis. (She does not stop to consider what Lorenzo Valla and other pioneers of modern scholarship on the biblical text may have owed to their humanist predecessors, most of whom—like Petrarch—were primarily intent on recovering the styles, voices, and 'living' presences of *classical* Latin writers.[3]) Regrettably, influential humanists had let themselves be distracted from God's 'True Word' by the mere words of the classics that they had undertaken to study for its sake, and so inadvertently founded the 'so-called humanities' of the modern university curriculum. 'The *studia humanitatis* have taken a long time to die,' Sister Bridget tells her audience, 'but now, at the end of the second millennium of our era, they are truly on their deathbed'. Though herself 'a daughter of the Catholic Church', she confesses that she cannot help applauding Martin Luther 'when he turns his back on Desiderius Erasmus, judging that his colleague, despite his immense gifts, has been seduced into branches of study that do not, by the standards of the ultimate, matter'.

Coetzee's nun's tale may not be wholly reliable as literary history, but neither is it perfect fiction. Francis Bacon, apocryphal addressee of the postscript to *Elizabeth Costello*, presses a similar charge against the cultivators of a double antiquity early in *The Advancement of Learning* (1605). Sparing Erasmus, Bacon makes Luther chiefly responsible for the latest outbreak of a 'distemper of learning' arising from 'affectionate study of eloquence and copy [facility] of speech':

> Martin Luther, conducted (no doubt) by an higher Providence, but in discourse of reason finding what a province he had undertaken against the Bishop of Rome and the degenerate traditions of the church... was enforced to awake all antiquity, and to call former times to his succours to make a party against the present time; *so that the ancient authors, both in divinity and in humanity, which had long slept in libraries, began generally to be read and revolved.* This by consequence did draw on a necessity of a more exquisite travail in the languages original wherein those authors did write, for the better understanding of those authors... And thereof grew again a delight in their manner and style of phrase, and an admiration of that kind of writing...[4]

In the *Advancement*, the Erasmus of the *Ciceronianus* stands up as a critic of humanist stylistic affectation and as the natural ally of Bacon, who next compares the vanities of literary classicism (as we would call it) to 'Pygmalion's frenzy', since 'words are but the images of matter, and except they have life of reason and invention, to fall in love with them is all one as to fall in love with a picture'. Bacon's experience of Reformation controversy led him to give a more sceptical account of the religious motivations for recourse to 'ancient authors, both in divinity and in humanity' than Sister Bridget would, but his critique anticipates hers. The surface delights of verbal artistry had diverted attention from the proper objects of learning. Even as he summoned the figure of Pygmalion, Bacon was attempting like others before and after him 'to separate a language of truth from the tropical languages of myth and rhetoric', in his case by setting 'rational discourse' against 'its supposedly non-serious twin'.[5]

As Waswo and Moss have shown, the 'linguistic turn' of the Renaissance humanists ran counter to the classical precept of *rem tene, verba sequentur* ('hold fast to the thing, and the words will follow').[6] Symptomatically, the title of a bestselling textbook by Erasmus that would nearly justify the reproaches of Coetzee's nun was *De Duplici Copia Verborum ac Rerum*, 'On the Double Provision of *Words* and *Things*'—in that order. Whereas in scholastic philosophy language was taken to be the bearer of mental concepts whose truth or correspondence to an objective reality was independent of the actual forms of verbal expression, in the new humanist discourse, 'meaning emerged from words in context, from cultural allusion, and from sophisticated judgements made on the basis of verbal competence, memory, and educated taste'.[7] As soon as language—in the first instance, Latin or Greek—was seen in this way as the ground of cognition, rather than as a window into a non-linguistic realm of concepts, philology and textual scholarship became privileged techniques for the transhistorical remaking of worlds of human experience.[8] Philosophical dismay like Bacon's at 'affectionate study of eloquence and copy of speech' was a corollary of the high value set by Renaissance humanists on rhetoric and rhetorical analysis as instruments of practical knowledge, including that most practical, 'saving' knowledge identified by nearly all of them with (Christian) religious truth.

Erasmus would not have quarrelled much with Coetzee's nun. Only in the text of the Christian Scriptures, he held, could the truth of Christ as divine 'Word' still be found incarnate, physically present, charged with the potentially transformative power of living speech (*sermo*, not *verbum*, in his controversial rendering of the *logos* of John 1: 1).[9] Erasmus' revision of the *textus receptus* of the Vulgate New Testament was designed to guarantee that the force of that saving discourse was felt again to the full in Latin, the common language of Western or Roman Christendom. From its first edition, under the title of *Novum Instrumentum* (1516), his New Testament was prefaced with an address 'To the Pious Reader', the *Paraclesis*, explaining how Christ as divine *auctor* was embodied in the text. 'Because he promised to be with us to the end of time,' Erasmus wrote, 'he is present most especially in these writings [in his *litteris praecipue praestat*] in which even now he lives, breathes, and speaks, more effectively [*efficacius*], I would almost say, than when he lived among human beings.'[10] This characteristically Erasmian, Christocentric theory of the power of written language to move individuals and thereby shape societies was to have wide resonance in early modern Europe, not least in England.

Apart from Dame Folly (in the *Encomium Moriae* or 'Praise of Folly'), herself a projection both of Christ and of her author, only one other figure in texts published by Erasmus competes with the second person of the Trinity in his (or its) power of self-presentation in writing, and that is the figure of Desiderius Erasmus, whose texts—as was claimed, in epigraphic Greek, on a famous portrait of him by Albrecht Dürer—set forth a livelier image of him than the artist could fashion.[11] This Erasmian self-figuration, building on poetic initiatives by humanists since Petrarch, would contribute to the prevalence in Renaissance England of the post-Augustan Latin idiom of the literary work as a 'living' monument of its author.[12] Erasmus' theory of the textually realized, historically *active* authorial image contested in advance the Baconian reduction of language and text to the status of mere reflections of reality. It also took for granted the existence of a plenary set of lively authorial works (classical, biblical, patristic, contemporary), understood by him and others as falling under a single, providentially Christian dispensation.[13]

Erasmus' exposition of a unified sphere of *bonae literae* (in his book, 'texts good for the soul') offers an imposing instance of the kind of 'imaginary library' that has been said to manifest the reality of 'literature' as a privileged set of discursive practices, before the invention of the corresponding late modern concept.[14] Yet there are obvious differences between Erasmian theory and the notions underpinning 'English literature' in our current sense. They chiefly relate to Erasmus' Christo-bibliocentrism, his Latinism, and his distinctly 'Renaissance' sense of epoch. (1) Erasmian theory defers to a higher law or truth that, while never identified by Erasmus himself solely with the canonical Christian Scriptures, was nonetheless consistently associated by him with the presence of Christ as textually incarnated in the Gospels. (2) Although he was an impassioned proponent of Greek studies and, for a time, of translation of the Bible into the vernaculars, Erasmus' best energies were devoted to bringing the resources of salutary learning within the orbit of humanist Latin. Although not unaware of post-classical, national 'proto-literatures' in Italian, French, and English, he held no brief for any such. (3) Erasmus' vision of the imaginary library of famous and approved authors was coordinated with a radically 'Renaissance'-minded literary and cultural history, in which a mythical 'dark age' intervened between the end of the Roman Empire in the West and the revival of *bonae literae* in quattrocento Italy.[15] As an editor and commentator of Christian texts, besides the New Testament and the Psalms, Erasmus concentrated on the writings of the church fathers from the period 200–500 CE. He especially honoured Jerome (*c*.347–419) for his exemplary combination of classical Latin eloquence, literacy in Greek, and Christ- and Bible-centred piety.[16] For the space of almost 1,000 years after Jerome, we could infer, there had been little if anything to admire in Latin letters. Erasmus, however, does not measure the Middle Ages. For him, philology seamlessly closed the gap in time.

Since Wellek broached the subject in the early 1949s, the relationship between emerging projections of English literature and trial constructions of English literary history in the sixteenth and seventeenth centuries has been studied from a number of angles.[17] This chapter offers another, by considering some of the terms in which sixteenth-century and later appeals to the authority of texts from Christian as well as classical antiquity were phrased by those with a special interest in the pasts, presents, and possible futures of 'letters' in England or Britain. Erasmus cannot provide the elusive thread that would guide our steps through this labyrinth, but his formative role with respect to the religious–educational ideologies and institutions of early modern England makes him a natural point of reference.[18] How was Christo-bibliocentric, Erasmian literary humanism—Latin in expression and founded upon a radically discontinuous, ultimately *un*historical narrative of the literary culture of post-Roman Christianity—accommodated by writers and readers of texts in English? If Coetzee's nun's tale is not to stand as the whole story, as assuredly it should not, what other tales can now be told?

It is too soon for anything like a comprehensive survey of the field. Scholarship on literary and broadly cultural aspects of the reception of ancient Christian texts in early modern England (with the exception of the Bible) is only now inching beyond the incunabular stage.[19] Other chapters below provide soundings for individual English authors whose œuvres have attracted some of the most intensive research in that area.[20] Here we focus attention on a number of scenes of insular literary history in the making, beginning with a late Elizabethan retrospect on the first Erasmian age in English letters, lingering over the most spectacular Jacobean instance of the religious 'writing of Britain', and closing with an array of poetic examples of Caroline or anti-Caroline divinity. In each case, our primary concern will be with figures and narratives of the reappropriation and representing of a living 'truth' (God, divine wisdom, saving knowledge) imagined as inhering in texts or verbal monuments.

The Last Great Clerks: The Erasmian Past of the Later Elizabethan Renaissance

> Towards Venice we progressed, and took Rotterdam in our way, that was clean out of our way. There we met with aged learning's chief ornament, that abundant and superingenious clerk Erasmus, as also with merry Sir Thomas More our countryman, who was come purposely over a little before us, to visit the said grave father Erasmus. What talk, what conference we had then, it were here superfluous to rehearse...

Paradox is the prevailing figure of thought in this page from a 'Chronicle of the King of Pages', Thomas Nashe's *The Unfortunate Traveller* (1594).[21] Rotterdam is on the way and out of it. Erasmus, master of *copia* both of words and matter, has nothing to say. He and More are intimates with 'contrary' opinions. Neither has yet written the work for which he will be best known (*Praise of Folly*, *Utopia*) and which the reader is presumed already to know. The significance of Erasmus and More for Nashe's travellers and their fellow 'countrymen' is taken for granted, but no more settled in the text than the two men's 'discontented studies'. The one certainty is that the next stop after Rotterdam on this Anglo-European itinerary will be Wittenberg: after the city of Erasmus, the city of Luther—and only then to Italy, cradle of the new (and 'aged') learning, as of the latest vernacular idioms. In the annals of print, *The Unfortunate Traveller* falls close to Sidney's *Defence of Poesy* (1595). Although Nashe claimed in his preface to the Earl of Southampton not to 'ascribe' himself among the 'sacred number' of poets, he plainly meant to contribute in some fashion to the newly re-professionalizing discourses of 'letters' in England and in English. Under the guise of travelogue, his 'Life of Jack Wilton' intervenes in a field of English literary reception and production, the frontiers and internal districts of which were still being adumbrated in the later sixteenth and earlier seventeenth centuries. The figure of 'Erasmus' was one of the devices temporarily used to structure that field.

For Roger Ascham in *The Scholemaster*, Erasmus had been 'the ornament of learning in our time'.[22] Thomas Campion in *Observations in the Art of English Poesie* (1602) gives a concise version of a literary–historical narrative that, in various forms, was presupposed by many other chroniclers:

> Learning, after the decline of the Roman Empire and the pollution of their language through the conquest of the barbarians, lay most pitifully deformed till the time of Erasmus, Reuchlin, Sir Thomas More, and other learned men of that age, who brought the Latin tongue again to light, redeeming it with much labour out of the hands of the illiterate monks and friars . . .[23]

The scheme of this narrative of redemption is that of the Renaissance itself, its plot motifs ones that Erasmus had done more than anyone else to popularize in northern Europe. Along with the habitual association of Erasmus with More, other customary features of the insular figuration of the Dutch humanist were an emphasis on his advocacy of poetry and a special interest in his prose declamation, the *Praise of Folly*. Part of Erasmus' rhetorical appeal, it is clear, lay in his Protean elusiveness with respect to the written genres of eloquence. Before English writers began systematically inventorying and exploiting the classically differentiated 'resources of kind', Erasmus was recognized as a resource beyond kind, an outstanding exponent of the *genus universum*, who, beginning with his collection of classical proverbial wisdom in the *Adagia* (much of it sourced from early Christian authors such as Jerome), 'attempt[ed] to perform the encyclopedia in the mode of *copia*'.[24]

Over time this figure of Erasmus lent itself to comic stylization. In a gloss on the February eclogue of Spenser's *Shepheardes Calender* 'E.K.' makes gentle fun of 'Erasmus a great clerk and good old father' by attributing to him the exegesis of an adage that was never included in the *Adagia* (Spenser, *Shorter Poems*, 51).[25] Nashe's evocation of Erasmus the 'abundant and superingenious clerk' is in the same vein. The shared term of these two descriptions is telling. In England and in print during the sixteenth century Erasmus was routinely hailed as 'clerk' (or 'clark'), usually with the addition of an epithet such as 'great', 'learned', or 'famous'. In Middle English, 'clerk' (< Old French *clerc* < Christian Latin *clericus*) meant (1) a member of the clergy; (2) a person with book learning, one who could read and write, a scholar; or (3) a scribe or notary. All three senses persisted into the early modern period, whereupon the second began to fade into archaism (*OED*). An Early English Books Online search reveals Erasmus to have been by some distance the named individual most often given the title of 'clerk' in extant printed English texts of the mid- to late sixteenth century. It also confirms that after the turn of the century the notarial sense of 'clerk' (3) quickly came to predominate. The Erasmian clerkly figure then disappears from sight. Nashe's epithets of 'abundant' and 'superingenious' were outliers for the time, signs of the archness of his deployment of a trope that was already losing its power to capture English styles of redeeming the textually accumulated wisdom of the Christian and classical past(s).

In the searchable records of printed English only two individuals step out as 'famous clerks' before the year 1529. First is the anonymous, disaffected Roman clerk who trained a dove to settle at the ear of the prophet Mohammed by putting food out for it. This anti-Islamic libel, appearing in three recensions of the English version of Ranulf Higden's fourteenth-century *Polychronicon*, the earliest from 1482 (STC 13438), parodied a figure of textual inspiration familiar to late medieval readers from the traditional iconography of the Evangelists and church fathers.[26] The accidental prototype of the 'famous clerk' in English travestied the prophet of Islam in the guise of the best accredited writers of the Christian biblical and post-biblical canon, the *viri illustres* ('famous men') who were the subjects of Christian encyclopedic bio-bibliographers from Jerome in the late fourth century to Johannes Trithemius in the late fifteenth and well beyond.[27] The next extant 'famous clerk' in English print is a *bona fide* member of the saintly company of Christian (reputed) writers, Dionysius the Areopagite, in Lydgate's *History of Troy* (1513; STC 5579).

These fugitive references point to the primary ground for the early modern figure of the 'famous clerk', which is the universal chronicle in English. Nashe's source for the literary–historical coordinates of the 'Life of Jack Wilton' was a chronicle to the time of Queen Elizabeth, which supplied, *inter alia permulta*, a piecemeal literary history of the Renaissance, including notices on 'the famous clerk Reuchlin [who] restored again the knowledge of the Hebrew tongue' and 'the famous and great learned man master Erasmus of Rotterdam . . . by whose benefit and diligence as well divine knowledge, as all other good learning was marvellously furthered and augmented'.[28] Universal chronicles were natural repositories for the bibliographically derived, biographically formulated, records of the men of letters who appear in sixteenth-century English contexts as 'great clerks' and who collectively—or, in the case of Erasmus, 'a man most learned in all departments' (*vir undecumque doctissimus*), singly—embodied the ideal of an erudition that defied distinctions of discipline and genre.[29]

When the title 'clerk' appeared with a proper name in English texts of the late fifteenth and early sixteenth centuries, the name was almost always that of one of the *auctores* of the combined classical-and-Christian tradition: Aristotle, Virgil, Ovid, Origen, Jerome, Augustine, Leo the Great, Boethius, Gregory the Great, Isidore, Bonaventure, Aquinas, Nicolas of Lyra, and so on. These were the illustrious dead of the Christian Latin annals of 'letters', which—following Jerome's expansion of the *Chronici Canones* (or 'Chronicle') of Eusebius of Caesarea with material from the Suetonian *De Viris Illustribus* ('On Famous Men')—incorporated the basic records of classical literary history. By contrast, the designation of contemporary writers as 'clerks' appears to have been rare before *c.*1529, when Thomas Berthelet announced Juan Luis Vives's *Instruction of a Christen Woman* (translated by Richard Hyrd) as by 'the right famous clerk master Lewes Vives' (STC 24856.5). Where Vives's English publisher led, Erasmus' soon followed. When the *Enchiridion Militis Christiani* ('Handbook [or Poiniard] of a Christian Soldier') was printed in English by Wynkyn de Worde in 1533, the title page described it as the work of 'the famous clerk Erasmus of Rotterdam' (STC 10479). Over the next decade and a half, a string of translations of other devotional works by Erasmus came off English presses, each one repeating the titular description of its author as a 'famous clerk', a phrase for which there was no equivalent on the title pages of the Latin editions.[30]

The titular presentation of Erasmus and Vives as 'famous clerks' implicitly co-opted two living writers, both with well-advertised English affiliations, to a company of ancient (and some later) *auctores*. These newly Englished modern Latin 'classics' quickly fell in with native company. In 1530, de Worde published an edition of the *Assemblie of Foules* 'compiled by the preclared [notable] and famous clerk Geoffrey Chaucer' (STC 5092). Illustrating this description of Chaucer on the title page was a portrait depicting him in his study, in a style popularized by French printers and deriving from a long tradition of Christian author portraits in which images of Jerome, Augustine, Gregory the Great, and other Latin church fathers were pre-eminent.[31] Erasmus had already merged his publishing persona with these prestigious exemplars. In England, meanwhile, long before Erasmus began to cut the figure of a 'Renaissance' Latin author, Chaucer had assumed the figure of the English 'clerk' as a way of representing his role as at once a student and a producer of poetry—most strikingly in his Oxford clerk's deference to that 'worthy clerk' and 'laureate poet' Petrarch, in the *Canterbury Tales* ('The Clerk's Prologue', ll. 27, 31). This transparently immodest Chaucerian trope of authorship had then been seized upon by his fifteenth-century imitators, becoming central 'to the ongoing invention and narration of English literary history'.[32] The woodcut author portrait for the 1530 *Assemblie of Foules* offered 'a visual realization of Chaucer's clerkly self-representation within his text'.[33]

De Worde was not the only English printer to hold stock in both Latin and vernacular clerkly idioms. In 1532, the year before De Worde issued the *Enchiridion*, Berthelet, publisher already of the 'famous clerk' Vives, produced the first collected *Workes of Chaucer*, in an edition by William Thynne. In his preface to Henry VIII, he presented Chaucer as a polymath whose true measure could now be taken for the first time. The king was invited 'to read and hear the books of that noble and famous clerk Geoffrey Chaucer, in whose works is so manifest comprobation of his excellent learning in all kinds of doctrines and sciences'. Chaucer's works were imagined as modelling a *genus universum*, the more precious for being by an Englishman and thus able to represent a larger whole comprising 'the works or memory of the famous and most excellent clerks in all kindes of sciences that [had] flourished' in Henry's realm.[34] In the absence of the national catalogue *De Scriptoribus Illustribus* ('On Famous Writers') that Leland had grandiloquently promised to the same monarch and that Bale had yet to produce, Chaucer—by himself, if required—might secure Britain's place in the new world of printed learning.[35] As if for subliminal reinforcement of its claims, the title-page border for the 1532 *Workes* was copied from Holbein's design for a 1518 Basle edition of Erasmus' *Epigrammata*, More's *Utopia*, and a selection of More's own Latin epigrams.[36]

These, then, were the remote antecedents of Nashe's fiction of an Erasmian age in English letters in *The Unfortunate Traveller*. As noted earlier, the literary–historical moment of that work is well defined. Nashe belonged to the generation of the 'Elizabethan prodigals' who broke open new paths for *non*-clerical literary professionals by repenting in print of their youthful failure to live up to the ideals of a Christian humanist education and by 'converting' from their former, licentious readerly and writerly pursuits (amorous poetry, romance) to higher, more serious, and godly endeavours, usually in prose.[37] The possibility of a reformation of 'letters' was thus staked on a personal project of penitence. While deeply influenced by the values of Erasmian humanism, this prodigal or 'conversional' narrative of a literary career departed sharply from the clerkly paradigm of an encyclopedic unity of good learning. It was in fact distinctly un-Erasmian. Nothing about Erasmus' career or the styling of his œuvre suggested a split within the classical-and-Christian universe of *bonae literae*. As far as Erasmus was concerned, Italian humanists of the previous century had already dispelled the illusion of a schism between Christian and classical professions, once famously hallucinated—in overtly penitential idioms—by Jerome.[38] If there was a patristic warrant for the Elizabethan literary conversion story, it was derived not from Jerome via Erasmus but from Augustine's *Confessions* via Petrarch.[39]

Just as it made possible new and productive alignments between Christian schemes of spiritual recovery and classical models of literary progress, so the conversional plot of a literary career posed the problem of insular literary history anew for the later English Renaissance. The problem was simultaneously one of language, genre, and periodization. Subsuming differences of language, discipline, and literary kind, the vernacular English clerkly model of scholarly authorship also largely effaced the distinction of times assumed by Erasmus and his fellow-humanists. Aristotle, Ovid, Augustine, Aquinas... Erasmus, Vives... Chaucer and other British writers writing in Latin, French, or English: all could be seen as belonging to one transhistorical, transdisciplinary, translinguistic company of famous men of letters. By contrast, the best articulated models of literary career, whether classical Latin (Virgil, Horace, Ovid) or Italian Renaissance ('Augustinian' Petrarch), were temporally selective, self-consciously poetical, strictly genre-observant.[40] Issues of cultural–historical and linguistic difference—the very issues that humanist philology had first raised—would henceforth need to be addressed on fresh terms.

As Nashe's travelogue bade farewell to the Erasmian clerk as local-and-universal culture hero, Sidney in the *Defence* joined E.K. in elegantly sublimating the anxieties of a new English literary vocation—carefully demarcating the domain of the 'right poet' with respect to other disciplines (including theology), checking off the classical poetic genres, querying the styles and trajectories of English poetry since the 'misty time' of Chaucer. With the partial exception of Spenser, whose maturer work lay beyond Sidney's view, no other English writer before Milton would formulate the challenge of a *poetic* renaissance of English letters so sharply. And, by the time of Milton's maturity, the national religio-political context had been transformed.

All the King's Books: The Library of a Christian Nation

In book 2 of *The Advancement of Learning* (1605), a work dedicated to King James I of England as monarch most 'learned in all literature and erudition, divine and human... since Christ's time', Bacon famously gave the brief for a new discipline that he called *historia literarum* or the 'history of learning' (*Major Works*, 121, 175–6).[41] The passage occurs as part of a general taxonomy of learning, the main divisions of which are history (as the work of memory), poetry (the work of imagination), and philosophy (the work of reason). Sidney had made the same classical division in the *Defence*, in order then to press the claims of poetry at the expense of the other two disciplines. While Bacon staked little directly on the powers of the poet, he did set a high value on history and was ready to award it a new province. 'History', he wrote,

> is Natural, Civil, Ecclesiastical, and Literary; whereof the first three I allow as extant, the fourth I note as deficient. For no man hath propounded to himself the general state of learning to be described and represented from age to age, as many have done the works of nature, and the state civil and ecclesiastical; without which the history of the world seemeth to me to be as the statua [statue] of Polyphemus with his eye out; that part being wanting which doth most show the spirit and life of the person.

In the corresponding passage of the expanded Latin version of the *Advancement*, Bacon would speak of conjuring the 'spirit of learning' (*spiritus literarius*) of past ages. As we have seen, however, there were limits to Bacon's philological enthusiasm. They applied as well to the new 'literary' historical science:

> The use and end of which work I do not so much design for curiosity or satisfaction of those that are the lovers of learning; but chiefly for a more serious and grave purpose,

> which is this in few words, that it will make men wise in the use and administration of learning. For it is not St Augustine's nor St Ambrose's works that will make so wise a divine, as ecclesiastical history, thoroughly read and observed; and the same reason is of learning.

When he had the whole of natural, civil, and ecclesiastical history at his disposal, why did Bacon single out the works of those famous Christian authors of antiquity, Augustine and Ambrose, in an order neither alphabetical nor chronological, as exemplary impediments of practical divinity? Circumstance may have played a part. As he was putting the finishing touches to the *Advancement*, another volume was published that accorded those two ecclesiastical writers a priority. This was the first printed catalogue of the University Library at Oxford, as recently refounded by Sir Thomas Bodley. In a room over the Divinity School, Bodley's first librarian, Thomas James, had set up two rows of book presses. Those on the south side of the building held works of theology, those on the north side books relating to the faculties of medicine, law, and arts. The Latin catalogue, compiled by Dr James and presented to the king during a royal visit to Oxford in the autumn of 1605, was arranged in the same order as the physical collection.[42] Its first entry is for the Erasmus–Froben edition of the *Opera Omnia* of Augustine; other editions of works by Augustine fill the remainder of that page and the first four lines of the next. Then come the works of Ambrose. A reader who entered the early seventeenth-century world of learning through the portals of the Bodleian collection or its catalogue thus immediately came face-to-face with the two church fathers cited as counterexamples by Bacon in his manifesto for a *historia literarum*, in the order in which he named them.

One of the inspirations for Bacon's idea of 'literary history', and a model for his description in *New Atlantis* of the laboratory-style division of tasks among Bensalemite experimenters in the natural sciences, was the multi-volume Lutheran *Historia Ecclesiae Christi* (also known as the 'Centuries of Magdeburg' because of its organization by epochs) published at Basle between 1559 and 1574.[43] The laboratory of the Magdeburg compilers was historical and documentary. Their object was to recover, authenticate, excerpt, and publish textual witnesses to a history of the original purity, later corruption, and eventual restoration of the 'true' church. Theirs was a confessional programme developed from the scheme of decline and renewal that Erasmus had propagated, but resulting in a discourse of ecclesiastical history that traversed—rather than eclipsing, as Erasmus' did—the centuries of the intermediate age. In the England of Bacon's day, other more or less Erasmian enterprises of textual recovery were under way, each with its own style of 'medievalism'. Thomas James set up *his* laboratory at the Bodleian, where he launched an ambitious project to purge current (especially 'Roman') printed editions of the Latin church fathers by having a team of assistants collate them against medieval manuscripts taken mainly from English monastic libraries.[44] While little came of these labours, they are another instance, alongside Bacon's proposals in the *Advancement* and related works, of a more general impulse in Jacobean Britain towards securing, enhancing, and realizing the textual resources of the realm.[45] The pre-eminent case for Christian letters in English is the 'King James' version of the Bible, which is also the period's most impressive literary monument of the reception of antiquity.[46]

Still the best commentary on the Jacobean Bible project is the preface of 'The Translators to the Reader', the unsigned work of Miles Smith, a member of the First Oxford Company for the translation and (from 1612) Bishop of Gloucester.[47] An accomplished classical and biblical scholar, Smith was also, as anonymous prefacer of the Bible, the author of a brief for English letters comparable with Sidney's *Defence*, Bacon's *Advancement*, or any other manifesto of the time.

The new translation had been ordained by a prince whom Smith paragons first with David and Solomon and then with a series of Roman emperors: Julius Caesar for correction of the calendar; Constantine for strengthening of the Empire and provision for the Church; Theodosius for peace-making; Justinian for lawmaking (p. liv). The opening paragraphs of the preface thus compound the title page's depiction of a succession of divine and human authors of the Bible with a biblical and (late) classical royal/imperial genealogy of the foundation, maintenance, and restoration of normative texts and, in the same acts, of polities. The publishing of this version is understood to be the promulgation of a Christian social and political order, at once anciently established and newly restored.

A calculus of times is crucial to the translation project as a whole. If the previously existing official English biblical text was satisfactory, why replace it? If it was defective, why had it been tolerated? The dilemma was as old as the Vulgate. The central and longest section of the preface catalogues texts and versions of Scripture from ancient Israel to Elizabethan England. To detractors who asked why a further translation should be called for, the translators (voiced by Smith) replied in the words of Jerome to Rufinus:

> *Do we condemn the ancient? In no case: but after the endeavours of them that were before us, we take the best pains we can in the house of God*... And to the same effect say we, that we are so far off from condemning any of their labours that travelled before us in this kind, either in this land or beyond sea... that we acknowledge them to have been raised up of God, for the building and furnishing of his Church, and that they deserve to be had of us and of posterity in everlasting remembrance. ('Translators to the Reader', p. lxi)

There may also be a reminiscence here of the preamble to Jerome's catalogue of Christian writers, the *De Viris Illustribus*.[48] The allusion would be pointed, since Smith, in his memorial of biblical translators 'in this land or beyond sea' (for which he relies upon Trithemius, with other bibliographers and chroniclers), has economically sketched the 'British' tradition in that kind from Bede to John Trevisa and beyond. Translations of biblical texts into the vernacular had been practised 'even from the first times of the conversion of any nation' (p. lx). There was now assurance of the continuity of English Scripture for the length of the history of the English—or indeed British—nation.

Chronologically continuous as it is in its review of the essentially collaborative work of biblical transmission, Smith's preface nonetheless bears the shadow of a certain 'middle' age. To possible 'Roman' objections to repeated revision of the biblical text, it responds with a list of humanist scholars who had been put on the Index for their pains: 'Valla, Stapulensis [Jacques Lefèvre d'Étaples], Erasmus and Vives' (p. lxiv). Erasmus' Latin New Testament is prominently cited in the same place, because it had once been endorsed by a pope. It was also, not incidentally, the primary model for humanist Bible retranslation as critical reappropriation of a complex array of texts, versions, and exegeses.[49] For Erasmus, the church fathers represented an earlier high point of classical eloquence in the service of biblical truth. The same (late) ancient Christian horizon was now graphically projected on behalf of the 1611 translators. In contrast to the biblical text itself, whose only annotation would be cross-referencing, the preface of 'The Translators to the Reader' makes an exhibition of its own intertextuality, piling up classical commonplaces and aphorisms in good humanist fashion, signalling them with a different font, and meticulously referencing most of them in the margins. Amid this *copia* of words and things, the church fathers loom large. The first in their file is ceremonially introduced as 'a great clerk' who uttered opinions 'in writing to remain to posterity' (p. liii). When the prefacer urges the Bible as the normative text for a Christian commonwealth, his short catena of biblical passages on searching the Scriptures gives way to a more substantial anthology of patristic commendations, beginning with the supernatural command 'Tolle, lege; tolle, lege' of Augustine's *Confessions*, translated 'Take up and read, take up and read the Scriptures' (p. lv). As the two most voluble, influential, and unimpeachably orthodox early theorists of biblical text and translation, Jerome and Augustine are the most heavily cited throughout the document, though well supported by other Greek and Latin writers of their age. Of the several companies of authors, translators, and scholars presented as collaborators in the production of the King James Bible, the church fathers play the most concerted role in accrediting it for English readers.[50]

Seen in the light of the translators' preface, the dedicatory fiction of the king's role as 'principal... author of the work' becomes a unifying figure for the emergent idea of *this* English Bible as a plenary text for the realm, one that simultaneously engrossed and refined the labours of all who had anywhere lent their hands to such an enterprise, from remote antiquity down to the present. As the Tetragrammaton surmounting the title page guaranteed the spiritual unity of the contents of the Old and New Testaments in their several books, so the king's name at the head of the volume would guarantee the literal integrity of the same as 'Imprinted at London by Robert Barker, printer to the king's most excellent majesty. Anno Dom. 1611'. If anything short of a royal institution for the advancement of learning in Britain could have satisfied Bacon's desire to see James I of England inaugurate 'some solid work, fixed memorial, and immortal monument, bearing a character or signature both of the power of a king and the difference and perfection of such a king', the 1611 Bible might have done.[51]

In the event, the most solid monument to the king's mastery 'as well of divine and sacred literature as of profane and human' would be raised in another medium. Before he died in 1613, Bodley put up the money to pay for the addition of a third storey to the new Schools building then under construction next to and adjoining his library in Oxford.[52] This is the building whose quadrangle one now crosses on entering the Bodleian. On its inner east facade rises the tower of the 'Five Orders of Architecture', into which, at a late stage, a canopied niche was inserted for a statue of James I, who is portrayed presenting copies of his Complete Works to Fame, on the one hand, and the university on the other. Inside the building, immediately below the level of the entablature supporting the royal state, the upper parts of the walls of the gallery of Bodley's third storey were painted with a frieze containing medallion portraits of famous men of learning, derived from recently published albums of images. The main division of the portraits recalls that of the book collection and the 1605 catalogue, theology separate from the other faculties. The south range displays the theologians in a chronological sequence beginning with Dionysius the pseudo-Areopagite and Philo of Alexandria, running through twenty-four church fathers of the second to eighth centuries, nineteen of their 'medieval' successors, and forty-four scholars and reformers from the sixteenth and early seventeenth centuries, Erasmus prominent among them, to conclude with John Rainolds (the original proposer and chief editor of the new Bible translation) in the company of other contemporary English divines. This section of the frieze was evidently designed to present the spectator with an 'impression of an uninterrupted tradition from the sub-apostolic age to the Jacobean church'.[53] A symmetrical (mixed) series of portraits for the faculties of law, medicine, and arts, in the north range, opens with Homer, includes all the major Greek and Latin 'classics', and closes with Sir Philip Sidney. The deviser of the programme as a whole was Thomas James, who saw the new extension and the tower completed before being succeeded as Bodley's Librarian by John Rous in 1620.[54]

With its effigy of the king-as-author and accompanying literary portrait series, the symbolism of the Bodleian Tower of the Five Orders recapitulates the preliminaries of the 1611 Bible in an idiom broadly consistent with Erasmus' Christological vision of a total 'order of books'. While neither biblical testament is physically presented in the Bodleian decor, the divine double book was presupposed by the gallery of Christian famous men of letters—beginning after the Apostles, ending with the latest English Bible translators. It is also allusively present in the figure of the king delivering his two books, an iconography that borrowed both from representations of previous monarchs on title pages of printed English versions of the Bible and from scenes of Roman imperial lawgiving or *traditio legis* long since adapted for images of Christ as lawgiver in late Roman visual and plastic art. James I's own literary works were given pride of place in the revised (1620) Bodleian catalogue.[55] Simultaneously, his even-handed gesture of benediction on the facade of the new building could be seen as proclaiming the ideal unity of a divine literary dispensation, at once secular and sacred, now (re)settled on the English or British nation.

And yet, behind the appearance of plenitude, the Bodleian decorative programme sheltered historical discontinuities and ideological tensions. On the side of secular letters, it displayed no English or British poet besides Chaucer and Sidney, nor is it certain that Sidney owed his place in the frieze to literary achievement alone. Conversely, on the side of sacred or Christian letters, the ornamental regime (like the intertextuality of the preface to the King James Bible) deliberately blurred the sharp distinctions between antiquity, intervening 'dark' or 'middle' age, and present times that Erasmus and English reformers from Thomas Cranmer to John Jewel—both depicted in the frieze—had made the basis for their patristically oriented programmes of reading, teaching, and preaching.[56] The question of what pre-authorized positions of honour might lie open in the field of *English* sacred letters would acquire some urgency for classically educated, devoutly Christian writers ambitious of the name of poet in the period after 1620. One type of response, as we shall see, was a new Christian 'classicism'.

Forms of Association: Christian Antiquities, Poetical Divinities

In the year that the new English Bible and Thomas James's *Treatise of the Corruption of Scripture, Councels and Fathers* were published, an edition by Sir Henry Savile of the works of the church father John Chrysostom (in the original Greek) was also coming off the press.[57] Complete, it would make eight stout folio volumes. No work of patristic—or classical—philology on that scale had been executed before in England or by an English scholar.[58] Savile was a collaborator on the King James Bible, a major benefactor of Bodley's library, and provost of an institution (Eton College) that Bacon would later covet as a laboratory for his new science. Though conceived as a contribution to European humanistic scholarship, his Chrysostom fits squarely within the Jacobean multidisciplinary project of national literary thesaurization.[59] The edition is dedicated to James I as exemplar of universal learning, discriminating reader of the church fathers, and one who accorded antiquity the reverence it deserved.

The measure of Christian antiquity, and of the reverence due to it, was carefully calibrated by English scholars and controversialists in this period. In his *Apologia Ecclesiae Anglicanae* (1562), John Jewel had staked the national church's claims to orthodoxy on the consistency of its beliefs and practices with those of 'the primitive church for the space of six hundred years after Christ', a recognizably Erasmian criterion that left the door open for equivocation over the Gregorian mission to the *Angli* in the year 597. Doubts about the lower limits of reliably 'ancient' Christianity and about the antiquity and apostolicity of the English (as opposed to British) church were key elements of the ecclesiological debates of the English Reformation. Recent research has shown how critical the early decades of the seventeenth century were for the elaboration of techniques of recourse to the textual witness of the church fathers that in the long run would be claimed as typically 'Anglican'.[60] It is now clear how far the refashioning of the identity of the Church of England that took place during the 1620s and 1630s—and that has been variously labelled 'Caroline', 'Laudian', 'Arminian', and 'conformist'—relied on 'an art of manipulating [textual] authorities, as part of . . . a technology of truth'.[61] While the intricacies of this new technology lie mainly in the field of theological reception, they also affected forms of literary reception and intertextuality. Most obviously, conformist ecclesiology encouraged new forms of association between contemporary exponents of rhetorical or poetic genres and their putative precursors among the orators and writers of the primitive church. As Erasmian compilers like Francis Meres and elegists like Ben Jonson matched English poets of their time with their generic equivalents in the classical pantheon, so comparisons would now also increasingly be made with famous Christian authors of antiquity. The main fame of Bishop John of Antioch and Constantinople, nicknamed Chrysostom ('Golden Mouth'), was as an orator, and Savile's edition appears around the midpoint of the golden age of English pulpit oratory exemplified by Lancelot Andrewes and John Donne.

Andrewes's use of the fathers and early church councils in his preaching combines historical and bibliographical precision with an air of personal familiarity.[62] 'One foot of our compass we fix in the Apostles' times,' he declared in an Easter Day sermon at Whitehall in 1618: 'The other, where? They [the Protestant reformers] appoint us Gelasius' time, who was fast upon the five hundredth year. Be it so.'[63] These coordinates established, primitive testimonies to the custom of Easter observance are then collated by period and genre. For the period of the 'peace' of the Church (fourth and fifth centuries), Andrewes begins reflexively with 'the homilies or sermons made purposely by [the fathers], to be preached on this day'. First he assembles the company:

> We have a full jury, Greek and Latin, of them; and that of the most chief and eminent among them. Saint Basil, Nazianzen, Chrysostom, Nyssen, Theophilus, Alexandrinus, Cyril, Chrysologus, Leo, etc. And yet I deal not with any of those [Easter sermons] in Ambrose, Augustine, Maximus, now extant; I know, they are questioned. I rely onely on the report of Saint Hierom [i.e. Jerome, *De Viris Illustribus*] and Gennadius [who extended Jerome's catalogue for the fifth century], who saw the right copies, and what they saw, have reported. (*XCVI Sermons*, 525)

Next he brings forward his main spokesman for the day: 'I will give you a taste of one. It shall be [Gregory] Nazianzen, surnamed the Divine, and so one that knew what belonged to divinity. Thus begins he a sermon of his upon it. Easter Day is come . . .' Whatever differences might subsist between East and West in the dating of Easter, the observance of the feast united Christians of all times and places; it was another reminder or instantiation, like the Eucharist, of their mystical unity in the body of Christ. From Easter sermons of the fathers, Andrewes passes to hymns composed for the day: 'By Prudentius that lived in Saint Ambrose's time. By Saint Ambrose himself. Before him by Saint Hilary. But, Paulinus [of Nola] I insist on . . . He lived with Saint Augustine. A pregnant record, for the church's custom then.'

After hymns or poems, 'writings' (commentaries, letters, treatises). After writings, the testimony of the fathers' actions in life. Deposed from the see of Constantinople, Chrysostom celebrated Easter '*in Thermas Constantini* (a spacious great building, for the public bath of the city)' (*XCVI Sermons*, 526). In Andrewes's preaching we see what Bacon meant by recommending 'ecclesiastical history, thoroughly read and observed' as a mode of practical divinity.

In the 1629 collection of his sermons, 'a commemorative folio edited (not unlike the first folio of Shakespeare) by admiring colleagues', Andrewes would be represented as 'a singular preacher, and a most famous writer', one who 'ever misliked often and loose preaching, without study of antiquity', and whose character was such that, 'had he lived among those ancient fathers, his virtue would have shined, even amongst those virtuous men'.[64] The sponsors of that volume, one of whom was William Laud, used the posthumous authority of Andrewes to buttress a project of liturgical reconstruction in the Church of England, for which patrons from Christian antiquity were by then also being actively recruited. The commemoration of Andrewes in the 1629 *XCVI Sermons* is an early instance of a kind of biography that proliferated in 'Laudian' or 'conformist' milieux between the 1630s and the Restoration, in which the godly lives—and *Lives*—of eminent churchmen were promoted as 'living' sermons or texts, according to the incarnational logic outlined (for the New Testament) by Erasmus in the *Paraclesis*.[65]

That tendency is especially marked in the memorialization of John Donne as poet and divine, a process that begins—if not with his own pre-posthumous performances—with the 'elegies on the author's death' collected for the first edition of his *Poems* (1633).[66] Although classical poetic references are not entirely absent there, the heavier accent falls on divinity and its patristic models. One admirer imagines Donne in the pulpit: 'Where we that heard him, to our selves did feign | Golden Chrysostom was alive again.' Another, Izaak Walton, asks rhetorically: 'Did he write hymns, for piety and wit | Equal to those that grave Prudentius writ?' A third epitaph, addressed by Thomas Browne to the late author 'Upon the promiscuous printing of his Poems, the looser sort, with the religious', predicts that wiser readers will 'dare read even thy wanton story, | As thy confession, not thy glory'.[67] The implicitly Augustinian, conversional model for this last tribute would be reinforced in the second edition (1635), the contents of which were so arranged that the profane part of Donne's poetic œuvre preceded the divine. It is possible that Walton had a hand in the reordering.[68] In any case, Walton's *Life of Donne*, first published with the *LXXX Sermons* (1640), perfected the patristic transformation of his subject. With Donne's ordination, his biographer affirmed, 'the English Church... gained a second St Austin; for I think none was so like him before his conversion, none so like St Ambrose after it'.[69]

Tendentious as it is, Walton's patristic analogy was also apt. Donne in his sermons is as familiar with the church fathers as Andrewes, whose patristic style he emulated, even if he could not match his erudition. Like Andrewes (and Erasmus), Donne took for granted the possibility of an experience of transcendence *in* time and *in* texts. In

Donne's case, the premiss was manifestly Augustinian. From Augustine's *Confessions* Donne learnt 'the symbolic importance of hermeneutic and providential time'; this father's work provided him with a model of 'the sustaining force of (inter)textual fictions, the power of interpretation to re-imagine the flow of time'.[70] Augustine gave Donne a licence to practise humanist philology in the key of poetry and call it divinity. His habits as a preacher suggest that he too was content to let the 'other' foot of his compass of the primitive church be set around 500 CE. Although the question raised in one of the Holy Sonnets ('Sleeps she [Christ's spouse, the church] a thousand, then peeps up one year?' (18. 5; *Poetical Works* I. 330)) was still a troubling one, the class of saintly 'Doctors' that Donne retained in his 'Litany', in succession to the Apostles, Martyrs, Confessors, and Virgins of the first centuries, was clearly confined to the church fathers.[71] (The *Book of Common Prayer* omitted the entire roll-call of saints from the Roman litany.) This poem, one of Donne's earliest on 'divine' themes, exemplified a style of paraliturgical verse that in other hands—notably George Herbert's and Henry Vaughan's—would justify further comparisons with Prudentius.

Herbert's ideal country parson had 'read the fathers', along with 'the schoolmen, and the later writers, or a good proportion of all'.[72] In his own will, Herbert left his curate 'Augustine's works' and a half-year's advance wages (*Works*, 382). Writing in the same spirit as Andrewes's and Donne's literary executors, the publishers of *The Temple: Sacred Poems and Private Ejaculations* 'by Mr George Herbert' (1633), considered that the author's service as a churchman made him 'justly a companion to the primitive saints, and a pattern or more for the age he lived in' (Herbert, *Works*, 3). It was left to his student and poetic disciple Henry Vaughan to turn the vicar of Bemerton into a Christian 'classic' in Walton's sense. Vaughan's conviction of the 'life' of literary *monumenta* is plainly of his age—which is to say, ultimately Erasmian. It is distilled in an elegy 'On Sir Thomas Bodley's Library' that sees 'old Palestine', 'Athens', and Rome co-located in a single pilgrimage site: 'Walsam [i.e. Walsingham] is in the midst of Oxford now.'[73] The first printed volume of Vaughan's poems (1646) was ballasted by a version of Juvenal's Tenth Satire suiting the 'distractions' of the time.[74] A subsequent one (1651) hailed Herbert as his Latin master ('Herbertus, Latiae gloria prima scholae', 'Herbert, pride of the Latin school'), and included translations from Ovid, Ausonius, and Boethius.[75] Only with the second edition of *Silex Scintillans* (1655; 1st edn, 1650) do the author's poetics become programmatically Christian and redemptive. The preface preaches poetic conversion in a late antique key. The kingdom was full of 'wits' possessed by 'a most vain, insatiable desire to be reputed poets', whose only reward or 'laureate crown' would be the death of their own souls. Of each of them it could be said, as Prudentius once said (in Latin) of the pagan senator Symmachus:

> A wit most worthy in tried gold to shine,
> Immortal gold, had he sung the divine
> Praise of his maker: to whom he preferr'd
> Obscene, vile fancies...[76]

The remedy for such abuses, of which Vaughan confesses himself to have been guilty in the past, lay not in official censorship of the press but in the writers' own 'wise exchange of vain and vicious subjects, for divine themes and celestial praise'. The first 'to excel in this kind of hagiography, or holy writing' in the present age was 'the blessed man, Mr George Herbert, whose holy life and verse gained many pious converts'.[77]

Vaughan's 'conformist' commemoration of Herbert as the pioneer of a new English hagiography and hymnography can be understood partly as a response to the banning of the *Book of Common Prayer* under the Protectorate.[78] It is also evidence, with Walton's *Lives* of Donne and Herbert, of a conscious effort on the part of proto-Anglican writers to construct a literary genealogy that put them in communion with their counterparts from the 'classical' age of the church. These linked liturgical and genealogical impulses are clearly in play in two of the prose works that Vaughan published in 1654 under the title of *Flores Solitudinis*. The first of them, *The World Contemned*, translated a short paraenetic work by the fifth-century monastic writer Eucherius of Lyon. The second, *Primitive Holiness Set Forth in the Life of Blessed Paulinus . . . of Nola*, translated a compilation made (in Latin) by a recent Jesuit editor of both Eucherius and Paulinus, Heribert Rosweyd.[79] Eucherius' *De Contemptu Mundi* was an exhortation to Christian–ascetic conversion, framed to appeal to a member of the late Roman social elite. It included a miniature catalogue of famous Greek and Roman men of letters who had turned their talents to the service of Christ, leaving 'monuments of their Christian learning' to posterity. Among them was 'Paulinus Bishop of Nola . . . a person of princely revenues, powerful eloquence, and most accomplished learning', who became a monk 'and afterward filled most part of the world with his elegant and pious writings'.[80] That notice is the cue for the *Life of Paulinus*, whose 'conversion' away from the practice of worldly poetry had been enacted in a famous exchange of verse with his former mentor Ausonius (duly rendered by Vaughan). Aside from the correspondence with Ausonius, the main poetic anthology in the *Life* comes in the section towards the end on 'works of piety', in which the narrator walks through the churches that Paulinus built, reciting the epigrams that he had composed for their walls. In case the reader was not already reminded of *The Temple*, twice in the closing pages of his version Vaughan cites 'Mr Herbert' in comparison.[81] By this point, fifth- and seventeenth-century poetic lives (Paulinus', Herbert's, Vaughan's, the contemporary reader's) have ideally conformed to each other.

The historical singularity of John Milton's career is thrown into still higher relief by the kind of survey that has been sketched here. We saw how the obsolescence of the English 'clerkly' paradigm of universal learning coincided with a rash of manifestos for new styles of English literary profession, including Sidney's for a poetic vocation that knew its own divinity. The mark set by Spenser in aspiring to that ideal would stand for decades. The great Jacobean national 'literary' projects staked out other grounds for their edifices, and it was in their precincts that John Milton grew up and pursued his studies. His family Bible was the king's English version.[82] The Bodleian Library lay within a day's ride of his house at Horton. Re-despatching his *Poems* (1645) to the librarian John Rous, he was pleased to imagine them being perused

> inter alta nomina
> Authorum, Graiae simul et Latinae
> Antiqua gentis lumina et verum decus
>
> (among the sublime names of authors who were the ancient lights and the true glory of the Greek and Latin race)
>
> (Milton, 'Ad Ioannem Rousium', 70–2; *Poems*, 302)

The same classical spirit of emulation suffuses several of the poems in point. Yet Milton's volume was for the most part still generically indistinguishable from the productions of other self-crowning laureates of the day, soon to be shamed by Vaughan for their failure to turn their wit to holier use.[83] Of no less literary–historical interest now are the eleven prose pamphlets that had been sent earlier to the Bodleian with the first copy of *Poems*. Much of the interest is biographical. The autobiographical passages in the tracts provide us with a clearer view of the author's literary–professional aspirations than do any of the minor poems. Milton was to prove the outstanding nonconforming self-memorialist in an age of conformist commemorations. As his nonconformity with the Laudian Church of England actuated the works of his 'left hand', the impossibility of his conforming his talents as a poet to any existing model in English 'letters'—not even, in the end, his admired Spenser—now justifies us in treating those prose writings as an intermittent commentary on the poetic œuvre.

Milton's life's ambition as he polemically represented it in a passage of *The Reason of Church-Government* (1642) was

> to be an interpreter and relater of the best and sagest things among mine own citizens throughout this island in the mother dialect. That what the greatest and choicest wits of Athens, Rome, or modern Italy, and those Hebrews of old did for their country, I in my proportion with this over and above of being a Christian, might do for mine.
>
> (Milton, *Complete Prose Works*, 811–12)

On this ground, he acknowledged no precursors. A twentieth-century scholar might write of 'Milton and the Christian tradition', but that assurance was unavailable to the man himself, who could no more use the word 'tradition' positively in a religious context than he could speak favourably of 'clerks' in reference to his own times.[84]

Laboratory Renaissance humanist that he was—more so than most of the insular clerks and career-converts who came before him—Milton collated other men's texts in view of a recension of his own. What Helgerson called the 'extraordinary delay' in his 'progress as a poet' encompassed, among other labours, the first serious reconnaissance of European, British, and ecclesiastical history ever undertaken by an

English poet of the first rank, as well as extensive reading in the Greek and Latin Church Fathers.[85] Milton was a better scholar of 'late antiquity' and of the 'Middle Ages' than all but the most learned of his British contemporaries.[86] Yet his national epic, when it appeared, would spend barely thirty lines on the course of historical events beyond the literal time of the biblical narrative. For the author of *Of Reformation* and *Paradise Lost*, as for Erasmus, the sovereign remedy for damage previously inflicted on a Christian *respublica literarum* by monks and other 'mechanical' or hireling writers was philological. It lay in the author's taking the biblical text in hand again for himself and faithfully interpreting it, in the light of his own lucubrations, for readers of his time and place, redeeming the truth:

> the truth
> With superstitions and traditions taint
> Left only in those written records pure,
> Though not but by the Spirit understood.
> (Milton, *Paradise Lost*, 12. 511–14; *Poems*, 1052)

Notes

1. J. M. Coetzee, *Elizabeth Costello* (2003), 122, in a chapter entitled 'The Humanities in Africa'. Quotations in this paragraph and the next are from pp. 119–25. See Michael Lambert, *The Classics and South African Identities* (Bristol, 2011), 126–32.
2. Jacques Derrida, 'Before the Law', in Jacques Derrida and Derek Attridge, *Acts of Literature* (New York, 1992), 183–220 (215, 217–20).
3. Ronald G. Witt, *In the Footsteps of the Ancients: The Origins of Humanism from Lovato to Bruni* (Leiden, 2000); Thomas M. Greene, *The Light in Troy: Imitation and Discovery in Renaissance Poetry* (New Haven, 1982).
4. Francis Bacon, *The Major Works*, ed. B. Vickers (Oxford, 2002), 138, emphasis added.
5. Terence Cave, *The Cornucopian Text: Problems of Writing in the French Renaissance* (Oxford, 1979), 333.
6. Richard Waswo, *Language and Meaning in the Renaissance* (Princeton, 1987); Ann Moss, *Renaissance Truth and the Latin Language Turn* (Oxford, 2003). See also Brian Cummings, *The Literary Culture of the Reformation: Grammar and Grace* (Oxford, 2002), esp. 137–42 on Erasmus on language and meaning.
7. Moss, *Renaissance Truth*, 274.
8. See in general Anthony Grafton, *Worlds Made by Words: Scholarship and Community in the Modern West* (Cambridge, MA, 2009).
9. Marjorie O'Rourke Boyle, *Erasmus on Language and Method in Theology* (Toronto, 1977).
10. Erasmus, *Paraclesis*, my translation. For context, see the full translation in *Christian Humanism and the Renaissance: Selected Writings of Erasmus*, ed. John C. Olin (New York, 1987), 97–108 (105), and, for implications, Cummings, *Literary Culture*, 105–10.
11. Andrée Hayum, 'Dürer's Portrait of Erasmus and the *Ars Typographorum*', *Renaissance Quarterly*, 38 (1985), 650–87; Lisa Jardine, *Erasmus, Man of Letters: The Construction of Charisma in Print* (Princeton, 1993), ch. 1.

12. James Kearney, '"Relics of the Mind": Erasmian Humanism and Textual Presence', in *The Incarnate Text: Imagining the Book in Reformation England* (Philadelphia, 2009), ch. 1; Mark Vessey, '*Vera et aeterna monumenta*: Jerome's Catalogue of Early Christian Writers and the Premises of Erasmian Humanism', in Gunther Frank, Thomas Leinkauf, and Markus Wriedt (eds), *Die Patristik in der frühen Neuzeit: Die Relektüre der Kirchenväter in den Wissenschaften des 15. Bis 18. Jahrhunderts* (Stuttgart, 2006), 351–75.
13. Mark Vessey, 'Erasmus' Lucubrations and the Renaissance Life of Texts', *Erasmus of Rotterdam Society Yearbook*, 24 (2004), 23–51 (esp. 49–51); Marjorie O'Rourke Boyle, *Christening Pagan Mysteries: Erasmus in Pursuit of Wisdom* (Toronto, 1981).
14. Alvin B. Kernan, *The Imaginary Library: An Essay on Literature and Society* (Princeton, 1982). See the introduction to Brian Cummings and James Simpson (eds), *Cultural Reformations: Medieval and Renaissance in Literary History* (Oxford, 2010), for a recent affirmation of the role of Erasmus and fellow humanists in formulating 'methods and concepts that are central to the practice of modern literary history: philology, textual criticism, and the idea of "literature" (or *bonae literae*) itself' (p. 4).
15. István Bejczy, *Erasmus and the Middle Ages: The Historical Consciousness of a Christian Humanist* (Leiden, 2001).
16. Jardine, *Erasmus, Man of Letters*, ch. 2; Benedetto Clausi, *Ridar voce all'antico Padre: L'edizione erasmiana delle Lettere di Gerolamo* (Soveria Mannelli, 2000); Hilmar M. Pabel, *Herculean Labours: Erasmus and the Editing of St Jerome's Letters in the Renaissance* (Leiden, 2008). On Erasmus and Augustine, see now Arnoud S. Q. Visser, *Reading Augustine in the Reformation: The Flexibility of Intellectual Authority in Europe, 1500–1620* (Oxford, 2011), ch. 2.
17. René Wellek, *The Rise of English Literary History* (Chapel Hill, NC, 1941), 2–44. See also, e.g. John N. King, *English Reformation Literature: The Tudor Origins of the Protestant Tradition* (Princeton, 1982), esp. ch. 1; Kevin Pask, *The Emergence of the English Author: Scripting the Life of the Poet in Early Modern England* (Cambridge, 1996), pts 1 and 2; Philip Schwyzer, *Literature, Nationalism and Memory in Early Modern England and Wales* (Cambridge, 2004); Seth Lerer, 'Literary Histories', and Gordon Teskey, '"Literature"', in Cummings and Simpson (eds), *Cultural Reformations*, 75–91, 379–95.
18. After T. W. Baldwin, *William Shakespeare's Small Latine & Lesse Greeke*, 2 vols (Urbana, IL, 1944), see esp. Anthony Grafton and Lisa Jardine, *From Humanism to the Humanities: Education and the Liberal Arts in Fifteenth- and Sixteenth-Century Europe* (1986), ch. 6; Brian Vickers (ed.), *English Renaissance Literary Criticism* (Oxford, 1999), 31–8 and *passim*; Stuart Gillespie, *Shakespeare's Books: A Dictionary of Shakespeare Sources* (2004), 152–60; and, for theological reception, Gregory D. Dodds, *Exploiting Erasmus: The Erasmian Legacy and Religious Change in Early Modern England* (Toronto, 2009).
19. Katrin Ettenhuber, *Donne's Augustine: Renaissance Cultures of Interpretation* (Oxford, 2011), sets a new standard.
20. See, notably, Richard McCabe, Chapter 25, and Thomas Luxon, Chapter 29, this volume.
21. Thomas Nashe, *The Unfortunate Traveller*, in Thomas Nashe, *Works*, ed. R. B. McKerrow, rev. F. P. Wilson, 5 vols (Oxford, 1958), 2. 245.
22. G. Gregory Smith (ed.), *Elizabethan Critical Essays*, 2 vols (Oxford, 1904), 1. 8.
23. Smith (ed.), *Elizabethan Critical Essays*, 2. 329.

24. Rosalie L. Colie, *The Resources of Kind: Genre-Theory in the Renaissance* (Berkeley and Los Angeles, 1973); Alastair Fowler, *Kinds of Literature: An Introduction to the Theory of Genres and Modes* (Cambridge, MA, 1982); Kathy Eden, *Friends Hold All Things in Common: Tradition, Intellectual Property, and the Adages of Erasmus* (New Haven, 2001); Cave, *Cornucopian Text*, 332.
25. William W. Barker, 'Erasmus, Desiderius', in A. C. Hamilton et al. (eds), *The Spenser Encyclopedia* (Toronto, 1990), 251–2 (252).
26. Paul Saenger, 'Silent Reading: Its Impact on Late Medieval Script and Society', *Viator*, 13 (1982), 367–414 (388).
27. Mary A. Rouse and Richard H. Rouse, 'Bibliography before Print: The Medieval *De viris illustribus*', in *Authentic Witnesses: Approaches to Medieval Texts and Manuscripts* (Notre Dame, IN, 1991), ch. 13; Richard Sharpe, *Titulus: Identifying Medieval Latin Texts: An Evidence-Based Approach* (Turnhout, 2003), 281–96.
28. Thomas Lanquet, *An Epitome of Chronicles* (1559; STC 15217.5), 272.
29. The description was applied to Erasmus on the title page of his *Lucubrationes* (Strasbourg, 1515). It had been conferred on Varro by Terentianus Maurus 2846, and then by Augustine, *City of God*, 6. 2.
30. STC 10504a, 10498, 10509, 10473.5, 10480, 10454, 10443, etc.
31. Roger Chartier, *The Order of Books: Readers, Authors, and Libraries in Europe between the Fourteenth and Eighteenth Centuries*, trans. Lydia G. Cochrane (Stanford, 1994), 52–3.
32. Seth Lerer, 'Writing like the Clerk: Laureate Poets and the Aureate World', in *Chaucer and his Readers: Imagining the Author in Late-Medieval England* (Princeton, 1993), ch. 1 (p. 56).
33. Alexandra Gillespie, *Print Culture and the Medieval Author: Chaucer, Lydgate, and Their Books, 1473–1557* (Oxford, 2006), 123.
34. *The Workes of Geffray Chaucer*, 2nd edn (1542; STC 5069), sigs. A2^{r}–A2^{v}.
35. On the projects of Leland and Bale, see James Simpson, 'The Melancholy of John Leland', in *Reform and Cultural Revolution* (*The Oxford English Literary History*, vol. 2: *1350–1547*) (Oxford, 2002), ch. 1; Richard Sharpe, 'The English Bibliographical Tradition from Kirkestede to Tanner', in Charles Burnett and Nicholas Mann (eds), *Britannia Latina: Latin in the Culture of Great Britain from the Middle Ages to the Twentieth Century* (2005), 86–128 (97–114); John Leland, *De Viris Illustribus/On Famous Men*, ed. and trans. James P. Carley with the assistance of Caroline Brett (Toronto, 2010).
36. Gillespie, *Print Culture and the Medieval Author*, 135.
37. Richard Helgerson, *The Elizabethan Prodigals* (Berkeley and Los Angeles, 1976).
38. Jerome's fevered 'dream' or vision of answering to a Christlike persecuting magistrate on the charge of being a Ciceronian not a Christian (*Epistula* 22. 30 in modern editions of his correspondence) was a *locus classicus* of humanist debate: Eugene F. Rice, *Saint Jerome in the Renaissance* (Baltimore, 1985), chs. 4–5.
39. See J. Christopher Warner, *Augustinian Epic, Petrarch to Milton* (Ann Arbor, 2005).
40. Patrick Cheney and Frederick de Armas (eds), *European Literary Careers: The Author from Antiquity to the Renaissance* (Toronto, 2002); Philip Hardie and Helen Moore (eds), *Classical Literary Careers and their Reception* (Cambridge, 2010).
41. For Bacon's idea of a 'history of learning' and its immediate sequels, see Arthur B. Ferguson, *Clio Unbound: Perception of the Social and Cultural Past in Renaissance England* (Durham, NC, 1979), 38–50; C. R. Ligota and J.-L. Quantin (eds), *History of Scholarship: A Selection of Papers from the Seminar on the History of Scholarship Held*

Annually at the Warburg Institute (Oxford, 2006), 22–5.

42. *Catalogus Librorum Bibliothecae Publicae Quam Vir Ornatissimus Thomas Bodleius... in Academia Oxoniensi nuper instituit... auctore Thoma James ibidem bibliothecario* (Oxford, 1605), 1–2. On relations between Bacon and Bodley, see Jennifer Summit, *Memory's Library: Medieval Books in Early Modern Britain* (Chicago, 2008), ch. 5.
43. Grafton, 'Where Was Solomon's House? Ecclesiastical History and the Intellectual Origins of Bacon's *New Atlantis*', in *Worlds Made by Words*, ch. 5. For the work of Thomas James and the Magdeburg centuriators in context, see Irena Backus, *Historical Method and Confessional Identity in the Era of the Reformation (1378–1615)* (Leiden, 2003), 237–43, 358–70.
44. Paul Nelles, 'The Uses of Orthodoxy and Jacobean Erudition: Thomas James and the Bodleian Library', *History of Universities*, 22 (2007), 21–70.
45. The process had of course begun earlier: Richard Helgerson, *Forms of Nationhood: The Elizabethan Writing of England* (Chicago, 1992); Schwyzer, *Literature, Nationalism and Memory*. See also Richard Ovenden, 'The Libraries of the Antiquaries (*c*.1580–1640) and the Idea of a National Collection', in Elisabeth Leedham-Green and Teresa Webber (eds), *The Cambridge History of Libraries in Britain and Ireland*, vol. 1: *To 1640* (Cambridge, 2006), 527–61.
46. Helen Moore and Julian Reid (eds), *Manifold Greatness: The Making of the King James Bible* (Oxford, 2011), is a good introduction to the scholarship. For the King James version as a work of cultural–linguistic reception, see Naomi Tadmor, *The Social Universe of the English Bible: Scripture, Society, and Culture in Early Modern England* (Cambridge, 2010).
47. David Norton, *A History of the Bible as Literature*, vol. 1: *From Antiquity to 1700* (Cambridge, 1993), 147–54. Quotations from the preface follow the text and pagination of the World's Classics edition of *The Bible: Authorized King James Version*, ed. Robert Carroll and Stephen Prickett (Oxford, 1997), which, however, omits the marginal references.
48. 'You have urged me... briefly to set before you all those who have published any memorable writing [*memoriae aliquid prodiderunt*] on the Holy Scriptures... Let [the enemies of Christianity] learn how many and what sort of men founded, built and adorned [*fundaverint, extruxerint, et ornaverint*] the church' (Philip Schaff and Henry Wace (eds), *A Select Library of Nicene and Post-Nicene Fathers of the Christian Church*, 2nd ser.,vol. 3 (Edinburgh, 1989), 359).
49. Erika Rummel, *Erasmus' Annotations on the New Testament: From Philologist to Theologian* (Toronto, 1986).
50. The 1611 preface thereby meant to counter the claims to patristic sanction advanced by Gregory Martin in the preamble to his Vulgate-based English rendering (Rheims, 1582) of the New Testament for (Roman) Catholic readers: text in Gerald Bray (ed.), *Documents of the English Reformation* (Cambridge, 1994), 364–96.
51. Bacon, *Major Works*, 121, from the preface to book 1 of *The Advancement of Learning*; the phrase quoted in the following sentence is from the same place.
52. Ian Philip, *The Bodleian Library in the Seventeenth and Eighteenth Centuries* (Oxford, 1983), 23–5.
53. J. N. L. Myres, 'Thomas James and the Painted Frieze', *Bodleian Library Record*, 4 (1952–3), 30–51 (38).
54. André Masson, *The Pictorial Catalogue: Mural Decoration in Libraries*, trans. David Gerard (Oxford, 1981), 4–6; M. R. A. Bullard, 'Talking Heads: The Bodleian

Frieze, its Inspiration, Sources, Designer and Significance', *Bodleian Library Record*, 19 (1994), 461–500.

55. James P. R. Lyell, 'King James I and the Bodleian Catalogue of 1620', *Bodleian Quarterly Record*, 7 (1923), 261–83.
56. Richard Hooker had already provided a humanistically inspired, cultural–historical rationale for the more inclusive—indeed 'Catholic'—sense of Christian 'tradition' that would be relied upon by William Laud and other conformist churchmen of the 1620s and 1630s: Ferguson, *Clio Unbound*, 207–22; Peter Lake, *Anglicans and Puritans? Presbyterianism and English Conformist Thought from Whitgift to Hooker* (1988); Anthony Milton, *Catholic and Reformed: The Roman and Protestant Churches in English Protestant Thought 1600–1640* (Cambridge, 1995).
57. *Τοῦ ἐν ἁγίοις πατρὸς ἡμῶν Ἰοάννου τοῦ Χρυσοστόμου τὰ εὑρισκόμενα*, 8 vols (Eton, 1610–12).
58. William P. Haugard, 'Renaissance Patristic Scholarship and Theology in Sixteenth-Century England', *Sixteenth Century Journal*, 10 (1979), 37–60; J. W. Binns, *Intellectual Culture in Elizabethan and Jacobean England: The Latin Writings of the Age* (Leeds, 1990), 218–28, on Latin translations of the Greek fathers; Mark Vessey, 'English Translations of the Latin Fathers, 1517–1611', in Irena Backus (ed.), *The Reception of the Church Fathers in the West: From the Carolingians to the Maurists*, 2 vols (Leiden, 1997), I. 775–835.
59. Jean-Louis Quantin, 'Du Chrysostome latin au Chrysostome grec: Un histoire européenne (1588-1613)', in Martin Wallraff and Rudolf Brändle (eds), *Chrysostomosbilder in 1600 Jahren: Facetten der Wirkungsgeschichte eines Kirchenvaters* (Berlin, 2008), 267–346 (311–40).
60. See Jean-Louis Quantin, *The Church of England and Christian Antiquity: The Construction of a Confessional Identity in the 17th Century* (Oxford, 2009), consolidating and extending recent revisionist study of the origins of 'Anglicanism'.
61. Quantin, *Church of England and Christian Antiquity*, 18.
62. On Andrewes's sense of the authority of the early church and his habits of patristic citation, see Nicholas Lossky, *Lancelot Andrewes the Preacher: The Origins of the Mystical Theology of the Church of England*, trans. Andrew Louth (Oxford, 1991), 336–50; Peter McCullough (ed.), *Lancelot Andrewes: Selected Sermons and Lectures* (Oxford, 2005), pp. lvi–lvii and *passim*.
63. *XCVI Sermons by the Right Honourable and Reverend Father in God, Lancelot Andrewes, Late Lord Bishop of Winchester*, 3rd edn (1635), 523.
64. McCullough, *Lancelot Andrewes: Selected Sermons and Letters*, 12; the descriptions appear in the funeral sermon for Andrewes preached by John Buckeridge, which was appended to the *XCVI Sermons* (and separately paginated), 18, 21, and in the dedicatory epistle to King Charles from Laud and Buckeridge, sig. A3^{v} (1635 edn).
65. Jessica Martin, *Walton's 'Lives': Conformist Commemorations and the Rise of Biography* (Oxford, 2001), with reference to the *Paraclesis* at pp. 90–1. See nn. 10–13.
66. David Novarr, *The Making of Walton's 'Lives'* (Ithaca, NY, 1958), 19–126; Martin, *Walton's 'Lives'*, 168–203.
67. John Donne, *Poetical Works*, ed. H. Grierson (1967), I. 386, 377, 372–3.
68. Mark Vessey, 'John Donne (1572–1631) in the Company of Augustine: Patristic Culture and Literary Profession in the English Renaissance', *Revue des études Augustiniennes*, 39 (1993), 173–201 (180–1), following Novarr. On Donne's conversion, see now Cummings, *Literary Culture*, 366–77; Molly Murray, *The Poetics of Conversion in Early Modern Literature: Verse and Change from Donne to Dryden* (Cambridge, 2009), ch. 2.

69. Walton, *The Life of Dr John Donne*, in John Donne, *LXXX Sermons* (1640), 47–8.
70. Ettenhuber, *Donne's Augustine*, 230–1, summarizing the argument of her book.
71. Donne, 'The Litanie', 109–17; *Poetical Works*, 1. 342–3.
72. *A Priest to the Temple, or The Country Parson* (1652), ch. 5; *The Works of George Herbert*, ed. F. E. Hutchinson (Oxford, 1941), 229.
73. 'On Sir Thomas Bodley's Library', 9–10, 13, 44; 45–7: 'Th'hast made us all thine heirs; whatever we | Hereafter write, 'tis thy posterity. This is thy monument!' (*The Works of Henry Vaughan*, ed. L. C. Martin (Oxford, 1957), 633–4).
74. *Poems with the Tenth Satire of Juvenal Englished*, 'To All Ingenious Lovers of Poetry'; Vaughan, *Works*, 2.
75. *Olor Iscanus*, 'Ad Posteros', 6; Vaughan, *Works*, 32.
76. Prudentius, *Contra Symmachum* 1. 632–7; Vaughan, *Works*, 389.
77. *Silex Scintillans: Sacred Poems and Private Ejaculations*, 'The Author's Preface to the Following Hymns'; Vaughan, *Works*, 388–9, 391–2. On Vaughan's 'poetics of conversion', see Jonathan F. S. Post, *Henry Vaughan: The Unfolding Vision* (Princeton, 1982), 70–115.
78. Judith Maltby, 'Suffering and Surviving: The Civil Wars, the Commonwealth and the Formation of "Anglicanism", 1642–60', in Christopher Durston and Judith Maltby (eds), *Religion in Revolutionary England* (Manchester, 2006), 158–80.
79. Vaughan, *Works*, 311–36, 337–85; Mary Jane Doherty, '*Flores Solitudinis*: The "Two Ways" and Vaughan's Patristic Hagiography', *George Herbert Journal*, 7 (1983–84), 25–50; Jonathan Nauman, 'Alternative Saints: Eucherius, Paulinus of Nola, and Henry Vaughan's *Silex Scintillans*', *Seventeenth Century*, 26 (2011), 264–78.
80. Vaughan, *Works*, 323–4.
81. Vaughan, *Works*, 377–9.
82. Barbara Kiefer Lewalski, *The Life of John Milton: A Critical Biography*, revised edn (Malden, MA, 2003), 5; Norton, *History of the Bible as Literature*, 1. 299–307.
83. Richard Helgerson, *Self-Crowned Laureates: Spenser, Jonson, Milton, and the Literary System* (Berkeley and Los Angeles, 1983), 268: 'Wherever one looks in the *Poems* of 1645, one finds Milton speaking the literary language of his generation.'
84. On Milton and 'tradition', see now Stephen Prickett, *Modernity and the Reinvention of Tradition: Backing into the Future* (Cambridge, 2009), 39–41.
85. Helgerson, *Self-Crowned Laureates*, 242.
86. For orientation, see Nicholas von Maltzahn, *Milton's History of Britain: Republican Historiography in the English Revolution* (Oxford, 1991); Thomas Fulton, *Historical Milton: Manuscript, Print, and Political Culture in Revolutionary England* (Amherst, MA, 2010).

CHAPTER 7

Women Writers and the Classics

JANE STEVENSON

you must know we read Plutarch now 'tis translated.[1]

On the whole, the study of classical texts has been a masculine province. Walter Ong observed that '[Latin] was a sexually specialized language used almost exclusively for communication between male and male'.[2] Further, Edmund Leach has suggested that the underlying purpose of a classical education is to create a class of bureaucrats who share a cultural background, and hence a language in the semiotic as well as a literal sense.[3] It is an idea that helps to explain why, for most of European history, women's participation in learned culture has been perceived as either an outrage or an irrelevance.

It also explains why it was sometimes insisted upon. In the tenth to twelfth centuries, when kings were rulers—not figureheads—of polities increasingly dependent on Latin literacy, their queens frequently acted as regents, and were educated accordingly.[4] For example, Matilda, wife of Henry I, quotes Cicero and mentions Pythagoras and Socrates in her Latin letters to Anselm in the early twelfth century.[5] The tale of women's involvement with high culture is not one of onward-and-upward progress. The next Queen of England who would have recognized the name of Pythagoras was probably Catherine of Aragon.

From the point of view of those involved with it, a high culture is entirely self-justifying, and has its own attractions. While post-medieval Western society did not *need* more than a very few women to acquire knowledge of the classics, it could not prevent daughters of the literate from being attracted. If their personal circumstances allowed them to pursue their interest, they found a variety of female figures to point their way. Above all, the classical tradition informed them of 'The Poetess'—Sappho, counterbalancing 'the Poet', Homer. But it is ominously relevant that, while Homer's life was proverbially obscure and his verse widely obtainable, Sappho's *verse* was almost completely lost while she was personally notorious for her sexual history.

Sappho was, therefore, a deeply problematic model for women writers. Even in antiquity, Martial complimented two separate women poets of his acquaintance by declaring that they were as talented as Sappho, *but chaster* (7. 69, 10. 35). Early modern men often follow Martial and use Sappho as the negative mirror of a positively represented female contemporary.[6] The early seventeenth-century François Sivvert writes of the Counter-Reformation Antwerp poet (and Latinist) Anna Bijns:

> Arte pares Lesbis Sappho et mea Binsia, distant
>   hoc solo, vitia haec dedocet, illa docet.
>
> (Lesbian Sappho and my [Anna] Bijns are equals in art,
>   Separate in this alone, that the one teaches vice, the other drives it away.) [7]

Other poems addressed by men to learned women poets rank their subject above her contemporaries, and above, beside, or immediately below Sappho. For example, in a poem by Franciscus Junius (the elder; the biblical scholar and theologian), addressed to Mildred Cecil, Lady Burleigh, in 1565,[8] the Muses declare that now she has come along,

>   Sappho ne perenne
> Lesbia nos inter sit meritura decus.
>
> (Lesbian Sappho may not always merit our praise.)[9]

Lady Burleigh was a student of Greek. Her reading included Hesiod, on the evidence of a poem she wrote in recommendation of Bartholo Silva's *Giardino Cosmografico* (*Cosmographic Garden*), which was included in a beautiful manuscript of this work, commissioned by Lady Burleigh and her sisters.[10] We know that she was also a student of Thucydides, since the well-known Ghent humanist Karel Utenhove wrote a letter to the Parisian Jean Morel in 1564, from London, reporting that he had given a public lecture on Thucydides, well attended by English scholars, with Lady Burleigh as guest of honour. He praises her writing in both Latin and Greek.[11] Evidently, she was one of the best-educated women of her generation, but, for all that Junius compares her to Sappho, she produced very little original writing, and the translations she undertook were from the Greek fathers.

Sappho is seldom cited by women themselves, as either a model, or a comparandum. The reason above all why they found her so unhelpful is 'Sappho to Phaon', attributed to Ovid.[12] Daniel Heinsius, in his edition of the *Heroides* of 1629, placed the poem fifteenth in series, where it has remained ever since, though the fifteenth-century editions of Ovid I have seen all print it as a free-standing work. While the *Heroides* all represent passionate women, 'Sappho to Phaon' is distinguished for its heroine's abandon, and for her sexual explicitness: it is notable that two recent commentators on *Heroides* were both drawn to use the word 'grotesque': 'the real Sappho...has degenerated into a grotesque pursuer of material luxury and corporeal lust';[13] 'she is pathetic, if not grotesque, in her vaunted skill in sexual performance'.[14] To Renaissance women writers, this crazy, ageing erotomaniac was worse than useless; and she stood squarely in the way of 'The Poetess'. With only the rarest exceptions, humanists approached Greek through Latin, which they learned first, and almost always more thoroughly. Since Ovid held his central cultural position into the Renaissance,[15] Sappho was inevitably perceived through 'Sappho to Phaon'.

The first woman to try and reclaim Sappho as a model for women writers is Madeleine de Scudéry, in *Les Femmes illustres*, written in partnership with her brother Georges and first published in Paris in 1642: her Sappho writes not to Phaon, but to a female pupil, Erinna. She is not a semi-legendary Muse, a nymphomaniac, or (in the modern sense) a Lesbian, but a reclamation of Sappho as a guide and example to women writers.[16] Interestingly, the endnote to 'Sapho à Erinne' cites the *Greek Anthology* for evidence that Erinna surpassed her teacher in hexameter verse: the Scudérys thus stake a claim to be re-creating the 'real' Sappho, rather than the Roman Sappho of Ovid.[17] The Scudérys' various writings were much read in England, and circulated both in French and in translation.[18]

A far commoner strategy for early modern women writers was to look for other kinds of precedent. A variety of stories from antiquity that were resurrected at the Renaissance associate female figures with literacy. For example, in Boccaccio's book on famous women (written 1355–9), Isis is credited with the invention of writing, Minerva with numbers, and Nicostrata or Carmenta invented both the Latin alphabet and grammar.[19] According to Plutarch, Rome's first laws were redacted by Numa Pompilius, but devised by the nymph Egeria.[20] These feminine personages frequently appear in the innumerable catalogues of learned and famous women that were written all over Europe from the fourteenth century onwards.

Compilers were also highly conscious of a small number of historical women who were remembered as both writers and as virtuous wives and mothers—notably Sulpicia, wife of Calenus (a poet in Martial's circle, praised by him in 10. 35 and 10. 38), Cornelia, mother of the Gracchi, and Proba. The argument from classical precedent was of huge importance to intellectually ambitious women, and these names are cited again and again. Rachel Speght, in a long polemical poem published in 1621, evokes Cornelia:

> A Roman matron that Cornelia hight [was called]
> An eloquent and learned style did write.
>
> ('The Dream', ll. 139–40;
> *Early Modern Women Poets*, 202–3)

A mid-seventeenth-century Irishwoman known only by her nom de plume, 'Philo-Philippa', praises Katherine Philips in 1667 with the words:

Those laws for which Numa did wise appear,
Wiser Egeria whispered in his ear,
The Gracchi's mother taught them eloquence,
From her breasts courage flowed, from her brain sense;
And the grave beards, who heard her speak in Rome,
Blushed not to be instructed, but o'ercome.
(ll. 93–9; *Early Modern Women Poets*, 402–7)

Numa, legendary Roman lawgiver, was said to have been instructed by the nymph Egeria, a story told by Plutarch in his *Life of Numa*. A more exotic version of the argument from precedent is mounted by an Elizabethan woman, Margaret Tyler, who translated a Spanish chivalric romance: she excuses herself by pointing out that, according to classical legend, some women used to be warriors: thus, she implies, there is nothing odd in a woman merely *writing* about war.[21]

Other female figures of considerable significance to creative women are the nine Muses.[22] Here, for instance, they are invoked by Martha Moulsworth (1577–after 1632):

My father was a man of spotless fame . . .
By him I was brought up in godly piety,
In modest cheerfulness, and sad sobriety.
Not only so, beyond my sex and kind
He did with learning Latin deck [my] mind.
And why not so? The muses females are,
And therefore of us females take some care.[23]

Elizabeth Jane Weston, in her Latin verse written in Prague in the late sixteenth century, is confident in presenting herself as a muse in the following stanza.

Gulielme, parce, te rogo,
Quod impolita carminis
Inusitati mî hactenus
Tibi loquatur Pieris.

(William, pardon me, I beg,
That an unpolished Muse has thus far
Spoken to you
in my unaccustomed song.)[24]

But Muses were not always entirely helpful to women writers. A variety of neo-Latin poets represented the relationship of Muse and poet as a sexual one, and anyone who shared this view inevitably had considerably more trouble with the relationship between a woman and the Muses.[25] Ben Jonson writes savagely on Cecelea Bulstrode in 1609 for daring to set pen to paper, even in the essentially playful and social activity of writing 'News':

What though with tribad [lesbian] lust she force a muse
And in an epicéne fury can write news

Equal with that, which for the best news goes?
As airy-light, and as like wit, as those?[26]

Women's writing is here represented as homosexual rape—an extreme position on Jonson's part, but, for that very reason, a reminder of how careful a Jacobean woman might have had to be if she were to avoid giving offence.

Translation

One of the most important issues that has to be addressed with respect to women and the classical tradition is language. A number of early modern women writers express a sense that classically educated men used their knowledge to assert a superiority that is arrived at unfairly by keeping women in ignorance, then blaming them for it. As the Scottish didactic poem attributed to 'Lady Lothian' (which was circulating by the 1630s) observes:

The weakness of a woman's wit
Is not to Nature's fault,
But lack of education fit
Makes Nature whiles to halt [sometimes to limp / stumble].
(ll. 61–4; *Early Modern Women Poets*, 228–30)

A generation later, 'Philo-Philippa' puts this point of view particularly crisply:

Ask me not then, why jealous men debar
Our sex from books in peace, from arms in war.
It is because our parts will soon demand
Tribunals for our persons, and command?
Shall it be our reproach, that we are weak,
And cannot fight, nor as the school-men speak?
Even men themselves are neither strong nor wise,
If limbs and parts they do not exercise,
Trained up to arms, we Amazons have been,
And Spartan virgins strong as Spartan men:
Breed women but as men, and they are these;
Whilst Sybarite men are women by their ease.
(ll. 55–66; *Early Modern Women Poets*, 403)

This is a note that is also struck by men who write in a female *persona*. For example, Geoffrey Chaucer uses Alysoun, his 'Wife of Bath', to express the view that knowledge is power. Janekyn, her fourth husband, possessed what she refers to indignantly as a 'book of wicked wives', which afforded him superior amusement.[27] Alysoun, angered and frustrated by her inability to produce counterexamples of equally despicable men, can only resort to violence: she tears the pages, whereupon Janekyn batters her. She is strongly aware that it would have been far more effective to answer Theophrastus in his own terms:

By god, if wommen hadde writen stories,
As clerkes han withinne hire oratories, [as clerk have within their oratories]
They wolde han writen of men moore wikkednesse
Than al the mark of Adam may redresse.

(ll. 693–6)[28]

John Skelton in 'Philip Sparrow' attributes to his mouthpiece Jane Scrope a bashful hesitancy about writing that derives from lack of classical knowledge:

I have but little skill
With Ovid or Virgil
Or with Plutarch,
Or Francis Petrarch,
Alcaeus or Sappho.
('Philip Sparrow',
ll. 754–9)[29]

However, Jane Scrope as voiced by Skelton has heard of a woman Latin poet, Sulpicia (147–53), and she knows the stories of Andromache, Attalus, Medea, Philip of Macedon, Actaeon, Penelope, Hannibal, Scipio, and Hector. Skelton is making a point that is important to understanding Renaissance Englishwomen's relationship with high culture: even before the Reformation, stories, themes, tropes, and characters originating in the classical tradition were accessible without Latin, redacted through the vernacular romances that were the principal entertainment of the nobly born.

As the sixteenth century wore on, life began to catch up with Skelton's fiction, and real-life women took advantage of it. The Wife of Bath would have been delighted by Isabella Whitney, who, in 1567, published a verse letter addressed to the lover who had jilted her. She is not likely to have been Latin-literate, but both the title and the content of her poem indicate that she intended her work to be read in relation to Ovid's *Heroides* (published in English translation that same year) rather than as a purely autobiographical complaint. Aeneas, Theseus, Paris, and Jason are marshalled into a rogue's gallery of defaulting males that would have made a very effective answer to Janekyn's 'wicked wives'.

Example take by many a one
whose falsehood now is plain.

As by Aeneas first of all,
who did poor Dido leave,
Causing the Queen, by his untruth,
with sword her heart to cleave.

Also I find that Theseus did
his faithful love forsake,
Stealing away during the night,
before she did awake.

Jason, that came of noble race,
two Ladies did beguile:
I wonder how he dared show his face,
to those that knew his wile. [treachery]
(The Copy of a Letter Lately Written in Meeter, by a Yonge Gentilwoman [1567], ll. 31–44; *Early Modern Women Poets*, 49–52)

Whitney's poem reveals that knowledge of Latin is not the only key to entering the world of shared values and assumptions that derives from familiarity with classical texts. It also suggests that, insofar as there is an aspect of male bonding in Renaissance teaching of Latin, as Walter Ong argued, women who managed to acquaint themselves with the classical tradition might quite deliberately challenge these values and assumptions.[30]

The output of the first fifty years or so of printing in England has something to tell us about English consumption of classical literature, notably, a preference for versions. The book generally known as *The Recuyell* (compendium) *of the Historyes of Troye* (it has an *incipit* rather than a title) was perhaps the first book to be published by William Caxton, translated from French,[31] and thereafter significant numbers of translations from French romances were printed in London.[32] Only in 1553 was an actual English translation of the *Aeneid* published (Gawain Douglas's, issued by William Copeland), and English printers were cautious about venturing on actual classical texts.[33]

Romance texts based on classical stories did at least introduce names and stories to a wider public. They thus widened the circle of readers aware that classical texts existed, and, as a result, as early as the mid-sixteenth century, when relatively few classical texts were as yet available in English, some women could, and did, get Latin-literate male relatives and friends to translate for them ad hoc.[34] Margaret, Countess of Cumberland, commissioned translations from Latin for her personal use in and after the 1580s: most of these were theological, but they also included Boethius and Seneca.[35]

Beyond such domestic commissions, the translation of classical texts was a major academic industry of the sixteenth century, especially after 1550.[36] The learned community as ordinarily defined was of Latinate ex-university men, and most major writers, such as Ben Jonson and Christopher Marlowe, who read Latin as fluently as English, could and sometimes did write in it, and were acquainted with Greek, belonged to it. However, some did not, including William Shakespeare, who clearly read Plutarch in Thomas North's translation, and read Ovid primarily through Arthur Golding (though he also read Ovid in Latin). But Shakespeare was not handicapped by his lack of university-level education, because Golding, North, and many another had placed the classical tradition within his reach. It was equally within reach of female contemporaries such as Aemilia Lanier.

Women's own contribution to the translation of classical texts was negligible in this period. Three Englishwomen translated from classical Latin and Greek texts: Elizabeth

I and the daughters of the twelfth Earl of Arundel.[37] Queen Elizabeth's translations from classical authors were a strictly private aspect of her adult life. They were swiftly composed rough versions that seem to have doubled as exercises in keeping her languages fluent,[38] and as some kind of relief from the tensions of her life. William Camden asserted that her 1593 translation of Boethius's *Consolation of Philosophy* was undertaken as a result of her grief over Henri IV's conversion to Catholicism.[39] Elizabeth wished it to be known to her subjects that she allowed herself very little leisure. But translation was difficult enough and engrossing enough to take her mind off the constant juggling of active rule, and relevant to it, since Elizabeth needed to play the part of the humanist princess. Few of her courtiers, with the possible exception of the Cecils, were as diligent in keeping their school Latin and Greek in repair.

Arundel's daughters wrote entirely for their father. Lady Jane, who became Lady Lumley, translated selections from Isocrates from Greek to Latin, and translated Euripides' *Iphigeneia at Aulis* into English, both at his behest.[40] Her sister Lady Mary, who died at 17, completed four translation exercises, presented to her father as successive New Year's gifts (now London, British Library Royal 12 A i–iv): the last of these was *sententiae* translated from Greek to Latin. Lady Mary's early death precluded her putting this linguistic ability to any use; and Lady Jane spent most of her married life nursing her father, who had a breakdown after the deaths of both his wife and Lady Mary in 1557.

Most early modern women writers are demonstrably the product of families in which there was some tradition of learning. And a university education did not necessarily produce a lifelong preference for reading in Latin. The Newdigates of Arbury, for example, were book-lovers. Personal notebooks belonging to John Newdigate survive from 1597–1610, in which he excerpts and makes notes on about fifty writers, including Lucan, Livy, Plutarch, Cicero, Seneca, Marcus Aurelius, Epictetus, and Pliny—almost entirely in translation: he returned time and time again to North's translation of Marcus Aurelius, for example.[41] His wife, Dame Alice, evidently had sufficient leisure to browse his library from time to time: a friend, Frances Beaumont, expects her to recognize allusions to the painter Timanthes, the Sphinx, and Pygmalion.

Few women were in a position to build up their own libraries, though they could certainly have a share, both as collectors and readers, in a family enterprise: Lady Jane Lumley is a case in point: the Lumley Library, built up by her husband, her father, and herself, became famous as one of the greatest private collections in England.[42] On a more humble social level, the 'List of my Books' in Lady Anne Southwell's commonplace book records a private library of 110 volumes, which included 'Pliny's Natural History, in folio... History of the Roman Emperors, in folio... Sallust's history in English, in folio... Suetonius, of the 12 Cæsars, in folio... Lucius Annæus Seneca... Seneca, his ten Tragedies', all very much standard texts.[43] The fact that the Sallust is specifically described as 'in English' casts a question upon whether all these classical texts were translations (that many were in folio format hints otherwise).

Another question, however, is which of the collection are Lady Anne's own books, since the list is compiled by her second husband, Henry Sibthorpe, and some, published after her death, are definitely his. However, material elsewhere in the manuscript, such as texts headed 'An Abstract of The Lives of the Roman Emperors; as They Have Been Related Unto Us by Pliny, Plutarch, and Suetonius' and 'A Paraphrase Upon Lucius Anneus Seneca on his Booke of Providence', suggests that it was Lady Anne who collected Seneca and the books on Roman history.[44] Dame Sarah Cowper (1644–1720), daughter of a Lord Mayor of London, left a memorandum of the 133 books she owned: these were in English or French, and include a variety of classical authors such as Seneca and Epictetus.[45]

The father of Lady Anne Clifford (1590–1676), the third Earl of Cumberland, forbade her mother, from whom he was estranged, to have her taught Latin. Her mother obeyed the letter but not the spirit of this injunction. She hired the poet Samuel Daniel as Lady Anne's tutor, and though he taught entirely through translations, he gave her a literary education. The so-called Great Picture of the Clifford family, which Lady Anne commissioned *c.*1646, shows books in all three panels of the triptych, presumably ones she considered particularly significant to her cultural formation: they include Ovid's *Metamorphoses*, Boethius, Seneca, Plutarch (in French), and Ammianus Marcellinus.[46]

Accessing classical texts through translations and secondary literature is obviously not ideal, but it is a great deal better than nothing. As Thomas Wilson observed in his 1570 translation of Demosthenes:

> Such as are annoyed with translated books, are like those who, eating fine white bread themselves, are angry with others that eat brown bread. And yet, God knows, those men would as gladly eat white bread as they, if they had it.[47]

Not every intellectually ambitious woman had the opportunity to learn Latin, but for all that, she was not necessarily excluded thereby from dipping into the well of Helicon.

It is also important to realize that English versus Latin is by no means the whole story of women's reception of Greek and Latin texts. French is an essential third term. In the course of the seventeenth century French gradually extended out from court circles to become an ordinary accomplishment of gentry-level women, and the enterprise of translation from Latin and Greek began in France just as early as in England.[48] It was already well underway in the sixteenth century, but the seventeenth century has been described (by Henri-Jean Martin) as 'the time of translations'. By the mid-seventeenth century, access to all classical texts of any importance could be achieved by someone who read French.[49] This florescence of translation had an obvious impact on women's access to classical texts—Lady Anne Clifford read Plutarch in French.

A number of other women demonstrably approached the classical tradition through French, such as Mary Sidney, Countess of Pembroke. In 1592, she published

Antonie, a Senecan closet drama on Anthony and Cleopatra that she had translated from Robert Garnier's *Marc Antoine*, in turn, based on Plutarch, Dio Cassius, Appian, and Josephus. The countess was content to follow her original closely, but drew on North's 1579 Plutarch translation alongside Garnier.[50] Another is Katherine Philips, who similarly translated classically themed plays, Corneille's *Pompée* and *Horace*.

More generally, we should ask whether the classical tradition was enabling or disabling to Renaissance women, and in what ways. As Chaucer demonstrated, its existence allowed learned men to patronize and discount the experience of Alysouns. But the vast ragbag of myth and semi-legendary history that comprises the classical tradition includes stories pointing in many different directions, some of which were seized on by women such as Isabella Whitney for their own distinct purposes. The sixteenth-century author of an overtly lesbian poem (perhaps Marie Maitland) written in Scots before 1586 compares her feelings for her unnamed woman friend with those of Pirithous for Theseus, Achilles for Patroclus, Orestes for Pylades, Achates for Aeneas, and Titus for Josephus; she is thus the first English-language writer I know of to assemble a canon of homosexual lovers.

> In amity Perithous
> to Theseus was not so traist [trustworthy]
> Nor, to Achilles, Patroclus,
> nor Pylades to true Orest[es]
> Nor yet Achates' love so lest [loyal]
> to good Æneas, nor such friendship
> David to Jonathan professed
> nor Titus true to kind Josip [Josephus].
> (ll. 25–32)[51]

For good measure, she also adds virtuous women of antiquity, Penelope and Portia, wife of Brutus, to her list. Since her concern is to marshal instances of fidelity, she naturally does not cite Sappho, though she is herself compared to Sappho by an anonymous contemporary.[52]

A surprisingly high proportion of seventeenth-century women poets were Latin-literate. This suggests that Latin had a very definite bearing on women's confidence as writers. Elizabeth Grymeston, a profoundly religious woman who died in 1603, was Latin-literate, and, though she was far more interested in Christian texts, nonetheless musing on fortune in the fourteenth of her *Miscellanea*, the *exempla* that come to her mind are Troy, Hecuba, Alexander the Great, Caesar, and Xerxes. She quotes in Latin (apparently from memory, since her citations are not entirely accurate) from standard works on fortune, possibly via a handbook, drawing on Seneca's *Troades*, Ovid's *Epistolae ex Ponto* 4, Manilius's *Astronomica* 4, and Juvenal's tenth *Satire*.[53]

However, by 1650, and probably by 1600, it was possible for an individual to write like an educated person on the basis of extensive reading in English and French, and many women poets of gentry or higher status deploy a wealth of classical references. Katherine Philips probably did not read Latin, but her poem 'On the Welsh language' alludes to the ruin of Troy, Athens, and Rome, and cites the stories of Boadicea and Caractacus from Tacitus' *Annals* and *Agricola*.[54] The *Annals* had been translated into English by William Fulbecke (1598) and R. Greneway (1604), and *Agricola* by Sir Henry Savile (1591). Both texts were also available in French.[55] Similarly, Lady Anne Southwell read classical texts in translation, if not in the original, and adorned her verse accordingly,[56] while Francellina Stapleton, writing a poem to her friend and neighbour John Newdigate in 1655, is another reader of Plutarch in translation, since she alludes to the Life of Dion; she seems also to have been familiar with Cicero's *De Amicitia*,[57] and, like Marie Maitland (if it is she), she knows the story of Pylades and Orestes.[58]

Hester Pulter (1605–78), a poet who deserves to be far better known, was profoundly acquainted with classical myth and history: her poem on Sir George Lisle's and Sir Charles Lucas's execution after the battle of Colchester is cast in the form of deliberations between Atropos, Lachesis, and Clotho, and mentions in passing Mars's trial on the Areopagus, Tantalus, Nessus, Hercules, Cambyses, and Brennus, among others, in a densely woven tissue of reference.[59] There is nothing strained or artificial about this: these stories and characters are simply available to her as aids to the shaping and framing of her discourse, as they are for a contemporary such as Andrew Marvell. A poem on watching her dearly-beloved daughter die of smallpox ends thus:

> But what a heart had I, when I did stand
> Holding her forehead with my trembling hand.
> My heart to heaven with her bright spirit flies,
> Whilst she (ah me!) closed up her lovely eyes
> Her soul being seated in her place of birth,
> I turned a Niobe as she turned earth.
> ('Upon the Death of my deare and lovely Daughter
> J.P. Jane Pulter', ll. 53–8; *Early Modern Women Poets*, 193)

For Pulter, the figure of Niobe, the epitome of bereaved motherhood, turned to stone by the intense pain of her loss, offers a summation of the intensity of her personal grief in a daring and paradoxical metaphor.

One woman whose relation to the classical tradition is boldly individual is 'the Tenth Muse lately sprung up in America', Anne Bradstreet (1613–72).[60] She was the daughter of the chief steward of the Earl of Lincoln, and, as a girl, she had free run of the library at Sempringham Castle. She went to Massachusetts with her father and husband in 1630, when she was 18. Her husband, Simon Bradstreet, was, like her father, an educated man; a disastrous fire at the Bradstreet's home in Massachusetts in 1666 destroyed more than 800 books, many of which, to judge from her writings, must have been works of history. It is clear from all her work that Bradstreet's mind was stocked with the heroes and villains of Greece and Rome. Her poem on Elizabeth I compares and contrasts the late queen with Thomyris, Semiramis, Dido, and

Zenobia; an Amazon and three female founders of cities. Her lament for Sir Philip Sidney alludes to the story of Augustus saluted by a crow,[61] Achilles and Hector, Scipio, Hercules, and the legend of Apollo and Phaethon.

I would also like to suggest that, in fashioning herself as a writer, she may have had a specific female precedent in mind. The Prologue to *The Tenth Muse* begins with a classic *recusatio*:

> To sing of wars, of captains, and of kings,
> Of cities founded, commonwealths begun,
> For my mean pen are too superior things,
> Or how they all, or each, their dates have run:
> Let poets and historians set these forth,
> My obscure verse shall not so dim their worth.[62]

It is worth setting this beside the opening of the prologue to the fourth-century Proba's *Cento* (similarly written in the aftermath of a civil war) to which it seems directly referential:

> Iam dudum temerasse duces pia foedera pacis,
> regnandi miseros tenuit quos dira cupido,
> diversasque neces, regum crudelia bella
> cognatasque acies, pollutos caede parentum
> insignis clipeos nulloque ex hoste tropaea,
> sanguine conspersos tulerat quos fama triumphos,
> innumeris totiens viduatas civibus urbes,
>
> confiteor, scripsi: satis est meminisse malorum.
> (I have for a long time now, I confess,
> been writing about how warlords broke pious peace-treaties
> wretched men whom a dire lust for dominion held in its grip;
> diverse slaughter, the cruel wars of kings,
> and of battle-lines of kinsmen, shields polluted by the slaughter of parents
> and trophies from no [external] enemy,
> bloodstained triumphs which Fame had reported,
> cities bereft so many times of innumerable citizens.
> That is enough of remembering evils!)[63]

The *Cento* was not available in translation. This raises the possibility that Bradstreet had some Latin—or, of course, her husband Simon Bradstreet could perfectly well have read over the text with her.[64]

Proba is in many respects a relevant *comparandum* for Bradstreet: a virtuous Christian wife and mother whose writings expressed strong scepticism towards the militaristic values of the Roman Empire, and refocused Virgil's narrative of imperial destiny upon the building of the kingdom of God. Centos, tiresome though they now seem, exercised the ingenuity of many early modern poets, and Proba attracted a great deal of attention.[65] She was, therefore, an available role model for women, and specifically legitimated writing Christian epic. Her work was used as a teaching text in late antiquity and again in the early modern period, because it was linguistically correct but neither pagan nor obscene: she appears, for example, as a curriculum author in Colet's 1518 statutes for St Paul's School.[66] Thus the Bradstreets may very well have taken a copy to the New World (by the time they set sail, there were at least twenty-seven editions in circulation).

Bradstreet's *recusatio* is less assertive than Proba's. Whereas Proba refers to the traditional male ranking of epic over pastoral, and boldly claims to supersede epic itself, Bradstreet disclaims a concern with the great epic themes of history and warfare on grounds of incapacity;—implying, it would seem, that her work is slight, intimate, and domestic. However, actual perusal of *The Tenth Muse* reveals that, far from being confined to suitable domestic topics, most of Bradstreet's œuvre consists of a series of very long poems, *The Four Elements, The Four Monarchies,* and the *Dialogue between Old England and New*. In fact, both the *Four Monarchies* and the *Dialogue* tackle precisely the same themes as Proba's lost poem on the civil wars of the fourth century, 'diversasque neces, regum crudelia bella, | cognatasque acies' (various kinds of slaughter, cruel wars between kings, battlelines of kinsmen).

In her long poems, Anne Bradstreet leans on secondary sources rather than researching Latin and Greek historians—Du Bartas's *Weeks*, translated by Joshua Sylvester, and Sir Walter Raleigh's *History of the World* were her principal source texts. But, if we are talking about classical *tradition*, dependence on secondary sources is not to be dismissed. The duty of parliament, according to her *Dialogue between Old England and New* (1642), is 'to crush the proud, and right to each man deal' (l. 164).[67] If that most familiar of formulations comes readily to a writer's mind, then that individual is clearly in a relationship with the classical tradition, whether or not she had read the *Aeneid* in Latin.

It is also worth comparing Bradstreet's enterprises with that of Proba. Versifying Walter Raleigh's *History* was anything but mechanical, since Bradstreet ignores Raleigh's book divisions and shapes her material with reference to the Bible, using the Book of Daniel's scheme of four world empires. What comes over in her text is hardline Calvinist contempt for the masculine world of conquest and empire-building. Historical facts derived from Raleigh are so presented as to appear simply as centuries of futile and meaningless struggle, with a strongly implied questioning of the value of monarchy. The last stanza of her poem is principally engaged with the rape of Lucretia by Tarquin, and the last lines of the entire project are:

> The government they change, a new one bring,
> And people swear ne'er to accept a King.[68]

Since this poem was written in the 1640s by a member of a group of refugees from the personal rule of Charles I who were attempting to set up a new kind of godly community in Massachusetts, it is quite hard to maintain the view that this abrupt conclusion is 'not political' merely because its author was female. While Bradstreet's *recusatio* deprecates her ability to engage with wars, captains, and kings, the actual content of her writing deals with these themes at length, and, precisely like that of Proba, *reverses* the value schemes of Virgil and the Roman historians, sweeps traditional epic away as so much rubble, and, in its stead, looks forward to the kingdom of the saints.

In this, she strongly resembles Lucy Hutchinson, another Calvinist epic poet and student of Latin.[69] Hutchinson similarly offers a *recusatio*, rejecting her own early study of Lucretius' *De Rerum Naturae* (which she translated into verse), and declaring in her prose introduction to *Order and Disorder*, a book-length poem on the Creation and Fall of Man, 'I found it necessary to have recourse to the fountain of Truth . . . and fortify my mind with a strong antidote against all the poison of human wit and wisdom that I had been dabbling withal'. Hutchinson may well have been a reader of Anne Bradstreet, since elsewhere in this introduction she declares: 'I know I am obnoxious to the censures of two sorts of people'—as she explains, literary critics on the one hand, and those who think verse an unsuitable medium for religious writing on the other.[70] Bradstreet, in the poem prefaced to *The Tenth Muse*, similarly excuses herself with the words:

> I am obnoxious to each carping tongue,
> Who says, my hand a needle better fits.[71]

Though 'obnoxious to . . .' was contemporary standard English, the similarity of phrasing is so striking as to suggest direct recollection.

In conclusion, it is hard to overestimate the importance of translation to intellectually aspirant women. I argued elsewhere that there is a profusion of anecdotal evidence to suggest that the number of women who could read Latin with ease and pleasure in sixteenth- and seventeenth-century England was greater than is generally assumed.[72] However, that may not be as important as the fact that, by 1650, one could travel a considerable distance in the realms of gold without the passport of a Latin education, and we must also take into account that the personal libraries of most country gentlemen, parsons, and London merchants who were literary in their tastes were full of translations, and nothing whatever prevented daughters from browsing there. Mary Evelyn, daughter of John Evelyn the diarist, is a case in point: she educated herself in her father's study, reading 'abundance of History, and all the best poets, even to Terence, Plautus, Homer, Virgil, Horace, Ovid ...' on a basis of having good French and some Italian, before her death at the age of 19, in 1665.[73]

Thus the sixteenth and, still more, the seventeenth century saw a significant democratization of the classical tradition. After the Reformation, a concatenation of social changes greatly increased the proportion of literates in the population. The book trade expanded enormously in the later sixteenth and seventeenth centuries. The proportion of Latin-literate gentry also increased, owing to the expansion of the universities. In Cambridge, Christ's, Emmanuel, St John's, Sidney

Sussex, and Trinity, in Oxford, Corpus Christi, St John's, Trinity, Christ Church, Brasenose, and Jesus, are all sixteenth-century foundations. Many of the men who attended Oxford and Cambridge came away with a taste formed by years of intensive education, but did not go on to lead lives that kept their Latin fluent. Many of them, therefore, preferred to do their leisure reading in English, and bought books that were potentially accessible to their wives and daughters.

It seems to me perfectly probable that poets as sophisticated as Hester Pulter and Anne Bradstreet could read Latin. But it is at least as important that women born after 1600, as they both were (in 1605 and 1612 respectively), did not actually need to, provided that they either shared their milieu with educated fathers, brothers, or husbands who bought books, or could afford to amass a library of their own.

Classical reference and a Latinate vocabulary remained central to cultivated discourse down to the twentieth century. Mrs Chapone (1727–1801), a very influential voice in girls' education, assumes as a matter of course that a properly educated woman would read seriously in classical literature, and says of Homer and Virgil in translation: 'everybody reads [them] that reads at all.'[74] However, she observes that Latin itself was no longer necessary. 'I respect the abilities and application of those ladies who have attained them [the classical languages]... yet I would by no means advise... [any] woman who is not strongly impelled by a particular genius to engage in such studies... the real knowledge that they supply is not essential, since the English, French, or Italian tongues afford tolerable translations of all the most valuable productions of antiquity'—a state of affairs that was already in place by 1660, and that radically altered the relationship between women and the classical tradition.

Notes

1. Elizabeth Rowe, *Poems on Several Occasions, Written by Philomela* (1696), preface by her friend Elizabeth Johnson, sig. A3^{v}: 'sometimes it pleases heaven to raise up some brighter genius to succour a distressed people—; an Epaminondas in Thebes; a Timoleon for Corinth; (for you must know we read Plutarch now 'tis translated)'.
2. Walter Ong, SJ, 'Latin and the Social Fabric', in *The Barbarian within and Other Fugitive Essays and Studies* (New York, 1962), 211.
3. Edmund Leach, *Culture and Nature, or La Femme Sauvage* (1968), 7.
4. On medieval queenship, John Carmi Parsons, *Medieval Queenship* (Stroud, 1993), and Pauline Stafford, *Queen Emma and Queen Edith: Queenship and Women's Power in Eleventh-Century England* (Oxford, 1997), are good starting points.
5. *Patrologia Latina* 159, col. 119 (Anselm's *epistolarium*, II 55). She commissioned William of Malmesbury's *Gesta Regum Anglorum* and a Latin *Life* of her mother, St Margaret of Scotland, and may herself have been a writer: Thomas Tanner, *Bibliotheca Britanno-Hibernica* (1748), attributes to her a Latin treatise, now lost, called *De Mundi Catastropho*.
6. For example, Madeleine de Scudéry, referred to as 'Sapho' by contemporaries, has that name with the rider that she 'eclipsed [Sappho] with her virtue' (Joan

DeJean, *Fictions of Sappho, 1546–1937* (Chicago, 1989), 105).

7. Hilarion de Coste, *Les Eloges et vies des reynes, Princesses, Ames et damoiselles illustres en pieté, courage et doctrine* (Paris, 1630), 590. On Bijns, see Kristiaan P. G. Aercke, 'Germanic Sappho: Anna Bijns', in Katharina M. Wilson (ed.), *Women Writers of the Renaissance and Reformation* (Athens, GA, 1987), 365–97.
8. London, Public Record Office SP 12/47, fos 14r–18: fos 17–18 contain poems from Franciscus Junius to Mildred Cecil, July 1565.
9. This poem invokes Sappho together with Perilla, a protégée of Ovid's whom he addresses in one of the *Tristia*.
10. Jane Stevenson and Peter Davidson (eds), *Early Modern Women Poets: An Anthology* (Oxford, 2001), 20.
11. Munich, Bayerische Staatsbibliothek, Clm lat. 10383, fo. 260r.
12. 'Sappho to Phaon' has a completely different textual transmission from the *Heroides*, and may not be by Ovid at all. L. D. Reynolds (ed.), *Texts and Transmission: A Survey of the Latin Classics* (Oxford, 1983), 272–3.
13. Howard Jacobson, *Ovid's Heroides* (Princeton, 1974), 297.
14. Florence Verducci, *Ovid's Toyshop of the Heart: Epistulae Heroidum* (Princeton, 1985), 137.
15. Caroline Jameson, 'Ovid in the Sixteenth Century', in *Ovid*, ed. J. W. Binns (Boston, 1973), 210–42 (esp. 213–14); Anne Moss, *Ovid in Renaissance France* (1982).
16. DeJean, *Fictions of Sappho*, 100–10.
17. [Madeleine] de Scudéry, in *Les Femmes illustres, ou les harangues heroïques*, 2 vols (Paris, 1655), 1. 391–409 (409). On the authorship, see Linda Timmermans, *L'Accès des femmes á la culture (1578–1715)* (Paris, 1993), 304–5.
18. *Les Femmes illustres* was translated into English in 1681 and published in Edinburgh (this translation was by James Innes, who moved in the circles of Mary of Modena). Another translation, first published in London in 1714, went through several editions.
19. Giovanni Boccaccio, *Concerning Famous Women*, trans. Guido A. Guarino (New Brunswick, 1963), Ceres, pp. 11–13, Minerva, pp. 14–15, Isis, pp. 18–19, Carmenta, pp. 52–3.
20. Alex Hardie, 'Juvenal, the *Phaedrus*, and the Truth about Rome', *Classical Quarterly* NS 48/1 (1998), 234–51.
21. Margaret Tyler, *The Mirrour of Princely Deedes and Vertues* (1578), sig. A iii.
22. Effrosini Spentzou and Don Fowler (eds), *Cultivating the Muse: Struggles for Power and Inspiration in Classical Literature* (Oxford, 2002).
23. *'My Name was Martha': A Renaissance Woman's Autobiographical Poem by Martha Moulsworth*, ed. Robert C. Evans and Barbara Wiedemann (West Cornwall, 1993), 5, ll. 21–2, 27–34.
24. 'To Wilhelm Friedrich von Pisnitz', *Elizabeth Jane Weston: Collected Writings*, ed. and trans. Donald Cheney and Brenda M. Hosington (Toronto, 2000), 30–1.
25. See Jane Stevenson, 'Johanna Otho (Othonia) and Women's Latin Poetry in Reformed Europe', in Laurie Churchill, Phyllis R. Brown, and Jane E. Jeffrey (eds), *Women Writing Latin from Roman Antiquity to Early Modern Europe*, 3 vols (New York, 2002), 3. 189–216.
26. *News of my Morning worke*, by Mist. B.', in the ninth edition of *The Conceited News of Thomas Overbury* (1609). See Barbara Lewalski, *Writing Women in Jacobean England* (Cambridge, MA, 1993), 109.
27. Jankyn's book was apparently a compilation of Walter Map, *Letter of Valerius*, Theophrastus, *On Marriage*, and St Jerome, *Against Jovinian*.
28. 'The Wife of Bath's Prologue', in *The Riverside Chaucer*, gen. ed. Larry D. Benson, 3rd edn (Boston, 1987), 114.

29. John Skelton, *The Complete English Poems*, ed. John Scattergood (Harmondsworth, 1983), 90.
30. W. J. Ong, SJ, 'Latin Language Study as a Renaissance Puberty Rite', *Studies in Philology*, 56 (1967), 103–24.
31. *Here Begynneth the Volume Intituled and Named the Recuyell of the Historyes of Troye*... Bruges, 1473 or 1474).
32. *Here Fynyssheth the Boke yf [sic] Eneydos, Compyled by Vyrgyle, which Hathe Be Translated oute of Latyne in to Frenshe, and oute of Frenshe Reduced in to Englysshe* (1490). Lotte Hellinga, 'Tradition and Renewal: Establishing the Chronology of Wynkyn de Worde's Early Work', in Kristian Jensen (ed.), *Incunabula and their Readers: Printing, Selling and Using Books in the Fifteenth Century* (2003), 13–30 (16).
33. *THE xvi. BUKES OF ENEADOS of the Famose Poete Virgill* (1553).
34. J. W. Saunders, 'From Manuscript to Print', *Transactions of the Leeds Philological Society*, 6 (1951), 507–28.
35. Richard T. Spence, *Lady Anne Clifford* (Stroud, 1997), 9.
36. For an overview, see Gordon Braden and Robert Cummings, *The Oxford History of Literary Translation in English*, vol. 2: *1550–1660* (Oxford, 2010).
37. Elizabeth I translated from Boethius, Horace, and Plutarch: see Janel Mueller and Joshua Scodel (eds), *Elizabeth I: Translations*, 2 vols (Chicago, 2009).
38. She was evidently highly conscious of the need to work at a language in order to maintain fluency: Victor von Klarwill (ed.), *Queen Elizabeth and Some Foreigners* (1928), 59, 187, 194.
39. William Camden, *The Historie of the Most Renowned and Victorious Princesse Elizabeth* (1630), 475.
40. In Diane Purkiss (ed.), *Three Tragedies by Renaissance Women* (Harmondsworth, 1998), 1–35.
41. Vivienne Larminie, *Wealth, Kinship and Culture: The Seventeenth Century Newdigates of Arbury* (Ipswich, 1995), 146–8 (121).
42. See Sears Jayne and Francis R. Johnson, *The Lumley Library: The Catalogue of 1609* (1956).
43. *The Southwell–Sibthorpe Commonplace Book*, ed. Jean Klene (Tempe, AZ, 1997), 98–101.
44. *Southwell–Sibthorpe*, 33–4, 48
45. Hertfordshire Record Office, D/EP F 36
46. Spence, *Lady Anne Clifford*, 189–94.
47. *The Three Orations of Demosthenes* (1570), quoted in Louis B. Wright, *Middle-Class Culture in Elizabethan England* (Chapel Hill, NC, 1935), 344.
48. The first woman of the Renaissance to translate from classical Latin is probably Marguerite Briet, who translated *Aeneid* 1–4. Her works were published in Paris from 1538 to 1542. See Kittye delle Robbins-Herring, 'Hélisienne de Crenne: Champion of Women's Rights', in Katharina M. Wilson (ed.), *Women Writers of the Renaissance and Reformation*, ed. (Athens, GA, 1987), 177–218.
49. H.-J. Martin, *Livre, pouvoir et société à Paris au xviie siècle (1598–1701)* (Geneva, 1969), 607.
50. *The Collected Works of Mary Sidney Herbert, Countess of Pembroke*, ed. Margaret P. Hannay, Noel J. Kinnamon, and Michael G. Brennan, 2 vols (Oxford, 1998), 139–40.
51. See *The Maitland Quarto Manuscript*, ed. W. A. Craigie, STS ns 9 (Edinburgh, 1920), 160–2, and Jane Farnsworth, 'Voicing Female Desire in "Poem XLIX"', *Studies in English Literature 1500–1700*, 36/1 (1996), 37–72.
52. In a poem, 'To your self' (in the same manuscript, Cambridge, Magdalene College, Pepys Library 2251, fo. 126), which makes considerable claims for her as a poet: stanza 1 compares her to Sappho,

stanza 2 to Olimpia Morata, Latin poet and polymath.

53. Elizabeth Grymeston, *Miscellanea, Memoratives* (1618), sig. E5^{v}–6^{r}.
54. *Early Modern Women Poets*, 329–30.
55. Étienne de la Planche translated the *Annals* in 1540, Nicolas Perrot d'Ablancourt published a translation of Tacitus' complete works in 1658.
56. *Southwell–Sibthorpe*, 24–7.
57. Translated by John Tiptoft, and published by William Caxton in 1481.
58. *Early Modern Women Poets*, 341.
59. *Early Modern Women Poets*, 193–5
60. *The Tenth Muse Lately Sprung up in America, Or Severall Poems* (1650).
61. From Macrobius' *Saturnalia*, retold by Erasmus in his *Apophthegmata*. See T. M. Parrott, 'Marlowe, Beaumont and Julius Caesar', *Modern Language Notes*, 44 (1929), 69–77 (71–2).
62. ll. 1–6, in Jane Stevenson, *Women Latin Poets* (Oxford, 2005), 233.
63. See *The Golden Bough, the Oaken Cross: The Virgilian Cento of Faltonia Betitia Proba*, ed and trans. Elizabeth A. Clark and Diane F. Hatch (Chico, 1981), 14–15. Three of these lines are adapted from Virgil: *Georgics* 1. 37 and 3. 32, and *Aeneid* 8. 571.
64. She quotes the tag 'bis pueri senes' ('old men are twice children') in 'Old Age', the last of her *The Four Ages* (*The Tenth Muse*, 52), and 'ne sutor ultra crepidam' ('let the cobbler stick to his last') in an epilogue to the third of *The Four Empires* (p. 174).
65. See Filippo Ermini, *Il centone di Proba e la poesia centonaria latina* (Rome, 1909); and Joseph Octave Delepierre, *Centoniana, ou Encyclopédie des Centos* (1866–8).
66. Printed in Joseph Hirst Lupton, *A Life of Dean Colet* (1887), 279.
67. *Early Modern Women Poets*, 240: 'parcere subiectis et debellare superbos' (*Aeneid* 6. 853).
68. *The Tenth Muse*, 179.
69. *The Works of Lucy Hutchinson* are being re-edited by David Norbrook et al. for Oxford University Press; *The Translation of Lucretius*, 2 vols, ed. Reid Barbour and David Norbrook, was published in 2012; *Order and Disorder* is forthcoming.
70. Lucy Hutchinson, *Order and Disorder*, ed. David Norbrook (Oxford, 2001), 3–5.
71. ll. 25–6; *The Tenth Muse*, 3–4
72. Stevenson, *Women Latin Poets*, 368–94.
73. *The Diary of John Evelyn*, ed. Guy de la Bedoyère (Ipswich, 2004), 279.
74. Josephine Kamm, *Hope Deferred: Girls' Education in English History* (1965), 105.

CHAPTER 8

Cultural Contexts

a. Politics and Nationalism

CURTIS PERRY

For early modern English writers, political thought was typically mediated by the dynamics of classical reception. Grammar-school curricula familiarized students with Latin authors (in most cases, Cicero, Horace, Ovid, Sallust, Terence, Virgil, and others) and inculcated in students an idea of classical letters as a storehouse of exempla and commonplaces useful both for generating arguments about contemporary questions and for garnering credibility with like-minded audiences. This training ensured familiarity with a range of classical texts, and it fostered a disposition towards classical learning that emphasized its practical utility for analysing current events. As a result, people read classical texts with an eye towards instructive parallels with the present, and knowledge of classical authorities could be seen as a prerequisite for politically oriented argumentation.[1]

Often, too, the categories within which early modern English writers understood politics were shaped within larger, European histories of classical reception, which were, therefore, sedimented within received habits of English political thought. Cicero's *De Officiis*—commonly studied in English schools and readily available in English translation from 1556 on—expressed assumptions about the virtue of active citizenship that were presupposed by most of the Tudor and early Stuart writers who attempted to comment upon political matters.[2] And even a book like Seneca's *De Clementia*, which was not part of any standard grammar-school curriculum and which was not available in translation until 1614, helped frame a conceptual vocabulary about the relationship between government and self-government that was fundamental to early modern European conceptions of monarchy.[3] Sir Thomas Smith's *De Republica Anglorum*, a treatise composed during the 1560s that purports (on the title page of its first printed edition, from 1583) to describe 'the manner of Government or policy of the Realm of England', opens with a taxonomy of constitutions derived from Aristotle's *Politics*, and then moves through eight introductory chapters defining key political terms via predominantly classical exempla before finally turning, in chapter nine, to specific discussion of England. This organizational logic makes manifest the prior, structuring importance of classical texts and stories for the constitutive categories of Elizabethan political thought.

A similar dynamic occurs at the level of form: prior histories of classical reception had a central, shaping influence on expectations about the political content of different kinds of writing. And, though the impact of classical writing upon literary genres is a product of the familiarity and cultural prestige of classical writers, the production of classically inflected kinds of literature could also have a patriotic aspect to it, as proof that the English could produce a vernacular literature to rival the cultural achievements of antiquity. Seen in this way, there is a close relationship between vernacular literatures produced in classically derived genres and the 'translation movement' characteristic of the first half of Elizabeth's reign, which saw numerous classical texts and authors translated into English for the first time.[4] Each is part of the development of a self-conscious national literary tradition.

We can sketch the relationship between politics, nationalism, and the reception of classical literary genres by considering, briefly, Edmund Spenser's *The Shepheardes Calender* (1579).[5] Spenser's book meditates upon the role of the poet within the political nation by means of its explicit self-consciousness concerning the relationship between classical and native precursors for pastoral form. Part of the book's self-presentation as pastoral has to do with the idea, based on the example of Virgil, that the composition of pastoral was a starting point for an epic poet's career. This presumption gives the pastoral an implied claim to national significance despite the ostensible rusticity of its settings and personae. *The Shepheardes Calender*, which also alludes to a native tradition of poetry highlighted by Chaucer and Skelton, uses the mode's Virgilian associations to present Spenser's poetry in terms of an English national tradition potentially on a par with Rome's. Spenser also draws upon a reception history that associated pastoral with oblique political commentary.[6] Accordingly, several of the eclogues comment upon controversies of ecclesiastical politics or the threat of Elizabeth's possible marriage to the French Duke of Anjou. Contemporaries—who shared the assumptions about pastoral's generic resources that Spenser exploits—seem to have understood the national and political stakes of Spenser's pastoral book. So much so that (in the words of David Norbrook) the poem 'established a political rhetoric that was to remain popular until the civil war', one linking the figure of the shepherd–poet with the memory of an Elizabethan style of Protestant nationalism.[7] This whole history—Virgil's complex and mediated influence upon an idea of pastoral that Spenser in turn takes up and transforms into a nativist political discourse with a significant English afterlife—is emblematic of the interplay between English political literature and inherited resources of genre and form shaped by the dynamics of classical reception.

Classicism and Counsel in the Elizabethan Polity

Each of these preconditions for the political importance of classical texts pre-dates the accession of Queen Elizabeth I. But humanistic learning played an especially important role in both the practice and the propaganda of the new queen's regime. Demonstrated mastery of classical learning was an important part of Elizabeth's persona, both domestically and on the international stage, because it offered a way of countering scepticism concerning the ability of a woman to rule. Hence, for instance, the publication of *Precationes Privatae Regiae E.R.* (1563), a book of prayers that also contains a collection of 259 Latin *sententiae*, culled mostly from classical authors and sorted into sections on rule, justice, mercy, counsel, peace, and war (*Translations*, I. 346–94). Such a publication makes a public demonstration of Elizabeth's godliness, of course, but also of her solid grounding in classical political wisdom. Roger Ascham, who had once been Elizabeth's tutor, frames *The Scholemaster* (1570) with a preface describing a dinner party in the chambers of Sir William Cecil—Elizabeth's principal secretary and the main architect of her new government—during which Ascham and the queen depart for a time to read, 'in the Greek tongue . . . that noble oration of Demosthenes against Aeschines for his false dealing in his embassage to King Philip of Macedonia'.[8] This oration evokes Athens's resistance to the imperial encroachment of Philip of Macedon, and English readers *c.*1570 were likely to understand a parallel with current worries about Philip II of Spain: this association, for instance, animates Thomas Wilson's English translation of Demosthenes' *Olynthiacs* and *Philippics*, likewise printed in 1570.[9] So the studious Elizabeth that Ascham publicizes is praised for her diligence in mastering a difficult classical author whose wisdom prepares her as a ruler to handle the current Spanish threat.

Cecil—to whom both Wilson's and Ascham's books were dedicated—brought to his administrative work a combination of committed Protestantism and pragmatic humanism, and he packed Elizabeth's government with like-minded associates.[10] Cecil's political beliefs have been described as paradoxical, in the following sense: 'he was a loyal servant of the crown who knew that government was too important to be left to kings and queens, a republican who believed passionately and forcefully in the survival of Elizabethan monarchy.'[11] He both epitomized and helped to create the early Elizabethan political praxis that has come to be known as 'monarchical republicanism': a happy amalgam of classically derived ideas about active citizenship joined to a native tradition of mixed government in which the monarch was thought to rule via common law and in tandem with Parliament.[12] This ethos (in which a royal councillor's first duty was to the good of the *res publica*), and the urgency of early Elizabethan political crises (uncertain succession, royal marriage, religious settlement, the threat of international Catholicism), sometimes caused members of the regime to attempt to influence policy via appeals to public audiences beyond the queen's inner circle. And this, in turn, created social conditions favourable to the production of politically engaged literary texts, which could be used to address a readership beyond the Elizabeth's inner circle but still be framed as counsel.[13]

A good example is *Gorboduc*, the earliest and best known of several politically oriented tragedies produced during Elizabeth's reign by members of the Inns of Court (the four residential societies for the study of law: Gray's Inn, Lincoln's Inn, the Middle Temple, and the Inner Temple). These Inns—ostensibly law schools, but also residential societies for ambitious young gentlemen—developed a distinctive and heavily classicizing literary culture and were, for instance, the epicentre of the early Elizabethan translation movement.[14] Since the Inns were home to a critical mass of well-connected and ambitious young men, armed with the requisite erudition and eager to secure advancement at court, their members played an especially important role in the production of politically engaged literature.

Gorboduc was written by Thomas Norton and Thomas Sackville for performance at the Inner Temple Christmas revels of 1561. The plot—in which old King Gorboduc's decision to divide his kingdom between his two sons leads to civil war—is designed to comment upon the uncertainty of succession, a major early Elizabethan political preoccupation. The story's political relevance would have been enhanced by the fact that it was taken from the legendary British history (derived from Geoffrey of Monmouth's twelfth-century *History of the Kings of England*), which depicts the line of ancient British kings as descendants of Brutus, himself a descendant of the Trojan hero Aeneas, founder of Rome. Dramatizing an episode from this history evokes a mythical genealogy of empire in which a united Britain is the natural inheritor of Roman grandeur: readers of Spenser's *The Faerie Queene* will remember that this same mythical history, with its attendant imperial fantasy, looms large within later formulations of Elizabethan nationalism.[15] Here, though, emphasis is placed upon the potentially disabling threat of disunion. The Inner Temple revels were presided over by Robert Dudley (later Earl of Leicester). Since he was a suitor to Elizabeth, and since the play inveighs against the 'unnatural thraldom of stranger's reign', it is likely that *Gorboduc* was meant to recommend that Elizabeth settle the succession by marrying the native-born Dudley, who may have had a hand in arranging for a second performance of the play before the queen at Whitehall in January of 1562.[16]

Gorboduc would have struck its original audiences as ostentatiously innovative at the level of form. At a time when most vernacular drama was written in fourteeners, Sackville and Norton wrote in blank verse, a metrical form that they would have known primarily from Henry Howard, Earl of Surrey's translations of Virgil's *Aeneid*. The play also makes use of Senecan tragedy in form as well as in its depiction of characters in the throes of violent, emotional extremity. It has been argued that the vogue for Seneca in the early Elizabethan Inns of Court had partly to do with the fact that Seneca himself had been both a playwright and a political advisor, and there is a thematic aspect to *Gorboduc*'s use of Senecan models in a play that stages failed counsel and that purports to offer political advice.[17] The play's innovative use of classical literary models has an authorizing function, in other words, establishing its authors' humanistic credentials and the importance of the Inner Templars' erudition. *Gorboduc*'s explicit political advice was probably tolerated by the queen only because the elite status of its authors and the restricted nature of its original audiences made it possible to understand the play as a form of counsel with limited circulation rather than as public political expression. Still, the play was printed in 1565 and reprinted in 1570 and 1590, so it did reach a broader public audience. This inherent tension—between literature as a form of counsel and literature as a mode of broader political appeal—is constantly renegotiated throughout the Elizabethan and early Stuart period.[18]

Elizabethan Disaffection and the Uses of Rome

Historians have recently described a transformation in the style of Elizabethan government during the 1580s and 1590s, as increasing conflict among the political elite, and a more withdrawn and autocratic mode of rule on the queen's part, undermined the conciliar ethos of monarchical republicanism.[19] In place of a political culture encouraging the production of literature-as-advice, the frustrations of the late Elizabethan period encouraged the development of modes of literature as outsider commentary. This change in the English political environment echoes a pan-European shift away from Ciceronian optimism about active political virtue. The key international figure here is the Belgian humanist Justus Lipsius, who in the last decades of the sixteenth century championed a brand of neo-stoicism derived primarily from Seneca and Tacitus that emphasized constancy and forbearance in the face of political turmoil as a potential alternative to engaged citizenship.[20] Introduced into the English scene by Sir Philip Sidney, who was himself an acquaintance and correspondent of Lipsius', these ideas became prominent in the 1590s: the sceptical pessimism of this new humanism offered a useful way of understanding events to those who felt disenfranchised, particularly associates of Robert Devereaux, second Earl of Essex, who wanted a more aggressive foreign policy and who increasingly felt that their rivals at court were leading the queen astray.[21] It is notable that in plays like Thomas Kyd's *Cornelia* (1594) and Shakespeare's *Julius Caesar* (1599), where Cicero appears as a character, he is represented as an ineffectual figure emblematic of a republican culture in decline.[22]

In part because the native political vocabulary associated with the ancient constitution was so conservative, Roman history became a crucial vehicle for exploring the mutability of political institutions. And, though Rome continued to serve as a benchmark for cultural achievement, late Elizabethan writers increasingly looked to Roman history for examples of imperial tyranny and corruption. This is one way to understand the fascination with the Roman republic and its collapse in the works of late Elizabethan writers such as Christopher Marlowe or Shakespeare.[23] These writers, and others like them, used Roman texts and stories in order to explore present-day concerns about domestic and foreign policy: the potential erosion of native liberties, instability associated with the colonial project in Ireland, the threat posed to Protestantism by international Roman Catholicism, and so on. Take *Julius Caesar,* a play that depicts factional intrigue and the dangers of succession in a manner designed to seem familiar to late Elizabethan audiences: by locating these contemporary issues in the context of the larger story of the end of the republic, the play touches upon deeply seated anxieties about irreversible cultural decline.

As part of this shift in emphasis, new classical authors came into fashion, especially post-Augustan writers such as Lucan and Juvenal whose works might be read as attacking or otherwise undermining Rome's exemplarity. Marlowe's translation of the first book of Lucan's *Pharsalia* was printed in 1600, and there are borrowings from Lucan in numerous late-Elizabethan depictions of British civil strife, including the Gray's Inn play *The Misfortunes of Arthur* (1588), Samuel Daniel's *First Four Books of the Civil Wars between the Two Houses of Lancaster and York* (1595) and Shakespeare's first tetralogy.[24] The cultural significance of Juvenal, meanwhile, is demonstrated by the Bishops Ban of 1599, an edict that attempted to curtail a vogue for Juvenalian satire.[25] Something similar might be said about the late Elizabethan interest in Tacitus, whose accounts of imperial court politics and *arcana imperii* provided a perspective that was broadly applicable to perceived court corruption and tyranny at home and abroad.[26]

Ben Jonson's harrowing play *Sejanus His Fall*—written during the last years of Elizabeth's reign, though not printed until 1605—distils the paranoid potential of Elizabethan Tacitism. Its depiction of the virtuous but disenfranchised followers of the late general Germanicus is designed to elicit comparison with Essex and his followers. Even more radically, its evocation of the absolutism of Tiberius and the impotence of his merely ornamental senate captures a distinctively late-Elizabethan worry about the potential loss of the native liberties.[27] Still, Jonson was no republican, as we can see by juxtaposing the political pessimism of *Sejanus* with the imperial model of authority that is held up as an ideal in his *Poetaster* (1601–2).[28] In this play, Jonson figures himself as Horace, and depicts Augustus and Virgil as cultural arbiters able to distinguish on merit between the scurrilous satire of writers like John Marston (figured in the play as Crispinus) and the 'free and wholesome sharpness' of Horace's/Jonson's writing (5. 1. 94).[29] Ovid—perhaps representing the pervasive Ovidianism of Elizabethan court culture—is depicted as erotically unruly, and is ultimately banished. Implicit is a model of cultural authority whose guarantee of liberty for the criticism provided by learned subjects is grounded ultimately in the judgement of the wise sovereign.

Augustan Style and Anti-Court Tacitism

The appeal of this neo-Augustan vision of cultural and political authority is partly responsible for Jonson's remarkable rise to prominence as a court poet under

King James I. And Jonson, who composed most of the Jacobean court's masques, was the single author most responsible for creating the literary image of the Jacobean regime. Because James (who had already been King James VI of Scotland) ruled England and Scotland at once, his accession seemed to raise the possibility that the ancient Britain linked genealogically to Troy and Rome in Monmouth's *History* might be reunited. When James signed a peace treaty with Spain in 1604, the parallel with Augustus' *pax romana* became unavoidable. Jonson's devices for the pageantry accompanying James's magnificent entry into the city of London in 1604 are saturated with imperial imagery, culminating in a prophecy that links James's reign to the 'lasting glory' of 'Augustus's state' (l. 763; *Works*, 7. 109). This Augustan vision proved to be a durable aspect of early Stuart court culture under both James and his son Charles I. A later example is Sir Richard Fanshawe's ode 'Upon Occasion of His Majesty's Proclamation in the Year 1630'. Fanshawe, himself a translator of both Horace and Virgil, celebrates Charles as the 'Augustus of our world' and casts England as a peaceable kingdom set apart from war-torn Europe.[30]

The cultural optimism associated with this Augustan vision of Britain could not, however, eradicate late-Elizabethan cynicism about rulers and courts. Tacitus' depictions of intrigue and corruption in the courts of imperial Rome remained influential throughout the entire early Stuart period and played a key role in shaping anti-court perspectives and stereotypes. Much of the evidence for such an argument resides in ephemera such as verse libels, letters, and pamphlet publications, but a Tacitean image of Jacobean corruption—emphasizing the wicked intrigues of all-powerful royal favourites, and the personal moral weakness of King James—was codified out of this material by anti-royalist writers such as Francis Osborne, Anthony Weldon, and Arthur Wilson in the 1640s and 1650s and has had a profound impact upon subsequent historiography. Wilson's *History of Great Britain, Being the Life and Reign of King James the First* (1653) presents itself as a Tacitean exposé of royal secrets, and offers the following as a summation of the king's character and his age: 'some paralleled him to Tiberius for dissimulation, yet peace was maintained by him as in the time of Augustus' (p. 289). George Villiers, the notorious Duke of Buckingham, whose status as favourite to both James and Charles occasioned enormous resentment, was compared to Sejanus in the context of impeachment proceedings against him in the Parliament of 1626. 'If the duke is Sejanus,' Charles is said to have commented, 'I must be Tiberius.' And, though Jonson's *Sejanus* was not popular in its own day, its influence can be detected in later Roman plays such as Philip Massinger's *The Roman Actor* (printed in 1629) and Thomas May's *Julia Agrippina* (1628, printed 1639).[31]

Lucan likewise grew in popularity during the early Stuart period, especially with those writers and readers worried about royal tyranny or the perceived failure of James and Charles to intervene effectively in international affairs on behalf of the Protestant nation.[32] In 1614, Sir Arthur Gorges published the first complete translation of *Lucan's Pharsalia*. This may originally have been intended as a dedication piece for James's eldest son, Henry, who died in 1612: Gorges is one of many early Jacobean figures who pinned their hopes for the future on the succession of the popular Prince Henry and who were, after his untimely death, ready to take a more oppositional stance with regard to James's pacific foreign policy. His *Pharsalia*, as printed in 1614, would have read like a rebuttal to the prevalent Augustan style of James as *rex pacificus*, particularly in the context of the political turmoil surrounding the so-called Addled Parliament that sat and was dissolved during the same year.[33] Thomas May's translation of Lucan's epic was first printed in 1627—at the height of opposition to the king's favourite Buckingham—with dedications to several noblemen known for their commitment to anti-Catholic militarism and/or antagonism to Buckingham.[34]

Classical Authority and Cultural Conflict

Buckingham was assassinated by John Felton in 1628. Felton was executed, but was also celebrated in numerous manuscript poems as both a martyr and a heroic, republican-minded 'Roman spirit'.[35] Hostility to Buckingham was symptomatic of a widening gap between the court and the rest of the political nation, and after 1629 that gap grew wider still: Charles decided to attempt to rule without Parliament, a resolution that held until 1640, when financial pressures associated with war in Scotland forced him to summon Parliament. The so-called Long Parliament, first assembled in November 1640, was almost immediately embroiled in conflict with Charles. Armed conflict between the king and Parliamentary forces began in earnest in 1642. The socio-political upheavals of the revolutionary era and the interregnum did away with many of the cultural and institutional frameworks that had once structured the use of classical materials within politically oriented literature. For instance, the relaxation of press censorship—which contributed to an unprecedented volume of polemical publication—and the eradication of the royal court as a centre for literary patronage each contributed to a radical shift in the basic dynamics of political address. It is emblematic of a transformation that Hobbes, in *De Cive* (1642), makes a specific point of eschewing argumentation based on classical history. In doing so, he responds to the fragmentation of English political culture by jettisoning the part of his rhetorical training that would have encouraged the use of classical commonplaces to ground argumentation in a shared intellectual framework.[36]

Historians and critics who attempt to survey the print cultures of the civil war and interregnum period often emphasize the unstable, improvisational quality of the period's ongoing renegotiation of literary genre and cultural authority.[37] We can see this in the sometimes dissonant or eclectic way writers redeploy once-authoritative classical forms. One example is Abraham Cowley's unfinished epic *The Civil War*, which sought to enlist the resources of Lucanian epic for a royalist representation of the English civil wars.[38] Another is Andrew Marvell's 'Horatian Ode upon Cromwell's Return from Ireland', which encodes moral ambivalence about the meaning of Cromwell's aggressive virtue by an ironic juxtaposition of Horatian and Lucanian allusion.[39] But literary classicism and formal regularity could also have profoundly nostalgic and socially conservative implications, as in Robert Herrick's 1647 poem 'To the King, upon his Welcome to Hampton-Court'.[40] Though the occasion for this poem is actually Charles's return to Hampton Court as a prisoner of the Parliamentary armies, it is written as if the king were returning to his palace in triumph. In Herrick's conceit, Charles is greeted as 'Great Augustus' (l. 18), and the poem is published with the headnote 'set and sung' as if it were part of some royal entry pageant. This is wishful thinking, and it goes hand-in-hand with the poem's Augustan mode of address because Herrick's intent is to gesture backwards in time towards a pre-revolutionary social order within which the current, distasteful situation would have seemed unthinkable.

In *Behemoth*, Thomas Hobbes takes up the question of how a settled monarchy like England's could so suddenly have come to ruin. One of his answers (elaborating on a theme discussed generally in *Leviathan* [1651]), is that

> there were an exceeding great number of men of the greater sort that had been so educated as that in their youth having read books written by famous men of the ancient Grecian and Roman commonwealths concerning their polity and great actions; in which books the popular government was extolled by the glorious name of liberty, and monarchy disgraced by the name of tyranny; they became thereby in love with their forms of government.[41]

Hobbes here describes a proto-republican bias, developed as part of the humanist education in classical literature, as an important motor for England's cultural transformation. Certainly, perspectives derived from reading both Greek and Roman writers also shaped the rapidly evolving political scene during the revolutionary and interregnum periods. The challenge of engineering a new mode of government after the execution of Charles I ushered in a brief golden age for explicitly governmental republican political thought, and there is a remarkable breadth and eclecticism of reference in the political writing of this period.[42] Scholars are hard-pressed, for instance, to disentangle Greek, Roman, Machiavellian, and Hobbesian strands of argument in the period's most ambitious piece of republican writing, James Harrington's *The Commonwealth of Oceana* (1656).[43] As late as 1660, in *The Ready and Easy Way*, Milton could describe the English republican project as evidence of 'a spirit in this nation no less noble and well fitted to the liberty of a Commonwealth, than in the ancient Greeks or Romans' (*Prose Works*, 7. 356). He was to be disappointed, of course, by the restoration of the monarchy later that same year.

Notes

1. Peter Mack, *Elizabethan Rhetoric: Theory and Practice* (Cambridge, 2002), 11–47; Lisa Jardine and Anthony Grafton, '"Studied for Action": How Gabriel Harvey Read his Livy', *Past and Present*, 129 (1990), 30–78.
2. See, e.g. Markku Peltonen, *Classical Humanism and Republicanism in English Political Thought, 1570–1640* (Cambridge, 1995), 1–53.
3. Peter Stacey, *Roman Monarchy and the Renaissance Prince* (Cambridge, 2007).
4. The phrase comes from C. H. Conley, *The First English Translators of the Classics* (New Haven, 1927), 18–33. On translation in this period more generally, see Gordon Braden, Robert Cummings, and Stuart Gillespie (eds), *The Oxford History of Literary Translation in English*, vol. 2: *1550–1660* (Oxford, 2011).
5. See also the more sustained discussion of *The Shepheardes Calender* in Richard McCabe, Chapter 25, this volume.
6. See, e.g. Annabel Patterson, *Pastoral and Ideology: Virgil to Valéry* (Berkeley and Los Angeles, 1987).
7. David Norbrook, *Poetry and Politics in the English Renaissance* (1984), 89.
8. Roger Ascham, *The Schoolmaster*, ed. Lawrence V. Ryan (Charlottesville, VA, 1967), 7.
9. Alastair J. R. Blanchard and Tracey A. Sowerby, 'Thomas Wilson's Demosthenes and the Politics of Tudor Translation', *International Journal of the Classical Tradition*, 12 (2005), 46–80.
10. On Cecil and his associates, see Stephen Alford, *The Early Elizabethan Polity: William Cecil and the British Succession Crisis, 1558–1569* (Cambridge, 1998), 9–42. On links between Tudor Protestantism and classical humanism, see Margo Todd, *Christian Humanism and the Puritan Social Order* (Cambridge, 1987).
11. Stephen Alford, 'The Political Creed of William Cecil', in John F. McDiarmid (ed.), *The Monarchical Republic of Early Modern England: Essays in Response to Patrick Collinson* (Aldershot, 2007), 75.
12. The phrase comes from Patrick Collinson, 'The Monarchical Republic of Queen Elizabeth I', *Bulletin of the John Rylands University Library of Manchester*, 69 (1987), 394–424 (repr. in Patrick Collinson, *Elizabethan Essays* (1994), 31–57).
13. Peter Lake, 'The Politics of "Popularity" and the Public Sphere: The "Monarchical Republic" of Elizabeth I Defends Itself', in Peter Lake and Steven Pincus (eds), *The Politics of the Public Sphere in Early Modern England* (Manchester, 2007), 59–94.
14. Conley, *The First English Translators*, 23–33.
15. Philip Schwyzer, *Literature, Nationalism and Memory in Early Modern England and Wales* (Cambridge, 2004), 1–48.
16. Thomas Sackville and Thomas Norton, *Gorboduc or Ferrex and Porrex*, ed. Irby B. Cauthen, Jr (Lincoln, NE, 1970) 5. 2. 177. On the play's politics, see, e.g. Greg Walker, *The Politics of Performance in Early Renaissance Drama* (Cambridge, 1998), 196–221.
17. Jessica Winston, 'Seneca in Early Elizabethan England', *Renaissance Quarterly*, 59 (2006), 29–58. See also Winston, 'Expanding the Political Nation: *Gorboduc* at the Inns of Court and Succession Revisited', *Early Theatre*, 8 (2005), 11–34.
18. See Lake and Pincus, *The Politics of the Public Sphere*.
19. See, e.g. John Guy (ed.), *The Reign of Elizabeth I: Court and Culture in the Last Decade* (Cambridge, 1995).
20. Richard Tuck, *Philosophy and Government, 1572–1651* (Cambridge, 1993), 31–119.
21. See F. J. Levy, 'Francis Bacon and the Style of Politics', *English Literary Renais-*

sance, 16 (1986), 101–22; and J. H. M. Salmon, 'Seneca and Tacitus in Jacobean England', in Linda Levy Peck (ed.), *The Mental World of the Jacobean Court* (Cambridge, 1991), 169–88.

22. See Curtis Perry, 'The Uneasy Republicanism of Thomas Kyd's *Cornelia*', *Criticism*, 48 (2007), 535–55; and Andrew Hadfield, *Shakespeare and Republicanism* (Cambridge, 2005), 168–83.
23. See Patrick Cheney, *Marlowe's Republican Authorship: Lucan, Liberty, and the Sublime* (Basingstoke, 2009); and Hadfield, *Shakespeare and Republicanism.*
24. Hadfield, *Shakespeare and Republicanism*, 103–29. See also Curtis Perry, 'British Empire on the Eve of the Armada: Revising *The Misfortunes of Arthur*', *Studies in Philology*, 108 (2011), 508–37. For a brief overview of Lucanism that cautions against assuming republican resonance, see Edward Paleit, 'Lucan in the Renaissance, pre-1625: An Introduction', *Literature Compass*, 1 (2004). See also Philip Hardie's discussion of the Lucanian tradition in Chapter 10, this volume.
25. William R. Jones, 'The Bishops' Ban of 1599 and the Ideology of English Satire', *Literature Compass*, 7/5 (2010), 332–46.
26. See Paulina Kewes, 'Savile's Tacitus and the Politics of Roman History in Late Elizabethan England', *Huntington Library Quarterly*, 74 (2011), 515–51, and Malcolm Smuts, 'Court-Centred Politics and the Uses of Roman Historians, *c.*1590-1630', in Kevin Sharpe and Peter Lake (eds), *Culture and Politics in Early Stuart England* (Stanford, 1993), 21–43. I am grateful to Dr Kewes for allowing me to see her article in advance of its publication.
27. Cf. Blair Worden, 'Ben Jonson among the Historians', in Sharpe and Lake (eds), *Culture and Politics*, 67–89.
28. On the complexity of Jonson's engagement with republican thought, see Julie Sanders, *Ben Jonson's Theatrical Republics* (Basingstoke, 1998), esp. 11–33.
29. Victoria Moul, *Jonson, Horace, and the Classical Tradition* (Cambridge, 2010), esp. 135–47
30. Peter Davidson (ed.), *The Poems and Translations of Sir Richard Fanshawe* (Oxford, 1997), I. 57. For an overview emphasizing the neo-Augustan imperial vision of Early Stuart culture, see Graham Parry, *The Golden Age Restor'd: The Culture of the Stuart Court, 1603–1642* (Manchester, 1981).
31. Curtis Perry, *Literature and Favoritism in Early Modern England* (Cambridge, 2006), 229–75; see p. 229 for Charles's quotation.
32. David Norbrook (*Writing the English Republic: Poetry, Rhetoric and Politics, 1627–1660* (Cambridge, 1999)) places special emphasis upon the importance of Lucan for republican or anti-monarchical writing. See esp. pp. 23–62, 83–92.
33. Jonathan Gibson, 'Civil War in 1614: Lucan, Gorges, and Prince Henry', in Stephen Clucas and Rosalind Davies (eds), *The Crisis of 1614 and the Addled Parliament: Literary and Historical Perspectives* (Aldershot, 2003), 161–76.
34. On Gorges and (especially) May, see Norbrook, *Writing the English Republic*, 34–62.
35. These poems are available online at 'Early Stuart Libels: An Edition of Poetry from Manuscript Sources', ed. Alastair Bellany and Andrew McRae, *Early Modern Literary Studies Text Series I* (2005), Pii <http://purl.oclc.org/emls/texts/libels/> (accessed 13 March 2015). I quote from Pii18, l. 5. On the classical, Lucanian tenor of the response to Felton see also Norbrook, *Writing the English Republic*, 53–8.
36. Quentin Skinner, *Reason and Rhetoric in the Philosophy of Hobbes* (Cambridge, 1996), 250–93.
37. e.g. Sharon Achinstein, *Milton and the Revolutionary Reader* (Princeton, 1994);

Nigel Smith (ed.), *Literature and Revolution in England, 1640–1660* (New Haven, 1994).

38. See Allan Pritchard's account in *Abraham Cowley: The Civil War* (Toronto, 1973), 11–51.
39. See Nigel Smith's notes on the poem's classical sources in *The Poems of Andrew Marvell*, rev. edn (Harlow, 2007), 267–70; Norbrook, *Writing the English Republic*, 243–71.
40. More generally, see Syrithe Pugh, *Herrick, Fanshawe and the Politics of Intertextuality: Classical Literature and Seventeenth-Century Royalism* (Farnham, 2010).
41. Thomas Hobbes, *Behemoth: The History of the Causes of the Civil-Wars of England* (1682), 5. See also Hobbes, *Leviathan, with Selected Variants from the Latin Edition of 1688*, ed. Edwin Curley (Indianapolis, IN, 1994), 214–15.
42. Jonathan Scott, *Commonwealth Principles: Republican Writing of the English Revolution* (Cambridge, 2004) provides an authoritative survey.
43. In addition to Scott, *Commonwealth Principles*, 284–93, see Eric Nelson, *The Greek Tradition in Republican Thought* (Cambridge, 2004), 87–126.

b. Sexuality and Desire

CORA FOX

Sexuality, arguably more than any other sphere of activity in Renaissance England, was generated by a web of classical intertexts. Influenced primarily by the Latin works of Rome in the age of Augustus, English Renaissance ideas about sexual practices and identity were formed in relation to the literary and philosophical works of a culture where, as Thomas Habinek has argued, a modern, urbanized form of sexuality was invented.[1] The most influential authors of the ancient world for Renaissance readers were Virgil and Ovid, and they participated in the sexual culture of Augustan Rome: Virgil during the formation of the Augustan principate, and Ovid in the early stages of empire when Augustus attempted to legislate sexual morality to contain the powers of the Roman elite at the empire's centre. According to Habinek, Rome's quick rise as a world city resulted not just in the adjustments to state power that accompany a growing empire, but also in the 'disembedding' of sexual practices from the more traditional regulations of shame and honour within the family. For the first time, sexuality was actively defined by the centralized state and became a focus of discussion outside other social relationships. In addition, rather than being characterized by the public and communal familial relationships of earlier Roman households, under Augustus a private, intimate union became the normative model of sexual relations.

In Renaissance literary circles, these inherited Latin works formed a rich intertextual web, and English writers drew upon them as they produced technologies of sex in the growing world city of London.[2] Responding to a Protestant and nationalistic focus on the importance of the married couple at the centre of social relations, Renaissance writers represented sexual practices through various classical narratives and tropes. They also participated in solidifying models of sexuality that reinforced the centrality of the intimate, heterosexual couple.[3] Just as Augustan literature reflected both state-sanctioned attempts to limit sexual behaviours and the challenges to those limits, however, Renaissance writers who were influenced by these classical texts defined both normative models of sexuality in Renaissance England and the trajectories of various transgressions.

In this chapter, I will address the ways a few repeated classical models of desire informed a literature of normative sexuality in Renaissance England and at the same time gave expression to alternative sexualities, some fully articulated and some gestured at through local classical allusions. Whether the classical sources were translated into English, circulated in translations in other modern languages, or were transmitted through continental works (or usually all of these), new editions and translations of classical authors were potentially set loose from the moralizing tradition of the medieval church (sometimes just in being printed without commentary). But, while translations and imitations proliferated, translators of classical works, as well as authors of works that were self-consciously classical in their sexual content, expressed anxiety about the morality of their pagan sources. In response to worries over the codes of sexual behaviour found in so much of their inherited literature, writers in the period often make the reader the site where the possible scandal of pagan narratives of desire is laid to rest or draws attention to its restlessness.

In the 'Epistle to the Earl of Leicester' of Arthur Golding's translation of Ovid's *Metamorphoses* (the first full translation of the poem into English, in 1567), for instance, Golding makes the case that 'the readers therefore earnestly admonished are to be | To seek a further meaning than the letter gives to see' (ll. 541–2). Once correctly—that is figuratively—read, Ovid's obscene and diverse poem will be filled with salutary models and precepts:

> The use of this same book therefore is this: that every man
> (Endeavouring for to know himself as nearly as he can,
> As though he in a chariot sat well ordered), should direct
> His mind by reason in the way of virtue, and correct
> His fierce affections with the bit of temperance, lest perchance,
> They taking bridle in the teeth like willful jades do prance
> Away, and headlong harry him upon the rocks of sin,
> And overthrowing forcibly the chariot he sits in,
> Do tear him worse than ever was Hippolytus, the son
> Of Theseus, when he went about his father's wrath to shun.[4]

Wittily invoking the classical imperative to 'know thyself' (written on the Delphic oracle), Golding stresses individual regulation of sexual will, but at the same time he undercuts the assumption that readers can control passionate relations. As attentive readers would realize, knowing oneself in *Metamorphoses* is difficult, especially when the self is sexually aroused. This Delphic principle is in fact mocked in Ovid's retelling of the tale of Narcissus, when his mother consults Tiresias and is told that Narcissus will live a long life only if he does not fully know himself (3. 339–58). Golding goes on to conflate the Platonic charioteer (reason leading the horses of passion) with Hippolytus' chariot. Since Hippolytus is the innocent victim of his stepmother's incestuous desire and his father's excessive anger (book 15), this conflation points to the ways we may actually be unable to control desires and passionate emotional states. While Golding seems to claim that classical texts and their transgressive representations can be safe when read 'correctly' using the will, the irony of his classical reference suggests otherwise. Classical texts are in fact capable of promoting immoral behaviour, and his didactic preface will have little effect on the salacious content represented in the translation. Golding concludes his 'Preface to the Reader' by comparing his translation of Ovid to the siren's song:

> If any stomach be so weak as that it cannot brook
> The lively setting forth of things described in this book,
> I give him counsel to abstain until he be more strong,
> And for to use Ulysses' feat against the Mermaid's song.
> (ll. 215–18)

Golding recognizes the specifically erotic beauty of his translation, but he also worries over the potential for sexual error that lurks in the tales.

Similarly, Spenser constructs the culminating episode of his encyclopedic analysis of chastity in *The Faerie Queene*, book 3, as a tale of earnest but dangerous reading of classical models of desire. Britomart, the cross-dressed, heroic female knight of book 3, reaches the culmination of her quest in a mysterious house of the evil enchanter, Busirane, who has imprisoned the conventional romance object of desire, Amoret. Through a clever pun on 'penned' (Scudamore, her knight, in canto 11, stanza 11, complains: 'my lady and my love is cruelly pen'd'), the poet presents the episode as an examination of the place of female characters in the inherited gender politics of the generic traditions of both epic and romance. Britomart enters into rooms that evoke the models of desire that her redefined Protestant virtue of chastity must defeat. Most of these models are classical.

In the first room, the walls are covered with an arras like Arachne's in *Metamorphoses* 6, depicting gods who transform themselves into various creatures to rape or seduce mortals—primarily though not exclusively women. While the catalogue is mainly Ovidian, characters from other metamorphic rape stories appear too. The room also contains a statue of Cupid and is the site of a masque depicting allegorical figures associated with desire. Within this house, the heroine spends most of her time misreading. She does not fully understand the meaning of the rooms that symbolically construct her position in the world of intertextual desire. She is instructed by writing on the walls to 'Be bold, be bold, and everywhere be bold', but then finally to 'Be not too bold' (*Faerie Queene*, 3. 11. 54). In her position of strength, but also confusion and wonder before the intertextual nature of sexuality, Britomart is cautioned like Golding's reader. She must find her desire in the classical intertexts that the room witnesses, but she must not be too bold and let excessive desires lead her beyond the moral codes of good Protestant behaviour. She must be wary of the potential for transgression depicted in the classical narratives, while boldly acknowledging the ways her desire is defined by classical sources.

To place responsibility for moral vigilance onto the reader of classical texts is to acknowledge the foundational status of these narratives. Existing as the backdrop for literary representations of desire, classical works are the anxiously acknowledged technologies for the production of Renaissance sex.

Petrarch and Normative Classical Narratives of Desire

The classical author most repeatedly associated with both normative and transgressive or licentious sexual material is Ovid, and primarily his *Metamorphoses, Ars Amatoria,* and *Amores.* Ovid, the witty self-described *praeceptor amoris* (love teacher), influenced the representations of sexuality in the period to such an extent that we can call an entire climate of erotic writings Ovidian.[5] It is also true that Ovidianism often stood in for classical culture more generally, especially in defining desire. As Leonard Barkan has argued, even when the actual source of a particular representation was not Ovid's works, Ovidian metamorphosis often signalled an engagement with the larger ideological heritage of antiquity, and particularly its sexual mores and values.[6] In addition to metamorphic representations of the body, Renaissance English Ovidianism is also generally characterized by the narrative of desire based on the subject–object binary model of the hunt, its repetitions of the rape/abduction narrative, and its consistently ironic, anti-authoritative, and self-questioning stance towards sexual morality and ethics. Ovid's particular works self-consciously defined the genres of early erotic and pastoral elegies, as well as the minor epic, but the intertextual influence of his œuvre extends beyond these forms to almost every context in which desire is represented in the period. In fact, as Lynn Enterline has shown, and as Goran Stanivukovic's recent collection on *Ovid and the Renaissance Body* attests, Ovidianism defined the sexual body itself.[7]

Ovid was not the only classical author to produce technologies of sex in the period, of course. In philosophical writings, for example, Plato, and especially the *Symposium*, initiated discussions of love and sex, and, as Jonathan Goldberg has shown, Lucretian works and their intertexts redefined the notion of sexual generativity.[8] Most notably, however, the many repetitions of Aeneas' abandonment of Dido in works of all genres reveal how this episode from Virgil's *Aeneid* regulated both male and female sexual behaviour.[9] As Philip Hardie has pointed out, the Dido episode in the *Aeneid* is the closest the poem comes to Ovid's later celebration of transformational grief and desire. Virgil's account of how male honour and duty must trump female despair enforced a hierarchy of sexual difference, and, in turn, this difference reinforced humoral conceptions of the female body as excessively sexual and in need of male control. At the same time, however, the episode memorialized the loss that Dido feels, affirming the tragedy of such desires. In a scene from

The Tempest, Shakespeare highlights the centrality of this narrative when Antonio and Sebastian, the play's two 'new' men who are also murderers, mock the good old counsellor, Gonzalo, for his offhanded reference to 'widow Dido' (2. 1. 77). The dialogue is difficult for contemporary readers and students because it involves such a commonplace understanding of Dido's sexual status. She is literally a widow, since her first husband has died, but Virgil never emphasizes that sexual relation because from the perspective of the epic of masculine heroism her place is to be left behind after her pseudo-marriage to Aeneas. Shakespeare's evil young men mock Gonzalo for euphemistically referring to Dido in relation to her previous marriage (or possibly siding with her in understanding her tryst with Aeneas as a marriage), rather than characterizing her as what she is: Aeneas' illegitimate lover. The short scene exemplifies how a classical character can represent an entire nexus of Renaissance codes of sexual behaviour, especially as they enforce certain models of heterosexual desire.

But, while such discrete erotic episodes and dominant philosophical works permeated Renaissance discourses on love in the same way that they shaped the entire literary landscape, Ovid's works held a position of singular importance in matters of sex. I will focus here on Ovidian erotic poetry, that vast textual arena where sexuality is most insistently defined. If we seek a literary history of normative Ovidian sexual desire in English Renaissance literature, however, we need to begin before Elizabethan England, as it emerges in response to Petrarch's *Rime Sparse*. Petrarchism as an erotic discourse is, in fact, often set in contrast to Ovidianism, but this dichotomy is highly problematic, since Petrarch insistently cites Ovid and forever inflects Petrarchism with Ovidianism.[10] In his *Rime*, Petrarch frequently alludes to the Ovidian myths of Daphne and Actaeon, for instance, and imitations of Petrarch in English utilize these myths repeatedly as well, but they also often draw on additional classical narratives to contrast with these famous stories. In this highly Ovidian discursive field, three striking tropes emerge, helping to redefine desire in English Petrarchism and post-Petrarchism.

First, at the thematic core of Ovid's great poem and Petrarch's definitional sonnet sequence is the idea that desire is like metamorphosis. This metaphor will be so compelling to English writers that it will mutate from emphasizing physical transformations into more figurative, psychological metamorphoses, a development suggested first in Ovid's *Metamorphoses* itself. In Petrarch's famous Song 23, for example, the speaker is at pains to translate his unrequited desire for Laura into repeated images of metamorphosis via direct allusions to Ovidian myths. Philip Hardie has called this song 'a miniature image of the *Canzoniere* as a whole' in its obsessive recirculations of the models of desire that dominate the collection.[11] Describing Cupid as a hunter of his heart, the speaker laments that Cupid and Laura 'transformed me into what I am, making me of a living man a green laurel that loses no leaf for all the cold season' (23. 38–40).[12] Rewriting the classical myth of Daphne to emphasize the speaker's subjugation, Petrarch here takes the central Ovidian motif of love as a hunt in a new direction, since it is the male subject who suffers metamorphosis, rather than the (usually female) object of desire. The speaker's transformations are repeated throughout the song, as he introduces a long series of metamorphosed figures to represent himself transformed by love. He is Byblis, for example, turned to a fountain in his frustrated tears over Laura's rejection and departure (ll. 112–20) ('Who ever heard of a spring being born from a real man?'). He is not Jupiter descending in a cloud of gold to Danae, but Semele consumed by fire during his visit (ll. 161–4). Then finally he is Daphne transformed to the laurel again, whose beauty he cannot leave behind (ll. 167–9). In this virtuoso use of Ovidian allusion, Petrarch insistently enforces the Renaissance trope, rooted in Ovid, of desire as metamorphosis, and this trope will go on to help define English love poetry and in many respects comedy on the stage.[13]

Shakespeare jokingly plays with this trope in *A Midsummer Night's Dream*, as Bottom is physically transformed into an Ass in order to experience loving the fairy queen. Similarly, Shakespeare names his most fickle and hypocritical lover in *Two Gentlemen of Verona* Proteus, suggesting the darker side to the trope that love involves a psychic transformation analogous to physical transformation. In a later response to this model of desire, and in an entirely different tone, Donne pushes the trope to its metaphysical limit in *A Nocturnal upon S. Lucie's Day,* when he describes his grief at losing his love as transforming him into the elixir of nothingness:

> Study me then, you who shall lovers be
>
> . . . . .
>
> For I am every dead thing,
> In whom love wrought new alchemy.
>
> . . . . .
>
> He ruined me, and I am re-begot
> of absence, darkness, death; things which are not.[14]

Of all the various metaphors for desire that Petrarchism encodes in Renaissance England, this one has the greatest currency for later generations as a particularly Ovidian way of representing desire.

The second major trope of English Ovidianism represents Cupid as the symbol for desire that is experienced as an attack from outside the self. Cupid is abundantly represented in medieval literature, but he takes on new status as a central trope of desire in the genre-defining lyrics of English Petrarchism.[15] He is a third player in most sonnet sequences, and Shakespeare, for instance, ends his sonnets with a re-mythologizing of Cupid as a figure, in which his powers transfer to Shakespeare's mistress. He becomes such a strong discursive presence within the sonnet tradition that Lady Mary Wroth, writing a deliberately anachronistic English sonnet sequence (the first published by a woman in 1621), will address her poems to him, rather than a lover.

In the later Anti-Petrarchists, Cupid is the focus of more bitter revision, such as when Robert Herrick literalizes Cupid's entrance into the speaker's body in 'Upon Cupid':

As lately I a garland bound,
'Mongst Roses, I there Cupid found:
I took him, put him in my cup,
And drunk with Wine, I drank him up.
Hence then it is, that my poor breast
Could never since find any rest.[16]

In this later incarnation, Cupid is humorously imagined as entering the body through drinking, rather than through the more violent means of metaphorical arrows. He produces heartburn, rather than anguish, and this is clearly an attempt to diminish his hold over the love poetry of the time. Over the course of the English Renaissance, Cupid will transform from the dangerous god of all gods to the laughing boy captured in the ubiquitous putti of European mannerist art, but within Petrarchism and its later responses he will remain a trope for the surprising, self-alienating force of desire.

Finally, the major metaphor of love as a hunt that pervades *Metamorphoses* will have implications that are wide-reaching, affecting not just the scripts of desire, but the dichotomous cultural constructions of self and other, subject and object, active and passive, male and female. Although the idea of love as a hunt circulates in medieval literature as well, it is reinforced when Ovid's *Metamorphoses* becomes central to Renaissance literature. This script is closely related to one in which desire is narrativized as rape or abduction, and this darker model often shares space with a more benign representation that still objectifies the female beloved and naturalizes violence to her person as part of sexual play.

Sir Thomas Wyatt's 'Whoso list to hunt' serves as an excellent example of how this model comes into English Petrarchism. Like many of Wyatt's lyrics, this is a translation of an Ovidian poem in the *Rime Sparse.* In *Rime* 190, Petrarch describes a mystical vision of a female deer, discovers that she wears a collar indicating that she is the property of Caesar, and then falls into the water as she disappears. Although Petrarch's lyric speaker expresses a Christian mysticism not found in his classical source, the poem retains its Ovidianism, importing the setting, mood, and sense of vulnerability from the Actaeon tale, as well as the specific dangers of the reflecting pool from the story of Narcissus. The model of desire in this poem is oblique, however, and the power dynamics multidirectional; while the deer is objectified as an animal hunted by Caesar, she is also powerful, and it is not clear that the speaker will be another hunter. Unlike most Ovidian lovers, Petrarch's desire is accidental, rather than immediately predatory. In 'Whoso List to Hunt', one of Wyatt's loose translations of a Petrarchan lyric (first published in *Tottel's Miscellany* of 1557), by contrast, Wyatt makes the power dichotomy between lover and mistress his primary concern and plays up the difficulties of being a hunter who is unable to obtain the deer/mistress who belongs to another and more powerful man:

Who list her hunt, I put him out of doubt,
As well as I, may spend his time in vain.
And graven with diamonds in letters plain

There is written, her fair neck round about,
'*Noli me tangere*, for Caesar's I am,
And wild for to hold, though I seem tame.'[17]

This poem emphasizes that the deer is not just prettified by the diamond collar; she is owned by another male figure for the purpose of his own hunting. While this idea is originally Petrarch's and references a classical tradition and moment (when Caesar owned such deer), the focus is Wyatt's and creates a poem that comments on the dangers for the male desirer of this particular homosocial paradigm. The potential for sexual violence inherent in this definition of heterosexual desire is complicated only slightly by the fact that the inscription on the beloved's collar seems to be the deer herself speaking, as she refers to herself in the first person and claims that she is 'wild'. Although Wyatt's speaker suggests his frustration and weakness in relation to other men engaged in the pursuit that defines desire, the poem supports a predatory model and a subject–animal binary that represents the mistress as a hunted thing.

In later English erotic poetry, the Ovidian hunt is transmuted into various models of desire that still objectify the beloved as something to be achieved but do not explicitly employ the hunting metaphor. In Donne's famous 'Elegy 19: To His Mistress Going to Bed', for example, the desiring speaker is a discoverer of new lands rather than a hunter: 'O my America! My new-found-land, | My kingdom, safeliest when with one man man'd' (ll. 27–8). This metaphysical twist on the model of predatory desire turns the beloved into a land to be conquered by the speaker. Donne complicates this model within the same poem, however, when he revises another classical model of desire closely related to the hunt: the race. He writes:

Gems which you women use
Are like Atalanta's balls, cast in men's views,
That when a fools eye lighteth on a gem,
His earthly soul may covet theirs, not them.
(ll. 35–8)

Through this allusion, Donne suggests that the male speaker is in the position of Atalanta, diverted from his race towards the union of their 'earthly souls'. Ovid's version of this myth in *Metamorphoses* 10 already implies that Atalanta and her desirer, Hippomenes, are potentially equals, until Venus assists Hippomenes in obtaining his desire by giving him the golden apples of the Hesperides to throw before Atalanta as a distraction. Donne takes up this suggestion in the classical narrative and ultimately supports a more equal relationship, since either sex in the footrace can apparently be distracted. In fact, a model of desire in which male and female are equals is frequently dominant in Donne's works, especially his major love lyrics in the *Songs and Sonnets*. In poems like *The Ecstasy* or *The Canonization*, for example, the predatory model is replaced by one still dominated by a male voice but insisting on a possible equality between gendered souls.

In most later English love poetry overall, the model of love as a hunt appears less frequently, replaced with various other permutations of a subject–object binary. The female beloved is still threatened with a violent form of desire, however, in such later poems as Robert Herrick's 'To Virgins':

> Hear ye virgins, and I'll teach
> What the time of old did preach.
> Rosamond was in a bower
> Kept, as Danae in a tower:
> But yet Love (who subtle is)
> Crept to that, and came to this.
> Be ye locked up like to these,
> Or the rich Hesperides;
> Or those Babies in your eyes,
> In their crystal nunneries;
> Notwithstanding love will win,
> Or else force a passage in:
> And as coy be, as you can,
> Gifts will get ye, or the man.[18]

While Herrick's poem does not represent a hunt, the predatory nature of desire is still the dominant theme. In fact, in this poem it seems to be both Cupid and the lover who will stealthily infiltrate the beloved's defences, as the last line suggests that either he or the gifts involved in courtship will 'get' her. While the hunt is gone, the underlying structure in which the beloved is an object to be won or obtained survives.

All three of these mainstream classical tropes of desire support a model of sexual relations between men and women that focuses on interpersonal power in the couple and is a reflection of the politicizing of sexuality itself, an intertexual transfer of the sexual technologies of Augustan Rome onto an English culture defining Protestant marriage. And it is notable that heterosexual desire is characterized by a loss of power for both desirer and desired. In these classical scripts of romantic love, desire first violently impacts the physical or emotional stability of the desirer and is experienced as transformation, with primarily negative results. It then leads to a predatory stance for the desirer that objectifies—or in more extreme cases does violence to—the beloved. Although it often exists alongside competing models of sexual relationships, this potentially debilitating model of romantic love is easy to trace in later permutations in Western culture. It also serves to reinforce the heterosexual couple (with the male as active and the female as passive) as the place where social power is found and negotiated, and it thus supports a focus on chaste Protestant marriage as the centre of sexual culture.

Alternate Desires and Alternate Classical Intertextualities

In addition to these paradigms defining a patriarchal heterosexual couple, classical Renaissance sexualities also challenged the dominance of male–female monogamous desire that defines Petrarchism and later love lyrics. As evidenced by the proliferation of marriage manuals, Protestant norms of marriage and chaste sexuality were seriously promoted in this era, but this cultural trend generated multiple arenas of debate and resistance surrounding the heterosexual couple. These other models of desire that were not explicitly sanctioned by the state or the church were also produced through explicit forms of classical intertextuality.[19] 'Sodomy', a term applied in Renaissance England to various sexual practices, for example, although primarily a crime developed through interpretations of biblical sources and the writings of the medieval church, was also defined by Greek and Roman myths, especially those of Orpheus, Ganymede, and Hyacinthus.[20] The Renaissance genre of pastoral elegy, in particular, which gave expression to various forms of homoerotic desire, was developed, as Stephen Guy-Bray has shown, through reference to classical texts of same-sex relationships.[21] Leonard Barkan has argued further that Renaissance Humanism was itself defined through a classically homoerotic poetics.[22] Similarly, Valerie Traub has traced the way the figure of Sappho, as well as Ovidian myths such as Iphis and Ianthe, reinvigorated a tradition of Renaissance writings about same-sex female desire.[23] And, in areas of culture that are more difficult to trace, appropriations of classical love lyrics occupied positions within a burgeoning proto-pornographic literature.[24] As Ian Moulton has shown, these were perhaps 'alternative' or 'deviant' textual arenas where sexuality was defined, but they were increasingly influential in Renaissance England, as these texts became more widely available through print and translation. In these ways, classical texts helped define multiple sexualities in the period, and their multiplicity suggests the ways the distinction between 'normative' and 'alternative' is a useful, but limited one, especially in the context of Ovidian models of desire.

Marlowe's *Hero and Leander* (published 1598) serves as an important illustration, because his Ovidian poetry, especially his translation of the *Amores*, titled *Ovid's Elegies* (probably published in the mid-1590s) modelled many kinds of desire for a generation of writers. While most of Ovid's elegies uphold heterosexual union as the goal of sexual intimacy, *Hero and Leander* multiplies the kinds of desire it represents, just as Ovid's own works do. Most of Ovid's narratives in *Metamorphoses*, for instance, involve the pursuit of a female figure by a male figure, but there are many and notable exceptions, and Ovid devotes his tenth book to the song of Orpheus, the singer who, according to Ovid's revision of the well-known myth, began the practice of men loving boys. What is most notable about this book is the way it frames tales of deviant or transgressive kinds of desire within a structure that does not condemn any of the various sexual expressions. In fact it equalizes their value and often celebrates them. Jove desires Hyacinthus. Cyparissus desires a stag. Pygmalion desires a statue. Even Myrrha's incestuous desire for her father is given a sympathetic or at least amoral rendering here. But then Hippomenes also desires Atalanta, and their otherwise prototypical heterosexual union in marriage (he literally wins her in a race) is punished when their desire exceeds proper limits and they have sex in Cybele's temple and are transformed into lions. The equanimity with which Ovid writes his tales of desires that transgress the social limits of behaviour here is exemplary of his works overall. All desire—normative, marginalized, ambiguously sexual—has the potential to be dangerous, and none more than any other.

Although modelled on a poem by the sixth-century poet, Musaeus, Marlowe's *Hero and Leander* is a tour de force of this particular kind of Ovidian eroticism. In fact, Marlowe portrays Leander's encounter with Neptune when swimming the Hellespont to meet Hero as a homoerotic narrative impeding a heterosexual one. When Neptune sees Leander, he mistakes him for Ganymede, almost drowns him, and then begins a highly erotic seduction:

> He clapped his plump cheeks, with his tresses played,
> And smiling wantonly, his loved betrayed.
> He watched his arms, and as they opened wide
> At every stroke, betwixt them he would slide,
> And steal a kiss, and then run out and dance,
> And as he turned, cast many a lustful glance,
> And threw him gawdy toys to please his eye,
> And dive into the water, and there pry
> Upon his breast, his thighs, and every limb,
> And up again, and close beside him swim,
> And talk of love: *leander* made reply,
> You are deceived, I am no woman I.
> Thereat smiled Neptune and then told a tale.[25]

Although Leander privileges consummation with Hero, the poem self-consciously does not privilege that sexual model. As James Bromley points out, the poem instead resists consummation, both in sexual relations and in narrative, suggesting the ways sexual practices can be constructed in multiple ways through multiple tales that do not necessarily lead to marriage.[26] In addition to levelling the social censure attached to multiple sexual relationships, as Ovid does in the book of Orpheus, Marlowe values various sexual practices as part of an erotics of deferral surrounding virginity. The poem also highlights the way sexual identity is the product of classical narratives, as Neptune hopes to correct Leander's misunderstanding of the sexual situation through telling a mythologically prototypical tale of a shepherd who desired a lovely boy. The poem's self-conscious classical context opens up arenas for alternate sexualities, repeating them as scripts of desire that a Renaissance audience can itself repeat.

Marlowe's poem also highlights the public social life that is at stake in classical technologies of sexuality. Patrick Cheney has called the poem an 'erotic counter-epic of empire', capturing as it does the national politics of the Hellespont, the place where East meets West and Greece meets Troy.[27] Although the poem privileges the intimate sphere of sexual practices, it does so within the larger cultural context of epic and empire, reflecting an Augustan approach to the values attached to genres of literature and the social practices of culture. Depicting muliplicitous desires framed within the demands of imperial destinies, *Hero and Leander* participates in the classical intertextual technologies of sexuality that are characteristic of Renaissance England.

Notes

1. Thomas Habinek, 'The Invention of Sexuality in the World-City of Rome', in Thomas Habinek and Alessandro Schiesaro (eds), *The Roman Cultural Revolution* (1996), 23–43.
2. Although many persuasive critiques of Foucault's historiography have been made, his fundamental insight in *The History of Sexuality*—that sexuality is not just regulated but generated by discourse—is crucial to seeing how intertexts work to define desire and sexuality in any period. I will, therefore, sometimes employ the Foucauldian term 'technology' to describe this web of texts and practices embedded in power relationships. See Michel Foucault, *The History of Sexuality*, vol. 1: *An Introduction*, trans. Robert Hurley (New York, 1978).
3. On the question of how intimacy is defined or to what extent it existed in the Renaissance period, however, see Daniel Juan Gil, *Before Intimacy: Asocial Sexuality in Early Modern England* (Minneapolis, 2006).
4. Ovid, *Metamorphoses: The Arthur Golding Translation, 1567*, ed. John Frederick Nims (New York, 1965), ll. 569–80.
5. Goran Stanivukovic argues, for instance, that Arthur Golding's 1567 translation of *Metamorphoses* 'was crucial to the emergence of the rhetoric of desire and sexuality in English erotic literature and that it therefore lies at the heart of a new, Ovidian conception of sexuality in the English Renaissance' ('Teaching Ovidian Sexualities in English Renaissance Literature', in Barbara Weiden Boyd and Cora Fox (eds), *Approaches to Teaching the Works of Ovid and the Ovidian Tradition* (New York, 2010), 194. On the role of the Ovidian epyllion in 'eroticizing English literature' in the 1590s, see Georgia Brown, 'Literature as Fetish', in *Redefining Elizabethan Literature* (2004), 102–77. See also the foundational arguments made by Leonard Barkan and Lynn Enterline on the ways Ovidian texts shaped rhetoric, and especially erotic representations, in the Renaissance: Barkan, *The Gods Made Flesh: Metamorphosis and the Pursuit of Paganism* (New Haven, 1990); Enterline, *The Rhetoric of the Body from Ovid to Shakespeare* (2006). On the persona of the *praeceptor amoris*, see Robert Durling, 'Ovid as *Praeceptor Amoris*', *Classical Journal*, 34 (1958), 157–67.
6. Barkan, *The Gods Made Flesh*, 18.
7. Enterline, *The Rhetoric of the Body*; Goran V. Stanivukovic (ed), *Ovid and the Renaissance Body* (Toronto, 2001).
8. See Jonathan Goldberg, *The Seeds of Things: Theorizing Sexuality and Materiality in Renaissance Representations* (New York, 2009).
9. See also John Watkins, *The Specter of Dido: Spenser and Virgilian Epic* (New Haven, 1995), and David Scott Wilson-Okamura, *Virgil in the Renaissance* (Cambridge, 2010).
10. For a discussion of Ovid's presence in Petrarch's *rime*, see Enterline, *The Rhetoric of the Body*, or Philip Hardie, *Ovid's Poetics of Illusion* (2002), 70–81.
11. Hardie, *Ovid's Poetics of Illusion*, 71.
12. Robert Durling (ed. and trans.), *Petrarch's Lyric Poems: The Rime Sparse and Other Lyrics* (Cambridge, 2001).
13. See William Carroll, *The Metamorphoses of Shakespearean Comedy* (Princeton, 1985).
14. John Donne, *Poetical Works*, ed. Sir Herbert Grierson (New York, 1967), ll. 10, 12–13, 17–18.
15. See Jane Kingsley-Smith, *Cupid in Early Modern Literature and Culture* (2010); or Thomas Hyde, *The Poetic Theology of*

Love: Cupid in Renaissance Literature (Newark, DE, 1986).

16. Robert Herrick, *The Complete Poetry of Robert Herrick*, ed. J. Max Patrick (New York, 1968).
17. I have chosen to cite this poem as it is often modernized and regularized for ease of use from *The Norton Anthology of English Literature*, vol. 1, 7th edn, ed. Stephen Greenblatt et al. (New York, 2000), although it has a complex transmission and editorial history.
18. Robert Herrick, *The Complete Poetry of Robert Herrick*, ed. J. Max Patrick (New York, 1968).
19. For a recent analysis of some particular Ovidian sites of sexual transgression, for example, see Sarah Carter, *Ovidian Myth and Sexual Deviance in Early Modern English Literature* (New York, 2011).
20. For a history of this term and its use, see Jonathan Goldberg, *Sodometries: Renaissance Texts, Modern Sexualities* (New York, 2010). The foundational work on the history of sexual practices between men in Renaissance England is Alan Bray, *Homosexuality in Renaissance England* (New York, 1995). Bruce Smith, in *Homosexual Desire in Shakespeare's England: A Cultural Poetics* (Chicago, 1995), uses classical literary characters as touchstones in his own foundational cultural history of same-sex eroticism between men.
21. Stephen Guy-Bray, *Homoerotic Space: The Poetics of Loss in Renaissance Literature* (Toronto, 2002). See also Smith, *Homosexual Desire in Shakespeare's England*.
22. See Leonard Barkan, *Transhuming Passion: Ganymede and the Erotics of Humanism* (Stanford, 1991).
23. See Valerie Traub, *The Renaissance of Lesbianism in Early Modern England* (2002). See also Henriette Andreadis, *Sappho in Early Modern England: Female Same-Sex Literary Erotics, 1550–1714* (Chicago, 2001).
24. For surveys and discussions of some of these early writings and a theorization of erotica before modern pornography, see Ian Moulton, *Before Pornography: Erotic Writing in Early Modern England* (2000).
25. Christopher Marlowe, 'Hero and Leander', in *The Complete Works of Christopher Marlowe*, ed. Roma Gill (1987), 1. 665–77.
26. James Bromley, '"Let it Suffise": Sexual and Narrative Structure in *Hero and Leander*', in Stephen Guy-Bray, Vin Nardizzi, and Will Stockton (eds), *Queer Renaissance Historiography: The Backward Gaze* (Burlington, VT, 2009), 72–3.
27. Patrick Cheney, 'Introduction: Authorship in Marlowe's Poems', in Patrick Cheney and Brian J. Striar (eds), *The Collected Poems of Christopher Marlowe* (2006), 17–18.

c. Literary Careers

PATRICK CHENEY

The 1671 volume printing Milton's *Paradise Regained* and *Samson Agonistes* provides a retrospective on a foundational legacy of classical literature to the English Renaissance: the idea of a literary career. To open his volume, Milton writes:

> I who erewhile the happy garden sung,
> By one man's disobedience lost, now sing
> Recovered Paradise to all mankind.
> (Milton, *Paradise Regained*, 1–3; *Poems*)

Here, Milton relates *Paradise Regained* to *Paradise Lost*, and puts the two into a sequence: he once wrote about the loss of 'the happy Garden' through one 'man's disobedience', but 'now' he 'sing[s]' of paradise 'Recovered' for 'all mankind'. Yet Milton does more than relate the two works: startlingly, he sees his long epic *succeeded* by his 'brief epic'.[1] He does so, most obviously, to create a *typological* relation between the loss and regaining of paradise, focused on the epic heroes Adam and Christ, in keeping with scriptural exegesis: the saviour fulfils the failed promise of the first father, recovering what Adam lost. Yet Milton transacts his unusual literary typology for his two Christian epics precisely by imitating a classical text, the famed opening four lines to classical, medieval, and Renaissance editions of Virgil's *Aeneid*:

> Ille ego, qui quondam gracili modulatus avena
> carmen, et egressus silvis vicina coegi
> ut quamvis avido parerent arva colono,
> gratum opus agricolis; at nunc horrentia Martis.

(I am he who once tuned my song on a slender reed, then, leaving the woodland, constrained the neighbouring fields to serve the husbandmen, however grasping—a work welcome to farmers: but now of Mars' bristling.)[2]

We do not know whether Virgil wrote these verses himself, or whether someone else had an insight about the significance of his works as a canon.[3] Each possibility gestures to an interpretative model important to criticism on the classical reception of literary careers in English: either a poet presents his own literary career to the public; or another individual reads the poet's works and sees such a career in them.

To begin, what matters is the idea itself. Written in the personal voice, the Virgilian verses present the poet making an announcement about the generic structure of his career: in the past, he has written a pastoral poem, the *Eclogues*, and a didactic poem about farming, the *Georgics*, but 'now' he produces an epic about war, the *Aeneid*. Such a tripartite structure corresponds to the social roles of shepherd, farmer, and warrior, with each represented through a developing style, from lower to middle to higher. For Virgil's readers, the three works have corresponding literary antecedents in major practitioners: Theocritus, who wrote the bucolic *Idylls*; Hesiod, who wrote the didactic *Works and Days*; and Homer, who wrote the epic *Iliad* and *Odyssey*. In this way, the Virgilian verses map the professional development of the poet onto a larger history of poetry, although they do so through a mirror-like reversal: ingeniously, the maturation of the Virgilian poet, culminating in the great epic of Rome, takes us back to the birth moment of Western epic poetry itself. Important to Milton, the Virgilian idea of a literary career, both in the three poems and in the *ille ego* verses, proceeds through a principle that anticipates Christian typology. According to John S. Coolidge, Virgil relies on a classical topos, 'great things in small', to develop a typological relation between lesser and greater works: 'Thus the idle shepherd carries the implicit promise of . . . the strenuous hero, to come; and the lowly pastoral kind looks forward towards epic.'[4] Milton, I suggest, imitates the Virgilian verses to open *Paradise Regained* in order to construct a typology for his Christian epic career.

Milton, of course, inherits a long reception history for the Virgilian career idea. To map it briefly here, we might see the history proceeding through four stages. First, in antiquity, Suetonius, Donatus, and Servius discuss the poet's career in their lives of Virgil. In particular, Donatus records Virgil's epitaph, which connects his works to his life pattern: 'Mantua gave birth to me, the Calabrians snatched me away . . . I sang of pastures, fields, and princes.'[5] Second, during the Middle Ages, John of Garland popularizes a *rota Vergiliana* or *Wheel of Virgil*: in a series of concentric circles, divided by three spokes corresponding to the three poems, John distinguishes sets of writing styles, life styles, social ranks, and imagery (plant, animal, implement).[6] Third, in his 1582 translation of Virgil's *Aeneid*, Richard Stanyhurst first Englishes the Virgilian verses:

> I that in old season with reeds oaten harmony whistled
> My rural sonnet; from forest flitted I
>
> . . . . .
>
> A labour and a travail to plowswains heartily welcome.
> Now manhood and garboils I chant, and martial horror.[7]

And, fourth, most important to Milton, Spenser opens his 1590 *The Faerie Queene* with a clear imitation of *ille ego*:

> Lo I the man, whose Muse whilome did maske,
> As time her taught in lowly Shepheards weeds,
> Am now enforst a far unfitter taske,
> For trumpets sterne to chaunge mine Oaten reeds,
> And sing of Knights and Ladies gentle deeds.
> (*Faerie Queene*, I. Proem. I. 1–5)[8]

Spenser compacts the three-part Virgilian progression to two genres, pastoral and epic, eliding didactic in keeping with sixteenth-century practice.[9] In particular, Spenser identifies himself as the anonymous poet who had written *The Shepheardes Calender* in 1579, and now presents himself as the national poet of English epic.

After Spenser, poets of the English Renaissance imitate the Virgilian verses, making the career move one of the most durable representations of the era. Hence, when Milton begins his last volume of verse with his own imitation, he self-consciously crowns a tradition reflecting on the classical origin to a literary career, one that for him was mediated through a fellow English Virgilian poet, Spenser. This is an important principle for thinking about the relation between classical and Renaissance, one that usually gets overlooked. Imitating Virgil via Spenser, Milton rewrites the Virgilian verses by making two important changes. First, he *reverses* the Virgilian progression from lower to higher forms by making his lower form, the brief epic, typologically fulfil his greater epic. As we shall see, the condensation of a literary career to a single genre, epic, has precedents in classical culture, especially Propertius and Tibullus, who confine their literary careers to elegy. Second, since Milton writes both his epics in a Christian register, taking as their subject not the national founding of Rome or London but the loss of Eden in the Book of Genesis and the wilderness temptation of Christ in the Gospels, Milton at once overgoes and recuperates the classical literary career by Christianizing it. These revisions constitute one of the last major authorial self-presentations of the English Renaissance.

The idea of a literary career may trace to classical culture, but formal criticism on 'literary careers' has emerged only in the last two decades of the twentieth century. The founding figures are Lawrence Lipking in *Life of the Poet: Beginning and Ending Poetic Careers*; and Richard Helgerson in *Self-Crowned Laureates: Spenser, Jonson, Milton, and the Literary System*.[10] Lipking's comparatist study linking Virgil to later European authors (from Dante to Blake to Rilke) focuses on three moments of *self-discovery* in a 'great poet's' career: 'the moment of initiation or breakthrough; the moment of summing up; and the moment of passage, when the legacy or soul of the poet's work is transmitted to the next generation.'[11] In particular, Lipking shows how 'every major Western poet after Homer . . . has left some work that records the principles of his own poetic development . . . [We need to accept] the testimony of poems as decisive evidence about the way that poets conceive, or invent, their careers.'[12] Equally important, 'the poet who lives with such a responsibility [of being a great poet] has only one way to meeting it: planning ahead... The master plan, like scaffolding, holds everything in place.'[13]

In contrast, Helgerson's study of English Renaissance writers focuses on *self-presentation*: Spenser, Jonson, and Milton use print to present themselves as laureate or national poets like Virgil. In particular, Helgerson locates self-presentation in three structural points in the texts themselves: 'I thus talk often of proems, prefaces, and prologues. Pressure falls too on endings and on intermediate passages of transition or challenge.'[14] Nonetheless, Helgerson shares with Lipking what has become a hallmark of career criticism: 'a holistic commentary on an individual writer's work'[15]—or what Philip Hardie and Helen Moore term 'the totality of an author's textual corpus'.[16]

In part because of Helgerson's influence, most criticism on literary careers has centred on Spenser, whom Helgerson christens 'England's first laureate poet'.[17] During the 1980s and 1990s, two books and several seminal essays examined Spenser's literary career, making it a 'growth industry'.[18] In the past few years, however, two collections of essays have expanded the coverage considerably: *European Literary Careers: The Author from Antiquity to the Renaissance* (eds Patrick Cheney and Frederick A. de Armas), which includes essays on Virgil, Statius, Petrarch, Spenser, and 'Renaissance Englishwomen'; and *Classical Literary Careers and their Reception* (eds Hardie and Moore), which includes essays on Virgil, Horace, Propertius, Ovid, Juvenal, Petrarch, Shakespeare, and Milton. The essays on classical authors in these collections are the first ever published, offering a sober reminder that 'career criticism' is still in its infancy.

The present essay cannot canvas such an extensive field; it aims, rather, to offer a critical orientation based on past and current research. Below, the first section defines 'literary career' and 'career criticism' further; the second section focuses on the major classical models underwriting English Renaissance careers; the third inventories the classical reception in Spenser, Marlowe, Jonson, Chapman, and Isabella Whitney; and the last section returns to Milton.

Definition

What, more precisely, is a literary career? Can we step back from the vast field of Western writing between antiquity and the Renaissance to formulate an idea of a literary career? These two questions are interlocked, for the second speaks to the role of the critic in answering the first. Because Virgil forms a beginning, we can extend what has been said about his idea of a career.

Virgil devoted his adult life to writing poetry; it was his vocation, his calling. His poetry in three major forms—pastoral, georgic, and epic—is major not only because each has a significant precursor but because together the three represent a large canvas of cultural ideas, from the pastoral fields of *otium* to the domestic farm of *labor* to the international landscape of civic duty. Since Virgil centres his career on Rome, with the *Aeneid* culminating in the epic founding of the city, the Virgilian career idea is at once political and nationalist, having a patriotic agenda (whether it critiques the Augustan regime or not). In turn, this agenda has a religious element, because Virgil presents Aeneas' founding of Rome as destined by the gods. It also has an underlying gender dynamic, for a male poet sings about *Roma*, gendered female in Latin, characterized in Aeneas' destined bride, Lavinia, an eponym for the Latin land. Finally, the Virgilian career pursues its most memorable *telos*, the acquisition of fame as a consolation for tragic suffering (*Aeneid*, 1. 461–3). *Vocation, genre, intertextuality, idea, nationalism, gender, destiny, fame*: these become the defining features of a Virgilian idea of a literary career—ones that get taken forward.[19]

For instance, in one of our earliest formulations of Virgil's career, the distich in Elegy 1. 15 of the *Amores*, Ovid turns a critical reading into an artistic representation:

> Tityrus et segetes Aeneiaque arma legentur,
>   Roma triumphati dum caput orbis erit.
>
> (Tityrus and the harvest, and the arms of Aeneas, will be read as long
> as Rome shall be capital of the world she triumphs o'er.)[20]

Here, Ovid *contains* the three-part Virgilian progression within a single line, and in the exact order Virgil composed them: pastoral, georgic, epic. In addition to outlining a progression of genres and the idea of each, Ovid includes a political context, a poetic *telos*, and a gender dynamic, and he envelopes the model with a sense of destiny. As scholars have determined, he also has his eye on Propertius' Elegy 2. 34. 61–86, which takes twenty-five lines to outline Virgil's career but scrambles the sacred order (*Aeneid, Eclogues, Georgics*).[21] For Ovid, the Virgilian triad divinely serves the feminized Empire in order to secure her fame and that of her male poet.[22]

While the Virgilian career idea is author-centred, ensuring that much career criticism follows suit,[23] we need not construe it this way. For, as Ovid intimates by emphasizing the process of reading, reception is tied to authorship. This principle helps explain the difference between Helgerson and Lipking, who write at the same time but pursue different methodologies: Lipking, focusing on the poet's inward maturation in the process of discovering his career; Helgerson, focusing on the poet's reliance on print to advertise his career. Nor is either critic much interested in genre patterning as the main frame of a career.[24]

From the available criticism, we can identify two corresponding sources of evidence for theorizing a literary career. The first, which we find in author-centred models, consists of career documents: these are an author's representations in his works, and they are valuable for *fictionalizing* a career model. The *ille ego* verses prefacing editions of Virgil, along with Ovid's distich, are examples. The second source, which we find in careers reticent about self-presentation, consists of canons of authors' works that the reader *interprets* as forming a literary career. The most well-known example is Shakespeare, who avoids self-presentation in his plays and poems (except the *Sonnets*).[25]

In short, career criticism is diverse in its interests, methodologies, and conclusions. Thus, the critic is free to determine whether a writer has a career or not. Most have been confident that Spenser, Jonson, and Milton have literary careers, but express doubt about Philip Sidney, Marlowe, and Donne, primarily because these three do not print their works themselves (although Donne does print the *Anniversaries*, as well as other works). Yet scholars might wish to look again at the canons of such writers, in part because they can form *proto-careers*, and then see such careers going on to form part of the reception of laureate careers in poets like Jonson or Milton.[26]

Classical Literary Careers

The two recent collections of essays on literary careers have opened up the research considerably. The conclusion is that many classical authors were deeply self-conscious about themselves, not just as authors but as authors with literary careers. At the head of the classical pantheon, Homer and Hesiod both present themselves as poets, but they do not outline a career structured by a pattern of works. In the *Iliad* and *Odyssey*, Homer uses the first-person voice to invoke the Muse at the outset, but thereafter remains reticent. Yet in the *Odyssey* readers have long seen a self-portrait in the blind singer Demodocus singing about the Trojan War, while in the *Iliad* Achilles is notable as the only hero to imitate Homer in the art of singing about heroes.[27] Importantly, Hesiod does name himself near the beginning of the *Theogony*:

> The Muses once taught Hesiod to sing
> Sweet songs, while he was shepherding his lambs
> On holy Helicon.
>
> (ll. 21–3)

Even though Virgil will make Hesiod's *Works and Days* the middle work of his triad, Hesiod himself never reflects on the generic shape of his career.

The first extant poet who does is Callimachus. In the prologue to *Aetia*, he reports that the Telchines foolishly complained that he 'did not accomplish one continuous poem of many thousands of lines on . . . kings or . . . heroes, but like a child I roll forth a short tale', and Callimachus goes on to defend 'short' poems because they are 'sweeter'. He concludes by telling how Apollo told him, ' "poet . . . keep the Muse slender . . . do not drive your chariot upon the common tracks of others . . . though your course be more narrow" ' (1. 1–29).[28] Here Callimachus scripts a *recusatio*, or a refusal to write in the higher genres, preferring to write in the lower genre of elegy. The *recusatio* becomes important to Roman poets, especially Horace, Ovid, Propertius, and Tibullus, who use it to defend their work in non-epic genres. Virgil in *Eclogue* 6, however, echoes Callimachus both to choose pastoral over epic and to use pastoral to predict epic.[29]

As indicated, Propertius and Tibullus both anticipate Milton by enclosing a literary career within a single genre, love elegy. As Stephen Heyworth shows, Propertius is an elegist who never breaks away from elegy in order to have a Virgilian-style career,[30] and we could say the same about Tibullus. Both elegists do so via *recusatio*: Propertius, habitually (1. 7, 2. 1, 3. 1, 3. 9, 2. 10, 3. 3); Tibullus, occasionally (1. 1, 1. 10). Neither poet rejects epic outright, but instead chooses to write in the lower form. The effect, especially prominent in Propertius, is to turn a collection of love elegies into a meditation on a literary career, focusing on a lower genre's relation to a higher one. As Apollo tells Propertius, '"Madman, what business have you at such a stream?... Not from here, Propertius, may you hope for any fame: small wheels must run upon soft grass"' (3. 3. 15–18). As we are beginning to see, a poet's fiction of his literary career depends on certain metaphors, one of the most important being the chariot, proceeding down a path or road.[31]

The Horatian career model is more complex, but curiously critics have described it only recently. Stephen Harrison surveys Horace's works—*Satires, Epodes, Carmen Saeculare* and *Odes, Epistles* 2, and *Ars Poetica*—to discover 'several patterns: ascent from humble *sermo* to higher lyric, engagement in different genres at the same time, and (ultimately) a parabolic move from lyric back to *sermo*'.[32] Whereas Virgil pursues a progressive structure, Horace 'represent[s a]... broad variety of genres', some of which he works on 'simultaneously'.[33] In this eclectic model, Horace begins in the lower genres of satire and iambus; he proceeds to higher genres in the odes; and then he 'come[s] full circle': 'This parabolic trajectory stands in contrast with the Virgilian model... and provides some precedent for Ovid's return... to a modified form of elegy in exile after the grand enterprise of the epic *Metamorphoses*.'[34]

Of all Roman poets, Ovid is arguably the most complicated, because his canon unfolds two distinct models, one represented in the *Amores* and one represented in the exile poems, *Tristia* and *Ex Ponto*.[35] In the *Amores*, Ovid composes five 'programmatic' poems (1. 1, 2. 1, 2. 18, 3. 1, 3. 14) that represent a generic structure designed to compete with the Virgilian one. In 1. 1 and 2. 1, Ovid tells how he attempted to write epic but then was compelled by Love to write elegy. In 2. 18, he adds tragedy, while in 3. 1 he writes that his rendezvous with Dame Elegy is interrupted by Dame Tragedy:

> Elegia came with hairs perfumed sweet,
> And one, I think, was longer of her feet;
>
> . . . . .
>
> Then with huge steps came violent Tragedy.
> (*Ovid's Elegies* 3. 1. 3, 6–11, trans. Marlowe)

At the end of the elegy, Ovid promises to write Tragedy a work if she will let him serve Elegy first. The *Amores* then ends with Ovid's move into the 'area maior' ('mightier field') of tragedy (3. 15. 18). Hence, in this first career model Ovid begins by writing elegy but finally moves into the higher genres of epic and tragedy. Yet, as

2. 18 shows, Ovid scrambles Virgil's progressive model through a principle of *oscillation*, revealing, for instance, that even before his so-called inaugural work he has written a tragedy, *Medea* (only two lines have been preserved of this work, which was famous in antiquity as the mark of Ovid's genius).[36]

In the second career model, Ovid moves from elegy to epic to exile poetry.[37] In the opening poem of the *Tristia*, he imagines three 'book-cases... arranged in order' back in Rome, corresponding to his early amatory poetry, the mature poems in the higher genres, and finally the exile poetry (1. 1. 105–17). In this model, Ovid regrets his love poetry and features the catastrophe of his attempt to be a national poet of Rome.[38]

Thus, Roman poets are important to a history of classical reception during the English Renaissance in part because they self-consciously represent various ideas of a literary career. As the examples above indicate, these ideas tend to be in dialogue with one another, especially with the foundational one, the Virgilian. Horace, Propertius, Tibullus, and Ovid do not only have literary careers because we see it today; each uses poetry to present himself as an author with a distinct career. Their importance as authors, we might say, depends on their power to invent models different from, but related to, their Virgilian predecessor.

Renaissance Literary Careers

English Renaissance poets read the Roman poets carefully, and four in particular define their authorship in terms of a single classical poet: Spenser, Virgil; Marlowe, Ovid; Jonson, Horace; and Chapman, Homer.[39] We have already glanced at the opening of *The Faerie Queene*, to see Spenser presenting himself as England's Virgil, becoming the first national poet to write in the canonical genres progressing from pastoral to epic. Imitating Virgil's *Eclogues*, Spenser had launched this career in the *Calender*. As the glossator E.K. puts it in his Dedicatory Epistle, 'this our new Poete' 'follow[s]... the best and most auncient Poetes... at the first to trye theyr habilities: and as young birdes, that be newly crept out of the nest, by little first to prove theyr tender wyngs, before they make a greater flyght'.[40]

In the *October* eclogue, Spenser presents the younger shepherd Cuddie and the older Piers carrying on a dialogue about literary careers. Cuddie complains that he has written 'dapper ditties... | To feede youths fancie' (ll. 13–14) but received no remuneration. Piers responds by telling Cuddie how to attract a wealthy patron: 'Abandon then the base and viler clowne, | ... | And sing of bloody Mars, of wars' (ll. 37–9)—turn from pastoral to epic. Piers's advice reminds Cuddie of 'the Romish Tityrus', who 'Through his Mecoenas left his Oaten reede... | And labored lands... | And eft did sing of warres' (ll. 55–9)—an allusion, says E.K., to Virgil's 'Aeglogues... Georgiques... and... Aeneis'.[41] Yet, in a revolutionary move Spenser presents Piers recognizing that a Virgilian epic may exhaust the poet, so the shepherd encourages Cuddie to 'slack...the tenor of [his]...string' and 'sing' of 'love' (ll. 50–1): 'So mought our Cuddies name to Heaven sownde' (l. 54). Here, Spenser becomes the first European poet to slot the Ovidian-based Petrarchan genre of erotic verse formally into the structure of the Virgilian career in order to secure renown: love poetry functions as a bridge between pastoral and epic.[42]

Accordingly, in his Petrarchan sequence, *Amoretti*, Spenser composes two sonnets fulfilling this prediction. In Sonnet 33, he tells Lodowick Bryskett that he has failed to 'finish' his Empress' 'Queene of faery', having become 'tost with troublous fit, | of a proud love' (ll. 2–12), reminiscent of Ovid in *Amores* 1. 1 and 1. 2. In Sonnet 80, Spenser then presents his sonnet sequence as a 'pleasant mew' that will 'give him leave... | To sport' his 'muse and sing' his 'loves sweet praise: | the contemplation of whose heavenly hew, | my spirit to an higher pitch will rayse'—the pitch of epic, praising 'the Faery Queene' (ll. 9–14). A 'mew' is a cage in which a young hawk molts or grows its feathers for higher flight: Spenser presents the Petrarchan genre as a form of epic regeneration. In this, Spenser manages to enfame and overgo Ovid and Virgil at once.

October gestures to a final genre when Piers suggests that at the end of his career the poet should 'flye backe to heaven apace' (l. 84)—turn away from courtly poetry to write devotional verse. Here, Spenser follows the career move advertised by the French poet Du Bartas in his 1574 *La Muse chrestiene*, and then in his 1578 *La Sepmaine; ou, Creation du monde*, a project indebted to St Augustine's *Confessions*, with its turn from classical literature to Christian faith.[43] Hence, Barnabe Barnes writes in his 1595 *A Divine Century of Spiritual Sonnets*:

> No more lewde laies of Lighter loves I sing
>
> . . . . . .
>
> But my Muse fethered with an Angels wing,
> Divinely mounts aloft unto the sky.[44]

The next year, Spenser publishes his own 'spiritual' work, *Fowre Hymnes*, which announces a turn from amatory to devotional poetry:

> Many lewd layes...
>
> . . . . . .
>
> I have in th'heat of youth made heretofore,
>
> . . . . . .
>
> But all those follies now I do reprove,
> And turned have the tenor of my string,
> The heavenly prayses of true love to sing.
> (*Hymne of Heavenly Love*, ll. 8–14)

In sum, Spenser's career model begins with pastoral, proceeds to epic, is interrupted by love lyric but finally bridged by it, and then concludes with hymn, in a remarkable suturing of Virgilian, Ovidian, and Augustinian forms. Notably, Spenser's model, which the poet himself presents, leaves out some of his poems: the 1591 *Complaints*, for instance, indebted primarily to the Chaucerian tradition. Thus, we can distinguish between a career that the poet himself bequeaths and one as it exists in his practice. A full analysis would include both.

While the Virgilian model of pastoral and epic serves as the exemplary model in England, and while some like Barnes turned from courtly to devotional poetry, others voice a third model: beginning a career with love poetry in preparation for epic. In *Virgidemiae*, Joseph Hall says, 'Her Arma Virum goes by two degrees'. The first is the 'nursery' of the 'sheep-coat', or pastoral; and the second is the 'Chamber' of 'Venus', or amatory verse: 'To play with Cupid... | Then was she fit for an Heroic place.'[45] As we have seen, this second 'degree' is Ovidian in origin. Among Elizabethans, Marlowe is first to adopt this model, when he translates Ovid's volume in the mid-1580s, and thus inscribes the Ovidian *cursus*, telling a fiction of the poet oscillating among elegy, epic, and tragedy. Just as Spenser presents his career developing from pastoral to epic to love lyric to hymn, so Marlowe's career includes love poetry (*Ovid's Elegies* and 'The Passionate Shepherd to his Love'), tragedy (from *Dido, Queene of Carthage* to *Doctor Faustus*), and epic or proto-epic (*Hero and Leander* and *Lucan's First Book*).[46]

Although T. S. Eliot called Jonson 'the legitimate heir of Marlowe',[47] Jonson himself adopts a Horatian rather than an Ovidian persona. Nonetheless, the contour of Jonson's career does not resemble the one identified by Harrison for Horace. As revealed in the 1616 folio edition of his *Works*, Jonson's career divides into three genres: poetry; masques; plays (both comedy and tragedy). In the *Ars Poetica*, which Jonson himself translated, Horace reflects widely on drama, especially tragedy, perhaps supplying Jonson with his dramatic cue. Jonson never wrote an epic, but he told Drummond of Hawthorndon that he planned to write one.[48] For the most part, then, Jonson adopts a Horatian persona not because of Horace's career but because of Horace's character: '*Horace*, an Author of much civility; and... the best master, both of virtue and wisdom.'[49] In short, Horace perfectly embodies the central Jonsonian edict that 'the good poet' must 'first be... a good man'.[50]

Arguably the most innovative model during the English Renaissance is Chapman's. In 'The Occasion of this Impos'd Crown', prefacing his 1616 *Whole Works of Homer*, Chapman outlines three parts to a Homeric *cursus*, which he himself has translated, and which he probably modelled on the Virgilian triad, yet effectively reversing the progression from lower to high. In the first phase are the epics, one tragedic and the other comedic, *Iliad* and *Odyssey*. In a second phase is mock epic, the *Batrachomyomachia* (*Battle of Frogs and Mice*), which was thought to be by Homer. And in a third phase are the hymns and epigrams, illustrated in the *Homeric Hymns* and the extant *Epigrams*. Chapman gives the Homeric triad a tragic cast, ending on an elevated note: the Gods 'env[y]' Homer so much that he 'liv'd unhonoured and needy till his death', but afterwards he acquired fame.[51]

In contrast to male writers, 'English Renaissance women writers', write Susanne Woods, Margaret P. Hannay, Elaine Beilin, and Anne Shaver, 'were not Virgilians who styled their lives from low to high, Horatians who taught by delighting... Yet women's voices and self-presentations were visible both in the more confined traditions of manuscript circulation and the increasing ubiquity of the printed book', which allowed women to 'present... themselves as authors'.[52] As Jane Stevenson shows (Chapter 7, this volume), some women authors include a clear imitation of classical sources in their self-presentation. Yet one women writer does use classical sources to present herself as having a literary career in competition with the Virgilian model.

We know little about Isabella Whitney beyond her two books of poetry: *The Copy of a Letter* (1567), which consists of four complaint poems, two spoken by women, two by men; and *A Sweet Nosegay* (1573), which consists of selected versifications of Hugh Plat's 1572 *Floures of Philosophy*, as well as verse letters to family and friends, concluding with Whitney's *The Maner of her Wyll*, which bids the reader farewell. In both books, Whitney adopts a persona that enters the binary of Ovidian and Virgilian careers. In *The Copy*, she models herself on the Ovid of the *Heroides*, evidently benefiting from George Turbervile's translation published that year, and adopting the voice of female complaint against masculine abuse. By remembering that Ovid's volume responds to Virgilian epic, we can see Whitney Englishing Ovid's career move, relying on the voice of the betrayed Dido to critique Virgilian imperial ambitions.

In *A Sweet Nosegay*, Whitney may be the first female English poet to adopt the classical *recusatio*:

> No Virgil this, nor Ovid eke may blame,
> For beauty pressing as the conduit flows,
> Was cause that Paris greatest love arose:
> Who lov'd before, though never touched so,
> As Ovid shows.[53]

In a companion piece, the anonymous 'T.B.' clarifies Whitney's *recusatio*:

> She doth not write the brute or force in Arms,
> Nor pleasure takes, to sing of others harms,
> But mustred hath, and wrapped in a pack
> A heap of Flowers of Philosophy.
> (ll. 34–7, B1[r]).

That is, Whitney writes neither Virgilian epic nor strictly Ovidian elegy but an English didactic verse designed to educate her family and friends, not the nation or its queen and courtiers.

Writing well in advance of Spenser and canonical Elizabethan literature, Whitney opens a door that a contemporary of Milton steps through toward the end of the English Renaissance. Writing from the shores of America, Anne Bradstreet opens her Christian defence of poetry, *The Tenth Muse* (1650), with a classical *recusatio*:

> To sing of wars, of captains, and of kings,
> Of cities founded, commonwealths begun,

For my mean pen arc too superior things,
Or how they all, or each, their dates have run:
Let poets and historians set these forth,
My obscure verse shall not so dim their worth.[54]

Milton

By recalling the English Renaissance tradition of *writing* a literary career, we can more fully gauge the significance of Milton's 1671 volume.[55] The opening lines to this volume, the prologue to *Paradise Regained*, are unusual in the Milton canon because they connect two of his poems. Relying on the Virgilian verses of *ille ego* imitated by Spenser, Milton makes the bold move of identifying his brief epic as more 'heroic' (l. 15) than his epic, because it regains lost paradise. Milton radically alters the career topos of 'great things and small' to offer a Christian correction to his Virgilian—and Spenserian—use of it back in his 1637 *Lycidas*, the use of pastoral to predict epic: 'Tomorrow to fresh woods, and pastures new' (l. 193).

While scholars recognize the career advertisement opening *Paradise Regained*, they neglect the corresponding advertisement concluding *Samson Agonistes*, a fourteen-line sonnet, spoken by the Chorus in Milton's preferred form, the Italian, the first quatrain of which reads,

All is best, though we oft doubt,
What the unsearchable dispose
Of highest wisdom brings about,
And ever best found in the close.[56]
(ll. 1745–8)

Editors gloss this conclusion with 'the closing choruses—virtually identical in every case—of Euripides' *Alcestis, Andromache, Bacchae, Helen*, and *Medea*'.[57] What has escaped attention is that Milton uses a rhyme scheme he has used in his earlier sonnets in order to offer an authorial signature to his otherwise third-person tragedy. This, I suggest, creates a *dramatic* correlate to the first-person signature that opens the 1671 volume in *Paradise Regained*.[58] Just as Milton alludes to the Virgilian verses opening his brief epic, so he alludes to Euripides to close his poetic tragedy. In the first work, he uses a classical allusion to represent the typological relation between his epic and brief epic, in a bid both to remember and to surpass Spenser and Virgil. In the second poem, he uses a classical allusion to represent the typological relation between his tragedy and his past lyric poetry, especially the sonnets. Sonnet and lyric; epic and brief epic; drama and tragedy: these constitute the major genres on which Milton grounds his poetic canon. In the 1671 volume, he offers a historically important retrospective on the classical origin of his Christian literary career.

Notes

1. Barbara Kiefer Lewalski, *Milton's Brief Epic: The Genre, Meaning, and Art of 'Paradise Regained'* (Providence, RI, 1966).
2. Reprinted in *Virgil*, trans. H. Rushton Fairclough, Loeb Classical Library (Cambridge, MA, 1935), I. 240–1. See Laura Lunger Knoppers (ed.), *The 1671 Poems* (Oxford, 2008), 121.
3. Gian Biagio Conte, *The Rhetoric of Imitation*, trans. Charles Segal (Ithaca, NY, 1986), 84–7. Although we lack certainty, classicists pretty much agree that Virgil did not write the verses.
4. John S. Coolidge, 'Great Things and Small: The Virgilian Progression', *Comparative Literature*, 17 (1965), 11.
5. Aelius Donatus, *Life of Virgil*, trans. David Scott Wilson-Okamura (2008), sect. 123 <www.virgil.org/vitae/a-donatus.htm> (accessed 13 March 2015). See Charles Martindale, 'Green Politics: The *Eclogues*', in Martindale (ed.), *The Cambridge Companion to Virgil* (Cambridge, 1997), 107.
6. John of Garland, *Parisiana Poetria*, trans. Traugott Lawler (New Haven, 1974), 38–41. For excerpts, diagrams, and discussion, see Jan M. Ziolkowski and Michael C. J. Putnam (eds), *The Virgilian Tradition* (New Haven, 2008), 744–50.
7. Richard Stanyhurst, *Thee First Foure Bookes of Virgil his Aeneis* (1582), sig. Biii^r.
8. For Milton's debt to Spenser, see Knoppers (ed.), *1671 Poems*, 240.
9. Alastair Fowler, *Kinds of Literature* (Cambridge, MA, 1982), 240.
10. Lawrence Lipking, *The Life of the Poet* (Chicago, 1981); Richard Helgerson, *Self-Crowned Laureates* (Berkeley and Los Angeles, 1983). See Patrick Cheney, 'Introduction', in Patrick Cheney and Frederick A. de Armas (eds), *European Literary Careers* (Toronto, 2002), 4–8.
11. Lipking, *Life of the Poet*, p. ix.
12. Lipking, *Life of the Poet*, pp. viii, x.
13. Lipking, *Life of the Poet*, 79–80.
14. Helgerson, *Self-Crowned Laureates*, 13.
15. Cheney, 'Introduction', 6.
16. Philip Hardie and Helen Moore, 'Introduction: Literary Careers—Classical Models', in Hardie and Moore (eds), *Classical Literary Careers* (Cambridge, 2010), 1.
17. Helgerson, *Self-Crowned Laureates*, 100.
18. The books are Richard Rambuss, *Spenser's Secret Career* (Cambridge, 1993); and Patrick Cheney, *Spenser's Famous Flight* (Toronto, 1993). Seminal essays include Richard Helgerson, 'The New Poet Presents Himself', *PMLA* 93 (1978), 893–911; David L. Miller, 'Spenser's Vocation, Spenser's Career', *English Litarary History*, 50 (1983), 197–231; Joseph F. Loewenstein, 'Echo's Ring: Orpheus and Spenser's Career', *English Literary Renaissance*, 16 (1986), 287–302; and Richard Rambuss, 'Spenser's Lives, Spenser's Careers', in Judith H. Anderson, Donald Cheney, and David A. Richardson (eds), *Spenser's Life and the Subject of Biography* (Amherst, MA, 1996), 1–17. The phrase 'growth industry' comes from Jerome S. Dees's review of Cheney's *Spenser's Famous Flight* in *Journal of English and Germanic Philology*, 96 (1997), 124.
19. Several of these features receive essays in this volume. On the genres of pastoral and georgic, see Helen Cooper, Chapter 9; on epic, Philip Hardie, Chapter 10; on intertextuality, Patrick Cheney and Philip Hardie, Chapter 1; on nationalism, Curtis Perry, Chapter 8a; on gender, both Jane Stevenson, Chapter 7, and Tanya Pollard, Chapter 18; and on destiny and fame, Philip Hardie, Chapter 8d.
20. Ovid, *Amores* I. 15. 25–6, in *Ovid*, trans. Frank Justus Miller, rev. G. P. Goold, Loeb Classical Library, 6 vols (Cambridge, MA, 1984), vol. I.

21. See D. W. T. Vessey, 'Elegy Eternal: Ovid, *Amores*, I.15', *Latomus*, 40 (1969), 80–97.
22. See Cheney, 'Introduction', 9–11. Two vectors not evident in Ovid's distich are emphasized by Hardie and Moore, 'Introduction': 'the extratextual conditions of production' (p. 1) and 'patronage' (p. 14).
23. Hardie and Moore, 'Introduction', 1.
24. This has become my own interest, and figures centrally in Hardie and Moore (eds), *Classical Literary Careers*.
25. See Patrick Cheney, 'Did Shakespeare Have a Literary Career?', in Hardie and Moore (eds), *Classical Literary Careers*, 160–78.
26. On Sidney, see Cheney, *Spenser's Famous Flight*, 262 n. 36; on Marlowe, see Patrick Cheney, *Marlowe's Counterfeit Profession* (Toronto, 1997); and on Donne, see Patrick Cheney, *Reading Sixteenth-Century Poetry* (Oxford, 2011), 280–7, as well as 'Donne's Literary Career', in Michael Schoenfeldt (ed.), *John Donne in Context* (Cambridge, 2019), 5–17.
27. Donald Lateiner, 'The *Iliad*: An Unpredictable Classic', in Robert Fowler (ed.), *Cambridge Companion to Homer* (Cambridge, 2004), 15 n. 11.
28. Cf. Alan Cameron, *Callimachus and his Critics* (Princeton, 1995), 266–7, 437, 454–83; and Benjamin Acosta-Hughes and Susan A. Stephens, 'Rereading Callimachus' "Aetia" Fragment 1', *Classical Philology*, 97 (2002), 238–55. Scholars debate whether Callimachus refers to epic or not.
29. On Callimachus' representation of his œuvre, see Joseph Farrell, 'Greek Lives and Roman Careers', in Cheney and de Armas (eds), *European Literary Careers*, 33; on Virgil in *Eclogue* 6, p. 25.
30. Stephen Heyworth, 'An Elegist's Career: from Cynthia to Cornelia', in Hardie and Moore (eds), *Classical Literary Careers*, 89–104.
31. See Philip Hardie, *The Epic Successors of Virgil* (Cambridge, 1993), 100–1; Hardie and Moore, 'Introduction', 3. The career path can refer to the trajectory a single genre follows, as with Propertius, or the trajectory of a poet's set of works, as with Virgil. On the word 'career' originating in the Latin *cursus*, chariot race course, and the Virgilian progression originating in the Roman *cursus honorum*, or progression through a political career, see Cheney, 'Introduction', 8–9.
32. Harrison, 'There and Back Again: Horace's Poetic Career', in Hardie and Moore (eds), *Classical Literary Careers*, 39.
33. Harrison, 'There and Back Again', 39.
34. Harrison, 'There and Back Again', 58.
35. See Cheney, *Marlowe's Counterfeit Profession*, esp. 31–48. Subsequently, see Philip Hardie, 'Introduction', in Hardie (ed.), *Cambridge Companion to Ovid* (Cambridge, 2002), 1–10; Stephen Harrison, 'Ovid and Genre: Evolutions of an Elegist', in Hardie (ed.), *Cambridge Companion to Ovid*, 79–94; and Philip Hardie and Alessandro Barchiesi, 'The Ovidian Career Model: Ovid, Gallus, Apuleius, Boccaccio', in Hardie and Moore (eds), *Classical Literary Careers*, 59–88.
36. See Cheney, *Marlowe's Counterfeit Profession*, 41–6, 89–98.
37. See Michael A. Calabrese, *Chaucer's Ovidian Arts of Love* (Gainesville, FL, 1994), 5.
38. See Maggie Kilgour, 'New Spins on Old Rotas: Virgil, Ovid, Milton', in Hardie and Moore (eds), *Classical Literary Careers*, 179–96.
39. This is not to say that other classical authors are not important to each: Ovid to Spenser, for instance (see Syrithe Pugh, *Spenser and Ovid* (Aldershot, 2005)).
40. E.K., Dedicatory Epistle, *Shepheardes Calender*, ll. 10, 144–50; Spenser, *Shorter Poems*.
41. Spenser, *Shorter Poems*, 135.
42. See Cheney, *Spenser's Famous Flight*, 27–38, including on how the Petrarchan genre responds to Ovid.
43. See Lily B. Campbell, *Divine Poetry and Drama in Sixteenth-Century England* (New York, 1972).

44. Barnabe Barnes, *A Divine Century of Spiritual Sonnets* (1595), 1. 1–6, repr. in Campbell, *Divine Poetry*, 137.
45. Joseph Hall, *Virgidemiae* 6. 268–80, in *Collected Poems of Joseph Hall*, ed. A. Davenport (Liverpool, 1949). For a variation on the Renaissance Virgilian model of pastoral and epic, see Girolamo Vida, *Art of Poetry* (1527), 1. 495–65, who sees the heroic poet preparing for epic by writing both pastoral and the juvenilia of the so-called 'Appendix Virgiliana' (noted by Colin Burrow, 'Spenser's Genres', in Richard McCabe (ed.), *The Oxford Handbook of Edmund Spenser* (Oxford, 2010), 408–9).
46. For a different view of Marlowe's career, see Charles Martindale, Chapter 26, this volume. Francis Davision assigns the three-part Ovidian model to Samuel Daniel: 'So if soft, pleasing lyrics some are skill'd, | In tragic some, some in heroical, | But thou alone art matchless in them all' ('To Samuel Daniel, Prince of English Poets', ll. 28–30, in Hyder E. Rollins and Herschel Baker (eds), *The Renaissance in England* (Lexington, MA, 1954), 245). On Daniel's literary career (and Michael Drayton's), see Cheney, *Marlowe's Counterfeit Profession*, 164–5.
47. T. S. Eliot, *Elizabethan Dramatists* (1963), 75.
48. In *Ben Jonson: The Complete Poems*, ed. George Parfitt (Harmondsworth, 1988), 461.
49. Jonson, *Timber*, in Jonson, *Works*, 8. 642. On Jonson's Horatian career, see Helgerson, *Self-Crowned Laureates*, 101–84. Helgerson (126–7) also discusses the Elizabethan invention of satire as both 'enmity' and 'erotic' poetry, as well as a 'displacement of the heroic', quoting John Weever, *Faunus and Melliflora*, ed. A. Davenport (Liverpool, 1948), 42–3. For a book-length study of the relation between Jonson and Horace, see Victoria Moul, *Jonson, Horace, and the Classical Tradition* (Cambridge, 2010).
50. *Volpone*, Dedicatory Epistle, 22–3 in Jonson, *Works*, 5. 17.
51. Chapman, 'The Occasion of this Impos'd Crowne', *Whole Works of Homer*, in *Chapman's Homer*, ed. Allardyce Nicholl, 2 vols (New York, 1956), 2. 511.
52. Susanne Woods, Margaret P. Hannay, Elaine Beilin, and Anne Shaver, 'Renaissance Englishwomen and the Literary Career', in Cheney and de Armas (eds), *European Literary Careers*, 302. Mary Wroth is the first Englishwoman to compose a sonnet sequence (*Pamphilia to Amphilanthus*) and an epic romance (*Urania*), and she adds a drama (*Love's Victory*). See Margaret P. Hannay, *Mary Sidney, Lady Wroth* (Burlington, VT, 2010).
53. Isabella Whitney, *Sweet Nosegay* (1573), ll. 17–21, sig. B1r. On Whitney's 'literary career', see Cheney, *Reading Sixteenth-Century Poetry*, pp. 231–40.
54. Anne Bradstreet, *Tenth Muse*, ll. 1–6, in Jane Stevenson and Peter Donaldson (eds), *Early Modern Women Poets* (Oxford, 2001), 233. I am grateful to Jane Stevenson for drawing my attention to Bradstreet's poem (see Chapter 7, this volume).
55. See Knoppers (ed.), *1671 Poems*, pp. xcvii–xcviii, lxxiv.
56. I am grateful to Linda Gregerson for directing me to the Chorus's sonnet.
57. Merritt Y. Hughes (ed.), *John Milton* (Indianapolis, 1957), 593.
58. On Milton's sonnets in his long poems, see Lee M. Johnson, 'Milton's Blank Verse Sonnets', *Milton Studies*, 5 (1973), 129–53. On *Samson* as a retrospective on Milton's poetry, see Ann Baynes Coiro, 'Fable and Old Song: *Samson Agonistes* and the Idea of a Poetic Career', *Milton Studies*, 36 (1998), 123–52.

d. Fame and Immortality

PHILIP HARDIE

The discourse of fame is central to Renaissance ideas about individual achievement, nationhood, and authorship, and it reveals the traces of a long history through pagan and Christian culture.[1] Classical conceptions of fame and of the immortality that an author can win for himself and for the objects of his praise form the main repertoire for Renaissance writers. Qualifications and reservations concerning the possibility of achieving lasting fame and the desirability of the ambition are fed both by classical pagan models for the imperilment or vanity of the pursuit and by a Christian critique of the desire for earthly fame, as opposed to divine glory, a critique whose authoritative formulation is owed to two late-antique authors, Augustine and Boethius, who were formed within an as yet uninterrupted classical culture and who draw on a pre-existing philosophical critique of the values of fame.

Key formulations of classical topics of the pursuit and achievement of fame are found in the Augustan poets Virgil, Horace, and Ovid. In the proem to the third *Georgic*, Virgil declares his ambition of setting off on a path of flight that will enable him to match his famous epic predecessor Ennius in 'flying victorious through the mouths of men' ('uictorque uirum uolitare per ora'). Virgil goes on to fantasize about a future triumph of poetry and the erection of a temple to celebrate the fame of Octavian and his ancestors; both as *triumphator* and as temple-builder, the poet adopts the roles of the emperor-to-be, Augustus, so asserting a partnership in fame and success between ruler and his poet, and reworking a Pindaric paradigm for the collaborative effort of victor and poet.[2] Horace outlines a career of successfully achieved 'laureation' in the first three books of *Odes*: an opening hope for elevation to the stars through canonization as one of the great lyric poets (*Odes* 1. 1. 35–6) is followed by a confident prediction in *Odes* 2. 20 of Horace's metamorphosis into a swan that will fly deathless to the ends of the earth, and is capped by the self-monumentalization of *Ode* 3. 30 ('exegi monumentum aere perennius' ('I have completed a monument longer-lasting than bronze')), as a lasting textual body exempt from death and capable of continued growth in fame ('usque ego postera | crescam laude recens' (ll. 7–8)), ending with a request to the Muse to crown the poet with laurel. *Odes* 4 contains two further influential formulations of the poet's power to confer a life in fame (4. 8, 9). Horace's proclamations of his own fame were imitated by the elegists Propertius and, above all, Ovid, who, in defiance of Envy, already makes the Horatian claim to survive the grave in his poetry at the end of his first book of *Amores*, having used the promise of worldwide and everlasting renown as a come-on for his girlfriend in 1. 3. Ovid's fullest reworking of Horace, *Odes* 3. 30, is reserved for the Epilogue to the *Metamorphoses* ('Iamque opus exegi ...' ('And now I have completed a work ...') (15. 871–9)), where the poet defies the anger and thunderbolts of Jupiter/the emperor, predicts a flight even higher than the stars, and looks forward to an everlasting fame coextensive with the Roman Empire. Emphatically closural, this epilogue will be recurrently revisited in the exile poetry, either to draw back from its bold certainties in the light of subsequent events, or to reassert its confidence in the teeth of the mutability of the poet's fortunes. The intratextualities of the *Metamorphoses* already establish a link between the flight of the poet in the Epilogue, reincarnated on the breath of future generations of readers, and the sky-wandering Pythagoras earlier in book 15, who rises superior to the tyrant who sent him into exile, and whose philosophical authority is based in part on his ability to recall his own previous incarnations.[3] But recollection of Pythagoras' doctrine of universal change ('omnia mutantur' (*Met.* 15. 165)) will leave us wondering how fixed and unchanging this poetic monument can really be. Ovid's reception of Horace's statements on fame, and his exilic reception of his own claim to undying fame at the end of his epic poem, inaugurate a long line, ancient and post-antique, of Horatian–Ovidian assertions of fame, made with greater or lesser confidence.

'Fame' in early modern English retains a wider range of meanings than that of 'renown' or 'celebrity', the only meaning current today. In Renaissance texts the pursuit of 'fame' in that narrow sense interacts with other kinds of 'fame': the evil fame of infamy, and 'fame' in the senses of 'report' or 'rumour'. For the articulation of the connections between these various meanings of fame, the major classical sources are the personifications of *Fama* in Virgil, *Aeneid* 4. 173–97, and Ovid, *Metamorphoses* 12. 39–63. In the *Aeneid*, 'Rumour' erupts to spread a distorted version of the 'wedding' in the cave of Dido and Aeneas; Virgil creates the monstrous person of *Fama*, her body covered with eyes, ears, and tongues, and flying swiftly through the air, which will appear countless times in Renaissance images of fame both good and bad. In the *Metamorphoses, Fama* appears at the beginning of Ovid's retelling of the Trojan War, and, among other things, she embodies the Greco-Roman tradition of epic as praise poetry. Ovid also gives *Fama* the allegorical house that she lacks in Virgil, the model for a series of later Houses or Temples of Fame. Decisive for English literature is Chaucer's *House of Fame*, which works the Virgilian and Ovidian personifications into the narrative form of a medieval dream vision that is also an encyclopedia of literary tradition as it stood in Chaucer's time. The close relationship of Ovid's *Fama* to another Ovidian personification, *Inuidia* 'Envy' (*Met.* 2. 760–805), registers the fact that envy has dogged the fame of men of action and poets alike since at least the time of Pindar. Renaissance writers are constantly aware of envy's tooth.

I explore the reception of classical texts on fame, rumour, envy, and literary immortality by four of the major English poets of the period, before turning to the role of fame in historiography.

Spenser

Edmund Spenser offers a full canvas of the workings of Renaissance fame in the classical tradition: the glorification of national achievement and of the nation's ruler; the poet's ambition for a personal immortality of fame; and the dangers that beset the poet in his quest to bestow immortal fame on himself and his glorious subjects. Spenser's project for a 'famous flight' (*October*, l. 88)[4] is pieced together largely out of classical materials. *The Ruines of Time* combines the vanity *topos*, largely a medieval development of a biblical text (Eccles. 1: 2), with Horatian topics (ll. 407–10, 421–7):

> In vain do earthly princes, then, in vain
> Seek with pyramids, to heaven aspired;
> Or huge colosses, built with costly pain;
> Or brazen pillars, never to be fired
>
> . . . . .
>
> But fame with golden wings aloft doth fly,
> Above the reach of ruinous decay,
> And with brave plumes doth beat the azure sky,
> Admir'd of base-born men from far away:
> Then who so will with virtuous deeds assay
> To mount to heaven, on Pegasus must ride,
> And with sweet poets' verse be glorified.

The contrast between poetry and pyramids and bronze comes from *Odes* 3. 30; flight, as of a bird, calls to mind *Odes* 2. 20, while the phrasing of 'beat the azure sky' might recall Horace's ambition in *Odes* 1. 1 to 'knock against [*feriam*] the stars with head held high'. The flight of Pegasus is a classical myth, but its use as an allegory for fame is medieval and Renaissance.[5] Swan and Pegasus are both used later in *Ruines* with reference to Sir Philip Sidney: the flight of swan–Sidney to heaven at ll. 589–602 is a flight both of fame and of a more literal, Christian, life after death, which is also figured in the application of Perseus' flight to heaven on Pegasus as an allegory for the death of Sidney (ll. 645–58). Sidney, like the Earl of Essex, is a cult figure around whom the imagery of fame gathers, as in an emblem in Geffrey Whitney's *Choice of Emblemes* (1586), 'Pennae gloria immortalis' 'the undying glory of the pen': Whitney takes from Hadrianus Junius' *Emblemata* (1565) a winged figure of (Virgilian) Fame with eyes all over his body, blowing a trumpet and with a quill pen slung over his shoulder, and flying through the clouds high above a (Horatian) pyramid, and applies it specifically to Sidney: an accompanying poem announces that a new poet is arising to take the place of the deceased Earl of Surrey.[6]

Fame's flight in *Ruines* unites virtue ('virtuous deeds') and glory ('with sweet poets' verse be glorified'), an unstable alliance, but one asserted in the classical tag that 'glory is the shadow of virtue' (e.g. Seneca, *Ep.* 79. 13). Sidney's flight to heaven combines poetic glory with a Christian ascent, a Christianization of classical models of fame and glory found also in *The Faerie Queene*, where the Mount of Contemplation is compared to both the Mount of Olives, 'Adorned with fruitful olives... as it were for endless memory | Of that dear Lord who oft thereon was found', and Mount Parnassus, 'that is for ay | Through famous poets' verse each where renowned' (1. 10. 54).[7] From the Mount of Contemplation the Red Crosse Knight has a vision of the celestial Jerusalem, whose splendour transcends but also includes the brightness and glory of Cleopolis ('fame-city'), the city of the Fairy Queen, and a mirror of London's glorious past. In other respects the panegyrical elements of *The Faerie Queene* are heavily indebted to an epideictic tradition, going back to classical antiquity, of reading and writing epic as a genre of praise.[8] Britomart's vision in the cave of Merlin of her 'famous progeny' down to Elizabeth (3. 3. 22) is one of many Renaissance reworkings of the Parade of Heroes viewed by Aeneas in the Underworld in *Aeneid* 6, and, like the Virgilian Parade, the Spenserian show is nuanced with negative moments.[9] Spenserian panegyric of Gloriana, the fairy queen and figure of Elizabeth, is part of the wider use of classical, and especially Virgilian, templates to celebrate the glory of Elizabeth and the Stuart kings.[10]

In *The Faerie Queene*, the pursuit of fame and glory on the part of both poet and his heroes is dogged by the gathering forces of envy and detraction, which become more threatening in the 1596 *The Faerie Queene* (with the additional books 4–6). The personifications Envy and Detraction, corresponding to the classical enemies of the poet and those he praises (Greek *Phthonos* 'Envy' and *Momos* 'Blame'; Latin *Inuidia* or *Liuor* 'Envy'), appear at the end of book 5, accompanied by the Blatant Beast, a monstrous hound of blame and detraction, led in chains by Calidore at the end of book 6, but which in the poet's day has now broken his chains to bark and bite without restraint. This closural monster answers to the hellish figure for the negative powers of the poet, Ate (companion of Duessa), who stands at the beginning of book 4, the first book of the second half of the six books of the poem. The ancestry of both monsters is complex: in Virgilian terms, Ate is a conflation of the Fury Allecto and the personification of *Fama*, in itself a comment on the close relationship of the two within the *Aeneid*. The Blatant Beast is also, among other things, a version of *Fama*; his association with Envy reflects the close connections between Ovid's Envy and Ovid's and Virgil's *Fama*. His intratextual link with the Fury-like Ate matches the close relationship of Ovid's Envy to Virgil's Allecto.

Shakespeare

Spenser's alertness to the complex inter- and intra-textual workings of his classical models is matched by Shakespeare. Shakespeare's *Sonnet* 55, 'Not marble, nor the gilded monuments | Of princes, shall outlive this pow'rful rhyme', is the most famous English Renaissance reworking of Horace's *Exegi monumentum* (*Odes* 3. 30) and of Ovid's imitation in the Epilogue to the *Metamorphoses*. Continuing life is assured not for the poet, but for the object of his love, one of many promises of immortality by Renaissance lover–poets to their beloveds, following Ovid's proud reversal of the association of the life of the love elegist with the lack of fame for worthy achievement, through the proclamation of his elegy's power to immortalize Corinna (*Am.* 1. 3, 2: 17. 27–34, 3. 12; cf. Prop. 3. 2. 17–26). The final couplet, 'So, till the judgement that yourself arise, | You live in this, and dwell in lovers' eyes', exemplifies a non-classical analogy between a continued life in poetry and the revival of the physical person at the Last Judgement.[11] The opening poem of Abraham Cowley's 1656 *Poems*, 'The Motto', in which the poet asks himself how he is to live up to the Virgilian motto on the title page (*Georgics* 3. 8–9), 'I must attempt a path on which I too may raise myself from the ground and fly victorious over the lips or men', includes a conceit on the trumpet of Fame (an attribute scarcely developed in antiquity) and the Last Trump, 14–6 'Sure I Fame's trumpets hear. | It sounds like the last trumpet; for it can | Raise up the buried man.'

Horace and Ovid are confident that their poetry can outlast the endless succession of the years and the tooth of antiquity. Cicero's *Dream of Scipio* (6. 27—8), followed by Boethius' *Consolation of Philosophy* (2. 7), warns that fame will perish through the forgetfulness of posterity and the obscurity of antiquity, in what Boethius calls a 'second death'. Fame triumphs over Death, but Time triumphs over Fame in Petrarch's *Trionfi*, a much read and imitated sequence in which Petrarch frames his own proto-humanist attempt to revive the fame of classical antiquity within Christian perspectives on time and eternity. Spenser's *The Ruines of Time* is a large-scale meditation on the power struggle between time and fame, a topic that concerns Spenser in many of his works.[12] Shakespeare calls on his Muse to undo the effects of time on his love's face, 'Give my love fame faster than Time wastes life, | So thou prevent'st his scythe and crooked knife' (*Sonnet* 100, ll. 13–14). In *Sonnet* 60 ('Like as the waves make towards the pebbled shore, | So do our minutes hasten to their end') Shakespeare uses the Ovidian Pythagoras' comparison of the flow of time to a flowing river or a succession of waves, but attempts to fix his poetry against the ineluctable onset of time, 'And yet to times in hope my verse shall stand, | Praising thy worth, despite his cruel hand' (ll. 13–14); Shakespeare comments on the connections between the figures of Pythagoras and the poet in *Metamorphoses* 15.[13]

Lucrece, in Shakespeare's *The Rape of Lucrece*, is a woman obsessed with shame and with her own good name and fame. In traditional societies, a woman's fame is based not on what she does, but on what she does *not* do—that is, compromise her chastity. Lucrece's action in killing herself to vindicate her good name against her rapist was taken by Valerius Maximus in his collection of *exempla* as the mark of a man's spirit in a woman's body (6. 1). In Lucrece, Shakespeare explores issues of female fame that Virgil had dramatized in the tragedy of Dido, another woman obsessed with fame and reputation, and, like Lucrece, in problematical ways.[14] The relationship between female chastity and masculine varieties of fame was a matter of urgency in a nation ruled by a female monarch, Elizabeth.

Shakespeare presents a case study in a self-destructive masculine obsession with name and fame in *Coriolanus*, the name that is attached to the protagonist, Martius Caius, to honour his victory at Corioles. Such *cognomina*, nicknames, were a very Roman way of marking out great military conquerors (for example, Scipio Africanus), who were also celebrated in that most famous of Roman rituals, the triumph, the frequent object of reconstruction and revival in Renaissance culture both in pageant and in text.[15] Coriolanus' inability to limit his desire for fame, and his solipsistic alienation from the popular voices that are the bearers of that fame, lead to the destruction of his civic and personal identity, in an example of a wider Shakespearean and Renaissance 'critique of honour' that in part replicates ancient, and especially, Roman anxieties about the excessive pursuit of individual fame at the expense of the cohesion of the state.[16] The Earl of Essex, the subject of much fame literature before and after his death (1601), was an object lesson in the dangers of an individualistic pursuit of glory.

In *Henry V* (1599) the chorus anticipates Henry's triumphal return to London from his French conquests, as in the past Julius Caesar returned in triumph to Rome, and as in the future the Earl of Essex will return to London (5. 0. 13–34). 'The Mayor and all his brethren' will come to meet Henry, as 'the senators of th'antique Rome | With the plebeians [i.e. Senatus Populusque Romanus] go forth and fetch their conqu'ring Caesar in'. These are images of national solidarity, the outstanding leader's victories at the service of, and celebrated by, the people as a whole. *Henry V* is much concerned with what Edwin Benjamin calls 'national fame'.[17] Henry bases his claim to France on glorious English victories in the past and on his own bloodline, and hopes for an undying place in English history: 'Either our history shall with full mouth | Speak freely of our acts, or else our grave, | Like Turkish mute, shall have a tongueless mouth' (*Henry V*, 1. 2. 233–5). Henry's vindication of his royal claims through the actions of his right hand, and the consolidation, however temporary, of national unity through his famous victories provide a resolution to a problematic of rumour and renown that runs throughout the tetralogy (sometimes known as the 'Henriad') of *Richard II*, *Henry IV* Parts 1 and 2, and *Henry V*, and which relates to the legitimation of monarch in a narrative of usurpation and civil war. At the beginning of the second half of the tetralogy, the Induction to *Henry IV* Part 2 (a 'proem in the middle'), enters the figure of Rumour, 'painted full of tongues', and one of the most elaborately developed descendants of the Virgilio-Ovidian *Fama*. Like his classical ancestors he has both an immediate dramatic function of shifting scene and of propagating a report, in this case a rumour that is the opposite, rather than merely a distortion, of the truth, and a metapoetic role of embodying the operations of the poet and playwright. Rumour is a figure both for fame ('I, from the Orient to the drooping West... still unfold | The acts commenced on this ball of earth') and for rumour ('Upon my tongues continual slanders ride'). And, as in the *Aeneid* and *Metamorphoses*, the discrete personification of Rumour/*Fama* is at the centre of concentric ripples of images and themes relating to fame, rumour, and report, that spread out to encompass the text (in this case the tetralogy) as a whole. These figures of fame include Falstaff, who comes out, as it were, as a personification of *Fama* on the field of Gaultre ('I have a whole school of tongues in this belly of mine' (*2 Henry* 4, 4. 1. 374)), after his famous version of the topos of the vanity of fame at Shrewsbury ('What is honour? A word. What is in that word "honour"? Air' (*1 Henry* 4, 5. 1. 132–3)).

Jonson

Ben Jonson combines a classicizing interest in the details of the classical texts on rumour and renown with a keen sense for the contemporary politics of fame and defamation. His occasional verse returns obsessively to Horatian lyric formulations of the poet's power to confer fame, as well as going directly to Horace's own models in Pindar.[18] A poem like the 'Epistle: To Elizabeth Countess of Rutland' is a tissue of Horatian reminiscences (ll. 41–8; Jonson, *Works*, 8. 114); cf. esp. Horace *Odes* 4. 8, 9):

> It is the Muse alone can raise to heaven,
> And, at her strong arm's end, hold up and even
> The souls she loves. Those other glorious notes,
> Inscribed in touch or marble, or the coats
> Painted or carved upon great men's tombs,
> Or in their windows, do but prove the wombs,
> That bred them, graves; when they were born, they died,
> That had no Muse to make their fame abide.

In *Poetaster* (1601) Jonson brings on stage the three Augustan poets Horace, Virgil, and Ovid, in a defence of Horatian (and Jonsonian) satire against the charge of slander and defamation, and dramatizes the aspiration of the poet to fame and immortality. The play is a manifesto for an English Augustanism as monumental as the illustrious products of Augustus' Rome. In the 'Induction' an Ovidian personification of Envy is trampled into the ground by an armed Prologue.[19] In the first scene, Ovid is found reading out his own proud defiance of Envy and boast of his poetic immortality in *Amores* 1. 15, in substantially the translation of Marlowe. Ovid will be disgraced and exiled in the play for adultery with Augustus' daughter, but the continued life of his poetry in English translation is proof of the validity of his claim to fame (and recognition by Jonson of his contemporary Marlowe's claim to a place in the poetic pantheon). Personification turns into reality later in the play when Virgil reads to Augustus (a translation of) his description of the slanderous *Fama* in *Aeneid* 4, to be interrupted by the entrance of an informer bearing a slanderous accusation against Horace. Earlier Augustus has praised the power of poetry to give life beyond the grave to Rome and her monuments, and Horace praises Virgil as supreme in this power:

> And, for his poesy, 'tis so rammed with life
> That it shall gather strength of life with being,
> And live hereafter more admired than now.
> (5. 1. 136–8; Jonson, *Works*, 4. 293)

The masque is one of those Renaissance forms of pageant whose business is praise and fame. Jonson's *The Masque of Queenes* (1609) stages the triumph of good fame, born of virtue and represented by eleven famous queens of legend and history capped by Bel-Anna (Anne of Denmark), over the 'opposites to good Fame', twelve witches embodying twelve vices; the flaming Hell of the witches vanishes and is replaced by the heavenly House of Fame. The published text is accompanied by Jonson's own dense scholarly annotation of the classical and post-classical sources for his and Inigo Jones's invention: Virgil, Ovid, Claudian, and many others enter the mix, including Chaucer's *House of Fame*. The binarism of the antimasque and masque format sharpens the dichotomies that already structure the Virgilian tradition of *fama*.

Milton

John Milton is as susceptible to the frenzy of renown as any author, and conscious of the need to discipline it within the value system of Christianity.[20] The frontispiece to the 1645 *Poems* contains a Virgilan motto averting envy from the poet's bid for fame (*Eclogue* 7. 27–8): 'baccare frontem | cingite, ne uati noceat mala lingua futura' ('garland the poet's head with baccar, so that the evil tongue does not harm the bard to be'). 'Lycidas', the poem that concludes the sequence of poems in English in the 1645 volume, contains a passage that attempts to translate the young poet's ambitions in the matter of earthly fame into a transcendentally anchored heavenly fame, and that includes perhaps the most famous book-of-quotations lines on fame:

> Fame is the spur that the clear spirit doth raise
> (That last infirmity of noble mind)
> To scorn delights, and live laborious days.
> ('Lycidas', ll. 70–2)

'Spur' and 'infirmity' both have classical parallels. 'Spur' (*calcar*) or 'goad' (*stimulus*) is used of the incentive to achieve literary greatness and immortality by Horace (*Ep.* 2. 1. 217–18) and the younger Pliny, for example in a letter to another wealthy *littéra-*

teur that ends: 'I know that you need no goading; but my love for you stirs me to spur you on even though you are already running, as you also do to me. It is a "good strife" when friends incite each other with mutual encouragement to a love for immortality' (*Ep.* 3. 7. 15). Tacitus credits the Stoic martyr Helvidius Priscus with a truly philosophical indifference to external goods, but reports that 'there were some who thought that he was rather too eager for fame, seeing that the desire for glory is last to be shed, even by the wise' (*Hist.* 4. 6. 1).

In his two biblical epics, Milton repeatedly distinguishes between false earthly glory and true heavenly glory, with the longest discrimination placed prominently at the beginning of book 3 of *Paradise Regained* (ll. 1–149). Satan presents the Son of God with classical examples of great fame, Alexander, Scipio, Pompey, Caesar. Jesus' reply is largely based on Christian tradition, but his critique of fame starts with a distinction between true glory and the worthless fame conferred by the 'miscellaneous rabble' that is found in philosophical discussions of fame by Cicero and the younger Seneca.

Milton's biblical tragedy, *Samson Agonistes*, is much concerned with the epic matter of fame. By the end of the play the Old Testament hero and his family have not attained to the sharp distinction between earthly glory and the glory sanctioned by God that is made in *Paradise Regained*. Dalila is not obviously worsted in her *agon* with Samson, and her statement of the relativism of reputation and renown in her personification of Fame has force:

> Fame if not double-faced is double-mouthed,
> And with contrary blast proclaims most deeds,
> On both his wings, one black, the other white,
> Bears greatest names in his wild aery flight.
> (*Samson Agonistes*, ll. 971–4)

The many-tongued flying monster, who had appeared in a more fully Virgilian incarnation, and in an Ovidian House, in the 17-year-old Milton's Latin poem on the Gunpowder Plot (*In quintum Novembris*), has been stripped down to a two-tongued version of herself, and the black/white contrast sums up the dichotomous tendencies of classical *Fama*. Details of Dalila's description are paralleled in Silius Italicus and Martial, but the classical *Fama* has also been filtered through Chaucer's *House of Fame* and Renaissance iconographies and emblem books. As often, Fame here reflects her own status as a figure for a complex literary tradition.

Historiography

Classical and Renaissance historians alike are much concerned with fame, in the shapes of the reputations, good or bad, that they confer on the actors in their histories; of their own fame as authors; and of the propagation and circulation of reports and rumours that often determine the course of history, a point emphasized by Francis Bacon in 'Of Fame, a Fragment', which offers a political reading of Virgil's personification of *Fama*.[21] The exemplary function of historiography, particularly important for the ancient Roman historian, carries over into the Renaissance historians' concern to use fame 'to establish the order of history',[22] working against the disorder of history that is threatened by the unaccountable workings of rumour and fame in Shakespeare's 'Henriad'. Milton observes that the civilizing conqueror 'hath recourse to the aid of eloquence...by whose immutable record his noble deeds...becoming fixed and durable against the forces of years and generations, he fails not to continue through all posterity, over envy, death, and time, also victorious' (*History of Britain*; *Prose Works*, 5. 40). The historian's duty to write nothing but 'an image of the truth' is urged by Edmund Bolton in *Hypercritica*, with the promise that such a historian 'shall thereby, both in present and to posterity, live with honour, through the justice of his monuments',[23] as proved by Cremutius Cordus, the Roman historian who defied Tiberius by calling the tyrannicide Cassius the last of the Romans, and whose work survived book-burning as a reproach to his accusers, an episode immortalized by Tacitus (*Annals* 4. 34–5) and by Ben Jonson in the translation of the Tacitean passage put in the mouth of Cordus in *Sejanus His Fall* (3. 407–60; l. 456 'Posterity pays every man his honour').

Ben Jonson's sonnet 'The Minde of the Front', accompanying the frontispiece to Walter Raleigh's *The History of the World* (1614), puts fame at the centre of the historian's task:

> From death and dark oblivion, (near the same)
> The mistress of man's life, grave history,
> Raising the world to good, or evil fame,
> Doth vindicate it to eternity.
>
> (Jonson, *Works*, 8. 175)

'Mistress of man's life' is the Ciceronian tag *magistra uitae* (Cic. *De oratore* 2. 36). At the top of the frontispiece are the two paired and opposing figures of *Fama Bona* and *Fama Mala*, the former in a burst of light, with wings adorned with ears, eyes, and tongues, the latter set amid dark clouds, with her whole body and dress covered in spots, derived from the eyes that frequently cover the person of *Fama*. Both are ultimately descended from the Virgilian *Fama*. 'Eternity' is represented by the eye of God, all-seeing and all-knowing, in a Christian order of things the final authority that pagan *Fama* never can be.

Notes

1. For fuller discussion of many of the topics in this chapter, see Philip Hardie, *Rumour and Renown: Representations of Fama in Western Literature* (Cambridge, 2012). Edwin B. Benjamin, 'Fame, Poetry, and the Order of History in the Literature of

the English Renaissance', *Studies in the Renaissance*, 6 (1959), 64–84, is a valuable survey. There is a wealth of material in Leo Braudy, *The Frenzy of Renown: Fame and its History* (With a New Afterword) (New York, 1997). For a wider survey of fame in early modern English culture, see Keith Thomas, 'Fame and the Afterlife', in *The Ends of Life: Roads to Fulfilment in Early Modern England* (Oxford, 2009), ch. 7.

2. Foreshadowing a favourite Renaissance comparison of the power of pen and sword: R. J. Clements, 'Pen and Sword in Renaissance Emblem Literature', *Modern Language Quarterly*, 5 (1944), 131–41.
3. On the longer history of metempsychosis as an image for poetic succession and for a claim to poetic fame equal to that of great poets of the past, see Stuart Gillespie, 'Literary Afterlives: Metempsychosis from Ennius to Jorge Luis Borges', in Philip Hardie and Helen Moore (eds), *Classical Literary Careers and their Reception* (Oxford, 2010), 209–25.
4. The phrase that supplies the title for Patrick Cheney, *Spenser's Famous Flight: A Renaissance Idea of a Literary Career* (Toronto and Buffalo, 1993), with major discussions of Spenser's dealings in fame.
5. See Mary Lascelles, 'The Rider on the Winged Horse', in H. Davis and H. Gardner (eds), *Elizabethan and Jacobean Studies Presented to Frank Percy Wilson in Honour of his Seventieth Birthday* (Oxford, 1959), 173–98 (189–95 on fame).
6. Robert J. Clements, 'The Cult of the Poet in Renaissance Emblem Literature', *PMLA* 59 (1944), 672–85 (680–1).
7. See Cheney, *Spenser's Famous Flight*, 8.
8. Thomas H. Cain, *Praise in The Faerie Queene* (Lincoln, NE, 1978); O. B. Hardison, *The Enduring Monument: A Study of the Idea of Praise in Renaissance Literary Theory and Practice* (Chapel Hill, NC, 1962). On the earlier tradition, see Craig Kallendorf, *In Praise of Aeneas: Virgil and Epideictic Rhetoric in the Early Italian Renaissance* (Hanover, NE, 1989).
9. Philip Hardie, 'Strategies of Praise: The *Aeneid* and Renaissance Epic', in G. Urso (ed.), *Dicere laudes: Elogio, Comunicazione e Creazione del Consenso* (Cividale del Friuli and Milan, 2011), 383–99.
10. See Frances A. Yates, *Astraea: The Imperial Theme in the Sixteenth Century* (1975).
11. On Shakespeare's negotiation of classical fame and Christian glory in *Sonnet* 55, see Patrick Cheney, *Shakespeare's Literary Authorship* (Cambridge, 2008), 228–30.
12. See Richard A. McCabe, *The Pillars of Eternity: Time and Providence in The Faerie Queene* (Blackrock, Co. Dublin, 1989), 72–9, 'Time vs Fame'. On Spenser's reworking of Ovidian themes of immortality and mutability, see Michael Holohan, '*Iamque opus exegi*: Ovid's Changes and Spenser's Brief Epic of Mutability', *English Literary Renaissance*, 6 (1976), 244–70.
13. Jonathan Bate, *Shakespeare and Ovid* (Oxford, 1993), 87–100, on Ovid in the *Sonnets*.
14. See Heather Dubrow, 'A Mirror for Complaints: Shakespeare's Lucrece and Generic Tradition', in Barbara K. Lewalski (ed.), *Renaissance Genres: Essays on Theory, History, and Interpretation* (Cambridge, MA, 1986), 399–417 (404–7, on the moral and emotional consequences of too deep an interest in fame).
15. See Anthony Miller, *Roman Triumphs and Early Modern English Culture* (Basingstoke, 2001).
16. D. J. Gordon, 'Name and Fame: Shakespeare's *Coriolanus*', in D. J. Gordon, *The Renaissance Imagination*, ed. S. Orgel (Berkeley and Los Angeles, 1975), 203–19.
17. Benjamin, 'Fame, Poetry and the Order of History', 64.
18. See Victoria Moul, *Jonson, Horace and the Classical Tradition* (Cambridge, 2010), ch. 1.
19. On the importance of envy for Jonson's sense of himself as an author, see

Lynn S. Meskell, *Ben Jonson and Envy* (Cambridge, 2009).

20. On Milton on fame and glory, see, e.g. Irene Samuel, *Plato and Milton* (Ithaca, NY 1947).
21. Martin Dzelzainis, '"The Feminine Part of Every Rebellion": Francis Bacon on Sedition and Libel and the Beginning of Ideology', *Huntington Library Quarterly*, 69 (2006), 139–52.
22. In the phrase of Benjamin, 'Fame, Poetry, and the Order of History', 76.
23. In Joel E. Spingarn (ed.), *Critical Essays of the Seventeenth Century* (Oxford, 1908), I. 93–4.

PART II

Genre

CHAPTER 9

Pastoral and Georgic

HELEN COOPER

Pastoral literature became an extraordinary phenomenon in the century covered by this chapter. All the great writers turned their attention to the mode at some point in their careers, in a wide variety of genres. Spenser and Milton wrote eclogues; Shakespeare and Jonson wrote pastoral plays; Sidney and Greene set romances in the shepherd world; an entire anthology, *Englands Helicon*, was devoted to pastoral lyrics, Marlowe's and Raleigh's among them; and scores of other writers added their own contributions. The degree of classical influence in all this varied widely, but two characteristics stand out. Almost every example showed some kind of nostalgia or desire for a Golden Age of innocence and contentment on the model drawn by Ovid's *Metamorphoses* and Virgil's *Georgics*, whether by imaginative recreation, or by lament or satire on its absence;[1] and a high proportion of the non-dramatic works placed the poet himself at the centre of his work, usually implicitly, sometimes explicitly, as Virgil had done in his *Eclogues*. Those same qualities, however, militated against an equal acceptance of georgic. Physical labour was all too harsh a part of the brazen or postlapsarian world, and it was too much present to make space for nostalgia or desire. It was easy for the shepherd–singer to become a metaphor for the courtly or urban poet within the world of the imagination, but the essentially non-fictional mode of georgic resisted any such treatment. No socially aspirant poet of the period wanted to be associated with the men who actually got their hands muddy, and the genre never found a distinctive English equivalent.

The expansion of the Renaissance interest in pastoral rapidly left ancient precedents far behind, but the quintessentially classical genre of the eclogue remained at its centre. It was that that sixteenth-century theorists had in mind when they discussed pastoral, and the classical eclogue meant Virgil. No poet, moreover, ever wrote an eclogue accidentally. Virgil himself was consciously working in a poetic tradition deriving from Theocritus, and early modern poets were equally consciously working in a tradition deriving from him. Their knowledge of the tradition behind him was more limited, and Greek pastoral had little influence compared with Latin.

The restriction of the classical pastoral tradition to Virgil did not, however, imply narrow imitation. The understanding of what his *Eclogues* meant had been altered and enlarged over the many centuries of commentary and composition that had intervened between the Augustan age and the Elizabethan. Commentators from Servius forward (fourth century CE) had variously emphasized his concern not only with poetry and the poet but with political panegyric and elegy, with the moral value of the simple life and the hardships of exile. Allegorical interpretations of the poems became increasingly standard, and that *Eclogue* 4 was a messianic prophecy came to be so generally accepted that Virgil himself was enlisted as a prophet of Christ alongside Moses and Isaiah. The mis-etymologizing of 'eclogue' (a choice or select poem) as 'aeglogue', deriving from αἰγ- and λογος, 'goatish speech', current by the ninth century, further encouraged a use of the genre for satire.[2] The neo-Latin eclogues of Baptista Spagnuolo Mantuanus, the 'good old Mantuan' cited by Holofernes in *Love's Labours Lost*, were a key text in transmitting such conceptions of the eclogue, as his *Adolescentia* (so called because he had started work on them in his youth, in the 1460s, though they were first printed only in 1498) became a standard text in schoolrooms well into the seventeenth century. Their pedagogic function stemmed from Mantuan's moralizing (often with a distinct antifeminist slant) as well as the comparative simplicity of his Latin, and his descriptions of harsh weather were more immediately recognizable than Virgil's idealized landscapes. Early modern poets thus found in the eclogue a pattern by which they could establish their own names, and a model for writing ambitious, wide-ranging, and politically engaged work, often giving a realistic surface to an allegorical or allusive core, which took them far beyond the classical tradition as Virgil would have understood it.

For all their declarations of homage, early modern eclogues are, therefore, not very like Virgil's. Such declarations are often coded in variants on the opening of his first eclogue, with the shepherd playing on a slender pipe under the shade of a tree, sometimes set in contrast with a herdsman suffering hardship; or of his fourth, his 'paulo maiora canamus', 'let us sing of somewhat greater things', which is commonly invoked to signal subject matter of major social significance. The shepherd world, in early modern pastoral, is always to some degree metaphorical, a way of simplifying a complex world or a complex society.[3] The nature of the metaphor had been influenced over many centuries not only by Virgil's praise of Augustus in his opening eclogue and what was universally taken as his elegy on Julius Caesar in the fifth, but by the influence of the Bible. For Christian writers, the shepherd was not primarily a singer, but a man who cared for a metaphorical flock: a pastor, or even Christ as the Good Shepherd. A high proportion of English Renaissance eclogues, including many of the best known—Spenser's *Shepheardes Calender* (1579), Milton's *Lycidas* (1635)—made the connection as a matter of course. The overlap between the biblical and the classical *pastor* changed the balance of the eclogue significantly. The biblical shepherd was based on the literal herdsman, with all his responsibilities and hardships. Looking after the sheep scarcely figures in Virgil, but the state of the flock becomes the crucial measure of the shepherd in a large number of the eclogues and related pastoral works written in both the Middle Ages and the Renaissance. When, in the run-up to the Civil War, Francis Quarles named the bad shepherds of his fourth eclogue Nullifidius and Pseudo-Catholicus, the effect was deliberately over the top, the poetic equivalent of a political cartoon, but his readers would not have been puzzled.[4] The opposite tendency, towards idyllic fantasy, became increasingly evident as the period progressed, and especially in genres beyond the eclogue. Pastoral romances and plays, strongly influenced by Italian and Spanish models, became increasingly fashionable from the end of the sixteenth century. The enlargement of the mode led Jacobean theorists to recognize the distinction between pastoral form and pastoral content that had been largely absent from their Elizabethan forebears.[5]

The history of georgic followed a very different trajectory. A ploughman carried none of the cachet of the literary herdsman.[6] The shepherd furthermore came to be not only the central metaphor for the poet, but the type of the contemplative life. The ploughman, by contrast, represented the active life, the life of labour. Tilling the soil, moreover, was inflicted on humankind by God as punishment for the Fall; and, in the generation after Adam, it was the shepherd Abel, not the ploughman Cain, who was the more acceptable to God. The counterpart to the shepherd swain was the altogether more derogatory rustic clown, and the classical literature of agriculture was not sufficient to counterbalance such perceptions. Hesiod was highly thought of by those who knew him: Richard Field, the Stratford-born publisher of *Venus and Adonis*, printed a Greek *Works and Days* in 1590, one of only a handful of Greek texts to be printed in England in the period, and George Chapman translated it in 1618 under the title *The Georgicks of Hesiod*. Neither that nor the *Georgics* themselves, however, affected the common image of the ploughman as the type of brute rusticity, not least because the life they describe remains so stubbornly literal. Two fourteenth-century poems known in the sixteenth century, Langland's *Piers Plowman* (printed under Edward VI) and Chaucer's portrait of the Ploughman in the General Prologue to the *Canterbury Tales* (available in multiple editions), presented the ploughman who works for the love of God and his neighbour as the bedrock of society, Langland going so far, in a break from the Good Shepherd tradition almost unprecedented before or since, as to make him a figure for Christ; but the early modern reaction to labourers was one of general disdain. Aestheticization was as rare as idealization: the maps to Michael Drayton's paean to the land and landscapes of Britain, *Poly-Olbion* (1612, 1622), decorate the country's uplands with shepherds and its forests with huntresses, but there is no comparable personification available to mark agricultural land.

Both the *Eclogues* and the *Georgics* were nonetheless translated several times, though pastoral predominated.[7] The *Eclogues* were often used as a school text, though usually only after the pupils had worked their way through Mantuan, and the translations were designed with the needs of learners in mind. They were first translated by Abraham Fleming in 1575, and in 1589 by 'A.F.'—fairly certainly Fleming again, though the translation is entirely new, into unrhymed instead of rhymed fourteeners and with different paratextual material. Further translations followed by John Brinsley (1620), William Lisle (1628), and John Biddle (1634). Translations of individual eclogues included William Webbe's translation of *Eclogues* 1 and 2, designed to illustrate the metrics of quantitative verse, in his *Discourse of English Poetry* of 1586; Abraham Fraunce's of *Eclogue* 2, made as a preamble to a logical analysis in his *Lawiers Logike* of 1588; and, in 1658, James Harrington's of the eclogues concerned with enforced exile, 1 and 9, together with a commentary on the best principles of government.[8] The *Georgics* were first translated by A.F. in his 1589 volume; Thomas May produced a free-standing translation of the work in 1628; and John Ogilby included both *Eclogues* and *Georgics* in his much-reprinted complete *Works of Publius Vergilius Maro*, first published in 1649 and revised in 1654. Translations of selected passages of the *Georgics* were made by Barnabe Googe, to supplement his translation of Conrad Heresbach's *Four Books of Husbandry* in 1577, and by Richard Crashaw (the coming of spring) and Sir Richard Fanshawe (the battle of the bulls) in the mid-seventeenth century.[9] Translations of the Greek eclogusts were more unusual. Three of the *Sixe Idillia* of 1588 are of poems wrongly ascribed to Theocritus, and Sir Edward Sherburne published translations of four of the *Idylls* (15, 20, 27, and 30) in 1651, but a full translation had to wait until after the Restoration. The year 1651 also saw translations from Moschus and Bion, including their pastoral elegies, by Thomas Stanley.[10]

The Eclogue Tradition

The first formal eclogues in English were written by Alexander Barclay in the very early years of Henry VIII's reign, and put into final shape around 1513–14. His choice of the eclogue is a sign of the new humanist interests, and he lists his illustrious predecessors in the genre in his Prologue: Theocritus, Virgil, Theodulus (the ninth- or tenth-century author of an eclogue that advocated Christian doctrine over Classical mythology, and that was still regularly used as a school text), Petrarch (who had written a set of Latin eclogues with a strong element of antipapal invective), and Mantuan. He is very unlikely to have known Theocritus at first hand, and not necessarily Petrarch either; and, although he probably knew Virgil, it does not show much. His primary model was Mantuan, with his readiness to incorporate a moral or satirical take on his society and a more realistic image of shepherd life, though Barclay's world is still harsher. In his winter, 'the fields be near intolerable', and his herdsmen are poor, with threadbare clothing and their hair growing through the holes in their hoods.[11] Barclay's poems were given fresh dissemination through a reprint in 1570, by which time interest in the eclogue form was becoming more widespread. Barnabe Googe published a set of eclogues in 1563 that together incorporate love, the rejection of love, and the horrors of the Marian burnings of Cranmer, Latimer, and

Ridley. The same decade saw three neo-Latin eclogues by Giles Fletcher, two of which are Protestant polemic and the third an allegory of college politics.[12] George Turberville translated Mantuan's *Adolescentia* in 1567, and Fleming produced his first version of Virgil's *Bucolics* in 1575. By the time Spenser turned his attention to the genre, therefore, he could expect to find a well-prepared readership.

Spenser's connection to Virgil goes well beyond his choice of an eclogue series as the form of *The Shepheardes Calender*.[13] The work owes more to the *Eclogues* than do any of its English predecessors, but his debts to Mantuan and the French Clément Marot are still more in evidence. His choice of genre nonetheless announces his intention of following a poetic career on the Virgilian model, by which pastoral is the first step on the road to epic.[14] For the first time in English poetry, an author presents poetry as his sole vocation, and Virgil is the exemplar by which he authorizes his declaration. The point is made first in E.K.'s dedicatory epistle, where it is pointed out that the eclogue has functioned for poets since classical times 'to prove theyr tender wyngs, before they make a greater flyght'.[15] The idea is taken up within the *Calender* itself, when in 'October' Piers urges Cuddie to raise his sights from 'the base and viler clowne' to write in heroic mode of 'bloody Mars' and 'doubted Knights', just as the 'Romish *Tityrus*' had done (ll. 37, 39, 41, 55). The Virgilian pattern is repeated again at the start of *The Faerie Queene*, which borrows the spurious opening of the *Aeneid* widespread in Renaissance editions:

> Lo I the man, whose Muse whylome did maske,
> As time her taught, in lowly Shephards weeds,
> Am now enforst a farre unfitter taske,
> For trumpets sterne to chaunge mine Oaten reeds.
> (1. Proem 1–4)

In book 6 Spenser introduces himself under his pastoral pseudonym of Colin Clout (deriving both from Marot's poetic persona of Colin, and Skelton's self-naming as the satirist Colin Clout); but, whereas the poet of the *Calender* could describe himself as 'Immerito', undeserving, and his poem as being of unknown parentage, Spenser can now ask triumphantly, 'who knowes not *Colin Clout*?' (6. 10. 16). As an epic poet, he has earned his fame, by his long apprenticeship from the *Calender* forwards.

That the eclogue is consciously written within a tradition is emphasized from the moment the reader opens the *Calender*. Like Barclay, and like a good many later poets, E.K. spells out the history and credentials of the genre, listing Spenser's precursors and explaining the etymology of *aeglogue*; he also justifies his archaic language on the grounds of rhetorical decorum, as being appropriately rustic, though others, including Sidney, were more sceptical. The format of the volume was likewise modelled on a number of editions of the *Eclogues*, with a woodcut at the head of each poem, and, for the first time for a poem written in English, a commentary that explained hard terms, pointed out rhetorical figures, and explained classical references. Virgilian commentaries similarly identified allusions to his own times, but here, whenever the material becomes contemporary and therefore dangerous, E.K. will refer darkly just to 'the party herein meant' ('September', introduction to Gloss) or that 'the personage is secrete, and to me altogether unknowne' ('November', Argument). This close engagement of the poems with concerns of greater weight than the overt shepherd subject matter was fully in keeping with the understanding of the genre presented by contemporary theorists—and theorizing on the eclogue was an even newer exercise in English at this date than composing them. Sidney, Webbe, and Puttenham, all writing in the 1580s, all make the same points: that the eclogue should never be dismissed as mere rustic poetry, and that the shepherd world is a disguise for higher matters, adopted to protect the poet. In Sidney's formulation:

> Is the poor pipe disdained, which sometimes out of Melibeus' mouth can show the misery of people under hard lords and ravening soldiers? And again by Tityrus, what blessedness is derived to them that lie lowest from the goodness of them that sit highest? Sometimes under the pretty tales of wolves and sheep, can include the whole consideration of wrongdoing and patience; sometimes show that contentions for trifles can get but a trifling victory.[16]

Virgil's first eclogue is easily recognizable from that description, and his singing-matches only slightly less so; but the idea that the eclogue is a good vehicle for allegorical beast fables comes from a more medieval tradition, represented in the *Calender* in 'May'. Webbe warns against taking eclogues at face value (as 'rude and homely, as the usual talk of simple clowns'), and stresses their usefulness as vehicles for praise or satire; Puttenham asserts that the genre was a late invention, 'not of purpose to counterfeit or represent the rustical matter of loves and communication, but under the veil of homely persons and in rude speeches to insinuate and glance at greater matters, and such as perchance had not been safe to have been disclosed in any other sort'.[17] The phrase 'greater matters' would have been immediately recognizable to his readers as an allusion to the 'paulo maiora' of Virgil's *Eclogue* 4, with its justification of the expansion of pastoral subject matter to high politics.

The Shepheardes Calender illustrates very clearly both how much the early modern eclogue owed to the classical tradition, and how much it broke away. The form of a shepherd monologue, dialogue, or, more rarely, a dialogue with a third framing speaker is taken from Virgil; so is the presence, inset within such poems, of a singing-match, or sometimes a song ascribed to an absent singer, representing the poet himself (most of the *Eclogues* are designed as containers for poetry of this kind, as are 'April', 'August', and 'November'). Unrequited love is a commonplace theme, in 'January' as in Virgil, *Eclogue* 2, though the love in Renaissance English is most often heterosexual; anything that appeared otherwise, including some lines from 'January' and Richard Barnfield's avowedly homoerotic *Affectionate Shepherd, containing the Love of Daphnis for Ganymede* (1594), was excused by an appeal to the classics.[18] The most consciously crafted poetry can take the form of elegy, and the elegies may well (like Virgil, *Eclogue* 5, and 'November'), shift from mourning to rejoicing halfway through. Political panegyric, authorized by the praise of Augustus in Virgil, *Eclogue* 1, is taken up and expanded in 'April'. And there are closer verbal allusions too, as in the opening to 'June', with its dialogue between one shepherd in an ideal landscape and another who is a homeless exile, as in the opening of Virgil, *Eclogue* 1:

> HOBBINOL. Lo *Colin*, here the place, whose pleasaunt syte
> From other shades hath weand my wandring mynde.
> Tell me, what wants me here, to worke delyte?...
>
> COLLIN. O happy *Hobbinoll*, I blesse thy state,
> That Paradise hast found, whych *Adam* lost.
> Here wander may thy flock early or late,
> Withouten dreade of Wolves to bene ytost:
> Thy lovely layes here mayst thou freely boste.
> But I unhappy man, whom cruell fate,
> And angry Gods pursue from coste to coste,
> Can nowhere fynd, to shroude my lucklesse pate.
>
> ('June' ll. 1–3, 9–16)

The differences are, however, as striking as the similarities. That the landscape is a mirror of the shepherd–poet's mind remains implicit in Virgil; here, it has come to the surface (and is commented on in 'January' l. 20), so that the shade and the wolves have become features of the imagination, and the world Colin inhabits is explicitly a fallen one, where age, disappointment, and moral concerns weigh heavy. The Muses, Pan, and Phoebus may potentially inhabit this landscape in place of Adam, but Virgil himself is explicitly displaced by a different 'God of shepheards, *Tityrus*' ('June', l. 81): not Virgil, despite the name, but Chaucer, the master-poet of the English tradition. He is the first poet to be cited within the *Calender* (in the first sentence of E.K.'s prefatory matter, and in 'February', ll. 91–9), and that Spenser gives him the place one would expect the classical poet to hold is a striking declaration of his dual allegiance, Latin and vernacular, for all his choice of the eclogue form.

The opening-up of the *Calender* to other influences apart from the Virgilian shows itself continually, in both form and content. 'March' is loosely based on Bion's fourth idyll, but its metre is the old-fashioned tail-rhyme; 'August' contains not only Colin's Italianate sestina, a new form in English, but the downward extension of the singing-match into the lightheartedness of folksong. The more satirical eclogues eschew fine poetry or recognized models of poetic language in favour of rougher, dialect-inflected modes of speech. From the early Middle Ages forwards, the singing-match had tended to be conflated with the debate;[19] here, 'July' continues that debate tradition, its opposing arguments for the virtues of hills or valleys being borrowed from Mantuan. And that the pastor has a potentially Christian function is invoked in poem after poem, most strongly in 'May', 'July', and 'September'. The paratextual material of the work may invoke Virgil in layout, but the woodcuts show a more contemporary world, with the shepherds equipped with bagpipes rather than panpipes or 'oaten reeds', and the pictures for summer include miniature vignettes of the labours of the months in the background. The shepherds' names, moreover—Hobbinol, Thenot, Morrell—are often not exactly English, but they are certainly not classical either.

The somewhat equivocal relationship of the *Calender* to the *Eclogues* is nicely illustrated by two translations of them back into Latin: one, the *Calendarium Pastorum* by John Dove, of *c.*1584, survives in a single presentation manuscript; the second, Theodore Bathurst's *Calendarium Pastorale,* written shortly after 1608, survives in five manuscripts and three prints.[20] Dove signals his debt to Spenser immediately by retaining the Diggons and Cuddies of the original, though he gives the names Latin endings; Bathurst reverts to Virgil's use of Theocritean names, with Colin becoming Alexis and Rosalind the hackneyed Phyllis. He retains the one Virgilian name that Spenser uses, 'Tityrus', for Chaucer, but its implications are largely lost against the background of similar nomenclature. Both use the quantitative hexameter as the basis of their versions, differentiating only 'March' and the songs, but in doing so they lose the virtuoso range of Spenser's stanzaic and metrical forms. The use of Latin also enforces not only a smoothing-out of the archaisms and oddities of the language of the original (Bathurst's version was indeed praised for making Spenser more comprehensible),[21] but the loss of the distinct vocabularies of different characters and different eclogues. Both translations were apparently made to impress patrons, but that it was Bathurst's version, more immediately recognizable in Virgilian terms, that acquired a significant reading public through to the eighteenth century is a measure of what Spenser's readers wanted to find in him but needed another writer to supply.

Dove's and Bathurst's reversion to hexameters is the inverse aspect of the debate in England over whether the best prosody consisted in classical quantitative or English stress- and syllable-based metres. This was at its most intense in the decade after the publication of the *Calender*, and both the brevity and the impeccable classical antecedents of the eclogue made it an especially appropriate form for experiment. Spenser was prepared to debate the issue, but if he ever tried quantitative verse, none of his attempts survives. Sidney, by contrast, used the interludes of pastoral poetry that divide up the narrative sections of his *Arcadia* for just such experimentation. The 'real' shepherds sing in English measures, and Sidney gives them some fine poems: they may not be high-born, but they are still good shepherd–poets. The aristocrats in disguise set themselves apart by choosing quantitative measure for their own poems. The increasingly obscure verse forms are named in both the manuscript and the printed versions—hexameters, asclepiadics, phaleuciacs, and so on—and symbols for the scansion are also given at the head of each poem in some of the manuscripts of Sidney's first version, the *Old Arcadia*. He did not, however, use classical metres for the poetry he wrote outside the quasi-Greek setting of the romance. Two attempts were made at eclogue series in quantitative verse: Abraham

Fraunce 'paraphrastically translated' Thomas Watson's Latin *Lamentations of Amyntas* into quantitative hexameters;[22] and Francis Sabie wrote an original set of eclogues, *Pans Pipes* (1595), basically in hexameters but incorporating a variety of other metres too.[23] At their best, both poets negotiate well the difficulties of transposing length-based metrics to a stress-based language, though both make some compromises between the two. Sabie, for instance, has an attractive account of fowling in winter:

> With milk-white snow when th'earth was all hidden
> Forth with a fowler he was, to the wellsprings and to the fountains
> And to the running lakes, whose ever moveable waters
> Frost never alter could, there for the long-billed hernshaw [heron]
> And little snipe did he set snares.
>
> (*Pans Pipes*, Eclogue 2. 59–63)

The winter setting, along with an openness to misogyny where love is concerned, a tendency to moralizing, and his choice of names nonetheless make clear that Sabie's model is as much Mantuan as Virgil. He claims in a prefatory address to his book that it is not only about, but intended for, country folk; but that the address is itself composed in Latin hexameters makes the pretence even more implausible than usual. Like Dove and Bathurst, he is out to show off.

The generation of eclogists after Spenser tended to move further away from immediate classical influence, with a generous element of social satire and unpleasant weather. Colin–Spenser is frequently cited as a poetic model, and Philisides–Sidney is much remembered; Tityrus–Virgil remains largely unmentioned, and Eliza–Elizabeth moves into the space created by Virgil for Augustus. The group of Spenserian poets led by Michael Drayton and writing largely under James I tended to write allusively, with their eyes increasingly on their fellow-poets. Drayton cast himself as Rowland, in his eclogue set first published in 1593 and revised in 1606; the choice of such a name indicates a commitment more to the Spenserian than the classical tradition. He was one of the most prolific pastoral poets of the era, and his address to the reader preceding the 1619 edition of his *Pastorals: Containing Eclogues* offers a clear summary of contemporary definitions.[24] He homes in on the paradox that, while the ostensible subject matter of pastorals should be 'base, or low', in practice 'the most high and most noble matters of the world may be shadowed in them, and for certain sometimes are'; and he claims to honour Virgil most, not as a poet, but as a prophet. On the problem of low style versus high matter, he notes that decorum, appropriateness of language, should be maintained, which is 'not to be exceeded without leave, or without at least fair warning', as authorized by Virgil, *Eclogue* 4. He also notes God's blessing bestowed on pastoral poetry in the angels' song to the shepherds at the Nativity. His later pastorals experiment with a variety of non-eclogue forms, and diverge into increasingly bitter political satire, on the one side, and idyllic fantasizing, on the other.

Classical Forms: The Pastoral Elegy

The one element that remained faithful to its classical roots through all this was the use of the eclogue itself. Even its political turn was taken as authorized by Virgil, as were, more obviously, some genres that he had incorporated within it—political panegyric, especially as focused on Elizabeth; discussions of patronage, or its lack; the birth song; singing-matches and inset songs; and the lament, the pastoral elegy. All of these, however, moved some way away from their Virgilian roots. Where panegyric was concerned, Spenser's 'April' tended to displace Virgil as the principal model for English poets, not least because it was more extensive than the summary panegyric of Octavian in *Eclogue* 1; Drayton's third eclogue, in praise of Beta, is one of many poems to follow its lead. The issue of patronage allowed both for complaint at its absence—a theme touched on in Virgil 9 and sounded recurrently from Mantuan and Barclay forwards—and for turning the eclogue to the topic of poetry and the poet himself, as in Spenser's 'October'. The messianic associations of Virgil 4 became almost inseparable from the birth song. Francis Quarles produced an eclogue on the Nativity itself as the one non-satirical poem of his *Shepheards Oracles* (*Eclogue* 5), to highlight the corruption of the clergy laid out in the surrounding poems. Robert Herrick's 'Pastoral on the Birth of Prince Charles' has two shepherds and a shepherdess compare the prince's birth to Christ's (it is greeted by the appearance of a star like that of the Wise Men, and 'golden angels' celebrate his birth with song), and they agree to bring him country gifts in the manner of the shepherds of the mystery plays: a garland, Virgilian 'oaten pipes', and a sheep-hook to symbolize that he is a shepherd of his people.[25] The singing-match took a more distinctively classical turn, as poetic contests returned to the eclogue alongside the debates that had almost entirely displaced them in medieval pastoral. Sidney has a particularly complex one in the *Arcadia*, 'Come, Dorus, Come', in which the best of the shepherd–singers challenges the prince disguised as a shepherd in an aggressively complex series of rhyme patterns;[26] Spenser's 'August' offers a thoroughly rustic duet, the 'Hey ho holiday' of Perigot and Willy, but follows it with Cuddy's singing of a magnificent sestina of Colin's. A high proportion of Drayton's eclogues contain inset songs; the ninth of the revised version gives two dialogue love songs, the first folksong style, the second more overtly poetic, and then a final song from Rowland himself, with the rest of the shepherds acting as chorus. His eighth eclogue (fourth in the revised version) follows up a eulogy of the long-gone 'Saturn's Reign', the Golden Age, with the tail-rhyme story of Dowsabell, a riff on Chaucer's romance parody 'Sir Thopas' now relocated to the shepherd world.

The pastoral elegy is probably the best-known form of the eclogue now, and it was the Virgilian form that was taken up with the most enthusiasm by early modern poets.[27] The first use of the term seems to have been Spenser's, in the subtitle given to 'Astrophel', his lament for Sidney, as 'a pastoral elegy'. His most imitated elegy, however, was 'November', on the death of the shepherdess Dido—clearly associated with Elizabeth, through its echoes of 'April' and Dido's alternative name of Elissa.[28] He takes an elegy of Clément Marot's as his immediate model, but both poets follow the pattern of Virgil's *Eclogue* 5, on the death of Daphnis, with mourning being superseded by rejoicing. Whatever the contemporary reference of 'November', its potential to serve as the basis for elegies when the queen did indeed die was picked up by other poets later.[29] One of the finest poems in Sidney's *Arcadia* is an elegy on the apparent death of the king Basilius, 'Since that to death is gone the shepherd high' (Sidney, *Poems*, 125–9): this takes the alternative movement of the elegy, derived more from Moschus' 'Lament for Bion' than Virgil, *Eclogue* 5, in its contrasting of the cycle of nature with the finality of death for nature's 'best child', man (and Sidney even builds into the imagery of the poem the irony that Basilius will in fact return to life). That Sidney had presented himself as the shepherd-knight Philisides encouraged an outpouring of pastoral elegies after his death. Others who inspired such elegies included Sir Francis Walsingham, the Earl of Essex, and Henry, Prince of Wales.[30] Rare exceptions to the insistently homosocial world of the eclogue and its poets can be found in some elegies. Elizabeth was exceptional by virtue of her office, but Spenser's *Daphnaida* is a lament for Lady Douglas Howard (a female counterpart to the deceased Daphnis of Theocritus and Virgil), and the 'Doleful Lay of Clorinda' inset within his 'Astrophel' is put in the mouth of, and may possibly have been written by, Sidney's sister Mary. William Drummond of Hawthornden also wrote a lament for a woman, in which the bereaved Damon grieves in thoroughly classical fashion that

> Woods cut again do grow,
> Bud doth the rose and daisy, winter done,
> But we, once dead, no more do see the sun.[31]

The exclusion of any Christian consolation is unusual; most of his contemporaries allow for resurrection, on the model of Daphnis's apotheosis in Virgil, *Eclogue* 5, even if the departed soul is conducted there by apparently pagan routes. Two seventeenth-century writers illustrate that process particularly clearly: Thomas Randolph and John Milton. They were contemporaries as students at Cambridge, but Randolph's early death, in 1635 at the age of 29, extinguished what was widely regarded at the time as the most promising poetic career in England. His 'Eclogue Occasioned by Two Doctors Disputing upon Predestination' does not sound the most promising place to look for evidence of classical reception, but in practice it manages to absorb many of the attributes the genre had acquired over the centuries—debate, an overt doctrinal element, allegorical wolves and foxes—into a genuinely Virgilian model of pastoral.[32] The debate between Tityrus and Alexis as to why Pan should allow one lamb to be born 'black as jet, the other white as snow' (that is, predestined to damnation, or as one of the elect) is rapidly put a stop to by Thyrsis, who points out that

> To your vain piping on so deep a reed
> The lambkins listen, but forget to feed:

the shift up from the *tenuis avena* to *paulo maiora* means that the main function of the good shepherd, to feed his sheep, is being overlooked by these over-subtle pastors. Rather, 'it gentle swains befits of Love to sing'—that is, of Christ. His birth offers the model for contentment with little, the shepherd garland is replaced by the crown of thorns, and the Golden Age life of plenty without labour is transformed into:

> He press'd no grapes, nor prun'd the fruitful vine,
> But could of water make a brisker wine.

The shepherdesses Amaryllis and 'sunburnt Thestylis' are summoned to repair their beauty in the balsam flowing from his side, and 'love-sick Amyntas', whom Watson had established as the type of the wretched lover, is promised healing. Randolph's account of Love's death gives way not to a Virgilian apotheosis but to the Resurrection:

> Now Love is dead; Oh no, he never dies;
> Three days he sleeps, and then again doth rise
> (Like fair Aurora from the eastern bay).

The eclogue ends, like so many eclogues, with nightfall, but very differently inflected:

> Good night to all; for the great night is come;
> Flocks to your folds, and shepherds hie you home!
> Tomorrow morning, when we all have slept,
> Pan's cornet's blown, and the great sheepshears kept.

The shearing feast in other pastoral texts is an occasion for merrymaking; here, it also has something of the *dies irae* about it too: the conventional nightfall is the prelude to an apocalyptic dawn. Despite Thyrsis' rejection of the deep reed, the eclogue's embrace of Christian doctrine shows Randolph navigating with remarkable subtlety the possibilities of classical pastoral to embrace the whole salvation of humankind.

Randolph's poem may have been one of the inspirations behind what must be the best-known pastoral elegy in the English language, Milton's *Lycidas*.[33]

This too uses the analogy of the sun rising from the sea for its image of resurrection, and, although the Christian elements occupy much less space, not least imaginative space, in Milton's poem than in Randolph's, ecclesiastical matters were an integral part of his conception: as the heading to the work that he added in 1645 puts it: 'In this monody the author bewails a learned friend, unfortunately drowned in his passage from Chester on the Irish Seas, 1637. And by occasion foretells the ruin of our corrupted clergy then in their height' (*Poems*, 239). In practice, both the nature of Lycidas' afterlife as imagined within the poem and the condemnation of the corrupted clergy play a subordinate role to the shaping of Milton's own poetic career. This is the major preoccupation too of his later Latin pastoral elegy on the death of his friend Charles Diodati, the *Epitaphium Damonis*. Both poems are written overtly within the tradition established by Theocritus 1, the 'Lament for Daphnis', and Moschus' 'Lament for Bion', and by the eclogue that had transmitted the tropes of both poems to the Latin West, Virgil's *Eclogue* 10, 'Gallus'; but Milton's elegies differ in making himself the central subject. Theocritus had enclosed his elegy as a song within the larger idyll, and it is sung by Daphnis himself, dying for unfulfilled love: it is an elegy both for Daphnis, and by him. Virgil's Gallus, also 'dying' of unrequited love, likewise sings his own lament, but it is enclosed within a first-person frame in which Virgil comes as close as he ever does to identifying himself with the shepherd–poet. The *Epitaphium Damonis* may be notionally sung by the shepherd Thyrsis, but the topic is more Milton's own grief than the death of his friend. It is Thyrsis–Milton, not Damon–Diodati, whom the nymphs and the other shepherds grieve for; and, by the time Thyrsis is describing his plans for a future epic poem, the distance between Milton and his pastoral persona is very thin indeed. *Lycidas* introduces the 'I' in the very first sentence, in words that relate the untimeliness of his writing to his own poetic career:

> I come to pluck your berries harsh and rude,
> And with forced fingers rude
> Shatter your leaves before the mellowing year.
> (ll. 3–5)

The elegy itself moves continually from its ostensible subject, the dead Lycidas, to the singer himself, to the thanklessness of the poetic vocation and the instability of earthly fame. The ending, where the 'I' is suddenly distanced into an 'uncouth swain' ('uncouth' being borrowed from the unknown Colin of *The Shepheardes Calender*), supplies a frame that no reader has had any idea was missing (Spenser, *Shorter Poems*, 25; *Lycidas*, l. 186). In the whole tradition of the eclogue, however, the last line is particularly telling. The poem ends not when the sun sets but by looking forward to its return, as had been foreshadowed in its earlier imagery for resurrection. 'Tomorrow to fresh woods, and pastures new' (l. 193) is not an ending but a new beginning, such as Milton later chose to conclude *Paradise Lost*.

Milton's elegies set themselves in dialogue with their classical predecessors in both form and content. The hexameters of the *Epitaphium* are broken up with refrain lines on the model of Theocritus and Moschus and the love laments of Virgil 8. *Lycidas* is written in a series of verse paragraphs of varying lengths and rhyme schemes, and it varies its pentameters with six-syllable lines in an effect that has been compared to the Italian *canzone*. Both poems end with a shift from death to the afterlife, on the model of Virgil, *Eclogue* 5: a transition almost inevitable in Christian elegies, though less usual in pagan ones. The poems are more similar in the tropes they use, not least the procession of gods and demi-gods that is found in both their Greek and Latin models. The 'Where were ye, nymphs?' of *Lycidas* (l. 50) is a direct translation from both the 'Lament for Daphnis' and 'Gallus'. The irruption among the figures from classical myth of Camus, the river-god of the Cam (who comes 'footing slow', l. 103, as is appropriate for a fenland river), and 'the pilot of the Galilean lake', St Peter (l. 109), may disrupt the familiar mythography, but they invoke instead very strongly the Renaissance–Reformation tradition of ecclesiastical satire. St Peter's berating the corruption of those clergy who care more for stuffing their own bellies than for feeding their sheep, and who can only 'grate on their scrannel [meagre] pipes of wretched straw' (l. 124) instead of meditating on an oaten reed, gives the poem a weight in keeping with the politically central place that the English eclogue had created for itself. Another of the poem's most striking characteristics, its wateriness, has more classical authorization, including Daphnis' death by water in Theocritus, but Milton takes this much further than his predecessors' references to the rivers of Greece and Sicily. The poem is in effect constructed out of water: the seas that drowned Lycidas, Orpheus' body sent 'down the swift Hebrus' (l. 63), the invocations of the fountain Arethuse and the Mincius and the Alpheus, Camus and the Galilean lake, and the final set of interwoven images that connect the drowned man's hair with the sun rising from the sea, Christ walking on the water, the risen Lycidas laving his 'oozy locks' in 'nectar pure' (l. 175), and the setting of the sun in the 'western bay' (l. 191). Milton also had more recent authorities for such a move away from the land-bound shepherd. Two of the pastoral elegies on the death of Sidney included in *Astrophel*, the mourning volume that opens with Spenser's own eclogue tribute, had similarly emphasized seas and rivers; and Sannazaro, in Italy, had invented the form of the piscatory eclogue, which substituted fishermen for shepherds, and which Phineas Fletcher had transported to the waters of the Cam.[34]

Nymphs and Swains: The End of Social Engagement

The distance of much English Renaissance pastoral literature from Virgil was the result not only of what had happened over the intervening sixteen centuries, but of what was happening more recently in continental Europe. The eclogue remained the locus for the closest classical imitation, however distant some of its variations might be from their original models; but a selective reading of the *Eclogues* could also produce the idyllic Arcadianism that came to characterize the treatment of pastoral in other modes, not least romance and drama. This fantasy version of the shepherd world draws generously on ideas of the Golden Age, with its absence of labour, its benign climate, and an abundance of nymphs, though the plots of the Renaissance works required a world that allows for more exciting things to happen too: innocence does not make for good narrative. Romance of this kind was further encouraged by the rediscovery of the late Greek *Longus and Chloe*, which was translated into English by Angel Day in 1587 by way of a French intermediary; but by that time pastoral romance was already following a newly fashionable course of its own, inspired more by continental European than classical models. Sannazaro's Italian

Arcadia (*c.*1489) and Montemayor's Spanish *Diana* (mid-sixteenth century, translated by Bartholomew Yong in 1598) exercised an increasing influence on English pastoral; they were supplemented from the end of the century by two Italian plays, Tasso's *Aminta* (1573) and Guarini's *Pastor Fido* (1590, translated by Fanshawe in 1647). The unreality of their worlds made them overdue for Cervantes' comment that the whole idea that shepherds had 'excellent voices' was a 'delicate and courtly invention', not an 'approved truth'.[35] Anything resembling a realistic herdsman was here at best marginalized, more often non-existent. The protagonists are typically aristocrats taking time out, or occasionally noble children lost at birth. Supposedly actual herdsmen are presented as figures either of implausible courtliness, or of almost equally implausible rusticity. The unabashed aristocratic basis of such literature helped to enforce the idea that shepherds are appropriate characters to treat in polite literature. An early romance such as Sidney's *Arcadia* resists the mythologizing of the landscape and maintains a stringent moral and political core to its story, in ways that show a profound attempt to bring together the two traditions, of imaginative fantasy and ethical engagement, but it was not an easy balance to hold. The first version of the work did not allow space for any 'art' shepherds within the main plot—the herdsmen with a function in the prose narrative were all clowns, the poetic shepherds confined to non-narrative eclogue interludes, and anyone with any higher aspirations was an aristocrat in disguise—but the revised version turned two of those aristocrats, Strephon and Claius, into native Arcadian shepherds with a high Neoplatonic reach to their minds. More generously inclusive is *As You Like It*, where the exiled aristocrats mix with country-born shepherds named Silvius and Corin—the former a lover whose love overrides his low status so far as to allow him to speak in blank verse, the latter an old shepherd who is the spokesman for pastoral contentment—but where the local inhabitants also include the barely articulate goatherd Audrey and her even less articulate suitor William. The Forest of Arden is reminiscent of Robin Hood and yet contains a lioness, Corin is threatened by economic disaster in the form of a grasping landlord, and Hymen appears at the close to celebrate the happy ending; but whether Hymen is a god or a local hired by Rosalind is left to the director.

As all these examples illustrate, the masculine society of both Virgil's shepherd world and the labouring good shepherds of biblical imagery was replaced in pastoral of this kind by a generously heterosexual set of *dramatis personae*. Narrative poems such as William Browne's *Britannia's Pastorals* or the many songs and lyrics that feature shepherdesses and nymphs have moved a long way from classical models, but they share a common conviction that the pastoral world is primarily one of the imagination, that it is aesthetically delightful, and that the sexuality of the female inhabitants is a key part of that delight, not least if it is not easily available. Shepherdesses had never been an English phenomenon, for all the reliance of the English economy on the wool industry ('shepherdess' is a literary, not a rural, term); their distance from reality is indicated by their increasing synonymy with nymphs. In such pastoral, male shepherds become swains, regularly rhyming with 'plains'—the undemanding landscape implicitly contrasted with hills, the 'downs' inhabited by 'clowns'. Here, love becomes the dominant subject, to the exclusion of ecclesiastical or political comment. Pastoral of this kind begins to appear under Elizabeth, and by the mid-seventeenth century had largely displaced the more socially engaged model. Petrarch the lover accordingly displaces Virgil as the covert model: the poet who writes about frustrated love as an excuse for rhetorical display.

Georgics

In contrast to pastoral, the georgic elicited comparatively little response before the later seventeenth century, and any rural poetry that might look similar was often not written with any connection with Virgil in mind.[36] There were no tag-lines from the *Georgics* comparable to Tityrus lying under the beech, or the singing of greater things, that signalled a relationship to the Virgilian model. Virgilian georgic differed most evidently from his pastoral writing on account of its factual basis: no one could use the *Eclogues* as a manual on keeping sheep, whereas the *Georgics* is ostensibly designed to serve as a guide to husbandry, with abundant advice on soil types, the right dates for planting different crops, the best locations for beehives, and so on. Sheep-keeping there becomes a matter of constant labour, in contrast to the *otium* on display in the *Eclogues*. Virgil's bid to be regarded as a major poet is evident throughout the *Georgics*—he insists many times that his own work in producing the poem is equivalent to the labour of the husbandman, and it concludes with a repetition of the first line of the *Eclogues* to confirm his poetic identity and help establish the growing canon of his works—but poetry is not its subject in the way that it forms the subject of the earlier poems. Its great poetic reach, which brings together the movements of the heavens with the techniques for grafting, landscapes instinct with gods and demi-gods with the capacities of different soils to sustain varying crops, never denies the literal labour that falls to the men who work the earth. It may have great poetic passages, on the Golden Age or the myth of Orpheus, but it remains primarily a work of non-fiction, whereas the *Eclogues* contains poems of the imagination. Sir John Harington's comment on how verse can transform even the most 'harsh and unacceptable' matter into 'pleasure and sweetness' encapsulates nicely both the admiration the *Georgics* elicited, and the reason why it was so little imitated:

> For mine own part I was never yet so good a husband to take any delight to hear one of my ploughmen tell how an acre of wheat must be fallowed and twyfallowed [ploughed and reploughed]...but when I hear one read Virgil [and he quotes *Georgics*, I. 84–8, 94–5]...with many other lessons of homely husbandry, but delivered in so good a verse...me thinks all that while I could find it in my heart to drive the plough.[37]

Virgilian georgic was one thing; actual labour was very different.

The Virgil that the Elizabethans were most likely to read into the *Georgics* was not a husbandman but a natural philosopher, not so far distant from the medieval view of him as a magician: a man who could read omens and who had an arcane knowledge of the stars.[38] The aspect of his subject matter that they were most ready to take up was the analogy he draws between his own labour as poet and labour on the land. Francis Bacon was thus happy to use the *Georgics* as a parallel for the intellectual effort he describes in *The Advancement of Learning*, where he advocates a 'Georgics of the mind';[39] Chapman dedicated his translation of the metaphor-resistant Hesiod to Bacon on the basis of such passages. A literal reading was almost always something of an embarrassment, however. In pastoral poetry, the shepherd is the metaphorical figure, who stands in for the literal poet; in the *Georgics*, the husbandman is literal, the poet metaphorical. Early modern poets will occasionally allow an agricultural metaphor into their verse, but it is always very clear that its status is rhetorical.[40] When agricultural similes occur independently of such intellectual or poetic contexts, or indeed when characters appear who actually till the land, the tone is predominantly disdainful. Poetry that regarded active participation in labour favourably began to emerge only with the approach of the Civil War, with its rebalancing of social, political, and therefore literary priorities.[41]

Elizabethan and early Stuart poets did on occasion write rural poetry that responded to the landscape, but their work rarely aimed at, or achieved, the kind of synthesis between the agricultural and the larger political and mythological project that Virgil offered. Agricultural verse is typified by Thomas Tusser's *Five Hundred Points of Good Husbandry* (as the edition of 1573 was called; the first, of 1557, had encompassed a mere 'hundred good points'). Webbe mentions it as the only example he knows of English georgic, but, although Tusser's skills as a chorister had given him an education that included St Paul's, Eton, and Trinity Hall, his work does not show any signs of familiarity with the *Georgics*.[42] He broke off a career in music to marry and take up farming, but for all his good advice to others his practice of husbandry proved disastrous. The core of the work is a month-by-month account of the year's labours, to which were added a 'book of huswifery', instruction in good manners, and various items of moral and religious instruction. In this it makes an agricultural parallel to the *Kalendrier des Bergers*, English editions of which appeared throughout the sixteenth century and which gave Spenser his title. It contributes rather more to our knowledge of early modern agricultural practices and terminology than to the English poetic tradition, as in a verse selected at random from its eighty-four-line list of 'husbandly furniture'.[43]

> Sharp cutting spade, for the dividing of mow,
> with skuppat and skavel, that marsh men allow;
> A sickle to cut with, a didall and crome
> for draining of ditches, that noyes thee at home.

The work encompasses too the kind of information found in modern gardening guides or cookery books. A later age would have written such a treatise in prose, but Tusser is not being merely old-fashioned in opting for verse: its jog-trot rhythms and regular rhymes have a genuine mnemonic function for a rural readership whose experience in literacy may have been minimal. Classicism would be out of place for such readers, and it is given none. The one sign of its appreciation as a literary work comes from the following century, from a poet whose primary interest was in Chaucer and Middle English romance rather than the classics, John Lane. His *Tritons Trumpet*, written in 1621 but never published, is a compendium of farming advice and stories arranged almanac-style by month, where the agricultural sections are explicitly designed to rewrite 'eastern Tussers husbandry' into Lane's own 'western' version, modernized into pentameter 'Georgic lays'.[44]

The one work that does draw together contemporary and classical views of agricultural work, and that offers an extensive apologia for a life lived close to the soil, is Barnabe Googe's translation of Conrad Heresbach's *Four Books of Husbandry* (which went through seven editions from 1577 to 1631), into which he interpolated a number of Englished extracts from the *Georgics*. Similar praise of agricultural work is found in Joshua Sylvester's translation of du Bartas's *Divine Weeks and Works*, though this is based on God's work in Creation rather than on Virgil's on his farm. It is especially notable for its readiness to assimilate the life of postlapsarian labour into the creation of the earth: it is 'th'almighty Voice' that sets in motion the cycle of the sowing of seed, harrowing, and harvest, so filling 'the husband-man with hope'.[45]

So far as descriptions of the rural world for its own sake are concerned, in 1626 Nicholas Breton published the counterintuitively entitled *Fantastics*, a prose work summarizing the labours and landscapes of the seasons, months, and hours, with some delightful vignettes of an unmistakably English countryside that idealize by selection rather than arcadianizing, but it does so with little influence from either the classics or Arcadianism.[46]

Tusser, for all his lack of success at farming, does not draw any distinction between himself and the yeoman farmers who are his implied readers. The literature that recent criticism has more often associated with georgic in the early modern period, the country-house poetry that flourished under the Stuarts, is aimed at a much higher class.[47] Such poems consistently elide Virgil's concern with the actual labour that goes into making the land fruitful, and his insistence that the active work of production could contribute to the good of the nation is almost entirely missing.[48] In early modern England, it was the ownership of land, not the farming of it, that carried social and political clout, and country-house poetry makes the distinction very clear. The earliest such poem appears in Geoffrey Whitney's *Choice of Emblems* of 1586,[49] where the perfectly functioning beehive is presented as an analogue both to the commonwealth and to Richard Cotton's estate at Combermere: an analogue with clear Virgilian potential (*Georgics* 4), not least because Whitney, like Virgil, is as interested in the bees as in the metaphor. It was, however, Ben Jonson who set the fashion for such poetry with the two major opening poems of his collection *The Forest*, 'To Penshurst' and 'To Sir Robert Wroth' (1616; Jonson, *Works*, 8. 93–6, 96–100). For all their classicism, these demonstrate the radical reinterpretation given to Virgilian georgic. Both poems are written as complimentary pieces to patrons, where the praise is focused through the great house and the kind of lifestyle, not least the ethical lifestyle, that it represents. Penshurst, home of the Sidneys since the 1550s, is praised for being a house designed for use, not for show: it is an 'ancient pile' most distinguished for its 'better marks, of soil, of air, | Of wood, of water' ('To Penshurst', ll. 7–8). The estate in which it is set is the haunt of the gods, of Pan and Bacchus, sylvans, fauns, and satyrs—a mythologizing made possible in part by the Reformation, which had obliterated the sense of the presence of the saints from the landscape and left a space ready for the Roman gods to fill.[50] The poet here is not the man who owns the land, and certainly not the man who tills it, but the guest who counts himself honoured by being given a place at the lord's table and invited to dine on the produce of an estate that appears to produce food without visible labour. Jonson describes how different sections of the estate nourish different produce—deer in the woods, fish in the river, sheep and cattle in the meadows, rabbits on the banks, pheasants in the copses—but all this abundance is not only self-producing, but eager to be eaten:

> The painted partridge lies in every field,
> And, for thy mess, is willing to be killed.
> (ll. 29–30)

When the inhabitants of the countryside ('the farmer, and the clown' (l. 48)) do eventually put in an appearance, they come carrying unsolicited gifts for 'the lord and lady', capons and cheeses and fruit: the portrayal is of an idealized feudal system, in which the lord's benevolence is reciprocated by the gratitude of the lower orders. Like the pastoral world, Penshurst is a place of moral value, where the lord's children are taught religion and learn 'the mysteries of manners, arms, and arts' from their virtuous parents (l. 98), but they would not dream of learning how to wield a spade.

'To Sir Robert Wroth' is closely similar in tenor, but Jonson there places more emphasis on the negatives, the vices whose absence makes the dedicatee and his estate ethically admirable. In its freedom from ambition, debt, money-grabbing, warfare, and lawyers, it is reminiscent of the Golden Age, 'Saturn's reign' ('To Sir Robert Wroth', l. 50), a description that carries almost as much satire as panegyric, and that brings in Juvenal as a model alongside *Georgics* 2 and Horace's Second *Epode* (which Jonson also translated). The gods inhabit here as they do Penshurst, and the countryside is even more markedly aestheticized, with 'curléd woods, and painted meads'. Other country-house poems deploy similar topoi, and similarly address patrons: Robert Herrick's 'Panegyric to Sir Lewis Pemberton' (before 1640), for instance, celebrates the 'ancient honesty' (l. 42) and hospitality that characterizes his house at Rushden. One outlier among these poems, since it ostensibly takes pastoral form even though its content is so closely allied with the country-house poem, is William Basse's third eclogue, on the subject of his patron Richard Wenman and his estate at Thame Park.[51] Influenced more by *The Shepheardes Calender* than by Jonson, the poem takes the form of a debate between a shepherd who speaks in favour of contentment and an ambitious neatherd; unsurprisingly, it is the shepherd who wins. When rural life is allowed space in these poems, it is usually in terms of holidays rather than working days, as Herrick's lyrics generously attest.

If political reality enters these poems at all, it is usually in order to be denied: the country house offers the kind of safety and contentment enjoyed by Tityrus. One rare moment when a real event impinges on this world comes in Sir Richard Fanshawe's 'Ode upon the Occasion of His Majesty's Proclamation in the year 1630, commanding the Gentry to reside upon their estates in the Country' (Fanshawe, *Poems*, I. 55–9). The date is still early enough for the shadow of civil war not yet to be visible, and England's peace is contrasted with the bloodshed across Europe. 'White peace', Fanshawe declares, has fixed her 'everlasting rest' here (ll. 37–8), as if Britain were the last home of the Golden Age. The English have, however, left 'the despised fields to clowns' (l. 50), and it is time to leave the choking air of the towns and return to the country:

> And if the fields as thankful prove
> For benefits receiv'd, as seed,
> They will, to quite so great a love,
> A Virgil breed;
>
> A Tityrus, that shall not cease
> Th'Augustus of our world to praise.
> (ll. 73–8)

Even so, he has to do some intense idealizing to make it sound attractive, and there is far more on nightingales and tulips than on the humdrum business of the soil. The casting of Charles I as Augustus is telling, however: the great landowners of the Stuart age were the aristocracy, and almost all these poems are written by poets with clear royalist sympathies. The one exception is Andrew Marvell's 'Upon Appleton House' (*c.*1651), written for General Fairfax after he had retired as head of Cromwell's armies. Nun Appleton, as its name implies, had originally been a nunnery, and the estate's origins give a different basis for its moral worth than the nostalgia for feudal values found in many of the earlier poems: here, it derives in part from the release of the house from the tyranny of the Catholic Church at the Reformation by an ancestor who had abducted one of the nuns. However committed the poem is in religious terms, its predominant ethos is moral rather than political, between the active life of warfare required by the times, and Fairfax's choice for Conscience over Ambition. The war is displaced into descriptions of how the gardens themselves form fortresses and battalions, or of the bloodshed of a rail killed by a reaper's scythe, almost as if writing about the innocence of the estate could be apotropaic, could keep worse anxieties and worse troubles at bay. Marvell delights in the similes and conceits he can spin from the estate, but that includes the productive land as well as the gardens. He devotes seven stanzas to mowing, though his distance from the labourers' viewpoint is indicated by his giving the name 'Thestylis' to the woman who brings the food (l. 401); the protagonist in his later sequence of 'mower' poems is comparably named Damon.[52] His own role in the poem is that of the contemplative, while the active life is left to others.

The Restoration marked a divide in the reception of pastoral and georgic, just as it served as a political divide.[53] Georgic became a more serious mode, pastoral more frivolous. There were occasional examples of politically committed eclogues written later, but satire was led by Juvenal rather than by any development from the *Eclogues*; and, before many decades had passed, it was possible to suggest that 'the morals of pastorals should particularly aim at regulating the lives of virgins and all young persons', or even, in Dr Johnson's notorious dismissal of *Lycidas* in his *Life of Milton*, that the mode was 'easy, vulgar, and therefore disgusting'.[54] Not only had a whole kind of poetry been lost: so too had the ability to understand it.

Notes

1. An ecocritical perspective on such nostalgia is explored by Robert N. Watson, *Back to Nature: The Green and the Real in the Late Renaissance* (Philadelphia, PA, 2006).
2. Helen Cooper, *Pastoral: Mediaeval into Renaissance* (Ipswich, 1977), 26.
3. William Empson, in a famous definition of the mode that goes far beyond the early modern association of pastoral with the shepherd world, defined it as 'putting the complex into the simple' (*Some Versions of Pastoral* (1935; repr. Harmondsworth, 1966), 25).
4. Francis Quarles, *The Shepheards Oracles* (published posthumously in 1646), 33–43.
5. Rosemary Laing, 'The Disintegration of Pastoral: Studies in Seventeenth-Century Theory and Practice', unpublished Ph.D. thesis (Oxford, 1982), 18–32. For a broad conspectus, see Sukanta Chaudhuri, *Renaissance Pastoral and its English Developments* (Oxford, 1989).
6. Anthony Low, *The Georgic Revolution* (Princeton, 1985), 13–34.
7. For fuller discussion, see Gordon Braden, Robert Cummings and Stuart Gillespie (eds), *The Oxford Handbook of Literary Translation in English*, vol. 2: *1550–1660* (Oxford, 2010), esp. 251–6 (the *Eclogues*, by G. W. Pigman III), and 197–9 (georgic, by Alastair Fowler).
8. James Harrington, *Essay upon Two of Virgil's Eclogues...* (1658), sig. A8^{r-v}.
9. Crashaw, from *Georgics* 2. 323–45, in *The Poems of Richard Crashaw*, ed. L. C. Martin (Oxford, 1957), 155–6; Fanshawe, from *Georgics* 3. 219–41, in *The Poems and Translations of Richard Fanshawe*, ed. Peter Davidson, 2 vols (Oxford, 1997), I. 234–5. Fanshawe's other translations included Guarini's *Pastor Fido*, which he read as an allegory of the state (I. 355–6), and a Latin version of Fletcher's tragicomedy *The Faithful Shepherdess*, *La Fida Pastora*.

10. *Thomas Stanley: Poems and Translations*, ed. Galbraith Miller Crump (Oxford, 1962), 102–16.
11. *The Eclogues of Alexander Barclay*, ed. Beatrice White, Early English Texts Society OS 175 (1928), 5. 2, 1. 146–56; Cooper, *Pastoral*, 118–23.
12. Printed in 1678 in *Poemata varii augmenti*, ed. William Dillingham, 184–207. On these and on the thin tradition of Anglo-Latin eclogue in this period, see Leicester Bradner, *Musae Anglicanae* (New York, 1940), 35–77.
13. For a more detailed discussion, especially of the work's political affiliations, see Richard McCabe, Chapter 25, this volume. Clare R. Kinney gives a good account of the pastoral background in '*The Shepheardes Calender*', in Richard McCabe (ed.), *The Oxford Handbook of Edmund Spenser* (Oxford, 2010), 160–77; and see also Cooper, *Pastoral*, 152–65. On the work's composition, see Andrew Hadfield, *Edmund Spenser: A Life* (Oxford, 2012), 83–8, 118–39.
14. For a discussion and refinement of the idea, see Patrick Cheney, *Spenser's Famous Flight: A Renaissance Idea of a Literary Career* (Toronto, 1993).
15. Spenser, *Shorter Poems*, 29.
16. Sir Philip Sidney, *Defence of Poesy*, in *Miscellaneous Prose of Sir Philip Sidney*, ed. Katherine Duncan-Jones and Jan van Dorsten (Oxford, 1973), 94–5.
17. William Webbe, *A Discourse of English Poetry*, in G. Gregory Smith (ed.), *Elizabethan Critical Essays* (1904; repr. 1967), 1. 265; George Puttenham, *The Art of English Poesy*, ed. Frank Whigham and Wayne A. Rebhorn (Ithaca, NY, 2007), 1. 18 (128).
18. E.K., in his notes to 'January', ll. 55–60, appeals to Plato; Webbe authorizes the passage by reference to Virgil, *Ecologue* 2 (Smith (ed.), *Elizabethan Critical Essays*, 1. 265); and Barnfield appeals to the same eclogue in the volume that followed the *Affectionate Shepherd* (Richard Barnfield, *The Complete Poems*, ed. George Klawitter (Selinsgrove, PA, 1990), 115–16).
19. Cooper, *Pastoral*, 13–15.
20. A full account is given by Tabitha Tuckett, 'Character, Moral Evaluation and Action in Virgilian and Elizabethan Pastoral', unpublished Ph.D. thesis (Oxford, 1996); and see also Leicester Bradner, 'The Latin Translations of Spenser's *Shepheardes Calender*', *Modern Philology*, 33 (1935), 21–6. The Dove manuscript survives in the library of Gonville and Caius College, Cambridge; Bathurst's work was twice printed in parallel with Spenser's English, in 1653 and 1732, and once at the end of the 1679 edition of Spenser's works.
21. Tuckett, 'Character', 234–5.
22. *Thomas Watson's Latin 'Amyntas'* (1585), ed. Walter F. Staton, Jr, and *Abraham Fraunce's 'The Lamentations of Amintas'* (1587), ed. Franklin M. Dickey (published as a single volume, Chicago, 1967).
23. J. W. Bright and W. P. Mustard (eds), '*Pans Pipe*, Three Pastoral Eclogues', *Modern Philology*, 7 (1910), 433–64. John Dickenson also incorporated a hexameter lament into his *Shepheardes Complaint* (?1596).
24. Michael Drayton, *Works*, ed. J. William Hebel, 5 vols (Oxford, 1961), 2. 517.
25. *The Complete Poetry of Robert Herrick*, ed. J. Max Patrick (New York, 1968), 120–1, ll. 23, 41.
26. Sir Philip Sidney, *Poems*, ed. William A. Ringler, Jr (Oxford, 1962), 14–20.
27. William C. Watterson, 'Nation and History: The Emergence of the English Pastoral Elegy', in Karen Weisman (ed.), *The Oxford Handbook of the Elegy* (Oxford, 2010), 135–52, provides a survey of the form in the early modern period.
28. The standard interpretation now relates the elegy to the metaphorical death

Elizabeth would undergo were she to marry the duke of Alençon, negotiations for which were under way in 1579: see McCabe's notes in Spenser, *Shorter Poems*.

29. In particular, John Lane and Henry Chettle: see Cooper, *Pastoral*, 209–11.
30. On Walsingham, Thomas Watson's *Meliboeus*, which he wrote in both Latin and English versions (1589, 1590); on Essex, an unpublished one printed in *Ballads from Manuscripts*, ed. W. R. Morfill (1873), 2. 217–38; on Henry, the lament in William Browne, *Britannia's Pastorals* (1616; facsimile, 1969), song 5, pp. 89–93.
31. *The Poetical Works of William Drummond of Hawthornden*, ed. L. E. Kastner, Scottish Texts Society 3–4 (1913), 1. 55–9, ll. 106–8.
32. *The Poems of Thomas Randolph*, ed. G. Thorn-Drury (1929), 101–4; no lineation supplied.
33. For a fine discussion that takes full account of the pastoral background of the poem, see Stella Revard, '*Lycidas*', in Thomas N. Corns (ed.), *A Companion to Milton* (Oxford, 2001), 246–60.
34. *Giles and Phineas Fletcher: Poetical Works*, ed. Frederick S. Boas, 2 vols (Oxford, 1909), 2. 175–22.
35. Thomas Shelton's translation, *The History of the Valourous and Wittie Knight-errant, Don-Quixote of the Mancha* (1612), 3. 13. 262.
36. For a complementary discussion of literature that might fall within the 'georgic' heading, see Reid Barbour and Claire Preston, Chapter 20, this volume, where the emphasis falls on the second half of the seventeenth century, and on gardening more than agriculture.
37. Harington, *A Brief Apology for Poetry*, in Smith (ed.), *Elizabethan Critical Essays*, 2. 206–7.
38. Margaret Tudeau-Clayton, *Jonson, Shakespeare and Early Modern Virgil* (Cambridge, 1998), 83–108.
39. *The Advancement of Learning*, ed. Michael Kiernan, in *The Oxford Francis Bacon*, 15 vols (Oxford, 1996–), 4.135; see also Annabel Patterson, *Pastoral and Ideology: Virgil to Valéry* (Berkeley and Los Angeles, 1988), 134–9.
40. See the discussion by Jane Tylus, 'Spenser, Virgil, and the Politics of Poetic Labor', *ELH* 55 (1988), 53–77.
41. Low, *Georgic Revolution*, 222–54.
42. Smith (ed.), *Elizabethan Critical Essays*, 1. 265; Tusser's life is outlined by Geoffrey Grigson in his edition of *Thomas Tusser: Five Hundred Points of Good Husbandry* (Oxford, 1984, based on the edition of 1580), pp. xi–xvii.
43. Grigson, *Thomas Tusser*, 31–3 (33).
44. *John Lane's 1621 Pastoral Poem Tritons Trumpet*, ed. Verne Underwood (Lewiston, NY, 2001), 'December's husbandry', 143–6; and see also Lane's address to the reader, p. 5.
45. Guillaume de Salluste Du Bartas, *The Divine Weeks and Works of Guillaume de Saluste, Sieur du Bartas*, trans. Joshua Sylvester, ed. Susan Snyder (Oxford, 1979), 1.195, ll. 817–28.
46. *The Complete Works in Prose and Verse of Nicholas Breton*, ed. Alexander B. Grosart, 39 parts (1875–8), pt 2; and see also his verse *Passionate Shepherd* (1604), pt 38.
47. The group was first identified by G. R. Hibbard in 'The Country House Poem of the Seventeenth Century', *Journal of the Warburg and Courtauld Institutes*, 19 (1956), 159–74; William A. McClung, *The Country House in English Renaissance Poetry* (Berkeley and Los Angeles, 1977), discusses their other classical sources, in particular Horace's *Epode* 2 and Martial 3. 58. Laing discusses a larger group: 'Disintegration', 91–143.
48. The point was first made forcefully by Raymond Williams, *The Country and the City* (1973), 24–34.

49. Geoffrey Whitney, *Choice of Emblems* (Leiden, 1586), 200–1.
50. Alexandra Walsham, *The Reformation of the Landscape: Religion, Identity, and Memory in Early Modern Britain and Ireland* (Oxford, 2011).
51. *The Poetical Works of William Basse*, ed. R. Warwick Bond (1893), 194–201.
52. *The Poems of Andrew Marvell*, ed. Nigel Smith (2003), 211–41. Although Marvell's 'Mower' poems are frequently described as pastoral, they are so idiosyncratic in terms of the larger traditions of both pastoral and georgic as to fall outside the more central traditions discussed here. Smith provides a generous discussion (pp. 128–45).
53. For a discussion of post-Restoration works, see Juan Christian Pellicer, 'Georgic and Pastoral', in David Hopkins and Charles Martindale (eds), *The Oxford History of Classical Reception in English Literature*, vol. 3 (Oxford, 2012).
54. Thomas Purney, *A Full Enquiry into the True Nature of Pastoral* (1717), ch. 4; Samuel Johnson, *Life of Milton*, in his *Lives of the English Poets*, ed. George Birkbeck Hill, 3 vols (Oxford, 1905), I. 163.

CHAPTER 10

Epic Poetry

PHILIP HARDIE

Latin epic was at the heart of English education in the Renaissance.[1] Virgil's *Aeneid* and Ovid's *Metamorphoses* were extensively read in grammar schools. Lucan's *Bellum Civile* maintained a canonical status that it lost in the nineteenth century; Statius and Claudian also had a higher profile than in more recent times. Homer in the original Greek was available to few, especially in the earlier part of the period. But the subject matters and voices of Latin epicists were a constantly available resource to English writers across a wide range of genres. Epic maintained the position it held in antiquity at the head of the generic hierarchy, and throughout the period the ambition was felt to produce an English epic to rival Homer and Virgil. Spenser's 'October' expresses a forlorn wish for an English poem to match the *Aeneid*. Ben Jonson told William Drummond 'that he had an intention to perfect an epic poem entitled *Herologia* of the worthies of his country, roused by fame, and was to dedicate it to his country' (Jonson, *Works*, 1. 132). Today the long narrative poems published during the period (up to 1660) are not generally regarded as its greatest literary monuments, with the exception of Spenser's *The Faerie Queene*, in form a very unclassical kind of epic, although profoundly indebted to both the *Aeneid* and the *Metamorphoses*. It has been claimed that, despite the pride and ambition of the times, 'no national poem worthy of England's greatness appeared. Or rather... the true national epic is the chronicle play',[2] and more specifically the history plays of Shakespeare. There is also a view that epic, expressive of the values of an aristocracy, was obsolescent in the sixteenth and seventeenth centuries, as the nobility found themselves squeezed between absolute monarchies and a newly powerful mercantile bourgeoisie.[3] This is to take too narrow a view of the nature even of Homeric epic, and the flexibility and versatility of the form were such as to allow of evolution and accommodation to changing social, historical, and ideological circumstances. The greatest, and most profoundly classicizing, of English epics, Milton's *Paradise Lost*, but significantly not an epic overtly on a British legendary or historical subject, was under way by the end of the period covered by this volume, and it emerged from an intensive engagement by

Milton with the traditions of epic in both the classical languages and the vernacular that goes back to the composition by the 17-year-old poet of *In Quintum Novembris* (1626), a late specimen of the subgenre of the Anglo-Latin gunpowder epic.[4] That brief epic has a very immediate connection with the history and politics of its time, and many of the other poems discussed in this chapter are deeply involved with contemporary history and politics, in a creative response to the engagement of the epics of Virgil, Ovid, and Lucan with the history of the early Roman principate.

No small part of the history of English Renaissance epic is constituted by the history of translation of classical epics, yielding a number of texts that are themselves major documents of English literature,[5] even if none of them quite reaches the status of classics accorded to Dryden's *Aeneid* or Pope's *Iliad* (although Coleridge considered Chapman's *Odyssey* 'as truly an original poem as the *The Faerie Queene*'[6]). These translations matter for the wider history of the reception of classical epic. Choices of metre, and the decision whether to use rhyme or not, show English poets searching for the most appropriate form to match the Latin hexameter, a quantitative form at once stately and flexible.[7] A later sixteenth-century vogue for finding an exact English equivalent to the Latin hexameter bore fruit in Richard Stanyhurst's 1582 hexameter translation of *Aeneid* 1–4, but such experiments did not take lasting root. A native metre that might be felt to carry the weight of the hexameter was the rhymed fourteener, a line balanced in two sections of eight and six syllables (the old four-line ballad stanza redivided as two lines), used by Thomas Phaer and Thomas Twyne in their translation of the *Aeneid* (1558/73); Arthur Golding in his translation of Ovid's *Metamorphoses* (1567); and George Chapman in his translation of the *Iliad* (1598, 1609, 1611). Chapman uses the force and drive of which the fourteener is capable to convey the 'free fury' of Homer, which Chapman contrasted with the 'courtly, laborious, and altogether imitatory spirit' of Virgil,[8] in a reversal of the usual Renaissance judgement, endorsed by Julius Caesar Scaliger, of the superiority of Virgil over Homer.[9] The native origin of the fourteener also made it accommodating of colloquial effects, stretching the distance between classical original and English imitation, exploited by Golding to give his own variants on Ovidian humour—see, for example, 3. 521–4 (Narcissus):

> For like a foolish noddy
> He thinks the shadow that he sees, to be a lively body.
> Astraughted ['distracted'] like an image made of marble stone he lies
> There gazing on his shadow still with fixed staring eyes,

where the vernacular 'foolish noddy' is at odds with the image as of a calm and noble classical statue that he sees in his own reflection.[10]

An experimental form that eventually took full root in English was the unrhymed iambic pentameter, or blank verse, first used by the Earl of Surrey (d.1547) in his translation of books 2 and 4 of the *Aeneid*, probably influenced by the *versi sciolti* 'free verse' of sixteenth-century Italian poets imitating the Latin hexameter. Christopher

Marlowe gave a decisive impulse to the naturalization of blank verse in both narrative verse and drama. His *Dido, Queen of Carthage* contains many translations or imitations of lines from the *Aeneid*, and his translation of book 1 of Lucan displays full mastery of the form in conveying the force and rhetoric of a poet for whom Marlowe had a natural affinity.[11] From here there is a direct road to the blank verse of Milton.

But the metre that was to dominate the English epic tradition was the rhymed iambic pentameter couplet, first used in a translation by Gavin Douglas in his version of the *Aeneid* (published 1553). Chapman chose it, rather than the fourteeners of his *Iliad*, for his translation of the *Odyssey* (1614, 1615), perhaps as more suitable for the quieter virtues of this epic, which Chapman contrasts with the 'predominant perturbation' of the *Iliad*.[12] The iambic pentameter couplet becomes standard in seventeenth-century translations of epic, in George Sandys's *Metamorphoses* (1626, 1632), and in the translations of the *Aeneid* that prepare the way for the regular heroic couplets of Dryden's version, including those by John Ogilby (1649, 1654) and Sir John Denham (book 2, 1656 (composed 1636), book 4, 1668),[13] an accomplished polisher of the balanced style to which the heroic couplet lends itself.[14]

As well as decisively influencing the development of English versification, translation from the ancient classics, and of Latin epic in particular, was a catalyst in the development of an aesthetic of 'Augustan' classicism in English literature of the seventeenth and eighteenth centuries, achieving a refined perfection in Dryden's handling of the heroic couplet.[15] An early document of this process is Ben Jonson's *Poetaster*, which stages a defence of an Augustan aesthetics and morality, personified in the poets Horace and Virgil, protected by the good emperor Augustus, against the envious attacks and stylistic excesses of backbiters and bad poets.[16] In the play Jonson champions his own brand of classicism, hopefully under the protection of a benevolent monarch. The character Horace stands for Jonson, but it is Virgil who embodies an almost transcendental ideal of poetic perfection. In putting in Virgil's mouth a translation of the scene of the storm and outburst of *Fama* in *Aeneid* 4, Jonson offers a specimen of his own 'Augustan' English poetry. Echoes of earlier translations by Surrey and Phaer position Jonson's classicism within the sixteenth-century tradition that he here refines.[17]

Other translators also filter their versions through the phrasings of their predecessors. Thus Dryden takes over unchanged the last line of Denham's partial translation of *Aeneid* 2, 'A headless carcass, and a nameless thing' (describing Priam's corpse).[18] Dryden himself annotates the borrowing, but his many borrowings from his earlier seventeenth-century predecessors mostly go unacknowledged. As well as easing the route of successive translators back to the original, translations also channel the ancient texts to authors, and a wider reading public, less than fluent in Greek and Latin or otherwise disinclined to go to the wellhead. Chapman made Homer available to a wider circle than the few with advanced Greek in sixteenth- and early seventeenth-century England. But Chapman himself is not engaged in a one-to-one encounter with Homer. He often cites the edition of Spondanus, which includes the neo-Latin hexameter translation of Andreas Divus, from which it is clear that Chapman largely worked, rather than from Homer's Greek; he also bases some of his quaint compound epithets on a literal translation of the entries in Scapula's Greek–Latin *Lexicon* (1580).[19] Even authors comfortable in the ancient languages may combine allusion to the originals with allusion to translations, in a bilingual example of what classicists label 'double allusion' or 'window reference' with reference to the multilayered allusive practice of ancient poets. Thus for Spenser Ovid's *Metamorphoses* means Golding as well as Ovid's Latin.[20]

The Renaissance is often characterized as returning directly to the ancient sources, but classical reception is usually mediated, if not through intermediate translations and imitations, then through the filters of practices of reading, commentary, and interpretation often quite alien to those familiar today. The link between epic and panegyric that goes back to antiquity has largely been severed by modern readers uneasy with what is perceived as flattery; so, for example, the *Aeneid*, one of whose two chief intentions was identified by the late-antique commentator Servius as 'to praise Augustus through his ancestors', is routinely now read as questioning or even subversive of the virtues of both Aeneas and his descendant Augustus. In the Renaissance, it is a commonplace that praise is a central goal of the *Aeneid*, and of epic in general.[21] This 'epideictic filter' on readings of the poem informs, for example, Maffeo Vegio's book 13 of the *Aeneid* (1428, in Latin), which continues the story after the death of Turnus with the funeral of Turnus and the wedding of Aeneas and Lavinia, down to the apotheosis of Aeneas, handing out praise for Aeneas and blame for Turnus.[22] The thirteenth book of the *Aeneid* was regularly printed in editions of Virgil until the later seventeenth century, and was included by Gavin Douglas and Thomas Twyne in their translations.[23] A reading of the *Aeneid* that includes book 13 gives a very different overall shape to the poem, and one that is perhaps reflected in the structure of book 1 of *The Faerie Queene*, when contrasted with the parallel history of the quest of an epic hero in book 2. While the latter ends with the sudden violence of Guyon's destruction of the Bower of Bliss, corresponding to the sudden and violent ending of *Aeneid* 12, book 1 follows the climactic killing of the dragon in canto xi with the celebration in canto xii of the betrothal of the Red Crosse Knight and Una, corresponding to the ceremonial conclusions of Vegio's *Aeneid* 13.

The late-antique epic poet Claudian (b. *c.* AD 370) had a higher profile in the Renaissance than in more recent times, partly because his epics of panegyric (or invective) were important models for an age that maintained tight links between epic and praise.[24] Thomas Elyot and James I recommended Claudian's panegyrics as mirrors for princes. Claudian was a source for Ben Jonson's celebration of James I's entry into London in 1604, and for Aurelian Townshend's masque *Albion's Triumph*. Panegyrical elements of classical epic—for example, the praise of Augustus in the Parade of Heroes in *Aeneid* 6, often combined with allusion to *Eclogue* 4—were deployed in the combined textual and visual media of pageant and masque.[25]

The epideictic reading of epic is closely linked to the pedagogical goal of presenting in the hero either a model of moral perfection to be imitated by the reader, or an image of the moral growth of the hero towards perfection. A view that this is a defining feature of epic could override formal generic markers: Xenophon's prose *Cyropaedia*, on the education of the perfect king, the Persian Cyrus, was labelled 'an absolute heroical poem' by Sir Philip Sidney in the *Defence of Poesy*.[26] Such readings rested on a tradition of moralizing and allegorizing interpretation of Homer that goes back to the beginnings of Homeric criticism in Greece.[27] Virgil drew on this tradition in rewriting the Homeric epics in the *Aeneid*, but, modern scholars would have it, in an intermittent rather than systematic way. A more far-reaching moralizing and allegorical interpretation of the *Aeneid* as the progress of the hero towards perfection and, in a Christian version, towards a vision of God dominated commentary on the *Aeneid* from late antiquity through the Middle Ages and into the Renaissance.[28] In the *Letter to Sir Walter Raleigh*, appended to *The Faerie Queene*, Spenser airs what had become commonplaces in this tradition of reading epic, particularly close to the material in prefaces to Counter-Reformation Italian epics: the poem is presented as 'a continued allegory, or dark conceit': 'The general end... of all the book is to fashion a gentleman or noble person in virtuous and gentle discipline.'[29] Spenser claims to be following 'all the antique poets historical: first Homer, who in the persons of Agamemnon and Ulysses hath ensampled a good governor and a virtuous man, the one in his Iliad, the other in his Odysseis; then Virgil, whose like intention was to do in the person of Aeneas'. Spenser then includes in his list Ariosto and Tasso. Sir John Harington's translation of *Orlando Furioso* includes allegorical glosses, based on the Italian commentaries such as that of Simone Fornari,[30] using a fourfold scheme divided into 'moral', 'history', 'allegory' (ethical–psychological, based on a reason versus passion model), and 'allusion'. Harington's translation of Ariosto pushes the poem more towards a quest for virtue, in which reason must overcome the passions.[31] Tasso provided his own 'Allegory of the Poem' (1581) to *Gerusalemme Liberata*, according to which the three main Christian heroes correspond to the parts of the Platonic tripartite soul (Godfrey = Understanding, Tancredi = Concupiscence, Rinaldo = Irascibility). In book 2 of *The Faerie Queene*, Spenser offers a version of this approaching more closely to the schematic flatness of personification allegory in the characters of Cymochles (sensual abandonment) and Pyrochles (fiery anger), opposed to the hero Guyon, the Knight of Temperance.

This interpretative tradition is strongly felt in Chapman's translations of Homer and paratexts (discussed by Jessica Wolfe, Chapter 21, this volume). Allegorization of Ovid's *Metamorphoses* does not go back to antiquity, but the medieval industry of which the *Ovide moralisé* is the major monument continues into the Renaissance. Golding, who later translated Protestant works by Calvin and du Plessis Mornay, prefaces his 1567 complete translation of the poem with a verse preface to the reader and a longer verse epistle to the Earl of Leicester, both of which offer a moralizing reading: for example,

in the tale of Daphne turned to bay,
A mirror of virginity appear unto us may,
Which yielding neither unto fear, nor force, nor flattery,
Doth purchase everlasting fame and immortality.[32]

These moralizations may be an insurance policy against hostile responses to the project of Englishing a poem so full of licentious and irreverent stories as the *Metamorphoses*, and the translation itself shows few examples of the moralizing expansions and reshapings found in Chapman's Homer.[33] There is even more of a disconnection between George Sandys's translation of the *Metamorphoses* and the commentary added to the 1632 edition,[34] the product of Sandys's attempt 'to collect out of sundry authors the philosophical sense of these fables of Ovid', including allegorical and exemplary readings, amid a host of much else. This is not an isolated example of the survival of the allegorical tradition well into the later part of our period; recent studies have shown the falsehood of a view that literary allegorism went into terminal decline by the end of the sixteenth century.[35]

How automatic and unthinking the application of such allegorical schemes could be is seen in Leonard Digges's 'Preface' to his 1617 translation of Claudian's 'The Rape of Proserpine', which briefly runs through three senses, 'historical' (a euhemerist, rationalizing reading), 'natural' (an allegory of sowing and reaping), and 'allegorical' (moralizing and providential). The Preface is lifted without acknowledgement from a 1586 Palermo translation of the poem.[36] Digges is perhaps more in earnest when he tells his sister, the dedicatee of the translation, that 'it was intended to you, as a pattern for a piece of needle-work...for which purpose...no poetical author will with more variety furnish you, than Claudian', with its implicit identification of the sister with Proserpine, whose cosmic tapestry is the subject of an ecphrasis in the poem.

Mediation may work through languages other than the classical. The English Renaissance epic was significantly shaped by Spenser's use of the Italian romance epics of Ariosto and Tasso, *Orlando furioso* and *Gerusalemme liberata*, which convey a Virgilianism and an Ovidianism of distinctive kinds and in varying combinations:[37] a heightening of the Ovidian marvellous, and the development of the Virgilian plot into a dynastic epic with a harmonious retuning of the Virgilian discord between erotic and nationalist–political ends. Another potent reworking of the Virgilian plot to create a foundation myth for the early modern Portuguese empire, Camões's *Os Lusíadas*, with striking passages such as the elemental spirit of the Cape of Good Hope, Adamastor, a relative of the Homeric and Virgilian Polyphemus, was translated by Sir Richard Fanshawe (*The Lusiad* (1655)). One of the routes for the transmission of Lucretian didactic epic into English literature was Josuah Sylvester's translation (1592–1621) of Du Bartas's *Divine Weeks*, a runaway success in both French and English.[38] Didactic poetry and heroic epic, both written in hexameters, were closely linked in antiquity, a link exploited by Lucretius to polemical ends in his *De Rerum Natura*, and further reinforced by a close engagement with Lucretian themes and language in Virgil's *Aeneid* and later Latin epic. The Renaissance belief that epic poems contained the secrets of the universe further encouraged the inclusion of Lucretian material in *The Faerie Queene* and *Paradise Lost*—for example, in Raphael's hexaëmeral account of creation (book 7), a prototype as it were for Du Bartas's *La Semaine ou création du monde* (1578).[39]

If mediation of various kinds widens the gap between the English reception of classical epic and the ancient texts, that gap is kept narrower through the continued vitality in our period of neo-Latin epic, whose shared language keeps it closer to the ancient models, although we should remember the mediation of earlier Renaissance, largely continental, Latin epic. Neo-Latin literature largely falls outside the scope of *OHCREL*, but a distorted view of writing in English results from a failure to register the bilingualism of many writers of the period. Phineas Fletcher's *Apollyonists*, in Spenserian stanzas, is the English tip of a Latin iceberg of anti-Catholic and nationalist poems on the Gunpowder Plot of 1605[40] (including Fletcher's Latin version of his own poem, the *Locustae*), following a series of poems celebrating the deliverance of the England of Elizabeth I from Papish plots (George Peele (?), *Pareus* (1585); William Alabaster, *Elisaeis*, projected in twelve books), and from the Armada (Thomas Campion, *Ad Thamesin* (1595). A central episode in most of these poems is a Council of Devils summoned by Satan, a feature of many Renaissance epics that stage a contest between the Christian God and his hellish adversaries, and for which the main ancient model is the Council of Furies called by Allecto in Claudian, *In Rufinum* 1. 27–117, with important Italian intermediaries in the Council of Devils in book 2 of Girolamo Vida's widely read neo-Latin *Christiad*, an epic on the last days of the life of Christ praised by Milton, and the Council of Satan in book 4 of Tasso's *Gerusalemme liberata*.[41] Milton's own short Gunpowder Plot epic, *In Quintum Novembris* (1626), does not have a set-piece Council of Satan, but in other respects conforms to the tradition. It models Satan's attack against James I's prosperous England and Scotland on the onslaught against the Trojans, safely arrived in Italy in accordance with Jupiter's plot of Fate, by Juno and the Fury Allecto in book 7 of Virgil's *Aeneid*, an episode that is the source for countless later epic stagings of a dualistic struggle between the forces of heaven and hell, including the Claudianic tradition of Councils of Devils.[42] A full-scale Council of Devils in English-language epic occurs in Abraham Cowley's unfinished *Civil War*. The most important product of this tradition lies just beyond our period, the Council of Satan in *Paradise Lost*, to which Thomas Warton described *In Quintum Novembris* as a 'promising prolusion', and whose wider debts to the Gunpowder epic are traced by David Quint, concluding that 'in the Gunpowder Plot Milton had found the plot of history itself'.[43]

Other authors whose English and Latin outputs are in dialogue with each other include Thomas May, who also combined the roles of translator and independent author. His accomplished translation in heroic couplets of Lucan's unfinished epic was followed by a continuation in both English and Latin versions, and he was the author of classicizing epics in English on medieval English historical subjects.

Abraham Cowley wrote a Latin version of the first book of his biblical epic the *Davideis*. William Slatyer's *Palae-Albion* (1621, updated 1630), narrates the history of Britain from the creation of man down to James I in facing texts of Latin hexameters and English octosyllabics. Finally, an example of a long neo-Latin narrative poem later translated into English, Christopher Ocland's *Anglorum Proelia* (1580), is a versified history of England from Edward III to Mary, comprising battle narratives and speeches, with a patchwork of Virgilian and Ovidian imitations, to which was added in 1582 a versified account of the life of Queen Elizabeth. Both poems were ordered to be read in grammar schools by the Privy Council, and were translated into fourteeners by John Sharrock (1585).[44]

The Homeric Tradition

Homer does not become fully naturalized in the English epic tradition until *Paradise Lost*, whose author was at home in the Greek texts in a way that his epic predecessors were not. Spenser knows enough about the Homeric poems to include Iliadic and Odyssean plotlines in book 2 of *The Faerie Queene*, 'a kind of analytical encyclopedia of the epic tradition, classical and modern':[45] the fiery Pyrochles represents a negative version of the anger of Achilles, which must be overcome by temperance. This is followed by a mini-Odyssey, in the journey of Guyon, knight of temperance, to Acrasia's Bower of Bliss, in which the hero proves superior to the temptations of a Circe or Calypso figure. Iliadic and Odyssean elements are interwoven with allusions to the prior reworking of the Homeric materials by Virgil (Turnus' Achillean fury) and Tasso (the Achillean hero Rinaldo and the Circean temptations of Armida). But authors of our period writing on Trojan subjects often take the easier route to the medieval tradition of the Trojan legend (Chaucer, Lydgate, Caxton), which depended largely on non-Homeric, Latin, sources (Dictys Cretensis, Dares Phrygius), rather than going to the Homeric wellhead. For example, there is still debate as to whether Shakespeare goes to Chapman's Homer for material for his Trojan drama, *Troilus and Cressida*.[46] This and other aspects of the reception of Homer and the Trojan story in the Renaissance are discussed more fully by Jessica Wolfe, Chapter 21, this volume.

The Virgilian Tradition

Renaissance writers readily found ways of making the classical epics relevant to contemporary history and politics. The epideictic–allegorical tradition of reading and writing epics put emphasis on the formation of the individual, and sometimes the aristocratic individual, harking back to a medieval ideal of noble heroism. Chapman dedicated his 1598 *Seaven Bookes of the Iliades* 'To the most honoured now living instance of the Achilleian virtues eternized by the divine Homer, the Earl of Essex', who three years later proved only too Achillean in his rebellious attitude towards his monarch.[47] The *Aeneid* shapes its hero Aeneas for service to a cause greater than himself, the fated foundation and world empire of Rome, and the successes of Aeneas do not so much serve his own glory (in which Aeneas, unlike his enemy Turnus, shows little interest) as ensure the survival of his bloodline, the Julian family, down to Augustus, who will found a new political order and a ruling dynasty after the decades of civil war that had torn apart the Roman state.[48] The 'Augustan myth' has affinities with the 'Tudor myth', which traced the emergence of a stable monarchy after the disruptions of civil war, the Wars of the Roses, and a concern that the country should not fall apart again through the lack of a successor, increasingly urgent towards the end of the childless Elizabeth's reign, is anticipated in the anxiety over the succession to Augustus, detectable already in the *Aeneid*.

The *Aeneid*, with its narrative of a legendary founder and ancestor, and its prophetic prolepses of future history down to the poet's own day, in episodes of pageant and ecphrasis, had provided a model for dynastic epic in *Orlando furioso* and *Gerusalemme liberata*.[49] Ariosto and Tasso celebrated the local Ferrarese house of the D'Este family; English epic poets could take as their subject the foundation of a nation and of a royal dynasty. Spenser articulates the relationship between the legendary past of *The Faerie Queene* and sixteenth-century England in ways that reflect in various ways the *Aeneid*'s aetiologies and foreshadowings of later Roman history down to the time of Augustus.[50] The myth of the Trojan origins of Britain (as of other European countries[51]) facilitates an immediate overlap between Virgilian and Spenserian narratives. But Trojan legend, the primary plot of the *Aeneid*, becomes a minor inset in *The Faerie Queene*, in Arthur's reading of the 'Briton moniments' in the library of Eumnestes in the House of Alma (2. 10), repeated briefly by Paridell (the descendant of Trojan Paris) in 3. 9, in answer to Britomart's reminder to him of Troynovant's (London's) foundation by the Trojan exile Brut, father of the Britons. Spenser footnotes his own debt to Virgil by pairing Paridell's brief history of Brute with Paridell's previous summary of the plotline of the *Aeneid*, from Aeneas' flight from Troy to Romulus' foundation of Rome (3. 9. 41–3), this too prompted by Britomart, moved by the tale of Troy's sack, 'from whose race of old | She heard that she was lineally extract' (3. 9. 38). Earlier in book 3 Britomart had received a verbal equivalent of the Parade of Heroes in *Aeneid* 6 when, with her nurse Glauce, she descends to the deep cave of Merlin, who prophesies the line from Britomart and Arthegall, down to Elizabeth, who will unite the nations in an age of peace after civil wars (3. 3). In the English Trojan myth, London (Troynovant) is Troy resurgent, and the Tudor dynasty is the restoration of 'Briton blood' (3. 3. 48) to their rightful crown, after long centuries of Saxon, Danish, and Norman rule (as the Julian family accedes to supreme power in Rome after the long centuries separating Aeneas from Virgil's own day).

The story of Brute is told in other long verse narratives, episodic poems that make as much use of tales from the *Metamorphoses* as they do of the *Aeneid*, and that, like the *Metamorphoses* and unlike the *Aeneid*, tell a continuous story from remote beginnings down to the present day. William Warner's *Albion's England* (1586, with seven subsequent editions down to 1612, reaching its final total of sixteen books in 1606), presents itself as 'A continued history of the same kingdom, from the originals of the first inhabitants thereof . . . unto . . . the happy reign of our now most gracious sovereign, Queen Elizabeth', in fourteeners;[52] Thomas Heywood's *Troia Britannica* (1609), seventeen books in ottava rima, narrates the history of the world from its beginning to the Sack of Troy and its legendary aftermath, with a 'brief epitomy of chronicles', from Brut to Norman William, and from Norman William to James I in the last two books. *Troia Britannica* is based on William Caxton's prose translation of Raoul Lefèvre's *Recuyell of the Historyes of Troye*, an influential medieval repository of classical matter, much of it transmitted via Ovid.[53] William Slatyer also tells the story of Brute in *Palae-Albion* 3. 4, and in song 1 of Michael Drayton's *Poly-Olbion* the river Dent tells of Brut's conquest of Albion.

From its beginnings, epic is concerned with the continuity or rupture of father–son bloodlines. For no ancient epic is this more important than for the *Aeneid*, which tells of the precarious survival of a people and a family on which depends the glorious future of Rome and its imperial house. Virgil, strikingly, marginalizes the role of marriage in his plot of generational continuity. The goal to which the second half of the poem is headed, the wedding of Aeneas and Lavinia, will happen only after the end of the *Aeneid*, and love does not enter into it. Aeneas' son Iulus, the eponymous ancestor of the Julian family of Augustus, is the offspring of the hero's previous, doomed, union with his Trojan wife Creusa. The major erotic interest of the *Aeneid* is invested in a 'wedding' that should never have happened, that of Dido and Aeneas, which leads not to a famous dynasty, but to death (Dido's) and war (between Rome and Carthage, realizing Dido's dying curse). The bleakness of the ending of the *Aeneid* contrasts strongly with the happy reunion of husband and wife at the end of the *Odyssey*. The medieval and Renaissance reception of the *Aeneid* compensated for Virgil's sidelining of love and marriage.[54] The twelfth-century *Roman d'Eneas* ends with a lengthy treatment of the courtship and marriage of Aeneas and Lavinia, and the wedding is circumstantially narrated in Maffeo Vegio's book 13 of the *Aeneid*. In the Renaissance dynastic epic there is a marked shift from disastrous love affairs that only get in the way of the hero's epic goals to the celebration of romantic loves rewarded after trials and wanderings with the consummation of marriage and the blessing of heirs (Ruggiero and Bradamante, Rinaldo and Armida). Spenser goes further than his Italian predecessors in integrating the disruptive and digressive force of love with the pursuit of a virtuous nobility. At the beginning of *The Faerie Queene*, the Red Crosse Knight and Una are forced by a storm to take shelter in a shady covert, but this will not lead to the scandalous union of *Aeneid* 4, and at the end of book 1 the couple are ceremoniously betrothed. As a youth Arthur had fallen in love with a vision of the Faery Queen, Gloriana, the embodiment of glory (1. 9. 13–15), and his own glorious deeds are carried out in the course of the 'labour and long tine ["trouble"]' with which he searches for her. This is one manifestation of what Colin Burrow calls the 'synthetic motive "love of fame"' in Spenser and his successors,[55] which works to heal the breach between the pursuits of (sexual) love and heroic achievement and fame that yawns in the *Aeneid*.

Spenser splits the complex and ambivalent figure of the Virgilian Dido into good and bad 'spectres of Dido',[56] a doubling that reflects the two Didos of tradition, Virgil's fallen queen and the chaste widow. In *The Faerie Queene*, Dido appears negatively as witch, seductress, luxurious queen, and Amazon, in the persons of Duessa, Lucifera, Acrasia, Malecasta, and Radigund; and positively in the hospitable and temperate Medina and Alma. The queen whose absent presence dominates Spenser's romance epic, and whom the poet himself is in the business of wooing for patronage and favour, is Queen Elizabeth. Gloriana, the Faery Queen, who shadows the person of Elizabeth in her person 'of a most royal queen or empress', never appears, but Belphoebe, who expresses Elizabeth's person 'of a most virtuous and beautiful lady', does, on several occasions that allude to the appearance to Aeneas in a wood outside Carthage of Venus looking like Diana or one of her nymphs (*Aeneid* 1. 314–20), an apparition that foreshadows the wondrous sight of Dido herself later in the book. The words with which Aeneas addresses his disguised mother, 'o quam te memorem, uirgo' 'what shall I call you, virgin', and 'o dea certe' 'a goddess to be sure', had been used as the emblems of the two shepherds in the 'April' eclogue of *The Shepheardes Calender*, in which Hobbinol had sung Colin Clout's 'lay | Of fair Elisa, Queen of shepherds all',[57] an example of the use of images of virginal and queenly beauty from the *Aeneid* in combination with elements of Virgil's fourth *Eclogue* that is found widely in the mythologization of Elizabeth in contemporary poetry and art.[58]

A positively valued eroticism in the context of dynastic epic is also found for example in William Warner's *Albion's England*, which includes Ovidian love exchanges between Catherine of Valois, widow of Henry V, and Owen Tudor:

> The Queen and this brave gentleman did marry, and their seed
> Began that royal race that did, doth, and may still succeed
> In happy empire of our throne, a famous line in deed.
>
> (6. 29)

In the following stanzas (6. 30–41) dynastic love is the excuse for the Queen's and Tudor's 'chat' of erotic stories about Vulcan and Venus, Pan, Mercury, Mars. In Hugh Holland's *Pancharis* (1603),[59] of which only the first book was written, 'containing the preparation of the love between Owen Tudor and the Queen', the plot of Dido and Aeneas is turned to the celebration of a wound of love that leads to the dynasty of the Tudors. Catherine, like Dido, is initially determined to preserve honour and fame by remaining faithful to her dead husband, but Venus' and Cupid's plot to make Owen fall in love with her will eventually win out, without tragic consequences. Spenserian in language, the poem self-consciously swerves from the martial subject matter of traditional epic, to sing of which Spenser had exchanged his pastoral oaten reed for 'trumpets stern' (*The Faerie Queene*, 1, prol. 1), *Pancharis* 36:

> That argument a louder trump doth ask,
> To sound a march too slender is my reed;
> Enough is it to tune a courtly masque.

The Ovidian is mingled with the Virgilian, and in the dedication to Queen Elizabeth a famous Ovidian tag is readjusted in line with this epic masque's harmonization of love with the proper exercise of royal power:

> And thou, O second sea-borne Queen of Love!
> In whose fair forehead love and majesty
> Still kiss each other

—unlike Jupiter's descent from his royal dignity to indulge his passion for Europa:

> Between the state of majesty and love is set such odds,
> As that they can not dwell in one.
> (Golding, *Metamorphoses*, 2. 1057–8)

The ultimate epic plot of a mutually fulfilling marital love, which manages to survive a fall even more tragic than Dido's, will be the story of Adam and Eve in *Paradise Lost*. Milton achieves this partly by incorporating Ovidian models for fulfilled love (Pomona and Vertumnus, Pyrrha and Deucalion) within a plot largely Homeric and Virgilian.[60] From this union will proceed not a dynasty, but the human race itself.

The Ovidian Tradition

Despite Spenser's adaptation of the four-line *ille ego* proem, regularly printed before *Arma uirumque cano* in Renaissance editions of Virgil's *Aeneid*,[61] in the Prologue to *The Faerie Queene* ('Lo! I, the man whose muse whilome did mask...'), in order to signal his ascent on the Virgilian career pattern from pastoral to epic,[62] the poem is often seen as more like Ovid's *Metamorphoses* than the *Aeneid*, in its episodic nature, its recurrent eroticism, its tales of marvels and metamorphoses, its set to the ecphrastic, and its use of personifications.[63] Much that is Ovidian in Spenser is mediated through the medieval and earlier Renaissance tradition, Ariosto in particular, but Spenser also responds directly to Ovid in ways that make him a congenial partner in discussion for modern critics of Ovidian poetics.[64] The usually destructive eroticism of the *Metamorphoses* is accommodated by Spenser to an epic that constructs models of personal and public improvement and fulfilment, in keeping with its moralizing and pedagogic drive. The 1590 *The Faerie Queene* ended with the application to the reunited Scudamour and Amoret, who find and lose themselves in mutual erotic bliss, of a positively valued interpretation of Ovid's Salmacis and Hermaphroditus.

The kaleidoscopic *Metamorphoses* offered itself to a wide variety of receptions in different genres, dramatic as well as narrative, in short poems as well as long, in the visual arts as well as literature (see Maggie Kilgour, Chapter 23, this volume, on Virgilianism and Ovidianism; and Lynn Enterline, Chapter 11, this volume, on epyllion).[65] Its status as an epic has been much contested. But, in its overall shape, Ovid's *perpetuum carmen*, telling the story of the world from creation down to the poet's—and Augustus'—own day, is an unpacking of the universal epic allusively contained within Virgil's *Aeneid*, and, with varying degrees of distance, a model for a fashion in the English Renaissance for encyclopedic and totalizing long narrative poems, whose outward forms are very different from any classical epic. I have looked briefly at William Warner's *Albions England*, and William Slatyer's *Palae-Albion: The History of Great Britanie*. A dedicatory poem by Slatyer to Michael Drayton attests the inspiration of the latter's *Poly-Olbion*:

> Thy *Poly-Olbion* did invite
> My *Palae-Albion*, thus to write.
>
> . . . . .
>
> Thine, ancient Albion's modern glories;
> Mine, modern Olbion's ancient stories.[66]

Drayton's *Poly-Olbion* is a description of Britain in thirty 'Songs', in which the poet's Muse moves from Cornwall to Cumberland (projected Songs on Scotland were never written), and which combines chorography with inset narratives that together make up a chronicle of the time from Brute's migration to Albion to Elizabeth. Its great variety within the unifying frame of a description of Britain may be compared to the *concors discordia* that is the *Metamorphoses*.[67] The disagreement between modern critics as to the balance in the poem between the sense of a unified nation and the liberty afforded a localism resistant to the monarchical centre[68] may be compared with modern Augustan and anti-Augustan readings of the *Metamorphoses*. *Poly-Olbion* is full of stories of the loves of rivers and streams, of geographical aetiologies and tales of metamorphosis. One of her nymphs consoles the river Lea in Hertfordshire for her diminution through the division of her streams with a message straight out of the mouth of the Ovidian Pythagoras:

> Your case is not alone, nor is (at all) so strange;
> Sith everything on earth subjects itself to change.
> Where rivers sometime ran, is firm and certain ground:
> And where before were hills, now standing lakes are found.
> (16. 301–4)

Cf. Golding, *Metamorphoses* 15. 288–9: 'For I have seen it sea which was substantial ground alate, Again where sea was, I have seen the same become dry land.' Drayton uses the conceit of reincarnation to express his wish to re-embody the 'sacred bards, that to your harps' melodious strings | Sung th'ancient heroes' deeds', but referring to the native British Druids for the doctrine not to Pythagoras, a clever example of Ovid Englished.

Pythagoras' long speech on mutability in *Metamorphoses* 15 embarrasses modern readers who feel that Ovid here forgets to be Ovidian, but it was one of the favourite episodes for Renaissance readers, for the same reason that Aeneas' descent to the Underworld in *Aeneid* 6 was the object of intensive interpretative activity, and creative imitation, from late antiquity through to the Renaissance,[69]—namely, that it spoke to readers conditioned to look for profound moral and philosophical truths in classical epic. Spenser combines imitation of the Virgilian Underworld and the Ovidian Speech of Pythagoras in the Garden of Adonis, with a Neoplatonic overlay (*Faerie Queene*, 3. 6), and returns to the themes of the Speech, now combined with Ovidian erotic and aetiological narrative, in the 'Mutabilitie Cantos', the fragments on the transience of things belonging to an unfinished book of *The Faerie Queene*.[70] Golding, in his Epistle to the Earl of Leicester, foregrounds the natural–philosophical themes of the *Metamorphoses*, themes

> specially...
> Discussed in the latter book in that oration where
> He bringeth in Pythagoras dissuading men from fear
> Of death, and preaching abstinence from flesh of living things.[71]

Allusions to Pythagoras on mutability are found widely in non-epic Renaissance texts—for example, in Shakespeare's *Sonnets*.[72] Another reason that attracted poets to the Ovidian Pythagoras was that his doctrine of metempsychosis, which he exemplifies from his own memories of earlier incarnations, became a favourite trope for the claim to be the modern incarnation of an ancient poet, as in Francis Meres's much-quoted dictum on Shakespeare: 'As the soul of Euphorbus was thought to live in Pythagoras: so the sweet witty soul of Ovid lives in mellifluous and honey-tongued Shakespeare.'[73]

It was left for Milton to write a universal epic that incorporated Ovidian (as well as many other) elements within the tightly unified and highly Virgilian structure of *Paradise Lost*.[74]

The Lucanian Tradition; Historical Epic

Lucan's *Civil War*, on the struggle for control of Rome between Pompey and Julius Caesar, held a central place in English Renaissance literature. This reflects the general popularity of the poem in the Middle Ages and the Renaissance,[75] but also the relevance of the theme of civil war for Tudor and Stuart England's construction of its own nationhood against the backdrop of past and future threats to national cohesion. Engagement with Lucan is a major preoccupation of some of the period's most prominent authors, Marlowe, Daniel, Drayton, May, Cowley, Marvell, preparing the ground for Milton's far-reaching use of Lucan in *Paradise Lost*.[76]

David Quint has influentially defined two rival traditions of epic, one the epic of imperial victors, in the line of Virgil's *Aeneid*, the other the epic of the defeated, 'whose resistance contains the germ of a broader republican or antimonarchical politics', in the line of Lucan's *Civil War*.[77] Lucan's narrator forces himself to tell the unspeakable tale of the destruction by Julius Caesar of Republican liberty, and the foundation of the Romans' perpetual slavery under their imperial masters, an 'anti-*Aeneid*' to counter the Virgilian plot of the foundation and growth of Rome culminating in the salvation of the state from the chaos of civil war by Augustus. But the politics of the Renaissance reception of Lucan is not simple. Indeed, a history of English Renaissance Lucanism could be plotted against the changing place of the idea or reality of civil war within English political life, from the 'Tudor myth', purveyed in Hall and Holinshed, of the restoration of order through the union of the two houses of Lancaster and York, through growing anxieties about the succession in the later years of Elizabeth I, to Protestant internationalist dissent from the policies of James I, to concern about the erosion of ancient liberties in the early years of Charles I, to the actual civil war of the 1640s.[78] Medieval manuscripts of Lucan most commonly give as the 'intention of the author' 'to describe the civil war and dissuade the Romans from civil war by showing the misfortunes of both sides', and this is repeated in the standard Renaissance commentary of Sulpitius.[79] An extreme example of a monarchical appropriation of Lucan is James VI/I's paraphrase of Lucan 5. 335–40, the episode in which Caesar tells the mutineers that they can make no difference to his onward momentum. The moral is drawn at ll. 25–6: 'So even suchlike: though subjects do conjure | For to rebel against their Prince and King...'[80] Norton and Sackville's *Gorboduc* (1561), an early example of the use of Lucan in English Renaissance drama, is a politically straightforward academic play on the dangers of dividing a kingdom between two heirs, and of listening to parasites rather than good counsellors like Eubulus, who poses the Lucanian question: 'O Jove, how are these people's hearts abus'd! | What blind fury thus headlong carries them?' (5. 11. 1–2; cf. Lucan 1. 8–9, trans. Thomas May: 'What fury, countrymen, what madness could | Move you to feast your foes with Roman blood?').

The two major English civil-war epics from the end of Elizabeth's reign, Samuel Daniel's *The Civil Wars* (on the Wars of the Roses, 1595–1609, in successive extensions and revisions) and Michael Drayton's *The Baron's Wars* (on Mortimer's rebellion against Edward II; 1603 revision of the 1596 *Mortimeriados*), both narrate the horrors of civil war as a contrast to the (hopefully) continuing stability and prosperity of the rule of Elizabeth I. In his third stanza Daniel reworks for Elizabeth Lucan's statement in his proem (*Bellum Civile*, 1. 33–45) that the civil wars were all worth it if that was the only way to bring about the rule of Nero (1. 3):

> Yet now what reason have we to complain?
> Since hereby came the calm we did enjoy;
> The bliss of thee, Eliza; happy gain
> For all our loss; when-as no other way
> The heavens could find, but to unite again
> The fatal severed families, that they

> Might bring forth thee; that in thy peace might grow
> That glory, which few times could ever show.

The (superficially) unqualified panegyric of Lucan's proem exercises modern readers, and Renaissance commentaries already flag the irony of this passage,[81] but irony is difficult to import into praise of a monarch that prefaces a civil-war narrative of the disorder that follows on the deposition of the rightful king. Daniel and Drayton both play Lucan's game of being reluctant to narrate, expressing an unease at writing epics of infamy on the subject of civil wars rather than epics of fame on glorious foreign conquests; Drayton complains, for example, that (*Barons Warres*, 5. 29) the 'hateful deed [the murder of Edward II by 'vile Gurney and Matrevers'] pollutes my maiden pen'. Yet both poets are buoyed up by the knowledge that, had they chosen, they *could* have

> rather glorious triumphs undertook,
> And registered in everlasting rimes
> The sacred trophies of Elizabeth.
> (Daniel, *Civil Wars*, 2. 127)[82]

Unlike Lucan, they are not the victims of a perverse itch to tell of a criminality that has led to the final death of a desirable form of polity.

Neither Daniel's nor Drayton's narrative manner strikes the modern reader as particularly Lucanian.[83] Their comparative restraint is conditioned by a greater or lesser commitment to the belief that Lucan is really more of a historian than a poet.[84] This debate, going back to criticism of Lucan in antiquity, was conducted vigorously in the Renaissance: the main issue was whether Lucan could be both a historian and a successful poet, rather than the reliability as such of his historical narrative. In his letter to the Countess of Pembroke in the 1609 edition of *The Civil Wars*, Daniel states that he has 'carefully followed that truth which is delivered in the history', that 'Famae rerum standum est' ('one must hold to the record of events') . For being more of a historian than a poet, Drayton passes adverse comment on Daniel in a poem 'To . . . Henry Reynolds':

> Samuel Daniel . . . some wise men him rehearse,
> To be too much historian in his verse;
> His rimes were smooth, his metres well did close,
> But yet his manner better fitted prose.[85]

Drayton himself revised the *Mortimeriados* in *The Barons Wars* in the direction of a more sober verse chronicle, and eliminates some of the verbal excess and conceits of the *Mortimeriados*.

Daniel eventually turned from writing poetry to prose history; the same is true of Thomas May, the translator and continuator of Lucan's *Bellum Civile*. May is careful to annotate his numerous historical sources for the narrative of the seven-book English *Continuation* (1630; rev. edn 1650; translated as the Latin *Supplementum* (1640)), written after his translation of Lucan's ten books (1627), and taking the story down to the assassination of Julius Caesar.[86] May skilfully weaves original Lucan into his *ersatz*-Lucan, but a concern for historical plausibility tones down the excessive in Lucan's matter and manner. In the dedicatory epistle to the 1627 translation, May describes Lucan's poem as 'a true history adorned and heightened with poetical raptures, which do not adulterate nor corrupt the truth, but give it a more sweet and pleasant relish'.[87] In his own continuation of Lucan, May avoids the kind of 'poetic rapture' that for many readers drives Lucan's poem beyond the realism of 'true history' into a realm of phantasy and grotesquerie. The politics of the various stages of May's Lucanian career have been the subject of debate. David Norbrook has traced the various stages in May's engagement with Lucan against a growing republicanism,[88] although the claim that the 1640 *Supplementum* represents a move away from the 1630 *Continuation* towards a greater hostility to Caesar and a more overt republicanism has been subjected to telling criticism;[89] Edward Paleit points to links between May and the circle of Ben Jonson, and argues that May's politics in the 1620s are rather those of an anxious supporter of constitutional monarchy than of a republican sympathizer.[90]

An excessive and transgressive poetics in the manner of Lucan is to be found in the tragedies of Marlowe rather than the epic narratives of Daniel and Drayton. Marlowe's translation of 'Lucan's First Book' is an important landmark in the history of English narrative blank verse; Julius Caesar, Lucan's hyperbolic antihero, is a model for the typical over-reaching Marlovian hero.[91] Lucan's subject matter and manner translate easily and early on to the English stage, in plays such as Norton and Sackville's *Gorboduc* (1561), Thomas Hughes's *The Misfortunes of Arthur* (1588), the anonymous *Caesars Revenge* (1592/6?), and Chapman's *Caesar and Pompey* (*c.*1604),[92] as well as the plays of Marlowe and, to a lesser extent, Shakespeare.[93] Ben Jonson incorporates some of the more historical passages of narrative and rhetoric in Lucan into his Roman plays *Sejanus* and *Catiline*, while the supernatural grotesque of Lucan's Erictho is at home in Jonson's *Masque of Queenes*, a very different stage genre.[94] Thomas May, like Jonson, was an admirer of Lucan's Erictho, but his own imitation is to be found not in the *Continuation* of Lucan, but in his tragedy *Antigone* (published 1631). Continental mediation plays its part: the battle narrative in Kyd's *The Spanish Tragedy*, Act 1, scene 2, is indebted to the Lucanian account of the battle of Thapsus by the French tragedian Robert Garnier (1544–90) in Act 5 of his *Cornélie*, a play that Kyd translated as *Cornelia* in 1594.[95] The line of translations of French Lucanian tragedies continues with Katherine Philips's *Pompey* (1662), a version of Corneille's *La Mort de Pompée* (1644/60), itself a deliberate exercise in transferring the thought and language of Lucan to the stage.

The most unconstrained of the narrative poems on English civil war is that closest in time to the events narrated, Abraham Cowley's *The Civil War*, written in Oxford contemporaneously with the events of summer and autumn 1643.[96] Cowley deploys

Lucan's cosmic imagery, to which his own sense of the need for order corresponded, and indulges in Lucanian conceits in battle descriptions,[97] for example:

> Through both his temples the hot bullet pressed,
> The sword at the same instant ripped his breast.
> Too much of death did make his end more slow,
> The spirit awhile doubted which way to go.
> (3. 419–22, death of John Towse at the Battle of Newbury)[98]

The greater freedom of Cowley's *The Civil War*, however, derives in no small part from the fact that it is at least as much a Virgilian as a Lucanian poem, with the full divine machinery of a hellish personification of Rebellion and Furies, derived from the intervention of Allecto in *Aeneid* 7 and later reworkings thereof by Seneca and Claudian. To read Lucan's epic as an 'anti-*Aeneid*' of course depends on a reading of the *Aeneid* as a poem of empire, but Virgil's epic can also be pressed for a less cheering view of the chances of finally chaining the fury of civil strife. Instead of looking for Renaissance rewritings of an opposition between Virgilian and Lucanian epic traditions, it might be as rewarding to look for examples of texts that read Virgil through Lucan. The first couplet of Cowley's *The Civil War* indeed blends Lucan's *quis furor?* and a Virgilian text, *Eclogue* 1. 66, 'et penitus toto diuisos orbe Britannos' ('the Britons utterly separated from the whole world'): 'What rage does England from it self divide | More than the seas do from all the world beside?'[99] If Cowley hoped to steer his poem to a royalist victory and the reimposition of an 'Augustan' order of things, he was to be disappointed, and the poem breaks off with the Battle of Newbury, when it became clear that things were not going the king's way.

Of all seventeenth-century essays in the Lucanian, Marvell's *An Horatian Ode* (June–July 1650) perhaps re-creates most successfully the power and sublimity of the *Bellum Civile*, in the image of Cromwell as a Caesarian thunderbolt, alluding to the famous simile at Lucan 1. 151–7 (9–24):[100]

> So restless Cromwell could not cease
> In the inglorious arts of peace,
> But through adventurous war
> Urgèd his active star:
>
> And like the three-forked lightning, first
> Breaking the clouds where it was nursed,
> Did thorough his own side
> His fiery way divide:
>
> (For 'tis all one to courage high,
> The emulous, or enemy;
> And with such, to enclose
> Is more than to oppose.)
>
> Then burning through the air he went
> And palaces and temples rent;

And Caesar's head at last
Did through his laurels blast.

Allusion not just to Lucan, but specifically to Thomas May's translation of Lucan, poses an implicit challenge to May as an adequate continuer of Lucan, a demolition job completed in *Tom May's Death* (late 1650), where the same Ben Jonson who had composed a commendatory poem to May's translation of Lucan now appears as a figure of authority 'amongst the chorus of old poets' in Elysium, sitting in judgment on May and finally hustling him out of the House of Fame. Marvell, through Jonson, accuses May of drawing false parallels between Roman and English history, as unjustified as May's claim to be a true continuer of Lucan: 'And who by Rome's example England lay, | Those but to Lucan do continue May' (ll. 53–4) As in *An Horatian Ode*, Marvell shows how it should be done, in the sudden flash of Lucanian cosmic imagery at ll. 67–9 ('He' is possibly Davenant):

He, when the wheel of empire whirleth back,
And though the world's disjointed axle crack,
Sings still of ancient rights and better times.

The immediate allusion here is not to May's translation of Lucan, but to Jonson's praise of the translation in his commendatory poem 'To My Chosen Friend, the Learned Translator of Lucan, Thomas May, Esquire', ll. 1–6:

When, Rome, I read thee in thy mighty pair,
And see both climbing up the slippery stair
Of Fortune's wheel by Lucan driven about,
And the world in it, I begin to doubt:
At every line some pin thereof should slack
At least, if not the general engine crack.

Marvell gives a lesson in the successful reanimation of a dead poet—of Jonson, but also of Lucan, the source for Jonson's own imagery of cosmic catastrophe (Lucan 1. 72–80).[101]

Thomas May also wrote long verse narratives in heroic couplets on medieval English historical subjects, 'The Reigne of King Henry the Second' (1633) and 'The Victorious Reigne of King Edward the Third' (1635), examples of a wider fashion for such subjects that includes Christopher Ocland's Latin 'Anglorum Praelia', and Charles Aleyn's 'The Battailes of Crescey and Poictiers' (1631, 1633) and 'The Historie of Henry the Seventh' (1638), both in heroic sextets. Together with the civil-war epics of Daniel and Drayton, these form part of a project to supply a native historical epic on formative years in the nation's history, a narrative parallel to Shakespeare's history plays. The classicizing May in particular is concerned to shape his materials into a form that could compete with ancient models,[102] incorporating imitation of models in Virgil, Ovid, and Lucan, and setting off national wars of conquest and self-defence against passages of civil war, and using the medieval histories to look forward to the 'halcyon days' of the Stuart kings, as the *Aeneid* looks through legendary Trojan and early Roman history to the Golden Age of Augustus. The martial and the erotic are combined in self-conscious contrast, with overt signalling of generic switching—for example, 'Edward the Third', book 5 (the Black Prince's love for the Countess of Kent):

> Forbear a while to sound the martial noise
> Calliope, and tune thy gentler voice
> Soft Erato; declare what princely love
> Did then th' heroic breast of Edward move.

Or, shifting to a different genre, 'Henry the Second', 5. 390–2:

> Oh tune thy heaviest notes, Melpomene,
> And to the world in fitting accents sound
> The tragic fate of fairest Rosamund

(cf. Milton, *Paradise Lost*, 9. 5–6, 'I now must change | Those notes to tragic'). Behind the tragic turns of the plots may also be discerned the tradition of the *Mirror for Magistrates*, which traces a longer route back to classical sources via Lydgate and Boccaccio. Thomas May was among those who wrote commendatory verses for Charles Aleyn's 'Battailes of Crescey and Poictiers'. Aleyn begins the 'Battaile of Crescey' with a modesty topos on his poetic inability 'unless Homer's soul | Were made by wondrous transmigration mine'.[103] His battle descriptions are full of grotesqueries and conceits in the manner of Ovid and Lucan, paralleled a decade later in the 'metaphysical' conceits of Cowley's *Civil War*.[104]

Neoclassical Epic

Neoclassical theorizing on epic does not really get under way in England until the middle of the seventeenth century. William Davenant's 'Preface' to *Gondibert* (1651), together with Thomas Hobbes's 'Answer', sets out Aristotelian prescriptions for the 'likelihoods of story' and the need for probable fictions, while maintaining the poet's duty to provide models by which to avert outstanding men from vice and incline them to virtuous actions.[105] *Gondibert* itself has a dramatic five-act structure, and is a generic hybrid that taken in the round looks very different from any classical epic. Another unfinished epic from the end of our period, Abraham Cowley's *Davideis* (composed probably in the 1650s), is accompanied by a 'Preface' and extensive notes by the author that together constitute a manifesto for what is the first fully neoclassical (in the sense of a conscious effort to reproduce the formal qualities of classical models) epic in English on a biblical subject.[106] Only four books of a projected Virgilian twelve were completed. In his notes, Cowley quotes from a wide range of classical epic, Homer, Apollonius, Ovid, Lucan, and Statius, as well as Senecan tragedy, but the *Aeneid* is the dominant model. In keeping with the Virgilian and Homeric model (approved by Aristotle) of narrating only a self-contained portion of the life of the hero, the *Davideis* launches *in medias res*, at the point where a temporary lessening of Saul's hostility to David is suddenly reversed by the intervention of the Devil and his agent, the personification of Envy. The ultimate model for Envy's mission from the Council of Devils to inspire the sleeping Saul with renewed enmity against David is the Juno and Allecto sequence at the beginning of the second half of the *Aeneid*. In what follows, the plot is not as tightly structured as in Virgil, but the various digressions, in the form of ecphrasis, inset narrative and song, and prophecy, express a drive to write an epic that, while ostensibly on a section of the life of a single biblical hero, in fact covers the whole of sacred history, from creation to the birth of Christ. This universal reach, culminating in the beginning of a new age with the coming of a saviour who is the lineal descendant of the eponymous hero of the epic, acknowledges Virgil's similar strategy in the *Aeneid*. Engagement with the Virgilian model extends to such details as the self-conscious use of half-lines. In the 'Preface' to his 1656 *Poems*, Cowley states of the four books: 'And I shall be ambitious of no other fruit from this weak and imperfect attempt of mine, but the opening of a way to the courage and industry of some other persons, who may be better able to perform it thoroughly and successfully.'[107] There are indeed striking analogies with, if not necessarily direct models for, many things in *Paradise Lost*,[108] that epic courageously brought to a conclusion by the strongest of poets, not the least of whose brave acts was to decide to write his epic in English, and abandon the wider European audience that he might have wooed with an epic in Latin, contenting himself with a readership of those Britons separated from the rest of the world (*Epitaphium Damonis* 161–78).[109] It is perhaps a sign of Cowley's timidity that he hedged his bets by producing a Latin version of the first (but only the first) of the four books of the English *Davideis*.

Notes

1. See Peter Mack, Chapter 2, this volume; T. W. Baldwin, *William Shakspere's Small Latine and Lesse Greek* (Urbana, IL, 1944), 417–96, on Ovid and Virgil; Jonathan Bate, *Shakespeare and Ovid* (Oxford, 1993), 19–32, on Ovid in the schoolroom, editions, and translations.
2. W. MacNeile Dixon, *English Epic and Heroic Poetry* (1912), 172–3. More generally on Shakespeare and the classical hero, see Reuben A. Brower, *Hero and Saint: Shakespeare and the Graeco-Roman Heroic Tradition* (Oxford, 1971).
3. See David Quint, *Epic and Empire: Politics and Generic Form from Virgil to Milton* (Princeton, 1993), 10.
4. Estelle Haan, 'Milton's *In Quintum Novembris* and the Anglo-Latin Gunpowder Epic', *Humanistica Lovaniensia*, 41 (1992), 221–95; 42 (1993), 368–402.
5. In general, see Gordon Braden, 'Epic Kinds', in Gordon Braden, Robert Cummings, and Stuart Gillespie (eds), *The Oxford History of Literary Translation in English* (Oxford, 2010), 167–93. On translations of Virgil's *Aeneid*, see Colin Burrow,

'Virgil in English Translation', in Charles Martindale (ed.), *The Cambridge Companion to Virgil* (Cambridge, 1997), 21–37; on translations of Ovid's *Metamorphoses*, see Raphael Lyne, *Ovid's Changing Worlds: English Metamorphoses 1567–1632* (Cambridge, 2001), and 'Ovid in English Translation', in Philip Hardie (ed.), *The Cambridge Companion to Ovid* (Cambridge, 2002), 249–63.

6. *The Collected Works of Samuel Taylor Coleridge*, ed. George Whalley (Princeton, 1984), *Marginalia* II. 1120.
7. On the sixteenth- and early seventeenth-century debate between supporters of quantitative verse and of rhyme, see Richard Helgerson, *Forms of Nationhood: The Elizabethan Writing of England* (Chicago, 1992), 25–40. See also Helen Cooper, Chapter 9, this volume. In general, on prosody, see George Sainstbury, *A History of English Prosody from the Twelfth Century to the Present Day*, 2nd edn (1923).
8. *Chapman's Homer: The Iliad*, ed. Allardyce Nicoll, with a new preface by Garry Wills (Princeton, 1998), 543.
9. David S. Wilson-Okamura, *Virgil in the Renaissance* (Cambridge, 2010), 124–41; Philip Ford, *De Troie à Ithaque: Réception des épopées homériques à la Renaissance* (Geneva, 2007), 275–83.
10. See Raphael Lyne, 'The Englishness of Golding's Ovid', in *Ovid's Changing Worlds*, 53–79.
11. Patrick Cheney, *Marlowe's Republican Authorship: Lucan, Liberty, and the Sublime* (Basingstoke, 2009); Charles Martindale, Chapter 26, this volume.
12. *Chapman's Homer: The Odyssey*, ed. Allardyce Nicoll, with a new preface by Garry Wills (Princeton, 2000), 4. On Chapman's Homer, see Jessica Wolfe, Chapter 21, this volume.
13. Robin Sowerby (ed.), *Early Augustan Virgil: Translations by Denham, Godolphin, and Waller* (Lewisburg, WV, 2010).
14. See Leslie Proudfoot, *Dryden's 'Aeneid' and its Seventeenth Century Predecessors* (Manchester, 1960).
15. Robin Sowerby, *The Augustan Art of Poetry: Augustan Translation of the Classics* (Oxford, 2006); Howard Erskine-Hill, *The Augustan Idea in English Literature* (1983).
16. Full discussion in Tom Cain (ed.), *Ben Jonson: Poetaster* (Manchester, 1995); see also Sean Keilen, Chapter 28, this volume.
17. Robert Cummings and Charles Martindale, 'Jonson's Virgil: Surrey and Phaer', *Translation & Literature*, 16 (2007), 66–75.
18. *Aeneis* 2. 763, in John Dryden, *The Works*, ed. E. N. Hooker, H. T. Swedenberg, and V. A. Dearing, 20 vols (Berkeley and Los Angeles, 1956–89), 5. 403.
19. See George deForest Lord, *Homeric Renaissance: The Odyssey of George Chapman* (1956), ch. 1. On the various Latin versions of Homer, see R. Sowerby, 'The Homeric *Versio Latina*', *Illinois Classical Studies*, 21 (1996), 161–202.
20. M. L. Stapleton, 'Spenser's Golding', in *Spenser's Ovidian Poetics* (Newark, DE, 2009), ch. 3.
21. In general, on epic, see O. B. Hardison, *The Enduring Monument: A Study of the Idea of Praise in Renaissance Literary Theory and Practice* (Chapel Hill, NC, 1962), 71–84. On *The Faerie Queene* and praise, see Thomas H. Cain, *Praise in The Faerie Queene* (Lincoln, NE, 1978); Brian Vickers, 'Epideictic and Epic in the Renaissance', *New Literary History*, 14 (1982–3), 497–537; and Philip Hardie, 'Strategies of Praise: The *Aeneid* and Renaissance Epic', in G. Urso (ed.), *Dicere laudes: Elogio, comunicazione e creazione del consenso*, ed. G. Urso (Pisa, 2011), 383–99.
22. Craig Kallendorf, *In Praise of Aeneas: Virgil and Epideictic Rhetoric in the Early Italian Renaissance* (Hanover, NH, 1989), ch. 5; Wilson-Okamura, *Virgil in the Renaissance*, 239–47.

23. On Douglas's translation of Vegio's *Aeneid* 13, see Robert Cummings, '"To the cart the fift quheill": Gavin Douglas's Humanist Supplement to the "Eneados"', *Translation & Literature*, 4 (1995), 133–56.
24. See Alan Cameron, *Claudian: Poetry and Propaganda at the Court of Honorius* (Oxford, 1970), 'Conclusion', on the reception, largely English, of Claudian; James D. Garrison, *Dryden and the Tradition of Panegyric* (Berkeley and Los Angeles, 1975), index, s.v. 'Claudian'.
25. See J. Peacock, 'The Image of Charles I as a Roman Emperor', in I. Atherton and J. Sanders (eds), *The 1630s: Interdisciplinary Essays on Culture and Politics in the Caroline Eras* (Manchester 2006), 50–73.
26. Sir Philip Sidney, *The Defence of Poesy*, in *Miscellaneous Prose of Sir Philip Sidney*, ed. Katharine Duncan-Jones and Jan van Dorsten (Oxford, 1973), 81.
27. Anthony Grafton, 'Renaissance Readers of Homer's Ancient Readers', in R. Lamberton and J. J. Keaney (eds), *Homer's Ancient Readers: The Hermeneutics of Greek Epic's Earliest Exegetes* (1992), 149–74.
28. Danilo L. Aguzzi, *Allegory in the Heroic Poetry of the Renaissance* (Ann Arbor, 1971); Mindele A. Treip, *Allegorical Poetics & the Epic: The Renaissance Tradition to Paradise Lost* (Lexington, KY, 1994); Kenneth Borris, *Allegory and Epic in English Renaissance Literature: Heroic Form in Sidney, Spenser, and Milton* (Cambridge, 2009).
29. *Letter to Sir Walter Ralegh*, in Edmund Spenser, *The Faerie Queene*, ed. A. C. Hamilton (Harlow, 2001), 737.
30. McNulty, in *Orlando Furioso, Translated into English Heroical Verse by Sir John Harington (1591)*, ed. Robert McNulty (Oxford, 1972), pp. xxvii–xxix; Treip, *Allegorical Poetics*, 36–41.
31. See Colin Burrow, *Epic Romance: Homer to Milton* (Oxford, 1993), 148–68.
32. *Ovid's Metamorphoses: The Arthur Golding Translation (1567)*, ed. J. F. Nims (New York, 1965), 407.
33. See Raphael Lyne, 'Ovid Moralized and Unmoralized', in *Ovid's Changing Worlds*, 29–53.
34. George Sandys, *Ovid's Metamorphosis: Englished, Mythologiz'd, and Represented in Figures* (Oxford, 1632).
35. e.g. Grafton, 'Renaissance Readers'; Borris, *Allegory and Epic*.
36. Translation by G. D. Bevilacqua, with 'arguments' and allegories provided by Antonino Cingale: information from *Claudian The Rape of Proserpine, translated by Leonard Digges*, ed. Herbert H. Huxley (Liverpool, 1959), p. xii.
37. See A. C. Hamilton (ed.), *The Spenser Encyclopedia* (Toronto, 1990), arts s.vv. 'Ariosto', 'Tasso', with further bibliography.
38. V. K. Whitaker, 'Du Bartas' Use of Lucretius', *Studies in Philology*, 33 (1936), 134–46.
39. Barbara K. Lewalski, *Paradise Lost and the Rhetoric of Literary Forms* (Princeton, 1985), 44–5, 133–5. For a review of earlier discussion of Spenser and Lucretius, see Anthony Esolen, 'Spenserian Chaos: Lucretius in *The Faerie Queene*', *Spenser Studies*, 11 (1994), 31–51 (at 49 n. 1). See also Ayesha Ramachandran, 'Mutabilitie's Lucretian Metaphysics: Skepticism and Cosmic Process in Spenser's Cantos', in Jane Grogan (ed.), *Celebrating Mutabilitie: Essays on Edmund Spenser's Mutabilitie Cantos* (Manchester, 2010), 220–45.
40. See Haan, 'Milton's *In Quintum Novembris*'.
41. Mason Hammond, '*Concilia Deorum* from Homer through Milton', *Studies in Philology*, 30 (1933), 1–16; O. H. Moore, 'The Infernal Council', *Modern Philology*, 16 (1918), 169–93.
42. For the earlier part of that history, see Philip Hardie, *The Epic Successors of Virgil: A Study in the Dynamics of a Tradition* (Cambridge, 1993), ch. 3.

43. David Quint, 'Milton, Fletcher and the Gunpowder Plot', *Journal of the Warburg and Courtauld Institutes*, 54 (1991), 261–8 (267).
44. See James W. Binns, *Intellectual Culture in Elizabethan and Jacobean England: The Latin Writings of the Age* (Leeds, 1990), 30.
45. David Quint, 'The Anatomy of Epic in Book 2 of *The Faerie Queene*', *Spenser Review*, 34 (2003), 28–45. Tania Demetriou ('"Essentially Circe": Spenser, Homer, and the Homeric Tradition', *Translation & Literature*, 15 (2006), 151–76) makes a persuasive case that Spenser combines detailed imitation of the text of the *Odyssey* with later reworkings and interpretations.
46. Convenient overview in Stuart Gillespie, *Shakespeare's Books: A Dictionary of Shakespeare's Sources* (New York, 2001), 83–6.
47. On the tension in *The Faerie Queene* between a romance ideal of independent aristocratic achievement and an epic model of heroism in the service of a centralized and absolutist monarchical state, see Richard Helgerson, 'The Politics of Chivalric Romance', in *Forms of Nationhood*, 40–59.
48. On the *Aeneid's* redefinition of the Roman epic tradition to provide a myth of the foundation of a unified state under a single ruler, in contrast to Ennius' polycentric epic celebrating the deeds of a traditional nobility, see Ingo Gildenhard, 'Virgil vs Ennius, or: the Undoing of the Annalist', in William Fitzgerald and Emily Gowers (eds), *Ennius Perennis: The Annals and Beyond* (Cambridge, 2007), 73–102.
49. See Andrew Fichter, *Poets Historical: Dynastic Epic in the Renaissance* (New Haven, 1982).
50. In general on *The Faerie Queene* and the *Aeneid*, see M. Y. Hughes, *Virgil and Spenser* (New York, 1929); V. Gentili, 'Spenser', in *Enciclopedia Virgiliana*, ed. F. della Corte (Rome, 1988), 2. 983–90; Philip Hardie, 'Spenser's Vergil: *The Faerie Queene* and the *Aeneid*', in Joseph Farrell and Michael C. J. Putnam (eds), *A Companion to Vergil's Aeneid and its Tradition* (Malden, MA, 2010), 173–85.
51. Ronsard's unfinished *Franciade* (1572) is an attempt at a national epic telling of the Trojan ancestor of the French, Francus (Astyanax, who survives the sack of Troy and is renamed); unlike *The Faerie Queene*, it sticks closely to Homeric and Virgilian models.
52. R. Birley, *Sunk without Trace: Some Forgotten Masterpieces Reconsidered* (1962), ch. 1; J. W. Mahon, *A Study of William Warner's Albion's England*, Ph.D. (Columbia, 1980).
53. Large portions of Heywood's *The Ages* (1611–32) are adaptations for the stage of *Troia Britannica*: A. Holaday, 'Thomas Heywoods *Troia Britannica* and the *Ages*', *Journal of English and Germanic Philology*, 45 (1946), 430–9.
54. Wilson-Okamura, *Virgil in the Renaissance*, 227–47, on the 'centrality of love in Renaissance epic' (pp. 228–9).
55. Burrow, *Epic Romance*, 180.
56. With reference to J. Watkins, *The Specter of Dido: Spenser and Virgilian Epic* (New Haven, 1995).
57. Spenser, *Shorter Poems*, 62. For a more troubled reading of the Virgilian emblems, see Richard McCabe, Chapter 25, this volume.
58. See Frances Yates, 'Queen Elizabeth as Astraea', in *Astraea: The Imperial Theme in the Sixteenth Century* (1975), 29–87.
59. Hugh Holland, *Pancharis* (1603; repr. New York, 1966).
60. Mandy Green, *Milton's Ovidian Eve* (Farnham, 2009).
61. 'I that my slender oaten pipe in verse was wont to sound | Of woods, and next to that I taught for husbandmen the ground | How fruit unto their greedy lust they might constrain to bring, | A work of

thanks; lo now of Mars and dreadful wars I sing...' (trans. Thomas Phaer).

62. On which see Patrick Cheney, *Spenser's Famous Flight: A Renaissance Idea of a Literary Career* (Toronto, 1993); Philip Hardie and Helen Moore (eds), *Classical Literary Careers and their Reception* (Oxford, 2010).
63. In general on *The Faerie Queene* and Ovid, see Syrithe Pugh, *Spenser and Ovid* (Aldershot, 2005); M. L. Stapleton, *Spenser's Ovidian Poetics* (Newark, DE, 2009); Colin Burrow, 'Original Fictions: Metamorphoses in *The Faerie Queene*', in Charles Martindale (ed.), *Ovid Renewed: Ovidian Influences on Literature and Art from the Middle Ages to the Twentieth Century* (Cambridge, 1988), 99–119. On the balance and dialogue of Virgilianism and Ovidianism in *The Faerie Queene*, see Maggie Kilgour, Chapter 23, and Richard McCabe, Chapter 25, this volume.
64. For example, Colin Burrow, '"Full of the maker's guile": Ovid on Imitating and on the Imitation of Ovid', in P. Hardie, A. Barchiesi, and S. Hinds (eds), *Ovidian Transformations* (Cambridge, 1999), 271–87.
65. On Ovid in the English Renaissance in general, there is much useful material in Bate, *Shakespeare and Ovid*.
66. William Slatyer, *The Historie of Great Britanie: from the First Peopling of this Iland to this Presant Raigne of K. Iames* (1621), ¶3, 4[r].
67. On the Ovidianism of *Poly-Olbion*, see Raphael Lyne, 'Drayton's Chorographical *Metamorphoses*', in *Ovid's Changing Worlds*, ch. 3; Barbara C. Ewell, 'Drayton's *Poly-Olbion*: England's Body Immortalized', *Studies in Philology*, 75 (1978), 297–315.
68. Helgerson, *Forms of Nationhood*, 140–1, emphasizing the multiplicity of the poem.
69. On the disproportionate attention paid to the Virgilian Underworld in the Renaissance, see Wilson-Okamura, *Virgil in the Renaissance*, ch. 5.
70. Michael Holahan, '*Iamque Opus Exegi*: Ovid's Changes and Spenser's Brief Epic of Mutability', *English Literary Renaissance*, 6 (1976), 244–70.
71. Golding, *Metamorphoses*, 405–6.
72. On the wider influence of the Speech of Pythagoras, see Bate, *Shakespeare and Ovid*, index, s.vv. 'Ovid, individual tales: Pythagoras & metempsychosis'.
73. Meeres, *Palladis Tamia*, in G. Gregory Smith (ed.), *Elizabethan Critical Essays* (Oxford, 1904), 2. 317; see Stuart Gillespie, 'Literary Afterlives: Metempsychosis from Ennius to Jorge Luis Borges', in Philip Hardie and Helen Moore (eds), *Classical Literary Careers and their Reception* (Oxford, 2010), 209–25 (216–18 for examples in the period covered by this volume).
74. On the longer history of the universal epic within which *Paradise Lost* is to be placed, see Lewalski, *Paradise Lost and the Rhetoric of Literary Forms*, 4–5.
75. But, for a revisionist account of Lucan's place in humanist pedagogy, see Edward Paleit, *War, Liberty, and Caesar: Responses to Lucan's Bellum Ciuile, ca. 1580–1660* (Oxford, 2013), ch. 1.
76. See *OHCREL*, vol. 3, Paul Davis, Chapter 5, pp. 139–41. For a fuller version of the material in the following paragraphs, see Philip Hardie, 'Lucan in the English Renaissance', in Paolo Asso (ed.), *Brill's Companion to Lucan* (Leiden, 2011), 491–506. Paleit, *War, Liberty, and Caesar*, is now the major treatment of the topic; see also G. M. Logan, 'Lucan in England: The Influence of the "Pharsalia" on English Letters from the Beginnings through the Sixteenth Century', Ph.D. (Harvard, 1967). On '*Paradise Lost* and the *Pharsalia*', see David Norbrook, *Writing the English Republic: Poetry, Rhetoric and Politics 1627–1660* (Cambridge, 1999), 438–67.

77. Quint, *Epic and Empire*, 8.
78. For an attempt to include Shakespeare as an important witness to this political history of English Lucanism, see Andrew Hadfield, *Shakespeare and Republicanism* (Cambridge, 2005), airing the possibility that the *Henry VI* tetralogy was designed to represent Henry's troubled reign as the English Civil War, a means of adapting Lucan on to the stage to suit the climate of Elizabeth's 'second reign'.
79. See E. M. Sanford, 'The Manuscripts of Lucan: *Accessus* and *Marginalia*', *Speculum*, 9 (1934), 278–95 (283–4).
80. J. Craigie (ed.), *The Poems of James VI of Scotland* (Edinburgh, 1955), I. 61–3.
81. Arthur Gorges notes in his 1614 translation 'This is mere ironical flattery.'
82. Cited from Samuel Daniel, *The Civil Wars*, ed. L. Michel (New Haven, 1958).
83. See David Galbraith, *Architectonics of Imitation in Spenser, Daniel, and Drayton* (Toronto and Buffalo, 2005), 84–6, on Daniel's 'consistent diminution of Lucan's hyperbolical rhetoric'.
84. See H.-D. Leidig, *Das Historiengedicht in der englischen Literaturtheorie: Die Rezeption von Lucan's Pharsalia von der Renaissance bis zum Ausgang der achtzehnten Jahrhunderts* (Frankfurt, 1975); Gerald M. Maclean, 'The Debate over Lucan's *Pharsalia*', in *Time's Witness: Historical Representation in English Poetry, 1603–1660* (Madison, WI, 1990), 26–44; Edward Paleit, 'Lucan in Controversy: Poetry, History and Truth', *War, Liberty, and Caesar*, ch. 2.
85. Michael Drayton, *Works*, ed. J. W. Hebel and K. Tillotson, 5 vols (Oxford, 1961), 3. 229.
86. On the *Continuation* and *Supplementum*, see R. T. Bruère, 'The Latin and English Versions of Thomas May's *Supplementum Lucani*', *Classical Philology*, 44 (1949), 145–63; B. Backhaus, *Das Supplementum Lucani von Thomas May: Einleitung, Edition, Übersetzung, Kommentar* (Trier, 2005); Paleit, *War, Liberty, and Caesar*, ch. 6.
87. *Lucan's Pharsalia, or, the Civill Warres of Rome betweene Pompey the Great and Iulius Caesar: Englished by Thomas May* (1627), a2^{v}.
88. Norbrook, *Writing the English Republic*, 34–62, 225–8.
89. Bruère, 'The Latin and English Versions', criticized by C. C. Cliff, 'Thomas May: The Changing Mind of Lucan's Translator', Ph.D. (Yale, 1999), 79–81; Backhaus, *Das Supplementum*, 69–74.
90. Paleit, *War, Liberty, and Caesar*, ch. 6.
91. Marlowe's affinities with Lucan are explored by Harry Levin, *The Overreacher: A Study of Christopher Marlowe* (Cambridge, MA, 1952). Cheney (*Marlowe's Republican Authorship*), argues that 'Lucan's First Book' is central to an understanding of Marlowe's tragedies, and that Marlowe's Lucanism is a crucial part of a 'Republican authorship'; see also Charles Martindale, Chapter 26, this volume.
92. See J. E. Ingledew, 'Chapman's Use of Lucan in *Caesar and Pompey*', *Review of English Studies*, 13 (1962), 283–8.
93. Lucan in Shakespeare: Gillespie, *Shakespeare's Books*, s.v. 'Lucan'; Hadfield, *Shakespeare and Republicanism*.
94. Lucan and Jonson: Logan, 'Lucan in England', 185 ff.
95. On the engagement of Kyd's *Cornelia* with contemporary political thought, see Curtis Perry, 'The Uneasy Republicanism of Thomas Kyd's Cornelia', *Criticism*, 48 (2006), 535–55.
96. Cited from Abraham Cowley, *The Civil War*, ed. A. Pritchard (Toronto and Buffalo, 1973).
97. Cowley's sense of order: R. Hinman, *Abraham Cowley's World of Order* (Cambridge, MA, 1960); on Cowley's Lucanian conceits, see Charles Martindale, 'Introduction', to *Lucan, The Civil*

War: Translated as Lucan's Pharsalia by Nicholas Rowe, ed. Sarah A. Brown and Charles Martindale (1998), pp. xxii–xxiii.

98. Indebted, it would seem, to Charles Aleyn 'The Battaile of Crescey', stanza 50: 'Here one, all of whose self was as one wound, | (Oftener transfixed than mighty Scaeva's shield) | Sometimes himself, sometimes he beats the ground, | Or clings so fast, as if he'd win the field. | So many ways to death, yet doth not die, | The soul uncertain which way it should fly.'
99. As noted by Henry Power, '"Teares breake off my Verse": The Virgilian Incompleteness of Abraham Cowley's *The Civil War*', *Translation & Literature*, 16/2 (2007), 141–59 (150).
100. On the allusions to Lucan and May, see Nigel Smith (ed.), *The Poems of Andrew Marvell* (2003), 268–9. For further discussion of 'An Horatian Ode', see Roland Greene, Chapter 14, and Charles Martindale, Chapter 26, this volume.
101. See Norbrook, *Writing the English Republic*, 278–80, for an insightful discussion of Marvell's dealings with the tropes of reviving the dead.
102. G. Schmitz (ed.), *Thomas May, The Reigne of King Henry the Second Written in Seauen Bookes* (Tempe, AZ, 1999), pp. xciii–c 'The influence of classical literature'; p. xcvi 'May aims at creating a national epic not far from the Virgilian scale'.
103. Charles Aleyn, *The Battailes of Crescey and Poictiers*, 2nd edn (1633), 2.
104. On seventeenth-century historical verse, see also Ross A. Kennedy, 'The Franciad of Joshua Barnes: A Previously Unstudied Anglo-Latin Epic', Ph.D. thesis (Cambridge, 2005), 115–30, on predecessors of the neo-Latin epic on the exploits of the Black Prince by Joshua Barnes (future Regius Professor of Greek at Cambridge), written in the 1670s.
105. 'Preface' and 'Answer' are both in J. E. Spingarn (ed.), *Critical Essays of the Seventeenth Century*, vol. 2: *1650–1685* (Oxford, 1908). See also H. T. Swedenberg, *The Theory of the Epic in England 1650–1800* (New York, 1944).
106. Gayle Shadduck, *A Critical Edition of Abraham Cowley's Davideis* (New York, 1987). On the longer history of biblical epic, including English examples, see Barbara Lewalski, *Milton's Brief Epic: The Genre, Meaning, and Art of Paradise Regained* (Providence, RI, 1966), chs 3–4.
107. Abraham Cowley, *Poems*, ed. A. R. Waller (Cambridge, 1905), 14.
108. According to Milton's widow, his three favourite poets were Spenser, Shakespeare, and Cowley.
109. v. 174, 'externo penitusque inglorius orbi' ('utterly without glory in the outside world') echoes the language of Virgil's description of the Britons (*Eclogue* 1. 66): 'et penitus toto diuisos orbe Britannos' ('and the Britons utterly divided from the whole world').

CHAPTER 11

Elizabethan Minor Epic

LYNN ENTERLINE

Poets and Lawyers

In the 1560s, English writers attested to the influence of humanist education with a steady stream of English translations of Ovid. The 1590s, in turn, saw an explosion of Ovidian imitations across a variety of literary genres. Both these discursive practices—translation and imitation—were inculcated early in a writer's life, as Tudor grammar-school masters felt they were crucial methods for acquiring good skills in Latin grammar and rhetoric. Self-conscious imitations of Ovid's stories, ranging from Shakespeare's *Titus Andronicus* to John Lyly's *Galathea*, rapidly found their way onto Tudor stages. But Ovid's work was equally influential among a young generation of aspiring narrative poets who were once Latin schoolboys trained in the techniques of Roman oratory. Some of these former schoolboys turned their rhetorical skills to the stage, some to the practice of law. Thomas Lodge, the poet who inaugurated the vogue for minor epics, attended the Merchant Taylors' Grammar School and Trinity College, Oxford, before entering the Inns of Court. He published *Scillaes Metamorphosis* in 1589: an erotic narrative based very loosely on Ovid's story of Glaucus and Scylla, Lodge's poem ignited an intense, but short-lived, trend for what scholars now call the Elizabethan 'epyllion' ('little epic'). At least twelve more epyllia followed close on the heels of *Scillaes Metamorphosis*.[1]

Whether or not the epyllion constitutes a 'genre' remains an open question: as this analysis suggests, we might plausibly group these narratives together with other poems of 'female complaint'.[2] Originally coined by nineteenth-century classicists, 'epyllion' is not an ancient term; it was invented to designate mythological narratives, popular from Theocritus to Ovid, of about 100–600 hexameter lines. Ancient epyllia display the kind of learned, polished style admired by Augustan poets; Catullus's poem 64, on the marriage of Peleus and Thetis, is perhaps the best-known example. In the early twentieth century, English scholars applied the term to the decade-long series of Elizabethan narrative poems that responded to one another through the mediation of mythological material drawn largely from Ovid's *Metamorphoses* and *Heroides*. Characterized by highly wrought displays of rhetorical skill, provocative depictions of desire ('wanton' being a favourite word), and depictions of extreme female 'passions', Elizabethan minor epics were an immensely popular, if short-lived, form.

Why did epyllia became popular so quickly and fade away almost as fast? To begin to answer that question requires an outline of the specific historical pressures, influences, and occasions that gave audiences a taste for them. Many, but not all, writers of minor epics were members of the Inns of Court; but the epyllia written by playwrights rather than lawyers also show considerable familiarity with the structures and tropes of forensic rhetoric.[3] The fact that dramatists shared a lawyer's ability to argue cases 'on either side of a question' (*in utramque partem*) attests to the influence of the institution they all knew well: the humanist grammar school. Extensive practice writing themes both 'pro' and 'con' was standard fare for young Latin scholars: for example, younger boys might compose themes around Erasmus's proposed topic, 'whether to take a wife or not to take a wife', while more advanced students were asked to practise the techniques of *legislatio* ('proposal of law').[4] The final lesson in the most popular rhetorical manual in English schools proposes the following debate: 'whether or not an adulterer should be killed if apprehended in the act.'[5] All the men who turned their hand to writing epyllia were once Latin grammar-school students, drilled in such exercises by humanist schoolmasters whose goal was to produce fluent speakers of Latin ready to turn their rhetorical skill to the service of the state (see Peter Mack, Chapter 4, this volume). Not surprisingly, the epyllia of former schoolboys frequently draw on debate structures: Lucrece versus Tarquin on who is to blame for the rape; Venus versus Adonis on the difference between 'love' and 'lust'; Oenone versus Paris on whether or not he should return to her.[6]

Beyond the ability to argue either side of a question, former grammar-school boys shared an identifiable curriculum prominently on display in epyllia. As I discuss later, Virgil's *Aeneid* and Ovid's *Metamorphoses* were culminating texts in the upper forms and were integral to the verbal 'plenitude', or *copia*, required for eloquence. Grammar-school training produced a ready-made audience of similarly educated peers, which helps explain why epylla were so popular. But it also helps explain why some contemporaries took Lodge's poem as an occasion to compose their own witty variations: the habit of inventing new ways to express the same 'theme' was engrained early in school exercises. The implicit competition between epyllia may well stem from past experience; schoolmasters were forthright about encouraging an agonistic environment among the boys: 'All things in Schools are to be done by emulation, and honest contention.'[7] Perhaps the most extreme case of rivalry is that of John Marston (member of Middle Temple). A 'barking satirist' who adjudicates the difference between 'wanton' and 'obscene' discourse in *The Metamorphosis of Pigmalions Image*, Marston's narrator flirts with pornography only to blame such thoughts on his audience: not the writer but the reader's 'gaping', 'wanton', and 'itching ear' is responsible for the 'loose lines' that 'from my pen do slip' (33. 1 and 38. 6). In other words, the way each poet adapts his Ovidian material in relation to the poems that precede his, or in relation to his audience, may reveal as much about the social and personal effects of humanist pedagogy as it does about the influence of literary history.

But several minor epic poets take up the challenge of imitation less to compete with peers than to interrogate the discursive and disciplinary practices of the institution that granted them the cultural capital of being a Latin-speaking 'gentleman'.[8] That is, epyllia do more than display the specific technical skills born of grammar-school instruction. Many of them pointedly place themselves in a pedagogical environment, draw on identifiable school exercises and habits, or take up the topic of 'learning' and its consequences. And, in so doing, they pose pointed questions about the social goals behind humanist pedagogy. In the following pages, I suggest that what has been relegated to the status of a 'minor' genre has much to tell us about the discursive and disciplinary practices of the Latin grammar school, the educational institution that initiated future poets, dramatists, and lawyers into the practices of Roman rhetoric, and profoundly affected experiences of masculinity in the period.

Pedagogy, Oratory, and Sexuality

Despite (or, I will argue, because of) the epyllion's overt challenges to normative sexual mores and the institution of marriage, one finds frequent echoes of the Tudor schoolroom and its distinctive forms of training in this verse. That boys who spent their years in puberty reading and imitating Roman precursors came to associate Latinity with sexuality can hardly surprise—particularly because many school exercises revolved around questions of marriage (whether to take a wife?) and sex (whether to kill an adulterer in the act?). Regardless of how provocative the sexual story in question, Elizabethan minor epics frequently bring the school and its Latin schoolmasters into view. In one particularly (in)famous case, Shakespeare's Venus tries to seduce Adonis by becoming his teacher. Indeed, her 'lesson' in 'love' replicates the humanist platform of learning through imitation; she begs Adonis to copy the actions of his lusty horse: 'O learn to love, the lesson is but plain' (*Venus and Adonis*, l. 407).[9] Adonis declines, but Venus' appeal allows Shakespeare's narrator to produce a memorable ekphrastic description of the horse that aspires to the kind of 'liveliness' (or *enargeia*) that school manuals told boys was the goal of this trope.[10] But, despite the rhetorical skill of either Venus or her narrator, the 'unripe' boy says he is an 'orator too green' to compete with her 'idle, overhandled theme' (ll. 806, 422). Venus' failed lesson in classical desire gives a salacious twist to the familiar role of schoolmaster: the first lesson in Lily's *Latin Grammar*—'amo magistrum' ('I love the master')—is one she would happily teach.[11]

But less pointed moments in these poems also draw on the discursive and material practices of sixteenth-century pedagogy. Where masters were narrowly focused on producing Latin 'eloquence' in young orators, epyllia often feature characters representing themselves as orators or define erotic protagonists in terms of their relation to verbal power (or lack of it). In the last poem generally categorized as an epyllion, James Shirley signals his interest in the nearly defunct genre by focusing on Echo's verbal predicament, dwelling at length on the kinds of 'Rhetorick' which might work even in her case (*Narcissus or the Self-Lover*, 5. 2). Marlowe's Leander, 'a bold sharp Sophister' (another word for sophist), uses 'words, with sighs and tears' to 'lead' Hero's 'thoughts' (ll. 193–201). And Hero gets the point: 'these words should I abhor, | And yet I like them for the Orator' (ll. 339–40). In *Oenone and Paris*, Heywood's Paris hears the nymph's plea that he leave Helen to return to her, his '*quondam* wife', in rhetorical terms as if she were challenging him to conduct a legal 'argument' (26. 5; 30. 4). Paris therefore portrays himself not as a lover, but as a lawyer pleading a case in court: 'Persist fair Nymph, attentively to hear me, | And thou shalt see how well as I can clear me' (33. 5–6). *The Rape of Lucrece* similarly emphasizes school training and the force, or impotence, of words: Lucrece asks Tarquin if he wants to make himself a 'school for lust', and worries her story will become a 'theme for disputation' in future schoolrooms (l. 820). Producing what amounts to a forensic defence of her case,[12] Lucrece finally despairs of success and portrays her frustration—'For me, I force not argument a straw | Since that my case is past the help of law'—by dismissing the verbal power that Tudor boys were busy trying to acquire in 'skill-contending schools' and brought to bear in legal careers (ll. 1018–22).

When epyllia do not directly describe characters as orators, they often accentuate verbal acts: prayers, vows, oaths, promises made and broken, and speeches designed to persuade substitute for action. Indeed speech acts often fuel the engine of what passes for a plot. For example, in Beaumont's *Salmacis and Hermaphroditus*, action follows words rather than the other way around: Apollo fatefully changes course when he calls to mind

> his promise lately past,
> And all the vows and oaths that he did pass
> Unto fair Salmacis.
>
> (ll. 617–19)

And so Salmacis catches a fateful glimpse of Hermaphroditus, not by accident, as in Ovid's poem, but because Apollo had earlier made a 'promise' to the nymph that in exchange for a favour she would 'enjoy | The heavenly sight of the most beauteous boy' (l. 535). Trained to focus like a laser beam on symbolic efficacy, Elizabethan schoolboys achieved not only verbal skill, but a place in their social milieu at school and beyond, by paying attention to what J. L. Austin (himself a graduate of Shrewsbury School), would call language's 'performative' dimension. Small wonder young orators were drawn to Ovid, a poet once trained in a lawyer's forensic skill, who gained fame in Rome as a declaimer, and wrote poetry that engages in meta-rhetorical reflections on the unpredictable power of speech acts and the human voice.[13]

In *Scillaes Metamorphosis*, the poem that inaugurated the vogue for erotic narratives, Lodge sets his scene on the banks of Oxford's 'lovely stream', Isis (1. 2). The city was home to the university and to Magdalen School, an influential institution because it monopolized the publication of textbooks for school use.[14] The opening conversation between Lodge's lovelorn narrator and Glaucus quickly turns to Ovid's main theme in the *Metamorphoses*—unending change—only to reveal that the narrator is not merely a disappointed lover. He is also a student. Glaucus, a character plucked from the fourteenth book of the poem all schoolboys knew well, berates Lodge's narrator for having forgotten the lesson he should have learned from 'schoolmen': that is, 'times change by course of fate' (7. 1–5). Glaucus develops Ovid's great topic, telling the narrator that 'inconstancy' is the only constant (4. 5) and condensing the general principal of metamorphosis into a specific lesson about the vagaries of love.

> Thy books have schooled thee from this fond repent,
> And thou canst talk by proof of wavering pelf:
> Unto the world such is inconstancy,
> As sap to tree, as apple to the eye.
>
> (4. 3–6)

The shifting nature of love goes hand in hand with a text from school in Glaucus's lesson, which is that, in a world of incessant change, one must discipline one's emotions: as he asks the narrator, 'why wandereth thy content | From forth his scope as wearied of itself?' (4. 1–2).

Once Glaucus narrows Ovid's sweeping idea of universal inconstancy into the channel of desire, he begins what sounds like an epic catalogue of learning:

> In searching then the schoolmen's cunning notes,
> Of heaven, of earth, of flowers, of springing trees,
> Of herbs, of metal, and of Thetis's floats,
> Of laws and nurture kept among the Bees...
>
> (7. 1–4)

But this stanza's final couplet swerves away from epic back to epyllion by returning from cosmology to desire. And it does so by way of a joke on this tutorial, because Glaucus reveals he has learned nothing from his own lesson.

> Conclude and know times change by course of fate,
> Then mourn no more, but moan my hapless state.
>
> (7. 5–6)

Lodge's humour presumes an audience not merely well 'schooled' enough to recognize the main topic of Ovid's *Metamorphoses*, but experienced in the stated aspirations of the humanist programme—which was, as one boy scrawled in his edition of Aphthonius, 'the mending of my youth'.[15] By stanza 7, Lodge prompts his audience to ask: what kind of instructor is this? What help can he offer to himself—or anyone else? The epyllion that inspired many others to witty imitation begins on the banks of a stream associated with a prominent educational institution; turns a character derived from a poem translated and imitated at school into a flawed teacher interpreting a text the narrator has forgotten; and undermines the lesson with a pointed question about the personal, or indeed social, efficacy of instruction in a classical curriculum.

Aesop's Cock

The editor of the standard collection of Elizabethan minor epics cannily points out that, while these poets were enamoured of Ovid's *Metamorphoses*, they 'endlessly elaborated' one line from the poem.[16] Realizing that the image before him is only that, an image, Narcissus laments 'inopem me copia fecit' ('my very wealth impoverishes me', Met. 3. 466). This line's appeal to writers of epyllia may be not merely, or not only, due to the power of Narcissus's story. Nor is it solely due to the evident Renaissance fascination with the paradoxes that the story poses for ideas about subjectivity and desire. The line's appeal may also stem from the fact that the noun Narcissus uses for wealth, *copia*, had a specific and urgent meaning in the daily life of students in Tudor grammar schools. Central to Erasmus's pedagogical theory and to his widely disseminated school text, *De Copia*, this noun came to signify for several generations of schoolboys, university students, and law students the kind of 'verbal plenitude' required for effective oratory.[17] To humanist pedagogues, *copia* was the fountain from which all else flowed.

That so many poets diligently trained in acquiring verbal abundance remember Narcissus' lament, 'my very *copia* makes me poor', suggests that at least some of them perceived a gap between what schoolmasters claimed about the utility of their programme and how students felt about such claims. While masters announced that eloquence equals wisdom, one former schoolboy is happy to suggest otherwise. With respect to *copia*, Shakespeare casts suspicion on a 'fantastical' character with 'a mint of phrases in his brain' (*Love's Labour's Lost*, 1. 1. 164). Another of his students puts the matter more curtly: the result of constant drilling in *copia* might not, in fact, be wisdom or social benefit but rather, as Hamlet observes, not 'matter' but 'words, words, words' (2. 2. 192–5). With respect to such suspicions, Colin Burrow aptly queries the potential drawbacks of humanist training:

> What was it for? If this question is asked at a merely instrumental level a number of problems immediately arise. It was to equip students with the *copia*, or fullness of language and knowledge, which would enable them to delight an audience, to persuade,

> to praise, or to obtain work as lawyers, secretaries to noblemen... But fullness of language has as its nightmarish double an ability to paraphrase, circumlocute, and ornament in a manner which serves no instrumental purpose at all.[18]

In *Hero and Leander*, Marlowe interrogates the school's investment in rhetoric's instrumental function in a mythological poem that prominently displays his Latin education—a virtuoso display of verbal and erotic abundance that has delighted readers for centuries. Critics have long been alert to the poem's ornamental and rhetorical self-consciousness. I suggest that Marlowe's performance of, and reflections on, rhetorical technique put the grammar school's founding theory—the personal and social efficacy of *copia*—to the test. In an evocative reading, Judith Haber argues that the narrator's elaborate ekphrases pose precisely the kinds of questions Burrow raises about language's instrumentality: detours into ekphrasis derail the poem's erotic plot so early and often that she suspects Marlowe of developing 'an aesthetic of pure pointlessness'. Haber argues that the narrator's visual tropes disrupt any direct path to the tragic end—even though he announces that ostensible 'end' in the first line: 'On Hellespont guilty of True-love's blood.' On her account, Marlowe purposely evades his own announced conclusion with ekphrastic indirection, a rhetorical choice that 'is paralleled by, and indeed equivalent to' the poem's 'disruption of end-directed sexuality'.[19]

Haber's argument about *Hero and Leander* is pertinent to other Elizabethan epyllia, since so many of them show two, interrelated impulses: a provocative habit of comparing rhetorical forms to sexual pleasure; and a propensity to indulge verbal skill in ways that interfere with hetero-normative sex/gender categories and plots.[20] In Marlowe's poem, for instance, the Petrarchan figure of the blazon applies to Hero but also to Leander; Marlowe's 'slack muse' can 'sing of Leander's eyes' as much as of Hero's. The gender categories traditionally associated with this trope become labile enough to prompt the narrator's remark, 'Some swore he was a maid in man's attire' (1. 71, 83). Shakespeare famously deploys a similar strategy, portraying Adonis as 'Stain to all nymphs, more lovely than a man' (l. 9). Marlowe's lovely Leander may protest that he is 'no maid', but, as Haber points out, Neptune's angry reaction threatens to 'wound' him just as much as Leander's desire threatens to wound Hero. Like the narrator's elaborate visual tropes, Neptune's sexual advances and *suasoria* interrupt the 'end' of heterosexual coitus; the plot, such as it is, shifts between the struggle over Hero's 'maidenhead' and Neptune's exuberant pleasure in feeling the naked Leander swimming the Hellespont.[21] Another blazon erupts as Neptune mistakes Leander for 'Ganymede': he 'clapped his plump cheeks, with his tresses played... Upon his breast, his thighs, and every limb' (2. 157). Finally, as Haber points out, modern editions emend the original line order of Leander's second visit to Hero's tower to produce 'the sense of an ending'; but the 1598 edition leaves heterosexual coitus a more open question than these editions suggest. Indeed, Marlowe's deferral seems to have goaded modern editors to try to tame the poem's unruly erotic energy by producing a sense of heterosexual narrative closure. The oblique line order of the 1598 edition, however, teases readers (just as the narrator has done throughout the poem) into asking, 'are we there yet?'[22]

The poem's considerable investment in endless rhetorical and sexual energy may reveal something of Marlowe's cheeky reaction to the social teleology laid down by schoolmasters who claimed that the texts and rhetorical techniques of the Latin past would turn boys into 'gentleman' who could, as Austin put it, 'do things with words'. If we understand Haber's account of the poem's 'pointlessness' in the light of the civic agenda of Tudor pedagogy, Marlowe appears to suggest that his own rhetorical skill is just as pointless as his poem's narrative and sexual economies.[23] Received ideas about what counts as useful eloquence, or indeed as a gentleman, no longer apply. Marlowe calls into question the humanist presumption about rhetoric's end-directed usefulness not only by suspending narrative momentum with dazzling ekphrases—convincing readers, as Aphthonius puts it, that they 'do not read so much as see'.[24] He also manages, in an extensive network of images for jewels and treasure, to perform and interrogate the general platform of verbal plenitude that suffused Erasmus's theory of education and governed institutional practice. Much as Shakespeare's 'mint of phrases', Marlowe's poem exploits *copia*'s two senses: 'verbal plenitude' and 'financial wealth'. Alongside his emphasis on rhetorical performance (his own and others), the narrator reifies the school's desideratum of verbal *copia* into cascading images of riches: gold, silver, jasper, coral, pearls, amber, diamonds, rather than, say, flowers or trees, are the chief images in the poem's 'blazons'. Hero's necklace consists of shells 'all silvered', pebbles like 'diamonds' (1. 26–32); Leander contrasts Hero, a 'diamond', to Venus's mere 'flaring glass' (1. 214), argues that women are a 'treasure' 'abused' only 'when misers keep it' (1. 234–6), and thinks of Hero's tower as a place 'wherein the liberal graces lock'd their wealth' (2. 17). And, of course, Hero's 'maidenhead' is 'the inestimable gem' (2. 78). But, true to the narrator's epicene work of distributing blazons across male and female bodies, male beauty also inspires images of wealth. When Neptune pulls Leander 'to the bottom' of the Hellespont, he describes a place 'where the ground | Was strewed with pearls':

> Sweet singing Mermaids sported with their loves
> On heaps of heavy gold, and took their great pleasure
> To spurn in careless sort the shipwrecked treasure.
>
> (2. 161–3)

'Pleasure' not 'treasure': Marlowe's pointed rhyme tells us that, instead of a useful store of classical *copia*, his linguistic skills create a world where characters 'spurn' wealth for love, where the only abundance is 'careless' erotic 'sport'.

The narrator soon extends *copia*'s economic sense beyond metaphors for physical beauty to metaphors for words. After another speech of seduction (Mercury's), the narrator remarks that plenitude is crucial to an orator's success: 'Maids are not won by brutish force and might, | But *speeches full* of pleasure and delight' (ll. 419–20, emphasis added). And, when Leander is 'moved' by his pain (1. 219), Neptune rushes off to the 'rich Ocean' because 'a gift prevails | When deep persuading Oratory fails' (I. 225–6). Gifts for words: in Marlowe's hands, fluctuations of value accrue to speech as much as bodies and things. A former grammar-school boy replete with *copia* understands that word in two intertwined senses, economic and verbal. But that is not all. Over the course of the poem, both kinds of wealth emerge as ends in themselves—not instrumental or in a useful relation to the world, but useful in so far as they self-reflexively glitter with 'pleasure' and 'delight'. In a telling moment that exceeds traditional epideixis, Leander develops his 'thesis' about why Hero should love him (I. 329): he 'argues' that beauty should earn interest, that her 'treasure' should be 'put to loan' because 'in time it will return us two for one' (I. 234–5). The metaphor asks us to entertain two competing ideas, neither of which cancels out the other: beauty's 'interest' is either physical reproduction or sheer aesthetic pleasure. The metaphorical vehicle exceeds the world of utility to suggest that beauty's *copia* can beget itself.

In the poem's longest digression, Marlowe associates endless wealth with verbal abundance once again only to return to the main plot after an abrupt aside about 'learning'. The digression itself suspends all sense of ending whatsoever because it explains why 'the everlasting Destinies' (I. 462), the ancient personification of teleology, do not get what they want (Mercury's love). When the narrator veers into his complex aetiology—a truly Ovidian touch—the reason given is that he will explain why Cupid's sorrow for Hero and Leander's plight does them no good. To capture the affective power, and futility, of the god's pity, the narrator decorates Cupid with jewels: 'And as she wept her tears to pearl he turned | And wound them on his arm and for her mourned' (I. 375–6). And when the narrator finally turns back from Mercury and the Fates to the main narrative, he does so only after pausing to explain why poverty accompanies 'Learning'. Bringing his meandering detour to a halt, Marlowe abruptly remarks: 'Learning, in despite of Fate' will 'mount aloft ... and enter heaven's gate' by paying the price that 'he and Poverty should always kiss' (I. 465–70). Now 'Learning', too, defies the ends of 'Fate' while acquiring significance in relation to the poem's performance of, and reflections on, *copia*. 'Gross gold ... runs' from scholars while a 'few great lords' will be 'enrich[d]' by keeping 'learning down' (I. 479–81). In part, Marlowe is rehearsing a standard humanist complaint born of the reality that 'learning' was a (generally low-born) pedagogue's only means of social advancement. Perhaps Marlowe sympathizes with scholarly poverty; certainly the poem's first part ends on a sour note: 'fruitful wits' will be 'discontent' while the 'servile clown' is rewarded with a 'Midas brood' of gold (I. 475–80). But is scholarly penury all that Marlowe's detour signifies? In the context of the poem's constant association between rhetorical plenitude, wealth, beauty, and delight, the narrator's allusion to learning's poverty prompts further questions. Given his bravura display of *copia*, what value is Marlowe attributing to the Latin learning that made his digression—and his poem—possible? To put the matter another way: what does the educational institution that gave him considerable cultural capital have to do with the relationship Marlowe forges among his poem's rhetorical, economic, and libidinal riches?

Here 'Aesop's cock' puts in his two cents (2. 51). When we read that their sex has not involved penetration, that Leander suspects 'some amorous rites or other were neglected', Marlowe turns Hero into yet one more gem.

> Like Aesop's cock, this jewel he enjoyed
> And as a brother with his sister toyed
> Supposing nothing else was to be done
> Now he her favour and good will had won.
> (ll. 51–4)

Aesop's *Fables* was the first ancient literary text sixteenth-century schoolboys encountered; and Aesop's cock very likely one of the first stories they translated.[25] On digging 'a jewel' out of a dunghill, the cock remarks that he would rather have found a kernel of corn. Like the mermaids sporting 'with their loves' while spurning 'heaps' of pearls and gold (i. 161–2), Aesop's cock has no interest in treasure. One schoolmaster reduced the constitutive ambiguity of fables by interpreting the story as a moral lesson about education: schoolboys are like cocks, plucking the jewel of 'learning' from the dunghill.[26] By contrast, Marlowe draws attention to 'learning's' connection with 'poverty' after a convoluted digression that threatens to run off with the poem's main story only to allude, in the next erotic encounter, to a founding educational text that poses the question of wealth and utility. Rather than give a moral about what the jewel means, Marlowe may be echoing the cock's question: 'what's the use of all this *copia*?' Querying the end-driven narrative humanists offered to justify their pedagogy (eloquence's social efficacy), Marlowe invents a rhetorically and sexually exuberant narrative in which repeated, energetic evasion rather than possession, or instrumental action, *is* the treasure afforded.

With learned nods to endless *copia*—sexual, rhetorical, economic—Marlowe declines to 'conclude' what contemporaries and modern scholars generally think of as a poetic 'fragment'. Instead, the poem returns once more to Hero's beauty before breaking off with the evocative comment 'Desunt nonnulla' ('not a few things are missing'). And in the final lines, 'heaps of gold' no longer signify Hero's beauty. Now it is 'Dis' who 'fixes' his gaze on gold; Leander takes 'more pleasure' from gazing on Hero herself. Caught rising naked from her bed, 'Hero's ruddy cheek Hero betrays' to Leander's 'admiring eyes' (2. 323–6). Her blush 'brings forth the day before the day was born' and inspires Apollo's 'golden harp' to make 'music to the Ocean' (2. 322–8). Marlowe's inconclusive, 'final' lines bring no new blazons to bear; no Petrarchan images convey what Shakespeare brands 'false compare'. Instead, the narrator attributes Hero's beauty only to herself. Like a loan's generation of 'interest' in Leander's argument, Hero's beauty begets more beauty, inspiring music, and a new day. The 'fullness' of 'pleasure', in this poem, derives from a kind of sexual and verbal abundance, or *copia*, that leads nowhere, produces nothing but attention to itself. Because of the light from Hero's cheek, Apollo sings and Hesperus brings light to the world early, overcoming '*ugly* night' (2. 329–34, emphasis added). Born from his critique of the literary and social teleology behind the humanist programme, Marlowe's intense engagement with his own medium produces, instead, a compelling meditation on the power of the aesthetic. Consonant with the question Aesop's cock raises about *copia*—could the 'jewel' of eloquence result in personal and communal masculine profit?—*Hero and Leander*'s sexual and rhetorical digressions anticipate those kinds of endless pleasures that Freud would come to call 'polymorphous perversity' and Kant designate as the aesthetic's 'purpose without a purpose'.

Not-so-Minor Epics

Both Lodge's and Marlowe's epyllia suggest that the turn to Ovidian desire in the 1590s carries within it an institutional critique with important consequences for how we understand early modern masculinity and the passions. Schoolmasters uniformly claimed that their instruction in acquiring Latin grammar and rhetorical facility would benefit the commonwealth by producing educated masculine subjects whose eloquence would be of considerable use to the emerging English nation. That so many former schoolboys used their rhetorical training to write deliberately scandalous erotic narratives—and that they found an eager audience for such performances—suggests that schoolmasters produced some effects they did not anticipate. Indeed, the preference for sexually provocative material and excessive ornamentation among the writers of epyllia calls into question the specific form of cultural capital bequeathed by a grammar-school education. Georgia Brown argues that this group of Latin-speaking poets promoted themselves as a 'generation of shame' by way of a deliberate triviality that stood against the serious tradition of masculine epic—a culturally significant literary distinction that, if viewed from the perspective of school training, suggests they were also styling themselves against their moralizing, civic-minded schoolmasters.[27] Their overt public posture could, in short, double as poetic self-advertising and as institutional critique.

With respect to their preference for Ovid, their choice stands in marked contrast to humanist theorists and schoolmasters, many of whom showed a decided preference not just for epic, but for epic in its Virgilian form, as the best exemplar for moulding a boy's conduct.[28] The ubiquitous Lily's *Grammar* puts the matter succinctly. In the lesson on the impersonal verb, boys learned 'Oportet me legere Vergilium' ('it is good for me to read Virgil'). Suspicion always clung to Ovid—some of his poetry was banned altogether—but Virgil required no defence. Thomas Wolsey wrote that a good curriculum requires students to imitate Virgil, 'the first among all poets'. In *The Governor*, Elyot recommends imitating Virgil because, like Homer, he is 'like to a good nurse'. Ovid is a necessary evil: he helps 'for understanding other authors' but has 'little other learning... concerning other virtuous manners of policy'.[29] As Baldwin discusses in detail, the class notes of a Winchester schoolboy indicate that his master followed similar advice from the humanist John Sturm, who preferred

Virgil for matter that is 'chaste, pious, elegant, liberal' and recommended that Ovid could be excluded from the classroom and left to reading at home.[30] Subject to Lily's maxim, 'it is good for me to read Virgil', schoolboys imbibed habits of imitation built around an ideal of devotion to the 'good of the commonwealth' like that of *pius* Aeneas. But poems written by former schoolboys rarely followed anything like the model of the *Aeneid*. Rather, the school's training encouraged an outpouring, not of epic poetry, but of epyllia with a distinctly Ovidian, erotic cast. Rejecting Virgil's theme of 'empire without end', these poets preferred to investigate questions of sexuality, emotion, and desire. Indeed, they invent voices for a series of wronged and abandoned women like Dido—characters whose complex relationship to eloquence has much to tell us about the institution whose social agenda dubbed Virgil 'the prince of poets' and exemplar for masculine civic virtue.

With respect to the move from epic to 'minor' epic, then, it is worth remembering that the story Lodge adapted—Ovid's version of Glaucus and Scylla—constitutes Ovid's pointed interruption of 'the translation of empire'. In books 13–15, Ovid reworks Virgil's story of Aeneas' journey by taking a meandering, meta-rhetorical route to Italy. Competing with the end-driven narrative of masculine duty triumphing over the temptations of desire—and ignoring Virgil's own dark hints that the end (Rome) may repeat the violence and betrayals of the beginning (Troy)—Ovid effectively derails Virgilian teleology. Rhetorical combat replaces martial action (the debate between Ulysses and Ajax); and, when Troy falls, it falls in half a line. In place of Aeneas' grief, Ovid puts stories of female despair: first Hecuba's, then Aurora's for her dead son—a nymph who 'has no time to be moved' by the city's fall (13. 840). He reduces the six books of Aeneas' wanderings to a mere thirty lines listing the names of places passed in the Aegean. That is, instead of Virgil's proto-romance plot of errant wandering, Ovid substitutes the kind of rhetorically self-conscious digressions he favours, showing off the 'ingenium' ('wit') that made Quintilian cross. Plucking Scylla out of Virgilian context—a prophecy directing Aeneas to find the Sibyl names Scylla as one of the dangerous places he must pass—Ovid changes a place obstructing Aeneas' goal into a nymph with an interesting romantic past. That story begets yet another love story as Scylla listens to the nymph, Galatea (opening up the digression on Polyphemus' unrequited longing); and her final transformation results from a third unrequited passion (Circe's for Glaucus). Only after this associative chain of disappointed desire does Ovid return to Virgil's plot—and, of course, we return to it with Dido.

From the *Metamorphoses*' hundreds of stories, Lodge selected Scylla's—one that begins Ovid's pointed interruption of Virgil's prophetic plot. His choice suggests that Lodge and the poets who seized on his example for their own further invention were happy to displace the *Aeneid*'s *telos* of masculine civic duty alongside the pedagogical agenda that gave it pride of place. Heywood and Marlowe understood and replicated Lodge's gesture. In *Oenone and Paris*, the nymph foretells the 'fatal end to Troy' if Paris does not forsake Helen; she then invites Paris to turn his back on fate—

'that burning fire-brand' of Troy and its 'thousand mourning widows'—by embracing her 'in these verdant meadows' (ll. 16–17). Oenone's verdant pastoral pleasures may well be Heywood's antidote for the terrible pressure Virgil's gods bring to bear on Aeneas to fulfil his civic destiny. *Hero and Leander* similarly tells an erotic story that, while set near Troy, has little to do with the privileged cultural narrative that excises female desire from the business of nation-building. The poem opens 'On Hellespont', with two cities standing 'opposite'; but, rather than evoke the war and 'fateful' ends associated with that river, Marlowe tells us instead that the Hellespont is 'guilty of True-love's blood'. And even that amatory plot remains incomplete. From the poem's first line, we know the love affair will end badly. But Marlowe never narrates the tragic end—an evasion I have been suggesting is deliberate—and gives us, instead, a fragment that offers as much of a formal and erotic challenge to epic teleology as does Ovid's penchant for derailing the story of a second Troy with meta-rhetorical digressions about female desire.

Echoing Nymphs

With regard to the unintended consequences of school training, *Scillaes Metamorphosis* pushes its critique of contemporary pedagogy well beyond the opening joke on the figure of the teacher. Lodge opens the poem with a male–male teacher–student relationship and a lesson from a well-known school text; but his ending appears to leave the all-male world of the grammar school, as well as its social agenda, behind. In the final stanzas, it is Scilla's pain that preoccupies the narrator; her 'piteous' lament constitutes the poem's final 'lesson'—one directed not to men, but to 'Ladies' (l. 117). Certainly one could say that the opening conversation (between two male characters about love) and the poem's final Envoy, admonishing 'Ladies' to 'yield' to 'faithful lovers', constitute the kind of homosocial discursive exchange that characterizes the literary history of Petrarchism.[31] But I would like to suggest that, much like Petrarch's own interest in Ovid's female voices, neither that exchange nor Scilla's place in it functions quite as smoothly as the term 'homosociality' implies.

Other writers of epyllia clearly appreciated Lodge's attempt to ventriloquize female emotion. Shakespeare's Venus and Lucrece, Heywood's Oenone, Edward's Cephalus, Beaumont's Salmacis, Shirley's Echo, and a throng of unnamed, unhappy nymphs give voice to a host of passions—love, grief, rage, despair. Heywood, for example, concludes the debate between Oenone and Paris with the nymph's 'lament', a 'well of woe' that fills fifteen stanzas (stanzas 121, 125). Much like Shakespeare's sorrowing yet talkative Lucrece, Oenone's emotions temporarily render her mute—'Her language stopped, as bird pent up in cage' (stanza 124)—only to burst out anew when she calls out to 'Ye ragged cliffs...rocks, and clowdy mountains', 'streams, wells, brooks, and lovely fountains' (stanzas 1289). Her situation (abandoned by the water's edge) and rhetorical and emotional predicament (no human audience) clearly draw upon and amplify Lodge's earlier scene. Where Scilla beats 'the weeping waves that for her mourned' and 'Echo herself' answers, 'returning' only 'words of sorrow, (*no love*)... Then fie on hope: *then fie on hope*' (stanzas 115–17), Heywood's Oenone extends the fantasy by projecting voices onto the inanimate world, asking rocks to 'howl, and lament' with her (stanza 128).

Both scenes of female woe clearly recall that of the abandoned Ariadne, and Ovid's *Heroides* was another text commonly imitated at school. When Ariadne runs down the shoreline after Theseus' ship, her voice brings the landscape to life: 'And all the while I cried out "Theseus!" along the entire shore, and the hollow rocks sent back your name to me (*reddebant nomen*); whenever I called to you, the place spoke the same word. The place itself wanted to feel my misery' (Her. 10. 21–3).[32] Ariadne's lament is a programmatic one on Ovid's part. It revisits one of his favourite dreams about language—the dream of a voice that can 'move' rocks and stones to pity, animate the inanimate.[33] As such, Ariadne's predicament was all the more memorable for the sixteenth-century students set to write in his style in order to become effective rhetoricians themselves. They seem to recognize that Ovid dwells on the power and limits of the voice because he wants to explore not merely intense affect, but the relationship *between* rhetoric and emotion.

A year before Heywood published his epyllion, Shakespeare also picked up Lodge's scene of Scilla's echoing woe; and his grieving, lonely Venus makes the allusion to Ovid's Ariadne more explicit still. Though Adonis leaves Venus alone in the woods, the narrator's simile removes her to the water's edge: 'after him she darts, as one on shore | Gazing upon a late embarked friend' (ll. 817–18). And Venus hears, like Ariadne and Scilla before her, only the sound of her own echo.

> And now she beats her heart, whereat it groans,
> That all the neighbour caves, as seeming troubled,
> *Make verbal repetition* of her moans;
> Passion on passion deeply is redoubled:
> 'Ay me!' she cries, and twenty times, 'Woe, woe!'
> And twenty echoes twenty times cry so.
> (ll. 829–34, emphasis added)

To 'make verbal repetition', of course, is exactly what Tudor schoolmasters, following Erasmus's theory of imitation, required of young boys. Perhaps the outpouring of echoing female complaint, and of implied universal sympathy, is as much a re-enactment as a critique of schoolroom training. For those who acquired rhetorical skill by imitating classical precursors, the humanist platform of instruction clearly proved profitable. But drilling in *imitatio* might have prompted some of them to empathize with Echo's quandary. As Narcissus asks on hearing her make verbal repetition, 'is anyone here?' Such a question moves beyond the critique of rhetoric's instrumental function to suggest that an educational programme based on imitation might well produce convincing fictions of rhetorical mastery and masculine identity, but such fictions would always be haunted by an indeterminate vacillation between Echo and echo.

Here the shifting allegiances and passions of Lodge's nymphs give further insight into problems of identity implicit in such training. Lodge begins the poem with male desire—the narrator's, Glaucus's—but closes with a crescendo of lamenting nymphs. At first they form a 'piteous' chorus, weeping 'so sore' for Glaucus' pain that 'their tears' form 'a pretty brook' (71. 1–6). This outpouring of shared feeling includes the narrator, who depicts his own act of writing as a transfer of affect. Addressing his Muse, he transforms his own lines of poetry into Ariadne's rocks, asking them to participate in and transmit sorrow:

> Yield me such feeling words, that whilst I write,
> My working lines may fill mine eyes with languish,
> And they to note my moans may melt with anguish.
> (73. 4–6)

'Feeling words': a phrase for rhetorical success, but it also raises the question, who (or what) is doing the 'feeling' here? Distinctions between speaker, text, and audience begin to blur. And they do so again when the nymphs start echoing Scilla: 'forced with tears for to assist her moan', they persist in piteous identification until the end (104. 6). For example, when Scilla cries out for Glaucus, 'all the Nymphs afflict the air with noise' (100. 6). And at this point, the narrator's grief also seems to 'melt' into Scilla's: 'Rue me that writes, for why her ruth deserves it' (109. 5). Scilla's woe acquires the kind of embodied, affective, and animating force that might make Orpheus envious:

> For every sigh, the rocks return a sigh;
>
> . . . . .
>
> Woods, and waves, and rocks, and hills *admire*
> *The wonderous force* of her untam'd desire
> (118. 1–6, emphasis added)

Nature itself is tamed by her 'untam'd' desire. From such transfers of affect between speaker and audience, yet further passions emerge: Lodge produces an allegorical parade worthy of Spenser—'Fury and Rage, Wan-hope, Despair, and Woe' (120. 1)—and these personifications 'assail' their subject, leading Scilla 'captive' to the island where she turns into 'that famous Isle', 'a hapless haunt' for weeping (stanzas 124–5). Even after Scilla is gone, the narrator remains afflicted with her emotion: he sits 'a-lonely' like the captive Scilla 'with many a sigh and heart full sad and sorry' (128. 5–6). At times uniting subjects and at others exceeding them, passions in Lodge's epyllion enable the poetic speaker to represent himself as a poet only by blurring the distinctions necessary to received categories of gender and identity.

Despite the evident similarity between Scilla's moving voice and that of Ariadne and Orpheus, Lodge does not quote her directly. Rather, he channels Scilla's words and passions through other parties: echoing nymphs, 'Echo herself', and the sound of waves, rocks, and fountains. It is as if the narrator's verse brings all these sounds together; and it is precisely the *detour* through other voices that allows him to find 'feeling words' capable of moving an audience. The energetic relay of vocal power and transfer of affective intensity exceeds the difference between animate and inanimate, which in turn allows Lodge to lay claim to a poetic voice rivalling that of Orpheus or Ariadne. But that relay of emotional and rhetorical force also exceeds the difference between genders necessary to the definition of a gentleman and around which the all-male school appeared to turn. Indeed, the crucial role that shared affect plays in Lodge's claim to poetic power carries a specific institutional resonance: as one schoolboy wrote in his commonplace book under the heading of 'Rhetoricke': 'Cicero Saith it is almost impossible for an orator to stir up a passion in his auditors except he be first affected with the same passion himself.'[34] Success at school was more than a matter of learning to imitate precedent authors; it meant learning to feel for oneself, and to convey to others, the many passions represented in them. The goal of rhetoric, this young student knows well, is to 'move' one's audience—and to do so in ways that mobilize quicksilver transmissions of feeling.

Schoolmasters felt themselves to be in the business of producing not just verbal skill in students, but socially acceptable affect and bodily deportment as well. And, as the moving 'force' of Scilla's sighs and tears suggests, humanists knew that rhetorical power requires more than verbal skill. It requires what one schoolboy called 'eloquence of the body', otherwise known as *actio*, an eloquence that he calls 'the shadow of affect'. Bodily and facial gestures are crucial to persuasion, and school archives suggest that masters devoted themselves to training their students accordingly. Lodge's Scilla and her echoing nymphs draw attention to the repeated rhetorical and institutional practices through which, as Judith Butler argues, conceptual frames guide the materialization of gendered bodies.[35] But cross-voiced epyllia suggest that what materialized did not always neatly coincide with normative definitions of a 'gentleman'.

Indeed, Lodge's desire for 'feeling words' to convey and transmit female passion owes much to the disciplinary practices schoolmasters used to inculcate rhetorical power. School archives suggest that becoming a Latin speaking *puer* involved a number of trans-gendered exercises, beginning with school theatricals. Training in gentlemanly behaviour included the displacements and emotional excesses of the theatre; whatever 'male' signifies in this context, it must be capacious enough to include the widespread practice of cross-dressing.[36] Schoolmasters were enthusiastic about theatricals because they believed acting was excellent preparation for oratory: it was 'conducive to fluency of expression and deportment' and taught boys 'to speak clearly and elegantly'.[37] But beyond theatricals, other exercises required boys to speak in the voices of women. Perhaps the most pertinent to epyllia—and the evident appeal of Ariadne's story—occurred at the Shrewsbury School in 1591. Gathered on a riverbank, the 'scholars of the free school', 'apparelled all in green' with 'green willows upon their heads', bid their patron farewell in the voices of nymphs. Like Lodge's scene, one 'nymph' reports the woe of others—'Their woe is great, great moan they make'—and a chorus of four more nymphs then takes up the tune of a 'woeful wretched time'. Whatever we may make of boys dressed in green crowned with willow boughs, contemporaries were moved by it: 'so pitifully and of such excellence' was the lament, a witness writes, 'that truly it made many both [those] in the barge upon the water as also people upon land to weep and my Lord himself to change countenance'.[38]

Dedicated to producing and policing socially acceptable speech, movement, and affect in their students, humanist grammar schools established rhetorically and institutionally specific parameters within which gender could be performed. But Elizabethan minor epics indicate that the path to eloquent masculinity sometimes took turns that schoolmasters did not anticipate. If read in the light of school practice, epyllia tell us that at least some former schoolboys either grasped the extent to which gender is a social and rhetorical script or identified with characters and passions at some distance from the script they were expected to adopt. Transmitting feelings of woe, grief, desire, and rage while laying claim to the kind of rhetorical power that might make a schoolmaster proud, Ariadne, Scilla, Venus, Oenone, and the sorrowing nymphs echoing in their wake indicate that achieving the identity of an eloquent 'gentleman' was a contradictory, unfinished process. Minor epics signal resistance to the school's social teleology through rhetorically skilled detours of intense feeling. If read carefully, these detours trouble any claim—whether early modern or modern—about the school's seamless production of 'male' identities in its undoubtedly eloquent gentlemen.

Notes

1. The standard collection of non-Shakespearean epyllia is Elizabeth Story Donno (ed.), *Elizabethan Minor Epics* (New York, 1963). All quotations are from this edition. Following *Scillaes Metamorphosis* (1589), epyllia were published as follows: in 1593, *Venus and Adonis*; in 1594, *The Rape of Lucrece* and Thomas Heywood, *Oenone and Paris*; in 1595, Thomas Edwards, *Cephalus and Procris*, Michael Drayton, *Endimion and Phoebe*, George Chapman, *Ovids Banquet of Sence*; in 1598, Christopher Marlowe, *Hero and Leander*, George Chapman, *Hero and Leander Completed*, and John Marston, *Metamorphosis of Pigmalions Image*; in 1600, John Weever, *Faunus and Melliflora*; in 1602, Francis Beaumont, *Salmacis and Hermaphroditus*; in 1616, Chapman, *The Divine Poem of Musaeus: Hero and Leander*. Two later poems, Phineas Fletcher, *Venus and Anchises: Brittain's Ida* (1628) and James Shirley, *Narcissus or the Self-Lover* (1646), returned to the trend but did not revive it.
2. See John Kerrigan (ed.), *The Motives of Woe: Shakespeare and 'Female Complaint': A Critical Anthology* (Oxford, 1991). The most important modern studies of Elizabethan epyllia are: Elizabeth Story

Donno, 'Introduction', in Donno (ed.), *Elizabethan Minor Epics*; William Keach, *Elizabethan Erotic Narratives: Irony and Pathos in the Ovidian Poetry of Shakespeare, Marlowe, and their Contemporaries* (New Brunswick, NJ, 1977); Clark Hulse, *Metamorphic Verse: The Elizabethan Minor Epic* (Princeton, 1981); James Ellis, *Sexuality and Citizenship: Metamorphosis in English Erotic Verse* (Toronto, 2004); Georgia Brown, *Redefining Elizabethan Literature* (Cambridge, 2009), ch. 3; William Weaver, *Untutored Lines: the Making of the English Epyllion* (Edinburgh, 2012).

3. For epyllia in relation to the 'well-defined cultural milieu' of the Inns of Court, see Ellis, *Sexuality and Citizenship*.
4. T. W. Baldwin, *Shakespere's Small Latine & Lesse Greeke* (Urbana, IL, 1944), I. 339–40.
5. *Aphthoniis sophistae progymnasmata . . . and Sum scholiis Reinhardi Lorichii Hamdaarii* (1592).
6. For the influence of humanist pedagogy and classical rhetorical training on drama in the period, see Emrys Jones, *The Origins of Shakespeare* (Oxford, 1977); Joel Altman, *The Tudor Play of Mind: Rhetorical Inquiry and the Development of Elizabethan Drama* (Berkeley and Los Angeles, 1978); Neil Rhodes, 'The Controversial Plot: Declamation and the Concept of the "Problem Play" ', *Modern Language Review*, 95/3 (2000), 609–22; Ursula Potter, 'Performing Arts in the Tudor Classroom', in Lloyd Kermode, Jason Scott-Warren, and Martine Van Elk (eds), *Tudor Drama before Shakespeare 1485–1590* (New York, 2004); and Lynn Enterline, *Shakespeare's Schoolroom Rhetoric, Discipline, Emotion* (Philadelphia, 2012).
7. John Brinsley, *Ludus Literarius* (1612), 49.
8. In *Untutored Lines*, William Weaver argues that the techniques of grammar-school training on display in epyllia mark the shift from lower to upper forms in the schools. I am indebted to his work, but my approach to the relationship between puberty and humanist practice differs from Weaver's; I build on a psychoanalytic theory of the psyche as a kind of palimpsest that resists narratives of progressive 'stages'.
9. For my account of pedagogy's impact on sexuality in *Venus and Adonis*, see Lynn Enterline, 'The Art of Loving Mastery', in *Shakespeare's Schoolroom*.
10. See the chapter on ekphrasis in *Aphthoniis sophistae progymnasmata*.
11. For Shakespeare's engagement with Ovid in *Venus and Adonis*, see Jonathan Bates, *Shakespeare and Ovid* (Oxford, 1994), ch. 2.
12. William Weaver, ' "O teach me how to make mine own excuse": Forensic Performance in Lucrece', *Shakespeare Quarterly*, 59 (2008), 421–49, outlines the rhetorical techniques and textbooks Lucrece deploys in what amounts to 'a formal oration in the judicial genre'.
13. See Lynn Enterline, *The Rhetoric of the Body from Ovid to Shakespeare* (Cambridge, 2005).
14. William Nelson, *A Fifteenth Century Schoolbook* (Oxford, 1956), 32.
15. Reinhard Lorich's translation of *Aphthoniis sophistae progymnasmata* went through over 150 editions in as many years.
16. Donno (ed.), *Elizabethan Minor Epics*, 19.
17. Erasmus culled the word from Quintilian (*copia rerum ac verborum*) but vastly extended its range. See *The Collected Works of Erasmus, Literary and Educational Writings*, vol. 1, ed. Craig R. Thomson (Toronto, 1978), p. xxxv. See Richard Halpern's account of the pertinence of *copia* to economic history (*The Poetics of Primitive Accumulation: English Renaissance Culture and the Genealogy of Capital* (Ithaca, NY, 1991)).
18. Colin Burrow, 'Shakespeare and Humanistic Culture', in Charles Martindale and

A. B. Taylor (eds), *Shakespeare and the Classics* (Cambridge, 2004), 9–27.

19. Judith Haber, *Desire and Dramatic Form in Early Modern England* (Cambridge, 2009), 39–43. James Bromley extends Haber's point in relation to Neptune's attempted seduction ('"Let it Suffise": Sexual Acts and Narrative Structure in Hero and Leander', in Stephen Guy-Bray and Stephen Nardizzi (eds), *Queer Renaissance Historiography: Backward Gaze* (Farnham, 2009), 67–84).
20. *Venus and Adonis* is a notable case in point. See Catherine Belsey, 'Love as Trompe-l'œil: Taxonomies of Desire in *Venus and Adonis*', *Shakespeare Quarterly*, 46/3 (1995), 257–76, and Richard Halpern, '"Pining their Maws": Female Readers and Erotic Ontology of the Text', in Philip C. Kolin (ed.), *Shakespeare's Venus and Adonis: Critical Essays* (New York, 1997), 377–88. For Marston's 'verbal fetishism', see Lynn Enterline, '"Be not obsceane though wanton": Marston's *Metamorphosis of Pigmalions Image*', in *The Rhetoric of the Body*, 125–51.
21. Bromley discusses non-teleological pleasures in Neptune's story of the shepherd and his boy ('"Let it Suffise"').
22. Haber, *Desire and Dramatic Form*, 45–8.
23. On Marlowe's training at the King's School in Canterbury, see David Riggs, *The World of Christopher Marlowe* (New York, 2004).
24. *Aphthoniis sophistae progymnasmata*, 281.
25. Baldwin, *Small Latine*, I. 608–40.
26. As quoted in Baldwin, *Small Latine*, I. 607.
27. Brown, *Redefining Elizabethan Literature*, 3.
28. I draw this paragraph from Enterline, *Shakespeare's Schoolroom*.
29. For Virgil's place in the schools, see Andrew Wallace, *Virgil's Schoolboys: the Poetics of Pedagogy in Renaissance England* (Oxford, 2011). For further details about the ongoing debate among schoolmasters about Ovid's value, see Enterline, *Shakespeare's Schoolroom*, 74–9.
30. Baldwin, *Small Latine*, I. 340–1.
31. Here I differ from Ellis's account (*Sexuality and Citizenship*, 51–64). Focusing on the work of Luce Irigaray and Monique Wittig, Ellis explores the 'socially productive' aspects of heterosexuality with intriguing consequences for epyllia. In my view, social constructionist arguments gloss over the fissures that psychoanalytic theorists find at the heart of an ostensibly efficient cultural system—a persisting nonsense that can unexpectedly resurface in performances of gendered 'identity'.
32. From Ovid, *Heroides and Amores* (Cambridge, MA, 1977).
33. For a full account of Ovid's 'phonographic imaginary', see Enterline, *The Rhetoric of the Body*.
34. Folger MS V.a.381, fo. 94.
35. See Judith Butler, *Bodies that Matter: On the Discursive Limits of Sex* (New York, 1993).
36. Harold Newcomb Hillebrand, *The Child Actors* (Urbana, IL, 1926). Critics have begun to reassess the proto-dramatic aspect of early grammar-school training; see Ursula Potter, 'Performing Arts in the Tudor Classroom', in Lloyd Kermode, Jason Scott-Warren, and Martine van Elk (eds), *Tudor Drama before Shakespeare, 1485–1590* (New York, 2004).
37. For the archival evidence, see Lynn Enterline, 'Imitate and Punish: The Theatricality of Everyday Life in Elizabethan Schoolrooms', in *Shakespeare's Schoolroom*, ch. 2.
38. *A History of Shrewsbury School* (Shrewsbury, 1889), 65–6.

CHAPTER 12

The Epistolary Tradition

WILLIAM FITZGERALD

Familiarity and the Familiar Letter

What we now know as the letter is the descendant of the 'familiar' letter of the Renaissance, itself modelled on the letters of Cicero, collected in the books known as the *Ad Familiares* (*To his Intimates*). Perhaps the most important bequest of ancient letter-writing to modern culture is the notion of familiarity itself, that combination of friendly intimacy with an appropriate style, which was practised and theorized during the Renaissance in the wake of the rediscovery of Cicero's letters. While it was the *Ad Familiares* that gave the Renaissance familiar letter its name, the sixteen books of letters by Cicero to his closest friend, Atticus, were equally important for the association between letters and intimacy. In fact, it is in one of the letters to Atticus that Cicero describes the difference between the broader term *amicitia* (friendship) and *familiaritas*. In *Ad Atticum* 1. 18. 1 Cicero complains that among the brilliant friendships that are on display to the world there is none that allows him 'to make an unguarded joke or release a private sigh [*suspirare familiariter*]', and in another letter to Atticus he speaks of the kind of letter in which he can write familiarly ('scribere familiariter' (*Ad Atticum* 9. 4. 1)).[1] When Cicero (*Ad Familiares* 2. 4) distinguished three types of letter, he identified one as the 'intimate and humorous' ('familiare et iocosum'), a connection that made relaxed humour an important ingredient of the familiar letter.

The story of the Renaissance familiar letter begins when Petrarch discovered Cicero's letters to Atticus in 1345 in the chapter library of Vercelli and made them widely known through his letters to dead authors, including one to Cicero himself. Petrarch also owned the complete letters of Seneca, a decisive influence on his early letters, later revised to reflect his reading of Cicero. Petrarch's five collections of letters in Latin are the fountainhead of the Renaissance epistolary tradition. In 1392 Coluccio Salutati discovered Cicero's *Ad Familiares* in the cathedral library at Verona. Like Petrarch, Salutati was inspired by the example of Cicero's books of letters to edit and publish his own letter collections.[2] Cicero's *Letters to his Friends* was among the first books printed in Italy, with printings in Venice in 1469 and in Rome in 1467 and 1470. By 1500 it had been printed at least fifty-two times. Of the other notable Latin letter-writers, Seneca's letters first appeared in print in 1470, and Pliny's in 1471.[3]

The rediscovery of Cicero's letters shifted the emphasis of letter-writing manuals away from the oratorical model that governed the medieval *ars dictaminis*, the art of writing (official) letters.[4] In the *ars dictaminis* the letter's structure was described in terms of the ancient rhetoricians' divisions of the parts of a speech, and strict attention was paid to the decorum appropriate to the relative status of writer and addressee. The transition from *ars dictaminis* to the theory of familiarity can be seen in Erasmus' *De Conscribendis Epistolis* (*How to Write Letters*) (1522), in which the first three of his four categories of letters—deliberative, demonstrative, judicial, and familiar—correspond to the three branches of ancient rhetoric, but the fourth one derives its name from Cicero's *Ad Familiares*. Erasmus also moves away from the rhetorical emphasis of the *ars dictaminis* when he describes the letter as 'a sort of conversation between absent friends' ('absentium amicorum quasi mutuus sermo').[5] Juan Luis Vives, in his influential *De Conscribendis Epistolis* (1534), goes further and denies the relevance of rhetorical categories altogether, for the letter is 'as it were a reflection of everyday speech and of continuous conversation' ('imago quaedam est quotidiani sermonis, ac colloquii cuijusdam perpetui').[6] This idea that the letter is a conversation between absent friends is the most important of several influential *topoi* of ancient letter-writing theory.[7] It comes with assumptions about the proper style for a 'familiar' letter. Seneca puts it as follows:

> Qualis sermo meus esset, si una sederemus aut ambularemus, inelaboratus et facilis, tales esse epistulas meas volo, quae nihil habent accersitum nec fictum.
>
> (I want my letters to be as my conversation would be if we were sitting or walking together, casual and easy, with nothing recherché or made-up about them.)
>
> (*Moral Epistles*, 75. 1)

Ironically, the familiar letter became implicated in the anti-Ciceronian movement, which rejected Cicero's oratory as a model for prose in favour of the more pithy style of Seneca.[8] The emphasis on conversation in ancient epistolary practice and theory encouraged the development of the plain style as a universal medium. As Wesley Trimpi pointed out, if the letter could encompass any matter or emotion (as theorists both ancient and modern declared), and the appropriate style for the letter was unelaborated and casual, then theories of decorum attached to a hierarchy of styles no longer held, and the plain style could accommodate any subject.[9]

A further consequence of the idea that the letter is a conversation, as ancient epistolographers insist, is that it should be written in the vernacular. It is under the pretext of this ancient *topos* that Renaissance English letter-writers explain their decision to write in English rather than Latin.[10] Most of them, as schoolboys, would have composed letters in Latin, an exercise that was part of the rhetorical education of all grammar schools; by the 1570s English publishers were producing school editions of Cicero's letters.[11] While continental letter collections and treatises on the letter, whether in Latin or in the vernacular, were disseminated in England, by the mid-sixteenth century England was beginning to produce its own vernacular epistolography.[12] Two important English treatises on the letter appeared in the second half of the century: William Fulwood's *The Enemie of Idleness* appeared in 1568 (and saw its seventh edition by 1598) and Angel Day's *The English Secretorie* appeared in 1586. The content of these treatises was heavily influenced by continental, and through them ancient, models. Day calls the letter 'the familiar and mutual talk of one absent friend to another', whose character 'should be simple, plain, and of the lowest, meanest style, utterly devoid of any shadow of high and lofty speeches' (*Secretorie*, 8). For Fulwood, this means that the appropriate style for letters was 'not that of a rare and diffused phrase, or inkhorn terms, scummed from the Latin, nor of too base terms and barbarous, or terms unknown except in certain places' (Fulwood, *Enemie*, 8). The letter is 'the messenger and familiar speech of the absent' (Day, *Secretorie*, 1) or 'a declaration, by writing of the minds of such as be absent, one of them to another, even as though they were present' (Fulwood, *Enemie*, 9).

Collections

Familiar letters might be published as a collection, in the manner of Cicero's *Ad Familiares*, and as a collection they might tend towards the narrative or historical by presenting an oblique history of the times in which the letter-writer was himself a player.

James Howell's familiar letters, collected under the title *Epistolae Ho-Elianae* (volumes appeared in 1645, 1647, 1650, and 1655) are a case in point.[13] They cover the experiences and reflections of a man who travelled widely on diplomatic or commercial missions during this turbulent period of history. Both a portrait or biography of their author and a historical survey, they would be inconceivable without the example of Cicero's letters.[14] The frontispieces of the 1645 and 1650 editions contain portraits of Seneca and Marcus Aurelius on the one side and Cicero and Caesar on the other, marking respectively the historico-political (Cicero) and philosophical (Seneca) streams of the Roman epistolary tradition. Howell declares, in the dedicatory letter of the 1645 edition (addressed to Charles I), that 'it is well known, that letters can treasure up, and transmit matters of state to posterity, with as much faith, and be as authentic registers, and safe repositories of truth, as any story whatsoever'. If this is well known, it is at least in part because of the remark of Cornelius Nepos that, thanks to Cicero's letters to Atticus, 'the reader would hardly need a continuous history of the period' (Nepos, *Life of Atticus*, 16). Howell's collection of familiar letters is deliberately constructed to do what the letters of Cicero were said to do. But

Howell is eclectic in his influences: though many of the letters contain that mixture of political news and personal trivia familiar to readers of Cicero's letters, others are more in the tradition of Pliny and Seneca in developing a single theme.

Howell is well aware of the potential of the letter to compose an image of the writer, and he echoes the influential statement of Demetrius (date unknown, perhaps second century BC) in the section on letters of his *De Elocutione* (227). Demetrius says: 'The letter should be strong on characterization, like the dialogue; everyone in writing a letter more or less composes an image of his own soul. One can indeed see the writer's character in any other kind of writing, but in none so clearly as in the letter.'[15] In the prefatory poem to his *Epistolae Ho-Elianae* (*To the Knowing Reader Touching Familiar Letters*), Howell writes:

> Speech is the index, letters ideas are
> Of the informing soul; they can declare,
> And show the inward man, as we behold
> A face reflecting in a crystal mould.

Many of Howell's letters are clearly composed for the collection, and his retrospective doctoring of history in this apparently eyewitness account tends towards fiction. Other collections are more transparently fictional, and have been seen as important precursors of the epistolary novel, which was itself to play a key role in the development of the modern genre par excellence.[16] Early forms of the fictional narrative in letters derive from the epistolographers' practice of providing model letters. In the treatise *On Letter Form* (*De Forma Epistolari*) attributed to Libanius (fourth century AD), the author gives specimens of the forty-one categories of letter he identifies, and so initiates an important tradition. Both Fulwood and Day had included model letters in their handbooks, but it was Nicolas Breton's enormously popular *Poste with a Madde Packet of Letters* (1602, with at least twelve editions in the seventeenth century) that took the genre of the model letter firmly in the direction of epistolary fiction by excluding anything but the letters themselves. *Poste* is an array of model letters of different kinds, whose variety is motivated by the fiction that they were contained in a lost bag of mail (a fiction whose transparency is underlined by the fact that many of the letters had replies). Letters with replies occur also among the model letters of Fulwood and Day. The closest ancient precedent for this kind of collection are the letter books of Alciphron, a Greek writer of the Second Sophistic (late second or early third century AD), who wrote four books of letters, some with replies, treating the life of ordinary people (the fourth book consists of courtesans' letters). Whether Alciphron was known to Breton is dubious. Though the *editio princeps* in Greek was a Venetian edition of 1499, the first Latin translation did not appear until 1606, and an English translation would not appear until 1791.[17] Breton's letters show a clearer relation to the rhetorical tradition, foregrounding the elegant use of rhetorical figures and epistolary formulae.

The Heroic Epistle

The Latin prose epistolary tradition is short on love letters, though the shortfall is made up by Ovid's highly influential *Heroides*, fictitious letters in verse in which mythical heroines write to their lovers, and in some cases vice versa. The *Heroides* is usually positioned first in early printings of Ovid's works. Important translations of the *Heroides* by Thomas Heywood (*Heroides* 6 and 17 (1609)), George Turberville (1567), and Wye Saltonstall (1630) made them available in English, and perhaps encouraged imitations, of which the most well known in our period are Michael Drayton's *Englands Heroicall Epistles* (1597).[18] These were the first English examples of a genre that would include Pope's *Eloisa to Abelard*. Following the example of Ovid's paired *Heroides* (*Heroides* 16–21), Drayton takes pairs of lovers from English history, beginning with Rosamond and Henry II, and gives them a letter each. Like Ovid, Drayton was concerned with the letter-writer's creation of a self through writing.[19] One aspect of this is that Drayton's lovers allude knowingly to their models in Ovid. Geraldine writing to Surrey, for instance, echoes the opening words of Penelope to Ulysses in the first of Ovid's *Heroides*. If Surrey is a wandering Ulysses, then she is the Penelope to whom he will return:

> Then, as Ulysses wife, write I to thee,
> Make no reply, but come thy self to me.[20]

The 1590s were particularly rich in imitations of the *Heroides*. Samuel Daniel's 'The Complaint of Rosamond' (1592) marries the complaint tradition to the Ovidian heroic epistle, and the fusion proves highly influential.[21] Many of these epistles, like Drayton's, are written in the voice of historical rather than mythical figures. Daniel's 'A Letter from Octavia to Marcus Antonius' (1599) was anticipated by the two epistles between Mark Antony and Octavia appended to Samuel Brandon's play 'The Tragi-Comoedi of the Vertuous Octavia' (1598).

In the heroic epistle the female voice, ventriloquized by a male author though it may be, presents a resisting perspective on the life that is allowed to women. Ovid's Hero had contrasted the varied pursuits of men (hunting, farming, wrestling, riding, fishing) with the confined monotony of the woman's life, for whom nothing remains but to love ('superest praeter amare nihil' (*Heroides* 19. 16)). Accordingly Hero loves with a love that Leander could never return ('plus quoque quam redidi quod mihi possit amo' (19. 18)). Drayton's Jane Shore complains that husbands, fearing the corrupting effect of city entertainments, keep their wives at home:

> What sports have we, whereon our minds to set?
> Our dog, our parrot, or our marmoset,
> Or once a week to walk into the field.
> ('The Epistle of Mistress Shore, to King Edward the Fourth', ll. 147–9)

Daniel's Octavia is more abstract, but closer to Ovid's psychological analysis:

> We, in this prison of ourselves confined,
> Must here shut up with our own passion live,
> Turned in upon us, and denied to find
> The vent of outward means that might relieve:
> That they alone must take up all our mind
> And no room leave us, but to think and grieve:
> Yet oft our narrowed thoughts look more direct
> Than your loose wisdoms born with wild neglect.
> (ll. 137–44)[22]

In Donne's 'Sappho to Philaenis' (1601?), the resisting female voice is directed not only at men but at the author of the genre.[23] Donne's Sappho quite deliberately answers Ovid's 'Sappho to Phaon' (*Heroides* 15, though Ovid's authorship is disputed) by making Sappho a Lesbian:

> Such was my Phao awhile, but shall be never,
> As thou wast, art, and, oh, mayst thou be ever.
> (ll. 25–6)[24]

Sappho's letter is a forceful persuasion to homosexual love and sexual emancipation from men.

But not all heroic epistles present us with a female voice ventriloquized by men. Ovid's *Heroides* was on the Renaissance school syllabus, and girls as well as boys might be required to construe the work. In Shakespeare's *Taming of the Shrew* Lucentio uses a lesson on *Heroides* 1 to woo his pupil Bianca. The fruits of the educational use of *Heroides* can be seen, for instance, in Isabella Whitley's 'Copy of a Letter, Lately Written in Metre, by a Young Gentlewoman; To Her Inconstant Lover' (*c.*1567).[25]

The Verse Epistle

A more distinctly male genre is the verse epistle, of which the two most important writers in the English Renaissance were Jonson and Donne. Horace had written two books of verse *Epistles*, addressed to various contemporaries, and these proved a valuable model for Renaissance authors looking to create new forms of intimate style, particularly with respect to the uneven relation between patron and poet that is such a central preoccupation of Horace. Horace's epistles negotiate the claims of *amicitia* and *libertas* (both freedom and freedom of speech) within a circle that includes superiors and inferiors as well as equals. Renaissance editors of Horace tended to see the *Satires* and *Epistles* as complementary, the one attacking vice and the other teaching virtue.[26] Since Horace gave the label *sermones* (conversations) to both his epistles and his satires, and both collections were also composed in hexameters, the Renaissance verse epistle draws freely on the manner and content of both the *Satires* and the *Epistles*. It is also the case that Horace's *Epistles* might infiltrate

English poems not attributed to the epistolary genre. While Jonson gave the title 'Epistle' to some of his poems, the influence of Horace's *Epistles* can be seen in his epigrams as well. One of the best known of these, *Epigram* 101 ('Inviting a Friend to Supper'), overlays Horace's invitation in *Epistles* 1. 5 on Jonson's more obvious model in Martial (10. 48).[27]

The verse epistle became an important locus for negotiating relations between poet and patron. *Epistles* 1. 18 of Horace, which deals with the question of how to strike the right balance between subservience and presumptuousness in dealings with the powerful, seems to have been particularly interesting to Jonson and his circle.[28] But Jonson can also play the role of the gracious patron, as in 'An Epistle Answering One that Asked to be Sealed in the Tribe of Ben'. Here Jonson rehearses the characteristics that he expects of a member of his circle in terms that are borrowed from Horace's descriptions of the circle of Maecenas in his *Satires*. He also discusses his own standing at court and then, in the final three lines of an epistle of nearly eighty lines, he turns to his addressee's request:

> I will take you so,
> As you have writ yourself. Now stand, and then,
> Sir, you are sealed of the tribe of Ben.
>
> (ll. 76–8)

Jonson's ending recalls an epistle of Horace in which the poet is in a quite different position. Writing to recommend a friend to Tiberius, the future emperor, Horace spends the bulk of this short poem negotiating the issue of his potentially presumptuous request, against which he cites the responsibilities of friendship. Finally, in the last three lines of the poem, he gets to the point:

> quodsi
> depositum laudas ob amici iussa pudorem.
> scribe tui gregis hunc et fortem crede bonumque.
>
> (So,
> If you approve me putting aside my embarrassment to gratify a friend
> Enroll him in your circle and take him for a good man and true.)
>
> (*Epistles* 1. 9. 11–13)

The echo reminds us that, by contrast with Horace, here it is Jonson who is in a position to grant or deny.

Donne writes to both patrons and friends in his verse epistles. Matters of relative position, prestige, and power are important, as they are in Horace. But the more reflective, philosophical aspect of Horace's *Epistles* is reflected in a poem such as 'To Mr Roland Woodward', which, like the first epistle of Horace's first book, outlines a new kind of poetry.[29] In the Horatian poem, the poet declares his intention to retire from the role of lyric love poet ('nunc iterum et versus et cetera ludicra pono' (*Epistles* 1. 1. 10)) and compares himself to a gladiator who has earned his release. Donne's comparison is still more surprising:

Like one who in her third widowhood doth profess
Herself a nun, tied to retiredness,
So affects my Muse now a chaste fallowness;

Since she to few, yet too many hath shown
How love-songs weeds and satiric thorns are grown
Where seeds of better arts were early sown.
(ll. 1–6)

The conceit that Donne's Muse is in retirement echoes Horace's notion that his *sermones* are not really poetry at all. Donne, in fact, is outlining a programme for a new kind of poetry, and he describes himself as 'betrothed to no one art', adapting Horace's declaration that he is a devotee of no particular philosophy ('nullius addictus iurare in verba magistri' (*Epistles*, I. I. 14)). He appropriates Horace's critique of the false freedom of travel (*Epistles*, I. II. 26–30) to his own promotion of 'retiredness':

So works retiredness in us: to roam
Giddily, and be everywhere, but at home,
Such freedom doth a banishment become.
(ll. 28–30)

But Donne goes one step beyond Horace in assigning Horace's new, more serious theme for the *Epistles* (virtue) to second place, behind religion:

There is no virtue but religion:
Wise, valiant sober, just, are names, which none
Want, which want not vice-covering discretion.
(ll. 16–18)

As with his reformulation of Ovid's letter of Sappho to Phaon, here too Donne subjects his model author to the kind of critique that the ancient author had himself initiated.

The Moral Epistle

Besides the familiar letter, the verse letter, and the heroic epistle, the Renaissance also recognized the category of the moral epistle, modelled on the Stoic letters of Seneca to Lucilius. The reputation of Seneca received a boost in the latter part of the sixteenth century from continental writers and scholars, notably Justus Lipsius (1547–1606), who expounded Stoic philosophy from a Christian angle and wrote in a Latin style heavily influenced by Seneca. Lipsius' 'hopping' style, abrupt in movement and terse in expression, combined features that were to become characteristic of the Senecan manner.[30] Its virtues are well described by Thomas Randolph ('To Master Feltham on his Book of Resolves'):

I mean the style being pure, and strong, and round;
Not long, but pithy; being short-breathed but sound,
Such as the grave, acute, wise Seneca sings,
That best of tutors to the worst of kings.
Not long and empty, lofty but not proud;
Subtle but sweet; high but without a cloud.
Well-settled, full of nerves, in brief 'tis such,
That in a little hath comprised much.[31]

(89–96)

Seneca played a decisive role in the emergence of the genre of the essay, and the term returned to bite him in the many modern characterizations of his moral epistles as essays rather than letters. The term derives from Montaigne, whose *Essais* (1580–92), widely read in England, were Senecan in both thought and manner. Descended from both Montaigne and Seneca are Bacon's *Essays* (1597, 1612, and 1625). As Bacon himself puts it, 'the word [essay] is late, but the thing is ancient: for Seneca's Epistles to Lucilius . . . are Essays, that is dispersed meditations'.[32] Bacon was the first to use the title 'Essay' in English. He was followed swiftly by Sir William Cornwallis (*Essayes* (1600, 1601)), Robert Johnson (*Essaies or Rather Imperfect Offers* (1601)), Daniel Turill (*Essaies Politick and Morall* (1608)), and Nicholas Breton (*Characters upon Essays* (1615)). The first complete translation of Seneca's prose works into English was that of Thomas Lodge in 1614.

Among the earliest non-fictional collections of letters in English were the *Epistles* of John Hall (instalments in 1607, 1608, and 1610). Hall gives titles to his individual epistles, as each focuses on a particular topic, like the letters of Seneca (and the essays of Montaigne); his tone is persuasive, rather than communicative, and the epistles often concern matters of religion. Thomas Fuller, in his *History of the Worthies of England* (1662), recounts that Hall was 'commonly called our English Seneca, for the pureness, plainness and fullness of his style' (p. 130). Indeed, Hall's style is recognizably Senecan, and nowhere more so than in his *Meditations* (1597), where he aspires to a brevity and directness that will have maximum impact on the reader:

> A man under God's affliction is like a bird in a net; the more he strives the more he is entangled. God's decree cannot be eluded with impatience. What I cannot avoid, I will learn to bear.
>
> ('The Second Century' no. 1)[33]

'A Letter Doesn't Blush'

I will conclude with a more detailed look at a couple of *topoi* from Latin letters that are absorbed by Renaissance English letter-writers of different generic character, illustrating some of the dimensions of epistolary familiarity. The first of these is that 'a letter does not blush' ('epistula non erubescit'), as Cicero puts it in a famous, and infamous, letter to the historian Lucceius, begging him to include in his histories an account of Cicero's consulship, which, Cicero urges, would make an exciting monograph of its own (*Ad Familiares* 5. 12).[34]

> Coram me tecum eadem haec agere saepe conantem deterruit pudor quidam paene subrusticus quae nunc expromam absens audacius; epistula enim non erubescit.
>
> (Though I have been trying to broach this subject with you face to face, a sort of clumsy shyness has held me back. In your absence I shall lay it out more boldly; for a letter doesn't blush.)
>
> (*Ad Familiares* 5. 12. 1)

Perhaps the best-known sentence in the whole of the ancient epistolary tradition, Cicero's opening gambit turns what is usually taken to be the lack that a letter must heal into its prime advantage. For the letter is, *as it were*, a conversation between absent friends, and here the fact that it is not actually a conversation becomes significant. Such is the currency of this tag in the Renaissance that we find it adduced by a suitor in (slightly modified) Latin as a privilege of the letter form that may be open to abuse. Timothy Hutton writes to the Archbishop of York: 'I must acknowledge that I have not deserved to obtain any suit of you; yet such is the nature of the necessity that it oftentimes presumes upon *non erubescunt literae.*'[35]

Cicero's opening sentence to Lucceius endowed the world with another tag that was almost as useful to the Renaissance suitor—namely, *subrusticus pudor* (clumsy shyness). Early in his correspondence with Anne Finch, Henry More writes to her:

> I think I shall not see London of a great while now, but let not my silence keep you back from writing to me, when ever you think I may do you any service this way, for although I have *a kind of a rustic aversation* (for I will not give anything in me so good a name as bashfulness) from adventuring to salute you by letters first, yet I am sure I am not so uncivil, as that I should ever dare to fail the answering of you.[36]

More substitutes a coy Latinism (aversation) for the closer, vernacular translation of the Latin *pudor* that he will not bestow on himself (bashfulness), enrolling his intellectual addressee in a sophisticated allusive play. The classical reference also serves to overlay the tone of the more equal relationship between Cicero and Lucceius on the deference of More to his social superior.

Deference of a different kind marks the use of Cicero's phrase in a letter by Richard Masters to the Swiss minister Rodolph Gualter. Masters excuses himself for not having replied to Gualter's letters and solicitations for a return: 'For I was afraid, unlearned as I am, to intrude upon a man so learned and accomplished as yourself with my unpolished letters. At length however, I have divested myself of this rustic shamefacedness, as I esteem your sincerity and candour more than I fear my own rudeness of style.'[37] The Ciceronian allusion comes to the rescue of Masters's Latinity: his Latin may be unpolished, but to be overcome by a *subrusticus pudor* would only compound the problem.

Characteristic of the Renaissance reception of the ancient letter is the contamination of different ancient authors and epistolary subgenres in their descendants. And so we find a little poem on the theme of Cicero's 'epistula non erubescit' in Drayton's *Englands Heroicall Epistles*. Towards the beginning of Edward the Black Prince's letter to Alice Countess of Salisbury:

> This cannot blush although you do refuse it,
> Nor will reply, however you shall use it;
> All's one to this, though you should bid despair,
> This still entreats you, this still bids you fair.
>
> (ll. 9–12)

Drayton's Edward seems to make the letter an emblem of the masochistic constancy of the lover, immune not to the shame that shrinks from an importunate request, but to the disappointment or anger that might shake the lover in the event of a rebuff. But Drayton's expansion of Cicero's phrase opens an array of potential meanings. Is the letter *like* Edward the Black Prince, constant in his love, despite the ill-treatment with which he may meet, or is it constant in the face of ill-treatment because it is *only* a letter, and *not* the lover himself? The repeated *this* might emphasize the deictic connection with the speaker or alternatively the thingness that *separates* it from the speaker. Is the blush, perhaps, one of anger rather than embarrassment? This ambiguity would serve the relation between suitor and patron as well as that between lover and beloved. Does Drayton have one eye on a different kind of suit, more relevant to the letter of Cicero he quotes in his love poem?

Before we leave Cicero's 'epistula non erubescit', a final example will serve to show how versatile a reflection on the letter Cicero's tag can prove to be. At the trial of the Earl of Essex, the accused cited Francis Bacon himself as a witness of his innocence. For had not Bacon written a letter on Essex's behalf to the queen? Bacon replies:

> since you have stirred up this point my Lord: I dare warrant you this letter will not blush: for I did but perform the part of an honest man, and ever laboured to have done you good if it might have been, and to no other end, for what I intended for your good was wished from the heart, without touch of any man's honour.[38]

The tag *epistula non erubescit* is so familiar that Bacon can use it to make a point that is almost the opposite of Cicero's. Bacon's crucial modification of the original ('*this* letter will not blush') suggests that a letter *can* blush, though this one will not. The letter is a trace of the man, tied to the moment, and to the exigencies of social duties, and yet as an object or text it may survive beyond the original context to be confronted with changed circumstances. (One might note, too, that it is not just in the dimension of time that the letter straddles two worlds. Bacon equivocates tellingly as he justifies his letter: he did but *perform the part* of an honest man, and yet what he intended was *wished from the heart*. Writing a letter may be a social duty, but it must trade in the rhetoric of sincerity.)

Bacon's allusion to Cicero in this particular context reminds us that Cicero had found himself in a similar predicament, engineered by the antagonist of his final years,

Mark Antony. In the *Second Philippic* (2. 4) he complains that Antony had read out to the senate a letter that Cicero had written to him. The letter (*Ad Atticum* 14. 13b) was a response to one of Antony's asking Cicero's acquiescence in the return from exile of Sextus Cloelius, an enemy of Cicero. Antony was making a show of paying Cicero respect, and Cicero wrote an unctuous reply disingenuously protesting his love and respect for Antony. He even opens the letter by expressing a characteristically epistolary wish that their communication were face to face, not through letters, so that Antony could read in his face and expression his love for Antony (the opposite, of course, was the case). In the *Second Philippic* Cicero berates Antony for having publicized this letter, failing to respect the fact that what transpires in a letter does not necessarily survive transplanting beyond the epistolary exchange and its decorum. Antony, he says, is deprived of *humanitas*, ignorant of the *vita communis*, and his action threatens 'the conversations of absent friends' ('amicorum colloquia absentium' (*Philippics* 2. 4)). But Demetrius, who quotes Artemon to the effect that a letter is like one of the two sides of a dialogue, reminds us that 'the letter should be somewhat more formal in its composition than the dialogue, as the latter represents someone speaking impromptu, whereas the former is written down and sent as a kind of gift' (*De Elocutione* 224). As a gift, the letter belongs to the receiver, and yet as a gift it also has a 'sentimental value', which requires it to be treated as in some ways a proxy of the sender. It is something to be displayed or used, and at the same time the token of a relationship between two people that cannot survive transplanting from its original context.

Another Renaissance equivalent of Antony's misuse of Cicero's letter would be the opening of Charles's personal letters to Henrietta Maria in 1645, which prompted a revolutionary pamphlet called *The King's Cabinet Opened*. This in turn elicited a satirical poem in response, attacking the abuse of the king's privacy. Since men, unlike angels, cannot communicate directly from soul to soul, nature provided them with 'two close safe paths':

> In presence, whisper, and at distance pen.
> Public decrees and thoughts were else the same,
> Nor were it to converse but to proclaim.
> Conceits were else but records, but by this care
> Our thoughts no commons, but enclosures are:
> What bold intruders then are they, who assail
> To cut their prince's hedge, and break his pale?
> That so unmanly gaze, and dare be seen
> Ev'n then, when he converses with his queen.[39]

'I Have Nothing to Say'

The letter is a conversation, or rather, it is *like* a conversation, but fortunately, and sometime unfortunately, it is not a conversation ('epistula enim non erubescit'). As to its purpose, Cicero, echoed by many a Renaissance epistolographer, tells us that it serves to inform the absent of matters that are of concern to them (*Ad Familiares* 2. 4. 1). And indeed Cicero's letters are famously newsy. But in a number of well-known passages, Cicero tells Atticus that he is writing even though he has nothing to say, or urges Atticus to do the same:

> There was nothing to write. For I had heard no news and had written back to all your letters yesterday. Since my distress not only deprived me of sleep, but didn't even let me stay awake without great pain, I started to write any old thing so that I could, so to speak, be with you in whom alone I have peace.
>
> (Cicero, *Ad Atticum* 9. 10. 1)

And

> I would have you write often to me. If you have nothing to say, write what comes into your head ['si rem nullam habebis, quod in buccam venerit scribito']
>
> (*Ad Atticum* 1. 12)

The latter passage was picked up by Seneca as the foil for his own, philosophical subject matter.

> Nor will I do what Cicero, that most eloquent of men, tells Atticus to do, that even 'if he has no message, to write what comes into his head'. There can never be a lack of material for my writing, even if I pass over all that [political] stuff that fills the letters of Cicero.
>
> (Seneca, *Moral Epistles*, 118. 1)

As Kathy Eden points out, the phrase 'whatever comes into your head' ('quidquid in buccam venerit'), or the sentiment it expresses, became a *topos* of letter-writing, and she cites, besides the ancient examples, passages from Petrarch and Erasmus.[40] Fulwood (*Enemie*, 53–4) even includes a section with advice on 'How to visit our Friend with Letters, not having any great matter to write'. So Cicero's statements and example confirm both that the letter communicates something and that it can also be the realm of the phatic, the foregrounding of communication itself, which, stripped of content, becomes the true medium of friendship.

The letters of Donne make much of their lack of news, as John Carey has pointed out, and this protestation often strays into the territory of the Ciceronian *topos*.[41] For instance, writing to Bridget Wright, Donne enquires politely about his previous letters. Have they, perhaps gone astray in the post?

> If you have had more before, this comes to ask how they were received; and if you have had none, it comes to try how they should be received. It comes to you like a bashful servant, who though he have an extreme desire to put himself in your presence, yet hath not much to say when he is come.[42]

Here is Donne the suitor concerned with the reception of his letters, and of himself. He is also the slave of love, the bashful rustic (victim of *subrusticus pudor*), and the friend who proves his devotion by having nothing to say and yet writing all the same.

John Carey denies that Donne had any authority for this 'functional emptiness' from the ancients.[43] As we have seen, not only was it a Ciceronian *topos* but, with Seneca it becomes the point at which the later letter-writer situates his relation to the great epistolary model, Cicero (what, asks Seneca, is it *really* to have something to say?). Seneca's aggressively sanguine approach contrasts with Pliny's concession of defeat.

> [You demand more frequent and longer letters from me]...I did not have at my command the subject matter to write more about. For I am not in the same situation as Cicero, whose example you encourage me to follow. He had abundantly at his disposal both the most fertile of natural talents, and the range and weight of subject matter to match it; even without my telling you, you can discern how narrow the limits are that confine me...
>
> (Pliny, *Letters*, 9. 2. 1–4)

One of the most notable occurrences of the 'nothing to say' *topos* in Donne can be found in a letter very much concerned with the ancients and with his own status as a letter-writer within the tradition. It is addressed to his Atticus, Sir Frances Goodyer, and its opening features Donne's famous remark about the letter that 'no other conveyance is better for knowledge or for love'.[44] But a long roll-call of the great letter-writers of the past, from Cicero to the Italians, leads to the conclusion that they have between them exhausted the capacity of letters for conveying knowledge. Donne must content himself, then, with the letter's other capacity, 'which must make mine acceptable, that they are also the best conveyors of love'. But now he rallies: 'Yet though all the knowledge be in those authors already, yet...much of the knowledge buried in books becomes ineffectual if it be not applied and refreshed by a companion or friend.' After this roll on the drums, Donne confesses that, having put himself on the stage, he has nothing to say, 'and it is well, for this letter is already long enough'. I will not follow up all the feints and dodges of this letter to their conclusion, but up to this point it is clear that Donne's letter is torn between two impulses. On the one hand, it concedes that the letter's capacity to convey knowledge has been pre-empted by the great writers of the past, leaving Donne to fall back on the love that is particular to his relationship with Goodyer. On the other hand, Donne has the advantage that those great letter-writers have themselves become books, and the knowledge buried in books becomes ineffectual if it is not applied and refreshed by a companion or friend. Let us call that the Senecan option, because it finds a way to pre-empt the great forebears.

For both Donne and Seneca, the knowledge contained in books can survive only in the context of *familiaritas*, which is the realm of the letter. But Donne then retreats from this position to bring his letter to its official close (there is a longish coda) with a self-consuming gesture that emphasizes his pure desire to set himself on the stage before Goodyer, without anything to say. One might compare Donne's gesture to the end of Pliny's short letter (from which I quoted above) in which he concedes Cicero's advantage in subject matter as an excuse for not writing at greater length as his friend has requested. Pliny's ending is as self-consuming as Donne's, which denies its own matter in order to bring forth the pure phatic pleasure of communication through the letter, conduit of *familiaritas*.

> This is my apology, and I think it is a legitimate one, yet I am not sure that I wish you to find it acceptable. For it is a mark of the closest friendship to refuse to pardon short letters from one's friends, even though you may know they have sound reasons. Farewell.
>
> (Pliny, *Letters*, 9. 2. 5)

I have been considering the reception of ancient letters in the English Renaissance letter. More might be said about the reception of ancient Greek letters and about other Renaissance genres. To take an example that brings together both of these areas I have neglected, one might cite the fact that the poets Jonson and Herrick both show that they know the *Love Letters* of Philostratus (a Greek author of uncertain date and identity). Jonson's 'To Celia' develops conceits from a number of the *Love Letters* of Philostratus, and the rosebuds of Herrick's 'To the Virgins' are put to much the same use as they are in Philostratus 55. The presence of ancient letters extends beyond the field of the Renaissance letter itself into other genres. Essays and other discursive forms; the lyric; the novel; satire; theories of friendship and of style—all of these are relevant to the reception of ancient letters in the English Renaissance and their influence is truly tentacular.

Notes

1. For more on familiarity in the Renaissance, see Kathy Eden, *The Renaissance Rediscovery of Intimacy* (Chicago, 2012).
2. On the rediscovery of Cicero's letters, see L. Reynolds and N. Wilson, *Scribes and Scholars: A Guide to the Transmission of Greek and Latin Literature*, 3rd edn (Oxford, 1990), 131, 135.
3. Cecil Clough, 'The Cult of Antiquity: Letters and Letter Collections', in Cecil Clough (ed.), *Cultural Aspects of the Italian Renaissance: Essays in Honour of Paul Kristeller* (Manchester, 1976), 33–87 (on early editions, pp. 43–4).
4. For a nuanced study of the relationship between medieval *ars dictaminis* and humanist epistolary theory, see Judith Rice Henderson, 'Erasmus on the Art of Letter-Writing', in James. M. Murphy (ed.), *Renaissance Eloquence: Studies in the Theory and Practice of Renaissance Rhetoric* (Berkeley and Los Angeles, 1983), 331–55.
5. Erasmus, *Opera Omnia Desiderii Erasmi* (Amsterdam, 1971), 1/2. 225.
6. Juan Luis Vives, *De Conscribendis Epistolis*, ed. C. Fantazzi (Leiden 1989), 96.
7. e.g. Cicero, *Ad Atticum* 12. 39. 2 ('adleuor cum loquor tecum absens'). A succinct account of the commonplaces of ancient epistolography and letter-writing can be found in Michael Trapp, *Greek and Latin Letters: An Anthology with Translations* (Cambridge, 2003), 38–46.
8. Gary Grund, 'From Formulary to Fiction: The Epistle and the English Anti-Ciceronian Movement', *Texas Studies in Language and Literature*, 17/2 (1975), 379–95.
9. Wesley Trimpi, *Ben Jonson's Poems: A Study of the Plain Style* (Stanford, 1962), 60–75.
10. For examples, see Gary Schneider, *The Culture of Epistolarity: Vernacular Letters and Letter Writing in Early Modern England, 1500–1700* (Newark, DE, 2005), 130–1.
11. Thomas W. Baldwin, *William Shakespeare's Small Latine and Lesse Greeke*, 2 vols (Urbana, IL, 1944), 1. 89–90, 99–101, 132–3, 155–63, 363, 402, 413.

12. For the continental context of the English epistolary tradition, see Claudio Guillen, 'Notes toward the Study of the Renaissance Letter', in Barbara Lewalski (ed.), *Renaissance Genres: Essays on Theory, History and Interpretation* (Cambridge, 1986), 70–110.
13. Besides Howell's collection and the *Epistles* of Joseph Hall, one might cite two collections by Joseph Markham (*Five Decades of Epistles of War* (1622), and *The Book of Honour: Five Decades of Epistles of Honour* (1625)), as well as Richard Flecknoe's *A Relation of Ten Years Travel in Europe, Asia, Africa and America* (1656). However, compared to the Continent, England produced relatively few collections of letters until the mid-seventeenth century. See Schneider, *Culture*, 183–5.
14. On Howell's letters, see Annabel Patterson, *Censorship and Interpretation: The Conditions of Writing and Reading in Early Modern England* (Madison, 1984), 218–26.
15. Translation from Trapp, *Greek and Latin Letters*, 181. On this *topos*, see Wolfgang Mueller, 'Der Brief als Spiegel der Seele', *Antike und Abendland*, 26 (1980), 138–57.
16. Robert Day, *Told in Letters: Epistolary Fiction before Richardson* (Ann Arbor, 1966), esp. 10–26.
17. A. Benner and F. Fobes (eds), *Alciphron, Aelian and Philostratus: The Letters* (Cambridge, MA, 1949), 32–3.
18. On the influence of Ovid's *Heroides* on English poetry in the Renaissance, see the articles collected in the special number of *Renaissance Studies*, 22/3 (2008), under the title *The Rhetoric of Complaint: Ovid's Heroides in the Renaissance and Restoration*. The articles of Danielle Clarke and Alison Thorne deal specifically with Drayton's Ovidian connection. John Kerrigan, *Motives of Woe: Shakespeare and 'Female Complaint': A Critical Anthology* (Oxford, 1991), 23–83, describes the genre of female complaint and its relation to its Ovidian cousin. There is a full history of the heroic epistle in a European context in Heinrich Dörrie, *Der Heroische Brief: Bestandaufnahme, Geschichte, Kritik einer humanistischen-barocken Literaturgattung* (Berlin, 1968).
19. Barbara Ewell, 'Unity and the Transformation of Drayton's Poetics in *England's Heroicall Epistles*: From Mirrored Ideals to "The Chaos in the Mind"', *Modern Language Quarterly*, 44 (1983), 234–5.
20. 'The Lady Geraldine to Henry Howard, Earle of Surey', 181–2, in *Englands Heroicall Epistles*, in Michael Drayton, *Works*, ed. J. William Hebel, 5 vols (Oxford, 1961), vol. 2. Cf. Ovid, *Heroides* 1. 1–2.
21. Georgia Brown, *Redefining Elizabethan Literature* (Cambridge, 2004), 195. Brown discusses Daniel and Drayton on pp. 193–223. Stephen Guy-Bray's article in *Renaissance Studies*, 22.3 (2008) (see n. 18) considers 'Rosamond's Complaint' in relation to the *Heroides*.
22. 'A Letter from Octavia to Marcus Antonius', in Samuel Daniel, *The Complete Works in Verse and Prose*, ed. Alexander B. Grosart, 5 vols (1885–96), 1. 127.
23. A character named Philaenis is mocked for Lesbian activities in two of Martial's epigrams (7. 67 and 7. 70).
24. John Donne, *Poetical Works*, ed. Sir Herbert Grierson (1967), 1. 125.
25. Kerrigan, *Motives of Woe*, 70.
26. Colin Burrow, 'Wyatt and Sixteenth-Century Horatianism', in Charles Martindale and David Hopkins (eds), *Horace Made New: Horatian Influences on British Writing from the Renaissance to the Twentieth Century* (Cambridge, 1993), 27–49 (esp. 42).
27. Victoria Moul, *Jonson, Horace and the Classical Tradition* (Cambridge, 2010), 54–63, who argues that Jonson's epigrams mediate the influence of Martial through Horace.
28. Moul, *Jonson, Horace and the Classical Tradition*, 193–200.

29. There is an excellent account of Donne's use of Horace in this poem in Victoria Moul, 'Donne's Horatian Means: Horatian Hexameter Verse in Donne's Satyres and Epistles', *John Donne Journal*, 27 (2008), 21–48 (esp. 39–47).
30. On the Senecan style in England, see George Williamson, 'Senecan Style in the Seventeenth Century', in Stanley Fish (ed.), *Seventeenth Century Prose: Modern Essays in Criticism* (Oxford, 1971), 112–46. For more on the influence of Seneca's prose, see Reid Barbour and Claire Preston, Chapter 20, this volume.
31. Thomas Randolph, 'To Master Feltham on his Book of Resolves', in *The Poems of Thomas Randolph*, ed. George Thorn-Dury (1929), ll. 89–96.
32. Francis Bacon, *The Essays or Counsells, Civill and Morall*, ed. Michael Kiernan (Oxford, 1985), 317.
33. Charles Sayle (ed.), *The Meditations and Vows of Joseph Hall* (1901), 59. On Hall's Senecan prose style, see Richard McCabe, *Joseph Hall: A Study in Satire and Meditation* (Oxford, 1982), 189–96.
34. For a brief survey of themes and *topoi* in Roman letters and epistolary theory, see Trapp, *Greek and Latin Letters*, 34–46. Some of the most important letters and theoretical pronouncements are contained in this anthology, with the original and facing translation. Schneider, *Culture*, 132–40, is an excellent treatment of the 'letter does not blush' *topos* in English Renaissance letters, and includes some of the passages I cite.
35. James Raine (ed.), *The Correspondence of Dr Matthew Hutton* (1843), 119 (quoted Schneider, *Culture*, 43–4).
36. Sarah Hutton (ed.), *The Conway Letters: Correspondence of Anne, Viscountess Conway, Henry More and their Friends* (Oxford, 1992), 52. Quoted Schneider, *Culture*, 135.
37. Hastings Robinson, *Original Letters Relative to the English Reformation* (Cambridge, 1846), 358–9. I have unfortunately not had the opportunity to read the letter in its original Latin.
38. *The Arraignment, Trial and Condemnation of Robert Earl of Essex and Henry Earl of Southampton* (1679), 20–1. Quoted Schneider, *Culture*, 32.
39. *Rump: Or an Exact Collection of the Choicest Poems and Songs Relating to the Late Times* (1662), I. 170, quoted by Patterson, *Censorship and Interpretation*, 217–18.
40. Kathy Eden, *The Renaissance Discovery of Intimacy* (Chicago, 2012), 78 n. 7.
41. John Carey, 'John Donne's Newsless Letters', *Essay and Studies*, 34 (1981), 46–65.
42. John Donne, *Select Letters*, ed. P. M. Oliver (Manchester, 2002), 52.
43. Carey, 'John Donne's Newsless Letters', 53.
44. Donne, *Select Letters*, 17–18.

CHAPTER 13

Prose Romance

HELEN MOORE

The reception of ancient romance in early modern England is framed, somewhat paradoxically, by two publications that are actually French. The first of these was the landmark translation of Heliodorus' *Aethiopica* by Jacques Amyot in 1547 that introduced Greek romance to a vernacular European readership.[1] The second French publication, Daniel Huet's seventeenth-century account of the origins of romance, *Traité de l'origine des romans* (1670), sought to defend modern romance as diverting, instructive, and with a heritage stretching back to antiquity. In doing so, Huet's treatise singles out the *Aethiopica* as the high point of romance-writing for being (in the words of the anonymous English translator) 'better designed' and 'more complete' than any previous romance, and for the chaste virtue of its lovers Theagenes and Chariclea.[2] The English translator further amplifies Huet's verdict, declaring in his preface that after Heliodorus romance 'degenerated', abandoning that which was 'natural, exact and probable' in favour of the 'wild, grotesque and chimerical' (sig. A4^{v}).

This narrative of a post-Heliodoran decline into (medieval, chivalric) fantasy, followed by a return to Heliodoran 'naturalness', or verisimilitude, had been first articulated by Amyot in the preface to his *Histoire Aethiopique*, and reached its apotheosis in the seventeenth-century promotion of French heroic romance—in which Huet's *Treatise* is a vocal participant—as a return to the foundational virtues of Greek romance. Heliodorus was also praised for presenting, as Huet's English translator puts it, 'Virtue crowned, and Vice punished' (sig. A4^{v}). This celebration of Heliodorus the moralist originates with Amyot, and was echoed by Thomas Underdowne, the first English translator of the full text of the *Aethiopica* (1569). In the second edition of his translation, Underdowne asserts that, unlike other well-known, vernacular examples of romance, the *Aethiopica* is legitimate reading because it 'punishes the faults of evil doers, and rewards the well livers'.[3]

Apart from the fourth-century *Aethiopica*, two other Greek romances were known in early modern England: *Leucippe and Klitophon* by Achilles Tatius (2nd century CE) and Longus' *Daphnis and Chloe* (2nd/3rd century CE). In addition, the inset romance of 'Cupid and Psyche' in Apuleius' *Metamorphoses* was available in Latin, French, and William Adlington's translation, *The Golden Asse* (1566). With the exception of Philip Sidney, who read Greek and had access to a Greek manuscript of *Daphnis and Chloe* through his friend the Huguenot scholar Henri Estienne, early modern English authors generally encountered Greek romance via translations made into Latin, French, or English.[4] Underdowne's translation of Heliodorus derived from the Latin of Stanislaus Warschewiczki (1551), and William Burton used the Latin of Annibale della Croce (1544) for his translation of Achilles Tatius, *The Most Delectable and Pleasant History of Clitiphon and Leucippe* (1597). The source text for Angel Day's *Daphnis and Chloe* (1587) was Amyot's *Les Amours pastorales de Daphnis and Chloe* (1559); Day's translation held sway for seventy years until displaced by George Thornley's version of 1657, which was based on the parallel Greek and Latin edition by Jungermann (1605).[5] The attractions of the *Aethiopica* for early modern readers were manifold. Its plot, encompassing the elemental romance tropes of love, loss, and restoration, provided rich opportunities for moral, philosophical, and political readings that were particularly drawn to questions of providence and ethical action, and its sophisticated layering of narratives commanded widespread attention and acclaim.[6] The modelling of mid-seventeenth-century English romances such as Roger Boyle's *Parthenissa* (1651–69) on French heroic romances that were themselves Heliodoran in conception meant that the fictional poetics of the *Aethiopica* dominated the period 1550–1660. Occasional irruptions of ancient romance (such as the painting of Psyche described in *Parthenissa* that triggers a mini-retelling of her story) are therefore still to be found in the mid-1600s, even as English fiction looked increasingly to the Continent rather than the classical past for inspiration.[7]

There is no word in ancient Greek or Latin that indicates a literary category to which ancient fictions belong, or that would equate to the terms 'novel' or 'romance'. The common ground of ancient romance lies in the depiction of an intensely erotic, young, reciprocated heterosexual love that nonetheless remains chaste until a socially sanctioned union in marriage is secured. In progressing towards this union, the lovers are typically separated by the interventions of Fortune and the lusts of others as expressed in an assortment of tricks, traps, and travails that espouse both comedy and tragedy. These interruptions allow the inclusion of material on subjects such as travel, ethnography, religion, and the marvellous, and facilitate narrative digressions and interpolations. The style of the Greek romances is typical of the period known as the Second Sophistic (*c.*50–230 CE, although these dates, and indeed the notion of this as a period, are subject to some qualification).[8] Hence these fictions manifest a knowing rhetoricity characterized by digression, antithesis, and modes of formal display such as ekphrasis. All the romances exhibit an intense interest in the articulation, performance, and formation of the self, especially but not exclusively in its sexual potentialities.[9] Informing this interest is a deep-seated fascination with the capacity of art (both pictorial and literary) to capture the self. So we find in ancient fictions, and the early modern romances that imitate them, artful verbal descriptions of beautiful beings and of the pictures that represent them. In the same way, both ancient and early modern romances show a marked fondness for overt, formal articulations of the self, typically expressed through soliloquy, disputation, and letter-writing.

Ancient romances are driven by a strong, unified narrative that is either performed in the first person, or contains one or more lengthy, nested first-person narratives. Unity is thus provided thematically through the emphasis on the binding love of the central couple, and narratively by the use of a single dominant narrator who either exists outside the plot but is nonetheless affected by it (as in Longus' encounter with a picture that begins *Daphnis and Chloe*), or is himself a participant (as in *Leucippe and Klitophon*, which is told by Klitophon to the speaker of the brief frame narrative). In modern criticism, the origin of these romances in Asia Minor, at the periphery of the Roman Empire, has been seized on as indicative of their oblique, even perhaps contrastive, relationship with empire (especially its political institutions; Achilles Tatius' 'mischievous' elevation of folklore over accepted learning and his evasion of Roman political terms is indicative here).[10] Within the romances themselves, Homeric quotation and allusion is frequently found as a marker of learning and overt Greek-ness, often in fruitful conjunction with the mythic (more often than the imperial) Ovid.[11] While the romances by Chariton (*Chaereas and Callirhoe*, *c*.50 CE) and Xenophon of Ephesus (*Ephesiaca*, 2nd century CE) do exhibit a concern with the social world of the *polis*, the accident of their loss to the sixteenth century means that English writers would have construed ancient romance through the pastoral mode of Longus, the epic ranginess typified by Heliodorus or the mythological otherness of Apuleius's 'Cupid and Psyche'. For these English writers, the civic life of the self was supplied by the matter of the Italian novella, a genre that combined frequently and fruitfully with Greek romance in the sixteenth century, in part, no doubt, thanks to its own (still obscure) sources in ancient fiction.

The matter and style of ancient romance as it was encountered from the 1550s accorded with the Elizabethan admiration for Ovid (see Maggie Kilgour, Chapter 23, this volume), whose reception history as both poet of married love and master of seduction, as well as his fondness for watching-moments and his skill in structuring tales within tales, all chimed with the characteristics of Greek romance.[12] This collision of interests, styles, and themes provided the opportunity in Elizabethan fiction for an energetic and creative recombining of the Ovidian sources with their Greek successors. Robert Greene's pastoral romance *Pandosto: The Triumph of Time* (earliest extant edition 1588), for example, contains a list of divine rapes that blurs the boundaries between the Ovidian and Greek texts that were equally fascinated by this subject; when this list is itself transferred into Shakespeare's *Winter's Tale* (1610), the 'art of precedent' being deployed is simultaneously and natively Greek, Roman, and English.[13] This exploitation and enhancement of the intertextualities of the ancient world provide the keystone for a style of English romance that is, on the one hand, amorous, witty, and knowing, and, on the other, sorrowful: it is haunted by inescapable mortal metamorphoses, preoccupied with what Arthur Kinney terms the 'fearful contingencies of life'.[14]

The fearful contingencies of death, violence, treachery, and ruin are not locally specific to the early modern world in the romances of Sidney, Lyly, and Greene (this achievement belongs rather to Shakespeare and Webster), but are trans-temporal and deliberately inter-cultural. The variously foreign, quasi-ancient, and hyper-literary worlds of early modern romance are indicative of the fact that *translatio* in this context means the transference not only of sense, meaning, and culture, but also of a body of paradigmatic human types and situations: the vigorous heroines of ancient romance and their intermittently boyish and majestic lovers are reanimated across early modern romance with many a nod to Ovid and elsewhere. This human *translatio* is achieved with particular deftness and directness by Sidney, whose revision of his pastoral *Old Arcadia* into specifically Heliodoran epicity as the *New Arcadia* elevates the suffering women of Greek romance to newly princely heights while updating their boy-men as gifted but overtrained and underemployed Renaissance aristocrats. Aspects of fictionality that are valued in the modern novel such as probability, realism, and character are less important to ancient and early modern romance than the reiterations of a continuous human experience. Thus the speechifying that is self-consciously derived from Greek romance and that has been intermittently praised and condemned in Sidney and Greene is indicative not of grandiloquence or sterility, but rather of a determination that the pathos and eloquence of the inhabitants of Greek tragedy, ancient romance, and Ovidian poetry could and should be realized in English fiction and in the English language. In this, as in so much else, Heliodorus provides the guiding principle: as Tim Whitmarsh notes, Heliodorus himself uses 'mythic paradigms' not just as a literary 'resource', but as the 'fundamental paradigm for life itself'.[15]

Another important act of combining—one that changed the course of English fiction—took place in Elizabethan romance as the ancient romances rubbed shoulders with the widely read neo-Arthurian fictions of the Spanish *libros de caballería*, such as *Amadís de Gaula* (1508), that had originated in the Iberian peninsula in the late fifteenth century as nascently modern versions of the medieval legends of Lancelot and Tristan. These were the post-antique romances that Amyot and Huet sought to write out of literary history as chimerical fictions, a blip in the narrative of Heliodoran continuity, but the reality was not so simple. Thanks to the efforts of the French translator Nicolas de Herberay in the 1540s and the French and Italian continuators of the Spanish original, the *Amadis* that was read outside Spain and the New World was very much a sixteenth-century affair that combined the traditions of ancient and medieval narrative with decidedly Renaissance conceptions of eloquence, love, monarchy, chivalry, and pastoralism.[16] Italian and Spanish romances such as *Amadis*, Sannazaro's *Arcadia* (1504), Ariosto's *Orlando Furioso* (1516), and Montemayor's *Diana* (?1559) all complicate the relationship between ancient and early modern English romance. The multiplicity of early modern English romance is exemplified in prose by Emanuel Ford's *Ornatus and Artesia* (?1599), in which Greek and Iberian romances are imitated separately and in combination, and much common ground—such as scenes of shipwreck and 'erotic contemplation'—is reworked.[17] In poetry, Spenser's *The Faerie Queene* (1590, 1596) stands as the archetype of romance intertextuality—for example, in the blending of Ovid with 'Cupid and Psyche' in the Garden of Adonis episode that addresses, as Robert Carver puts it, the perennial 'problem of pleasure'.[18]

The lack of any ancient, medieval, or early modern treatises explicitly addressed to the art of prose fiction renders the identification of reception relationships for ancient romance very difficult, as even those English fictions that seem closest to the matter and sentiment of Greek fiction, like William Warner's *Pan his Syrinx, or Pipe, Compact of Seven Reedes* (1584), cannot be proven to know exactly what they were aiming at. *Pan his Syrinx*, despite its collation of narrative *topoi* from ancient romance, such as fractured families, grotesque violence, and an inconstant Fortune, is not really a romance at all, being a collection of six stories within a frame narrative, gathered together to demonstrate 'something of the vain, wanton, proud, and inconstant course of the world', according to its title page.

The classicism of most early modern English romance, therefore, is much more likely to be diffuse and allusive than it is to be an act of considered imitation like Sidney's homage to Heliodorus in the deliberately 'philhellene' *New Arcadia*. Sidney apart, this classicism is not exclusively, or even primarily, an elite practice, and it often involves acts of internal recycling and imitation located within the English tradition. Such generic self-quotation occurs, for example, in the repeated use of the Actaeon myth or the rape of Europa in the popular prose romances of Robert Parry and Richard Johnson published in the 1590s. These romances contain many moments of notionally classical reception that actually invoke the naturalized English tradition as much as the classical one. When Priscus sees Florida bathing in Parry's *Moderatus* (1595), for instance, the sight 'so benumbed his senses that he remained in a trembling fear', anticipating a fate like that of Actaeon.[19] The English intertext is Sidney's *New Arcadia*, specifically the scene in which the princesses bathe, watched with different forms of covertness by prince Pyrocles disguised as the Amazon Zelmane, and their cousin Amphialus, hidden in the bushes.[20]

The simultaneously direct and indirect transmission of ancient romance into the English Renaissance is typified by its presence in drama. Direct transmission takes place in various guises, such as Thomas Heywood's allegorical masque *Love's Mistress* (printed 1636; a version of 'Cupid and Psyche') and John Gough's *The Strange Discovery* (1640), which is the only extant printed dramatization of Heliodorus. (There is a manuscript play, *The White Ethiopian*, dating from perhaps the 1650s, and reports of a performance at court of a play called *Theagines and Chariclea* in 1572 and of *The Queen of Ethiopica* (perhaps the same play) in Bristol in 1578.)[21] Several dramatizations of 'Cupid and Psyche' have been lost: the anti-theatricalist Stephen Gosson referred contemptuously in 1582 to works such as *The Golden Ass* and *Amadis* being 'ransacked' for the stage, and a play of 'The golden Ass & Cupid & Psiches' by Dekker, Day, and Chettle was written around 1600.[22]

The Strange Discovery was probably written in the 1630s, in the aftermath, it would seem, of William Lisle's versification of Heliodorus as *The Fair Ethiopian* (1631). Gough's play is notable for its concentration on the overwhelming power of love, whether admirable (Theagenes and Chariclea) or dangerous (Dementa and Arsace); for its organization of the *Aethiopica*'s famously tangled narrative into a chronological order; and for its heightening of Heliodorus' already extensive dramatic allusions to include aspects of early modern dramaturgy such as the use of a bed as a stage prop.

Shakespeare's use of ancient romance is notoriously hard to pin down. There is one direct allusion, to Heliodorus: 'th'Egyptian thief' Thyamis is referenced in *Twelfth Night* (5. 1. 118). The sixth-century Latin romance *Apollonius of Tyre* mediates the tropes of ancient fiction into *Pericles*, and Titania's love for Bottom in *A Midsummer Night's Dream* probably glances at Apuleius. But in general Shakespeare's 'Greek effects', as A. D. Nuttall puts it, operate on the large scale—in the 'structures', 'dynamics', and 'pattern[s]' of plays such as *Cymbeline*, with its balancing of the grotesque and the tragic, its sexual violence and fake deaths.[23]

Learning to Love

The ancient romance is a knowingly learned genre. It espouses the elite principles of *paideia* (education, civilization), and in foregrounding the amorous career of a young couple it casts love as an area of youthful instruction and initiation. The flowering of Greek romance in the early centuries CE in part explains this interest in education: it was at this time that the art of declamation (public speaking) shifted from a primarily pedagogical activity to a literary one, bringing with it rhetorical techniques such as *controversia* (a speech in character) and *suasoria* (a speech advising a course of action) that continued to underpin the rhetorical practice of many a Renaissance text such as Marlowe's *Hero and Leander* (first published 1598)—itself, of course, a wittily precocious exercise in attempted sexual initiation.[24]

Intertextuality is another learned aspect of the Greek romances, which frequently display a detailed knowledge of Attic and Roman New Comedy as well as of Homer. The writers' learnedness is not just a matter of allusion, however: according to Simon Goldhill, the intertextuality of *Daphnis and Chloe* is a means of display and transformation, an 'allusive layering of language and narrative' that fits into a broader manipulation of readerly knowingness (both literary and erotic) throughout the romance.[25] The most famous conjunction of eroticism and education in Greek romance occurs in book three of *Daphnis and Chloe*, in the episode of Lycaenion's lesson in sex given to Daphnis. The detail of this account meant that it was suppressed by Amyot and so was unknown to English writers and translators other than Sidney.[26]

While the idea that sex has to be taught is, no doubt, a witty joke levelled at the cultural capital of *paideia* and the pedagogical exertions of the Second Sophistic, it also raises more serious questions about what it is that distinguishes men from beasts: why are we not like them? worries Daphnis incessantly. The very first allusion to learning in *Daphnis and Chloe* makes this unmistakably apparent through a comic inversion of the accepted hierarchy of sentience and sentiment: on finding the baby Chloe, the shepherd Dryas *learns* to love it from his ewe, who is 'acting in a human way' by suckling the child (*CAGN* 291). Learning is inherent to the life of man in Longus, and it is, ultimately, shown to be the bedrock of the differentiation of man and beast. Whereas the beasts are driven by instinct, man is saddled with the simultaneous blessing and curse of knowledge.

The progress of the lovers in Greek romance towards sexual knowledge in marriage is mirrored by and entwined with a parallel narrative of social maturation. Ironically, the apex of this social progress is reached by a narrative regression, a return to origins achieved through the conventional revelation of royal birth at the end of the story. This trope of identity revelation is one of the enduring contributions made by ancient romance to English fiction; much of its success lies in the effectiveness with which it unites these two themes of sexual and social maturation. In the final revelation of identity, any remaining barriers to marriage are removed, and a previously authoritarian parental generation is narratively recast in its youthful folly in order to be forgiven, like a prodigal child, by the child(ren) it abandoned. Social order is affirmed, and the primacy of chaste marriage is asserted.[27]

For all these reasons, ancient romances fell onto particularly fertile soil once they began to be read and translated by English authors trained in the humanist grammar schools and skilled in the practices of rhetorical imitation and invention that underpinned both late antique and Tudor pedagogy.[28] Indeed, the practice of education features thematically in many works from this period, most popularly in the guise of the prodigal play that was imitated from Latin but became naturalized in English literature. One writer in particular, John Lyly, made full use of the education and maturation narratives he found in Roman New Comedy, ancient fiction, prodigal plays, and the Italian novella. Lyly himself came from impeccable pedagogic stock: his grandfather William Lily was high master of the first humanist grammar school, St Paul's, and co-author of *A Short Introduction of Grammar* (*c.*1548), the standard schoolroom text used by English grammar schools throughout the early modern period. Grandfather William's *Grammar* is woven into the rhetorical fabric of *Euphues: The Anatomy of Wit* (1578), Lyly's courtly fiction set in Naples that tells the story of how Euphues (a Greek) deceives his friend Philautus by wooing his beloved Lucilla, but is then himself cast off and turns his wit to learning rather than love. It was followed in 1580 by a sequel, *Euphues and his*

England, in which a reconciled Euphues and Philautus travel to England. The slender narrative, in which Philautus falls in love with Camilla and then Frances, whom he marries, provides further opportunities for debates and discourses on love, as well as travelogue material on the customs and history of England. Although there are no direct allusions to ancient romance in Lyly's works, they manifest a comparably self-conscious erudition, and ally themselves overtly to a highly rhetoricized educational and courtly culture of debate.[29] Euphuistic fiction also prepared the ground for the flowering of Elizabethan pastoral romance in the 1580s and 1590s.

The name of Lyly's protagonist, meaning 'one who is apt for learning', is taken from *The Scholemaster* (1570) by the humanist Richard Ascham (who himself borrowed it from Plato). In *Euphues*, Lyly assembles a hodge-podge of humanist material drawn from Lily's *Grammar* and *The Scholemaster*, similes and sayings lifted from Erasmus' *Similia* and *Adagia*, and allusions and precepts from schoolroom favourites such as Ovid and Plutarch. A striking point of contact between the Greek romancers and Lyly lies in their shared love of (often unnatural) natural history, which tends to be deployed in a leisured and splendid manner in Greek (for example, the digression on crocodiles, reminiscent of Herodotus, that closes book four of *Leucippe and Klitophon*), but in Lyly is terse and epithetical, operating as precept drawn from the natural world rather than marvel: 'the bird Trochilus liveth by the mouth of the crocodile and is not spoiled,' declares Euphues (referencing Pliny) as he rejects the voice of caution.[30] In *Euphues and his England*, the rhetoric of ethnographic expertise and enquiry derived from Greek romance and Herodotus is turned on England and melded with the contemporary discourses of travel-writing upon which early English fiction fed with such enthusiasm.[31] Specifically, Lyly uses William Harrison's *Description of Britain* as prefixed to Holinshed's *Chronicles* (1577). 'The attire they [the English] use', notes Euphues (following Harrison), 'is rather led by the imitation of others, than their own invention' (*Euphues*; Lyly, *Complete Works*, 2. 194). Here England itself has become the subject of an ancient yet simultaneously very modern kind of ethnographic erudition.

The oppositional nature of Lyly's plot that pits the Athens of Euphues (a figuration of Oxford) against the Naples of Philautus (London), as well as Euphues against his friend, makes it unsurprising that, of the rhetorical figures favoured in Greek romance, antithesis is the one upon which Lyly may have drawn most directly. Antithesis has long been identified as the major stylistic vehicle of Euphuism, the literary style derived from Lyly that was fashionable in English prose throughout the 1580s. Many of the favoured rhetorical techniques of this style, such as *isocolon* (phrases of balanced length and structure) and *similia* (comparison), can be characterized as figures of balance and/or opposition stemming from a structural commitment to antithesis: John Carey puts it well in noting how in Euphuistic fictions the 'perception of opposites' becomes a way of 'apprehend[ing] the world'.[32] In *Euphues*, the apprehension of the world is more conflicted than cooperative, so Lyly's antitheses are decorative, but also steely and confrontational; they are often bitingly ironic, especially when afforced by alliteration or rhyme, as, for example, when Philautus, unaware he is being played by Euphues, answers his friend's 'forged gloze' with a 'friendly close' (Lyly, *Complete Works*, I. 214).

As Samuel Wolff pointed out a century ago, the interest of Greek romance lies 'not in the ethical choices and avoidances of life' but in the 'rhetorical expression' of emotion through set speeches.[33] The same could be said of much early Elizabethan fiction, such as George Pettie's novella collection *A Petite Palace of Pettie his Pleasure* (*c.*1576). This accords with the priority given in humanist education to the para-fictional rhetorical devices of *prosopographia* (speaking as a person from history) and *prosopopoeia* (speaking as a fictional person), and their capacity for evoking the passions. The sublimation of feeling as talk in Pettie and Lyly contrasts both with the racy bodiliness of the Italian novella, and the eroticism of Greek romance: in Lyly there is a particularly marked absence of that warm-blooded yet philosophical aspect of ancient romance Wolff perceptively describes as the 'worship of the kiss'.[34] The mouth still figures in *Euphues*, but it operates only as a speaking agent: desire is articulated verbally, not bodily, as sex retreats behind a wall of learned precept, and even the implication of bodily contact is metaphorized as speech, such as 'agreement' (Lyly, *Complete Works*, I. 220). Mouths are only for talking, and the body is treated in terms that are bookish and citational: witness the empty reference to the mole on Venus' cheek, or the scar on Helen's chin, sexually charged details that are possessed intellectually by the writer, but not imaginatively by the reader (I. 184). Whereas Daphnis and Chloe thrill to the sight of uncovered skin, 'naked' in Lyly is a literary–linguistic term meaning plain and unadorned (*OED*, senses 17 and 18), as in the proverbial observation cited in his dedicatory epistle, that 'a naked tale doth most truly set forth the naked truth' (I. 181). So all-eclipsing is the role of speech in Lyly that the distinction between speech acts and physical actions collapses: when Philautus promises to gain access for Euphues to Lucilla's household, words operate as a means of violent physical entry as he declares his plan to 'flap Ferardo [Lucilla's father] in the mouth with some conceit' (I. 214).

Given the absence of sexual contact and marriage in *Euphues*, the educative theme in Lyly is at several removes from the erotic pedagogy of Greek romance. Lyly inverts the trope of sexual attainment into one of sexual failure, and substitutes a narrative of moral, rather than sexual, maturation in which, gradually (and mostly in the continuation), Euphues learns greater wisdom through experience and his study of divinity. The mutuality and sympathy of the lovers in Greek fiction—their 'symmetry'[35]—and the trials to which that symmetry is put, are found not in the relationship of Euphues and Lucilla, but in his friendship with Philautus; the two remain 'companions' even in their rupture, having 'both drunk of one cup', as Lucilla puts it, in being rejected by her (I. 238). Following her marriage to Curio, they are reconciled, the 'conjunction of their minds' (I. 246) being perpetuated through letters.

Time and Triumphs

This male mutuality, reminiscent of the discussions of sex in ancient romance and typical of English prodigal plays and mid-sixteenth-century fiction, gradually gives way in the works of Robert Greene, Lyly's successor and imitator, to an emphasis on singular, especially female, passion. At the same time, and under the influence of Greek romance combined with Ovid's *Heroides*, the casual misogyny typical of the novella and Euphuistic fiction starts to recede, and the rhetorical roles available to women within English fiction are expanded.[36] Thus the female soliloquy—already present in the novella collections of the 1570s, and voiced memorably in the *Euphues* narratives by Lucilla and Camilla—emerges as the dominant rhetorical mode of English romance. It is a mode that particularly favours another trope of Greek romance: the divided mind, or conflict of emotions. Mixing 'laughter and tears', this feature of ancient romance 'imitates and rivals' Greek theatre, and is one reason—along with the publication of Guarini's pastoral tragicomedy *Il Pastor Fido* in 1590—why pastoral prose romance and tragicomedy enjoyed a common popularity in Stuart England.[37]

A key scenario for the exercising of this newly powerful female rhetoric is the virtuous resisting of Fortune and its manifestations such as, in Greene's fictions, 'the murderous inconstancy of... royal men'.[38] The ancient romances' characterization of an all-powerful Fortune, capricious at best and hostile at worst, was embraced enthusiastically by early modern writers, particularly Greene, who responded eagerly to the questions it raises about human agency. As Walter Davis notes, the 'point of contact' between Fortune and love is that both are 'chaotic and irrational': from this principle Greene's romances develop a universe in which the 'pure chance or accident' found in Greek romance is succeeded by a deep-seated irony that leads to 'the constant falsification of expectations and overturn of intentions'. In such a world, the efficacy of human character and action is brought into question: are moral states 'irrelevant', or are they the means by which mutable Fortune can itself be overturned?[39] Greene's *Pandosto* deals directly with this problem by allying Fortune and her agent Pandosto, king of Bohemia, as comparably jealous entities, and by using Pandosto's virtuous queen, Bellaria, as a force of opposition and resistance to that jealousy. Envious of Pandosto's happiness, Fortune turns her wheel and summons up not pirates or an invading army, but his friend Egistus, king of Sicilia. The symmetrical and mutual virtue of Egistus and Bellaria torments Pandosto with jealousy; he accuses Bellaria (who later dies just as an oracle proves her innocence), and abandons their newborn daughter to Fortune in a boat. That daughter, Fawnia, is raised by shepherds and loved by a prince, Dorastus, the son of Egistus. Years later, the lovers arrive in Pandosto's court and are faced with a new problem in the guise of the king's incestuous desire for his unrecognized daughter. The revelation of her identity averts the disaster of incest but initiates that of suicide, as Pandosto kills himself for his jealousy and lust.

Although it takes her life, Time is Bellaria's ally. The romance's subtitle is 'The Triumph of Time' and, as the title page states, the concealing of truth by 'sinister fortune' is 'by time . . . most manifestly revealed'.[40] A Latin motto also used on the title page, 'Temporis filia veritas' ('Truth is the daughter of time'), goes one stage further by tying up the traditional plot of identity revelation with this rebuttal of Fortune, thereby making Fawnia the agent of truth and time, and the vanquisher of Fortune. In the light of this, there is more subtlety to the incestuous ending of *Pandosto* than is typically acknowledged. Far from being an excrescence of romance plotting—moderated by Shakespeare in *The Winter's Tale*, who keeps Leontes alive and reanimates Hermione—it locates a young woman in direct resistance to patriarchy, just as the rape plots of Greek romance, the incest narrative as represented by the romance of *Apollonius of Tyre*, and early Christian hagiography had always done.[41] Within the harsh moral world of this 'triumph of time' over Fortune's envy, there is, therefore, a suitable and symmetrical justice in the death of Pandosto at his own hand.

Another aspect of *Pandosto* that deserves greater recognition is the remarkable—and, until this point in Greene's career, uncharacteristic—restraint Greene exercises in the field of talk. Gone is the verbal ping-pong of Euphuistic fiction, to be replaced instead by pages of reported speech and psychological analysis delivered by the narrator, but very few set pieces of rhetoric. The first formal speech, in fact, is delivered not by Bellaria or Pandosto, but by Pandosto's cupbearer, Franion, whom he has instructed to murder Egistus. It is a classic of conflicted emotionality, spinning around and around the agonized question 'What shalt thou do?', a soliloquy in which the servant identity of Franion imparts new force to the age-old problem of righteous disobedience.[42]

If Franion initiates the rhetorical performances of *Pandosto*, Bellaria surely holds centre-stage, being granted three oratorical moments: of complaint against injustice (Greene, *Life and Complete Works*, 4. 249–50); lament for a lost child (4. 252–3), and courtroom self-defence (4. 260–1). Not until Bellaria is dead does Pandosto get to speak his own words, and it is then, tellingly, a verbal rampage against jealousy that almost ends with the king's attempted suicide. This act is prevented by his courtiers, who remind him that the sheep of his commonwealth 'could not but perish that wanted a shepherd' (4. 263). They thus deflect this hitherto novella-like narrative from its natural ending in a tragic *quid pro quo*, and effect a generic modulation into a redemptive, but as it turns out, also retributive, pastoral.

The possibilities of English pastoral romance were similarly stretched and restitched by Sir Philip Sidney in his *Arcadia*, a work that Greene had potentially seen in manuscript.[43] Sidney began his five-act pastoral fiction in 1577, but wrote most of it in 1580–1. From 1582 he reworked it as the *New Arcadia*, and this incomplete revision, interrupted by his death in 1586, was printed along with the ending of the *Old Arcadia* in 1593 as *The Countess of Pembroke's Arcadia*. The core plot of the *Arcadia* concerns Duke Basilius, who retreats into pastoral seclusion with his wife Gynecia and daughters Pamela and Philoclea, in order to evade the consequences of an oracle foretelling a succession of perplexing familial upheavals and the seeming loss of his kingdom. These foretold dangers pursue him, however, in the form of the princes Musidorus and Pyrocles, who take on disguises as the shepherd Dorus and the Amazon Cleophila respectively, in order to woo the princesses. Both Basilius and Gynecia fall in love with Pyrocles/Cleophila, leading to a tragi-comic denouement in which Basilius appears to have been killed by a mistakenly administered love potion, but is restored to life during the trial of Gynecia and the princes for their part in his apparent murder and the subsequent disturbances afflicting Arcadia.

Sidney's relationship with ancient romance is the closest of any early modern English writer; only he can be said to have made 'a conscious attempt to domesticate the genre'.[44] Wolff and, more recently, Skretkowicz have described Sidney's use of aspects both general and specific drawn from Greek romance, such as Basilius' oracle, the inset travel narratives, and the closing trial scene imitated from Achilles Tatius. The concentrated manipulation of Heliodoran matter and plotting that characterizes the *New Arcadia* is manifested in elements such as its opening *in medias res* at the scene of a shipwreck; the rewriting of Heliodorus' tale of Calasiris, Petosiris, and Thyamis as the tale of the Paphlagonian king and his two sons, a story that then finds its way into *King Lear* as the Gloucester subplot; and the combining of Heliodorus' amorous women Demaenete and Arsace in the persona of Andromana.[45] Sidney routinely amalgamates Greek romance with other literary traditions: the five-act structure of the *Old Arcadia* (each book is called an 'Act') is derived from Terence; Pyrocles' disguise as the Amazon Cleophila is from books 8 and 11 of *Amadis de Gaule*, and the comic plot of both father and mother falling in love with their daughter's disguised suitor occurs in books 11 to 12; Musidorus' disguise as a shepherd is based on that of Florisel in *Amadis* book 9; and from the *Arcadia* of Sannazaro and the *Diana* of Montemayor comes the convention of using a prose romance plot as the narrative link between verses, in Sidney's case the four sets of Eclogues sung by the Arcadian shepherds.[46] Allusions to the *Metamorphoses* of Apuleius are threaded throughout both *Arcadias*, from the oracle and associated *curiositas* that initiates Sidney's plot, to the 'convergence of malice and wonder', as Carver puts it, that is imitated from 'Cupid and Psyche' in the comic subplot, to the lustful *matronae* Gynecia and Andromana.[47]

The versions of love played out in the *Old Arcadia* are demonstrative of this mixed mode of romance writing that melds ancient and modern. The Greek motif of love at first sight via a picture is used to initiate the passion of Pyrocles for Philoclea, but that love is inflected differently in the *Arcadia* as a consequence of the Amadisian female disguise the prince adopts, a disguise that as well as creating the intergenerational sexual comedy also amplifies the range of agonies induced by love. For much of the romance, Philoclea, unlike her classical counterparts, is forced into complex self-negotiations and analyses about what seems to be an inadmissible inclining towards another woman; 'mutual' and 'impossible' are adjectives frequently used by protagonists and narrator. The symmetry and mutuality of the lovers in ancient romance is thus recalibrated into a same-sex rhetoric of affinity, self-mirroring, and sorority that is also, on Philoclea's part, intermittently self-exculpatory. Until Pyrocles reveals his male identity, the lovers' mutuality is expressed through a dramatically altered courtly discourse that turns the heterosexual Petrarchan tropes of distance and difference into homosexual tropes of proximity and same-ness—for example, in the compliments the lovers exchange regarding their mirroring beauty ('You are so acquainted with your own beauty that it makes you easily fall into the discourse of beauty,' smiles Philoclea (*Old Arcadia*, 38)). Pyrocles' Amazon disguise facilitates an interplay of innocence and knowingness that is strikingly similar to *Daphnis and Chloe* (albeit there is no direct citation of Longus by Sidney). When the knowing reader is told of Basilius being 'transported with delight' at this scene, or encounters the loaded innuendo of Philoclea's awareness that 'Cleophila might well want power, but not will, to please her' (p. 111), he (and at moments like this I think it is very much a 'he') is being 'framed' and 'implicated', just like Longus' reader, as lasciviously engaged in the unveiling of euphemism.[48]

Similar generic interplay is seen in the depiction of Gynecia, who combines elements of the sexually masterful matron (notably Achilles Tatius' Melite) with the lustful stepmother of book 10 of Apuleius's *Metamorphoses*, and who exhibits a Euripidean sense of herself as a tragic protagonist embracing evil and infamy in the pursuit of her desire. It is, indeed, only the sudden return to life of Basilius in the restorative, romance denouement that saves her from a charge of murderess. The Euripidean strain is shared across both *Old* and *New Arcadias*, first because it underpins the words of tragic women throughout Greek romance, and secondly because the characterization of Gynecia remains constant across both *Arcadias*. In a speech at the beginning of book II that appears in both versions she contemplates, rhetorically at least, the murder of her own child who stands in the way of her passion: 'the life I have given thee, ungrateful Philoclea, I will sooner with these hands bereave thee of than my birth shall glory she hath bereaved me of my desires' (p. 92).

Although Gynecia's role remains largely unchanged in the *New Arcadia*, in respect of the sisters Pamela and Philoclea Sidney performs a notable retrenchment back to the celebration of *sophrosune* (chastity, self-control) typical of the Greek romances. Whereas, in the *Old Arcadia*, courtly eroticism prevails (Musidorus nearly effects a successful assault on the sleeping Pamela's chastity, and Pyrocles makes love to Philoclea), there are no consummations in the *New Arcadia*. Instead, the revised version develops a sustained alliance of eroticism and violence, the centrepiece of which is the immurement of the princesses in a castle by their aunt Cecropia, who hopes to secure the Arcadian throne by marrying one of them to her son Amphialus. This 'Captivity Episode' provides scope for Sidney's amplification of the 'erotic sufferings' (*erotika pathemata*) of ancient romance. Ironically, however, the text Sidney imitates for his celebration of a princely, Christian *sophrosune* under torture is Achilles Tatius' *Leucippe and Klitophon*, notable for its tonal slipperiness in this regard: '*Sophrosune*, sexual control, truth-telling, self-knowledge, the central terms of contemporary philosophical *askesis* [self-denial] are all objects of Achilles' sly rewriting,' observes Goldhill. Goldhill goes on to remark the over-riding importance of Leucippe in this respect: 'Cleitophon's life history may be *sophron*, but it is the beaten, shorn and misused body of Leucippe that evinces—like a martyr—the acme of *sophrosune*.'[49] This comment is remarkably pertinent to the *New Arcadia*. Much of Sidney's revised version is taken up with fleshing out the *sophron* life histories of Musidorus and Pyrocles through the inset digressions outlining their heroic deeds, to the extent that it has often been read as an attempted recuperation of the unchaste, deceitful strategizing of the princes in the *Old* version. The captive princesses, however, are at the heart of the romance's new ethic of self-control, and their beautiful pain, like that of Leucippe, admits of a complicated degree of voyeuristic eroticism at the same time as it reanimates the foundational virtue of Greek romance—a heroic, female *sophrosune*.

Besieged by Basilius' troops, Cecropia displays the princesses and the disguised Pyrocles (who is called Zelmane in the *New Arcadia*) on a scaffold, threatening to stage their decapitation: in the event no heads are lost, but the scene is nonetheless soaked in blood, whether the 'pretty fear' that 'came up to endamask' Philoclea's rosy cheeks (blushing being a traditional indicator also of sexual passion) or the swelling courage of Zelmane that made 'the blood burst out at her nose' (*New Arcadia*, 415). Erotic violence, like erotic love, is inflected through female same-ness, as Cecropia escalates the princesses' suffering. With a rod and accompanied by a strange group of wicked 'old women' she 'fell to scourge that most beautiful body' of Philoclea (p. 420) and then, in a direct rewriting of the fake deaths meted out to Leucippe, first Pamela's and then Philoclea's executions are staged. For the latter, Zelmane is even treated to a gruesome mini-ekphrasis with the sight of 'a basin of gold pitifully enamelled with blood, and in the midst of it, the head of the most beautiful Philoclea' (p. 431). The 'executions' are achieved through a real death (that of Artesia), and a fake one, a theatrical sleight of hand (pushing Philoclea's head through the basin), just like the apparent beheading of Leucippe (*Old Arcadia*, 436; *CAGN* 236).

Disturbance and Disruption

Surveys of the influence of ancient romance in English literature typically characterize that relationship as rooted in elements of disruptive plotting, such as shipwrecks and familial separations, all of which are resolved (and even forgotten) in the final scenes of revelation, judgement, and reconciliation. Although some of these disruptions emanate from forces external to the rural world, such as the pirates, the sexual predator Gnathon and the rich young men from Methymna in *Daphnis and Chloe*, disruption is also inherent to the countryside. As Suzanne Saïd has shown, the elite and urban perspective of ancient romance means that, while the countryside itself can be a source of pleasure, and nature (especially when cultivated as a garden) can be restorative, truly rural inhabitants are inherently disruptive, being essentially comic or dangerous.[50] Furthermore, love and violence are perpetually intertwined, through amorous competition (cf. Dorcan's trap and wolf disguise in *Daphnis and Chloe*) and mythological precedent: 'stories of love stir feelings of lust', as Klitophon puts it (*CAGN* 180). When English romance incorporated from Italian pastoral the notion of shepherd-as-poet, this tradition of erotic rural competition was intensified to include poetical competition as well: Greene's pastoral romance *Menaphon* (1589), for example, copies Sidney in having the rival shepherd–poets Menaphon and Melicertus compete in verse (Greene, *Life and Complete Works*, 6. 122–8).

The attitudes of early modern English romance towards rural-dwellers are similarly urban and elite, although it also draws on the energetic traditions of allegory, satire, and political commentary intrinsic to medieval pastoral writing.[51] Thanks to what Louis Montrose terms the 'formal indirections' thus encoded in English pastoral, romance rusticity becomes topical—a means, for example, of introducing that particular kind of 'cruel laughter' influentially characterized by Stephen Greenblatt as attempting to 'inscribe ineradicable differences' between lords and clowns in order to suppress rebellion and protect property.[52] The two *Arcadias* are thus punctuated by eruptions of rusticity that evoke simultaneously the ancient motif of rural banditry and the Elizabethan elite's distaste for the populace (for example, the clownish rebels who are talked down by Pyrocles in his feminine persona of Cleophila (*Old Arcadia*, 126–32)). On the other hand, there is also space within the English tradition for the equally politicized depiction of an idealized and obedient rural populace, seen notably in Day's interpolation into his *Daphnis and Chloe* of 'The Shepherds Holiday', a collection of shepherd songs performed at a festival in honour of their queen, Eliza.[53]

Seventeenth-century romances perpetuate this distrust of what is termed in John Barclay's *Argenis* (1621) the 'unruly vulgar', at the same time as they extend the agents of unruliness to include rebellious magnates, devious courtiers—and, in some respects, women, whose role is dramatically expanded in Jacobean romance.[54] *Argenis*, written originally in Latin and translated into English first in 1625, is both like and unlike ancient romance. Credited with initiating the seventeenth-century category of the political romance, *Argenis* blends together classical political dialogue (especially Xenophon's *Cyropaedia*) with a post-Sidneian imitation of Heliodoran plotting. The result is a family narrative detailing the domestic and political 'tumults' (p. 11) endured by Meleander, the troubled king of Sicily, as a consequence of internal rebellion and external aggression by Radirobanes, king of Sardinia, who desires to marry Argenis, Meleander's daughter. In some significant respects *Argenis* is consciously imitative of ancient romance: it is set in a pseudo-classical Sicily; there are shipwrecks and pirates; complex use is made of flashbacks; it includes *ekphraseis*, such as the fountain carved by Daedalus (p. 25); and it is punctuated by digressions on laws, customs, and religion (such as the cult of Pallas in which Argenis is a priestess, pp. 57–8). But at the same time *Argenis* is underpinned by a resolutely modern and devoutly monarchist sensibility. Barclay's familiarity with the Stuart court and his closeness to James I mean that the priorities of *Argenis* are unlike those of Elizabethan prose romance: it is far more concerned with anatomizing government than love or wit, and, like Spenser's heavily allegorical verse romance *The Faerie Queene*, it casts many sideways, satirical glances at contemporary politics such as the Overbury scandal (p. 15). Indeed, the relative lack of direct contact between its pair of lovers, Argenis and the French king Poliarchus, is striking. Although couched in the traditional language of love, their alliance owes little to the *eros* of ancient fiction: it is imperially, intellectually, strategically virtuous and powerful—but not sexual. The private tumults of love and grief, and the public tumults of war are both categorized as 'broils' (pp. 334, 336), and they are emblematically combined in the person of Argenis. Like Greene in *Pandosto* (and, indeed, the older Shakespeare), Barclay's interest seems to lie primarily in the nexus of dynastic and sexual anxieties focused by a father on his daughter, his attempts to control her sexuality, and the personal and imperial unruliness that stems from this generational tension. As a result, the resolution of *Argenis* as a political, rather than erotic, fiction necessitates (unusually) the *effacement*, not the exposure, of its heroine in the climactic *anagnorisis*. Argenis' erstwhile suitor Archombrotus is revealed to be her half-brother, at which point 'she, that not long was so bold, so almost rebellious against her father... now remembered she was a virgin' (p. 395).

Another romance published in 1621, *The Countess of Montgomery's Urania* by Sidney's niece, Lady Mary Wroth, examines in detail the unruliness of love as it is focused through the passionate sufferings of women. The first English romance that can genuinely lay claim to being written for women,[55] the *Urania* combines material taken from ancient Greek, English, French, and Spanish romances with contemporary political anxiety about the fate of the kingdom of Bohemia into which James's daughter Elizabeth had married. To this is added *roman à clef* material that, primarily through the narrative of the lovers Pamphilia and Amphilanthus, reimagines Wroth's affair with her cousin William Herbert, Earl of Pembroke.[56] The undertow of this relationship is widely felt, not least in the fact that it transforms the mutuality of ancient romance into 'mismatch', because Amphilanthus is an inconstant lover.[57]

Wroth's simultaneous deference to and disruption of the Heliodoran mode naturalized by her uncle in the *Arcadia* is evident in the opening incidents of the *Urania*. It begins *in medias res*, with the laments of the shepherdess Urania who has just learned that she is not the child of her supposed parents: thus identity revelation is used as a trope of initiatory sorrow ('I am lost' (p. 16)), rather than terminal rejoicing. Urania then encounters Perissus, whose ego-narrative, reminiscent of Achilles Tatius, tells a sombre tale of his love for Limena, married 'dutifully, though unwillingly' at the command of her father and whom he believes murdered by her jealous husband (pp. 5, 17). This narrative foregrounds virtue, once again, but makes it extra-marital: as Philargus, the husband, points out, the issue in Limena's refusal to participate in his trap for Perissus is that she is being faithful and virtuous 'to one besides your husband' (p. 12). This theme of female constancy as manifested in unconventional and unhappy circumstances is often reprised. It is treated emblematically when Pamphilia receives a set of keys from Constancy during the adventure of the Throne of Love, at which point 'Constancy vanished, as metamorphosing her self into her breast' (p. 169). Wroth's reification of constancy in the person of Pamphilia is only one of many classically inspired metamorphoses in early modern romance, and it suits the simultaneously abstract and topical significations of the *Urania* very well. Indeed, one could go so far as to characterize the multifaceted English receptions of ancient romance in comparable terms, as acts of metamorphosis in which literary traditions both ancient and modern are incorporated into a new form such that they may even, at times, appear to vanish.

Notes

1. In what follows, I refer to ancient 'fictions' and 'romances' rather than 'novels', the term that has become normalized among classicists since the 1980s (although 'romance' continues to be used in some contexts). 'Novel' is applied to ancient fiction partly as a 'label of convenience', partly as a 'valorization' of these fictions in the face of Victorian contempt, but neither 'novel' nor 'romance' is a native classical category (Tim Whitmarsh, 'Introduction', and Simon Goldhill, 'Genre', in Tim Whitmarsh (ed.), *The Cambridge Companion to the Greek and Roman Novel* (Cambridge, 2008), 1–14 (3) and 185–200 (193) respectively). One justification of the use of 'novel' for ancient fiction is to collapse the distinction between romance and novel: this is the import of Margaret Anne Doody, *The True Story of the Novel* (1996), but the validity of the distinction has been powerfully reasserted by James Grantham Turner, '"Romance" and Novel in Restoration England', *Review of English Studies*, 63 (2012), 58–85. Generic self-designation in ancient fiction is the subject of ongoing research: for one indicative aspect, see Tim Whitmarsh, 'The Greek Novel: Titles and Genre', *American Journal of Philology*, 126 (2005), 587–611. Surveys of the relationship of ancient romance to early modern fiction are provided in Samuel Lee Wolff, *The Greek Romances in Elizabethan Prose Fiction* (New York, 1912); Steve Mentz, *Romance for Sale in Early Modern England: The Rise of Prose Fiction* (Aldershot, 2006); Viktor Skretkowicz, *European Erotic Romance: Philhellene Protestantism, Renaissance Translation and English Literary Politics* (Manchester, 2010).
2. Daniel Huet, *A Treatise of Romances and their Original* (1672), 38–9. See further April Shelford, *Transforming the Republic of Letters: Pierre-Daniel Huet and European Intellectual Life, 1650–1720* (Rochester, NY, 2007), 108–12.
3. Thomas Underdowne, *An Ethiopian History*, 2nd edn (1577), sig. ¶3r.
4. On Sidney, see Skretkowicz, *European Erotic Romance*, 206–7.
5. Laurence Plazenet, *L'Ébahissement et la délectation: Réception comparée et poétiques du Roman Grec en France et en Angleterre aux XVIe et XVIIe Siècles* (Paris, 1997); and 'Jacques Amyot and the Greek Novel: The Invention of the French Novel', in Gerald Sandy (ed.), *The Classical Heritage in France* (Leiden, 2002), 237–80.

6. See Skretkowicz, *European Erotic Romance*, 21–6, 111–65 (with an emphasis on political allegory); and Mentz, *Romance for Sale*, 47–71 (on heroism and human agency).
7. Robert H. F. Carver, *The Protean Ass: The 'Metamorphoses' of Apuleius from Antiquity to the Renaissance* (Oxford, 2007), 357–8.
8. Tim Whitmarsh, *The Second Sophistic* (Oxford, 2005), 5.
9. Cf. Michel Foucault, *The Care of the Self* (*The History of Sexuality*, vol. 3) (Harmondsworth, 1986 (originally in French, 1984)), and, in riposte, Simon Goldhill, *Foucault's Virginity: Ancient Erotic Fiction and the History of Sexuality* (Cambridge, 1995).
10. See the note by John J. Winkler in *Collected Ancient Greek Novels*, ed. B. P. Reardon (Berkeley and Los Angeles, 1989), 223 (hereafter cited as *CAGN*).
11. The intertwining of Homer with romance continues into the Renaissance: see Colin Burrow, *Epic Romance: Homer to Milton* (Oxford, 1993).
12. Charles Martindale, 'Introduction', in Charles Martindale (ed.), *Ovid Renewed: Ovidian Influences on Literature and Art from the Middle Ages to the Twentieth Century* (Cambridge, 1988), 1–20 (13).
13. Jonathan Bate, *Shakespeare and Ovid* (Oxford, 1993), 35, 84.
14. Arthur F. Kinney, *Humanist Poetics: Thought, Rhetoric and Fiction in Sixteenth-Century England* (Amherst, MA, 1986), 219.
15. Tim Whitmarsh, *Narrative and Identity in the Ancient Greek Novel: Returning Romance* (Cambridge, 2011), 112.
16. Nicole Cazauran and Michel Bideaux (eds), *Les Amadis en France au XVI*[e] *Siècle* (Paris, 2000).
17. Goran Stanivukovic, 'Introduction', in Emanuel Ford, *The Most Pleasant History of Ornatus and Artesia*, ed. Goran Stanivukovic (Ottawa, 2003), 11–105, esp. 17–24 (19).
18. Spenser, *The Faerie Queene*, 3. 6. 50–1; Carver, *The Protean Ass*, 384–428 (384).
19. Robert Parry, *Moderatus*, ed. John Simons (Aldershot, 2002), 46.
20. *The Countess of Pembroke's Arcadia: The New Arcadia*, ed. Viktor Skretkowicz (Oxford, 1987), 189–96.
21. Gerald Eades Bentley, *The Jacobean and Caroline Stage*, 7 vols (Oxford, 1941–68), 4. 515–16, 5. 1439–40; Carol Gesner, *Shakespeare and the Greek Romance: A Study of Origins* (Lexington, KY, 1970), 47.
22. Carver, *The Protean Ass*, 331, 337–9, 349–55.
23. A. D. Nuttall, 'Action at a Distance: Shakespeare and the Greeks', and Stuart Gillespie, 'Shakespeare and Greek Romance: "Like an old tale still"', in Charles Martindale and A. B. Taylor (eds), *Shakespeare and the Classics* (Cambridge, 2004), 209–22 (215–17), 225–37; Tanya Pollard, 'Romancing the Greeks: *Cymbeline*'s Genres and Models', in Laurie Maguire (ed.), *How to Do Things with Shakespeare: New Approaches, New Essays* (Oxford, 2008), 34–53.
24. For the parallel movement of oratory into fiction in the sixteenth century, see Arthur F. Kinney, 'Rhetoric and Fiction in Elizabethan England', in James J. Murphy (ed.), *Renaissance Eloquence: Studies in the Theory and Practice of Renaissance Rhetoric* (Berkeley and Los Angeles, 1983), 385–93.
25. Goldhill, *Foucault's Virginity*, 3.
26. Skretkowicz, *European Erotic Romance*, 206.
27. On Greek romance as a means of praising chaste marriage, see Darlene C. Greenhalgh, 'Love, Chastity and Women's Erotic Power: Greek Romance in Elizabethan and Jacobean Contexts', in Goran Stanivukovic and Constance C. Relihan (eds), *Prose Fiction and Early Modern Sexualities in England, 1570–1640* (New York, 2003), 15–42.
28. The literary impact of this grammar-school training—particularly as it affects

Shakespeare's articulation of love and woe—is explored in Lynn Enterline, *Shakespeare's Schoolroom: Rhetoric, Discipline, Emotion* (Philadelphia, 2012).

29. Judith Rice Henderson, 'Euphues and his Erasmus', *English Literary Renaissance*, 12 (1982), 135–61.
30. *The Complete Works of John Lyly*, ed. R. Warwick Bond, 3 vols (Oxford, 1902), 1. 193.
31. On this subject, see *Travel and Prose Fiction in Early Modern England, Yearbook of English Studies*, 41 (2011).
32. Jonas Barish, 'The Prose Style of John Lyly', *Journal of English Literary History*, 23 (1956), 14–35; John Carey, 'Sixteenth- and Seventeenth-Century Prose', in Christopher Ricks (ed.), *English Poetry and Prose, 1540–1674* (1970), 339–431 (364).
33. Wolff, *Greek Romances*, 144.
34. Wolff, *Greek Romances*, 134.
35. David Konstan, *Sexual Symmetry: Love in the Ancient Novel and Related Genres* (Princeton, 1994).
36. The Greek romances themselves play a part in this misogyny—e.g. Clinias' invective against women from *Leucippe and Klitophon* is reused in Greene's euphuistic romance *The Carde of Fancie* (1584) (Wolff, *Greek Romances*, 396–7). I discuss the role of the *Heroides* further in 'Elizabethan Fiction and Ovid's *Heroides*', *Translation and Literature*, 9 (2000), 40–64.
37. Masimo Fusillo, 'The Conflict of Emotions: A *Topos* in the Greek Erotic Novel', in Simon Swain (ed.), *Oxford Readings in the Greek Novel* (Oxford, 1999), 60–82.
38 R. W. Maslen, 'Greene and the Uses of Time', in Kirk Melnikoff and Edward Gieskes (eds), *Writing Robert Greene: Essays on England's First Notorious Professional Writer* (Aldershot, 2008), 157–88 (166).
39. Walter Davis, *Idea and Act in Elizabethan Fiction* (Princeton, 1969), 144, 178.
40. On the changing titular identities of Greene's romance as *Pandosto* and then *Dorastus and Fawnia*, see Lori Humphrey Newcomb, *Reading Popular Romance in Early Modern England* (New York, 2002).
41. For the Latin romance *Apollonius of Tyre*, perhaps of the sixth century CE but with possible Greek antecedents, see Elizabeth Archibald, *Apollonius of Tyre: Medieval and Renaissance Themes and Variations* (Woodbridge, 1991). On the link between romance and early Christian hagiography, see Judith Perkins, 'Representation in Greek Saints' Lives', in J. R. Morgan and Richard Stoneman (eds), *Greek Fiction: The Greek Novel in Context* (1994), 255–71.
42. *The Life and Complete Works in Prose and Verse of Robert Greene, MA*, ed. A. B. Grosart, 12 vols (1881–3), 4. 241.
43. Newcomb, *Reading Popular Romance*, 63–5.
44. Wolff, *Greek Romances*, 353, referring to the *New Arcadia*.
45. Wolff, *Greek Romances*, 312–14; and Skretkowicz, *European Erotic Romance*, 168–224.
46. Clark L. Chalifour, 'Sir Philip Sidney's *Old Arcadia* as Terentian Comedy', *Studies in English Literature 1500–1900*, 16 (1976), 51–63; *The Countess of Pembroke's Arcadia (The Old Arcadia)*, ed. Jean Robertson (Oxford, 1973), pp. xx–xxii; John J. O'Connor, *'Amadis de Gaule' and its Influence on Elizabethan Literature* (New Brunswick, 1970), 183–201.
47. Carver, *The Protean Ass*, 365–83 (370).
48. Goldhill, *Foucault's Virginity*, 27.
49. Goldhill, *Foucault's Virginity*, 100–1.
50. Suzanne Saïd, 'Rural Society in the Greek Novel, or the Country Seen from the Town', in Swain (ed.), *Oxford Readings in the Greek Novel*, 83–107.
51. Helen Cooper, *Pastoral: Mediaeval into Renaissance* (Cambridge, 1977).
52. Louis Montrose, 'Spenser and the Elizabethan Political Imaginary', *Journal of English Literary History*, 69 (2002), 907–46 (914); Stephen Greenblatt, 'Murdering Peasants: Status, Genre and the

Representation of Rebellion', *Representations*, 1 (1983), 1–29 (17).

53. Angel Day, *Daphnis and Chloe* (1587), sigs K1^{v}–M1^{v}.
54. John Barclay, *Barclay his Argenis: or, the Loves of Poliarchus and Argenis*, trans. Kingsmill Long (1625), 247. The Latin text and a translation based on that of Long are available in *Argenis*, ed. Mark Riley and Dorothy Pritchard Huber, 2 vols (Assen, 2004).
55. On this vexed question of female readership in classical and early modern cultures, see Katharine Haynes, *Fashioning the Feminine in the Greek Novel* (2003) and Helen Hackett, *Women and Romance Fiction in the English Renaissance* (Cambridge, 2000).
56. *The First Part of the Countess of Montgomery's Urania*, ed. Josephine Roberts (Tempe, AZ, 1995), pp. xviii–xxix, xxxix–xlv, lxxxvi–lxxxvii; Margaret P. Hannay, *Mary Sidney, Lady Wroth* (Farnham, 2010), 189–96.
57. Skretkowicz, *European Erotic Romance*, 278.

CHAPTER 14

Elegy, Hymn, Epithalamium, Ode

Some Renaissance Reinterpretations

ROLAND GREENE

Early modern European poetry is written in a zone between the authoritative examples of classical verse—represented here by four forms and genres, the elegy, the epithalamium, the ode, and the hymn—and vernacular poetics as the site of expansive, often unscripted, possibilities. This chapter describes how that zone is redrawn over the Renaissance, as the classical genres, of which these four represent strikingly different instances, become absorbed into the practice of poetry in English. While there are many other such instances, these four are something like cardinal directions, indicating varying but complementary models for rendering classical models into the vernacular.

The premiss of the present chapter is that the adaptation of classical models into the vernacular entails a process of reinterpretation, which is masked by a common nomenclature. In one sense, 'elegy', 'hymn', 'epithalamium', and 'ode' are available more or less continuously from antiquity through the Middle Ages and the Renaissance, and in searching out the terms we may recover the patterns of their usages. In the era of early modern humanism, however, each term is not only the register of received meanings but a metonymy of the negotiation between past and present, especially where the reach of a genre has come to accommodate new circumstances. Sometimes, as in the case of elegy, the classical sense of a term is more capacious, while the Renaissance meaning becomes more closely circumscribed over time; in other cases, such as the epithalamium, the pre-modern and modern meanings are ostensibly the same—a poem celebrating a wedding—but Renaissance poets and readers tend to see a more complex problem that such a poem addresses—namely, the rendering of an act (such as a marriage) into an event (such as a wedding). In a sense this is to imagine that these stock genres are more than legacies of classical poetry adapted into English: it is to suppose that they participate in the social, ethical, and phenomenal questions that figure in Renaissance thought. During this period theologians such as Martin Luther, historians such as Francesco Guicciardini, and philosophers such as Niccolò Machiavelli address (among many other topics) the nature of private experience, the pull of the invisible past on the present, and the removal between a deed and how it is received. In their own ways, these genres respond such questions within the compass of poetic representation.

In antiquity 'elegy' means only poems in elegiac couplets, but in its reception by Renaissance writers the term has a penumbra that extends further: while the canonical Greek elegists such as Archilochus, Callinus, Tyrtaeus, Theognis, and Simonides were known irregularly or not at all, many Renaissance poets assembled canons of 'elegies' that responded more to their ambitions than to classical criteria.[1] For many writers, such a canon might include the idylls of Theocritus, the eclogues of Virgil, and especially the Roman love elegies of Catullus and his successors Tibullus, Propertius, and Ovid. Ancient Greek elegies address a great deal more than the motifs familiar to modern readers of honouring the dead and finding consolation after grief: they speak of love, war, history, pleasure, and much more.[2] More circumscribed in its reach as well as in the period of its composition, Roman elegy tends towards love in all its complexities.[3] When Renaissance poets read the Greek and Roman elegists, they saw a poetry of lamentation and love but noticed a rich complement of ways of registering absence, including that of persons no longer present or living as well as the loss of formerly powerful ideas, relations, and values. Even when the speaker's lover is physically available in a love elegy, something else may yet be absent: self-understanding, a true commerce between the lovers, or a correspondence between mythological precedents and present reality. Renaissance elegy might be understood, then, not in its restricted sense of an expression of grief but expansively, as a way of recovering things below the surface of present reality. When Renaissance poets adapted Catullus and especially Ovid, they recovered a broad mandate for the genre to treat discursively those things that are nearly unthinkable in other amatory genres of the time: for example, not how it feels to be in love—in the fashion of a sonnet—but what we think about how it feels to be in love. Once we recognize it on its own terms, the Renaissance elegy becomes legible for a reinterpretation of its antecedents conditioned to its own age.[4]

The hymn presents another purchase on contemporaneous reality.[5] Its classical precursors are as various as those of the elegy, notably including songs of worship, praise, and lyric reflection; they are still more varied in metre.[6] The Renaissance receives a history of the hymn that fuses classical instances with the understandings of hymnody promoted by the Greek and Latin church fathers of the early centuries CE. Sometimes treated as closely related to the psalm or the ode, the hymn is universally extolled in the Renaissance as the highest form of poetry. And yet its power entails untouchability or at least a certain version of difficulty: the genre offers up the challenge of representing sheer presence—of God, of faith, of love—despite intellectual and cultural pressures (of reformed religion, of Protestant poetics, of Petrarchism) that make such presence a problematic concept.[7]

The epithalamium and the ode offer complementary approaches to another task of Renaissance poetry, to fuse public life and private experience into an occasional poetics adapted to the courtly and ceremonial culture of the period. While these genres are often incompletely understood by the Renaissance as varieties of largely public poetry—in antiquity the reality was, of course, more complex—their adaptation to the vernacular grants them an interior, not in the fashion of later Romantic poetry, where 'the interweaving of thought, feeling, and perceptual detail' often infuses poems outwardly based on classical models, but in the peculiar way natural to the sixteenth century, when figures and occasions were explored for the relations between insides and outsides.[8] Such early modern poems, we will see, exist not so much to record the subjectivity of a speaker but to show the private within the public, the motives inside the gesture, the affect behind the ceremony. A great deal of influential thought of the period is devoted to this kind of unmasking—consider Castiglione's *Book of the Courtier* and Machiavelli's *The Prince*—and it makes sense that, in the poetry as well, poets and readers expect to see genres such as the epithalamium and the ode reweighed in this inquisitive spirit.

The early modern epithalamium can be construed as a wedding poem, much in the way that the contemporaneous elegy might be seen as a lament for the dead.[9] But classically inflected poetry of this period, I will suggest, is often motivated by a problem of poetics that extends beyond the genre at hand: in the case of the epithalamium, as I have noted, to discern the difference between the act of marriage and the event of the wedding. Poems such as John Donne's 'Epithalamion, or Marriage Song on the Lady Elizabeth, and Count Palatine Being Married on St Valentines Day' and Robert Herrick's 'Epithalamie to Sir Thomas Southwell and his Ladie' locate themselves in the crease between these two kinds of occasion, and deserve the epithet 'occasional' not for addressing a particular occasion—although they do that—but for enquiring into the making of occasions within human life.[10]

Ode, the fourth of these genres received from antiquity, has perhaps the most complex descent, with two streams of influence, the Pindaric and the Horatian (not to mention the tributary called the Anacreontic), which are often explored by Renaissance poets in a thoroughgoing way.[11] Following a complicated history in antiquity that overlaps that of the hymn, the ode enters the early modern period as a vessel for a balanced, harmonious comment on figures or occasions. Within these formal or tonal dispositions, however, the Renaissance ode often subscribes to a programme that corresponds to the workings of the elegy, the hymn, and the epithalamium: that is, the ode appeals to early modern poets and readers because it addresses figures or occasions in view of the fit (or lack thereof) between deeds and their significance. Praising heroic acts while parsing the nature of heroism, or celebrating and analysing at once great occasions, Renaissance odes manage to infuse the models received from antiquity with a measure of humanist self-consciousness about the making of history in modern culture. They disclose the strata of meaning-making even in what may seem the most monumental of literary celebrations.[12]

This chapter will examine the four genres through several representative examples, seeking to render legible those challenges and expedients by which the elegy, the hymn, the epithalamium, and the ode were remade in English. In this setting the classicism of Renaissance English poets is most profitably construed as their way of finding expressive but also explanatory power in the available genres of classical poetry. Each genre will be discussed through a few principal instances that demonstrate what I argue is the constitutive problem of that genre in the Renaissance: conjuring what is latent or absent, representing presence, rendering an act into an event, or distinguishing a deed and its significance. As we shall see, elegy, one of the most multifarious early modern genres, tends to treat absence and latency; hymn is often about the challenge of representing sheer presence; epithalamium represents how an act is transmuted into an event; and ode explores the distinction between a deed and its significance. Each genre is considered through examples that demonstrate the relevant problem in action, as a dynamic instance of classical reception that takes place through and beside the kind of reception that entails imitation and allusion. The poems chiefly under discussion—including John Donne's elegy 'On his Mistress', Edmund Spenser's *Fowre Hymnes*, Ben Jonson's epithalamia on two marriages of 1608 and 1632, and Andrew Marvell's 'Horatian Ode upon Cromwell's Return from Ireland'—tend to demonstrate their genres in self-conscious fashion, serving as definitions and commentaries even while they seem to exist as discrete works of poetic art. They remind us that even the most authoritative literary terms represent compromises between past and present, and develop new justifications as circumstances change—or do not, and disappear with their original contexts.

Elegy

Of the Renaissance genres that show themselves as survivors across diverse contexts, elegy is one of the hardiest. Classical elegy is a highly uneven terrain that extends from the laments of Archilochus to the frankly erotic lyrics of Tibullus, Propertius, and Ovid; Renaissance readers conceive the genre still more widely to include the pastoral laments of Theocritus, Moschus, and Virgil.[13] The basis of elegy is elegiac metre, which consists of a distich or couplet, one line of hexameter followed by a line of pentameter.[14] Horace called these 'versibus impariter iunctis' ('verses unequally joined') (*Ars Poetica* 75) because of the instability built into the pairing, a rising line of six feet matched with a falling line of five. While the couplets often resolve into units of sense, the asymmetry in the metre propels each couplet into the next, and the resulting poem is a vehicle for many sorts of seeking. Propertius applies the form to descry the perfection of the naked form within the adorned body:

Qvid iuvat ornato procedere, vita, capillo
　et tenuis Coa veste movere sinus,
aut quid Orontea crines perfundere murra,
　teque peregrinis vendere muneribus,
naturaeque decus mercato perdere cultu,
　nec sinere in propriis membra nitere bonis?

(What avails it, my love, to step out with ornate hair and flutter the sheer folds of a Coan dress? What avails it to drench your locks with Syrian perfume and to vaunt yourself in foreign finery, to destroy your natural charm with purchased ornament, preventing your figure from displaying its own true merits?)

(Propertius, *Elegies* 1.2.1–6, translation modified)

In the *Amores*, Ovid elevates the quotient of narrative to depict, within the story of a confounding love affair, many discrete events that lend concrete form to the problem of attaining a fulfilment that is close at hand but in many ways unreachable:

Vir tuus est epulas nobis aditurus easdem—
　ultima cena tuo sit, precor, illa viro!
ergo ego dilectam tantum conviva puellam
　adspiciam?

(That husband of yours will attend the same banquet with us—may that dinner, I pray, be your husband's last! Must I then merely look upon the girl I love, be merely a fellow guest?)

(Ovid, *Amores* 1.4.1–4)

While this orientation of form and attitude finds many versions in classical poetry, it becomes a central bequest from antiquity to the European vernaculars, especially English. Readers and writers of the later Middle Ages and the Renaissance seem to understand that elegy is a kind of poetry in which metrical, psychic, and fictional elements converge around the problem of addressing something not present in or to the poem. Towards the end of the seventeenth century, the problem is made regular in a modern generic disposition: elegy as lament for the dead. But, for the preceding two or three centuries, early modern elegy can be that sort of lament or many other things: praise for an unattainable model of conduct, flirtation with a woman who withholds body or mind, meditation on death as a human concern. The modern notion of elegy that has been anatomized by Peter Sacks, Jahan Ramazani, and other critics is not inapt for this era, but it does not tell the entire story of a set of conventions that struggles to define itself as a genre.[15]

John Skelton's *Philip Sparrow* is a curiosity in the history of English elegy, a founding instance that carries its own counterexample within it. The first section of the poem is over 800 lines of lament for the dead sparrow Philip in the voice of his mistress Jane Scrope, closely following the Office for the Dead that appears among the prayers in the Roman Catholic Book of Hours and, more distantly, exploding Catullus 3, a compact lament for Lesbia's dead bird. Then follows this transitional remark:

But for my sparrow's sake
Yet as a woman may,
My wit I shall assay
An epitaph to write
In Latin plain and light,
Whereof the elegy
Followeth by and by.[16]

Are the two literary terms used here as synonyms? Or does Skelton promise an epitaph 'whereof' there will follow an elegy? I believe the latter reading comes closer to his meaning: notice that the elegy comes not immediately but 'by and by', presumably as the epitaph winds down. The distinction seems to be between mere epitaph and something greater and of wider implications: perhaps not only a lament for the dead but a reflection on an object that could not be possessed in any event, dead or alive. George Puttenham addresses this criterion when he writes that 'an epitaph is but a kind of epigram, only applied to the report of the dead person's estate and degree, or of his other good or bad parts, to his commendation or reproach... So as if it exceed the measure of an epigram, it is then (if the verse be correspondent) rather an elegy than an epitaph.'[17] Skelton implies that the epitaph and the elegy in part coincide but in another part are disposed one following the other. If Skelton did not mark the boundary and apply the labels, would we know that we were watching epitaph shade into elegy? And, in Puttenham's terms, do we know where the 'measure' of an epigram ends and elegy begins?

I suggest that these appeals to objective measure and visceral distinction between the terms mask a supple sense of elegy that comes to define the term for Renaissance poets and readers. If epitaph exists to honour what is gone, elegy comes into its own to celebrate what is not merely gone but latent, unavailable, hidden, or lost—and we see how an epitaph with a certain degree of ambition may become an elegy.[18] Philip Sidney alludes to this expansive sense of the elegist as one 'who bewails with the great philosopher Heraclitus the weakness of mankind and the wretchedness of the world'.[19] Short, concentrated lamentations as in epitaphs have little in common with the philosophical canon of becoming that Renaissance humanists believed to originate in Heraclitus; but what Puttenham calls the 'long lamentation' in elegy is searching rather than circumscribed, and easily extends beyond a conventional object (a dead friend, an absent lover) to consider what else is missing from the world as we find it. Puttenham's chapter on lamentation adduces a startling list of what might be latent, lost, or unavailable and therefore apt for elegy: 'the overthrows and discomforts in battle; the subversions of towns and cities; the desolations of countries; the loss of goods and worldly promotions, honour and good renown; finally, the travails and torments of love forlorn or ill-bestowed, either by disgrace, denial, delay, and twenty other ways that well-experienced lovers could recite.'[20] Likewise, John Harington defends elegy (among several genres) from the charge of 'lightness and wantonness' with this terse observation: too preoccupied for trifles, 'the Elegy is still mourning'.[21] Puttenham, Sidney, and Harington share a sense of elegy as 'long' not only in literal length—though this is a factor in distinguishing elegy from epitaph—but in reach and implication. This sense of the term explains the usages that confound Morton Bloomfield, who rehearses the classical definition but then observes that, in the Renaissance,

> Latin elegies written in an artificial and reconstructed classical Latin flourished . . . The word in English, however, tended to be used primarily to indicate lamentation or, later, various mood poems . . . Elegy enjoyed an exuberant growth which has never been explained, except perhaps with general reference to the revival of the classics, especially Latin.[22]

Perhaps the explanation Bloomfield seeks is that, in domesticating the programmatically unsettled quality of the classical elegy into English verse, poets such as Skelton see the form as bringing classical authority to the project of disclosing what is not manifest or otherwise disturbing the surface of things. What was in the first instance a metrical criterion for classical elegy becomes something compound in English, a fusion of stance, tone, and mood. The unfixed form of English elegy allows the investigation of a topic to extend past the conventional bounds of a sonnet or any other stanza, into new fields of discursive and even self-reflexive commentary.

When Thomas Campion introduces his *Elegiarum Liber* (1595), he acknowledges this aspect of elegiac writing:

> Ite procul tetrici, moneo, procul ite severi,
> Ludit censuras pagina nostra graves.
> Ite senes nisi forte aliquis torpente medulla
> Carminibus flammas credit inesse meis.
> Aptior ad teneros lusus florentior aetas,
> Vel iuvenis, vel me docta puella legat.
> Et vatem celebrent Bruti de nomine primum
> Qui molles elegos et sua furta canat.

> (Go far away, gloomy men; I warn you, go far off, stern men, our page makes sport of serious judgements. Go, old men, unless by chance someone with sluggish marrow believes there are flames in my songs. A more vigorous age is better suited to gentle sports; let a youth or a learned girl read me. And let them celebrate the first poet of the name of Brut to sing sweet elegies and his own hidden acts.)[23]

Campion's appeal to a juvenescent, hot-blooded readership shades into the recognition that, much as acts of love are sweeter for being hidden from unfitting eyes, elegies gain their sweetness from disclosing what is hidden, the *furta* that cannot be spoken elsewhere with the same directness or charm.

Despite Campion's self-designation as the first English elegist, the central event in the development of English Renaissance elegy is probably John Donne's set of poems of that genre.[24] Likely written in 1593–6 when Donne was a law student at Lincoln's Inn, this loose collection, which some critics believe to have circulated as a book, includes between thirteen and twenty poems about love.[25] In form they are made of rhymed couplets varying in number from the 114 lines of 'The Bracelet' to the 20 lines of 'His Picture'. Donne turns to elegy in counterpoint to (and perhaps in chronological overlay with) his *Songs and Sonnets*, in which the experience of love is more often tangible and ripe for enjoyment; in the more philosophical (and of course longer) *Elegies*, Donne reflects on those elements of love that defy possession. Even Elegy 19, 'Going to Bed', with its famous lines of erotic analogy,

> License my roving hands, and let them go,
> Before, behind, between, above, below.
> O my America! My new-found-land...[26]

declares the joys of a hypothetical undressing to 'full nakedness'. At the end of that elegy, the speaker, the only one of the couple who is naked ('To teach thee, I am naked first' (l. 47)), is still cajoling the woman to disrobe. Perhaps the most famous bedroom scene in English verse is more a fantasy than a reality in its own fictional world.

'On his Mistress' says a number of vivid, astonishing things but holds in reserve a measure of dramatic irony, to mean more than what it says; and the figures of speech employed to make the argument far exceed the rational need for such figuration. The poem is an appeal to a lover to remain in England while the speaker goes abroad, but nonetheless to keep him in mind throughout his travels.[27] From the first lines, however, the poem broaches a set of contexts that seem about to break out of that condition and become texts themselves:

> By our first strange and fatal interview
>
> . . . . .
>
> by that remorse,
> Which my words masculine persuasive force
> Begot in thee, and by the memory
> Of hurts, which spies and rivals threatened me...
> (Donne, Elegy 16, 1, 3–6; *Poems*, I. 111)

Each of these clauses is a pinhole through which we see an entire history, and after five of them we reach the main clause of the sentence, 'I calmly beg'. But no sooner does it appear than that main clause is overwritten by two more subordinate clauses, each one a condensed history, followed by a new main clause, 'I conjure thee'. Calmly beg what? Conjure thee to do what? Before completing the thoughts, the speaker revokes 'all the oaths' to constancy he has sworn in the past so that he can 'overswear' them again in the service of an exhortation: not to accompany him on his journey. If elegies often respond to latency or absence, what sort of elegy starts from the lovers' presence to one another and argues for their separation?

The poem captures a property of these lovers' mutual involvement that is named in the first line: 'strange and fatal'. Fatal because, like their first encounter or 'interview', every conversation seems endowed with ultimate significance; there is no trivial talk between them. And strange because, while the poem talks around a fairly simple appeal with a dazzling array of condensed recollections, hypothetical statements, and vivid digressions, it is estranged from its category. 'On his Mistress' turns the elegy inside out to disclose what is really at stake in the genre. Mere physical presence and absence are token conditions that may seem to define elegy but only mask the lovers' state of 'constancy' to one another; while close to each other in person, they may nonetheless be at risk of danger or dissemblance, while 'absent Lovers' may truly 'one in th'other be' (l. 26). He would rather keep her true at a distance than expose her to danger or duplicity while they are together. In arguing for what is unconventional in their relationship but true in a deeper sense than proximity, the speaker reveals what is unexpected but true about elegy itself: that the issue is latency and loss, not merely presence or absence. And thus a 'strange' conversation and a strange elegy are not strange at all. 'Strange' is the word that anchors the elegy, from the first line that characterizes not only the lovers' first interview but this one and probably every conversation as well. The speaker urges the woman not to disguise herself as a boy in order to accompany him as a page ('be my true Mistress still, not my feigned Page' (l. 14)), and then at the exact midpoint of the lyric adds this injunction:

> be not strange
> To thy self only; all will spy in thy face
> A blushing womanly discovering grace.
> (Donne, Elegy 16, 28–30; *Poems*, I. 112)

At the most literal level 'be not strange to thyself only' seems to say that her disguise will fool no one, but of course it implies more than that: once the legibility of a woman poorly disguised as a man is thrown off, is the woman legible or illegible as herself; is she strange or unstrange? Does being not strange to thyself only entail being strange to no one or being strange to everyone? The command at the centre of the passage and the elegy suggests that being strange to oneself and to everyone else is the threshold condition from which we ought not to decline. Once abroad in the elegy, questions such as these cannot be put back into any sort of fictional or formal box. They remain exposed to the light.

The final episode in the elegy occurs after line 43, where the speaker winds into his final appeal:

> O stay here, for, for thee
> England is only a worthy Gallery,
> To walk in expectation, till from thence
> Our greatest King call thee to his presence.
> When I am gone, dream me some happiness,
> Nor let thy looks our long hid love confess,
> Nor praise, nor dispraise me, nor bless nor curse
> Openly loves force, nor in bed fright thy Nurse

With midnight's startings, crying out, oh, oh
Nurse, o my love is slain, I saw him go
O'r the white Alps alone; I saw him I,
Assail'd, fight, taken, stabb'd, bleed, fall, and die.
(Donne, Elegy 16, 43–54; *Poems*, I. 112)

The power of this final passage is that it does not speak of their strange love in a strange world but demonstrates that property in action: England is an apt stage for her desires, because the passing show of persons who make themselves spectacles sets off not only her beauty but her intellect (that is, she appears in the gallery but also observes it); all of this passing strangeness will dissolve only when God calls her to heaven and his presence, a translation from one reality to another emphasized by the startling usage of a trochaic foot at the end of line 46, 'presence' as a rhyme for 'thence'. Nothing about God's presence rhymes with our world here below.

The last injunction to the woman—do not frighten your nurse with 'startings' such as the curiously detailed raving that begins 'oh, oh Nurse, o my love is slain'—confirms that the project of the elegy's concluding phase is not to use the word 'strange' but to make us think it, and say it, as if closing a semantic triptych: our interviews as lovers are strange, our self-acquaintance as human beings is strange, and finally, accordingly, this elegy is strange. The speaker represents a property of their love—strangeness—that has implications for not only the course of love but their self-understandings as human beings. And in addressing this highly mobile and transitive strangeness, he fashions a strange poem, bringing to light the property he can otherwise only name. Compared to the compact love lyrics in the *Songs and Sonnets* and the socially and divinely directed poems of the *Satires* and *Holy Sonnets*, elegies such as 'On his Mistress' range discursively around a problem without resolving it, and deliver to the surface perspectives that might go unspoken in a different poem—that is, something shorter, or with a stronger formal mandate or a higher measure of artifice. Pursuing that which is not present in or to the poem, Renaissance elegists grant the genre a licence to explore those *furta* that make reality as we recognize it. On a broad scale, this is a version of the capacity that in English poetry comes to be called wit: that is, the finding of resemblances and the development of extended metaphor, the disposition of paradoxes, and the absorption of new knowledge, all into a vividly rhetorical verse. Donne's elegies (and early modern elegy in general) receive too little acknowledgement as a site for wit because the genre often opens issues without closing them, or exposes the incongruities among received learning and lived reality without quite telling us what to think about them. Sidney glances at this property of elegy in *The Defence of Poesy* when he observes that the genre 'bewails... the weakness of mankind and the wretchedness of the world'; Sidney, who produces a few elegies (as 'eclogues') only within the confines of his fictional *Arcadia*, probably takes the view that elegy investigates too much and resolves too little, leaving the world more strange to us than a well-made poem should.[28] But this too is wit, played out on a wide field linking classicism with early modernism and in the service of a more intellectually complex project than the briefer, so-called metaphysical poems.

Hymn

If the elegy entails a negotiation between classical authority and contemporaneous invention, the hymn involves a conversation between divine authority and the poetic imperatives of the present. These are different challenges with distinctive results for the production of poetry. Where the elegy is an equivocal category for sixteenth-century theorists such as Puttenham and Sidney, the hymn is widely extolled as the chief among poetic genres. The Greek term *hymnos* was applied both to a poem of praise to the gods or quasi-divine mortals that served a liturgical function in worship and to a more literary kind of hymn, often in hexameters or elegiac couplets; since few instances of the former survived into the Renaissance, the literary hymn—exemplified for early modern readers by the *Orphic Hymns*, the *Homeric Hymns*, and the *Hymns* of Callimachus—became the dominant Greek model. When Roman poets such as Horace and Catullus imitated the Greek hymns in their *carmina*, they tended to reinterpret the genre for their own purposes, developing the literary dimension; and when in turn St Ambrose adapted the liturgical hymn for the Roman Church (*c.*375 CE) and Prudentius 'Christianized the Horatian tradition' (*c.*405 CE),[29] they bequeathed to Renaissance poets a story of evolution within continuity as well as an emphatic turn towards a Christian application of the received elements of the classical hymn. Where Greek or Roman poets often extolled gods, narrated mythological events, and concluded with apostrophe and prayer, Christian hymnists adapted these features to the praise of saints and martyrs. As classicists, many Renaissance poets were attracted to the continuity in the history of the hymn; as Christians, however, they see the turn, and often re-enact it in their accounts of the genre. Some poetic theorists find in the Christian hymn a continuity with its classical antecedents, however coloured by divine revelation, while others see an insuperable difference in the Christian God's capacity for absorbing praise, and many stake out an ambiguous position. This passage from Richard Willes's *De Re Poetica* (1573) is typical:

> did [ancient divines] not celebrate sacred and divine subjects in poems: the mysteries, precepts, and foundations of our faith and religion?... It is the same in later ages, since the birth of Christ and the transmission of the New Law of the Gospel, as is demonstrated by the constant hymns and praises, written in the form of poetry, which Christians, both in church and in the greatest assemblies, sing to God the Almighty Creator.[30]

And Puttenham:

> The gods of the gentiles were honoured by their poets in hymns, which is an extraordinary and divine praise, extolling and magnifying them for their great powers and

> excellency of nature in the highest degree of laud, and yet therein their poets were after a sort restrained, so as they could not with their credit untruly praise their own gods...But with us Christians, who be better disciplined and do acknowledge but one God, almighty, everlasting, and in every respect self-sufficient...: to him we cannot exhibit overmuch praise, nor belie him any ways, unless it be in abasing his excellency by scarcity of praise.[31]

While the poetics of the early modern hymn traces a sinuous line from antiquity to the early medieval Christians and then to the present, we notice that comparatively few vernacular poems of the early modern period carry the title of hymn. In English the category is observed more in theory than in practice, and even some poems that might be classified as hymns, such as Milton's 'L'Allegro' and 'Il Penseroso' or the song within the frame of Marvell's 'Bermudas', do not assume the label,[32] or, like Sidney's 'Ye Goat-Herd Gods' among the Fourth Eclogues of the *Arcadia*, accept it only retrospectively: the last line of Sidney's double sestina is 'Our morning hymn this is, and song at evening'.[33] If the hymn is one of the most exalted kinds of poetry, and lives on through many neo-Latin instances of the fifteenth and sixteenth centuries, why does it not have a more prominent and unequivocal place in the vernacular? Several available answers to this question direct us to major issues in the reception of this classical genre. Neo-Latin hymns by the Italian poet Giovanni Pontano, the Greek expatriate Michele Marullo, and their younger contemporary Marco Girolamo Vida take various positions as to whether early modern hymns should adopt classical (that is, pre-Christian) subjects and attitudes along with the genre itself; this debate was more easily staged in neo-Latin than in the vernaculars, because the language of Horace or Catullus could be invoked or parodied according to an early modern poet's disposition. For many vernacular poets, a related issue is how to stake a claim for original composition in the face of a scriptural corpus that includes exemplary instances of all the devotional modes such as lamentation, self-examination, and paean; in this context the models for post-scriptural hymns are often those vernacular poems that hew closely to the psalms, as either translations or adaptations.[34] Moreover, whether they write in neo-Latin or the vernacular, Renaissance poets recognize the challenge of composing new hymns that fall along the spectrum from paraphrase to imitation to innovation. Does a modern hymn extend and annotate a classical or scriptural model? Is it a new poem or a new rendering of an ancient original? And where does the Renaissance poet stand among these questions: as an accessory of Callimachus or Horace, a singer of old songs, a new David, or a hymnist reimagined for an era of religious schism and polemic? Each hymn of the period answers these questions in its way, adjusted to sects and generations. Thus, in poems as different as George Chapman's two hymns in *The Shadow of Night* (1594) and in Richard Crashaw's 'Hymn of the Nativity' one notices the outlines of a common problem within drastically different solutions.

Enveloped in these religious issues is another trial for Renaissance hymnists, that of writing totality and sheer presence into a vernacular poem. Like the elegy's task of making what is absent available, the hymn's office of making divinity legible has implications beyond the genre itself; both elegy and hymn are limit cases of problems that appear elsewhere, even in secular poetry. These animating problems of absence and presence are everywhere in the period, but these two genres are workshops in which they are confronted directly. When an occasional poem ventures to offer praise of a distant object that falls short of elegy, or a love poem endows a beloved lady with a vividness that recalls divine presence, these tactics are often the legacy of what the elegists and hymnists have developed in the pursuit of their particular genres.

Edmund Spenser's *Fowre Hymnes* (1596) is perhaps the era's most daring assay against the difficulties of divine presence because the poems demonstrate the nature of the problems while offering Spenser's solution; not so much a sequence in any narrative sense as a set of hymn versions in which each instalment exposes the limits of the preceding one, the *Fowre Hymnes* shows hymnody as a process of making totality perceptible and presence bearable within the confines of a vernacular poem.[35] While they offer four versions of these qualities in action, their attention to the process is the story of these poems. That process, we shall see, depends upon a vacillating representation of classical ideas of love and beauty from abstract deities to a Spenserian fixation on the emotional centre of a specifically Christian love and beauty.

The first of the series, 'An Hymne in Honour of Love', seems at first to render the conventional outlook of Petrarchan and Neoplatonic love lyric into the genre of hymn.[36] The god Love lurks in many Petrarchan sonnets as a proximate force and sometime addressee, alongside the lady who is most often celebrated and addressed; and it might seem a trivial adjustment to shift the terms to where Love is recognized directly as a divine force:

> Great god of might, that reignest in the mind,
> And all the body to thy hest dost frame,
> Victor of gods, subduer of mankind,
> That dost the Lions and fell Tigers tame,
>
> . . . . .
>
> Who can express the glory of thy might?
> (Spenser, 'An Hymne in Honour of Love',
> ll. 43–6, 49; *Shorter Poems*, 454)

However, the shift from sonnet to Neoplatonic hymn as the carrier of this kind of feeling exposes the limited perspective of the former, in which Love can be imagined as a godlike force without confronting what that view supposes. Sonnets may make gods hyperbolically or figuratively, but hymns must examine the nature of divinity, the workings of faith, and the dispensation of justice, among other aspects of godly manifestation. When the 'Hymne in Honour of Love' turns to these questions, the speaker addresses Love exactly as any other hymnist would the Christian God, and the inadequacy of the former as the object of this sort of poem is starkly visible:

Why then do I this honour unto thee,
Thus to ennoble thy victorious name,
Since thou dost show no favour unto me,
Ne once move ruth in that rebellious Dame,
Somewhat to slack the rigour of my flame?
(Spenser, 'An Hymne in Honour of Love',
ll. 148–52; *Shorter Poems*, 457)

The questions provide their own answers: that a god who expends his favour on undeserving acolytes—who grants 'furious fervour' (l. 158) to unworthy or even random followers—oversees a religion based on passion rather than understanding, delusion rather than self-knowledge. 'Glory' (l. 162) is lent back to this god by his faithful in tribute to his choosing of them, and the divine 'grace' (l. 164) that results amounts to a compact of mutual convenience, not an expression of faith in the manner of a true religion. When the speaker carries the hymn to its conclusion, he remains unaware of how the genre of the hymn compromises the matter of the sonnet, but every reader notices the dramatic irony that comes to occlude the subject:

Ay me, dear Lord, that ever I might hope,
For all the pains and woes that I endure,
To come at length unto the wished scope
Of my desire...

. . . . .

Then would I sing of thine immortal praise
An heavenly Hymne, such as the Angels sing.
(Spenser, 'An Hymne in Honour of Love',
ll. 294–7, 301–2; *Shorter Poems*, 461–2)

The next episode in the series, 'An Hymne in Honour of Beautie', implicitly concedes the shortcoming of 'Love' by taking as its object a quality that enjoys less association with concupiscence and an equally exalted philosophical genealogy. Two generations before Spenser, Castiglione's *Book of the Courtier* reflects a long tradition of Neoplatonic thought in its avowal that beauty is a transcendent property to which Love is only a response. The second hymn, then, has raised its sights, inviting us to ask again whether the occasion warrants the classically original genre.

Again, we notice that, where blazons and other epideictic poems describe and celebrate beauty, a hymn is obliged to conduct us from outward manifestations back to divine origins, and to reason its way to faith. The Neoplatonic and Petrarchan platitudes with which this hymn begins necessarily develop into logical statements that become impossible to credit as soon as they are spoken:

So every spirit, as it is most pure,
And hath in it the more of heavenly light,

So it the fairer body doth procure
To habit in, and it more fairly dight
With cheerful grace and amiable sight.
For of the soul the body form doth take:
For soul is form, and doth the body make.

Therefore where ever that thou dost behold
A comely corpse, with beauty faire endewed,
Know this for certain, that the same doth hold
A beauteous soul, with faire conditions thewed,
Fit to receive the seed of virtue strewed.
(Spenser, 'An Hymne in Honour of Beautie',
ll. 127–38; *Shorter Poems*, 466–7)

We know from *The Faerie Queene* that Spenser would consider anyone who accepted this conclusion dangerously obtuse, and yet this is where the logic of the hymn takes us, to the point of its own undoing. The hymn reaches back to its forerunner, drawing love into Neoplatonic philosophy as an effect of beauty, as though revising the 'An Hymne in Honour of Love' in light of new information. Again, however, the conclusions are faulty inasmuch as the object does not suffice for the genre:

For Love is a celestial harmony,
Of likely hearts composed of starres consent,
Which join together in sweet sympathy,
To work each other's joy and true content,

. . . . .

But they which love indeed, look otherwise,
With pure regard and spotless true intent,
Drawing out of the object of their eyes,
A more refined form, which they present
Unto their mind, void of all blemishment;
Which it reducing to her first perfection,
Beholdeth free from flesh's frail infection.
(Spenser, 'An Hymne in Honour of Beautie',
ll. 197–200, 211–17; *Shorter Poems*, 468–9)

The argument is closely woven, with one proposition following another, and the passage is difficult to reduce to paraphrase or excerpt—a condition that is far from common in Spenser, and that generally signals world views of which we should be wary. We emerge from these stanzas as though from a dream that makes sense on its own terms, not by the light of day.

Spenser's own *Amoretti* is implicated here, as the speaker observes how lovers see beauty through eyes acclimated to 'armies of loues still flying too and fro' (l. 240). He asks us here to do what the *Amoretti* never proposes (and is sometimes at pains to disavow as a project): to worship beauty itself rather than the non-corporeal perfection to which it imperfectly alludes, and to imagine a world ruled by that value:

> Then *Iö triumph*, O great beauty's Queen,
> Advance the banner of thy conquest hie,
> That all this world, the which thy vassals been,
> May draw to thee, and with due fealty,
> Adore the power of thy great Majesty,
> Singing this Hymn in honour of thy name,
> Compiled by me, which thy poor liegeman am.
> (Spenser, 'An Hymne in Honour of Beautie',
> ll. 267–73; *Shorter Poems*, 470)

Will we choose to live in such a world? The hymn delivers us to the threshold of a condition from which most contemporaneous readers will recoil, as we did in the 'Hymne in Honour of Love'; and what survives from this self-criticizing poem, again, is the urgency of finding the proper object for the genre.

With two gorgeous but hollow shells behind him, Spenser attacks these questions afresh in the two remaining poems of the series, 'An Hymne of Heavenly Love' and 'An Hymne of Heavenly Beautie'. The impulse of the previous poems was flawed but not irrecoverable, the sequence seems to say here; what now seems in retrospect to be the disabling condition of the preceding hymns is that they were implicitly investigations of earthly love and beauty, ideals that cannot be honoured and understood in the medium of a hymn without distorting the nature of that genre. When these ideals are relocated in the immortal sphere of the Christian heaven, much of the same classical hymnic machinery can be preserved—as he does between the *Amoretti* and *Epithalamion*, Spenser makes these poems track the language and thought of their corresponding numbers—but with the difference that here the key terms (grace, immortality, glory) make a new sense from being gathered into a new order:

> Before this world's great frame, in which all things
> Are now contained, found any being place,
>
> . . . . .
>
> That high eternal power, which now doth move
> In all these things, mov'd in it self by love.
>
> It lov'd itself, because itself was fair;
> (For fair is lov'd;) and of it self begot
> Like to it self his eldest son and heire,
> Eternal, pure.
> (Spenser, 'An Hymne of Heavenly Love',
> ll. 22–3, 27–32; *Shorter Poems*, 472–3)

Here love is not a god but a condition employed by a god to know himself, and the paronomastic nature of the term—which is acknowledged everywhere that Spenser intends to show self-understanding in his works and ignored where he depicts delusion—is duly discovered by the operations of the hymn: divine and earthly, charitable and cupidinous, investigative and illusory are all readily available dimensions of this term, and this revised hymn shows us how to live among them productively. Once demoted from its status as a classical god in the first hymn, love may finally be understood and (properly) celebrated, the purpose of this 'Hymne of Heavenly Love'. The final lines prepare for the 'Hymne of Heavenly Beautie' by proposing a condition in which, with earthly desire extinguished, we love our creator as the fruit of this new understanding:

> Thenceforth all worlds desire will in thee die,
> And all earths glory on which men do gaze,
> Seem dirt and dross in thy pure sighted eye,
> Compar'd to that celestial beauty's blaze,
> Whose glorious beams all fleshly sense doth daze
> With admiration of their passing light,
> Blinding the eyes and lumining the sprite.
> (Spenser, 'An Hymne of Heavenly Love', ll. 274–80;
> *Shorter Poems*, 480)

The concluding 'Hymne of Heavenly Beautie' revels in the recalibration that has taken place across the series, here seen in the possibilities that come from joining an epideictic imperative to a hymnic purpose. But that reorientation brings a cost in poetic terms, which is already visible in the rapturous lines that conclude 'Heavenly Love':

> Then shall thy ravished soul inspired be
> With heavenly thoughts, far above human skill,
> And thy bright radiant eyes shall plainly see
> Th'Idea of his pure glory present still,
> Before thy face.
> (Spenser, 'An Hymne of Heavenly Love',
> ll. 281–5; *Shorter Poems*, 480)

How will we 'plainly see' God's 'pure glory present'? This poem's provisional hedge is to insert the Neoplatonic term 'idea': we see 'Th'Idea of his pure glory present still', not the sheer presence itself. But where sonnets and epideictic lyrics are likely to change the subject or avert their gaze from a fully present object, a hymn should confront the poetic challenge of getting such an object into the poem and moreover allowing it to extend into subject and origin. Many classical and Christian hymns involve the acknowledgement that the speaker has taken on an object that exceeds the confines of the particular poem, and that the genre itself contains resources that permit us to confront divine plenitude without being subsumed into it. These resources include the forms of investigation—past compared to present, ideals considered in philosophical context, or values assayed for implications—that keep the poem under the speaker's control by showing us divinity but marking out a path around it, behind it, before and after it.

Spenser's 'Hymne of Heavenly Beautie' draws such a path by stages: first by providing an orderly itinerary through creation that includes direct apprehension of totality (ll. 29–35), next by moving to the celestial bodies (ll. 57–63) and then to the sphere of the primum mobile (ll. 71–4), and finally claiming its own power of hymnic investigation, though a concession of mortal limits (ll. 104–5) harnessed to the power of the genre to explain:

> Thence gathering plumes of perfect speculation,
> To imp the wings of thy high flying mind,
> Mount up aloft through heavenly contemplation,
> From this dark world, whose damps the soul do blind,
> And like the native brood of Eagles kind,
> On that bright Sun of glory fixes thine eyes,
> Clear'd from gross mists of frail infirmities.
>
> (Spenser, 'An Hymne of Heavenly Beautie',
> ll. 134-40; *Shorter Poems*, 485)

Look, interpret, contemplate: indebted to the long history linking classicism to Christianity, poems of this kind ultimately put us in a position to register divine presence. Segmenting our encounter with presence into discrete acts that we know from profane experience, they bring us to a state of understanding that makes the illegible legible and the unknowable knowable. With divinity in sight and totality encircled by strategy, the limits on human capacity transposed into order and the cover of scriptural authority cast over the entire project, these hymns confront with vivid measures some of the period's fundamental problems of poetic representation. Spenser's series is exemplary because it takes us into the making of the Renaissance hymn as both a problem and a project, characteristically offering up lovely poems such as the hymns in honour of love and beauty that are nonetheless unsatisfactory to this project. How better to conceive a poem containing presence than to see it imperfectly made? Or to understand the nature of divinity than to see it mistakenly apprehended? Arriving at the conclusion of the final hymn, we have been educated to the character and limits of the genre. This is a venturesome and hazardous kind of classical reception, in which an ancient genre is brought back to life for a changed world, enabled and then disabled again, and ultimately made the object of what we might call speculative adaptation, raising the question whether the original genre and its modern applications can still be aligned with each other. Spenser and several of his successors (notably Milton, whose ode 'On the Morning of Christ's Nativity' contains a hymn to be discussed shortly) tend to answer this question affirmatively, but with enough implicit reservations that the hymn does not become as firmly re-established in the Renaissance as do several other classical genres.

Epithalamium

If the Renaissance hymn comes in the wake of nearly unapproachable models, the epithalamium might have too many models. While there are alternatives in Theocritus, Statius, and Claudian, the salient template for Renaissance epithalamia is a tradition of wedding songs derived from Catullus 61, 62, and 64 and, more distantly, from Sappho. Principal Renaissance examples include neo-Latin epithalamia by Giovanni Pontano, Ludovico Ariosto, Diogo de Teive, and George Buchanan; experiments by the Italian poets Torquato Tasso and Giambattista Marino and the Spanish Francisco de Quevedo; and the widely imitated poems called *Epithalame* by the French poets Pierre de Ronsard and Joachim Du Bellay. In an unsurpassed essay, Thomas M. Greene locates many of these examples against one another and describes the elements of the Sapphic–Catullan convention, which attains its apex in English in Spenser's *Epithalamion* (1595). The dispositive elements are that the poet–speaker should depict a web of social connections that renders legible where he stands in relation to the often aristocratic bride and bridegroom; the poem should accept 'a stockpile of *topoi*, commonplaces, similes, [and] epithets', especially those that evoke leading precursors such as Catullus 61; the epithalamium 'implies a social context—an actual wedding with festivities appropriate to the setting—and must refer to a specific day, fictive or real...Thus the poem acquires dramatic impetus not from an institution—marriage—but from a series of concrete actions—a wedding'; and, finally, the poet–speaker enacts a role that straddles the wedding and the poem that represents it. As Greene shows, this latter element is largely a Catullan innovation that comes to define the genre for many of its Renaissance adapters.[37] In Spenser's middle-class version, the poet–speaker sings of his own wedding, an unprecedented joining of roles. Noticeably and with considerable charm, all of the other elements shift in response to this condition. In *Epithalamion* the received *topoi* come off differently in the light of the poet–speaker's own wedding, the tributes to the bride's beauty need not suggest a strictly vicarious distance, and the typical gestures of welcome to the guests carry a current of anxiety within a general hospitality. The provision of a distinctive stanza form—nineteen lines mostly of pentameter with three lines of trimeter (ll. 6, 11, and 17) and one final line of hexameter (l. 19)—and the publication of the poem alongside his sonnet sequence, the *Amoretti*, fulfil Spenser's domestication of the classical epithalamium in a vernacular setting.[38]

Implicit in Greene's anatomy of the genre is the summons that early modern poets tend to see in the genre: to explore the powers and devices that render an act, such as marriage, into an event like a wedding. The social motive for such a poem is to celebrate a wedding, with the possibilities of social reconciliation that entails; but the poetic motive is to demonstrate the poem's capacity to locate itself in the gap between act and event, shaping the former into the latter.[39] The distinction between an act and an event may seem abstract, but, when the scholar Julius Caesar Scaliger turns to the epithalamium in his *Poetics*, much of his exposition is devoted to the rituals and gestures that bridge act and event: for instance, the strewing of nuts outside the bedroom that is mentioned in both Virgil's eighth Eclogue and Catullus 61. Is this a practical expedient to muffle the sound of the bride's cries during intercourse? Or is it that, 'because nuts protect their kernel', the casting of them 'provides a good omen of the parents' sheltering their offspring with equal protection'?[40] The first explanation belongs to an act, and makes only literal sense, while the second implies an event, in which the central act enjoys a meaning beyond itself. Scaliger presents the two explanations alongside one another but then proposes a third: that, as children give up playing with nuts when they enter adulthood, the revellers throw nuts to mark the end of childhood. The version he prefers, in other words, fuses act and event by making literal and symbolic meaning in a single gesture. Scaliger and many of his contemporaries posit an epithalamium that would conjoin the two kinds of occasion and accept for poetry the office of moving between them.

When Puttenham describes the classical epithalamium as a poem performed in three episodes during wedding festivities, his investment in what he calls 'the mystery of the whole matter' seems connected not to the particulars of the genre but to its role in disposing a social act into parts, veiling the physical rigors that occur in the act with reflection on its meaning, and establishing moods for participants and spectators:

> This epithalamie was divided by breaches into three parts to serve for three several fits or times to be sung. The first breach was sung at the first part of the night when the spouse and her husband were brought to their bed and at the very chamber door, where in a large outer room used to be (besides the musicians) good store of ladies or gentlewomen of their kinfolk and others who came to honour the marriage, and the tunes of the songs were very loud and shrill, to the intent there might no noise be heard out of the bedchamber by the screaking and outcry of the young damsel feeling the first forces of her stiff and rigorous young man... The tenor of that part of the song was to congratulate the first acquaintance and meeting of the young couple, allowing of their parents' good discretions in making the match, then afterward to sound cheerfully to the onset and first encounters of that amorous battle, to declare the comfort of children and increase of love by that means chiefly caused...
>
> [The second] part of the ballad was to refresh the faint and wearied bodies and spirits, and to animate new appetites with cheerful words, encouraging them to the recontinuance of the same entertainments...[that] they should persist in all good appetite with an invincible courage to the end.
>
> In the morning...the same musicians came again with this last part and greeted them both with a psalm of new applausions, for that they had either of them so well behaved themselves that night, the husband to rob his spouse of her maidenhead and save her life, the bride so lustily to satisfy her husband's love and escape with so little danger of her person, for which good chance that they should make a lovely truce and abstinence of that war till next night, sealing the placard of that lovely league with twenty manner of sweet kisses, then by good admonitions informed them to the frugal and thrifty life all the rest of their days.[41]

In this spirit, Katherine Philips begins her epithalamium to Lady Mary Butler on her marriage with Lord Cavendish with this quatrain that naturalizes spectatorship into part of a new whole, act and event fused together by what she calls concernment:

> At such a time as this, when all conclude
> Nothing but unconcernment can be rude,
> The muses, Madam, will not be deny'd
> To be the bride maids where you are the bride.[42]

What Philips names and Puttenham describes is not exactly the making of a private act public—those adjectives apply unsatisfactorily to aristocratic weddings in the period—but the enlargement of the circle of sharers until the bride and groom can seem merely two among many. Puttenham tells us why the involvement of the spectators matters, while Philips fuses their participation and that of the couple into a new idea of what they hold in common.

More ambitious, Ben Jonson's epithalamium on the marriage of John Ramsey, Viscount Hadington, and Lady Elizabeth Ratcliffe revels in its capacity to show how 'state'—in the sense of rank and the display associated with it—is made necessary, behind the curtain of ceremony, by countless gestures of intimacy:

> The solemn state of this one night
> Were fit to last an age's light;
> But there are rites behind
> Have less of state, but more of kind:
> Love's wealthy crop of kisses,
> And fruitful harvest of his mother's blisses.[43]
> (Jonson, 'The Haddington Masque',
> ll. 393–8; *Works*, 7. 262)

Only a poem of this sort, with its license to move across the curtain, confers the sight of the personal domain transposed into the public by a code of reference known to a small circle of contemporaries; and only the epithalamium wrings ideality from these intimate acts while urging it on the reader, here in the short lines of each stanza:

> Two of your troop, that, with the morn were free.
> Are, now, wag'd to [Hymen's] war.
> And what they are,
> If you'll perfection see,
> Your selves must be.
>
> . . . . .
>
> Live what they are,
> And long perfection see:
> And such ours be.
>
> . . . . .
>
> They sweeten Hymen's war,

And, in that jar,
Make all, that married be,
Perfection see.
(Jonson, 'The Haddington Masque',
ll. 376–80, 389–91, 410–13; *Works*, 7. 262)

Twenty-four years later, Jonson's 'Epithalamion' celebrating the wedding of Jerome, the son of Lord Treasurer Richard Weston, and Lady Frances Stuart, the daughter of Jonson's patron Esmé Stuart, Duke of Lennox, makes vivid the conventional link between the immediate occasion and the fate of humanity:

It is the kindly season of the time,
The month of youth, which calls all creatures forth
To do their offices in nature's chime,
And celebrate (perfection at the worth)
Marriage, the end of life,
That holy strife,
And the allowed war:
Through which not only we, but all our species are.
(Jonson, 'Epithalamion', ll. 25–32; *Works*, 8. 253)

The consciousness of time is a necessary condition for turning an act into an event, of course, but it belongs to the special capacity of this kind of poem to do more, to open the most intimate reaches of experience to an awareness of their import:

Till you behold a race to fill your hall,
A Richard, and a Hierome, by their names
Upon a Thomas, or a Francis call;
A Kate, a Frank, to honour their grand-dames,
And 'tween their grandsire's thighs,
Like pretty spies,
Peep forth a gem; to see
How each one plays his part, of the large pedigree.

And never may there want one of the stem,
To be a watchful servant for this state.
(Jonson, 'Epithalamion', ll. 169–78; *Works*, 8. 258)

This act of marriage becomes an event in its reference to a pattern of past acts, each one personal or familial in its own context but all together making a history inseparable from the state. Where but in this poem may our gaze move from the loins of the actors to the destiny of a family and a nation?[44] In these epithalamia Jonson writes not only of two marriages of 1608 and 1632, but of the potential of a received classical genre to adapt to present conditions and notably to develop the poetic faculty of turning act into event. Following the common investments in this faculty cultivated by Spenser, Puttenham, Philips, Jonson, and many other early modern epithalamists, we notice that the reception of the classics in the Renaissance is a great deal more than who read whom and which new poem refers to which old one. If we take the term 'reception' seriously, we are obliged to record what an antecedent is received *as* or *for*: in this case, how the remaking of an ancient genre such as the epithalamium becomes intellectually challenging or compelling. For these early modern poets, a kind of poem ostensibly about a wedding becomes an exploration of the received but poorly theorized category of 'occasional' poetry, and the more searching poets find themselves modelling to one another—in a conversation that takes place within the poems themselves—the rendering of occasions out of contributing terms such as 'act' and 'event' and the relating of poetic occasions to cultural ideas such as ceremony and state. Among their tributes to celebrants and families, many if not most Renaissance epithalamia declare poetry's power to find new problems in the poetry of the antique past.

Ode

In an age that prizes those literary genres that represent subjective experience, a franchise was granted to those classical genres that had managed the fusion of public and private in an indivisible container. The ode is one of the principal vessels of this sort, and in the Renaissance, balance is its criterion. Renaissance odes cultivate in their Horatian instances a general balance that arises out of mature contemplation, and in their Pindaric versions a resolution achieved often against sharp swings of topic or tone. Puttenham associates this principle of balance with the technopaegnion—or visual shape on the page—of the square:

> Into this figure may ye reduce your ditties by using no more verses than your verse is of syllables, which will make him fall out square... in good art all your ditties, odes, and epigrams should keep and not exceed the number of twelve verses, and the longest verse to be of twelve syllables, and not above, but under that number as much as ye will.[45]

But what is kept in balance? And how much variance does the genre tolerate among the elements under balance? In its Horatian model, the ode is made of stanzas of two or four lines, while the atmosphere is 'tranquil rather than intense, contemplative rather than brilliant'.[46] The Pindaric ode, by contrast, is made of two isostrophic units, the strophe and antistrophe, that can vary wildly in outlook and tone, and the concluding epode of a different metrical footprint in which the topic of the ode comes to rest, if not resolution. In English, the Pindaric tradition is often expressed in 'a magniloquent poem with abrupt transitions written either in irregular stanzas or in regular stanzaic triads'.[47] Odes of Horatian or Pindaric genealogies achieve balance on different terms: the former often finds balance in a considered stance or attitude that radiates across the poem, while the latter may arrive at it from drastic shifts in stance or attitude that address, criticize, or cancel each other.

In some ways the inner motion of the genre is the inverse of epithalamium in that it starts from public events and persons and finds private significance in them; but the ode as received into the Renaissance tends to seek out a formally and politically impeccable balance between these modes. The poets who adapt the ode are interested not so much in attaching the private to the public—as though the former is the first condition of the genre—as in developing practices that maintain that balance: cultivating second voices within a nominally univocal poem, telling an abstract story alongside a concrete one, or employing the hypothetical mode to criticize and undo the actual. Perhaps 'private' is inapt as a term for what develops in the Renaissance ode. Its distinctiveness might be better understood as a self-conscious mode that is not counter or opposite to the public mode but necessary to it, as self-reflection is indispensable to a life of action.[48] The most influential early modern odes are those that demonstrate the inseparability of deeds or occurrences and the ideas they entail in the achievement of self-knowledge. How is history made, in the sense not of historical events themselves but of the reflection on those events? How are great deeds not only achieved but remembered, glossed, and interpreted? How does significance trail action? These are the kinds of questions that draw into the ode poets such as Pierre de Ronsard in French, Bernardo Tasso in Italian, and John Milton and Abraham Cowley in English.

Milton's 'On the Morning of Christ's Nativity' demonstrates these principles almost to its own disadvantage—or so have said some commentators who have remarked on the ode's structure, which can seem dilatory or hurried from one section to another.[49] Four stanzas of seven lines establish the occasion at hand: 'This is the month, and this the happy morn' of Christ's birth (l. 1; *Complete Shorter Poems*, 101). The body of the poem, twenty-seven stanzas of eight lines designated a 'hymn', tells of the gathering celestial harmony and the flight of the pagan gods, both in view of the nativity; but the true subject of the poem is the moment, made elastic in the telling, between the end of pagan antiquity and the beginning of Christian history. The fact that many stanzas are suffused with classical allusions—for instance in stanza 14, 'For if such holy song | Enwrap our fancy long, | Time will run back, and fetch the age of gold' (ll. 133–5) with its allusion to Virgil's fourth eclogue—only emphasizes the ode's capacity to refashion the received corpus of ancient poetry into something with a startling, revelatory relation to Christian myth.[50] What is called a hymn here is a beautiful meditation on the divine presence not as seen by direct gaze—we see the child only indirectly—but as registered through its reverberations from the earthly landscape to the heavens. That hymn in turn fills a prolonged hiatus between the Incarnation conceived as an occurrence starting from one instant and the discursive responses to that occurrence: thus, when the wise men are on the threshold of the manger, the poem must conclude, having fulfilled its project of opening the gap between an occurrence and its significance. The entire assemblage, four stanzas of preamble and the hymn, is Milton's 'humble ode' (l. 24). Renaissance odes sometimes omit the rehearsal of the conventional significance following a deed or event, as Milton leaves the life and influence of Christ out of this poem, showing the capacity of this kind of poem to force these elements apart in order to reflect on how significance is made. We readers know the significance of the nativity, goes the ode's justification, but we might not have considered it apart from the occurrence until we were obliged to linger in the long moment before anyone on earth put the one and the other together to begin Christian history.

Andrew Marvell's 'An Horatian Ode upon Cromwell's Return from Ireland' takes what may seem nearly the opposite tack, treating the significance of deeds as inseparable from the deeds themselves.[51] Nonetheless, Marvell shares the period's understanding of the ode as reflecting on the making of historical and cultural significance, and demonstrates in his Horatian ode a provocative handling of that significance no less decisive than Milton's.[52] Marvell's topic, the heroic career of Oliver Cromwell seen from the vantage of a particular moment in its unfolding in 1650, between invasions of Ireland and Scotland, grants Marvell the scope to develop the complex attitudes towards Cromwell's exercise of temporal power that characterize several of his poems; the ode differs from other poetic expressions of ambivalence in that topical events and the portrayal of the feelings they occasion appear mutually entwined.[53] For instance, a celebratory poem such as 'Upon the Hill and Grove at Bilbrough', addressed like several others to Lord Fairfax, treats the landscape as a hieroglyph of history and politics:

> Upon its crest this mountain grave
> A plump of aged trees does wave.
> No hostile hand durst ere invade
> With impious steel the sacred shade.
> For something always did appear
> Of the great Master's terror there:
> And men could hear his armour still
> Rattling through all the grove and hill.[54]

Classical and neo-Latin antecedents that depict hills and groves (for example, Mantuan's eighth Eclogue and Ovid's *Amores* 3.1, respectively) surely lend resonance to the landscape at Bilbrough, but, in passages such as this, events and their interpretations are held at a distance or evoked in freighted terms such as 'terror'. Concomitantly, a lyric of disconcerting intimacy such as 'Young Love', based on a convention represented by Philodemus and Horace, lets simile convey the otherwise inexpressible urge to see a king crowned:

> Thus as kingdoms, frustrating
> Other titles to their crown,
> In the cradle crown their king,
> So all foreign claims to drown,
> So, to make all rivals vain,
> Now I crown thee with my love.
> (Marvell, 'Young Love', ll. 25–30;
> *Poems and Letters*, 27)

The 'Horatian Ode' takes a different approach in its first lines, which are easily recognizable as Marvell's in the manner of those poems that begin with prosaic observations or anonymous persons whose importance will be revealed by stages:

> The forward youth that would appear
> Must now forsake his muses dear,
> Nor in the shadows sing
> His numbers languishing.
>
> 'Tis time to leave the books in dust,
> And oil th'unused armor's rust:
> Removing from the wall
> The corslet of the hall.
> (Marvell, 'Horatian Ode', ll. 1–8;
> *Poems and Letters*, 91)

Who is this youth? A blank model of the puissant man who moves wilfully out of domestic retirement into action, he establishes an abstract domain for the ode before it has a literal one. He is like the hypothetical figures who appear in other poems, but with the difference—seemingly native to the ode as a genre, and seen in authoritative cases such as Ben Jonson's ode on Lucius Cary and Henry Morison—that he will shortly have a counterpart in the highly public figure of Cromwell:

> So restless Cromwell could not cease
> In the inglorious arts of peace,
> But through adventurous war
> Urged his active star.
> (Marvell, 'Horatian Ode', ll. 9–12;
> *Poems and Letters* 91)

Showing us the abstract figure before the concrete one, Marvell (like Jonson and others) broaches the import before what it attaches to, as though to make literal and figurative change their conventional places. From this point the ode exists in two dimensions at once, its similes seeming not contrived or secondary but natural to this poem:

> And like the three-forked lightning, first
> Breaking the clouds where it was nursed,
> Did through his own side
> His fiery way divide.

And abstract principles deduced from Cromwell's conduct are so fully worked into the ode that he and his deeds seem to pertain to them rather than they to him:

> For 'tis all one to courage high,
> The emulous or enemy;

And with such to enclose
Is more than to oppose.)
(Marvell, 'Horatian Ode', ll. 13–16,
17–20; *Poems and Letters*, 91, 92)

These highly abstract lines may mean that Cromwell achieves as much in encouraging his friends as in countering his enemies, or that the containment of one's opponents counts for more than direct conflict; but, whatever they mean, the lines continue the ode's frictionless alternation of figurative and literal until even the boldest comparisons seem natural:

Then burning through the air he went,
And palaces and temples rent;
  And Caesar's head at last
  Did through his laurels blast.

This habit of thinking abstractly and concretely together prepares for the body of the ode, where Marvell proposes a sensitive assessment of the roles of Cromwell and King Charles in the events leading to the regicide:

What field of all the civil wars
Where his were not the deepest scars?
  And Hampton shows what part
  He had of wiser art.
Where, twining subtle fears with hope,
He wove a net of such a scope,
  That Charles himself might chase
  To Caresbrook's narrow case:
That thence the royal actor born
The tragic scaffold might adorn,
  While round the armed bands
  Did clap their bloody hands.
He nothing common did or mean
Upon that memorable scene;
  But with his keener eye
  The axe's edge did try.
Nor called the Gods with vulgar spite
To vindicate his helpless right,
  But bowed his comely head,
  Down as upon a bed.
This was that memorable hour,
Which first assured the forced power.
(Marvell, ''Horatian Ode', ll. 21–4,
45–66; *Poems and Letters*, 92, 93)

The balance of sympathy for the king and admiration for Cromwell casts the two figures as counterpart actors in a 'tragic' episode. While both are historical figures, the structure of thought established from the ode's first lines allows that we will continually see the literal in the figurative and vice versa, which raises the question of how these figures are yoked together. We are obliged to consider how significance is constructed out of the facts of historical deeds and a quantum of interpretation. Marvell remains fairly self-effacing as he broaches these questions, probably because the significance of the deeds involved in the Revolution was negotiated by the body politic, and his place as poet—though hardly unimportant—was to frame both deeds and significance within the balanced structure of the ode.[55]

In some odes, such as Jonson's on Cary and Morison, the poet acknowledges his decisive role in building significance: Jonson's speaker urges the living Cary to 'accept this garland, plant it on thy head', obviously from Jonson himself, and, in case anyone overlooks his role as arbiter, he peeks out from backstage even while he relates the dead Morison's reputation in heaven:

> we priests, and poets say
> Such truths, as we expect for happy men,
> And there he lives with memory; and Ben.
> (Jonson, 'Cary and Morison', ll. 83–4; *Works*, 8. 245–6)

So ends the third antistrophe, to be completed by an epode that provides the rest of the poet's name and his place in the proceedings: 'who sung this of him, ere he went | Himself to rest' (ll. 85–6). Jonson cannot resist the implication that in establishing the significance of the deeds of his addressees, he is making his own. That symbiotic relation is not uncommon in Renaissance odes, though not always expressed in such an unvarnished way. In the end, it augments the mission of the post-classical genre to reflect on the constructedness of culture, not to discredit human interpretations but to understand them, and of course to marshal them again in the service of achievements that are, or can be rendered, notable.

The fate of these four genres might be taken as corresponding to the fate of vernacular poetry in the Renaissance, but in fact they are among the prestigious genres that come into the period with a heavy legacy of classical authority and example. In his survey of the kinds of poetry least vulnerable to criticism as socially expendable, for instance, Willes mentions three of the genres treated here, omitting epithalamium. The most compelling story of these genres in the period—on which the present chapter is a meditation—must put the received definitions of 'elegy', 'hymn', 'epithalamium', and 'ode' in dialogue with the motives and problems that animate these terms for the poets and readers who try to make them new.

Notes

1. On the elegy broadly, see Gordon Braden and Elizabeth Fowler, 'Elegy', in Roland Greene and Stephen Cushman (eds), *Princeton Encyclopedia of Poetry and Poetics*, 4th edn (Princeton, 2012), 397–9; Karen Weisman (ed.), *Oxford Handbook of the Elegy* (Oxford, 2010); and David Kennedy, *Elegy, New Critical Idiom* (New York, 2007). For the English elegy, see Melissa Zeiger, 'Elegy', in David Scott Kastan (ed.), *Oxford Encyclopedia of British Literature*, 5 vols (Oxford, 2006), I. 243–8.
2. Martin L. West, 'Elegiac Poetry, Greek', in Simon Hornblower and Antony Spawforth (eds), *Oxford Classical Dictionary*, 3rd rev. edn (Oxford, 2003), 517–18. See also Gregory Nagy, 'Ancient Greek Elegy', in Weisman (ed.), *Oxford Handbook of the Elegy*, 13–45.
3. Edward John Kenney and Stephen E. Hinds, 'Elegiac Poetry, Latin', in Hornblower and Spawforth (eds), *Oxford Classical Dictionary*, 518–19. See also Joshua Scodel, 'Elegy', in Anthony Grafton, Glenn W. Most, and Salvatore Settis (eds), *The Classical Tradition* (Cambridge, MA, 2010), 303–6; Paul Allen Miller, '"What's Love got to Do with it": The Peculiar Story of Elegy in Rome', in Weisman (ed.), *Oxford Handbook of the Elegy*, 46–66; and Michael J. Roberts, 'Late Roman Elegy', in Weisman (ed.), *Oxford Handbook of the Elegy*, 85–100.
4. Criticism links love elegy with funeral elegy through the topic of loss (classical collections of love elegies often contain at least one funeral elegy); this topic is important not just to a Western poetry of death but also to Petrarchism, which becomes an important element of English Renaissance love elegy, along with Ovidianism. By far, most of the criticism is on the funeral elegy, which concentrates on a history of the form (Greek, Roman, medieval, Renaissance), its lyric mode, its conventions or generic markers (e.g. apostrophe, exclamation, pathetic fallacy, epideixis, pastoralism, allusion), its moods (ranging from sorrow to shock, longing to melancholy). The seminal works have been Peter M. Sacks, *The English Elegy: Studies in the Genre from Spenser to Yeats* (Baltimore, 1985), and G.W. Pigman III, *Grief and Renaissance Elegy* (Cambridge, 1985), which follow methodologies of psychoanalysis and literary history, respectively, and focus on either 'the work of mourning' (Sacks) or 'the process of mourning' (Pigman), whether emphasizing elegy's personal or its cultural instrumentality. See also Ellen Z. Lambert, *Placing Sorrow: A Study of the Pastoral Elegy Convention from Theocritus to Milton* (Chapel Hill, NC, 1976); and Dennis Kay, *Melodious Tears: The English Funeral Elegy from Spenser to Milton* (Oxford, 1990). R. Clifton Spargo, *The Ethics of Mourning: Grief and Responsibility in Elegiac Literature* (Baltimore, 2004), shifts elegy into the ethical sphere. Relevant essays in Weisman (ed.), *The Oxford Handbook of Elegy*, include: William C. Watterson, 'Nation and History: The Emergence of the English Pastoral Elegy', pp. 135–52; Lorna Clymer, 'The Funeral Elegy in Early Modern Britain: A Brief History', pp. 170–86; Lauren Shohet, 'Women's Elegy', pp. 433–41; Lisa J. Schnell, '"Lett me not Pyne for Poverty": Maternal Elegy in Early Modern England', pp. 481–97; Jonathan Goldberg, 'Between Men: Literary History and the Works of Mourning', pp. 498–517; and

Jonathan Crewe, 'Elegy in English Drama, 1590–1640', pp. 518–32. For love elegy, similar attention to genre history, form, convention, and topic obtains. Especially important has been the way in which the elegies of Marlowe, Donne, and others respond vociferously to Petrarchism, replacing an often delicate idealism of desire with the realities of sexual play and trauma. Important as well has been the role of the poet as an author of desire, featuring the literariness of love as a topic of poetry. For a recent overview, see Gordon Braden, 'Classical Love Elegy in the Renaissance (and After)', in Weisman (ed.), *Oxford Handbook of the Elegy*, 153–69. See also R. V. Young, 'The Elegy', in Jeanne Shami, Dennis Flynn, and M. Thomas Hester (eds), *Oxford Handbook of John Donne* (Oxford, 2011), 134–8; and Patrick Cheney, *Reading Sixteenth-Century Poetry* (Oxford, 2011), 95–8, 208–11.

5. On the hymn generally, see Philip Rollinson, 'Hymn', in Greene and Cushman (eds), *Princeton Encyclopedia of Poetry and Poetics*, 645–47. For the hymn in English, see Louis F. Benson, *The English Hymn: Its Development and Use in Worship* (Richmond, VA, 1962); and J. R. Watson, *The English Hymn: A Critical and Historical Study* (Oxford, 1997).

6. On the Greek hymn, see C. M. Bowra, 'Aristotle's "Hymn to Virtue"', *Classical Quarterly*, 32 (1938), 182–9, and *Greek Lyric Poetry from Alcman to Simonides*, 2nd edn (Oxford, 1961); W. D. Furley, 'Praise and Persuasion in Greek Hymns', *Journal of Hellenic Studies*, 115 (1995), 29–46; M. Depew, 'Enacted and Represented Dedications: Genre and Greek Hymn', in M. Depew and D. D. Oblink (eds), *Matrices of Genre* (Cambridge, MA, 2000), 59–80; and Robert Christopher Towneley Parker, 'hymns (Greek)', in Hornblower and Spawforth (eds), *Oxford Classical Dictionary*, 735–6. On the Roman hymn, see J. Szoverffy, *Latin Hymns* (Turnhout, 1989); and 'hymns (Roman)' [no author], in Hornblower and Spawforth (eds), *Oxford Classical Dictionary*, 736.

7. On the Renaissance hymn as a genre, very little criticism exists, and even less that is recent. The main topics have been a history of the genre, its conventions (such as the main topics, gods and heroes), its metres, its function (whether religious or literary), its connection to epic; and its structure (an opening invocation or apostrophe to the subject; the story about the subject, usually praiseworthy; and a closing prayer or farewell). Critics also distinguish between Prudentian hymn, which is Christian but includes classicism; and secular, which is fully classical (philosophical rather than religious). While there are currently no burning debates, much of the work has been done on individual hymnists, such as Spenser. The major critic remains Philip Rollinson; in addition to the article listed in n. 5, see 'The Renaissance of the Literary Hymn', in George Walton Williams (ed.), *Renaissance Papers 1968* (Durham, NC, 1969), 11–20; 'A Generic View of Spenser's *Four Hymns*', *Studies in Philology*, 68 (1971), 292–304; and 'hymn', in A. C. Hamilton (ed.), *Spenser Encyclopedia* (Toronto, 1990), 385. See also Francis C. Blessington, '"That Undisturbed Song of Pure Concent": *Paradise Lost* and the Epic-Hymn', in Barbara Kiefer Lewalski (ed.), *Renaissance Genres: Essays on Theory, History, and Interpretation* (Cambridge, MA, 1986), 468–95.

8. M. H. Abrams, 'Structure and Style in the Greater Romantic Lyric', in Frederick W. Hilles and Harold Bloom (eds), *From Sensibility to Romanticism: Essays Presented to Frederick A. Pottle* (New York, 1965), 538.

9. On the epithalamium as a genre, see Heather Dubrow, 'Epithalamium', in Greene and Cushman (eds), *Princeton*

Encyclopedia of Poetry and Poetics, 452–3; and Virginia Tufte, *The Poetry of Marriage: The Epithalamium in Europe and its Development in England* (Los Angeles, 1970). On the classical genre, see D. A. Russell, 'Rhetors at the Wedding', *Proceedings of the Cambridge Philosophical Society*, 25 (1979), 104–17; and Eveline Krummen and D. A. Russell, 'epithalamium', in Hornblower and Spawforth (eds), *Oxford Classical Dictionary*, 548.

10. On the epithalamium in the Renaissance, see Thomas M. Greene, 'Spenser and the Epithalamic Convention', *Comparative Literature*, 9 (1957), 215–28; M. M. McGowan, '"As through a Looking-glass": Donne's Epithalamia and their Courtly Context', in A. J. Smith (ed.), *John Donne: Essays in Celebration* (1972), 175–218; Heather Dubrow, *A Happier Eden: The Politics of Marriage in the Stuart Epithalamium* (Ithaca, NY, 1990); and Camille Wells Slights, 'The Epithalamion', in Shami et al. (eds), *Oxford Handbook of John Donne*, 298–307. Most of the critical conversation has been intent on defining the genre, its history, its verse forms, its relation between public ceremony and private intimacy, the role of the poet in celebrating someone else's intimacy (with the exception of Spenser), and often the adaptation of the classical genre (to an extent, the biblical one, e.g. Song of Songs) to early modern circumstances. Like the hymn, the epithalamium has been understudied, especially of late.

11. For a recent overview of the ode, see Stephen F. Fogle and Paul H. Fry, 'Ode', in Greene and Cushman (eds), *Princeton Encyclopedia of Poetry and Poetics*, 971–3. See also C. Maddison, *Apollo and the Nine: A History of the Ode* (Baltimore, 1960); J. Heath-Stubbs, *The Ode* (Oxford, 1969); J. D. Jump, *The Ode* (1974); and William Fitzgerald, *Agonistic Poetry: The Pindaric Mode in Pindar, Horace, Hölderlin, and the English Ode* (Berkeley and Los Angeles, 1987).

12. On the Renaissance ode, see Paul H. Fry, *The Poet's Calling in the English Ode* (New Haven, 1980); and Stella P. Revard, *Pindar and the Renaissance Hymn-Ode, 1450–1700* (Tempe, AZ, 2001). As with the other genres, criticism focuses on a history of the genre (Greek, Roman, Renaissance), especially its dual forms of Pindaric and Horatian ode, including their structures, moods, and modes, but also their centralizing relation between public and private, on the one hand, and their political and individual function, on the other.

13. Georg Luck, *The Latin Love Elegy*, 2nd edn (1969); Paul Veyne, *Roman Erotic Elegy: Love, Poetry, and the West*, trans. David Pellauer (Chicago, 1988); Philip Hardie, *Virgil* (Oxford, 1998), esp. 13–18; and, more variously, Philip Hardie (ed.), *Virgil: Critical Assessments of Classical Authors*, 4 vols (1999), vol. 1.

14. Bruno Gentili and Liana Lomiento, *Metrics and Rhythmics: History of Poetic Forms in Ancient Greece*, trans. E. Christian Kopff (Pisa, 2008), 55–6, 266–7.

15. In addition to Sacks and others (already cited), see Jahan Ramazani, *Poetry of Mourning: The Modern Elegy from Hardy to Heaney* (Chicago, 1994).

16. John Skelton, *Philip Sparrow*, ll. 819–25, in *John Skelton: The Complete English Poems*, ed. John Scattergood (Harmondsworth, 1983), 92.

17. George Puttenham, *The Art of English Poesy*, ed. Frank Whigham and Wayne A. Rebhorn (Ithaca, NY, 2007), 144. On Skelton's elegy, including its classicism and his practice of the form more broadly, see Cheney, *Reading Sixteenth-Century Poetry*, 29–34, 53–6, 95–8.

18. Cf. Georgia Brown, *Redefining Elizabethan Literature* (Cambridge, 2004), 176, on 'memory, rhetoric, and sex as ways of overcoming loss', as well as the usages

recorded in Francis White Weitzmann, 'Notes on the Elizabethan Elegie', *PMLA* 50 (1935), 435–43.

19. Sir Philip Sidney, *The Defence of Poesy*, in *Miscellaneous Prose of Sir Philip Sidney*, ed. Katherine Duncan-Jones and Jan van Dorsten (Oxford, 1973), 95.
20. Puttenham, *The Art of English Poesy*, ed. Whigham and Rebhorn, 136.
21. John Harington, in G. Gregory Smith (ed.), *Elizabethan Critical Essays* (Oxford, 1904), 2. 209.
22. Morton W. Bloomfield, 'The Elegy and the Elegiac Mode: Praise and Alienation', in Lewalski (ed.), *Renaissance Genres*, 150, 152.
23. Thomas Campion, 'Elegy I', in *Works*, ed. Walter R. Davis (New York, 1970), 402–3; I have modified Davis's translation.
24. For an introduction, see Young, 'The Elegy', in Shami et al. (eds), *Oxford Handbook of John Donne*, 134–48.
25. Helen Gardner in her edition of *The Elegies* and *The Songs and Sonnets* (Oxford, 1965), pp. xxxi–xxxiii, argues for a 'book of Elegies' modelled on Campion that circulated as a set of poems; Arthur Marotti, *John Donne, Coterie Poet* (Madison, 1986), 44–53, disagrees. *The Variorum Edition of the Poetry of John Donne*, ed. Gary A. Stringer (Bloomington, 1995–), 2. 448–53, summarizes a range of positions on the dating of the poems.
26. Donne, Elegy 19, ll. 25–7, in *The Variorum Edition*, 1. 120.
27. For the classical models of Propertius, *Elegies* 1.8 ,and especially Ovid, *Amores* 2.11, see R. D. Bedford, 'Ovid Metamorphosed: Donne's "Elegy XVI"', *Essays in Criticism*, 32/3 (1982), 222.
28. Sidney, *The Defence of Poesy*, 95.
29. Rollinson, 'Literary Hymn', 15.
30. Richard Will[e]s, *De Re Poetica*, ed. and trans. A. D. S. Fowler (Oxford, 1953), 83.
31. Puttenham, *The Art of English Poesy*, ed. Whigham and Rebhorn, 117, 118.
32. Stella P. Revard, '"L'Allegro" and "Il Penseroso": Classical Tradition and Renaissance Mythography', *PMLA* 101 (1986), 338–50; Heather Dubrow, *The Challenges of Orpheus: Lyric Poetry and Early Modern England* (Baltimore, 2008), 142–5.
33. Sir Philip Sidney, 'Ye Goat-herd gods', 75, in Sir Philip Sidney, *The Countess of Pembroke's Arcadia: The Old Arcadia*, ed. Katherine Duncan-Jones (Oxford, 1985), 287.
34. Coburn Freer, *Music for a King: George Herbert's Style and Metrical Psalms* (Baltimore, 1971), 14, speculates that 'the vogue for psalm translation generally redirected efforts' at the vernacular hymn.
35. On Spenser's *Fowre Hymnes*, see Richard McCabe, Chapter 25, this volume; and David Lee Miller, '*Fowre Hymnes* and *Prothalamion* (1596)', in Richard A. McCabe (ed.), *Oxford Handbook of Edmund Spenser* (Oxford, 2010), 293–313.
36. On Plato in Spenser, see Elizabeth Jane Bellamy, Chapter 22, this volume. Studies of Spenser's Platonism (or Neoplatonism) are legion; for seminal studies, see Robert Ellrodt, *Neoplatonism in Spenser's Poetry* (Geneva, 1960); Elizabeth Bieman, *Plato Baptized: Towards the Interpretation of Spenser's Mimetic Fictions* (Toronto, 1988); Jon Quitslund, *Spenser's Supreme Fictions: Platonic Natural Philosophy and 'The Faerie Queene'* (Toronto, 2001); and the recent number of *Spenser Studies* devoted to the topic (vol. 24 (2009)), with several essays on *Fowre Hymnes*.
37. Thomas M. Greene, 'Spenser and the Epithalamic Convention', 218, 219.
38. For notable studies of Renaissance epithalamia, in addition to those already cited, see Louis A. Montrose, 'Spenser's Domestic Domain: Poetry, Property, and the Early Modern Subject', in Margreta de Grazia, Maureen Quilligan, and Peter Stallybrass (eds), *Subject and Object in Renaissance Culture* (Cambridge, 1996), 83–130. On Spenser's, see Roland Greene, 'Amoretti

and Epithalamion (1595)', in McCabe (ed.), *Oxford Handbook of Spenser*, 265–8.

39. On the event in the Renaissance, see Jacques Lezra, *Unspeakable Subjects: The Genealogy of the Event in Early Modern Europe* (Stanford, 1997).
40. Julius Caesar Scaliger, *Poetices Libri Septem (Lyon, 1561)*, intro. August Buck (Stuttgart-Bad Cannstatt, 1964), 153; the translation of the relevant chapter by Jackson Bryce appears as an appendix to Dubrow, *A Happier Eden*, 285.
41. Puttenham, *The Art of English Poesy*, ed. Whigham and Rebhorn, 139–41.
42. Katherine Philips, *Collected Works*, ed. Patrick Thomas, 2 vols (Stump Cross, 1990), I. 250.
43. According to David Lindley, 'The narrative [of *The Haddington Masque*] is derived from Moschus' *Idyll*, "The Runaway Love", a poem much imitated in the period'; the *Masque* also shares the comic and satiric spirit of Lucian's *Dialogues of the Gods*, to which Jonson makes several allusions (*Cambridge Edition of the Works of Ben Jonson* (Cambridge, 2012), 3. 253–5). Jonson, of course, himself adds marginal comments to *The Masque* that record a number of classical allusions.
44. In his annotation on this poem, Colin Burrow identifies allusions to several classical poems: Catullus, *Odes* 61 and 62; Statius, *Silvae* 1.2; Claudian, *Epithalamium of Honorius*; Lucan, *Pharsalia* (*Cambridge Edition of the Works of Ben Jonson*, 7. 232–40).
45. Puttenham, *The Art of English Poesy*, ed. Whigham and Rebhorn, 189.
46. Fogle and Fry, 'Ode', in Greene and Cushman (eds), *Princeton Encyclopedia of Poetry and Poetics*, 971.
47. Fry, *The Poet's Calling in the English Ode*, 5.
48. Hence perhaps the association of 'ode' and 'lyric' noted by Dubrow, *The Challenges of Orpheus*, 11.
49. Thus E. M. W. Tillyard, *Milton* (1930), 37–8, and Don Cameron Allen, *The Harmonious Vision: Studies in Milton's Poetry* (Baltimore, 1954), 24–9.
50. John K. Hale, 'Milton Meditates the Ode', *Classical and Modern Literature*, 16 (1996), 341–58, provides classical context for Milton's odes; David Quint, 'Expectation and Prematurity in Milton's *Nativity Ode*', *Modern Philology*, 97 (1999), 195–219, argues for a Euripidean subtext to this ode.
51. For further discussion of 'An Horatian Ode', see Charles Martindale, Chapter 26, this volume, (with further bibliography on the classical sources) and Philip Hardie, Chapter 10, this volume (on Marvell's use of Lucan).
52. John C. Coolidge, 'Marvell and Horace', *Modern Philology*, 63 (1965), 111–20.
53. On the attitudes towards the King and Cromwell expressed in this ode, see several classic statements: Cleanth Brooks, 'Marvell's 'Horatian Ode', *English Institute Essays 1946* (New York, 1947), 127–58; Douglas Bush, 'Marvell's "Horatian Ode"', *Sewanee Review*, 60 (1952), 363–76; Cleanth Brooks, 'A Note on the Limits of "History" and the Limits of "Criticism"', *Sewanee Review*, 61 (1953), 129–35; R. H. Syfret, 'Marvell's "Horatian Ode"', *Review of English Studies*, ns 12 (1961), 160–72; Rosalie Colie, *'My Ecchoing Song': Andrew Marvell's Poetry of Criticism* (Princeton, 1970), 62–71.
54. Andrew Marvell, 'Upon the Hill and Grove at Bilbrough', ll. 34–40, in *The Poems and Letters of Andrew Marvell*, ed. H. M. Margoliouth, 2 vols (Oxford, 1971), I. 61.
55. Thomas M. Greene, 'The Balance of Power in Marvell's "Horatian Ode"', *English Literary History*, 60 (1993), 379–96.

CHAPTER 15

Complaint, Epigram, and Satire

SUSANNA BRAUND

Classicizing Epigram and Satire: A Sudden Bloom

In a poem dating from the end of our period, 'The Apparition of his Mistress Calling Him to Elysium' (1648), Robert Herrick imagines meeting his classical models, including 'Catullus, sharp-fanged Martial', Horace, Juvenal, and 'snaky Persius'.[1] This collocation of Rome's epigrammatists (Catullus and Martial) and satirists (Horace, Persius, and Juvenal) in effect chronicles the sudden efflorescence during the late sixteenth and early seventeenth centuries of classically rooted epigram and satire in the English literary repertoire. The deployment and adaptations of classical models in these genres had lasting effects on both genres into the seventeenth century and on down to the present day. In studying complaint, epigram, and satire in this period we have an intriguing chance to see English poetry at work self-consciously inventing itself. In this chapter, I shall focus on the appropriations of the Latin satirists and epigrammatists, Horace, Persius, Martial, and Juvenal, by a range of English poets, some well known and some lesser known. These appropriations, which are generally explicitly self-conscious adaptations, mostly date from the turn of the sixteenth into the seventeenth century. The inevitable consequences of my specific focus are that I will neglect some authors who are less evidently dependent on the Latin texts and that I will omit discussion of the later decades in this period.[2]

Epigram and satire arrive relatively suddenly on a literary scene in which the chief vehicle of criticism was the medieval form we can call 'complaint'. Complaint was not so much a genre as a mode and it reflected the medieval Christian mindset. John Peter argues that Christian complaint displaced pagan satire during the early Middle Ages and, once established, maintained its salient features constantly until the shifting social and religious circumstances of the sixteenth century saw it eclipsed by more personal and pointed modes of criticism.[3] Complaint is marked by its allegorical simplifications and conceptual generalizations, its unspecific targets, its limited range, and its lack of authorial personality; by contrast, classically based satire is marked by the concrete and the particular, in terms of both the objects of attack and the details with which the attack is performed, by its flexibility, which encompassed 'urbanity, malevolence, raillery, scurrility, cynicism and so on', and by a marked sense of authorial personality and virtuosity.[4]

To talk of a satirical explosion in the late sixteenth century is not to deny familiarity with the Latin satirical writers at earlier periods. There had been for many years what Peter calls 'a slow seepage' from the works of the Latin satirists into English.[5] This 'seepage' came directly from the original Latin, since the earliest translations of Persius and Juvenal were not done until the seventeenth century, or was mediated by continental translations and imitations, or both. Three examples: (1) Alexander Barclay, translating Sebastian Brant's *The Ship of Fools* in 1509, quotes Juvenal, *Satire* 1. 85–6, with approbation in his prologue. (2) Sir Thomas Wyatt wrote three poems, now usually labelled satires, in which he deploys material from the Latin satirists. The first of these poems, 'Of the Meane and Sure Estate Written to John Poins' (published posthumously in 1557 in Tottel's *Songes and Sonettes*), reworks the fable of the city mouse and the country mouse from Horace, *Satires* 2. 6, and concludes with an elaboration of Persius, *Satire* 3. 35–8.[6] And (3) Thomas Drant in the first part of *A Medicinable Morall* (1566) translates Horace's *Satires* along with Jeremiah's *Lamentations*.[7] Drant is a particularly illuminating case: in his juxtaposition of Horace with Jeremiah he looks both forwards and backwards, backwards to the medieval complaint tradition and forwards to the appropriation of the Latin satirists by English poets.[8] But none of these delivers satire as we know it—that is, the self-consciously vicious aggression and harsh obscurity that is the mark of the Elizabethan satirists.

Before I turn to epigram and satire on the Roman model, which exploded on to the literary scene at the end of the century, I will briefly mention earlier works called epigrams that lack what is for us the characteristic feature of the epigram—namely, the 'point' delivered at the end of the poem. The classical model for epigrammatic point was Martial, as we will see, even though a good number of Martial's poems do not exhibit this feature. In 1550 Robert Crowley, a printer, published *One and Thyrtye Epigrammes*, and the dramatist John Heywood published *An hundred Epigrammes*.[9] There is nothing of Martial recognizable here, although Crowley does deploy the canine imagery that will be so important in the satires of fifty years later—for example:

> I bark at your faults, but loath I am to bite,
> If by this barking aught might be won.[10]

This was not yet Martial's moment.[11]

Edmund Spenser too tried his hand at 'Epigrams', but these were actually translations of a Petrarch canzone (*Rime Sparse* 323, on the death of Laura), published anonymously in van der Noot's *Theatre for Worldlings* (1569).[12] Here we see the influence of the short poems in Greek with which Spenser was familiar, the *Anacreontea* (1554) and *Planudean Anthology* (1556), which inspired Renaissance lyric poetry, including the sonnet.[13] (The larger Palatine Anthology was not discovered until 1606 and not published until the late eighteenth century.) By the last decade of the sixteenth century, it appears that the growing differentiation between epigram and sonnet moved Spenser to rework these poems into sonnets and to alter their title to 'The Visions of Petrarch' for publication in his *Complaints* (1591). This is an odd collection, or, better, a collection of poetic oddities. At this point in his career, Spenser had traversed the Virgilian arc from pastoral to epic with the publication of the first part of *The Faerie Queene* in 1590. In the absence of a classical model for a post-epic poetic trajectory,[14] Spenser reverts to publishing poems written at earlier dates, including a translation of the pseudo-Virgilian poem *Culex*, called 'Virgil's Gnat', and a mock-epic poem 'Muiopotmos' on the death of a butterfly called Clarion at the hands of the spiteful spider Aragnoll. Other poems in *Complaints* maintain the theme of lament and add critique of the world's vanities and the anatomy of decay. What we see here is a renewal of the medieval tradition of the complaint combined with the pathological dwelling upon grief that is the mark of Ovid's exile poetry, for example. In contrast with elegy, 'complaint is poetry of unconsoled grief' and, one might add, unconsolable grief;[15] hence its characteristic extensiveness and repetition. Spenser, in his deployment of the complaint, displays his familiarity with classical literature but has little in common with his contemporaries, who see such possibilities in the concision and aggression of epigram and satire as treated by Martial, Persius, and Juvenal.[16]

Classicizing epigram emerges earlier than satire. This can be attributed to the encouragement in some schools to write epigrams in both Latin and English.[17] Epigrams translated from Martial appeared in collections including *Tottel's Miscellany*, an important and popular work that was reprinted, with changes in contents, eight times during the thirty years from 1557 onwards. Timothy Kendall's anthology *Flowers of Epigrams* (1577) marks a further important step in the arrival of Martial, both in some astute translations and in the deployment of point in original poems. Kendall introduces the poems of Martial to his 'courteous reader' saying that 'of all sorts of poems, & poesies, none (me thinketh) are more pithy and pleasant, than pretty, short, witty, quick and quipping epigrams'.[18] Consider, for example, the excellent translation of Martial 1. 10 in the volume:

> Gemellus, Maronilla fain
> would have unto his wife:
> He longs, he likes, he loves, he craves
> with her to lead his life.
> What? Is she of such beauty brave?
> Nay, none more foul may be:
> What then is in her to be liked
> or loved? Still cougheth she.

The author reproduces all the effects of the Latin—for example, his third line captures well the list of verbs in the Latin (*et cupit et instat et precatur et donat*)–and he delivers the same cynical punch in the final word (in the Latin *tussit*, 'she coughs'), a great example of epigrammatic 'point'. But it is still not Martial's moment.

Silencing Satire: The Bishops' Ban

Martial's moment, and the moment of the Latin satirists too, comes in the final years of the century. That moment, which will occupy most of the rest of this chapter, seems to have prompted an astonishing move by the Archbishop of Canterbury and the Bishop of London to ban and burn various epigrams and satires in June 1599. First, a glance at the document and its context:

> Satyres tearmed HALLES Satyres viz virgidemiarum or his tootheles or bitinge Satyres
> PIGMALION with certaine other Satyres
> The scourge of villanye
> The Shadowe of truthe in Epigrams and Satyres
> Snarlinge Satyres
> Caltha Poetarum
> DAVYES *Epigrams*, with MARLOWES *Elegyes*
> The booke againste woemen viz, *of marriage and wyvinge*
> The XV ioyes of marriage
> That noe *Satyres* or *Epigrams* be printed hereafter...
> Suche bookes as can be found or are allready taken of the Argumentes aforesaid or any of the bookes aboue expressed lett them bee presentlye broughte to the Bishop of LONDON to be burnte...[19]

With this Order of Conflagration, issued on 1 June 1599, John Whitgift, Archbishop of Canterbury, and Richard Bancroft, Bishop of London, burned and attempted to ban a number of satirical and erotic texts, as well as 'Englishe historyes', 'playes' (except as permitted by the relevant authorities), and everything written by Nashe and Harvey.[20] Richard McCabe shows that the bishops were not interested in banning pornography (as has been assumed) but were nervous about the concentrated production of satire and epigram with its political innuendo and social commentary at a time of uncertainty and anxiety caused by Queen Elizabeth's declining health.[21] Cliff Forshaw offers a convincing interpretation of the bishops over-reaching themselves in acting against verse satire, a target less seditious than drama, which reached much wider audiences.[22]

In discussing the history of the reception of classical satire and epigram, it would almost be possible to write this chapter entirely by drawing on works published in the four years 1598–1601. The bishops' list headlines five works of verse satire, along with the epigrams of Sir John Davies (1599): the six books of Joseph Hall's *Virgidemiarum* (1597), comprising both 'Tooth-lesse' and 'Byting Satyres', John Marston's *Certaine Satyres* (1598) and *The Scourge of Villainy* (1598, 2nd edn 1599), Edward (or Everard) Guilpin's *Skialethia, or a Shadowe of Truth in Certaine Epigrams and Satyres* (1598, comprising seventy epigrams and six satires), *Micro-cynicon, Six Snarling Satyres* by 'T. M. Gentleman', usually taken to be the dramatist Thomas Middleton (1599); to these I add the so-called *Whipper Pamphlets* of 1601. What we see targeted in the short-lived ban of 1599 is a sudden frenzy of productivity in these genres, well before the first complete translations of their Latin models. This is an important clue as to what is going on. Unlike the medieval complaint associated especially with clerics and disseminated widely in a range of genres, and unlike the rapidly developing genres of drama that found a broadly mixed audience including the uneducated populace, the genres of epigram and satire were being taken up by the cognoscenti, by students from Oxford and Cambridge and the Inns of Court. The authors were educated men writing for educated men, often precocious and competitive young men who were self-consciously inventing new poetic *personae* for themselves: 'young men's Rhetoric', as John Weever describes it in a passage from his *Epigrammes in the Oldest Cut and Newest Fashion* (1599).[23] Within their coteries they are vying with one another for attention and esteem. Their competitiveness runs even to the extent of a possibly fabricated quarrel (discussed later in this chapter).

Martial's Moment(um): The Epigrams of Bastard, Weever, and Davies

I shall first explore the ways in which the epigrammatists sought to appropriate Martial for Elizabethan England at the turn of the century, and then move to assimilations and imitations of the Roman satirists. The Latin epigrammatist Martial (*c.*38–104 CE) published fifteen books of epigrams from 80 CE onwards, starting with his 'Book of the Shows' (*Liber De Spectaculis*) celebrating the Emperor Titus' hundred-day long extravaganza of public entertainments, and then two books of 'Guest-Gifts' (*Xenia* and *Apophoreta*, numbered as books 13 and 14), consisting entirely of two-line poetic labels for gifts. The publication in 85 CE of books 1 and 2 of his epigrams gave his career the necessary boost, and he flourished until the political chill of the post-Flavian era (the Emperor Domitian died in 96) drove him back to his native Spain. Variety is the key to Martial's content, metrical form, and arrangement. He rightly says that his poetry is rooted in realism: 'my page tastes of humankind' (10. 4. 10, 'hominem pagina nostra sapit'). He switches effortlessly between praise and blame, between the panegyrical and the scoptic modes. He praises patrons and friends; he satirizes greed, meanness, ostentatious display, hypocrisy, and self-delusion. He talks about his own poetry, about the poetry of others, and about others who pass off his poetry as their own (he gives us the word 'plagiarism'). He imagines figures of myth and early history, respectfully and less respectfully. He mocks men and women for their disgusting practices, sexual and otherwise—for example, 1. 83: 'Manneia, your little dog licks your face and lips. Small wonder that a dog likes eating dung.' Immediately in the prose preface to book 1 Martial explicitly asserts that he does not attack real individuals in his poems and that his use of vivid and graphic language is sanctioned by generic precedent. He is anxious not to be misunderstood: at 10. 33. 10 he says that it his books' practice 'to spare persons, to speak of vices' ('parcere personis, dicere de uitiis'). In terms of arrangement, he offers provocative juxtapositions and antitheses, sometimes developing cycles on a single topic that are either grouped or distributed. Poems complimentary to the emperor and to Martial's patrons prevail at the start of books, while obscene material tends to be placed later in books. Possibly the single most important characteristic of Martial's epigrams is 'point', the delivery of a witty or obscene barb in the final word or line.[24]

The sheer variety of Martial's material, tone, and organization offered a wealth of inspiration for the English epigrammatists.[25] My first exhibit is the Reverend Thomas Bastard, whose *Chrestoleros* (1598) consists of seven books of epigrams, explicitly offered as a tribute to the Latin poet in 1. 17 'De Poeta Martiali' ('On the Poet Martial'):

> Martial, in sooth none should presume to write,
> Since time hath brought thy Epigrams to light:
> For through our writing, thine, so praised before,
> Have this obtained, to be commended more:
> Yet to ourselves although we win no fame,
> We please, which get our master a good name.

It is customary to impugn Bastard's epigrams; yet among the several hundred poems there are plenty with fine turns of phrase and witty point worthy of his model. For example (and the Latin title is typical and telling), 7. 19 'De naeuo in facie Faustinae' ('On the Spot on Faustina's face'):

> Faustina hath a spot upon her face,
> Mixt with sweet beauty making for her grace.
> By what sweet influence it was begot,
> I know not, but it is a spotless spot.

Particularly fine are the last two lines of 4. 32, a longer poem in which he imagines himself looking at the tombstones of the great in Westminster Abbey:

> Life is a frost of cold felicity.
> Death the thaw of all our vanity.

Like Martial in his prefaces and poems, Bastard frequently addresses his reader and describes his project:

> 1. 7 'Ad curiosum lectorem' ['To the Curious Reader']
> Methinks some curious reader, I hear say,
> What epigrams in English? 'tis not fit.
> My book is plain, and would have if it may,
> An English reader but a Latin wit.

Like Martial, and like contemporary poets engaged in criticism, Bastard offers reassurance of his good intentions—for example, in 2. 16 'Ad Lectorem' ('To the Reader'):

> Reader, there is no biting in my verse;
> No gall, no wormwood, no cause of offence.
> And yet there is a biting I confess

And sharpness tempered to a wholesome sense.
　　Such are my epigrams well understood,
　　As salt which bites the wound, but doth it good.

Bastard arranges his books with the same kind of eye to variety as does Martial, offering a range of topics, tones, tactics, forms, and recurring themes. Interspersed with the caustic poems are poems praising Queen Elizabeth and other named individuals. He uses recurring Latin names such as Matho, Cacus, Scilla, Quintus, Severus, for criticism and he also addresses Momus ('Blame') in several poems. Particularly appealing are a number of extremely self-conscious poems in which he emphasizes how much work goes into writing even tiny poems—for example, 7. 40 'Ad lectorem' ('To the Reader'):

If my books easy of digestion be,
Thank not my matter reader but thank me;
How many verses have I cancelled?
How many lumps of meaning seasoned!
I suffer epigrams to sprout forth, when
I use mine art, and prune them with my pen,
　　For he that will write epigrams indeed,
　　Must use to wring the meaning till it bleed.

Exhibit two is John Weever (1576—1632), whose seven books of epigrams, called 'The First Week', 'The Second Week', and so on, were published in 1599 (evidently after the bishops' ban, since they praise men knighted in July 1599), though probably written earlier.[26] C. S. Lewis did not have a high opinion of Weever's epigrams, saying that they fail to 'rise so high as mediocrity'.[27] This is unfair to some of the shorter poems, which manipulate language and ideas in ways that Martial might have appreciated—for example, 1. 9 'De Ingenio, Fortuna, Fama' ('On Wit, Fortune, Fame'):

Wit scorned fortune, followed after fame,
That through the world she might extol his name;
Fortune scorned wit, and gave him this therefore,
He might have fame, but ever with it poor.

or 1. 20 'In Nigellum' ('Against Nigellus'):

Dogs thou dost love, dogs thou dost feed,
Thy wife thou hat'st in time of need;
And still with her thou art at strife,
Better to be thy dog than wife.

Other poems satirize physical traits—for example, 5. 2 'In Rufum' ('Against Rufus'):

Some say the soul within the brain close lies,
Some in the head, in th'heart some, some in the eyes,
Others affirm it harbours in the breast,
Others will have it in the blood to rest:

'Gainst all philosophers I do suppose,
Rufus' red soul lies hid in his red nose.

Or pretentiousness—for example, 7. 10 'In Cacum' ('Against Cacus'):

Cacus is angry he hath not a place
Amongst the worthies of our Faërie land,
Nor doth the peasant think himself too base,
Among the bravest of the lords to stand:
He wears brave clothes; but what wears he within?
An ass an ass is in a lion's skin.

Weever is perhaps too fond of puns (1. 5 has a terrible pun on meddler/medlar), especially puns on names, but he also has fine poems praising Shakespeare (4. 22) and Spenser (6. 23):

Colin's gone home, the glory of his clime,
The Muses' mirror, and the shepherds' saint;
Spenser is ruin'd, of our latter time
The fairest ruin, Faëries foulest want:
Then his time-ruins did our ruin show,
Which by his ruin we untimely know:
Spenser therefore thy ruins were call'd in,
Too soon to sorrow lest we should begin.

He is well aware of his debt to Martial (explicitly translating Martial 1. 32 in 3. 20), and in the dedication of book 3 he addresses Sir Richard Mallineux with an invitation to relax while reading the poems, which are described as 'trifles' and as 'pills which will purge melancholy', in terms borrowed directly from Martial's preface to book 1, saying 'the gravest *Cato* would have his festival day to frolic in'. Martial explicitly debars the censorious Cato from his 'theatre' unless he is prepared to watch in the same spirit of licence as the rest of the audience.

Exhibit three is the poet most often accorded the soubriquet of 'the English Martial' (though, as we shall see there was competition for this title), Sir John Davies (1569–1626). The identification is made by Edward Guilpin in *Skialetheia* (1598), in 'Epigram 20 To Candidus':

Friend Candidus, thou often dost demand
What humours men by gulling understand:
Our English Martial hath full pleasantly,
In his close nips described a gull to thee...
(ll. 1–4)[28]

referring back to Davies's poem 'Of a Gull', which ends thus:

But to define a gull in terms precise,—
A gull is he which seems, and is not wise.
(ll. 17–18)[29]

Although Davies's output is relatively slender (just forty-eight poems), it vividly evokes London life, matching Martial's evocation of Rome: the theatres, the revels, gamblers and whores, poets and lawyers, social etiquette and embarrassment (for example, at farting in public (l. 14), incomprehensible Northern speech (l. 16), or Friesian vocabulary (l. 24)). There are personal attacks, and, though a modern audience sometimes needs the commentator's notes to understand the complicated social and literary contexts, we can be confident that Davies's original audience was in the know.

Some of the personal satire vividly recalls poems by Catullus and Martial—for example, 11 'In Gellam' ('Against Gella'):

> Gella, if thou dost love thyself, take heed,
> Lest thou my rhymes unto thy lover read;
> For straight thou grinn'st, and then the lover seeth
> Thy canker-eaten gums and rotten teeth.

Sensitivity to status is the subject of 31 'In Priscum' ('Against Priscus'):

> When Priscus, rais'd from low to high estate,
> Rode through the street in pompous jollity;
> Caius, his poor familiar friend of late,
> Bespake him thus: 'Sir, now you know not me.'
> 'Tis likely friend,' (quoth Priscus) 'to be so,
> For at this time myself I do not know.'

Poem 34 'In Castorem' ('Against Castor') puns on the meanings of 'speaking well' and 'speaking ill':

> Of speaking well why do we learn the skill,
> Hoping thereby honour and wealth to gain;
> Sith railing Castor doth, by speaking ill,
> Opinion of much wit and gold obtain?[30]

His longer poem 'Of Tobacco' (36) is wit writ large. It starts by mentioning Homer's praise of Moly (the herb mentioned in *Odyssey* 10) and Nepenthe (a medicine for sorrow mentioned in *Odyssey* 4), then:

> But this our age another world hath found,
> From whence an herb of heavenly power is brought;
> Moly is not so sovereign for a wound,
> Nor hath nepenthe so great wonders wrought:
> It is tobacco, whose sweet substantial fume
> The hellish torment of the teeth doth ease…
>
> (ll. 5–10)

Three times more (ll. 13, 17, 19) he starts a line with 'It is tobacco…' before he boldly asserts (ll. 33–4):

> Yet would I use none of these terms before;
> I would but say, that it the pox will cure.

This, the guarantee of the allure of tobacco to 'all our brave gallants in the town', is the witty climax of the poem.

This is not the end of the story of classical epigram in this period. In the early years of the seventeenth century, John Owen (?1563–1622), another candidate for the title 'the English Martial', published three books of Latin epigrams (1607), which were translated into English and other European languages. Another important Jacobean epigrammatist, Sir John Harington (1560–1612), based at least 80 of his 430 epigrams on Martial.[31] A third important name, to which I shall return, is Ben Jonson. For now, though, the chief point to acknowledge is the importance of epigram, despite its slightness and its miscellaneity as a genre, for the development of English poetry. J. P. Sullivan in his valuable paper 'Martial and English Poetry' is emphatic on the point: 'Martial, through his English admirers and imitators, affected the development of English verse until it culminated in the wit and polish of the heroic couplets of Dryden, Pope, and Augustan verse in general' (p. 149).[32] Again: 'the wit and the metrical and linguistic conciseness of Martial's Latin *forced* his English admirers and translators to try to reproduce in English similar wit and a similarly economic form' (p. 159); and again: 'early Elizabethan writing was undisciplined and rambunctious. The Classical formalism of Martial pared down this expansiveness' (p. 160). Whether or not Alastair Fowler is correct in saying that poets who chose to work in this kind of genre were turning away from the 'fat' Virgilian–Ciceronian genres to 'thin' or pithy forms based on Callimachus, Seneca, and Persius,[33] it is clear that poets who responded to Martial enjoyed the challenge of matching his satirical concision in English.[34]

Hall, Marston, and Fellow Combatants: 'Jerking Rime' and the 'Barking Satyrist'

The bishops' ban of June 1599 certainly targeted epigrams for the *ad hominem* attacks that lurked behind the Latin names used by Davies and his predecessors, but the chief target of the ban was the explosion of satire during the years 1597–9. I use the word explosion deliberately, to pick up on the imagery deployed by one of the authors affected by the ban, the satirist and epigrammatist Edward Guilpin (1572–1601), whose *Skialetheia* (*A Shadow of Truth*) was published in 1598 (*Satire* 1. 50–3):

> Thou must have words compact of fire and rage:
> Terms of quick camphire and salt-peter phrases,
> As in a mine to blow up the world's graces,
> And blast her antick apish complements.[35]

All the authors affected by the ban were young men: at 30, the epigrammatist Davies was the oldest; Guilpin was 27, Hall 25, Marston 23, and Middleton just 19. The aggression and destructiveness in this quotation typifies the satire of these years: the satirists present themselves as angry young men, assimilating the satiric *personae* presented by Persius and Juvenal. Before we look at the use made of these two Roman satirists, it makes sense to glance at their most salient features.[36]

Persius (34–62 CE) presents himself as isolated from society by his moral disgust, articulated in terms that borrow heavily from Stoic philosophy and laced with vivid physical imagery. For example, in *Satire* 1 poetry is frequently represented as food (for example, supposedly poetic diction is reduced to hash served up in a frying-pan (ll. 80–2)) and in *Satire* 4 the dominant metaphor compares the politician to a male prostitute.[37] His brief, probably unfinished, book of *Satires* consists of just six poems, preceded by a prologue in which he explicitly dissociates himself from other 'bards' by coining a word to call himself 'a half-caste' (*semipaganus* (prol. 6)). His fierce independence from the corrupt standards of contemporary taste is maintained in the first *Satire*, in which he professes not to care if his audience is tiny (or non-existent), provided it is an audience immersed in the satire of Old Comedy (Aristophanes & Co.) that will appreciate 'something rather boiled down' ('aliquid decoctius' (1. 125)), an acknowledgement of his obscure, compressed style. His aloof detachment attains a physical reality in the sixth *Satire* with his withdrawal from Rome and from the obligations of Roman society. Juvenal, writing about sixty years after Persius, probably during the first three decades of the second century CE, adopts Persius' angry voice but situates his satiric *persona* right in the middle of Rome, standing at a crossroads with 'a roomy notebook' ('ceras . . . capaces' (1. 63)), like a documentary film-maker, to record every instance of behaviour that perverts or inverts Roman morality. The first two of his five books of *Satires* maintain the pose of indignation established in his opening shout for revenge ('numquamne reponam . . . ?' ('shall I never retaliate . . . ?') (1. 1)), as he lambasts greedy patrons and clients (*Satires* 1, 3, 5), hypocritical moralists and effeminate men (*Satire* 2), the crooks and foreigners who drive out ordinary honest Romans (*Satire* 3), the Emperor Domitian for his abuse of power (*Satire* 4) and in *Satire* 6, a massive poem that occupies all of book 2, the appalling behaviour of Roman wives. In his later Satires he modulates into more ironic tones, but the first two books establish his *saeva indignatio* ('savage indignation', Scaliger's phrase) that has permanently shaped the English concept of satire.

Joseph Hall (1574–1656) was the first of this group of classicizing satirists to be published. He immediately stakes his claim to be called the first English satirist in the opening lines of the prologue to book 1 of his *Virgidemiae*:

> I first adventure, with foolhardy might
> To tread the steps the perilous despite:
> I first adventure: follow me who list,
> And be the second English satirist.
>
> (ll. 1–4)[38]

Scholars have challenged his claim by referring to earlier poets who criticized vice and folly, including Skelton, Wyatt, and Lodge.[39] But the claim stands firm once we realize that Hall sees himself as bringing the genre of Latin hexameter verse satire into English, and that Hall and his contemporaries find in Persius and Juvenal the root and justification for the new features of their satire: aggression and obscurity.

Hall's six books of satires substantially imitate, rework, and develop material and stylistic features from Juvenal and Persius. For example, in *Virgidemiae* 1. 1 Hall savages the frivolity of contemporary literary efforts and affectations in a programmatic satire modelled on the opening six lines of Juvenal's first *Satire* and inspired by Persius' attack on Neronian literary faults in his first *Satire*; as well Hall almost quotes the image of poets' statues twined with foliage from Persius' prologue (ll. 5–6: 'quorum imagines lambunt | hederae sequaces' ('people with their statues licked by clinging ivy'); Hall 5. 1. 1. 20–1: 'whose statues wand'ring twine | Of ivy, mixed with bays, circlen around'). At the end of *Virgidemiae* 5. 2, he incorporates features of Juvenal *Satire* 5, the depiction of the humiliation of the lowly guest Trebius when invited to dinner by his patron Virro.

John Marston likewise flags his purpose of re-creating Latin satire by giving Latin titles to the five poems of *Certaine Satyres* and to some of the poems in *The Scourge of Villanie* (henceforth *SV*).[40] The first two poems of *SV* book 1 proclaim their bloodline most clearly. *SV* 1. 1 is called 'Fronti nulla fides', a (mis)quotation of the key phrase at Juvenal *Sat.* 2. 8 (it should be *frontis*), 'there's no trusting appearances', and makes substantial use of Juvenal's attack on hypocrisy throughout—for example, lines 24–30:

> Mystagogus, what means this prodigy?
> When Hiadolgo speaks 'gainst usury.
> When Verres rails 'gainst thieves. Mylo doth hate
> Murder, Clodius cuckolds, Marius the gate
> Of squinting Ianus shuts? run beyond bound
> Of Nil ultra, and hang me when on's found
> Will be himself.

These lines rework Juvenal 2. 25–8, where Verres, Milo, and Clodius are all named. The next poem takes its title from Juvenal *Sat.* 1. 30: 'Difficile est Satyram non scribere' ('It is hard not to write satire'). And at *Virgidemiae* 4. 7. 9–12 Hall invokes the indignation of Juvenal's ghost at all the ostentatious pomp practised in sixteenth-century Rome, in a passage indebted to Juvenal's description of the early philosopher Democritus' reaction if he were to be transported to ancient Rome (*Sat.* 10. 33–46):

> When once I think if carping Aquines [Juvenal] spright
> To see now Rome, were licenc'd to the light;
> How his enraged ghost would stamp and stare
> That Caesar's throne is turn'd to Peter's chair.

In other words, both Hall and Marston clearly advertise their project as the appropriation of Latin verse satire for the Elizabethan age.

Hall called his satires *Virgidemiae*, literally, 'a harvest of rods', a rare Latin word,[41] immediately indicating the intent of physical violence. The work consists of six books, 'First Three Books of Tooth-lesse Satyres' (1597) and a further three books of 'Byting Satyres' (1598). The first three books abound in Hall's characteristic aggression; their toothlessness is only relative to the three books that follow, in that books 1–3 deal largely with the lamentable state of literature, while books 4–5 deal with immorality, ambition, greed, corruption; book 6 is a mock recantation of everything that has preceded. John Marston (1576–1634) takes up Hall's image of the rod when he calls his second book of satires *The Scourge of Villanie* (1598), while the author of *Micro-cynicon, Six Snarling Satyres* (1599), probably Thomas Middleton, develops Hall's idea of the biting dog by having his satires 'snarl'. When the publication of classically informed satire resumes after the short-lived bishops' ban, the physicality is still there in the titles of the three works comprised in the so-called *Whipper Pamplets* (1601). *The Whipping of the Satyre*, an anonymous pamphlet usually attributed to the epigrammatist John Weever (discussed above), attacks three figures referred to as the Epigrammatist, the Satirist, and the Humorist, probably Guilpin, Marston, and Ben Jonson respectively. Guilpin responds to this in *The Whipper of the Satyre His Pennance*, a defence of satirists (or specifically of Marston) so long as they are dealing in truth. Nicholas Breton's *No Whippinge* (in full *No Whippinge, nor trippinge: but a kinde friendly snippinge*) attempts to defuse the violence of the poets' attacks on one another.

This overview of satiric productions during these years indicates the close acquaintance of these poets and their fierce rivalries. Marston criticizes Hall; Hall allegedly responds with an epigram pasted into copies of Marston's book in the Stationer's Office at Cambridge; Marston draws attention to this epigram by quoting it in *The Scourge of Villanie*; Guilpin supports Marston in his *Skialetheia*; then in *The Whipping of the Satyre* Weever takes Hall's side, and Guilpin rallies to Marston in *The Whipper of the Satyre His Pennance*. T. F. Wharton brilliantly demonstrates how Marston manufactured a quarrel with Hall, which, though it could never give him the coveted status of 'first' satirist chronologically, nevertheless managed to give him equal airtime.[42]

Two of the most important characteristics of this outburst of satire are the violence of the imagery deployed and the obscurity of the language, features for which there was some precedent in Latin satire. The Elizabethan satirists are self-conscious and assertive in both matters, addressing these issues head-on, usually in prefatory material. Hall prefixes his collection with a prefatory poem 'His Defiance to Envie', which functions in the same way as epigrams addressed to Momus (for example, Bastard's dismissal of Momus (1. 6)).[43] Other satirists follow Hall's lead, with Marston's 'To Detraction' prefixed to *The Scourge of Villanie* and Middleton's 'His Defiance to Envy' prefixed to his *Micro-Cynicon*. The satirists probably drew inspiration and precedent for this from the *apologiae* offered by the Roman satirists, Horace in *Satires* 1. 4, 1. 10, and especially 2. 1, Persius in *Satire* 1 and Juvenal in *Satire* 1.[44] This bears out Peter's observation that, by the end of the sixteenth century, poetry of criticism 'is no longer reformative but self-indulgent'.[45]

One of the most shocking features of Elizabethan satire is the sheer physical violence that is threatened. Hall opens *Virgidemiae* 5. 3 thus:

> The satyre should be like a porcupine,
> That shoots sharp quills out in each angry line,
> And wounds the blushing cheek, and fiery eye,
> Of him that hears, and readeth guiltily.

The passage is clearly inspired by lines from the close of Juvenal's programmatic satire, where the satirist's interlocutor imagines the consequences when a listener 'whose mind is chilled with crime goes red and his heartstrings sweat with silent guilt' (*Satire* 1. 166–7). But where Juvenal's satirist is imagined as a heroic warrior with a sword (a nod towards satire's appropriation of the metre of martial epic), Hall innovates with the image of a porcupine on the attack. This is typical of the late-sixteenth-century satirists, and is plausibly attributed to the false etymological identification of 'satire' with 'satyr', which I will discuss shortly: although the Roman satirists seldom threaten physical attack, the fierce indignation of Juvenal along with the vivid imagery of Persius is taken as justification for this approach.

I will return to animal imagery shortly, but for now let us stay with the language of physical attack initiated in the title *Virgidemiae*. At the end of the prologue to the second book of *Virgidemiae* Hall declares:

> but angry Nemesis,
> Whose scourge doth follow all that done amiss:
> That scourge I bear, albe in ruder fist,
> And wound, and strike, and pardon whom she list.
> (ll. 9-12)

He closes his third book with these two lines:

> Hold out ye guilty, and ye galled hides,
> And meet my far-fetch'd stripes with waiting sides.

The Proemium to book 1 of Marston's *The Scourge of Villanie*, in its opening and closing words, could hardly present a more explicit statement of the satirist's role:

> I bear the scourge of just Rhamnusia [a name for Nemesis],
> Lashing the lewdness of Britannia.
>
> . . . . .
>
> Quake guzzell [gutter] dogs, that live on putrid slime,
> Skud from the lashes of my jerking [lashing] rime.
> (ll. 1–2, 19–20)

It is no surprise, then, that Marston characterizes himself as 'Theriomastix' ('Beast-scourger') at the very end of *Scourge of Villanie*. The satirist is depicted likewise in *The Whipping of the Satyre*:

He scourgeth villanies in young and old,
As boys scourge tops for sport on Lenten day;
So scourges he the great town-top[46] of sin,
And puts his wits' felicity therein.

(ll. 525–8)

Another major source of physical imagery represents the satirist as a doctor or surgeon, using treatments such as the emetic and the scalpel to cure sickness or to remove diseased limbs. The inspiration for this may come from the close of Persius' third satire, where there is an extended passage depicting the satirist as moral physician (*Sat.* 3. 107–18). Invasive surgery is developed into a prominent image by the Elizabethan satirists, as shown by M. C. Randolph in her classic study;[47] one brief example, taken from *The Whipping of the Satyre*, will suffice here:

As once I serv'd a friend of mine I wisse,
Healing his bile by lancing of the sore.

(ll. 453–4)

Another of the favoured images is that of the snarling or biting dog. There is some basis for this in Roman satire, but it is developed beyond bounds in the English satirists. Lucilius, the founder of Roman verse satire writing in the second century BCE, apparently wishes to attack 'with a dog's grin and glare' ('canino rictu oculisque') (ll. 1000–1 W); a hundred years later Horace wonders if he appears 'vicious' ('mordax' (*Sat.* 1. 4. 93)) and defends the satirist who 'barks' ('latrauerit') at a public menace (*Sat.* 2. 1. 85). Writing under the emperor Nero in the mid-first century CE, Persius has his interlocutor ask him why he needs 'to scrape delicate ears with biting truth' ('mordaci . . . uero' (*Sat.* 1. 107)) and gives a warning about 'the dog's letter' ('canina littera' (1. 109–10))—that is, a snarl, an idea taken from Lucilius (3–4 and 389–90). A few lines later he attributes to Lucilius more than a snarl (*Sat.* 1. 114–15): 'Lucilius ripped into [*secuit*] Rome—you, Lupus, you, Mucius—and broke a molar [*genuinum fregit*] on them.' Marston in particular represents himself as a dog in countless passages in *Certaine Satyres* and *Scourge of Villanie*—for example:

I'll snarl at those, which do the world beguile
With masked shows. Ye changing Proteans list,[48]
And tremble at a barking satyrist.

('The Author in Praise of
his Pigmalion', ll. 44–6)

The dog provides far and away the most common animal image for these satirists, partly because of the link between the dog and the Cynic (Greek *kuōn* furnishes the word *kunikos*, 'Cynic') and hence with the satirist, via the figure of Menippus, the third-century BCE Cynic philosopher and originator of prose satirical works called 'Menippean satire'. The Greek prose satirist Lucian, writing in the same tradition during the second century CE, described Menippus as 'a prehistoric dog, with a very loud bark, it seems, and sharp fangs, a really dreadful dog who bites unexpectedly because he grins when he bites' (*The Double Indictment*, l. 33). Whether transmitted indirectly or directly (and it is clear that at least some Elizabethan poets and dramatists, including Shakespeare and Jonson, were familiar with some of Lucian's works[49]), the association of satire and dogs had a basis in classical literature.

Dogs bark; dogs bite; dogs also piss. Marston writes:

> What then? must straight some shameless satyrist
> With odious and opprobrious terms insist [persevere]
> To blast so high resolv'd intention
> With a malignant vile detraction?
> So have I seen a cur dog in the street
> Piss 'gainst the fairest posts he still could meet.
>
> (*Certaine Satyres* 4. 115–20)[50]

Satire according to this imagery is any kind of bodily discharge: urine, belch,[51] vomit,[52] or excretion. The Roman satirists had already deployed this imagery. Horace's interlocutor declares: 'And when he has smeared some dirt [*illeuerit*] on his page, he is bursting to pass it on' (*Sat.* 1. 4. 36–7, trans. N. Rudd[53]). Most explicit is Persius, who portrays the satirist as a potential sacrilegious offender, defiling sacred ground, when he addresses his interlocutor at *Sat.* 1. 112–14: '"Defecation prohibited [*ueto quisquam faxit oletum*] here,' you say. Paint up two snakes: "Lads, this place is off limits—piss outside [*extra* | *meiite*]."' But typically, the Elizabethan satirists go much further. Here is Marston wallowing in excrement:

> He slinks away, leaving but reeching steams
> Of dungy slime behind, all as ingrate
> He useth it, as when I satiate
> My spaniel's paunch, who straight perfumes the room,
> With his tail's filth: so this uncivil groom,
> Ill-tutor'd pedant, Mortimer's numbers[54]
> With muck-pit esculine filth bescumbers [befouls].
>
> (*Scourge of Villanie* 9. 28–34)

The other dominant feature of the satirists of this explosive moment is their self-willed 'darkness' or obscurity. Hall appears to strive in this direction, but to admit failure, in the prologue to *Virgidemiae*:

> Some say my satyrs over-loosely flow,
> Nor hide their gall enough from open show:
> Nor riddle-like obscuring their intent:
> But pack-staff [a pedlar's staff] plain utt'ring what thing they meant:
> Contrary to the Roman ancients,
> Whose words were short, & darksome was their sense:
> Who reads one line of their harsh poesies,
> Thrice must he take his wind, & breath him thrice.
>
> (3. 1–8)

Marston claims to reject obscurity, but his poems are at least as impenetrable as Hall's. In his *persona* as 'W. Kinsayder'[55] in 'To those that seeme iudiciall perusers', prefixed to *SV*, he claims:

> Know I hate to affect too much obscurity, and harshness, because they profit no sense... Yet there are some, (too many) that think nothing good, that is so courteous, as to come within their reach. Terming all satyres (bastard) which are not palpable dark, and so rough writ, that the hearing of them read, would set a man's teeth on edge. For whose unseason'd palate I wrote the first Satyre in some places too obscure, in all places misliking me. (ll. 1–11)

He goes on to argue that Persius, though 'crabby' and with 'dusky' 'jerks', and Juvenal, though 'gloomy', proceed at a good pace, 'not stumbling, shuffling' and were readily understandable in their own times. That said, he cultivates obscurity himself in what Wharton has nicely called 'a dedication to excess': 'He alone has the true moral indignation that roughens both the content and the surface texture of his verse... The more roughly he handles vice, and the more extremely he expresses his hatred of it, the more he evinces his inspirational quality.'[56]

'Shaggy satyres': A False Etymology

Both these characteristics of Elizabethan satire, vicious aggression and harsh obscurity, can be attributed in part to the confusion of the derivation of the word 'satire'.[57] One of the most fascinating background documents is a poem prefaced to Thomas Drant's *A Medicinable Morall* (1566),[58] which offers four possible derivations, including (1) an Arabic word for a swordlike weapon; (2) 'the mossy rude, | Uncivil god' Satyrus (meaning the Greek and Latin priapic deities known as satyrs); (3) another god, 'writhled waspish Saturn'; (4) the Latin word *satur*, meaning 'full'. Of these it was the second that held sway over the sixteenth-century consciousness; it was not until 1605 that Isaac Casaubon undermined the connection between satire and 'satyr'.[59] Thus William Rankins introduces his *Seaven Satyres* (1598) (which are not at all Juvenalian) with an 'Induction' that makes the derivation clear:

> Of love, of courtships and of fancies force,
> Some gilded Braggadochio may discourse:
> My shaggy satyres do forsake the woods,
> Their beds of moss, their unfrequented floods.
> Their marble cells, their quiet forest life,
> To view the manner of this humane strife.
> Whose skin is touch'd, and will in gall revert,
> My satyres vow to gall them at the heart.

In the hands of Hall and Marston, the uncouth primitive rustic spirits of this favoured derivation offer all the justification needed for aggression and obscurity.

Donne: None of the Above

There is one major satirist that I have not yet mentioned, and that is John Donne (1572–1631). Donne was writing his five *Satyres* at the same time as the satirists discussed above (probably 1593–9) and the poems were circulating in those years, but were not published until 1633, after his death. Donne was clearly familiar with the two major Roman satirists Horace and Juvenal. For example, he uses the framework offered by Horace's encounter with the awful social climber in *Satires* 1. 9 twice, in *Satyres* 1 and 4, and blends it with Juvenal's vivid portrayal of walking the streets of Rome in *Satires* 1 and 3.[60] Yet he is much more independent of the Roman satirists than the authors discussed above; in both ideas and syntax, his poems are more complex and more demanding of the reader.[61] From Horace he takes the dialogic mode, but instead of adopting Horace's humble *persona*, he tends to offer criticism and invective from a position of Juvenalian superiority without the self-critique that characterizes Horace.[62] Donne's targets often differ from those of Hall, Marston, and Guilpin, and so does his style. He is especially critical of court life, which he attacks in *Satyres* 4 and 5, for example:

> No, no, thou which since yesterday hast been
> Almost about the whole world, hast thou seen,
> O sun, in all thy journey, vanity,
> Such as swells the bladder of our court?[63]

He devotes an entire poem, *Satyre* 3, to an impassioned lament about the state of religion ('Seek true religion. O where?' (l. 43)), which starts in a Juvenalian tone of voice but has more moral substance than the voices of Hall or Marston:

> Kind pity chokes my spleen; brave scorn forbids
> Those tears to issue which sell my eye-lids;
> I must not laugh, nor weep sins, and be wise,
> Can railing then cure these worn maladies?
> Is not our mistress faire religion,
> As worthy of all our souls' devotion,
> As virtue was to the first blinded age?
>
> (*Satyre* 3. 1–7)

In contrast with Hall and Marston, Donne is much less concerned with the state of contemporary literature, the abuse of Coscus the Poet in *Satyre* 2 being the only extended passage on poetry, and that is a mere preliminary to the attack on Coscus the Lawyer. As Heather Dubrow points out, while the other satirists of the 1590s are 'intensely self-conscious about their experimental and highly controversial genre', Donne offers 'no such theoretical apologia'.[64] He does not baulk at the kind of bodily imagery favoured by the likes of Marston—for example, *Satyre* 2. 25–30, attacking a plagiarist:

> But he is worst, who (beggarly) doth chaw
> Others wits fruits, and in his ravenous maw

Rankly digested, doth those things out-spew,
As his own things; 'and they are his own, 'tis true,
For if one eat my meat, though it be known
The meat was mine, th'excrement is his own.

Yet in one of the few passages directly inspired by Juvenal (*Sat.* 13. 28–30), we hear also echoes of the insistence that judges must judge justly from *Deuteronomy* 16: 18–20:[65]

O age of rusty iron! Some better wit
Call it some worse name, if ought equal it;
Th'iron age *that* was, when justice was sold; now
Injustice is sold dearer far.

(*Satyre* 5. 35–8)

Donne's *Satyres*, then, are not a prime site for the study of the reception of classical literature but more an exhibit that displays the competing influences on sixteenth-century poets from sources both religious and humanistic.

Jonson: Horace Impersonated, Martial Moralized

While Donne is clearly entirely his own man, the concept of impersonation or metempsychosis might usefully be invoked when considering the relation between Hall and Marston and the Latin satirists Juvenal and Persius. And it is clearly a powerful tool for analysing the relationship between Ben Jonson and Horace: Jonson's identification with Horace is systemic and deep-seated.[66] Starting with his play *Poetaster* (performed in 1601 and published in 1602; the third of his three 'comical satires',[67] as he called these plays, after *Every Man out of his Humour* (1599) and *Cynthia's Revels* (1600)) Jonson (1572–1637) developed a Horatianism that was both ethical and aesthetic.

In the play, the poet 'Horace', who represents Jonson himself, is attacked by social climbers and envious poetasters. In Act III, scene i, Jonson incorporates a clever adaptation of Horace, *Satires* 1. 9, the famous poem in which Horace is assailed by a dreadful social climber, often referred to in the scholarship as 'the bore' or 'the pest'. The main action of the play, set in the court of the Roman emperor Augustus, involves a conspiracy against Horace by the poetaster Crispinus, who represents John Marston, and his sidekick Demetrius, who represents Marston's collaborator Thomas Dekker. By the end of the play Horace has been vindicated and his enemies have had the tables turned on them. Jonson assimilates into the play apologetic material from Horace, *Satires* 1. 4, 1. 10, and 2. 1, and, with a stroke of genius, borrows the plot of the Greek satirist Lucian's *Lexiphanes* in Act V, scene iii, to have Crispinus purged of his bombast by being given pills that cause him to vomit up gobbets of verbiage.[68] The immediate response of Marston and Dekker suggests that Jonson hit his target: their play *Satiromastix, or The Untrussing of the Humorous Poet* (likewise 1601/2) features the same characters and culminates with Horace being crowned with nettles.[69]

Jonson's Horatianism is maintained in his *Epigrammes*, a collection of 134 poems first published in 1616 in his *Works*. Here we see a fascinating blend: Martial's genre, a genre that took off exponentially in the 1590s in the hands of Bastard, Weever, and Davies (already discussed), becomes substantially moral. Jonson makes this move in the dedicatory epistle to the Earl of Pembroke, where he describes his *Epigrammes* as 'the ripest of my Studies' and asserts that 'in my Theatre... C A T O, if he liv'd, might enter without scandal', a contrast with Martial, who excludes Cato from his 'theatre' (preface to book 1). The same moral position is spelled out in the second poem in the book:

It will be look'd for, book, when some but see
    Thy Title, Epigrammes, and nam'd of me,
Thou should'st be bold, licentious, full of gall;
    Wormwood, and sulphur, sharp, and tooth'd withal;
Become a petulant thing, hurl ink, and wit,
    As mad-men stones: not caring whom they hit.
Deceive their malice, who could wish it so.
    And by thy wiser temper, let men know
Thou art not covetous of least self-fame,
    Made from the hazard of another's shame.
Much less with lewd, profane, and beastly phrase,
    To catch the world's loose laughter, or vain gaze.
He that departs with his own honesty
    For vulgar praise, doth it too dearly buy.[70]

Jonson's *Epigrammes* proceed to cover at least some of the same ground as Martial, but with fewer poems attacking people's social follies, and in a less acerbic tone than the satires and epigrams of the late 1590s. A poem such as 118, 'To Gut', is as strong as it gets in the castigation of vice:

GUT eats all day, and lechers all the night,
    So all his meat he tasteth over, twice:
And, striving so to double his delight,
        He makes himself a thorough-fare of vice.
Thus, in his belly, can he change a sin,
        Lust it comes out, that gluttony went in.

There are also, following Martial's lead in book 1,[71] several poems attacking plagiarists, a pet hate of all poets, for example, 56 on the poet-ape and 100, against 'Playwright'. And there are poems full of pathos marking the premature deaths of his first daughter (22) and his first son (45). The end of the first of these—

This grave partakes the fleshly birth.
    Which cover lightly, gentle earth.
                (22. 11–12)

—directly reworks the last two lines of Martial's lament for the death of the slave girl Erotion (5. 34. 9–10): 'Not hard be the turf that covers her soft bones, be not heavy upon her, earth; she was not heavy upon you.' Poem 45 includes the heartfelt lines:

> Rest in soft peace, and ask'd, say here doth lie
> BEN JONSON his best piece of poetry.
> (ll. 9–10)[72]

Alongside the epigrams of criticism, comprising about half of the collection and concentrated near the start, are numerous poems of praise celebrating contemporary poets, including Donne (23, 96), and lauding the constancy and virtue of his powerful friends, expressed in 'lapidary couplet' after 'lapidary couplet'.[73] A fine example is addressed to the ghost of Martial but aimed at King James (36):

> MARTIAL, thou gav'st far nobler Epigrammes
> To thy DOMITIAN, than I can my JAMES:
> But in my royal subject I pass thee,
> Thou flattered'st thine, mine cannot flatter'd be.

Many more are addressed directly to his patrons. These poems serve to imply, as Stanley Fish suggested, an audience of the like-minded, a 'community of the same', which is flattering to all concerned.[74]

And it is in his celebration of his friends and of friendship in the *Epigrams* that Jonson is most markedly Horatian.[75] A powerful example is *Epigram* 101, 'Inviting a Friend to Supper'. Victoria Moul argues that this poem is indebted in particular to three of Martial's invitation poems, 5. 78, 10. 48, and 11. 52, and so it is, but Horace and also Juvenal are much more to the fore than Martial.[76] The poem is a brilliant blend of Horace's epistolary *persona*, as manifested in his invitation to Torquatus in *Epistles* 1. 5, and the mellower Juvenal of *Satire* 11 (itself modelled on Horace, *Epistle* 1. 5), in which Persicus is invited to a simple meal (11. 56–208). Juvenal perhaps inspires Jonson's promise of edifying entertainment in his undertaking (*Satire* 11. 179–81) that instead of exotic erotic dancers the entertainment at the simple dinner will consist of recitations from the *Iliad* and *Aeneid*:

> How so ere, my man
> Shall read a piece of VIRGIL, TACITUS,
> LIVY, or of some better book to us,
> Of which we'll speak our minds, amidst our meat...
> (*Epigramme* 101. 20–3)

And Horace's celebration of wine and the civilized release it brings at *Epistle* 1. 5. 16–20, along with other passages throughout the *Satires* and *Epistles* commending commensality, seems to lie behind *Epigram* 101—for example, lines 27–32:

> Digestive cheese, and fruit there sure will bee;
> But that, which most doth take my Muse, and me,
> Is a pure cup of rich Canary-wine,

Which is the Mermaid's [a tavern], now, but shall be mine:
Of which had HORACE, or ANACREON tasted,
Their lives, as do their lines, till now had lasted.

Jonson's commendation of simplicity, innocence, and liberty makes him sound very like Horace in his *Epistles* negotiating his relationships with the powerful men in the Emperor Augustus' entourage.

Jonson's Coprological Turn

This moral turn is in marked contrast to the final poem in the collection of *Epigrammes*, a longer, mock-heroic, scatological poem entitled 'The Voyage It Selfe', which Richard Helgerson calls 'among the filthiest, the most deliberately and insistently disgusting poems in the language'.[77] It is introduced in *Epigramme* 133, 'On the Famous Voyage', as a modern-day coprological equivalent to Greek and Latin stories of journeys to the underworld by heroes such as Hercules, Theseus, and (especially) Aeneas:

All, that they boast of STYX, of ACHERON,
COCYTUS, PHLEGETON, our have prov'd in one;
The filth, stench, noise: save only what was there
Subtly distinguish'd, was confused here.
Their wherry had no sail, too; ours had none:
And in it, two more horrid knaves, than CHARON.
Arses were heard to croak, in stead of frogs;
And for one CERBERUS, the whole coast was dogs.
(*Epigramme* 133. 7–14)

In the mock-heroic 'The Voyage It Selfe', just shy of 200 lines long, Jonson's 'two wights' have a 'brave adventure' when they take a water taxi ride along Fleet Ditch from Bridewell Dock, just outside the city wall, upstream to Holborn, a passage undertaken as a lark after drinking in a tavern (ll. 37–8).[78] Since Fleet Ditch was actually an open sewer, Jonson in effect 'maps a journey through a grotesque urban body' steeped in excrement (here called 'Mud'), interweaving 'strains of satire and saturnalia'.[79] This journey is clearly a burlesque version of Aeneas' entry through the jaws of the Underworld.[80]

At the same time, we can also see here the influence of Lucian, the second-century CE Greek satirist who among his many satirical prose works wrote imaginary journeys that appealed to Renaissance readers, *Icaromenippus* and *A True Story*.[81] We know that Jonson possessed his own copy of Lucian in Greek;[82] in his 1600 play *Cynthia's Revels* he has the character Amorphus refer to Lucian in this particular regard: 'I will believe mine own travels before all the Lucians of Europe' (1. 4. 10). Lucian's *Icaromenippus* is an extraterrestrial journey that clearly exercised an influence on Jonson's 1620 masque *News from the New World Discovered in the Moon*, while *A True Story* (which would later influence Swift in *Gulliver's Travels*) parodies terrestrial journeys in higher literary genres.

'The Voyage It Selfe' is a good place to end this chapter on Elizabethan and Jacobean epigram and satire. The travellers' journey continues with turds raining down on them (ll. 90–102) and ghosts of farts flitting around (ll. 124–5). On the banks of 'Fleet-lane' they see 'grease, and hair of measled [worm-infested] hogs, | The heads, houghs, entrails, and the hides of dogs' (ll. 145–6). As McRae rightly observes: 'The catalogue reads as a parody of Jonson's eminently civilized menu in "Inviting a Friend to Supper" (*Epigrammes* 101).'[83] In other words, while Jonson in the *Epigrammes* generally displays his wholesale embrace of Horatianism, he shows himself capable of yielding to delight in satirizing the grotesque features of the underbelly of London in the 'tumultuous . . . distended epigram'[84] with which the collection closes. In this poem, Jonson goes further than anything in Martial or Juvenal and comes closest to the satirical vision of Hall and especially Marston. The difference is that their Juvenalian *personae* are grim and lacking in humour, while in 'The Voyage It Selfe' Jonson follows Lucian in his positive enjoyment of exposing the sordid reality lurking beneath the fine façade of city life. In this way, Jonson paved the way for the supreme satirists of the early eighteenth century, such as Pope and Swift. By then, the unruly vehemence and self-willed obscurity of Hall and Marston was contained by formal discipline crucially shaped by the concision and point of Martial's epigrams.[85]

Notes

1. ll. 43–5, in *The Complete Poetry of Robert Herrick*, ed. J. Max Patrick (New York, 1963).
2. The largest neglect I perpetrate here is of John Donne, whom I will discuss only briefly. His satires, penned during the 1590s, are of course thoroughly imbued with knowledge of Roman satire. But since these poems are 'the most innovative of the group' (that is, of late-sixteenth-century satirists) and 'the most thoroughly transformative', according to Stuart Gillespie, 'Imperial Satire in the English Renaissance', in S. Braund and J. Osgood (eds), *A Companion to Persius and Juvenal* (Malden, MA, 2012), 396) they do not fall within my ambit. See Gillespie's discussion of Donne, 'Imperial Satire in the English Renaissance', 396–8, with further bibliography.

   During the seventeenth century, the central issue for translators and adapters of Roman satire is the debate between Horatianism and Juvenalianism. This debate began as early as Scaliger, who in 1561 established the persisting binary opposition between Horace, on the one hand, and Juvenal and Persius, on the other. Dryden in his *Discourse Concerning the Original and Progress of Satire*, dated 1693, was still grappling with the Horace versus Juvenal dichotomy. For further discussion of these two models, see Charles Martindale, 'The Horatian and Juvenalesque in English Letters', in Kirk Freudenburg (ed.), *The Cambridge*

Companion to Roman Satire (Cambridge, 2005), 284–98; Gillespie 'Imperial Satire in the English Renaissance', 388–9; and Josiah Osgood and Susanna Braund, 'Imperial Satire Theorized: Dryden's *Discourse of Satire*', in Braund and Osgood (eds), *Companion to Persius and Juvenal*, 409–35.

For fuller studies of seventeenth-century English satire, see G. L. Broderson, 'Sixteenth Century Translation of Juvenal', *Phoenix*, 7 (1953), 57–76; William Kupersmith, *Roman Satirists in Seventeenth-Century England* (Lincoln, NE, 1985); and especially Angela J. Wheeler, *English Verse Satire from Donne to Dryden: Imitation of Classical Models* (Heidelberg, 1992). Martin Winkler, *Juvenal in English* (2001), has examples primarily of translations; for discussion of seventeenth-century translations, including those of Holyday (1616) and Stapylton (1640s), see Dan Hooley, 'Imperial Satire Reiterated: Late Antiquity through the Twentieth Century', in Braund and Osgood (eds), *Companion to Persius and Juvenal*, 347, and the following section on the long eighteenth century, pp. 347–57; and Gillespie 'Imperial Satire in the English Renaissance', 402–7.

3. John Peter, *Complaint and Satire in Early English Literature* (Oxford, 1956), 14.
4. See Peter, *Complaint*, 9–13 (with quotation from p. 10), 14–22; also p. 59.
5. Peter, *Complaint*, 107.
6. For discussion, see Catherine Bates, '"A mild admonisher": Sir Thomas Wyatt and Sixteenth-Century Satire', *Huntington Library Quarterly*, 56 (1993), 243–58, e.g. 244: the three poems blend elements of Chaucerian satire, late medieval anti-court lampoon, and contemporary *terza rima* from the Continent with ideas from Horace and Juvenal.
7. On Wyatt's and Drant's relation to Horace, ahead of the rise of Horatianism in the seventeenth century, see Colin Burrow, 'Horace at Home and Abroad: Wyatt and Sixteenth-Century Horatianism', in Charles Martindale and David Hopkins (eds), *Horace Made New: Horatian Influences on British Writing from the Renaissance to the Twentieth Century* (Cambridge, 1993), 27–49. Victoria Moul, Chapter 24, this volume, also addresses Horace's presence in the second half of the sixteenth century and into the seventeenth century.
8. Thus, Peter, *Complaint*, 123.
9. J. P. Sullivan, 'Martial and English Poetry', *Classical Antiquity*, 9 (1990), 157.
10. Quoted from *The Select Works of Robert Crowley*, ed. J. M. Cowper (1872), 55.
11. See Sullivan, 'Martial and English Poetry', 157–9.
12. See Mark David Rasmussen, '*Complaints* and *Daphnaïda* (1591)', in Richard A. McCabe (ed.), *The Oxford Handbook of Edmund Spenser* (Oxford, 2010), 229–30.
13. The *Planudean Anthology* exercised considerable influence on the Continent, both in neo-Latin and in the vernaculars, but was less important for English literary culture: see Joshua Scodel in G. Braden, R. Cummings, and S. Gillespie (eds), *The Oxford History of Literary Translation in English*, vol. 2: *1550–1660* (Oxford 2010), 233–4; for Greek epigram on the Continent, see James Hutton's rich treatments, not yet superseded, in *The Greek Anthology in Italy to the Year 1800* (Ithaca, NY, 1935), and *The Greek Anthology in France and in the Latin Writers of the Netherlands to the Year 1800* (Ithaca, NY, 1946). I am grateful to Gideon Nisbet for his help on this topic.
14. On the risks involved in a regression from epic and romance to complaint and satire, see Katharine A. Craik, 'Spenser's *Complaints* and The New Poets', *Huntington Library Quarterly*, 64 (2001), 63–79 (66–71).

15. Quotation from Mark David Rasmussen, 'Complaints and Daphnaïda (1591)', in McCabe (ed.), *The Oxford Handbook of Edmund Spenser*, p. 223.
16. On Spenser as a 'new' poet, see Richard McCabe, Chapter 25, this volume.
17. Alastair Fowler, 'Genre and Tradition', in Thomas N. Corns (ed.), *A Cambridge Companion to English Poetry: Donne to Marvell* (Cambridge, 1993), 81–2; Sullivan, 'Martial and English Poetry', 152.
18. Timothy Kendall, *Flowers of Epigrammes*, repr. from original edition of 1577 by Spenser Society (Manchester, 1874), 9.
19. For orthography, I follow Davenport in his edition of Hall, App 3, pp. 293–4; see also Richard A. McCabe, 'Elizabethan Satire and the Bishops' Ban of 1599', *Yearbook of English Studies*, 11 (1981), 188–93, whose orthography differs slightly. I am grateful to the editors for exempting me for this item from the requirement of the volume that the text be modernized. I use the spelling 'Satyre' throughout as a title, as a reminder of the false etymologies current at the time; see p. 361 with n. 57.
20. In the event, there were a couple of reprieves (Hall's satires and the obscene volume, Cutwode's *Caltha Poetarum* ('Marigold of Poets')); that fact, and the strange ragbag of targets, and the notable breach of the ban by printers and publishers within just a few months, and the lack of lasting consequences for at least one of the targets (Davies rose to be Attorney General in Ireland a few years later), suggest a more complex story than is usually told.
21. McCabe, 'Elizabethan Satire'.
22. Cliff Forshaw, '"Cease Cease to bawle, thou wasp-stung Satyrist": Writers, Printers and the Bishops' Ban of 1599', *EnterText*, 3/1 (2003), 101–31.
23. The quotation comes from 3. 8, where in a highly defensive poem Weever apologizes for his obscurity, which he has just displayed in the remarkable tour de force of recherché classical learning, 3. 7 'Ad fatorum dominum' ('To the lord of the fates'). The competitive impulse of the young scholar–poets of the age is certainly on display there.
24. For a brief overview of Martial's life and works, see J. P. Sullivan in *Epigrams of Martial Englished by Divers Hands*, ed. J. P. Sullivan and Peter Whigham (Berkeley and Los Angeles, 1987), 1–21; at greater length J. P. Sullivan, *Martial, The Unexpected Classic: A Literary and Historical Study* (Cambridge, 1991). Art L. Spisak, *Martial: A Social Guide* (2007), explores the social setting in depth; William Fitzgerald, *Martial: The World of the Epigram* (Chicago, 2007), 68–105, offers an excellent unfolding reading of book 1.
25. For an excellent discussion of translations of Martial in this period, by Surrey, Kendall, Guilpin, Weever, Davison, Harington, Owen, Jonson, Herrick, May, and Fletcher, see Joshua Scodel's discussion in *The Oxford History of Literary Translation in English*, vol. 2: *1550–1660*, 225–31. On p. 226 he includes Davison's fine 1608 translation of Martial 1. 83: 'I muse not that your dog turds oft doth eat, | To a tongue that licks your lips, a turd's sweet meat.'
26. Weever accessed via EEBO durable URL: http://gateway.proquest.com/openurl?ctx_ver=Z39.88-2003&res_id=xri:eebo&rft_id=xri:eebo:citation:99838812.
27. *Oxford History of English Literature* (Oxford, 1954), 478.
28. Guilpin's *Skialetheia* accessed online via EEBO at http://gateway.proquest.com/openurl?ctx_ver=Z39.88-2003&res_id=xri:eebo&rft_id=xri:eebo:image:6161.
29. Davies accessed via EEBO durable URL: http://gateway.proquest.com.ezproxy.library.ubc.ca/openurl?ctx_ver=Z39.88-2003&res_id=xri:eebo&rft_id=xri:eebo:image:14064:4.

30. Davies's pun recalls Horace's pun on *bona carmina* and *mala carmina* ('good' and 'bad' 'poems'/'spells') at *Satires* 2. 1. 82–6.
31. Sullivan, 'Martial and English Poetry', has an excellent discussion of these and other epigrammatists: on Owen, see pp. 151–2 and 154–5; on Harington, see p. 162.
32. Sullivan cites Paul Nixon, *Martial and the Modern Epigram* (New York, 1927), and W. B. Piper, *The Heroic Couplet* (1969).
33. See Fowler, 'Genre and Tradition', 90, for these evaluations.
34. My comments are directed specifically at the satirical genres, which is why I privilege Martial's role; of course it was Ovid's honing of the elegiac couplet that exercised the most important single influence upon the development of pith and polish in the English Augustan poets in general. This process was under way as early as Marlowe's translations of Ovid's *Amores*, thought to have been written during the 1580s.
35. Guilpin, *Skialetheia* accessed online via EEBO at http://gateway.proquest.com/openurl?ctx_ver=Z39.88-2003&res_id=xri:eebo&rft_id=xri:eebo:image:6161: images 18–19. The opening of Guilpin's first Satire is closely modelled on Juvenal *Satire* 1.
36. The other major Roman satirist, Horace, writing at the very end of the Roman Republic just as Octavian, the future Emperor Augustus, was coming to power, exercised a significant influence on Donne and Jonson, as discussed on pp. 362–6.
37. C. S. Dessen, *The Satires of Persius: 'Iunctura Callidus Acri'*, 2nd edn (1996), remains crucial reading on the imagery in Persius; on *Satire* 4 see pp. 66–70. For an in-depth study of the imagery of *Satire* 1, see J. C. Bramble, *Persius and the Programmatic Satire* (Cambridge, 1974).
38. Joseph Hall, *The Collected Poems of Joseph Hall*, ed. Arnold Davenport (Liverpool, 1949).
39. See, e.g. Davenport's edition of Hall, pp. xxiv–xxv.
40. John Marston, *The Poems of John Marston*, ed. Arnold Davenport (Liverpool, 1961).
41. It occurs only in the comic dramatist Plautus (*Rudens* 636) and in Varro's prose satires (*Men.* 8); the form *Virgidemiarum* is the genitive plural after 'Books'.
42. T. F. Wharton, *The Critical Fall and Rise of John Marston* (Columbia, SC, 1994), 1–17; for more details, see Davenport's edition of Hall, pp. xxviii–xxxiv.
43. Cf. Thomas Lodge's collection, *A Fig to Momus* (1595), which contains satirical poems more in the mode of complaint than on the Juvenalian model.
44. For discussion of this tradition of apologia, evidently initiated by Lucilius, see Susanna Morton Braund, '*Libertas* or *licentia*? Freedom and Criticism in Roman Satire', in Ineke Sluiter and Ralph Rosen (eds), *Free Speech in Classical Antiquity* (Leiden, 2004), 409–28, especially 418–21.
45. Peter, *Complaint*, 113.
46. Cf. the 'parish-top' mentioned by Shakespeare at *Twelfth Night*, I. iii. 43.
47. M. C. Randolph, 'The Medical Concept in English Renaissance Satiric Theory', *Studies in Philology*, 38 (1941), 121–57.
48. Meaning, people like the shape-changing god Proteus.
49. Christopher Robinson, *Lucian and his Influence in Europe* (1979), 95–163.
50. For the same accusation against Marston, of 'lifting up your leg and pissing against the world', in the contemporary *Parnassus* plays, see *The Selected Plays of John Marston*, ed. Arnold Davenport (Liverpool, 1961), 15.
51. e.g. Middleton's *Micro-Cynicon*, quoted by Peter, *Complaint*, 147.
52. e.g. *The Whipping of the Satyre*, 491.
53. *Horace Satires and Epistles, Persius Satires*, trans. N. Rudd (repr. with revisions, 1987).

54. A reference to Drayton's *Mortimeriados.*
55. Literally 'Castrator's Song', probably a play on Mar-stone's name = Ball-Breaker.
56. T. F. Wharton, *The Critical Fall and Rise of John Marston* (Columbia, SC, 1994), 9.
57. For useful discussion, see I. De Smet, 'Giants on the Shoulders of Dwarfs? Considerations on the Value of Renaissance and Early Modern Scholarship for Today's Classicists', in S. Harrison (ed.), *Texts, Ideas, and the Classics: Scholarship, Theory, and Classical Literature* (Oxford, 2001), 252–64 (255–6).
58. Valuably quoted by Peter, *Complaint*, at app. A, pp. 301–3.
59. Isaac Casaubon, *De Satyrica Graecorum Poesi et Romanorum Satira Libri Duo* (Paris, 1605).
60. See Heather Dubrow, '"No Man Is an Island": Donne's Satires and Satiric Traditions', *Studies in English Literature 1500–1900*, 19 (1979), 71–83 (71–6); M. Thomas Hester, *Kinde Pitty and Brave Scorn: John Donne's Satyres* (Durham, NC, 1982), 128–33. On Donne and Horace, see too Victoria Moul, Chapter 24, this volume.
61. For some astute comparisons, see Dubrow, 'No Man'.
62. See Dubrow, 'No Man', esp. 75, on the failure of Donne's blend: the Horatian dialogue cannot easily accommodate Juvenalian insults. Horace's characteristic self-critique is motivated by his relatively low status, as the son of a former slave.
63. John Donne, *Poetical Works*, ed. H. Grierson (1967), *Satyre* 4. 165–8.
64. Dubrow, 'No Man', pp. 81–2.
65. See Achsah Guibbory, 'John Donne', in Claude Rawson (ed.), *The Cambridge Companion to English Poets* (Cambridge, 2011), 110.
66. See Joanna Martindale, 'The Horace of Ben Jonson and his Heirs', in Martindale and Hopkins, *Horace Made New*, 50–85, esp. 50–67; Susanna Braund, 'The Metempsychosis of Horace: The Reception of the Satires and Epistles', in Gregson Davis (ed.), *A Companion to Horace* (Malden, MA, 2010), 382–9; Victoria Moul, *Jonson, Horace and the Classical Tradition* (Cambridge, 2010), 135–72. Sean Keilen (Chapter 28, this volume), sees Horace as crucial in shaping Jonson's poetic vocation.
67. On the 'comical satires', see Richard Dutton, 'Jonson's Satiric Styles', in Richard Harp and Stanley Stewart (eds), *The Cambridge Companion to Ben Jonson* (Cambridge, 2000), 60–5, and Sean Keilen, Chapter 28, this volume.
68. See Braund, 'The Metempsychosis of Horace', 388.
69. I cannot discuss here the so-called War of the Theatres of these years, but it involved many of the authors mentioned in this chapter.
70. For sensitive discussion of how Jonson Horatianizes this and other poems of Martial, see Moul, *Jonson, Horace*, 63–70.
71. Martial seems especially concerned with plagiarism in book 1: 38, 52, 53, 63, 66, and 72. For discussion, see Fitzgerald, *Martial*, 91, 93–7.
72. On Jonson's adaptations of classical form to Christian purpose in these poems, see R. V. Young, 'Jonson and Learning', in Harp and Stewart (eds), *Cambridge Companion to Ben Jonson*, 52–3.
73. Richard Helgerson, 'Ben Jonson', in Corns (ed.), *Cambridge Companion to English Poetry: Donne to Marvell*, 153; his whole discussion of Jonson (pp. 148–70) is excellent.
74. See Ian Donaldson, 'Jonson's Poetry', in Harp and Stewart (eds), *Cambridge Companion to Ben Jonson*, 119–28, citing Fish at p. 123.
75. Katharine Eisaman Maus has a full discussion of Jonson's sympathy with Roman ideology in *Ben Jonson and the Roman Frame of Mind* (Princeton, 1984);

Moul, *Jonson, Horace*, 54–93, is crucial reading.

76. Moul, *Jonson, Horace*, 54–63.
77. Richard Helgerson, 'Ben Jonson', in Corns (ed.), *Cambridge Companion to English Poetry: Donne to Marvell*, 152.
78. On the significance of Bridewell, see Andrew McRae, '"On the Famous Voyage": Ben Jonson and Civic Space', *Early Modern Literary Studies*, Special Issue 3 (1998), 8. 1–31 <http://purl.oclc.org/emls/04-2/mcraonth.htm> (accessed 22 February 2012), at para. 13.
79. McRae, 'Famous Voyage', para. 3.
80. Compare 'The Voyage It Selfe', 61–72, with *Aeneid* 6. 273–81, where Aeneas, like Jonson's travellers, sees Grief, Cares, Diseases, Age, Fear, Famine, Want, Death, and Distress.
81. Robinson, *Lucian*, 129–44.
82. See Robinson, *Lucian*, 104, referring to *Works*, I. 266.
83. McRae, 'Famous Voyage', para. 25.
84. McRae, 'Famous Voyage', para. 30.
85. Profound thanks to my colleague Rob Cousland for his editing skills, to Ace Krupkin for library help, to the editors for their patience, and to the series editors for their comments. The essays by Dan Hooley ('Imperial Satire Reiterated: Late Antiquity through the Twentieth Century') and Stuart Gillespie ('Imperial Satire in the English Renaissance') in Braund and Osgood (eds), *A Companion to Persius and Juvenal*, were inspiring and are recommended reading for a larger overview. Raman Selden, *English Verse Satire 1590–1765* (1978); William Kupersmith, *Roman Satirists in Seventeenth-Century England*; and especially Angela J. Wheeler, *English Verse Satire from Donne to Dryden: Imitation of Classical Models* (Heidelberg, 1992), are all valuable resources on this topic.

CHAPTER 16

Tragedy

GORDON BRADEN

Genre Theory

Tragedy is one of the most important generic categories passed on from classical literature, with a prestige second only to epic. In the English Renaissance, the most exemplary and self-conscious career of classical imitation, that of John Milton, climaxes in the later seventeenth century with studied and unprecedentedly successful re-creations of each type: *Paradise Lost* and *Samson Agonistes*. The achievement is such as to exert a powerfully teleological pull on any literary history of the topic; it would misrepresent the record to resist that pull entirely. The achievement is also, however, an almost uniquely lonely one—*Samson* especially, which neither draws on nor establishes much of a tradition among other English writers. To treat it as a *telos* is to miss most of what happens along the way.

The genre's name survives the lapse of classical theatre and the loss of any memory or understanding of theatrical performance; its specific reference gone, the word seeks for other meanings. The great Islamic philosopher Averroes, writing a commentary on Aristotle's *Poetics* in twelfth-century Andalusia, takes the odd terms 'tragedy' and 'comedy' to refer respectively to eulogy and satire, the poetry of praise and blame.[1] Christendom is not much more successful. Dante identifies comedy and tragedy as genres of *poetica narratio* (along with pastoral, elegy, satire, and hymns of thanksgiving), defined by contrasting narrative arcs: the distinguishing characteristic of tragedy is that it 'is tranquil and conducive to wonder at the beginning, but foul and conducive to horror [*foetida et horribilis*] at the end'.[2] Dante is explaining among other things why he entitles his own visionary allegory *Commedia*; within it Virgil refers to his *Aeneid* as 'l'alta mia tragedìa', my high Tragedy.[3] The first occurrence of 'tragedy' in English appears to be in Chaucer, in his translation of Boethius and in characterizing his own verse narrative, *Troilus and Creseyde*: 'litel myn tragedye'.[4] Such usage is partly confusion and partly a generalization of meaning that is still with us. Some confusion persists even as scholarship begins to scrutinize the scripts of actual classical tragedies; the work usually identified as the first Renaissance tragedy, Albertino Mussato's *Ecerinis* (1315), contains what appear to be versified stage directions, evidence that the performance that the author had in mind was declamatory recitation by a single speaker.

Properly theatrical performances of some of the ancient scripts begin in the late fifteenth century (they become a feature of university life throughout Europe), and the distinctions between narrative and dramatic form are sorted out; even as that happens, though, tragedy continues to be defined to a great extent by its content, and often in the vein of Dante's 'foul and conducive to horror': 'The subjects of tragedy are grand, appalling, the commands of kings, massacres, acts of desperation, hangings, banishments, the loss of parents, the killing of parents, acts of incest, conflagrations, fights, putting people's eyes out, weeping, wailing, lamenting, funerals, funeral speeches, funeral odes.'[5] The writer here is the esteemed theorist Julius Caesar Scaliger, though his list also serves the needs of anti-theatrical polemicists in England; John Greene might as well have had it in front of him: 'The matter of tragedies is haughtiness, arrogancy, ambition, pride...murder, cruelty, rapine, incest...hewing, stabbing, dagger-drawing, fighting, butchery, treachery, villainy, etc., and all kind of heroic evils whatsoever.'[6] Horatio's summary of what just happened in *Hamlet* breathes a surprisingly similar spirit:

So shall you hear
Of carnal, bloody, and unnatural acts,
Of accidental judgments, casual slaughters,
Of deaths put on by cunning and forc'd cause,
And in this upshot, purposes mistook
Fall'n on th' inventor's heads.
(*Hamlet*, 5. 2. 380–5)

Earlier, the Ghost had paused in relating his 'foul and most unnatural murther' for a succinct, 'O, horrible, O, horrible, most horrible!' (1. 5. 25, 80).

Criticism in our own time can be receptive to characterizations of tragedy in such a key,[7] but in the Renaissance they have the disadvantage of being the naive common wisdom. A more sophisticated theory of the genre gains authority in the sixteenth century, aided by the belated recovery (in which Scaliger, when not listing the hair-raising subjects of tragedy, plays a part) of Aristotle's *Poetics*. The *Poetics* is translated into Latin in the thirteenth century (as is Averroes' commentary) and printed (in a newer translation) in 1498, but it only gets traction after the publication of yet another translation in 1549 and of a series of new commentaries that take their place in the flowering of literary criticism in the late Italian Renaissance. These commentaries among other things search Aristotle for rules for an austere and dignified dramaturgy, and that of Lodovico Castelvetro (1570) gives definitive formulation to the influential concept of the 'three unities' of action, place, and time (the last now cut from Aristotle's twenty-four hours to twelve). The idea of this and related prescriptions has a privileged place in thinking about dramatic form for at least another century; their promulgators become known as *i regolisti*, the rule-makers. Their influence is most significant in France, where an often public and acrimonious debate about the classically correct way to write plays figures in the development of a genuinely successful and enduring tradition of new drama.

That success, of course, is not simply a matter of applying theory to practice. In the sixteenth century, a line of fairly direct transfers of classical form, chorus and all, to the contemporary stage—beginning with Étienne Jodelle's *Cléopâtre captive* (1553)—acquires a measure of prestige; towards the end of the century, the collected plays of Robert Garnier (composed between 1568 and 1583) come to stand, in France and elsewhere, as an exemplary corpus of what classical imitation in drama can and should be. In the long run, though, none of this would count for very much if it were not for a more volatile encounter in the seventeenth century with contemporary theatrical savvy. The breakthrough production, Corneille's *Le Cid* (1637), is fiercely attacked by the newly established Académie for its supposed irregularities. Corneille stands by his play but makes changes in later printed versions of the text; when the dust settles, the polemics turn out to have obscured what was actually happening, the creation of a vital dramatic mode in which potentially anarchic passion and austere formal control address each other in something like equal measure. That mode is not identical to that of ancient tragedy—no more chorus, for one thing—but it lays claim to a *gravitas* sufficient to earn the rubric *Classicisme*. The plays of Corneille and his successor Racine are regularly published with authorial *examens* analysing and defending their observance of the supposed rules of proper dramaturgy, often with specific reference to classical precedent. A parallel development, guided by the plays of Terence, results in a comparable model for comedy, though an important part of the theory is a vigilant separation of the two genres; one of the objections to *Le Cid* is Corneille's designation of it as *tragicomédie*. In later printings it is *tragédie*, pure and simple.

Despite widespread admiration for the French achievement, nothing comparable to this stunning metamorphosis of ancient tragic form into new theatrical reality happens elsewhere; no similar attempt rises beyond the level of 'neoclassicism'. An English translation of *Le Cid* is performed in London within a month of the play's debut in Paris, but the play is much altered in the process and makes no special impression. Other translations of Corneille are printed during the closing of the theatres under the Commonwealth, and Katherine Philips's version of *La Mort de Pompée*, with dialogue in pentameter couplets that mimic *alexandrins* (the dodecasyllabic couplets that were standard in French theatre), reaches the stage in Dublin in 1663. Such efforts feed into the modestly successful attempt in the Restoration to create an English neoclassical theatre somewhat along French lines; this, like the very different one-time achievement of *Samson Agonistes* (which Milton explicitly announces is *not* for the stage), is discussed in the next volume of this *History*. During the period that concerns us here, though, the English story is mainly one of contrast, with neo-Aristotelian theorizing at most a spectral presence. The spectre has some claim on the literary conscience; Philip Sidney, in his *Defence of Poesy* (*c*.1583), scorns the English stage for 'observing rules neither of honest civility nor of skilful poetry'; he singles out violation of the three unities, mandated 'both by Aristotle's precept and common reason', and the promiscuous mingling of tragedy and comedy—the instinct to 'match hornpipes and funerals'—for which the Elizabethan theatre was famous.[8] Such criticisms were on the minds of at least some practising playwrights. Ben Jonson, in a preface to the printed text of his *Sejanus* (1605), concedes: 'if it be objected, that what I publish is no true poem, in the strict laws of time, I confess it: as also in the want of a proper chorus.' Jonson's self-justification is simple: the rules do not work on the modern stage. It is neither 'needful, or almost possible, in these our times, and to such auditors, as commonly things are presented, to observe the old state and splendour of dramatic poems, with preservation of any popular delight' (*Works*, 4. 350).[9] Castelvetro himself might have understood; one agenda of his commentary on the *Poetics*, in addition to defining the three unities, was to advance an extreme theory that the originating and sole purpose of poetry, dramatic and otherwise, was 'to provide pleasure and recreation to the souls of the common people and the rude multitude'.[10]

Classical Scripts and English Dramatic Form

By and large, the impact of classical tragedy on the English Renaissance stage happens outside the matrix of any controlling theory; it mostly consists of response, some of it quite scattered, to the specifics of available classical texts. As elsewhere in Europe, Greek tragedy is at a serious disadvantage. Access to it is mainly through translation, primarily the various Latin translations that became available (not all of them by continental scholars; a Latin version of Sophocles's *Antigone* by the English poet Thomas Watson was printed in London in 1581). We know that Jonson—who did know Greek, and was a tireless propagandist for classical literature of all stripes—owned an anthology of Greek drama providing Latin translations *en face* with the Greek; we also know that he was willing to lend his books, and it is possible that they circulated among friends and colleagues.[11] Two lost plays by Henry Chettle and Thomas Dekker, *Agamemnon* and *Orestes' Furies* (1599), might well have been based on the abbreviated two-play version of Aeschylus' *Oresteia* that was current in the sixteenth century (and was included in the bilingual anthology that Jonson owned). If so, they would have been the only translations, more or less, of classical tragedies known to have been acted on the public stage during the English Renaissance.[12] Surviving English translations of Greek tragedy are scant. Sometime in the early 1550s Lady Jane Lumley produced an English version of Euripides' *Iphigenia in Aulis*, apparently from the Latin translation by Erasmus. It is, unusually for the period, a prose version of a verse original, and edits that original aggressively, with severe compromise to the ancient form. The choruses are eliminated, mythological and rhetorical elaborations are curtailed, and some local additions emphasize the poignancy and outrage of a father's sacrifice of his own daughter to political necessity.[13] It remained in manuscript until the twentieth century. A script by George Gascoigne and Francis Kinwelmersh identified as a version of Euripides' *Phoenician Women* when performed at Gray's Inn in 1566 and when published by Gascoigne in 1573 is actually a translation of Lodovico Dolce's *Jocasta* (1549), indeed based on Euripides but revised in the direction of Seneca and contemporary taste. An English translation of Sophocles' *Electra* by Christopher Wase was published at The Hague during the Interregnum (1649); it is scholarly in its presentation, though framed as a Royalist polemic, celebrating successful vengeance against regicides. The widest diffusion of Greek tragedy in England is through quotations by other authors; we can be sure that Shakespeare read a couple of lines from the opening of *Oedipus Tyrannus* because they are quoted in Plutarch's life of Antony.

Until Milton, Seneca is the dominant figure in all English dealings with classical tragedy.[14] That the original texts in this case are in Latin made them accessible to a wider audience than those in Greek, but there was clearly something to their ethos that resonated more readily with Renaissance readers than did Greek tragedy. Scaliger's lurid catalogue is not exactly incongruent with the texts of the Greek plays, but it does make an easier fit with Seneca's. It is also possible that, despite its famously horrific content, Seneca's plays were easier to come to terms with, less challenging emotionally for a Christian readership. Their most disturbing claim is probably that of the second chorus in *The Trojan Women* on the absence of any kind of afterlife: 'Post mortem nihil est, ipsaque mors nihil' ('After death is nothing, and death itself is nothing') (l. 397). That is bleak, but it is nihilism with an aura of heroic endurance. The sentiment's opposite number in Greek is more harrowing:

μὴ φῦναι τὸν ἅπαντα νι-
κᾷ λόγον·τό δ', ἐπεὶ φανῇ,
βῆναι κεῖθεν ὅθεν περ ἥ-
κει πολὺ δεύτερον ὡς τάχιστα.

(*Oedipus at Colonus*, ll. 1224–7)

(Not to be born comes first by every reckoning; and once one has appeared, to go back where one came from as soon as possible is the next best thing.)

The tragic fact is not mortality but the irredeemable torment of life itself. That 'archaic insight' has been posited as the benchmark set by Attic tragedy, a vision that its descendants achieve only rarely and with great difficulty.[15] We meet its like on the Renaissance stage in a few extraordinary works: 'we came crying hither. | Thou know'st, the first time that we smell the air | We wawl and cry' (*King Lear*, 4. 6. 178–80). Even those lines, however, are introduced with a hint of Stoic affirmation: 'Thou must be patient.'

Interest in Seneca's plays is indeed connected to interest in his philosophical works, and both have much to do with interest in a classically Roman style of dignity: lofty, imperious, self-possessed; a suitable presence, not to be trifled with, for the corridors of power. (Seneca's own experiences in those corridors, part of the subject of the pseudo-Senecan *Octavia*, are staged in English in an anonymous *Tragedy of Nero* (1624).) English translations of individual Senecan plays by young men associated with the Inns of Court—London's law schools and de facto university, an urban focus of ambition in many areas—begin to appear in print in 1559. They are collected and rounded out by Thomas Newton into a complete collection in 1581. The translators accommodate the plays to contemporary taste with cuts and substitutions for the most part clearly identified to the reader. They are also of their historical moment in (with the exception of Thomas Nuce's *Octavia*) putting their dialogue and some of their lyrics into fourteener couplets, a decision that seriously hobbles them for later readers and was the likely target of Shakespeare's mockery in the last act of *A Midsummer's Night's Dream*: 'Hippolytus (aye, woe is me!) is slain by doleful death.'[16] But there is trace evidence that Shakespeare and others read them carefully and took things over from them ('One hurly-burly done, another doth begin' (*Macbeth*, 1. 1. 3); 'O coward, peasant slave' (*Hamlet*, 2. 2. 550)),[17] and there is no question that Seneca's tragedies were common currency in the Elizabethan literary world, both as source and as standard, a name with which to conjure. That name figures in the advertising copy of the Players in *Hamlet*: 'Seneca cannot be too heavy, nor Plautus too light' (2. 2. 400–1; the Greek dramatists are mentioned nowhere in Shakespeare). The joke is that if anything Seneca is the first refuge of the ambitious theatrical hack: 'English Seneca read by candlelight yields many good sentences, as *Blood is a beggar* and so forth; and if you entreat him fair in a frosty morning, he will afford you whole Hamlets, I should say handfuls of tragical speeches.'[18]

One result of this regard for Senecan drama is Renaissance England's own small run of 'neoclassical' tragedies. The first of these, *Gorboduc*, by Thomas Sackville and Thomas Norton, two members of the Inner Temple (and of Elizabeth's first Parliament), received a lavish debut there, after a banquet, on Twelfth Night in 1562; a command performance at Whitehall followed less than two weeks later. It was an appropriately ceremonious way of beginning the history of Elizabethan tragedy. The play does not take any of its text directly from Seneca, but it is Senecan in form and to a great extent in spirit: composed mostly of lengthy, highly wrought speeches with minimal give-and-take in the dialogue (the brothers Ferrex and Porrex, whose contention sets the plot in motion, are never on stage at the same time), sectioned into five acts by the odes of a Chorus ('four ancient and sage men of Britain') that never interacts with the characters, and involving a good deal of violent action that takes place offstage and in one case is reported by a character with no other name than Nuntius. This is the play that Sidney exempts from his otherwise sweeping scorn for English tragedy: 'it is full of stately speeches and well-sounding phrases, climbing to the height of Seneca's style.' He does complain of its carelessness about the unities: 'it is faulty both in place and time'—a sign that the authors were being guided by mimicry of the Senecan dramatic texts rather than the kind of detailed theoretical thinking that flourished on the Continent. Sidney was right, though for the wrong reason, in saying the play 'might not remain as an exact model of all tragedies' (*Defence*, 113). He was 7 years old at the time of the play's two known performances and probably never saw it staged; his enthusiasm was one based on reading, not theatrical experience. Especially with the hindsight provided by Elizabethan drama at its height, it is only necessary to describe the dramaturgy of *Gorboduc* to know that, aside from a prescient decision to use unrhymed iambic pentameters for the dialogue, this was not going to do.

Sidney's enthusiasm was nevertheless not merely eccentric or deluded; it was shared within circles where performability was not the criterion. Fulke Greville, Sidney's lifelong friend, wrote unapologetically of his own dramatic efforts (as Milton did of *Samson*): 'I have made these tragedies no plays for the stage.'[19] The example of neo-Senecan dramatic form attracts some genuine talent—such as Greville's—for a limited but serious line of works that has very little connection with the public stage but gains a following. *Gorboduc* has a succession of similar plays at the Inns of Court: the Gascoigne–Kinwelmersh *Jocasta* already mentioned, the anonymous *Gismond of Salerne* (1567–8; from a story in Boccaccio), and Thomas Hughes's *The Misfortunes of Arthur* (1588).[20] The tradition is given new energy when Seneca's example is joined by the more stringent one of Garnier.[21] Two of his plays are translated into English: *Marc Antoine* by Sidney's sister, the Countess of Pembroke (*Antonius* (1592)), and *Cornélie* (*Cornelia* (1593)) by, surprisingly, Thomas Kyd, already author of the popular and stageworthy *Spanish Tragedy* (*c.*1587) and possibly of the pre-Shakespearean *Hamlet*. Cornelia was the wife of Pompey, whom Julius Caesar defeated in the Roman Civil War before beginning his liaison with Cleopatra; original plays in this mode cluster around this historical moment. Samuel Daniel, a poet with ties to Pembroke, produced a *Cleopatra* (1594) that complements her *Antonius*,[22] as does Samuel Brandon's *The Virtuous Octavia* (1598; labelled a tragicomedy by its author), about the Roman wife that Antony divorced on Cleopatra's behalf. Sir William Alexander published a *Julius Caesar* (1607), which climaxes in the assassination; Elizabeth Cary's *Mariam* (1613, based on a story in Josephus) takes place in the aftermath of Octavian's defeat of Antony and Cleopatra. Greville wrote his own *Antony and Cleopatra*, which he says he destroyed, and two plays set in the recent history of the Middle East, *Mustapha* and *Alaham* (published posthumously in 1633); Alexander published three other 'monarchic tragedies': *Darius* (1603), *Croesus* (1604), and *The Alexandrian Tragedy* (1607); Daniel also wrote the one play of this type, *Philotas* (1604), that apparently was performed on the public stage. Even Jonson, experienced and successfully writing for the playhouses, feels the pull of the genre in his own two tragedies, *Sejanus* (performed in 1603) and *Catiline* (1611). They have passages of lively dialogue and even downscale humour, but they also have an uncharacteristic stiffness to them, and a propensity for lengthy set speeches. *Catiline* includes substantial portions of Cicero's *First Catilinarian* translated into blank verse; and, despite Jonson's seemingly confident defence of the absence of a neoclassical Chorus in the first play, he adds one to the second. To his longstanding indignation, neither is a hit.

These plays are worth listing to make clear the extent to which they follow the precedent set by *Ecerinis* in taking subjects not from the world of ancient mythology—the site of almost all surviving classical tragedies—but from history. With *Gorboduc* and *The Misfortunes of Arthur*, it is somewhat legendary history, but most of the others concern events and persons firmly in the historical record (Jonson's are researched with particular care), with a notable interest in the violent return of monarchical rule to classical Rome. The felt presence in Seneca's works of imperial Rome, indeed of Rome under Nero at a point of extreme political and moral crisis, seems to have been part of what caused Renaissance readers to respond to them in a way in which they did not respond to Greek tragedy even when they had access to it. The great political event arching over the European Renaissance, from the fourteenth into the seventeenth centuries, is the rise of a new strain of monarchical absolutism, and neo-Senecan tragedy participates in the encounter with that overwhelming and sometimes terrifying reality. (*Ecerinis* is about Ezzelino da Romano, one of the first of the new breed of Italian despots, and one of Neronian pathology.) Greville, defining the purpose of his own tragedies, distinguishes their purpose from that of the ancient writers 'to exemplify the disastrous miseries of man's life . . . and so, out of that melancholy vision, stir horror or murmur against divine providence', and from the modern desire 'to point out God's revenging aspect upon every particular sin, to the despair or confusion of mortality', by identifying them as fundamentally political parables about the lust for power, intended 'to trace out the highways of ambitious governors, and to show in the practice of life that the more audacity, advantage and good success such sovereignties have, the more they hasten to their own desolation and ruin' (Greville, *Prose Works*, 133). Contemporary relevance makes unstageability irrelevant: 'he that will behold these acts upon their true stage, let him look on that stage whereon himself is an actor, even the state he lives in, and for every part he may perchance find a player, and for every line (it may be) an instance of life beyond the author's intention or application . . . which whosoever readeth with this apprehension will not perchance think the scenes too long' (Greville, *Prose Works*, 135). Look about you; these plays are being performed in the real world.

The political focus most suitable to neo-Senecan dramaturgy is the court, a central institution of monarchical rule, but an incurably tricky one. It is presided over by a ruler of putatively total authority who is also reliant on an elite circle of highly competitive and alert subordinates with their own instinct for power. This was an environment that aristocrats knew well, some of them (like Greville) intimately. What remains compelling in *Gorboduc* is the play's taut, almost mathematical demonstration of such a circle flying apart by its own logic, with catastrophic consequences throughout society. The two princes generate a civil war through basically accurate assessments (mimicking the logic of Seneca's Atreus in *Thyestes*, ll. 192–204) of what the other has in mind, through the cascading dynamics of what in modern strategic planning is known as FUD (Fear Uncertainty Doubt). Ferrex quite sensibly reasons:

> sith I fear my younger brother's rage,
> And sith, perhaps, some other man may give
> Some like advice, to move his grudging head
> At mine estate—which counsel may perchance
> Take greater force with him than this with me—
> I will in secret so prepare myself,
> As if his malice or his lust to reign
> Break forth in arms or sudden violence,
> I may withstand his rage and keep mine own.
> (2. 1. 185–93)[23]

Porrex reacts to just these pre-emptive arrangements:

> And is it thus? And doth he so prepare
> Against his brother as his mortal foe?
> And now, while yet his aged father lives?
> Neither regards he him nor fears he me?
> War would he have? And he shall have it so!
> (2. 2. 1–5)

Porrex kill Ferrex, their mother kills Porrex, the commons in revolt kills both king and queen, and the Duke of Albany manœuvres cynically to exploit the chaos to his own advantage; the prospect in the last act is desolate:

> Lo, here the end of Brutus' royal line,
> And lo, the entry to the woeful wreck
> And utter ruin of this noble realm.
> (5. 2. 180–2)

All of this follows (as in *King Lear*) from the decision, unassailable at the time, of the king himself to divide his inheritance: 'Hereto it comes when kings will not consent | To grave advice, but follow wilful will' (5. 2. 234–5). The play's last lines anachronistically and not very hopefully suggest the importance of Parliament's having a say in the succession.

The spectacle clearly bore on the succession question in contemporary England, already an issue in the early years of Elizabeth's reign.[24] There is no evidence that she took offence, despite her documented sensitivity to possible references to her in contemporary drama. A touchier connection to the business of sovereign and courtier manifests itself at the end of the century. Greville, by his own account, destroys his *Antony and Cleopatra* because of its possibly perceived reference to Elizabeth and the Earl of Essex. We can only guess at how accurate such perceptions might have been, but Daniel's *Philotas*, the story (taken from Plutarch and Curtius) of a fatally ambitious member of the inner circle of Alexander the Great, displays striking and complex parallels with the same events at court.[25] By his own account, Daniel had written the first three acts before Essex's rebellion and execution, and finished the play with some trepidation afterwards; he prudently kept it from the public until after the accession of James. There is an impressive, if uncomfortable, multi-sidedness to the treatment. Philotas himself, confident of his special relationship with his king, is pre-emptively suspicious and competitive with his fellow courtiers, despite advice from his own father to ease up:

> Shall I let go the hold I have of grace,
> Gained with so hard adventures of my blood,
> And suffer others mount into my place,
> And from below look up to where I stood?
>
> . . . . .
>
> As if such men as I had any place
> To stay betwixt their ruin and their grace.
> Can any go beyond me, but they will
> Go over me, and trample on my state,
> And make their fortunes good upon my ill,
> Whilst fear hath power to wound me worse than hate?[26]

The hate his arrogance inspires proves lethally resourceful, as his rivals exploit a Hotspur-like recklessness to engineer a charge of treason. He is not exactly guilty, but he is incomplete in his commitment to the style of monarchy towards which his king is moving, with the self-serving consent of the rest of his court:

> Nor can I patiently endure this fond
> And strange proceeding of authority
> That hath engrossed up all into their hand
> By idol-living feeble majesty,
> And impiously do labor all they can
> To make the king forget he is a man.
>
> (*Philotas*, ll. 69–74; Daniel, *Complete Works*, 3. 109)

This defect of devotion on Philotas' part, combined with his delay in reporting a regicidal conspiracy of which he had heard, is sufficient to convince Alexander that the charge of treason is just. The end is unexpectedly unheroic; under torture Philotas loses all resolution, confesses to more overtly treasonous thoughts, implicates others, and astonishes Alexander all the more: 'I never thought a man that had a mind | T'attempt so much had had a heart so weak!' (*Philotas*, ll. 2172–3; Daniel, *Complete Works*, 3. 175).

This action is framed by an unusually provocative Chorus, a shade more active than usual, engaging the Nuntius directly in dialogue in the last act; at its entrance it proclaims itself the voice of independent judgement from below:

> We, as the Chorus of the vulgar, stand
> Spectators here to see these great men play
> Their parts both of obedience and command,

And censure all they do, and all they say.
(*Philotas*, ll. 407–10; Daniel,
Complete Works, 3. 121)

They are, moreover, a multicultural Chorus—'Three Grecians and a Persian'—and at the start of the last act the Persian speaks separately with a scathing evaluation of the political pretensions of the West:

Well, then I see there is small difference
Betwixt your state and ours, you civil Greeks,
You great contrivers of free governments,
Whose skill the world from out all countries seeks.
Those whom you call your kings are but the same
As are our sovereign tyrants of the East.

. . . . .

Only herein they differ, that your prince
Proceeds by form of law t' effect his end.
Our Persian monarch makes his frown convince
The strongest truth; his sword the process ends
With present death, and makes no more ado.
He never stands to give a gloss unto
His violence, to make it to appear
In other hue than that it ought to bear.
(*Philotas*, ll. 1790–5, 1802–9; Daniel,
Complete Works, 3. 166)

The Greeks are not vigorous in defending their culture's ways; the judgement on view is that what they all have just witnessed has been the exposure of Alexander as a hypocritical tyrant. Daniel includes with the printed text of the play a sceptical comment on the *vox populi* in this regard; readers should bear in mind that the Chorus judges 'vulgarly' and 'according to their affections, carried rather with compassion on great men's misfortunes than with the consideration of the cause' (*Complete Works*, 3. 106)—a remark in key with other signals that the author does not want to be identified with a position that could be construed as a defence of Essex. But the text of the play stands, and the Chorus has the last word in every act. The cultural *cachet* and ostentatious dignity of neo-Senecan dramaturgy sheltered a venue for exploring and engaging extremely sensitive aspects of contemporary power politics.[27]

The English Public Stage

The influence of classical tragedy on the public stage generally follows different paths. There is very little formal imitation at the level of the play as a whole. The five-act structure is an inheritance from comedy. Some of the formal terminology of classical drama is taken over; it is often being used in new ways, sometimes metaphorically ('What's past is prologue' (*Tempest*, 2. 1. 253)), though when Kyd opens *The Spanish Tragedy* with a dialogue between Andrea and the spirit of Revenge, he is specifically mimicking the prologue of Seneca's *Thyestes*. At the end of that scene Revenge says, 'Here sit we down to see the mystery, | And serve for Chorus in this Tragedy';[28] playwrights occcasionally include a character named Chorus, though its function is usually that of a presenter or master of ceremonies (as in *Henry V*). Patches of rapidly contentious dialogue look very much like an imitation of classical *stichomythia*:

> BASSANIO. Do all men kill the things they do not love?
>
> SHYLOCK. Hates any man the thing he would not kill?
>
> BASSANIO. Every offence is not a hate at first.
>
> SHYLOCK. What, wouldst thou have a serpent sting thee twice?
>
> (*Merchant of Venice*, 4. 1. 66–9)

(This in a play catalogued as a comedy.) The terms 'tragedy' and 'comedy' are, of course, in wide circulation, as is the sense that a play needs to be accompanied by an overt designation of its genre, though it is also clear that the simple classical binary does not meet all needs. Shakespeare's plays in the First Folio are grouped by genre, with Comedy first and Tragedy last, though between them is a third category, History (also a Greek word, but not in antiquity the designation of a dramatic genre). Samuel Johnson refused to use the traditional taxonomies for Shakespeare's plays and preferred the term 'mingled drama'.[29] Shakespeare himself recognized something funny about the determination to classify; the proliferation of categories is one of the metatheatrical jokes in *Hamlet*: 'tragedy, comedy, history, pastoral, pastoral–comical, historical–pastoral, tragical–historical, tragical–comical–historical–pastoral' (2. 2. 396–9). The most consequential of the new terms is 'tragicomedy' (see Tanya Pollard, Chapter 18, this volume). It has modest classical pedigree—Plautus applies it to his *Amphitryon*—and it becomes the focus of an innovative strain of Italian thinking about drama, culminating in Giambattista Guarini's widely read *Il compendio della poesia tragicomica* (1601); by way of John Fletcher's preface to *The Faithful Shepherdess* (1610) it becomes one of the most advanced developments of continental dramatic theory to gain a foothold in England. Sidney acknowledges the term, but plays it down, and is sure in any case that it cannot be used to authorize matching hornpipes and funerals; had Thomas Nashe seen the *Defence* in manuscript, he may have been twitting Sidney when he called *Astrophil and Stella* 'the tragicomedy of love . . . performed by starlight'.[30]

Identifiable quotations from the texts of classical tragedies are, unsurprisingly, from Seneca, and are scattered about the English dramatic corpus. In the usual way of these things, they are often not much more than something well said in one context that proves useful in another, though some of them testify to deeper affinities.

The bravura, not met with in Greek tragedy, with which Senecan characters boast of living up to their own names—'Medea superest' ('Medea remains') (*Medea* 166)—finds a natural home on the Renaissance stage: 'I am Duchess of Malfi still' (*Duchess of Malfi*, 4. 2. 139; Webster, *Works*, 1. 542).[31] So does the sinister aura that accompanies this Senecan motif. Medea is one of Seneca's villain heroes; the self-possession to which she is laying claim will enable her to requite the wrongs done to her through, first, the gruesome murder of her ex-husband's new wife and father-in-law, and then, to more chilling effect, the killing of her own two children—after which she escapes unhindered in a chariot drawn by a dragon. She is joined in this category by Atreus, who dominates Seneca's *Thyestes* and makes its last scene, which also involves the murder of innocent offspring, an even more extreme spectacle of unconstrained vindictive satisfaction. Newton is probably thinking mainly of Atreus when he expresses concern that some 'squeamish' readers of Seneca's tragedies might find them 'literally tending (at the first sight) sometime to the praise of ambition, sometime to the maintenance of cruelty, now and then to the approbation of incontinency, and here and there to the ratification of tyranny' (*Seneca His Ten Tragedies*, fo. A3^{v}). The translation of *Thyestes* in his collection has a new epilogue that ends the play with a call, only feebly heard in the original, for Atreus himself to receive due punishment.

The English stage still largely in the future when Newton wrote was to have its own portion of, in John Greene's hostile phrase, 'heroic evils'. Playwrights are (almost) always careful to see to it that their villains are punished in the end, but they regularly allow them a good deal of open space before that happens, and the opportunity to make themselves the most intelligent and interesting characters in sight. The dominant genre of the revenge tragedy is engineered to secure the audience's sympathy and identification with characters whose actions almost inevitably lead them to mortal sin and death, often by suicide or at the hands of justice. Seneca's tragedies do much to authorize such figures, and give them voice. It is Seneca's Clytemnestra who formulates the classic rationale for the villainous career: 'per scelera semper sceleribus semper est iter' ('For crimes the safest path is always through crimes') (*Agamemnon*, l. 115). Kyd quotes the line in Latin, slightly altered, in *The Spanish Tragedy* (3. 13. 6); in John Marston's *The Malcontent* the Latin is bandied stychomythically against its translation:

> MENDOZA. Black deed only through black deed safely flies.
>
> MALEVOLE. Pew! *Per scelera semper sceleribus tutum est iter*.[32]

Shakespeare's Richard III seems to have this playbook in mind, even as he shows signs of losing heart: 'Uncertain way of gain! But I am in | So far in blood that sin will pluck on sin' (*Richard III*, 4. 2. 63–4). Macbeth effectively translates Seneca's line: 'Things bad begun make strong themselves by ill' (*Macbeth*, 3. 2. 55). As the play progresses, we watch the sentiment drain of its energy: 'I am in blood | Stepp'd in so far that, should I wade no more, | Returning were as tedious as go o'er' (3. 4. 135–7).

Probably the most important contribution of Senecan drama to the public stage, however, is to its expansive rhetoric.[33] Discovery of the power of such rhetoric, especially as deployed through the resources of unrhymed iambic pentameter, is arguably the foundational event of Elizabethan tragedy in its mature phase; the Prologue to the first *Tamburlaine* seems to announce as much, linking the military might of the title character to the verbal skill of the actor speaking with power such as English theatre audiences had never heard before:

> From jigging veins of rhyming mother wits
> And such conceits as clownage keeps in pay,
> We'll lead you to the stately tent of war,
> Where you shall hear the Scythian Tamburlaine
> Threat'ning the world with high astounding terms
> And scourging kingdoms with his conquering sword.[34]

Several traditions, and a strong measure of original talent, feed into this new medium. Senecan dramatic declamation is one of these, its distinctive contribution being its cosmic sweep, by which at a stretch the actor's words are an assault on the universe itself. Atreus at his moment of fulfilment touches the heavens: 'Aequalis astris gradior et cunctos super | altum superbo vertice attingens polum' ('Peer of the stars I stride, out-topping all, my proud head reaching to the lofty sky') (*Thyestes*, ll. 885–6). The previous Chorus announces that Atreus' actions have in fact driven the stars from the sky; the night is utterly dark, filled by the avenger's triumph. Tamburlaine's rhetoric seeks a similar end:

> Our quivering lances shaking in the air,
> And bullets like Jove's dreadful thunderbolts,
> Enrolled in flames and fiery smoldering mists,
> Shall threat the gods more than Cyclopean wars,
> And with our sun-bright armor as we march
> We'll chase the stars from heaven, and dim their eyes
> That stand and muse at our admirèd arms.
>
> (*1 Tamburlaine*, 2. 3. 18–24)

The drama of such rhetoric is not only its success; its failure is just as telling, as in Hieronimo's frustration in *The Spanish Tragedy*:

> still tormented is my tortured soul
> With broken sighs and restless passions
> That winged mount and, hovering in the air,
> Beat at the windows of the brightest heavens,
> Soliciting for justice and revenge.
> But they are placed in those empyreal heights,
> Where, countermured with walls of diamond,
> I find the place impregnable, and they
> Resist my woes, and give my words no way.
>
> (3. 7. 10–18)

At some of Renaissance tragedy's supreme moments, language like this is unbearably contrary to fact:

> Howl, howl, howl! O, you are men of stones!
> Had I your tongues and eyes, I'ld use them so
> That heaven's vault should crack. She's gone for ever!
> I know when one is dead, and when one lives;
> She's dead as earth.
>
> (*King Lear*, 5. 3. 258–62)

Specific Senecan moments have their own history. A geographical trope reaches to the borders of the Roman Empire and beyond to dramatize the speaker's sense of inexpiable guilt:

> quis Tanais aut quis Nilus aut quis Persica
> violentus unda Tigris aut Rhenus ferox
> Tagusve Hibera turbidus gaza fluens
> abluere dextram poterit? Arctoum licet
> Maeotis in me gelida transfundat mare
> et tota Tethys per meas currat manus,
> haerebit altum facinus.
>
> (*Hercules*, ll. 1323–9; also at *Phaedra*, ll. 715–18)

(What Tanais or what Nile or what Persian Tigris with its violent waters or fierce Rhine or Tagus, turbid with Spanish treasure, can wash my right hand clean? Though chill Maeotis should pour its northern seas over me and all the Ocean stream across my hands, the deed will stay deeply ingrained.)

John Marston imitates this passage closely in *The Insatiate Countess*;[35] Shakespeare condenses it and then answers the rhetorical question in a way that extends the hyperbole:

> Will all great Neptune's ocean wash this blood
> Clean from my hand? No; this my hand will rather
> The multitudinous seas incarnadine,
> Making the green one red.
>
> (*Macbeth*, 2. 2. 57–60)[36]

The guilt is now itself a grand act of aggression against the outside world.

The guilt in Hercules' case is that of a genuine hero, but one whose speech of victory over the play's initial villain had—in a prime example of what Bottom the Weaver calls 'Ercles' vein, a tyrant's vein' (*Midsummer Night's Dream*, 1. 2. 40)—graded into a madness in which he murdered his own wife and children.[37] When he woke into sanity, he beheld the evidence of what he had done, and the rest of the play is his response to that tragic knowledge. The beginning of that return to consciousness is one of Senecan drama's famous moments:

Quis hic locus, quae regio, quae mundi plaga?
ubi sum? sub ortu solis, an sub cardine
glacialis Ursae? numquid Hesperii maris
extrema tellus hunc dat Oceano modum?
quas trahimus auras? quod solum fesso subest?
certe redimus.

(*Hercules*, ll. 1138–43)

(What place is this, what region, what tract of the earth? Where am I? Beneath the sun's rising, or beneath the turning point of the icy Bear? Can this be the limit set to Ocean's waters by the farthest land on the western sea? What air do I breathe? What ground lies under my weary body? Certainly I have returned.)

The first words of the main character in George Chapman's *The Conspiracy of Charles, Duke of Byron* unmistakably quote the first line of that speech before moving on, seemingly, to something different:

What place is this? what air? what region?
In which a man may hear the harmony
Of all things moving? Hymen marries here
Their ends and uses, and makes me his temple.[38]

Dazzled by the magnificence of the court of Archduke Albert, Byron feels that he is coming in contact with something fine and wonderful beyond his experience. In fact, as we know from the play's first scene, Byron—another stage character likely to make the original audience think of Essex—is the target of a conspiracy to seduce him away from his loyalty to the King of France; the drug entering his bloodstream to megalomaniac effect is the first flush of that exhilarating derangement that will lead to his treason and eventual execution. Not only does Seneca's line serve Chapman's immediate purposes, but recognizing the original context gives the moment new depth and power. The same is even more the case with Shakespeare's version of mad Hercules waking to reality:

Where have I been? Where am I? Fair daylight?
I am mightily abus'd; I should ev'n die with pity
To see another thus. I know not what to say.
I will not swear these are my hands.

(*King Lear*, 4. 7. 51–4)

The language is much simpler, less showy—not in fact anything that you would call Senecan rhetoric. But the deep connection is there, though the meaning of the connection is precisely in the unbelievably blessed reversal of what Lear thought he would and should awake to. He has not in fact deprived himself of the child whom he has come to feel is everything. Seeing Cordelia, he assumes that she is dead, and he is in a hell of eternal torment for what he has done:

> Thou art a soul in bliss, but I am bound
> Upon a wheel of fire, that mine own tears
> Do scald like molten lead.
>
> (4. 7. 45–7)

But it is not so. Despite everything he had a right to expect, she is not lost, and he is not damned—a miraculous redemption whose very beauty sets up the most devastating of Shakespeare's tragic conclusions.[39]

Shakespeare's Career

Shakespeare's name keeps coming up here; it is the one that still—properly—counts the most for us, and it has attracted the most sophisticated scholarly attention on a topic that cannot be searched quickly but relies on sustained and patient attention to achieve results. Those results are not necessarily a measure of the importance of classical literature for Shakespeare in comparison with other playwrights (for Jonson and Chapman it unquestionably ranks higher), or of the importance of classical tragedy within his own work. (For a discussion of Shakespeare's classicism generally, see Colin Burrow, Chapter 27, this volume.) By all counts, the most significant classical writers for Shakespeare were, by a considerable margin, Ovid and Plutarch. There does seem to have been some self-consciousness in the way in which Shakespeare (probably) began his career as a tragic playwright with a conspicuously 'Senecan' tragedy, *Titus Andronicus*; but that play does not resemble a Senecan play to anything like the degree to which its opposite number in the alternate genre, *The Comedy of Errors*, resembles a play of Plautus. *Titus* does include brief quotations in Latin from Seneca's *Phaedra* (and from Ovid's *Metamorphoses* and Horace's *Odes*), and there are patches of rhetoric in the hyperbolic Senecan style. The feature that most marks the play as 'Senecan' in the memory is the climactic outrage of what is usually called a Thyestean banquet. There is a similar banquet, however, in the story of Philomela in Ovid, and the storyline there is a significantly closer match; Titus's daughter earlier endures a rape and mutilation modelled on Philomela's, and she later tells her father what has happened with the help, onstage, of a copy of the *Metamorphoses*. Nor does the play, despite what seems to have been considerable success with audiences, set much of a pattern for Shakespeare's mature tragedies. Those begin with *Julius Caesar*, midwived by fresh and extensive use of Plutarch's *Lives*; Shakespeare mines that source even more aggressively for his last works in the genre.[40] Even on the local level of verbal echoes from available English translations, Golding's Ovid and North's Plutarch are far more of a presence in Shakespeare's language throughout his career than is *Seneca His Ten Tragedies*. The relevance of Senecan drama to Shakespeare's work is by now well established, and may have aspects and details still to be revealed, but it does not need to be overstated.

Still, it is possible that, at the end of Shakespeare's career, Senecan drama, though not Seneca's own text, plays a part in the haunting valedictories of *The Tempest*. Scholarly unhappiness with the tradition of seeing Prospero as Shakespeare's self-portrait and the play as his farewell to the stage has not made that tradition go away; whatever the intended autobiographical reference, the psychology of leave-taking is written too deeply into the play itself. Part of the leave-taking is literary. The play contains Shakespeare's longest sustained imitation of a specific passage in Ovid, Prospero's summoning of the magical spirits at his command at the beginning of the last act; he summons those powers in preparation to dismissing them by, he says at the end of the speech, drowning the book that has been the source of all his magic. More than one critic has been unable to resist the implication that that book is a copy of the *Metamorphoses*. In the play's Epilogue, there is a briefer speech in which the character Prospero, praying for God's mercy, merges into the actor playing him, asking for applause; whoever he is, he must do so because he has now surrendered his magic: 'Now my charms are all o'erthrown, | And what strength I have's mine own, | Which is most faint' (ll. 1–3). The speech is not usually thought to have any particular source, but it does have precedent.

On 8 February 1592 Seneca's *Phaedra* (here called *Hippolytus*) was performed in Latin at Christ Church, Oxford, in a text with additions by the well-known neo-Latin dramatist and poet (and defender of the theatre against the puritan John Rainolds) William Gager.[41] It was the culmination of something of a festival in Gager's honour; two of his other plays had been performed on the previous two days. The additions were published later the same year in the appendix to an edition of Gager's *Meleager*. One of them is an epilogue in which the speaker asks for the audience's approval with a nautical metaphor:

Videte quaeso, vestra cui nostrum freto
Humanitatis aura commisit gregem.
Huc usque vela dedimus, hic terra procul,
Tenemur alto.

(ll. 1–4)

(Behold, I pray, what sea the breath of your kindness has committed my troop to. To this point we have set sail till now; here, far from land, we are held in the deep.)

It is a metaphor that Prospero will use; the wind in my sails must now come from your applause:

I must be here confin'd by you,
Or sent to Naples.

. . . . .

Gentle breath of yours my sails
Must fill, or else my project fails,
Which was to please.

(Epilogue, ll. 4–5, 11–13)

In a shift also anticipating Prospero—'Let your indulgence set me free' (l. 20)—Gager's epilogue suddenly heightens approval into forgiveness—'Veniam precari iussit obnixe Chorus; | date quaeso veniam' ('The Chorus has urged strenuously that your pardon should be entreated. Grant indulgence I beseech you'). And suddenly the moment gets startlingly personal:

> hanc etiam dari
> Unam labori postulat stipem ultimo,
> Qui saepe fecit fabulas vobis dari.
> Sed hic habebit barbiton paries suum,
> Hic arma figit, hic equum solvit senem,
> Artemque, caestusque hic reponit ludicros.
> (ll. 14–19)

(He who has often caused plays to be given to you, asks this one reward for his latest labour. But here, the wall will have his lyre, here, he hangs up his arms, here, he frees his aged horse. Here he lays aside his art and the comic gloves.)

Gager was to live another thirty years, but this was indeed his last work for the theatre. The authorial gesture widely intuited in Prospero's epilogue is here overt.

Notes

1. See Charles E. Butterworth, *Averroes' Middle Commentary on Aristotle's Poetics* (Princeton, 1986), 59, 66–7. As Borges tells the story in 'Averroës' Search' (1949), the learned Arab cannot grasp what a theatrical performance is even when he hears one described by a world traveller: Jorge Luis Borges, *Collected Fictions*, trans. Andrew Hurley (New York, 1998), 235–41. The fortunes of 'tragedy' in the Middle Ages are detailed by Henry Ansgar Kelly, *Ideas and Forms of Tragedy from Aristotle to the Middle Ages* (Cambridge, 1993).
2. Robert S. Haller (ed. and trans.), *Literary Criticism of Dante Alighieri* (Lincoln, NE, 1973), 100.
3. *Inferno* 20. 113; *The Divine Comedy*, ed. and trans. Charles S. Singleton (Princeton, 1970–5), 1. 210–11.
4. *Troilus and Criseyde*, 5. 1786, in Geoffrey Chaucer, *The Riverside Chaucer*, gen. ed. Larry D. Benson, 3rd edn (Boston, 1987).
5. Julius Caesar Scaliger, *Poetices Libri Septem* (Lyons, 1561), 144 (bk 3, ch. 97); my translation.
6. John Greene, *A Refutation of the Apology for Actors* (1615), 55–6.
7. e. g. Simon Critchley, approaching Racine by way of Heidegger and Levinas: 'The mood that accompanies this experience of being riveted to existence is not anxiety or fear, but rather *horror*' ('Phaedra's Malaise', in Rita Felski (ed.), *Rethinking Tragedy* (Baltimore, 2008), 181).
8. Sir Philip Sidney, *Defence of Poesy*, in *Miscellaneous Prose of Sir Philip Sidney*, ed. Katherine Duncan-Jones and Jan van Dorsten (Oxford, 1973), 112–13, 115.
9. So also John Webster in his introduction to *The White Devil* (1612): 'If it be objected this is no true dramatic poem, I shall easily confess it . . . willingly and not ignorantly in this kind have I faulted; for should a man present to such an auditory

the most sententious tragedy that ever was written, observing all the critical laws, as height of style and gravity of person, enrich it with the sententious Chorus, and as it were liven death in the passionate and weighty Nuntius, yet after all this divine rapture ... the breath that comes from the uncapable multitude is able to poison it' (*Works of John Webster*, ed. David Gunby et al., 3 vols (Cambridge, 1995–2007), 1. 140).

10. *Castelvetro on the Art of Poetry*, ed. and trans. Andrew Bongiorno (Binghamton, NY, 1984), 19; see Bongiorno's introduction, pp. xvii–xx.
11. I draw here and below on the information and speculations of Louise Schleiner, 'Latinized Greek Drama in Shakespeare's Writing of *Hamlet*', *Shakespeare Quarterly*, 41 (1990), 29–48. Her arguments for Shakespeare's direct access to Greek tragedy by way of such translations are intelligent but necessarily inferential; she makes a particularly striking case that the closet scene in *Hamlet* is prompted by some lines in Euripides's *Orestes* (ll. 287–91); see p. 37. Other strong claims for Shakespeare's direct use of Euripides are made by Emrys Jones, *The Origins of Shakespeare* (Oxford, 1977), 85–118; on larger affinities, however mediated, between Shakespeare and his Attic predecessors, see Michael Silk, 'Shakespeare and Greek Tragedy: Strange Relationship', in Charles Martindale and A. B. Taylor (eds), *Shakespeare and the Classics* (Cambridge, 2004), 241–57.
12. For a comprehensive view of English translations of classical tragedy, Greek and Latin, during the Renaissance, see Gordon Braden, 'Tragedy', in Peter France and Stuart Gillespie (eds), *The Oxford History of Literary Translation in English* (Oxford, 2005–), 2. 262–72.
13. The translation may have been informed by the similar fate of Lady Jane Gray, Lumley's namesake and first cousin; see Lorraine Helms, *Seneca by Candlelight and Other Stories of Renaissance Drama* (Philadelphia, 1997), 66–75.
14. The first systematic study was that of John W. Cunliffe, *The Influence of Seneca on Elizabethan Tragedy* (1893). Vigorous arguments that Cunliffe and others seriously overstated that influence were advanced by Howard Baker, *Induction to Tragedy* (Baton Rouge, LA, 1930), 30–41, 107–53; and G. K. Hunter, 'Seneca and the Elizabethans: A Case Study in "Influence"' (1967), in *Dramatic Identities and Cultural Tradition* (Liverpool, 1978), 159–73; the principal counter-statements have been Gordon Braden, *Renaissance Tragedy and the Senecan Tradition: Anger's Privilege* (New Haven, 1985), and Robert S. Miola, *Shakespeare and Classical Tragedy: The Influence of Seneca* (Oxford, 1992).
15. George Steiner, '"Tragedy," Reconsidered', in Felski (ed.), *Rethinking Tragedy*, 31–2; also 'Tragedy, Pure and Simple', in Michael Silk (ed.), *Tragedy and the Tragic* (Oxford, 1996), 535–6. The sentiment, first attested in the elegiacs of Theognis (ll. 425–8), is widely quoted in Greek literature and becomes proverbial.
16. *Seneca, His Tenne Tragedies*, ed. Thomas Newton (1581; fac. repr. New York, 1967), fo. 70^{v}.
17. *Seneca, His Ten Tragedies*, fos 142^{r}, 214^{r}. In the case of *Hamlet*, the phrase that Shakespeare appears to take over is generated by a misprint; see A. B. Taylor, 'Two Notes on Shakespeare and the Translators', *Review of English Studies*, NS 38 (1987), 522–4.
18. Thomas Nashe, in his preface to Robert Greene's *Menaphon* (1589), in Thomas Nashe, *Works*, ed. Ronald B. McKerrow, rev. F. P. Wilson, 5 vols (Oxford, 1958), 3. 315. 'Blood is a beggar' is often thought to be a quotation—one of two to survive—from the so-called *Ur-Hamlet* from which Shakespeare started.

19. Fulke Greville, *A Dedication to Sir Philip Sidney*; in *The Prose Works of Fulke Greville, Lord Brooke*, ed. John Gouws (Oxford, 1986), 134.
20. Hughes's play is almost parodically larded with direct translations of passages in Seneca; they are the main exhibit in Cunliffe, *The Influence of Seneca*, 130–55.
21. Systematically surveyed by Alexander Maclaren Witherspoon, *The Influence of Robert Garnier on Elizabethan Drama* (New Haven, 1924), though attempts to use the resulting plays as evidence of a well-defined literary movement centred on Mary Sidney now seem unfounded: see Mary Ellen Lamb, 'The Myth of the Countess of Pembroke: The Dramatic Circle', *Yearbook of English Studies*, 11 (1981), 194–202.
22. Shakespeare seems to have known Daniel's play; see Geoffrey Bullough, *Narrative and Dramatic Sources of Shakespeare* (1957–75), 5. 231–6.
23. I quote from *Gorboduc; or, Ferrex and Porrex*, ed. Irby B. Cauthen, Jr (Lincoln, NE, 1970).
24. The connection is somewhat oblique in the published text of the play, but a recently discovered eyewitness account reports more explicit dialogue on the subject in the first performance; see Greg Walker, *The Politics of Performance in Early Renaissance Drama* (Cambridge, 1998), 210–21.
25. See *The Tragedy of Philotas by Samuel Daniel*, ed. Laurence Michel, 2nd edn (Hamden, CT, 1970), 36–66; with recent refinements by Hugh Gazzard, '"Those Graue Presentments of Antiquitie": Samuel Daniel's *Philotas* and the Earl of Essex', *Review of English Studies*, NS 51 (2000), 423–50, and Kevin Curran, 'Treasonous Silence: *The Tragedy of Philotas* and Legal Epistemology', *English Literary Renaissance*, 42 (2012), 58–89.
26. *Philotas*, ll. 7–10, 15–20, in Samuel Daniel, *The Complete Works in Verse and Prose*, ed. Alexander B. Grosart, 5 vols (1885–96), 3. 107–8.
27. Cary's *Mariam*, the first original dramatic text by a woman to be published in England, deals with gender relations in a charged political context. The story is that of a queen killed by an irrationally, uncontrollably jealous monarch: *Othello* with Desdemona as the main character and a husband who is also king. In a subplot the unhappily married Cary dramatizes what is said to be the first Jewish divorce initiated by the wife; the divorcee in question is also the play's most resourceful villain—her machinations see to it that her ex-husband does not live to the end of day—but she does get away with it. There is a critical edition by Barry Weller and Margaret W. Ferguson (Berkeley and Los Angeles, 1994); see also Marta Straznicky, '"Profane Stoical Paradoxes": *The Tragedie of Mariam* and Sidneian Closet Drama', *English Literary Renaissance*, 24 (1994), 104–34.
28. *The Spanish Tragedy*, 1. 1. 90–1, in *The Works of Thomas Kyd*, ed. Frederick S. Boas (Oxford, 1967), 7.
29. See *Johnson on Shakespere*, ed. Walter Raleigh (Oxford, 1925), 15–18.
30. *Sir P. S. His Astrophel and Stella* (1591), sig. A3[r].
31. See Braden, *Renaissance Tragedy and the Senecan Tradition*, 33–4, 67–9.
32. John Marston, *The Malcontent*, 5. 3. 15–17, in *The Selected Plays of John Marston*, ed. MacDonald P. Jackson and Michael Neill (Cambridge, 1986), 274.
33. I put this case in Braden, *Renaissance Tragedy and the Senecan Tradition*, 175 ff. The subject has received extended treatment within a broadly literary and philosophical context by Christopher D. Johnson, *Hyperboles: The Rhetoric of Excess in Baroque Literature and Thought* (Cambridge, MA, 2010), 279–333.

34. 1 *Tamburlaine*, Prologue 1–6, in *The Complete Works of Christopher Marlowe*, ed. Roma Gill et al., 5 vols (Oxford, 1987–98), 5. 6.
35. John Marston, *The Insatiate Countess*, 5. 1. 40–4, in *The Works of John Marston*, ed. A. H. Bullen, 3 vols (1887), 3. 225.
36. The twist may have been suggested to Shakespeare by another passage in Seneca (*Phaedra* 551–2), or by lines in Anthony Munday and Henry Chettle's Robin Hood plays; see Kenneth Muir's note in his edition of *Macbeth* (1953), 57–8.
37. For an overview of English Renaissance interest in the story, see Rolf Soellner, 'The Madness of Hercules and the Elizabethans', *Comparative Literature*, 10 (1958), 309–24. This interest contaminates reporting of a horrifically similar happening in contemporary Yorkshire, where a respectable country gentleman murdered two of his sons and tried to murder his wife and another son. The killer had used his dagger, but the title page of the pamphlet telling the story (*Two Most Unnatural and Bloody Murders* (1605)) shows him, like Hercules, swinging a club against his family. The anonymous short play based on the pamphlet, *A Yorkshire Tragedy*, has sometimes been attributed to Shakespeare.
38. *The Works of George Chapman*, ed. R. H. Shepherd and A. C. Swinburne (1904–24), 1. 218. See Gunilla Florby, *Echoing Texts: George Chapman's Conspiracy and Tragedy of Charles Duke of Byron* (Lund, 2004), 41–2.
39. As far as I know, the first critic to note the connection is Miola, *Shakespeare and Classical Tragedy*, 165–9; see also Gordon Braden, 'Herakles and Hercules: Survival in Greek and Roman Tragedy (with a Coda on *King Lear*)', in Ruth Scodel (ed.), *Theater and Society in the Classical World* (Ann Arbor, 1993), 257–61. T. S. Eliot quotes the first line of the Senecan speech in Latin as the epigraph to his 'Marina', a poem of mysterious Lear-like waking.
40. Strong claims have been made in this connection: 'I believe that it was from Plutarch that Shakespeare learned how to make a tragedy of the kind exemplified in *Hamlet* and *Othello, Macbeth* and *Lear*. It was, I think, in the course of writing *Julius Caesar* that he learned it' (J. A. K. Thomson, *Shakespeare and the Classics* (1952), 242). Plutarch himself, of course, was more familiar than we can be with Greek tragedy, and scholars have come to appreciate how his own artfulness in narrative and characterization is linked to that tradition. Reading Plutarch may have put Shakespeare in touch with Greek tragedy in ways that went beyond the numerous brief quotations in the *Lives*; see C. B. R. Pelling, 'Seeing a Roman Tragedy through Greek Eyes: Shakespeare's *Julius Caesar*', in Simon Goldhill and Edith Hall (eds), *Sophocles and the Greek Tragic Tradition* (Cambridge, 2009), 264–88.
41. See J. W. Binns, 'William Gager's Additions to Seneca's *Hippolytus*', *Studies in the Renaissance*, 17 (1970), 153–91; the text and translation quoted are on pp. 182–3.

CHAPTER 17

Comedy

BRUCE R. SMITH

'Laughable' is a category of experience recognized in cultures all over the world, throughout time. In fact, according to Aristotle, laughter is one of the things that make humans *human*. Susceptibility to tickling is another. 'That man alone is affected by tickling is due firstly to the delicacy of his skin,' Aristotle observes in *Parts of Animals*, 'and secondly to his being the only animal that laughs'.[1] Earlier in the same treatise Aristotle has noted that 'flesh is softer in man than in any other animal'—hence man's possession of 'the most delicate sense of touch' among all animals (660^{a}11–14). And hence Aristotle's astonishing conclusion in *The Soul*: 'That is why man is the most intelligent of animals' (421^{a}22).[2]

Intellect, touch, laughter: the connections among these three aspects of human experience provide a promising route for exploring the reception of Greek and Latin comedy in England from 1558 to 1660. The importance of laughter and intellect in this enterprise should be obvious. But *touch*? Fundamental to Aristotle's notion of *katharsis* in the *Poetics* is synergy between the feelings (*pathê*) experienced by the characters in the fiction and the feelings experienced by spectators and listeners. The responses that drama touches off are *visceral*: someone who is merely 'hearing the events unroll *shudders* with fear and *feels* pity at what happens'.[3] Aristotle is anxious to detach *katharsis* from the masks, costumes, vociferations, and gestures of live performance, but it is nonetheless a vicarious sense of touch that explains why fictional events exert such imaginative power. And when those events *are* witnessed in person—in a theatre, in a marketplace, in the great hall of a palace, in a college chapel—the power is all the greater.[4] To account for the interplay of laughter, intellect, and touch, we might define 'tickled minds' as the object of our search in these pages.

Comedy with a Twist

In its universality 'laughable' would seem to be different from 'pitiable-and-fearful', the latter a category of experience quite specific to the culture of Athens in the fifth century BCE and to the cultures, including Rome, that took up 'goat-song' (from *tragos* goat + *oide* song) as their own measure of human aspiration and human limitation.[5] It would be a mistake, however, to equate 'laughable' and 'comic' and assume that 'comic' is likewise universal. Susceptibility to the 'laughable' may, as Aristotle claims, be a fact of human biology, but 'village-song' (from *kṓmē* village + *oidos* singer (*OED*, 'comedy, *n.*[1]', etymology)) is no less a social construct than 'goat-song'?

The artefacted nature of comedy—its status as a made thing, something specific to Greek and Latin culture—is captured in the two definitions of *comedia* supplied by the fourth-century grammarian Aelius Donatus in the *Excerpt on Comedy* that was printed in most editions of Terence in the fifteenth, sixteenth, and seventeenth centuries. The first definition Donatus takes from his contemporary Diomedes: '*Comoedia* is a story made up of diverse matters concerning civil and private passions ['diuersa instituta continens affectuum ciuilium ac priuatorum'], by which are distinguished what is useful in life and what should be avoided.'[6] Note the interface here between 'civil' and 'private', precisely with respect to passions or (as we would now say) emotions or (as I would say with Aristotle) touch. Comedy in Diomedes' definition is located just where society and the individual touch. Hamlet captures the tactile immediacy of the relationship between society and the individual when he enumerates the purposes of play-acting: 'to hold as 'twere the mirror up to nature: to show Virtue her feature, Scorn her own image, and the very age and body of the time his form and pressure' (*Hamlet*, 3. 2. 21–4). Quoting from a text by Cicero that seems not to have survived today, Donatus anticipates Hamlet in offering a second definition of *comedia* as an 'imitation of life, mirror of custom, image of truth' ('imitationem uitae, speculum consuetudinis, imaginem ueritatis'). 'Imitation', 'mirror', 'image': the hand of a craftsman is implicit in all three objects. 'Life' may seem to gesture towards an unchanging phenomenon, but 'custom' certainly changes with place and time, perhaps calling into question the universal status of 'truth'.

So familiar have certain precepts from Donatus become—an opposition between tragedy and comedy, a register of stock character types, division of stage time into five acts, a narrative move from exposition to complication to resolution, even the moral seriousness of comedy—that it may be hard for us to appreciate what an odd intrusion the texts of Aristophanes, Plautus, and Terence were in western Europe's already established culture of laughter. Anglo-Saxon riddles, 'The Miller's Tale', the *Second Shepherds' Play*, the Vice that romps through morality plays, even the conceptual schemes of *The Divine Comedy* and *Troilus and Creseyde* should make us realize that the denizens of England in the fifteenth and early sixteenth centuries hardly needed Aristophanes, Plautus, and Terence to teach them how to laugh.

If not how to laugh, Terence taught sixteenth- and seventeenth-century Europeans how to think about what they were laughing at. Terence owed that influence to the central place his plays assumed in humanist schemes of education. Cicero gave humanist educators their cue. Cicero is always quoting Terence, praising his stylistic elegance, and commending his memorable formulations of moral truths. 'My familiar Terence said in his comedy Andria, that soothing [*obsequium*, flattery] getteth friends, and truth doth purchase hatred,' Cicero declares in John Harington's 1562 translation of Cicero's dialogue *On Friendship*.[7] (A marginal tag supplied by Harington explains, 'Familiar because he used to read his books' (sig. H1).) A few lines later Cicero is quoting Terence's *obsequium* again, 'because I delight to use Terence['s] word' (sig. H1^{v}). After such a recommendation, it should come as no surprise that Erasmus in his treatise *On the Plan of Study* (*De Ratione Studii* (1512)) gives pride of place among Latin writers to Terence: 'He is pure, concise, and closest to everyday speech.'[8] In this short sentence are contained three reasons why Roman comedy became much more important than it had been in the Middle Ages: not only did it offer the models of style and ethical formulations that Cicero had commended but it facilitated learning to speak the pure Latin of antiquity and to put that language to use in the here-and-now.[9]

The reception of Greek and Latin comedy, in England as all over Europe, took shape, in Robert Miola's apt phrase, as a 'project of domestication' in which influences can be seen to run both ways.[10] Plautus and Terence had been engaged in just such an exercise vis-à-vis Greek comedy, in particular the plays of Menander. Plautus' own word for what he did to his Greek originals was *uertere*, literally 'to turn'. As Erich Segal notes, the notion survives in the English word 'version'.[11] A less formal word might be 'twist'. Plautus and Terence offer their own twists on Greek comedy, just as English writers, in turn, offer their twists on Plautus and Terence. The challenge for a literary historian is to discern the patterns in those movements.

Chronologically, three stages in the domestication of classical comedy in English Renaissance culture suggest themselves: (1) an early period, from 1558 to about 1580, in which continental humanist culture determined how classical comedy was studied in schools and colleges, performed at court, and cited by authors, (2) a middle period beginning in the 1580s when a distinctively British tradition took shape in which classical comedy was thoroughly naturalized in translations and Plautus- and Terence-inspired plays in London's public theatres, and (3) a later period, beginning in the late 1640s, when hostility to performance, even in schools and colleges, turned classical drama back into closet drama and the debate between 'ancients' and 'moderns' reframed Greek and Latin scripts as things set apart from contemporary English culture. We might describe these three periods in terms supplied by Donatus, as a story with a prologue (enacted in this introduction), a beginning (*protasis*) from 1558 to 1580, a middle (*epitasis*) from the 1580s to the late 1640s, and an end (*catastrophe*) from the late 1640s to the 1660s.[12]

Using either way of dividing up the story, we can follow the domestication of classical comedy in England on three fronts: publication, performance, and criticism. While it would be easy to assume that criticism is something that evolved within the pages of books, I have purposefully put it third, because criticism was always in dialogue—sometimes in hostile dialogue—with the visceral experience of live performance. Laughter, intellect, and the forms of emotional engagement that I have been calling touch give us three continuing reference points for gauging a shift from deference to assimilation to perspective-distancing in the reception of classical comedy.

Protasis: Humanist Harmony

Unlike Anglo-Saxon riddles told in person, unlike outdoor performances of the *Second Shepherds' Play*, unlike 'The Miller's Tale' or *Troilus and Creseyde* read aloud to audiences assembled in great halls and merchants' houses, classical comedy presented itself, in the first instance, as a book. The very touch of editions of Terence in schoolboys' hands is captured in one of the dialogues in Mathurin Cordier's *Colloquia Scholastica* (1564, first English translation 1584):

> [*Austine.*] What new gilded book is this, which thou makest ostentation of so highly [*Rodig.*] Terence. *A.* Where [was it] printed. *R.* At Paris. *A.* Who gave it thee? *R.* I bought it with my money . . . *A.* . . . of whom hast thou bought this Terence? *R.* Of Clement. *A* What of that book-seller that goeth about from market to market? *R.* Yea verely. *A.* How much cost it? *R.* Ten pence. *A.* Nothing more? *R.* Nothing at all. *A.* Truly the price [is] cheap enough. *R.* Especially seeing it is gilded, and so finely bound up. *A.* Were there not other books like? *R.* Two or three. *A.* I pray thee bring me to him. *R.* Let us go.[13]

The edition of Terence being described in this dialogue from the 1560s was small enough to be taken in hand and carried around, but behind it lay much larger and heavier books: manuscripts that kept Terence's texts in circulation throughout the Middle Ages and printed folios that redacted Terence's texts according to modern ideas of editing. What gave both sorts of books, the manuscripts and the folios, their weight were introductions and passage-by-passage commentaries that turned 1,000-line scripts into 300-page tomes. In spirit and in substance these books were *scholastic* enterprises: introductions like Donatus' *Excerpt on Comedy* and marginal *scholia* on words, lines, and speeches brought to Terence's plays the same close attention that Thomas Aquinas brought to bear on Aristotle's treatises.

From the beginning of print in England, when Richard Pynson issued separate runs of Terence's comedies in 1495 and 1497 and Wynkyn de Worde published Terence's collected plays in 1504, English printings followed continental exemplars including not only Donatus' paraphernalia but treatises and running commentaries by modern scholars.[14] De Worde's 1504 edition includes the introduction and commentary of Jodocus Badius Ascensius (aka Josse Bade), heavily indebted to Donatus, that had first been published at Lyons in 1493. In their marginal notes commentators like Badius were interested in three things in particular: philology (in this context *this* word means *that*), aesthetics (note the elegant way Terence orders this speech), and ethics (this speech describes the duties of sons to fathers). By contrast, Richard Pynson's quarto printings of Terence's plays as separate jobs in 1495 and 1497, though probably designed to be bound together into a collected works, can be credited with inaugurating a second printing tradition in England: small-scale plain texts designed for use in schools. Schoolmasters could crib their knowledge from the likes of de Worde's folio; their students honed their skills on cheaper plain texts. This downsizing and streamlining must have been handy in more ways than one: it could easily be carried around by schoolboys such as Austine and Rodig. In the enterprise of printing classical comedy in England in the sixteenth century, Terence enjoyed a monopoly. Between 1558 and 1660 not a single Latin edition of Plautus was printed in England or Scotland and only one edition of the Greek text of just one of Aristophanes' plays, *Hippeis* (*The Knights*).[15]

Erasmus in his treatise *On the Method of Study* sets an agenda for reading and interpreting Roman comedy that takes note of the aesthetics of style and structure but, in terms of touch, would seem to admit, in the last analysis, only two responses: sober approbation of the moral lesson and ridicule of the characters' moral depravity. Take, for example, the maxim from Terence's *Andria* that Cicero quotes in the dialogue *On Friendship*: 'soothing getteth friends, and truth doth purchase hatred.' Erasmus' agenda offers two ways of taking that. The readiest way is to extract the statement from the play and set it off as a universal truth, as Cicero does. In the dramatic context, however, the maxim is spoken directly to the audience, as an aside, by the freed slave Sosia, who, true to his type, offers an ironic commentary on his social betters (in this case, the blocking father-figure Simo) and serves as an intermediary between the audience and the play. The point of the whole enterprise is ethical judgement, including the self-affirming ridicule provoked by that judgement.

Boys such as Austin and Rodig did not just *read* Terence; they learned to *speak* him. The full title of John Brinsley's translation of Cordier emphasizes that the dialogues are devised to foster '*the more speedy attaining to the knowledge of the Latin tongue, for writing and speaking Latin*'. Learning to speak Latin like one's native tongue was fundamental to the way Plautus and Terence were taught. Printed aids to gaining this oral proficiency suggest three stages of increasingly intense engagement: from idiomatic phrases (Nicholas Udall's *Floures for Latine Speakyng Selected and Gathered Oute of Terence*, eight editions 1534 to 1581) to selected speeches (*Sententiæ Ciceronis, Demosthenis, ac Terentii* (*Aphorisms of Cicero, Demosthenes, and Terence*), seven editions 1575 to 1648) to declamations of entire scripts.[16] How far along this path a given student might go depended very much on which school or college he attended, and when. By 1558 academic productions of classical comedy had been going on in England for almost half a century.[17]

Some schools, St Paul's in London and Westminster School in particular, became famous for their productions of classical drama, as did certain colleges—Christ

Church, Oxford, for example, and St John's College, Cambridge. Queen Elizabeth's statutes for the refounding of Westminster School in 1560 specifically require that the scholars put on two plays each Christmas, one in Latin and one in English—a frugal move on the queen's part, since some years the Latin production was brought to court. In the festivities of 1564–5 it was Plautus's *Miles Gloriosus*.[18] The previous summer the queen and her courtiers had witnessed a production of Plautus' *Aulularia* as part of an inspection visit to Cambridge.[19]

Display of academic skills, especially bravura speech-making, was ostensibly the motive for these academic productions. Lest we imagine two hours or more of staid declamation on these occasions, we should note an exchange in George Chapman's comedy *The Gentleman Usher* (printed 1606) in which Sarpego boasts,

> when I in Padua schooled it,
> I played in one of Plautus' comedies,
> Namely, *Curculio*, where his part I acted,
> Projecting from the poor sum of four lines,
> Forty fair actions.[20]

Taking Sarpego's cue, we should imagine extemporaneous fun in these productions, not to mention, from the spectators' point of view, the inescapably ironic effect of boys playing old men and prostitutes. That ironic effect would, in fact, have been apparent in the original performances of *The Gentleman Usher*, acted by the Children of the Chapel Royal in 1602. For the boys doing the performing, the irony would have been of a different sort: seeing one's fellows dressed up in other people's clothes and hearing them mouth other people's words. Ridicule does not adequately cover an effect that could have included admiration, envy, and sheer delight.

The extremes in the range of responses that Plautus' and Terence's scripts invite are encoded in the implied stage directions. Donatus' juxtaposition of civil and private passions is physically mapped on the stage. Terence's *Andria* is typical of Roman comedy in situating the action at the pressure point where public space and private space converge, on a street backed by houses belonging to two or three of the protagonists. It is out of these houses and into them that the characters make most of their entrances and exits. In the case of *Andria* the houses are two: one belonging to the upstanding father Simo, the other to Glycerium, a young woman of mysterious origin who has been raped by Simo's son Pamphilus. Two other possibilities for entrances and exits, stage left and stage right, complete the boundaries of the comedy's fictional world. Stage left is imagined to lead to the forum, stage right to foreign parts.[21] *Andria* begins with the entrance of servants who carry provisions, presumably just purchased in the forum, and take them into Simo's house. If not here, the specificity of stage left is made explicit at the beginning of Act Two, when two characters in mid-conversation make their entrance from that direction. How do you know Pamphilus is marrying Glycerium, one asks. 'I heard it of Davus but a little while since, at the market place,' the other replies in Maurice Kyffin's translation of 1588.[22]

It is from stage right, from foreign parts (in this case the Aegean island of Andros), that a mysterious stranger makes his entrance at the end of Act Four, with news that clarifies Glycerium's true identity and opens the way for the comedy's happy ending. Has Glycerium found the parents she came to seek, Crito asks the first citizen he meets. If not, 'Then in an ill hour am I come hither. For in good faith if I had known this, I would never have set foot forward in this journey' (sig. I1^{v}). Thus is Roman comedy framed by quotidian realities on the left and romantic possibilities on the right. Events originating on each side touch the spectators differently: quotidian realities invite satiric laughter; romantic possibilities invite surprise, pleasure, and delight. What we know about stage productions of Plautus and Terence in the sixteenth century suggests that romance was often heightened. On occasion the plot might be censored or tweaked so as to play up the love interest, as it was in the *Aulularia* acted before Elizabeth at Cambridge 1564. The fortunate loss of the ending of Plautus' script allowed the adaptor to present the lovers at the end as about to be married, not as tricksters who have already consummated their passion and produced a child.[23] In terms of touch, the evidence of early productions suggests a measure of confusion. How was romantic gratification to be reconciled with the satiric ridicule that Plautus' and Terence's plays, according to Erasmus, were supposed to invite? For some people, by suppressing the gratification.

Beginning in the 1560s, the pathway from phrases to speeches to stagings seemed, in the eyes of some, to lead to perdition: a line was crossed when students did not just declaim selected speeches but dressed up and acted out the fiction. John Rainolds, who played the part of Hippolyta in Richard Edwards's tragedy *Palamon and Arcite* on the occasion of Queen Elizabeth's visit to Oxford in 1566, went on to make his reputation as reader in Greek at Oxford with lectures on Aristotle's *Rhetoric* in 1572–3, but by the 1590s he had embraced hardline Protestantism and regarded 'Theatre sights and stage plays', even in academic settings, as 'hurtful and pernicious', especially males cross-dressing as females.[24] From his experience as Hippolyta, Rainolds must have known whereof he spoke. Rainolds's trajectory from amateur thespian in the 1560s to anti-theatrical polemicist in the 1590s charts a general trend in sixteenth-century English culture with the rise of Puritanism, first as a movement within the Church of England and then as a separatist religion. In the ears—and on the flesh—of these objectors laughter and touch were deeply suspect.

Epitasis: Accommodation and Conflict

Donatus' word for what happens in the epitasis of a Terentian comedy is *turba*, 'tumult', specifically a disturbance to the happy state of affairs that obtained in the protasis.[25] The uniformity of approach to classical comedy in humanism underwent changes and challenges beginning in the 1580s. For a start, there were changes in the printed format of editions. Annotation as a form of intellectual distraction certainly did not cease in the later sixteenth century, but in editions of Terence printed in England the proportion of commentary to text began to shrink. Beginning in the 1580s, a distinctively British tradition flourished as presses in London, Oxford, Cambridge, and Edinburgh issued anthologies, editions, and translations. One London press in particular, Thomas Marsh's, seems to have specialized in such publications.[26]

It was during the same decade, the 1580s, that a steady demand seems to have materialized for English translations.[27] Although a translation of *Andria* had been printed as early as 1520 as *Terence in English* (were other translations planned, on the order of Pynson's separate issues of each play?), it was in the 1580s that Englishings of classical comedy began to proliferate. These translations follow two curved trajectories: one inwards towards the Latin texts and reading and one outwards towards English idioms and performance.

The inward trajectory propels Richard Bernard's *Terence in English* (1598, with reprints in 1607, 1614, and 1629) and William Webbe's *The First Comedy of Pub[lius] Terentius, Called Andria, or, The Woman of Andros, English and Latin* (1629). Erasmus' poise between ridicule and moral seriousness is registered in *Terence in English*. Bernard, better known for his religious writings, offers literal, rather pedestrian translations of all six plays, with Latin and English on facing pages in the first edition and in sequent sections in later editions, along with marginal tags as in Thomas Marsh's editions of the Latin text, a catalogue of idiomatic phrases like Udall's, and a compendium of memorable passages in the manner of *Sententiæ Ciceronis, Demosthenis, ac Terentii*. Included among Bernard's aphorisms is, of course, Sosia's '*obsequium amicos, ueritas odium parit*', '*plausibleness gains friends, and truth gets foes*' (sig. B1, italics in original).[28] In dedicating the volume to Sir William Wray's sons, Bernard notes how Terence 'can play craftily the cozener, and cunningly the clown', all with the purpose of showing how 'men might become wise to avoid such vices, and learn to practice virtue' (sigs. ¶2–¶2^{v}). Despite the subtitle of William Webbe's translation of *Andria*—'claused for such as would write or speak the pure language of this author'—the emphasis falls heavily on writing, on diagramming Terence's Latin.[29] Webbe is a man with a system, and the word 'claused' provides the master key: Webbe turns the entire text into a series of tables that reduce the play to a series of clauses, English on the left, Latin on the right, act/scene/line references in the middle.

The other trajectory, outwards into English, can be witnessed in Maurice Kyffin's *Andria* (1588), W. W.'s *Menaecmi* (1595), and Thomas Newman's *The Two First Comedies of Terence* (1627). The trajectory in these cases leads not to pedantry but to pleasure. 'Your old acquaintance *Pub[lius] Tere[n]tius*' is the familiar way Maurice Kyffin invokes Terence in dedicating his translation of *Andria* to William Sackville, son of Sir Thomas Sackville of *Gorboduc* fame. Terence comes to Sackville, in Kyffin's words, 'in such and so much, English attire, as my poor judgment found fittest for him to be clad withal' (sig. ¶3). That means, it turns out, in idiomatic English prose (sig. ¶4). Pleasure is likewise registered in the front matter to *Menaecmi A Pleasant and Fine Conceited Comedy, Taken out of the Most Excellent Witty Poet Plautus* (1595) by one

'W.W.', whom Katharine Craik plausibly takes to be William Webbe, author of *A Discourse of English Poetry* (1586).[30] W.W. reports that he has translated several of Plautus' comedies 'for the use and delight of his private friends, who in Plautus's own words are not able to understand them' (sig. A3). Domesticating Roman comedy to English circumstances is likewise Thomas Newton's agenda in *The Two First Comedies of Terence called Andria, and the Eunuch Newly Englished* (1627).

> Many things were in Athens in Menander's time, which Terence had not seen [Newman observes], there were as many in Rome in Terence his time, which no Englishman knoweth. Shall I be driven to give names of things not extant? If I put in things now in being to supply the place of other things long since lost, so the understanding of my reader and sufficient expression of my author, I hope I can be no further required.[31]

The subtitle of the volume, 'Fitted for scholar[s'] private action in their schools', underscores Newman's dedication of the translation to the scholars of St Paul's School, with their established tradition of donning costumes and impersonating Plautus' and Terence's youths, whores, fathers, and slaves. The insistence on *private* action may be an anxious response to increasing criticism of this tradition by the likes of John Rainolds.

By the time Newman published his translations in 1627, the stage-worthiness of Plautus and Terence had been demonstrated, many times over, outside academia as well as within. With the establishment of permanent public theatres in London in the late 1570s and the enormous demand those theatres created for scripts, a second phase in the domestication of classical comedy was reached. Plays such as Shakespeare's *The Comedy of Errors* (1592, adapted from Plautus' *Menaechmi* and *Amphitruo*), Jonson's *The Case Is Altered* (1597, adapted from Plautus' *Captivi* and *Aulularia*), and Chapman's *All Fools* (1604, adapted from Terence's *Heauton Timorumenos* and *Adelphoe*) show that the domestication begun in school plays like *Jack Juggler* (published 1565 and 1570) had taken a radical new direction in which English mores and English voices came to dominate Roman mores and Roman voices. Thomas Heywood's *The Captives, or The Lost Recovered* (1624, adapted from Plautus' *Rudens*) and *The English Traveller* (1625, adapted from Plautus' *Mostellaria*) show this domestication at its self-confident extreme.

Of the three plays, Shakespeare's adheres closest to the Latin originals. Partly that may be a function of the academic circumstances in which the first known performance occurred, as part of the Gray's Inn Christmas revels of 1594. The fictional setting remains classical, or at least oriental: the Epidamnus of *Menaechmi* becomes Ephesus, which humanists in the audience would know as the centre of a cult of Diana and all members of the audience as the site of the early Christian community addressed in St Paul's Epistle to the Ephesians. Openings in the screen of the great hall at Gray's Inn provided practicable equivalents for two of the houses called for in *Menaechmi*, one belonging to Menaechmus of Epidamnus (called in Shakespeare 'The Phoenix') and one belonging to the courtesan Erotium (Shakespeare's 'The Porpentine'), plus a third house ('The Abbey', belonging to Aemilia). The addition of the third house indicates the chief change Shakespeare makes in Plautus' two plays: he heightens the importance of stage right and endows the story with romance. The result is a rounding and complicating of the characters, particularly the questing brother, Antipholus of Syracuse.[32]

In *The Case is Altered*, debuted under unknown auspices in 1597–8 but later performed by the Children of the Blackfriars, Jonson likewise heightens the romance element by setting the play in Italy, where a count's persecuted slave can plausibly turn out to be his long-lost son (in the plot adapted from *Captivi*) and an outcast miser who guards his daughter as closely as his pot of gold (in the plot adapted from *Aulularia*) can be revealed as a former steward of the king of France and his daughter as the stolen child of a French nobleman who, of course, turns up towards the end. Through it all, the satiric ridicule for which Jonson became famous sorts oddly with the impulse towards romance. In the last scene the chief knave Onion is unmasked as knaves always are in Jonson's later, more famous comedies ('Onion, you will now be peeled', taunts one of the noblemen), but the French lord Chaumont, who has the last word, strikes a note that sounds very much like Duke Senior in *As You Like It*: 'Lovers to your nuptials, lordings to your dances. March fair all' (sc. 13, ll. 26, 66–7; Jonson, *Works*, 3. 188). Or is it the final note? In his *very* last words Chaumont turns a satirist's eye on gold, on the miser's horde and the ransoms that have been paid for the noble prisoners' release: 'for a fair march is worth a king's ransom' (sc. 13, l. 67). It was only when Jonson shifted the setting of *Everyman in his Humour* from Italy (1598 version) to London (1616 version) that he found his footing between stage left and stage right in Roman comedy.

'Tart Aristophanes, | Neat Terence, witty Plautus': Jonson's formulation in his poem 'To the Memory of my Beloved, The Author Master William Shakespeare: And what he hath left us' nicely catches the sixteenth- and seventeenth-century reputations of the three ancient playwrights (ll. 51–2; *Works*, 8. 392). Between the two Romans, Plautus was regarded as the clever plotter, Terence as the elegant stylist. It is worth noting how much more popular Plautus was with playwrights for the public stage such as Shakespeare, Jonson, and Heywood.[33] Chapman's *All Fools*, acted by the Children of the Queen's Revels at court on New Year's Day 1605 and probably also at the Blackfriars Theatre, illustrates what happens when Terence, not Plautus, becomes the inspiration for a vernacular play. From Terence's *Heauton Timorumenos* and *Adelphoe* comes Chapman's main plot, with its contrast between two fathers, the tyrannical Gostanzo and the lenient Marc Antonio, and the resulting complications in the love lives of their children, who in various combinations are in love with each other. (Like Jonson's *The Case is Altered*, Chapman's *All Fools* finds in Italy an English equivalent for the Romans' free-wheeling Greece.) In both of Terence's plays it is the stern *pater familias* who ends up carrying the day. In Chapman's play *both* fathers are fooled, and it is their children, particularly Gostanzo's son Valerio and Marc Antonio's son Rinaldo, who engineer the happy ending. A notable difference from Terence's two plays is Chapman's insistence that the protagonists work out their own destiny without the help of a cunning servant. In *Heauton Timorumenos* and *Adelphoe* it is a wily slave with the same name, Syrus, who is largely responsible for the denouements. The closest Chapman comes to Syrus is the pert page Curio, whose part is all about style, not plotting. In defence of women Curio delivers a long set speech: 'let us endure their bad qualities for their good; allow the prickle for the rose; the brack [flaw in weaving] for the velvet; the paring for the cheese, and so forth.'[34] And so forth, for 776 words. Chapman reproduces the stylistic flair for which Terence was famous without hewing too closely to Terence's plots.

By the 1620s, when Thomas Heywood wrote two Plautus-inspired plays for Christopher Beeston's companies at the Drury Lane Cockpit, the domestication of Roman comedy was so complete that Plautus and Terence are hardly discernible in the result. Heywood's pillages of Plautus's *Rudens* in *The Captives* (1624) and Plautus' *Mostellaria* in *The English Traveller* (1625) are a far cry from Shakespeare's close adherence to Plautus' *Menaechmi* thirty-five years earlier. Updating the settings, dramatizing events that are narrated only in Plautus, multiplying the number of characters, adding episodes not mentioned in Plautus, above all darkening the narrative circumstances so as to turn the endings into tragicomedies, Heywood thoroughly remodels Plautus to suit the tastes of the 1620s.[35] In this radical domestication he follows the example of Shakespeare and Jonson in their later comedies. The twins business in *Menaechmi* and *The Comedy of Errors* has become thoroughly assimilated in *Twelfth Night* (1602), the miser guarding his gold and his daughter in *Aulularia* appears in a new guise as Shylock, and the haunted house in *Mostellaria* gets remodelled, unobtrusively, as Lovewit's London townhouse in *The Alchemist* (1610).

Heywood may have erased obvious traces of Plautus in the two plays he wrote for the Drury Lane Cockpit, but the humanist legacy of Latin comedy figures prominently in the *Apology for Actors* that Heywood contributed to the controversy that raged around plays and play-acting in the early seventeenth century. 'In the time of my residence in *Cambridge*,' he reports, referring to the 1590s, 'I have seen tragedies, comedies, histories, pastorals and shows, publicly acted, in which graduates of good place and reputation, have been specially parted.'[36] By the time Heywood published his *Apology* in 1612, grumblings against play-acting that had first been heard in the 1560s had become a noisy thunderhead, brooding over a full-fledged culture war of the sort witnessed in the United States in the 1980s. Attackers of play-acting would have liked to have play-acting, or at least public play-acting, banned altogether. Thirty years later, with the establishment of the republic, they succeeded. In the meantime, Heywood mounted against the attackers three lines of defence, all of them grounded in the humanist framing of classical drama: (1) play-acting was prized in the public life of ancient Greece and Rome, (2) accordingly actors were esteemed, and (3) public performances of tragedies and comedies serve a useful purpose by teaching morality.

At issue here is not only politics but the nature of poetry: what it is, how it relates to philosophy and history, how it works its effects. An example is the stand-off between Stephen Gosson and Sir Philip Sidney in 1579–80, just as the controversy was heating up. On the proper functions of poetry Gosson in *The Schoole of Abuse* (1579) adopts Plato's line: 'The right use of ancient poetry' was to set forth the noble deeds of heroes and 'the wholesome counsels of good fathers' so that listeners might be inspired to emulate them.[37] By this criterion, poets who write for theatres are an outrage, precisely because their works appeal to passions, not intellect:

> There set[ ]they abroach strange consorts of melody, to tickle the ear; costly apparel, to flatter the sight; effeminate gesture, to ravish the sense; and wanton speech, to whet desire to inordinate lust . . . these by the privy entries of the ear, slip down into the heart, & with gunshot of affection gaul the mind, where reason and virtue should rule the roost. (sig. B6^{v})

Apologists for theatre, Gosson acknowledges, will claim that Greek and Latin 'new comedy' is not like that: the satiric libels of Greek old comedy, they say, have been 'altered and changed to the love of young men; force, to friendship; rapes, too [*sic*] marriage; wooing allowed by assurance of wedding' (sig. B5)—all very proper. Gosson will have none of it.

Sidney's rebuttal of Gosson in *A Defence of Poesy* (possibly written as early as 1580, one year after Gosson had presumed to dedicate *The School of Abuse* to Sidney) takes Aristotle's line on how poetry works and refutes Gosson on his own terms.[38] Just as Aristotle in the *Poetics* locates the communicative power of tragedy in the affects of pity and fear, not (as Plato thought) in ideas, Sidney argues that poetry is superior to philosophy precisely *because* it works on the consumers' passions. And what it touches off is not just ridicule, as Erasmus and other humanist critics would have it, but delight. Sidney manages to acknowledge and to celebrate the pleasure that we have observed among many of Plautus' and Terence's translators. Sidney's delight is a generous, outgoing response that contrasts markedly with the judgemental drawing-back of ridicule. 'Delight hath a joy in it, either permanent or present,' Sidney observes. 'Laughter hath only a scornful tickling.'[39]

For all that, Sidney is not so generous with English drama of the 1570s, 'observing rules neither of honest civility nor skillful poetry' (*Miscellaneous Prose*, 112–13), nor is his position clear on live performance in general. In setting an example of how classical precepts could be put into practice in English, Sidney himself did not write classical comedies, as, for example, Edmund Spenser is supposed to have done, but adopted the five-act structure of Terentian comedy to lay out the sections of his prose romance *Arcadia*.[40] As Sidney's editor Jean Robertson suggests, the pastoral eclogues that separate the five acts may be modelled on the mythological *intermezzi* that the Italians were fond of performing between the acts of comedies by Plautus and Terence and their modern imitators.[41] Comedy, Sidney implies in word and deed, is not limited to drama. Even if Sidney approved performances of comedy, he might not have approved performances of comedy in public by people who made their living as performers.

Beneath the philosophical disputes about classical comedy pulse early modern political prejudices. Heywood's *Apology* is, after all, a defence of *actors*. What he was reacting against can be witnessed in Robert Greene's famous put-down of Shakespeare as 'an upstart crow, beautified with our feathers' in *Green's Groatsworth of Wit*.[42] (The 'our' here refers to Greene, Christopher Marlowe, Thomas Nashe, and George Peele, all university graduates. According to several of his title pages Greene was 'Utruisq[ue] Academiae in Artibus Magister' ('master of arts in both universities').[43]) Not so famous is Greene's dress rehearsal for the insult two years earlier in *Francesco's Fortunes: Or, The Second Part of Green's Never Too Late*. In that pamphlet Greene tells the story of what happened when Cicero and the famous actor Roscius met at a dinner party hosted by the poet Archias. Roscius dared to compare himself with Cicero, 'which insolency made the learned orator to grow into these terms: "Why, Roscius, art thou proud with Aesop's crow, being pranked with the glory of others' feathers? Of thyself thou canst say nothing"'. Whatever Roscius utters on the stage is, Cicero insists, the product of 'our' wit. If people applaud some *sententia* or conceit, it is the produce of 'our' knowledge, not Roscius'. 'I grant your action, though it be a kind of mechanical labour, yet well done, 'tis worthy of praise: but you worthless, if for so small a toy you wax proud' (*Complete Works*, 8. 132). What Greene found wanting in Shakespeare, as in Roscius, was not just education; it was the social status that education conferred.

Greene's anecdote concerns an actor, but there was a three-way slippage among actor, playwright, and slave that went back to ancient times. Erasmus advises schoolmasters to tell their pupils about the life of the playwright they are studying. In the case of Terence, what the schoolboys seem to have remembered best is that he was a freed slave. In their preface 'To the readers' the publishers of *Five New Plays* by Richard Brome (1659) take note of this fact, along with the lowly origins of other Latin authors:

> none versed in letters but know the wise Aesop was born and bred a wretched slave, Lucian a stone-cutter, Virgil himself begotten by a basket-maker, born in a ditch, and then preferred to an undergroom in the stable, nay (to instance in our author's own order) Naevius the comedian a captain's man's man, Plautus servant to a poor baker, Terence a slave as well as Aesop.

A more recent example is Brome's own master, Ben Jonson, who 'handled the trowel before he grew acquainted with *Sejanus* or *Catiline*'.[44] According to Alison Sharrock in *Reading Roman Comedy*, the clever slave assumed such a central role in Plautus and Terence precisely because he acts out the playwright's precarious position in the world at large. As the author, 'The playwright is the god of his fictive world', but he exercises his fiction-making powers through the figure of the conniving slave. Indeed, vis-à-vis the audience the playwright *is* a slave: 'Like a god and a slave, the playwright both controls the play and is also dependent on the audience's response.'[45]

Technically William Shakespeare and his fellows were servants, first to the Lord Chamberlain and later to King James I. If Sharrock is correct, we would expect the anxieties of that position to be played out in the Dromio twins of *The Comedy of Errors* or perhaps in the Feste of *Twelfth Night*. Perhaps to a degree they are. What is more remarkable, however, is the way agency is shifted in Shakespeare to characters of middling or ambiguous social status such as the Antipholus twins or Sebastian and Viola. That Shakespeare is not alone in this shift is witnessed in the diminution of the servant's role in Chapman's *All Fools*. Jonson, though legally no one's servant, develops servants' roles more in line with Sharrock's observations about Plautus and Terence. Consider Jeremy/'Captain Face' in *The Alchemist* and Mosca in *Volpone*. Compared with Shakespeare, Jonson is more at home among the social realities of stage left, and servant figures are one sign of his domestic comfort there.

Catastrophe: A Truce in the Quarrel of Ancients and Moderns

If the catastrophe of a Terentian comedy turns on knowledge—Donatus describes it as a 'throwing-open' of knowledge to all parties involved—we can distinguish the third and final phase in the domestication of classical comedy as a time when knowledge fostered an estrangement from plays that had once been regarded as close at hand. We can observe that perspective shift in printed editions. A new state of knowledge about classical comedy is found in William DuGard's 1651 printing of an octavo edition of Terence's plays edited by the Dutch scholar Daniel Heinsius, with additional annotations by the schoolmaster and Greek and Latin grammarian Thomas Farnaby.[46] What Heinsius' treatise *On the Making of Tragedy* (*De Tragoediae Constitutione* (1611)) did for tragedy his 'Dissertation concerning the Judgment of Horace on Plautus and Terence', reprinted in DuGard's Terence, did for comedy. In particular, Heinsius used Aristotle to question ridicule as the only passion touched off by comedy.[47] By bringing Aristotle's *Poetics* to bear on both tragedy and comedy Heinsius demonstrated that classical authorities did *not* constitute a single unified theory of tragedy and comedy, as earlier humanists had assumed. What Plato meant by *imitatio*, for example, was not the same thing that Aristotle meant. *Imitatio* in Cicero and Quintilian was something else again. One result of Heinsius' scholarship was a new appreciation for the heterogeneity of classical texts, a cultural relativity that explains the *neo-* in the neo-classicism of the late seventeenth and early eighteenth centuries. Another factor, paradoxically perhaps, was the suspension of play-acting in England from 1642 to 1660.

A premonition of 1642 is registered in Jonson's *The Staple of News*, acted by The King's Men in 1625. In the 'intermean' between Acts Three and Four Jonson gets together Censure, Mirth, Tattle, and Expectation, who exchange the latest news, including the story of a certain schoolmaster who is supposed to have left out a conjuring book that was discovered by one of his pupils. Censure can well believe it:

'They make all their scholars play-boys! Is't not a fine sight, to see all our children made interluders? Do we pay our money for this? We send them to learn their grammar and their Terence, and they learn their play-books?' ('The third Intermeane', ll. 46–56; *Works*, 6. 344–5). Seven years later the record of expenditures for performances of classical plays at Westminster School, Jonson's alma mater, comes to an end, not to be resumed until the late seventeenth century.[48] 'Well, they talk we shall have no more Parliaments (God bless us),' Censure goes on to say (ll. 56–7), 'but an'we have, I hope, *Zeal-of-the-Land Busy* and my gossip *Rabby Trouble-Truth* will start up, and see we shall have painful good ministers to keep school and catechize our youth, and not teach 'hem to speak plays and act fables of false news' (ll. 56–8). Seventeen years later that was exactly what happened. The 1642 parliamentary 'Order for stage plays to cease' and its confirmations and extensions in 1647 and 1648 put an end to play-acting. The last of these ordinances settles the argument about the legitimacy of Greek and Latin drama, at least as it was performed in ancient theatres, by stating explicitly that the acting of plays was 'condemned by ancient heathens', hence 'much less to be tolerated amongst professors of the Christian religion'.[49]

As a result, classical comedy went undercover—literally, under the wraps and leather bindings of printed books. Classical scripts became the closet dramas they had been at the beginning of the sixteenth century—the 'books' that Harington imagined Cicero reading in 1562. It is as books, as printed texts, that Plautus and Terence figure in John Milton's *Areopagitica* (1644). Milton uses Greek and Roman precedents to argue that only blasphemy and libel should be censored, but comedy comes in for particularly close scrutiny. When Attic culture first arrived in Rome in the persons of Carneades, Critolaus, and Diogenes, there was a move in the Senate by Cato the Censor 'to banish all such Attic babblers out of Italy'. In the event, Cato was outvoted and in old age studied the very texts he had hoped to ban. But the plays of Naevius and Plautus, which 'had filled the city with all the borrowed scenes of Menander and Philemon', raised the question of 'what was to be done to libellous books and authors'. Naevius, so Milton relates, was briefly imprisoned 'for his unbridled pen' (*Prose Works*, 2. 722). Later in *Areopagitica* Milton marvels that St Jerome was admonished in a vision for reading Cicero 'and not for scurril Plautus whom he confesses to have been reading not long before' (*Prose Works*, 2. 726).

Nostalgia for what had been lost as a result of the parliamentary ordnance of 1642 is registered in the publishers' preface to the edition of five previously unprinted plays by Brome in 1659, seventeen years after the prohibition went into effect and just one year before it was rescinded with the downfall of the republican government. The preface is addressed 'To the readers. Or rather *to the spectators*, if the Fates so pleased, these comedies exactly being dressed for the stage' (sig. A3). Five years earlier, in the very midst of the prohibition, Richard Whitlock, physician and fellow of All Souls, Oxford, singled out antipathy to plays as one of the topics in his *Zootomia, or, Observations of the Present Manners of the English* (1654). A cross among Montaigne's essays, Burton's *Anatomy of Melancholy*, and Sir Thomas Browne's *Pseudodoxia*

Epidemica or *Vulgar Errors*, Whitlock's book aims to correct the 'false principles, errors, and causes of miscarriage' thoughtlessly entertained by English society.[50] Although Whitlock will 'enter not the lists with any *Histriomastix*, to maintain the stage's quarrel, as to the presentments on [it]', he does defend 'writings and pennings for it', and he begins his defence with the wit of Plautus and his followers. From their achievements the stage derives not only 'its quickenings and heights' but its moral probity:

> Nay, wisdom is debtor no less to the sock and buskin, nor is it such a paradox as it may seem to sound to some half-witted ears, for I dare aver what hath been writ for the stage (ancient or modern) is not inferior to any writings on the same theme (excepting the advantages of Christianity and our better schoolmasters for heaven) of never so severe an authority. (sigs. HH4^{v}–HH5)

Why, in 1654, Whitlock refused to meddle with William Prynne's *Histriomastix*: *The Player's Scourge or Actor's Tragedy* (1632) is open to question, but Whitlock's appreciation for drama's quickenings and heights, as well as his fondness throughout *Zootomia* for the conceit 'All the world's a stage', indicate imaginative sympathies that ran counter to the prejudices of his age. He could find no better exemplar of those sympathies than Plautus.

One result of book-based dramatic culture in the mid-seventeenth century was at last bringing 'tart Aristophanes' to the fore. Throughout the sixteenth and early seventeenth centuries knowledge of Aristophanes in England had largely been confined to books. An *editio princeps* of the Greek text had appeared from the Aldine Press as early as 1498, and editions with a Latin trot and Latin commentaries soon followed from other presses on the Continent, but several factors conspired to keep Aristophanes in the shadow cast by Plautus and Terence: Aristophanes' texts were written in none-too-easy Greek, his *ad hominem* attacks cried out for footnotes, his loose plots were little more than excuses for bringing on a parade of satiric victims, above all his endings lacked the romance that modern audiences craved.[51] *Ploutos*, with its adolescent protagonist, its major domo servant, its attack on the corrupting power of money, and its redistribution of wealth at the end, seemed to be an exception. It was probably these new-comedy features that recommended the play for performance, in Greek, at St John's College, Cambridge, in 1536.[52] (The previous year at St John's the play had been one of Terence's.[53]) John Dee's spectacular production of *Eirene* (*Pax*) at Queen's College, Cambridge, ten years later was the last recorded performance of a play by Aristophanes in England until Thomas Randolph adapted *Ploutos* sometime between 1626 and 1628, probably for performance at Trinity College, Cambridge—a gap of nearly a hundred years. In the interim, Aristophanes was, for most English readers and play-goers, little more than a name, a place-holder for Greek old comedy and its satiric excesses. An exception is Ben Jonson, whose library included an edition of Aristophanes with Greek and Latin texts published in Geneva in 1607.[54] *Bartholomew Fair* shows that Jonson appreciated not only Aristophanes' tartness but his serial plots.

Perhaps it was as a 'son of Ben' and fellow graduate of Westminster School that Randolph came to Aristophanes. The only record of his version of *Ploutos*, however, is a further adaptation published in 1651, sixteen years after his death. By the time Francis Jacques took in hand Randolph's text and 'augmented and published' it as *Hey for Honesty, Down with Knavery*, stage productions were a thing of the past.[55] Jacques registers that situation when he says of the play's plot that his gentleman readers 'had rather see it performed in men's lives than personated on the stage, rather represented in action than acted in speculative representations' (sig. A2). For Jacques, the honesty in question belongs to royalists; the knavery, to roundheads. By adding a preface, assorted speeches, and an epilogue to Randolph's twenty-five-year-old text Jacques creates a physical and cultural palimpsest.[56] Typical of the added speeches is this one given to Poverty or Penia, as she is called in the play: 'In the City many that go in gay clothes know me; in the country I am known for taxes, excise and contributions: besides I have an army royal of royalists that now live under the sequestration-planet, I shall muster them up if need be...I hope to give these round—a breakfast, for all they vapor now; I hope to bring 'em under my dominion shortly' (sig. C4). The dash after 'round', the presence of only the initials 'F.J.' on the title page, and the absence of a printer's name suggest that the publication of *Hey for Honesty, Down with Knavery* came with political risks. Combining Randolph's script for performance at Cambridge in the 1620s with Jacques's satire of the republic in the 1650s, *Hey for Honesty, Down with Knavery* stands as a monument to two cultures: one that relished classical comedy in performance and one that abhorred the very idea.

The re-consignment of classical comedy to book culture from 1642 to 1660 is exemplified in Thomas Stanley's translation of Aristophanes' *Nephelai* (*The Clouds*) in his *History of Philosophy* (1655) and a translation of *Ploutos* by 'H.H.B.' printed in 1659. In both of these publications the texts are enshrined in print; both turn Aristophanes' plays into curiosities, objects of study that belong to another culture. For Stanley, Aristophanes' *The Clouds* is interesting primarily for its portrayal of Socrates, head of the original 'Think Tank' (*Phrontisterion*), the patron goddesses of which are clouds. Stanley emphasizes the gap between ancient Greece and contemporary Britain when he insists that his translation of the play is 'added, not as a comical divertissement for the reader, who can expect little in that kind from a subject so ancient and particular, but as a necessary supplement to the life of Socrates'.[57] Indeed, Stanley goes out of his way to note that Socrates was not a fan of the theatre: 'Socrates came seldom to the theatre, unless when Euripides contested with any new tragedian there...He was so far from esteeming comedians that he contemned them, as lying, abusive, and unprofitable, whereat they were much displeased' (sig. YY1^{v}). Indeed, Aristophanes returned the insult in *The Clouds*. In contrast to Randolph, stage performance is very far from the mind of H.H.B. in his translation of *Ploutos*. The 'short discourse' promised on the title page reads Aristophanes' play typologically, as an anticipation of Christian revelation. 'The wisdom of the world in all ages and their precepts of life', H.H.B. observes, 'lies wrapped up in their mythology, even as ours at this present is contained in the Holy Scriptures... Now amongst the ancient fables, I find none that better unfolds the nature and state of mankind than this, which Aristophanus takes for the subject of his comedy.'[58] The position taken here might seem to be that of humanism, but the translator insists on the cultural strangeness of the text he has taken in hand. His understanding of fables and mythology anticipate modern anthropology.

When drama returned to the stage with the restoration of the monarchy in 1660, Greek and Latin comedy was put on an altogether new footing vis-à-vis English comedy. The 'quarrel of the ancients and the moderns' is usually regarded as one of the imports from France brought over with Charles II in 1660.[59] Cultural conditions in Britain, however, were ripe for a rethinking of the humanist idea that classical texts and modern experience were compatible. The closing of public theatres in 1642 put an end to the cultural cross-fertilization that produced plays such as Shakespeare's *The Comedy of Errors*, Jonson's *The Alchemist*, and Heywood's *The English Traveller*. Some performances of scripts by Plautus and Terence may have continued in schools and colleges, but outside those venues consumption of classical comedy was exclusively a matter of print. Unless one were a scholar or a student, encounters with *Menaechmi*, *Eunuchus*, and *Phormio* came through books like Heinsius' 1651 edition of Terence.

It is against spectrophobia of the English republic as well as the artistic rules of France that we should read Dryden's *Of Dramatic Poesie, An Essay*, published eight years outside the chronological range of this volume but usefully epitomizing the third phase of criticism, from 1642 to 1660. In Dryden's account, 'ancients' and 'moderns' figure as two separate entities. All four speakers in Dryden's dialogue, mouthpieces for Dryden and three friends, get a good hearing, but on the subject of ancients versus moderns Crites (apologist for the ancients, modelled on Sir Robert Howard) is ultimately out-argued by Eugenius (champion of the moderns, modelled on Sir William Davenant). With all due respect to the ancients, Eugenius asserts: 'We draw not therefore after their lines, but those of nature; and having the life before us, besides the experience of all they knew, it is no wonder if we hit some airs and features which they have missed.'[60] What the moderns hit in particular, says Neander (Dryden's own spokesman), is character. In old comedy one encounters only ridiculous exaggerations like Socrates in Aristophanes' *The Clouds*; in new comedy, 'only the general characters of men and manners, as old men, lovers, servingmen, courtesans, parasites, and such other persons as we see in their comedies, all which they made alike: that is, one old man or father, one lover, one courtesan so like another as if the first of them had begot the rest of every sort' (*Works*, 17. 60). By contrast, English comic characters typically display a distinctive humour, 'some extravagant habit, passion, or affection; particular... to some one person: by the oddness of which, he is immediately distinguished from the rest of men' (*Works*, 17. 60–1). Shakespeare's Falstaff and Jonson's Morose are offered as examples. The result, in terms of touch, is not just the laughter of ridicule but aesthetic pleasure at 'imitation of what is natural' (*Works*, 17. 61).

Epilogue

Intellect, touch, laughter: between 1558 and 1660 these fundamental elements of classical *comoedia* were combined in varied ways as scripts by Aristophanes, Plautus, and Terence were domesticated in English culture. The written record, one has to admit, makes it seem as if the whole process were a matter of intellect. More fugitive, harder for a historian to put a finger on, are the private and civic affects that Donatus specifies as the very essence of comedy. More fugitive still is the private and civil experience of laughter. Laughter, as Bergson insists, is inarticulate. It may be occasioned by words—a quip by a slave from stage left, unexpected good news from stage right—but laughter abandons words. The last word, the word that connects intellect, touch, and laughter, is supplied by Plautus and Terence: *plaudite*.

Notes

1. Aristotle, *Parts of Animals*, book 3, chapter 10 (673^{a}4–6), in *The Complete Works of Aristotle*, ed. Jonathan Barnes (Princeton, 1984), 1. 1049. Further quotations from Aristotle (with the exception of the *Poetics*) are taken from this edition and are cited in the text by Bekker reference number.
2. The implications of Aristotle's observations are pursued in Daniel Heller-Roazen, *The Inner Touch: Archaeology of a Sensation* (New York, 2007).
3. Aristotle, *Poetics*, trans. Gerald F. Else (Ann Arbor, 1966), 53^{b}1–5, emphases added.
4. I pursue this argument more largely in Bruce R. Smith, 'Touching Moments', in *Phenomenal Shakespeare* (Oxford, 2010), 132–76.
5. Etymology as given at 'tragedy, *n.*', *Oxford English Dictionary Online*, 2nd edn (Oxford, 1989) <http://www.oed.com> (accessed January 2012). Further quotations from the *OED* are cited in the text.
6. *Evanthii de comoedia excerpta*, my translation, from the edited text on the website 'Hyperdonat' curated by Bruno Bureau, Maud Ingarao, Christian Nicolas, and Emmanuelle Raymond (director) of the Centre d'Études et de Recherches sur l'Occident Romain, the Université Lyon III, and the École Normale Superieur de Lyon <http://hyperdonat.ens-lyon.fr> (accessed January 2012). Now attributed to Donatus, the *Excerpta de comedia* appears in most fifteenth- and sixteenth-century printings of Terence as an appendage to a treatise *De fabula* that is now assigned to another fourth-century grammarian, Evanthius. A full account of these fourth-century treatises and their influence in the sixteenth century is provided in Marvin T. Herrick, *Comic Theory in the Sixteenth Century* (Urbana, IL, 1964), 58–60.
7. Cicero, *The Booke of Freendeship of Marcus Tullie Cicero*, trans. John Harington (1562), sig. H1. The quotation from *Andria* is spoken by the servant Sosia, 1. 1. 67–8, in *Terence* 1: 56. Further quotations from Terence's Latin are cited in the text by act, scene, and line numbers.
8. Erasmus, *On the Method of Study (De Ratione Studii)*, trans. Brian McGregor, in *Collected Works of Erasmus*, gen. ed. Craig R. Thompson (Toronto, 1978), 24. 669. Further quotations from this treatise are

taken from this translation and are cited by page number. The importance of drama in Erasmus' scheme is considered by Howard Norland, 'The Role of Drama in Erasmus' Literary Thought', *Medieval & Renaissance Texts & Studies*, 37 (1985), 549–57.

9. On humanist schemes of education, with particular reference to England, see Ian Green, *Humanism and Protestantism in Early Modern English Education* (Farnham, 2009); David Cressy, *Education in Tudor and Stuart England* (New York, 1975); M. L. Clarke, *Classical Education in Britain, 1500–1900* (Cambridge, 1959); and T. W. Baldwin, *William Shakspere's Small Latine & Lesse Greeke* (Urbana, IL, 1944).

10. Robert S. Miola, *Shakespeare and Classical Comedy: The Influence of Plautus and Terence* (Oxford, 1994), 9. In addition to Miola, I have been anticipated in my endeavours here by Wolfgang Riehle, 'Shakespeare's Reception of Plautus Reconsidered', in Charles Martindale and A. B. Taylor (eds), *Shakespeare and the Classics* (Cambridge, 2004), 109–21; and Raphael Lyne, 'Shakespeare, Plautus, and the Discovery of New Comic Space', in Martindale and Taylor (eds), *Shakespeare and the Classics*, 122–40; Charles and Michelle Martindale, *Shakespeare and the Uses of Antiquity* (1998); Wolfgang Riehle, *Shakespeare, Plautus, and the Humanist Tradition* (Cambridge, 1990); Eugene M. Waith, 'Aristophanes, Plautus, Terence, and the Refinement of English Comedy', *Studies in the Literary Imagination*, 10/1 (1977), 91–108; and Richard Hosley, 'The Formal Influence of Plautus and Terence', in John Russell Brown (ed.), *Elizabethan Theatre* (1966), 131–45.

11. Erich Segal, 'Introduction', in *Oxford Readings in Menander, Plautus, and Terence* (Oxford, 2000), p. xx.

12. Donatus in *Evanthii de Fabula* 4. 5 explains the terms thus: 'Comedy is divided into four parts: prologue, protasis, epitasis, catastrophe. The prologue is a kind of preface to the piece; it is the only moment where, apart from the intrigue, it is permissible to say something about the poet, the piece, or the actor. The protasis is the first act and the beginning of the drama; the epitasis is the development and progress of the commotion and, one might say, the node of the confusions ['epitasis incrementum processusque turbarum ac totius, ut ita dixerim, nodus erroris']. The catastrophe is the return to the happy situation at the beginning, an occasion when knowledge is thrown open to all the actors' (my translation).

13. Mathurin Cordier, *Corderius Dialogues Translated Grammatically. For the More Speedy Attaining to the Knowledge of the Latine Tongue, for Writing and Speaking Latine. Done Chiefly for the Good of Schools*, trans. John Brinsley (1636), sigs C6^v–C7. Further quotation from Cordier is taken from this edition and is cited in the text. Earlier English-language editions had been published in 1584, 1592, 1607, 1608, 1614, 1618, 1624, and 1625; later editions continued into the early nineteenth century.

14. A census of these editions is provided in Joseph William Moss, *A Manual of Classical Bibliography*, 2nd edn (1837).

15. *Aristophanous Ippeis. Aristophanis Equites* (Oxford, 1593).

16. Udall isolates, act by act, scene by scene, key phrases that will provide young learners with 'formulas for speaking Latin according to the use and variety of everyday speech' (my translation), in Nicholas Udall, *Floures for Latine Speakyng Selected and Gathered oute of Terence* (1560), sig. A4. The anonymously collected *Sententiæ Ciceronis, Demosthenis, ac Terentii* is devoted mostly to memorable speeches in Cicero's orations and dialogues, with passages from Terence and

Plautus added in an appended section 'Certain famous *sententiae* selected from other distinguished authors' (my translation), in *Sententiæ Ciceronis, Demosthenis, ac Terentii* (1575), sigs Q2[v] ff.

17. The earliest can be dated to 1510–11, when the accounts of King's Hall, Cambridge, record a payment of six shillings and eight pence 'pro Commedia Terentij in ludo' ('for a comedy of Terence in play') (Alan H. Nelson (ed.), *Cambridge*, Records of Early English Drama (Toronto, 1989), 1. 84). Surviving evidence of academic stagings of Latin comedy is surveyed in Bruce R. Smith, *Ancient Scripts and Modern Experience on the English Stage 1500–1700* (Princeton, 1988), 134–98.
18. A tradition of acting Latin comedy was already well established at Westminster School. Prologues for productions of Terence's *Adelphoe* and *Eunuchus* in 1545 survive among the papers of the headmaster, Alexander Nowell. On the 1560 statutes and the tradition of play-acting at Westminster School, see Lawrence E. Tanner, *Westminster School: A History* (1934), 55–9. Nowell's prologues are translated and discussed in Smith, *Ancient Scripts*, 141–7.
19. Details are discussed in Smith, *Ancient Scripts*, 157–8.
20. George Chapman, *The Gentleman Usher* (1606), sig. A4[v].
21. C. W. Marshall, *The Stagecraft and Performance of Roman Comedy* (Cambridge, 2006), 49–56.
22. Terence, *Andria the First Comoedie of Terence, in English*, trans. Maurice Kyffin (1588), sig. D3[v].
23. The eyewitness accounts of the production are discussed in Smith, *Ancient Scripts*, 157–9.
24. John Rainolds, *Th'overthrow of Stage-Playes, by the Way of Controversie betwixt D. Gager and D. Rainoldes* (Middleburg, NL, 1599), sig. B1.
25. See n. 12.
26. Marsh was the publisher of the first edition of *Sententiæ Ciceronis, Demosthenis, ac Terentii* in 1575. Six years later he issued an updating of Udall's *Flowers for Latin Speaking*, this time covering all six surviving plays. Then, in 1583 and 1585, came two editions of the complete Terence. The first, an octavo printing of Marc-Antoine Muret's carefully edited text, includes Donatus' complete introduction but reduces the running commentary of the earlier folio editions to marginal tags and to notes before and after each scene. In effect, Terence's text looms larger in the reader's experience. Handier still is Marsh's sexdecimo reprinting of Muret's text two years later (just three by four and a half inches in Eton College's copy), this time with a shorter introduction and sparser notes but with the marginal tags preserved intact. Muret's text was reissued in this format by an array of British printers for use as a school text fourteen times down to 1656.
27. Gordon Braden, 'Tragedy' and 'Comedy', in Gordon Braden, Robert Cummings, and Stuart Gillespie (eds), *Oxford History of Literary Translation in English*, 2 (Oxford, 2011), 262–92.
28. *Terence in English*, trans. Richard Bernard (Cambridge, 1598), sig. AA5, spelling and orthography modernized. This translation was published by Legat in the same year he issued a Latin edition of Terence. Further quotations are cited in the text by signature number.
29. *The First Comedy of Pub. Terentius, Called Andria, or, The Woman of Andros, English and Latine: Claused for Such as Would Write or Speake the Pure Language of this Author, after Any Method Whatsoeuer, But Especially after the Method of Dr Webbe*, trans. William Webbe (1629).
30. Katharine A. Craik, 'Warner, William (1558/9–1609)', *Oxford Dictionary of*

National Biography (Oxford, 2004) <http://www.oxforddnb.com.libproxy.usc.edu/view/article/28770> (accessed 18 January 2012).

31. *The Two First Comedies of Terence Called Andria, and the Eunuch Newly Englished by Thomas Newman. Fitted for Scholler Priuate Action in their Schools* (1627), sig. A5^{v}. Further quotation is cited in the text by signature number.
32. On the likely staging arrangements of *The Comedy of Errors* at Grays Inn, see R. A. Foakes's introduction to William Shakespeare, *The Comedy of Errors*, Arden Two (1962).
33. Riehle discusses this distinction in *Shakespeare, Plautus, and the Humanist Tradition*, 14–43.
34. George Chapman, *Al Fooles a Comedy* (1605), sig. F2^{v}.
35. A full account of these changes is offered in Smith, *Ancient Scripts*, 177–83.
36. Thomas Heywood, *An Apology for Actors* (1612), sig. C3^{v}.
37. Stephen Gosson, *The Schoole of Abuse Conteining a Plesaunt Inuectiue against Pœts, Pipers, Plaiers, Iesters, and such like Caterpillers of a Co[m]monwelth* (1579), sig. A7^{v}.
38. In citing Aristotle, Sidney is being remarkably up to date. Aristotle's *Poetics* became influential only in the later sixteenth century, after Francesco Robortello in 1548 had begun the process of reconciling Aristotle's cryptic comments on comedy with the much more substantial rhetorical tradition set in place by Cicero. Until then, Giorgio Valla's Latin translation of 1498, the Aldine edition of the original Greek text in 1508, and Alessandro Pazzi's proto-Loeb edition of the Greek text with a Latin translation on facing pages in 1536 had had surprisingly little impact. On the reception of Aristotle's *Poetics* in the sixteenth and seventeenth centuries, see Bernard Weinberg, *A History of Literary Criticism in the Italian Renaissance* (Chicago, 1961), 1. 349–634, 2. 635–714; and Martin T. Herrick, *The Poetics of Aristotle in England* (New Haven, 1930), 8–79.
39. *Miscellaneous Prose of Sir Philip Sidney*, ed. Katherine Duncan-Jones and Jan van Dorsten (Oxford, 1973), 112–13, 115.
40. In *Three Proper, and Wittie, Familiar Letters: Lately Passed betvveene Tvvo Vniuersitie Men* (1580), Gabriel Harvey reminds Spenser of 'your *Nine Comedies*, whereunto in imitation of *Herodotus*, you give the names of the *Nine Muses*, (and in one man's fancy not unworthily) come not nearer *Ariosto's Comedies*, either for the fineness of plausible Elocution, or the rareness of Poetical Invention, than that *Elvish Queen* doth to his *Orlando Furioso*, which notwithstanding, you will needs seem to emulate, and hope to overgo, as you flatly professed your self in one of your last Letters' (in Gabriel Harvey, *Works*, ed. Alexander B. Grosart (n.d.), 1. 95).
41. Jean Robertson, 'General Introduction', in *The Countess of Pembroke's Arcadia (Old Arcadia)* (Oxford, 1973), p. xxxvii. A general consideration of Sidney's adoption of Terence's five-act structure is provided by Robert Parker, 'Terentian Structure and Sidney's Original *Arcadia*', *English Literary Renaissance*, 2/2 (1972), 61–78.
42. *The Life and Complete Works in Prose and Verse of Robert Greene*, ed. Alexander B. Grosart (1881–6), 12. 144.
43. Greene's rather peripatetic academic career is summarized in L. H. Newcomb, 'Greene, Robert (bap. 1558, d.1592)', *Oxford Dictionary of National Biography* (Oxford, 2004) <http://www.oxforddnb.com.libproxy.usc.edu/view/article/11418> (accessed 6 February 2012).
44. Richard Brome, *Five Nevv Playes* (1659), sigs A5–A5^{v}.
45. Alison Sharrock, *Reading Roman Comedy: Poetics and Playfulness in Plautus and Terence*

(Cambridge, 2009), 132–3. See also Douglas Bruster, 'Comedy and Control: Shakespeare and the Plautine Poeta', *Comparative Drama*, 24/3 (1990), 217–31.

46. Terence, *Comediae Sex* (1651), sigs A5^{v}–aa5^{v}.
47. An edition of Heinsius' treatise, with critical introduction, has been provided by Jean-Marc Civardi, 'La Dissertation de Heinsius sur le jugement d'Horace au sujet de Plaute et de Térence', *Litteratures Classiques*, 27 (1996), 67–116. On Jonson's debt to Heinsius' treatise in *Discoveries*, see Herrick, *Comic Theory*, 55–6.
48. Tanner, *Westminster School*, 55–9.
49. 'February 1648: An Ordinance for the utter suppression and abolishing of all Stage-Plays and Interludes, within the Penalties to be inflicted on the Actors and Spectators therein expressed', in *Acts and Ordinances of the Interregnum, 1642–1660* (1911), 1070–2 <http://www.british-history.ac.uk/report.aspx?compid=56247&strquery=stage> (accessed February 2012).
50. Richard Whitlock, *Zootomia, or, Observations of the present Manners of the English: Briefly Anatomizing the Living by the Dead* (1654), sig. A2^{v}. Further quotations are cited in the text. On Whitlock's career and writings, see Christopher Bentley, '*The Anatomy of Melancholy* and Richard Whitlock's *Zootomia*', *Renaissance & Modern Studies*, 13 (1969), 88–105; Christopher Bentley, 'The Life of Richard Whitlock', *English Language Notes*, 10 (1972), 111–15; and George Williamson, 'Richard Whitlock, Learning's Apologist', *Philological Quarterly*, 25 (1936), 254–72.
51. Aristophanes' fortunes in England in the sixteenth and seventeenth centuries are detailed in Smith, *Ancient Scripts*, 169–77.
52. Nelson, *Cambridge*, 1. 111, as reported in Thomas Smith, *De Recta et Emendata Linguae Graeciae Pronuntatione* (Paris, 1568).
53. Nelson, *Cambridge*, 1. 109.
54. David McPherson, *Ben Jonson's Library and Marginalia: An Annotated Catalogue, Studies in Philology*, 71 (1974), 25–6.
55. Thomas Randolph and Francis Jacques, *Ploutophthalmia Ploutogamia: A Pleasant Comedie, Entituled Hey for Honesty, Down with Knavery* (1651), title page.
56. The hands of Randolph and Jacques in the text are sorted out in G. E. Bentley, *The Jacobean and Caroline Stage* (Oxford, 1956), 4. 980–2; and Cyrus L. Day, 'Thomas Randolph's Part in the Authorship of *Hey for Honesty*', *PMLA* 46 (1926), 325–34.
57. Aristophanes, *The Clouds*, trans. Thomas Stanley, in *The History of Philosophy*, 2nd edn (1656), sig. HHH1.
58. Aristophanes, *Plutus a Comedy Written in Greek by Aristophanes, Translated by H.H.B. Together with his Notes, and a Short Discourse upon It* (W.G. for Richard Skelton, Isaac Pridmore, and H. Marsh, 1659), sig. F1, spelling and orthography modernized. H.H.B. is identified as H. H. Burnell in the English Short Title Catalogue <http://estc.bl.uk> (accessed 23 January 2012) and as the playwright Henry Burnell in the *Oxford Dictionary of National Biography* <http://www.oxforddnb.com> (accessed 23 January 2012).
59. The fullest account of how this French quarrel was played out in England is provided by Joseph M. Levine, *Between the Ancients and the Moderns: Baroque Culture in Restoration England* (New Haven, 1999), and *The Battle of the Books: History and Literature in the Augustan Age* (Ithaca, NY, 1991). The battle did not rage in England until the very end of the seventeenth century.
60. John Dryden, *The Works*, gen. eds Edward Niles Hooker, H. T. Swedenberg, Jr., and Vinton A. Dearing, 20 vols (Berkeley and Los Angeles, 1956), 17. 22.

CHAPTER 18

Tragicomedy

TANYA POLLARD

Is tragicomedy a classical genre? Most English Renaissance critics suggested that it lacked the dignity, unity, and ancient authority implied by the term. Famously, Philip Sidney's complaints about his contemporaries' unhappy distance from classical theatre focused on 'their mongrel tragi-comedy', which he described as 'mingling kings and clowns... with neither decency nor discretion',[1] and George Whetstone similarly fretted over the 'gross indecorum' of his peers who 'to make mirth... make a clown companion with a king'.[2] Although more recent critics have tended to reverse these aesthetic judgements, typically celebrating tragicomedy for its unconventional hybridity, for the most part they have similarly seen the genre as new and iconoclastic, representing a daring break from classical precedent. Yet the development of tragicomedy in the sixteenth century was firmly rooted in engagement with classical texts. The authority conferred by classical precedents was crucial to establishing the genre's legitimacy and success, but they provided more than simply justification. Perhaps surprisingly, they also offered specific structural models for the conventions that made tragicomedy so popular with audiences. Even when playwrights diverged from their theoretical and practical models, tragicomic plays evolved in intimate relationship to the classical dramatic genres from which they drew their name.

The curious status of tragicomedy requires us to consider more closely what it means to be a classical genre. To critics writing on this period, the term classical is typically allied with the academic, conservative, and rule-bound, in contrast with popular, native, and playful literary styles and strategies.[3] Recent attempts to revive interest in tragicomedy, in fact, have increasingly emphasized its roots in native traditions such as miracle plays and medieval romances.[4] Yet we do not have to overlook native roots to see that engagement with classical texts played a crucial role in tragicomedy's development. Recent scholarship has demonstrated that classical reception was an active process by which writers reread and rewrote the past, a process that Bruce Smith has aptly termed 'confluence', rather than as 'influence', because of the reciprocity by which early moderns shaped what they read.[5] If we take seriously the extent to which classical genres were constructed by their later readers, tragicomedy is a classical genre precisely because it was understood, invented, and shaped in classical terms. We might even go further and propose that, in the Renaissance, tragicomedy was—paradoxically—the quintessential classical genre. Designed precisely to fulfil mandates widely understood as the primary legacy of classical genre theory, tragicomedy is a striking example of the period's creative classicism at its best.

Tragicomedy from Antiquity

As Renaissance genre theorists frequently observed, the term tragicomedy first appeared in antiquity, in Plautus' *Amphitryo*. 'I will make it a mixture [*commixta*],' Mercury announces of the play; 'let it be a tragicomedy [*tragico[co]moedia*]. I don't think it would do to make it entirely a comedy, when we have gods and kings here' (Prologue, 59–61).[6] Plautus' wry coinage offered a crucial foundation for Renaissance discussions of the genre, but the idea of tragicomedy began far earlier. As a number of sixteenth-century writers observed, Aristotle offered models for the genre by classifying tragedies as ending either unhappily, happily, or with a double ending (happy for some and unhappy for others).[7] Mixed and happy-ending tragedies had an ambivalent status for Aristotle, as for later writers. 'The well-made plot, then,' he wrote, 'ought to be single rather than double, as some maintain, with a change not to prosperity from adversity, but on the contrary from prosperity to adversity' (*Poetics* 1453^{a}12–15). Although Aristotle found unhappy endings preferable because of their greater capacity for producing pity and fear, his discussion identified tragedy with a happy or mixed ending as a legitimate dramatic form.

In fact, despite his stated disapproval, Aristotle provided some of the most important ammunition for later defences of tragicomedy. 'Second-best', he wrote,

> is the structure held the best by some people: the kind with a double structure like the *Odyssey* and with opposite outcomes for good and bad characters. It is thought to be best because of the weakness of the audience: the poets follow, and pander to the taste of, the spectators. Yet this is not the pleasure to expect from tragedy, but is more appropriate to comedy... (*Poetics* 1453^{a}30–6)

Even in the act of dismissing tragedy with a happy ending, then, Aristotle implicitly offers two defences: Homeric authority and audience mandate. His characterization of the *Odyssey*'s ending as comic is intriguing, particularly because of his earlier claim that the *Odyssey* and *Iliad* both offer models for tragedy.[8] If such a primary source of literary authority can model both tragedy and comedy, the two genres must be capable of a successful coexistence. Aristotle's characterization of Homer was influential, but his offhand reference to audiences' preference proved even more important in establishing the terms of later debates. He concedes that happy endings are thought by some people to be best because of the weakness (*astheneian*) of the audience (*theatrōn*), since poets aim to please audiences. Yet his criticism of pandering playwrights sits uneasily with his claim that Euripides is 'the most tragic of the poets [*tragikōtatos*]' (*Poetics* 1453^{a}29). Euripides was notorious for his mixed and happy endings in plays such as *Cyclops* (categorized today as a satyr play), *Ion*, *Helen*, *Iphigenia in Tauris*, and *Alcestis*, many of which became key models for tragicomedy, and Aristotle's praise resonated with Renaissance printers, translators, audiences, and readers, with whom Euripides found an especially warm reception.[9] More broadly, Aristotle's dismissal of an audience-pleasing form struck at least some early readers as being at odds with his emphasis on the primacy of audience response as a measure of tragic success.[10] Famously, he defined tragedy as 'through pity and fear accomplishing the catharsis of such emotions [*pathēmatōn katharsin*]' (*Poetics* 1449^{b}23–8), and he justified his structural recommendations—specifically, plots that feature a reversal of fortunes (*peripeteia*) alongside recognition (*anagnōrisis*)—in terms of their effectiveness at moving audiences' emotions. For Aristotle's Renaissance readers, the idea that tragedy's *telos* involved conjuring intense emotion through structural devices formed the centrepiece of the genre theory they constructed in his name.[11]

Aristotle's observations about audiences' preferences for comic endings resonate throughout the development of tragicomedy. In the prologue to *Amphitryo*, Mercury rests his offer to make the play a tragicomedy on the grounds that this is what the audience wants:

> What? You're frowning because I said this was going to be a tragedy? I'm a god, I'll change it. If you want, I'll immediately turn this same play from a tragedy into a comedy with all the same verses. Do you want it to be one or not? But I'm being silly, as if I didn't know that you want it; after all, I'm a god. I know what your feelings in this matter are. (Prologue, ll. 52–8)

Mercury justifies his decision to change the play's genre with the assertion that he knows what audiences want, and it is the pleasure of comedy.[12] In the context of a long-standing identification of comic prologues as mouthpieces for the playwright, Mercury's confident assumption implicitly suggests Plautus' own beliefs about audiences' preferences. And hindsight suggests that Mercury and Plautus were right: of Plautus' twenty extant plays, *Amphitryo* ranks fourth in documented postclassical performances before 1600, following only *Menaechmi*, *Aulularia*, and *Miles Gloriosus*.[13] And although the play differed considerably from the structural conventions that ultimately came to define Renaissance tragicomedy, its dramatization of Amphitryo losing his wife to a disguised Jupiter before recovering her, through a divinely facilitated reconciliation, suggests a playful revision of Euripides' loss-and-recovery dramas, mediated through the Greek comedies that Plautus imitated.[14]

If *Amphitryo* offered a conspicuous vehicle for transmitting Euripides' exploration of rescues and recoveries to later audiences, so did the nondramatic *Aethiopica* of Heliodorus, usually dated to the third century CE (on its Renaissance reception see also Helen Moore, Chapter 13, this volume). Like Euripides' *Alcestis*, the *Aethiopica* depicts (among a myriad of related plots) the restoration of an apparently dead beautiful woman to her lover.[15] Beyond this quintessentially tragicomic plot, Heliodorus adopted self-consciously theatrical language in order to identify his story with the mixing of dramatic genres. At the story's climactic denouement, when lovers, brothers, parents, and child all tearfully rediscover and embrace each other, the narrator stands back from the events and explicitly describes the turnabout as tragicomic:

> To be short, all that part . . . was full of such wonderful affections, as is commonly represented in comedies. The wicked battle between the two brothers was ended, and that which men thought should be finished with blood, had of a tragical beginning, a comical ending [*eis kōmikon ek tragikou to telos katestrephe*).[16]

Despite the text's nondramatic status, the narrator's account of its development from tragedy to comedy explicitly evoked theatrical form to describe its pleasures, which proved considerable. Like *Amphitryo*, the *Aethiopica* was strikingly popular in the sixteenth century—the 1534 *editio princeps* was quickly followed by translations into Latin and five vernacular languages, and Thomas Underdowne's 1569 English translation was reprinted six times within a handful of decades.[17] By 1620, the satirist Joseph Hall could ask, rhetorically, 'What school-boy, what apprentice knows not Heliodorus?'[18] Its immediate success with both readers and critics would appear to confirm the claim—demonstrated by Euripides, observed by Aristotle, and echoed by Plautus—that fusing a tragic beginning with a comic ending offered a reliable formula for pleasing audiences.

Tragicomedy in Sixteenth-Century Continental Europe

The classically rooted idea that tragicomedy represented a concession to audience desires proved a central weapon for both sides in contentious sixteenth-century debates about the genre. Taking their cue from Aristotle's focus in the *Poetics*, the period's writers began their deliberations on genre theory primarily with tragedy, but some soon turned to tragicomedy as an attractive way to combine tragedy's prestige with comedy's appeal to audiences.[19] A number of critics followed Aristotle in expressing doubts about the form: Lodovico Castelvetro, for instance, found that 'experience confirms what reason has discovered, that the unhappy ending is of very great efficacy in arousing pity and fear. In fact experience attests that a tragedy with a happy ending does not and cannot produce these emotions.'[20] Yet Giraldi Cinthio, whose plays were the first in the period to achieve popular success onstage, argued that he wrote tragedies with happy endings, despite Aristotle's objections, 'as a concession to the spectators and to make the plays appear more pleasing on the stage'.[21] While acknowledging his divergence from Aristotle, then, he justified it through

Aristotle's own emphasis on audience response, thinking it wrong 'to displease those for whose pleasure the play is put on the stage'. He accordingly identified the form with the public realm of performance, as opposed to the private realm of reading: 'Plots that are terrible because they end unhappily (if it appears the spirits of the spectators abhor them) can serve for closet dramas; those that end happily for the stage' (Cinthio, *Composition*, 256). Despite explicit recommendations to the contrary, then, Aristotle's underlying emphasis on audiences and their responses directed Giraldi to see tragicomedy as the ideal dramatic genre.

Although Giraldi justified the genre of tragedy with a happy ending despite Aristotle, and only implicitly claimed an Aristotelian justification for its authority, Giambattista Guarini went a step further to argue that tragicomedy embodied the logical culmination of Aristotle's goals for dramatic poetry. Guarini cited the classical precedents of Euripides' *Cyclops* and Plautus' *Amphitryo* as justification for combining comic and tragic elements, and noted that in practice all classical tragedies mix generic registers, since servants appear onstage with those of high rank.[22] Primarily, though, he upheld the genre's value by linking it to Aristotle's most influential claim, arguing that tragicomedy offered the most perfect version of catharsis. Christianity, he held, made earlier versions of tragic catharsis superfluous: 'what need have we today to purge terror and pity with tragic sights, since we have the precepts of our most holy religion which teaches us with the word of the gospel?' (Guarini, *Compendium*, 523). Instead, he claimed that tragicomedy could fulfil comedy's most valuable function, 'to purge the mind from the evil affection of melancholy' (Guarini, Compendium, 522), while avoiding the vulgarity that threatened to undermine its moral impact. Reaping the best of both genres, tragicomedy offered a 'mingling of tragic and comic pleasure which does not allow hearers to fall into excessive tragic melancholy or comic relaxation' (Guarini, *Compendium*, 512). Aristotle, Guarini implies, would have come to this conclusion himself, had he lived in Christendom.

Although Guarini drew heavily on medical and affective arguments, his defence of tragicomedy also turned to politics. Drawing on Aristotle's identification of comedy with the lower sort and tragedy with kings, he compared tragicomedy to the political form of the republic, in which noble and common social classes mixed together. 'Why cannot poetry make the mixture,' he asked, 'if politics can do it?' (Guarini, *Compendium*, 511). According to Guarini, the temperate and tempering function the genre brought to its catharsis worked similarly as a medicine for the body politic.[23] His explicit attention to the form's political analogue drew on other writers' identification of tragedy and comedy with their origins in Greek democracy—one critiquing rulers, and the other celebrating the common people—and pointed towards a way that the sixteenth century's very different political configurations might benefit from uniting these politically coded genres.

Between Cinthio's defences and Guarini's manifesto, tragicomedy came to hold a central place in sixteenth-century genre theory. Not only did these writers, along with those who debated them, turn to classical precedents to frame and support their arguments, but printed editions of the plays themselves both reflected and contributed to broader interest in the genre. The plays identified most explicitly with tragicomedy—*Amphitryo, Cyclops*, and *Alcestis*—were especially popular in the period, attracting substantial numbers of vernacular translations, individual printed editions, and performances.[24] They also prompted editorial commentary on the genre. Florent Chrestien's Latin translation of *Cyclops*, published in 1605 but completed before Chrestien's death in 1596, presented the play as an example of classical tragicomedy. At the start of the notes to his translation, Chrestien wrote:

> I do not know whether to call this play a tragedy, for it does not have a sad ending, according to the common definition... and in fact the characters are mixed from tragic and comic examples... And so, as Plautus prefaced his *Amphitryo*, I think that this play could be called a tragic comedy (tragico comoediam [*sic*]).[25]

Attached to these classical precedents, tragicomedy, or tragedy with a happy ending, thrived in European dramatic practice at least as much as in its theory. Cinthio achieved considerable popular success with tragicomic plays such as *Altile, Arrenopia*, and *Epitia*, as well as with *novelle* based on tragicomic narratives in his *Hecatommithi*; the pastoral dramas of Tasso's *Aminta* (1580) and Guarini's *Il Pastor Fido* (first published 1590) similarly sparked conversations, controversies, translations, and imitations.[26] These plays, which dramatized the passions and stratagems of pastoral Arcadians, were attacked for their blatant eroticism, as well as for what many saw as their shocking novelty.[27] Yet, despite or perhaps precisely because of the surrounding scandals, they captured the imagination of readers, audiences, and other writers, and went on to prove influential to the development of tragicomedy not only in Italy but beyond. By the early seventeenth century tragicomedy was becoming popular in France and Spain as well, but it was the genre's earlier rise in Italy that set the tone for both the conversations and generic conventions that developed in England.

Tragicomedy in Early Modern England

As interest in tragicomedy made its way to England, the genre not only flourished, but eventually went on to dominate the stage. Dryden later claimed that the English 'had invented, increased, and perfected a more pleasing way than was ever known to the ancients or moderns of any nation—which is tragi-comedy'.[28] Although English writers were less self-consciously classicizing than their continental counterparts, genre theory by writers such as George Puttenham, Philip Sidney, Ben Jonson, and John Fletcher drew explicitly on both classical texts and their contemporary continental critics.[29] Tragicomedy's popularity in England's commercial playhouses offers a striking example of the unexpected ways that the classical dramatic tradition offered both rhetoric and templates for the complex hybrid forms that are often seen as challenging its mandates.

As in Italy, the earliest English plays to describe themselves as tragicomedies were written by scholars steeped in the classics, and were performed—like other early classically inspired plays—by students or children's companies. The first English play to label itself in these mixed generic terms—as a 'comoedia tragica, sacra, et nova'—was the *Christus Redivivus* (1543) of Nicholas Grimald, a classically trained Oxford fellow, which partook of the neo-Latin biblical tradition that dominated early humanist versions of tragicomedy.[30] Richard Edwards, master of the Chapel Children, used a version of the term in the prologue of his *Damon and Pythias* (1563–4): 'Which matter mixed with mirth and care, a just name to apply, | As seems most fit we have it termed a "tragical comedy".'[31] Similarly, Richard Bower, the previous master of the Chapel Children, wrote a play titled *The New Tragical Comedy of Appius and Virginia* (entered in the Stationers' Register in 1567–8, printed 1575). As these titles suggest, both plays drew on classical material in order to dramatize tragedies happily averted and/or redeemed by transformative consequences. Similarly, George Gascoigne, who with Francis Kinwelmershe had earlier translated Euripides' *Phoenician Women*, described his *Glass of Government* (1575) as 'a wofull tragicall comedie'.[32] George Whetstone turned to classical structure and Italianate tragicomic romance in his *Promos and Cassandra* (1578), which drew its plot from Cinthio's *Hecatommithi* and possibly his tragicomic play *Epitia*. John Lyly's *Gallathea* and George Peele's *Arraignment of Paris* (both *c.*1584) similarly shaped classical plots into tragicomic form. Each of these early experiments with fusing tragedy and comedy actively engaged with classical literary traditions, and/or continental mediating forms.

As tragicomic plays became more visible, and moved into the arena of adult commercial playing companies, the genre attracted more attention, both positive and negative. Although sceptics attacked it as formally incoherent, they acknowledged and even exploited the genre's substantial appeal for audience. Whetstone's complaints, cited earlier, appeared in the preface to his own tragicomic play *Promos and Cassandra* (1578), suggesting gaps between his theory and his practice. Sidney countered his own criticisms of mixing kings and clowns by acknowledging, 'I know the ancients have one or two examples of tragi-comedies, as Plautus hath *Amphitryo*' (*Defence*; *Miscellaneous Prose*, 115), and even observing that 'some poesies have coupled together two or three kinds, as the tragical and comical, whereupon is risen the tragi-comical... if severed they be good, the conjunction cannot be hurtful' (*Defence*; *Miscellaneous Prose*, 94). Sidney must have seen for himself how popular the mixed form was with audiences. His prose romance, *The Arcadia*, embodied the pleasures of the mixed form in its tragicomic structure, modelled on the *Aethiopica*, in which separations, losses, and apparent deaths give way to rediscoveries and reunions.[33]

Although tragicomic terminology, form, and theory had appeared in England by the middle of the sixteenth century, increasing literary traffic with Italy intensified and reshaped its impact sharply towards the end of the century, after the appearance of Guarini's first critical defence of tragicomedy (1588), Abraham Fraunce's English translation of Tasso's *Aminta* (1591), and the printing of Guarini's *Pastor Fido* in

England (1591).[34] The following years saw more pastoral tragicomic plays in the Italian model, as well as more experiments in tragicomedy and pastoral separately. Robert Greene's plays, including *The Honourable History of Friar Bacon and Friar Bungay* (1594) and *The Pleasant Conceited Comedy of George A Greene* (1599), toyed with tragicomic structures, as did Lyly's *Midas* (1592) and Chapman's *Blind Beggar of Alexandria* (1598). The first English translation of *Il Pastor Fido* (1602) drew further responses. Shakespeare wrote arguably the first of his tragicomedies (as they are now usually labelled), *Measure for Measure* and *All's Well That Ends Well*, in 1604–5; the same years saw Marston's satiric tragicomedy *The Malcontent* and *Dutch Courtezan*, and Samuel Daniel's *The Queen's Arcadia*, a pastoral tragicomedy with obvious debts to Guarini. By 1607 Ben Jonson was parodying English interest in Guarini and *Il Pastor Fido* via Lady Politic Would-Be in his *Volpone*, itself a dark mix of tragedy and comedy.

These Italian-influenced plays in many ways laid the groundwork for a significant turning-point in the development of English tragicomedy. John Fletcher's pastoral tragicomedy *The Faithful Shepherdess* (1608) nodded explicitly to Guarini's *Il Pastor Fido*, not only in its title but in its bawdy nymphs, shepherds, and satyrs, who similarly if less directly paid homage to the tragicomic satyrs of Euripides' *Cyclops*. With its almost parodically pastoral setting, the play offered an exaggerated caricature of Italy's rewriting of Greek literary shepherds; it has been widely credited with introducing formal Italian pastoral tragicomedy to English audiences. It also alludes, similarly ironically, to Greek romance. Fletcher's choice of the names Daphnis and Cloe for a love-stricken shepherd and shepherdess evokes Longus' *Daphnis and Chloe*—another tragicomic Greek romance that came close to rivalling the *Aethiopica*'s popularity in the period—yet parodies them by making Cloe desperate to be ravished, while a lukewarm Daphnis leaves her chastity intact despite her ardent encouragement.[35]

Fletcher signalled his debts to Guarini not only in his play but in his account of tragicomedy in the play's preface, which rebukes English readers and audiences for their misconceptions of the genre's nature. Fletcher defines pastoral as 'a representation of shepherds and shepherdesses, with their actions and passions' ('To the Reader', 10–11), and goes on memorably to summarize the genre's defining characteristics:

> a tragi-comedy is not so called in respect of mirth and killing, but in respect it wants deaths, which is enough to make it no tragedy, yet brings some near it, which is enough to make it no comedy: which must be a representation of familiar people, with such kind of trouble as no life be questioned, so that a God is as lawful in this as in a tragedy, and mean people as in a comedy.
>
> ('To the Reader', 20–6)

Fletcher's brief account of the genre draws on Renaissance understandings of Aristotle's 'better' and 'worse' kinds of people to refer to courtly and common ('mean') classes, and also on the distinction between unhappy endings (deaths) and happy ones. He distinguishes the genre from comedy by its proximity to death, and from tragedy by its lack of actual death. Fletcher's claims do not reliably describe all of the period's tragicomedies, many of which feature actual deaths alongside averted ones.[36] Yet his self-conscious reflections on the genre's structure and underlying logic point to his close engagement with continental genre theory's responses to Aristotle, and their consequences for the evolution of tragicomedy on the English stage.

Although it was a failure onstage, *The Faithful Shepherdess* led to the highly successful tragicomedies that Fletcher co-wrote with Francis Beaumont, beginning especially with *Philaster* (1609) and *King and No King* (1610–11). It also influenced Shakespeare's best-known tragicomedies, *The Winter's Tale* (*c.*1610), *Cymbeline* (1610–11), and *The Tempest* (1611). The chorus of satyrs in Jonson's masque *Oberon* (1611) seem to have responded to the play as well. Jonson self-consciously drew on both classical antecedents and their mediating forms in the masque; in his notes for its printed edition, he acknowledged a debt to Euripides' *Cyclops*, and additional notes referring to Isaac Casaubon's *de Satyrica poesi*, which was printed alongside Chrestien's translation of the play in 1605, indicate his familiarity with the edition.[37]

As this very schematic overview suggests, tragicomedy emerged as an official genre in England in response to conversations between playwrights and theorists across far-flung countries and time periods. Challenging critical tendencies to identify the genre's English beginnings with Fletcher, Lucy Munro has argued for an expanded genealogy, observing that its development in England during the crucially lively period between 1603 and 1613 was 'propelled by the collaborative practices of the playing companies, and one group in particular: the Children of the Queen's Revels'.[38] Building on this claim, I would suggest that this local collaborative practice had roots in more far-ranging literary conversations, both transnationally among contemporary continental writers and diachronically with the classical texts that inspired and legitimized the period's generic experimentation. The process of negotiating and fashioning the genre was protracted, and the range of plays that identified themselves as tragicomedies is broad enough to make any definition necessarily partial and incomplete. Yet through the genre's development, particular themes and conventions came to recur more consistently and forcefully than others, eventually arriving at some relatively recognizable outlines.

The traits that came most insistently to define early modern English tragicomedy, and to mark its debts to what we might call classical tragicomedy, include the mixing of social classes; distressing threats, transformed to unexpected happy endings; and apparent corpses, miraculously reanimated. The pleasures of tragicomedy also came to be associated with the freedom of pastoral realms, sometimes populated by satyrs, nymphs, and shepherds, and the sensual licence unleashed by these settings. These features responded both to classical precedents and to genre theory that largely followed Aristotle in identifying the roots of successful emotional response in plot structure. It is fitting, then, that tragicomedies relied heavily on sudden and unexpected reversals of fortune, *peripeteia*, and especially those brought about by moments of recognition, *anagnorisis*.

Aristotle's privileging of *anagnorisis*, or recognition, surfaces in tragicomedy's fascination with disguise, mistaken identity, and sudden revelation, often brought about by an identifying mark or object. In *Cymbeline*, the mole under Imogen's breast, and Guiderius' birthmark, catalyse crucial plot twists by sparking emotional recognitions; in *The Winter's Tale* the bag of treasure left with the infant Perdita in Bohemia reveals her status as Leontes' daughter, and leads to the play's astonishing reunions and restorations. The genre's dependence on these visual forms of proof suggests an interweaving of classical literary legacies with practical theatrical factors. Tiffany Stern has identified the appeal of 'miniaturizing' motifs such as birthmarks with the intimate size of the coterie theatres where these plays were staged.[39] Yet they also revisit climactic moments in classical tragicomic texts such as Heliodorus' *Aethiopica*, where identifying marks lead to the culminating reunions, and the *Odyssey*, in which the nurse's recognition of Odysseus's scar begins the process that eventually leads Odysseus back into the arms of his wife.

The reversals brought about by these recognitions for the most part follow a consistent pattern: children are restored to their grieving parents, and wives are restored to their grieving husbands (or, less frequently, vice versa). In its most extreme form, this pattern takes the form of resurrecting characters who seem to have been lost to death. Critics have identified this trope with the resurrection of Christ in mystery plays, but, particularly in the light of the fact that these characters are usually female, these moments more directly evoke the wife's return from the dead in Euripides' *Alcestis*, and the discovery in the *Aethiopica* that Chariclea, long believed dead, is still alive. Early modern recoveries often hinged on the theatrically congenial device of a sleeping potion.[40] Some of the most well known are *Cymbeline*, in which Imogen's apparent death turns out to have been merely a deep sleep brought about by a sleeping potion that the doctor passed off to the wicked queen as a poison, and the comitragedy of *Romeo and Juliet*, in which Juliet's false death is meant to enable her escape to Romeo's waiting arms. Barabas successfully tries the same trick to escape punishment in Marlowe's *Jew of Malta*: 'I drank poppy and cold mandrake juice; | And being asleep, belike they thought me dead',[41] and failed poisonings lead to unexpected happy endings in Edward Sharpham's *The Fleire* (1606), John Day's *Law Tricks* (1608), and Dekker's *Match Me in London* (1611). But deaths are forged without chemical enhancement as well; Hero in *Much Ado About Nothing* (1598–99), Hermione in *The Winter's Tale*, and Ferdinand in *The Tempest* are only a few of those who are taken for dead before eventually being restored to those who love them. In each of these plays, the pleasures of embracing a lost beloved are intensified by the grief that has come first.

As these last examples suggest, although Shakespeare's tragicomedies echo Heliodorus in their frequently tongue-in-cheek irony, they juxtapose it with an emotional intensity offering sentimental appeal. Later plays, influenced by the success of satiric city comedy, went further in playing up the artifice intrinsic in tragicomedy's often implausible reversals. Middleton, best known for his city comedies as well as for his dark, often satiric revenge plays, struck a rich vein of satiric parody in tragicomedies including *The Witch* (*c.*1616), in which supernatural and pharmaceutical interventions suddenly and implausibly resolve various crises (including no fewer than three false deaths) at the end of the play, parodying the rapid resolutions typical of the genre. Other later tragicomedies followed *The Witch* in escalating the genre's raciness and ludicrousness for comic effect.[42] *The Custom of the Country* by Fletcher and Massinger (*c.*1619–23) features young lovers fleeing from a rapacious governor pursuing the bride's maidenhead, only to find the groom aggressively pursued by a lusty older woman, while his older brother delights in being enlisted to serve as a male prostitute but finds women's demands debilitating, until all are finally, and implausibly, rescued;[43] Dryden claimed that there was more bawdry in this play than in all later plays combined.[44] Tragicomedy's appeal to audiences' pleasure shifted as those audiences became acclimatized to different sorts of irony and erotic playfulness.

Conclusion: Tragicomedy as Classical Reception

Tragicomedy developed in England in response to literary conversations—inspired in large part by the newly visible classical dramatic tradition—about what audiences wanted, and what they should get. Despite widespread claims that the genre's hybridity challenged received conventions, tragicomedy drew on the authority of classical plays and genre theory both for claims to legitimacy, and for strategies of cultivating audience pleasure through recognitions, reversals, and happy endings. Acknowledging this engagement with the classical literary past requires us to reconsider the impact of the period's classical reception, and in particular to appreciate the ways that classical precedents modelled complexity, hybridity, and attention to audience pleasure. Writers such as Euripides, Heliodorus, and Plautus offered Renaissance writers valuable challenges to restrictive ideas about generic rules, and compelling models for manipulating audiences' emotions and prompting pleasures. Early modern writers by no means consistently agreed on their readings of the classical dramatic tradition, but their varying forms of engagement with its texts show clear responses to their complexity and fertility.

Notes

1. *A Defence of Poetry*, in *Miscellaneous Prose of Sir Philip Sidney*, ed. Katharine Duncan-Jones and Jan van Dorsten (Oxford, 1973), 114.
2. George Whetstone, *Promos and Cassandra* (1578), 'Epistle Dedicatory'.
3. For another account, and critique, of this opposition, see Kent Cartwright, *Theatre and Humanism: English Drama in the Sixteenth Century* (1999).
4. See, e.g. Mimi Still Dixon, 'Tragicomic Recognitions: Medieval Miracles and

Shakespearean Romance', in Nancy Klein Maguire (ed.), *Renaissance Tragicomedy: Explorations in Genre and Politics* (New York, 1987), 56–79, and Valerie Forman, *Tragicomic Redemptions: Global Economics and the Early Modern English Stage* (Philadelphia, 2008).

5. See Charles Martindale, 'Thinking through Reception', in Charles Martindale and Richard F. Thomas (eds), *Classics and the Uses of Reception* (Oxford, 2006), 1–13, and Bruce R. Smith, *Ancient Scripts and Modern Experience on the English Stage 1500–1700* (Princeton, 1988), 6.
6. Intriguingly, from the very beginning the term itself was fraught: the play's 1495 and 1499 editions printed the term as 'tragico comoedia', but later editions came to settle on the single word 'tragicomoedia'. See Marvin T. Herrick, *Tragicomedy: Its Origin and Development in Italy, France, and England* (Urbana, IL, 1955), 1.
7. See Herrick, *Tragicomedy*; Frank Ristine, *English Tragicomedy: Its Origin and History* (New York, 1963); and Sarah Dewar-Watson, 'Aristotle and Tragicomedy', in Subha Mukherji and Raphael Lyne (eds), *Early Modern Tragicomedy* (Cambridge, 2007), 15–27.
8. See *Poetics* $1448^{b}38–1449^{a}1$; also Sarah Dewar-Watson, 'Shakespeare's Dramatic Odysseys: Homer as a Tragicomic Model in *Pericles* and *The Tempest*', *Classical and Modern Literature*, 25/1 (2005), 23–40 (25–8).
9. For tables and lists on the breakdown of early printed Greek plays, see Rudolf Hirsch, 'The Printing Tradition of Aeschylus, Euripides, Sophocles and Aristophanes', *Gutenberg Jahrbuch* 39 (1964), 138–46; Jean Christophe Saladin, 'Euripide Luthérien?', in *Mélanges de l'Ecole française de Rome*, 108/1 (1996), 155–70; and R. R. Bolgar, *The Classical Heritage and its Beneficiaries* (Cambridge, 1954), 512–15.
10. Aristotle, of course, had distinctive criteria for the kinds of pleasure that audience should experience, but his early modern interpreters frequently took his mandate as justification for prioritizing audiences' own preferences, as will be discussed further below.
11. See Stephen Orgel, 'Shakespeare and the Kinds of Drama', *Critical Inquiry*, 6/1 (1979), 107–23; Nicholas Cronk, 'Aristotle, Horace, and Longinus: The Conception of Reader Response', in Glyn Norton (ed.), *The Cambridge History of Literary Criticism*, vol. 3: *The Renaissance* (Cambridge, 1999), 199–204; and Timothy J. Reiss, 'Renaissance Theatre and the Theory of Tragedy', in Norton (ed.), *Cambridge History*, 3, esp. p. 242.
12. See Timothy J. Moore, 'Tragicomedy as a Running Joke: Plautus' *Amphitruo* in Performance', *Didaskalia*, supplement 1 (1995) <http://www.didaskalia.net/issues/supplement1/moore.html> (accessed April 2015).
13. There were 9 recorded stagings of *Amphitryo* before 1600; *Menaechmi* had 24, *Aulularia* 11, and *Miles Gloriosus* 10. Other Plautus plays average 3 performances each before 1600. See Archive of Performance of Greek and Roman Drama (APGRD) Database, University of Oxford <http://www.apgrd.ox.ac.uk/research-collections/performance-database/productions> (accessed April 2015).
14. On Plautus's engagement with Greek literary models, see Jeffrey Henderson, 'Introduction', Loeb *Plautus* 1, pp. xvii–xxx, lxxvi–lxxxi.
15. On Heliodorus' use of Euripides, see James Pletcher, 'Euripides in Heliodorus' *Aethiopika* 7–8', *Groningen Colloquia on the Novel*, 9 (1998), 17–27; and Anna Lefteratou, 'Myth and Narrative in the Greek Novel', D.Phil. thesis (Oxford, 2000).
16. Thomas Underdowne, *An Aethiopian History of Heliodorus* (1587), p. 174; 7.7–7.8. On Heliodorus's theatricality, see J. W. H. Walden, 'Stage-Terms in Heliodorus's

Aethiopica', *Harvard Studies in Classical Philology*, 5 (1894), 1–43; Stuart Gillespie, 'Shakespeare and Greek Romance: "Like an old tale still"', in *Shakespeare and the Classics*, ed. Charles Martindale and A. B. Taylor (Cambridge, 2004), pp. 225–37, 233; and Tanya Pollard, 'Romancing the Greeks: *Cymbeline*'s Genres and Models', in *How To Do Things with Shakespeare*, ed. Laurie Maguire (Oxford, 2007), pp. 34–53.

17. For an overview of Heliodorus' reception in Europe, see Alban K. Forcione, *Cervantes, Aristotle, and the Persiles* (Princeton, 1970); on his reception in England, see Pollard, 'Romancing the Greeks'.
18. Joseph Hall, *The Honour of the Married Clergy* (1620), 175.
19. On the complexity of the period's genre theory and its responses to Aristotle, see, e.g. Daniel Javitch, 'The Emergence of Poetic Genre Theory in the Sixteenth Century', *Modern Language Quarterly*, 59/2 (1998), 139–69; and Kristine Louise Haugen, 'The Birth of Tragedy in the Cinquecento: Humanism and Literary History', *Journal of the History of Ideas*, 72/3 (2011), 351–70.
20. Castelvetro, *Castelvetro on the Art of Poetry*, ed. and trans. Andrew Bongiorno (Binghamton, NY, 1984), 144–5.
21. Giraldi Cinthio, *On the Composition of Comedies and Tragedies* (1543), trans. Allan Gilbert, in Allan Gilbert (ed.), *Literary Criticism: Plato to Dryden* (New York, 1940), 256.
22. Giambattista Guarini, *The Compendium of Tragicomic Poetry* (1599), trans. Allan Gilbert, in Gilbert (ed.), *Literary Criticism*, 508.
23. See James J. Yoch, 'The Renaissance Dramatization of Temperance: The Italian Revival of Tragicomedy, and *The Faithful Shepherdess*', in Nancy Klein Maguire (ed.), *Renaissance Tragicomedy: Explorations in Genre and Politics* (New York, 1987), 115–38; also Zachary Lesser, 'Mixed Government and Mixed Marriage in *A King and No King*: Sir Henry Neville Reads Beaumont and Fletcher', *English Literary History*, 69 (2002), 947–77.
24. With 11 individual or partial printed editions before 1600, *Alcestis* was one of the 4 most frequently printed of Euripides' 18 plays in the period, following *Hecuba, Iphigenia in Aulis*, and *Medea*; *Cyclops* was 6th, with 4 individual or partial printed editions. For details of Greek plays, see Hirsch, 'The Printing Tradition'; Saladin, 'Euripide Luthérien?'; and Bolgar, *The Classical Heritage*.
25. *Euripidis Cyclops Tragoedia Q. Septimo Florente Christiano Interprete*, 32 (Paris: 1605), Aii^{r}. See also Dana F. Sutton's 1998 hypertext critical edition of the play <http://www.philological.bham.ac.uk/chrestien/> (accessed 26 July 2011).
26. The play circulated in manuscript and was first performed in 1581, published in 1589, and reprinted in final form in 1602.
27. On *Il Pastor Fido* and its controversies, see especially Robert Henke, *Pastoral Transformations: Italian Tragicomedy and Shakespeare's Late Plays* (Newark, DE, 1997); and Matthew Treherne, 'The Difficult Emergence of Pastoral Tragicomedy: Guarini's *Il Pastor Fido* and its Critical Reception in Italy, 1586–1601', in Mukherji and Lyne (eds), *Early Modern Tragicomedy*, 28–42.
28. John Dryden, 'An Essay on Dramatic Poesy', in John Dryden, *The Works*, gen. eds Edward Niles Hooker, H. T. Swedenberg, Jr, and Vinton A. Dearing, 20 vols (Berkeley and Los Angeles, 1956), 17. 46.
29. On Sidney's substantial intellectual debts to Castelvetro, Minturno, and Scaliger, see Joel Spingarn, *Literary Criticism in the Renaissance* (New York, 1908), 268; and Marvin Herrick, *The Poetics of Aristotle in England* (New Haven, 1930), 24–9. On Puttenham's engagement with Scaliger, see Frank Whigham and Wayne A. Reborn,

'Introduction', in *The Art of English Poesy by George Puttenham: A Critical Edition* (Ithaca, NY, 2007), 1–87 (esp. 38–40). Ben Jonson's voracious readings in classical and humanist scholarship have been well documented; see, e.g., Robert Evans, *Habits of Mind: Evidence and Effects of Ben Jonson's Reading* (Lewisburg, PA, 1995). On Fletcher's responses to continental writers, see Florence Ada Kirk, 'Introduction', in John Fletcher, *The Faithful Shepherdess*, ed. Kirk (New York, 1980).

30. Herrick describes this body of quasi-tragicomic plays as the 'Christian Terence'; see Herrick, *Tragicomedy*, 16–62. The label 'comoedia tragica, sacra et nova' appears on the play's title page.
31. Richard Edwards, *Damon and Pythias*, in *The Works of Richard Edwards*, ed. Ros King (Manchester, 2001), prologue, 35–8.
32. George Gascoigne, *Complete Works*, ed. John W. Cunliffe, 2 vols (New York, 1969), 2. 88.
33. See Steven Mentz, *Romance for Sale in Early Modern England: The Rise of Prose Fiction* (Aldershot, 2006).
34. G. K. Hunter has pointed out the conspicuous intensity of English responses to Italian tragicomic experimentation. Noting the substantial and unparalleled number of English translations of Tasso's *Aminta* and Guarini's *Il Pastor Fido*, he points out that, although these responses continued through the seventeenth century, it is striking how early they began: '*Aminta* was first published in 1580; *Il Pastor Fido*, first published in 1590, did not reach its final revision till 1602, in the twentieth edition. But as early as 1591 Italian texts of both plays were published in London, from the press of John Wolfe.' G. K. Hunter, 'Italian Tragicomedy on the English Stage', *Renaissance Drama*, ns 6 (1973), 123–48 (126). On the timeline of attacks on and defences of Guarini's *Il Pastor Fido*, see especially Ristine, *English Tragicomedy*, and Henke, *Pastoral Transformations*.
35. On this irony, see Richard F. Hardin, *Love in a Green Shade: Idyllic Romances Ancient to Modern* (Lincoln, NE, 2000), 44.
36. On the limitations of Fletcher's preface as a definition of tragicomedy, see Gordon McMullan and Jonathan Hope, 'Introduction: The Politics of Tragicomedy, 1610–50', in McMullan and Hope (eds), *The Politics of Tragicomedy: Shakespeare and After* (New York, 1992), 1–20 (esp. 1–7).
37. Jonson, *Oberon, The Faery Prince*, in *Works*, 7. 341–2.
38. Lucy Munro, *Children of the Queen's Revels: A Jacobean Theatre Repertory* (Cambridge, 2005), 96.
39. Tiffany Stern, 'Actors and Audience on the stage at Blackfriars', in Paul Menzer (ed.), *Inside Shakespeare: Essays on the Blackfriars Stage* (Selinsgrove, 2006), 35–53 (46).
40. On this phenomenon and the following examples, see Tanya Pollard, '"A Thing like Death": Poisons and Sleeping Potions', in *Romeo and Juliet* and *Antony and Cleopatra*', *Renaissance Drama*, 32 (2003), 95–121.
41. Jew of Malta, 5. 1. 81–2, in *The Complete Works of Christopher Marlowe*, ed. Roma Gill, 5 vols (Oxford, 1987–98), vol. 4.
42. On Middleton's underexplored satiric tragicomedies, see Inga-Stina Ewbank, 'The Middle of Middleton', in Murray Biggs et al. (eds), *The Arts of Performance in Elizabethan and Early Stuart Drama* (Edinburgh, 1991), 156–72; and Lucy Munro, 'Middleton and Caroline Theatre', in Gary Taylor and Trish Thomas Henley (eds), *The Oxford Handbook of Thomas Middleton* (Oxford, 2012), 164–80.
43. The play's sources show the influence of continental tragicomic romance; it took its plot from *Los Trabajos de Persiles y Sigismunda*, a romance by Cervantes (translated into English 1619), and Cinthio's *Hecatommithi*.
44. Dryden, 'Preface to the Fables' (1700), in *Essays of John Dryden*, 2 vols, ed. W. P. Ker (New York, 1961), 2. 273.

CHAPTER 19

Historiography and Biography

BART VAN ES

Ben Jonson and Sallust: Setting the Stage

Ben Jonson's copy of the works of the Roman historian Sallust survives in Clare College at the University of Cambridge. It is a 1564 Basle edition that has been heavily marked by lines and crosses in pencil in its margins and looks very much like the working source text from which *Catiline* was composed. Although we cannot be entirely certain that the marks are Jonson's, they relate very closely to this drama, highlighting all the key passages that the poet made use of in the course of writing the play.[1] *Catiline*, performed in 1611 by The King's Men, is thus an exemplary case of the impact of classical historiography on English drama. Here, still preserved in its white vellum binding with 'Salustius l. 24' across the cut outer edge in Jonson's inked hand, is a concrete remnant of a body of literature that had a profound and transformative influence on the nature of early modern literary thought.

It is worth beginning this account of the reception of classical historiography and biography with the case of Jonson's Sallust. This is because the situation here is an unusually precise one: a specific edition used by an exceptionally learned literary author to produce a single, purely historical and biographical play. All of Jonson's *Catiline* can be related in some way to the Basle volume. There is in this instance clarity to the categories of 'history' and 'literature'. Very little else in this chapter will meet such exacting standards of precision: for this reason Jonson provides a useful point of reference as well as a test case whose complexities are greater than they might at first seem.

The impression that Sallust made on Jonson's *Catiline* is as substantial as the folio volume. In parts, the play could be called a translation of Sallust's account of the life of Lucius Sergius Catilína, whose conspiracy and attempted revolution against the state of Rome played out in the years 63–62 BCE. Repeatedly, long sections of Sallust's speeches are rendered into English. Indeed, Jonson's verse retains traces of its rendering from the Latin, as in 'use me your general' ('imperatore me utimini') (1. 1. 416; *Works*, 5. 448) or 'I cannot fear the war but to succeed well' ('vereri non possum quin...') (4. 6. 1; *Works*, 5. 523).[2] His final scene scrupulously follows the Roman historian's account of the pivotal debate in the Senate on the fate of the captured conspirators. Taking Julius Caesar's oration as an example, we discover a consistent pattern of Jonson's closeness to the classical text that is worth examining in detail, not only to typify the playwright's practise but also to illustrate the kind of material that Renaissance readers routinely drew from accounts of the classical past. First, there is what, in isolation, could be extracted as legal precedent, as in Caesar's judgement on the punishment of traitors:

If there could be found
A pain or punishment equal to their crimes,
I would devise and help; but if the greatness
Of what they ha' done exceed all man's invention,
I think it fit to stay where our laws do.
(*Catiline* 5. 6. 39–43; *Works*, 5. 541)

This edict is taken directly from the *Bellum Catilinae*, where Sallust records Caesar speaking as follows:

> Nam si digna poena pro factis eorum reperitur, novum consilium approbo; sin magnitudo sceleris omnium ingenia exsuperat, eis utendum censeo quae legibus comparata sunt.
>
> (If a punishment commensurate with their crimes can be found, I favour a departure from precedent; but if the enormity of their guilt surpasses all men's imagination, I should advise limiting ourselves to such penalties as the law has established.)
>
> (*Bellum Catilinae* 51. 8)

Here the bald political facts are rendered by Jonson as clean-lined blank verse.

Second, it was not merely the facts but also rhetorical construction through figures such as *epanorthosis* ('sententia eius mihi non crudelis... sed aliena a re publica nostra') and *erotesis* ('quid enim... crudele fieri potest?') that appealed to Jonson, as is clear from the continuation of Caesar's speech:

Nor do I think his sentence cruel, for
'Gainst such delinquents what can be too bloody,
But that it is abhorring from our state.
(*Catiline* 5. 6. 58–60; *Works*, 5. 542)

'Abhoring from' as an Englishing of *aliena a* is especially telling because it contains in one phrase both a Latinate mindset and a characteristically Roman sense of the moral integrity of the state itself.

Third, at a political level, there is the strategic working practice of the statesman, the thing more than anything else that sent young Renaissance courtiers to the pages of Roman historiography:

> How then? Set free, and increase Catiline's army?
> So will they, being but banish'd. No, grave Fathers,
> I judge 'em first to have their states confiscate;
> Then that their persons remain prisoners
> I'the free towns far off from Rome, and sever'd.
>
> (*Catiline* 5. 6. 75–9; *Works*, 5. 542)

Placet igitur eos dimitti et augeri exercitum Catilinae? Minume. Sed ita censeo, publicandas eorum pecunias, ipsos in vinculis habendos per municipia quae maxume opibus valent.

(Do I then recommend that the prisoners be allowed to depart and swell Catiline's forces? By no means! This, rather, is my advice: that their goods be confiscated and that they themselves be kept imprisoned in the strongest of the free towns.)

(Sallust, *Bellum Catilinae* 51. 43)

What these passages show goes beyond accurate translation. Jonson's English verse is Latinate—a deliberate attempt to convey the brevity and somewhat archaic diction of Sallust's prose. The difficulty that the modern reader of Latin sometimes experiences in detecting main verbs and objects in sentences is here also experienced in the English ('I would devise and help'; 'so will they, being but banished'). As a result, there is a profound sense of being transported, not so much to the actual world of the Roman Empire in the first century BCE as to the literary mode of classical politic history.

Exemplum, rhetoric, and politic statecraft: these are the staples of the reception of early modern historiography in Renaissance England.[3] The influence of Sallust is so strong in these and countless other instances that it appears to imprint not merely a historical narrative but also an entire political and moral system. Jonson's tragedy is in many ways scrupulously consistent in its adoption of the classical era, taking great care to replicate the details of Roman custom such as pagan sacrifice or senatorial procedure. His drama, moreover, also seems to internalize the ethical convictions of its historical source text (there can, for example, be no doubt in *Catiline* as to the rightness of the preservation of empire as an all-consuming cause). All the same, this reconstructive notion of influence (the idea that Jonson is merely dramatizing classical historiography) is misleading and becomes more so the closer we look.

The more variegated imprint of the 1564 Basle Sallust on *Catiline* becomes evident when we consider the passages from the *Bellum Catilinae* that are not taken up into the closing senate scene of Jonson's drama. The protagonists' reference to other events from Rome's past, for example, is almost entirely excluded. Jonson is remarkably uninterested in Rome's constitutional or social development, topics that are of great prominence in Sallust's original work. Commensurate with this, the whole picture of Rome's decline from its ancient ethos of self-denial and public service (so central to Sallust's authorial presence as a narrator) is missing from Jonson's version of Catiline's conspiracy. Even the emphasis on stoic control of the passions, which one might imagine would appeal to Jonson as a moralist, is radically downplayed in the work for the Jacobean stage. What, we might ask, is the impetus behind this change in the shape of events?

One answer to this question is to be found in the 1564 Basle Sallust itself, because the Renaissance *Sallustii Latinorum Historicorum Praestantissimi quae quidem extant Omnia (All the Surviving Works of Sallust, Most Outstanding of Roman Historians)* is something very different from Sallust's *Bellum Catilinae* as a standalone text. The Basle volume is a product of Renaissance humanism, an intellectual movement whose priorities (for all its commitment to accuracy) differ markedly from those of a Roman statesman in the first century BCE. Any attempt to assess the reception of classical historiography and biography in Renaissance English literature must take account of this mediating influence. In the Basle edition Sallust's account of the conspiracy is dwarfed by the commentaries of nine separate Renaissance scholars. As well as the *Bellum Jugurthinum* and an epitome of Sallust's lost *Histories* (left unmarked by the pencil of the annotator), the volume also contains extensive supplementary material to the Catiline history. These include Cicero's four Catilinarian orations (heavily marked in the Clare College copy and heavily used in *Catiline*) plus the dubiously attributed invectives exchanged between Sallust and Cicero (remaining unmarked and unused).

Jonson's sound scholarly choice of edition shaped the way he accessed his history. Characteristic sixteenth-century features of the volume include marginal commentaries that signpost subject matter and highlight rhetorical features ('amplificat ab exemplis Demosthenis sententiam' ('he amplifies Demosthenes' thought with examples'), for example, or 'pulchra similitudo' ('beautiful simile') and 'comparatio' ('comparison')). The scholarly commentary does much to expand upon and substantiate the historical detail of the *Bellum Catilinae*: one passage where the commentary particularly fascinated the annotator concerns the inception of Catiline's plot (XVI 4, Basle 150), which is marked as 'occasio, et temporis opportunitas' ('opportunity and favourable moment') in the marginal note to the main text (Basle 146). We find reference to corroborating evidence of Catiline's ambition in Cicero and Plutarch. This commentary was as important as Sallust's original to Jonson: nineteen separate pencil stripes and crosses in the margin mark the scholarly commentary concerning ambition and hope.

The nature of the commentary in the Basle text shaped Jonson's understanding of Sallust, making it more focused on the action of individuals (in the tradition of Machiavelli) and more programmatic in its stylistic imitation (following the Erasmian model of rhetoric). On top of this, the supplementary material in the Basle volume expanded Jonson's understanding of what counts as classical historiography and biography. Modern readers might not automatically include Cicero's Catilinarian orations under that heading, but they were clearly just as influential as Sallust in shaping the historical and moral design of Jonson's play. Cicero, who is a relatively minor figure in the *Bellum Catilinae* on account of Sallust's hostility to the anti-Caesarian party, is the hero of Jonson's tragedy: it is his eloquence, his subtle awareness of the limits of his own power, and his downright political cunning in getting the best out of ill-motivated people that ends up saving the state.

When we start to read beyond the localized instances of translation in *Catiline*, the picture of classical reception becomes increasingly complicated. At first it may seem that Jonson is simply dramatizing a source in Roman history, but the more closely one looks the less like Sallust the play becomes. The fundamental drive of Sallust's *Bellum Catilinae* is an almost elegiac lament for the lost virtues of a martial, morally severe Rome. This is the purpose of its preamble on the ancient kings and constitution of the city; it is also the logic according to which Sallust makes Gaius Caesar and Marcus Cato the great men of his story (the former for his generous public spirit; the latter for his incorruptible restraint). Neither this temporal scheme nor these characters make their way into Jonson's drama (his Caesar is a direct opposite of Sallust's and Cato becomes less important to the plot). For all its accuracy in historical setting, *Catiline* has a seventeenth-century agenda. As David Norbrook has shown, Jonson was hostile to puritanism even in its classical version and he was much more positive than the ancient historians themselves about the value of political cunning.[4] His primary focus was on statecraft (the prudence of Justus Lipsius), and in this he confronted the moral and practical issues of the Stuart age.[5] It was this, rather than any practical motivation of dramaturgy, that made Cicero a hero and Caesar a villain. The eloquence, judgement, and forensic intelligence of Cicero made him a model for Renaissance courtiers, whose own education was founded upon his books. The idea of defending an empire by means of rhetorical brilliance was a humanist dream, whereas Julius Caesar, by contrast, with his populism and assault on the constitution, was always likely to fare poorly in translation to the Stuart court.[6]

The relation between *Catiline* and the works of Sallust is a salutary example on which to begin an account of the reception of classical historiography and biography in English literature. Compared to many others, the case for influence is strong and also relatively simple, with the vast majority of narrative detail being drawn from an identifiable single text. Yet that clarity proves deceptive. Not only is the Roman history fused with numerous directly literary influences (such as Senecan tragedy, the satires of Juvenal, and Lucan's *Pharsalia*); it is also distorted through the lens of humanist statecraft, which (further to complicate matters) was itself initially shaped by the reading of classical historical texts. A reliable account of reception, from direct translation to more diffuse, but no less important, intellectual and ideological influence, must take account of this complex, layered, presence of the classical past in the early modern mind.

In the period covered by this volume, Ben Jonson stands out as the apogee of comprehensive absorption—from *sequi* through *imitari*, to *aemulari*, ending with the ideal of complete absorption to produce an original whole.[7] His pre-eminence in this respect makes him a useful starting point, but there are also dangers in this evaluative perspective. First, it is misleading to think of Jonson as 'advanced' from a modern standpoint: he was undoubtedly deeply read in the work of contemporary commentators upon classical historiography (most obviously the work of Lipsius), but this does not mean that his thinking sits further along a line of progression towards a twenty-first century understanding of these texts. Jonson was not, for example, in any noticeable way sceptical of the political motivation of those men who produced his sources, and nor, for all his precision about ritual, did he think critically about the experience of religion in the classical world. Second, it is a mistake to assume that Jonson's laborious intellectual approach was shared by many of his contemporaries. No playwright of this period stuck as closely as Jonson did to the form in which classical historiography reached him. John Marston explicitly opposed the agenda set by his rival and in the preface to his Roman tragedy, *Sophonisba* (1606), stated that he had 'not laboured in this poem to tie my self to relate any thing as an historian but to enlarge everything as a poet'.[8] 'To transcribe authors, quote authorities, and translate Latin prose orations into English blank verse', he pointedly declared, 'hath in this subject been the least aim of my studies'. Third, even where scholarly labour was considerable, it did not necessarily translate into a reverential attitude to historical truth. A more oppositional formulation of the relationship between historical writing and poetry was not uncommon in the period. Sir Philip Sidney and Edmund Spenser, in both their critical pronouncements and their literary practice, were strong in their rejection of historians as models. All the same, their multi-plotted romances are equally important texts in which to examine the impact of classical historiography, even if we do not find in them the neat connection to specific editions that we find in the case of Jonson's *Catiline.*

This chapter will highlight what is new and distinctive about the early modern literary reception of classical history and biography. That question is usefully begun by considering early modern editions, translations, and the annotations of readers. Ultimately, however, reception becomes a more attenuated process—something that can take us to the complex interdependence of vernacular historiography and drama in this period. The question of what we call literary and what historiographical is at times a fraught one, but humanist histories such as John Hayward's *First Part of the Raigne of King Henry the IIII* and Francis Bacon's *The History of the Reign of King Henry VII* (strongly modelled on the work of Tacitus and Thucydides) are now commonly understood to reward analysis as creative works in their own right. Such books were influenced by and proved an influence on English tragedy: a play like Samuel Daniel's *Philotas,* depicting the fall of one of Alexander the Great's generals, is typical of this two-way influence. The 'Apology' appended to its first printed edition records this work's genesis as a response to discussions at St John's College, Cambridge, and describes its reception in academic circles. Daniel clearly conceived *Philotas* as a contribution to historiographical debate. The ripples of classical reception are thus multiply refracted: from simple source use they take us to questions of identity and political allegiance. It is no exaggeration to say that a change in the understanding of what history meant must lie at the heart of any understanding of the cultural and ontological impact of the Renaissance. Humanism would look very different without Livy, Tacitus, and Plutarch. The big picture of the literary reception of classical historiography and biography is thus inseparable from wider questions about the emergence of a modern sensibility: even Jonson's faithful translation of passages of the *Bellum Catilinae* is a less familiar process than it might at first seem.

Although it is always difficult to draw divisions between kinds of texts and kinds of reception, it makes sense to divide this chapter into three sections and to include a chronological element in each. Section One, 'Statehood', will look principally at humanism's reaction to Livy, using his work as a focal point for the reception of republican ideas. Section Two, 'Policy', is concerned mainly with Tacitus and the associated political thinking of Machiavelli and Lipsius, going on to examine the reaction against Tacitus in the latter stages of Stuart rule. Finally, Section Three is concerned with biography: both classical writing of lives, such as those of Plutarch, and the wider treatment of character in this period. Across all these sections it is also important to bear in mind the presence of early modern antiquarianism. Writers such as Camden were providing a more clear-sighted picture of classical culture (especially during the Roman colonization of Britain).[9] They learnt their methods in part from classical predecessors such as Varo and Herodotus; in this way too, classical texts helped to change the way that the ancient past was understood. The increasingly sharp distinctions that these men drew between ancient and modern modes of living had a profound impact on Renaissance authors, and they have also shaped the way we today look on the classical and early modern past. In the light of this thinking, the close of this chapter will return once more to Jonson's *Catiline*, this time to examine its techniques of characterization. Here too, in spite of close connections, Jonson's priorities are more radically different from classical historiography than we might expect.

Statehood: Livy and the Republican Ideal

By the time that Jonson completed *Catiline* it was, above all, an interest in Tacitus that was the marker of a new sophisticated political thinking. The worldly *realpolitik* calculations of Tacitus' *Histories* and *Annals*, even if not a narrative source for Jonson on this occasion, cast a long shadow over Catiline's rebellion. Indeed we could say that Jonson carves out of Sallust's moralistic *Bellum Catilinae* a decidedly Tacitean plot. Yet Tacitus had not at first been the most important classical historian for the humanist movement. In the fifteenth and early sixteenth centuries pride of place was held by Livy's *History of Rome*.

J. H. Whitfield wrote most emphatically against the assumption that there was a constant and even presence of the classical historians in Renaissance culture.[10] The first generation of humanists, Petrarch foremost among them, were interested in Livy because it was in his *History* that the ethical and constitutional foundations of a successful republic were to be seen. Livy, especially in his early books, provided a template of the balanced constitution as well as a set of iconic stories (such as the upbringing of Romulus and Remus; the capture of the Sabines; and the framing of Numa's laws) on which a myth of statehood could be built. That primary focus remained in force among the thinkers who followed. In Machiavelli, Whitfield states, 'references are 99 to 1 in favour of Livy' because Livy's picture of the early history of Rome was much more relevant to the make-up and aspirations of Florence than was Tacitus' forensic analysis of the state's moral decline. The full surviving body of Tacitus' work did not become available until the first decades of the sixteenth century, and even then the courts of the dictatorial Caesars that they described were of less interest to the intellectual culture of the Italian city states. It was perhaps only the trauma of Charles V's wars in the period 1527–30 (resulting in the crushing of the Florentine republic and the imposition of Medici rule) that made Tacitean post-Republican Rome directly relevant to contemporary politics. Until that point at least, Livy's *History* had been dominant. The pre-Imperial Rome of its surviving books offered lessons for the preservation of legal institutions, spelled out the duties of citizens, analysed the competing claims of aristocracy and popular interest, and set out the conditions necessary for successful colonial enterprise. Livy's Rome, therefore, offered a mirror for any ambitious early modern state.

The theme of tyranny might well have had earlier relevance to Tudor England, especially under Henry VIII's reign of terror, but in spite of this it was again the work of Livy that spearheaded the entry of a new body of classical historiography. His *History* was carried across the channel directly by Italian scholars who were spreading the new learning to the North. Among these was Polydore Vergil, who began his *Anglica Historia* around 1506 for Henry VII. Although Caesar's *Commentarii de Bello Gallico* and Tacitus' *Agricola* were important sources for Virgil's account of the Kingdom's origins it was Livy's comprehensive state history, as taken up by Italians such as Leonardo Bruni, that was the primary model for his work. Virgil was an influence on English writers, including Sir Thomas More, who knew him personally. As with the adoption of the Roman republic as a point of self-comparison for the independent states of Italy, so too it is evident that English writers felt confident in taking Livy's narrative as a source of moral and practical instruction for their own monarchical commonwealth. Antony Cope's *Anniball and Scipio* (1544), which was in large part sourced in books 21 to 38 of Livy's *History*, was the earliest English history explicitly to use this comparison as its justification. Thomas Berthelet's prefatory verse epistle to the volume writes of 'profit at time of need' to be gained from this history, a point that Cope drives home in his opening address to his sovereign. Declaring the present a 'time of war' and observing 'the manifold injuries, done to your majesty, and to your subjects of this realm, by your unnatural and unkind enemies on sundry parties', Cope suggests the utility of his material in the following way:

> Wherefore well pondering the time of war to be now in hand, as a thing so much needful for many considerations, I (for my poor part) thought that I should do not only your

> highness acceptable service but also to all noble men and gentlemen of the realm great pleasure and commodity, if gathering together out of Titus Livius and other authors, the lives, the policies, and the martial acts of two the most worthy captains, of the two most renowned empires of the world, that is to say of Anniball of Carthage, and Scipio of Rome, I would bring the same into our English tongue, whereby beside the pleasant bestowing of time, in the reading thereof, men also may learn both to do displeasure to their enemies, and to avoid the crafty and dangerous baits, which shall be laid for them.
>
> (*Anniball and Scipio* A3[a])

Cope, who was an arch-loyalist to Henry's rule (taking an active part in both foreign wars and in the suppression of domestic risings) was evidently interested in applying his learning to the practicalities of warfare. This was also the position of Gabriel Harvey, who commended Cope's work for its application of political lessons and whose celebrated annotations of Livy were designed for use by the Sidney family in the pursuit of Irish policy.[11] Cope was a pioneer in the use of Livy in English for the practical purpose of governance and characteristic of his time in selecting Livy above all others for this purpose.

In 1580, when Harvey was working with a new intensity on the annotation of Livy, the pre-eminence of his author as a schoolbook for the courtier and commander was an established fact. He notes that eminent figures including Nicholas Throckmorton prefer Livy to other classical historians. Handwriting a summative account at the close of the volume of the 1555 Basle text with commentaries by Joannes Velcurio and Henricus Glareanus, Harvey confirms this justified preference among men of affairs:

> The notablest men that first commended the often and advised reading of Livy unto me were these five: Doctor Henry Harvey, Mr Roger Ascham, Sir Thomas Smyth, Sir Walter Mildmay, Sir Philip Sidney (all learned, expert, and very judicious in the greatest matters of private or public quality). Once I heard Mr Secretary Wilson & Doctor Binge prefer the Roman history before the Greek, or other and Livy before any other Roman history. But, of all other, Sir Philip Sidney, Colonel Smyth [i.e. Smith junior], and Monsieur Bodin won my heart to Livy. Sir Philip Sidney esteems no general History like Justine's abridgement of Trogus, nor any special Roman history like Livy, nor any particular history, Roman, or other, like the singular life, and actions of Caesar.[12]

This remarkable paragraph tells us a great deal about what might be called the first phase of the reception of classical historiography in Renaissance England. Harvey commends the best examples of the three best kinds of history: general history (the abridgement of Trogus); special Roman history (Livy); and particular history (all accounts of the life of Caesar, including the work of Sallust, Plutarch, and Caesar's own *Commentaries*). Here a body of prominent English humanist thinkers with close connections to government concur in what Jardine and Grafton term the 'pragmatic' reading of this body of material. In this context, the supplementing of Livy with Caesar (whose narrative is much more specific in military detail while lacking in constitutional depth) is revealing. It illustrates an operating assumption that Roman colonial governance (much more than the mixed constitutions of city states) provides an immediate reference point for English statecraft. In the case of Cope and also for the coterie inhabited by Gabriel Harvey, this is most immediately the case when looking at Ireland, where England was attempting something along the lines of imperial rule. Sir Thomas Smith thus repeatedly draws on information from Livy and Caesar's *Commentaries* (generally without acknowledgement) in *De Republica Anglorum*, which he completed in 1565, and his prospectus for Irish colonization, *A Letter Sent by I. B. Gentleman unto His Very Friend Master R. C.* (1572).[13] When Harvey's protégé, Edmund Spenser, came to write his brutally militaristic *View of the Present State of Ireland*, the poet operated under the influence of such thinking, so that his policies for the island's systematic colonization were based explicitly on Roman precedent as set out in Caesar's account of the Gallic Wars and Tacitus' *Agricola*.[14]

Jardine and Grafton show how Harvey read and reread Livy in the company of a series of politically active patrons—the Sidneys and the Earl of Leicester most prominent among them. In part, this is straightforwardly a matter of extracting methods of governance, as was the case in 1571 when Harvey took part in a debate at the house of Sir Thomas Smith. On that occasion, Smith and his son took opposing characters from Livy's *History* (Fabius and Marcellus) in order to test the respective validity of more measured and more aggressive strategies for the maintenance of control. Here history translated directly into Irish policy, but Harvey's reading was not always of this kind. In addition to 'pragmatic' reading, Jardine and Grafton define 'moral', 'politique', and, thirdly 'positioning' methods of interpretation, which translate approximately to courtly and academic milieus. In these cases, we have something more complex than the extraction of precedent. For at the heart of Jardine and Grafton's account of early modern historiographical reading sits the emblematic object of the book-wheel: a physical instrument that allows the reader to access tens of volumes (open at specific passages) at the same time. It is this that ultimately provides the true picture of Harvey as a reader: supplementing Livy with works as far apart as Augustine's *City of God* (in the edition of Juan Luis Vives) and Machiavelli's *Art of War*. 'Supplementing', in fact, gives a misleading sense of hierarchy: often it is difficult to determine whether any text takes precedence in a mode of reading that is topic-centred rather than focused on any individual book.

Sir Philip Sidney, a particularly well-attuned reader of Livy through personal contact with Lipsius, provides an exemplary instance of this polyphonous engagement with the classical past and in particular with the notion of the ideal commonwealth. Sidney's letters are replete with examples of his analytical contact with classical history, but in the *Arcadia* too the conception of aristocratic right, law, and the limits of sovereignty make use of touchstone episodes from Rome's early years. The romance is richly allusive in its engagement with the first three books of Livy's *History*, which, as we have seen, the poet was reading with particular attention in the early 1580s. At the heart of these early books stands Rome's break with monarchy and the establishment of its republic. Among the most famous episodes dealt with in these early volumes are, first, the rape of Lucretia, and, second, a conspiracy against the new state by a party of young men of the equestrian class. Livy describes the assault on Lucretia towards the end of the opening book of his *History*: it is this act of sexual violence that sparks a rebellion against the rule of the Tarquins, which leaves Lucius Junius Brutus as one of the two first consuls of a newly republican Rome at the book's close. Book 2 begins the history of the republic with an act of treason that involves the sons of Brutus: young men who look for 'freer rein to their appetites and to live the dissolute and irresponsible life of the court' (2. 3). Brutus, as bearer of the rods of justice, fights this attempt to reimpose monarchy. He tries his sons and stands by, unbending but suffering 'a father's anguish', as they are stripped, flogged, and beheaded on his orders, thereby providing an absolute exemplum of even-handed judgment in the new non-monarchical state. These episodes, dominating Livy's account of the birth of the Roman republic, were a source of fascination in Elizabethan England and provide Sidney with a complex ethical matrix, which he exploited to great effect in the denouement of the *Arcadia*.

Rape, concupiscent monarchs, attempted revolution, and the exercise of unrelenting justice on young men by their relatives are all key constituents of the plot of Sidney's romance. Yet what Sidney gives us is not Roman history in any straightforward sense. As Debora Shuger has demonstrated, Euarchus' judgement on Sidney's heroes at the book's denouement both replicates and reverses the judgment of Brutus in book 2 of the *History*.[15] Like Brutus, Euarchus reluctantly passes judgment on young men (one of them his son) who are tainted by unlicensed sexual acts and political rebellion. In relating this incident, however, Sidney's narrator alludes not to Brutus (the founding figure of the republic) but to Cato of Utica (the opponent of Caesar whose noble suicide marked the Republic's final collapse):

> But Euarchus, that felt his own misery more than they, and yet loved goodness more than himself, with such a sad assured behaviour as Cato killed himself withal, when he had heard the uttermost of that their speech tended unto, he commanded again they should be carried away, rising up from the seat (which he would much rather have wished should have been his grave), and looking who would take the charge, whereto everyone was exceeding backward.[16]

This is a complex double allusion, pairing rationalistic self-sacrifice with its doom-laden end. Its political complexity is heightened by the continuation of the story, which (through the most last minute of last-minute revelations) turns away from classical precedent. Not only does Duke Basilius revive at the providential moment, he also saves the princes with monarchical equity, opposing the mechanics of republican law. Arguably this conclusion critiques rather than adopts Livy's ethics; it certainly subsumes the *History*'s dictums within a larger pool of *topoi*, leaving questions about clemency, noble nature, and models of civic governance open to debate.

Sidney's *Arcadia* thus repeatedly interrogates, contests, and even parodies the ethical assumptions of Livy's *History*. After Pyrocles takes Philoclea's virginity, for example, he himself (to borrow a phrase as well as an argument from Debora Shuger) 'plays Lucretia' in attempting to kill himself so that his body may testify to the chastity of his beloved.[17] The irony of that situation is then further heightened when the woman he has wronged responds with arguments against suicide that are taken from Saint Augustine's examination of Lucretia's self-murder in *The City of God*. There is intellectual wit in such engagements not just with Roman history but with the different traditions of commentary upon it. Such wit depended on an author's wide frame of reference; still more importantly, it depended on a reader's familiarity with these stories and their associations, so that innovative combinations had a meaningful effect. Decades of humanist reading of classical history made this possible. Sidney's *Arcadia* is thus just one example of the way Livy's influence blended with other literary and philosophical sources among poets of the sixteenth century, especially in response to Lucretia's rape.

Shakespeare's *Rape of Lucrece* is among the most complex of these cases. Colin Burrow has written about the way that Livy's version of the history (which is made prominent in the prose Argument that prefaces the poem in its first edition) differs in important ways from the poet's own.[18] Shakespeare, he demonstrates, was not merely inventing his version, but drawing on other retellings, possibly including that of Livy's contemporary, Dionysius of Halicarnassus, whose *Roman Antiquities* covered the same ground. Most intriguingly, Burrow suggests that Shakespeare may have read Livy's *History* in the edition of Ovid's *Fasti* prepared by Paulus Marsus. This text includes massive quotations from Livy's narrative of Lucretia, which Marsus believed to be Ovid's main source. Such a rich body of historical and quasi-historical versions of the same story, combined with various traditions of commentary, offered extraordinary literary potential. The example of Marsus' edition gives us a picture of Renaissance engagement with classical history that is distinct from the pragmatic model so influentially forwarded by Jardine and Grafton. As well as reading for practical political purpose, early modern readers (including poets) could work comparatively, seeking out difference between rival accounts. This notion somewhat modifies Arnaldo Momigliano's influential claim that the factual content of ancient history was very little questioned by early modern readers.[19] A poem like *The Rape of Lucrece* is implicitly sceptical about the truth of any single version of classical history: through its numerous acts of retelling it indicates that there is something partial about every account. More than this, literary readers, with Shakespeare as the most spectacular example, could hybridize Livy with other sources, producing what Burrow terms 'rhetorical cross-dressing'—a deliberate mixing of well-known historical material with unstable, reactive elements, such as the poetry of erotic persuasion or religious belief. The categories of history and poetry became inextricably intertwined as a result.[20]

This mixing of narratives was an occasion for wit, but it also had a political aspect. For, while the reception of historical writing always involved an engagement with politics, the conjunction of certain stories could add a polemical edge. In the case of *The Rape of Lucrece* the combination of rhyme royal with male erotic persuasion would inevitably have recalled Samuel Daniel's *Complaint of Rosalind* (a poem that is pointed in condemning the abuse of monarchical power). That connection strengthened the domestic application of lessons from Livy's *History*. As a result, some scholars are prepared to call this a 'republican' poem. For work produced before the outbreak of the Civil War this term rarely if ever denotes anything programmatic, if by 'programmatic' we mean the desire to establish a state that is permanently without a king. Yet the praise of republican rule could imply criticism of present conditions. As Quentin Skinner has shown, ideas of liberty in this period were profoundly informed by classical precedent, so resistance to tyranny, insistence that monarchs take advice, and pressure surrounding uncertain succession could all be expressed using republican language.[21] An apparently neutral account of classical government could thus become a medium for dissent.

Andrew Hadfield provides a checklist of factors that, in combination, constitute what he calls republicanism: (1) rhetoric against tyranny, (2) commitment to humanist education, (3) stress on virtue in government officials, often linked to critique of hereditary monarchy and praise of republics, (4) keen interest in histories of the republic and enthusiasm for Livy, (5) the language of natural rights, and (6) emphasis on the importance of offices held by ordinary citizens.[22] Classical historiography is the key ingredient of this cocktail, and, in consequence, Hadfield discovers republicanism in early modern drama, including Thomas Lodge's *Wounds of Civil War*, the anonymous *Tragedy of Claudius Tiberius Nero, Rome's Greatest Tyrant*, and George Chapman's *Caesar and Pompey, a Roman Tragedy*. The strongest polemical element in such work tends to come from Lucan's *Pharsalia* rather than from Roman historiography directly.[23] If we are to call these plays republican in sympathy, then this refers to republicanism in what Patrick Cheney terms its 'imaginative', 'linguistic', and 'pre-practical' phase.[24] For Cheney this means that even plays without classical subject matter can evoke the rhetoric of particular historiographic traditions: for example, a Tacitean *realpolitik* in Marlowe's *Edward II* that exists in tension with a Lucan-inspired republican sublime.

It is precisely because they have no direct historical source that Shakespeare and his likely collaborator George Peele are able to exploit such competing political valences in *Titus Andronicus*.[25] As Hadfield has shown, the play is indebted to different strata of Roman history. Given its concern with the last days of the empire, *Titus* relates to Herodian's *History*, which charts the fates of a series of unfortunate emperors from the death of Marcus Aurelius to AD 238. The names Saturninus and Bassianus can be traced to Herodian, even if they lack direct parallels in Shakespeare's plot. On top of this, the play has connections to Sallust's *Bellum Iugurthinum*, where excoriating rhetoric about Roman decline sits alongside a barbarian threat. Finally, the protagonists of *Titus Andronicus* are themselves aware of precedents in republican history, thus making the rape of Lavinia a political act. Seen in the context of anxieties around the succession in the early 1590s, the alternative systems of governance presented in the play—free election, military might, foreign marriage, inherited monarchy—have direct policy implications. Such systems are sourced in classical history even if they are not restricted to a particular period of classical time.

The multiplicity of historical parallels in *Titus Andronicus* bears comparison with Sidney's *Arcadia*: the work is well attuned to the sensibilities of an educated audience, and it is unsurprising that this should have been the first Shakespeare play to reach print in 1594. Alongside the *Arcadia*, published 1593, and *Lucrece* (1594), it forms part of a cluster of publications in this period that seem to comment on the succession by means of republican history, especially that of Livy's Rome. In the years that followed such history became less prominent. Erudite attention switched to Tacitus and Lucan, even though Livy continued to provide material for the public stage. This late reception of Livy is arguably more programmatically republican in character, especially when seen in the context of growing resentment about Stuart rule. John Webster and Thomas Heywood's *Appius and Virginia*, first performed between the mid-1620s and the mid-1630s but unpublished until the advent of the Commonwealth, is characteristic of a more strident language of liberty, unthinkable in England a few decades before. Here the sin of attempted rape is the direct outcome of a corrupt non-democratic system. The dramatists seize on the reign of the Decemvirs, described in book three of Livy's *History* and also accessible through Painter's *Palace of Pleasure.* This is the part of Livy's book that is most strident in its defence of constitutional government, and Webster and Heywood do nothing at all to curb that edge. The closing lines of this tragedy are, as a result, far more programmatically republican than any performed in Elizabeth's reign:

ICILIUS: The Life of the *Decemviri*
Expires in them. *Rome* thou at length art free,
Restored unto thine ancient liberty.
MINUTIUS: Of Consuls: which bold *Junius Brutus* first
Begun in *Tarquins* fall. *Virginius* you
And young *Icilius* shall his place succeed,
So by the peoples suffrage 'tis decreed.[26]

Closing reference to the rape of Lucretia caps this republican apology. Although the speech can hardly be counted as an allusion to James or his son, the potential for such application was always there. As Paulina Kewes has illustrated, in the run-up to the Civil War direct parallels were indeed made between Charles I and Tarquin. The revivals and republications of Heywood's *Rape of Lucrece* in the 1630s and 1640s are thus very likely to be connected to Charles's personal rule.[27] This feels a long way from the pragmatic reading of Gabriel Harvey, even if some of the ideals of the Roman republic had always been there.

Livy was the dominant classical historical influence in England from the early sixteenth century until the beginning of the 1590s. By the time that Philemon Holland's translation of the *History* was published in 1600, scores of literary works had already been based on Livy, and his availability in English would stimulate many more.[28] At the same time, however, a more exact study of *ars historica* was gaining in prominence. This scholarly trend did not displace Livy, but it did gradually make his work less fashionable among the elites. For those connected to the Earl of Essex especially, from the mid-1590s onwards a purer form of high political history (concentrated on the courts of emperors more than the battlefields of the republic) came to be prized. Those preferences made Tacitus newly important: it was the sceptical, analytic, political thinking of his *Agricola, Annals*, and *Histories* that would prove the shaping presence for the new classical tragedies of Samuel Daniel and Ben Jonson as well as the kind of prose history written by Hayward or Bacon.[29] The thinking that is often crudely characterized as 'Machiavellian' is in fact better traced to the Tacitean historiography of imperial Rome.

Policy: Tacitean Readers from the 1590s to the Civil War

It would be a mistake to think of Livy as a conservative influence or to contrast his stable civic ethics straightforwardly with the scepticism of Tacitus. In obvious ways Livy's *History* provided the more radical political model. Its concentration on the life of the Republic offered readers an alternative vision of statecraft: a sober, meritocratic, militaristic culture that contrasted with the vagaries of a monarch's personal rule. This republican *virtù* had attracted Livy's most influential continental exponent, Niccolò Machiavelli, whose *Discourses on the First Ten Books of Titus Livy* (*c*.1517) reflected on the character of Roman constitutional government and applied his stark pragmatic conclusions to Italian states.[30] Adventurous republican thinking, therefore, could be shaped by Livy and Machiavelli at the same time. All the same, the fashion for this kind of thinking did not come into force in England until the 1590s, and it was associated with Tacitus much more than with Livy's work. It was sparked above all by Henry Savile's celebrated translation of the first four books of the *Histories* plus the *Life of Agricola*, which was printed in 1591. With their account of the chaotic 'year of the four emperors' following Nero's suicide, the *Histories* must have felt prescient at the start of what is often called the Elizabethan 'succession crisis'. They were made still more explosive thanks to Savile's addition of his own original piece of history writing, 'The End of Nero and Beginning of Galba', which preceded the translations themselves.

Savile's book is in several ways a highpoint in the reception of classical historiography and biography in Renaissance England.[31] His linguistic ability allowed him to translate the knotty Latin into a terse, aphoristic English equivalent and also to provide learned commentary on such subjects as Roman warfare. In addition, Savile's

'End of Nero' was in its own right a model for a new kind of prose in the vernacular: based on research across multiple sources, this was argument-driven history that focused on the analysis of political power. But the work has historical significance also because of its connections to the Earl of Essex's faction. Its mysterious preface by 'A.B. to the Reader' was said by Jonson and Edmund Bolton to be by the earl himself. The preface warned that 'in Galba thou mayest learn that a good Prince governed by evil ministers is as dangerous as if he were evil himself' (¶3[a]). Even though the book was dedicated to Queen Elizabeth, its Machiavellian logic disavowed unconditional loyalty to the sovereign and Savile's concluding Judgment on Julius Vindex, the first instigator of the rebellion against Nero, is worth citing in full:

> This end had Julius Vindex, a man in the course of this action more virtuous then fortunate; who having no army provided, no legion, no soldier in charge, whiles others more able looked on, first entered the lists, challenging a Prince upholden with thirty legions, rooted in the Empire by four descendants of ancestors, and fourteen years continuance of reign, not upon private despair to set in combustion the state, not to revenge, disgrace, or dishonour, not to establish his own sovereignty, things which have moved most men to attempt, but to redeem his country from tyranny and bondage, which only respect he regarded so much, that in respect he regarded nothing his own life or security.[32]

Not only does Savile here celebrate one who conspired against his sovereign; he attributes the success of the rebellion to the political guile of Julius Vindex rather than any divine judgement on the evils of Nero's reign.

Savile himself was a proficient servant of monarchy who was successful in his pursuit of patronage under both Elizabeth and James. Through the Essex circle, however, Tacitus came increasingly to be associated with subversion. In 1598 Richard Greenway dedicated his (less accomplished) translation of the *Annals* to Essex, starting with the historian's 'Proem', which expressed regret that when the imperial rule of Augustus was established 'there was no sign of the old laudable customs to be seen: but contrary, equality taken away as every man endeavoured to obey the prince'.[33] Still more dangerously, Sir John Hayward prefaced his Tacitean *First Part of the Life and Raigne of King Henrie IIII* (1599) with an address to the earl in Latin. Paired with a history that focused on the overthrow of a monarch and the establishment of an alternative government, this dedication was incendiary. The preface was suppressed, the second edition burned, and, even before Essex's failed uprising, Hayward was interrogated and detained by the authorities. The *First Part of the Life* featured prominently in Essex's trial for treason, and its author remained in prison for the rest of the reign. Because the principal instigator of the rebellion, Essex's secretary Henry Cuff, was a student of classical history and a protégé of Savile's, the association of Tacitus with dangerous politics became stronger still.

The reception of Livy had centred on a series of iconic narrative episodes; the model of a socially balanced constitution; and the ideal of republican liberty. Tacitus, in contrast, offered a way of thinking: his working methods created an 'ism' of a kind that exists for no other classical historian.[34] The narrative content of the *Annals*, *Histories*, and *Germania* was relatively less important. When Savile described Vindex's strategy for sparking rebellion, it was his method, not his information, that came from Tacitus. Vindex sent conspiratorial letters to numerous parties knowing that most recipients would report these to Nero. It was Galba's failure to report his letter that tied him (somewhat unwillingly) to the rebellion, and *this* was what Savile identified as Vindex's skill. This emphasis on fear, on mixed and uncertain motivation, and on communication rather than military prowess was what made the account a Tacitean one.

With the exception of Sir Thomas More (in his abandoned account of *Richard III*), no sixteenth-century historian before Savile had written in English according to the methods of a classical historian, but in the last decades of the sixteenth century this changed. Savile's *End of Nero*, though brief, was the first of a series of politic histories—Hayward's *Henry IIII* (1599), Bacon's *Henry VII* (1622), and the Earl of Clarendon's *History of the Rebellion* (1646–72) being the most prominent.[35] In the tradition of classical historians such as Thucydides, Sallust, and Tacitus, these were books written by men with personal experience in the administration of government: they focused on specific events such as the loss or seizure of political control. Tacitean or Machiavellian concepts such as 'skill', 'seasonableness', and 'dexterity' were important in their vocabulary. Although these authors might serve their monarchs, they placed little reliance on the intrinsic authority of rulers because history was there to be made by able men. It was this pragmatism, as well as the seductiveness of liberty, that Thomas Hobbes had in mind when he wrote that 'books written by famous men of ancient Grecian and Roman Commonwealths, concerning their policy and great actions' should be counted as contributory causes of the Civil War.[36]

Paradoxically, however, the immediate literary effect of Tacitism at the turn of the century was not a culture of political action, but its exact reverse. Daniel's *Philotas* and Jonson's *Sejanus* are characteristic of the tense, wordy, dramas of tyranny in this period that grew directly from the intellectual culture of the Essex circle. They present the moral ideal of a resigned stoicism, rather than commitment to or against the cause of a prince. The trials of Essex and Sir Walter Ralegh provide one backdrop to this culture. Many of those associated with these fallen heroes of the late Elizabethan era were readers of Tacitus and they responded to recent events with a literature of cynicism and unease. Daniel's *Small Poems* (1605) was largely concerned with classical history, and, even if Plutarch was his principal source, the emphasis on policy across many of its parts was Tacitean. *Philotas* (the play that was printed as part of the volume) tells the story of a man whose sense of his own dignity prevents him from paying proper homage to his newly deified leader. Whether Philotas is guilty of anything more than arrogance and a failure to pass on the details of a rumoured conspiracy remains uncertain, but for his nemesis Craterus that question is ultimately an immaterial one. This wily counsellor exemplifies the relentless suspicion that characterizes the Tacitean world view, in which the potential for rebellion is as legitimate a target as open rebellion itself. In his words:

> Men in their private dangers may be stout,
> But in th'occasions and the fears of kings,
> We ought not to be credulous, but doubt
> The intimation of the vainest things.[37]

Just as in *Sejanus*, it is a possible plot rather than an actual one that is ruthlessly crushed at the play's conclusion, a queasy victory being achieved by an emperor who remains hidden from view. Although both Daniel and Jonson were called in for questioning and suspected of inserting subversive references, their plays were not actually revolutionary in the sense of promoting an anti-monarchic cause. They reported the ancient past without any obvious modern intrusions, and their message, if anything, endorsed the prudent loyalism found in Justus Lipsius' edition of Tacitus. At heart, it was their utterly sober perspective on the political process that was the cause of concern.

Politic history had always been a source of unease in early modern England, but the opposition to this way of thinking became more strident and sophisticated in the 1620s and 1630s. Edmund Bolton, a Catholic client of the Duke of Buckingham, was among the strongest of the anti-Taciteans. His *Nero Caesar or Monarchy Depraved* (1624) was written with King James's approval in order to critique Tacitean assumptions about monarchy. He, like many strong loyalists to the Stuarts, preferred Polybius and also promoted Lucius Florus, a translation of whose *Epitome* he had published in 1619. In Bolton's work we see the emergence of a professional language of historical disputation, most remarkably so in his manuscript *Averunci, or The Skowrers* (1634), which defends Tiberius from alleged bias in the Tacitean account.[38] By this point in intellectual history, educated men came more clearly to see that there were ideological implications to certain historiographical methods. It was thus, again, to provide a methodological alternative to Tacitean thinking about kingship that Thomas Hobbes produced his translation of Thucydides.

Two things thus develop in reaction to Tacitus: an increased awareness of the political implications of any historical method and a more concrete sense of what historical argument (as distinct from rhetorical *inventio*) involves at an intellectual level. Diagory Wheare, the first Camden Professor of History at Oxford, is a characteristic product of those intellectual pressures. He was (like Bolton) an exponent of Florus and a detractor of Tacitus. His *De Ratione et Methodo Legendi Historias Dissertatio* (*Dissertation on the System and Method of Reading Histories* (1623)) was the most distinguished example of the *ars historica* thus far published in England. It was scrupulous in avoiding contentious references to contemporary politics and, as such, an indication that the study of history could become a more exclusively academic discipline.[39]

As D. R. Woolf has argued, the catalyst of political conflict transformed the writing of history in the last few decades before the outbreak of Civil War. Thus, in sharp contrast to Wheare at Oxford, Isaac Dorislaus lectured on Tacitus as the first incumbent of the chair in history that Fulke Greville established at Cambridge in 1628. Before the third could be delivered, Dorislaus' lectures caused uproar and were suppressed as a threat to monarchical government. That furore can in retrospect be understood as a pre-tremor of the conflicts of the English Civil War. At the same time, the establishment of chairs in history at Oxford and Cambridge was also a marker of a new scholarly clarity about historiography, a development that made the *literary* reception of classical history more marginal. Increased theoretical focus on the study of history was corrosive to old practices because history and poetry were now more distinct as categories. Daniel's abandonment of his grand poetic account of the Wars of the Roses in favour of the prose *History* was a product of this shift in thinking. To compose *The Civil Wars* Daniel had drawn on classical historians in addition to Lucan, but that had become an unstable mix. The elegiac treatment of past events could now be confined to works like Thomas May's translation and continuation of the *Pharsalia*. Politic history, in contrast, had become prosaic, and its influence was destined to shape narratives like Clarendon's *History* or Hobbes's *Behemoth*. The notion that Tacitean 'policy' was a fit subject for literature, while important, was short-lived.

Biography: Plutarch and the Concept of Character

Shakespeare, from his earliest history plays onwards, was profoundly affected by Roman historians. Whether directly or indirectly, they underpin not just the core narratives but also the conception of statehood and the language of politics in his works. But Shakespeare's favourite historian was the Greek Plutarch: had his folio copy of Sir Thomas North's English translation survived, we would presumably find it to be still more heavily marked with underlinings than Jonson's copy of Sallust at Clare. Almost as much as Jonson, Shakespeare was willing to versify classical history: substantial direct borrowing from Plutarch is to be found in *Julius Caesar, Antony and Cleopatra, Coriolanus*, and *Timon of Athens*, and his influence also extends beyond the historical works. The playwright was unusual in this preference. It reflects a way of approaching character that is also unusual in this period. In spite of a surface similarity in their borrowing of whole passages, there is in fact a profound difference between Jonson and Shakespeare when we look in detail at how they read the classical past.

As noted in this chapter's opening section, Jonson was uninterested in many of the intellectual 'virtues' of Roman political history, to the point of excluding their emphasis on characterization and constitutional change. Above all, internal conflict (which is important in Tacitus and still more so in Plutarch) was problematic for Jonson. As Philip Ayres has shown, in both *Sejanus* and *Catiline* there is a conscious drive towards moral schematization on the part of the author.[40] Extraordinarily,

Jonson's *Sejanus* depicts even Caligula as unambiguously good because, within the instructive template of the play, he must stand as part of a coherent grouping of the oppressed Germanican faction—a body characterized by neo-Stoical virtue. The same is true of the blanching of Julius Caesar's character in *Catiline*, where Sallust's account is the primary source. Sallust saw Caesar as part of a populist political faction, and he understood the actions of Marius as a response to the pressures of the republic's mixed constitution (which was the subject of Livy's analysis and Lipsius' commentaries). Jonson, however, chooses to make Caesar a ruthless Machiavellian careerist (and Jonson's Machiavellianism is a much simpler thing than the constitutional thinking we find in the Italian's original). Jonson is celebrated for creating an English version of the Latin elegance of the Augustan age, but this Ciceronean clarity is something quite different from Tacitus' strained syntax. Tacitus had depicted the Emperor Tiberius as a very complex character—not just deceiving others but often deceiving himself. Jonson makes Tiberius much more goal oriented and steely: conflicted character is not an aesthetic virtue for his art.

Jonson is also much less concerned with epoch—he has little interest in the constitutional rifts or competing conceptions of justice that so fascinated Sidney. In *Catiline* the dramatist can accept Brutus or Cassius as honourable men (as active citizens of a republic, prepared to kill in order to preserve their rights). In *Sejanus*, however, there exists a completely different code of honour (that of neo-Stoical acceptance), which is deemed appropriate to imperial Rome. Jonson's drama is not concerned with the movement between these two different moral positions as a diachronic process. An audience is required to accept the ground rules of the state in which the action takes place and to judge in simple terms on that basis. There is thus no doubt that the Germanicans in *Sejanus* are doing the right thing in sticking to their policy of sufferance, because Jonson did all he could to make Tiberius' claims more like those of a hereditary monarch. Jonson's ethics are thus always personal and historically contingent rather than being based on any transcendent political ideals. At the same time, Jonson is unconcerned with the opacity of the record (his Cordatus is confident that history will survive in spite of his own suppression). Again, this is something that flows from his moral agenda: the editorial apparatus surrounding the printed text of *Sejanus* is intended to protect Jonson from accusations of political allusion, but it is also a moral assertion that the verdict of history on actions past and present is accurate and just.

All this is different in Shakespeare. *Coriolanus*, for example, is a play concerned both with the internal contradictions of its hero and with the conflicts between the equestrian and plebeian class. For this double perspective its author drew simultaneously on Plutarch and Livy, thereby acquiring a developmental perspective on both the individual and the nation.[41] The Rome of this play is a city state but also contains the germ of an empire. Shakespeare exploits the tensions that result from such transitional moments, which also lie at the centre of *Julius Caesar* and *Antony and Cleopatra*, in which Plutarch again sits alongside other material as a narrative source. The playwright's tendency to hybridize so as to complicate character is the reverse of Jonson's, and it is a consistent feature across his classical historical work.

It has been argued that Shakespeare's reading of Plutarch had a direct impact on his development of complex characterization. This is not only because the Greek biographer is so intensely focused on the nature of individual characters but also because of the comparative structure of the *Lives*. Ernst Honigmann maintained that Shakespeare studied the Greek parallel lives even where these were not germane to his story, so that Plutarch's stand-alone 'Comparisons' (for example, of Brutus with Dion or of Alcibiades with Martius Coriolanus) subtly colour his Roman world.[42] These moments of connection are fleeting but suggestive: for instance, that at which Shakespeare's Brutus confesses he has 'no personal cause to spurn' Caesar but fears that his friend's coronation 'might change his nature' so as to become tyrannous (*Julius Caesar*, 2. 1. 11–13). There is no hint of such thinking in the main body of Plutarch's life of Brutus (where we find only a principled republican), but it does emerge in the comparison with Dion, whose motivations are more driven by the 'private cause' of distrust. While for any specific set of paired lives such verbal parallels remain inconclusive, it is undeniable that across the span of his Roman plays Shakespeare allows cross-comparisons to soften Plutarch's moral exempla, so that Antony—most spectacularly—is given an aspect of erotic grandeur even as we hear the moralist's condemnation of his decline.

Ultimately, it is too absolute to claim that Shakespeare's concept of character was transformed by Plutarch. Internal conflict and comparison are there in plays written earlier than those sourced in the *Lives*. This, however, is not to devalue the impact of classical historiography on his thinking. An early play like *Richard III* may take its plot from Holinshed rather than Plutarch, but its methods of characterization are still rooted in classical historical work. There is an exchange in this play that has become an emblematic one in the recent discussion of Renaissance ideas on the transmission of historical record. As an entry point to a conclusion about the presence of classical historians in this period, it is worth citing at length. The exchange takes place while Buckingham conducts the princes to their secret death in the Tower of London, a location that becomes the object of a dialogue on the roots of the period's beliefs:

PRINCE: I do not like the Tower, of any place.
Did Julius Caesar build that place, my lord?

BUCKINGHAM: He did, my gracious lord, begin that place,
Which since, succeeding ages have re-edified.

PRINCE: Is it upon record, or else reported
Successively from age to age, he built it?

BUCKINGHAM: Upon record, my gracious lord.

PRINCE: But say, my lord, it were not register'd,
Methinks the truth should live from age to age.

(Shakespeare, *Richard III*, 3. 1. 68–76)

The discussion concludes, as it began, on Julius Caesar, who was wise enough to have written his own history: 'his wit set down to make his valour live' (3. 1. 86).

The scene provides a perspective on the sources of history writing in the early modern period. The prince, as a good humanist schoolboy before his time, is aware of Caesar's *Gallic Wars* as an authority (although clearly not of its lack of reference to the building of the Tower of London). We can take this question as a cue for a more modern kind of historicism: the kind championed by Camden in the *Britannia* of 1586, which asked more probing questions about the nature of the Roman world and its mark upon the sixteenth-century present. Yet we can also, in a wider sense, see the scene as representative of a mood and way of thinking that is more pervasive in *Richard III*. In Act 3 scene 1, and in the play more generally, we find a conception of politics and subterfuge, an emphasis on the imaginative reconstruction of lost historical speeches, a characterization of despotism, and a pessimism about the recoverability of truth under dictatorship that bespeaks a more deep-seated—yet also more nebulous—presence of classical historiography in Renaissance England. This is a presence that has its origins in Livy's *History* and later Tacitus' *Histories* and *Annals*, is filtered through the commentaries of Machiavelli and Lipsius, and comes to inform the most sophisticated literary writing of the sixteenth and seventeenth centuries: a layered and sometimes disputable presence that 'succeeding ages have re-edified'.

If *Richard III* has connections with this culture, the foundations for such a connection must lie with Sir Thomas More. More's *History of Richard III* is a seminal entry point for classical historiography in the early modern period. Even incomplete, the text is one of the most thoroughgoing absorptions of classical history writing in the period. The single-minded character of Gloucester; the coherent narrative of his rise to power; the exclusive high political focus of this account: these are continuities across More's and Shakespeare's two works. As has long been recognized, the world of More's Ricardian court is that of first-century Rome as much as of fifteenth-century England. Key elements in More's portrayal include: the orchestrated appearance of reluctance on Richard's part to take up the crown; a continual sense of a ruler who works by proxy; and a situation where outward appearance is almost certainly false. Alongside this there stands the idea of the populace as a body that can be manipulated. There is also a subtle sense of multiple motivations (Richard, like Tiberius, is a successful general serving a regime that has imposed order after a period of civil war). This is a world of high politics, in which the conventional elements of medieval chronicle (monstrous births, notorious murders, unusual weather) are excluded. It provides a coherent account of causation, and a perspective on the maintenance of power that is not (at a day-to-day level) marked by divine action or providence.

A Richard who, as More says, 'was close and secret, a deep dissembler, lowly of countenance, arrogant of heart, outwardly companionable where he inwardly hated, not letting to kiss whom he thought to kill: despitious and cruel, not for evil will always, but other for ambition, and either for the surety or increase of his estate' is very close to Tacitus' Tiberius, and the author himself made this comparison.[43]

More had carefully studied Thucydides, Livy, Sallust, and Tacitus, and knew Suetonius and Plutarch well. His *History of Richard III* is so different from almost any of the writing of English historians before the 1590s as a direct result of this influence. As Richard Sylvester has demonstrated, More's Richard is a complex fusion of classical influences: Sallust's *Jugurtha* and *Catiline* were required reading of More's schooldays; and he frequently echoes them in Richard's speeches. In Sylvester's assessment, 'Sallust provides the framework, he sets the genre, and he outlines the plot', but 'for Richard's character, and for a closer analogue to the atmosphere of dissimulation and deceit that hung over his reign, More turned to Suetonius and Tacitus'.[44] More's fusion of influences is so thoroughgoing that it is seldom reducible to one-for-one parallel. Given that the first six books of the *Annals* were not found until the early sixteenth century, appearing in the Rome Folio of 1515, it is likely that More continued to modify his *History* as he absorbed the new books of the *Annals* and extended his own account.[45]

It is unsurprising that Shakespeare's Richard, unlike the protagonists of his earlier histories, should be a consistently subtle political thinker: that characterization was More's, and it was a unique one in the record of English history. The attitude of subtle positioning and emerging fear is palpably there in the conversations around the Tower of London scene upon which I opened, but a more direct parallel can be found in the manœuvrings on Richard's assumption of power. Tiberius' feigned reluctance to take on the role of emperor is a central feature of both Suetonius' and Tacitus' opening characterizations. It is a performance that nobody credits, but that none dares openly to dismiss. With the murder of Agrippa Postumus already effected, in Tacitus *Annals* I, the persuasion in the Senate takes several hundred words, until Tiberius,

> wearied at last by the universal outcry and by individual appeals...gradually gave ground, up to the point, *not* of acknowledging that he assumed the sovereignty, but of ceasing to refuse and to be entreated.
>
> (Fessusque clamore omnium, expostulatione singulorum flexit paulatim, non ut fateretur suscipi a se imperium, sed ut negare et rogari desineret.)
>
> (*Annals*, I. 13)

In More's *History* Richard's evasion of the crown is likewise protracted—a process that More famously compares to the customary refusal of episcopal office:

> For at the consecration of a bishop, every man wot well, by the paying for his bulls, that he purposes to be one, and though he pay for nothing else. And yet must he be twice asked whether he will be bishop or no, and he must twice say nay, and at the third time take it as compelled thereunto by his own will.[46]

These are devices that More famously calls 'kings' games, as it were stage plays' (pinpointing a dramatic plotting in classical historiography that relates closely to the working of drama).

It is these 'kings' games' that we find in both More and Shakespeare. Tiberius' complaints about the burdens of office and his unwillingness to take them on, find a close equivalent in *Richard III*:

> Alas, why would you heap this care on me?
> I am unfit for state and majesty.
> I do beseech you, take it not amiss;
> I cannot, nor I will not, yield to you.
> (*Richard III*, 3. 7. 203–6)

A case could be made for this as a direct verbal borrowing, but Shakespeare is unlikely to have read Tacitus in the Latin, and Greenway's 1598 translation of the *Annals* and the *Germania* was to come well after Shakespeare's play.[47] In all likelihood, the stemma of descent for this kind of *intellectual conception* of the workings of power is much more diffuse. More's *History* was itself not directly encountered by Shakespeare (although it is ultimately his principal source). It found its way through various conduits (including *The Chronicle of John Hardyng*) before being taken up by Grafton and incorporated (and acknowledged) in Edward Hall's *Union* and also melded into Holinshed's *Chronicles*.[48]

The influence of classical historiography on *Richard III* is thus highly attenuated. That fact, however, makes the play all the more suitable as a point of conclusion. The recovery of classical history and biography was pivotal to the humanist Renaissance. If there was a 'discovery of anachronism' or an 'invention of the human' in this period, then such developments can be traced at least as much to the reading of ancient history as to the reading of drama or verse.[49] But such thinking permeated only gradually and often ran into channels very different from those of its origins. It was 'upon record' but also that which 'succeeding ages have re-edified'.

Notes

1. The markings consistently highlight those passages of relevance to Jonson's source text and therefore look highly likely to have been made by the poet. The only reason for doubt comes from the fact that they are in pencil, which is unusual, although not unheard of, in this period. If they are of later date, then they are testament to a deep scholarly engagement with sources in one early reader of the play.
2. These examples are listed in Alice P. Wright, 'A Study of Ben Jonson's *Catiline* with Special Reference to its Sources', unpublished Ph.D. thesis (University of Yale, 1907), 279, and repeated in *Catiline*, ed. W. F. Bolton and Jane F. Gardner, Regents Renaissance Drama Series (1972).
3. The principles on the utility of history were themselves also drawn from classical theorists and practioners—e.g. Dionysius of Halicarnassus (fl. 30 BCE), whose focus was on rhetorical and moral exemplarity.
4. David Norbrook, *Poetry and Politics in the English Renaissance* (1984), 153–62.

5. See F. J. Levy, 'Hayward, Daniel, and the Beginnings of Politic History in England', *Huntington Library Quarterly*, 50 (1987), 1–34 (7). Patricia J. Osmond (in '"Princeps Historiae Romanae": Sallust in Renaissance Political Thought', *Memoirs of the American Academy of Rome*, 40 (1995), 101–43) shows that Sallust's popularity was much less affected than that of Livy or Tacitus by changes in the political climate. She argues that Jonson used him as a politically safe source after the reception of *Sejanus* (p. 127).
6. Caesar's reputation as one who 'so successfully blinded the masses' that he made them 'unaware of the yoke which they themselves had placed on their necks' is traced by Quentin Skinner in *The Foundations of Modern Political Thought*, 2 vols (Cambridge, 1978), I. 55, 83, 161–2. Depending on their political orientation, sixteenth- and seventeenth-century commentators could characterize Julius Caesar as anything from secular saint to demonic tyrant. On this reception, see, e.g. Louisa MacKenzie, 'Imitation Gone Wrong: the "Pestilentially Ambitious" Figure of Julius Caesar in Michel de Montaigne's *Essais*', in Maria Wyke (ed.), *Julius Caesar in Western Culture* (Oxford, 2006), 131–47, and Maria Wyke, *Caesar: A Life in Western Culture* (2007).
7. On this progression, see Ricci's *De Imitatione Libri Tres* (Venice, 1545), which distinguishes between following, imitating, and emulation. The ideal of complete absorption is most famously expressed in Lucius Seneca's example of the honey bee, widely cited in the period. On doctrines of imitation, see Patrick Cheney and Philip Hardie, Chapter 1, this volume.
8. John Marston, *Sophonisba* (1606), $A2^{a}$.
9. On the transformative impact of Camden's *Britannia* on the perception of Britain's past, see Graham Parry, *The Trophies of Time: English Antiquarians of the Seventeenth Century* (Oxford, 1995), 1–37.
10. J. H. Whitfield, 'Livy > Tacitus', in R. R. Bolgar (ed.), *Classical Influences on European Culture AD 1500–1700* (Cambridge, 1976), 281–94. For a broader survey of Livy's reception and its political resonance, see Peter Culhane, 'Livy in Early Jacobean Drama', *Translation and Literature*, 14 (2005), 21–44.
11. See Lisa Jardine and A. T. Grafton, '"Studied for Action": How Gabriel Harvey Read his Livy', *Past and Present*, 126 (1990), 30–78; on the discussion of Cope, see pp. 57–8.
12. Princeton University Library, *T. Livii Patavini, Romanae Historiae Principis, Decades Tres, cum Dimidia* (Basle, 1555), $P1^{r}$, transcribed in Jardine and Grafton, 'Studied', 55. Jardine and Grafton date the note between 1580 and 1586.
13. Smith's authorship is nowhere mentioned, but can be inferred because the letter exchange backs the scheme he was proposing and matches his style and intellectual preferences. Such pseudonymous publication was common in writing about Irish colonization.
14. See Bart van Es, *Spenser's Forms of History* (Oxford, 2002), 95–102.
15. Debora Shuger, 'Castigating Livy: The Rape of Lucretia and *The Old Arcadia*', *Renaissance Quarterly*, 51 (1998), 526–48.
16. Sir Philip Sidney, *The Countess of Pembroke's Arcadia: The Old Arcadia*, ed. Katherine Duncan-Jones (Oxford, 1985), 358–9.
17. Shuger, 'Castigating Livy', 527. The point about allusions to St Augustine, discussed in the next sentence, is also hers.
18. Colin Burrow, in William Shakespeare, *Complete Sonnets and Poems*, ed. Colin Burrow (Oxford, 2002), 45–66.
19. See Arnaldo Momigliano, 'Ancient History and the Antiquarian', in Momigliano, *Studies in Historiography* (1966), 1–39.

20. See Heather Dubrow, 'The Rape of Clio: Attitude to History in Shakespeare's *Lucrece*', *English Literary Renaissance*, 16 (1986), 425–41.
21. Skinner's scholarship on this subject spans decades; among his more recent contributions see Quentin Skinner, 'Classical Liberty, Renaissance Translation and the English Civil War', in *Visions of Politics*, 3 vols (Cambridge, 2002), vol. II: *Renaissance Virtues*, 308–43.
22. Andrew Hadfield, *Shakespeare and Republicanism* (Cambridge, 2005), pp. 52–3.
23. The dominant study here is David Norbrook, *Writing the English Republic: Poetry, Rhetoric and Politics 1627–1660* (Cambridge, 1999); prose historiography is relatively unimportant in Norbrook's account.
24. Patrick Cheney, *Marlowe's Republican Authorship: Lucan, Liberty, and the Sublime* (Basingstoke, 2009), 5.
25. Paul Hammond (in 'Shakespeare as Collaborator: The Case of *Titus Andronicus*', in Paul Scott (ed.), *Collaboration and Interdisciplinarity in the Republic of Letters: Essays in Honour of Richard G. Maber* (Manchester, 2010), 195–210) argues that Shakespeare and his co-author have a subtly different perspective on Roman history. In Act I, attributed to George Peele, Rome is 'a political space, poised between monarchy and republic, between civic values and tyranny, a place of ancestral monuments and public buildings'; in contrast, for the rest of the play (where Shakespeare had the dominant input) Rome is 'a symbolic, mythologized space' (p. 209).
26. John Webster [and Thomas Heywood], *Appius and Virginia* 5. 3. 167–73, in *The Works of John Webster*, ed. David Gunby et al., 3 vols (Cambridge, 1995–2007), 2. 577–8.
27. Paulina Kewes, 'Roman History and the Early Stuart Drama: Thomas Heywood's *The Rape of Lucrece*', *English Literary Renaissance*, 32 (2002), 239–67 (266).
28. For these and later examples, see Peter Culhane, 'Livy in Early Jacobean Drama', *Translation and Literature*, 14 (2005), 21–44. Holland's prodigious industry as a translator, not only of Livy but also of Suetonius and Xenophon, made classical historiography accessible to a non-elite audience in the new century and beyond.
29. See, e.g. Edwin B. Benjamin, 'Sir John Hayward and Tacitus', *Review of English Studies*, 31 (1957), 275–6, and 'Bacon and Tacitus', *Classical Philology*, 60 (1965), 102–10.
30. For more detail, see J. H. Whitfield, 'Machiavelli's Use of Livy', in *Livy*, ed. T. A. Dorey (1971), 73–96.
31. See David Womersley, 'Sir Henry Savile's Translation of Tacitus and the Political Interpretation of Elizabethan Texts', *Review of English Studies*, 42 (1991), 313–42, to which the following account is indebted.
32. Savile, *The End of Nero* [1591], 6.
33. Richard Greenway, trans., Cornelius Tacitus, *Annals* (1598), 2.
34. The scholarship on Tacitism at the turn of the sixteenth century is too voluminous for even an attempt at summary. One erudite overview, however, is provided in J. H. M. Salmon, 'Seneca and Tacitus in Jacobean England', in Linda Levy Peck (ed.), *The Mental World of the Jacobean Court* (Cambridge, 1991), 169–90.
35. The *History of the Rebellion* by Henry Hyde, first Earl of Clarendon, was not published until 1702, but work on it began after the first stage of the Civil War. Another important work of this kind was Camden's *Annals* of the reign of Elizabeth, but, like Camden's *Britannia*, the work was written in Latin and not translated by the author himself. On Clarendon's connections with the Jonson circle in the context of reading Tacitus, see Paul Seaward, 'Clarendon, Tacitism, and the Civil Wars of Europe', *Huntington Library Quarterly*, 68 (2005), 289–311.

36. Thomas Hobbes, *Behemoth* (1679), 3.
37. Samuel Daniel, *The Complete Works*, ed. A. B. Grosart, 5 vols (1885–96), 3. 139.
38. Patricia J. Osmond, 'Edmund Bolton's Vindication of Tiberius Caesar: A "Lost" Manuscript Comes to Light', *International Journal of the Classical Tradition*, 11 (2005), 329–43.
39. J. H. M. Salmon, 'Precept, Example, and Truth: Degory Wheare and the *ars historica*', in Donald R. Kelley and David Harris Sacks (eds), *The Historical Imagination in Early Modern Britain: History, Rhetoric, and Fiction, 1500–1800* (Cambridge, 1997), 11–36. This is not, of course, to say that history had become an independent subject: Wheare's lectures still fitted in to a generalist undergraduate curriculum.
40. Philip J. Ayres, 'The Nature of Jonson's Roman History', *English Literary Renaissance*, 16 (1986), 166–81.
41. See Anne Barton, 'Livy, Machiavelli, and Shakespeare's *Coriolanus*', in Catherine M. S. Alexander (ed.), *Shakespeare and Politics* (Cambridge, 2004), 67–90.
42. E. A. J. Honigmann, 'Shakespeare's Plutarch', *Shakespeare Quarterly*, 10 (1959), 25–33.
43. St Thomas More, *Richard III*, in *The Complete Works of St Thomas More*, ed. Richard S. Sylvester (New Haven, 1963), 2. 7. On More's comparisons between King Richard and Tiberius, see Sylvester, in More, *Works*, 2, p. lxxxix.
44. Sylvesteer, in More, *Works*, 2, p. lxxxviii.
45. See Sylvester, in More, *Works*, 2, p. xc.
46. More, *Works*, 2. 81.
47. David Womersley, '*3 Henry VI*: Shakespeare, Tacitus, and Parricide', *Notes & Queries* (1985), 468–73, argues that Shakespeare had already read Savile's translation of the *Histories* by 1592.
48. See David Womersley, 'Sir Thomas More's History of King Richard III: A New Theory of the English Texts', *Renaissance Studies: Journal of the Society for Renaissance Studies*, 7 (1993), 272–90.
49. On the development of a new sense of anachronism in the period, see Peter Burke, *The Renaissance Sense of the Past* (1969), 1–2. The notion that a new sense of the particularity of human existence develops in Shakespeare's writing is put forward in Harold Bloom, *Shakespeare: the Invention of the Human* (New York, 1998).

CHAPTER 20

Discursive and Speculative Writing

REID BARBOUR AND CLAIRE PRESTON

The Classical Inheritance

Because its classical models and their Renaissance inheritors were utterly diverse, generically, formally, and thematically, 'discursive' writing in the early modern period can be neither rigorously defined nor insisted upon as a generic category. Broadly speaking, however, the ancient and early modern discursive must comprehend any kind of didactic, speculative, ideational, polemical, meditative, or factual (as opposed to fictional) writing, either in prose or in verse, and include Plato's dialogues 'wherein he feigns many honest burgesses of Athens' speaking of philosophical matters, Virgil's mythic and didactic *Georgics*, and the dialogic fiction of Seneca's letters to Lucilius, as well as early modern works as diverse as Francis Bacon's parabolic *New Atlantis* (1624/1627), Rooke Church's dramatic dialogue *An Old Thrift Newly Reviv'd* (1612) on farming and enclosure, Henry Butts's stories and 'table-talk' of herbs, fruits, and animal husbandry (*Dyets Dry Dinner* (1599)), Margaret Cavendish's utopian/scientific fantasy *A Blazing World* (1666), Izaak Walton's extended narrative of angling and friendship, and the dramatic fictions of Boyle's scientific dialogues.[1] Poetry in its most limited definition ('verse') is, of course, the vehicle of ancient factual/didactic writers such as Lucretius, Empedocles, and Virgil, as well as early modern imitations such as Thomas Tusser's versified agricultural advice (*Five Hundreth Pointes of Good Husbandrie* (1585)), Cavendish's atomic poems (*Poems and Fancies* (1653)), and Abraham Cowley's lively *Sex Libri Plantarum* (1668). Thus, although it is possible to maintain some sort of thematic category for both ancient and early modern discursive writing, the forms in which it appears are highly variable and cross the generic boundaries between fiction and non-fiction, and between verse and prose.

The range of ancient discursive poetry and prose available to late Tudor and early Stuart readers was astonishingly diverse. It included 'scientific' poetry—from writers as diverse as Hesiod, Aratus, Lucretius, Virgil, Manilius, Nicander, and Oppian,—and the prose of Sextus Empiricus, Pliny the Elder, Theophrastus, Dioscorides, Galen, and of course Aristotle. As Thomas Browne explained to his son, 'while much is lacking in Aristotle, much wrong, much self-contradictory, yet not a little is valuable. Do not then bid farewell to his entire work; but while you hardly touch the Physics and read the Metaphysics superficially, make much of all the rest and study them unwearyingly.'[2] Browne's readiness to pick and choose within the classical heritage is characteristic of the early modern embrace of eclecticism, accretion, and hybridity, qualities that played into an emerging English discursive tradition. This trend is not very surprising: the habit of (sometimes idiosyncratic) selection was dynamic, and did not set out to conquer but rather to reinvent Aristotle and indeed many other classical precursors. It was a habit that must have found encouragement in the particular formal structures through which the words of the great ancient philosophers were transmitted: in cumulative centos or the miscellanies, anthologies, and lexicons or encyclopaedias of Aulus Gellius, Stobaeus, Suidas, Pliny the Elder, and Diogenes Laertius, as well as in the works of Plutarch, Cicero, and Sextus Empiricus, the sense of hybridity, inclusion, even formlessness in the structure of such compilations must have reinforced the openness to generic diversity of the early modern essay.

The early modern reception of Seneca's dialogues and moral epistles, for example, was especially rich, decisive, and controversial, and epitomized a tension in contemporary meanings of the word 'discursive'/'discoursive' itself: it could refer to a narration or account, to wide-ranging and encyclopaedic scope, to conversation, to a treatment or dissertation, or to rational argument, especially the inductive process of moving from premiss to conclusion. Pejoratively it could signal irregularity and digressiveness, as well as a random and undigested meaning.[3] These qualities, both of thought and of expression, sometimes mutually exclusive, further suggest the appeal of boundlessness, unconventionality, and psychological or experiential verisimilitude of early modern prose that spoke to Elizabethan and Stuart intellectuals and ultimately yielded that baggy and supremely versatile form, the English essay.

The following discussion is therefore necessarily highly selective within the vast field of philosophy, theology, natural philosophy, utilitarian and practical writing, political, polemical, and controversial writing, sermons, and historical and antiquarian writing. Within the arbitrary limits of what follows, Plato's dialogues inaugurate attention to discursive styles and structures for speculative writing in English that were already available in the great triumvirate of Cicero, Plutarch, and above all Seneca. With Plato the four, and Seneca in particular, are examined as the bases of certain categories of early modern speculative writing, which include works by Bacon, John Donne, Robert Burton, Browne, and Robert Boyle; meanwhile, Virgil, and Lucretius, together with

Columella, Varro, and Hesiod, serve as the influential sources of less speculative genres broadly encompassed under the category of 'georgic' writing, and informing early moderns such as John Evelyn, Ralph Austen, Walton, and Cowley.

Plato

Plato's fictional representation of open philosophical enquiry exemplifies some of the ways in which sixteenth- and seventeenth-century English discursive writing adapted classical precedents. Despite the rise of Greek studies in the sixteenth century and the proliferation of vernacular translations of classical texts, Plato's works were encountered in Latin translation, especially those by Marsilio Ficino (1484) and Jean de Serres (1578). Platonic thought and style of argument also came indirectly through English translations of Italian works such as Baldassare Castiglione's *Book of the Courtier* (1528; trans. 1561) and Stefano Guazzo's *Civile Conversations* (1574; trans. 1581–6). Platonic and quasi-Platonic ideas—the immortality and pre-existence of the soul, and its meditative up-reaching to a realm of ideas, as well as the notion of a providential cosmic order—are central to Edmund Spenser's *Fowre Hymnes*, to the Cambridge Platonists, to Sir Thomas Browne, to influential compilations of conventional wisdom like La Primaudaye's *French Academy*, and to Caroline court masques and plays celebrating the royal cult of Platonic love. They were filtered through Neoplatonists such as Plotinus and affiliated with the quasi-divine wisdom of the 'ancient theologians' Moses, Zoroaster, they were the legendary Hermes Trismegistus; and enhanced by Plato's reputation as an allegorist whose fables, conceits, or 'likely stories' communicated transcendent mysteries.[4] Early modern enthusiasm for certain examples of Plato's Socratic dialogues, where interlocutors proceed from uncertainty to discovery and thence to conversion (quite different from the more historically situated and equilibrious Ciceronian dialogues[5]), initiated a fundamental openness to styles of speculative writing that emphasized the tentative, the unsystematic, and the heuristic, features highly attractive to seventeenth-century natural–philosophical writing.

The Platonic dialogue, Torquato Tasso had argued, was situated midway between poetry and dialectic,[6] not only embodying a transcendent idea but also moving readers to live according to that idea; its Socratic form was thus an instrument of moral and spiritual conversion, both a model for and a means of Christian education. In early modern adaptations, however, dialogue could assume a form more fixed than that of the Platonic originals. In Sir Thomas Elyot's 'Platonick' dialogue *Of the Knowledge whiche maketh a wise man* (1533), the Socratic teacher (named Plato) holds forth on wisdom and goodness rather than initiating a process of discovery through questions. And in Walton's *Compleat Angler* (1653), the wise and modest Christian fisherman 'Piscator' is only a remote avatar of Socrates, a figure designed to mitigate the woes of war-wracked England. Walton's inspiration from Platonic/Socratic practice was probably transmitted to him by George Herbert and Herbert's literary executor Nicholas Ferrar. Herbert identified the Socratic master-and-pupil dialectic as a pagan type of Christian catechism, which lays the groundwork for Christian experience by 'infus[ing] a competent knowledge of salvation' so that this knowledge can be translated into practice; it can be adjusted to suit the recipient pupil and enhance intellectual development rather than rote learning.[7] 'Socrates,' he says, 'did thus in philosophy, who held that the seeds of all truths lay in everybody, and accordingly by questions well ordered he found philosophy in silly tradesmen... The secret of [its] good consists in this, that... when one is questioned, he must discover what he is.'[8] Nicholas Ferrar and his family performed the most fascinating early Stuart imitation of Platonic dialogues as a 'little academy' in Little Gidding in the 1630s, where dialogues spoken in assumed fictional identities and guided by a 'Chief' conducted them on the passionate process of spiritual discovery by way of Socratic questioning.[9]

Henry More and the Cambridge Platonists in the mid-seventeenth century used Platonic ideas to resist the threat of Epicurean materialism that seemed to undermine essential Christian verities. Yet there were signs at mid-century that the arbiters of philosophical culture were ready to move beyond the mystical dreams of Platonic absolutes. Although Socrates and Plato received full attention as late as Stanley's *History of Philosophy* (1655–62), it was to be Epicurus who prevailed in England, particularly from the 1650s, a focus that Stanley adopted from Pierre Gassendi. And, although the foremost English Epicurean, Walter Charleton, published a translation of Plato in 1675, Platonic philosophy had already been sent packing a decade earlier as 'an ungrounded and Fanatick Fancy', hardly distinguished in this phrase from Quakers, Diggers, and Ranters.[10]

Cicero, Plutarch, Seneca

Nothing in the ancient discursive legacy made more difference, in both form and content, to the cultural brokers of late-sixteenth- and seventeenth-century England, than the generically varied moral prose of Cicero, Plutarch, and Seneca. The moral explorations and exhortations of this ancient triumvirate laid the groundwork for the early modern essay form to develop in ways that suited controversial writers, scientific practitioners, and the peculiar moral/pragmatic blend of georgic writing. In particular, the influence of Cicero's *De Officiis* in early humanist England was a powerful one. Cicero's style was already slavishly imitated as the gold standard of Renaissance Latinity; thematically and philosophically, *De Officiis* offered readers 'virtually the whole framework for civic humanist discussions of the active life' and an incomparable guide to their 'highest earthly duty... to place [their] talents in the service of [their] community'.[11] However, Cicero's philosophical dialogues were eclectic in their thought, conveying Stoic and Epicurean ideas couched in a productive scepticism not easily reducible to 'duty' alone.[12] If Cicero's style had already secured him dominance in English letters, the anti-reductive quality of his work, a practical wisdom equally blended with a formal eloquence, was deeply refreshing to humanist thinkers and writers militantly eschewing Scholasticism, and this is his signal influence on the development of English speculative writing.[13]

By the turn of the seventeenth century, *De Officiis*'s earlier prominence as a model for the philosophical reconciliation of honesty and duty began to share ground with the rhetorical and philosophical liberty of the essay, a new form that responded to the weakness of certain ancient discursive forms as practical interventions in the affairs of early modernity. Yet Cicero's dialogues remained influential on the new form: as with the essay, their moral directives were not monolithic—they represented speaking, reacting characters whose voices could insist on competing opinions to enhance the provisional, probable, and speculative, and they aimed less at moral regulation than at navigating between the moral theory and workaday reality of the man of action.[14] It was this synthesis of personal virtue and social obligation, one sensitive and adaptable to context and circumstances, that maintained *De Officiis* as an essential document for Stuart readers.

In 1556 Nicholas Grimald characterized Cicero's aim as the *use* of the self. With obligations both to conscience and society, 'it beseemeth most to use ourselves: our part, without doubt, and our duty shall we do best if we employ the using of ourselves to deeds that be honest and commendable'.[15] To 'use' the self is to implement one's potential; but in its Ciceronian inflection self-use entails the decorous *adaptation* of self 'with respect to the circumstances of times, places, and persons'. 'Use' takes on a secondary meaning of 'accustom'. Ciceronian constancy is not a strict Stoic consistency but rather a consistent duty in virtuously moulding the self to meet circumstances. Cicero's legacy is thus largely prudential and instrumental, neither a Boethian, philosophical aid to rebuking and rejecting the vicissitudes of fortune, nor a Senecan mode, where vicissitude is instructive if properly meditated and productive of resolve. In *De Officiis* Cicero is singularly accommodating: honesty (in the profound Stoic sense of constant virtue founded in universal natural law and right reason) is indispensable, but so too are life's successes and commodities, and Ciceronian 'duty' productively reconciles utility and rectitude. This Ciceronian mean—between regulation and suggestion, between prescription and description of conduct—enables the prized distinction (mainly Baconian and post-Baconian) between the conclusive scholastic treatise or system and the inconclusive, contingent early modern essay, reflection, or experimental narrative. Cicero's mean provides a model for early modern conceptions of self-use that would influence Donne, Burton, Browne, Boyle, and many more.

Equally germinative in Tudor and Stuart moral writings were Plutarch's *Moralia*, his moral essays. Despite that generic designation, only a few (if highly influential) of the writings in the miscellany were straightforward 'morals'. Philemon Holland's translation lists seventy-two items, referred to as 'Morals and mixt works'.[16] Some focused on the diffuse subject of conversation at table, others on virtually the entire range of ancient learning, history, and culture (including natural studies, music, oratory, government, vegetarianism, usury, oracles, and glosses on difficult passages in Plato), while others addressed problems of specific addressees—on identifying flatterers, consolation on the death of a child. Of this intimate and pragmatic quality, Erasmus remarked that 'Socrates drew philosophy down from heaven to earth [but] Plutarch brought it into men's chambers and private apartments and bedrooms'.[17] Holland's catalogue of Plutarch's subjects also indicates their influence on the early modern essay: 'Of Fortune', 'Of the Nouriture and Education of Children', 'Of the oracles that have ceased to give answer', and 'Of the primitive or First Cold' are among many Plutarchan subject headings that sound very much like Montaigne, Bacon, and Browne, and it is hardly surprising that Montaigne and Bacon cited Plutarch in their intellectual formation. English generic labels for Plutarch's various 'morals' ('dialogue', 'discourse', 'letter', 'declamation', 'treatise', 'apothegm', 'symposiac') continue a terminological variety initially generated by those medieval scholars who lacked the term or the concept 'essay' (Seneca's essays were, for example, designated as 'dialogues', 'epistles', and even 'books'), and suggest quite how unfixed and pliable the classical models were in early modern minds.

It is clear that early modern readers valued Plutarch as a supremely useful educator of gentle virtues, not a random assortment but carefully sequenced to follow moral development from infancy onwards, unfolding mental growth 'by good order and with great reason'.[18] The *Moralia* mediated between transcendent Platonic truth (with which Plutarch assailed Epicurean and Stoic materialism) and the practical, experiential domain of worldly affairs. Holland singles out Plutarch's lively use of similitudes, exempla, and 'such like ornaments' as his chief vehicles of moral instruction, as though the moralist were not just a guide to poetry but a poet himself.[19] With his command of *enargeia*, Plutarch resembles the mythologizing and fabling Plato himself or the dialogist Xenophon, whose *Cyropaedia* or education of a prince in compelling images of virtue was so approved by Sir Philip Sidney. The *Moralia* particularly influenced early modern drama and poetry, precisely because high notions of goodness and truth are most powerfully accommodated within the literary;[20] and Plutarch was also a source and a model for the sermons of such English divines as Jeremy Taylor. Yet Holland reminds the Christian reader that Plutarch was a pagan without benefit of the divine word or grace, and warns (for example) against the infection from Greek sexual mores in the same vein that Plutarch has cautioned against the seductions of poetry.[21] But Holland commends Plutarch's powerful attacks on Epicureanism, a philosophy all too flourishing in Holland's era.[22] The early modern reception of Plutarch extends from Ben Jonson's quip that the tedium of the *Moralia* will 'spoil [a reader's] wit utterly' (*Epicoene or The Silent Woman*, I. 2. 62–4; *Works*, I. 166) to Montaigne's celebration of Plutarch's comparisons as 'excellent and commendable' in those essays where 'the faithfulnesse and sinceritie of his judgement equalleth their depth and weight'.[23] Plutarch's discursive writing is thus both the bane and the boon of wit.

That Seneca's moral writings, often essayistic epistles cast mainly as addresses to named individuals, were categorized in the Middle Ages as dialogues suggests their generic kinship with the works of Plato and Cicero. It is a kinship that ramified throughout humanist dialogic culture from Erasmus' early humanist *Convivium Religiosum* (1518) to the *convivium philosophicum* at Little Gidding (*c.*1620s–30s), and even to the dialogic colloquy of Boyle's *Sceptical Chymist* (1661).[24] Although hardly dialogic in the strict sense of *prosopopoeia*, of representing or recounting conversation,[25] the dialogic qualities of Seneca's moral works—the persistent address to an interaction with an implied interlocutor, dramatization of exploratory mental processes, as well as the heavy use of diatribe and debate—are embedded in the prose itself.[26] And Seneca's moral philosophy was far more divisive, volatile, and even more productive of discursive innovation in English prose than Cicero's and Plutarch's had been. Seneca's potent combination of moral authority and irregular, complex rhetorical processes prompted much of the generic experimentation that flourished in late-Elizabethan and early Stuart discursive prose. If the essay is 'a manner of writing well befitting undigested motions, or a head not knowing his strength like a circumspect runner trying for a start',[27] its Senecan heritage allows it to transform thoughts and inner experience into concrete expression, and to formulate resolves that will translate virtuous thought into right action. Seneca's 'everyday Stoicism' is essayistic in emphasizing process, the 'constantly mediated and realized truth'[28] that arises from the marshalling of complex, often dramatic, interior processes. 'Without showiness, without luxuriance, without the Tullian [i.e. Ciceronian] concinnities', condensed, 'something more to be understood...than was actually painted'[29]—this was Justus Lipsius's praise of Seneca; and this emphasis further pointed early modern Stoicism away from moral absolutism and towards self-exploration and preparation.

Senecan style promoted its own moral heft: Lipsius had confidently contrasted it with the barren old Scholastic discourse, the latter a mere 'divertissement' that converted 'the most serious instrument of life, into a sportage with trifles'.[30] Seneca's diction was by contrast 'choice, suitable and significant'; his meanings exceeded their linguistic conveyances and brought strength, clarity, and fluency to the interaction between mind and subject.[31] In a burgeoning variety of forms, including the resolve and the meditation, English essayists enthusiastically adopted these bracing Senecan effects.[32] Nicholas Breton's essays offer 'in 'few words, great worth';[33] William Cornwallis said that the brain might 'dance a jig at the hearing a *Tullian* sound' but it would 'sit in counsel' before the style of Seneca.[34] Bacon had admired Seneca's aphorisms (part of the contemporary reverence for two other Stoics, Epictetus and Marcus Aurelius); and Owen Feltham cited Seneca for 'fit words...that lead the mind to something besides the naked term' or bare semantic definition.[35] Thomas Randolph praised a style that was 'pure and strong and round' as well as 'pithy... sound...grave...[and] acute...',

> Not long and empty; lofty, but not proud;
> Subtle but sweet; high but without a cloud.

Well settled full of nerves—in brief 'tis such
That in a little hath comprised much.[36]

'Seneca's Epistles to Lucilius, if one mark them well, are but essays,' said Bacon, a remark that epitomizes Seneca's part in the Renaissance pursuit of mixed modes. Montaigne's 'I cannot settle my object; it goeth so unquietly and staggering, with a natural drunkenness' ('Of Repenting'; *Essayes* (1613), 451), indicating the radically unmoored style that enacts the early modern essay's uncertain undertakings (repentance, or discovery, or speculative exploration), encapsulates the shift that begins with Cicero's confident and yet unauthoritarian aid to the *process* of achieving virtuous action, continues with Plutarch's 'scatteringly and loosely handled' topics (Montaigne, 'Of Books'; *Essayes* (1613), 228),[37] and evolves into the later Senecan style, which more dynamically emphasizes the framing, preparing, or resolving of the self. Generic permeability and hybridity—for example, that Seneca's epistles are dialogic but might as well be essays—are analogues of the waywardness of human experience against moral and rational fashioning and control. The evolving Montaignean/Baconian essay capitalized on that generic uncertainty and tonal freedom, and swiftly established itself during the seventeenth century as an ideal mode for speculative investigations and especially for experimental narratives.[38]

If early modern readers were increasingly accustomed to Plutarchan eclecticism and generic 'variety', to Ciceronian inspection of the self, and to moral writing as an experience rather than as dogma, Seneca's dialogues and epistles confirmed these developing tendencies: their pithy syntax (Jonson detected his 'compression' in succinctness, brevity, concision, and abruptness (*Works*, 8. 623)) seemed stylistically to support his armoured honesty. Yet his hortatory Stoicism is significantly more fixed and absolute (at least in its purposes and conclusions) than the restless, exploratory brokenness of the early modern essay. For the English essayists, character writers, aphorists, and authors of resolves such as Feltham, Senecan moral works situated fixed, practical, ethical guidance in an uneven, informal process that led to the possibility of moral clarity, and shaped the English understanding and adaptation of complex rhetorical, syntactical, and formal productions of meaning. Bacon, having disparaged humanist idolatry of copious and periodic Ciceronian elocution, was equally critical of what had 'succeeded this copy and superfluity of speech', namely an anti-Ciceronian (or Attic) style he called 'aculeate'—that is, sharp, pointed, or stinging—with 'sentences concise, and the whole contexture of the speech and discourse, rather rounding into itself, than spread and dilated'. Where the finish and elegance of shapely Ciceronian periods and *copia* might suggest highly systematic and comprehensive works, the aculeate style moved instead towards discursive fragmentation, each part appearing 'more witty and weighty than indeed it was', and not necessarily more productive of real knowledge than the Ciceronian period.[39] The aculeate manner in English was potentially startling to ears conditioned to appreciate Ciceronian concinnities;[40] and, to Bacon, it seemed a style suited to those 'meaner capacities' who lacked 'the more exact judgements' required to adapt discourse accurately to the individual phenomena of real or 'broken' experience. Ben Jonson jestingly criticized the 'raw, and undigested' quality of the essay and the Senecan and Plutarchan offering of 'a few loose sentences, and that's all';[41] but his epigrammatic ideal of much in little owed a great deal to the contemporary resurrection of Senecan discourse. Such formal and rhetorical fluctuation and versatility, moral vigour, and febrile self-inspection in different measures are qualities clearly evident in works as diverse as Robert Burton's *Anatomy of Melancholy* (1621) and Thomas Browne's *Religio Medici* (1642), where we discover Plutarch's idiosyncratic mixture of topics, Seneca's gravely diffident authority, and Cicero's auto-examination of the spirit and the intellect, a productive *contaminatio* generated by this tripartite influence.

Early modern reactions to the competing and perhaps antithetical classical styles available to them were mixed and inconsistent.[42] Ciceronian *copia*, although it was the stylistic antipode of the Senecan penchant for more fragmented style and structure, seemed in its attention to linguistic surface to be dangerously suggestive of the scholastic hairsplitting subtleties and 'niggling minutiae' so despised by humanism, and especially by the post-Baconian speculative stylists, rhetorical features that could have no appreciable or legitimate moral impact on readers.[43] Bacon noted that the rhetorically questionable moral philosophy of the Stoics attempted 'to thrust virtue upon men by concise and sharp maxims and conclusions' without the necessary 'sympathy with the imagination and will of man',[44] and cavils at 'a high speech of Seneca' in 'Of Adversity' that 'would have done better in poesy; where transcendences are more allowed' (*Essayes*; *Works*, 12. 94). Even staunch admirers such as Lipsius and Thomas Gataker admitted that Seneca was frequently irregular, inconsistent, haphazard, and informal, and his complex, unfixed authorial persona open to criticism. Gataker thought that, despite his many good points, he was 'variable and often inconsistent'. In *The Golden Meane* (1613) the tragedian John Ford resolved these competing Senecas by fusing a Ciceronian meditation on the four cardinal virtues with a Stoic commitment to resolution, and drew especially on Seneca's *Consolatio ad Marciam* for his promotion of the 'resolved and prepared mind' or its 'settled and well governed resolution', achieved through the practical and uneven processes of preparation. He enlisted Senecan rhetorical questions, an auditor or silent second-person interlocutor, an eclectic ensemble of moral philosophers, and the vividness of *exempla*.[45] Democritus Jr's banter with his reader in *The Anatomy of Melancholy* operates as a kind of Senecan dialogue, and its zany and abruptly shifting tendencies recall Montaigne's fascination with the 'unconstant, unsettled mind'. Here as well as in his digressions Democritus Jr advertises and practises a kind of discursive atomism that makes his prose resemble the Epicurean universe—limitless, fragmentary, haphazard, and indecorous in its erasure of the boundary between the sacred and profane.

Montaigne admired Seneca's moral clarity, and like Joseph Hall appreciated the brevity of 'disconnected pieces, which do not require lengthy study' and accommodate 'moods and circumstances'.[46] Feltham could read densely packed Senecan moral thought only a little at a time.[47] Burton found Seneca's Stoic wisdom both immune to rhetorical influence but stylistically variable according to mood and moment.[48] The Senecan alternation of 'beautiful and lofty' parts and repetitious and confusing ones were an apt model for the early modern essay,[49] and English writers developed new prose forms in which to reinvent and adapt ancient philosophies and styles. Sir William Cornwallis sought to define the modern essay against the ancient modes: 'I hold neither *Plutarch's* nor none of those ancient short manner of writings nor *Montaigne's* nor such of this latter time to be rightly termed essays,' he explained, the reason being that, their brevity notwithstanding, these writings featured a moral strength and fortitude wholly at odds with the essay's proper focus on human fluctuations, on the trial and error of a 'newly bound prentice to the inquisition of knowledge' who would 'use these papers as a painter's boy a board, that is trying to bring his hand and his fancy acquainted' (Cornwallis, *Essayes* (1601), Gg8v and Hh3r). He approves Seneca, however, or at least Senecanism, because it is 'easy to be understood and easily digested to the nourishment of virtue', which is a very different thing from a focus on human fluctuations.

Essayistic self-exploration was especially attractive to courtiers: it carefully signalled to the ruler that the decorative class posed no threat to the regime and advanced no morally charged opposition.[50] An indication only of internal liberty, the essay could hardly trouble the commonwealth; and various English courtly translations of the Roman moralists were posed as blameless, peaceful, and disengaged. The examples of Seneca, Plutarch, and Cicero kept English courtiers out of trouble.[51] Haly Heron (*A Newe Discourse of Morall Philosophie* (1569)) and William Paulet, Marquis of Winchester (*The Lord Marques Idlenes* (1586/7)) found relief in the solitary idleness of moral essaying from the pressures and compromises of courtliness. But this pose was ultimately untenable: Stoic moral improvement, however framed as wholly internal and apolitical, tended towards an inner absolutism and righteous indignation.[52] Thus, Stoicism as a *modus philosophicus* could be sustained only in the most fortunate of circumstances. John Evelyn, though not a courtier, and never either seriously disfavoured or caressed by either side of the English Civil War, could enact his self-fashioned classicism with the aid of a private income and an almost self-sufficient estate, and did so pragmatically in the 1650s and by inclination until the end of his long life in 1706. From his splendid garden retreat and his translation of Lucretius, he could solemnly refer to salad-dressing as *oxybaphon* ('vinegar cruet'), and waggishly explain that 'goodwife Hecate entertained Theseus with a sallet. See sowthistle.'[53] Bacon remarked that the Stoics were known for troubling ancient states; Charles I responded that he still preferred the Stoics to the profane Epicureans.[54] Charles's retort epitomizes the extremely vexed politics of neo-Stoicism: it was apparently far more dangerous to authority than pacific, apolitical Epicureanism, and yet some Epicureans presented a different danger in their exposure of the sham of state religion and their denial of a potentially penal afterlife. The Stoic attitude is clearly related to late-sixteenth-century English would-be political players, for whom it was an instrumental, tactical, and pragmatic mode of surviving the vicissitudes of absolute and potentially persecuting monarchy, a Senecan survivalism that was neither quietism nor truculence, but rather a brave, if passive, fortitude whose very resilience threatened the tyrant or persecutor.

To secure or implement the self is an objective rendered inventively and complexly in much of the classically shaped discursive prose of the early seventeenth century, and literary self-scrutiny had a particularly Senecan and Stoic character; but such self-examination is extant as early as the Platonic representation of Socrates, and for Renaissance readers Augustine's *Confessions* was probably the most influential example. The Augustine-inspired spiritual autobiography was a genre closely related to the essay, and popularized by Marcus Aurelius. Bacon, however, explained to Buckingham that his essays 'of all my other works, have been most current: for that, as seems, they come home to men's business and bosoms' (*Essayes*; *Works*, 12. 77), and this commitment to interventions in the business as much as the bosoms of his readers orients the essays away from the hyper-self-regulation and self-preparation that he often criticized in Stoic writings. Although Bacon's essays employ Seneca's rhetorical patterns of exhortation (a second-person addressee, for instance, or the use of rhetorical questions), in 'Of Anger' he criticizes the 'bravery'—the ostentatious absolutism—of the Stoics in rejecting anger (*Essayes*; *Works*, 12. 271); and in 'Of Delays' he offers political counsel without recourse to Senecan self-assessment or self-improvement. In the shadow of Cicero's *De Officiis*, the Baconian essay is meant to help readers mediate 'between self-love, and society'; and Bacon is constantly alert for potential narcissism (thematic and rhetorical) in the literary representation of retreat into the self, a narcissism that would not contribute fruitfully or actively to the advancement of learning: 'It is a poor centre of a man's actions, *himself*. It is right earth. For that only stands fast upon his own center; whereas all things that have affinity with the heavens move upon the center of another, which they benefit' (Bacon, *Essayes*; *Works*, 12. 158).

Early modern imitators of Seneca like Ford attempted 'to affirm selfhood at the very moment of the dissolution of the self' at death,[55] as well as to shore up the fixity of moral resolution in the face of those vicissitudes, distractions, and seductions that threaten always to dissolve or subvert human constancy. 'Certainly, the Stoics bestowed too much cost upon death,' Bacon complained, 'and by their great preparations, made it appear more fearful' (*Essayes*; *Works*, 12. 86). That Stoic obsession with the moment of dissolution, and its attendant resolutions and revelations, inform Donne's *Devotions upon Emergent Occasions* (1624) and even a late work like Robert Boyle's *Accidents of an Ague* (1669). In each of these philosophical–theological responses to sudden illness the Senecan inspiration from *occasionality*, from specific circumstance with its slings and arrows, is thematically dominant.

Lucretius, Ancient Science, and English Georgics

The Anatomy of Melancholy (1621), with its coupling of science and rhetoric, prompted the English recognition that Lucretian atomism had to be assessed both as a world view and as a model of discourse and intellection. This coupling is the essential breakthrough in locating the rise of English natural philosophy in association with the emergence of the English essay. Centre stage in this drama—both liberating and menacing—was the 'rehabilitation' of the *De Rerum Natura*, Lucretius's first-century BC argument for Epicurean physics and moral philosophy,[56] which took place over the course of the sixteenth century, when Lucretius' great philosophical themes—the fear of death and eternal punishment, and the rejection of disturbing passions—were acknowledged alongside his atomic principles. Lucretius joined moral and natural philosophy in the application of atomism to theories of the mind, the soul, and perception, and most radically in the atomic denial of divine providence. His combination of cosmic epic with passionate and instructive didacticism was widely imitated in the Renaissance, as was the language of the poem itself, even by those opposed to the threatening 'atheism' of Lucretius' world view. His translators had to decide how the discourse of atomism might shift the literary properties of English. Lucretius analogised atoms and letters of the alphabet (small differences in atomic combinations determine species as 'fire' and 'fir' (*ignis* and *lignis*) are distinguished by one letter), but admitted 'the scantness of the tongue' to translate 'Greek obscurities' out of Greek natural philosophy.[57] That Lucretian scantness, a natural-philosophical problem and a literary–linguistic one that also plagued early modern scientific writers, required great care in vernacular transmission.

The Lucretian combination of moral and natural philosophy was generically and intellectually troubling. Robert Burton worried that 'being a divine [I] have meddled with physic' (*Anatomy of Melancholy*, 1. 20), even though this transgression licensed him to engage in a liberty of philosophizing that amounts to a discursive analogy with the haphazard, fortuitous behaviour of Epicurean atoms, a likening of prose and physics. In 'The Digression of the Air', the displacement of the earth from the centre of the cosmos, the breaking-open of what had been a finite cosmos, is rhetorically enacted by Seneca's own discourse, immethodically proceeding in a 'negligent and remiss' manner (Burton, *Anatomy of Melancholy*, 2. 33–67). The macaronic cento of Burton's own apparently chaotic prose invited readers in the 1620s and 1630s to rethink not just relations between ancient and modern philosophy but also the ways in which discourse was shaped by, as well as constitutive of, the boundaries of experience.

Although some seventeenth-century translators rendered Lucretian verse as prose, Lucy Hutchinson (*c.*1650s–1675) chose couplets—so too would Edward Sherburne, John Dryden, and John Evelyn—as the best English means of wedding its poetic qualities to its moral and scientific didacticism. By the time Hutchinson undertook her translation, Lucretius' heroic introduction of epic subjects[58] was especially significant: as a poet marked by the civil wars of his own time, Lucretius thought of atomic collisions as armies clashing in internecine strife (a notion adapted by Milton, Clarendon, and others in the seventeenth century), and his atomic theory served as the physical basis for an ethics of tranquillity aimed at endurance of and resistance to a violent culture. But constancy and a certain regularity of activity are also features of the Lucretian atom, and the counterpoise to its apparent violence and disorder was the idea that regular and predictable atomic processes morally embodied a supreme, universal, and indivisible constant. Although by the mid-seventeenth century Lucretius was a leading discursive writer of antiquity, he was by no means pre-eminent—Aristotle's account of causation remained of great value to Browne in *Religio Medici* and to William Harvey in his treatise on generation. But the need to reassert eternal providence was a crucial *donnée* of mid-century discursive prose and poetry, and, to delineate order in apparent atomic fortuity, some early modern Lucretian inheritors read the predictable properties of his atoms as yet another defence against a chaotic world.

In the *Anatomy of Melancholy*, Burton argues for a life of tranquillity partly by locating his persona, Democritus Jr, in a lineal descent, via Seneca and Epicurus, from the garden-dwelling Democritus. Burton ballasts himself against anxiety and disturbance by recourse to Seneca, who borrowed the Epicurean lesson of constant and unperturbed life (although he is not an Epicurean) and was the heir of Democritean peace and seclusion. Seneca voluntarily retired from public life; Cicero was put to death for his role in the affairs of state. These exemplary Roman figures, together with the model of the ironical Greek philosopher–scientist, provided a dual impulse to retreat from the early modern public sphere. A peculiarly late-Renaissance English response to the quandaries produced by an extreme national political dichotomy, and to the rapidly developing culture of observation and experimentation, was a species of georgic writing that married Stoic virtues to the new philosophy and its intellectual outriders.

A late-sixteenth-century verse treatise on farming declares that 'The Plough is the Lord's pen',[59] an analogy that animates the extraordinarily lively and varied category of georgic writing in early modern literature, a category, according to George Puttenham, 'wherein honest and profitable arts and sciences are treated'.[60] Montaigne declared Virgil's *Georgics* 'the most accomplished piece of work of poesy' ('Of Books'; Montaigne, *Essayes* (1613), 227),[61] and Bacon modelled *The Advancement of Learning* as a kind of intellectual cultivation that he styled 'georgics of the mind' (*Advancement of Learning*; *Works*, 6. 811).[62] The impulse to explain and advise on agricultural and related matters of food provision, and to do so in an unusual range of literary genres and styles, was an exercise prompted by the powerful examples of Hesiod, Columella, Nicander, the Oppians (*Halieutica* and *Cynegetica*), Varro, and, above all, Virgil. By the mid-seventeenth century, as the fashion for pastoral declined into 'idealized emptiness'[63] and empirical, observational prose developed, Virgil's *Georgics* were held in higher esteem than the *Eclogues*. As Stuart political pastoral vanished in the 1640s, as various forms of political retirement and retreat generated a rising interest in georgic topics and practices in the 1650s, and as agricultural and horticultural efficiency became an economic necessity with the calamity of foreign wars and of trade's increase in the 1660s, practical discussions of sowing, rearing, cultivating, irrigating, hybridizing, fertilizing, and distribution of agricultural products occupied literary, scientific, and pragmatic writers alike.

The rise of English georgic has traditionally been associated with the eighteenth century and the late Augustans;[64] and even recently it has been argued that it was a response to John Dryden's 1697 translation of Virgil, or to the 1707 Act of Union.[65] But, as Alastair Fowler notes, a less imitative and less formulaic approach to georgic by English writers of the period from at least the 1550s onwards places this kind of writing (in verse and prose) much earlier. 'The Renaissance conception of georgic,' observes Fowler, 'was distinctly loose',[66] and even Addison, an early Augustan who naturally disparaged the base style of many of the more homely English georgical writers who preceded him, allowed that the genre was comprehended in 'that class of poetry which consists in giving plain and direct instructions to the reader', and that such instructions could be on either moral or speculative subjects, or on 'rules of practice' such as those of Hesiod and Virgil.[67]

English georgic includes a very wide range of writing. Thomas Tusser's best-selling *A Hundreth Good Pointes of Husbandrie* (1557), a hugely popular black-letter collection of aphoristic verse advice that went through successive expansions, conveyed general topics like 'the ladder to thrift' as well as 'good husbandly lessons' on the tasks of the seasons, and digressions on housekeeping and hospitality, in rustically thumping demotic verse that belies Tusser's Eton and Cambridge training.[68] By contrast, Robert Sharrock's *The History of Propagation* (1659) is a learned prose work dedicated to Robert Boyle by a self-described Baconian. Midway between these are an apparently pastoral exercise like Spenser's *The Shepheardes Calender* (1579), with an unusual concentration on georgic tasks (an emphasis signalled in the authorially sanctioned woodcuts as well as in the verse), Michael Drayton's *Poly-Olbion* (1612/22), the country estate poems of Jonson, John Denham, Aemelia Lanyer, and Andrew Marvell, the retirement works of country life and its labours by Robert Herrick, Charles Cotton, and Walton, and more idiosyncratic items such as Evelyn's incomplete *Elysium Britannicum* (1650s–1706) and Browne's *Garden of Cyrus* (1658). Still another kind of pragmatic georgic is the legal, antiquarian labour of Sir William Dugdale's *History of Imbanking and Drayning* (1662) on behalf of land economy and soil science. To this can be added a host of other practical works on all aspects of husbandry and soil improvement, and on household arts and arboriculture and horticulture—brewing, grafting, fruit trees and cider-making, forestry, beekeeping, silkworm cultivation, salad leaves, flower- and kitchen-gardening—in prose and in verse, in high and low style, many of them structured calendrically, like Evelyn's *Kalendarium Hortense* (1666).This interesting mixture of the pragmatic and the literary, and of the most elevated and the most homely writers, illustrates 'a widespread shift...from the cultivation of mimetic to the cultivation of didactic forms' during this period.[69]

All these productions owe something to their classical exemplars—Virgil, Hesiod, Varro, Columella, among others—and this distinguished heritage ought to have smoothed the way for vernacular georgic in the British Isles. But instead, the georgic mode was a puzzle to the theorists of genre. Sidney described the work of poets of this 'second kind' as 'the sweet food of sweetly uttered knowledge', but was not persuaded that georgic writers 'properly be poets'.[70] It is probably an overstatement to say that the literary–didactic mix of georgic writing caused 'confusion' in the period before Dryden's 1697 translation of Virgil,[71] but fears of debasement of Virgil's 'rustic majesty, like that of a Roman dictator at the plough-tail' (Addison, 'Essay on the Georgics', in Dryden, *The Works*, 5. 151) were latent in earlier seventeenth-century georgic, from which majesty was often quite absent. The banausic verse of Tusser, or the homiletic prose advice of Ralph Austen, or the wholly utilitarian works of Samuel Hartlib seemed to mimic Hesiod himself, 'the first poet of the world' who chose to write of husbandry, but was condescendingly approved by Addison as 'more a husbandman than a poet...[who] does not stir out of the field once' but has at least given us 'the first rough *sketch* of a georgic' ('Essay on the Georgics'; in Dryden, *The Works*, 5. 150). From the mid-sixteenth century, literary and poetic English georgic coexisted with more workmanly, less ostentatiously literary, and usually prose 'georgical' writings; and even this distinction is not rigid when homiletic and demotic writers like Austen and John Beale write their practical country knowledge of horticulture from deeply learned backgrounds and thorough acquaintance with the classical agricultural writers.[72] In the category of classical literary georgic fall Virgil himself, along with Columella, Hesiod, and English imitators such as Drayton, Walton, Browne, Henry Vaughan, Rooke Church, and William Temple; the less self-consciously literary georgical would include Varro, Cato Major, Palladius, Tusser, Gervase Markham, Ralph Austen, Walter Blith, and much of the work of John Evelyn.

The (poetic) georgic and the (practical) georgical, taken together as a vibrant and popular English genre, tell a great deal about seventeenth-century social and economic history, superbly documented by Andrew MacRae, among others.[73] The georgic(al) impulse is, however, much more than simply the reiteration and imitation of classical precedents in the manner of the English Augustans in the next century, or the self-conscious identification of early modern writers with classical forebears. It encodes the complex Ciceronian–Senecan–Lucretian–Epicurean ideology of retirement, contemplation, country pursuits, and self-cultivation that was uniquely the product of the seventeenth century.[74]

The georgical John Evelyn thought a garden was a type of heaven, and the 'best representation of our lost felicity...we all came out of this parsley bed', and in his plan for a royal garden, Evelyn described it as a residual memory of that Edenic origin, and emblematic of a deep-seated characteristic of humanity—'from thence we came, and thither we tend'.[75] In a fine definition of the georgic impulse, he noted that 'Men began...to recover that by art and industry, which was before produced to them spontaneously'.[76] The early modern georgical mode was symptomatic of the prevailing ideology of Baconian reparative intellectual projects to restore or reconvene the broken knowledge of the natural world, a knowledge destroyed, damaged, or lost with the fall of man and only to be recuperated *in sudore vultus* ('by the sweat of his brow'), just as man's ability to know good from evil (and his consequent eligibility to be saved with the coming of Christ) followed happily, if paradoxically, from the fall. Baconian science was thus animated by the sense of the fall as an intellectual *felix culpa*: seventeenth-century pastoral indolence, leisure, and plenty faded and gave way to georgic labours and the satisfactions of useful, productive toil ('it does, like grace, the fallen tree restore, | to its blessed state of paradise before', said Cowley[77]), and English georgic garden books reinvent the Edenic by strenuously reconvening horticultural felicity. Such works resituate us in an intellectual garden by showing us how to construct a real one, and, although they are framed in profound engagement with the literary georgic inheritance from Virgil, they are above all practical and instructive. Evelyn's portrait as a young man of 28 bears a solemn Senecan inscription on preparation for death, but his major work, as an expert advising gardener, was devoted to the life of plants,[78] a combination of an intensely practical interest in horticulture with a highly developed sense of the classical precedents for his various horticultural and natural–philosophical activities.

Within georgic literary and social practice there is a significant confluence of, on the one hand, Stoic–Democritean–Epicurean retirement (via Seneca, Cicero, and Lucretius and natural–philosophical seclusion), as demonstrated by Boyle's apolitical retreat to a remote laboratory in Dorset in the late 1640s, and the relatively sequestered Oxford group in the 1650s (retirement as avoidance), and, on the other hand, John Evelyn's and Abraham Cowley's cultivation of specifically pragmatic retirement from the political sphere in their gardens in the 1650s and later (retirement as escape). The powerful influence of Cicero's *De Officiis* is latent here, of retreat as productive and actively attentive to duty. Such retirement, in either category, was rarely permanent or absolute, as Evelyn's essay on public employment and Boyle's essential participation in the new Royal Society indicate.

If the sweat of some seventeenth-century brows was expended on purely scientific, technological, and agricultural undertakings in response to the Baconian rationale for the new learning, at the same time the georgic impulse coupled that labour with a retreat from public affairs, often to the country or to a garden, a re-enactment of the classical models of actual or imagined retirement by Seneca, Martial, Horace, and Cicero, among others, and marking the actors of such retreat as part of a more specialized withdrawal into a friendly space for recuperative science. In other words, Senecan, Stoic contemplation together with Epicurean/Democritean philosophy was inflected by what Røstvig calls 'ecstatic Hortulan[ism]';[79] intellectual and private self-cultivation was yoked with a more disinterested cultivation of the natural world in the form of georgic and georgical activities, and thence with the cultivation of improved and extended knowledge of the natural world. That hortulanism could take the form of a Senecan 'herby diet' (Evelyn's term for vegetarianism[80]) or John Beale's vigorous proselytizing for the growing of apples and of cider-making for health and national well-being or William Temple's anti-scientific praise of retirement from public affairs. These distinct and occasionally antithetical enterprises had, in some measure, their inspiration from the Senecan and Epicurean sense that 'If Eden be on earth at all, | 'Tis that, which we the country call'.[81]

Cowley quoted Columella on country life, 'the nearest neighbour, or rather next kindred in philosophy' ('Of Agriculture'; *Several Discourses*, in *Works*, 98), but the classical ideal of retirement was more often a decision forced upon those whose fortunes during the Commonwealth were damaged by loss of favour or actual sequestration of property; even after the Restoration, with fewer extant threats of this sort, the ideal remained. It was conveniently embodied in the Epicurean principle of *ataraxia*, calmness promoted by seclusion and the avoidance of public affairs and private passion. The most famous of Evelyn's gardens, Sayes Court on the banks of the Thames near Deptford, was designedly constructed as the Epicurean retreat of a *literatus* (indeed, all his gardens were self-consciously Epicurean in their references),[82] and Jeremy Taylor likened Sayes Court to Pliny's villa.[83] Evelyn wanted this, and his other gardens, to become the locus of philosophical discussion among the learned gentlemen he styled *paradisi cultores* or 'hortulan saints',[84] but fretted that, by inviting friends to visit and admire it, even if under the rubric of what he called a 'deipnosophisse' [*sic*], a re-enactment of Athenaeus' philosophical supper,[85] he was violating the spirit of Epicurean withdrawal.[86] That impulse, 'nostalgically fixated on sustained sociability', is a holding action *against* the admission and recognition of loss,[87] and Evelyn (along with Cowley, Boyle, Browne, and others) is partly enchanted by the thought of practised forgetfulness in the midst of civil war, foreign altercations, and a disappointingly hedonistic court culture. But Evelyn's powerful sense of public duty never allowed him to become wholly retired, and his garden life was truly georgical, based not only on the sense of recovered memory of Edenic felicity and the human disobedience whose penalty was the hard labour of reacquisition, but on an outward-looking dedication to national prosperity and military dominance. Worried in the 1640s that he might become 'wrapped in moss', he framed his enforced absence from English public life thereafter as a specifically Roman, political retirement rather than an idealized one, and styled himself a 'mere planter of Coleworts',[88] in the manner of Cato Major, the Roman statesman who wrote *De Agricultura* when he retreated from politics and military service.

His friend Abraham Cowley wrote a long Latin poem, *Plantarum Libra Sex* (1662), after a decade in exile or under arrest,[89] informed by Virgil's *Georgics* and by his study in retirement of medical botany and natural philosophy.[90] The impulse of his proposal to establish an institution for the advancement of experimental philosophy is meshed with his interests in and essays on gardens and on farming, and the specialization of his proposed university professorships (tillage, pasturage, arboriculture, and animal husbandry) was based on Virgil's *Georgics* (Cowley, 'Of Agriculture'; *Several Discourses*, in *Works*, 101; McRae, *God Speed the Plough*, 298). The essay 'Of Agriculture' (*c*.1650s) recapitulates the Virgilian georgic virtues: the farmer is a natural aristocrat whose heraldic achievement would show 'a plough in a field arable' (Cowley, 'Of Agriculture'; *Several Discourses*, in *Works*, 101); and he is the most civil and irenic of all beings. Cowley says he is unable to remember a single farmer who took part in the late wars; he regrets that 'we have no men now fetched from the plough to be made lords, as they were in Rome to be made consuls and dictators' ('Of Agriculture'; *Several Discourses*, in *Works*, 99–101).

But such philosophically inspired agriculture and retreat are often more inviting in conceit than in reality: Evelyn's garden at Albury proved to be not wholly benign when a grotto collapsed and nearly killed the mathematician William Oughtred and the Earl of Arundel as they discussed 'high matters',[91] and likewise Cowley found the georgic conditions of his rural life rather less to his taste than he had imagined, confined to a hired house and garden 'among weeds and rubbish' ('The Garden'; *Several Discourses*, in *Works*, 114). Cowley nevertheless celebrated the Baconian advancement of learning and the birth of the Royal Society with a georgic image of reclaimed Edenic innocence and fruitfulness:

> The orchard's open now, and free;
> *Bacon* has broke the scarecrow deity.
> Behold the ripen'd fruit, and gather now your fill.[92]
> ('To the Royal Society'; *Verses Written on Several Occasions*, in *Works*, 39)

Conclusion

Classical models of discursive writing guided early modern self-exploration and self-preparation and were the best instruments for examining and explaining the nature of the universe. But the ancient models had to be edited, refashioned, and expurgated for their Christian audience—it was typical of Sherburne to leave out bits of Seneca's dialogue on providence that were dangerous;[93] and of John Evelyn to be unable, ultimately, to countenance the heretical aspects of Lucretius's cosmology and physics. The ultimate version of this selective reception was the ongoing tendency to transmit ancient wisdom in commonplace books, in which aphoristic extracts were rearranged thematically and out of their original contexts. By 1679 Roger L'Estrange deemed Seneca's 'frequent repetitions' and 'rhapsod[ies] of divine, and extraordinary hints, and notions, [rather] than in any regulated method of discourse' too eccentric to warrant straight translation. Instead, L'Estrange opted for an 'abstract' by means of which Seneca's 'scatter'd ethics' could be gathered and placed beneath 'their proper heads'.[94] But, at the outset of the century, Thomas Lodge had left this sort of thematic editing to the reader, who was instructed

> to pretend this translation to be a garden, wherein though thou mayest find many wholesome herbs, goodly flowers, and rich medicines; yet can it not be but some weeds may rankly shoot out, which may smother or obscure the light and lustre of the better. Play the good gardener, I pray thee, and pulling up the weeds, make thy profit of the flowers.[95]

Another factor in the reception and transmission of ancient discursive writing was more pressing than ever: whether to choose verse or prose, and the contingent decision, whether the philosophical and the scientific in English were best served by the Renaissance arsenal of literary tropes and genres. Bacon and Boyle, to name only two major voices in the debate, deeply considered the propriety of the literary as a vehicle of scientific writing. Bacon associated the poetic with certain kinds of discursive, natural-philosophical writing and banned it categorically from others, while Boyle concluded in Sidneian fashion that, if literary conceits could make meaning clearest and most persuasive, they were to be embraced.[96]

These concerns did not entirely disappear with the advent of early Enlightenment mathematical expression and the last unspooling of the Renaissance recovery of classical texts; but, as Newton's cosmology and optics were converted into poetic conceits by eighteenth-century poets, as the pragmatic georgics of Beale and Austen were appropriated for nationalist purposes in Phillips's *Cyder* (1708), and as Boyle's style was sent up by Butler and Swift, eighteenth- and nineteenth-century thinkers and writers had to modify what Isaac Barrow had called 'the exercise of our mind in ... rational discursiveness',[97] a mode of thinking that Milton had located just below the angels in degree but also acknowledged to be sorely fallen as 'process of speech'.[98] This modification would take many forms, from periodical journalism and Romantic meditative poetry through the social–aesthetic criticism of Ruskin. The subsequent history of English writing shows that ancient discursivities continued to exert a profound influence.

Notes

1. On early modern scientific poetry and its relation to Aristotle and classical exemplars, see Robert M. Schuler, 'Francis Bacon and Scientific Poetry', *Transactions of the American Philosophical Society*, NS 82/2 (1992), 1–65.
2. *The Works of Sir Thomas Browne*, ed. Geoffrey Keynes, 4 vols, rev. edn (Chicago, 1964), 3. 206.
3. *OED* A.1–3. Its modern use as the adjectival form of 'discourse' was used only, and then rarely, from the last quarter of the seventeenth century.
4. See Kathryn Murphy, '"A Likely Story": Plato's *Timaeus* in the *Garden of Cyrus*', in Reid Barbour and Claire Preston (eds), *Sir Thomas Browne: The World Proposed* (Oxford, 2008), 242–57.

5. See K. J. Wilson, *Incomplete Fictions: The Formation of English Renaissance Dialogue* (Washington, 1985), 23–45; and Donald Douglas Wells, 'Political Platonism in the English Renaissance', Ph.D. thesis, University of North Carolina (2007).
6. Torquato Tasso, 'Discourse on the Art of Dialogue', in *Tasso's Dialogues: A Selection*, trans. and ed. Carnes Lord and Dain A. Trafton (Berkeley and Los Angeles, 1982), 41.
7. George Herbert, *A Priest to the Temple* (written 1632, published 1652), 81.
8. Herbert, *A Priest to the Temple*, 85–7.
9. See *Conversations at Little Gidding*, ed. A. M. Williams (Cambridge, 1970), pp. xx, 51–60.
10. Samuel Parker, *A Free and Impartial Censure of the Platonick Philosophy* (1666), 2.
11. Quentin Skinner, *Visions of Politics*, 3 vols (Cambridge, 2002), 2 (*Renaissance Virtues*), 218–19.
12. Charles Schmitt, *Cicero Skepticus: A Study of the Influence of the Academia in the Renaissance* (The Hague, 1972), and Howard Jones, *Master Tully: Cicero in Tudor England* (Nieuwkoop, 1998).
13. *Gabriel Harvey's Ciceronianus* (1577), intro. Harold S. Wilson, trans. Clarence A. Forbes (Lincoln, NE, 1945), and Jones, *Master Tully*, 268–70.
14. To be sure, anyone with the slightest knowledge of Cicero understood that his own career had belied this confidence, and that the relationship between philosophical *otium* and political *negotium* was a highly vexed one for him.
15. Nicholas Grimald, *Marcus Tullius Ciceroes Thre Bokes of Duties* (1556), ed. Gerald O'Gorman (Washington, 1990), 40.
16. *The Philosophie, Commonlie Called, The Morals Written by the learned Philosopher Plutarch*, trans. Philemon Holland (1603), 1.
17. Erasmus' letter to Alexius Turzo (1525), quoted in Fred Schurink, 'Print, Patronage, and Occasion: Translations of Plutarch's *Moralia* in Tudor England', *Yearbook of English Studies*, 38 (2008), 88.
18. Plutarch, *The Morals*, trans. Holland, 83.
19. Plutarch, *The Morals*, trans. Holland, 1. Holland borrows his summaries from annotations by Plutarch's French translator Simon Goulart (1581).
20. Cf. Robert Lamberton, *Plutarch* (New Haven, 2001), 37.
21. Plutarch, *The Morals*, trans. Holland, 1130.
22. Plutarch, *The Morals*, trans. Holland, 538.
23. 'A Defence of Seneca and Plutarke', in *The Essayes or, Moral, Politike, and Militarie Discourses of Lord Michael de Montaigne*, trans. John Florio (1613), 406.
24. *Conversations at Little Gidding*, ed. A. M. Williams (Cambridge, 1970); B. Blackstone (ed.), *The Ferrar Papers* (Cambridge, 1938); E. Cruwys Sharland (ed.), *The Story Books of Little Gidding* (1899). Their complex ethical meditations are discussed in Reid Barbour, *Literature and Religious Culture in Seventeenth-Century England* (Cambridge, 2003), ch. 1.
25. Quintilian had already listed his writings as *orationes, poemata, epistulae, dialogi*. See L. D. Reynolds, 'The Medieval Tradition of Seneca's Dialogues', *Classical Quarterly*, NS 18 (1968), 355–72.
26. See C. D. N. Costa (ed.), *Seneca: Four Dialogues* (Boston, 1974); J. R. G. Wright, 'Form and Content in the *Moral Essays*', in Costa (ed.), *Seneca*, 39–65 (esp. 45); Anna Lydia Motto, *Seneca* (New York, 1973), 50.
27. *Essayes by Sir William Cornwallis*, ed. Don Cameron Allen (Baltimore, 1946), 190, 192, 209.
28. Mireille Armisen-Marchetti, 'Imagination and Meditation in Seneca: The Example of Praemeditatio', in John G. Fitch (ed.), *Oxford Readings in Classical Studies: Seneca* (Oxford, 2008), 102.
29. For Lipsius' *Quaestiones Epistolicae* (1575), see G. Williamson, *Senecan Amble: A*

Study in the Prose Form from Bacon to Collier (Chicago, 1932), 123.

30. *Two Bookes of Constancie, Written in Latine by Justus Lipsius, Englished by Sir John Stradling*, ed. and intro. Rudolf Kirk (New Brunswick, NJ, 1939), 205–6.
31. Justus Lipsius, *Manuductio ad Stoicam Philosophiam*, quoted in Williamson, *Senecan Amble*, 111–12.
32. For the forms, see John L. Lievsay (ed.), *The Seventeenth-Century Resolve: A Historical Anthology of a Literary Form* (Lexington, KY, 1980), 1–7.
33. Nicholas Breton, 'Characters upon Essaies: Morall and Divine', in *The Works in Verse and Prose*, ed. Alexander B. Grosart, 2 vols (repr. edn, Hildesheim, 1969), 2. 4.
34. William Cornwallis, 'Of Vanity', in *Essayes*, 175.
35. Feltham, 'Of Preaching', in *Resolves*, in Lievsay (ed.), *Seventeenth-Century Resolve*, 86.
36. Thomas Randolph, *The Poems and Amyntas of Thomas Randolph*, ed. John Jay Parry (New Haven, 1917), 126.
37. These epithets are at first applied by Montaigne to both Seneca and Plutarch; but later in the same essay he distinguishes Plutarch as 'more uniforme and constant' from the 'more waving and diverse Seneca' (pp. 228–9).
38. See Michael Hall, 'The Emergence of the Essay and the Idea of Discovery', in Alexander J. Butrym (ed.), *Essays on the Essay: Redefining the Genre* (Athens, GA, 1989), 73–91; Peter Dear, 'Narratives, Anecdotes, and Experiments: Turning Experiments into Science in the Seventeenth Century', and Frederic Holmes, 'Argument and Narrative in Scientific Writing', both in Peter Dear (ed.), *The Literary Structure of Scientific Argument* (Philadelphia, 1991); Steven Shapin and Simon Schaffer, *Leviathan and the Air-Pump: Hobbes, Boyle, and the Experimental Life* (Princeton, 1985).
39. *Of the Advancement of Learning*, trans. Gilbert Wat (1640), bk 1, ch. 4, sect. 2 (p. 29).
40. On this style, see David Burchell, '"A Plain Blunt Man": Hobbes, Science, and Rhetoric Revisited', in Juliet Cummins and David Burchell (eds), *Science, Literature and Rhetoric in Early Modern England* (Aldershot, 2007), 60.
41. Williamson, *Senecan Amble*, 202–3. The criticism of Seneca and Plutarch ('mere essayists') is voiced by the character Jack Daw in *Epicoene* (2. 2).
42. See Williamson, *Senecan Amble*; and quoted in G. M. Ross, 'Seneca's Philosophical Influence,' in Costa (ed.), *Seneca*, 146.
43. See Williamson, *Senecan Amble*, 190, 194, 170, 174.
44. Francis Bacon, *De Augmentis*, 6. 3, in *The Works of Francis Bacon*, ed. James Spedding, Robert Leslie Ellis, and Douglas Denon Heath http://onlinebooks.library.upenn.edu/webbin/metabook?id=worksfbacon (accessed April 2015), 2.133.
45. *The Nondramatic Works of John Ford*, ed. L. E. Stock et al., p. 245; see also the introduction to this work by Gilles D. Monsarrat and L. E. Stock, 220–8.
46. Montaigne's autobiography, as quoted by G. M. Ross in Costa (ed.), *Seneca*, 147; Joseph Hall, *Epistles, Containing Two Decades* (1611), 107–8.
47. Owen Feltham, 'Of the Worship of Admiration', in *Resolves: A Duple Century*, 3rd edn (1628), 43.
48. Robert Burton, *The Anatomy of Melancholy*, ed. Thomas C. Faulkner et al., 6 vols (Oxford, 1989–), 1. 4, 1. 18.
49. *De Ira ad Novatum*, in *L. Annæi Senecæ Philosophi Opera Quæ Exstant Omnia*, ed. Justus Lipsius (Antwerp, 1652), 1.
50. David R. Carlson, 'Morley's Translations from Roman Philosophers and English Courtier Literature', in Marie Axton and James P. Carley (eds), David Starkey

(intro.), *Triumphs of English: Henry Parker, Lord Morley, Translator to the Tudor Court: New Essays in Interpretation* (2000), 131–51.

51. Carlson, 'Morleys' Translations', 137.
52. For this argument, see Gordon Braden, *Renaissance Tragedy and the Senecan Tradition: Anger's Privilege* (New Haven, 1985).
53. John Evelyn, *Acetaria, or A Discourse of Sallets* (1699), 5, 23.
54. See Reid Barbour, *English Epicures and Stoics: Ancient Legacies in Early Stuart Culture* (Amherst, MA, 1998), ch. 4.
55. John G. Fitch (ed.), *Oxford Readings in Classical Studies: Seneca* (Oxford, 2008), 1.
56. Don Cameron Allen, 'The Rehabilitation of Epicurus and his Theory of Pleasure in the Early Renaissance', *Studies in Philology*, 41 (1944), 1–15.
57. Lucretius, *De Rerum Natura*, trans. W. H. D. Rouse (Cambridge, MA, 1959), 1. 907–14, 136–45.
58. The ancient inclusion of both hexameter heroic narrative and hexameter didactic under the heading 'epic' allowed J. C. Scaliger to assert that *De Rerum Natura* and other scientific subject matter qualified as epic.
59. John Kay, 'A Fatherly Farewell', Folger Library MS W.b.484, p. 3 (quoted in Andrew McRae, *God Speed the Plough: The Representation of Agrarian England, 1500–1660* (Cambridge, 1996), 210).
60. George Puttenham, *The Art of English Poesy*, ed. Gladys Doidge Willcock and Alice Walker (Cambridge, 1936; repr. 1970), 44.
61. Montaigne considers the *Aeneid* in need of revision.
62. See also Annabel Patterson, 'Pastoral Versus Georgic: The Politics of Virgilian Quotation', in Barbara K. Lewalski (ed.), *Renaissance Genres: Essays on Theory, History, and Interpretation*, Harvard Studies in English 14 (1986), 241–67 (esp. 242–3).
63. Ralph Cohen, *Innovation and Variation: Literary Change and Georgic Poetry*, Literature and History Papers Read at a Clark Library Seminar March 3, 1973 (Berkeley and Los Angeles, 1973), 24–5.
64. See, e.g. John Chalker, *The English Georgic: A Study of the Development of a Form* (1969).
65. See, e.g. Rachel Crawford, *Poetry, Enclosure, and the Vernacular English Landscape, 1700–1880* (Cambridge, 2002), 92. McRae observes that the aesthetics of agricultural production did not really develop until the eighteenth century (*God Speed the Plough*, 241).
66. Alastair Fowler, 'The Beginnings of English Georgic', in Lewalski, *Renaissance Genres*, 105–25 (109).
67. Addison, 'Essay on the Georgics', in John Dryden, *The Works*, gen. eds Edward Niles Hook, H. T. Swedenberg, Jr, and Vinton A. Dearing, 20 vols (Berkeley and Los Angeles, 1956), 5. 146.
68. See the discussion of Tusser in Helen Cooper, Chapter 9, this volume.
69. R. S. Crane, quoted in Cohen, *Innovation*, 23.
70. Sir Philip Sidney, *Defence of Poesy*, in *Miscellaneous Prose of Sir Philip Sidney*, ed. Katharine Duncan-Jones and Jan van Dorsten (Oxford, 1973), 80.
71. McRae, *God Speed the Plough*, 200.
72. Austen rattles off numerous classical sources on fruit trees (*A Dialogue or Familiar Discourse and Conference between the Husbandman and Fruit Trees* (1676), 18); and Beale's Herefordshire family cider-making expertise survived a Cambridge fellowship and entry into holy orders (see Mayling Stubbs, 'John Beale, Philosophical Gardener of Herefordshire', *Annals of Science*, 394 (1982), 88).
73. See also Michael Leslie and Timothy Raylor (eds), *Culture and Cultivation in Early Modern England: Writing and the Land* (Leicester, 1992); and Douglas Chambers, *Planters of the English Landscape: Botany, Trees, and the Georgics* (New Haven, 1993).

74. See Maren-Sofie Røstvig, who observes that the georgical writers of the seventeeth and early eighteenth centuries were referencing their classical antecedents in order to reconfigure rather than imitate them, quoted in Cohen, *Innovation*, 5–6.
75. John Evelyn, *Elysium Britannicum or The Royal Gardens*, ed. John E. Ingram (Philadelphia, 2001), 31.
76. Evelyn, *Elysium Britannicum*, 29. On this theme, see Anthony Low, *The Georgic Revolution* (Princeton, 1985).
77. Abraham Cowley, 'The Garden'; *Several Discourses*, in *The Works of Mr Abraham Cowley* (1688), 119.
78. The portrait, by Robert Walker in 1648, is inscribed 'Mortem venientem nemo hilaris excipit [nisi] qui se ad [eam] [diu] composuerat' ('he cannot with cheerfulness and joy receive his death unless he bestowed much time and care in preparations against that sad calamity'). Seneca, *Epistle* 30 (discussed in John Ingamells, *Later Stuart Portraits, 1685–1714* (2009), 86–8).
79. Røstvig, cited in Cohen, *Innovation*, 28–30.
80. See Seneca, *Epistle* 108.
81. Vaughan, 'Retirement IV', *Thalia Rediviva* (1678), 309.
82. See Carola Small and Alastair Small, 'John Evelyn and the Garden of Epicurus', *Journal of the Warburg and Courtauld Institutes*, 60 (1997), 194 ff.
83. Joseph M. Levine, 'John Evelyn: Between the Ancients and the Moderns', in Therese O'Malley and Joachim Wolschke-Bulmahn (eds), *John Evelyn's Elysium Britannicum and European Gardening* (Washington, 1998), 70.
84. John Evelyn to Thomas Browne, 28 Jan 1659/60 (in Keynes, *Works*, 4. 275).
85. Evelyn to Samuel Pepys, 1 March 1686 and 7 January 1695, in Guy de la Bédoyère (ed.), *Particular Friends: The Correspondence of Samuel Pepys and John Evelyn* (Woodbridge, 1997), 167, 256.
86. Evelyn thought of his earlier garden at Wotton as the place where he and his friends could discuss tulips; and a dinner in 1656 given to Taylor, Wilkins, and Boyle prompted his worry about publicity (see Gillian Darley, *John Evelyn: Living for Ingenuity* (New Haven, 2006), 130, 139).
87. Karen Edwards, 'Engaging with Pygmies: Thomas Browne and John Milton', in Barbour and Preston, *Sir Thomas Browne: The World Proposed*, 112–13.
88. Evelyn to Samuel Pepys, 26 August 1689, in de la Bédoyère (ed.), *Particular Friends*, 189.
89. Though probably mistakenly, even though he was a known Royalist and facilitator of correspondence in the exiled court.
90. Cowley is an unusual example of a truly bilingual poet, equally at ease in Latin and in English.
91. Darley, *John Evelyn*, 119. The garden was the Earl of Arundel's at Albury: Aubrey, 'William Oughtred', in *Brief Lives*, 224.
92. In 'To the Royal Society' Cowley mitigates this praise, however, when he adds: 'Yet still, methinks, we fain would be | Catching at the Forbidden-Tree; | We would be like the Deity.'
93. *Senecas Answer to Lucilius his Quære; Why Good Men Suffer Misfortunes Seeing There Is a Divine Providence*, trans. Edward Sherburne (London, 1648), 30.
94. Roger l'Estrange, *Senecas Morals Abstracted* (1679), ii–iii.
95. *The Workes of Lucius Annæus Seneca*, trans. Thomas Lodge (1620), b1r.
96. See Claire Preston, 'English Scientific Prose: Bacon, Browne, Boyle', in Andrew Hadfield (ed.), *The Oxford Handbook of Early-Modern Prose* (Oxford, 2012).
97. Isaac Barrow, *Works* (1686), 3. 252.
98. Milton, *Paradise Lost*, 5. 480, 7. 178.

PART III
Authors

CHAPTER 21

Homer

JESSICA WOLFE

Texts, Translations, and Apparatus

England produced few editions and translations of the Homeric poems before the Restoration. Only two Greek texts of Homer were printed in England prior to 1660: a Greek-only text of books 1 through 10 of the *Iliad* (*Homerou Ilias, Id Est, De Rebus Ad Troiam Gestis*), printed in 1591 by George Bishop, and a 1648 Greek–Latin edition of the *Iliad*, printed by Roger Daniel and possibly edited by James Duport.

Before 1598, when George Chapman began to publish his English translation of the *Iliad*, only two other editions of Homer associated with English scholars are worthy of note. Lawrence Humphrey, future president of Magdalen College, Oxford, wrote the dedication to Hadrianus Junius' *Copiae Cornu Sive Oceanus Enarrationum Homericarum* (1558), a Greek edition of the *Iliad* and *Odyssey* containing the abridged commentaries of Eustathius. In 1581, the first English translation of Homer appeared in print, Arthur Hall's *Ten Bookes of Homers Iliades*.[1] Based heavily on Hugh Salel's French translation of the poem, Hall's translation is in rhyming fourteeners and contains a smattering of marginal notes, most of them consecrated to identifying rhetorical devices or moral and political allegories.

George Chapman published his English translations of the *Iliad* and *Odyssey* in seven instalments between 1598 and 1616.[2] Chapman consulted several prior editions of the Homeric poems, including those of Lorenzo Valla, Eobanus Hessus, and Johannes Spondanus; he also borrowed liberally from the poems and orations of Angelo Poliziano. Yet Chapman is often highly critical of Homer's earlier editors and translators, a habit upon which Ben Jonson comments sardonically in his own copy of Chapman's 1616 *Whole Works*.[3] One refrain of Chapman's commentary is that Homer has been either maligned by prior editors or simply misunderstood by 'prosers' whose 'affected expositions' are 'spent in mere presumptuous guess at this inaccessible poet'.[4]

Chapman's revisions to his Homeric translations reflect his changing attitude towards Homer as well as the changing political and literary landscape in which he worked: a new monarch, new patrons, and an emerging interest in neo-Stoicism all help reshape the translation over two decades. Between 1598 and 1609, Henry, Prince of Wales replaces the Earl of Essex as the dedicatee of the *Iliad*. Between 1609 and 1611, when Chapman publishes his first complete edition of the *Iliad*, he adds a substantial commentary, a prose preface, and an essay on the life of Homer. After Chapman's *Whole Works* appeared in 1616, no English translation of either poem appeared until 1660, a year that marked two new English translations of the *Iliad*, both produced by loyalists to Charles II: Thomas Grantham's translations of books 1 and 3 of the *Iliad* and John Ogilby's lavish *Homer his Iliads Translated, Adorn'd with Sculpture, and Illustrated with Annotations*.

Despite the paucity of English editions and translations of Homer, continental editions were widely available in university and private libraries. Homer was taught at Oxford from 1549 onwards; by 1605, the Bodleian library owned the Camerarius–Micyllus (1551) and Spondanus (1583) editions of Homer as well as numerous ancient commentaries.[5] Although library catalogues rarely identify specific editions of Homer's *Iliad* and *Odyssey*, the inventories of private libraries during the period suggest that Tudor and Stuart readers preferred editions of Homer produced in the Protestant north; that most readers encountered Homer in Greek–Latin editions, and that many libraries contained multiple editions of both poems.[6]

A handful of scholarly works concerning Homer were produced in England prior to 1660, including the *Clavis Homerica*, a Homeric lexicon and Greek grammar first printed at Douai in 1636 and reprinted several times in London.[7] In the 1650s, several English scholars produced concordances of Homer and the Scriptures, and, in 1659, Meric Casaubon published two dissertations on Homer under the title *De Nupera Homeri Editione*, the first a review of a 1656 Dutch edition of the *Iliad* and *Odyssey* and the second a treatise on Homeric theology.[8] But English scholars relied heavily on Homeric commentaries printed on the continent; many of these, including a *Life of Homer* attributed to Plutarch, the *Homeric Problems* ascribed to Heraclides, and several works by Porphyry, were available in Latin translation by the middle of the sixteenth century.[9]

Moral and Allegorical Interpretations of Homer

The majority of early modern English readers look to Homeric heroes such as Achilles and Odysseus as ethical models. The *Odyssey* was commonly read as an epic of moderation that exemplifies Aristotelian ideals of the virtuous mean. Scylla and Charybdis provide a lesson about the 'mediocrity' that requires keeping an 'even course' between 'two dangerous gulfs', an allegory that is occasionally given a Christian twist as the twin obstacles turn into the 'rock of presumption' and the pool of 'desperation'.[10] Chapman praises Odysseus' 'self-sufficient strength of virtue', describing his mind as an 'inward, constant, and unconquerd Empire', or what the ancient Greeks called *sophrosune* (self-mastery).[11] But 'much-enduring' (*polutlas*) Odysseus is also, at times, granted a distinctly Christian capacity to forbear 'afflictions and crosses' or to weather hardships and impediments.[12]

Ethically, the *Iliad* was a more challenging text for its English Renaissance readers than the *Odyssey*, for, while the latter poem appears to privilege emotional restraint and *metriopatheia*, the former provides in Achilles and in the Olympian gods figures of passionate excess whose susceptibility to anger, grief, laughter, jealousy, and pity had been criticized by Homer's commentators since antiquity.[13] As they imitate the *Iliad* in their respective epic poems, these questions grip Spenser and Milton as each explores the possibility that indignation (*nemesis*) and pity (*eleos*) might be more refined than other passions (as Aristotle had argued) and also more congenial to Christian ethics. Despite his Stoic interpretation of Odysseus, Chapman adheres to a more peripatetic view of the passions in his *Iliad*, defending Achilles' tears 'as tears of manliness and magnanimity' that earn comparison to Christ, 'who wept for Lazarus'.[14]

Despite the nervousness that attends upon certain episodes of intense affection in the *Iliad*, including the laughter of Zeus and the extravagant grief of Andromache, Hecuba, and Priam, English Renaissance interpretations of Homer often heighten and ennoble Iliadic passions by giving their own renditions of Homeric heroes a greater cue for passion than they possess in Homer's actual poem. In late Elizabethan complaints, the grieving widows of the *Iliad* take centre stage in works such as *Hecubaes Mishaps* (1590), a dream vision in which Hecuba mourns her 'manifold miseries, wonderful calamities, and lamentable chances', *The Lamentation of Troy for the Death of Hector* (1594), in which the Ghost of Troy's 'sad complaint' is followed by a series of lamentations by Trojan heroes and heroines, and *Penelopes Complaint* (1596), an epistolary romance featuring the 'lovesick motions' of Homer's heroine as she corresponds with her absent husband.[15] In the last two decades of the sixteenth century, the university wits and members of the Inns of Court used motifs from the *Iliad* and *Odyssey* for both ethical and generic experimentation. Both *Penelopes Complaint* and Sir John Davies's *Orchestra* (1596) assimilate Homeric episodes to the conventions of the late Elizabethan seduction poem, casting Antinous as a witty libertine and Penelope as his equally witty adversary. These and other works, such as Greene's *Penelope's Web* (1587), often focus on Homer's female characters, typically treating Penelope as a 'rare pattern of chastity and continence', a paragon of uxorial obedience.[16] But, if the *Odyssey* idealizes domestic bliss, the *Iliad* does quite the opposite for some Elizabethan readers: Nashe jokingly observes that Homer persistently represents Juno 'brawling and jarring with *Jupiter*' in order to show how 'irksome' women are.[17]

The allegorical traditions surrounding Homer were extremely familiar to Tudor and Stuart writers, and they circulated in various forms.[18] Mythographers often conflated Homeric and post-Homeric accounts of various myths; this problem often makes it difficult to distinguish Homeric from non-Homeric representations of characters or episodes. English writers inherited from classical antiquity the habit of interpreting various episodes in the *Iliad* and *Odyssey* as cosmological or moral allegories about the interplay between strife (*eris* or *neikos*) and love or harmony (*philia*).[19] In his dedication to *Achilles' Shield*, Chapman explains that the shield represents the *recto* and *verso* of a 'universal world' and he also interprets it as an allegory of the four elements, symbolized by its four types of metal.[20] Abraham Fraunce and Alexander Ross detect a similar allegory at work in the figure of Circe and her four handmaidens, who represent the contrary forces of the 'four elements'.[21] Allegories of elemental strife could be useful for explaining the poems' more indecorous representations of conflict. For instance, the strife between Zeus and Hera was commonly interpreted as a veiled account of 'the distemperature and struggling contention of the elements'—a conflict deemed cosmically productive in ways that the bickering of Olympian gods was not.[22]

English Renaissance writers also inherited the Platonic tradition of interpreting Homer's chains, nets, and bands as *desmoi* or cosmic bonds, an interpretation reinvigorated by Reformation theology. Spenser makes the golden chain a master metaphor for the ethical and narrative structure of *The Faerie Queene*. Appearing *in bono et in malo* throughout the poem, chains symbolize theological error and orthodoxy (*Faerie Queene*, 1. 5. 25; 1. 9. 1), the mutually supportive forces of divine grace and human will, and the interlacement and cooperation among the poem's titular virtues (4. 1. 30).[23] Many readers interpret the golden chain of *Iliad* 8. 5–28 as evidence of Homer's monotheism, as a lesson in theological accommodation (as Francis Bacon does), or as proof that 'all things are connected with [God] and depend upon him' (as Ralph Cudworth does).[24]

For Protestants such as Spenser and Bacon, the inclination to locate in Homeric epic seeds of their own religious doctrines is licensed by the commonplace that Homer is the source of all knowledge and his poems an *enkyklios paideia* or microcosm of human learning that contain all cosmological and philosophical doctrines.[25] In his *Defence of Poesy*, Philip Sidney affirms Homer's encyclopaedism when he describes how 'under the veil of fables' the poet 'give[s] us all knowledge' while Chapman describes Homer as 'captain' to many different philosophical schools, asserting that 'Socrates was Homer's scholar' but also asserting that Empedocles, Heraclitus, and Protagoras were likewise 'of Homer's part'.[26] One especially popular allegory links Homer's *Okeanos*, the oldest of all the gods, to the doctrines of Thales, since the god's primacy illustrates how Homer 'reduceth all things to Water'.[27] While most readers interpret such dark conceits as proof of Homer's primeval wisdom, a few find such allegories perilously heterodox. Cudworth protests that Homer's representation of 'Ocean (or fluid matter)' is 'the ancientest of all atheisms', a form of 'Hylopathian' materialism that holds everything to be generated from matter.[28] But other writers find Homeric allegories of form and matter more congenial to Christian metaphysics. Spenser borrows from the Homeric allegory tradition to dramatize a Christian Platonism in which the 'outward fashion' of matter decays while its 'substance' (*Faerie Queene*, 3. 6. 38) endures. The 'double gates' (*Faerie Queene*, 3. 6. 31) of the Garden of Adonis, an imitation of the double-doored cave of *Odyssey* 13.109–12 and its explication by Porphyry (*De Antro Nympharum*), acquire various meanings as Spenser transforms this allegory into lessons about the fecundity of created nature, the limits of mortal life, or the power of art. The Homeric allegory tradition also informs Spenser's depiction of Proteus, a god whose capacity for transformation had long been glossed as the imposition of form upon primal matter.

Like Proteus, Circe was frequently interpreted during the period as an allegory for various cosmological principles pertaining to change. She crops up in works of magic and alchemy such as Michael Maier's *Arcana Arcanissima* (1614), a treatise that interprets six Homeric myths according to alchemical principles, and she is a frequent interlocutor in philosophical dialogues with Homeric themes.[29] Circe's capacity for metamorphosis makes her (and her throng of beasts) ready-made for the court masque, a form in which change governs both dramaturgical and ethical structure. Several early seventeenth-century masques, including William Browne's *The Inner Temple Masque* (1614), Aurelian Townshend's *Tempe Restor'd* (1632), and John Milton's *Comus* (1634), cast Circe or her offspring as a personification of the concupiscible passions whose enticements must be resisted by an Odyssean hero (or heroine) with the help of right reason, heroic virtue, or divine beauty.

Homeric myths also feature on the English stage, although the most popular dramatic myth, the Judgment of Paris, derives not from the *Iliad* but rather from later classical and medieval Troy legends. George Peele, in his 1584 *Arraignment of Paris*, is one of several Elizabethan writers who transforms the myth into a piece of propaganda that celebrates the queen both as a figure of justice and as a composite of the three classical goddesses among whom Paris is obliged to arbitrate. The oft-conflated Homeric deities *Atê* and *Eris*—the first primarily associated with moral blindness or ruin, and the second a personification of strife who arouses passion on the battlefield—are frequent intruders in English plays and poems. Atê is prologue to Peele's *Arraignment* and to the 1591 *Locrine*; she instigates conflict in the 1582 *Rare Triumphs of Love and Fortune* and leads a troop of discordant antimasquers in Ben Jonson's 1609 *Masque of Queenes* until she is displaced by *Fama Bona*.[30] A similarly Homeric pantheon of strife inhabits Spenser's *The Faerie Queene*, populated by male and female versions of Homer's goddess of discord, including Atin (2. 4. 41–42), Atê (4. 1. 18–30), and Mutability.

Although English Renaissance readers generally agree that Homer's poems may fruitfully be interpreted as moral or cosmological allegories, they are divided as to the implications of the claim that Homer 'hid the mysteries of his doctrine . . . within the folds and involvements of fables'.[31] While Sidney, Chapman, and Reynolds each claim that the 'mysteries' contained in Homer's poems 'of purpose were written darkly', Francis Bacon's 1609 *De Sapientia Veterum* counters this position by arguing that the fables of ancient poets such as Homer and Hesiod were intended to reveal, rather than to conceal, physical and ethical wisdom.[32] Although many of Bacon's interpretations are highly conventional—the Sirens represent the temptation of pleasure, while Scylla and Charybdis symbolize the Baconian middle way between 'the rocks of distinctions and the gulfes of universalities'—Bacon is suspicious of the tendency to interpret Homer as a 'Greek oracle'.[33] And, while some allegorical interpretations of Homer turn the poet into a prophet or domesticate the subversive aspects of his poems, others have the opposite effect, making Homer speak for heterodox values such as Epicureanism or Republicanism.[34]

Even as the allegorical tradition began, in the middle of the seventeenth century, to give way to more philological and historical methods of interpreting Homer, English scholars continued to forge theological allegories of the *Iliad* and *Odyssey*, comparing Homeric verses to passages in the Scriptures.[35] Zachary Bogan (*Homerus Hebraizon* (1658)) and James Duport (*Homeri Gnomologia* (1660)) both compiled hefty concordances of Homer and the Bible, collating Homeric lines with 'parallel' verses from the Old and New Testaments. A similar mindset is evident in seventeenth-century theologians such as Henry Hammond, who refutes the error that God is 'the author of sin' by citing Zeus' self-defence in the opening scene of the *Odyssey*, arguing that the 'complaint of the Gods in *Homer* will best shut up this' intractable heresy.[36] Eleven years earlier, in his *Doctrine and Discipline of Divorce*, Milton appears to have the same speech in mind when he argues that 'man's own freewill self-corrupted is the adequate and sufficient cause of his disobedience *besides Fate*; as Homer also wanted not to express', and the perception that Homer effectively justifies the ways of god to men would later shape Milton's complex imitation of Homeric epic in *Paradise Lost*.[37] Not all seventeenth-century writers regarded Homer as a model of proto-Christian piety, however. Cudworth rails against Homer's 'wild and extravagant conceit' that 'God himself is a servant of necessity', a heresy illustrated by Zeus' admission that he is incapable of preserving his son Sarpedon, and he condemns Homer for not representing the Olympian gods as 'eternal, unmade, and self-existent'.[38]

The seventeenth-century inclination to trace the sympathies between Homeric and Judaeo-Christian wisdom was motivated not only by the syncretism of the era but also by the common perception that Homer's particular brand of wisdom came tidily packaged in maxims. Although some readers did read the *Iliad* and *Odyssey* from beginning to end, many others familiarized themselves with Homer via collections of Latin *sententiae* such as Erasmus' *Adages*, which gathered together more than 300 Homeric sayings in a discrete section with its own preface, or Alciati's *Emblemata*, which added pictures and morals to familiar proverbs.[39] Not everyone was pleased that Homer's epics were minced up into proverbs. Chapman protests that Homer must not be read 'for a few lines with leaves turned over capriciously in dismembered fractions', while, in an epigram published in 1656, John Collop mocks the practice of fitting Homer's *Iliad* into a 'nutshell' by compressing his poems into maxims: 'The Gods know all; wise men sleep not all night, | One man must govern; many can't do right.'[40]

Homer and Political Philosophy

Tudor writers appreciate Homer for his political and military wisdom, and the political applications of Homer expand over the course of the sixteenth century as readers consult his poems for their insight into tyranny and rebellion, civil strife and the politics of counsel, and what William Webbe calls 'discretion... and policy'.[41] The Reformation, the French wars of religion, and the English Civil War each intensify and alter the significance of the aborted rebellion against Zeus (*Iliad* 1. 395–403), a fable often interpreted through the lens of contemporary political events. The internecine strife of Homer's Olympian gods is often moralized as a warning about 'seditious and rebellious subjects in a commonwealth or schismatical and heretical seducers in a church'.[42] The *Odyssey*, too, yields political lessons for its Renaissance readers. In 1648, Alexander Ross extracts from Polyphemus a timely allegorical lesson about the perils of 'a Commonwealth without a king', arguing that a country without a monarch produces 'nothing but intestine wars and broils'.[43]

The commonplace that Homer's epics are 'full of government and direction to all estates', as Chapman puts it in his 1598 dedication to the Earl of Essex, does not preclude a certain interpretive flexibility. The *Iliad* and *Odyssey* were used to defend both republicanism and monarchy, both regicide and unwavering obedience to authority.[44] Arguments on both sides often focused on Achilles' rebuke of Agamemnon in the opening book of the *Iliad* and on Odysseus' defence of kingship at *Iliad* 2. 204, a passage read during the period as a 'necessary and admirable strategy in upholding monarchy', as a 'betrayal of the true rhetorician's love of liberty', or both at once in the case of Shakespeare's Ulysses, who extends Homer's half-verse into a sixty-three-line harangue.[45] Chapman changes his mind about the political implications of both scenes as his work on the *Iliad* progresses. His 1598 Achilles vilifies Agamemnon in the strongest possible terms, but subsequent revisions tone down his speeches, perhaps reflecting Chapman's prudence after the trial and execution of the Earl of Essex, a figure closely associated with Achilles in Chapman's earlier translations.[46]

Questions about Homer's representation of the origin and nature of kingly authority intensify during the Civil War period. In 1649–51, Claude Salmasius and John Milton debate the legitimacy of the regicide by offering competing interpretations of 'Homer's account of kings being descended from Jove'.[47] Milton's efforts to make Homer speak for English Republicans provides a counter-offensive to the staunchly Royalist editions and interpretations of the *Iliad* that abound at mid-century, including Ogilby's 1660 English translation, commissioned by and dedicated to King Charles II, and Roger Daniel's 1648 Greek–Latin edition of the *Iliad*, which capitalizes the initial words of lines asserting Agamemnon's supremacy so that readers might better construe them as Royalist *sententiae*.[48]

In England, as in Italy, writers interpret various Homeric heroes according to the standards of the Renaissance court: Phoenix is the model courtier and Ithaca's greedy suitors his negative counterparts.[49] In emblem books and books of adages,

Odysseus and Diomedes, Achilles and Patroclus, and Hector and Polydamas model the related virtues of cooperation (*philophrosune*), friendship (*philia*), and good counsel (*euboulia*), while the Homeric concept of *mêtis*, or cunning, is translated into the quintessentially sixteenth-century virtue of prudence in the 1587 *Nestor his Antilochus*, a fictional oration that closely imitates *Iliad* 23. 306–48. The cross-fertilization of classical epic and chivalric romance in the works of Ariosto and Spenser helps to adapt Homeric episodes into politically useful lessons about the value of honour (*timê*), shame (*aidôs*), or friendship, the danger of flattery, or the importance of hospitality. Typical of this melding of literary traditions is Robert Greene's 1587 *Euphues his Censure to Philautus*, a 'philosophical combat' between Hector and Achilles that praises gentlemanly virtues such as wisdom, fortitude, and liberality in the form of long, euphuistic speeches delivered by Homeric heroes.[50] But even as writers such as Greene, George Peele (in his 1589 *Tale of Troy*), and Spenser (in the Paridell–Malbecco–Hellenore episodes of *The Faerie Queene*, 3. 9–10) work to accommodate Homeric heroism to the Elizabethan court, there is a lingering suspicion that Achilles (and to a lesser extent Odysseus) exhibits a 'reckless individualism' at odds with the communalistic values of Christian chivalry.[51]

The Homeric Texts and their Style

Although many readers experienced Homer solely or principally in Latin translation, and although these Latin translations were often highly imitative of Virgilian syntax and diction, Homer's defenders and detractors alike considered Homer to possess a distinctive style. Homer's style was largely understood in contradistinction to that of Virgil, whose imitations of and deviations from Homeric conventions had been surveyed by Macrobius' *Saturnalia* (early fifth century CE), a work that shaped the sixteenth-century critical tendency to compare the two poets in order to demonstrate how Virgil improved upon Homer both stylistically and ethically.[52] In England, as on the continent, preference for Virgil over Homer was formulaic: the Greek poet was copious, rough, and indecent—an 'old tedious prolix ass', as Sir John Daw in Jonson's *Epicoene* puts it—whereas the Latin one was restrained, refined, and discreet.[53] Yet a small cadre of Elizabethan and Jacobean writers admired the naturalness of Homer's style, the realistic imperfection of his characters, and his obliquity and irony. Countering the commonplace that Virgil's economy and modesty are superior to Homer's coarse abundance, Chapman praises the Greek poet's 'free fury, an absolute & full soul' while condemning Virgil's 'courtly, laborious, and altogether imitatory spirit' and defending the Greek poet against the 'senseless reprehensions' of Julius Scaliger and Marco Girolamo Vida.[54]

English Renaissance readers champion Homer as a repository of different rhetorical styles, a master of *copia* or variety. Readers often mark rhetorical devices in printed editions and manuscripts of the *Iliad* and the *Odyssey*, and they interpret various Homeric episodes as displays of oratorical excellence. Accordingly, Homeric *exempla* are frequently included in rhetorical handbooks such as Fraunce's 1588 *Arcadian Rhetorike*, which cites verses from the *Iliad* to illustrate metonymy, irony, *praeteritio* (praetermission), and *paronomasia* (punning).[55] English Renaissance writers also take interest in the various rhetorical styles exemplified by different Homeric characters, often contrasting the laconic Menelaus, who 'spake little', with Thersites, whom Homer 'blamed…for too much speaking'.[56] Guided by the conviction that speech reveals character, Chapman indulges in lengthy commentaries on the voices of Menelaus and Odysseus at *Iliad* 2. 355 and 3. 233–44.[57]

As is evident from Chapman's evolving metre—he switched from fourteeners in the *Iliad* to iambic pentameter for his *Odyssey*—it was challenging for would-be translators to render Greek dactylic hexameters into English verse. Thomas Nashe admits that hexameter 'cannot thrive' in the English 'clime' because it 'goes twitching and hopping in our language like a man running upon quagmires'.[58] Faced with the prospect of translating Homeric verse a few years later, Chapman justifies his 'paraphrastical' method of translation by explaining that Greek and English 'in sounds, | and letters, shun one form'.[59] Befuddled about how best to translate Homer into English, Tudor and Stuart writers are also at odds about which contemporary poet best merits the title of 'English Homer'. Nashe dubs Chaucer England's Homer, Meres awards the title to Spenser, and Gabriel Harvey compares Sidney's *Arcadia* to Homer's 'furious Iliads, and cunning Odysses', each bestowing the title variously on the basis of rusticity of style, originality, and sheer volume.[60]

Few Homeric scholars during the English Renaissance concerned themselves greatly with the textual history of the poems. It was generally recognized that the individual books, or rhapsodies, of the *Iliad* and *Odyssey* were assembled centuries after their composition, that the text had been emended and in certain cases corrupted by various Alexandrian editors, and that there existed a vast ancient commentary tradition on Homer, who, according to Francis Bacon, was 'made a kind of Scripture' by the 'later schools of the Grecians'.[61]

Chapman seeks mainly to establish consistency and coherence both within and between the *Iliad* and *Odyssey*. Following Poliziano's reasoning that Homer 'loves to maintain an even tenor, true to himself' ('tenorem | semper amat meminitque sui'), Chapman uses various methods to explain the apparent contradictions in Homer, proposing (as Homer's ancient scholiasts did before him) that while Homer asserts 'contrary' (*enantia*) things through different speakers, what the narrator speaks in his own voice does not contradict itself.[62] Chapman's commentary also emphasizes how the disparate perspectives of speakers (or of speaker and narrator) produce irony, a rhetorical device he delights in identifying wherever it appears (and, at times, where it does not appear).[63] Commenting on a passage (*Iliad* 13. 556) in which Menelaus claims that Helen was still a virgin when he married her, Chapman observes that it is no 'rare credulity in men to believe they marry maids when they do not' and that the reader should not assume that the narrator shares the same blindnesses as his characters.[64]

Homeric Genres

The *Iliad* and *Odyssey* were predominantly regarded as epic poems, and although Virgil and his Latin successors were the chief epic models for the heroic poets of Renaissance England, Homer's readers still discerned in his poems many of the epic conventions that characterized the genre: catalogues, invocations to the muses, delayed encounters between adversaries, contrafactuals, prolepses and analepses, theomachies, battlefield speeches, sea voyages and shipwrecks, *peripeteias* (reversals of fortune), *anagnorisis*, ekphrasis, *nekyias* (underworld visits), prophecies, portents, and dreams.

Yet English Renaissance writers also stressed the generic range and variety of the Homeric corpus. Although few in the period claimed, like the ancient *chorizontes* (separators), that the two works were composed by different poets, many readers perceived certain tensions or ironies arising out of the difference between the two poems, even as they also interpret various passages in the *Iliad* as motivating or preparing for corresponding passages in the *Odyssey*. The *Iliad* and the *Odyssey* were commonly defined in contradistinction to each other: consecrated, respectively, to public and private virtue, to force and cunning, to *pathos* and *ethos*, or, as Chapman has it, to 'predominant perturbation' and 'over-ruling wisdom'.[65] While the *Iliad* was conventionally associated with tragedy, the genre of the *Odyssey* was a more complicated matter, sometimes identified as a tragedy with a happy ending or as a generic hybrid akin to romance. Both poems could, moreover, appear joco-serious to English Renaissance eyes, an unsettling combination of grim violence and witty jest.

The enormous popularity of the pseudo-Homeric *Batrachomyomachia* (*The Battle of the Frogs and the Mice*) heightened the sense that Homer was, at least intermittently, a comic poet. Prior to 1660 in England, the poem was translated (into Latin and English) more often than both the *Iliad* and the *Odyssey* combined. Although several scholars, including Isaac Casaubon, did question the poem's attribution to Homer, Chapman insists in his translation of the *Batrachomyomachia* that it derives 'from one self distaff's stuff' as the *Iliad* and *Odyssey*.[66] By the middle of the sixteenth century, moreover, the poem had been sealed with the stamp of Protestant piety, translated into Latin by more than a half-dozen German reformers, including Johannes Reuchlin in Vienna (1510) and his grandnephew Philip Melanchthon in Paris (1542). In England, Christopher Johnson (1580), William Gager (late sixteenth century), and Huntingdon Plumptre (1629) all produced Latin translations of the poem; there were also two English translations, by William Fowldes (1603) and George Chapman (1624).[67]

The *Batrachomyomachia* was read and translated for its ability 'covertly [to] deciphe[r]' contemporary conflicts, as Fowldes writes in his *ottava rima* translation, whose marginal notes caution against the effects of 'trifling iarres and foolish enmity'.[68] The poem was often (albeit erroneously) associated with the genre of the paradoxical encomium: both Thomas Nashe (in his 1599 *Lenten Stuffe*) and Sir John Harington (in his 1596 *A New Discourse of a Stale Subject, Called the Metamorphosis of Ajax*) invoke

Homer as a literary ancestor, while other contemporaries imagine Homer as a 'poore, blind, rhyming rascal' whose peripatetic life and repudiation of social norms link him to both cynic and apostolic ideals of poverty and humility.[69] Such a reading helps to turn the lowest and most ridiculous episodes in the *Odyssey*—the entrapment of Ares and Aphrodite by the lame Hephaestus, or the scenes featuring Odysseus and his old swineherd Eumaeus—into demonstrations of Christian piety.

Dramatic adaptations of Homer from the period tend to emphasize comic elements at the expense of tragic possibilities or to mix the two in unconventional ways. In the prologue to his *Ulysses Redux*, a Latin play performed at Christ Church, Oxford, in February 1591/2 and printed by Joseph Barnes later that same year, William Gager apologizes for the play's comic diction and the 'beggarliness of its material' ('materiae quadam mendicitate').[70] If Gager's play tentatively calls attention to the risible dimensions of its Homeric source, then Shakespeare's *Troilus and Cressida* (*c.*1601–2; printed 1609) lurches between bawdy comedy and the grimmest of tragedies, turning the *Iliad* into an 'academic... burlesque' that links Homer to the traditions of learned jest and 'world-upside-down *sottie*' or joke.[71] The play subjects to ridicule not just particular characters but also the entire history of the Trojan war, a history that Shakespeare treats with suspicion by 'refus[ing] to adjudicate' between rival accounts.[72]

This tendency to mistrust the veracity of Homer's Greeks grew partly out of Virgil's critical treatment of Sinon in book 2 of the *Aeneid* and partly out of the medieval literary corpus of Troy romances. Two early medieval Latin works, Dictys Cretensis' *Ephemeris de Historia Belli Trojani* (fourth century AD) and Dares Phrygius' *De Excidio Trojae Historia* (fifth or sixth century AD), both claimed to offer eyewitness accounts of the Trojan war, the former by a Cretan soldier and the latter by a Trojan priest of Hephaestus whose Phoenician manuscript, according to the prologue of *De Excidio*, was supposedly exhumed by an earthquake during the reign of the Emperor Nero and subsequently translated into Greek. Both works were translated and adapted with great frequency by later medieval writers, including Benoît de Sainte-Maure (*Roman de Troie, c.*1154–60), Guido delle Colonne (*Historia destructionis Trojae*, late thirteenth century), John Lydgate's *Troy Book* (1420; first printed in 1513 as *The hystorye, sege, and dystruccyon of Troye*), and Raoul Lefèvre (*Recuyell of the historyes of Troye*, first printed by William Caxton, in Bruges, 1473 or 1474). In the Middle Ages, the 'matter of Troy' rivalled the Alexander romances, the 'matter of Britain' (Arthurian romance), and the 'matter of Rome' (Charlemagne) for popularity. Particularly for the English, who claimed a Trojan heritage through Brut (or Brutus), the son of Hector, the continued appeal of these works through the seventeenth century resides largely in the fact that they narrate the destruction of Troy from a Trojan rather than a Greek perspective, as well as an attempt to retrieve the reputation of heroes (such as Palamedes and Troilus) who had been unduly neglected or disparaged by Homer.

Chaucer was medieval England's greatest adapter of the matter of Troy, and Shakespeare's *Troilus and Cressida* is often viewed as the pre-eminent early modern adaptation of the medieval Troy Book tradition, indebted principally to Chaucer's *Troilus and*

Criseyde (in turn indebted to Giovanni Boccaccio's *Il Filostrato*), Lydgate's *Troy Book*, and Caxton's translation of the *Recuyell*. Shakespeare's possible debts to Chapman's 1598 translations of the *Iliad* have, by contrast, been the subject of some debate. Most critics assume both Shakespeare's familiarity and his hostility towards Chapman's text, arguing that he strove to debase the 'moral altitude' of Chapman's *Seaven Books* by 'contaminat[ing]' those values that Chapman had sought to reify.[73] Yet the two works are united by their unusually arcane vocabulary and by their pervasive blame and rebuke. Chapman's *Seaven Bookes* is filled with thunderous volleys of verbal insult, chiding, and railing; Shakespeare follows suit, amplifying the character of Thersites in duration and amplitude. But, while Chapman's interest in Homeric railing is motivated by a desire to legitimate satirical discourse as a species of righteous anger, Shakespeare recasts the 'abusive quarrel' between Ajax and Thersites as a parody of the 'meaningless wrangling' between playwrights during the War of the Theatres.[74]

Notes

1. Homer, *Ten Bookes of Homers Iliades, Translated out of French by Arthur Hall* (1581).
2. The seven instalments are: *Achilles Shield Translated as the Other Seven Bookes of Homer* (1598); *Seaven bookes of the Iliades of Homer* (1598), a translation of books 1, 2, and 7–11; *Iliad; Homer Prince of Poets* (1609), which contains the first 12 books; *The Iliads of Homer Prince of Poets. Never before in any Language Truely Translated* (1611), a complete translation of the *Iliad* with marginal notes and commentary; *Homer's Odysses* (1614), a translation of books 1 through 12; *Homer's Odysses* (1615), containing all 24 books; *The Whole Works of Homer; Prince of Poets* (1616), containing complete translations of both poems. On Chapman's revisions to his translations of Homer, see Robin Sowerby, 'Chapman's Discovery of Homer', *Translation and Literature*, 1/1 (1992), 26–51.
3. On Jonson's copies of Chapman's Homer, see David McPherson, 'Ben Jonson's Library and Marginalia: An Annotated Catalogue,' *Studies in Philology*, 71/5 (1974), 3–106 (52); on Jonson's annotated copy of Chapman's 1616 *Whole Works* and his objections to Chapman's treatment of Scaliger on pp. 47–8 of that volume, see Percy Simpson, 'Ben Jonson on Chapman', *TLS*, 3 March 1932, 155. For examples of Chapman's attacks against 'translators and commentors,' see his marginal notes to *Odyssey* 10. 111 and 11. 694–700. On Chapman's sources for his translations of Homer, see George Forest de Lord, *Homeric Renaissance: The* Odyssey *of George Chapman* (New Haven, 1956); Phyllis B. Bartlett, 'The Heroes of Chapman's Homer', *Review of English Studies*, 17/3 (1941), 257–80; H. C. Fay, 'Chapman's Materials for his Translation of Homer', *Review of English Studies*, NS 2/6 (1951), 121–8 (121–2); and Franck L. Schoell, *études sur l'humanisme continentale en Angleterre à la fin de la Renaissance* (Paris, 1926), 147–52, 170–2.
4. Chapman, *The Whole Works of Homer* (1616), 181, marginal note to *Odyssey* 12. 101. All citations of Chapman's Homer are from this edition unless otherwise noted.
5. On the study of Homer at Oxford, see J. W. Binns, *Intellectual Culture in Elizabethan and Jacobean England: The Latin Writings*

of the Age (Leeds, 1990), 217; N. R. Ker, 'Oxford College Libraries in the Sixteenth Century', *Bodleian Library Record*, 6/3 (1959), 459–515 (475–6, 487). On the 1605 holdings of the Bodleian, see Thomas James, *Catalogus Librorum Bibliothecae Publicae Quam Vir Ornatissimus Thomas Bodleius* (Oxford, 1605), 296, 334, 338.

6. See R. J. Fehrenbach and E. S. Leedham-Green, *Private Libraries in Renaissance England*, 5 vols (Binghamton, 1992–8). On Elizabethan and Jacobean readers of Homer, see Philip Ford, *De Troie à Ithaque: Réception des épopées homériques à la Renaissance* (Geneva, 2007), 95.
7. Antonius Roberti, *Clavis Homerica Reserans Significationes, Etymologias, Derivationes, Compositiones, & Dialectos Omnium Ferè Vocabulorum, Quae In Viginti Quatuor Libris Iliadis Homeri Continentur* (1638; repr. 1647, 1656).
8. Meric Casaubon, *De Nupera Homeri Editione* (1659).
9. The first Greek and Latin editions of each work are: Plutarch (Greek: Florence, 1488; Latin by Conrad Heresbach: Cologne, 1537); Heraclides (Greek: Venice, 1505; Latin by Conrad Gesner, *Allegoriae In Homeri Fabulas De Diis*: Basle, 1544); Porphyry (Greek: 1518; Latin by Gesner, *De Antro Nympharum In XIII Libro Odysseae Homericae*: Basle, 1542). The commentaries of Eustathius were first printed at Rome, 1542–50.
10. This interpretation originates with Aristotle, *Nicomathean Ethics* II. ix. 3, in *Aristotle 19*, p. 111 (on *Odyssey* 12.214). On Odyssean 'Mediocritie', see Thomas Randolph, *The Muses Looking-Glasse* (1643), 78; on Scylla and Charybdis as the extremes of pride and despair, see Alexander Ross, *Mystagogus Poeticus or the Muses Interpreter*, 2nd edn (1648; repr. New York, 1976), 414.
11. Richard S. Ide, 'Exemplary Heroism in Chapman's *Odysses*', *Studies in English Literature 1500–1900*, 22 (1982), 121–36 (128). Chapman, *Odysses* (1614), 'To the Most Worthily Honored... Robert, Earle of Somerset', sig. A4^r.
12. Ross, *Mystagogus Poeticus*, 414.
13. For classical and late antique treatments of the passions in the *Iliad* familiar to Renaissance readers, see Plutarch, *Essay on the Life of Homer*, ed. J. J. Keaney and Robert Lamberton (Atlanta, 1996), 209, 211–15 (on Homer's Stoic view of the passions); Aristotle, *Rhetoric* 1386^b (on refined versus unrefined emotions in Homer).
14. Chapman, *Whole Works*, 15, commentary to *Iliad* 1. 359; Chapman, 'Euthymiae Raptus', l. 185, in *Poems*, ed. Phyllis Bartlett (New York, 1941), 177.
15. *Hecubaes Mishaps*, in Thomas Fenne, *Fennes Frutes* (1590); John Ogle, *The Lamentation of Troy for the Death of Hector* (1594), sig. A4^r; Peter Colse, *Penelopes Complaint: Or, A Mirrour for Wanton Minions. Taken out of Homers Odissea* (1596), sig. C2^r.
16. Ross, *Mystagogus Poeticus*, 357; Natale Conti, *Mythologiae*, ed. and trans. John Mulryan and Steven Browne, 2 vols (Tempe, AZ, 2006), 2. 801–3, defends Penelope against charges of adultery. Robert Greene, *Penelopes Web* (1587), in *Life and Complete Works in Verse and Prose*, ed. Alexander B. Grosart, 15 vols (New York, 1964), 6.
17. Thomas Nashe, *The Anatomie of Absurditie* (1589), in *Works*, ed. Ronald B. McKerrow, 5 vols (London, 1910), 1. 15.
18. On the allegorical interpretation of ancient myth in the Renaissance, see Don Cameron Allen, *Mysteriously Meant: The Rediscovery of Pagan Symbolism and Allegorical Interpretation in the Renaissance* (Baltimore, 1970); Jean Seznec, *The Survival of the Pagan Gods: The Mythological Tradition and Its Place in Renaissance Humanism and Art*, trans. Barbara Sessions (New York, 1953); Luc Brisson, *How Philosophers Saved Myths: Allegorical Interpretation and Classical*

Mythology (Chicago, 2004); Michael Murrin, *The Allegorical Epic: Essays in its Rise and Decline* (Chicago, 1980); Edgar Wind, *Pagan Mysteries in the Renaissance*, 2nd edn (1967).

19. On allegories of love and strife in Homeric epic, see Gesner, *Allegoriae*, 62, and Heraclides, *Homeric Problems*, ed. and trans. Donald A. Russell and David Konstan (Leiden, 2005), 87, 111; Llewellyn Morgan, *Patterns of Redemption in Virgil's Georgics* (Cambridge, 1999), 95.
20. Chapman, *Achilles Shield*, sig. A2[r].
21. Abraham Fraunce, *The Third Part of the Countesse of Pembrokes Yuychurch: Entitled, Amintas Dale* (1592), 47[r]; Ross, *Mystagogus Poeticus*, 75.
22. Richard Linche, *The Fountaine Of Ancient Fiction. Wherein Is Lively Depictured the Images and Statues of The Gods of the Ancients* (1599), sig. M[r]; Henry Reynolds, *Mythomystes*, in J. E. Spingarn, *Critical Essays of the Seventeenth Century*, 3 vols (Bloomington, IN, 1957), I. 171. On Homeric allegories of the four elements, see S. K. Heninger, *Touches of Sweet Harmony* (Pasadena, 1974), 176; Murrin, *The Allegorical Epic*, 4–5, 12–15.
23. Richard Mallette, *Spenser and the Discourses of Reformation England* (Lincoln, NE, 1997), 3.
24. Francis Bacon, *Advancement of Learning*, ed. Michael Kiernan, *Oxford Francis Bacon* 4 (Oxford, 2000), 79; Ralph Cudworth, *The True Intellectual System of the Universe: The First Part, Wherein all the Reason and Philosophy of Atheism is Confuted, and its Impossibility Demonstrated* (1678), 446.
25. Heninger, *Touches of Sweet Harmony*, 379–80; *Ovids Metamorphosis English'd, Mythologiz'd, and Represented in Figures*, trans. George Sandys (Oxford, 1632), 445, argues that Achilles' Shield represents 'the whole world'. On classical allegories of Achilles' shield, see P. R. Hardie, 'Imago Mundi: Cosmographical and Ideological Aspects of the Shield of Achilles', *Journal of Hellenic Studies* 105 (1985), 11–31.
26. Sir Philip Sidney, *A Defence of Poesy*, in *Miscellaneous Prose of Sir Philip Sidney*, ed. Katherine Duncan-Jones and Jan van Dorsten (Oxford, 1973), 121; Chapman, *Iliads* (1611), 'Of Homer', sig. A5[v]; *Odysses* (1614), Dedication to the Earl of Somerset, l. 92.
27. Philip de Mornay, *A Worke Concerning the Trewnesse of the Christian Religion*, trans. Philip Sidney and Arthur Golding (1587), 132; cf. Spenser, *The Faerie Queene*, 4. 11. 18, where Ocean and Tethys are 'th'oldest two of all the [gods]'. On Homeric and Virgilian allegories of *Okeanos*, see Morgan, *Patterns of Redemption*, 67–73, and Philip Hardie, *Virgil's Aeneid: Cosmos and Imperium* (Oxford, 1986), 23, 36–7, 51–2.
28. Cudworth, *True Intellectual System*, 102.
29. See, e.g. Giovanni Battista Gelli, *Circe*, trans. Henry Iden (1557); Giordano Bruno, *Cantus Circaeus* (1582), and Fortunio Liceti, *Ulysses Apud Circem* (1636).
30. For other instances of Atê or Discord in English plays and masques, see *Caesar and Pompey* (*c*.1592–6), John Lyly, *Woman in the Moon* (1593), Richard Brome, *Antipodes* (1638), and William Davenant's 1640 *Salmacida Spolia*.
31. Reynolds, *Mythomystes*, in Spingarn, *Critical Essays*, I. 156.
32. Sidney, *Defence*, 121; cf. Reynolds, *Mythomystes*, in Spingarn, *Critical Essays*, I. 156. On Chapman's understanding of the mysteries of Homer, see Gerald Snare, *The Mystification of George Chapman* (Durham, NC, 1989), and Raymond Waddington, *The Mind's Empire: Myth and Form in George Chapman's Narrative Poems* (Baltimore, 1974), 45–9, 183–5.
33. Bacon, *De Sapientia Veterum* (1609), trans. Arthur Gorges as *The Wisdome of the Ancients* (1619), ed. Stephen Orgel (New York, 1976), 169, 147.
34. On this point, see David Dawson, *Allegorical Readers and Cultural Revision in*

Ancient Alexandria (Berkeley and Los Angeles, 1992), 35.

35. On early modern allegorical interpretations of Homeric epic, see Anthony Grafton, 'Renaissance Readers of Homer's Ancient Readers', in R. Lamberton and J. J. Keaney (eds), *Homer's Ancient Readers: The Hermeneutics of Greek Epic's Earliest Exegetes* (1992), 149–74.
36. Henry Hammond, *Of Fundamentals in a Notion Referring to Practise* (1654), 177, 184–5.
37. Milton, *Doctrine and Discipline of Divorce* (1643), in *Complete Prose*, 8 vols, ed. Don M. Wolfe (New Haven, 1953–82), 2. 294.
38. Cudworth, *True Intellectual System*, 5, 358.
39. Erasmus added 273 Homeric adages (3.8.1 through 3.10.75) in 1508, separated by a preface ('Some Proverbial Lines from Homer'). See *Collected Works of Erasmus*, ed. John Grant and trans. Denis L. Drysdall (Toronto, 2005),35. 281–2.
40. Chapman, *Achilles Shield*, sigs A2^{v}–A3^{r}; John Collop, 'On Homer', ll. 3–6, in *Poems of John Collop*, ed. Conrad Hilberry (Madison, WI, 1962), 108.
41. Sir Thomas Elyot, *The Boke Named The Governour* (1531), 2 vols, ed. Henry Herbert Croft (New York, 1967), 1. 58–60; William Webbe, *A Discourse of English Poetrie* (1586), in G. Gregory Smith (ed.), *Elizabethan Critical Essays*, 2 vols (Oxford, 1904), 1. 234–5.
42. Fraunce, *Amintas Dale*, 9; on the Olympians as counsellors in senate, see Vincenzo Cartari, *Les Images des Dieux des Anciens* (Lyon, 1581), 5. According to Malcolm Bull, *The Mirror of the Gods* (Oxford, 2005), 150–3, the Giants and Titans were frequently confused during the Renaissance, and sometimes the Giants, rather than Zeus, were given heroic roles.
43. Ross, *Mystagogus Poeticus*, 87.
44. Chapman, *Achilles Shield*, 'To . . . Earle Marshall', sig. B2^{v}.
45. David Norbrook, 'Rhetoric, Ideology, and the Elizabethan World Picture', in Peter Mack (ed.), *Renaissance Rhetoric* (London, 1994), 145.
46. On Chapman's revisions to Achilles' character, see John Channing Briggs, 'Chapman's *Seaven Bookes of the Iliades*: Mirror for Essex', *Studies in English Literature 1500–1900*, 21 (1981), 59–73 (68–72); Norbrook, 'Rhetoric', 164 n. 58.
47. Milton, *Defence of the English People* (1651), in *Complete Prose*, 4 (1). 437, 441.
48. See, e.g. *Homerou Ilias* (1648), 41 (at *Iliad* 2. 204): 'non bona res est multorum dominatus; unus princeps esto.' On royalist interpretations of Homer, see Craig Kallendorf, *The Other Virgil: 'Pessimistic' Readings of the 'Aeneid' in Early Modern Culture* (Oxford, 2007), 141; Gregory Machacek, 'Royalist Homer', *Transactions of the Cambridge Bibliographical Society*, 12 (2002), 331–2.
49. Baldassar Castiglione, *Boke of the Courtier*, trans. Thomas Hoby (1561), 233.
50. Greene, *Euphues his Censure to Philautus. Wherein is Presented a Philosophicall Combat betweene Hector and Achylles, Discovering in Foure Discourses, Interlaced with Diverse Delightfull Tragedies, The Vertues Necessary to be Incident in Every Gentleman* (1587), in *Works*, ed. Grosart, 6. 152.
51. David Quint, *Epic and Empire: Politics and Generic Form from Virgil to Milton* (Princeton, 1993), 90–2; cf. George de Forest Lord, *Heroic Mockery: Variations on Epic Themes from Homer to Joyce* (Newark, DE, 1977), 17.
52. On the relationship between Virgil and Homer in the Renaissance, see David Scott Wilson-Okamura, *Virgil in the Renaissance* (Cambridge, 2010), 124–34.
53. Jonson, *Epicoene*, 2.3.62–3, in *Works*, 5. 185.
54. Chapman, *Achilles Shield*, sigs A2^{v}–A3^{v}; *Whole Works*, 87, marginal note at *Iliad* 6. 148–222.
55. Abraham Fraunce, *The Arcadian Rhetorike* (1588), ed. Ethel Seaton (Oxford, 1950), 4, 10–13.

56. Robert Albott, *Wits Theater of the Little World* (1599), 84; cf. Ben Jonson, *Timber: Or, Discoveries; Made upon Men and Matter*, in *Works*, 8. 574.
57. See Chapman, *Whole Works*, 35, 48–9, commentary on *Iliad* 2. 355 and 3. 233–44.
58. Nashe, *Strange Newes* (1592), in *Works*, ed. McKerrow, 1. 298–9.
59. Chapman, *Whole Works*, 'To the Reader', sigs. A[r], A4[r].
60. Nashe, *Strange Newes*; Meres, *Palladis Tamia*, sig. Oo2[v]; Gabriel Harvey, *Pierces Supererogation* (1593), in *Works*, ed. Alexander B. Grosart, 3 vols (New York, 1966), 2. 101.
61. Bacon, *Advancement of Learning*, ed. Kiernan, 4. 75.
62. Poliziano, *Ambra*, ll. 507–8, in *Silvae*, ed. and trans. Charles Fantazzi (Cambridge, MA, 2004), 100–1; Chapman is following Porphyry, *Homeric Questions on the Iliad*, ed. and trans. John A. MacPhail (New York, 2011), 83, 116–17.
63. On the early modern interpretation of Homer as a rhetorical handbook, and on ironic interpretations of Homer, see Jessica Wolfe, 'Chapman's Ironic Homer', *College Literature* 35/4 (2008), 151–86.
64. Chapman, *Whole Works*, 187, commentary on *Iliad* 13. 556.
65. Chapman, *Odysses* (1614), Dedication to Somerset, sig. A4[r].
66. Chapman, *Crowne of all Homers Workes Batrachomyomachia or the Battaile of Frogs and Mise. His Hymn's—and Epigrams* (1624), Preface, 'The Occasion of this Impos'd Crowne', sig. ¶2[r].
67. Christopher Johnson's translation into Latin hexameters appeared as *Batrachomymachia. Id Est. Ranarum & Murium Pugna, Latino Versu Donata Ex Homero* (1580). Gager's Latin translation is preserved in British Library Add. MS 22583, fos 1–8. Plumptre's Latin translation was printed in G4[r]–I2[r] of *Epigrammatôn Opusculum Duobus Libellis Distinctum* (1629); another Latin translation of the *Batrachomyomachia* appeared (with Greek text) in *Fabulae Aesopi Graece Ac Latine: Quibus Adduntur Ranarum Muriumq[ue], Pugna & Epigrammata* (1657). Fowldes's translation was printed as *The Strange, Wonderfull, and Bloudy Battell... Covertly Decyphering the Estate of these Times* (1603).
68. Homer, *The Strange, Wonderfull, and Bloudy Battell*, trans. Fowldes, sig. H3[v].
69. Jonson, *Poetaster*, 1. 2. 84, in *Works*, 4. 211.
70. On Gager, see Binns, *Intellectual Culture*, 127–9. Gager is paraphrasing Horace, *Ars Poetica*, l. 95, which argues that comedy may use elevated language on occasion and conversely that tragic heroes may fitly express their grief in pedestrian language ('sermone pedestri').
71. W. R. Elton, *Shakespeare's Troilus and Cressida and the Inns of Court Revels* (Aldershot, 2000), 167, 28.
72. Heather James, *Shakespeare's Troy: Drama, Politics, and the Translation of Empire* (Cambridge, 1997), 89.
73. Arthur Acheson, *Shakespeare and the Rival Poet* (1903), 202; James, *Shakespeare's Troy*, 113. For discussions of Shakespeare's debts to Chapman, see G. K. Hunter, 'Troilus and Cressida: A Tragic Satire', *Shakespeare Studies* (Tokyo), 13 (1974–5), 1–23 (7); Geoffrey Bullough, *Narrative and Dramatic Sources of Shakespeare*, 8 vols (1957–75), 6, 87–8; Robert Presson, *Troilus and Cressida and the Legends of Troy* (Madison, WI, 1953), 9; Stuart Gillespie, *Shakespeare's Books* (2001), 252–3.
74. James P. Bednarz, *Shakespeare and the Poets' War* (New York, 2001), 257, 47. On Shakespeare's treatment of the Troy legend, see also Charles Martindale and Michelle Martindale, 'Shakespeare's Troy', in Martindale and Martindale, *Shakespeare and the Uses of Antiquity: An Introductory Essay* (1994), ch. 3.

CHAPTER 22

Plato

ELIZABETH JANE BELLAMY

On the Difficulties of Locating Plato in Late Renaissance England

The task of locating an 'essential' Plato in later Renaissance England is daunting. In Christopher Marlowe's *Tamburlaine*, the protagonist boasts that his conquest of Bajazeth will long be talked about, 'Even from this day to Plato's wondrous years'.[1] Tamburlaine echoes the *Timaeus*' claim that in the future all planets will return to their original alignment. But Marlowe's in-depth study of the *Timaeus* is doubtful. He was more likely to have been moved to cite 'Plato' as one of later Renaissance England's more frequent ciphers of ancient wisdom. In the first year of James's reign, the question persists: how closely was Plato read—or, rather, how many Platonic aphorisms were culled from, say, Philemon Holland's 1603 translation of Plutarch's *Moralia*, particularly its culling from the *Timaeus*.[2] In Richard Crashaw's 1648 'In the Glorious Epiphany of our Lord God', the subject is elevated from sensuality to pure contemplation. But how reliably can the soul's ascent be read through a Platonic lens? Or, rather, should it be read through the lens of Crashaw's Counter-Reformation, baroque extravagances, one of many instances in later Renaissance England's devotional poetry of the ambiguous distinctions among religion, mysticism, and Neoplatonism—boundaries far easier to recognize than define?

As a context for locating Plato in later Renaissance England, it is necessary to backtrack to the Florentine Neoplatonism of the later *quattrocento*. Marsilio Ficino's knowledge of Greek inaugurated a more philologically grounded stage in Western receptions of Plato—receptions that were also misconceptions. Ficino's 1464 *Phaedrus* commentary *De amore* erroneously dated the dialogue as Plato's first—hence, foregrounding divine rapture as central to Plato's metaphysics.[3] Ficino's acontextual focus on two speeches from the *Symposium*, Phaedrus' praise of love as the oldest of the gods, and Diotima's speech on the ladder of love leading to absolute beauty, exaggerated the centrality of love in Platonic thought. Ficino's decontextualization became, nevertheless, a tenet of Renaissance Neoplatonism—that is, love as the desire for beauty.[4] This definition was destined to render *De amore* particularly influential. Ficino elevated love and beauty to the status of epistemological concepts: beauty is Being itself, and love is the desire for a beauty that is not merely aesthetic but rather a divine manifestation apprehended by the intellect.

Despite Ficino's decontextualized Plato, his concepts of love and beauty cohered into a compelling system of thought. So influential was Ficino's treatise that it spawned a new Italian genre, the *trattati d'amore*, generally written in the vernacular, and hovering between philosophy and literature.[5] But the most popular of the *trattati d'amore*, Baldassare Castiglione's 1528 *Il libro del cortegiano*, was also the least philosophically rigorous. Essentially a handbook for courtiers, Castiglione's treatise transmuted Ficino's cosmic love into the more personal love of the courtier for the truly chaste woman. But so distant from Florentine Neoplatonism was *Il cortegiano* that at times it bordered on satire, as when Bembo's oration on love's ravishment of the soul is gently mocked by Emilia. In time, the genre of the *trattati d'amore* played itself out, but not until, in Erwin Panofsky's words, 'what had been an esoteric philosophy became a kind of social game' for lovelorn courtiers expected to pose as 'Platonic' poets.[6]

In mid-sixteenth-century France, the *trattati d'amore*'s increasingly thinned-out theory of 'Platonic love' was inherited by the court poets, nurtured in the salons of Marguerite de Navarre, who encouraged a cult of intellectual love based on not altogether scholarly readings of *De amore*. In 1578 La Boderie published an influential translation of *De amore*, contributing to a vogue for Ficino evident everywhere in the works of the Pléiade poets. But the Platonic love poetry of the Pléiade often mirrored the *trattati d'amore*'s struggles to sustain the integrity of Ficino's intelligible beauty, at times degenerating into a superficial Petrarchism.[7]

Late-Sixteenth-Century England: Shakespeare, Bruno, Sidney, Spenser

Later-sixteenth-century England was without any formal Platonic academies. (A young Elizabeth Tudor had translated Marguerite de Navarre's 1531 *Mirror of the Sinful Souls*, a personal narrative that recounts the wayward soul's passion for Christ as intimate lover and filial companion. But the queen was uninterested in encouraging a specifically Platonic cult at court.) And, thus, England was even further distanced than France from an 'essential' Plato. To be sure, broad gestures towards the Platonic themes of spiritual love and beauty can be found almost everywhere in later English Renaissance literature, from Sir Philip Sidney to Abraham Cowley. But, in fact, Plato was little read at Oxford, which rarely acquired copies during 1558–78, a significant falling-off from Colet's, Linacre's, and Erasmus' engagement with Plato at early sixteenth-century Oxford, as well as a striking contrast to France, where, during the same period, many editions of Plato had been published. If England lacked an 'essential' Plato, it also, not surprisingly, lacked an 'essential' Ficino. Between 1465 and 1578, there were no recorded English translations of Ficino (though he was read in numerous continental editions), let alone of Plato.[8] In fact, the most widely read of the *trattati d'amore* was *Il cortegiano*, translated by Sir Thomas Hoby into English in 1561 and indicative of Elizabethan preferences for more popular versions of Neoplatonism.

Shakespeare, that most canonical representative of English Renaissance literature, has long been expected to serve as all things to all critical temperaments; and those inclined to identify him as a Neoplatonist have been no exception. But Shakespeare's plays, though offering 'Platonizing' glimpses, reveal no deep-seated Platonic influences. Theseus' reference, in *A Midsummer Night's Dream*, to 'The lunatic, the lover, and the poet | ... of imagination all compact' (5. 1. 7–8) recalls *De amore*'s commentary on Plato's types of divine furor. *The Merchant of Venice*'s Lorenzo offers Pythagorean praise of music's 'touches of sweet harmony' (5. 1. 57). But the satire in such popular forms of the *trattati d'amore* as *Il cortegiano* is evident in Shakespeare's ironic distance from the extravagances of continental Platonism. In *Love's Labour's Lost*, Ferdinand founds a love cult at Navarre: 'Our court shall be a little academe' devoted solely to the contemplation of spiritual love (1. 1. 13). Shakespeare's 'Navarre' is a thinly veiled satire on Marguerite de Navarre's French cult of the courtier–lover–poet.[9]

Despite the sparse evidence of Ficino's direct influence in the latter half of the English Renaissance, the philosopher–poet Giordano Bruno imported from the Continent his version of Neoplatonism. In 1583 Bruno visited England; and his *Gli eroici furori*, a collection of mystical love sonnets and commentaries, was written and published in London in 1585, with a dedication to Sir Philip Sidney. Bruno also admired Elizabeth, depicting the queen as the eternal form of the One, thus contributing to the massive cult of Elizabeth. Bruno's Ficinian preface attacked Petrarchism's decline into sensual love, and its focus on earthly over heavenly beauty. Among Bruno's more frequent emblem conceits were his idealized mistress's eyes as radiant stars upon which the lover gazes. Sidney's sonnet sequence, *Astrophel and Stella*, written in the early 1580s, during or just after Bruno's visit, often centred on star imagery, the eyes of the mistress Stella piercing the soul of the star-gazer Astrophel.[10]

But the highly theatrical Astrophel also invites readers to spectate his falls from the Platonic ladder of love. In Sonnet 5, for example, he praises the virtue of true beauty even as he confesses, 'and yet true that I must Stella love'.[11] The Elizabethan sonnet sequence (not only Sidney, but also Spenser, Shakespeare, Greville, Constable, Lodge, Barnes, Daniel, Drayton, and many others) was one of the nation's greatest literary genres. But, when viewed through a Neoplatonic lens, these sonnet sequences are largely derivative. The ancestor of the Elizabethan sonnet sequence, then, was not so much Ficino as the poetry of the French Pléiade.[12] The title and subject matter of Scève's sonnet sequence *Délie*, for example, was anagrammatically echoed in Michael Drayton's *Idea's Mirrour* (1594). All of which is to point out that the

Elizabethan sonnet sequence also inherited Pléiade ambivalences towards an idealized mistress who was more often the 'cruel fair' entrapping tormented lovers in a prison house of stock Petrarchan conceits.

Sidney's 1595 prose *Defence of Poesy* focuses some attention on Plato,[13] but in ways that tend to compete with one another. Sidney alludes to the *Phaedrus, Ion, Timaeus,* and *Republic*; but these diverse dialogues reveal a Plato divided as to whether poets are divine cosmographers (*Phaedrus* 238 D), or deceptive imitators (*Republic* X. 600 E). At one point, Sidney, echoing the Neoplatonic doctrine of the *prisci theologi*, or ancient purveyors of a divine wisdom, praises David, Orpheus, and Amphion, divine poets who wrote in 'heart-ravishing' metres.[14] But he also distances himself from the Plato of divine furor, 'especially since he attributeth unto poesy more than myself do, namely to be a very inspiring of a divine force, far above man's wit' (p. 109).

The question arises, then, as to whether Sidney's *Defence* has a 'Platonic content' in and of itself, or whether it is yet another telling document of the unevenness of Plato's transmission throughout later-sixteenth-century England. His claim that, 'if the saying of Plato and Tully be true, that who could see virtue would be wonderfully ravished with the love of her beauty' (p. 98) is, in some form, indebted to Ficino's *De amore*. And Sidney's oft-cited claim that the literary idea is antecedent to the work itself ('the skill of the artificer standeth in that idea or fore-conceit of the work and not in the work itself') can also be traced to *De amore*'s example of the architect conceiving an idea of the building, like an idea in the soul. But Sidney may have been more directly indebted to the sixteenth-century Italian literary critic Julius Caesar Scaliger's 1586 *Poetices Libri Septem* on the poet as an imitator of divine ideas.[15]

Sidney's familiarity with French Protestantism traces how unevenly not only Platonism but also Florentine Neoplatonism was transmitted to him. Sidney was in frequent contact with French Protestant apologists, with consequences for how to read the *Defence*'s Protestant poetics through the lens of French Protestant receptions of Platonism. Sidney's knowledge of Ficino was most likely mediated through his French Protestant colleague Philippe de Mornay. Written in London in 1577, Mornay's *De la vérité de la religion chrestienne* was the first scholarly account of the theological aspects of Plato's thought written in England, demonstrating a high regard for the late antique Plotinus and Florentine Neoplatonism. The extent of Mornay's impact on Sidney is reflected in the fact that Sidney began translating Mornay's treatise in 1581.

Another French Protestant purveyor of Plato in England was the Geneva-based Huguenot Henri Estienne, who, in 1578, published a three-volume folio of Plato's *Opera*. Estienne edited the Greek text, and his colleague Jean de Serres provided a Latin translation (known as the 'Serranus' Plato). The text was ambitiously intended to replace Ficino's long-dominant Latin translation. With significance for Elizabethan England, the first volume of the Serranus was dedicated to Elizabeth, in gratitude for her support of Huguenot exiles. Moreover, in a 1579 letter written from Cologne, Hubert Languet wrote that, at Estienne's urging, de Serres had sent Sidney a complimentary set of his Plato.[16]

De Serres introduced each of Plato's dialogues with an *argumentum* that commented on what he judged the dialogues' most important passages. Sidney had read portions of de Serres's Plato shortly before writing the *Defence*, and similarities between Sidney's treatise and de Serres's commentaries are striking. For example, Sidney's aforementioned claim that Plato 'attributeth unto poesy more than myself do' may also have been borrowed from de Serres's commentary on the *Ion*, specifically its claim that 'Plato attributeth poetry to a certain divine spirit'.[17]

A continued focus on the Serranus Plato provides a transition to Sidney's colleague Edmund Spenser. Sidney received his copy of the Serranus Plato while residing at the house of his uncle the Earl of Leicester. Spenser was then serving as the earl's secretary; and he had completed *The Shepheardes Calender*, which he dedicated to Sidney around the same time that his dedicatee had introduced him to the Serranus Plato. *The Shepheardes Calender* inaugurated an experimental phase of English poetry. But it is unclear whether England's 'new poete' was also an authentically Platonic poet. While reading the Serranus Plato at Leicester House, Spenser was also preoccupied with final editorial changes to the glosses of 'E.K.'s that introduced each of the eclogues. He may have been prompted to add Platonic references from the newly introduced Serranus Plato—that is, *October*'s and *November*'s citings of passages from, respectively, the *Laws* and the *Phaedrus*. Spenser's last-minute allusions to Plato were probably intended to impress not only Sidney but also Elizabeth. But these additions may have been hastily culled from the Serranus Plato, because neither of his references to Plato actually appears in the dialogues.[18]

The concepts of love, beauty, the soul's ascent, divine rapture, and so on are so embedded in Spenser's poetry that a large segment of Spenser scholarship has, with greater or lesser accuracy, identified the poet as a Neoplatonist. More than any other Elizabethan sonnet sequence, Spenser's *Amoretti* (1595) is inherently Neoplatonic, lifting eros from the mire of Petrarchan excess and reinserting it into the framework of spiritual love. (A notable exception is Sonnet 88, where the poet laments his 'love-famished heart', thus revisiting Astrophel's aformentioned failed Platonic ascents.) *The Fowre Hymnes* (1596) traces the ascent from earthly to heavenly love, culminating in the soul's reunion with its origin. Though ascending from the cruel Cupid to the realm of celestial love, the quartet is also interlaced, each poem participating in the *Hymnes*' overall design.[19] Ficinian in scope is Spenser's use of the earthly and celestial Venuses, who are as complementary as they are contradictory. The Venus of *The Hymne to Earthly Love* is not simply cast aside but anticipates the epiphany of the celestial Venus of *The Hymne to Heavenly Beauty*. Thus, Spenser's two Venuses trace the Ficinian *circuitus spiritualis*, the cycle of emanation from and reversion to True Beauty as the highest goal.[20]

A tradition of Neoplatonic interpretation has accrued around *The Faerie Queene* (1590–6), placing its fictive Faerie land 'in perspective with the Platonic doctrine of Ideas'.[21] The expansive vision of Plato's cosmogony is evident almost everywhere in the epic's mythic structure, particularly the notion of the poet as imitating the creative process of the cosmos. When an enraptured Colin pipes to the maidens 'raunged in a ring' on Mt Acidale (*Faerie Queene*, 6. 10. 12), or when *Mutabilitie*'s Jove becomes a kind of Plotinian World Soul mediating between earth and heaven on Arlo Hill, we are securely positioned within what Bennett termed Spenser's 'Platonic doctrine of Ideas'. The epic's most significant locus of a Platonic cosmogony is book 3's Garden of Adonis, 'The first seminarie | Of all things' (3. 6. 42), where the Platonic theme of the soul's immortality is explicitly played out—namely, the cycle of life processes, the cycle of return to everlasting forms.

But two influential scholars have warned against overestimating Spenser's knowledge of Neoplatonism's syncretism, its complex layering of Orphica, the Cabbala, and Gnostic and early Christian thought. Edgar Wind singled out a passage from *The Faerie Queene*, 4, as evidence of an oversimplified Neoplatonism. The three brothers Priamond, Diamond, and Triamond are miraculously bound to one another 'As if one soul in them did dwell | Which did her [Agape's] power into three parts divide' (4. 2. 42). Wind argues that this passage is 'no more than a didactic exercise', a perfunctory 'schoolroom lesson in mystical "explication"'.[22]

Robert Ellrodt published the first in-depth study of Neoplatonic influences on the poetry of Spenser. Although acknowledging some parallels with Ficino in *The Fowre Hymnes*, he was also concerned with the many source ambivalences of the *Hymnes*' supposedly Neoplatonic passages. Commenting on the *Hymne of Heavenly Beauty*'s celebration of the soul's 'perfect end | Of purest beauty' (ll. 46–7), Ellrodt asserted that the ascent of the *Hymne*'s human spirit is not inherently Neoplatonic but rather an ambiguous 'blend' of Christianity and Neoplatonism that one could find in Dante, Augustine, or St Thomas, even in his more Aristotelian moments. Ellrodt interpreted the Garden of Adonis as less Platonic than patristic, mediated by Boethius or by Augustine's *De Genesi Ad Litteram*.[23]

Early Seventeenth Century: Donne, Jonson, Jacobean Court Masques, and Poetry

Uneven receptions of Plato and Florentine Neoplatonism continued into the seventeenth century, challenging our understanding of some of John Donne's startling metaphysical conceits. To be sure, Donne occasionally falls in lockstep with an outmoded Petrarchism, as in his verse letter 'To the Countesse of Bedford'. Here, Donne praises the countess, patroness of the Petrarchans Drayton and Daniel, as 'the transcript, and original of goodness',[24] demonstrating his skill in praising a woman wholly accustomed to the courtly cult of praise. But, overall, Donne's poetry represents an epistemic break with the love clichés so overused by an earlier era; and the poet was often moved to use Platonic equatings of love, beauty, and goodness to breathe new life into old Petrarchisms. In 'The Undertaking or Platonic Love', the poet repudiates the flesh, praising 'He who loveliness within | Hath found all outward loathes' (ll. 13–14). Neoplatonic themes can readily be found in many of Donne's *Songs and Sonets* (1633), such as 'A Valediction: Forbidding Mourning', its contempt for 'Dull sublunary lovers' love' (l. 13).

But the split between a secular and a spiritual Donne prompts the question of whether Donne was authentically Platonic. To be sure, a recurring theme in Donne's poetry is an account of the soul's departure from the body.[25] In the 'First Anniversarie', the poet traces the departure of the soul from the deceased body of Elizabeth Drury, his paragon of ideal womanhood. The fusion of lovers' souls in an extracorporeal union (also an Ovidian theme) is the subject of 'The Extasie', which recounts the exodus of the soul of the two lovers from their bodies. But is the poet a mystic, adept, or a seducer? Perhaps the poet's reference to the soul's journey to the Absolute was taken from Plotinus' *Enneads* (6. 9. 11), widely available in Ficino's translation. But in 'The Extasie', the union of the lovers' souls may be, rather, one among many instances of Donne's poetic wit—namely, a parody of the Thomist doctrine of hypostases (a scholastic defence of the Trinity as subsisting in a single divine substance), as understood by Donne's contemporaries.[26]

Elsewhere, a focus on Neoplatonic themes in Jacobean literature leads directly to the court. Although Platonism never achieved the status of an organized courtly cult under Elizabeth, that changed with her successor James's marriage to Anne of Denmark, who actively encouraged celebrations of Platonic love at court. William Drummond wrote poems idealizing Platonic love and heavenly beauty for the entertainment of the new queen.[27] His Sonnet 4 is conventionally addressed to Plato, 'that learned Grecian, who did excel | in knowledge passing sense' (ll. 1–2). But the genre that flourished the most was the court masque and its idealizations of her court's perfections. Ben Jonson owned a copy of the Serranus Plato; and at least two of his court masques, the 1605 *Masque of Blacknesse* and the 1608 *Masque of Beautie*, were laden with Platonic motifs. One of the *Masque of Beautie*'s expositions on Love and Beauty ('It was for Beauty that the World was made' (l. 289)) is accompanied by Jonson's note, 'an agreeing opinion, both with the *Diuines* and *Philosophers*', most likely referring to the Florentine Neoplatonists. Giovanni Pierio Valeriano's 1595 *Hieroglyphica*, heavily influenced by the first-century *Hieroglyphica* of 'Horapollo' (presumably an ancient Egyptian, but actually medieval), helped spawn a long-standing vogue of ancient Egypt as the source of hieroglyphs, esoteric ciphers of the universe, both on the Continent and in England.[28] *The Masque of Blacknesse* readily partook of this vogue to praise the court. The Aethiopian nymphs who make their way to Albion in search of true beauty are arranged in pairs, each carrying a fan adorned with 'a *mute* hieroglyphick, expressing their mixed qualities'.[29]

But Jonson was also ambivalent about Platonism's allied phenomenon of hermeticism and veneration of ancient Egyptian learning; and his trenchant social satire inevitably subjected this esoterica to ridicule. In *The Alchemist* (1610), Subtle instructs the druggist Able Drugger to devise a shop sign featuring 'a bell' (as in 'Abel'), next to 'one named Dee, | In a rug gown' (hence, d-rug or 'drug'), and a dog 'snarling "er"' (2. 6. 19–24). Subtle satirically contends that Able Drugger's sign should be a hieroglyph ('a bell dee-rug-er'), an arcane hinting at his name that only the adept could decipher. Such is the scope of Jonson's satire on hermeticism that it also encompasses the (in)famous figure of the Elizabethan John Dee, author of the 1564 *Monas Hieroglyphica*, and either a hierophant or a practitioner of black magic, depending on whether one embraced or rejected his hermetic writings.

Caroline Poetry and Drama

Following the popularity of Anne's Platonic love cult, a second wave of Platonic court fashion shaped the cultural context of the reign of Charles I (1625–42), with elaborate debates on love flourishing before the civil wars. Again, the Platonic wave originated in France. In 1625, Charles married Henrietta Maria, who was schooled in France's salons of 'platonic love'. The new queen was eager to import the French Platonic love cults into the English court, and many Caroline poets—William Habington, Thomas Carew, Edward Lord Herbert of Cherbury, John Suckling, and Abraham Cowley—catered to her interests, praising the divinity of a beautiful woman. Such poems as Carew's 'To My Mistress in Absence' and Cowley's 'Friendship in Absence' constituted a subgenre, idealizing love as a union of soul and essence. But many poets, including Cowley, also demonstrated how easily Henrietta Maria's love cults could deteriorate into outright satire on their extravagances, such as William Cartwright's 'No Platonic Love' and Cowley's 'Answer to the Platonicks'.

Platonic court drama also flourished under Henrietta Maria, and even an ageing Jonson tried his hand at the genre, composing *The New Inn* (1625), where Lovel proclaims Love as a spiritual coupling of two souls. In William D'Avenant's *The Temple of Love*, the Magician speaks wondrously of a new love cult at court: the courtiers

> Raise strange doctrines, and new sects of Love
> Which must not woo or court the person,
> But the mind.[30]

But, like Caroline Platonic verse, such 'Love doctrines' could easily be parodied, their *préciosité* deteriorating into vulgar burlesque, such as Phillip Massinger's *The Guardian*, which declares wives obsolete.[31]

In much Caroline verse and drama, then, nothing remained either of Plato or of Ficino and his elevation of love to an epistemological concept. And thus John Norris, disciple of the prestigious Cambridge Platonist Henry More, was moved to observe: '*Platonic Love* is a thing in everybody's mouth... But why this should be call'd by the name *Platonic* Love, the best reason that I know of, is because people will have it so.'[32]

Mid-Seventeenth Century: Vaughan and Milton

By mid-century, several devotional poems by Henry Vaughan showed signs of more far-reaching engagements with Platonism, particularly the concept of *anamnesis* (recollection of prior events.) (Vaughan had probably become interested in Platonism through the hermetic writings of his brother.) In 'The World', Vaughan traces the soul's flight to immortality. 'The Retreat' expresses a longing to return to the soul's origin (its 'Angell-Infancy' (l. 2)), possibly alluding to the *Phaedo*.[33]

But the mid-century's closest engagement with Plato is the writing of John Milton. He read Plato in the original Greek; and Platonic references were almost as numerous as his biblical references.[34] The tone of many of the young Milton's poems written during his Cambridge years is difficult to assess, with consequences for reading his references to Plato. *Il Penseroso* (*c*.1631) expresses a longing to know 'thrice-great *Hermes*, or unsphere | The spirit of *Plato*' (ll. 88–9). Milton's Hermes and Plato can strike us as conventional Platonizing. But his satire on Aristotle, *De Idea Platonica* (1628–30), reveals an affinity for Plato. The poet is sufficiently confident in his knowledge of Plato to intimate that Aristotle had misread Plato's theory of an archetypal man made in a divine image, probably reflecting dissatisfaction with Cambridge, which, despite its excellence in Greek studies, virtually ignored Plato.

The topics so central to Milton's prose—education, right rule, law, rhetoric, marriage, and so on—lead directly to Plato. In *The Treatise on Christian Doctrine* (1652), Milton singles out the *Timaeus*' doctrine of the creation of the world out of formless matter (*Prose Works*, 6. 305–11). In the 1641 *Apology for Smectymnuus*, Milton praises Plato's mythic island in the *Critias* for teaching sound government (*Prose Works*, 1. 881). In *The Readie and Easie Way* (1660), Milton pointedly agrees with the *Republic* and the *Laws*' call for government by specially trained magistrates (*Prose Works*, 7. 432–4). At times, Milton disagrees with Plato. In *Tetrachordon* (1645), Milton is at odds with Plato's advocacy of censorship (*Prose Works*, 2. 655). But, elsewhere in the treatise, Milton generally regarded Plato as an expert on matters of the law, agreeing with the *Laws*' identification of marriage as beneficial to the state (*Prose Works*, 2. 593); and his *Doctrine and Discipline of Divorce* poses the question 'what would Plato have deemed' of England's conflicting marriage law (*Prose Works*, 2. 310). More than almost any other early modern English writer, Milton skillfully read Plato's elusive tone. In *Prolusions* 6 (*Prose Works*, 1. 272–3) and in his *Pro Se Defensio* (*Prose Works*, 4. 77), he separated Plato's more serious points from Socrates' jesting indulgences.

Milton makes no mention of the Florentine Neoplatonists, surprisingly given his frequent contacts with the Italian academies of the 1620s. But Milton's oft-analysed representation of chastity in his 1634 *Ludlow Masque* is a test case for exploring some possible mediating influences of Ficino on the Milton who never cited him. Plato's direct influence on Milton is evident in lines 463–75, which are almost literally translated from the *Phaedo* 81. But the masque may also be explicitly Neoplatonic. Although chastity is not an inherently Platonic concept, Plato's *Charmides* expounds on the importance of teaching young nobility *sophrosyne*, involving not only temperance but also power of contemplation. In his 1484 translation of this dialogue, Ficino had translated *sophrosyne* as a divine harmony, which possibly influenced Milton's complex concept of chastity.[35]

The Cambridge Platonists

The philosophical movement of the Cambridge Platonism represented an anti-Aristotelian revival of a virtually unread Plato at Cambridge. The Cambridge Platonism, shaped during a period of sectarian disputes and revolution, was a systematic corpus of religious and philosophical thought, in the form of sermons, treatises, and poems. Unlike the Puritan proponents of an 'active' religion, the Cambridge Platonists practised a contemplative ethics, valuing the intelligible as much as the physical world. With their knowledge of Greek, they drew directly from Plato's dialogues. John Smith's *The Excellency and Nobleness of True Religion* drew on the *Phaedrus* and *Timaeus*. Ralph Cudworth's *The True Intellectual System of the Universe* quoted frequently from the *Laws*, as well as the *Timaeus*.

The Cambridge Platonists also became seventeenth-century England's most profound inheritors of late antique Neoplatonism. More than Plato's dialogues, the Cambridge Platonists were indebted to Plotinus' *Enneads*, which gained 'an almost canonical validity'.[36] Its doctrine of the intuitive hypostases of Mind, Soul, and the One structures Henry More's mystical poem 'Pyschozoia' and its parallels between the Neoplatonic and Christian Trinities.[37] In his 1659 *The Immortality of the Soul*, More expanded on the Plotinian concept of the immortal World Soul. Smith's aforementioned *True Religion* was indebted to Plotinus' theory of emanation—that is, God as radiating through all creation and containing the archetypal Ideas.

Ironically, several poems by Thomas Traherne, educated at Aristotle-dominated Oxford, are explicitly Neoplatonic. 'The Vision', 'Sight', and 'An Infant-Ey' all demonstrate a familiarity with Ficino's coupling of the eye and soul.[38] Of note is Traherne's interest in Hermes. His commonplace book quotes from John Everard's 1657 English translation of Hermes, the *Divine Pymander* (the first of the treatises in the Corpus Hermeticum), particularly the passages on man's dignity.[39]

The Decline of Neoplatonism in Renaissance England

As early as the year of Elizabeth's death, there were indications that Neoplatonism would not survive the oncoming decades' emergence of the new science. To be sure, Robert Burton's *Anatomy of Melancholy* alludes frequently to Ficino's translation of the *Corpus Hermeticum* (*c.*1464), as well as to his *De Vita* (1489). But a gap between medical discourse and Neoplatonism steadily widened. By mid-century,

Neoplatonism's veneration of ancient Hermetic wisdom began to fade amid the new science's emphasis on the physical over the intuitive. The origin of an epistemic shift away from Neoplatonism was the Geneva-born scholar of antiquity Isaac Casaubon's 1614 dating of the *Hermetica* (published as *De Rebus Sacris et Ecclesiasticiis Exercitationes XVI*) as not the work of an Egyptian priest but forgeries written after the birth of Christ. Henry More extensively corresponded with Descartes. But overall the Cambridge Platonists laboured in the shadow of Casaubon. Although More's 1653 *Conjectura Cabbalistica* praised Moses' influence on Christianity, it felt compelled to mention Casaubon's dating of the *Hermetica*.[40]

Paul Oskar Kristeller has cogently warned: 'The term Platonism does not lend itself very well as a middle term in the arithmetic or syllogistics of sources and influences.'[41] This is especially apt for the England of 1558–1660, where Plato was most often accessed via translations, commentaries, and commonplace books. The Elizabethan sonnet sequences are documents of a derivative Platonic love inherited not from Plato but from the continental *trattati d'amore*, themselves mediated through the Pléiade—or, in the case of Sidney's prose, through the Latin commentaries of de Serres. Even the often Neoplatonic Spenser offers evidence of highly mediated borrowings not only from Plato but also from the more nearly contemporary Ficino. To be sure, in the otherwise politically diverse Jacobean, Caroline, and Interregnum periods, the poetry of Donne, Vaughan, Traherne, and Milton at times directly engaged with Florentine Neoplatonism—and, in Milton's case, with Plato himself. But the trend under James and Charles was a largely superficial 'Platonizing'. Not even the philological discipline of Milton and the Cambridge Platonists could prevent the waning influence of Platonism and Neoplatonism in the face of the new science, when such hitherto privileged concepts of Platonic *anamnesis* were replaced by a strict duality of body and soul.

Notes

1. *Tamburlaine*, 4. 2. 96, in *The Complete Works of Christopher Marlowe*, ed. Roma Gill, 5 vols (Oxford, 1987–98), vol. 5.
2. Holland's translation is reprinted in Leeds Barroll, 'Some Versions of Plato in the English Renaissance', *Shakespeare Studies*, 2 (1966), 228–95.
3. For this misdating, see Michael J. B. Allen, *The Platonism of Marsilio Ficino: A Study of his Phaedrus Commentary, its Sources and Genesis* (Berkeley and Los Angeles, 1984), 5.
4. Partial to Plato's *Phaedrus* and *Symposium*, Walter Pater argues that Plato is 'before all things from first to last, unalterably a lover' (quoted from Walter Pater, *Plato and Platonism: A Series of Lectures* (1910), 134).
5. For a definitive survey of the *trattati d'amore*, see J. C. Nelson, *Renaissance Theory of Love* (1955).
6. Erwin Panofsky, *Studies in Iconology: Humanistic Themes in the Art of the Renaissance* (1939; repr. New York, 1962), 146.
7. W. A. R. Kerr, 'The Pleiade and Platonism', *Modern Philology*, 5 (1908), 407–21.
8. See C. H. Conley, *The First English Translations of the Classics* (New Haven, 1927);

A. B. Emden, *Bibliographical Register of the University of Oxford, 1501–40* (Oxford, 1974); N. R. Ker, *Oxford College Libraries in 1556* (Oxford, 1956). For a downplaying of Ficino's influence in early modern England, see Sears Jayne, 'Ficino and the Platonism of the English Renaissance', *Comparative Literature*, 4 (1952), 214–38.

9. For Neoplatonism in *The Merchant of Venice*, see Lawrence Danson, *Harmonies of 'The Merchant of Venice'* (New Haven, 1978), 185–9. For Shakespeare's explicit refusal to see himself as a Neoplatonist, see Richard Cody, *The Landscape of the Mind: Pastoralism and Platonic Theory in Tasso's Aminta and Shakespeare's The Early Comedies* (Oxford, 1969), 16.
10. For Bruno in England, see Frances Yates, *Giordano Bruno and the Hermetic Tradition* (Chicago, 1964), 235–56.
11. *Astrophil and Stella*, 5. 14, in Sir Philip Sidney, *Poems*, ed. William A. Ringler, Jr (Oxford, 1962).
12. Alfred Upham, *French Influence in English Literature from the Accession of Elizabeth to the Restoration* (1965).
13. See, e.g. M. F. Krouse, 'Plato and Sidney's *Defence of Poesie*', *Comparative Literature*, 6 (1954), 138–47.
14. Sir Philip Sidney, *The Defence of Poesy*, in *Miscellaneous Prose of Sir Phiip Sidney*, ed. Katherine Duncan-Jones and Jan van Dorsten (Oxford, 1973), 76. 25. On the *prisci theologi*, see D. P. Walker, *The Ancient Theology: Studies in Christian Platonism from the Fifteenth to the Eighteenth Century* (New York, 1972).
15. For sources of the early modern poet as divine maker, see J. E. Spingarn, *A History of Literary Criticism in the Renaissance* (1924).
16. This letter is quoted in S. K. Heninger, 'Sidney and Serranus' *Plato*', *English Literary Renaissance*, 13 (1983), 148.
17. The translation is by Heninger, who points out the *Defence*'s many echoes of de Serres.
18. Sears Jayne, *Plato in Renaissance England* (1995), 115–16.
19. T. Comito, 'A Dialectic of Images in Spenser's *Fowre Hymnes*', *Studies in Philology*, 4 (1977), 301–21.
20. For the Neoplatonic vision of Spenser's pastoral persona Colin Clout, see Patrick Cheney, '*Colin Clouts Come Home Againe, Astrophel*, and *The Doleful Lay of Clorinda* (1595)', in Richard McCabe (ed.), *The Oxford Handbook of Edmund Spenser* (Oxford, 2010), 241–6.
21. J. W. Bennett, *The Evolution of 'The Faerie Queene'* (1960), 136. Two key recent studies are Elizabeth Bieman, *Plato Baptized: Towards the Interpretation of Spenser's Mimetic Fictions* (Toronto, 1988), and Jon Quitslund, *Spenser's Supreme Fiction: Platonic Natural Philosophy and* The Faerie Queene (2001).
22. Edgar Wind, *Pagan Mysteries in the Renaissance* (New Haven, 1958), 209–10.
23. Robert Ellrodt, *Neoplatonism in the Poetry of Spenser* (Geneva, 1960), 8.
24. 'To the Countesse of Bedford', l. 56, in *The Variorum Edition of the Poems of John Donne*, gen. ed. Gary A. Stringer (Bloomington, IN, 1995–), vol. 3.
25. Merritt Y. Hughes, 'Some of Donne's "Ecstasies"', *PMLA*, 75 (1960), 509–18.
26. A. J. Smith, 'Donne in his Time: A Reading of "The Extasie"', *Rivista di Letterature Moderne e Comparate*, 10 (1957), 274.
27. French Fogel, *William Drummond* (New York, 1952).
28. For the Renaissance vogue of hieroglyphics, see Mario Praz, *Studies in Seventeenth Century Imagery* (1939).
29. For Valeriano's influence on Jonson, see D. J. Gordon, 'The Imagery of Jonson's *The Masque of Blacknesse* and *The Masque of Beautie*', *Journal of the*

Warburg and Courtauld Institutes, 6 (1943), 122–41.

30. *The Temple of Love*, I. 292–3, in *The Dramatic Works of Sir William D'Avenant*, ed. W. Paterson, 5 vols (Edinburgh, 1872–74).
31. G. F. Sensabaugh, 'Love Ethics in Platonic Court Drama, 1625–1642', *Huntington Library Quarterly*, 1 (1938), 277–304.
32. Quoted from 'An Account of Plato's Idea, and of Platonic Love' by J. S. Harrison, *Platonism in English Poetry of the Sixteenth and Seventeenth Centuries* (New York, 1903), 157.
33. *George Herbert and Henry Vaughan*, ed. Louis Martz (Oxford, 1986). See Louis Martz, *The Paradise Within: Studies in Vaughan, Traherne, and Milton* (New Haven, 1964), 29–30.
34. Irene Samuel, *Plato and Milton* (Ithaca, NY, 1947), 13.
35. On *sophrosyne* in Milton's masque, see John Arthos, 'Milton, Ficino, and the *Charmides*', *Studies in the Renaissance*, 6 (1959), 261–74.
36. Ernst Cassirer, *The Platonic Renaissance in England*, trans. James. P. Pettegrove (Austin, TX, 1953), 25.
37. For these parallels, see Basil Willey, *The English Moralists* (1964), 172.
38. Sarah Hutton, 'Platonism in some Metaphysical Poets', in Anna Baldwin and Sarah Hutton (eds), *Platonism and the English Imagination* (Cambridge, 1994), 172.
39. For Hermetic and Neoplatonic echoes in Traherne's Commonplace Book, see C. A. Marks, 'Thomas Traherne and Hermes Trismegistus', *Renaissance News*, 19 (1966), 119–31.
40. On Casaubon's dating, see Yates, *Giordano Bruno*, 398–403. For Cambridge Platonists' disagreements with Cartesian rationalism and Hobbesian materialism, see G. R. Cragg's introduction to his edition *The Cambridge Platonists* (Oxford, 1968), 19–26.
41. Paul Oskar Kristeller, *Renaissance Thought and Its Sources* (New York, 1979), 33.

CHAPTER 23

Virgil and Ovid

MAGGIE KILGOUR

Although the entire classical tradition provided the material through which English artists thought and created, Virgil and Ovid played especially important roles. This chapter cannot hope to cover all the aspects of their influence, and will complement discussions in this volume of specific genres and authors. It will consider some of the reasons for the two poets' prominence, discuss how they were used generally, and then focus on three major authors they shaped and by whom they were shaped: Spenser, Shakespeare, and Milton.

The centrality of Virgil and Ovid in the development of English literature is partly due to their place in Renaissance pedagogy. Virgil's position in education was long established; he had been a school text from his own lifetime on. While Ovid took longer to become part of the curriculum, by the Middle Ages his works had become essential to the learning of Latin. During their grammar-school education, students in Renaissance England were exposed to at least selections from the entire corpus of both writers as part of the process of mastering both the Latin language and the arts of rhetoric and logic. While individual school practices vary, most curricula outline a sequence that begins with Ovid's *Tristia, Ex Ponto*, and *Heroides*, used to teach letter-writing and the arts of persuasion, and then proceeds in following years through Virgil's *Eclogues* and *Georgics*, and finally to the epics, the *Metamorphoses* and *Aeneid* (see Peter Mack, Chapter 2, this volume). Virgil and Ovid were also seen as particularly important for students who were beginning to write poetry themselves. Chapter 14 of John Brinsley's influential *Ludus Literarius: Or, the Grammar School* (1612) is dedicated to showing 'How to enter to make verses with delight and certainty without botching; and to train up scholars to imitate and express Ovid or Virgil, both their phrase and style' (p. 190). The two authors were deeply entwined with the experience and practice of writing verse. It is hardly surprising then that, as students matured (or, as some of their contemporaries would have said, degenerated) into writers, Virgil and Ovid provided the matter, themes, rhetorical formulae, and figures for their works. Formative in education, they were formative in the broader development of literature as a whole. At the level of form itself, they were seminal in the directions English literature would take, as translating their works helped produce the two verse forms that dominated English poetry until the twentieth century: blank verse, which Surrey used for his translation of the *Aeneid*, and the heroic couplet, polished and popularized by Marlowe in his translation of the *Amores* (see Philip Hardie, Chapter 9, and Charles Martindale, Chapter 26, this volume). More importantly, the two authors provided material for central themes of Renaissance art: alienation, mutability, desire, illusion, and art itself and its relation to political power. They also supplied key terms and images for thinking about the transmission and metamorphoses of the classical tradition as a whole.

In recent years, the general assumption has been, however, that in the Renaissance these two authors were viewed as opposites: the 'Prince of Poets and Lord of Misrule'.[1] Twentieth-century criticism tended to foreground the differences between the two authors, treating Virgil as the poet of empire, supporter of an authoritarian regime, and Ovid as a counter-authority, an apolitical aesthete or, more recently, a cunning critic of power. They are clearly very different types in terms of genres and values. Virgil famously began his career with pastoral poetry, then moved to the georgic and epic, a sequence of progression from lesser to greater genres that, known as the Virgilian rota or wheel, may have influenced later poets, including Spenser and Milton (see Patrick Cheney, Chapter 8c, this volume). At a time when Greek literature was still much less familiar than Latin, Virgil was the central model for the classical epic as a serious form that represented national values. He praises hard work and service to one's country and ruler, and shows the destructive effects of desire. While Ovid experimented with different genres, including tragedy (his lost *Medea*), he did not progress through a linear generic sequence, and at the end of his career returned to the elegy with which he began. Moreover, his epic is a very different kind from that of Virgil; in Renaissance debates, the *Aeneid* and *Metamorphoses* were often used to present antithetical theories of the epic, or to differentiate the linear and unified epic from the looser and errant romance. Romance and Ovid are linked in other ways, as he celebrates the desire that Virgil distrusts. Furthermore, Ovid elevates art and the poet himself over social responsibilities and even political power: 'carmina morte carent. | cedant carminibus reges regumque triumphi' (*Amores* I. 15. 32–3; in Marlowe's version: 'Verse is immortal, and shall ne'er decay, | To verse let kings give place, and kingly shows').[2]

The two poets' lives as well as their works seem antithetical. The widely read hagiographic life of Virgil written by Donatus stressed Virgil's rise through patronage and his active role as counsellor to Augustus.[3] He was the ideal poet, one whose influence on Augustus encouragingly showed that poetry could be a palpable force in the world. Ovid's life provides a stark contrast with this Horatio Alger success story. Many Renaissance editions and translations of Ovid's works included a potted biography of the poet based on the account he himself gives in the exilic poetry. Born into affluence, he was an instantly and enormously popular poet, but his life was ruined when he was suddenly banished to the Black Sea. Ovid left the exact cause of his banishment tantalizingly unexplained, saying only that it was because of 'carmen et error' ('a poem and a blunder') (*Tristia* 2. 207). A popular, if historically inaccurate, myth, the basis for Ben Jonson's *Poetaster*, reported that Ovid's fatal error was an affair with Augustus' banished daughter Julia. Ovid himself identifies the *carmen* as his *Ars Amatoria*, which had, quite unjustly he complains, offended the *princeps*, who misread its playful poetic licence as endorsing adultery. Despite his claims of omnipotence, the poet was destroyed by his reader, an ominous lesson that later writers would remember.

As Jonson's *Poetaster*, which contrasts the exalted Virgil with the disgraced Ovid, shows, the two Romans suggested antithetical career patterns for aspiring English artists. Virgil is the laureate poet, representative of an official order, whose art is central to his culture, as it guides and informs its leaders.[4] While for Virgil poetry is a means to power, for Ovid it leads to disgrace and punishment. The exiled Ovid seems the archetypal outsider, the alienated artist who is persecuted for challenging authority and setting himself up as a rival to the ruler. It has, therefore, sometimes been assumed that writers who follow Virgil are politically conservative, while Ovid is the choice of rebels on the margins, troublemakers like Marlowe. Virgil is the ancestor of serious literary *labour* with a social and particularly nationalist agenda; his georgic vision was compatible with the Protestant ethic of hard work, and his epic, with its strong sense of teleology and insistence on the subordination of individual desire to the general good and divine destiny, translated well into Christian and especially Protestant terms.[5] Ovid appeals to a different side of the Renaissance world: its spirit of individualism, even narcissistic egotism. He inspired writing that is obsessed with the glories and miseries of the self: love elegy, complaint, romance, romantic comedies, and that structurally as well as morally licentious form, the epyllion—in short, the kinds of asocial and immoral poetry that always gets poets into trouble.

The two authors were certainly recognized as very different types of poets. Virgil was the more admired and prestigious poet, though Ovid was usually the poet writers wanted to spend time with. As essays by Philip Hardie and Helen Cooper show (Chapters 9 and 10, this volume), Virgil was the central model for epic and pastoral. Love poets, notably Donne, turned to Ovid. For the new generation of writers of the late 1500s, Ovid was the prime source for complaints and the epyllia, in which writers expanded playfully on Ovidian tales and focused on erotic themes.[6] Women writers generally were also drawn to Ovid, whose presentation of female perspectives and voices in the *Heroides* especially offered them an important model.[7] Yet, despite these differences, it is misleading to treat the two poets as founders of totally separate poetic traditions and to assume that their works are inevitably aligned with any single political position or poetical form. The language, figures, and stories of both Virgil and Ovid were used to praise and to criticize Elizabeth and the Stuarts. Although Virgil provided the imagery for James I's succession and Charles II's restoration, his works have always appealed also to the politically marginalized, and he himself had made the pastoral a form of social criticism.[8] Georgics were used to celebrate Cromwell (though this is typical of the broader appropriation of royalist forms for the Protectorate). Ovid was also a staple for the court masques that reinforced the authority of the monarchy. If Ovid was a favourite of the new generation of commercial writers of the 1590s, he was equally a source of inspiration for the aristocrats of the Caroline court; lyrics of the 1620–30s draw on Ovid's erotic verse, and his exilic poetry has a grim relevance for Royalists after the 1640s.[9]

Renaissance students would not have first encountered the two writers as stark antitheses.[10] For one thing, in schools, classical works were not studied as entire texts but through isolated extracts, often printed in collections of classical excerpts or *florilegia*, which were used to illustrate a particular point or theme. Students may thus have read select episodes in the *Aeneid* and *Metamorphoses* with no knowledge of what came before or after, though teachers often stressed that students could understand the meaning of a passage only by knowing its context. However, detached from their own works, the authors entered a new system of relations when they became bound up with each other in handbooks where they were united under a common topic that encouraged comparison as well as contrast. This juxtaposition of authors was continued by readers in their own commonplace books, in which they put together different authors in ways that made them part of single discourse, created by the reader himself.[11]

It does not seem surprising, therefore, that Renaissance works often combine elements from Virgil and Ovid. In the evolution of pastoral away from its ancient origins that Cooper notes, Ovidian elements, primarily related to love and seduction, sneak in. While, as I suggested above, the epyllion looks back to Ovid, it sees through him to Virgil, known in the Renaissance as the author of the epyllia *Ciris* and *Culex*, as well as the story of Aristaeus and Orpheus in *Georgic* 4.[12] Charles Martindale's essay in this volume (Chapter 26) shows how the Ovidian Marlowe is also an excellent reader and reworker of Virgil. As Philip Hardie's essay (Chapter 9) also shows, Renaissance dynastic epic looked back primarily to Virgil for its themes, characters, and structure, but turned to Ovid to reconcile heroic questing with romantic love; similarly, English historical narratives that told the Virgilian story of England's descent from Troy included numerous Ovidian passages and motifs.[13] Poets do not always identify simply with one or the other of the authors. Cowley's unfinished *Davideis* follows 'the *Pattern* of our Master *Virgil*'.[14] The poem's opening 'I sing the Man who Judah's sceptre bore | In that right hand which held the Crook before' (Cowley, *English Writings*, 1. 1–2) makes David's transformation from shepherd to king a mirror of Cowley's own Virgilian progression from minor to major keys. Yet Cowley also sees himself as the exiled Ovid, whose *Tristia* he quotes in the preface to the volume (Cowley, *English Writings*, 1. 7–8). In *Poetaster*, Jonson's direct association with his ideal Horace is complicated by his admiration for Virgil and sympathy for Ovid.[15] The most popular episodes from the *Aeneid*—especially the fall of Troy in book 2, the love story in book 4, and the description of the underworld in book 6—

are often elaborated with passages from Ovid. The effect of such interweaving is not homogenous or predictable. It does not necessarily create a tension between an official Virgilian account and a subversive Ovidian one. It may simply be a means of supplementation. At times, however, the combination can produce a fruitful friction between different perspectives and treatments that challenged the idea of a single and original authoritative account, and freed up a space in which the new writer could insert his own version.

Such juxtapositions may also suggest continuity rather than contrast, by drawing attention to places where Ovid himself is interpreting Virgil. Trained to write by imitating classical writers, Renaissance authors had learned also how classical writers had imitated each other. Roger Ascham especially had urged students to study attentively the ways in which one ancient author transformed his source—adding new materials, eliminating old, changing order and emphasis—as a model for their own metamorphosis of the past.[16] Editions of Virgil listed parallel passages in Homer, through which readers might see how a writer had reworked earlier material.[17] It was recognized that in the *Metamorphoses* Ovid retells in his own fashion Virgil's *Aeneid*, while *Heroides* 7 (Dido to Aeneas) rewrites Virgilian epic from the perspective of the women marginalized in the grand march of nationhood. Today it is often assumed that the revisionary relation here is one of opposition, even subversion, as Ovid revises to overturn Virgilian ideas. But that too does not seem to have been the assumption of Renaissance readers, nor Ovid's practice. In focusing on the victims of history, Ovid builds on Virgil's sympathy for figures such Meliboeus, Orpheus, Dido, and Turnus. Moreover, reading his exilic poetry early in their schooling, students first encountered Ovid as the poet not of desire but of exile. The theme no doubt resonated with adolescents and with writers who felt alienated professionally, politically, erotically, or spiritually, and Ovid's last works are echoed frequently throughout this period. But allusions to Ovid are impossible to differentiate entirely from references to Virgil, for the reason that Ovid's representation of exile draws on Virgil for whom also, from *Eclogue* 1 on, exile is a central theme. Ovid's art and indeed life had already been shaped by Virgil, whose representation of the transformation of Trojans into Romans lies behind Ovid's broader treatment of forms of change. Ovid was, of course, known as the great poet of change; Pythagoras' description in *Metamorphoses* 15 of a world of constant flux and the author's final assertion that he will himself conquer change through his art were resonant for a period obsessed with mutability and the dream of immortality through art. But, in Renaissance works, echoes of Pythagoras' vision are often mixed with elements from Anchises' speech in *Aeneid* 6, which is one of Ovid's chief sources.

Classical writers had commonly used 'double allusions', in which they simultaneously alluded to both an early work and its later imitation to draw attention to their own genealogies.[18] The interweaving of sources was one way for Renaissance authors also to construct their own *translatio studii* and literary family trees. The idea of *translatio*, the transmission of learning from the ancient to the modern worlds, is itself influenced by Virgil's representation of the carrying-over of the Trojan past to Rome, though it draws also on images of Ovidian transformation. As an aetiological genre, the epyllion is especially useful for representing the beginnings of English literature as the transplantation of classical figures to England, where they take new mythological and poetic forms. The earliest English epyllion, Thomas Lodge's 1589 *Glaucus and Scylla*, uses the coming of the Ovidian Glaucus to England to show the metamorphosis of the Ovidian complaint into the epyllion itself. John Weever's 1600 *Faunus and Melliflora*, written at the end of the craze for this new genre, imagines the emergence of the next generation as the immigration of the generic heir of epyllion, satire, in the figures of satyrs.[19] In both works, the main characters and mood are basically Ovidian, but the overall plot, with the theme of *translatio*, is also Virgilian; in fact, Weever's hero Faunus is the son of Picus, who looks back to *Aeneid* 7–8 through Ovid's transformation of Virgil in *Metamorphoses* 14. In Weever's aetiology, furthermore, satyrs come to England with the Trojan Brut, England's version of Aeneas. Classical myths are a means of describing the development of English literature as stages in the remaking of classical forms handed down through a line that includes both Virgil and Ovid.

For a complex and learned author like Andrew Marvell, equally at home in English and in Latin, the well-wrought genre of pastoral with its long history of intertextual echoes and allusions is especially congenial to the shaping of his classical genealogy. Though Marvell is particularly fond of Ovid, his allusions are layered and multidimensional, and place him in a tradition that reaches past Ovid to Virgil and beyond. 'Damon the Mower' looks back to Ovid's Polyphemus (*Metamorphoses* 13. 740–897), but beyond that to Virgil's Corydon (*Eclogue* 2), behind whom lies the Cyclops of Theocritus's *Idyll* 11 (who, of course, is taken from Homer). 'The Nymph Complaining for the Death of her Fawn' brings together a number of Ovidian forms and figures. Recalling Ovid's elegy for the dead parrot in *Amores* 2. 6 (a poem that itself parrots Catullus 2), the use of the genre of Ovidian complaint, derived from the *Heroides*, gives away the poem's concern with the speaker's abandonment by her faithless lover. The killing of the beloved deer also has analogues with several scenes in the *Metamorphoses*.[20] Behind these, however, lurks the slaying of the pet deer that begins the war in Italy in *Aeneid* 7, an action that itself recalls Aeneas' abandonment of Dido, who in 4. 68–73 is compared to a stricken doe. Superimposing an Ovidian study of female psychology on a Virgilian narrative of civil war, the poem reads Ovidian erotic narratives as a revision of Virgilian epic from a female perspective.

As Marvell's example suggests, Virgilian and Ovidian elements cannot completely be separated from those of the classical authors whom they themselves had imitated. They are further mediated through later rewritings and interpretations. Commentaries on Virgil beginning with Servius and Fulgentius, and allegorical readings of Ovid, popular in the late Middle Ages and perpetuated through the translations of Arthur Golding and George Sandys, established models of interpretations through and against which authors read the texts.[21] Even more important, however, were the examples of other writers. Several other chapters have noted the role of continental works in the transmission of classicism to England. English epic was especially influenced by Ariosto's and Tasso's reworking of Virgil and Ovid; pastoral recalled Virgil through Mantuan and Sannazaro; love poetry absorbed Ovid by means of Dante, Petrarch, and Marino; Ovid's exilic verse was channelled to Spenser through Du Bellay. Moreover, in the competitive and fast-changing market of Elizabethan England, writers watched each other closely, copying their rivals' translations and reworkings and sometimes viciously attacking them to offer their own counter-versions. Weever's *Faunus and Melliflora* is a pastiche of motifs from Marlowe, Spenser, and, especially, Shakespeare, whose *Venus and Adonis* epitomized 1590s Ovidianism. In *Poetaster*, the parting scene between Ovid and Julia echoes both the *Tristia* and *Romeo and Juliet*. Like many of this generation, Shakespeare reads Ovid with one eye on Golding's translation, from which he learns how to capture Ovidian wit in English. When Drayton copies Ovid, it is through Spenser.[22] Donne's reimagining of Ovid's erotic poetry (probably itself influenced by Marlowe's translation of the *Amores*) shapes the next generation of writers such as Carew, Suckling, Randolph, and Cowley. As Cooper shows above, later Virgilian pastoral is shaped by Spenser. Renaissance Virgilianisms and Ovidianisms are complex because they are frequently entangled with each other, other classical authors, and with the later writers who had reworked them, above all with the transformative examples of Spenser, Shakespeare, and Milton.

Spenser

Spenser has sometimes been described as a Virgilian author who ends up as an Ovidian: seeking patronage from the court, and hoping to use poetry to counsel his ruler, he is instead neglected and sent out into exile in Ireland.[23] But from the beginning of his career the two classical writers are intertwined in his works. Their mixture helps him express his ambivalence towards his 'dearest dread' (*Faerie Queene*, 1. Proem. 4. 9), who was at the same time Virgilian ruler and Ovidian mistress, and whose authority both generates his poetic power and potentially silences it.[24] They help him imagine also a new kind of epic. The proem to *The Faerie Queene*,

> Lo, I the man, whose Muse whilom did masque,
> As time her taught, in lowly Shepherds' weeds,
> Am now enforced a far unfitter task,
> For trumpets stern to change mine Oaten reeds
> (1. Proem. 1. 1–4)

copies the *ille ego* proem, which opens standard Renaissance editions of Virgil, and therefore seems to announce Spenser's allegiance to a Virgilian model of both career and epic (see Patrick Cheney, Chapter 8c, this volume).[25] But, as the proem also explains, *The Faerie Queene* celebrates not just the traditional epic subject of war but also love: 'Fierce wars and faithful loves shall moralize my song' (1. Proem. 1. 9). Like other Renaissance epic writers, Spenser needs Ovid in order to make a place for the romantic love that Virgil banishes with Dido. While many of Spenser's heroes are modelled on Aeneas, the digressive and complex structure of the work and his interest in change of all kinds look back, through Italian romance, to Ovid.[26] As Richard McCabe argues (Chapter 25, this volume) his works show a 'sophisticated fusion of Virgilian and Ovidian motifs'. Furthermore, as Raphael Lyne has shown, 'Spenser seems to play upon the intertextuality between Ovid and Virgil, and on his ability to see through Ovid to Virgil'.[27] Virgil's voice may in fact be heard in Spenser's echoes of Ovid's exilic works, discussed by McCabe.[28] The double allusions reveal Spenser's complex inheritance but also suggest his sensitivity to the fine line between Virgil and Ovid, beneficiary and victim of princely power.

The presence of both authors is apparent in *The Shepheardes Calender*, in which Spenser presents himself as a budding writer of Virgilian eclogues. While the form and shepherds are Virgilian, the calendrical structure looks back to Ovid's poetic calendar, the *Fasti*. Spenser also sends off his work quoting the last lines of the *Metamorphoses* in which Ovid claims to have conquered time through art (Spenser, *Shorter Poems*, 156). Like the different voices in the poems, the allusions enable Spenser to contemplate alternative poetic identities. In the *October* eclogue, two poets debate the kind of poetry appropriate to the present. Piers tells Cuddie to stop singing rustic ditties and move from pastoral poetry to epic: 'Abandon then the base and viler clown, | Lift up thy self out of the lowly dust: | And sing of bloody Mars, of wars, of jousts' (*October*, ll. 36–9). While Cuddie notes that this is what Virgil did, he laments that England lacks the patronage system that supported Augustan writers (*October*, ll. 55–78). Past models are of limited use in new social and poetical circumstances. Piers's punningly self-centred reply, 'O pierless Poesy, where is then thy place?' (*October*, l. 79), raises what is in many ways the central question of Spenser's work. What is the place of poetry in this modern world? In such an age, what kind of poetry should Spenser write? While the pastoral genre suggests that Virgil is the poet's guide towards an epic future, the eclogue ends with an epigram from Ovid's *Fasti*, which asserts the divinity of the inspired poet: 'est deus in nobis | Agitante calescimus illo ...' ('There is a god within us. It is when he stirs that our bosom warms') (*Fasti* 6. 5). Ovid offers Spenser a route to immortality in a calendar that 'shall continue till the worlds dissolution' (Spenser, *Shorter Poems*, 156).

The two classical sources thus seem potentially at odds, confirming a common perception that Spenser is himself a house divided between an (Ovidian) love of the sensual and a (Virgilian) commitment to the ethical. The short poem *Muipotomos* (1590) especially seems to dramatize this psychological tension as the conflict between the two sources. Generically the work allies Spenser with Ovid, and with the popular Ovidian traditions of the complaint and the epyllion. Ovid provides the centre of the story, which tells of the murder of the beautiful butterfly Clarion by the spiteful spider Aragnoll, who is descended from Ovid's Arachne. However, this Ovidian tale is framed by Virgilian language, which envelops it like the spider's deadly web that traps the fatally carefree Clarion. It begins with an announcement of an epic battle between two mighty forces that reworks *Aeneid* 1. 11's famous 'tantaene animis caelestibus irae?' ('Can resentment so fierce dwell in heavenly hearts?') as 'And is there then | Such rancour in the hearts of mighty men?' (*Muiopotmos*, ll. 15–16). The wrath of Juno, which opens the *Aeneid*, becomes now that of the spiteful Aragnoll. Virgil also brings the poem to a close: the last lines replay the abrupt flight of Turnus' shade to the underworld at the end of the *Aeneid* (12. 951–2), as Clarion's 'deep groaning spright | In bloody streams forth fled into the air' (*Muiopotmos*, ll. 438–9). The Ovidian Clarion finds out too late that he is in a Virgilian story.[29]

The first books of *The Faerie Queene* also seem to oppose Virgilian and Ovidian paths for poetry. While books 1 and 2 of Spenser's epic are particularly Virgilian, this Virgil has been filtered through the allegorical tradition that read Aeneas' journey as the good man's conquest of the passions, embodied in Dido and Turnus (see also Richard McCabe, Chapter 25, this volume). From this perspective, desire is deadly, as Spenser's story of the aptly named Amavia and Mordante indicates. Book 2 especially is full of versions of Dido and Turnus—Amavia, Pyrochles, Cymochles, Acrasia—who represent the passions that the new Aeneas, Guyon, must defeat to fulfil his quest and destroy the Bower of Bliss. In book 1, the opening storm recalls another frequently copied Virgilian episode, that of *Aeneid* 1, in which Aeneas' ship is blown off course to Carthage by Juno's tempest. During the storm Redcrosse and Una take refuge in the wood of Error, just as in *Aeneid* 4 Dido and Aeneas take shelter in the fatal cave in which they consummate their love. But, modelled on Ovid's Scylla, who is part of Ovid's reimagining of the *Aeneid* in *Metamorphoses* 13–14, Error also represents the erotic and narrative seductions of specifically Ovidian romance, which threaten to distract the hero from his quest. While Redcrosse destroys the monster, he becomes entangled in a series of events that lead him astray and eventually to his Dido, Duessa. The first books thus associate Ovid with the passions that impede Virgilian heroic questing and that the heroes must overcome.

In book 3, however, Ovidian passion is given a new role. The narrative itself begins to wander and become more Ovidian in its digressions and multiplication of heroes. The book still has many Virgilian parallels, such as Paridell's account of the fall of Troy and the rise of Troy's other descendant, Britain (*Faerie Queene*, 3. 9. 33–43). But, as his name suggests, Paridell is a parody of Paris, a debased version of his ancestor who indicates how in the process of transmission classical figures can degenerate into caricatures of themselves. Some commentators had feared that, in slaying Turnus, Aeneas was not conquering his passions, but giving in to them;[30] the new Aeneas and knight of Temperance, Guyon, seems even more intemperate when he razes the Bower of Bliss. In the figure of Britomart in book 3, Spenser imagines a hero for whom love is not the enemy of heroism, as it was for Aeneas and Guyon, but the motive. The figure of the female warrior draws, of course, on Ariosto and Tasso, who transformed Virgil's Camilla, a fierce virgin warrior whose role is peripheral to the plot proper (she never meets Aeneas), into a central element of dynastic romance. Some aspects of the original Camilla are retained for Spenser's virginal Belphoebe. But Britomart is at the centre of the epic, both as the ancestor of Elizabeth, and thus a female Aeneas who foretells the future English Augusta, and as a figure for the reconciliation of Virgilian and Ovidian values. Her love for Artegall is first described through allusions to Ovid's tales of Narcissus and Myrrha, as well as to the pseudo-Virgilian *Ciris* (*Faerie Queene*, 3. 2. 18–44). As Syrithe Pugh has argued, her quest in book 3 to free Amoret involves overthrowing not Ovidian desire itself but a sterile Ovidianism that has been fossilized in courtly love and Petrarch, thus 'Rescuing Ovid from the Ovidian Tradition'.[31] At the same time, Britomart enables Spenser to release Virgil from the restrictive Virgilian tradition of the first books, which created a false opposition between desire and heroism. The disappearance of the allegorists' Virgil and the amorists' Ovid frees the poet to imagine his own version of both poets, who are absorbed into the eternally generative Garden of Adonis, which represents the origins of art and which draws on both *Aeneid* 6 and *Metamorphoses* 15, as well as many other sources.[32] For Spenser, the fact that there is no single authoritative story opens a space in which he can create a new vision of endless re-creation.

However, the existence of multiple versions of any story poses increasing problems. How do you tell which is true? In book 2, Archimago claims that Guyon is the perpetrator of what we would call elder abuse; in book 3 Britomart tests Artegall's reputation by representing him as a rapist, while Paridell retells Aeneas' account of his history to Dido as a version of the arts of seduction from the *Ars Amatoria*. The doubling of Una and Florimell in books 1 and 3 shows also how imitation creates competing versions, in which the difference between true and false, original and copy, may be lost. In the final books, the proliferation of stories as well as characters increases the interpretative problem. In book 5, Britomart's earlier innocent fiction about her beloved takes on a grim reality when Artegall becomes the target of forms of verbal abuse embodied in Envy, Slander, and the Blatant Beast. Such figures recall Virgil's *Fama* in *Aeneid* 4, who spreads news of the love of Dido and Aeneas. In Virgil, *Fama* is a figure for the author himself, who Renaissance authors thought had invented the love story that destroyed the reputation of a queen previously known for her fidelity and chastity. Ovid's revision of *Fama* in *Metamorphoses* 12. 39–63 shows how the retelling of stories enables creative expansion, but also the introduction of error and even deliberate lies.[33] The poet may himself be a perpetrator of verbal abuse and slander, as the figure of Bon/Malfont, the poet punished for 'wicked slanders', suggests (*Faerie Queene*, 5. 9. 26. 9). But Bon/Malfont's crime is never stated: has he himself been a victim of the very slander of which he has been accused? The mood at the end of book 6 recalls Ovid's exilic verse, with its portrayal of a poet ruined by misrepresentation.[34]

From the start, moreover, the Virgilian and Ovidian subtexts call into question the status of the poem. The two authors provide the central stories and motifs for

Renaissance artists like Spenser for whom distinguishing appearances from reality, idolatrous images from the truth, is a pressing religious as well as philosophical question. In Virgil, Aeneas stops to look at the images of Troy in the Temple of Juno in Carthage (1. 453–93), and the miniature Troy created by Andromache and Helenus (3. 349–51) makes him long to end his quest. Do such images propel or impede his journey? The question of the power of images is also developed into a central theme of Ovid, whose Narcissus pines away with longing for his own reflection. The story was a favourite one for Renaissance artists concerned with the danger as well as the delight of illusion.[35] But Ovid's story of Pygmalion shows how art can become real—a motif also in the love poetry where Ovid claims that if we fake love we may actually feel it (*Ars* 1. 615–18). Desire and illusion are deeply linked, and, while desire may lead us into error, it may also reveal the truth, as false dreams do in the story of Ceyx and Alcyone (*Metamorphoses* 11. 410 ff.). This last episode was important for Ovid himself, who in exile claims his own stories have become real, and for Spenser's representation of the Cave of Morpheus (*Faerie Queene*, 1. 1. 39–44), as well as for many other Renaissance treatments of dreams and visions.[36] The question of the moral and ontological status of images runs through *The Faerie Queene* from the never-realized dream of Arthur, which inspires his quest and is parodied by the false dreams sent to Redcrosse (1. 1–2), to the visions on Mt Acidale and of Mutabilitie in the last books. As in Virgil and Ovid, repeated ekphrases both comment on and momentarily stop the action, potentially trapping the reader and the story itself. Spenser's use of allegorical figures causes further problems: are events really happening or just figures for internal processes? Redcrosse's failure to see the relevance of the story of Fradubio (*Faerie Queene*, 1. 2. 30–45), in an encounter based on Virgil's highly Ovidian account of Aeneas' meeting with the murdered and metamorphosed Polydorus (*Aeneid* 3), suggests further that we do not learn from the stories of others but simply replay the past.[37]

Shakespeare

As part of the new generation of commercial dramatists, Shakespeare does not seek patronage as a Virgilian author as Spenser had. Moreover, when he presents himself as a poet who seeks courtly support, he identifies himself as an Ovidian.[38] His first published poem, the 1593 *Venus and Adonis*, dedicated to the Earl of Southampton, is prefaced with an epigraph from *Amores* 1. 15. 35–6. While his bid for patronage seems to have been a flop, the work was a commercial hit. It fuelled the vogue for Ovidian erotic poetry that had been building from the 1560s on. It showed others how to transform Ovidian stories (here that of *Metamorphoses* 10) and, even more importantly, how to 'English' Ovidian wit and paradox. Ovid is the presiding genius (or demon) of Shakespeare's poetry: he is the source for his other epyllion, *The Rape of Lucrece*, based on *Fasti* 2, while the sonnets are full of Ovidian imagery, themes, and figures. Ovid is a frequent resource in the plays as well, especially, but not exclusively, the comedies and romances. While Shakespeare is familiar with the range of Ovid's works, he seems most drawn to the *Metamorphoses*, and in particular *Metamorphoses* 2–4 (Phaethon, Actaeon, Narcissus, Hermaphroditus, Pyramus and Thisbe), *Metamorphoses* 10 (the stories told by Orpheus, most notably those of Pygmalion, and Venus and Adonis), and *Metamorphoses* 15 (Pythagoras' vision of eternal flux as well as the poet's final claim of immortality in art). He studied Ovid's use of dramatic soliloquy, filtered through the Senecan tradition, to present characters in the act of making transformative decisions.[39] He inherits Ovid's love of puns and witty wordplay, and his obsession with dynamic words, images, and characters that at any time can turn into something else. Francis Meres seems right when he famously observed that: 'as the soul of *Euphorbus* was thought to live in *Pythagoras*: so the sweet witty soul of *Ovid* lives in mellifluous and honey-tongued *Shakespeare*.'[40]

Virgil's role in Shakespeare's imagination is harder to trace and assess. Shortly after his death, Shakespeare was hailed as England's great national poet and therefore memorialized officially in a statue at Stratford as *arte Maronem* ('in art a Virgil').[41] He clearly had read Virgil, though he draws mostly on the first half of the *Aeneid*.[42] However, Charles Martindale concludes that 'Shakespeare is not usefully to be described as a Virgilian poet' as 'his reading of Virgil did not result in a profound modification of his sensibility and imagination in the way that his reading of other books did'.[43] In fact, when Shakespeare uses Virgil, it is almost always in conjunction with Ovid, as if he sees Virgil best from an Ovidian perspective.

A good example of Shakespeare's method is the account of the fall of Troy in *Hamlet* 2. 2. 450–518, which, like many other versions written at this time, elaborates *Aeneid* 2 using *Metamorphoses* 13 (with a dose of Marlowe's *Dido, Queen of Carthage*). The two sources are divided sequentially. Beginning with Virgil's scene, the speech is focused on the figure of Pyrrhus, who has just killed Priam's remaining son and is about to slay Priam himself. The end switches to an Ovidian view from the margins rather than centre of power, showing the action through the eyes of a woman, Hecuba, who watches in helpless horror as her family are destroyed.

The lengthy speech momentarily stops the action and reflects on it. The general focus on father–son relations in *Aeneid* 2, and the centrality of the murder of a father, is obviously significant for Shakespeare's tragedy.[44] But the correspondences between set piece and main action are unclear. Is Pyrrhus, who is avenging the death of his father Achilles, supposed to be a role model for Hamlet? Or, as murderer of a father/king, does Pyrrhus stand for Claudius? Hecuba's relation to the central action is also ambiguous. She is usually interpreted as a model of appropriate grief who reflects Hamlet's horror at his father's death, and implicitly rebukes Gertrude for her lack of sorrow. However, her presence opens up more disturbing possibilities in the play, especially for Hamlet himself. The opening description, spoken by Hamlet, makes Pyrrhus a diabolical monster who is 'with blood of fathers, mothers, daughters, sons, | Baked and impasted' (2. 2. 458–9). Even as he strikes the blow that will win the war for the Greeks, Pyrrhus is dehumanized by the act of violence. In Ovid's continuation of the story as part of his retelling of the *Aeneid* in *Metamorphoses* 13–14, however, the consequences of violence for the victim are equally disturbing. Introduced as an innocent victim of war, Hecuba takes action when, in revenge for the killing of her last son by the Thracian king Polymestor, she tears the king's eyes out. Deeply sympathetic to her plight (he comments that 'illius Troasque suos hostesque Pelasgos, | illius fortuna deos quoque moverat omnes' ('Her sad fortune touched her own Trojans and her Grecian foes and all the gods as well') (13. 572–3)), Ovid still shows how the violence of revenge dehumanizes the victim too: in the end Hecuba becomes a barking bitch. Her story thus has a particular and chilling relevance for Hamlet, who is caught in his own revenge cycle, especially as the player's speech is often seen as the turning point that prompts him into action. What kind of action do the classics inspire here? The dual reference of Pyrrhus—pointing simultaneously to both Hamlet and Claudius—suggests that, in committing revenge, Hamlet is becoming the new perpetrator of violence and so a version of Claudius.

Ovid's description of Hecuba was both praised as a model for the creation of emotion, and censured as an example of rhetorical excess. Richard Rainholde's *The Foundation of Rhetorike* (1563) recommends as a school exercise the task of imagining 'What lamentable Oration Hecuba Queen of Troy might make, Troy being destroyed' (sig. 50^{v}).[45] Drummed into students' minds, Hecuba appears frequently in Elizabethan literature, most often to illustrate the tragic fall of the mighty. Shakespeare typically transforms this stock figure into a complex network of ideas that builds on Ovid's reworking of Virgil. In the 1595 epyllion, *The Rape of Lucrece*, written to continue the momentum of *Venus and Adonis* while showing that the epyllion could encompass a graver subject, Hecuba is a figure of sympathy for the raped Lucrece. Using as a model complaints from Ovid's other works, Shakespeare elaborates Ovid's succinct account in *Fasti* 2, in which Lucrece is surprisingly quiet. As well, he draws upon elements from Virgil's representation of the fall of Troy, especially in the description of the painting of the Trojan war, which the raped Lucrece contemplates at length (1366–1569). Moreover, as Lucrece stares at the images, she takes up the position of Aeneas who, in *Aeneid* 1. 453–93, gazes on his own history engraved on Juno's Carthaginian temple. Juxtaposing Virgil's hero and Ovid's heroine, Shakespeare makes evident their likeness as Roman icons. However, Lucrece's identification with the Trojan Hecuba (1447–98) conjoins these two characters associated with the restraint of the passions with one who gives in to them fiercely. Grieving over the mute image, Lucrece wants to make the Trojan woman speak, just as Shakespeare gives a voice to Ovid's silent Lucrece. The subtexts create a myth of generic metamorphoses, in which, as in other epyllia and in Marvell, Virgilian epic turns out to be Ovidian complaint.

Shakespeare's Lucrece is identified with another Ovidian heroine, Philomela (*Rape of Lucrece*, ll. 1079–80, 1128–9), who begins as an innocent victim and ends as a ruthless murderer. The three figures of Lucrece, Philomela, and Hecuba are linked also in the early *Titus Andronicus*, co-authored with George Peele, which develops an Ovidian pattern in which victims perpetuate the violence they have suffered.[46] As often noted, the play, like *Hamlet*, questions the influence of classical models; it seems a nightmare version of humanist education in which ancient authors make students savages, as combatants fight equally with allusions and knives.[47] The *Metamorphoses* plays a central role, appearing on stage both as a text (*Titus Andronicus*, 4. 1) and as the weapon with which the characters attack each other. Like competing Elizabethan authors, Titus and Tamora present rival versions of the story of Philomela, topping each other until the final gleefully macabre climax in which Titus feeds Tamora her sons 'bakèd in this pie' (5. 3. 59).[48] However, the opening sets this battle of Ovidian authors in a Virgilian frame of reference: Titus is 'surnamèd Pius' (1. 1. 23); he names his daughter Lavinia, and references to Dido abound in the first acts. If Spenser's Clarion is an Ovidian trapped in a Virgilian plot, Titus inversely believes he inhabits a Virgilian world, only to discover that he is in the *Metamorphoses*. But, from the beginning, the boundary between the two texts seems fluid, as Shakespeare treats Ovid's works as a group of connected episodes that comment not only on each other, but also on Virgil. In both Ovid and Shakespeare, Virgil's Lavinia, that silent and opaque figure, easily turns into Philomela, silenced completely. If Tamora literally eats her children, *pius* Titus does so symbolically, sacrificing his sons to the glory of Rome, slaying Mutius (1. 1) and finally killing Lavinia (5. 3). Tamora's complaint that Titus' sacrifice of her sons (which recalls Aeneas' slaying of hostages to avenge the death of Pallas) is 'cruel irreligious piety' (1. 1. 130) translates a favourite Ovidian paradox; in the *Metamorphoses*, Althaea, who murders her son to appease the shades of her brothers, is 'impietate pia' ('pious in impiety') (8. 477).[49] In Ovid, Roman piety, incarnated in Virgil's *pius* Aeneas, produces its opposite. The fragility of the boundary between antitheses is suggested in the play's identification of both Tamora and Lavinia, Goth and Roman, victor and victim, with Hecuba (1. 1. 135–41; 4. 1. 20–1), the suffering victim who becomes bestial. The re-establishment of Virgilian order at the end of the play, when Lucius becomes a new Aeneas (5. 3. 79–86), does not end an Ovidian nightmare but brings us back to its source to start the cycle over again. The play makes Virgil and Ovid part of a single literary family tree—though unfortunately one in which parents devour their children.

At the end of his career, however, Shakespeare draws on the relation between Virgil and Ovid to create a very different vision in *The Tempest*. The Virgilian elements, mostly drawn from *Aeneid* 1–4, have been long noted, and today are often interpreted in the light of Shakespeare's concern with colonization and empire.[50] There are a number of specific allusions: Ferdinand's greeting to Miranda, 'Most sure, the goddess' (*Tempest*, 1. 2. 423), echoes Aeneas' address to his disguised mother 'O dea certe' (*Aeneid*, 1. 328)—another popular passage that is reworked in many other Renaissance works; the description of Iris's wings in the masque (4. 1. 78–9) recalls *Aeneid* 4. 700; and Ariel's appearance as a harpy who snatches food from the conspirators (3. 3. 52) is based on *Aeneid*, 3. 225–8. As in *The Faerie Queene*, 1. 1, the opening storm scene invokes *Aeneid* 1. The early debate over 'widow Dido' (2. 1. 73–81) and Gonzalo's claim that 'This Tunis, sir, was Carthage' (2. 1. 82) makes it appear as if the action is being literally mapped on top of Virgil's plot. While the characters are very different, in some ways the development of Prospero through the play mirrors that of the allegorized Aeneas.[51]

However, as usual in Shakespeare, such Virgilian paradigms are presented through a story that, in its general mood, imagery, and focus on the author's creative powers, is highly Ovidian. Both Ovid and Shakespeare are fascinated by the artist's ability to make something out of nothing. When Hamlet puzzles over the fact that he is worked up 'And all for nothing, | For Hecuba!' (2. 2. 557–8), he recognizes the power that fiction has to become more real and substantial than the real world itself. Art re-creates the world; *The Winter's Tale* uses Ovid's story of the artist Pygmalion to imagine an art that can bring the dead back to life. In Prospero, who conjures up both the storm and the plot and who has traditionally been read as Shakespeare himself, Shakespeare looks back also to Ovid's habit of creating authorial doubles of himself as a means of meditating on his own artistry.[52] The final scene in which Prospero renounces his powers (5. 1. 33–57) is based on Medea's summoning of her powers in *Metamorphoses* 7. 192–219 (channelled partly through Golding's recent translation). Medea is an artist in whom Ovid is especially interested. He tells three versions of her story: in *Heroides* 12, in his lost play, *Medea*, as well as in *Metamorphoses* 7.[53] In Ovid, Medea's arts, like those the poet claims for himself at the end of his epic, conquer time and even death itself. But they also generate death and destruction. Beginning as a heroic rescuer who saves Jason from a savage death, she herself becomes a savage who (like Pyrrhus) kills fathers and even children, including (like Procne) her own.

The relation between Prospero and Medea is an ambiguous one: the allusion makes us consider likenesses while also stressing difference, as Prospero renounces the powers that Medea embraces, and so breaks from the revenge cycle to establish a new, less cannibalistic, family and dynasty, centred on the next generation of Miranda and Ferdinand. Moreover, in the end, the omnipotent artist who plotted the action and authors his own story turns out to be himself a mere actor, who steps forward and asks the audience's favour: 'Let your indulgence set me free' (Epilogue, l. 20). The author's power is limited; like *The Faerie Queene*, the play draws attention to the fact that stories exist in multiple versions. The opening debate over 'widow Dido' shows that there are different accounts of her story—even Virgil's was not definitive.

Milton

While Milton was familiar from an early age with a wide range of ancient authors who informed his thinking, Virgil and Ovid have central roles throughout his career, and are especially significant in his early development as a writer. His identification with Virgil is prominent in his first collection of *Poems* published in 1645. Many critics have noted how the *Poems* narrate the emergence of what Louis Martz described as 'the rising poet, the predestined bard' who sets out on a Virgilian career.[54] Virgil provides the motto for the volume (from *Eclogue* 7. 27–8) as well as many of the characters, themes, and images. Each half of Milton's *gemellus liber* ('double book') ('Ad Joannem Rousium', 1) opens and closes with a work that appears to mark stages in the development of a Virgilian poet. The first English poem is the 'Nativity Ode', which draws on Virgil's *Eclogue* 4 to celebrate not only the birth of Christ but Milton's own poetic beginning. The Latin section also opens with a poem that places the poet in the Virgilian sequence, as the topic of exile in *Elegia* 1 recalls *Eclogue* 1—though playfully, as Milton's pleasant exile from school makes poetry possible. Two Virgilian pastoral elegies, *Lycidas* and *Epitaphium Damonis*, bring each half to a close, and announce the poet's next move up the *rota* towards epic. From the start Milton seems a serious and ambitious poet who aspires to Virgilian authority.

Yet the presence of Ovid is equally displayed in both halves of the volume, pointing the young poet in a different direction. Milton seems familiar early on with the entire spectrum of Ovid's poetry. He is especially drawn to the exilic verse, which, even more than Virgil's *Eclogue* 1, provides him with models for his own rustication in the Latin *Elegia* 1, as well as for the 'exile' in Germany of his tutor Thomas Young in *Elegia* 4.[55] In the Latin elegies, there are many echoes also of Ovid's early erotic works, which suggest a neat correspondence between the two young poets. *Elegia* 5, which celebrates the coming of spring in lush images that link natural fertility and creativity, captures particularly well an Ovidian spirit of careless rapture. The presence of the hybrid Sylvanus, 'Semicaperque Deus, semideusque caper' ('a half-goat god and a half-god goat') (l. 122), adds an Ovidian touch, recalling *Ars Amatoria* 2. 24, *Metamorphoses* 14. 515, and *Fasti* 4. 752.[56] The English verse shows him struggling to transform such Ovidianisms into his emerging English voice. In the 1673 edition of these poems, Milton added a work that he claimed to have been his first poem in English, 'On the Death of a Fair Infant Dying of a Cough', written when he was 17. Drawing on Ovidian figures and images of metamorphosis, it is also indebted to rewritings of Ovid in allegories and epyllia. Particular echoes of Spenser and Shakespeare show Milton's early study of his greatest native predecessors' appropriation and transformation of Ovid.[57] While the 'Nativity Ode' announces Milton's birth as a Virgilian, it is pre-dated by a work that traces Milton's English career to Ovid and his English reception.

Like others of this period, Milton is interested in the relation between the two authors. This is especially evident in the Latin poetry, in which Milton sometimes uses a double allusion, in which he imitates phrases in which Ovid imitates Virgil. For example, when he notes in *Elegia* 6 that 'Carmen amat Bacchum, Carmina Bacchus amat' ('Song loves Bacchus; Bacchus loves songs') (l. 14) he looks back to *Fasti* 5. 345 ('Bacchus amat flores'), which in turn reworks *Georgics* 2. 113 ('Bacchus amat colles'). Elsewhere he combines an Ovidian line with a Virgilian one. I noted above that, in *Elegia* 5. 122, Milton includes the characteristically Ovidian figure of 'Semicaperque Deus, semideusque caper' ('a half-goat god and a half-god goat') (l. 122). However, the preceding line in the couplet, naming 'Sylvanusque suâ Cyparissi fronde revinctus' ('Sylvanus also, crowned with his own Cypress') (l. 121), recalls Virgil's *Georgics* 1. 20 ('et teneram ab radice ferens, Silvane, cupressum' ('and you, Silvanus, with a young uprooted cypress in thy hand')). The effect of the juxtaposition is to give a Virgilian character an Ovidian form; even more, it shows Milton's metamorphosis of Virgil's pastoral figure into Ovid's satyr. Creating a hybrid poetics that yokes together Virgil and Ovid in a single couplet, Milton shows the transmission and transformation of classical genres at work at the level of form.

A more complex thematic as well as formal combination of sources is central to Milton's *Mask Presented at Ludlow Castle*. Like other masques of the time, it draws heavily on both Virgil and Ovid, and is concerned with the relation between poetry and power. However, while masques traditionally celebrate the ruler, whose authority guarantees both social and cosmic order, the King has no role in the resolution of the plot of *A Mask*. Nor does the Earl of Bridgewater, for whom the work was written. The power to free the Lady comes entirely from figures associated with poetry itself: Sabrina and the Attendant Spirit. The longest piece in the 1645 volume, and a shift to a completely new genre, drama, *A Mask* shows Milton's most serious early thinking about the transformative power of the poet. The work is an encapsulation of the classical and English literary traditions, a retrospective on Milton's poetic progress so far, and a map for his future development. The masque genre can barely mask Milton's eagerness to get to this next stage of his career, and epic elements keep pushing the boundaries of the drama. The Lady is a version of the typical epic questor, whose journey is impeded by evil forces. She recalls Odysseus, who resisted Comus' mother Circe, Spenser's Guyon, and especially his Britomart, who is similarly on a path of chaste womanhood. Yet her journey is particularly like that of Aeneas, especially read allegorically as embodying the conquest of the passions through temperance. Like Aeneas, and unlike Odysseus, she is going not to an old home but to a new one: she leaves England for Wales in a journey that is both a story of personal growth and part of the expansion of empire.[58]

The focus on journeying suggests that, like the epyllia of Lodge and Weever, the masque is about the movement of classical sources to the new world, figured most explicitly as the coming of Comus to the wild wood. Milton had already drawn attention to the idea of *translatio* in an earlier masque, *Arcades*, in which classical nymphs are invited to abandon the old world and come to a new English Arcadia where 'A better soil shall give ye thanks' (l. 101). In *Comus*, transmission is imagined also in terms of familial succession. Both heroine and villain are introduced in terms of their lineage, as the Lady is the daughter of the Earl of Bridgewater (ll. 31–6), and Comus the son of Circe and Bacchus (ll. 46–57). They offer alternative genealogies to a young poet eager to position himself as a member of the best family. The Lady is aided by the Spenserian Sabrina, taken from the history of Britain in *The Faerie Queene* 2. 10, who is a descendant of the Trojans who settled in England. Introduced also through her family, as 'Virgin, daughter of *Locrine* | Sprung of old *Anchises* line' (ll. 922–3), Milton's Sabrina is part of the Virgilian *translatio*, and creates a prestigious literary line that stretches from Homer, through Virgil and Spenser, to Milton. Threatening the Lady's journey and chastity is the enchanting and seductive Comus. He comes from the sinister side of the family tree, which begins again with Homer, but continues through Ovid, with his many scenes of seduction and rape, and descends (temporally, morally, and aesthetically) through Ovid's witty but licentious heirs, most notably Shakespeare and the Caroline poets.[59]

Like the battle between Spenser's Clarion and Aragnoll, the conflict between the Lady and Comus suggests a moral and poetical incompatibility between Virgilian and Ovidian traditions. In the end the two main characters are separated: the Lady returns home safely to her parents, while the irrepressible Comus escapes. But, with these stark antitheses now out of the picture, Milton absorbs both Virgil and Ovid into the paradise to which the Attendant Spirit returns at the end of the play. Like Spenser's Garden of Adonis, Milton's garden leaves behind the Virgil of the allegorists and the Ovid of the love poets. At the same time, Milton also moves beyond Spenser and the Shakespeare of *Venus and Adonis*, as the Spirit imagines himself rising above a garden inhabited by Venus and Adonis. His goal is a higher paradise centred on a different couple who demonstrate that the reward for heroic questing can indeed be married love: Venus' son, Cupid, and his bride Psyche.

By placing Cupid above his mother, Milton elevates the next generation and new forms of Virgilianism and Ovidianism. The description of the happy couple anticipates the much more extended examination of married love in *Paradise Lost*, to which I want to turn briefly as a fitting end point for the development of Milton's poetics and the larger process of Englishing Virgil and Ovid. From Virgil, Milton gets his structure, especially the twelve-book version published in 1674, and the georgic mood of Eden. The wrath of Juno that propels Virgil's epic is turned into the wrath of Satan, and parallels link Aeneas to Satan, Adam, the Son, and even the narrator.[60] At the same time, the primary motive in Milton's poem is not wrath but love, and the work is filled with Ovidian figures, including Narcissus, Flora, Pomona, Deucalion, and Pyrrha.[61] While Satan especially is an Ovidian shapeshifter, whose final transformation in book 10 draws on that of Cadmus in *Metamorphoses* 4, mediated through Dante's *Inferno* 26, Ovidianism is not associated only with fallen characters. Eden is itself a place of metamorphosis and Ovidian sexuality and abundance. Like Spenser and other Renaissance epic writers, Milton needs to transform Virgilian epic through Ovidian desire. He sets at the centre of his epic, not an isolated hero, but a couple whose happy and explicitly sexual relationship, 'Imparadis't in one anothers arms' (*Paradise Lost*, 4. 506), embodies his idea of heaven. While the poem ends where Virgil's career began and Ovid's ended, with exile, the wandering hero is not alone on his journey. The exodus from paradise of Adam and Eve 'hand in hand' begins the *translatio* of not only Genesis but also Virgil and Ovid into the domestic heroism of the novel.

Notes

1. Heather James, *Shakespeare's Troy: Drama, Politics, and the Translation of Empire* (Cambridge, 1997), 30.
2. *The Complete Works of Christopher Marlowe*, ed. Roma Gill, 5 vols (Oxford, 1987–98), I. 35
3. See David Scott Wilson-Okamura, *Virgil in the Renaissance* (Cambridge, 2010), 50–6.
4. On the laureate author, see Richard Helgerson, *Self-Crowned Laureates: Spenser, Jonson, Milton, and the Literary System* (Berkeley and Los Angeles, 1983).
5. On the development of new 'georgic' values and poetics in the Renaissance and the eighteenth century, see Anthony Low, *The Georgic Revolution* (Princeton, 1985).
6. On the epyllion, see Lynn Enterline, Chapter 11, this volume; also William Keach, *Elizabethan Erotic Narratives: Irony and Pathos in the Ovidian Poetry of Shakespeare, Marlowe, and their Contemporaries* (New Brunswick, 1977); Clark Hulse, *Metamorphic Verse: The Elizabethan Minor Epic* (Princeton, 1981). For Ovid's impact on sixteenth-century English poetry, see Georgia Brown, *Redefining Elizabethan Literature* (Cambridge, 2004), 36–52; Raphael Lyne, *Ovid's Changing Worlds: English Metamorphoses 1567–1632* (Oxford, 2001).
7. See Heather James, 'Ovid in Renaissance English Literature', in Peter E. Knox (ed.), *A Companion to Ovid* (Oxford, 2009), 423–41; Jane Stevenson (Chapter 7, this volume) notes Isabella Whitney's relation to the *Heroides*.
8. See Helen Cooper, Chapter 9, this volume; Annabel Patterson, 'Pastoral versus Georgic: The Politics of Virgilian Quotation', in Barbara Kiefer Lewalski (ed.), *Renaissance Genres: Essays on Theory, History, and Interpretation* (Cambridge, MA, 1986), 241–67; Colin Burrow, 'Virgil in English Translation', and 'Virgils, from Dante to Milton', both in Charles Martindale (ed.), *The Cambridge Companion to Virgil* (Cambridge, 1997), 21–37, 79–90.
9. See esp. Syrithe Pugh's reading of Herrick in *Herrick, Fanshawe and the Politics of Intertextuality: Classical Literature and Seventeenth-Century Royalism* (Farnham, 2010), 21–38, 57–83.
10. See also David Wilson-Okamura, 'Errors about Ovid and Romance', *Spenser Studies*, 23 (2008), 215–34.
11. See also Wilson-Okamura, *Virgil in the Renaissance*, 204–6, 212–15; Peter Mack, *Elizabethan Rhetoric: Theory and Practice* (Cambridge, 2004), 44–5.
12. See Colin Burrow, 'English Renaissance Readers and the *Appendix Vergiliana*', *Proceedings of the Virgil Society*, 26 (2008), 1–16. As Burrow also notes, the acceptance of the *Appendix* as Virgil's early work means that the Virgilian career model may have appeared less linear and distinct to Renaissance readers than we often assume.
13. See also Wilson-Okamura, *Virgil in the Renaissance*, 227–47.
14. *The English Writings of Abraham Cowley*, ed. A. R. Waller, 2 vols (Cambridge, 1905), II.
15. See further Philip Hardie, *Ovid's Poetics of Illusion* (Cambridge, 2002), 97–105.
16. Roger Ascham, *The Scholemaster*, in *English Works*, ed. William Aldis Wright (Cambridge, 1904; repr. 1970), 268. See also Peter Mack, Chapter 2, this volume.

17. See Wilson-Okamura, *Virgil in the Renaissance*, 66–9, 204–5.
18. See Philip Hardie, 'The Speech of Pythagoras in Ovid *Metamorphoses* 15: Empedoclean *Epos*', *Classical Quarterly*, 45 (1995), 204–14 (208); also Richard F. Thomas's discussion of 'window reference', in *Reading Virgil and his Texts: Studies in Intertextuality* (Ann Arbor, 1999), 130–2.
19. See Keach, *Elizabethan Erotic Narratives*, 37–51, 162–88.
20. See the notes in *The Poems of Andrew Marvell*, ed. Nigel Smith (New Haven, 2006), 65–71.
21. On the allegorical tradition, see also Philip Hardie, Chapter 10, this volume.
22. See Lyne, *Ovid's Changing Worlds*, 146.
23. Andrew Hadfield, *Literature, Politics and National Identity* (Cambridge, 1994), pp. 177–8.
24. As Spenser would have known, for Ovid also, the roles of ruler and mistress are linked: Ovid's exilic verse rewrites his earlier erotic poetry, placing the ruler in the role of the distant and immovable lover.
25. See Richard McCabe, Chapter 25, this volume; Patrick Cheney, *Spenser's Famous Flight: A Renaissance Idea of a Literary Career* (Toronto, 1993); John Watkins, *The Specter of Dido: Spenser and Virgilian Epic* (New Haven, 1995).
26. See Syrithe Pugh, *Spenser and Ovid* (Aldershot, 2005); M. L. Stapleton, *Spenser's Ovidian Poetics* (Newark, DE 2009); Michael Holahan, '*Iamque opus exegi*: Ovid's Changes and Spenser's Brief Epic of Mutability', *English Literary Renaissance*, 6 (1976), 244–70.
27. Lyne, *Ovid's Changing Worlds*, 121; see also Theresa M. Krier, *Gazing on Secret Sights: Spenser, Classical Imitation, and the Decorums of Vision* (Ithaca, NY, 1990).
28. As also suggested by Wilson-Okamura, 'Errors about Ovid', 220–2.
29. The fact that he is a bug should have given him a clue to his fate, as Virgil is, of course, a source of much Renaissance insect imagery. Spenser translated the *Culex* (which also tells of insecticide), and the description of the bees in *Georgics* 4 is important for the didactic tradition.
30. Wilson-Okamura, *Virgil in the Renaissance*, 198–202.
31. Pugh, *Spenser and Ovid*, 145–9.
32. While the number of texts invoked in the episode has frustrated critics who want to identify one distinct source, the poetic plenitude mirrors the fertility of the garden; see esp. Jon Quitsland, *Spenser's Supreme Fiction: Platonic Natural Philosophy and* The Faerie Queene (Toronto, 2001), 184–90.
33. On the figure of Fama in Virgil and Ovid, see Philip Hardie, *Rumour and Renown: Studies in the History of Fama* (Cambridge, 2012), 106–12, 150–74.
34. See Pugh, *Spenser and Ovid*, 240–43.
35. See my discussion in Maggie Kilgour, *Milton and the Metamorphosis of Ovid* (Oxford, 2012), 184–96.
36. On the episode in Ovid, including its role in his exilic works, see Philip Hardie, *Ovid's Poetics of Illusion*, 272–82, 285–92; Garth Tissol, *The Face of Nature: Wit, Narrative, and Cosmic Origins in Ovid's* Metamorphoses (Princeton, 1997), 72–84. Colin Burrow notes the influence of this episode, which itself looks back to the descent into the underworld in *Aeneid* 6, on later thinking on imitation: '"Full of the maker's guile": Ovid on Imitating and on the Imitation of Ovid', in Philip Hardie, Alessandro Barchiesi, and Stephen Hinds (eds), *Ovidian Transformations: Essays on the* Metamorphoses *and its Reception* (Cambridge, 1999), 271–87.
37. Dante had used Virgil's episode similarly in *Inferno*, 13, where Virgil makes Dante repeat Aeneas' breaking of the tree's

branch saying that otherwise Dante, who thought the *Aeneid* pure fiction, would never have believed that this kind of metamorphosis was true: 'la cosa incredibile mi fece | indurlo ad ovra ch'a me stesso pesa' ('the incredible thing made me prompt him to a deed that grieves me') (13. 50–1). The episode becomes a set scene for thinking about relations to past sources, repeated in *Orlando furioso*, 6, where Ruggiero disregards the story of the arboreal Astolfo, and in *Gerusalemme liberate*, 13.

38. See Colin Burrow, Chapter 27, this volume, and Jonathan Bate, *Shakespeare and Ovid* (Oxford, 1994).
39. John W. Velz, 'The Ovidian Soliloquy in Shakespeare', *Shakespeare Studies*, 18 (1986), 1–24.
40. Francis Meres, *Palladis Tamia: Wits Treasury: Being the Second Part of Wits Common Wealth* (1598), Oo^{v}–Oo2^{r}. On the influence of Meres's comparison, see Charles Martindale, 'Shakespeare's Ovid, Ovid's Shakespeare: A Methodological Postscript', in A. B. Taylor (ed.), *Shakespeare's Ovid: The* Metamorphoses *in the Plays and Poems* (Cambridge, 2000), 198–215.
41. Cited from Margaret Tudeau-Clayton, *Jonson, Shakespeare and Early Modern Virgil* (Cambridge, 1998), 3. Tudeau-Clayton argues, therefore, that, in terms of his cultural role, Shakespeare should be seen as England's Virgil rather than its Ovid.
42. The most extensive examination is still that of Baldwin, who tries, not completely convincingly, to make a case also for the *Eclogues* and *Georgics*: T. W. Baldwin, *William Shakspere's Small Latine & Lesse Greeke*, 2 vols (Urbana, IL, 1944), 2. 456–96.
43. Charles Martindale, 'Shakespeare and Virgil', in Charles Martindale and A. B. Taylor (eds), *Shakespeare and the Classics* (Cambridge, 2004), 89–90.
44. Shakespeare's use of Virgil may be influenced by his close attention to Thomas Kyd's hit *The Spanish Tragedy*, which opens with a descent into the underworld that draws on *Aeneid* 6, and is concerned with the Virgilian themes of revenge, father–son relations, and the catastrophe of premature death.
45. See further Lizette I. Westney, 'Hecuba in Sixteenth-Century Literature', *College Language Association Journal*, 27/4 (1984), 436–59.
46. On the question of Shakespeare's collaboration with Peele, see Brian Vickers, *Shakespeare, Co-Author: A Historical Study of Five Collaborative Plays* (Oxford, 2002).
47. See Colin Burrow, Chapter 27, this volume; Bate, *Shakespeare and Ovid*, 104; Grace Starry West, 'Going By the Book: Classical Allusions in Shakespeare's *Titus Andronicus*', *Studies in Philology*, 79 (1982), 62–77; Vernon Guy Dickson, '"A pattern, precedent, and lively warrant": Emulation, Rhetoric, and Cruel Propriety in *Titus Andronicus*', *Renaissance Quarterly*, 62/2 (2009), 376–409.
48. The competition may also take place between the two co-authors of the play; it is generally believed that Peele wrote the opening of the play (1.1–2.2) as well as 4.1, setting in motion the Virgilian and Ovidian plots that Shakespeare then tops. Collaboration in this case may be itself a kind of Virgilian singing match.
49. Ovid's Procne also claims 'scelus est pietas in coniuge Tereo' ('piety is a crime to such a husband as Tereus') (6. 635); see also *Metamorphoses* 7. 339–40, 10. 321–3.
50. Donna B. Hamilton, *Virgil and* The Tempest: *The Politics of Imitation* (Columbus, 1990); Craig Kallendorf, *The Other Virgil: 'Pessimistic' Readings of the* Aeneid *in Early Modern Culture* (Oxford, 2007).
51. See Kallendorf, *The Other Virgil*, 107; both he and Tudeau-Clayton suggest also that Prospero recalls the medieval myth of Virgil as magician: Tudeau-Clayton, *Jonson, Shakespeare and Early Modern Virgil*, 4–10.

52. See, especially, Eleanor Leach, 'Ekphrasis and the Theme of Artistic Failure in Ovid's *Metamorphoses*', *Ramus*, 3 (1974), 102–42; Patricia J. Johnson, *Ovid before Exile: Art and Punishment in the* Metamorphoses (Madison, WI, 2008); and Joseph Solodow, *The World of Ovid's* Metamorphoses (Chapel Hill, NC, 1988).
53. See Stephen Hinds, 'Medea in Ovid: Scenes from the Life of an Intertextual Heroine', *Materiali e discussioni*, 30 (1993), 9–47.
54. Louis Martz, *Poet of Exile: A Study of Milton's Poetry* (New Haven, 1980), 59. See also John K. Hale, 'Milton's Self-Presentation in *Poems 1965*', *Milton Quarterly*, 25/2 (1991), 39; Stella Purce Revard, *Milton and the Tangles of Neaera's Hair: The Making of the 1645* Poems (Columbia, 1997).
55. See *A Variorum Commentary on the Poems of John Milton*, 5 vols (1970–5), vol. 1: *The Latin and Greek Poems*, ed. Douglas Bush, and *The Italian Poems*, ed. J. E. Shaw and A. Bartlett Giamatti, 47; Revard, *Milton and the Tangles of Neaera's Hair*, 222 n. 34; and Ralph Condee, 'The Latin Poetry of John Milton', in J. W. Binns (ed.), *The Latin Poetry of the English Poets* (1974), 58–92.
56. I discuss this Ovidian phrase further in Kilgour, *Milton and the Metamorphosis*, 38–9, 50.
57. See further Kilgour, *Milton and the Metamorphosis*, 54–74.
58. On the political subtext, and relation between England and Wales at the time, see Michael Wilding, *Dragon's Teeth: Literature in the English Revolution* (Oxford, 1987).
59. For the role of Shakespeare in *A Mask*, see especially Paul Stevens, *Imagination and the Presence of Shakespeare in* Paradise Lost (Madison, 1985); and Kilgour, *Milton and the Metamorphosis*, in which I note also the relation of Comus to Milton's contemporaries.
60. On the Virgilian elements, see especially Charles Martindale, *John Milton and the Transformation of Ancient Epic* (Totowa, NJ, 1986), 107–52; and Kallendorf, *The Other Virgil*, 138–69. I discuss Virgil's relevance for Milton's last works further in Maggie Kilgour, 'Heroic Contradictions: Samson and the Death of Turnus', *Texas Studies in Literature and Language*, 50/2 (2008), 201–34; 'Satan and the Wrath of Juno', *English Literary History*, 75 (2008), 653–71.
61. Richard J. DuRocher, *Milton and Ovid* (Ithaca, NY, 1985); Mandy Green, *Milton's Ovidian Eve* (Farnham, 2009); Kilgour, *Milton and the Metamorphosis*.

CHAPTER 24

Horace

VICTORIA MOUL

(with a contribution by Charles Martindale)

In the preface to his influential *Songes and Sonnettes*, published on the very verge of our period in 1557, Richard Tottel writes:

> That to have well written in verse, yea and in small parcels, deserveth great praise, the works of diverse Latins, Italians, and other, do prove sufficiently. That our tongue is able in that kind to do as praiseworthily as the rest, the honourable style of the noble Earl of Surrey, and the weightiness of the deep-witted Sir Thomas Wyatt the elder's verse, with several graces in sundry good English writers, do show abundantly. It resteth now (gentle reader) that thou think it not evil done, to publish, to the honour of the English tongue, and for profit of the studious of English eloquence, those works which the ungentle hoarders up of such treasure, have heretofore envied thee. And for this point (good reader) thine own profit and pleasure, in these presently, and in more hereafter, shall answer for my defence.

Tottel's miscellany, containing material reaching back to Chaucer, was revised and reprinted eight times between 1557 and 1587, and inaugurated a trend for similar collections, typically incorporating a mixture of translated, imitated, and original lyrics.[1] Like many prefaces to literary works in the period, this introductory statement is built around an Horatian tag: 'Thine own profit and pleasure' invokes Horace's well-known lines on the dual aims of the poet:

> omne tulit punctum qui miscuit utile dulci,
> lectorem delectando pariterque monendo.

> (The man who has blended what is useful with what is sweet has won every vote, by both delighting and instructing the reader.)
>
> (*Ars Poetica*, 343–4)

It is a commonplace of criticism that Renaissance literary theory was heavily indebted to Horace's *Ars Poetica*, and in particular to its blend of aesthetic and ethical concerns. But the Horatianism of Tottel's miscellany is not confined to the preface, nor to the *Ars Poetica*. *Songes and Sonnettes* contains a variety of poems indebted to Horace for their ethical flavour, including Wyatt's imitations of Horatian hexameter verse ('Of the Mean and Sure Estate', 'Mine Own John Poynz', and 'A Spending Hand'). The collection also includes four translations from the *Odes*, although none is marked as such—a version of *Odes* 4. 7 entitled 'All Worldly Pleasures Vade' and three separate translations of *Odes* 2. 10, titled, in a pragmatic summary of their ethical content, 'Praise of Mean and Constant Estate', 'Of the Golden Mean', and 'The Mean Estate is to be Accounted the Best'. The first of these is by Henry Howard, Earl of Surrey, although the printed text gives no indication of authorship. None of these translations is well known, and the two anonymous versions of *Odes* 2. 10, marked by dense alliteration, seem alien even in comparison to the Horatian imitations of Surrey and Wyatt. Nevertheless, this most influential of sixteenth-century anthologies offered the Elizabethan reader models for the imitation of Horace in both modes—the lyric and the hexameter.

In the history of Horatian reception, our period is often passed over, via a brief mention of Ben Jonson's strident Horatian self-fashioning or the verse satire of the 1590s, on the way from Ronsard and Wyatt to the large-scale and well-known appropriation of certain kinds of Horatian voice—especially in satire—after the Restoration.[2] Some Horatian aspects of even major poets of the period have been surprisingly overlooked. We tend not to think of Donne as Horatian, but his considerable collection of satires and epistles, closely related to those of Ben Jonson and many more minor contemporaries, are marked by a sustained intertextual conversation with Horace's hexameter poetry.[3] A guiding principle of this brief survey of Horatianism in the latter part of the sixteenth and first half of the seventeenth century is to attend not only to the obvious Horatian 'high points' of canonical English verse of the period—especially that of Jonson and Marvell—but also to neglected or less familiar aspects of the engagement with Horace, including neo-Latin odes, translations, and material published or circulated only in manuscript.[4]

Colin Burrow has shown how ethical choices—and the freedom to make and express them—are central to Wyatt's reworking of Horace in his verse epistles: poems dating from before our period, but included in Tottel's *Miscellany*.[5] This observation holds true for many of the Horatian authors of our period, although with varied inflections: in *Medicinable Morall* (1566), for instance, Thomas Drant emphasized Horace's moral authority by juxtaposing translations of the *Satires* (the first in English) and of the book of Jeremiah; whereas both Richard Fanshawe and John Polwhele achieved something similar by setting translations of Horace's odes alongside versions of the metrical portions of Boethius' *Consolation of Philosophy*.[6] The freedom in question in Donne's profoundly Horatian *Satyres* is principally moral and religious; while Jonson's satires and epistles, by contrast, are concerned primarily with artistic freedom and the possibilities of free speech.

Working within this tradition, an early piece of Fanshawe, found at the beginning of a notebook (now in the British Library) that also includes early versions of his translations from Horace, uses Horatian lyric form and conventions to explore the constraints of his life as a student of law:

> My quenched and discontinued Muse
> Her idle fires again renews,
> Which from my course do me withdraw,
> The thriving law.
> Oh! whether rapt in waking dreams,
> Through hills, through dales, by tumbling streams,
> (Places which sad fancy loves)
> And silent groves![7]

The metre here echoes the verse structure of Horace's Sapphic stanza; the conceit is related to that of *Odes* 4. 1 (the late return of love); and lines 5–6 are a version of the end of that poem, as the poet recounts his desire for the boy Ligurinus:

> nocturnis ego somniis
> iam captum teneo, iam volucrem sequor
> te per gramina Martii
> campi, te per aquas, dure, volubilis.
> (*Odes* 4. 1. 33–40)

(At night, in dreams, at one moment I hold you, caught, at another I follow you as you flit through the grasses of the Campus Martius, follow you, hard-hearted, through the rolling waters.)

Horace's Ligurinus, the boy who tempts the poet back from hexameter poetry to lyric, has become Fanshawe's Muse. The youthful Fanshawe uses the ageing Horace to express a dilemma of his own, to emotive effect, and Ligurinus' erotic charge is transferred to poetry itself: the lure of art that draws Fanshawe from the law.

Fanshawe's *Selected Poems of Horace, Prince of Lyrics* (1652) is rightly mentioned, alongside a cluster of similar seventeenth-century translation collections, in any account of the *Odes* in England.[8] But to discuss Fanshawe's Horatianism only in light of his translation would be to miss the profound Horatianism of 'My quench't and discontinu'd Muse', which is neither, precisely, an imitation nor a translation. Perhaps even less obvious is the evidence of Horatianism offered by manuscript entries of this sort:

> As a friend, friendlike: to a friend far absent
> I, thy friend, friendlike, to thee send a present
> That we friends friendlike may abide i'friendship
> Friendly together.

This rather clumsy stanza (the first of twelve) has, unsurprisingly, found no place in anthologies of any kind. The poem to which it belongs is neither a translation nor, exactly, an imitation, though we recognize a blend of Horatian elements alongside the unHoratian insistent repetition and alliteration. The theme—'letters mingle souls' as Donne has it—is one derived above all, in verse letters, from Horace's first book of *Epistles*.[9] The piece does in fact seem to have been written for a friend of the author, but it is composed in English sapphics, and subtitled 'Carmina Saphica'.[10] Both Fanshawe's accomplished ode and the punning near-doggerel of 'As a friend, friend-like' demonstrate the ease with which educated men of this period could engage with Horace, and the personal force to which this kind of 'Horatianism' could be put.[11]

We find a similar range of responses if we trace the fortunes of a single Horatian poem, in this case *Odes* 2. 10. The importance of this poem—which was perhaps exacerbated by the three translations in Tottel's volume—is derived from its combination of ethical advice, personal force, and a fertile suggestion of political metaphor. In the first stanza and the final lines of Horace's ode, the moral ideal of the 'golden mean' is explored with a metaphor taken from sailing:

> rectius vives, Licini, neque altum
> semper urgendo neque, dum procellas
> cautus horrescis, nimium premendo
>   litus iniquum.
>
> . . . . .
>
> rebus angustis animosus atque
> fortis appare; sapienter idem
> contrahes vento nimium secundo
>   turgida vela.
>
> (*Odes* 2. 10, 1–4 and 21–4)

(You can live correctly, Licinius, by neither always daring the deep nor—when you shudder in fear at storms—by clinging to the dangerous shore . . . In tight circumstances show courage and fortitude; but be wise and shorten your swelling sails in too brisk a wind.)

The addressee of the ode, Licinius, is advised to avoid both treacherous shallows and dangerous deeps; to be neither too bold nor too cautious; not to hope for excessive wealth and good fortune; and to remember that neither good fortune nor bad lasts indefinitely. Such a summary reduces to bland aphorism a poem that works partly by association with Horace's wide-ranging use of the imagery of sailing and of storm in other contexts—including, notably, for epic adventures and delays (e.g. *Odes* 1. 15, on the Trojan war), the trials of love (as in *Odes* 1. 5) and of politics (the 'ship of state' ode, 1. 14, widely read as a comment upon the Roman civil war).

Perhaps the best translation is that of Sir Philip Sidney ('You Better Sure Shall Live, Not Evermore'); among imitations, Richard Lovelace's poem 'Advice to my Best Brother', published posthumously in 1659, starts from *Odes* 2. 10 and tracks it closely, although Lovelace's expansive response to Horace turns every couple of Latin lines into the starting point for an English verse paragraph. The effect is somewhat like reading *Odes* 2. 10 rewritten as a verse epistle:

Frank, wil't live unhandsomely? trust not too far
Thy self to waving seas: for what thy star,
Calculated by sure event, must be,
Look in the glassy-epithet [the sea, here compared to a looking-glass], and see.
Yet settle here your rest, and take your state,
And in calm halcyon's nest ev'n build your fate;
Prithee lie down securely, Frank, and keep
With as much no noise the inconstant deep
As its inhabitants...

. . . . .

Nor be too confident, fix'd on the shore:
For even that too borrows from the store
Of her rich neighbour, since now wisest know
(And this to Galileo's judgement owe),
The palsy earth itself is every jot
As frail, inconstant, waving, as that blot
We lay upon the deep, that sometimes lies
Chang'd, you would think, with's bottoms properties;
But this eternal, strange Ixion's wheel
Of giddy earth ne'er whirling leaves to reel,
Till all things are inverted, till they are
Turn'd to that antick confus'd state they were.

('Advice to My Best Brother', 1–9; 17–30)

Writing to very different effect, Andrew Marvell incorporates an allusion to *Odes* 2. 10 into his description—and defence—of Cromwell's ascent to power in his 'The First Anniversary of the Government under His Highness the Lord Protector, 1655'. In a striking dramatization, Marvell's Cromwell remembers Horace's advice: 'don't cling to the dangerous shore when you shudder in fear at storms.' Horace's 'iniquum litus' becomes 'the fatal shore':

Therefore first growing to thyself a law,
Th' ambitious shrubs thou in just time didst awe.
So have I seen at sea, when whirling winds,
Hurry the bark, but more the seamen's minds,
Who with mistaken course salute the sand,
And threatening rocks misapprehend for land,
While baleful Tritons to the shipwreck guide,
And corposants [balls of lightning; St Elmo's fire] along the tackling slide,
The passengers all wearied out before,
Giddy, and wishing for the fatal shore,
Some lusty mate, who with more careful eye
Counted the hours, and every star did spy,
The helm does from the artless steersman strain,
And doubles back unto the safer main.
What though a while they grumble discontent,

> Saving himself, he does their loss prevent.
> 'Tis not a freedom, that where all command;
> Nor tyranny, where one does them withstand...[12]

Horace's advocacy of moderation is transformed, to rather uneasy effect, to praise Cromwell's moment of decisive intervention; and the appropriation of *Odes* 2. 10 depends for its force upon an association, too, with *Odes* 1. 14, the 'ship of state', a poem traditionally interpreted as a comment upon the Roman civil war and a hope for the future in its aftermath. *Odes* 1. 14 ends with a similar image of careful and endangered steersmanship, upon which the fate of the ship—and, by implication, the state—depends.

In Marvell's poem Cromwell steers the ship away from disaster; for some of his contemporaries, the protectorate itself constituted the 'fatal shore'. I quote the royalist John Polwhele's translation of the close of *Odes* 1. 14, one of a sequence of translations he made in 1649 expressing his grief over the regicide and his hopes for his country in the aftermath of the civil war:

> Distressed Galley, though wert late my fear,
> But now my joyful hope, and tender care.
> Veer, o veer ho! the straits and seas
> between aspiring Cyclades.[13]

The translation is followed by a piece in the same form entitled 'The Scope of the Allegory', which makes the political implications of the translation still more plain:

> Most miserable Romans, late my fear
> but now my joyful hope, and tender care,
> avoid great factions, boldly say
> this is my path, the good liege way.[14]

A 'liege man' denotes at this period specifically one who is loyal to the king. Polwhele's translation of *Odes* 1. 14 is of almost identical form and length to the Latin original, but he makes it the speech of a despairing Royalist. Both Marvell and Polwhele make sharply political Horace's advice to avoid stormy extremes, but they do so to quite different effect.

Reading Lovelace's response to *Odes* 2. 10, Herrick's sprawling verse epistle to his friend Mr Wickes (which begins from *Odes* 2. 14), or even 'As a friend, friendlike', we are struck by the easy slippage between—in Latin terms—lyric and 'hexameter' verse; between the sort of English poem we associate with the odes and that which we associate with the satires and epistles. This is partly a reflection of an early modern perception of Horace's achievement as one centred upon the ethical. 'The best master, both of virtue and wisdom', as Jonson put it; a version of Horace that tends to elide, rather than emphasize, the distinctions between genres. But it reflects, too, the Horatian tendency to express the same idea—albeit in a different style and tone—in a range of generic contexts. *Odes* 2. 10 advocates an ethical mean—'rectius vives, Licini'—that avoids either ostentation or degradation, and that takes neither good nor bad fortune too seriously. The opening of *Epistles* 1. 18, a poem almost as influential as *Odes* 2. 10, explores the same idea—'virtue is a mid-point between vices, equidistant from either' (1. 18. 9)—but applies it to friendship; or, rather, to the flexible range of relationships, everything from patron to dependant, described by the Latin term *amicitia*: 'si bene te novi, metues, liberrime Lolli, | scurrantis speciem praebere, professus amicum' ('If I know you well, Lollius, frankest of men, you'll be wary of seeming like a parasite, when you've professed yourself a friend') (1. 18. 1–2).

Much of *Epistles* 1 is concerned with the negotation of power and freedom between the poet and those to whom he writes, including younger writers, servants, and above all his social superiors and patrons. *Epistles* 1. 18 goes on to consider in particular the difficulties of maintaining good relations with a wealthy patron, without sacrificing the virtuous 'mid-point' between flattery and outright insult:

> You will never pry into your patron's secrets, and if one is entrusted to you, you will keep it, though you may be tormented by wine or anger. You will neither praise your own tastes, nor find fault with those of others; nor, when your friend wishes to go hunting, will you stay in to write poems. (1. 18. 37–40)

Like *Odes* 2. 10, *Epistles* 1. 18 is a popular focus of allusion for writers of our period, many of whom faced similar challenges in preserving their ethical and artistic autonomy in a climate of patronage. Sir John Roe seems to have had *Epistles* 1. 18, and especially lines 37–40, in mind in one of his surviving verse letters to his close friend Ben Jonson:

> Write, but touch not the more descending race
> Of Lords' houses, so settled in worth's place,
> As but themselves none think them usurpers.
> It is no fault in thee to suffer theirs.
> If the Queen masque, or King a-hunting go,
> Though all the court follow, let them. We know
> Like them in goodness that court ne'r will be,
> For that were virtue, and not flattery.[15]

Roe's epistle to Jonson, like that of Horace to Lollius, advises his friend on how best to handle his relationships to the great, and assures him that tactful silence on his part is appropriate behaviour, rather than any moral failing ('It is no fault in thee to suffer theirs').

In 'Ungathered Verse' 49 ('Censure not sharply then, but me advise') Jonson himself alludes to *Epistles* 1. 18. Jonson's poem incorporates a version of the opening of the Latin poem, and, as in Horace, describes the extremes (of both restraint and or licence) to be avoided in successful friendship. The phrase 'profess amity' translates the Latin 'professus amicum':

> Little know they, that profess amity,
> And seek to scant her comely liberty,
> How much they lame her in her property.

And less they know, who being free to use
That friendship which no chance but love did choose,
Will unto licence that fair leave abuse.
('Ungathered Verse' 49, ll. 12–17; Jonson, *Works*, 8. 421–2;
see also *The Underwood*, 37; Jonson, *Works*, 8. 189–90)

'Ungathered Verse' 49 is titled simply 'An Epistle to a Friend'; I think it is very likely that it was meant for Roe, and the content—which, although elliptical, seems to constitute Jonson's apology for losing his temper—may even have been meant as a reply to Roe's epistle. In one manuscript, a version of Jonson's poem immediately precedes copies of Roe's two epistles for Jonson, strengthening the likelihood that they are associated with one another.[16]

More than any other genre, Elizabethan and Jacobean verse epistles, of which Donne and Jonson were only the most accomplished authors, were the medium for exploring conflicts of freedom and obligation of this sort. Verse epistles in this specifically Horatian tradition—distinct, that is, from prose letters or from imaginary letters between historical or mythological lovers, in the tradition of Ovid's *Heroides*—have suffered in particular from a lack of nuanced critical attention, although manuscript miscellanies of the period are full of unpublished examples.[17]

Studies of late Elizabethan satire—of which Donne's *Satires* are perhaps the most accomplished example—generally distinguish clearly between satires and epistles in order to discount the latter. But, insofar as this material is Horatian, the distinction is porous. The Latin word *satira* appears only twice in Horace; his usual term, for satires and epistles alike, is *sermo*, or 'conversation': this is the sense in which Ben Jonson uses 'speech' in his poem 'A Speech According to *Horace*' (*The Underwood*, 44; *Works*, 8. 213–16). Elizabethan writers of verse satire show a similar tendency to combine and juxtapose these forms: Lodge's 1595 volume *A Fig for Momus*, for instance, includes eight epistles alongside the satires for which it is best known. A very large number of Jonson's longer poems combine moral or stylistic advice with some kind of personal address and are best understood more broadly as 'hexameter' poems in this tradition.[18] Even Jonson's *Poetaster*, which puts Horace on stage as a character in dramatized versions of his own satires, is in fact made up of a dense patchwork of translation, imitation, and allusion stretching across every Horatian genre.[19]

In many cases, the ethical advice found in epistles and the ethical condemnation typical of satires overlap in both theme and vocabulary. Donne's first satire, for instance, is above all a witty, and even rather tender, exploration of the conflicting attractions of studious retirement and worldly adventure in a cityscape marked by lust and greed, with poetry itself occupying a noticeably liminal position:

Here [in the study] gathering chroniclers, and by them stand
Giddy fantastic poets of each land.
Shall I leave all this constant company,
And follow headlong, wild uncertain thee?
('Satire 1', ll. 9–12)

There is a joke here: 'giddy fantastic poets' can hardly constitute a 'constant company'. In fact, the speaker is surrounded by 'giddiness', not least that of his own indecision and the dense tumbling of the verse itself. The wayward 'motley humorist' of Donne's poem achieves a closing moment of Horatian constancy only in disgrace:

> He quarrelled, fought, bled; and turned out of door
> Directly came to me hanging the head,
> And constantly a while must keep his bed.
> (ll. 110–12, final lines of the poem)

Donne's *Satyres* are indebted to Horace in particular—*Satires* 1. 9 stands behind both his first and his fourth satires. But the choice between a kind of Stoic retirement and the restless wandering of ambition is one that animates, too, his equally Horatian epistles. Donne's verse letter 'To Mr Roland Woodward', for instance, begins by announcing—in a version of *Epistles* 1. 1—the author's transition from lighter genres ('love-song weeds' and 'Satyrique thorns' (l. 4)) to the serious concerns of ethics and religion. The conclusion of the poem employs Horatian vocabulary close to that found in *Satyres* 1:

> So works retiredness in us. To roam
> Giddily, and be everywhere, but at home,
> Such freedom doth a banishment become.
> ('To Mr Roland Woodward', ll. 28–30)

This is a version of the end of *Epistles* 1. 11:

> Those who rush across the sea change the weather, not their hearts. Busy idleness exhausts us: we seek the good life in ships and carriages. But what you seek is here—or it's Ulubrae—if only your balanced mind does not desert you.
> (Horace, *Epistles* 1. 11. 26–30)

The ethical message at the heart of these poems—the critique of 'giddiness' found even in Marvell's version of the Horatian ship from *Odes* 2. 10 ('Giddy, and wishing for the fatal shore')—is common to both satires and epistles. Whether addressing an imaginary audience or interlocutor in a satire, or a real friend or contemporary in an epistle, early modern English poets, like Horace, were concerned in both cases with potential conflict between social and moral demands:

> Believe me Sir, in my youths giddiest days,
> When to be like the court, was a play's praise,
> Plays were not so like courts, as courts are like plays.
> (Donne, 'To Sir Henry Wotton', ll. 19–21)

Satiric disapproval or epistolary advice are not, however, the only modes of engagement that Horace offers. Marvell's 'The First Anniversary'—mentioned above for its memorable adaption of the Horatian ship from *Odes* 2. 10 and 1. 14—sets the foolish giddy passengers as only a passing foil to the assurance of the 'lusty mate' who saves all on board (apparently rather against their will). Although far from satiric in effect, this remarkable poem shares many of its qualities with the best verse satires of the period, including considerable length (at 402 lines), metaphorical energy, and rhetorical force. It incorporates elements of narrative, but not to a sufficient extent to suggest epic or epyllion; it has a cumulative argumentative force, but proceeds by a succession of indirect steps and tangentially related ideas, including long similes and the narration of related myths (of Amphion, ll. 49–66; of Gideon, ll. 249–56). Many of the transitions from one section to another are marked by epigrammatic gnomic remarks ('All other matter yields, and may be ruled; | But who the minds of stubborn men can build?' (ll. 77–8)). We find, too, a vivid use of imagery and metaphor, including a remarkable negative image of the decline of man in the opening lines—a marked contrast to the celebration of Cromwell that follows. But, above all, this is a poem of sustained praise—sometimes of an explicitly Horatian form (ll. 167–74, for instance, list Cromwell's virtues in a form derived from the opening of *Odes* 3. 3). Despite its considerable length, this combination of features associates it not with satire or epistle but with the major panegyric odes of Horace's third and fourth books (and, indeed, with Pindar, who stands behind Horace's achievement). In this, it has much in common with Marvell's earlier poem 'An Horatian Ode upon Cromwell's Return from Ireland', dating from June–July 1650.

This, the most famous early modern lyric inspired by Horace, is also the most perplexing and elusive.[20] On the occasion of Cromwell's homecoming from his now notorious Irish victories, the Ode looks back to his rise to pre-eminence among his parliamentary colleagues, the regicide, and creation of the Republic, and forwards to the expected campaign against the Scots. The professed model is the lyric Horace, but the poem is packed more generally with Roman images, ideas, terminology, and allusions. Imitations of Horace are two a penny in the period, but it is highly unusual to have 'Horatian' in the title in this way (though some poems with Horatian forebears indicate the particular poem or poems imitated), but a sense of how odd the title is has been lost through familiarity; scholars have offered little in the way of convincing explanation (the effect seems a distancing, an increased self-consciousness, even a faint flavour of irony, as if the poem were placed in 'scare quotes'). By foregrounding one source, Marvell conceals others ('A Machiavellian Ode'? 'A Lucanian Ode'?[21]). In the twentieth century the Ode became something of a critical battleground in disputes about poetic ambiguity and irony and about how poetry works, disputes in which the complex classical presences necessarily played their part. In 1946 Cleanth Brooks published his influential New Critical reading of the Ode, which alleged irony at Cromwell's expense, but was arguably guilty of complacent liberalism and a distaste for politics; it received a historicist reply from Douglas Bush in 1952.[22] The Ode has been read as supporting Cromwell and the Republic, or Charles and monarchy, as vacillating between the two, or just sitting on the fence; today it is most often seen as an endorsement of apocalyptic Protestant imperialism, but doubtless the whirligig of time will soon again bring in his revenges.[23] It is puzzling that the poem should have been published first during the Restoration (1681, but then immediately cancelled from most copies[24]). Historical and biographical data external to the Ode cannot resolve the issues about the poet's precise political allegiance (there is evidence that the Ode was known in Royalist circles, and a few months later, in 'Tom May's Death', Marvell—if indeed he is the author[25]—ventriloquized the Royalist Ben Jonson in satiric mockery of the Republican translator of Lucan's *Pharsalia*). But, if there is dubiety, the cool, detached style, and unruffled surface, of the poem, what T. S. Eliot in his classic essay on Marvell called his 'bright, hard precision',[26] scarcely suggest significant anxiety or perturbation.

Title aside, the elements from Horace are not hard to locate. The metre (two tetrameters followed by two trimeters) had previously been used by Sir Richard Fanshawe for versions of Horace's Odes and serves well to suggest the weight of Alcaics (though the snap of the rhyme introduces a neatness that is more Marvellian than Horatian); Fanshawe's Horace had not yet been published but Marvell could have seen the poems in manuscript.[27] The opening stanzas recall the Iccius Ode (1. 29) where Horace twits a friend for exchanging Socratic books for Spanish breastplates to go on a lucrative military expedition; Marvell captures the concreteness of Horace's style and his tendency to argue in images, not abstractly. The Ode adheres to a lyric subgenre (*prosphonetikon* in the terminology of the rhetoricians), in which the poet praises a general returning victorious from a campaign. Horatian examples include 3.14 and 4.4, the latter in particular being a model for major aspects of both 'An Horatian Ode' and 'The First Anniversary'.[28] But arguably Marvell's principal Horatian model is the so-called 'Cleopatra Ode' (1. 37) celebrating the battle of Actium and its aftermath, though Cleopatra is never named, simply termed, in sinister gendered opposition to the victorious Octavian, *regina*, 'queen'. Horace likes to begin an Ode with a translation or motto taken from one of his Greek predecessors; so Marvell's 'now' (l. 2), acting as a signal, translates Horace's opening 'nunc' ('now we must drink') and ''tis time' (l. 5) his 'tempus erat'. The hunting imagery was probably suggested by Horace's simile of hawk and doves. But, more importantly, the memorable lines describing Charles' execution (ll. 53–64) reproduce the turn in Horace's poem whereby abuse of Cleopatra gives place to a measure of admiration for her Stoical courage in defeat. There is no undue pathos, but Charles shows dignity at his execution, and history becomes a stage where great deeds are done and fine words spoken. Both poets correctly identify a historical turning point (in Rome from Republic to one-man rule, in England the reverse) and oppose two principal figures involved in it, in the process turning history into a sort of resonant poetic myth. Early modern panegyrics tended to undue extravagance, like Marvell's own 'First Anniversary'; Horace provided him with a more controlled, measured, even prosaic classical mode (good examples are Odes 2.1 and 4.9). And in all this there is a measure of ideological revision. The Odes themselves, various in tone and subject matter, reveal a tension between a drive to sublimity and classical stature, and a preference, in the manner of Callimachus, for the small-scale, arty, and refined. Horace, usually associated, especially by Royalist poets, with retirement and quietude, is reclaimed in the Ode for the poetry of political action (Horace's gendered contrast between Octavian and Cleopatra is reapplied to Republicanism and monarchy).

The Horatian elements in the Ode are part of a wider *color Romanus*. Marvell is usually termed a 'Metaphysical' poet, but it is equally plausible to see him, like his friend Milton, as a classicist.[29] Like Milton's, his world is radically bilingual. We have two pairs of poems (*Ros*, 'On a Drop of Dew'; *Hortus*, 'The Garden') where scholars are not sure which is the 'original', which the 'translation', and where each pair tests the differences as well as the compatibilities between Latin and English. Marvell, like Milton, loves translingual puns. In 'The Garden' (another poem strongly indebted to the lyric Horace, poet of the Sabine farm) the Ovidian metamorphoses play on the fact that in Latin *ut* clauses with the subjunctive can express purpose or result: 'Apollo hunted Daphne so, | Only that she might laurel grow' (ll. 29-30; *ut fieret laurus*). In the Ode Charles's courageous testing of the axe ('But with his keener eye | The axe's edge did try' (ll. 59–60)) exploits the double meaning of the noun *acies* in Latin, 'keen eyesight' as well as 'sharp edge of a weapon'. *Pictus* is Latin for 'painted' or 'tattooed', but also 'deceptive', 'vain', a play activated in the lines on the Scots ('The Pict no shelter now shall find | Within his parti-coloured mind' (ll. 105–6)), where 'parti-coloured' describes persons united in a cause while also alluding to the colours of the tartan and the deviousness of the partisan. These puns and wordplays can be seen as 'Horatian'. But Marvell's classicism is of a special kind, not quite the mainstream inheritance of classical 'equipoise' in the manner of Ben Jonson, 'a balance and proportion of tones', for which Eliot sought to claim him. We might call it rather that form of mannerism, by which the classicism takes a partly unclassical turn to the bizarre. In common with earlier early modern poets Marvell imitated classical models, but he did so in ways that are paradoxical or involve an unusual twist or an idiosyncratic use of genre: gardens that both are and are not utopias; pastoral in which mowers replace shepherds and where there is a surprising element of violence ('For Death thou art a mower too'); an increasingly febrile *carpe diem* poem 'To his Coy Mistress' deriving from Catullus and Horace, in which there are strange and again violent pressures just offstage; and in the Ode a panegyric that has also been read as an attack. The protagonist of 'Damon the Mower' sees himself reflected in a scythe, therefore subject to distortion ('Nor am I so deformed to sight, | If in my scythe I lookèd right: | In which I see my picture done, | As in a crescent moon the sun' (ll. 57–60)), where in his classical models, Virgil and Theocritus, the reflection is in water; since reflection is a possible figure for imitating, associated with the myth of Narcissus, the passage may suggest a metapoetic reading acknowledging the mannerist twist. The almost 'pat' surface of Marvell's verse—he is perhaps the supreme English master of the short line—is at odds with the never-quite-fathomable or not fully articulated possibilities that lie, or may lie, beneath.[30] The Ode's melding of ancient and modern, and its deployment of divergent authorities, chiefly Horace supporter of Caesar Augustus the first emperor and the extravagantly Republican Lucan, create a two-way traffic of signification, in which—as in translation—a complete fit is never possible and where consequently there are constant slippages. So first Charles and then Cromwell are figured as Caesar (ll. 23, 101). Cromwell's velocity and generalship align him with Julius Caesar the energetic mould-breaker in the *Pharsalia* who, however, is the villain of Lucan's poem for subverting, not sustaining, the Republic. And for Marvell is Augustus the benign father of his people as in Horace, or the tyrant and destroyer of liberty as in Tacitus and Lucan ('cum domino pax ista venit' ('with a master comes that peace') (*Pharsalia* 1. 670))? The classical framework occludes some contemporary issues: we read of 'angry heaven's flame', 'fate', 'the gods' (ll. 26, 37, 61), but not of God (*pace* some scholars, Cromwell can hardly be holding his erect sword by the blade to make a sign of the Cross at the poem's end), and this allows a world, almost unspeakable in Christian terms, in which power might be self-legitimating and God might care nothing for 'ancient rights' (l. 38), or even for virtue. The cool, almost toneless surface in which there is no protest or compassion is a world away from such engaged political lyrics as Milton's Sonnet 'On the late Massacre in Piedmont' or Yeats' 'Easter, 1916'. 'The Horatian Ode' is hard to love but impossible not to admire; it may even be the finest political poem in the language. In the end we may decide that the Ode is as much, or more, unHoratian than Horatian (it is, for example, considerably more intellectual and analytic), but without Horace Marvell could never have conceived it.

Abraham Cowley, another careful student of Jonson's Horace, uses another late Horatian ode, *Odes* 4. 2, to celebrate not Cromwell, but the Restoration:

> Aureus portis Aries superne
> Exit auratis quadriformis Anni,
> Verque formosum radiante portat
> (Plaudite) dorso.
> Verque dum procedit (Io Triumphe!)
> Floreo procedit (Io!) Triumpho,
> Ferculum primum venio superbae
> Nobile pompae.

(The Golden Ram on high leaves via the golden gates of the four-part year, and bears the beautiful spring on his glowing back (applaud!). And while the spring comes on (Io triumph!), comes on (Io!) with flowery triumph, I come, the first noble offering of the proud procession.)

('Viola', ll. 1–8)[31]

The second stanza here is a close imitation of Horace, *Odes* 4. 2. 49–52, except that the celebration in Rome of Augustus' military triumphs abroad is here transferred to the Violet, the first of a procession of flowers, celebrated for their medicinal uses, who have returned to England in triumph following the Restoration of Charles II in 1660:[32]

> terque, dum procedis, io Triumphe,
> non semel dicemus, io Triumphe,

civitas omnis, dabimusque divis
tura benignis.
(*Odes* 4. 2. 49–52)

(And as you lead the way, the entire state shall cry, 'io Triumph!', three times, not just once; and we shall offer incense to the kindly gods.)

For both Cowley and Marvell, the grand panegyric odes of book 4 offer a model not only of substantial—and poetically ambitious—praise; but also of a nuanced freedom of perspective. The glimpses of royal power as seen from the perspective of the conquered flatter Cromwell as they do Augustus—since it is more impressive to have defeated an eloquent and formidable opponent than a mere barbarian—but they also leave room for humour or uncertainty: Marvell's evasive tone is widely remarked, and Cowley's poem suggests ultimately that the medicinal qualities of everyday plants are a greater 'victory' than that of Actium.

Conclusion

Any account in the twenty-first century of Horatianism in English literature can be only partial at best—not least because much primary research remains to be done. But even a brief survey suggests the range and depth of interaction with Horace to be found across genres, and in a variety of contexts. For all that variety, the Horatianism that emerges is remarkably cohesive: a poetic mode concerned more with (male) friendship than with romantic love; rooted—even at its lightest—in moral seriousness; very often politically inflected (even when marked by retreat); and concerned above all with an autonomy of expression, whether political, religious, or artistic. That version of Horace was, undoubtedly, greatly influenced by a handful of major authors, Wyatt, Donne, and Jonson chief among them; but it was a source of inspiration, expression, and even comfort for a host of more minor or now unfashionable poets, from Abraham Cowley and Richard Lovelace to John Roe and John Polwhele, whose work demonstrates their love and knowledge of the great English imitators of Horace as much as of Horace himself—a group who found, in Horace and in each other, something of that combined profit and pleasure with which we began.

Notes

1. Examples in the subsequent decades include Timothy Kendall's *Flowres of Epigrammes* (1577), *The Phoenix Next* (1593), and *Englands Helicon* (1600). For a fine introduction to the role of translation in these collections, see Joshua Scodel, 'Lyric', in Gordon Braden, Robert Cummings, and Stuart Gillespie (eds), *The Oxford History of Literary Translation in English: Volume 2: 1550–1600* (Oxford, 2011), 212–47.
2. Essays that cover more than one author of our period include: Joanna Martindale,

'The Best Master of Virtue and Wisdom: The Horace of Ben Jonson and his Heirs', in Charles Martindale and David Hopkins (eds), *Horace Made New: Horatian Influences on British Writing from the Renaissance to the Twentiethy Century* (Cambridge, 1993), 50–85; Michael J. McGann, 'The Reception of Horace in the Renaissance', in S. J. Harrison (ed.), *The Cambridge Companion to Horace* (Cambridge, 2007), 305–17; Glenn W. Most, 'Horatian and Pindaric Lyric in England', in Ernst A. Schmidt (ed.), *Zeitgenosse Horaz: Der Dichter und seine Leser seit zwei Jahrtausenden* (Tübingen, 1996), 117–52. On translations, see Robert M. Ogilvie, 'Translations of Horace in the 17th and 18th Centuries', in Walther Killy (ed.), *Geschichte des Textverständnisses am Beispiel von Pindar und Horaz*, Wolfenbütteler Forschungen 12 (Munich, 1981), 71–80. On Marvell, see A. D. Nuttall, 'Marvell and Horace: Colour and Translucency', in Martindale and Hopkins (eds), *Horace Made New*, 86–102. On Jonson, see Victoria Moul, *Jonson, Horace and the Classical Tradition* (Cambridge, 2006), and Sean Keilen, Chapter 28, this volume. David Money, 'The Reception of Horace in the Seventeenth and Eighteenth Centuries', in Harrison, *The Cambridge Companion to Horace*, 318–33, is especially strong on eighteenth-century material.

3. See also William Fitzgerald, Chapter 12, this volume.
4. Neo-Latin Horatian (and Pindaric) odes are found very widely both in manuscript sources and in printed Latin verse of the period, and are often associated closely with English versions—for example, Marvell's 'Garden', 'Hortus', and his early Latin 'parody' of *Odes* 1. 2; Cowley's fine ode 'Quid Relinquendos, Moriture, Nummos', the English version of which is published as part of his essay on 'The Shortness of Life and the Uncertainty of Riches', in Abraham Cowley, *The Works of Mr Abraham Cowley, Consisting of Those which were Formerly Printed: And Those which he Design'd for the Press* (1668), 138–9.
5. Colin Burrow, 'Horace at Home and Abroad: Wyatt and Sixteenth-Century Horatianism', in Martindale and Hopkins, *Horace Made New*, 27–49. See also Catherine Bates, '"A mild admonisher": Sir Thomas Wyatt and Sixteenth-Century Satire', *Huntington Library Quarterly*, 56 (1993), 243–58.
6. John Polwhele's translations of Horace and Boethius have not been published aside from some extracts published here and in Moul, *Jonson, Horace and the Classical Tradition*. They are to be found in Bodleian MS Eng. poet. f.16.
7. Sir Richard Fanshawe, *The Poems and Translations of Sir Richard Fanshawe: Volume 1*, ed. Peter Davidson (Oxford, 1997), 37–8. See also BL MS Add 15228, 30^{r-v}.
8. John Ashmore, *Certain Selected Odes of Horace* (1621); Thomas Hawkins, *Odes of Horace: The Best of Lyrick Poets* (1625); Henry Rider, *All the Odes and Epodes* (1638); John Smith, *The Lyrick Poet* (1649; includes some satires and epistles); *All Horace his Lyrics* (1653) (anonymous); Sir Richard Fanshawe, *Selected Poems of Horace, Prince of Lyrics* (1652, includes some satires and epistles).
9. On this tradition of letters as conversation between absent friends, see William Fitzgerald, Chapter 12, this volume.
10. It is titled 'Jacobus Res[hou]lde Amico suo T. M.'. The manuscript is Bodleian MS Rawlinson poet 85, fos 53^{r}–54^{v}. The notebook includes a good deal of Latin verse as well as English poetry, various topical speeches and libels, a translation of the first of Ovid's *Amores*, and two examples of English hexameters. It is undated, but of the late sixteenth century,

including several poems and songs found printed in verse collections of the period.

11. Better-known examples of this kind of Horatian response include the many odes addressed to Ben Jonson by Cavalier poets (including examples by Herrick, Carew, and Feltham) and Herrick's much anthologized long poem to Mr Wickes, which begins with an expansive version of *Odes* 2. 14 but incorporates allusions to a wide range of other Horatian odes ('His age, dedicated to his peculiar friend, M. John Wickes, under the name of Posthumus').
12. 'The First Anniversary', ll. 263–80, in *The Poems and Letters of Andrew Marvell*, ed. M. H. Margoliouth, 2 vols (Oxford, 1971). This allusion to *Odes* 2. 10 is discussed briefly but effectively by Joanna Martindale, 'The Best Master of Virtue and Wisdom', in Martindale and Hopkins, *Horace Made New*, 50–85.
13. *Odes* 1. 14. 15–20, in Bodleian MS English poet f. 16, 51[v]. It is followed by a version of *Epodes* 7 and 16, on the Roman civil war, in a way that stresses their application to the English political situation. For further discussion, see Moul, *Jonson, Horace and the Classical Tradition*, 198–202.
14. Bodleian MS English poet f. 16, 52[r].
15. 'To Ben. Johnson, 6 Jan. 1603', ll. 3–8, printed along with eight other poems attributed to Roe, three of them verse epistles, in Appendix B of John Donne, *Poetical Works*, ed. Sir Herbert Grierson, 8 vols (New York, 1967), 1. 371–86. John Roe was the eldest son of William Roe of Higham Hill in Essex; he inherited the estate of Higham-Bensted at Walthamstow upon his father's death in 1596, and was probably knighted in 1603. He died, allegedly in Jonson's arms, around 1606. See Alvaro Ribeiro, 'Sir John Roe: Ben Jonson's Friend', *Review of English Studies*, 24 (1973), 153–64.
16. Bodleian MS Rawlinson Poetry 31. This manuscript (and a related one, BL Harley 4064) also preserves an otherwise unrecorded translation of the latter part of *Epistles* 1. 18, in which Italian placenames are replaced by 'Low-Layton' and 'Hackney brook'—both close to the Roe family estate in Essex. This interesting translation may well be the work of Roe himself.
17. Several older articles remain useful, including: Clay Hunt, 'The Elizabethan Background of Neo-Classic Polite Verse', *ELH*, 8 (1941), 263–304; Jay Arnold Levine, 'The Status of the Verse Epistle before Pope', *Studies in Philology*, 59 (1962), 659–82; and D. J. Palmer, 'The Verse Epistle', in M. Bradbury and D. Palmer (eds), *Metaphysical Poetry* (New York, 1970), 73–99.
18. 'The generic ambivalence of epistle and satire derives ultimately from the satires of Horace' (Claudio Guillén, 'Notes toward the Study of the Renaissance Letter', in Barbara K. Lewalski (ed.), *Renaissance Genres: Essays on Theory, History, and Interpretation* (Cambridge, MA., 1976), 70–101).
19. Discussed in Moul, *Jonson, Horace and the Classical Tradition*, 135–72.
20. The following discussion of 'An Horatian Ode' (pp. 548–51) is by Charles Martindale, while Victoria Moul was in ill health. The poem is also discussed from other angles by Roland Greene, Chapter 14, this volume.
21. The relevant sources and analogues are assembled in Nigel Smith's Longman Annotated English Poets edition and commentary, *The Poems of Andrew Marvell* (2003). Machiavelli: Cromwell corresponds to the *nuovo principe*, who displays *virtù* and *industria* and seizes the occasion; the theme reaches its climax when Cromwell 'wove a net' (l. 50) tricking Charles into fleeing to the Isle

of Wight (a claim doubted by historians). Lucan: various passages are pressed into service, chief among them the lightning simile (ll. 21–4); Marvell was doubtless familiar with the Latin text, but also used May's translation. For further discussion of the Lucanian model, see Philip Hardie, Chapter 8d, this volume. Pindar, the lyric poet of the sublime, is sometimes invoked as another analogue, but of course for a number of his grander odes Horace himself imitates Pindar. There is also a prevailing Romanitas throughout; for example, the 'bleeding head' (l. 69) foretelling that Rome will be the capital (*caput*) of empire comes from Livy and Pliny the Elder.

22. This classic exchange is reprinted in John Carey (ed.), *Andrew Marvell: A Critical Anthology* (Harmondsworth, 1969), 179–210.

23. Significant discussions include: Anthony Miller, '"The English Hunter": Marvell's Cromwell and Tacitus' Agricola', *Classical and Modern Literature*, 20 (2000), 67–72; J. M. Newton, 'What Do We Know About Andrew Marvell?', *Cambridge Quarterly*, 6 (1972–3), 33–42, 125–43 (esp. 125–33); David Norbrook, *Writing the English Republic: Poetry, Rhetoric, and Politics 1627–1660* (Cambridge, 1999), 245–71; R. H. Syfret, 'Marvell's "Horatian Ode"', *Review of English Studies*, 12 (1961), 160–72 (on the interplay between Horace and Lucan); A. J. A. Wilson, 'An Horatian Ode on Cromwell's Return from Ireland: The Thread of the Poem and its Use of Classical Allusion', *Critical Quarterly*, 11 (1969), 325–41; Blair Worden, 'Andrew Marvell, Oliver Cromwell, and the Horatian Ode', in Kevin Sharpe and Steven N. Zwicker (eds), *Politics of Discourse: The Literature and History of Seventeenth-Century England* (Berkeley and Los Angeles, 1987), 147–80. See also the bibliography in Smith's edition.

24. For a possible explanation, see Paul Hammond, *The Making of Restoration Poetry* (Cambridge, 2006), 21–4.

25. See the concise discussion in Smith's edition.

26. This influential essay, entitled 'Andrew Marvell', was first published in the *TLS*, 31 March 1921, and has been often reprinted, e.g. in *Selected Essays: 1917–32* (1932); the quotations are on pp. 285 and 288.

27. See William Simeone, 'A Probable Antecedent of Marvell's Horation Ode', *Notes and Queries*, 197 (1952), 317–18; Barbara Everett, 'The Shooting of the Bears: Poetry and Politics in Andrew Marvell', in R. L. Brett (ed.), *Andrew Marvell: Essays on the Tercentenary of his Death* (Oxford, 1979), 74–7.

28. The final third of Horace *Odes* 4. 4 (50–72) is given over to the speech of Hannibal, forced to admit the unconquerable power of Rome. The second half of 'An Horatian Ode' offers a view of Cromwell's might as seen through the eyes of his defeated enemies (in this case the Irish): 'They can affirm his praises best, | And have, though overcome, confessed | How good he is, how just, | And fit for highest trust' (ll. 77–80). Similarly, the closing movement of 'The First Anniversary' is dominated by the speech of a rival 'prince', incredulous at Cromwell's courage and command: 'But let them write his praise that love him best, | It grieves me sore to have thus much confessed' (ll. 393–4). 'An Horatian Ode' also borrows many of the images that associate Cromwell with divine power from *Odes* 4. 4, and concludes with a list of the defeated enemies indebted in particular to *Odes* 4. 14 (another major ode in praise of the military victories of Augustus and his adopted sons). 'The First Anniversary'

repeatedly compares Cromwell with the returning sun, another feature shared with Horace's panegyric odes (cf., e.g. *Odes* 4. 5 and 4. 14).

29. On Marvell's classicism in general, see Paul Davis, 'Marvel and the Literary Past', in David Hurst and Steven N. Zwicker (eds), *The Cambridge Companion to Andrew Marvel* (Cambridge, 2011), 26–45; J. B. Leishman, *The Art of Marvell's Poetry* (1968).

30. This point, and this way of formulating it, Charles Martindale owes to an email exchange with David Hopkins.

31. As there is no modern edition of the *Plantarum*, the text is cited directly from *Poemata Latina* (1668), 162–4.

32. The ode goes on to incorporate allusions to *Odes* 4. 14 and 3. 3, also major panegyric odes in celebration of Augustus and his regime.

CHAPTER 25

Spenser

RICHARD A. MCCABE

Mimesis

Writing in the 1970s, René Girard asserted that 'there is nothing, or next to nothing, in human behaviour that is not learned, and all learning is based on imitation. If human beings suddenly ceased imitating, all forms of culture would vanish.' But, mindful of what he regarded as the undue emphasis that Modernism placed on 'originality', he added that 'our art and literature take great pains to resemble nothing and no one—mimetically. We have little idea of the possibilities for conflict contained in imitation.' The argument of the present chapter is that recognition of such possibilities was one of the major factors that recommended literary mimesis to Spenser and early modern writers generally. Mere imitation could reduce *mimesis* to the production of empty simulacra or plagiarism, but 'mimésis de l'antagonisme', the urge not only to emulate but to refute, or refute through emulation, afforded limitless opportunities for generic development and experimentation.[1]

It was evident to early modern authors that many of the social and moral values encoded in classical epic—and indeed in ancient pastoral, epideictic, and amatory verse—were incompatible with the ethos of Christianity.[2] The allegorical interpretation of Homer and Virgil represents, in part at least, an attempt to alleviate the anxiety of the alien by extrapolating a familiar 'moral' against the grain of a disquieting tale.[3] Cristoforo Landino's Aeneas, for example, is a moral agent virtually indistinguishable from Spenser's Red Crosse Knight: 'For the poet does not imagine him as one wise and adorned with true virtue from the beginning, but as one who, desirous of freeing his soul from disturbances, gradually redeems himself from vices, and after various wanderings, reaches Italy, that is, true wisdom.'[4] The evident similarity serves to remind us that what Spenser imitates is not 'Virgil' per se, but Virgil *in reception* from early commentators such as Fulgentius and Bernardus Silvestris to their Renaissance successors. What Spenser received was the annotated Virgil, 'complete', thanks to Maphaeus Vegetius, in thirteen books.[5] Repeated attempts to produce a truly 'Christian' epic are best regarded as attempts to realize the moral potential of the form supposedly identified by the allegorizers, a potential adumbrated but never quite realized in the original texts. 'Just as the divine Scriptures themselves do not bear much fruit if you persist in adhering to the letter,' wrote Erasmus in *Enchiridion Militis Christiani* (1503), 'the poetry of Homer and Virgil is of no little profit if you remember that it is entirely allegorical'.[6]

The implications for a would-be writer of Christian epic such as Spenser were considerable. In *The Faerie Queene*, as in Ariosto, Trissino, and Tasso, warfare becomes crusade, warriors become knights, travel becomes quest, and fate becomes providence. Yet readerly experience continued to suggest that the essence of classical epic was intrinsically resistant to Christian redaction. Such anxieties led to the full-scale revision of the heroic *Gerusalemme Liberata* into the homiletic *Gerusalemme Conquistata*.[7] Dryden, who feared that Milton's 'Devil' might become his readers' hero, toyed with the explanation 'that Christianity is not capable of those Embellishments which are afforded in the Belief of those Ancient Heathens'.[8] There was a pervasive sense, that is to say, that the only mimesis allowable to Christians was what Kempis identified as 'the Imitation of Christ'. But such imitation was fraught with difficulty. To the extent that St George—the saint that the Red Crosse Knight is destined to become—functions allegorically as a type or figure of Christ, he must be distinguished from Christ at every stage of the primary narrative. All of the elements of classical heroism evident in his make-up must be denied even as they are recorded because, properly considered, everything is achieved 'thorough grace' and 'all the good is Gods, both power and eke [also] will' (*Faerie Queene*, I. 10. 1). Ultimately the major effort required of the Christian hero, as Spenser conceives of him in the first book of *The Faerie Queene*, is the denial of his own heroism in favour of God's election. How compatible that conception is with the different varieties of 'heroism' presented in the remaining five books remains unclear. If a Christian epic begins with holiness, where does it go from there? Ideally the six virtues of the extant *The Faerie Queene* constitute a 'goodly golden chayne' (I. 9. 1), not just mutually compatible but morally complementary. But if book one manifests resolved Christian epic, as John Watkins has claimed, what is the effect of placing it in the context of a wider and more secular romance, particularly when Spenser's peculiar structure—a projected twelve books each with a separate hero operating in a distinct terrain—affords the possibility of radically competing visions of heroism that would be difficult, if not impossible, to synthesize in the one common protagonist, Prince Arthur?[9] George's vision of the New Jerusalem in book one is afforded by divine grace, but the poetic vision enjoyed by Colin Clout in book six centres upon the classical Graces. It was, of course, theoretically possible to reconcile the two at the level of allegory, as Edgar Wind and others have demonstrated, and the commentary to *The Shepheardes Calender* shows that Spenser was well aware of the fact.[10] The question, rather, is whether the sensuous poetics of book six facilitates or impedes such a possibility. The effect of Colin's vision on Sir Calidore, who watches covertly as though consciously indulging in voyeurism, is not immediately 'moral':

> There did he see, that pleased much his sight,
> That even he him selfe his eyes enuyde [envied],
> An hundred naked maidens lilly white,
> All raunged in a ring, and dauncing in delight.
>
> (6. 10. 11)

The problem is exacerbated by the fact that the 'classical' is often apprehended in the poem as artefact—whether tapestry, ekphrasis, icon, or 'idol'—and the seductively compelling experience of the encounter replicates the early modern fascination with recovered items of pagan art. Only the most naively reductionist employment of 'allegory' could ignore the discordance in literary ethos between the Mount of Contemplation and Mount Acidale, even though, or perhaps even because, the former is specifically compared not only to Mount Sinai and the Mount of Olives but to Parnassus, 'On which the thrise three learned Ladies play | Their hevenly notes, and make full many a lovely lay' (1. 10. 54). This final, unexpected choice of simile locates the uneasy relationship between the classical and the Christian at the heart of Spenser's epic, but the same tension also pervades the rest of the canon.

Pastoral

Spenser first signalled his epic intentions in *The Shepheardes Calender* (1579), in what is generally regarded as a gesture towards the Virgilian 'rota', the movement from pastoral through georgic to epic, but actually constitutes a far more complex exercise in authorial self-presentation.[11] What the *Calender* imitates is not just Virgil's *Eclogues*, but a scholarly edition of the eclogues: in other words, it imitates Virgil in humanist reception, complete with woodcuts and elaborate scholarly apparatus. The paratexts and commentary supplied by the unidentified 'E.K.' account for a third of the whole volume and function to contextualize the poems in the manner of Servius, the ancient Virgilian commentator whose annotations were incorporated into all major Renaissance editions.[12] But, whereas Servius laboured some 300 years after the fact upon an established 'classic', E.K. fabricates a form of pseudo-Servian commentary to lend 'classical' status to a contemporary work. The capacity to generate commentary was commonly regarded as a mark of a writer's 'authority'. By pretending to respond to interpretations made by previous readers, E.K. lends the brand new *Calender* a fictive history—doubtless to be imagined in terms of extensive manuscript circulation (for which, however, no substantiating evidence is extant). His commentary, like that of Servius, emphasizes Spenser's 'scientia' and rhetorical skill, while at the same time alerting the reader to the work's political dimension.[13]

By plausibly identifying implicit critique beneath overt praise, Servius suggested that Virgil's attitude to Augustus was ambivalent (in the sense that genuine gratitude for personal favours was at odds with deep resentment against the public policies that harmed all but the favoured) and infused the aesthetics of pastoral with expectations of the covert.[14] According to George Puttenham, for example, pastoral was designed 'not of purpose to counterfeit or represent the rustical manner of loves and communication: but under the veil of homely persons, and in rude speeches to insinuate and glance at greater matters, and such as perchance had not been safe to have been disclosed in any other sort'.[15] Servius regarded this as a Virgilian innovation: for political purposes, he argued, Virgil sometimes spoke figuratively ('aliquibus locis miscet figuras') where Theocritus had spoken simply ('simpliciter').[16] Such was the impact of the Servian commentary that politically neutral readings of the eclogues became virtually impossible in the early modern period and E.K.'s commentary brilliantly exploits that phenomenon by contriving a complex interaction between verse and annotation. From its dedication to Philip Sidney on the title page onwards, the *Calender* allies itself with the forces opposed to Queen Elizabeth's proposed marriage to the Catholic Duc d' Alençon (later Anjou), and affords its readers the frisson of dangerous matter.[17] Its pseudonymous editor frequently calls attention to his anonymous author's covert intentions—most successfully, perhaps, by gratuitously denying them and thereby generating a hermeneutics of acute suspicion—on the grounds that 'I was made privie to his counsell and secret meaning' ('Epistle', l. 178). As a result, while very few of Spenser's eclogues are directly modelled on those of Virgil (*Aprill* being a marked exception), the ethos of the collection is intensely 'Virgilian' in the Servian sense—a sense adapted and developed by, among others, Petrarch, Boccaccio, Mantuan, Sannazaro, and Marot.

Drawing equal inspiration from humanist verse and humanist scholarship, Spenser attained a unique fusion of the two by rendering the *Calender*'s commentary integral to its poetics. Thus *November*'s lament for an inescapably Virgilian 'Dido' is closely modelled on Clement Marot's *Eglogue sur le trépas de ma Dame Loyse de Savoye* (1531), which in turn harks back to Virgil's elegy for Daphnis (eclogue 5), generally interpreted, following Servius, as a lament for Julius Caesar.[18] It is written, that is to say, in the Virgilian tradition of national elegy to which E.K. alludes only by way of overt denial. Equating the queen with Dido, who perished for love of a faithless, foreign prince, at the time of her plans to marry a French Catholic (faithless and foreign by definition for many Englishmen) was intensely dangerous, and the commentary notes that the lady's father 'is . . . not as some vainely suppose God Pan. The person both of the shephearde and of Dido is unknowen and closely buried in the Authors conceipt' (*November*, l. 38). But this is calculated to prompt the very speculation it pretends to dismiss because E.K. had previously identified 'Pan' in the gloss to *Aprill* as 'her highnesse Father, late of worthy memorye K. Henry the eyght' (l. 50). The location of the earlier gloss is also highly significant. *Aprill* contains the famous 'laye | Of fayre *Elisa*, Queene of sheepheardes all' (ll. 33–4), and

Elissa is Dido's alternative name in the *Aeneid*. There is consequently every reason to suspect that readers intent on discovering the covert intentions that E.K. has elsewhere directed them to seek would find political significance in the Virgilian allusions of *November*. Read out of context (and it was sometimes anthologized as a separate poem), the 'laye' might appear to afford unqualified royal praise if not propaganda, but the combination of its original context and Virgilian connotations tells a different story.[19] As the fourth eclogue of the *Calender, Aprill* is written in imitation of Virgil's fourth eclogue, the poem that foretells the birth of an exceptional child and the dawn of a new Golden Age. Christian interpreters identified the child as Christ, thereby elevating Virgil to the status of prophet that he enjoys in Dante.[20] To fashion the queen's praise on such a model might, therefore, be regarded as paying her the highest compliment possible—were it not for the uncomfortable fact that it is precisely the choice of model that militates against her. The prevalent Messianic interpretation of the fourth eclogue necessitates a refusal of blasphemy by association:

> But I will not match her with *Latonaes* seede.
> Such follie great sorrow to *Niobe* did breede.
> Now she is a stone,
> And makes dayly mone,
> Warning all other to take heede.
>
> (*Aprill*, ll. 86–90)

The eclogue concludes with two emblems borrowed from Virgil that strongly warn the reader to 'take heede': 'O quam te memorem virgo?' and 'O dea certe' (*Aeneid*, I. 327–8). E.K. explains that

> this Poesye is taken out of Virgile, and there of him used in the person of Æneas to his mother Venus, appearing to him in the likenesse of one of Dianaes damosells... To which similitude of divinitie Hobbinoll comparing the excellency of Elisa, and being through the worthynes of Colins song, as it were, overcome with the hugenesse of his imagination, brusteth out in great admiration, (O quam te memorem virgo?) being otherwise unhable, then by soddein silence, to expresse the worthinesse of his conceipt. Whom Thenot answereth with another part of the like verse, as confirming by his graunt and approvaunce, that Elisa is no whit inferiour to the Maiestie of her, of whome the Poete so boldly pronounced, O dea certe.[21]

This is as much an appreciation of artistic licence—the 'worthynes' of Colin's song and the 'hugenesse' of his creator's 'imagination'—as it is of Elizabeth, whose 'divinity', unlike that of Christ, is purely a matter of poetic 'conceipt'. Elisa is a man-made, personalized 'goddess' who delivers little comfort:

> shee is my goddesse plaine,
> And I her shepherds swayne,
> Albee forswonck and forswatt I am.
>
> (ll. 97–9)

In his very first annotation to the *Calender*, written in direct imitation of Servius' first annotation to Virgil's eclogues, E.K. identifies Colin as the name under which 'this Poete secretly shadoweth himself, as sometime did Virgil under the name of Tityrus'. It is all the more remarkable, then, that Colin is absent from the *Aprill* eclogue, being described as too 'alienate and withdrawn' to sing Elisa's praise, and even more remarkable still that the voice attributed to Colin in the *Januarye* eclogue resembles not that of Virgil's Tityrus but his Meliboeus, the dispossessed victim of Augustus' policies whom Tityrus vainly tries to console in the first eclogue. The *Calender* responds more powerfully to Virgil's sense of social injustice and (poetic) impotence in the face of violence and intimidation (eclogues 1 and 9) than to its glorification of the powers that be. The *Aprill* eclogue lets Eliza know that she is a 'goddess' only in poetic conceipt; the *November* eclogue warns Elisa / Dido that the only apotheosis she will ever enjoy is by election through the grace of God: 'Dido nis [is not] dead, but into heaven hent' (l. 169). The classical 'conceipt' of deification must give way to the Christian truth of redemption, but only for those deemed worthy, only for the chaste Dido who remained faithful to her husband, as Elisa must remain faithful to the England she claimed to have 'married'.

But is Elisa worthy? What E.K. terms the *Calender*'s 'moral' eclogues (*Maye, Julye*, and *September*) blend biblical with classical pastoral to lament the state of the Church of England, of which the queen was the supreme governor, in imitation of the bitter, ecclesiastical pastorals of Petrarch and Mantuan.[22] Symptomatic of the malaise is the fact that the 'Queene of shepheardes all' has destroyed the good shepherd 'Algrind', a transparent anagram for Grindal, the Archbishop of Canterbury sequestered from his office by Elizabeth in a dispute about the extent of royal authority over the Church (*Julye*, ll. 213–32). Grindal was a former Master of Spenser's Cambridge College and just a few years earlier had circulated an open letter to the queen reminding her of her mortality—a letter unwisely modelled on Ambrose's excommunication of Theodosius and, in terms of its political consequences, one of the most unfortunate imitations of a late classical work.[23] The precedent would have been in Spenser's mind as he too tackled contemporary politics through classical imitation. Part of his solution was to contrive a disquieting, if implicit, tension between two discordant modes of pastoral vision, panegyrical and satiric.

Throughout the *Calender*, Colin Clout displays an attitude of alienation from the pastoral community of which he is technically a member. His persona less resembles that of Virgil's Tityrus than Ovid's exile. Spenser's calendrical structure, absent from Virgil, has been related to Ovid's *Fasti*, a poem broken off, according to Ovid, as a consequence of the author's banishment (*Tristia*, 2. 549–52). Evoking the same tradition, 'Colin' conspicuously abandons his pipes at the close of *December*.[24] Indeed the entire *Calender* is framed by Ovidian reference: the author's opening address 'To his Booke' echoes Ovid in imagining that the volume will venture where its author dare not (a frequent topos in the *Tristia* and *Epistulae ex Ponto*), and in advising it to give a false name when asked of its creator (*Ex Ponto*, 4. 5. 11–14)—just as the anonymous Spenser supplies the pseudonym 'Immeritô'. The *Calender*'s final emblem (mis)quotes lines from the concluding passage of the *Metamorphoses* (15. 871–2): 'Grande opus exegi quod nec Iovis ira nec ignis, | Nec ferrum poterit nec edax abolere vetustas', setting it off against Horace's 'Exegi monumentum ære perennius' (*Odes*, 3. 30. 1–3). The pairing is consciously problematical in the light of *October*'s debate on Elizabethan patronage: both poets assert their achievement, but one wrote with Augustus' support, the other despite him. What would be Spenser's fate? Reflecting on the possibility of modern epic in *October*, Cuddie (identified by E.K. as a persona for Colin) concludes that, whereas 'the Romish *Tityrus*... Through his *Mecœnas* left his Oaten reede', the classical exemplum is now irrelevant because '*Mecœnas* is yclad in claye, | And great *Augustus* long ygoe is dead' (ll. 55–62). Piers, his opponent, holds out the prospect of royal or aristocratic patronage, but 'Immeritô' leaves the matter to the reader.

Colin's pervasively Ovidian tone is greatly exacerbated in *Colin Clouts Come Home Againe* (1595), Spenser's unexpected return to pastoral in mid-epic career (appearing as it did between the first and second instalments of *The Faerie Queene*) in defiance of the Virgilian rota. The word 'home' that figures so prominently in the title lends emphasis to the work's sophisticated fusion of Virgilian and Ovidian motifs. 'Ite domum' is the last injunction of Virgil's eclogues (10. 77), and the desperate leitmotif of the *Tristia* and *Epistulae Ex Ponto*. Indeed the many echoes of the latter works in *Colin Clouts Come Home Againe* indicate that Spenser read them as a form of 'anti-pastoral', poetry written from a 'barbarous' landscape antithetical to traditional pastoral contentment and the values of literary community. The Colin of *The Shepheardes Calender* is a denizen of Elisa's England, that of the later poem is a denizen of Ireland, which he describes very much as Ovid describes Tomis: remote, barbarous, and violent.[25] Much has been made of Colin's apparent contentment among his fellow Irish shepherds, but that is only part of the complex picture that emerges; Ovid, one needs to remember, takes little comfort from the 'honour' accorded him by the Tomitae (*Ex Ponto*, 4. 9. 97–104; 14. 49–62).[26] While on one level Colin is regarded as native to Ireland, the words of the 'Shepherd of the Ocean' (Sir Walter Ralegh) suggest a very different perspective:

> He gan to cast great lyking to my lore,
> And great dislyking to my lucklesse lot:
> That banisht had my selfe, like wight forlore,
> Into that waste, where I was quite forgot.
> The which to leave, thenceforth he counseld mee...
>
> (*Colin Clouts*, ll. 180–4)

These words remind the reader that Colin's 'home' was not Spenser's. The term 'banisht' has a distinctly Ovidian ring, particularly in view of the opinion expressed by contemporary commentators that Spenser had fled to Ireland in 1591 after the banning of his *Complaints* for their attacks on Lord Burghley.[27] One of the things that Ovid most laments is the loss of his life ('communia sacra') among the Latin poets

(*Ex Ponto*, 3. 4. 65–72; 5. 21–32), and it is the equivalent loss of literary community that the Shepheard of the Ocean decries. From this stage onwards Spenser engineers a complicated counterpoint with Ovid's writings from exile. Colin's voyage to England echoes Ovid's voyage into exile, while simultaneously recording how his creator 'came home' at least briefly. But 'home', as represented by Elizabeth's court, proves to be as vicious and inhospitable as Ovid's place of exile, and 'Colin' forsakes Spenser's 'home' (identified as London the following year in *Prothalamion*) to go 'home againe'. Elizabeth is praised, certainly, but pastoral epideictic lies inert in pastoral satire. No previous English poet had used an Ovidian subtext with such complexity or finesse.

Spenser's experimentation with the pastoral genre brought even greater surprises the following year when Colin Clout was introduced into *The Faerie Queene* in defiance of generic convention. Aeneas' sojourn among the Arcadians of Latium temporarily shifts Virgil's epic into a bucolic setting, but the last person one would expect to meet there would be Tityrus, the poet's own pastoral persona (6. 10. 5–32). The Virgilian rota collapses as Spenser reverts to pastoral not just between epic instalments but within epic. And the breach of Virgilian convention is further underscored by Sir Calidore's meeting, in the same canto, with 'old Melibœ', a version of the figure driven into exile in the first eclogue by Augustus' policies. This Melibœ has taken to pastoral retirement in contempt of the court and eloquently advocates the contentment of private life (6. 9. 13–34). At first it seems as if the tale left unfinished in Virgil has been brought to a happy resolution, until the old man is killed by marauding brigands, his community scattered, and Calidore's vain hopes of a simple bucolic life shown to be naive (11. 18). What Calidore learns to his cost is that pastoral cannot be the 'answer' to epic. *The Faerie Queene* has returned him to the landscape of Virgil's ninth eclogue, where terrified shepherd-poets await the onslaught of invasion and Lycidas wonders if any man could be guilty of such a crime ('cadit in quemquam tantum scelus?' (l. 17)). Both Virgil and Spenser answer in the affirmative, the latter in a very personal key: 'Ne may this homely verse, of many meanest, | Hope to escape his venomous despite' (6. 12. 41). The distinctive feature of Spenser's use of pastoral, then, is that he uses it not just as a prelude to epic but as a means of interrogating epic: published ten years before *The Faerie Queene, The Shepheades Calender* debates the possibility of attaining epic vision in Elizabeth's England; issued between the epic's two instalments, *Colin Clouts Come Home Againe* challenges its viability and, perhaps, even its honesty; located within *The Faerie Queene*, Calidore's pastoral diversion exposes poetry's acute vulnerability to rebarbative forces within the very society it seeks to render heroic. Ultimately Spenserian pastoral writes the epitaph for Spenserian epic.

Epic

Or should it be romance? *The Faerie Queene* is hard to categorize, and intentionally so. Its opening lines imitate the quatrain commonly appended to the opening of the

Aeneid—'Ille ego, qui quondam gracili modulatus avena...' ('I am he who once tuned my song on a slender reed...')—only to subvert them with reminiscences of Ariosto:

> Lo I the man, whose Muse whylome did maske,
> As time her taught, in lowly Shephards weeds,
> Am now enforst a farre unfitter taske,
> From trumpets sterne to chaunge mine Oaten reeds:
> And sing of knights and Ladies gentle deeds...
> (I. Proem. I)

The rediscovery of Aristotle's *Poetics* inspired a vigorous debate among early modern neoclassicists about the relationship between Virgilian epic and Ariostan romance that raises fundamental questions about the generic implications of Spenser's avowed intention (at least according to Gabriel Harvey's account of it) to 'overgo' Ariosto.[28] In structural terms, Spenser's poem, with its multiple protagonists and division into *both* books and cantos, is as far from Virgil as it might be thought possible to go. Indeed, it conforms most closely to one of the varieties of narrative identified by Giraldi Cinthio as legitimate within what he regarded as the distinct, autonomous form of romance.[29] Which is to say that Spenser's poem is consciously innovative, intent on exploring the relationship between classical and Christian heroism through the medium of hybrid forms.

The Faerie Queene begins with holiness, and the hero learns from the most authoritative moral teacher in the book that 'blood can nought but sin, and wars but sorrows yield' (I. 10. 60). Yet the same teacher refuses to allow him to abandon his quest and sends him forth to slay the dragon. The episode hinges upon a contradiction in the make-up of Red Crosse that is marked from the outset. As his name indicates, he wishes to serve Christ, but he also wishes to serve Gloriana for less spiritual reasons, 'to winne him worshippe, and her grace to have, | Which of all earthly thinges he most did crave' (I. I. 3).[30] The potential conflict between worshipping God and winning personal 'worshippe' pervades the book. On the Mount of Contemplation, Red Crosse recognizes that the City of Cleopolis (the City of Fame) is nothing in comparison with the New Jerusalem, and that the fame for which he is destined is spiritual not 'earthly'—'thou Saint *George* shalt called bee' (I. 10. 61). He responds by asserting his eventual intention to renounce knighthood and become a 'pilgrim' (I. 10. 64). Yet, according to both the *October* eclogue and *The Teares of the Muses*, the function of epic, as evidenced by its classical paradigms, is to produce and promote fame—and the City of Cleopolis is where Gloriana lives. In this manner, book one interrogates both the integrity of classical heroism and the viability of Christian epic. Properly regarded, George is a hero by grace alone, and, according to the narrator, that is the only heroism possible:

> What man is he, that boasts of fleshly might,
> And vaine assurance of mortality,

> Which all too soone, as it doth come to fight,
> Against spirituall foes, yields by and by,
> Or from the fielde most cowardly doth fly?
> Ne let the man ascribe it to his skill,
> That thorough grace hath gained victory.
> If any strength we have, it is to ill,
> But all the good is Gods, both power and eke will.
>
> (I. 10. I)[31]

The operative phrase here is 'against spirituall foes': misunderstanding the nature of the quest, Red Crosse sets out 'to prove his puissance in battell brave | Upon his foe, and his new force to learne' (I. I. 3). But what he actually learns is that he has no 'force' independent of 'grace'. Denial of personal 'puissance' is the debt that Spenser's epic pays to allegory. Classical heroism can be reinscribed only at the expense of the Christian 'moral'.

The Virgilian influence in book one is in constant tension with that of Revelation, as Spenser effectively rewrites his earliest work. While still a schoolboy at Merchant Taylors, he had contributed to Jan van der Noot's *Theatre for Voluptuous Worldlings* (1569) English translations of eleven sonnets from the *Songe* appended to Joachim Du Bellay's *Les Antiquitez de Rome contenant une generale description de sa grandeur, et comme une deploration de sa ruine* (1558), a work he later translated in his *Complaints* as *The Ruines of Rome*.[32] In Noot's version of the *Songe*, Du Bellay's poems lead the reader to four original sonnets inspired by the Book of Revelation foretelling the fall of Rome and the coming of the New Jerusalem. Each of the Du Bellay sonnets is illustrated with a woodcut displaying simultaneous double visions of Rome in glory (Du Bellay's 'grandeur') and desolation (Du Bellay's 'ruine'). Noot's elaborate commentary on these 'visions' is designed to set the City of Rome (the Cleopolis of the ancient world) firmly in the context of the City of God; he is far less ambivalent in his response to the aesthetics of ruination than his original.[33] Spenser, then, first handled the Myth of Rome, the key classical myth underpinning his reception of the ancient world, in the context of Apocalyptic caution.[34] Virgil's Aeneas must reject Dido in order to found Rome and fulfil his destiny, but Red Crosse must reject Rome in the person of Duessa—'double', like Noot's Roman images, in disguising moral depravity in outward allure—to achieve personal, spiritual, and national identity (*Faerie Queene*, I. 10. 61).

When she first appears in the poem, Duessa associates herself with classical Rome (I. 2. 22) but later reveals herself as the Whore of Babylon or papal Rome (I. 8. 6), far worse than its predecessor in its determination to enslave the soul as well as the body. Under her guidance, Red Crosse is led first to the House of Pride under which all the great Romans from Romulus to Julius Caesar lie as 'caytive wretched thralls' (I. 5. 45, 49), and next to the Dungeon of Ignaro (spiritual ignorance), where he becomes 'a caytive thrall' himself (I. 7. 19). In *The Ruines of Time*, published the following year in the *Complaints* (1591), the speaker Verlame, representing the old Roman city of

Verulamium, solipsistically laments the fall of Roman Britain and, as she believes, her subsequent loss of identity. But book one allegorizes Henry VIII's break with Rome as marking the emergence of an independent English 'empire': Rome is therefore both an essential component of English identity and fatally antagonistic to it. It is only in books two and three, after George's quest has finished, that the Matter of Troy is developed through the myth of Brutus into the Matter of Troynovant, ideally denoting continuity between the classical and 'British' traditions of heroism.[35] But that notion of continuity is itself disjointed by the fragmentation of the embedded narrative, couched as 'antiquity' in the House of Alma (2. 10. 1–69), prophecy in the Cave of Merlin (3. 3. 22–50), and erotized legend in the House of Malbecco (3. 9. 32–51).[36] It is as though the poem is in conflict with its own ideology, employing fragmented forms to expose its own myth of origin as fiction.

The first book of *The Faerie Queene* might seem to create a major dilemma for an author intent on working in what was commonly regarded, *pace* Lucan, as an imperial genre. But the history of Virgilian reception to which Spenser responded transformed that dilemma into an aesthetic opportunity. For Christian humanists such as Du Bellay, Rome provided the supreme paradigm for both imperial aspiration and imperial corruption, and Virgilian commentators from Servius onwards noted their author's ambivalence towards the political ideas that supposedly lay at the heart of his epic.[37] As Michael Murrin points out, Aeneas descends to the underworld to receive instruction from his father by way of the elm of 'empty dreams' ('somnia ... vana') and bears the message back to the world, not, as might be expected, through the Gate of Horn (the gate of true dreams), but through the Gate of Ivory 'through which the shades send false dreams to the world above' ('falsa ad caelum mittunt insomnia Manes'). Servius concluded that the message is wholly feigned 'since both the entrance and the exit are counterfeit and false' ('quae res haec omnia indicat esse simulata, si et ingressus et exitus simulatus est et falsus').[38] Virgil's choice of the Gate of Ivory was extraordinary by any standards and risks, if not promotes, the perception of imperial vision as imperial delusion. For a writer such as Spenser, who addresses his poem to the 'Empresse' Elizabeth, derives her ancestry, like that of Aeneas, from Troy, and was actively engaged in the Irish colonial enterprise, the passage must surely have given pause for reflection. The 'dream' that inspires Prince Arthur to seek Gloriana, and ideally underpins the poem's commitment to 'glory' in all its many senses, is rendered similarly problematical to Virgil's by being drawn from the parodic adventures of Chaucer's *Sir Thopas* (1. 9. 13–15). Both authors explore the fine line between the heroic and the Quixotic.

Both Homer and Virgil were reputed to have written mock-epics, and the *Appendix Virgiliana*, which appeared in all major Renaissance editions, contained the *Culex*, which Spenser translated as *Virgil's Gnat*.[39] It was understood, of course, that 'mock-epic' did not necessarily mock epic, but it was equally evident that it had a powerful potential to do so. On the Mount of Contemplation the seer reconciles Red Crosse's potentially contradictory ambitions to serve God and Gloriana by lending semi-divine status to the latter: 'for she is hevenly borne, and heaven may justly vaunt' (1. 10. 59). He solves the dilemma by holding the mirror up to grace rather than nature. But Belphoebe, the character intended, according to the 'Letter to Ralegh' that accompanied the first instalment of the poem, to represent the queen's private person, seems like a different being entirely. Her initial encounter with Braggadocchio (2. 3. 20–46), later described as a 'mock-knight' (4. 4. 13), breathes pure mock epic, as though Spenser were using parody to demystify his own idealizations of monarchy and infuse scepticism into the practice of deification previously problematized in the *Aprill* eclogue. Similarly, the figure of False Florimell, who preoccupies so much attention in *The Faerie Queene* 3–4, is modelled on the myth of the phantom Helen, whose presence at Troy threatened to reduce even the *Iliad* to the sort of travesty that Shakespeare constructed in *Troilus and Cressida*.[40] The advantage of Ariostan romance over Virgilian epic for Spenser was that it could more readily accommodate, and even combine, both forms.[41]

At the close of book one Red Crosse's quest is apparently accomplished and his identity secure until the first of Spenser's famous 'deferrals of closure' sends him back into the world of the poem, a newly Ovidian world. The poetics of metamorphosis that inform the central episodes of books two and three, the Bowre of Blisse and the Gardens of Adonis, call in question the possibility of ever achieving a stable identity, of gaining the sort of 'rest' towards which the speakers of both the *Fowre Hymnes* (*Hymne of Heavenly Beautie*, 301) and the *Mutabilitie Cantos* (7. 8. 2) aspire. It has long been noted that Sir Guyon's voyage to the Bowre of Blisse reproduces Homer's *Odyssey* in miniature, but what has not been properly recognized is that this particular *Odyssey* concludes not in Ithaca and 'home' but on the Island of Circe—and there are those on the island who, like Plutarch's Gryllus, prefer loss of identity over recovery (2. 12. 86–7).[42] The episode is far less morally comforting than that of the transformed Fraudubio of book one (ultimately based on Virgil's tale of Polydorus (*Aeneid* 3. 22–68)), who assures Red Crosse that he expects redemption.[43] Similarly, while not wholly incompatible with the religious vision of book one, the relentlessly transformative cycles of birth, life, death, and renewal described in the Gardens of Adonis—touching on, if never expressly endorsing, the 'pagan' doctrines of metempsychosis expounded in the sixth book of the *Aeneid* (713–51) and the fifteenth book of the *Metamorphoses* (60–478)—reflect a very different ethos. Though present in books two and three, Red Crosse has remarkably little to do in either, because there is not much that his sort of heroism can accomplish in secular epic. His moral compass had always pointed east towards Eden, where he slays the dragon, but it is far harder to gain any sense of direction when linear narrative gives way to a web of intersecting storylines. Red Crosse had rejected Duessa as Aeneas rejected Dido, but the driving force of Spenser's poem from book two onwards is sexual desire: Arthur's pursuit of Gloriana, Florimell's pursuit of Marinell, Britomart's pursuit of Artegall, Timias' pursuit of Belphoebe, and Calidore's pursuit of Pastorella.[44] If Virgil dissociates heroism from desire, Spenser increasingly implicates the two.

There are signs that such growing adherence to Ovid did not pass unnoticed. The proem to the fourth book of *The Faerie Queene*, first published in the second edition of 1596, might indeed have been written *ex Ponto*:

> The rugged forhead that with grave foresight
> Welds kingdoms causes, and affaires of state,
> My looser rimes (I wote) doth sharply wite,
> For praising love, as I have done of late,
> And magnifying lovers deare debate;
> By which fraile youth is oft to folllie led,
> Through false allurement of that pleasing baite,
> That better were in vertues discipled,
> Then with vaine poemes weeds to have their fancies fed.
>
> (4. Proem. 1)

Spenser is attacked not for 'carmen et error' but for 'carmen' as 'error', and his response is highly Ovidian. In the manner of *Tristia* 2, which draws attention to the love interest in Homer and Virgil, he defends the link between *eros* and *heros* and turns from Lord Burghley ('the rugged forhead') to Elizabeth as 'Queene of love', much as Ovid reminds Augustus of his kinship, through Aeneas, to Cupid (*Ex Ponto*, 3. 3. 59–64). But, just as Ovid remarks that his life in exile obsessively constitutes its own theme (*Tristia*, 5. 1. 9–10), the narrator of *The Faerie Queene* grows increasingly self-referential and circumspect. The dedicatory sonnets to the first edition had noted that the poem was written from the margins of empire, but that sense of distance and dislocation is now exacerbated. Spenser's perception of the poem's poor reception at court and the rapidly worsening conditions in Ireland, where the Nine Years' War had already begun, lend a sense of urgency and even desperation to the narrative. In the episodes of Bonfont and Malfont (5. 9. 25–6), and the eventual escape of the Blatant Beast (6. 12. 38–41), the issue of censorship bears as heavily on Spenser as it does on the exiled Ovid, and there is the same sense that both authors have been injured by their own talent (*Tristia*, 2. 1–14; *Ex Ponto*, 3. 5. 1–4).

The description of the native Irish supplied in the *View of the Present State of Ireland*, completed about the same time, repeatedly echoes Ovid's description of the 'Scythians' from whom Spenser imagined the Gaelic Irish to be descended.[45] Eudoxus, one of the parties to the *View*'s dialogue, directly quotes Ovid's contention that learning softens character and dispels barbarity, but the context of this quotation is remarkable ('emollit mores nec sinit esse feros' (*Ex Ponto*, 2. 9. 48)).[46] Ovid was addressing King Cotys of Thrace, a poet like himself, who is represented as civil and humane despite his race. Spenser's Irenius opposes Eudoxus by arguing that the Irish constitute a counter-example to the general rule that Ovid expounds: despite their possession of letters, the Irish remain 'wilde' and violent and their poets promote barbarity. Essential to the argument of the *View* is that only military force will make Ireland civil, that policies of reform must be replaced by plans for suppression. The effect on Spenser's epic is profound. The second instalment of *The Faerie Queene* becomes the first epic poem in the Western tradition written to promote a military campaign, in marked contrast, for example, to the later editions of the *Orlando Furioso*, which manifest an increasing hostility to war.[47] Spenser models his exhortation to empire (*Faerie Queene*, 4. 11. 22) directly on that of Virgil (*Aeneid*, 6. 851–3), but the imperial imperative is perpetually at odds with the moral. The attempt to represent Elizabeth's expedient foreign policy under the rubric of 'Justice' in book five places not just the poem's moral allegory but its generic identity under severe strain.

The major instrument of justice in book five is Talus, an iron man incongruously imported into heroic poetics from the pseudo-Platonic *Minos*. More appropriately an 'it' than a 'he', Talus displays a mechanized violence that conflicts equally with the traditions of heroic hand-to-hand combat described in Homer and Virgil, and the chivalric endeavour of Christian knights in Ariosto and Tasso. Commentators had long detected a measure of disquiet with the human cost of empire even in Virgil, but those fault lines in the heroic tradition deepen to fracture the vision of *The Faerie Queene*.[48] The Virgilian eclogue upon which *Aprill*'s 'laye of fayre Elisa' is based had promised that the Virgin Astraea would return and bring back the Golden Age ('Iam redit et Virgo, redeunt Saturnia regna' (4. 6)). This is the crucial Virgilian connotation that most commentators miss in interpreting Thenot's question 'o quam te memorem virgo?' In effect he is asking Elisa if she will indeed prove to be Astraea and restore justice: 'shall I call you *Virgo*?' By contrast, at the outset of the *Legend of Justice*, the book in which the vision of Elizabeth as Astraea should ideally be fulfilled, Astraea forsakes the world and leaves Talus to operate in a fallen, violent, iron age (5. 1. 11). We have passed from Virgilian optimism to Ovidian despair: the heroic ages ended, according to the *Metamorphoses*, when 'piety lay vanquished and the maiden Astraea, last of the immortals, abandoned the blood-soaked earth' ('victa iacet pietas, et virgo caede madentis | ultima caelestum terras Astraea reliquit' (1. 149–50)). Spenser had previously employed this incident as a prelude to satire at the outset of *Mother Hubberds Tale* (1591), and its repetition at the outset of a professedly heroic poem signals the shift in outlook between the first and second instalments of *The Faerie Queene*. The emphasis of the second half of the *Aeneid* is on the union of Trojans and Latins to form one Roman people, but both the politics of the *View* and the poetics of *The Faerie Queene* 4–6 lay greater stress on division and difference: the 'salvages' of book six, for example, can never be civilized, and the one apparent exception, the 'salvage man' who pities Serena, is a foundling of 'noble blood' (6. 5. 2).[49] But most telling of all is the narrator's pervasive sense of betrayal, indicative of a changed relationship between poet and prince. It is the court that undermines Artegall at the close of book five and the narrator himself at the close of book six (5. 12. 27–43; 6. 12. 38–41). Perhaps responding to the irony that Ovid's praise of Augustus was never so fulsome as when it was at its most obviously self-serving in the exile poetry, *The Faerie Queene*'s narrator bitterly concludes that the only way forward is to flatter: 'therfore do you my rimes keep better measure, | And seeke to please, that now is counted wisemans threasure' (6. 12. 41).

Epithalamion and Epic's Mutability

What holds the whole massive framework of *The Faerie Queene* together is marital desire, Arthur's quest for the elusive Gloriana. That, at least, is what Spenser claims in the 'Letter to Ralegh'. Ideally conceived, all the subsidiary quests test the groom's character and bring him closer to his goal.[50] Ideally conceived, epic will culminate in epithalamion. But all such expectations are conspicuously frustrated, marriage being foremost of the many 'closures' that Spenserian narratology perpetually defers: Arthur never weds (or beds) his Gloriana, nor George his Una, nor Marinell his Florimell, nor Scudamour his Amoret, nor Britomart her Artegall. Marriage is ever present as a tantalizing ideal—for example, in the richly symbolic union of Thames and Medway (4. 12. 8–52)—and procreation as a biological necessity—for example, in the Gardens of Adonis (3. 6. 29–50)—but on the primary level of narrative they never occur. And Spenserian pastoral operates in the same manner as Spenserian epic: neither in *The Shepheardes Calender* nor in *Colin Clouts Come Home Againe* does Colin gain his Rosalind. By concluding his *Amoretti* (1595) with an *Epithalamion*, therefore, Spenser was springing upon his readers perhaps his greatest generic surprise. Petrarchan sonnet sequences never concluded in such a manner. Never before had the two modes been brought together. Generally speaking, amorous sequences ended in loss, disappointment, or irresolution—as in Petrarch's *Rime Sparse*, Sidney's *Astrophil and Stella*, or Shakespeare's *Sonnets*. The last thing anyone would have expected in 1595 was an epithalamion.

Readers familiar with the form in Catullus, Statius, and Claudian would notice from the outset that Spenser handles it in a uniquely personal way.[51] Contrary to all classical precedent, the poet celebrates his own marriage, and the studied distance that characterizes the classical speaker collapses. Spenser defends the procedure by citing classical myth against classical precedent:

> Helpe me mine owne loves prayses to resound,
> Ne let the same of any be enuide,
> So Orpheus did for his owne bride.
>
> (ll. 14–16)

The allusion is probably to Ovid, who, however, recounts the singular inefficacy of the example. An epithalamium was supposed to call down blessings on the married couple, but, while Hymen was summoned by Orpheus' song, it was 'all in vain. He was present, it is true; but he brought neither the hallowed words, not joyous faces, nor lucky omen.' In Ovid, as in Spenser, the landscape itself is dangerous: 'for while the bride was strolling through the grass with a group of naids, she fell dead, smitten in the ankle by a serpent's tooth' (*Metamorphoses*, 10. 1–10). Despite its classicizing features, Spenser's poem is set in the perilous Irish landscape of *Colin Clouts Come Home Againe* and *The Two Cantoes of Mutability*. As in Catullus, and epithalamion generally, the community is summoned to celebrate the couple's union, but it is a community under siege: the Nymphs of Mulla (Spenser's name for the Irish River Awbeg) who are called upon to 'bind up' the bride's locks are normally to be found deploying 'steele darts' against the 'wilde wolves' that seek to 'devoure' the local deer. In the *Amoretti* itself, as previously in Petrarch, the bride is figured as such a deer (sonnet 67).

The poem traces the couple's progress through the day in the conventional manner, but as darkness falls the sense of menace—never far from the surface through allusions to the myths of Tithonus, Medusa, and Endymion—increases:

> let no false treason seeke us to entrap
> Nor any dread disquiet once annoy
> The safety of our joy.
>
> (ll. 323–5)

Warding off evil was the poet's function, but, as the choice of language indicates, this is somewhat different. The tone is at once more personal—since the speaker is subject to the danger—and correspondingly paranoic: one does not expect to hear of 'false treason' or 'dread disquiet', nor indeed of how 'sad affray' may destroy the quite of the night (l. 327). We are back in the landscape of 'nightly bodrags (raids)' and 'hue and cries' described in *Colin Clouts Come Home Againe* (l. 315) as the antithesis to civil life. And then, as if itself the victim of such violence, the poem ends abruptly in mid-stanza, cut off 'through hasty accidents'. The charm has not worked, and classical form ends as classical fragment. But that, of course, is the point. Spenser, elsewhere such a master of symmetrical patterning, is once again exploiting the aesthetic functionality of the fragment. There is nothing accidental in his recourse to 'hasty accidents'. Incompletion is his choice. And the *Amoretti* twice suggests that the great epic project may also end by failing to end, that Gloriana's epithalamion, all of it, may be 'cut off'. The matter is left consciously ambiguous; it remains unclear whether amorous verse will impede (sonnet 33) or inspire (sonnet 80) a return to the heroic. But one point is surely suggestive: by concluding the *Amoretti* with an epithalamion written to celebrate personal love, Spenser signals a transition from dynastic epic to dynastic lyric. It is with the future of his own descendants, not those of the Tudors, that he is now concerned, and the childless Cynthia who 'peepes', perhaps enviously, through his bedroom windows highlights the incongruity of Elizabeth as the subject of a national epic that demands 'succession' and 'generation', that necessitates deferral of the sort of closure virginity entails (*Epithalamion*, ll. 372–423). The eclipse of Cynthia in the *Mutabilitie Cantos* points in the same direction and belatedly returns us to the death of *November*'s Dido (7. 6. 8–16).

The *Two Cantos of Mutabilitie* posthumously published in 1609—a fragment comprising cantos 6, 7, and two stanzas of canto 8 from an otherwise unknown book—constitute a sort of Ovidian epyllion, of which the unlikely 'hero' is the process of metamorphosis itself. Although they discard both 'fierce warres' and 'faithful loves', the *Cantos* have deep roots in *The Faerie Queene*'s intellectual structure, where allegorical 'meaning' often struggles for articulation through a welter of contradictory details and incompatible influences. What is at stake in the debate between Mutability and Jove is the viability of interpretation itself, the possibility of identifying meaning in so variable a world or so polyvalent a poem. The relentless cycles of creation and destruction described by Virgil's Anchises and Ovid's Pythagoras were previously reflected in book three's Garden of Adonis and book five's proem, but Mutability's marshalling of the arguments for change raises more fundamental issues about the relationship between transience and identity, including authorial identity. At the outset of the *Tristia*, Ovid remarks on the irony that, having written 'thrice five rolls about changing forms' ('mutatae, ter quinque volumina, formae'), he must now himself 'be reckoned amongst those transformed figures' ('inter mutata referri | fortunae vultum corpora posse meae') (*Tristia*, I. I. 117–20). 'What', he asks, 'but prayer is left' ('quid enim nisi vota supersunt?') (*Tristia*, I. 2. I). Spenser borrows a myriad details from Ovid in the course of the *Mutabilitie Cantos*, but is nowhere more 'Ovidian' than in the narrator's sense of entrapment in a bewilderingly metastasizing universe from which prayer affords the only possibility of escape: 'O that great Sabbaoth God, graunt me that Sabaoth's sight' (7. 8. 2).[52] The authorial detachment recommended for epic by Aristotle has been replaced by the intense personal intrusion of Ovid's later works. Not only is Cynthia on the point of dying, but she has, in any case, cursed the land of Ireland and abandoned all who live in it, including the narrator (7. 6. 37–55). The crime that brings about this catastrophe—Faunus' spying upon the naked goddess—is based upon Ovid's tale of Actaeon and Diana, the myth used in the *Tristia* as a metaphor for the unwitting 'error' that caused the poet's banishment. Its implications lead him to speculate on the inexplicable lack of mercy among 'the gods' and (presumably) all who resemble them on earth (2. 103–8). At the outset of Spenser's career the *Aprill* eclogue had expressed disquiet at the practice of deifying mortals, but the *Mutabilitie Cantos* register the imminent death of all such divinities. In so doing they gesture beyond epic to some higher genre for want of which the Virgilian rota remains as 'unperfite' as the cantos themselves. The incompletion of epic acts as an invitation to the inauguration of hymn.

Hymn

Published in 1596, the same year as the second edition of *The Faerie Queene*, the *Fowre Hymnes* represents the culmination of Spenser's negotiation between the classical and the Christian. Like the epic, the hymn was originally a pagan genre and generated similar debates about the possibility, or advisability, of its appropriation to Christian use.[53] The very structure of the *Fowre Hymnes* serves as a synopsis of the critical debate: the first two, allegedly written in Spenser's youth, are addressed to Cupid and Venus, the final pair to Christ and Sapience. If the six books of *The Faerie Queene* represent a progressive reimagining of the heroic, the *Fowre Hymnes* attempt its redefinition in terms of the self-sacrificial (*Hymne in Honour of Love*, ll. 225–37) with Christ as the supreme hero (*Hymne of Heavenly Love*, ll. 126–75), a motif Spenser bequeathed to Milton. But perceptive readers would note that Spenser actually produced five hymns in 1596 not four. One of the most surprising inclusions in the second instalment of *The Faerie Queene* is an extended paraphrase, the earliest of its kind in English literature, of Lucretius' famous invocation or 'hymn' to Venus (*De Rerum Natura*, 1. 1–49). Its immediate context, however, is highly un-Lucretian: Scudamours's description of the idolatrous worship of the goddess's statue in the Temple of Venus (*Faerie Queene*, 4. 10. 44–7). Lucretius' Venus symbolizes the force of Nature; Scudamour's is an artefact to which 'tormented' lovers attribute the powers of Nature in the hope of gaining personal contentment. The inclusion of this element allows Spenser to raise the issue of the relationship between hymn and epic in much the same way as the introduction of Colin Clout to book six raises that of the relationship between epic and pastoral. Whereas the proem to the fourth book alleges that Spenser's work was criticized, like Ovid's, for indulging love and misleading the young, the dedicatory epistle to the *Fowre Hymnes* levels the same charges against the two early hymns but undertakes to 'reforme' them by Augustinian 'retractation', 'making instead of those two Hymnes of earthly or naturall love and beautie, two others of heavenlie and celestiall'.[54] A similar process of 'retractation' is evident in Spenser's figuration of the 'great goddesse' Nature of the *Mutabilitie Cantos*, where unmistakably Lucretian elements are informed by intimations of transcendence, thereby implying an ultimately supernatural resolution to all debates 'de rerum natura' (7. 7. 5–13).

The mode of 'retractation' envisaged in the *Fowre Hymnes* may stand as a paradigm for Spenser's mature understanding of the reception of the classical into the Christian. The two 'pagan' hymns are not discarded but recontextualized, so that the Cupid of the first hymn ('Love') is made to adumbrate the Christ of the third ('Heavenly Love'), and the Venus ('Beautie') of the second hymn to adumbrate the Lady Sapience of the fourth ('Heavenly Beautie'). The danger incident to such a procedure, however, is that the elaborate system of linguistic echoes and structural coincidences that informs the quartet threatens to reveal the residual paganism of Christianity as powerfully as the incipient Christianity of the pagan. Marvell's fear that Milton 'would ruin (for I saw him strong) | The sacred truths to fable and old song' attests to similar anxieties.[55] Such is the spirituality attributed to the sensual in the hymns to Cupid and Venus, and the sensuality attributed to the spiritual in the hymns to Christ and Sapience, that all four components remain locked in a tense dynamic that facilitates patterns of descent as readily as those of ascent. From an aesthetic viewpoint, the Cupid and Venus of the hymns are no less mesmerizing in and of themselves than the cruel, blindfolded idol of the House of Busyrane (*Faerie Queene*, 3. 12. 22–3), or the sculpted hermaphrodite of Scudamour's temple, which outshone 'all other Idoles, which the heathen adore' (4. 10. 39–41).[56] The *Fowre Hymnes* thus constitutes an epitome of the problems of classical reception in the early modern period generally: what appears to be formally resolved through 'retractation' remains inherently unstable—as Erasmus, in opposing the new 'paganism', had always feared.[57] It was, after all, the papacy's resemblance to the empire it supposedly succeeded that made it vulnerable to the charge of 'paganism'. The element of Girardian *antagonisme* in early modern mimesis was a vital component of an aesthetic that sought to articulate an independent identity. In retrospect, one can see that what *The Shepheardes Calender* strove to herald was a poet quite unlike Virgil or Ovid, a really 'new' poet.

Notes

1. René Girard, *Things Hidden since the Foundation of the World*, trans. Stephen Bann and Michael Metteer (2003), 7, 17, 26. 'Mimésis de l'antagonisme', as I conceive it, goes well beyond the 'heuristic' imitation defined in Thomas M. Greene, *The Light in Troy: Imitation and Discovery in Renaissance Poetry* (New Haven, 1982).
2. See Teresa Krier, *Gazing on Secret Sights: Spenser, Classical Imitation, and the Decorums of Vision* (Ithaca, NY, 1990). See also the very useful H. G. Lotspeich, *Classical Mythology in the Poetry of Edmund Spenser* (Princeton, 1932).
3. See D. C. Allen, *Mysteriously Meant: the Rediscovery of Pagan Symbolism and Allegorical Interpretation in the Renaissance* (Baltimore, 1970); Michael Murrin, *The Allegorical Epic: Essays in its Rise and Decline* (Chicago, 1980); Robert Lamberton, *Homer, The Theologian* (Berkeley and Los Angeles, 1989).
4. Quoted in Murrin, *The Allegorical Epic*, 197–8.
5. See *Maphaeus Vegius and his Thirteenth Book of the 'Aeneid'*, ed. Anna Cox Brinton (2002; first pub. 1930).
6. *Collected Works of Erasmus*, 86 vols (Toronto, 1974–),66 (1988), 33.
7. See C. P. Brand, *Torquato Tasso: A Study of the Poet and his Contribution to English Literature* (Cambridge, 1965), 123–32.
8. *The Works of John Dryden*, ed. H. T. Swedenberg et al., 20 vols (Berkeley and Los Angeles, 1956–2000), 4. 16; 5. 276.
9. John Watkins, *The Specter of Dido: Spenser and Virgilian Epic* (New Haven, 1995), 90–112.
10. See Jean Seznec, *The Survival of the Pagan Gods: The Mythological Tradition and Its Place in Renaissance Humanism and Art*, Bollingen Series 38 (Princeton, 1972; first pub. 1953); Edgar Wind, *Pagan Mysteries in the Renaissance*, 2nd edn (1967); Malcolm Bull, *The Mirror of the Gods: Classical Mythology in Renaissance Art* (2005). See E.K.'s gloss to *Aprill*, l. 109.
11. M. L. Donnelly, 'The Life of Virgil and the Aspiration of the "New Poet"', *Spenser Studies*, 17 (2003), 1–35. See also Jane Tylus, 'Spenser, Virgil, and the Politics of Poetic Labour', *English Literary History*, 55 (1988), 53–77.
12. See *Servii Grammatici qui feruntur in Virgilii Carmina Commentarii*, ed. G. Thilo and H. Hagen, 3 vols (Leipzig, 1881–1902).
13. For E. K. and Servius, see Richard A. McCabe, 'Annotating Anonymity, or Putting a Gloss on *The Shepheardes Calender*', in Joe Bray, Miriam Handley, and Anne C. Henry (eds), *Ma[r]king the Text: The Presentation of Meaning on the Literary Page* (Aldershot, 2000), 35–54 (41–7). For the importance of commentary, see

W. J. Kennedy, *Authorizing Petrarch* (Ithaca, NY, 1995), 27–8.

14. See, e.g. Servius' comment on *Eclogues* I. 27, 70. *Commentarii* III, pt 1, pp. 8, 16.
15. George Puttenham, *The Art of English Poesy*, ed. Frank Whigham and Wayne A. Rebhorn (Ithaca, NY, 2007), 128.
16. Servius, *Commentarii* III, pt 1, p. 2.
17. See Richard A. McCabe, '"Little booke, thy selfe present": The Politics of Presentation in *The Shepheardes Calender*', in H. Erskine-Hill and R. A. McCabe (eds), *Presenting Poetry: Composition, Publication, Reception* (Cambridge, 1995), 15–40.
18. Servius, *Commentarii* III, pt 1, pp. 56–7. Clement Marot, *Œuvres*, ed. George Guiffrey and Jean Plattard, 5 vols (Geneva, 1969; first pub. 1911), 4. 399–407 (406). See Annabel Patterson, 'Re-Opening the Green Cabinet: Clement Marot and Edmund Spenser', *English Literary Renaissance*, 16 (1986), 44–70.
19. For de-contextualization of the 'laye', see William Wells (ed.), *Spenser Allusions in the Sixteenth and Seventeenth Centuries*, 2 pts, *Studies in Philology*, Texts and Studies 68, 69 (Chapel Hill, NC, 1971–2), pt 1, p. 71.
20. Frances A. Yates, *Astraea: The Imperial Theme in the Sixteenth Century* (Harmondsworth, 1977; first pub. 1975), 34–5.
21. See A. DiMatteo, 'Spenser's Venus-Virgo: The Poetics and Interpretative History of a Dissembling Figure', *Spenser Studies*, 10 (1989), 37–70.
22. See Helen Cooper, *Pastoral: Medieval into Renaissance* (Ipswich, 1977), 36–46, 108–11.
23. McCabe, '"Little booke: thy selfe present"', 30–2; *The Remains of Edmund Grindal*, ed. William Nicholson (Cambridge, 1843), 376–90.
24. See Syrithe Pugh, *Spenser and Ovid* (Aldershot, 2005), 12–41. See also L. Kelsey and R. S. Peterson, 'Rereading Colin's Broken Pipe: Spenser and the Problem of Patronage', *Spenser Studies*, 14 (2000), 233–72.
25. See Richard A. McCabe, 'Edmund Spenser: Poet of Exile', *Proceedings of the British Academy*, 80 (1993), 73–103 (89–94).
26. See Sue Petitt Starke, 'Briton Knight or Irish Bard? Spenser's Pastoral Persona and the Epic Project in *A View of the Present State of Ireland* and *Colin Clouts Come Home Againe*', *Spenser Studies*, 12 (1998 for 1991), 133–50.
27. See R. S. Peterson, 'Laurel Crown and Ape's Tail: New Light on Spenser's Career from Sir Thomas Tresham', *Spenser Studies*, 12 (1998), 1–35.
28. See Bernard Weinberg, *A History of Literary Criticism in the Italian Renaissance*, 2 vols (Chicago, 1961), 2. 635–714. Harvey is quoted from *The Works of Edmund Spenser*, ed. Edwin Greenlaw et al., Variorum Edition, 11 vols (Baltimore, 1932–58), 9: *Prose* (1949), 471–2. For the genre of *The Faerie Queene*, see John Arthos, *On the Poetry of Spenser and the Form of Romances* (1956); Colin Burrow, *Epic Romance: Homer to Milton* (Oxford, 1993).
29. Giraldi Cinthio, *On Romances*, trans. Henry L. Snuggs (Lexington, KY, 1968), 11, 23.
30. For some of the issues involved, see Michael West, 'Spenser and the Renaissance Ideal of Christian Heroism', *PMLA* 88 (1973), 1013–32.
31. See also *The Faerie Queene*, 1. 10. 64.
32. For Du Bellay, see George Hugo Tucker, *The Poet's Odyssey: Joachim Du Bellay and the 'Antiquitez de Rome'* (Oxford, 1990); Margaret M. McGowan, *The Vision of Rome in Late Renaissance France* (New Haven, 2000), 187–226.
33. For Noot, see J. A. Van Dorsten, *The Radical Arts: The First Decade of the Elizabethan Renaissance* (Leiden, 1970); Carl J. Rasmussen, '"Quietnesse of minde": *A Theatre for Worldlings* as a Protestant Poetics', *Spenser Studies*, 1 (1980), 3–27; Tom MacFaul, '*A Theatre for Worldlings* (1569)', in Richard A. McCabe (ed.), *The*

Oxford Handbook of Edmund Spenser (Oxford, 2010), 149–59.

34. See M. W. Ferguson, '"The Afflatus of Ruin": Meditations on Rome by Du Bellay, Spenser, and Stevens', in A. Patterson (ed.), *Roman Images*, Selected Papers from the English Institute 8 (Baltimore, 1984), 23–50; A. Fichter, '"And nought of *Rome* in *Rome* perceiu'st at all": Spenser's *Ruines of Rome*', *Spenser Studies*, 2 (1981), 183–92.
35. See S. K. Heninger, 'The Tudor Myth of Troy-novant', *South Atlantic Quarterly*, 61 (1962), 378–87. See also Heather James, *Shakespeare's Troy: Drama, Politics and the Translation of Empire* (Cambridge, 1997), 7–41.
36. See Harry Berger, Jr, 'The Structure of Merlin's Chronicle in *The Faerie Queene* III (iii)', *Studies in English Literature*, 9 (1969), 39–51; Heather Dubrow, 'The Arraignment of Paridell: Tudor Historiography in *The Faerie Queene*, III, ix', *Studies in Philology*, 87 (1990), 312–27; Stanley Stewart, 'Spenser and the Judgement of Paris', *Spenser Studies*, 9 (1991), 161–209.
37. See McGowan, *The Vision of Rome*, 187–226.
38. Murrin, *The Allegorical Epic*, 39–40. Servius, *Commentarii* II. 49, 122–3.
39. See Colin Burrow, 'English Renaissance Readers and the *Appendix Vergiliana*', *Proceedings of the Virgil Society*, 26 (2008), 1–16; H. G. Lotspeich, 'Spenser's *Virgil's Gnat* and its Latin Original', *English Literary History*, 2 (1935), 235–41.
40. For Helen, see T. P. Roche, Jr, *The Kindly Flame: A Study of the Third and Fourth Books of Spenser's 'Faerie Queene'* (Princeton, 1964), 152–62.
41. See Richard A. McCabe, 'Parody, Sympathy and Self: A Response to Donald Cheney', *Connotations*, 13/1–2 (2003–4), 5–22.
42. For Spenser's use of Homer, see T. Demetriou, '"Essentially Circe": Spenser, Homer, and the Homeric Tradition', *Translation and Literature*, 15 (2006), 151–76.
43. See S. C. Scott, 'From Polydorus to Fraudubio: The History of a Topos', *Spenser Studies*, 7 (1986), 27–57.
44. M. L. Stapleton, 'Devoid of Guilty Shame: Ovidian Tendencies in Spenser's Erotic Poetry', *Modern Philology*, 105 (2007), 271–99.
45. Richard A. McCabe, *Spenser's Monstrous Regiment: Elizabethan Ireland and the Poetics of Difference* (Oxford, 2002), 194–5, 263–4.
46. *Works*, ed. Greenlaw, 9: *Prose*, 87.
47. See R. M. Durling, *The Figure of the Poet in Renaissance Epic* (Cambridge, MA, 1965), 138–45.
48. See C. Kallendorf, *The Other Virgil: Pessimistic Readings of the* Aeneid *in Early Modern Culture* (Oxford, 2007).
49. McCabe, *Spenser's Monstrous Regiment*, 232–51.
50. See Richard McCabe, 'Prince Arthur's "Vertuous and Gentle Discipline"', in Eilean Ní Chuilleanáin and J. D. Pheifer (eds), *Noble and Joyous Histories: English Romances, 1375–1650* (Dublin, 1993), 221–43.
51. For Spenser's sources, see James A. S. McPeek, 'The Major Sources of Spenser's *Epithalamion*', *Journal of English and Germanic Philology*, 35 (1936), 183–213; Thomas M. Greene, 'Spenser and the Epithalmic Convention', *Comparative Literature*, 9 (1957), 215–28.
52. For details of Spenser's borrowings and adaptations, see Pugh, *Spenser and Ovid*, 246–77.
53. See P. Rollinson, 'The Renaissance of the Literary Hymn', *Renaissance Papers* (1968), 11–20, and 'A Generic View of Spenser's *Four Hymns*', *Studies in Philology*, 68 (1971), 292–304; Patrick Cheney, *Spenser's Famous Flight: A Renaissance Idea of a Literary Career* (Toronto, 1993), 201–5.
54. For a discussion of the relationship of the *Fowre Hymnes* to Spenser's canon, see Richard A. McCabe, 'Spenser, Plato, and the Poetics of State', *Spenser Studies*, 24 (2009), 433–52. For Augustinian

'retractation', see also David Lee Miller, *The Poem's Two Bodies: The Poetics of the 1590 'Faerie Queene'* (Princeton, 1988), 9–14.

55. John Milton, *Paradise Lost*, ed. Alastair Fowler (1968), 38.

56. For Spenser's Cupids, see C. S. Lewis, *Spenser's Images of Life*, ed. Alastair Fowler (Cambridge, 1967), 18–44.

57. Erasmus, *Complete Works*, 84 (2005), pp. xlvii, 35, 62.

CHAPTER 26

Marlowe

CHARLES MARTINDALE

Lucan's First Book Translated Line for Line, by Christopher Marlowe was published, apparently for the first time, in 1600. It had been entered in the *Stationers' Register* in 1593, a few months after Marlowe's death, on the same day as *Hero and Leander*, and there may even have been plans to publish the two works (both possibly composed towards the end of the poet's short career) in a single volume. One an accomplished version of a demanding Latin author as yet not satisfactorily Englished, the other the most assured example of the mythological short epic so fashionable throughout the 1590s (its subject taken from Musaeus, its main stylistic affiliations Ovidian), together they constitute a truly remarkable demonstration of Marlowe's pioneering achievements as a classicist.[1] It will indeed be the main argument of this chapter that it is precisely Marlowe's classicism that made him in his day so radical and influential a figure, one who launched a *poetic* revolution.

Contemporaries might well have been struck by the analogies between Lucan and Marlowe. Certainly there is a convergence in the 'myths' that have grown up around them. Both were precociously talented, marvellous boys; both died young, and violently, Lucan in his mid, Marlowe in his late twenties, the one by his own hand a victim of the imperial tyrant Nero against whom, in a bid for liberty, he had conspired, the other stabbed by Ingram Frizer, supposedly in a dispute over 'the reckoning', possibly (though this is highly speculative) as a result of his involvement in espionage. Both left works that have traditionally been regarded as unfinished in a way that appropriately symbolizes genius prematurely cut short: Lucan's *Pharsalia* ends abruptly in the middle of Caesar's Egyptian escapade; in the first edition of *Hero and Leander* (1598) the text is followed by the words (presumably editorial, unless we imagine Marlowe as a sort of Coleridge *avant la lettre*, knowingly constructing a poetic fragment) 'desunt nonnulla' ('quite a lot is missing'). Intriguingly, in both instances some (post)modern students of Lucan and Marlowe have argued—though quite independently—that, contrary to superficial appearance, the works are complete, justly (in view of their subject matter) lacking the sense of an ending desired by the conventional.[2]

Andrew Hadfield argues that it was Lucan's Republicanism that particularly attracted Marlowe to him; while admitting that 'Marlowe's works do not amount to an articulate political theory', he sees them as 'relentlessly hostile' to monarchical rule.[3] But the late Elizabethan interest in Lucan (shown also in Shakespeare's *Henry VI* plays, where at the battle of Towton the King witnesses, and moralizes on, the Lucanian figures of 'a son that hath killed his father' and 'a father that hath killed his son'[4]) can as readily be linked to fears about political instability (the *Pharsalia* was commonly read in the Middle Ages as a warning against civil war). The first book is anyway less outspoken in its Republicanism than some of its successors. And Marlowe quite glosses over its most overtly Republican line (l. 670), which presents the Augustan settlement as a form of universal slavery ('cum domino pax ista venit' ('when peace comes, a master will come with it')).[5] He seems more interested in the figure of the Superman beyond good and evil, the glittering over-reacher,[6] a figure who is so conspicuous a feature of the plays and whom we can connect with what Hazlitt famously called the 'lust of power in his writings, a hunger and thirst after unrighteousness, a glow of the imagination, unhallowed by anything but its own energies'.[7] So Tamburlaine in his chariot presents us with a visual image that recalls the Ovidian aspirer Phaethon,[8] though, in this like Lucan's Caesar, he suffers no immediate downfall.

Given that the context and occasions of Marlowe's works are unknown, his immediate purposes are necessarily obscured. However, Hadfield's view of Marlowe's Lucan chimes with a dominant modern picture of Marlowe that values him as radical, homosexual, with subversive views on gender, race, politics, and the humanist subject (by contrast contemporaries were inclined to dissociate his greatness as a poet from his supposed moral deficiencies). It is hard to think that this picture is not unduly influenced by the biographical tradition and in particular the notorious memorandum submitted to the Privy Council by the informer Richard Baines close to the time of Marlowe's death, which attributes to him various transgressive statements (of the kind associated with characters in the plays);[9] accusations of this kind from so disreputable a source are, however, poor foundation for sober history. We know little for certain about Marlowe's life (though you would not guess this from the numerous biographies).[10] Problems about authorship and the state of the text affect most of the plays. For example, in the 1594 quarto of *Dido, Queen of Carthage* the name of Thomas Nashe appears on the title page as well as that of Marlowe; we have two very different posthumous editions of *Faustus*, and we cannot tell whether either conforms to anything performed in Marlowe's lifetime; there is evidence for lost comic scenes in *Tamburlaine* (first explicitly published as Marlowe's in 1820), while the Latin act and scene divisions may or may not be authorial.[11] In *The Jew of Malta* (for which our first surviving text was published in 1633) the slave Ithamore unexpectedly delivers his version of the Marlovian grand manner with its classical flourishes in expressing his love for the prostitute Bellamira:

> Content, but we will leave this paltry land,
> And sail from hence to Greece, to lovely Greece.

> I'll be thy Jason, thou my golden fleece.
> Where painted carpets o'er the meads are hurled,
> And Bacchus' vineyards overspread the world,
> Where woods and forests go in goodly green,
> I'll be Adonis, thou shalt be Love's queen.
> The meads, the orchards, and the primrose lanes,
> Instead of sedge and reed, bear sugar-canes.
> Thou in those groves, by Dis above,
> Shalt live with me and be my love.
> (*Jew of Malta*, 4. 2. 99–109)

If Marlowe is the writer, and if we assume that the attribution to him of 'The Passionate Shepherd' is secure, the autocitation is slyly self-reflexive in a way that might be called 'Ovidian', as Marlowe 'authors' Ithamore's words. The writing has an alluring swagger, but there are curious touches: the somewhat inappropriate metaphor in 'hurled', the incongruous mention of 'sugar-cane' in connection with Greece, the oath 'by Dis above' (when Dis is the god of the Underworld). Is Marlowe then archly parodying, in advance of Pistol, what Ben Jonson in *Discoveries* (ll. 778–9; *Works*, 8. 587) termed his 'scenical strutting, and furious vociferation'? Or is some later poet attempting (incompetently, or wittily?) to create the 'Marlowe effect'? We can only guess.

There is no secure basis for a chronology of Marlowe's works (the translations and *Dido* are usually assigned an early date, but without decisive evidence, partly perhaps because translation is anachronistically regarded as inferior to 'original' poetry). This complicates the claim by Patrick Cheney that Marlowe, in conscious opposition to Spenser's aspiration to become England's Virgil, espoused a 'counter-Virgilian' conception of authorship modelled on the poetic career of Ovid.[12] Contemporaries certainly saw Marlowe as the modern equivalent of a classical *auctor* ('authority' as well as 'author'). Modern notions of literature and poetry as independent spheres of permanent importance are to an extent creations of the Early Modern period under classical influence. In *As You Like It* (3. 5. 81–2), Marlowe is invoked in Shakespeare's pastoral world as 'dead shepherd', an authority on love, and the author of *Hero and Leander*, a line from which is quoted ('Whoever loved that loved not at first sight?'), just as Virgil had inscribed both himself and contemporaries as shepherds into his *Eclogues*. But a view such as Cheney's requires a degree of security about the chronology to establish the 'Ovidian' trajectory from elegy through tragedy to epic (quite apart from the weight it gives to Ovid's lost play *Medea* for the shape of his career, as well as the question whether *Hero and Leander* is properly described as an epic).

Marlowe's classical preferences are not necessarily in themselves radical. 'The classical authors that Marlowe chose to translate and/or imitate in his poems, including Ovid, Lucan, Musaeus, and, in "The Passionate Shepherd", Callimachus,' writes Georgia E. Brown, 'were all recognized as dissident writers both by their contemporaries and by the Renaissance'.[13] Without very considerable qualification, this is seriously misleading (the word 'dissident' suggests a rather different cultural milieu). Callimachus was certainly caviar to the general, but is listed by Virgil in Jonson's *Poetaster* (5. 3. 543–8) as among 'the best Greeks', worthy of imitation, along with Orpheus, Musaeus, Pindar, 'high' Homer, and others (only 'dark' Lycophron is to be shunned). Musaeus's *Hero and Leander* was the first Greek work to be included in the Aldine classics (*c.*1494), and was regarded by J. C. Scaliger as more polished in style than Homer. The great scholar Isaac Casaubon showed in 1583 that it was a work of late antiquity, but the semi-mythical Musaeus ('he of the Muses'), like Orpheus, continued to be regarded as a primal poet of the most distant ancientry (mentioned as such by Virgil in *Aeneid* 6. 667), and as such much imitated throughout Europe. In all probability that was what drew Marlowe to him; in *Faustus* (*A-Text*, 1. 1. 117–18) he imagines Musaeus singing in Orphic fashion to 'the infernal spirits'. Ovid and Lucan are both central canonical authors, widely studied throughout the Middle Ages[14] and Renaissance. It is true that Ovid was exiled by Augustus for writing immoral verses, but many readers sided with the poet against the emperor. It is also true that Ovid was too licentious for more sober tastes (Sir Thomas Elyot in *The Governor* condemns his work, finding in the elegies 'nothing contained but incitation to lechery',[15] as to an extent does Jonson in *Poetaster*). But he remained the most imitated poet of the age (a taste that the influential Marlowe no doubt helped to foster), and known in Latin to every Elizabethan schoolboy. Admittedly in the *Amores* Marlowe chose one of the most overtly erotic of Ovid's texts to translate in full (his is the first translation of all three books in any modern language, though the poems were widely known in Latin), and in 1599 a published selection from his translations was burned on the orders of the Bishops (though the main target may have been the satiric epigrams of Sir John Davies in the same volume). And certainly the *Amores*, though readily available in complete editions of Ovid, was not a grammar-school text. Yet Erasmus, greatest of the humanists, singles out as praiseworthy the youthful achievements of Ovid and Lucan when comparing education past and present at the conclusion of *De Pueris Statim ac Liberaliter Educandis*, explicitly mentioning the *Amores*; perhaps the passage helped inspire the timely happy Marlowe's unusual choice.[16]

Marlowe, Ovid, and Virgil

There is little doubt that Ovid was Marlowe's favourite classical poet (as he was Shakespeare's, perhaps in a process of mutual engagement and rivalry). The association is picked up in *Poetaster*, 1. 1. 43 ff., where Jonson has his Ovid declaim Marlowe's version of *Amores* 1. 15, with some slight adjustments in the interests of greater 'correctness'[17] (the play is very much a meditation on translating, good and bad). Mythological references in Marlowe's plays usually derive specifically from Ovid. For example, in *Tamburlaine Part 2*, 1. 2. 38–9, 'As fair as was Pygmalion's ivory girl | Or lovely Io metamorphosed', 'ivory girl' translates Ovid's *eburnea virgo* (*Met.* 10. 275), while 'metamorphosed' gestures towards the title of Ovid's poem. In his use of Ovid, Marlowe can demand considerable alertness in his auditors. Gaveston plans to stage erotic Italianate masques for his royal lover (Italy is associated with sophisticated decadence also in respect of Lightborn's murderous skills in *Edward II*, 5. 4. 31–7). The one he describes at length has an Ovidian subject:

> Sometime a lovely boy in Dian's shape,
> With hair that gilds the water as it glides,
> Crownets of pearl about his naked arms,
> And in his sportful hands an olive tree
> To hide those parts which men delight to see,
> Shall bathe him in a spring, and there hard by
> One like Actaeon peeping through the grove
> Shall by the angry goddess be transformed,
> And running in the likeness of an hart
> By yelping hounds pulled down and seem to die.
> (*Edward II*, 1. 1. 61–70)

The passage with its sadistic transgressive eroticism (note the staged doubleness about which parts men desire to see) foreshadows Edward's destruction by his own subjects. And Marlowe exploits the complex ways in which the myth had previously been read, as a warning against prying into the secrets of princes, for example, or of the dangers of destructive desires, of wasting one's patrimony, and of the depredations of servants and favourites.[18] Of Gaveston and the King sitting side by side, Mortimer Senior observes, 'quam male conveniunt!' ('how ill they go together') (*Edward II*, 1. 4. 13); fully to understand the point you need to know how the Ovidian passage to which Mortimer alludes continues: 'non bene conveniunt nec in una sede morantur | maiestas et amor' ('majesty and love do not go well together or tarry in the same seat') (*Met.* 2. 846–7)—of the indignity of Jupiter in taking the form of a bull to seduce Europa. Faustus in his final speech quotes in Latin a line from *Amores* 1, 'lente currite, noctis equi' ('run slowly, horses of the night') (13. 40) in intensified form: 'o lente, lente, currite, noctis equi!' (*A-Text*, 5. 2. 74). The stark change of context—from the lover desiring more time in bed with his girl before the sun rises to Faustus on the verge of damnation begging for delay—creates an extraordinarily powerful *frisson* for those in the know (with similarly pointed incongruity Faustus had quoted Christ's words from the cross 'consummatum est' when signing his pact with the devil in 2. 1. 74).[19]

But Marlowe also translated, and imitated, Virgil's *Aeneid*. Scholars often work with an over-schematic opposition between a humourless, rigidly imperial, conservative Virgil and a subversive, witty Ovid. The Renaissance Virgil was also the author of poems in the *Appendix*, now regarded as post-Virgilian, including the *Ciris* and *Culex*, that are 'Ovidian' in style and subject matter.[20] And more generally it is easy to construct a more 'Ovidian' Virgil (or indeed a more 'Virgilian' Ovid); the reception of the two authors involves complex, and shifting, combinations. The common modern view that *Dido, Queen of Carthage*, is simply a parody, or Ovidian deconstruction, of Virgil is reductive. It is true that it is hard to imagine Virgil (or Ovid for that matter) directly representing Jupiter 'dandling Ganymede upon his knee' (as the stage direction for 1. 1 has it) and engaging in love play with him, but the rape of Ganymede is given as a key reason for Juno's hatred of the Trojans in *Aeneid* 1. 28. The comically erotic scene between Cupid and the old Nurse (4. 5) is also too frivolous for Virgil (or even Ovid), and burlesque would be a good term for it. But Marlowe's knowing treatment of the scheming goddesses Juno and Venus is perfectly convincing as a reading of Virgil's text. 'Marlowe's play follows Ovid by placing Dido centre stage,' writes one critic.[21] But Dido is centre stage throughout *Aeneid* 4, with Aeneas given only one speech in reply to her, which many readers have found cold and unimpressive. Indeed, Dido has repeatedly been seen over the ages as compromising, or at least complicating, the poem's imperial message, and Aeneas as somewhat of a cad. Certainly in the Middle Ages many had been sympathetic; in Helen Waddell's words: 'Dido they took to their hearts, wrote lament after lament for her, cried over her as the young men of the eighteenth century cried over Manon Lescaut.'[22] The play as a whole is better seen as a tremendous tribute to Virgil (even if inevitably it falls short of its model).

In the final act Marlowe directly quotes Virgil's Latin words, in an extreme example of what Thomas Greene has called 'sacramental' imitation, where the original is followed with quasi-religious fidelity.[23] Elsewhere lines gain power for those who can hear Virgil's resonant Latin echoing behind them: 'Sometime I was a Trojan, mighty queen' (*Dido, Queen of Carthage*, 2. 1. 75); *fuimus Troes, fuit Ilium* (*Aeneid* 2. 325). Stylistically the play is more accomplished and more varied than is generally recognized (there is no reason to presuppose a very early date).[24] The Queen when lovestruck by Cupid starts to employ a musical, lyricized, 'feminine' version of the 'mighty line' of Tamburlaine (this famous characterization of Marlowe's style is from Jonson's poem on Shakespeare in the first folio (l. 30)). These speeches are predominantly end-stopped, aggregates of individual fine lines rather than Virgilian verse paragraphs (this high lyric mode begins at 3. 1. 81, and the finest example is at 3. 1. 113 ff.; Aeneas falls into it at 5. 1. 1). The manner is classicizing, but not especially Virgilian (or even Ovidian, except in the rather generalized sense of being showily rhetorical, or evoking myths out of Ovid):

> I'll frame me wings of wax, like Icarus;
> And o'er his ships will soar unto the sun,
> That they may melt, and I fall in his arms.
> (5. 1. 243–5)

By contrast, Aeneas' retrospective narrative, sometimes closely translating passages from the *Aeneid*, eschews any lyric glitter in favour of a responsible epic mode that depends on rhythm and syntax rather than exotic lexis or poetic conceits (at 1. 2. 25 there is even a Virgilian half-line):

Then buckled I mine armour, drew my sword,
And thinking to go down, came Hector's ghost
With ashy visage, blueish sulphur eyes,
His arms torn from his shoulders, and his breast
Furrowed with wounds, and—that which made me weep—
Thongs at his heels, by which Achilles' horse
Drew him in triumph through the Greekish camp,
Burst from the earth, crying, 'Aeneas, fly!
Troy is a-fire, the Grecians have the town'.

(2. 1. 200–8)

Here we have skilfully deployed enjambment and a variety of verse movement that moves to a highly effective climax; Virgil's epic style had perhaps never before been represented so convincingly and so fluently in English verse.

Marlowe's Classicism

I agree with Marlowe's modern admirers about his radicalism. However, I see this not so much in terms of his supposed anticipation of (post)modern concerns; rather, it is because he was a leader of what it is not too much to call a poetic revolution. And that achievement is closely connected with the humanist education he received at King's School, Canterbury, and Corpus Christi, Cambridge, and with his enthusiasm for classical poetry. It is Marlowe's misfortune, and his glory, that he was born too early and died too young; he was killed not only by Ingram Frizer but by Shakespeare, who learned from him but eclipsed his achievements.[25] But, as contemporaries such as Chapman and Drayton saw,[26] he was prodigiously gifted with that capacity for creative origination outside the rules that Kant called 'genius'. For James Russell Lowell in 1887 he was 'an original man', for Swinburne 'the true Apollo of our dawn', 'the greatest discoverer, the most daring and inspired pioneer, in all our poetic literature', the first to write poetry in English that can truly be called 'sublime'.[27] With some help from 'sporting' Kyd, Marlowe established true blank verse as the natural metre for the drama, as well as setting a standard for the heroic couplet that prepared the ground for the Augustans, twin achievements that reflected his immersion in classical prosody and experience as a translator; out of the poetry of Virgil, Ovid, Lucan, and Seneca, he created a mode of English verse that displayed, in its 'high astounding terms' (prologue to *Tamburlaine 1*), sustained magnificence (even if at times this tips over into a monotonous and excessive grandiloquence). This is not infrequently achieved, as later by Milton, through the sounding resonance of exotic, often trisyllabic proper names (as C. S. Lewis observes, 'we forget Tamburlaine and Mortimer... and think only of Rhodope and Persepolis').[28] An extended epic simile, modelled after Homer and Virgil with appropriate syntactical structure, describes Agydas' response to Tamburlaine's wrath:

As when the seaman sees the Hyades
Gather an army of Cimmerian clouds
(Auster and Aquilon, with winged steeds
All sweating, tilt about the watery heavens
With shivering spears enforcing thunderclaps,
And from their shields strike flames of lightening)
All-fearful folds his sails, and sounds the main,
Lifting his prayers to the heavens for aid
Against the terror of the winds and waves:
So fares Agydas for the late-felt frowns...
(*Part 1*, 3. 2. 76–85)

The vigorous treatment of the epic trope of the battle of the winds with the riot of high-sounding, classical names anticipates the manner of *Paradise Lost* (Milton's debt to Marlowe merits fuller exploration[29]). Marlowe was not a scholar like Milton, or even Ben Jonson, but he received a better and more extended education than Shakespeare, which left its mark everywhere in his work. Leander, when he tries to persuade Hero to yield her maidenhead because virginity has no essence or form, is termed 'a bold, sharp sophister' (l. 197); 'sophister' was the word used to describe a 2nd- or 3rd-year Cambridge undergraduate, and Marlowe is here exemplifying, and parodying, the kind of argumentative declamatory exercise he had been taught to perform at university.[30] It is difficult to exaggerate the excitement in this period of what Adrian Poole calls 'the mass immigration from Greece and Rome into English culture, on a scale that would have taken Chaucer's breath away, of stories, ideas and language that have shaped the way we feel, think and communicate' in 'a whole great process transforming the very fabric of our culture'.[31] Within this bilingual context (which allows for difference), it is in the balance between the virtues of English, already well-developed, and the increased superimposition of a foreign language and culture, promoted by an educational system based largely on the study of classical Latin, that the distinctive greatness of Renaissance literature seems to reside. There was a dual response to this Latin influence; an eclectic response that stresses gorgeousness and glamour, which is evident in a particularly pure form in Marlowe, and a response of an opposite kind that imitates the supposed austerity and purity of Latin writing, characteristic of Jonson. But in general it was the eclectic that predominated, so that Latin influence brought greater richness—for example, in the grand rhetorical schemes and opulent mythological references so characteristic of Marlowe's plays.[32]

With the changed styles went new contents. The classics open up, and license, endless fresh possibilities, and present potential clashes with other aspects of the culture (if Marlowe really said that 'all the New Testament is filthily written',[33] that would reflect a taste nurtured on the virtues of the kinds of ancient prose favoured by the humanists). *Tamburlaine* tests, to destruction, the ancient philosophical idea that virtue was not a matter of parentage. Tamburlaine cites Jupiter's overthrow of his father Saturn as a justification for action: 'What better precedent than mighty

Jove?' (*Part* 1, 2. 7. 12–17). Mortimer Senior sets out examples from antiquity for acceptable homosexual desire[34]:

> Great Alexander loved Hephaestion,
> The conquering Hercules for Hylas wept,
> And for Patroclus stern Achilles drooped.
> (*Edward II*, 1. 4. 392–4)

Classical stories are an important way that characters in the drama, and its auditors and readers, can think about themselves and others, and can mediate situations. Barabas positions himself, with ominous implications for his future actions, within a classical model of patriarchy when he says:

> I have no charge, nor many children,
> But one sole daughter, whom I hold as dear
> As Agamenon did his Iphigen;
> And all I have is hers.
> (*Jew of Malta*, 1. 1. 133–6)

Shakespeare is the undisputed master here,[35] but Marlowe, rather less subtle, pointed the way.

Marlowe the Translator

The unwary could be excused for thinking that Marlowe was simply the author of seven plays (and only five of those worth reading); even the excellent *Cambridge Companion to Marlowe* devotes a single chapter out of seventeen to the poems and translations. But Marlowe translated four complete books of Latin poetry, a remarkable proportion of his total œuvre, representing a substantial input of time and effort. Few English poets of the first rank have devoted so much attention to translating (only Dryden, Pope, Shelley, Rossetti, Pound, and Hughes), and, whatever is thought of their merits, Marlowe's translations are of great historical importance. Marlowe showed an insight of genius about which English metres can operate most comfortably as equivalents for Latin metres: blank verse for hexameters; closed rhyming couplets for elegiac couplets (admittedly at the price of not reproducing the combination of a longer (hexameter) first and a shorter (pentameter) second line, something still unachieved in a credible English imitation). There were antecedents in Tottel's *Miscellany* (1557), the Earl of Surrey for epic (translations of *Aeneid* 2 and 4), Nicolas Grimald for elegy, but they remained isolated experiments, subsequently ignored. With the closed couplet Marlowe's choice was immediately decisive, and within a century, after 'numbers learned to flow' (Pope, 'Epistle to Augustus', l. 266) as a result of the metrical refinements introduced by Waller and Denham, quite minor poets could turn out couplets that were more polished and 'Ovidian' than

Marlowe's. With epic the matter was not settled until Milton wrote *Paradise Lost* (even thereafter some continued to feel that such verse with its lack of rhyme and frequent enjambment was too prosaic for high poetry).[36]

All Ovid's Elegies (perhaps not published until the early seventeenth century) was popular in its time, but subsequently found fewer friends. A. C. Bradley, in a generally positive account of Marlowe in 1880, wrote that 'it would have been no loss if all the copies had perished'[37] (a volume containing a selection of the poems was ordered to be burned in 1599, as we have seen). This is to overlook the real merits of a pathbreaking endeavour.[38] It is true that, constrained by the requirements of rhyme in a line-for-line version, Marlowe often produces clumsy and contorted syntax, with inert inversions and so forth (e.g. 2. 9. 7–8; 2. 11. 7–8; 3. 2. 29–30). Sometimes one has to look at the Latin to understand the English, as in 2. 7. 3–4 'If on the marble theatre I look, | One among many is to grieve thee took' ('eligis e multis unde dolore velis'). It is also true that Marlowe not infrequently misses what modern scholarship takes to be Ovid's meaning (not all these mistakes can be assigned to his use of a text that has differences from today's, or to the views of the commentators he consulted).[39] 'Ida, the seat of groves, did sing with corn' (3. 9. 39) is what used to be called a 'schoolboy howler', where Marlowe has confused *cāneo* 'be white' with *căno* 'sing' (the result is more exuberant than the original, perhaps under the influence of Psalm 65: 14;[40] Lucretius could have employed so bold a metaphor, but the more classical Ovid would never have done so).

Certainly few of the poems are successful as a whole; an exception is the sultry (and short) 1. 5, which describes love with Corinna in the afternoon, where Marlowe sustains an ongoing sense of erotic excitement and of a convincing speaking voice, in a way that anticipates the love poetry of Donne.[41] (Marlowe is perhaps especially comfortable with narrative, as here and in the crisply phrased opening of 3. 1.) But he often effectively Englishes the 'turns', balanced rhetoric, panache, wit, and polish of Ovid's style (with the added crisp snap of the rhyme):

> A white wench thralls me, so doth golden yellow;
> And nut-brown girls in doing hath no fellow.
>
> (2. 4. 39–40)

> What flies I follow, what follows me I shun.
>
> (2. 19. 36)

> My mistress hath her wish, my wish remain;
> He holds the palm, my palm is yet to gain.
>
> (3. 2. 81–2)

> Jove, being admonished gold had sovereign power,
> To win the maid came in a golden shower;
> Till then, rough was her father, she severe,
> The posts of brass, the walls of iron were;
> But when in gifts the wise adulterer came,
> She held her lap ope to receive the same.
>
> (3. 7. 29–34)

In this last example the cynical reading of the myth of Danae as an allegory of the power of money, the irreverent treatment of Jupiter ('the wise adulterer'), the sexual innuendo in the final line (with the ambiguity about whether 'the same' refers to the gold or the god, as Danae both opens herself to her lover and receives his gifts)—in all this Marlowe follows Ovid closely, with in this case lucid syntax and firmly controlled rhetoric, reinforced by the rhymes. Another of Marlowe's notorious mistranslations, 'snakes leap by verse from caves of broken mountains' (2. 1. 25), occurs in a passage where the syntactic and rhetorical organization depends on repetition of *carmen* (meaning both 'verse' and 'magic spell') in various different cases (which Marlowe, unable to reproduce the pun, imitates with 'verses', 'by verse', 'verses', 'to verses'). In such instances Marlowe is training himself in how to write in the rhetorically disciplined manner of a Latin poet, to the enormous benefit of his own and others' 'original' poetry. In the words of one critic, Marlowe's use of the heroic couplet shows 'deep understanding of the way two languages work, of the effects realized in one and of the possibilities latent in the other'.[42]

It is significant in that regard that Marlowe not only translated from Latin but also wrote in it (by contrast there is no indication that Shakespeare composed anything in Latin after his grammar-school years). Two late Latin works, one in hexameter verse, one in prose, are very plausibly assigned to Marlowe, even if his authorship cannot be established beyond all dispute.[43] The laudatory epitaph for judge and fellow Kentishman Sir Roger Manwood (who died in 1592), preserved in the commonplace book of Henry Oxenden from *c.*1650, is accomplished and smoothly versified, with the generic tropes deployed with wit and considerable skill.[44] Less successful are the somewhat tumid Ciceronian periods of the dedication of his friend Thomas Watson's *Amintae Gaudia* to Mary Sidney (1592). There are Ovidian references in this dedicatory epistle that specifically present the writer ('CM') as an Ovidian poet.

Lucan's First Book is altogether more consistently successful than the Ovid translations, whether because Marlowe had greater experience when he wrote it, or because he did not have to combine fidelity with the constraint of rhyme, or because he had a special affinity with this author. It won plaudits from Swinburne and from C. S. Lewis, who oddly doubted its ascription to Marlowe.[45] Indeed, this often overlooked near-masterpiece is one of the most accomplished of all Elizabethan translations from the classics, the majority of which are marred by clotted writing and passages that only skirt intelligibility. As a version of the *Pharsalia* it has never been surpassed, and its only equal is Nicholas Rowe's complete version of 1719, rightly admired by Dr Johnson, where, however, the balanced Augustan rhetoric is rather too orderly to represent Lucan's jagged brilliance.[46] Marlowe responds with enthusiasm to Lucanian hyperbole, but Lucanian paradox tends to elude him. 'Even so, the city left, | All rise in arms' (*Lucan's First Book*, ll. 501–2) misses the paradoxical force of 'sic urbe relicta | in bellum fugitur' ('one normally flees from war, not to it'). 'Each side had great partakers: Caesar's cause | The gods abetted, Cato liked the other' (ll. 128–9) is wordily flaccid as a rendering of Lucan's most famous *sententia*: 'victrix causa deis placuit sed victa Catoni', and fails to convey its implication of bitter protest. But Marlowe renders with exemplary vigour the comparison of the implosion of civil war to the dissolution of the cosmos (ll. 70–80), or the portents announcing civil war, including the gruesome description of the examination of entrails (ll. 520 ff.).

The opening description of Caesar, spare and energetic, gives a good measure of the translation's quality:

> Caesar's renown for war was less, he restless,
> Shaming to strive but where he did subdue,
> When ire or hope provoked, heady and bold,
> At all times charging home, and making havoc,
> Urging his fortune, trusting in the gods,
> Destroying what withstood his proud desires,
> And glad when blood and ruin made him way:
> So thunder which the wind tears from the clouds,
> With crack of riven air and hideous sound
> Filling the world, leaps out and throws forth fire,
> Affrights poor fearful men, and blasts their eyes
> With overthwarting flames, and raging shoots
> Alongst the air, and, nought resisting it,
> Falls, and returns, and shivers where it lights.
>
> (ll. 145–58)

The comparison of the power-driven Caesar with a lightning flash associates him both with a resistless and destructive force of nature and (paradoxically given his amorality) with the omnipotence of Jupiter, whose weapon it is, and which is supposed to punish wrongdoers. The vocabulary is plain, even prosaic (in this like Lucan); the effect is achieved by taut syntax and carefully placed caesuras, with three cases of enjambment, creating a varied verse movement. The weight falls first on a string of participles, then on a series of powerful verbs (many of them monosyllabic), culminating with four in the closing line, two of which involve effective verbal play: 'shivers' meaning both 'splits' and 'causes to shake', 'lights' both 'alights' and 'lights up'.[47] The writing is under complete control, each word precisely placed, the stresses and emphases falling invariably where they are most effective. More than Chaucer in Eustace Deschamps's designation of him, Marlowe deserves to be called 'grand translateur'.

'Translation'—carrying across—is a good trope with which to think about Marlowe's poetic practice (as 'imitation' is about Jonson's). *Dido* both contains local translations from Virgil's *Aeneid* and translates epic narration into tragic performance. *Hero and Leander*, Marlowe's single most fully achieved work and in the early seventeenth century his most popular one (with at least nine editions by 1637), might profitably be seen as the translation of a non-existent Ovidian original; Ovid included an exchange of letters between the lovers in the *Heroides* (18–19), but left no narrative version of the story.[48] For that Marlowe used 'divine Musaeus' (evoked as the source in l. 52), whom he read either in the original Greek, or in Latin translation (or most likely a combination), and to whom he owes the odd local detail.[49] But it is Ovid, not 'Musaeus', who is principally recalled, as Marlowe sought to re-create in English the bright erotic world of the *Metamorphoses*, and to make the reader, whether male or female,[50] feel at home there. (As C. S. Lewis in a classic essay puts it: 'In that world there are boys so beautiful that they can never drink in safety from a fountain: the water nymphs would pull them in.[51]) We have the interest in the psychology and paradoxes and contradictions of love (seen as polymorphous and as a universal solvent), and brilliant imitations of witty Ovidian effects, such as an aetiology in sprightly mock-heroic vein: 'Since Hero's time hath half the world been black' (l. 50). We have digression (explicitly signalled as Ovidian with the reference to the story of Io), delaying Leander's desire for consummation and the reader's for narrative closure.[52] We have an unreliable narrator, who patronizes the inexperienced lovers and is free with misogynistic comment (which allows us to posit an author of greater sophistication and more elusive views).

Spenser had already naturalized the Ovidian ecphrasis in English in *The Faerie Queene*, where it helped serve his larger moral purposes. In a prominent position early in the poem Marlowe places an ecphrasis that is equally emblematic of his own very differently Ovidian poetry, as he describes the temple where Hero serves as 'Venus's nun' ('nun' was a slang term for a prostitute, so its use here of a virgin votary of the goddess of sex is a piquant one).[53] There is an Ovidian emphasis on artificiality and illusion, as Marlowe constructs Ovid's mythological world in terms wholly opposed to those of the *Ovide moralisé*, in a passage that has all the glitter, panache, and iconoclasm one associates with him at his best:

> So fair a church as this had Venus none:
> The walls were of discoloured jasper stone,
> Wherein was Proteus carved, and o'erhead
> A lively vine of green sea agate spread,
> Where by one hand light-headed Bacchus hung,
> And with the other wine from grapes outwrung.
> Of crystal shining fair the pavement was,
> The town of Sestos called it Venus' glass.
> There might you see the gods in sundry shapes,
> Committing heady riots, incest, rapes:
> For know that underneath this radiant floor
> Was Danae's statue in a brazen tower,
> Jove slyly stealing from his sister's bed,
> To dally with Idalian Ganymede,
> Or for his love Europa bellowing loud,
> Or tumbling with the Rainbow in a cloud;
> Blood-quaffing Mars, heaving the iron net,
> Which limping Vulcan and his Cyclops set;
> Love kindling fire, to burn such towns as Troy,

> Sylvanus weeping for the lovely boy
> That now is turned into a cypress tree,
> Under whose shade the wood-gods love to be.
>
> (*Sestiad* 1. 135–56)[54]

The shape-shifting Proteus appropriately presides over the metamorphic whole (nothing here is single, even the variegated walls). Ovid loves to play on the dual nature of his divinities, whereby, for example, Aurora is both a goddess in human form and the dawn itself (figured as her blush in *Amores*, 1. 13. 47–8). So when Neptune tries to seduce Leander (*Hero and Leander*, 2. 181–92), he is both the anthropomorphic god of the sea and the waters of the Hellespont sliding round Leander's body, the passage contriving to be an accurate and sensuous description at once of swimming and of love-making, licensing our, as Neptune's, roving hands. Bacchus (regularly used in Latin poetry as a metonymy for wine) is 'light-headed' because wine makes us so, and he hangs on the vine like the grapes.[55] Jupiter (the rain god) coupling with Iris (the rainbow) mutates into a meteorological phenomenon. The passage provocatively details the amorous antics of the gods and points to the destructive power of sex (recalling, without naming her, Marlowe's favourite Helen, the face who burned Ilium's topless towers). The lines on Ganymede, for example, pointedly remind us that the philandering Jupiter is guilty of both incest and pederasty. 'Hero', writes Lewis, 'is compared to diamonds, and the whole work has something of their hardness and brightness'.[56] Only the lines on Sylvanus (again the homosexual theme) achieve a delicacy and elegiac wistfulness that evoke other facets of Ovid's poem. But in all this the dangerous eroticism of the classical gods has been in part defused by its transformation into art, the art on display in Venus' church—and in Marlowe's poetry about it. And this art is lavished on subject matter that sober readers would see at best as trivial (*abydena* from Leander of Abydos are glossed as 'trifles' and 'wanton toys' in Cooper's *Thesaurus*).[57]

There was a particular vogue for short mythological narrative poems of a broadly Ovidian character in the 1590s. *Hero and Leander* may have been written at the same time as Shakespeare's *Venus and Adonis* following the closure of the theatres in 1592, and indeed perhaps in some sort of dialogue with it. Both poems are today often styled *epyllia*; *epyllion* is a term unknown to either antiquity or the Renaissance, but that is no reason to deny relevant generic continuities. In 1595–6 Richard Carew links 'Marlowe's fragment' and Shakespeare (presumably, given the date, the hugely popular *Venus and Adonis*) with Catullus; he must surely be thinking of Catullus 64, the short epic (which entwines the stories of Peleus and Thetis and Ariadne), and treating the modern poems as works of the same type.[58] Ovid's *Metamorphoses* combines a series of such *epyllia* into a continuous poem. And uniquely in this kind Marlowe surpassed his rival, as Bradley, Swinburne, and C. S. Lewis all agree.[59] Perhaps this was because he was the better classicist, and thus better able to inhabit the appropriate form and style a poem of this type requires for full success. 'What is the peculiar sensation, what is the peculiar quality, which his work has the property of exciting in us, and which we cannot get elsewhere?'—that, according to Walter Pater, is the question about any artist with which the aesthetic critic must be concerned.[60] Marlowe's singularity is closely bound up with his love for the Latin poets, especially Ovid. Quite lacking Shakespeare's negative capability and centripetal interests,[61] he appropriates them, single-mindedly, for that glow of the imagination hallowed only by its own energies which he shares with his protagonists, and for his mighty line:

> O, thou art fairer than the evening air,
> Clad in the beauty of a thousand stars.
> Brighter art thou than flaming Jupiter
> When he appeared to hapless Semele,
> More lovely than the monarch of the sky
> In wanton Arethusa's azured arms:
> And none but thou shalt be my paramour.
> (*Faustus A-Text*, 5. 1. 104–10)

Notes

1. There is no comprehensive treatment of Marlowe and the classics (as there is for Shakespeare). Much basic spadework still needs to be done. The commentators offer most guidance, esp. Roma Gill (ed.), *The Complete Works of Christopher Marlowe: Vol. 1* (Oxford, 1987), and Patrick Cheney and Brian J. Striar (eds), *The Collected Poems of Christopher Marlowe* (New York and Oxford, 2006). For the influence of the grammar school, see T. W. Baldwin, *William Shakspere's Small Latine and Lesse Greeke*, 2 vols (Urbana, IL, 1944). Much of value about Marlowe's classicism will be found in Jonathan Bate, *Shakespeare and Ovid* (Oxford, 1993) and Neil Rhodes, *The Power of Eloquence and English Renaissance Literature* (New York, 1992), esp. ch. 2, 'Marlowe's Fascinations'. Two good introductions to Marlowe are Thomas Healy, *Christopher Marlowe, Writers and their Work* (Plymouth, 1994), and Patrick Cheney (ed.), *The Cambridge Companion to Christopher Marlowe* (Cambridge, 2004).
2. See, e.g. Marion Campbell, '"Desunt Nonnulla": The Construction of Marlowe's *Hero and Leander* as an Unfinished Poem', *ELH* 51 (1984), 241–68. By contrast, contemporaries saw the poem as unfinished (it certainly ends very abruptly), and it was completed by a great poet, Chapman, and a very minor one, Henry Petowe, who (perhaps in an implied comparison of Marlowe with Orpheus) compares it to 'a head separated from the body' (Cheney and Striar (eds), *Collected Poems*, 269). For Lucan's *Pharsalia* as complete, see Jamie Masters, *Poetry and Civil War in Lucan's Bellum Civile* (Cambridge, 1992), ch. 7.
3. Andrew Hadfield, *Shakespeare and Republicanism* (Cambridge, 2005), 65. Much subtler is Patrick Cheney, *Marlowe's Republican Authorship: Lucan, Liberty, and the Sublime* (Basingstoke, 2008). Cheney is careful to talk of 'Republican authorship', rather than Republican politics, arguing that Marlowe rewrites Lucan's complex fiction of the defeat of the Republic by Caesar and Empire. Cheney's concern is not with Republicanism as a political programme, but

with Republican discourse and the reception of that discourse. But Lucan was not always read as a Republican text, and was admired by many supporters of monarchy. It is important too not to be seduced by the idea of a teleological Republican trajectory leading to the Civil War.

4. *Henry VI, Part Three*, 2. 5 (direction in Folio).
5. I owe this point to Edward J. Paleit, who is sceptical about Republican readings; see *War, Liberty, and Caesar: Responses to Lucan's 'Bellum Civile', ca. 1580–1650* (Oxford, 2013).
6. See William Blissett, 'Lucan's Caesar and the Elizabethan Villain', *Studies in Philology*, 53 (1956), 553–75, and 'Caesar and Satan', *Journal of the History of Ideas*, 18 (1957), 221–32.
7. Millar MacLure (ed)., *Marlowe: The Critical Heritage 1588–1896* (1979), 78 (from *Lectures Chiefly on the Dramatic Literature of the Age of Elizabeth* (1820)).
8. Bate, *Shakespeare and Ovid*, 40–1.
9. Text in MacLure, *Marlowe: The Critical Heritage*, 36–8. On the issues, see Roy Kendall, 'Richard Baines and Christopher Marlowe's Milieu', *English Literary Renaissance*, 24 (1994), 507–52.
10. Most helpful for our subject is David Riggs, *The World of Christopher Marlowe* (2004), with useful material on Marlowe's education, from petty school to the University of Cambridge. For important reminders about how little we know for sure, see, e.g. Lukas Erne, 'Biography, Mythography, and Criticism: The Life and Works of Christopher Marlowe', *Modern Philology*, 103 (2005), 28–50; J. A. Downie, 'Reviewing what we Think we Know about Christopher Marlowe, Again', in Sarah K. Scott and M. L. Stapleton (eds), *Christopher Marlowe the Craftsman: Lives, Stage, and Page* (Farnham, 2010), 343–6.
11. Laurie E. Maguire, 'Marlovian Texts and Authorship', in Cheney (ed.), *The Cambridge Companion to Marlowe*, 41–54 (42).
12. Patrick Cheney, *Marlowe's Counterfeit Profession: Ovid, Spenser, Counter-Nationhood* (Toronto, 1997). It is true that Cheney stresses oscillation rather than trajectory from lower to higher forms as the hallmark of an Ovidian career; but the idea of a career does imply a chronology (even if that chronology has primarily symbolic force). That we do not know in what order Marlowe wrote his works makes constructing a *cursus* for him highly problematic.
13. Georgia E. Brown, 'Marlowe's Poems and Classicism', in Cheney (ed.), *The Cambridge Companion to Marlowe*, 106–26 (106).
14. For the later Middle Ages, when Ovid is everywhere, not least in the schoolroom, and when lines from the *Amores* could be quoted in sermons, see James G. Clark, Frank T. Coulson, and Kathryn L. McKinley (eds), *Ovid in the Middle Ages* (Cambridge, 2011), with full bibliography.
15. Brian Vickers, *English Renaissance Literary Criticism* (Oxford, 1999), 65; cf. p. 60 on the *Metamorphoses*.
16. So Eric Jacobsen, *Translation a Traditional Craft: An Introductory Sketch with a Study of Marlowe's Elegies* (Copenhagen, 1958), 116–17. Shakespeare uses a couplet from *Amores*, 1. 15 (35–6) as an epigraph for *Venus and Adonis*.
17. For example, Jonson (assuming he is the corrector) replaces Marlowe's energetic final lines 'Then, though death rakes my bones in funeral fire, | I'll live, and as he pulls me down mount higher' (where the image of Death with a rake is not in Ovid and is indeed strikingly unOvidian) with the smoother but flatter 'Then, when this body falls in funeral fire, | My name shall live, and my best part aspire', with its final Latinate 'aspire' (though Marlowe's 'I'll live' retains the immediacy of Ovid's *vivam*). For *Poetaster* as a play about translation, see Victoria Moul,

'Ben Jonson's *Poetaster*: Classical Translation and the Location of Cultural Authority', *Translation and Literature*, 16 (2006), 21–50.

18. Bate, *Shakespeare and Ovid*, 38–9; Healy, *Christopher Marlowe*, 7–9; Heather James, 'The Poet's Toys: Christopher Marlowe and the Liberties of Erotic Elegy', *Modern Language Quarterly*, 67 (2006), 103–27 (121–4); François Laroque, 'Ovidian V(o)ices in Marlowe and Shakespeare: the Actaeon Variations', in A. B. Taylor (ed.), *Shakespeare's Ovid: The Metamorphoses in the Plays and Poems* (Cambridge, 2000), 165–77.
19. Bate, *Shakespeare and Ovid*, 44–5.
20. Colin Burrow, 'English Renaissance Readers and the *Appendix Vergiliana*', *Proceedings of the Virgil Society*, 26 (2008), 1–16. For an implausibly extreme version of the view that the play is an Ovidian deconstruction of the *Aeneid* see Emma Buckley, '"Live false Aeneas!" Marlowe's *Dido, Queen of Carthage* and the Limits of Translation', *Classical Receptions Journal* 3 (2011), 129–147, with a full bibliography for previous views.
21. Sara Munson Deats, '*Dido, Queen of Carthage* and *The Massacre of Paris*', in Cheney (ed.), *The Cambridge Companion to Marlowe*, 193–206 (196).
22. Helen Waddell, *The Wandering Scholars* (1934), xxiii.
23. Thomas M. Greene, *The Light in Troy: Imitation and Discovery in Renaissance Poetry* (New Haven, 1982), 38–43.
24. The fact that the play was apparently performed by the child actors of 'her Majesty's Chapel' (original title page) suggests a date of 1584–5 (see Riggs, *World of Marlowe*, 113), but there can be no certainty.
25. For Marlowe and Shakespeare, see Jonathan Bate, *The Genius of Shakespeare* (1997), ch. 4, pp. 101–32; Robert A. Logan, *Shakespeare's Marlowe: The Influence of Christopher Marlowe on Shakespeare's Artistry* (Aldershot, 2007); A. D. Nuttall, *Shakespeare the Thinker* (New Haven, 2007), 82–6.
26. MacLure (ed.), *Marlowe: The Critical Heritage*, 44–5, 47 (Drayton: 'Marlowe... | Had in him those brave translunary things, | That the first poets had').
27. MacLure (ed.), *Marlowe: The Critical Heritage*, 159, 175, 184, 177.
28. C. S. Lewis, *English Literature in the Sixteenth Century Excluding Drama* (Oxford, 1954), 481.
29. A good start is made by Patrick Cheney, 'Milton, Marlowe and Lucan: The English Authorship of Republican Liberty', *Milton Studies*, 49 (2009), 1–19.
30. For a lively sense of what Cambridge university education was like, if for a slightly later period, see John K. Hale, *Milton's Cambridge Latin: Performing in the Genres 1625–1632* (Tempe, AZ, 2005), 1–31.
31. Adrian Poole, 'Confundering the Past' (review of Charles Martindale and A. B. Taylor (eds), *Shakespeare and the Classics*), *TLS*, 29 July 2005, 10–11 (10).
32. See further Russ McDonald, 'Marlowe and Style', in Cheney (ed.), *The Cambridge Companion to Marlowe*, 55–69.
33. MacLure (ed.), *Marlowe: The Critical Heritage*, 37 (from the Baines Memorandum).
34. For Marlowe, homosexuality, and the classics, see Alan Stewart, '*Edward II* and Male Same-Sex Desire', in Garrett A. Sullivan, Jr, Patrick Cheney, and Andrew Hadfield (eds), *Early Modern English Drama: A Critical Companion* (Oxford and New York, 2006), 82–95; for the context, see Bruce R. Smith, *Homosexual Desire in Shakespeare's England: A Cultural Poetics* (Chicago, 1991).
35. Poole, 'Confundering the Past'; Colin Burrow, 'Shakespeare and Humanistic Culture', in Charles Martindale and A. B. Taylor (eds), *Shakespeare and the Classics* (Cambridge, 2004), 9–27, esp. 22–4.
36. For a full account, see Robin Sowerby, *The Augustan Art of Poetry: Augustan*

Translation of the Classics (Oxford and New York, 2006), esp. ch. 2.

37. MacLure (ed.), *Marlowe: The Critical Heritage*, 129 (from *The English Poets, Selections*, 1880).
38. Five largely sympathetic accounts are Jacobsen, *Translation a Traditional Craft*, esp. 162–86; Lee T. Pearcy, *The Mediated Muse: English Translations of Ovid, 1560–1700* (Hamden, CT, 1984), esp. chs 1 and 2; Robin Sowerby, *The Classical Legacy in Renaissance Poetry* (1994), 276–86; M. L. Stapleton, *Harmful Eloquence: Ovid's Amores from Antiquity to Shakespeare* (Ann Arbor, 1996), esp. ch. 6. M. L. Stapleton, *Marlowe's Ovid: The 'Elegies' in the Marlowe Canon* (Farnham and Burlington, VT, 2014). For the selected elegies of 1599, see M. L. Stapleton, 'Marlowe's First Ovid: *Certaine of Ovids Elegies*', in Scott and Stapleton (eds), *Marlowe the Craftsman*, 137–48.
39. See Roma Gill, 'Snakes Leape By Verse', in Brian Morris (ed.), *Christopher Marlowe: Mermaid Critical Commentaries* (1968), 135–50.
40. So Cheney and Striar (eds), *Collected Poems*, 127.
41. See Sowerby, *Augustan Art of Poetry*, 72–3: 'It may be doubted whether anyone had written couplets in English before with such neat parallelism, such elegant precision, such terse definition, and such witty and teasing verbal play' (p. 73). Other particularly successful translations are 1. 1; 1. 9; 2. 5; 2. 10.
42. Pearcy, *The Mediated Muse*, 13–14.
43. For a sceptical view, see Tucker Brooke, 'The Marlowe Canon', *PMLA* 37 (1922), 367–417 (esp. 414–17) (though he did not know about the Folger MS of the elegy, and ignores the known connection between Marlowe and Watson).
44. Georgia E. Brown would dispute my 'laudatory', on the grounds that the poem is throughout 'ambivalent' (*The Cambridge Companion to Marlowe*, 108–10); so for her in the final line (an elegant version of a particularly well-worn *topos*) *fama* means 'ill repute' as well as 'fame'. Her analysis is ingenious, but to my thinking implausible (for her and many modern critics Marlowe has always and everywhere to be oppositional). More convincing is Dympna Callaghan, 'Marlowe's Last Poem: Elegiac Aesthetics and the Epitaph on Sir Roger Manwood', in Scott and Stapleton (eds), *Marlowe the Craftsman*, 159–76.
45. MacLure (ed.), *Marlowe: The Critical Heritage*, 183; Lewis, *English Literature in the Sixteenth Century*, 486. See also James Shapiro, '"Metre meete to furnish Lucans style": Reconsidering Marlowe's *Lucan*', in Kenneth Friedenreich, Roma Gill, and Constance B. Kuriyama (eds), *'A Poet and a Filthy Play-maker': New Essays on Christopher Marlowe* (New York, 1988), 315–25; Dan Hooley, 'Raising the Dead: Marlowe's Lucan', in Alexandra Lianeri and Vanda Zajko (eds), *Translation and the Classic: Identity as Change in the History of Culture* (Oxford, 2008), 243–60. For Lucan's influence beyond the translation, see Allyna E. Ward, 'Lucanic Irony in Marlowe's *Tamburlaine*', *Modern Language Review*, 103 (2008), 311–29.
46. See *Lucan: The Civil War, Translated by Nicholas Rowe*, ed. Sarah Annes Brown and Charles Martindale (1998); Sowerby, *Augustan Art of Poetry*, 174–209.
47. Sowerby, *Augustan Art of Poetry*, 182.
48. The many good discussions of this poem include: William Keach, *Elizabethan Erotic Narratives: Irony and Pathos in the Ovidian Poetry of Shakespeare, Marlowe, and their Contemporaries* (Hassocks, 1977), esp. ch. 4; Clark Hulse, *Metamorphic Verse: The Elizabethan Minor Epic* (Princeton, 1981); John Roe, 'Ovid "Renascent" in *Venus and Adonis* and *Hero and Leander*', in Taylor, *Shakespeare's Ovid*, 31–46;

Claude J. Summers, '*Hero and Leander*: The Arbitrariness of Desire', and Georgia E. Brown, 'Gender and Voice in *Hero and Leander*', in J. A. Downie and J. T. Parnell (eds), *Constructing Christopher Marlowe* (Cambridge, 2000), 133–47, 148–63; Georgia Brown, *Redefining Elizabethan Literature* (Cambridge, 2004), esp. ch. 3.

49. See Gordon Braden, *The Classics and English Renaissance Poetry: Three Case Studies* (New Haven, 1978), ch. 2.

50. For women readers, putative and actual, see Sasha Roberts, *Reading Shakespeare's Poems in Early Modern England* (Basingstoke and New York, 2003). In Middleton's *A Mad World My Masters* (1608), *Hero and Leander* and *Venus and Adonis* are described as 'two luscious mary-bone pies for a young married wife' (1. 2. 43–7).

51. C. S. Lewis, 'Hero and Leander', *Proceedings of the British Academy*, 38 (1952), 23–37 (25).

52. See Charles Martindale, *Redeeming the Text: Latin Poetry and the Hermeneutics of Reception* (Cambridge, 1993), 56–60.

53. Sowerby, *Classical Legacy*, 287–9

54. The classicizing term sestiad is not Marlowe's, but the more learned Chapman's; Chapman finished what he certainly regarded as a poetic fragment, dividing it into two sestiads, before adding four more of his own.

55. So Roe, 'Ovid "Renascent"', 38.

56. Lewis, 'Hero and Leander', 26.

57. See James, 'The Poet's Toys', 103.

58. Richard Carew, *The Excellency of the English Tongue*, composed in 1595–6, and first printed in William Camden's *Remains, Concerning Britain* (1614), 44: 'Will you read Virgil? Take the Earl of Surrey, Catullus? Shakespeare and Marlowe's fragment, Ovid? Daniel.' I am grateful to Dr Tania Demetriou for this reference.

59. MacLure (ed.), *Marlowe: The Critical Heritage*, 129–30, 174, 183; C. S. Lewis, 'Hero and Leander', 24.

60. Walter Pater, 'Sandro Botticelli', in *The Renaissance: Studies in Art and Poetry: The 1893 Text*, ed. Donald L. Hill (Berkeley and Los Angeles, 1980), 39.

61. See the excellent comparison in Heather James, 'Shakespeare's Learned Heroines in Ovid's Schoolroom', in Martindale and Taylor (eds), *Shakespeare and the Classics*, 66–85 (esp. 80–1).

CHAPTER 27

Shakespeare

COLIN BURROW

It would be possible to give a convincing and continuous narrative about the reception of the classics in the sixteenth and seventeenth centuries without mentioning Shakespeare at all. Unlike Christopher Marlowe, Ben Jonson, or John Dryden, Shakespeare did not write translations of classical verse. He did not bring about significant changes in the relationship between vernacular and classical writing, or establish a new and distinctive interpretation of any particular text. Within a few years of Shakespeare's death Jonson—who was not on oath—famously said that Shakespeare had 'small Latin and less Greek'. This effectively wrote Shakespeare out of the history of classical learning in England for centuries. From the 1630s onwards he came to be seen as a writer who showed the triumph of the vernacular rather than the power of classical influence to push the vernacular to new heights.

Despite his reputation for small or moderate classical learning, Shakespeare by modern standards knew a great deal of Latin.[1] His knowledge of Greek was indeed probably small, or at least 'less' than his Latin. Most grammar schools aimed no higher than enabling their charges to work through the Greek New Testament, which was a low target: students might already have much of the English translation by heart, and its Greek is relatively simple. Some schools did not aim even that high. Shakespeare's extensive use of Plutarch in the Roman plays came not via the Greek but from Thomas North's translation of Jacques Amyot's French version, and he probably read Homer principally in George Chapman's translation. If he read any of the Greek tragedians, he is likely to have done so in Latin translations.[2] This does not mean that it is pointless to look for analogies between Greek tragedy and Shakespeare's works: in Plutarch's *Lives* he could have found discussion of Homeric thought about the freedom of the will, a large number of quotations from Sophocles and Euripides, as well as at least one spectacular account of the staging of a tragedy.[3] But he would have left Stratford Grammar School at the age of about 15 principally a Latinist, well versed in Ovid, with some Virgil, a grasp of Terence and Plautus, and perhaps a smidgeon of Seneca. He would also have read (and learnt much) from works in the rhetorical tradition, such as Cicero's *De Oratore*, the anonymous *Rhetorica ad Herennium*, and passages from Quintilian. If a few years later one of his London friends had put a Latin text in front of him, he could have laughed at the jokes, admired the similes, and learnt from the plot.

Judging by the evidence of his works, Shakespeare seems chiefly to have read Latin drama and narrative poetry rather than lyric. He sometimes read translations as well as the originals, though this is often hard to determine. There are tantalizingly slight signs that he ventured into Horace's *Odes* or the lyrics of Catullus, and, unlike many of his contemporaries, including Ben Jonson, he does not seem to have had much interest in the epigrams of Martial or Juvenal's satires—though Juvenal might be the 'satirical rogue' whose 'words, words, words' Hamlet paraphrases in order to insult the prying Polonius (2. 2. 196). Unlike several of his contemporaries—notably Christopher Marlowe and Ben Jonson—Shakespeare left behind no Latin verse. He was trained in a good school that had a string of Oxford graduates as its principal masters (including at least one competent neo-Latin poet), but it was relatively small and certainly provincial.[4] Although Ben Jonson also left school in his mid-teens, the school he left was Westminster, in which pupils might act in Latin plays and compose Latin verse from an early age. Westminster was worlds apart from the cramped rows of desks above the Guildhall in Stratford where Shakespeare learnt Lily's Grammar and pored over Ovid.

It is naive to suppose, however, that Shakespeare's school taught him all he knew about Latin literature, or indeed that simply knowing what he read will tell us what he did with that reading. There was no simple two-way relationship between Shakespeare and his books. His uses of classical learning were determined by a many-sided relationship between his reading, his audiences, the genres in which he worked, and his contemporaries. When he began to write for the professional stage at some point in the late 1580s or early 1590s, the most successful playwrights had university degrees. This gave Robert Greene, George Peele, and the young Christopher Marlowe major advantages in the struggle to win cheers from audiences and fees from theatrical impresarios such as Philip Henslowe. They had seen the classically inspired dramas that were performed during the Christmas season in the universities 'to recreate ourselves . . . to be well acquainted with Seneca or Plautus',[5] and they knew how to appeal both to university men and to the wealthy group of young theatre-goers who were training as lawyers in the Inns of Court. Classical tastes were socially and generationally specific in this period.[6] Thomas Kyd and Peele, both born within a decade of Shakespeare, were near enough in age to inspire admiration, emulation, and perhaps a measure of envy. Their ability to please an audience with plays lightened by flashes of Seneca and technicolour displays of rhetoric left a strong imprint on Shakespeare's early responses to classical writing.

'The Sweet Witty Soul of Ovid'

The precise dating and sequence of Shakespeare's early works is relatively uncertain, but *Titus Andronicus*, *The Comedy of Errors*, and *The Taming of the Shrew* were composed and performed in the early 1590s. Those works are the products of an aspiring grammar-school boy who was using what he knew of classical texts to please a learned audience. Indeed *Titus* and *Shrew* are both extremely self-conscious about learning and teaching the classics. One of the oafish rapists in *Titus* recognizes a Latin tag from Horace with 'I read it in the grammar long ago' (4. 2. 23). After Lavinia has been raped, she chases a Roman grammar-school boy called Lucius across the stage, and points to the story of Philomela in the copy of Ovid's *Metamorphoses* that he is carrying in order to reveal what has happened to her (4. 1).[7] These plays show an acute awareness that classical learning can be used in a wide range of ways. In *Shrew*, Lucentio disguises himself as a Latin master, with a copy of the *Heroides* in hand (which was a popular work from which to learn Latin), and huddles with Bianca over the text in order to pursue his love affair (3. 1. 26–44).

Titus Andronicus (1594?), Shakespeare's most Ovidian play, was probably a collaborative drama.[8] There are strong stylistic grounds for believing that George Peele (several of whose title pages boast that he was a 'Master of Arts') composed the first act, which establishes a Roman historical setting, with funerary processions and arguments about the role of heredity, *pietas*, and virtue in the succession to the imperial throne. Shakespeare composed most of the rest of the play, drawing extensively on the tale of Tereus and Philomela from the *Metamorphoses*. We do not know if the two authors worked in tandem or sequentially, but Shakespeare's sections clearly display, and may initiate, a particular kind of 'classical' drama that was to become his hallmark in the early to mid-1590s. He adapted the Ovidian topos of a rape in a wood to give emotional, rhetorical, and personal force to Peele's picture of a Roman Empire in decline. He repeatedly exceeds the violence in Ovid (Lavinia has her hands cut off so that she cannot imitate Philomela and weave her story into a tapestry) and then invokes Ovid as a key to communicating and understanding passion which is so extreme that it lies on the boundaries of comprehension. When Lavinia is raped, the eloquent and learned Marcus painfully attempts to use his classical learning to respond to her bleeding distress ('sure some Tereus hath deflow'red thee ... A craftier Tereus, cousin, hast thou met' (2. 4. 26–41)). The effect is to link Ovid at once with excess (this is worse than the *Metamorphoses*) and with failed attempts to comprehend the experiences of another person. The excess of violence in *Titus*, which until recently dominated responses to the play, is not just the result of Shakespeare's reading in Seneca's *Thyestes* or Ovid. It is partly a consequence of its authors working to overgo each other, and to overgo Ovid. Shakespeare in *Titus* sought not to 'out-Herod Herod', but to out-Ovid Ovid and perhaps to out-Peele Peele. He was showing that he could produce a classically informed tragedy of revenge that went well beyond even Kyd's *Spanish Tragedy*, with its striking climax of mute passion in which the hero bites out his own tongue.

Shakespeare's reception of classical texts always has to be triangulated against his relations to other writers. It also has to be considered in relation to the milieu for which he was writing. His earliest works were in a sense social translations: they attempted to transform his own grammar-school classical learning into a shape that might appeal to a more socially elevated audience. By the time he was working in theatrical circles in London he would have known that writing comedy modelled on Plautus could make a poet's name. George Gascoigne, a master self-publicist in print, had translated Ariosto's *I Suppositi*, itself based on plays by Terence and Plautus, for the Inns of Court in 1566. Shakespeare's *Comedy of Errors* was performed at Gray's Inn in 1594, where it was described as 'a Comedy of Errors (like to Plautus his *Menaechmus*)'.[9] The relationship to Plautus was meant to be noticed. *Errors* is, like *Titus*, classical to excess: Plautus has one set of twins, so Shakespeare doubles up the doubles to two sets. This may be an artful attempt to make Plautus more like Terence, who regularly combines several plots. Shakespeare also adds a background of shipwrecks at sea to Plautus's fly cityscape, bringing to Roman comedy a strong flavour of Greek romance, while his description of the storm that leads to the shipwreck with which the plot begins shows traces of Virgil's *Aeneid*.[10] The play is an example of what Terence called *contaminatio*, in which several sources are fused together in ways that are visible to audiences who knew each of them.[11] *The Comedy of Errors*, performed before the slick audiences of the Inns, was designed to associate Shakespeare with upmarket Latinate and Italianate drama.

These early plays are closely connected with Shakespeare's narrative poems, although it is not certain which came first. When *Venus and Adonis* appeared in 1593—and it was the first printed work to which Shakespeare's name was attached—it was an instant hit. That was because it was brilliant, but also because of the way that it was positioned in relation to both English and classical authors. At roughly the time Christopher Marlowe was at work on *Hero and Leander*, which was based on a Greek narrative poem believed in this period to be by one of the earliest surviving poets, Musaeus.[12] The two poets vie with each other to create strikingly luxuriant poems that were instantly recognizable for their relationship to classical texts. Shakespeare's poem brings the rhetorical copiosity instilled in both grammar schools and universities in the sixteenth century to a retelling of Ovid's story from *Metamorphoses* 10. With *Lucrece* the following year Shakespeare moved into territory described in the dedication to *Venus and Adonis* as 'graver': an Ovidian story (this time from the *Fasti*) is fused with traces of Roman history deriving from Livy, and is prefixed by a prose narrative that relates the action of the poem to the advent of the Roman republic. Quite possibly Shakespeare found all these materials in a single annotated edition of Ovid,[13] but the way he combined them made *Lucrece* the sexiest book of the year. And they mark the poem as recognizably cognate with the approach to the classical world in *Titus*: a surrounding frame of political corruption and change puts extreme pressure on Ovidian passions. *Titus* may have preceded *Lucrece* by a few months, since Henslowe gives the earliest record of its performance in January 1594, while *Lucrece* was registered for publication in May.[14] In the poem Shakespeare perhaps learnt to incorporate Peele's historical 'frame' for the action of *Titus* into his own version of Ovidianism. In 1593–4 Shakespeare was making his reputation as someone who wrote classically derived works in which Ovidian violations occur in historical settings of tyranny.

Within five years Shakespeare was established as an English poet who could be compared to the big names in the classical canon: in 1598 Francis Meres declared 'as the soul of *Euphorbus* was thought to live in *Pythagoras*: so the sweet witty soul of *Ovid* lives in mellifluous and honey-tongued *Shakespeare*'.[15] Significantly, Meres linked Shakespeare not just with Ovid, but with a constellation of other fashionable English poets whom he also compared to classical figures. Shakespeare had arrived, and was in the company that he had been seeking since the start of his career.

To represent Shakespeare as simply an ambitious grammar-school boy who used what he knew of classical literature to outstrip his seniors would be misleading. This was how he was depicted in 1592 by the envious university graduate Robert Greene ('an upstart crow, beautified with our feathers'), but envy is rarely a good guide to the truth.[16] Even Shakespeare's earliest imitations of classical texts go far beyond a simple display of plumage, borrowed or not. Classical texts and actions based upon them tend to give rise to a variety of different points of view, and they are often presented in deliberately partial or ambiguous ways. The 'Ovidian' play within the play put on by the rude mechanicals in *A Midsummer Night's Dream* (1594–5?) is the most intriguing case in point. Their play is based on the story of Pyramus and Thisbe from the *Metamorphoses*. As every schoolboy who read Rudolph Agricola's edition of Aphthonius's *Progymnasmata* (and that was most schoolboys) would have known, this was a moral fable illustrating the value of obedience to parents and the dangers of lust.[17] That schoolroom moral reading may float mockingly in the background of *Dream*, in which children disobey their father's wishes, and in which the Queen of the Fairies herself is made to fall in love with an ass. But the Ovidian tale and its moral are transformed, translated indeed, by performance: a group of artisans muff their lines and turn Ovid's story into a theatrical muddle in a rumble-tumble theatrically old-fashioned style, put on before a group of wealthy Athenians. Critics have argued heatedly whether the style of the play mocks that of the English translation of the *Metamorphoses* by Arthur Golding, or, more probably, a ballad version of the story:[18] certainly someone is being laughed at, and possibly more or less everyone, from the snooty Hippolyta who criticizes the performance to Peter Quince, with his very small Latin, who is presumably its author. How you see the relationship of Ovid's story to the whole play depends, almost literally, on where you sit. The courtly audience fails to see its connection to the changes and dangers they have themselves been through in the wood, while the offstage audience might enjoy a knowledge of Ovid that places them above all those onstage. The guiding principle of Shakespearean drama is over-determination: there are always more possible explanations for the phenomena he presents onstage than the one that you presently see. That over-determination extends to his treatment of classical texts. The play of Pyramus and Thisbe comes from many places as well as Ovid: it shows traces of Shakespeare's own social unease about mediating a classical text to his superiors, hints of traditional moral interpretations of the *Metamorphoses*, as well, perhaps, as a kind of game with Shakespeare's own memory of reading Ovid at school. Can he quite remember his lines? Can he translate it into drama without making something ridiculous? Can he bring it onstage in a form suitable for a learned audience?

There were some large-scale changes in the ways Shakespeare treats Latin literature in the course of his career, as we shall see. But his treatment of different sources also varied in different genres. In the later romances, *Cymbeline*, *The Winter's Tale*, and *The Tempest*, Ovid is no longer the source of bloody violations in the woods, and references to his works tend to be oblique or even metaphorical. This is partly a consequence of genre. Romances often allude to texts from other genres (epic, tragedy) in ways that are designed to confuse and complicate readers' responses. Allusions to the conventions of epic or tragedy might create expectations that a particular narrative outcome—imperial splendour, painful death—will follow. Very often these outcomes remain possibilities (alternative dummy plots, as it were) rather than actualities. This has consequences for Shakespeare's imitations of Ovid in his romances. The late plays often introduce Ovidian allusions at narrative turning-points, where the plot could move in a variety of different directions. When the deceitful Iachimo in *Cymbeline* climbs out of the trunk in Imogen's chamber, he finds that 'She hath been reading late, | The tale of Tereus: here the leaf's turn'd down | Where Philomele gave up' (2. 2. 44–5). The strong association between Ovid and sexual violation that Shakespeare had explored early in his career charges this moment with particular danger: a man is alone with a sleeping woman, with Ovid. The 'rape' that follows, however, is ocular and metaphorical rather than physical, as Iachimo destroys Imogen's reputation and her marriage.

Ovid was, of course, himself a master at giving off conflicting generic signals, and he was a master of rhetoric pitched on the line between tragedy and comedy. That made him a particularly appropriate author to invoke at moments when the action onstage could move in any one of several directions. The extraordinary climax of *The Winter's Tale*, in which the statue of Hermione is brought to life, has somewhere near the foreground of its genealogy Ovid's story of Pygmalion, the artist who makes a statue that lives. A variety of perspectives encircle this Ovidian scene, however: illusion-making, outright deceit, wish-fulfilment, redemption, and witchcraft are all part of the range of theatrical possibilities. Paulina's 'magic' may be dangerous necromancy, as she (sounding almost like a priest at a magical wedding) urges 'those that think it is unlawful business | I am about, let them depart' (5. 3. 96–7). Ovid also brings uncertain undertones to the final act of *The Tempest*. Prospero invokes 'Ye elves of hills, brooks, standing lakes and groves' (5. 1. 33–57) in a speech closely modelled on Medea's invocation of spirits to assist her in the death and rejuvenation of Aeson (*Metamorphoses* 7. 197–219). Shakespeare's phrasing strongly suggests that Arthur Golding's translation was either on his desk or at the forefront of his mind as he wrote, but it is more than a simple quotation.[19] Medea not only rejuvenates Jason's father Aeson but goes on to destroy Pelias by a very similar method, and will then proceed to avenge herself on Jason. Prospero echoes her at the point when all his enemies are in his power. How much of her story might come along with that echo, and how far is Prospero simply a benign inversion of Medea? Charles Martindale has rapped 'ingenious critics' over the knuckles for assuming that there is 'complex interplay' between Ovid and Shakespeare's plot at this point, but the ingenious critics surely have a point.[20] *The Tempest* is not simply a redemptive romance. It is rather a kind of revenge tragedy gone wrong, which is deflected late on, and unsteadily, from vengeance to what Prospero calls 'virtue'. One way it keeps the possibility of revenge open is by alluding to Ovid's *Metamorphoses*, a text so generically inclusive and tonally slippery that it seems to have been strongly associated by Shakespeare with a variety of tragicomic effects, from the gory laughter of *Titus* through to the delicate structural interplay between comic and tragic forms and outcomes in the later plays.

Virgil

Virgil is sometimes said not to have meant much to Shakespeare.[21] He clearly knew the early books of the *Aeneid* (particularly books 2, the destruction of Troy, and 4, the episode with Dido), as well as Aeneas' visions in the underworld in book 6, while the *Georgics* and *Eclogues* left relatively little impression. Shakespeare's allusions to the *Aeneid* follow broadly the same pattern as his allusions to Ovid. Early set pieces, designed perhaps to flag his learning and to show poetic ambition, turn into more oblique references in the later works. His earliest major allusion to the *Aeneid* occurs in *Lucrece*, that early showpiece of his learning, when the heroine searches after her rape for a vehicle on which to project her misery. She 'calls to mind' a 'piece | Of skilful painting' (*Rape of Lucrece*, ll. 1366–7) that represents the fall of Troy and the grief of Hecuba. She then focuses her rage on the figure of the deceptive Sinon, and tears at the picture with her nails. This is a typical moment of early Shakespearean classicism. The Virgilian underpresence is meant to be noticed by his readers, and is the source of complex and unsettling effects. Lucrece is implicitly compared to Aeneas, since the scene is an oblique rewriting of the moment when Aeneas sees the representations of the sack of Troy in Carthage, and with those pictures experiences 'lacrimae rerum' (1. 462), the tears of things. But the emotion that Lucrece brings to the picture means that it provides a frustratingly inexact analogy rather than a direct parallel to her experience. The classical text is not brought back to life, in simple humanist fashion, as a means of articulating emotion in the present: the fall of Troy seems a long time ago, and to be just slightly askew from the emotions and experiences of the heroine. There is a gap, an area of discomfort, between Lucrece and Aeneas and between Shakespeare and Virgil. This implies at the level of character that Lucrece has had an experience that exceeds even the grandest literary vehicle. At the level of artistry, it might modestly suggest that Virgilian epic is just a little beyond Shakespeare's reach, a proximate vehicle for woe rather than a work that he could quite aspire to replicate.

This constellation of concerns continues to surround Virgil in Shakespeare's work up until roughly the end of the sixteenth century. In *Hamlet* (*c.*1600) the first player delivers a long speech about the death of Priam and the sufferings of Hecuba (2. 2. 450–520), which again recalls the early books of the *Aeneid*. It is written in an archaic style that has sometimes been seen as a teasing allusion to Christopher Marlowe's earlier play inspired by Virgil, *Dido Queen of Carthage*.[22] It might also exploit the fact that by the time Shakespeare wrote the play many English translations of classical works in general and of Virgil in particular were, by the standards of the deeply fashion-conscious literary *cognoscenti*, sounding distinctly old-fashioned. Either way, 'Virgil' is presented as something antique, partially recalled through an old-fashioned-sounding poem that the prince himself can barely remember. The Hecuba speech comes right from the same zone as *Lucrece* and *Titus*: intense and all-but inarticulable passion is figured forth by an extended allusion to a classical text, which is held up to view within the play as though in a frame, and which becomes the source of a range of interpretations. The professional player performs it with a weeping vividness. The complacent humanist Polonius appreciates its unusual epithets ('the mobbled queen is good' (2. 2. 504)). But Hamlet is prompted by the grief of Hecuba to reflect on his own incapacity to feel emotion ('What would he do | Had he the motive and the cue for passion | That I have?' (2. 2. 560–2)). 'Virgilian' passion is held up as a historically distant ideal from which the modern observer falls short.

Virgil, like Ovid, is treated differently in different theatrical genres. In *The Tempest*, allusions to the *Aeneid* are oblique, buried, and slightly mystifying, weaving in and out of the narrative in ways that can seem at some moments to be significant and at others to be almost whimsical. The courtiers banter about Carthage and 'Widow Dido' (*Tempest*, 2. 1. 76–86). Ariel creates a feast and then disguised as a harpy destroys it (3. 3. 53–82), in a direct allusion to *Aeneid* 3. 209–57, while the larger structures of the plot—a storm, an exiled leader, a marriage, a new kingdom—seem to display shadows of an imperial narrative, but that, in the characteristic manner of romance, never quite fulfil the epic expectations created by these allusions. The work of piecing together a version of the *Aeneid* is delegated to the audience.[23] Similar oblique hints at Virgilian narratives run through *Antony and Cleopatra*, where an apparent inversion of the story of Dido and Aeneas, in which the hero just keeps on coming back to his lover, seems to crystalize in Antony's final vision of the afterlife in which (contrary to the version told by Virgil) Dido and Aeneas are united in the underworld: 'Dido and her Aeneas shall want troops' (*Antony and Cleopatra*, 4. 14. 53).[24]

Shakespeare was quite capable of making indirect allusions to the plot of the *Aeneid* early in his career (Lavinia, the victim of rape in *Titus*, shares a name with the eventual partner of Virgil's Aeneas, which is a deliberate irony in a play that relates the unstitching of an empire rather than its foundation).[25] But in the later works that teasing obliquity becomes the rule rather than the exception.

Every aspect of Shakespeare's dramaturgy moved on with an almost incredible rapidity in the years around 1598–1603. His classicism was no exception. In 1599, by which point Kyd, Peele, and Marlowe were all dead, Shakespeare became part-owner of the Globe theatre and was well established as the leading playwright of his company. The need to impress what Gabriel Harvey called 'the wiser sort'[26] by visible citation of classical works may well have been less pressing after that date. By the accession of James I in 1603, in the wake of which Shakespeare's company became 'The King's Men', there were some less narrowly personal reasons why he should begin to allude to Virgil in new ways. Panegyrists of James VI and I made frequent reference to his role as a clement imperial peacemaker, and often supported that view of the King by references to Virgil. That shadowy underpresences of Virgilian imperial visions should become more pronounced in Shakespeare's Jacobean plays is not surprising. It *is* surprising, however, quite how dark the shadows that surround them can be. The imperial visions that Aeneas sees in book 6 culminate in the dead Marcellus, nephew and heir to Augustus, and the hero leaves the underworld by the gate of dreams. *Macbeth* is, like many Renaissance responses to the *Aeneid*, sensitive to the darkness beneath Virgil's imperial prophecies.[27] When the witches show to Macbeth the line of kings descended from Banquo stretching out to the crack of doom (4. 1. 63–134), the imperial vision is spectacularly dark: for Macbeth, the unending line of Banquo is a disaster for his own broken lineage. Meanwhile the offstage audience, subjects of a king descended from Banquo's line, and even the King himself, might see flickers of glory emerging darkly through the witches' vision. But this is no simple panegyric: throughout the play the prophecies of the weird sisters have not been kind to those for whom they predict triumph. In *Cymbeline* too there are fragments of Virgil—a headless trunk, distantly recalling the dead body of King Priam, a series of imperial prophecies—which suggest a larger narrative of empire at the edges of which the play positions itself.[28] In the Jacobean period, oblique allusions to the broken limbs of Virgil could do more work—political, emotional, multi-perspectival—than the kind of overtly displayed allusions found in *Lucrece* and *Hamlet*.

Events in Shakespeare's more immediate milieu also had an effect on his treatments of classical literature after about 1600. *Troilus and Cressida*, a play set in the world of the Trojan war and probably composed *c.*1601–2, marks a particularly significant stage in the evolution of Shakespeare's classicism. *Troilus* has often been associated with 'the war of the theatres', or 'the poets' war'.[29] This was less a war than a squabble, which began with exchanges of mutually satirical portraits by John Marston and Ben Jonson, and surged to a climax with Jonson's *Poetaster* (1601), which was set in the literary world of Augustan Rome, and which made transparent connections between a number of ancient and modern authors. The literary landscape of 'Rome' in *Poetaster* is that of the London theatres, in which rival authors steal each other's texts, and from which Horace and Virgil emerge as figures of particular literary authority. Jonson brought questions about literary property, about authorship, and about the nature and ethics of literary imitation to the foreground of an explicitly Roman drama laced with translations from classical poets. The 'prologue arm'd' (Prologue, l. 23) with which *Troilus* begins alludes to this series of literary battles, but the play may respond in rather deeper ways to the links forged by Jonson between classicism, imitation, plagiarism, and professional rivalry. *Troilus* is unusual in the Shakespearean canon because it seems to have fed richly on the vocabulary used by classical and Renaissance critics to describe how one author imitated another. Seneca urged that imitators should 'digest' their reading and turn it into bodily substance, rather than serving it up raw and uncooked (*Epistles* 84)—a passage that Francis Meres himself digested into 'Bees out of diverse flowers draw diverse juices, but they temper and digest them by their own virtue'.[30] Quintilian frequently made comparisons between imitation and military encounters with an adversary (e.g. 10. 1. 105). These metaphors may well be queasily replicated in the orts, relics, and semi-digested meals that run through the imagery of *Troilus and Cressida*, as well as in the battles great and small that occur during its action. In writing *Troilus*, Shakespeare read and digested at least some of Homer's *Iliad* (probably in the translation by George Chapman), as well as versions of the Troy story by Chaucer, Lydgate, Henryson, and others.[31]

A tiny clue in the text of *Troilus* may also indicate that Shakespeare had recently read and thought afresh about the theory and practice of literary imitation. Hector makes a famously anachronistic comment that his brothers have spoken like 'young men, whom Aristotle thought | Unfit to hear moral philosophy' (2. 2. 166–7). Aristotle (4th century BC) could not have been read by a Homeric hero who was fighting at Troy during the Bronze Age. Hector also does not seem to have read Aristotle very well, since the *Nicomachaean Ethics* (1. 3. 5) declare that young men should not study political, rather than moral, philosophy. Shakespeare's error could have come from a number of sources, but one possibility is Johann Sturm's *Nobilitas Literata* (1549), which was translated into English in 1570 as *A Rich Storehouse or Treasure for Nobilitye and Gentlemen*.[32] This includes an extended discussion of how one author should imitate another, in the course of which Sturm declares that imitation is not a childish activity, but is indeed suitable only for grown-ups: 'as Aristotle did exclude young boys from his *Ethics*: so I also remove from this artificial practice [of imitation] not only children and boys, but also those men which know not the precepts of rhetoric.'[33] That embeds Aristotle's remark in a rhetorical setting that fits the formal *disputatio* between Hector and Troilus in 2. 2. Sturm was an unusually enthusiastic advocate of a kind of imitation that has been called 'dissimulative', in which 'an imitator must hide all similitude and likeness'.[34] He is also keen on disguising classical heroes in unheroic dress: 'Therefore they give good advice, which will us to follow Minerva in Homer, who often changeth Ulysses into sundry forms, and sometimes maketh him a wrinkled, little, ill-favoured fellow.'[35] Greek heroes can have many forms, even shabby ones, in dissimulative imitation.

Whether or not the 'war of the theatres' or reading Sturm, or both, is the explanation, *Troilus and Cressida* is a 'classical' work in a rather different way from either *Lucrece* or *Hamlet*. Almost every classical text and mythological figure in this play seems to be a hybrid of several different sources: Ariadne (who was abandoned by Theseus) is fused with 'Arachne' (who challenged Minerva to a weaving competition and was turned to a spider) in Troilus's phrase 'Ariachne's broken woof' (5. 2. 152). The volume of philosophy that Ulysses is reading when he meets Achilles is, unlike the texts of Ovid that appear in *Titus*, *Shrew*, and *Cymbeline*, an unidentifiable hybrid. He paraphrases from this 'strange fellow' (3. 3. 95) an account of the social aspects of virtue that could variously be derived from Plato or from Cicero, or from any one of a dozen Renaissance imitations of those sources.[36] *Troilus* flashes classical texts before the eyes of its audience in forms that blend together the earliest texts with their later imitations, and promiscuously mingles imitation and archetype. In the language and action of the play, 'imitation' and reductive mimicry are barely distinguishable. Ulysses describes Patroclus pretending to be Agamemnon 'like a strutting player', 'which, slanderer, he imitation calls' (1. 3. 146–66). The classical sources of the action are inseparable from their 'imitations', which are at once pieces of theatrical mimicry and textual responses to a rich and confusing literary tradition. The increasingly indirect ways in which Shakespeare alludes to Virgil and Ovid in his later plays has a variety of origins, but the pressure put on ideas of imitation in Jonson's *Poetaster* and in the war of the theatres more generally certainly belongs among them.

Classical Drama: 'Most Excellent in Both Kinds'

There is widespread agreement about how much Latin poetry Shakespeare knew, although individual critics differ in their views of what he did with his reading.[37] There are some areas of uncertainty and disagreement: Lucan's *Pharsalia*, for example, has been seen by some as bringing republican overtones to Shakespeare's writing in the 1590s, and by others as a text that Shakespeare did not know very well, and that was in any case interpreted in the period in a range of ways, among which republican readings were only one possibility.[38]

The nature and extent of Shakespeare's debt to classical drama, however, have always been a more contentious area. Francis Meres, who was not very discriminating in his comparisons between English and ancient poets, compared Shakespeare not only to Ovid, but also to Plautus and Seneca, declaring that he was 'most excellent in both kinds' (that is, for both tragedy and comedy).[39] But his encomium does not answer the question 'how much did Shakespeare know of classical drama?' This question instantly comes up against a methodological stumbling block. The study of reception history is closely linked with hermeneutic principles that emphasize the openness of texts to interpretation.[40] It therefore tends to focus on responses to classical texts that imply a large-scale interpretation of an earlier work. Traditional source study, on the other hand, tended to focus on exact verbal parallels. Between these two methods lie a wide range of phenomena that are the main engines of literary history, and indeed are central to early modern theories about literary imitation, which emphasized that a poet should learn techniques and methods from an earlier writer rather than simply echoing ancient texts. Much of what Shakespeare took from his reading in classical drama in particular falls into this hinterland. He took from Seneca, Plautus, and Terence a set of techniques and skills—how to structure speeches and scenes, how to interrelate plot and subplot, how to unify a play around a core of metaphors. He also learned many of these things from his contemporaries, and as a result it is particularly difficult to give an exact account of his debts to classical drama.

Shakespeare's knowledge of Seneca has been long argued over. In the 1890s, J. W. Cunliffe found dozens of Senecan echoes reverberating throughout Shakespeare's works.[41] T. W. Baldwin, and after him G. K. Hunter, responded by claiming that most of what sounds like Seneca actually came to Shakespeare filtered through the 'Senecan' drama of his predecessors and contemporaries, or through Ovid.[42] These claims sprang from a variety of prejudices. There was a widespread dislike of Senecan drama among twentieth-century critics. Baldwin did not believe (despite good evidence to the contrary) that Seneca was read at grammar schools, and in any case tended to suppose that once a Tudor pupil had left school he threw away his books with a delighted cheer, and read no further in classical literature. In fact, reading at least parts of Seneca (probably choruses and speeches from the plays) does seem to have been an element in grammar-school training, and several English translations of classical dramas present themselves as cribs to help self-teachers and self-improvers to work through the Latin.[43]

More recent critics have brought out pervasive debts to Seneca in Shakespeare, from the 'Senecan' equation of high passion with high rhetoric, through to Seneca's association between the passion of an individual character and cosmic turmoil.[44] The rage of King Lear on the heath (3. 2), despite its very English weather and setting, could not have been written without the example of Seneca, for whom the cosmos often roars in sympathy with the passions of his heroes and heroines. Running through the scene are echoes of Seneca's Hippolytus, who calls on the universe to punish him: 'in me tona, me fige, me velox cremet | transactus ignis: sum nocens, merui mori' ('Hurl your thunder at me, transfix me, let the swift fire pierce and consume me. I am guilty, I deserve to die' (ll. 683–4)). 'Thought-executing fires', 'a man more sinned against than sinning': those Shakespearean phrases do not simply emerge from this Senecan speech, but without doubt they took their fire from those punitive Senecan lightnings.

Modern editors (some of whom do perhaps have 'small Latin and less Greek') often fail to record these strong parallels to Seneca, although he was the main exemplar of classical tragedy for Shakespeare and the principal model for the most successful Elizabethan dramatists of the immediately preceding generation. This did not mean, however, that splashing Senecan *sententiae* over a play was a ready and easy way to literary success. As early as 1589 Thomas Nashe complained that 'English Seneca read by candlelight yields many good sentences, as "Blood is a beggar", and so forth; and, if you entreat him fair in a frosty morning, he will afford you whole *Hamlets*, I should say handfuls of tragical speeches'.[45] This was a shrewd observation about literary history: at the very start of Shakespeare's theatrical career a 'Senecan' style was already *démodé*. Shakespeare was sensitive to everything, including criticism and Nashe. He either absorbed Senecan language deeply into the texture of his scenes (as he did in the case of *Lear*, and, more visibly, in *Richard III*) or used a 'Senecan' style in ways that show a profound awareness that being 'Senecan' is potentially a dangerous matter, both morally for a character, and stylistically for a playwright. His *Hamlet* (probably a descendant of the play criticized by Nashe) is not going to make the mistake of rewriting English Seneca:

> 'Tis now the very witching time of night,
> When churchyards yawn and hell itself breathes out
> Contagion to this world. Now could I drink hot blood,
> And do such bitter business as the day
> Would quake to look on.
>
> (3. 2. 388–92)

Hamlet's hot blood is distinctly *réchauffé*, harking back to the idiom of Kyd, and perhaps even beyond that to the translations of Seneca from the 1550s and 1560s. It is also an allusion to a 'Senecan' style that deliberately wrong-foots an audience. Hamlet ends his 'Senecan' speech on drinking hot blood, with 'Soft, now to my mother... I will speak daggers to her, but use none'. Unfortunately for Polonius, of course, the prince does not quite keep his word; but nonetheless there is an almost comical divergence between Hamlet's Senecan talk and his activities as a rat-killer in the next scene, in which he stabs Polonius in error through an arras.

These moments of 'Senecan' rhetoric followed by non-Senecan actions are part of the pulse of Shakespeare's *Hamlet*. Immediately after the player's Virgilian speech about Hecuba, Hamlet rebukes himself in language that strongly recalls the opening of Act 2 of Seneca's *Thyestes*:

> Why, what an ass am I! This is most brave,
> That I, the son of a dear father murthered,
> Prompted to my revenge by heaven and hell,
> Must like a whore unpack my heart with words,
> And fall a-cursing like a very drab,
> A stallion! Fie upon't, foh!
>
> (*Hamlet*, 2. 2. 551–6)

Atreus addresses himself as:

> Ignave, iners, enervis et (quod maximum
> Probrum tyranno rebus in summis reor)
> Inulte, post tot scelera, post fratris dolos
> Fasque omne ruptum questibus vanis agis
> Iratus Atreus? Fremere iam totus tuis
> Debebat armis orbis, et geminum mare
> Utrimque classes agree . . .

(Idle, inert, impotent, and (what I count the greatest reproach for a tyrant in high matters) unavenged: after so many crimes, after your brother's treachery and the breaking of every principle, do you act with futile complaints—you, Atreus in anger? By now the whole world should be resounding to your weapons, fleets on each coast should be stirring up the twin seas . . .)

(*Thyestes* 176–82)

Shakespeare read Seneca with a very keen ear. Seneca's characters, including Atreus here, frequently urge the world to respond to their passions. Often they do so in grammar that is optative or imperative rather than simply indicative, or they use modal verbs to describe what ought to happen rather than what is actually occurring ('the whole world *should be* resounding'). Hamlet replicates this rhetoric of hypothetical action ('now *could I* drink hot blood'), but in his case, famously, action does not follow. An analogous rhetorical tic runs through the Senecan emotional highs of *King Lear*: King Lear orders the winds to blow, the world to collapse. But the world does not collapse, and, if the winds do blow, it is probably not because Lear has ordered them to do so.

This disjunction between 'Senecan' language and action, which can create effects ranging from near comedy to painful irony, could be a sign that Shakespeare read rather than saw Seneca's plays. That is a reasonable assumption, since most of the performances of Seneca in and around Shakespeare's lifetime were in social spheres that lay on the edges of his ken. *Hippolytus* was adapted for university performance in 1592 by William Gager, while *The Misfortunes of Arthur*, which splices extended translations of Seneca into the texture of an English historical play, was performed at court in 1588. There are, however, some tantalizing signs that Shakespeare 'saw' some Senecan scenes, at least in his mind's eye. In *Hippolytus* 703–12 the hero's stepmother Phaedra kneels and invites Hippolytus to kill her with his sword if he does not respond to her passionate desire. This scene influences the moment in Shakespeare's early and most Senecan play, *Richard III* (*c.*1592), when Richard woos Anne by—theatrically, pointedly—kneeling to her and offering her his breast to stab (1. 2. 174–80).[46] *Hippolytus* provides some Latin (mis)quotations in *Titus* (2. 1. 135 and 4. 1. 81–2), as well as some mythological details in *Dream*. Lear on the heath, as we have seen, echoes Seneca's hero, and Macbeth too produces an oblique transformation of Hippolytus' cry of shame:

Will all great Neptune's ocean wash this blood
Clean from my hand? No; this my hand will rather
The multitudinous seas incarnadine,
Making the green one red.

(2. 2. 57–60)

The far-fetched words (this is the first usage of 'incarnadine' in the *OED*, and one of the earliest examples of 'multitudinous') are equivalents for the literally remote places invoked by Seneca's Hippolytus:

quis eluet me Tanais aut quae barbaris
Maeotis undis Pontico incumbens mari?
non ipse toto magnus Oceano pater
tantum expiarit sceleris.

(What water in the Tanais sea will cleanse me, or the Maeotis pouring its barbarous waters into the Pontic sea? Not the great father himself could expiate such a crime with the entire ocean.)

(ll. 715–18)

Hippolytus stayed with Shakespeare throughout his career. It is quite likely that he reread the play soon after his company became The King's Men: the former tutor of King James VI and I, George Buchanan, was noted both for his work on Scottish history and for his neo-Latin imitations of Seneca's plays.[47]

The evidence for Shakespeare's knowledge of the comedies of Plautus is more explicit. He certainly knew both the *Menaechmi* of Plautus and the *Amphitryon*, both of which are such clear influences on *The Comedy of Errors* that the driest of traditional source-hunters would be satisfied by the parallels. The *Menaechmi* is the ultimate origin of the separated-twin plot of *Twelfth Night*, as John Manningham of the Middle Temple noted in his diary record of the performance of that play in February 1601,[48] although it is fused with elements from Greek romance, which probably came to Shakespeare through English prose adaptations of that extremely fashionable genre. How far, though, did classical comedy influence Shakespeare's own theatrical practice?

The old orthodoxy was, more or less, that Shakespeare rapidly learnt to go beyond the early stilted imitation of classical comedy in *Errors*, putting aside childish things, end-stopped lines, and classical comedy at about the same time. Shakespeare's classical reading, though, does not simply go away as his career advances. It tends to grow subterraneously. Plautine comedy, absorbed and transformed, underlies some of the most central and pervasive features of Shakespearean drama. In *Amphitryon*, Jove and Mercury disguise themselves as Amphitryon and his slave so that Jove can sleep with Amphitryon's wife. The real slave Sosia meets his divine double, and wonders if he is himself who he believes himself to be. 'Egomet mihi non credo' ('I can't believe my own eyes' (l. 416)), he wonders, as he meets his 'imago' or mirror-like double, who is later described as being as like him as two drops of milk. Plautus generally associates such doubts over personal identity with material, even materialistic, causes, and links them with the loss or presence of physical tokens, such as necklaces or money. It is often said that Shakespeare's fluid representations of personal identity, steeped in Renaissance scepticism and the magic of the imagination, is quite distinct from the down-to-earth confusions of Roman comedy. The fragile illusions inhabited by Shakespearean characters—Titania's love of Bottom, Orsino's wonder at the 'natural perspective' (*Twelfth Night*, 5. 1. 216–17) that shows 'One face, one voice, one habit, and two persons', that sense of a time 'When no man was his own' (*The Tempest*, 5. 1. 213)—do indeed suggest a view of personal identity that emphasizes the role of the imaginary over the material. But the primary stimulus behind Shakespeare's interest in how deception can mine itself into the mind and result in gentle bewilderment, misplaced erotic passion, or the outright dissolution of personal identity lay in classical comedy. Plautine comedy was not a simple source for that aspect of Shakespeare, but it was certainly a central component in a complex genealogy, which includes long and tangled conversations between Shakespeare and classical drama, and between Shakespeare and his own and others' responses to that drama.

Shakespeare's interest in the ways in which imagination and belief shape people's self-conceptions and relationships with each other had a major effect on his treatment of genre. Indeed, it is perhaps the principal reason for what came to be regarded as his 'unclassical' willingness to mingle tragedy and comedy, which Samuel Johnson was to commend, but which severe advocates of French neoclassical drama were to condemn. A love that is founded on imagination and belief can develop in either tragic or comic directions. An imaginary self-deception can lead to a temporary loss of self or a suspension of social role that is comic (Titania loves an ass). But if someone for whom trust in a lover is foundational to their being is made to believe that their trust is misplaced, then their entire world can be destroyed. Again *Troilus and Cressida* (a play that is satirical or tragic or comic, rooted at once in Homer and in the *Miles Gloriosus* of Plautus, as well as in much of the complex literary tradition of the Troy story) is a pivotal play. When Troilus sees Cressida betraying him with Diomed, he echoes Plautus' 'Etsi east, non est ea' ('she is and yet she isn't' (*Miles Gloriosus*, l. 532)) in 'this is, and is not, Cressid' (5. 2. 146). Shakespeare could be, as Meres put it, 'most excellent in both kinds' partly because he explored how people's desires and beliefs construct their worlds. That has roots in classical comedy, but has the potential to ignite explosively into tragedy. The opening scenes of *Othello* are squarely positioned in the realm of comic drama: the enraged father, the elopement by night, and even the arguments put forward by Brabantio about the grounds on which testimony should be believed, all belong within the conventions of classical comic theory. But, when Othello's sustaining beliefs about Desdemona are broken down by Iago, Shakespeare shifts register from a comic realm into a rhetoric of Senecan rage:

Like to the Pontic Sea,
Whose icy current and compulsive course
Nev'r feels retiring ebb, but keeps due on

To the Propontic and the Hellespont,
Even so my bloody thoughts, with violent pace,
Shall nev'r look back, nev'r ebb to humble love,
Till that a capable and wide revenge
Swallow them up.

(3. 3. 453–60)

Othello moves with terrifying speed from the nocturnal landscape of a comedy of errors to the self-propulsive violence of Senecan tragedy. Meres could not have been thinking about this play when he praised Shakespeare for his excellence in both kinds, since it lay about five years in the future. But Shakespeare developed from classical comedy a range of interests that could enable him (unlike any surviving classical dramatist) to operate with equal comfort in the high uplands of Senecan rage and the gentle woodlands of pastoral comedy, and to move, in the course of a single play, from one to the other. There are many sources and forces behind Shakespeare's interest in the ways in which people structure their worlds by belief (including a whole range of legal and rhetorical arguments about 'ethical proof' and about the relationship between character and action).[49] But one of the central influences on this aspect of his writing was Plautus, whose *Amphitryon*, significantly enough, was the only classical drama to refer to itself as a 'tragicomoedia'.

The influence of Terence on Shakespeare is more elusive than that of Plautus, but may, nonetheless, be more pervasive.[50] Shakespeare never based a play or even a scene on any of Terence's surviving comedies, and yet Terence would have been right beside him from the moment he learnt to read Latin. Terence's plays were mined by educationalists for phrases that schoolboys could translate and learn to use in their own writing. Editions of Terence also provided early modern readers with the most accessible and extensive analyses of the theory of comedy. Terence's plays contain self-defensive critical prologues, in which the playwright discusses his sources, and (sometimes irascibly) his relationships to other dramatists. These made Terence one of the biggest influences, not on individual lines and scenes in early modern theatre, but on the structures and strategies that individual authors used to position themselves in relation to their sources and their contemporaries. He showed that it was possible to base a new play on a much older drama in a different language, to hybridize it with other texts, and to defend that imitation of ancient drama against contemporary rivals.

Terence could also have had a more humdrum influence on early modern drama. He made even clearer distinctions than Plautus between the idioms of clever slaves and smart young men about town, whose grammar and vocabulary are in turn differentiated from those of old men and matrons. It would be an exaggeration, as well as perhaps an unstomachable paradox, to claim that it was partly from classical drama that early modern dramatists learned to make their characters speak sharp, colloquial, vernacular English, since medieval mystery plays crackle with the rhythms of 'ordinary' speech, and early Tudor household plays create a variety of stylistic registers for different characters; but Terence may well have indirectly influenced even this aspect of Shakespeare's art. When Shakespeare represented people of different social classes in an English tavern having an exchange in the vernacular, as he does in *1 Henry IV*, 2. 4, he was not simply being 'popular', or defiantly unclassical. He may well have had his ears opened to the stylistic registers of the English he heard around him partly as a result of reading Terence. This would, pleasingly perhaps, take arguments for the influence of classical literature on Shakespeare to their logical vanishing point, and perhaps to their *reductio ad absurdum*: Shakespeare's much vaunted 'Englishness' may well partly derive from his reading in the classics.

This chapter began by saying that a history of classical reception in England could be told without mentioning Shakespeare at all. Why did it take so long to appreciate the nature and extent of Shakespeare's engagement with classical literature? This was partly because Shakespeare's kind of classicism was not one thing. It evolved throughout his career. It was also reactive. He looked back to and frequently played games with the spectacular classicism of his immediate predecessors. This made his earlier plays tend to associate 'classical' moments with stylistic unease, with an edge of social uncertainty, or even with anachronism. Very often an allusion to a classical text brings with it a set of questions: What does this piece of Virgil mean to Hamlet? What is this bungled Ovidian play doing within this courtly milieu? What might this allusion to Seneca mean for other characters onstage, or for what happens next? These quizzical treatments of classical texts are critically fascinating because they are so difficult to interpret, but they do not constitute a 'classical style' or a set of critical principles that later writers could emulate. This meant that, although Shakespeare had imitators in many areas of his theatrical practice—notably John Fletcher, John Webster, and even, more privily, Ben Jonson—there was no tradition of Shakespearean classicism.

Shakespeare also had the misfortune to be born eight years before Ben Jonson. Shakespeare attempted to make the classicism of his predecessors seem old-fashioned at the same time as he transformed it; Jonson matched him and raised the stakes. He developed methods of incorporating classical texts into poems and plays that instantly seemed more 'modern' than Shakespeare's. Jonson, who was a master of both the literal and the virtual footnote, could show his learning as he adapted a classical text. He followed Terence in providing critical prologues (and even literary-critical interludes) for his own plays. He explored the full range of responses to Latin poetry and drama, from bone-crunchingly literal translation to free-ranging imitation, through to high-level attempts to identify himself with Horace.[51] And so, when asked to write an elegy to Shakespeare for the first folio, Jonson, at the height of his fame and at the ripe old age (for this period) of 51, managed to present himself as the new Kyd on the block:

> For if I thought my judgement were of years
> I should commit thee surely with thy peers,
> And tell how far thou didst our Lyly outshine,

Or sporting Kyd, or Marlowe's mighty line.
And, though thou hadst small Latin and less Greek,
From thence to honour thee I would not seek
For names, but call forth thundering Aeschylus,
Euripides and Sophocles to us...

(ll. 27–34)

'For if I thought my judgement were of years' is not the phrase that is generally picked out of this passage, but it is crucial to its rhetorical effect: it means 'if only my judgement were mature enough to make such comparisons'. It suggests that Jonson was a stripling when he wrote his elegy, although in 1623 he was in fact just one year younger than Shakespeare had been when he died. Jonson tried to make it sound as though he was the voice of the new age, a man able to invoke the Greek playwrights, and to look back with gentle patronage on Shakespeare—old, dead, highly respectable but possibly just a tiny bit provincial Shakespeare—who represented a kind of classicism that belonged to a past age. Jonson's strategy was so effective that Shakespeare is only now being brought back to his rightful place within the history of English classicism. Methods for exploring the reception of classical texts and traditions have become increasingly tolerant of the plural and the unresolved. Shakespeare's notably plural and unresolved responses to classical authors have come, as a result, to seem more and more central to an understanding of the classical tradition—so central, indeed, that a history of that subject today that did not include a chapter on Shakespeare would be almost unthinkable.

Notes

1. See T. W. Baldwin, *William Shakespere's Small Latine and Lesse Greeke* (Urbana, IL, 1944); Charles Martindale and Michelle Martindale, *Shakespeare and the Uses of Antiquity: An Introductory Essay* (New York, 1990); Charles Martindale and A. B. Taylor (eds), *Shakespeare and the Classics* (Cambridge, 2004); Robert S. Miola, *Shakespeare and Classical Tragedy: The Influence of Seneca* (Oxford, 1992); Robert S. Miola, *Shakespeare and Classical Comedy: The Influence of Plautus and Terence* (Oxford, 1994); Lynne Enterline, *Shakespeare's Schoolroom: Rhetonc, Discipline, Emotion* (Philadelphia, 2013). Robert S. Miola, *Shakespeare's Reading* (Oxford, 2000); Colin Burrow, *Shakespeare and Classical Antiquity* (Oxford, 2013). Valuable summaries of Shakespeare's knowledge of classical authors are in Stuart Gillespie, *Shakespeare's Books: A Dictionary of Shakespeare's Sources* (New Brunswick, NJ, 2001).
2. Emrys Jones, *The Origins of Shakespeare* (Oxford, 1977), 85–118.
3. Plutarch, *Plutarch's Lives of the Noble Grecians and Romans*, ed. George Wyndham (1895), 2. 180–1 (in the 'Life of Coriolanus'); 3. 89 for the performance of Euripides' *Bacchae*.
4. Mark Eccles, *Shakespeare in Warwickshire* (Madison, WI, 1961), 54–62.
5. William Gager's 'Letter to John Rainolds', quoted in F. S. Boas, *University Drama in the Tudor Age* (Oxford, 1914), 235–6.
6. Carey Herbert Conley, *The First English Translators of the Classics* (New Haven,

1927), 26–7, notes that around half of identifiable translators in the period 1558–72 were connected with the Inns.

7. On Shakespeare's relationship to Ovid, see Leonard Barkan, *The Gods Made Flesh: Metamorphosis and the Pursuit of Paganism* (New Haven, 1986); Jonathan Bate, *Shakespeare and Ovid* (Oxford, 1993); Lynn Enterline, *Rhetoric of the Body from Ovid to Shakespeare* (Cambridge, 2000); A. B. Taylor (ed.), *Shakespeare's Ovid: The Metamorphoses in the Plays and Poems* (Cambridge, 2000).
8. Brian Vickers, *Shakespeare, Co-Author: A Historical Study of Five Collaborative Plays* (Oxford, 2002), 148–243; cf. Paul Hammond, 'Shakespeare as Collaborator: The Case of *Titus Andronicus*', in Paul Scott (ed.), *Collaboration and Interdisciplinarity in the Republic of Letters: Essays* in Honour of Richard G. Maber (Manchester, 2010), 193–208.
9. Henry Helmes, *Gesta Grayorum, or, the History of the High and Mighty Prince Henry, Prince of Purpoole, Anno Domini 1594*, ed. Desmond Bland (Liverpool, 1968), 32.
10. Cf. *Errors* 1. 1. 31–139 and *Aeneid* 2. 1–267, 1. 88–91.
11. *Heauton Timorumenos*, 17.
12. Gordon Braden, *The Classics and English Renaissance Poetry: Three Case Studies* (New Haven, 1978), 55–154.
13. William Shakespeare, *The Complete Poems and Sonnets*, ed. Colin Burrow (Oxford, 2002), 45–50.
14. Philip Henslowe, *Henslowe's Diary*, ed. R. A. Foakes (Cambridge, 2002), 21; E. Arber (ed.), *A Transcript of the Registers of the Company of Stationers of London*, 5 vols (1875–94), 2. 307.
15. Francis Meres, *Palladis Tamia* (1598), fo. 281v; MacDonald P. Jackson, 'Francis Meres and the Cultural Contexts of Shakespeare's Rival Poet Sonnets', *Review of English Studies*, 56 (2005), 224–46; Patrick Cheney, *Shakespeare, National Poet-Playwright* (Cambridge, 2004), 49–73.
16. Robert Greene and Henry Chettle, *Greenes, Groats-Worth of Witte, Bought with a Million of Repentance* (1592), sig. F1v.
17. Aphthonius, *Aphthonii Sophistae Progymnasmata, Partim a Rodolpho Agricola, Partim a Ioanne Maria Catanæo Latinitate Donata*, ed. Rodolphus Agricola (1580), 19.
18. See, e.g. Madeleine Forey, '"Bless Thee, Bottom, Bless Thee! Thou Art Translated!": Ovid, Golding, and *a Midsummer Night's Dream*', *Modern Language Review*, 93 (1998), 321–9, A. B. Taylor, 'Golding's Ovid, Shakespeare's "Small Latin", and the Real Object of Mockery in "Pyramus and Thisbe"', *Shakespeare Survey*, 42 (1990), 53–64.
19. Raphael Lyne, 'Ovid, Golding, and the "Rough Magic" of *The Tempest*', in A. B. Taylor, *Shakespeare's Ovid*, 150–64.
20. Martindale and Martindale, *Uses of Antiquity*, 23.
21. Notably by Charles Martindale, in Martindale and Martindale, *Uses of Antiquity*, 53, and in 'Shakespeare and Virgil', in Martindale and Taylor (eds), *Shakespeare and the Classics*, 89–106. For general discussion of Shakespeare and Virgil, see Barbara Bono, *Literary Transvaluation: From Vergilian Epic to Shakespearean Tragicomedy* (Berkeley and Los Angeles, 1984); Donna B. Hamilton, *Virgil and the Tempest: The Politics of Imitation* (Columbus, OH, 1990); Margaret Tudeau-Clayton, *Jonson, Shakespeare and Early Modern Virgil* (Cambridge, 1998); Robert S. Miola, 'Vergil in Shakespeare'; Heather James, 'Dido's Ear: Tragedy and the Politics of Response', *Shakespeare Quarterly*, 52 (2001), 360–82; David Scott Wilson-Okamura, 'Virgilian Models of Colonization in Shakespeare's *Tempest*', *ELH* 70 (2003), 709–37; David Scott Wilson-

Okamura, *Virgil in the Renaissance* (Cambridge, 2010).

22. Margaret Tudeau-Clayton, 'Scenes of Translation in Jonson and Shakespeare: *Poetaster, Hamlet,* and *A Midsummer Night's Dream*', *Translation and Literature,* 11 (2002), 1–23.
23. See Martindale and Martindale, *Uses of Antiquity*, 76.
24. Bono, *Literary Transvaluation*.
25. Miola, 'Vergil in Shakespeare', 242–4.
26. Gabriel Harvey, *Gabriel Harvey's Marginalia*, ed. G. C. Moore Smith (Stratford-upon-Avon, 1913), 232.
27. Craig Kallendorf, *The Other Virgil: 'Pessimistic' Readings of the Aeneid in Early Modern Culture* (Oxford, 2007), esp. 102–26.
28. Patricia Parker, 'Romance and Empire: Anachronistic Cymbeline', in George M. Logan and Gordon Teskey (eds), *Unfolded Tales: Essays on Renaissance Romance* (Ithaca, NY, 1989), 189–207.
29. James P. Bednarz, *Shakespeare and the Poets' War* (New York, 2001).
30. Meres, *Palladis Tamia*, fo. 268^{v}.
31. On the contamination of sources, see esp. Heather James, *Shakespeare's Troy* (Cambridge, 1997).
32. For the widespread error, see William Shakespeare, *Troilus and Cressida*, ed. Harold N. Hillebrand (Philadelphia, 1953), 106–8. Hamilton, *Politics of Imitation*, 11–18, discusses Sturm in connection with Shakespeare.
33. Johannes Sturm, *A Ritch Storehouse or Treasure for Nobilitye and Gentlemen* (1570), fo. 36^{v}.
34. G. W. Pigman, 'Versions of Imitation in the Renaissance', *Renaissance Quarterly*, 33 (1980), 1–32.
35. Sturm, *Storehouse*, sigs H5^{v}–H6^{r}.
36. See further Colin Burrow, 'Shakespeare and Humanistic Culture', in Martindale and Taylor (eds), *Shakespeare and the Classics*, 9–27 (21–2).
37. Contrast Miola, 'Vergil in Shakespeare', and Martindale, 'Shakespeare and Virgil', and see Charles Martindale, Chapter 26, this volume.
38. Andrew Hadfield, *Shakespeare and Republicanism* (Cambridge, 2005); Patrick Cheney, *Marlowe's Republican Authorship: Lucan, Liberty, and the Sublime* (Basingstoke, 2009), 42–9; cf. Colin Burrow, *Epic Romance: Homer to Milton* (Oxford, 1993), 180–9, Edward Paleit, 'The "Caesarist" Reader and Lucan's *Bellum Ciuile, ca.* 1590 to 1610', *Review of English Studies*, 62 (2011), 212–40; see also Jones, *Origins*, 273–7.
39. Meres, *Palladis Tamia*, fo. 282^{r}.
40. Charles Martindale, *Redeeming the Text: Latin Poetry and the Hermeneutics of Reception* (Cambridge, 1993).
41. John William Cunliffe, *The Influence of Seneca on Elizabethan Tragedy: An Essay* (1893); F. L. Lucas, *Seneca and Elizabethan Tragedy* (Cambridge, 1922).
42. Baldwin, *Small Latine*, 2. 553–60; G. K. Hunter, *Dramatic Identities and Cultural Tradition: Studies in Shakespeare and His Contemporaries: Critical Essays* (Liverpool, 1978), 159–213.
43. Charles Hoole, *A New Discovery of the Old Art of Teaching Schoole* (1659), 198; Jasper Heywood's 1561 translation of *Hercules Furens* is described on the title page as 'for the profit of young scholars'.
44. Gordon Braden, *Renaissance Tragedy and the Senecan Tradition: Anger's Privilege* (New Haven, 1985); Miola, *Seneca*; Jones, *Origins*, 267–72.
45. Thomas Nashe, *Works*, ed. Ronald B. McKerrow and F. P. Wilson, 5 vols (Oxford, 1958), 3. 315.
46. Harold F. Brooks, '"Richard III", Unhistorical Amplifications: The Women's Scenes and Seneca', *Modern Language Review*, 75 (1980), 721–37, notes this and parallels with *Troades* and *Hercules Furens*.
47. David Norbrook, '*Macbeth* and the Politics of Historiography', in Kevin Sharpe

and Steven N. Zwicker (eds), *Politics of Discourse: The Literature and History of Seventeenth-Century England* (Berkeley and Los Angeles, 1987), 78–166.

48. John Manningham, *The Diary of John Manningham of the Middle Temple, 1602–1603*, ed. Robert Parker Sorlien (Hanover, NH, 1976), 48.
49. Lorna Hutson, *The Invention of Suspicion: Law and Mimesis in Shakespeare and Renaissance Drama* (Oxford, 2007); and Joel Altman, *The Improbability of Othello: Rhetorical Anthropology and Shakespearean Selfhood* (Chicago, 2010).
50. See Thomas Whitfield Baldwin, *Shakspere's Five-Act Structure: Shakspere's Early Plays on the Background of Renaissance Theories of Five-Act Structure from 1470* (Urbana, IL, 1947); Miola, *Plautus and Terence*; Joel B. Altman, *The Tudor Play of Mind: Rhetorical Inquiry and the Development of Elizabethan Drama* (Berkeley and Los Angeles, 1978), 130–47; Lorna Hutson, *The Usurer's Daughter: Male Friendship and Fictions of Women in Sixteenth-Century England* (1994), 163–223.
51. Victoria Moul, *Jonson, Horace and the Classical Tradition* (Cambridge, 2010).

CHAPTER 28

Jonson

SEAN KEILEN

Ben Jonson's encounter with classical literature began in a Renaissance grammar school, and the influence of his formal education at Westminster is evident throughout his career as a playwright, poet, and critic. Marlowe and Shakespeare also absorbed the classics at school. However, the way that they manifest the experience of schooling does not have much in common with Jonson's works. Teachers and teaching come under harsh scrutiny in *Doctor Faustus*, for example—a play where learning is little more than the form desire takes, in order to persuade itself that what it wants is truth. In *Titus Andronicus*, Shakespeare associates the study and imitation of Roman texts with shocking acts of violence that bring civilization to the brink of ending. These plays see classical education, and the authority of learned men, through the lens of adolescent rebellion and sobering disenchantment. Jonson's works, by contrast, express a reverence for the books and teachers that taught him how to read and live, and also an earnestness about the benefits of classical studies that borders on idealization. Of course, Jonson's sense of human fallibility was no less keen than Marlowe's or Shakespeare's; like them, he makes hay of errant masters, inapt pupils, and ignorance disguised as knowledge. But the criticism he lavishes on bad teaching never adds up to a sceptical outlook on classical education or the wisdom to be found in ancient texts. Jonson was a believer. Scholarly and diligent in a literary culture that relished creative insubordination, he devoted himself to the idea that the classics are the best foundation for good judgement, legitimate authority, and a happy life. These beliefs set his classicism apart from other writers who admired ancient texts intensely, but also doubted the wisdom of what they had to say.

Jonson's dedication to the classics, and to the idea that poets are duty-bound to share what they learn from the past, is ordinarily regarded as a weakness of his writing, rather than a strength. Referring to Jonson's familiarity with Greek and Latin writing, T. S. Eliot reflects that his reputation is 'afflicted by the imputation of the virtues that excite the least pleasure'.[1] By the same token, Jonson's love of the classics is said to have prevented him from becoming a truly great artist, like Shakespeare.

Milton, despite being an advocate of classical education, inadvertently provides an early context for this invidious comparison when he juxtaposes 'the learned sock' and erudite footwork of Jonson's comedies with the sweetness of Shakespeare's warbling 'wood-notes wild' ('L'Allegro', ll. 132–4).[2] Dryden enlarges Milton's comparison when he describes Shakespeare as having 'the largest and most comprehensive soul' of all ancient and modern poets, and Jonson as 'the most learned and judicious writer which any theatre ever had'. This means that Jonson, by virtue of his prodigious learning, is 'more correct', but Shakespeare is 'the greater wit'—a Homer to Jonson's Virgil—because he was 'naturally learned' and 'needed not the spectacles of books to read nature'.[3] Ironically, when Dryden argues that 'those who accuse [Shakespeare] to have wanted learning, give him the greater commendation', he may be alluding to Jonson's elegy for Shakespeare: the well-known text that claims that, although Shakespeare himself had 'small Latin, and less Greek', his works are nevertheless 'for all time' (*Essay of Dramatic Poesy*; Dryden, 17. 55; 'To the Memory of My Beloved, the Author Mr William Shakespeare', 31, 43; Jonson, *Works*, 8. 391).

The reception of Jonson's work since the Renaissance follows in the steps of these early responses to a remarkable degree. In an influential essay about Jonson's life and art, Swinburne infers that 'the unequalled breadth and depth of [Jonson's] reading could not but enrich as well as encumber his writings'. He weighs the 'ponderous mass of illustrative superfluity' that Jonson borrows from classical literature, history, and philosophy, against the untutored subtleties that he finds in Shakespearean texts. On this basis, he concludes what Shakespeare knew as a birthright, Jonson could never learn, however wide or deep his classical studies went. 'The case of Ben Jonson is the greatest standing example of a truth which should never be forgotten or overlooked,' writes Swinburne: 'no amount of learning or labour, or of culture will supply the place of natural taste and native judgement—will avail in the slightest degree to confer the critical faculty upon a man to whom nature has denied it.'[4] Where Swinburne blames Jonson's inferiority to Shakespeare on an inborn lack of discernment, G. Gregory Smith argues that Jonson's nature is to be entirely too critical. It was his 'misfortune... that, being more than an Ascham or a Harvey [a schoolmaster and a Cambridge don], he so often allowed himself to gratify this ardour of intellect at the expense of the imagination'. For Smith, the root of Jonson's artistic failure lies in a 'tyrannical conscience' that indulges itself by judging others according to standards that Jonson himself did not uphold. Having 'encouraged himself to the performance of a public duty rather of the schoolmasterly kind', Jonson could not 'deny himself the further gratification of discoursing on the general purpose of art and of explaining his own efforts'. With Shakespeare, 'we feel that the subject is left to take care of itself, or is allowed a freer development', but with Jonson, who cannot help but explain the meaning of his works, literature becomes 'lessons of the class-room kind', forced upon a 'pupil-audience'.[5]

Because familiarity with the classics was synonymous with education in Jonson's period, it is not surprising that the anti-pedagogical tradition in Jonson studies should culminate in a statement of disapproval for classicism too. '[It] is the Nemesis of the classical habit', writes Smith, that, although classicizing texts 'should . . . offer to literature . . . a wholesome discipline [and] the only competent aid to the understanding of its own mysteries', nevertheless, they secure these benefits 'with the loss of that vitality by which alone the best things are sustained'. It follows that Jonson's writing has 'importance in our literary perspective' because it possesses 'the qualities expressed by the epithet ["classical"]', but it is precisely those classical qualities that have 'reduced [Jonson's] claims to higher individual honour'.[6] It would appear to be the case that to talk about Jonson's art at all is to talk about his classicism, and, for some readers, the poet's greatest asset will always be his worst liability. Fortunately, there are alternatives to this way of understanding Jonson's classicism and his pedagogical ambitions. They begin with questions that earlier critics rarely ask. What did Jonson learn from the classics, and what did he hope to teach?

Jonson's 'Wise Crafts': Constancy, Liberty, Friendship

Jonson's wide reading, proficiency in Latin and Greek, and skilful adaptations of ancient literary genres deserve pride of place in the long list of achievements that were commemorated in two folio editions of his *Works* (1616, 1640). His imitations of Martial revitalize the epigram in English. He imposes strict limits on the genre's erotic preoccupations and greatly extends its philosophical scope. Referring to the 'theatre' of his epigrams as 'the ripest of my studies', Jonson reflects that 'Cato, if he lived, might enter without scandal' (*Epigrams*, 'To the Earl of Pembroke'; Jonson, *Works*, 8. 25–6).[7] His odes bring Horace into the centre of vernacular literary culture, while the verse epistles that he models on both Horace's and Seneca's letters combine the resources of lyric poetry and moral philosophy, a bold attempt to show the affinity of these ostensibly antithetical modes. *Sejanus* (1603) and *Catiline* (1611), the Roman tragedies of Jonson's mid-career, translate long passages from Tacitus and other ancient historians, sometimes for the first time. He raises the status of satire—arguing, as Juvenal had done, that satire is not an abuse of freedom, but the essence of a free society, the discerning eye that developed cultures turn upon themselves. Jonson is the first English translator of Horace's *Ars Poetica* and the author of England's first Pindaric ode. His court masques give ancient mythology the currency of popular entertainment. Other classicizing projects are more academic than literary. Jonson writes a grammar that he hopes will 'free our Language from the opinion of rudeness and barbarism, wherewith it is mistaken to be diseased' and 'show the copy ['richness'] of it, and matchableness' with the languages of ancient Greece and Rome (*An English Grammar*; Jonson, *Works*, 8. 465). His commonplace book, combining passages of ancient literature, rhetoric, and moral philosophy, with excerpts from classical scholarship, humanist pedagogy, and his own commentary, was published, after his death, as *Timber, or Discoveries*. All of these endeavours tell us something about the nature and extraordinary range of Jonson's classical interests, but his classicism is still more than the sum of its outstanding parts.

There are many excellent studies of Jonson's formal achievements as an imitator and translator of classical texts,[8] but it makes sense to think of his classicism not only as the work he did, but also as the spirit in which he did that work. 'The crucial assumption on which [Jonson's] classicism depends' is, according to one scholar, 'the conviction that thorough immersion in a lost culture is a prerequisite for comprehension of, and contribution to, one's own culture'.[9] This conviction about the classics leads Jonson to an expansive vision of poetry as a socially consequential act of self-invention. 'All study of philosophy and all reading should be applied to the idea of living the happy life,' writes Seneca, in a letter that shapes Jonson's perception of the ancients and his own writing; 'we should not hunt out archaic or far-fetched words and eccentric metaphors and figures of speech, but... seek precepts which will help us, utterances of courage and spirit which may at once be turned into facts' (*Epistles*, 108. 35). Quintilian makes a similar point about the inextricability of character and style, arguing that, before one can write well, one must learn to be good, by reading and imitating the best books.

> Since the orator is a good man [he writes], and the concept of a good man is unintelligible apart from virtue, and since virtue, though it derives some impulses from nature, has none the less to be perfected by teaching, the orator must... develop his moral character by study, and undergo a thorough training in the honourable and just, because without this no one can be either a good man or a skilled speaker.
>
> (*Instituto Oratoria*, 12. 2. 1)

To steep oneself in these ideas, as Jonson did, is to believe that literature exemplifies good living, and that good lives are exemplary texts worth imitating, in both art and life. 'A good life is a main argument', he writes (*Timber*, ll. 91–2; Jonson, *Works*, 8. 566).

It follows that one's prospects for becoming the kind of model that others ought to imitate depend entirely on the attitude one takes towards reading and writing. For, in reading and writing, one discovers the extent to which one can make good choices in ambiguous circumstances; form honest and loving relationships with people of different points of view; and bring life to a happy conclusion, like a well-made work of art. Jonson's investment in this kind of ethical thinking gives his work its unmistakably didactic tone, but, far from handing down his own judgements as incontestable laws, he hopes that the education he provides through art will lead readers to share the ethos of independent decision-making that all his works exemplify. 'I will have no man addict himself to me,' writes Jonson, for 'it profits not me to have any man fence, or fight for me, to flourish, or take a side' (*Timber*, ll. 154–8; Jonson, *Works*, 8. 568).[10] In this context, a Jonsonian poem or play is an appeal to readers and audiences, rather than a command; his authority as a teacher reaches no farther than their desire to learn. If ancient precepts are to become modern facts—and modern facts, future classics—it is up to Jonson's audience to apply his principles for living to the complexity of their own experience in a changing world.

What are the principles of Jonson's classicism? In an era when Ovid inspired English poets to blur the boundaries that made social life coherent—self and other, male and female, civilized and wild, high and low—Jonson believed that it was necessary for poetry 'to draw true lines', distinguishing one thing from another, especially happiness from unhappiness, achievement from failure, and right from wrong ('Epistle to Katharine, Lady Aubigny', l. 20; Jonson, *Works*, 8. 117). Only in that way would poets contribute to the making of good men, whom Jonson called 'the stars, the planets of the ages wherein they live' (*Timber*, ll. 1100–1; Jonson, *Works*, 8. 597). Although Jonson read omnivorously, it was Horace, more than any other ancient writer, who furnished him with the precepts that he himself longed to bring into practice in his life and work. Especially in the satires and verse epistles that Jonson studied closely, Horace sets forth ideas about poetry and the good life from which Jonson builds the edifice of his vocation.[11] Horace describes the ideal poet as a temperate man and passionate teacher, as a loyal and earnest friend, and as advocate of both self-sufficiency and the common good. He also argues that poets should be unflinching critics, of themselves and others, and fulfil their duty to communicate the wisdom that comes down from the past. Under this influence, Jonson's classicism takes shape as an ethos of reading and writing that places him between his ancient models and his modern readers, as a participant in the free exchange of points of view on which education, art, and friendship all depend.

The classics taught Jonson that a constant character and imperturbable mind are the bases for discernment, and thus for the good life that good judgements alone make possible. 'The wise man is joyful, happy and calm, unshaken,' writes Seneca of constancy; likewise Horace, who urges a friend to seek the good life not in making changes of scenery, but in the stillness of well-ordered thoughts (*Epistles*, 59. 14; *Epistles*, 1. 11).[12] Jonson continues the stoical tradition that links constancy and discernment by commending steadfastness to others as a principle for making difficult choices about the best way to live. 'Be always to thy gathered self the same,' he advises Thomas Roe, 'And study conscience, more than thou wouldst fame. | Though both be good, the latter yet is worst' ('To Sir Thomas Roe', ll. 9–11; Jonson, *Works*, 8. 63).[13] He also practises what he preaches, writing of hard times that 'though forsook | of Fortune, [I] have not altered yet my look, | Or...myself abandoned' ('Epistle to Katharine, Lady Aubigny', ll. 15–17; Jonson, *Works*, 8. 117). By the same token, Jonson presents each poem and play he writes as the final and immutable form of a judgement about virtue and vice that he has formed after long study. The 'turning world...cannot see | Right, the right way', he writes, because it 'studies spectacles, and shows, | And after fresh objects goes, | Giddy with change'. By contrast, his writing is a mirror that 'takes, and gives the beauties of the mind'. It sees clearly but it changes nothing, and its own meaning remains the same, no matter how it is read, or by whom. 'Be bold to use this truest glass,' writes Jonson to a patron, of the poem that praises her for virtue: 'your form, you still the same shall find; | Because nor it can change, nor such a mind' ('Epistle to Katharine, Lady Aubigny', *passim*; Jonson, *Works*, 8. 117–20).

The benefit of being constant is being free. It is liberty, meaning independence from one's own desires and passions, and therefore from exigency of circumstance and exploitation by powerful people.[14] 'Men that are safe, and sure, in all they do, | Care not what trials they are put unto; | They meet the fire, the test, as martyrs would,' he writes ('An Epistle Answering to One that Asked to Be Sealed of the Tribe of Ben', ll. 1–3; Jonson, *Works*, 8. 218). In fact, liberty is constancy by another name, as Jonson implies in a translation of Martial. Explaining that a 'quiet mind' and 'free powers' are both prerequisites for living well, he intimates that liberty is not free action *per se*, but an equilibrium of character that makes free action possible: a 'will to be, what thou art; and nothing more' ('Martial. Epigram XLVII, Book X', 6, 12; Jonson, *Works*, 8. 295). Closely related to this first sense of freedom is *libertas*, the Roman idea that compasses political freedom and freedom of speech, including the freedom to criticize others candidly. Jonson conjoins them in the prologue to *Bartholomew Fair* (1614), encouraging everyone in the audience both to 'exercise his own judgement' and 'be fixed and settled in his censure' ('The Induction', ll. 97–101; Jonson, *Works*, 6. 16).

Because Jonson made his money by writing for patrons and the theatre-going public, assertions of independence are prominent features of his poems and plays. At every point in his career, the credibility of his teaching stands or falls with the idea that there is only one kind of authority worth submitting to: the authority of the classics, which frees one to engage it critically, as Jonson instructs his readers to engage him. 'I do not desire to be equal to those that went before, but to have my reason examined with theirs,' he writes, under the heading 'Non mihi cedendum, sed veritati' ('You should not yield to me, but to the truth') (*Timber*, ll. 151–2; Jonson, *Works*, 8. 567). An epigram for William Camden makes this point in a different way. Expressing the 'free truth' of Jonson's gratitude to his teacher at Westminster, this poem acknowledges Camden as the source of 'all that I am in arts, all that I know'. However, in giving back the 'all' of Camden's teaching to its source, in the form of gratitude and 'piety', Jonson reaps those benefits again, for they constitute the 'all' he has become ('To William Camden', *passim*; Jonson, *Works*, 8. 31). In the widening circle of the classical tradition that Jonson receives from Camden and passes on by writing, critical appraisal inspires gratitude, and gratitude stimulates the free play of critical and creative powers. 'I thank those that have taught me, and will ever,' writes Jonson, in an apposite passage, but '[I] dare not think the scope of their labour and enquiry was to envy their posterity, what they also could add and find out' (*Timber*, ll. 146–9; Jonson, *Works*, 8. 567). Or even more succinctly: 'Nothing is more ridiculous than to make an author a dictator' (*Timber*, l. 2096; Jonson, *Works*, 8. 627).

The man who is steadfast, freely speaks his mind, and has no fear of being criticized is in a position to become a friend to other, like-minded souls. Friendship is a third hallmark of Jonson's classicism, a major preoccupation of his poetry, and a rare relationship that he extends to every reader through the experience of discovering, in critical dialogue with Jonson himself, what one really stands for, and thus of learning to be free.[15]

Certainly, Jonson can be contentious and self-assured; even in small differences of opinion, he is an unyielding opponent. Those traits go a long way towards explaining the fierce resistance that his work arouses, even in admiring audiences. But are they contrary to friendship and the other 'wise crafts, on which the flatterer ventures not': 'Freedom, and truth; with love from those begot' ('To a Friend and Son', ll. 5–6; Jonson, *Works*, 241)? Quarrelsome though he could be, Jonson explicitly distinguishes between the kind of argument that arises from bad motives, and the better kind that promotes a love of clarity and truth. 'Study the separation of opinions, find the errors [that] have intervened, awake antiquity, call former times into question, he writes, 'but make no parties with the present, nor follow any fierce undertakers, mingle no matter of doubtful credit with the simplicity of truth, but gently stir the mould about the root of the question, and avoid all digladiations [fencing with words, wrangling]' (*Timber*, ll. 2108–13; Jonson, *Works*, 8. 627). Reflecting on his own tenacity in discourse, Jonson writes, 'I take this labour in teaching others that they should not be always to be taught; and I would bring my precepts into practice' (*Timber*, 1755–7; Jonson, *Works*, 8. 617). Of teaching, he believes that 'a master should temper his own powers, and descend to the other's infirmity', for 'to their capacity they will all receive, and be full' (*Timber*, 1791–6; Jonson, *Works*, 8. 618). Elsewhere, Jonson argues a writer is as much a recipient of special potency as the source of it. Because the writer stands in relation to the reader 'as an ambassador to his master, or a subject to a sovereign', those who would teach others how to live must 'beget love in the persons we counsel'—not by dominating them with eloquence, but by 'dissembling our knowledge of ability in ourselves', 'avoiding all suspicion of arrogance', and 'seasoning all with humanity and sweetness, only expressing care and solicitude' (*Timber*, ll. 93–8; Jonson, *Works*, 8. 566). This is essential, because the love of readers is the only authority that poets and playwrights can ever have.[16] These passages suggest that what appears to be a blindness to the limits of his own perspective, and an arrogant lack of interest in other points of view, is actually a gesture of goodwill, fully consonant with an older theory of friendship that, for the most part, has faded from our view. Swinburne blamed Jonson's classical studies for ruining his art, but even this stern critic understands that Jonson's adversarial behaviour, as a 'consummate and indefatigable scholar', is consistent with his nature as a 'generous and enthusiastic friend'.[17]

Long before William Blake supposes that opposition is true friendship, Jonson argues that a vigorous appraisal of oneself and others is friendship's special office. The Roman moralists, whom he preferred as models to Homer, Virgil, and Ovid, believed that the friend is another self, and friendship a technique for seeing the self critically. Friends are the best critics because they know the truth about the self—as it were, from the inside—and, unlike flatterers, their motives are above reproach. It follows that, because friends want what is best for the self, for the self's own sake, they reveal errors to which the self is blind, and therefore friendship is a form of judgement, leading to self-knowledge. But because it falls to friends to expose the very flaws that the self keeps hidden, conflict is as much friendship's métier as harmony. It is the risk that friends are willing to take in order to achieve a lasting unity. Seneca believes, for example, that 'good men are mutually helpful' and '[give] practice to [each] other's virtues'. For him, the friendship of wise souls is productive strife, like athletic competition or the rivalry of artists, without which one's capacity for goodness and wisdom cannot develop fully: 'Skilled wrestlers are kept up to the mark by practice; a musician is stirred to action by one of equal proficiency' (*Epistles*, 109. 1–2). Jonson's contemporary, Francis Bacon, argues, in the same spirit, that 'the best receipt [prescription]' for irrationality and vice is 'the admonition of a friend', for it 'is a strange thing to behold what gross errors and extreme absurdities many... do commit, for want of a friend to tell of them'.

Other ancient writers, supposing that friendship is the model for the best society, find in the unsparing criticism that friends bestow upon each other's faults the essence of freedom itself. 'We live in one way with a tyrant and in another with a friend,' writes Cicero; 'friends frequently must not only be advised [*monendi*] but also rebuked [*obiurgandi*]' (*De Amicitia*, 24. 89–90). Jonson echoes this passage when writing to a friend who seeks criticism about art and life. Asked to pull his punches and 'censure not sharply', Jonson states unequivocally that friendship *is* criticism. He concedes that 'wholly to reprove' is as an 'Act of Tyranny, not Love', but he also argues that 'Amity' demands the full exercise of 'Liberty' in discourse. Every man will 'sometimes... be tempted to obey | his fury', but, should he do so, 'no friendship he betray[s]' ('An Epistle to a Friend', *passim*; Jonson, *Works*, 8. 420–1). Even a furious critique can be a building-up, rather than a tearing-down, of autonomy, freedom, and happiness, provided that one is devoted to helping one's friend to see right the right way. 'No simple word, | That shall be uttered at our mirthful board, | Shall make us sad next morning', he promises a friend whom he invites to dinner, nor 'affright | The liberty, that we'll enjoy tonight' ('Inviting a Friend to Supper', ll. 39–42; Jonson, *Works*, 8. 65).

Self-Creating Jonson

At the start of his career, Jonson wrote three 'comical satires', professing his commitment to these classical ideals.[18] These plays are contributions to the *Poetomachia*, or Poets' War—a bitter, public quarrel in which John Marston and Thomas Dekker ridiculed Jonson as a hypocrite and pedant. Each play focuses on a well-read protagonist who, like Jonson himself, comes under attack, by a group of rivals, for the way that he lives, makes judgements, and writes. Taken together, they tell a story about the growth of Jonson's creative powers from his critical faculties, and chart a course between self-discovery and self-vindication. They also argue that Jonson's classicism makes his work different from the work of other poets; more specifically, that the way that Jonson reads and imitates the ancients makes him a better poet and a better man than Marston and Dekker. The first play, *Every Man out of his Humour* (1599), establishes a framework for making those claims. The second, *Cynthia's Revels* (1600), explores the evolution of Jonson's classicism in an Ovidian literary environment that is at odds with his creative and critical values. The third play, *Poetaster* (1601), decisively confirms Jonson's personal identification with Horace, rather than Ovid, and calls upon other writers to follow his example.

Jonson declares that his comedies chastise vice, in the tradition of ancient Greek comedy. He makes this claim with full awareness that good choices are difficult to make, even for one who has had a classical education. Therefore as an acknowledgement that he stands beside his audience (like a human being and a friend), rather than above them (like a god or master), Jonson puts himself in the middle of his plots. It is a strategy that courts solipsism and arouses suspicion and resistance. Dekker specifically condemns Jonson's self-projections. 'You must have three or four suits of names, when like a lousy pediculous vermin, th'ast but one suit to thy back,' he writes in *Satiromastix, or The Untrussing of the Humorous Poet* (1601); 'you must be called Asper, and Criticus, and Horace, thy title's longer a reading than the style [of] the big Turk's'. Elsewhere, he lampoons him as a 'self-creating Horace'.[19] There is no denying that Jonson's plays and poems are, formally speaking, self-centred, but his decision to write this way might be understood, more charitably, as a refusal to exempt himself from the moral and aesthetic teachings that his classicism recommends to others. Show me a passage in which Jonson argues that his point of view is superior to others, and I will show you a text in which he also takes pains to clarify that his perspective is exactly that and nothing more: one man's perception of the way that things are and should be, supported by learning but open to scrutiny and subject to change. 'If I err,' he writes, 'pardon me: *Nulla ars simul et inventa est, et absoluta*' ['No art was ever perfect at the start'] (*Timber*, ll. 150–1; Jonson, *Works*, 8. 567).

In the opening scene of *Every Man out of his Humour*, for example, a character named Asper promises two friends, Cordatus and Mitis, that the play that he has written for them will 'oppose a mirror' to their eyes, 'as large as is the stage whereon we act'. He says that they shall see 'the times deformity | Anatomized in every nerve, and sinew, | With constant courage and contempt of fear' (*Every Man out of his Humor*, 'Induction', ll. 118–22; Jonson, *Works*, 3. 432). Asper also invites these friends to criticize him, and his vision, unsparingly.

> Let me be censured, by th'austerest brow,
> Where I want art or judgment, tax me freely:
> Let envious censors, with their broadest eyes,
> Look through and through me, I pursue no favor.
> ('Induction', ll. 60–3; Jonson, *Works*, 3. 430)

In expressing his willingness to be censured for his faults, by critics who know the difference between the good and the bad, Asper makes an important point about the basis of discernment itself. His credibility as playwright and satirist, like the credibility of Mitis and Cordatus as critics, depends not only on familiarity with ancient literature and moral philosophy, but also on the fact that he is involved in the community that he proposes to evaluate, knows it intimately, and observes its strengths and weaknesses from within. The mirror that Asper holds up to life captures his reflection too, but that is because Jonson aims to make equals of his audience, and believes that no lesson can become a work of art unless it is also an experience that author and audience share.

Mitis worries that Asper is too confident in making the claims that he makes about his art, and too bold in taking on the mantle of the social critic. Cordatus reserves judgement. By contrast, he observes that, while Asper's play is 'somewhat like *Vetus Comoedia* [old comedy]', it is also 'strange, and of a particular kind by it self', an idea that is consistent with the way that Cordatus describes the comic tradition a moment later ('Induction', ll. 231–3; Jonson, *Works*, 3. 436). 'Every man in the dignity of his spirit and judgement, supplied something', he says of the ancient comedians, and therefore Asper, too, 'should enjoy the same licence, or free power, to illustrate and heighten our invention as they did; and not be tied to those strict and regular forms, which the niceness of a few... would thrust upon us' ('Induction', ll. 257–70; Jonson, *Works*, 3. 437). By articulating this rather liberal theory of tradition, Cordatus approves the creative and critical latitude than Asper claims, and confirms that it is not self-serving. The play, as a whole, affirms Cordatus' judgement by showing that the greater the playwright's scope becomes to imagine art and life the way he wants them to be, the more strictly his vision and his life are subject to examination by his own teachings. Asper leaves the stage once the play within the play begins, but, in the final scene, he unmasks himself as the character Macilente, who earlier fell 'into such an envious apoplexy... that he grows violently impatient of any opposite happiness in another' ('Names of the Actors', ll. 10–13; Jonson, *Works*, 3. 423). It is only because Asper has participated in the drama that he set in motion that he can say, at the end, 'Why here's a change! Now is my soul at peace. | I am as empty of all envy now, | As they of merit to be envied at' (5. 11. 54–6; Jonson, *Works*, 3. 596). The experience that he examines in these lines is his proof that his teaching is credible and transformative, and, as the play comes to an end, he places himself in the hands of his audience and shifts the responsibility for passing judgement to them: 'I stand wholly to your kind approbation, and am nothing so peremptory as I was at the beginning' (5. 11. 80–2; Jonson, *Works*, 3. 597). This act of deference echoes the submission to ancient literature and philosophy that the play enacts as a whole—the submission that Jonson encourages the audience to make, by following his example and becoming good judges of character and art.

In *Every Man out of his Humour*, Jonson establishes a balance between asserting his classical learning as a source of moral authority and acknowledging his own human finitude. This balance is a promise that his audiences can trust him, but it is also a lesson that, in doing so, they must preserve their independence to judge for themselves what is good and bad. Jonson invites them to adopt the attitude towards him and his writing that he adopts towards the literary and philosophical traditions from which he draws his teaching. In *Timber*, for example, under the heading 'Non nimium credendum antiquitati' ('We should not believe antiquity too much'), Jonson writes: 'I know *Nothing* can conduce more to letters, than to examine the writings of the *Ancients*, and not to rest in their sole Authority, or take all upon trust from them, provided the plagues of judging, and pronouncing against them, be away; such as envy, bitterness, precipitation, impudence, and scurrilous scoffing.' He continues: 'For to all observations of the *Ancients*, we have our own experience: which, if we will use, and apply, we have better means to pronounce. It is true they opened the gates, and made the way, that went before us; but as Guides, not Commanders... Truth lies open to all; it is no man's several' (*Timber*, ll. 129–40; Jonson, *Works*, 8. 567). This brief essay about originality is a paradox, in the sense that it imitates a number of ancient statements commending intellectual and creative independence from one's sources. On the other hand, and like the epigram that Jonson wrote for Camden, it demonstrates the validity of Jonson's own experience, as a context for understanding what the classics mean, by acknowledging the enduring contribution that the classics make to the perspective that he turned on art and life. Jonson's classicism implies that everyone is free to seek the truth in his or her own way, but the corollary to this thought is that each person is accountable for the results of that search—Jonson no less than the person who sees his plays or reads his poems.

Think of Jonson's classicism in *Every Man out of his Humor* as an evolving critical and creative stance towards ancient authors, modern audiences, and himself. His next satirical comedy, *Cynthia's Revels*, tests the adequacy of that stance, by asking whether it can cope with Ovidian myth, a literary context that is especially inhospitable to Jonsonian discernment. In portraying himself as Crites ('Criticus' in another version of the play), Jonson seems less ready to acknowledge the limitations of his own perspective than he was as Macilente. This time, there is no question that Crites' philosophy is superior to its rivals. Nevertheless, Jonson's presence on stage, at the very centre of the plot, is an important reminder of his commitment to being challenged by the very audience that he would instruct.

Jonson sets his scene in Gargaphy, at the place where Cynthia (Diana) proclaims the 'solemn revels' in which she hopes to refute 'black and envious slanders hourly breath'd against her' for the 'divine justice' that she imposed upon Actaeon (*Cynthia's Revels*, 1. 1. 92–5; Jonson, *Works*, 4. 47). This point in space is formed by the intersection of the Actaeon myth with two other plots, also drawn from Ovid's *Metamorphoses*. The spot where Actaeon was 'torn | By Cynthia's wrath' is also the resting place of Niobe, another victim of Cynthia's anger (1. 2. 82–3; Jonson, *Works*, 4. 51). As a weeping stone, Niobe feeds the pool in which Narcissus fell in love with his own reflection, the 'Fountain of self-Love' that gives the play its subtitle, a single drop of which causes those who drink from it to 'grow dotingly enamor'd on themselves' (1. 2. 100, 104; Jonson, *Works*, 4. 51). The combination of these different myths into one story expresses the ethical problem that the play explores in relation to Jonson's classicism. Actaeon, Niobe, and Narcissus are all exemplars of looking at oneself and others in the wrong way, but what is the right way to look, and who is qualified to judge the difference?

Into this environment, steps Crites, who contemplates the Ovidian framework of the text through a Horatian lens, like Jonson's. His first lines, quoting Horace's verses to the effect that water drinkers never write good poems, bring him into conflict with a group of courtiers, who have drunk from the fountain and lost the capacity to see themselves and the world apart from their desires (1. 4. 4–5; Jonson, *Works*, 4. 54).[20] Later, Crites makes a second judgement about Ovidian poetry and the people who imbibe it. This time, he imitates a passage from Seneca's epistles, in order to condemn the courtiers' self-love as an intoxicated ignorance of the very things that make for lasting joy (1. 5. *passim*; Jonson, *Works*, 4. 61–3).[21] Cupid and Mercury, who disguise themselves as pages, watch the dispute between Crites and the courtiers unfold, and Cupid vows to enflame Crites with desire. Mercury, however, praises Crites for having a 'most perfect and divine temper'. He says that Crites 'strives rather to be what men call judicious, than to be thought so'[22] and has 'a most ingenuous and sweet spirit, a sharp and season'd wit, a straight judgment, and a strong mind', slow to anger and resilient to misfortune (2. 3. *passim*; Jonson, *Works*, 4. 74). Crites himself exhibits all the qualities that Mercury ascribes to him in a soliloquy that weighs the censures of the courtiers against him and judges that they are slanderous. Comparing the courtiers to Proteus, who 'can change, and vary with all forms he sees; | Be anything but honest', Crites also points out the difference between superficial changes of character, such as the play associates with the hypocrisy of courtiers drunk on self-love, and the deeper transformations, as from bad to good character, that Crites' own writing will soon put into effect as a demonstration of what Jonson's Horatian theatre can do (3. 4. 43–4; Jonson, *Works*, 4. 90).

Crites' speech earns him the friendship and support of Arete, a lady in waiting to Cynthia; her name means virtue, or excellence, in the sense of fulfilment of potential. With her help, and Mercury's, Crites grows from a 'Truchman', or interpreter, of the courtiers' behaviour, into the author of a masque that vindicates Cynthia's reputation as a just goddess. His masque also reforms the courtiers—all of whom are obliged to experience it as spectators and participants (5. 4. 11; Jonson, *Works*, 4. 139). At the end of *Cynthia's Revels*, Cupid remains opposed to Crites, but Mercury explains that, as a result of his experiences during the play, Crites is now 'shot-proof' against his arrows (5. 10. 110; Jonson, *Works*, 4. 175). Confirming this conclusion, Cynthia delegates her divine authority to determine what is right and wrong to Crites. He judges that the courtiers should mortify their pride before 'Niobe's stone', then wash themselves in Helicon, 'the well of knowledge' that serves to distinguish the sources of Jonson's classicism from the draughts that other poets drink from Ovid's fountain of self-love (5. 11. 144, 153; Jonson, *Works*, 4. 180). In a final gesture of vindication, of both Crites' acumen and Jonson's classicism, Cynthia approves the verdict. The courtiers depart to transform themselves in the wholesome waters of Helicon, while Jonson, of one mind with the goddess whose chastity he embraces as the spirit of his judgement, both approves his own text and recognizes that others will reject it, with an epigraph drawn from Martial: 'Ecce rubet quidam, pallet, stupet, oscitat, odit. | Hoc volo: nunc nobis carmina nostra placent' ('Look, somebody turns red, turns pale, is dazed, yawns, is disgusted. | This I want. Now my poems please me') ('Epilogue', ll. 22–3; Jonson, *Works*, 4. 183).[23]

In *Cynthia's Revels*, Jonson takes the position that there is nothing wrong with writing like Ovid, provided that one reads and thinks like Horace. (He will strike the same note in *Volpone*, a play that revels in the antics of its protean anti-hero before unmasking him and bringing him to justice.) His next comedy, *Poetaster*, presents the difference between these Roman authors in starker terms, while evoking the plot of the earlier play in the shape of its own narrative. *Cynthia's Revels* starts at the pool of Narcissus and ends in Cynthia's court. Between these points, Jonson charts a course from self-love to self-knowledge, and from the lawlessness of immoderate desires to a lawful order, founded in the self-control that Crites embodies, 'like a circle bounded in itself' (*Cynthia's Revels*, 5. 8. 19; Jonson, *Works*, 4. 168). Likewise, *Poetaster* opens with self-love and ends with law. As the play begins, the pleasure that Ovid takes in verses that he has just written—a translation of *Amores* 1.15 that Jonson loosely adapts from Marlowe—persuades him to abandon the study of the law (*Poetaster*, 1. 1. 43–84; Jonson, *Works*, 4. 207–8). Later, Jonson concludes the play with an arraignment of slanderers and bad poets in the imperial court, where Horace presides as judge. Between these scenes, Ovid falls from a position of influence as the lover of Augustus' daughter, and goes into exile. Horace, by contrast, rises steadily above his enemies, and, having overcome the stigma of low birth, arrives at a place of authority and privilege at the centre of Roman civilization, alongside Caesar himself.

Poetaster approaches Ovid and Horace not only as backgrounds for Jonson's art, but also as models for different types of poetic vocation. Furthermore, because Jonson believes that poets have an important role to play in teaching the difference between virtue and vice to the societies in which they live,[24] the implications of choosing one model rather than the other are social as well as personal. The difference between Ovid and Horace, in this sense, reaches a head in *Poetaster*'s final acts. As this play revisits the questions that Jonson asked about himself in the earlier comedies, there is a sense of a decision being made. In Act 4, Ovid stages a 'poetical banquet' that decisively identifies his writing with intoxication, self-indulgence, and the loss of distinction between oneself and others (4. 2. 31; Jonson, *Works*, 4. 264). Swept away by imagination's power to usurp reality, Ovid announces that he is Jupiter, the god who figures all of the authorities that the poet brazenly rejects when he demands a 'thank-offering' from Augustus (4. 5. 204; Jonson, *Works*, 4. 279). 'Oh, who shall follow Virtue and embrace her', scolds Caesar; 'you, that teach and should eternize her, | Live as she were no law unto your lives— | Nor lived herself, but with your idle breaths' (4. 6. 39–47; Jonson, *Works*, 4. 281). In the next act, Horace's vision of the social order takes precedence over Ovid's unruly way of seeing Rome, and through the intervention of a judicious poetic sensibility, that Jonson embraces as his own, Horace sets about constructing an ideal community, in which 'each man has his place, | And to his merit, his reward of grace, | Which with a mutual love they all embrace' (3. 1. 257–9; Jonson, *Works*, 4. 242). At the arraignment of his enemies, Horace is measured, sobering, and medicinal, in contrast to now-banished Ovid. Ovid's poem-banquet, as a form of excessive consumption, caters to immoderate appetites, but, in the trial over which Horace presides, language is purgative and emetic. Under the influence of the pill that Horace gives him, a slanderer and poetaster called Crispinus vomits up the 'wild, outlandish terms' that he uses in scurrilous poems against the poet (5. 3. 549; Jonson, *Works*, 4. 314). The sentence that Horace passes on the vices of his enemies is Jonson's verdict about the excesses of a literary culture that tunes itself to Ovid's music. It ends this period of self-exploration and articulates a pattern for development in the work that follows.

Life and Art in Jonson's Works

Jonson's earliest professions of ethical and creative values leave an indelible mark on all his work. Despite setbacks, and periodic reassessments of his goals and methods, he never retreats from the basic ideas that he articulates during the *Poetomachia*. Yet, as Jonson takes the measure of himself and his art in these plays, he seems to recognize that his classicism falls short of achieving what he wants most to accomplish: to inspire readers and theatre-goers to become living re-creations of ancient virtues, and to establish a community of friendship with them, united not by blind obedience, but by love and gratitude for one another, creative independence, and a fierce dedication to discerning what makes truth different from error. A dialogue he appends to the folio edition of *Poetaster* makes his disappointment clear enough. There, Jonson acknowledges that audiences have not responded to the lessons of his comical satires as he had imagined they would. Two odes that he wrote later, 'To Himself', are further evidence of the unwillingness of audiences to embrace the programme of his classicism and become his friends.[25] Evidently, they did not understand that Jonson 'never writ [a] piece | More innocent, or empty of offence', or that, despite the 'salt' it had, 'there is neither tooth nor gall, | Nor was there in it any circumstance, | Which, in the setting down, I could suspect | Might be perverted by an enemy's tongue' (*Poetaster*, 'Apologetical Dialogue', ll. 74–9; Jonson, *Works*, 4. 319). Although few Renaissance poets worked harder than Jonson at self-portraiture, following the Poets' War, the perception of the artist and his work arguably owes more to Dekker than to Jonson himself. In *Satiromastix* (1601), the final volley of the conflict, Dekker brings Horace back on stage, but this time, he—that is to say,

Jonson—'is represented as a social hanger-on and toady, desperate to establish himself as an independent moralist but fearful of being held responsible for his judgements' and 'his verse is concocted to exploit social possibilities, though he presents it as an essential part of a well-regulated state (like Augustan Rome)'.[26]

The experience of failing to persuade others to embrace what he himself had learned from the classics also made its mark on Jonson and his art. In *Sejanus* and *Catiline*, the classical tragedies where he hoped to find 'a more kind aspect' in the audience, his approach to playwriting is much less personal; he removes himself from scrutiny, shifts the focus from the story of his own development, and from defences of his moral and aesthetic choices, to well-respected themes of humanist classical scholarship (*Poetaster*, 'To the Reader', l. 224; Jonson, *Works*, 4. 324). Jonson's court masques work in a similar way. In these erudite texts, which are concerned with moral crises of one kind or another, Jonson focuses on the choices other people make, and on the challenge of demonstrating that the masque is a form of serious literature, at least when classical studies enrich it. The rarefied knowledge of ancient myth and iconography that Jonson's masques exhibit may suggest a retreat from intimacy with spectators, and a diffidence towards the prospect of befriending them, but just the opposite is true. Through its classicism, the Jonsonian masque reaches out for relationship with new resources, and, according to one scholar, 'involves its audience in ways that are impossible for the drama', because, where 'drama is properly a form of entertainment, and involves its audience vicariously', the 'masque is a form of play, and includes its audience directly' in the dance in which it culminates. In this context, the Jonsonian masque 'not only allowed the unmediated confrontation of actor and spectator, but demanded it'.[27]

Perhaps it would be better to say that, following *Every Man out of his Humor*, *Cynthia's Revels*, and *Poetaster*, Jonson's writing becomes personal in unexpected ways, rather than impersonal. In *The Forest* (1616) and *The Underwoods* (1640), two anthologies of short poems that Jonson modelled on Statius' *Sylvae*, and in the many verses that were ungathered at the time of his death, Jonson sets out to establish relationships with the aristocrats whose lives, for him, exemplify the classical virtues that he teaches. His desire for a larger group of friends endures—in *The Forest*, Jonson boasts that 'the notes that I . . . shall sing, | Will prove old Orpheus' act no tale to be: | For I shall move stocks, stones, no less than he'—but he changes tack, and mostly leaves it to the readers of his poetry to infer, as it were by eavesdropping on the love he shares with his patrons, what befriending him would mean ('To Elizabeth, Countess of Rutland', ll. 6–8; Jonson, *Works*, 8. 115). At the same time, rejecting the false-friendship of drunkards, lechers, flatterers, and scandalmongers, Jonson holds fast in *Underwoods* to his vocation as a didactic writer and to the concepts that the classics furnished him. 'I study other friendships, and more one, | Than these can ever be; or else wish none' ('An Epistle Answering to One that Asked to Be Sealed of the Tribe of Ben', l. 29–30; Jonson, *Works*, 8. 219). Other poems in these anthologies suggest what the benefits of this other friendship are. In England's first Pindaric ode, Jonson stellifies the friendship of Lucius Cary and Henry Morison, 'this bright asterism' ('To the Immortal Memory and Friendship of that Noble Pair, Sir Lucius Cary and Sir H. Morison', l. 89; Jonson, *Works*, 8. 246). Now that Morison is dead, this text is all that remains of the loving 'law' that they embodied 'in deeds... not in words' (ll. 120–3, *passim*; Jonson, *Works*, 8. 247). It is also all that is left of Jonson's judgement that their friendship should be imitated. But Jonson is no historian or biographer. As a poet, he is less interested in recording the lives and relationships that he cherishes than he is in re-creating them, as living memories that extend and renew the friendship of Cary and Morison indefinitely—a new classical tradition, arising from modern exemplars of ancient virtues, in which Jonson's poetry plays a pivotal role. For the life that this poem imparts to the future is also Jonson's. As he had done earlier, in his epigram 'On My First Son', the poet writes his own name into his text, as the joint that holds together the entire framework of living well that Cary and Morison exemplify.[28] Even in the context of meditations on death, life and art, and the lessons that they teach, prove to be inseparable for Jonson, who is, as ever, both artist and work of art.

There are consequences to implicating oneself in one's art to the extent that Jonson does. One risk that his classicism takes, by insisting on the unity of life and art, is that it makes art vulnerable to criticism on the basis of the artist's human fallibility. Eliot is sanguine about this prospect, reflecting that, 'if we grasp the fact that the knowledge required of the reader is not archaeology but knowledge of Jonson, we can derive not only instruction in non-Euclidean humanity—but enjoyment'.[29] Jonson's own disciples, the so-called Tribe of Ben, also felt confident that Jonson's life was a credit to his art, and vice versa. In *Jonsonus Virbius* (1638), the collection of elegies that seeks to resurrect Jonson by interpolating him into the canon of Ovidian mythology[30]—presumably, without irony—these younger writers call upon future generations to 'survey him in his works, and know him there', the poet 'who dead's my wonder, living was my friend'.[31] Yet William Drummond, who met Jonson in 1619, takes a different view of him at the conclusion of the notes from the one he took on their conversations. 'He is a great lover and praiser of himself,' writes Drummond,

> a contemner and scorner of others, given rather to lose a friend than a jest, jealous of every word and action of those about him (especially after drink, which is one of the elements in which he liveth), a dissembler of ill parts which reign in him, a bragger of some good that he wanteth, thinketh him nothing well but what either he himself or some of his friends and countrymen hath said or done, he is passionately kind and angry, careless either to gain or keep, vindictive, but if he be well answered, at himself. (*Ben Jonson's Conversations with William Drummond of Hawthornden*, 680–9; Jonson, *Works*, 1. 151)

It cannot be denied that Jonson believed that a good life was the only basis for sound teaching and good art. 'If men will impartially, and not asquint, look towards the offices, and function of a poet,' he writes in *Volpone*, 'they will easily conclude to themselves, the impossibility of any man's being the good poet, without first being a good man' (*Volpone*, 'To the Two Famous Universities', 21–3; Jonson, *Works*, 5. 17). There is also no denying that, in Drummond's *Conversations*, everything that Jonson sought to accomplish through his classicism seems to be undone by the memory of the folly and imperfection of his volatile humanity. It would be wise to be as sceptical of these judgements as Jonson encourages us to be about his own. Perhaps the unruly return of Jonson's life to the centre of our attention suggests that a final comparison with Shakespeare is in order.

As we have seen, it is a commonplace of criticism that Shakespeare's works are divine and everlasting, while Jonson's merely mortal writing tends to perish over time. That idea goes hand in hand with the perception that, while Jonson is bent on telling us how to read, Shakespeare asks that we imagine what we want—that Jonson holds us in his power and Shakespeare sets us free. The invidious comparison begins to turn to Jonson's advantage when we consider that Shakespeare's immortality, and his willingness to let us do what we want with his poems and plays, is related to other godlike aspects of his works: his absence and indifference. In the texts that Shakespeare left behind, the author is nowhere to be found. He takes no position whatsoever on any of the questions that his works explore, and therefore his own answers, whatever they may be, are unknown, mysterious, and incontestable. Jonson's writing, by contrast, is a declaration of presence. He grabs us by the collar, shepherds our attention forcefully, and demands that we engage and question him until his meaning is clear. Shakespeare's disappearance behind the veil of writing gives his writing what authority it has. The authority of Jonson's work comes from somewhere else: from his presence—which is, in turn, the essence and the guarantee of his humanity. Where does one feel freer: in the company of Jonson or the absence of Shakespeare? The experience of reading and imitating the classics brought these writers to very different perceptions of what it means to be an author, and, consequently, different ideas about reading issue from their works. The fact that we tend not to like it when Jonson confronts us with our shortcomings, and prefer to be taken in, and left alone, by Shakespeare, may suggest how profoundly we would rather be enthralled by art than be free to call it to account for itself. Shakespeare will never tell us that we are wrong, but, unlike Jonson, he will also never be our friend.

Notes

1. T. S. Eliot, 'Ben Jonson', in *The Sacred Wood: Essays on Poetry and Criticism* (1920), 104.
2. Milton, *Complete Shorter Poems*, ed. J. Carey, 2nd edn (1997), 143 (cited hereafter as Milton, *Shorter Poems*).
3. *Essay of Dramatic Poesy*, in John Dryden, *The Works*, ed. Edward Niles Hooker, H. T. Swedenburg, Jr, and Vinton A. Dearing, 20 vols (Berkeley and Los Angeles, 1956), 17. 55 (cited hereafter as Dryden).
4. Charles Algernon Swinburne, *A Study of Ben Jonson* (1889), 114.
5. G. Gregory Smith, *Ben Jonson* (1919), 56, 60.
6. Smith, *Ben Jonson*, 63.
7. Jonson alludes to, and changes the sense of, Martial, *Epigrams*, 1. *praef.* 16–17: 'non

intret Cato theatrum meum, aut si intraverit, spectet' ('Let Cato keep out of my theatre; or if he comes in, let him watch').

8. Katharine Eisaman Maus, *Ben Jonson and the Roman Frame of Mind* (1984), is the best book-length introduction to Jonson's classicism. Other excellent studies include: Colin Burrow, 'Ben Jonson', in Claude Rawson (ed.), *Cambridge Companion to English Poets* (Cambridge, 2011), 122–38; Richard Helgerson, 'Ben Jonson', in *Cambridge Companion to English Poetry*, ed. Thomas Corns (1993), 148–70; Victoria Moul, *Jonson, Horace, and the Classical Tradition* (2010); George Parfitt, 'Jonson and Classicism', in *Ben Jonson: Public Poet and Private Man* (1976), 104–23; R. S. Peterson, *Imitation and Praise in the Poetry of Ben Jonson*, 2nd edn (2011); Wesley Trimpi, *Ben Jonson's Poetry: A Study of the Plain Style* (1962); and R. V. Young, 'Ben Jonson and Learning', in *Cambridge Companion to Ben Jonson*, ed. Richard Harp and Stanley Stewart (2000), 43–57.
9. Maus, *Roman Frame of Mind*, 4.
10. Jonson alludes to Horace, *Epistles*, 1. 1. 14: 'nullius addictus iurare in verba magistri' ('I am not bound over to swear allegiance to any master').
11. See *Epistles* 1. 19, 2. 1, and 2. 2.
12. In addition to texts by Cicero, Marcus Aurelius, Plutarch, and Seneca, Justus Lipsius' treatise *De Constantia* (1584) was an important influence on Jonson's understanding of ancient Stoicism and the virtue of constancy. An English translation, by John Stradling, appeared in 1594. For this text, and a useful introduction to Renaissance Stoicism in England, see *Two Books of Constancy*, ed. Rudolf Kirk (New Brunswick, 1939), 3–62. Lipsius defines 'constancy' in book one, chapter three.
13. On this passage, and the development of Jonson's ideal of bounded, self-reliant subjectivity, see Thomas Greene, 'Ben Jonson and the Centered Self', *Studies in English Literature, 1500–1900* 10/2 (1970), 325–48.
14. For Horace's understanding of liberty, see W. Ralph Johnson, *Horace and the Dialectic of Freedom: Readings in Epistles 1* (Ithaca, NY, 1993).
15. Friendship was a topic of great importance in Roman literature and philosophy. Jonson's own thoughts about it were shaped by Cicero's dialogue, *On Friendship*, and Seneca's *Epistles* (especially 9, 52, and 53), along with Horace's *Odes* and *Epistles*. For Horatian ideas about friendship, see Ross S. Kilpatrick, *The Poetry of Friendship: Horace, Epistles 1* (Edmonton, 1986).
16. 'No poet's verses yet did ever move, | Whose readers did not think he was in love' ('An Elegy', ll. 3–4; Jonson, *Works*, 8. 199).
17. Swinburne, *Study*, 115.
18. The first instance of Jonson's usage of 'comical satire' to describe his plays occurs on the 1599 title page of *Every Man out of his Humour* (Jonson, *Works*, 3. 419–20).
19. Thomas Dekker, *Satiromastix*, 1. 2. 311–14 and 5. 2. 138, in *The Dramatic Works of Thomas Dekker*, ed. Fredson Bowers (1953–61), 1. 325, 377.
20. See Horace, *Epistles* 1. 19. 2–3: 'nulla placere diu nec vivere carmina possunt, | quae scribuntur aquae potoribus' ('no poems can please long, nor live, which are written by water-drinkers').
21. See Seneca, *Epistles* 59. 15: 'omnes istos oblectamenta fallacia et brevia decipiunt, sicut ebrietas' ('all these men [hedonists] are led astray by delights which are deceptive and short-lived, like drunkenness').
22. Jonson alludes to Cicero, *On Friendship*, 98: 'Virtute enim ipsa non tam multi praediti esse quam videri volunt' ('For many wish not so much to be, as to seem to be, endowed with real virtue').
23. See Martial, *Epigrams* 6. 60. 3–4.

24. Jonson has this to say about the role of poets as teachers: 'He that is said to be able to inform young men to all good disciplines, inflame grown men to all great virtues, keep old men in their best and supreme state, or as they decline to childhood, recover them to their first strength; that comes forth the interpreter and arbiter of nature, a teacher of things divine, no less than human, a master in manners; and can alone (or with a few) effect the business of mankind: this, I take him, is no subject for pride and ignorance to exercise their railing rhetoric upon' (*Volpone*, 'To the Two Famous Universities', ll. 23–31; Jonson, *Works*, 5. 17).
25. For these odes, see Jonson, *Works*, 8. 174–5 and 6. 492–4.
26. G. K. Hunter, *English Drama 1586–1642* (Oxford, 1997), 300.
27. Stephen Orgel (ed.), *Ben Jonson: Selected Masques* (New Haven, 1970), 2.
28. 'To the Immortal Memory . . .', ll. 84–5; Jonson, *Works*, 8. 246: 'And there he lives with memory; and Ben | Jonson, who sung this of him, ere he went . . .'; 'On My First Son', ll. 9–10; *Works*, 8. 41: 'Rest in soft peace, and, asked, say here doth lie | Ben Jonson his best piece of poetry.'
29. T. S. Eliot, 'Ben Jonson', in *Sacred Wood*, 121.
30. In the title *Jonsonus Virbius; or The Memory of Ben Jonson*, the name 'Virbius' ('twice-man') is an allusion to an episode in the fifteenth book of Ovid's *Metamorphoses*, in which Diana brings Hippolytus back to life as the tutelary god, Virbius (*Met.* 15. 544).
31. John Ford, 'On the Best of English Poets, Ben Jonson, Deceased', l. 46, and John Beaumont, 'To the Memory of Him who can Never be Forgotten, Master Benjamin Jonson', l. 62, in *Jonsonus Virbius* (1638), 51, 13.

CHAPTER 29

Early Milton

THOMAS H. LUXON

For several decades, scholars have focused renewed attention to Milton as a radical reformer of Church and State. This has enhanced our understanding of his poetry, of course, but it has also prompted fresh attention to Milton's understandings of classical texts and the uses to which he put them as a reformer.

Scripture and Reason

Milton's commitment to reformation stood on two pillars—scripture and reason. 'I resolved', he proclaimed in his 1642 *Apology*, 'to stand on that side where I saw the plain authority of Scripture leading, and the reason of justice and equity persuading; with this opinion which esteems it more unlike a Christian to be a cold neuter in the cause of the Church, then the law of *Solon* made it punishable after a sedition in the state' (*Apology*; *Prose Works*, I. 868). The authority of Scripture *leading*, and the reason of justice and equity *persuading*. And from what fount of learning did Milton drink the 'reason of justice and equity'? From what we now call the classics.[1]

Another seventeenth-century Puritan, John Bunyan, was proud to claim that he had no other learning except what he gathered from Bible reading, but the 'wearisome labors and studious watchings, wherein' Milton 'spent and tired out almost a whole youth' refer principally to his classical education in Latin and Greek literature, philosophy, and history (*Prose Works*, I. 869). Of course he learned Hebrew as well, for Erasmus' famous injunction to resort *ad fontes* in all matters of learning meant reading the Bible in Hebrew, Aramaic, and Greek.[2] Indeed, few, if any, graduates of John Colet's Erasmian academy, St Paul's School, could be said better to embody the spirit of Renaissance Christian humanism than John Milton.

'The end then of learning', Milton wrote in *Of Education* (1644), 'is to repair the ruins of our first parents by regaining to know God aright, and out of that knowledge to love him, to imitate him, to be like him, as we may the nearest by possessing our souls of true virtue, which being united to the heavenly grace of faith makes up the highest perfection' (*Prose Works*, 2. 366–7). For Milton, learning was either a lifelong practice aimed at moral development, or it was worse than useless. The reason for studying ancient authors was not, he insisted, to be able to cultivate the flowers of rhetoric, or to adorn one's own compositions with classical references (though, of course, Milton excelled at both of these); it was because Latin and Greek are 'the languages of those people who have at any time been most industrious after wisdom; so that language is but the Instrument conveying to us *things useful* to be known'.

> And though a linguist should pride himself to have all the tongues that Babel cleft the world into, yet, if he have not studied the solid things in them as well as the words and lexicons, he were nothing so much to be esteemed a learned man, as any yeoman or tradesman competently wise in his mother dialect only.
>
> (*Of Education*; *Prose Works* 2. 369–70; emphases added)

Solid *things*, *things* useful to be known.[3] We may gloss Milton's *things* here as ideas, but more than that, ideas gain solidity and usefulness, so he thought, when they are put into conversation across authors, ages, and convictions, especially when ancient pagan wisdom could be put into conversation with Scripture, and both into conversation with men intent on reforming Christ's church and the English civil polity.

Milton often answered his detractors by ridiculing the errors and barbarisms in their Latin and Greek (see especially *An Apology* and *Colasterion*), but his most trenchant criticisms took deadly aim at displays of learning devoid of reason and wisdom, the 'solid things' of classical learning. One such he derides with the epithet 'Carnal textman!' (*Prose Works*, 1. 951). For similar reasons, he detested reading the records of the church councils from late antiquity to the Council of Trent, even though many at the universities regarded doing so as the centre of the undergraduate curriculum: 'For be not deceived, readers, by men that would overawe your ears with big names and huge tomes that contradict and repeal one another... Do but winnow their chaff from their wheat, ye shall see their great heap shrink and wax thin past belief' (*Prose Works*, 1. 945). Milton regarded Oxford and Cambridge, like the church for which they trained clergy, just as insufficiently reformed in pedagogy as the church was in government, doctrine, and liturgy. Though 'intended to be the seed plots of piety and the liberal arts', they had 'become the nurseries of superstition, and empty speculation' (*Prose Works*, 1. 923). True eloquence, in both the learned tongues and in English, achieves a naturalness and displays an intimate familiarity with 'regenerate reason' ('those unwritten laws and ideas which nature hath ingraven in us' (*Reason of Church Government*)) that can emerge only after long and careful 'reading and observing... and copious invention' attending more to the ideas, the 'solid things', than to imitations of style and diction, so often the tasks set to schoolboys long before they were ripe enough to know what they were about. 'So that how he should be truly eloquent who is not withal a good man, I see not' (*Prose Works*, 1. 874). Learning that did not serve self-reformation more than self-fashioning could never, Milton believed, achieve education's proper outcome—repairing the 'ruins of our first parents'.

Conversations

Both before and after his university days (1625–32) Milton pursued something very like this self-reforming discipline of learning. His father, a successful scrivener, financier, and musician, spared no expense for his son's education. Before and during his time at St Paul's School, private tutors introduced him to Latin, Greek, Hebrew, French, and Italian. Of these tutors, one stands out—Thomas Young (1587–1655), a Presbyterian Scot from St Andrews University and in 1641 the principal author of the anti-prelatical pamphlet Milton defended in his *Apology for Smectymnuus*—the 'ty' in the pseudonymous author, Smectymnuus. At age 18, Milton addressed his fourth Latin elegy to this beloved teacher, employing the discourse of classical friendship he may first have learned with Young, along with a tone of nostalgic loss reminiscent of Cicero's praise for Scipio in *De Amicitia*. Speaking as if to his letter, 'mea littera', he celebrates Young first as a friend and then as his teacher:

> That man is more to me than one half of my soul; I am forced, now, to love only a half-life. Ah! How many seas and mountains are thrust between us, to keep me apart from the other half of myself! He is dearer to me than you, most learned of the Greeks, were to Alcibiades, Telamon's descendant: dearer than the great Stagirite was to his noble pupil, the son whom that bountiful girl from Chaonia bore to Libyan Jove. To me he is as Amyntor's son and the heroic son of Philyra were to the Myrmidons' king. I was the first to wander under his guidance through the Aonian retreats and over the forked mountain's sacred, grassy slopes. There I drank Pieria's waters and, through the goodness of Clio, three times I made my happy mouth wet with Castalian wine.
>
> (Elegy 4, ll. 19–32)[4]

As Socrates to Alcibiades, Aristotle to Alexander, or Phoenix and Chiron to Achilles, so Milton thought of Young to himself. Along with the youthful arrogance displayed here, we may also detect a kind of hierarchy of classical wisdom that lists Socrates first, especially the Socrates of Plato's *Symposium*. More to the point, however, is that Young encouraged Milton to regard reading the classics as a kind of conversation, cemented by love, between teacher and pupil, ancients and moderns.

Milton's high master at St Paul's School, Alexander Gil, continued this practice. 'Paul's pigeons', as the students were sometimes called, spoke only in Latin while at school. They practised translating Latin and Greek into English and back again, as well as Psalms from Hebrew into Greek and English; Milton continued to translate Psalms well into adulthood and collected many of these in his 1673 *Poems*. But Gil was far more than a classicist and theologian. He also implanted in his students, certainly in Milton, a love of English and its Renaissance poets. Barbara Lewalski reminds us that, in his *Logonomia Anglica* (1619), Gil illustrated classical schemes and tropes with examples from English poets: 'Spenser ("our Homer"), George Wither ("our Juvenal"), Samuel Daniel ("our Lucan"), Philip Sidney ("our Anacreon"), John Harington ("our Martial").'[5] Gil invited his students to place English humanism in conversation with Greek and Latin authors. As early as 1641, Milton had decided that his most ambitious poetic project would be in English; he aimed to take Spenser's place in Gil's list, and many would say he succeeded.

> I applied myself to that resolution which *Arisoto* followed against the persuasions of *Bembo*, to fix all the industry and art I could unite to the adorning of my native tongue; not to make verbal curiosities the end, that were a toilsome vanity, but to be an interpreter and relater of the best and sagest things among mine own Citizens... in the mother dialect. That what the greatest and choicest wits of *Athens, Rome,* or modern *Italy,* and those Hebrew of old did for their country, I in my proportion with this over and above of being a Christian, might do for mine. (*Reason of Church Government*; *Prose Works*, I. 812)

'The best and sagest things' is another version of the 'solid things' that must, for Milton, be at the centre of any useful study of Milton's classicism.

Milton studied the classics, not only for the 'solid things' to be found there, but to provoke and nurture a conversation on these enduring things between ancients and moderns. His goal, not entirely unlike Clifford Geertz's as a semiotic ethnographer, was to gain access not only to the languages, but to 'the conceptual world in which our subjects live so that we can, in some extended sense of the term, converse with them'.[6] This is why, in his most mature work, he does not use Bible stories as did Dryden in *Absolom and Achitophel*—as a vehicle for contemporary politics and satire—but rather leaves us feeling that we have witnessed Adam in conversation with Galileo and Lucretius, Samson with Seneca and the New Model Army preachers, and Jesus with Socrates. Milton mines the classics not just for rhetorical flowers, or 'dialectical imitation', but for something more intimate, even erotic: conversation.[7]

'He who would not be frustrate of his hope to write well hereafter in laudable things, ought himself to be a true Poem, that is, a composition, and pattern of the best and honourablest things; not presuming to sing high praises of heroic men, or famous cities, unless he have in himself the experience and the practice of all that which is praise-worthy' (*Prose Works*, I. 890). It is tempting to regard such a manifesto as the worst sort of cynical self-fashioning—to make one's self a 'poem', a 'composition', a performance, but that would be a mistake. Ambitious, perhaps even overweeningly so, Milton had an unattainable goal to put himself in conversation with those authors who, he believed, had the most compelling things to say about laudable, honourable, and 'solid' things, matters that persistently occupy human beings. Where do we come from and why? What is love? What is liberty, justice, or true piety? Does the long arc of the universe and human history tend towards justice or self-annihilation?

We have precious few records of Milton's early education, classical or otherwise. 'Only through the Cambridge admissions register do we know he attended St Paul's

School' and studied with Alexander Gil.[8] The great fire of 1666 destroyed whatever school records once existed. Even the surviving records of Milton's time at Cambridge leave what Edward Jones calls 'a patchy account of a seven-year period'[9] that included a fairly lengthy suspension in the spring of 1627 and, of course, several vacations. We can, however, glean quite a bit about his studies from what he wrote. From the pre-Cambridge years, we have a Latin and Greek epigram (*Philosophus ad Regem*) that alludes to Virgil's *Aeneid*, a Latin fable in imitation of Mantuan (*Apologus de Rustico et Hero*), and a Latin prose theme on early rising that quotes from the *Idylls* of Theocritus and Homer's *Iliad*.[10] Nothing too surprising here for any student of the humanist curriculum for which St Paul's School was famous.

The Cambridge years, 1625–32, leave a far richer record. Besides seven academic exercises ('Prolusions') and four Latin letters (two each to his former teachers Young and Gill), the following poems probably belong to this period: Latin Elegies 1–7, two Latin obsequies (for John Gostlin and Nicholas Felton), two poems on 'the University Carrier', four epigrams on the Gunpowder Plot, and the longer *In Quintum Novembris*, Sonnet 1, 'Song: On May Morning', 'On Shakespeare', *Naturam non Pati Senium, De Idea Platonica*, and 'On the Death of a Fair Infant Dying of a Cough'. Though arguments still persist, most scholars accept that the Nativity Ode and 'On the Passion' belong to the period before Milton commenced Master of Arts in July 1632. The Latin poems demonstrate the young poet's remarkable facility with classical forms and tropes. The English poems, especially 'On a Fair Infant', can tell us much about a poet committed to a meaningful conversation between modern Christian convictions and classical pagan understandings of human suffering and painful change. What could be more daring than to invite us to consider the death by plague of an infant girl using Ovid's tropes of rape and transformation?

Between 1632 and May 1638, when he left for a fifteen-month tour of Europe, Milton pursued a self-designed course of intense study while staying at family homes in Hammersmith and Horton, Buckinghamshire. 'I devoted myself entirely to the study of Greek and Latin writers,' he wrote in *A Second Defense* (1654), but he also notes that he developed keen interests in new discoveries in music and mathematics (*Prose Works*, 4. 614). This would, no doubt, have included astronomy. Indeed, Carlo Dati, who befriended Milton during his travels in Italy, paid this tribute to young Milton's learning:

> To a man in whose memory the whole wide world is lodged, in whose intellect wisdom, in whose affections an ardent passion for glory, in whose mouth eloquence, who, with astronomy as his guide, hears the harmonies of the heavenly spheres, with philosophy as his teacher reads and interprets the true meaning of those marvels of nature by which the greatness of God is portrayed, who, with incessant reading of these authors as his comrade, probes the hidden mysteries of bygone days, restores whatever the distance of time has obscured, and covers all the intricacies of learning.
>
> Seeking, restoring, running through
> For what purpose this work of duty?[11]

Milton's arduous task is to restore to the English people a reputation for sound learning. Others of his Italian admirers understood that Milton planned to undertake a restoration of learning as a prophetic poet of epic ambitions. The Romans Giovanni Salsilli and Selvaggi praised Milton's poetic powers as above Homer's, Virgil's, and Tasso's. Antonio Francini of Naples praised him as a prophet, 'half-divine', who had already 'treasured up' in his prodigious memory ages of 'learned pages', actively 'communing with them in their works'.[12]

Evidence of communing with ancient authors appears very early in Milton's poetry. Elegy 4, as we have seen, takes the form of a verse letter to his beloved teacher Young. We should also note how cleverly he calls attention to this as an Ovidian practice. His speaker begins with an apostrophe to the letter—'Away, my letter, speed through the boundless sea'—that echoes Ovid's *Tristia* 3. 7: 'Go, greet Perilla, quickly written letter.' Ovid wrote from exile to his stepdaughter and protégé; Milton writes from London to his teacher in exile. This is either one of the clumsiest allusive gestures imaginable, or very early evidence of what Maggie Kilgour explores as Milton's signature practice of metamorphosing Ovid.[13] Though still under 20 and in his second year at Cambridge, Milton already knows how to use allusion to provoke not just memory and recognition, but also difficult conversation, and, most importantly, a conversation that engages his readers as well as his interlocutor. The poem provokes many questions worthy of long discussion, such as how do teachers and pupils switch roles in conversation over time? How do conversation partners resemble lovers and even spouses (Penelope and Odysseus in l. 56)? What distinguishes voluntary exile from involuntary? How do people come to share souls through the conversation of friends and lovers, even across ages, languages, and cultures (ll. 19–28)?

Graver Subjects

A year later, in a letter to his other beloved teacher, Gil, Milton refers to some of the oratorical exercises undertaken by Cambridge students as 'light-minded nonsense' of a sort he can excel at, but does not consider part of the 'serious things' he would rather be about as a poet, researcher, and reformer (*Prose Works*, I. 314). Though he refers to Cambridge as 'Athens itself ... the very Academy', he does so ironically, for he experiences residence there as a kind of exile from the 'almost constant conversations' with a teacher whom he 'never left ... without a visible increase and growth of Knowledge, quite as if I had been to some Market of Learning' (*Prose Works*, I. 314). In what ought to have been the English version of the Academy, he found instead 'almost no intellectual companions' and looked 'longingly' towards London. That said, Milton's academic prolusions and accompanying 'act verses' display a command of classical learning even his Cambridge colleagues admired. John K. Hale's extensive study of them details how useful these were to his later career as controversialist and poet.[14] At Cambridge, students were expected to show off their classical learning in set orations on the most prosaic required topics: whether day is to be preferred to night, or ignorance to learning. Prolusion Six concerns the claim that sportive exercises are not inconsistent with philosophical studies. The Latin oration is full of 'dirty jokes' and clever references to the undergraduates present and their tawdry exploits.[15] But, even in the midst of such performances, Milton raises his voice in English towards higher aspirations:

> Yet had I rather, if I were to choose,
> Thy service in some graver subject use,
> Such as may make thee search thy coffers round,
> Before thou clothe my fancy in fit sound:
> Such where the deep transported mind may soar
> Above the wheeling poles, and at heaven's door
> Look in, and see each blissful deity
> How he before the thunderous throne doth lie,
> Listening to what unshorn Apollo sings
> To the touch of golden wires, while Hebe brings
> Immortal nectar to her kingly sire:
> Then passing through the spheres of watchful fire,
> And misty regions of wide air next under,
> And hills of snow and lofts of piled thunder,
> May tell at length how green-eyed Neptune raves,
> In heavens defiance mustering all his waves;
> Then sing of secret things that came to pass
> When beldam Nature in her cradle was.
>
> ('At A Vacation Exercise in the College', ll. 29–46)

To do for English what Homer did for Greek, Virgil and Ovid for Latin, and Ariosto for Italian, Milton searched his wits for graver subjects, subjects pondered by the ancients, and still of pressing concern to seventeenth-century English men and women.

Beginning with his *Nativity Ode*, probably composed in 1629, graver subjects dominate Milton's verse throughout his post-Cambridge years until he departs for the Continent in 1638 and returns to serve his *patria* as a controversialist and schoolmaster. The year 1629 marked his twenty-first birthday and his commencement as a bachelor of arts. He also renewed his friendship with Charles Diodati, exchanging letters in Greek and Latin. Charles apparently joined the ranks of his former teachers as a principal companion in conversation about 'the best and honourablest things'. Milton tells Diodati that he 'cannot help loving people like you', people who dare 'to feel and speak and be that which the greatest wisdom throughout all ages has taught to be best' (*Prose Works*, I. 327). To this period belong his aristocratic masques, *Arcades* and *A Maske Presented at Ludlow Castle*, and probably the lyrics 'At a Solemn Music', 'Upon the Circumcision', 'On Time', Sonnet 7, as well as the companion poems 'L'Allegro' and 'Il Penseroso'.[16] *Lycidas* was composed and published just months before Milton left England for his only trip abroad.

Like Virgil's Fourth *Eclogue*, Milton's 'Ode on the Morning of Christ's Nativity' introduces within a lyric mode a 'loftier strain', as if deliberately challenging a humble choric hymn to contain, if not successfully, a prophetic 'graver subject'. Both poems announce the immanent fulfilment of an ancient prophecy, and both assign the poet himself a role in that announcement. In his Nativity Ode, the poet challenges his muse to outrun the 'Star-led' wise men and be the first to present a gift to the Christ child, in the form of a 'humble ode' (ll. 23–4).[17] Milton's characteristic mix of audacious ambition and pious humility appear throughout this poem. It begins with a four-stanza heroic proem, which points to the rest of the poem as a 'hymn' or 'humble ode'. The 'hymn' is both elegantly choric and yet like a childish sing-song. The themes are apocalyptically epic in scope, but the speaker refers to his song as 'tedious' (l. 239). Critics still argue about how successfully Milton has appropriated a pagan Virgilian voice for his Christian theme, or whether the message of Christ's incarnation suffers some inevitable pollution from the formal and thematic echoes of a 'pagan nativity hymn'.[18] These arguments will get nowhere, for they miss the genius of Milton's point, the same point that his Italian admirers so perfectly understood. Milton *is* reformed Christianity's Virgil, much as Dante was medieval Christianity's Virgil. It is a matter not of blending traditions, but of superseding one with another. And supersession requires remembering, repeating, and reinterpreting what is superseded, not ignoring or rejecting it. Christianity may aim at annihilating Jews and Judaism, but not the Hebrew Scriptures and their legacy. The same is true for remembering and reinterpreting the classics. Virgil's eclogue expresses confidence in both the Cumaean Sybil's prophecy and the poet's own capacity to render a vision of its fulfillment (*Eclogue* 4. 54–9). By echoing Virgil's poem, Milton invests himself with much the same confidence as he celebrates the advent of Messiah—'This is the month, and this the happy morn'—but he puts this borrowed confidence to at least two new uses. First, he announces that all pagan oracles and prophecies ended with the advent of Christ, some forty years after Virgil's song was first sung (*Nativity Ode*, stanzas 19–25). Perhaps out of some deference to his forerunner, he does not specifically mention the Cumaean Sybil in this list of defeated oracles, but, if Delphos crumbles before 'the dreaded infant's hand', surely Cumae does as well (l. 222). Second, Milton's prophetic voice stitches a thread of modesty into the bardic mantle he borrows from Virgil. Though nature, stars, and the sun itself all bow before the new-born Christ just as Virgil predicted the world's 'massive dome' would bow to another baby boy, Milton's 'tedious song' does not claim the power of the 'holy song' that will usher in the reign of Truth and Justice (stanzas 14–15). Instead it simply stands at the ready among the angels ranged 'in order serviceable' (l. 244). By echoing Virgil's song and borrowing his mantle, Milton can say more about the glory of Christ's advent than would otherwise be possible.

In the years between Cambridge and his continental tour, Milton immersed himself in classical study, probably in ways more reminiscent of his endless conversations with Young, Gil, and Diodati than of his university education. He also agreed to compose two aristocratic entertainments, the most important of these being *A Maske Presented at Ludlow Castle* in celebration of John Edgerton's installation as Lord President of Wales. As Maggie Kilgour has recently written, 'there are many forms of Ovid jostling together in Milton's masque: the Spenserian, Shakespearean, Marlovian, libertine, courtly, and no doubt others'.[19] Taking her cue from Charles Martindale's path-breaking work, she reminds us that Ovidian forms, themes, and images were recruited not just for poetic, but inevitably political work, and this is particularly evident in that most politically charged form of Caroline verse—the masque.[20]

A Chaste Erotics

The 'graver subject' that dominates the masque was already on Milton's mind in the *Elegies*, especially *Elegy* 6: are Eros and Chastity inevitably enemies, or is there some kind of love, procreative both intellectually and physically, that comprehends them both? Comus, the Lady, her brothers, and her saviours (the Attendant Spirit and Sabrina) all bring different Ovidian attitudes towards *amor* to a reader's mind, and they each trim to the various political winds of Caroline court culture. Milton had not, by 1634, explicitly announced his devotion to chastity as he does in the 1642 *Apology for a Pamphlet*, but, by substituting Chastity for Paul's *agape* in 1 Corinthians 13: 13's 'faith, hope and love', he moves in that direction. The end of the mask invites readers to 'imagine a world which is both erotic and chaste, and in which love motivates the highest form of action: poetry itself'.[21] I would add one important aspect to Kilgour's claim: Milton invites us to imagine an erotic practice that is both chaste and reproductive, both in body and in spirit:

> But far above in spangled sheen
> Celestial Cupid her famed son advanced,
> Holds his dear Psyche sweet entranced
> After her wandering labours long,
> Till free consent the gods among
> Make her his eternal bride,
> And from her fair unspotted side
> Two blissful twins are to be born,
> Youth and Joy; so Jove hath sworn.
>
> (*A Maske*, ll. 1003–11)

'List mortals, if your ears be true', as the poem's final lines describe an Elysium where Adonis reposes 'waxing well of his deep wound', where Eros entrances Psyche and together they bring forth 'blissful twins' from an 'unspotted side'. In such a world, Comus' libertine *carpe diem*, the brothers' moralized Ovid, and the Lady's 'rapt spirits' responding to attempted seduction and rape are all metamorphosed into a chaste erotics that enjoy 'free consent' among the gods. Rape gives way to chaste erotic rapture.

Long before he set himself the task of representing a chaste erotic love of prelapsarian Eden, Milton speculated about a chaste erotics in heaven. When he imagines his friend Diodati in heaven, it is a place of Dionysiac and Bacchic revels raging under 'the thyrsus of Zion' (*Epitaphium Damonis*, ll. 218–19). Bruce Boehrer even suggests that we can hear in 'the unexpressive nuptial song' of Lycidas's heaven a version of 'the voice of a love that dare not speak its name' (*Lycidas*, ll. 176–7)—that is, a love that not only embraces the fundamentals of the body but can enjoy those fundamentals in a place where the body and the spirit pass back and forth into each other in ways that stimulate more than our imaginations.[22]

Milton claims that he learned about love from many sources, ancient and modern, but he traces his moment of revelation to Plato's *Symposium*, in particular to what Socrates 'fained to have learnt from the prophetess *Diotima*, how Love was the Son of Penury, begot of Plenty in the Garden of Jupiter. Which divinely sorts with that which in effect Moses tells us, that Love was the son of Loneliness, begot in Paradise by that sociable and helpful aptitude which God implanted between man and woman toward each other. The same also is that burning mentioned by St Paul, whereof marriage ought to be the remedy' (*The Doctrine and Discipline of Divorce*; *Prose Works*, 2. 252). The conversation imagined here—a symposium including Socrates, Diotima, Moses, and Paul—demands of readers an active role, for it is not at all obvious how Diotima's allegory of the birth of Eros 'divinely sorts' with Genesis 2's account of man's loneliness or the 'rational burning' Milton says Paul addresses in his first Corinthian letter.[23] Milton challenges his readers to sort out, to divine, the 'things useful to be known' from such a conversation.

In his *Apology against a Pamphlet*, Milton claims that Socrates and Diotima, from Plato's *Symposium*, first taught him how eros and chastity cohere:

> Where if I should tell ye what I learnt, of chastity and love, I mean that which is truly so, whose charming cup is only virtue which she bears in her hand to those who are worthy. The rest are cheated with a thick intoxicating potion which a certain Sorceress the abuser of loves name carries about; and how the first and chiefest office of love, begins and ends in the soul, producing those happy twins of her divine generation knowledge and virtue, with such abstracted sublimities as these, it might be worth your listening, readers. (*Prose Works*, 1. 891–2)

Plato's Diotima teaches Socrates (or so he claims) that 'all human beings are pregnant... both in body and soul' (*Symposium* 206c). Bodily reproduction and soulful reproduction exist on a continuum, and both reach towards immortality by 'giving birth in beauty' (*Symposium* 206e). Soul pregnancy leads men to engage 'in many conversations... about virtue, about what a good man should be like, and what he should make it his business to do' (*Symposium* 209c), in short, about 'things useful to be known'. And these conversations 'give birth' to yet more conversations—'the sort of conversations that make young men better' (*Symposium* 210c). Milton invites us to join a conversation that began for him in Plato's *Symposium*, engages with Moses' story of beginnings, and even reinterprets Paul's teaching on love in 1 Corinthians. Along the way, others join this conversation, including Theocritus, Ovid, and Virgil. This conversation on the 'best and sagest things' said about love threads its way through all of Milton's work, early and late, weaving together the Bible, the classics, and his own deeply personal experiences. In *Paradise Lost*, Milton invites us to imagine Adam learning all he knows of the world and of love in conversations with his creator, himself, and his partner, but most of all with Raphael, the 'sociable archangel' whose conversation weaves together all these threads.

Lycidas

Lycidas, which Barbara Lewalski has dubbed 'at once the most derivative and most original of elegies', can be profitably read as an exercise in layered conversations.[24] The poem bristles with echoes of every pastoral poet from Theocritus to Spenser.[25] Unlike the schoolboy and undergraduate exercises that encouraged displays of classical learning for its own sake, *Lycidas* invites readers to overhear a number of conversations: between Greek, Roman, and Renaissance pastoral voices, between pastoral idylls and the interruptive voices of 'higher mood' (epic) and 'dread voices' (prophetic), and even between the two voices that speak the poem, one an 'uncouth Swain', naively committed to a fond old dream of pastoral peace on earth, and the oddly backgrounded but gradually emergent voice of the poet who sings instead of the 'sweet Societies' and 'nuptial song' of 'the blest kingdoms meek of joy and love' (ll. 87, 132, 176–9).[26] Critics generally agree that the pastoral mode had run itself out of fashion well before 1637. Even Spenser's *Shepheardes Calender* sounds self-consciously antique. *Lycidas* evokes ancient and modern pastoral images of a golden age in which human life and death can be harmonized with nature and its seasons and some kind of cosmic dance, but the poem evokes such images only to dramatize their failure.[27] Nymphs, bards, fellow shepherds, even the local muses of rivers and mountain steeps—all the demigods and voices of classical pastoral vision—collapse into failure in the face of Edward King's demise.

Lines 25–36 evoke the good old days of pastoral fellowship: King as Lycidas, John Milton as the 'uncouth swain', and William Chappel, their tutor at Christ's, as 'old Damoetas'. For shepherds, please read young poets and aspiring clergymen; for pastures, the 'high lawns' of Cambridge University; for 'flocks', fellow students and, perhaps one day, parishioners hungry for the word of God. But, even in this nostalgic reverie, the shepherds themselves appear somewhat 'silly', or what we might call clueless, like the 'Shepherds on the Lawn' in the Nativity Ode (ll. 85–92). They sing

'Rural ditties' to the 'oaten flute', while 'Rough satyrs and fauns with cloven heel' dance in time. It is hard to square these rough shepherds and their songs with the higher pastoral task of spiritual feeding and advancing a biblically based reform of a corrupted church. The poem does not even try; instead it reminds us just how ineffectual rural ditties and pastoral demi-gods really are in the face of death:

> Where were ye Nymphs when the remorseless deep
> Closed o're the head of your loved Lycidas?
> For neither were ye playing on the steep,
> Where your old bards, the famous Druids, lie,
> Nor on the shaggy top of Mona high,
> Nor yet where Deva spreads her wizard stream:
> Ay me, I fondly dream!
> Had ye been there . . . for what could that have done?
>
> (ll. 50–7)

Even 'the muse her self that Orpheus bore' is useless in the struggle against death and corruption (l. 58). She could not save even Orpheus, a singer whose enchanting lyre and voice could stop stones and spears in their tracks, from the 'hideous roar' that easily drowned out idyllic song and dealt destruction and death to pastoral harmonies of any sort (l. 61). In Ovid's story (*Metamorphoses*, 11), Orpheus rejoins Eurydice on the Stygian shore and loves again, but *Lycidas* takes the story no further than the point where we follow his severed head 'Down the swift Hebrus to the Lesbian shore' (l. 63)—there is little or no consolation in that.

Other voices of a distinctly unpastoral mood obtrude themselves on the 'uncouth swain'. Phoebus Apollo interrupts (much as the Cynthian god plucked Virgil's ear in *Eclogue* 6) with a heaven-centred definition of fame in a bid to displace the pastoral speaker's more limited sense (ll. 76–84). The stubborn swain calls on Arethuse and 'smooth-sliding Mincius' to return to a more pastoral mode, but his pipe channels voices like Aeolus and Triton, eager to learn what caused his friend's death. Aeolus pleads ignorance; Triton pleads innocence. In the end blame falls on the cursed ship—'that fatal and perfidious bark' (l. 10). Even Camus, a latter-day river god, can do no more than ask in vain: 'Who hath reft . . . my dearest pledge' (l. 107)? St Peter next interrupts in a prophetic jeremiad against a corrupt and ignorant clergy that allows Catholics to make dangerous inroads against reformation, with 'little' or 'nothing said' to stop them.[28] Presumably, Edward King, Cambridge's 'dearest pledge', might have raised a voice in protest; once he returned from Italy in 1639, Milton certainly did. But, again, the 'uncouth swain', the naive pastoral voice, would rather listen to Alpheus and traditional consolations, to the 'little ease' afforded by pastoral images of a flower-bedecked hearse (ll. 132–53). When all is said, however, the swain acknowledges that to do so is but to 'dally with false surmise' (l. 153).

The poem's final movement represents a heroic, but incomplete, effort to bring traditional pastoral consolations into fruitful conversation with a wider epic and Christian vision of a redeemed *locus amoenus* in 'blest kingdoms meek of joy and love', where one may hear and join the yet 'unexpressive nuptial song' in 'sweet societies' of saints and angels (ll. 175–80), a consolation more satisfying and more fitting than Orpheus reunited with Eurydice on the Stygian shore. But this conversation is barely begun; the poet and the 'uncouth swain' still speak in different modes and different tongues. In *Paradise Lost*, Milton finally puts pastoral and heroic, earth and heaven, angels and humans, into harmonic conversations.

Milton detested doctrine for doctrine's sake and erudition for its own sake. Instead he believed all learning should be put in the service of self-reformation—'to repair the ruins of our first Parents', Adam and Eve—and for the reformation of Christ's church on earth, and that reformation was political as well as ecclesiastical. His method was to put the 'solid things', the 'useful things', the concepts and ideas pursued by those 'who have at any time been most industrious after wisdom' into conversation with each other and with his contemporaries. Such conversations, he believed, were both the practice and the fruit of truly chaste love like that described by Diotima and embraced by Socrates. He believed that England, full of such conversations, would become a 'Nation of Prophets, of Sages, and of Worthies' (*Areopagitica*; *Prose Works*, 2. 554). One strain of Puritan reformers turned its back on anything but biblical learning. Quakers and Baptists wanted nothing to do with anything pre-Christian pagans might have thought or said. Even the days of the week and the names of months they thought should be purged of their pagan associations. Milton imagined quite another sort of reformation, of both Church and State, one founded on the twin pillars of Scripture and reason, reason informed by ages of writers industrious after wisdom.

Notes

1. For Milton and the classics, see Charles Martindale, *John Milton and the Transformation of Ancient Epic* (Sydney, 1986; 2nd edn, 2002), with chapters on Homer, Virgil, Ovid, and Lucan; for Virgil, see André Verbart, *Fellowship in Paradise Lost: Vergil, Milton, Wordsworth* (Amsterdam and Atlanta, GA, 1995), with a useful list of parallels pp. 253–302; Craig Kallendorf, *The Other Virgil: 'Pessimistic' Readings of the Aeneid in Early Modern Culture* (Oxford, 2007), 138–69; for Ovid, Davis P. Harding, *Milton and the Renaissance Ovid* (Urbana, IL, 1946); Richard J. DuRocher, *Milton and Ovid* (Ithaca, NY, 1985); John K. Hale, 'Milton Playing with Ovid', *Milton Studies*, 25 (1989), 3–19; Mandy Green, *Milton's Ovidian Eve* (Farnham, 2009); Maggie Kilgour, *Milton and the Metamorphosis of Ovid* (Oxford, 2012); for Lucan, David Norbrook, *Writing the English Republic: Poetry, Rhetoric and Politics 1627–1660* (Cambridge, 1999), esp. 438–67. General studies include: Davis P. Harding, *The Club of Hercules: Studies in the Classical Background of Paradise Lost* (Urbana, IL, 1962); Francis C. Blessington, *Paradise Lost and the Classical Epic* (Boston, 1979); Thomas M. Greene, *The Descent from Heaven: A Study in Epic Continuity* (New Haven, 1982); Claes Schaar, *The Full Voic'd Quire Below: Vertical Context Systems in Paradise Lost*, Lund

Studies in English 60 (Lund, 1982); Colin Burrow, *Epic Romance: Homer to Milton* (Oxford, 1993); William M. Porter, *Reading the Classics and Paradise Lost* (Lincoln, NE, 1993); David Quint, *Epic and Empire: Politics and Generic Form from Virgil to Milton* (Princeton, 1993); John K. Hale, *Milton's Languages: The Impact of Multilingualism on Style* (Cambridge, 1997); John K. Hale, 'The Classical Literary Tradition', in Thomas N. Corns (ed.), *A Companion to Milton* (Malden and Oxford, 2001), 22–36; Neil Forsyth, *The Satanic Epic* (Princeton and Oxford, 2003); David Hopkins, 'Milton and the Classics', in Paul Hammond and Blair Worden (eds), *John Milton 1608–2008: Life, Work, and Reputation* (Oxford, 2010), 23–41. Many of the above items include discussion of Milton's early works; on Milton's classical education, see Donald Lemen Clark, *John Milton at St Paul's School: A Study of Ancient Rhetoric in English Renaissance Education* (New York, 1948); Richard J. DuRocher, *Milton among the Romans: The Pedagogy and Influence of Milton's Latin Curriculum* (Pittsburgh, 2001). On the early poetry, including *Lycidas*, see also Watson Kirkconnell, *Awake the Courteous Echo: The Themes and Prosody of Comus, Lycidas, and Paradise Regained in World Literature with Translations of the Major Analogues* (Toronto, 1973); Stella Purce Revard, *Milton and the Tangles of Neaera's Hair: The Making of the 1645 Poems* (Columbia, MO, 1997). On *Lycidas* and the pastoral tradition, see E. Z. Lambert, *Placing Sorrow: A Study of the Pastoral Elegy Tradition from Theocritus to Milton* (Chapel Hill, NC, 1976); Thomas K. Hubbard, *The Pipes of Pan: Intertextuality and Literary Filiation from Theocritus to Milton* (Ann Arbor, 1998).

2. Erasmus, 'On the Method of Study and Reading and Interpreting Authors', *De Ratione Studii ac Legendi Interpretandique Auctores* (Paris, 1511), in *Desiderii Erasmi Roterodami Opera Omnia* (Amsterdam, 1971), 2. 79–151.
3. Richard J. DuRocher makes much the same point in his study of schoolmaster Milton's Latin curriculum: 'In contrast with the standard grammar school curriculum built around the trivium of grammar, logic, and rhetoric, Milton's program emphasizes *res* instead of *verba*, things rather than words' (*Milton among the Romans: The Pedagogy and Influence of Milton's Latin Curriculum* 4). Milton was a schoolmaster from 1640 until 1646.
4. Translated by John Carey in *Milton: The Complete Shorter Poems*, ed. John Carey, 2nd edn (Harlow, 1997), 59. All quotations from Milton's poetry come from this edition.
5. Barbara K. Lewalski, *The Life of John Milton* (Oxford, 2000), 8.
6. Clifford Geertz, *The Interpretation of Cultures* (New York, 1973), 24. I do not mean to recast Milton as a post-modern ethnographer. Milton, like any other Englishman of his day, believed Christian truths trumped all others, but we should also recognize, and many recent studies of Milton's heterodoxies point out, that what Milton hears Jesus saying in the Gospels about marriage and divorce is not unaffected by conversation with Plato and Aristotle. See chapter 10 of *Doctrine and Discipline of Divorce*, book 1.
7. The quoted phrase is Thomas M. Greene's in *The Light in Troy: Imitation and Discovery in Renaissance Poetry* (New Haven, 1982). See also Richard J. DuRocher's *Milton and Ovid*.
8. Edward Jones, 'Milton's Life, 1608–1640', in *The Oxford Handbook of Milton*, ed. Nicholas McDowell (Oxford, 2009), 8
9. Jones, 'Milton's Life', 10.
10. For the prose theme, see Alfred J. Horwood (ed.), *A Common-place Book of*

John Milton, rev. edn (1877), 61–2. For a good translation and helpful notes, see *Prose Works*, I. 1036–9.

11. *The Riverside Milton*, trans. Roy Flannagan (Boston, 1998), 178.
12. *Riverside Milton*, trans. Flannagan, 175.
13. Kilgour, *Milton and the Metamorphosis of Ovid*. Kilgour's analysis of Milton's first English verse, 'On the Death of a Fair Infant Dying of a Cough', explains how young Milton could 'use a poet of rape [Ovid] to create a poetry that celebrates the power of chastity' (p. 61). This skill becomes even more evident in *A Maske*. Stella Revard, in her recent edition of the *Complete Shorter Poems* (Oxford, 2009), includes a particularly useful bibliography of major editions, scholarly resources, and critical books and studies of Milton's shorter poems, and particularly his earlier verse (pp. 547–51).
14. *Milton's Cambridge Latin: Performing in the Genres 1625–1632* (Tempe, AZ, 2005).
15. Carey, *Shorter Poems*, 76.
16. See Jones, 'Milton's Life', 15.
17. Carey, *Shorter Poems*, 105.
18. Most recently, David Quint worries this point in 'Expectation and Prematurity in Milton's Nativity Ode', *Modern Philology*, 97 (1999), 195–219. For the older, supersessionist reading, see Rosemund Tuve, *Images and Themes in Five Poems by Milton* (Cambridge, 1957), 15–36.
19. Kilgour, *Milton and the Metamorphosis of Ovid*, 149–50.
20. Charles Martindale, *John Milton and the Transformation of Ancient Epic*, 160.
21. Kilgour, *Milton and the Metamorphosis of Ovid*, 163.
22. Bruce Boehrer, '"Lycidas": The Pastoral Elegy as Same-Sex Epithalamium', *PMLA*, 117 (2002), 234.
23. 1 Corinthians 7: 9.
24. Lewalski, *Life of Milton*, 82.
25. See *A Variorum Commentary on the Poems of John Milton*, vol. 2, part 2, ed. A. S. P. Woodhouse and Douglas Bush (New York, 1972), 544–734. This article also contains a good thumbnail history of pastoral conventions and practices from Theocritus to Spenser.
26. l. 177, 'In the blest kingdoms meek of joy and love', did not appear in the 1638 volume in which the poem originally appeared (*Justa Eduardo King Naufrago* (Cambridge, 1638)). It was added for the 1645 publication of *Poems of Mr John Milton*. The 'uncouth swain' takes comfort in imagining Lycidas transformed into the 'Genius of the shore', a distinctly pastoral consolation, but the emerging epic voice seems to insist that the only *truly* pastoral realm is Paradise or Heaven.
27. Lewalski, *Life of Milton*, 82.
28. In 1637, l. 129 read 'little said'; in the 1645 *Poems*, it was changed to 'nothing said'.

Classical Reception in English Literature, 1558–1660: An Annotated Bibliography

CRAIG KALLENDORF

1. KEY THEMES

1.1 General and Reference

Bate, Walter Jackson, *The Burden of the Past and the English Poet* (Cambridge, MA, 1970).

Bolgar, R. R. (ed.), *Classical Influences on Western Thought AD 1650–1870* (Cambridge, 1979). [A classic account, with useful information for this period as well as others.]

Brown, Huntingdon, 'The Classical Tradition in English Literature: A Bibliography', *Harvard Studies and Notes in Philology and Literature*, 18 (1935), 7–46. [Offers excellent access to older material.]

Carlsen, Hanne, *A Bibliography to the Classical Tradition in English Literature* (Copenhagen, 1985).

Clarke, G. W., *Rediscovering Hellenism: The Hellenic Inheritance and the English Imagination* (Cambridge, 1989).

Gillespie, Stuart, *The Poets on the Classics: An Anthology of English Poets' Writings on Classical Poets and Dramatists from Chaucer to the Present* (London and New York, 1988). [An important collection of source material.]

Grafton, Anthony, Most, Glenn W., and Settis, Salvatore (eds), *The Classical Tradition* (Cambridge, MA, 2010). [Far wider in scope than the present volume, but contains much discussion of Renaissance material *passim*.]

Haynes, Kenneth, *English Literature and Ancient Languages* (Oxford, 2007). [A stimulating study focused primarily on the linguistic level.]

Highet, Gilbert, *The Classical Tradition: Greek and Roman Influences on Western Literature* (Oxford, 1949). [The classic treatment, still of great value.]

Hopkins, David, *Conversing with Antiquity: English Poets and the Classics, from Shakespeare to Pope* (Oxford, 2010).

Kallendorf, Craig, *Latin Influences on English Literature from the Middle Ages to the Eighteenth Century: An Annotated Bibliography of Scholarship, 1945–79* (New York, 1982). [Chapters

4–6 cover Renaissance literature, the early seventeenth century, and drama from these periods.]

Kallendorf, Craig (ed.), *A Companion to the Classical Tradition* (Oxford, 2010). [Includes a chapter on the Renaissance by the editor.]

Lord, George deForest, *Classical Presences in Seventeenth-Century English Poetry* (New Haven, 1987).

Mason, Tom, 'Is There a Classical Tradition in English Poetry?', *Translation and Literature*, 5 (1996), 203–19.

Ogilvie, Robert M., *Latin and Greek: A History of the Influence of the Classics on English Life from 1600 to 1918* (Hamden, CT, 1964).

Sowerby, Robin, *The Classical Legacy in Renaissance Poetry* (London and New York, 1994). [An introduction to the topic, arranged by genre.]

Spencer, T. J. B., *Fair Greece! Sad Relic; Literary Philhellenism from Shakespeare to Byron* (1954).

Starnes, DeWitt T., *Classical Myth and Legend in Renaissance Dictionaries: A Study of Renaissance Dictionaries in their Relation to the Classical Learning of Contemporary English Writers* (Chapel Hill, NC, 1955). [Still the standard study of an unduly neglected topic.]

1.2. Humanism, Scholarship, and Education in the Classics

Ascham, R., *English Works*, ed. W. A. Wright (Cambridge, 1904).

Augustijn, C., *Erasmus: His Life, Works and Influence* (Toronto, 1991).

Baldwin, T. W., *Shakspere's Small Latine and Lesse Greeke*, 2 vols (Urbana, IL, 1944). [A valuable, detailed survey of Shakespeare's knowledge of the classical world.]

Baldwin, T. W., *Shakspere's Five-Act Structure: Shakspere's Early Plays on the Background of Renaissance Theories of Five-Act Structure from 1470* (Urbana, IL, 1947).

Barker, N., 'The Polyglot Bible', in Barnard and McKenzie (2002), 648–51.

Barnard, J., and McKenzie, D. F. (eds), *The Cambridge History of the Book in Britain*, vol. 4: *1557–1695* (Cambridge, 2002).

Besomi, O., and Caruso, C. (eds), *Il commento ai testi* (Basle, 1992).

Binns, J. W., *Intellectual Culture in Elizabethan and Jacobean England* (Leeds, 1990).

Bolgar, R. R. (ed.), *Classical Influences on European Culture 1500–1700* (Cambridge, 1976). [A valuable collection of essays, many focused on the UK.]

Brink, C. O., *English Classical Scholarship* (Cambridge, 1986).

Buck, A., and Herding, O. (eds), *Der Kommentar in der Renaissance* (Boppard, 1975). [A widely cited collection of essays.]

Case, John, *Summa Veterum Interpretum in Universam Dialecticam* (1584).

Chomarat, J., *Grammaire et rhétorique chez Erasme* (Paris, 1981). [An important book whose findings extend far beyond Erasmus.]

Clark, D. L., *John Milton at St Paul's School* (New York, 1948). [A valuable study of what a great poet could learn about classical antiquity at school.]

Crane, M. T., *Framing Authority: Sayings, Self and Society in Sixteenth-Century England* (Princeton, 1993). [An analysis of commonplaces as windows into Renaissance society.]

Documents Relating to the University and Colleges of Cambridge, 3 vols (1852).

Feingold, Mordechai, *The Mathematicians' Apprenticeship: Science, Universities and Society in England 1560–1640* (Cambridge, 1984).

Feingold, Mordechai, 'The Humanities', in Tyacke (1997), 211–448.

Fincham, K., 'Oxford and the Early Stuart Polity', in Tyacke (1997), 179–210.

Fletcher, H. F., *The Intellectual Development of John Milton*, 2 vols (Urbana, IL, 1956–61).

Gibson, Strickland (ed.), *Statuta Antiqua Universitatis Oxoniensis* (Oxford, 1931).

Grafton, A., 'Renaissance Readers and Ancient Texts: Comments on Some Commentaries', *Renaissance Quarterly*, 38 (1985), 615–49.

Grafton, A., and Jardine, L., *From Humanism to the Humanities* (Cambridge, MA, 1986). [A provocative book, claiming that humanist educational practice did not always live up to its ideals.]

Green, L. D., *John Rainolds's Oxford Lectures on Aristotle's Rhetoric* (Newark, DE, 1986).

Hoole, C., *A New Discovery of the Old Art of Teaching School* (Syracuse, NY, 1912).

Johnson, Ralph, *The Scholar's Guide* (1665; repr. Menston, 1971).

Kempe, W., *The Education of Children in Learning* (1588).

Kraye, J. (ed.), *The Cambridge Companion to Renaissance Humanism* (Cambridge, 1996). [A valuable, often-cited collection of essays.]

Kristeller, P. O., *Renaissance Thought and its Sources* (New York, 1979). [A classic study of the ancient roots of Renaissance thought.]

Leedham-Green, Elisabeth, *Books in Cambridge Inventories*, 2 vols (Cambridge, 1986).

Leedham-Green, Elisabeth, and McKitterick, D., 'Ownership: Private and Public Libraries', in Barnard and McKenzie (2002), 323–38.

McConica, J. K. (ed.), *A History of the University of Oxford*, vol. 3: *The Collegiate University* (Oxford, 1986).

Mack, P., 'Rhetoric and the Essay', *Rhetoric Society Quarterly*, 23/2 (Spring 1993), 41–9.

Mack, P., 'Ramus Reading: The Commentaries', *Journal of the Warburg and Courtauld Institutes*, 61 (1998), 111–41.

Mack, P., *Elizabethan Rhetoric: Theory and Practice* (Cambridge, 2002a). [An important study of how rhetorical training in the schools affected broader cultural life in Renaissance England.]

Mack, P., 'Melanchthon's Commentaries on Latin Literature', in G. Frank and K. Meerhoff (eds), *Melanchthon und Europa II* (Stuttgart, 2002b), 29–52.

Mallet, C. E., *A History of the University of Oxford*, 3 vols (New York, 1924–8).

Melanchthon, Philipp, *Enarratio Comoediarum Terentii*, in *Opera Omnia*, ed. C. Bretschneider, Corpus Reformatorum 19 (Brunswick, 1834–60).

Michael, Ian, *The Teaching of English from the Sixteenth Century to 1870* (Cambridge, 1987).

Moss, A., *Ovid in Renaissance France* (Oxford, 1982). [Contains material that is also useful in the English environment.]

Mullinger, James Bass, *The University of Cambridge*, 3 vols (Cambridge, 1873–1911).

Nichols, J. G. (ed.), *The Progresses of Queen Elizabeth*, 3 vols (1788–1823).

O'Day, Rosemary, *Education and Society 1500–1800* (London and New York, 1982).

Ong, W., 'Commonplace Rhapsody: Ravisius Textor, Zwinger and Shakespeare', in Bolgar (1976), 91–126.

Pade, M. (ed.), *On Renaissance Commentaries* (Hildesheim, 2005).

Pepper, R. D. (ed.), *Four Tudor Books on Education* (Gainesville, FL, 1966).

Philipps, J. T., *A Compendious Way of Teaching Antient and Modern Languages* (1750).

Rabil, A., Jr (ed.), *Renaissance Humanism: Foundations, Forms and Legacy*, 3 vols (Philadelphia, 1988). [A broad survey of how the effort to revive antiquity influenced Renaissance culture; somewhat dated by now but still valuable.]

Roberts, J. 'The Latin Trade', in Barnard and McKenzie (1992), 141–73.

Sabbadini, R., *Il metodo degli umanisti* (Florence, 1920).

Sanderson, Robert, *Logicae Artis Compendium*, ed. E. J. Ashworth (Bologna, 1985).

Serjeantson, R. W., 'Thomas Farnaby (1575?–1647)', in E. Malone (ed.), *British Rhetoricians and Logicians, 1500–1600, First series*, Dictionary of Literary Biography 236 (Columbia, SC, 2003), 108–16.

Spitz, L. W., and Tinsley, B. S., *Johann Sturm on Education* (St Louis, 1995).

Stone, L., 'The Size and Composition of the Oxford Student Body 1580-1909', in L. Stone, *The University in Society* (Princeton, 1974), 3–110.

Toomer, G. J., *John Selden: A Life in Scholarship*, 2 vols (Oxford, 2009).

Tyacke, N. (ed.), *The History of the University of Oxford*, vol. 4: *Seventeenth Century Oxford* (Oxford, 1997).

Virgil, *Opera. Notis a Thomae Farnabii* (1634).

Williams, Penry, 'Church State and University 1558–1603', in McConica (1986), 397–440.

Witt, R., *In the Footsteps of the Ancients: The Origins of Humanism from Lovati to Bruni* (Leiden, 2000). [An important effort to push the origins of humanism back to the generations before Petrarch.]

1.3. Rhetoric and Literary Criticism

1.3.A. Authorship and the Literary Career

Acosta-Hughes, Benjamin, and Stephens, Susan A., 'Rereading Callimachus' "Aetia" Fragment 1', *Classical Philology*, 97 (2002), 238–55.

Calabrese, Michael A., *Chaucer's Ovidian Arts of Love* (Gainesville, FL, 1994).

Cameron, Alan, *Callimachus and his Critics* (Princeton, 1995).

Campbell, Lily B., *Divine Poetry and Drama in Sixteenth-Century England* (New York, 1972).

Cheney, Patrick, *Spenser's Famous Flight: A Renaissance Idea of a Literary Career* (Toronto, 1993). [An often-cited book on a key *topos* in Renaissance literature.]

Cheney, Patrick, *Marlowe's Counterfeit Profession: Ovid, Spenser, Counter-Nationhood* (Toronto, 1997).

Cheney, Patrick, 'Introduction', in Cheney and de Armas (2002), 3–23.

Cheney, Patrick, 'Did Shakespeare Have a Literary Career?' in Hardie and Moore (2010), 160–78.

Cheney, Patrick, and de Armas, Frederick A. (eds), *European Literary Careers: The Author from Antiquity to the Renaissance* (Toronto, 2002).

Coiro, Ann Baynes, 'Fable and Old Song: *Samson Agonistes* and the Idea of a Poetic Career', *Milton Studies*, 36 (1998), 123–52.

Conte, Gian Biagio, *The Rhetoric of Imitation: Genre and Poetic Memory in Virgil and Other Latin Poets*, trans. Charles Segal (Ithaca, NY, 1986). [An important study of intertextuality that helped classicists develop a more sophisticated approach to this field.]

Coolidge, John S., 'Great Things and Small: The Virgilian Progression', *Comparative Literature*, 17 (1965), 1–23.

Eliot, T. S., *Elizabethan Dramatists* (1963).

Farrell, Joseph, 'Greek Lives and Roman Careers', in Cheney and de Armas (2002), 24–46.

Fowler, Alastair, *The Kinds of Literature: An Introduction to the Theory of Genres and Modes* (Cambridge, MA, 1982). [A classic study of Renaissance genre theory.]

Hannay, Margaret P., *Mary Sidney, Lady Wroth* (Burlington, VT, 2010).

Hardie, Philip, *The Epic Successors of Virgil: A Study in the Dynamics of a Tradition* (Cambridge, 1993). [An important study of later Latin epic.]

Hardie, Philip, 'Introduction' (Cambridge, 2000a), in Hardie (2000b), 1–10.

Hardie, Philip (ed.), *Cambridge Companion to Ovid* (Cambridge, 2002b).

Hardie, Philip, 'Introduction: Literary Careers—Classical Models', in Hardie and Moore (2010), 1–16.

Hardie, Philip, and Barchiesi, Alessandro, 'The Ovidian Career Model: Ovid, Gallus, Apuleius, Boccaccio', in Hardie and Moore (2010), 59–88.

Hardie, Philip, and Moore, Helen (eds), *Classical Literary Careers and their Reception* (Cambridge, 2010). [The fundamental collection of essays on this topic.]

Harrison, Stephen, 'Ovid and Genre: Evolutions of an Elegist', in Hardie (2002b), 79–94.

Harrison, Stephen, 'There and Back Again: Horace's Poetic Career', in Hardie and Moore (2010), 39–58.

Helgerson, Richard, 'The New Poet Presents Himself', *PMLA*, 93 (1978), 893–911.

Helgerson, Richard, *Self-Crowned Laureates: Spenser, Jonson, Milton, and the Literary System* (Berkeley and Los Angeles, 1983). [An excellent, widely cited study of the literary career in Renaissance England.]

Johnson, Lee M., 'Milton's Blank Verse Sonnets', *Milton Studies*, 5 (1973), 129–53.

Kilgour, Maggie, 'New Spins on Old Rotas: Virgil, Ovid, Milton', in Hardie and Moore (2010), 179–96.

Knoppers, Laura Lunger (ed.), *The 1671 Poems: 'Paradise Regain'd' and 'Samson Agonistes'* (Oxford, 2008).

Lateiner, Donald, 'The *Iliad*: An Unpredictable Classic', in Robert Fowler (ed.), *The Cambridge Companion to Homer* (Cambridge, 2004).

Lewalski, Barbara Kiefer, *Milton's Brief Epic: The Genre, Meaning, and Art of 'Paradise Regained'* (Providence, RI, 1966).

Lipking, Lawrence, *The Life of the Poet: Beginning and Ending Poetic Careers* (Chicago, 1981).

Loewenstein, Joseph F., 'Echo's Ring: Orpheus and Spenser's Career', *English Literary Renaissance*, 16 (1986), 287–302.

Martindale, Charles, 'Green Politics: The *Eclogues*' (Cambridge, 1997a), in Martindale (1997b).

Martindale, Charles (ed.), *The Cambridge Companion to Virgil* (Cambridge, 1997b).

Miller, David L., 'Spenser's Vocation, Spenser's Career', *English Literary History*, 50 (1983), 197–231.

Neuse, Richard, 'Milton and Spenser: The Virgilian Triad Revisited', *English Literary History*, 35 (1978), 606–39.

Rambuss, Richard, *Spenser's Secret Career* (Cambridge, 1993).

Rambuss, Richard, 'Spenser's Lives, Spenser's Careers', in Judith H. Anderson, Donald Cheney, and David A. Richardson (eds), *Spenser's Life and the Subject of Biography* (Amherst, MA, 1996), 1–17.

Vessey, D. W. T., 'Elegy Eternal: Ovid, *Amores*, I.15', *Latomus*, 40 (1969), 80–97.

Woods, Susanne, Hannay, Margaret, Beilin, Elaine, and Shaver, Anne, 'Renaissance Englishwomen and the Literary Career', in Cheney and de Armas (2002), 302–24.

1.3.B. Fame and Immortality

Bate, Jonathan, *Shakespeare and Ovid* (Oxford, 1993). [The proper beginning place for work on this relationship.]

Benjamin, Edwin B., 'Fame, Poetry, and the Order of History in the Literature of the English Renaissance', *Studies in the Renaissance*, 6 (1959), 64–84.

Braden, Gordon, 'Ovid, Petrarch, and Shakespeare's Sonnets', in A. B. Taylor (ed.), *Shakespeare's Ovid: The 'Metamorphoses' in the Plays and Poems* (Cambridge, 2000), 96–112.

Cain, Thomas H., *Praise in The Faerie Queene* (Lincoln, NE, 1978). [Analyses *The Faerie Queene* as an epic written in accordance with the norms of epideictic rhetoric.]

Cheney (1993): see 1.3.A.

Clements, Robert J., 'Pen and Sword in Renaissance Emblem Literature', *Modern Language Quarterly*, 5 (1944a), 131–41.

Clements, Robert J., 'The Cult of the Poet in Renaissance Emblem Literature', *PMLA*, 59 (1944b), 672–85.

Dubrow, Heather, 'A Mirror for Complaints: Shakespeare's *Lucrece* and Generic Tradition', in Lewalski (1986), 399–417.

Dzelzainis, Martin, '"The Feminine Part of Every Rebellion": Francis Bacon on Sedition and Libel and the Beginning of Ideology', *Huntington Library Quarterly*, 69 (2006), 139–52.

Gillespie, Stuart, 'Literary Afterlives: Metempsychosis from Ennius to Jorge Luis Borges', in Hardie and Moore (2010), 209–25: see 1.3.A.

Gordon, D. J., 'Name and Fame: Shakespeare's *Coriolanus*', in D. J. Gordon, *The Renaissance Imagination*, ed. Stephen Orgel (Berkeley and Los Angeles, 1975), 203–19.

Hardie, Philip, 'Strategies of Praise: The *Aeneid* and Renaissance Epic', in G. Urso (ed.), *Dicere laudes* (Pisa, 2011), 383–99.

Hardie, Philip, *Rumour and Renown: Representations of Fama in Western Literature* (Cambridge, 2012).

Hardison, O. B., Jr., *The Enduring Monument: A Study of the Idea of Praise in Renaissance Literary Theory and Practice* (Chapel Hill, NC, 1962). [Clarifies the importance of epideictic rhetoric in Renaissance literary theory.]

Holohan, Michael, '*Iamque opus exegi*: Ovid's Changes and Spenser's Brief Epic of Mutability', *English Literary Renaissance*, 6 (1976), 244–70.

Lascelles, Mary, 'The Rider on the Winged Horse', in H. Davis and H. Gardner (eds), *Elizabethan and Jacobean Studies Presented to Frank Percy Wilson in Honour of his Seventieth Birthday* (Oxford, 1959), 173–98.

Lewalski, Barbara (ed.), *Renaissance Genres: Essays on Theory, History, and Interpretation* (Cambridge, MA, and London, 1986). [An important series of essays, collected by her generation's expert on genre theory.]

McCabe, Richard A., *The Pillars of Eternity: Time and Providence in* The Faerie Queene (Blackrock, 1989).

Meskell, Lynn S., *Ben Jonson and Envy* (Cambridge, 2009).

Miller, Anthony, *Roman Triumphs and Early Modern English Culture* (Basingstoke, 2001).

Moul, Victoria, *Jonson, Horace and the Classical Tradition* (Cambridge, 2010). [An important new book, with broad implications for the study of the classical tradition in this period.]

Samuel, I., *Plato and Milton* (Ithaca, NY, 1947). [A classic study, still worth consulting.]

Spingarn, Joel E. (ed.), *Critical Essays of the Seventeenth Century* (Oxford, 1908).

Yates, Frances A., *Astraea: The Imperial Theme in the Sixteenth Century* (1975).

1.3.C. Rhetoric

Adlington, H., McCullough, P., and Rhatigan, E. (eds), *The Oxford Handbook of the Early Modern Sermon* (Oxford, 2011).

Green, L. D., and Murphy, J. J. (eds), *Renaissance Rhetoric Short-Title Catalogue 1460–1700*, 2nd edn (Aldershot, 2006). [The standard bibliography of primary sources.]

Harwood, J. T. (ed.), *The Rhetorics of Thomas Hobbes and Bernard Lamy* (Carbondale, IL, 1986).

Hornbeak, K. G., 'The Complete Letter-Writer in English', *Smith College Studies in Modern Languages*, 15 (1934), 1–150.

Hoskins, John, *Directions for Speech and Style*, ed. H. H. Hudson (Princeton, 1935).

Howell, W. S., *Logic and Rhetoric in England 1500–1700* (Princeton, 1956). [Partially superseded by Mack (2002a), but still valuable.]

Hunt, A., *The Art of Hearing* (Cambridge, 2010).

Joseph, M., *Shakespeare's Use of the Arts of Language* (New York, 1947). [A classic study, still valuable for its detailed treatment.]

Keller, Stefan Daniel, *The Development of Shakespeare's Rhetoric* (Tübingen, 2009).

Mack (2002a): see 1.2.

Mack, P. *Reading and Rhetoric in Montaigne and Shakespeare* (2010).

Mack, P. 'Ramus and Ramism: Rhetoric and Dialectic', in S. J. Reid and E. Wilson (eds), *Ramus, Pedagogy and the Liberal Arts* (Farnham, 2011a), 7–23.

Mack, P., *A History of Renaissance Rhetoric 1380–1620* (Oxford, 2011b). [The long-awaited synthesis of its field, magisterial in its coverage, with detailed analysis of the influence of classical rhetoric on Renaissance culture.]

Magnusson, Lynne, *Shakespeare and Social Dialogue* (Cambridge, 1999).

Medine, P., *Thomas Wilson* (Boston, 1986).

Morrissey, Mary, 'Scripture, Style and Persuasion in Seventeenth-Century English Theories of Preaching', *Journal of Ecclesiastical History*, 53 (2002), 686–706.

Morrissey, Mary, *Politics and the Paul's Cross Sermons 1558–1642* (Oxford, 2011).

Payne, Paula H., 'The Poet Orator's Praise: Epideictic Discourse in Sidney's *Astrophil and Stella*,' *Sidney Newsletter*, 9 (1988), 11–21.

Pennacchia, Maddalena, 'Antony's Ring: Remediating Ancient Rhetoric on the Elizabethan Stage', in Maria Del Sapio Garbero (ed.), *Identity, Otherness and Empire in Shakespeare's Rome* (Surrey, 2009), 49–59.

Pettegree, A., *Reformation and the Culture of Persuasion* (Cambridge, 2005).

Plett, H. F., *English Renaissance Rhetoric and Poetics: A Systematic Bibliography* (Leiden, 1995). [An invaluable orientation to work in the field.]

Plett, H. F., *Rhetoric and Renaissance Culture* (Berlin, 2004).

Rhodes, N., *The Power of Eloquence and English Renaissance Literature* (Basingstoke, 1992).

Robertson, J., *The Art of Letter Writing* (1942).

Sloane, Thomas O., and Waddington, R. B. (eds), *The Rhetoric of Renaissance Poetry* (Berkeley and Los Angeles, 1974).

Vickers, B., *Classical Rhetoric in English Poetry* (1970).

Vickers, B., 'Shakespeare's Use of Rhetoric', in K. Muir and S. Schoenbaum (eds), *A New Companion to Shakespeare Studies* (Cambridge, 1971), 83–98.

Vickers, B., *In Defence of Rhetoric* (Oxford, 1988).

Wilson, Thomas, *The Art of Rhetoric (1560)*, ed. P. Medine (University Park, PA, 1994).

1.4. Gender and Sexuality

1.4.A. Women as Readers and Writers

Aercke, Kristiaan P. G., 'Germanic Sappho: Anna Bijns', in Wilson (1987), 365–97.

Boccaccio, Giovanni, *Concerning Famous Women*, trans. Guido A. Guarino (New Brunswick, NJ, 1963).

Clanchy, Michael, *From Memory to Written Record: England 1066–1307* (Oxford and Cambridge, MA, 1979).

Clark, Elizabeth A., and Hatch, Diane F. (eds and trans.), *The Golden Bough, the Oaken Cross: The Virgilian Cento of Faltonia Betitia Proba* (Chico, 1981). [A thoughtful study of a work that exercised a surprising influence on Renaissance culture.]

Craigie, W. A. (ed.), *The Maitland Quarto Manuscript*, STS NS 9 (Edinburgh, 1920).

Dane, Joseph A., '"Wanting the First Blank": The Frontispiece to the Huntington Copy of Caxton's *Recuyell of the Historyes of Troy*', *Huntington Library Quarterly*, 67/2 (2004), 315–25.

de Coste, Hilarion, *Les Eloges et vies des reynes, princesses, ames et damoiselles illustres en pieté, courage et doctrine* (Paris, 1630).

DeJean, Joan, *Fictions of Sappho, 1546–1937* (Chicago, 1989).

Delepierre, Joseph Octave, *Centoniana, ou Encyclopédie des centos* (1866–8).

Dulac, Liliane, and Reno, Christine, 'L'Humanisme vers 1400, essai d'exploration à partir d'un cas marginal: Christine de Pizan traductrice de Thomas d'Aquin', in Monique Ornato and Nicole Pons (eds), *Pratiques de la culture écrite en France au XVe siècle* (Louvain-la-Neuve, 1995), 160–78.

Ermini, Filippo, *Il centone di Proba e la poesia centonaria latina* (Rome, 1909).

Evans, Robert C., and Wiedemann, Barbara, *'My Name was Martha': A Renaissance Woman's Autobiographical Poem by Martha Moulsworth* (West Cornwall, CT, 1993).

Farnsworth, Jane, 'Voicing Female Desire in "Poem XLIX"', *Studies in English Literature 1500–1900*, 36/1 (1996), 37–72.

Les Femmes illustres, ou les harangues heroïques, avec les veritables portraits de ces heroines, tirés des medailles antiques, 2 vols (Paris, 1655).

Hannay, Margaret P., Kinnamon, Noel J., and Brennan, Michael G. (eds), *The Collected Works of Mary Sidney Herbert I* (Oxford, 1998).

Hardie, Alex, 'Juvenal, the *Phaedrus*, and the Truth about Rome', *Classical Quarterly*, NS 48/1 (1998), 234–51.

Hellinga, Lotte, 'Tradition and Renewal: Establishing the Chronology of Wynkyn de Worde's Early Work', in Kristian Jensen (ed.), *Incunabula and their Readers: Printing, Selling and Using Books in the Fifteenth Century* (London, 2003), 13–30.

Jacobson, Howard, *Ovid's Heroides* (Princeton, 1974).

Jameson, Caroline, 'Ovid in the Sixteenth Century', in *Ovid*, ed. J. W. Binns (Boston, 1973), 210–42.

Jayne, Sears, and Johnson, Francis R., *The Lumley Library: The Catalogue of 1609* (1956).

Jones, Ann Rosalind, 'Contentious Readings: Urban Humanism and Gender Differences in *La Puce de Madame des-Roches* (1582)', *Renaissance Quarterly*, 48/1 (1995), 109–28.

Kamm, Josephine, *Hope Deferred: Girls' Education in English History* (1965).

Klene, Jean (ed.), *The Southwell–Sibthorpe Commonplace Book, Folger Shakespeare Library MS V b 198* (Tempe, 1997).

Larminie, Vivienne, *Wealth, Kinship and Culture: The Seventeenth Century Newdigates of Arbury and their World* (Ipswich, 1995).

Lathrop, Henry Burrowes, *Translations from the Classics into English, From Caxton to Chapman, 1477–1620* (Madison, 1933). [An old but still-valuable study.]

Leach, Edmund, *Culture and Nature, or La Femme Sauvage* (1968).

Lewalski, Barbara, *Writing Women in Jacobean England* (Cambridge, MA, 1993).

Lloyd-Jones, Hugh, *Blood for the Ghosts: Classical Influences in the Nineteenth and Twentieth Centuries* (1982).

Lupton, Joseph Hirst, *A Life of John Colet, DD, Dean of St Paul's and Founder of St Paul's School* (Hamden, CT, 1961).

Martin, Henri-Jean, *Livre, pouvoir et société à Paris au XVIIe siècle (1598–1701)* (Geneva, 1969). [An important study in book history, with implications for England.]

Moss, Anne, *Ovid in Renaissance France: A Survey of the Latin Editions of Ovid and Commentaries Printed in France before 1600* (1982).

Ong, Walter, SJ, 'Latin and the Social Fabric', in Walter Ong, SJ, *The Barbarian Within and Other Fugitive Essays and Studies* (New York, 1962), 206–19.

Ong, Walter, SJ, 'Latin Language Study as a Renaissance Puberty Rite', *Studies in Philology*, 56 (1967), 103–24. [An often-cited article that positions the study of Latin as a rite of passage in Renaissance culture.]

Parrott, T. M., 'Marlowe, Beaumont and Julius Caesar', *Modern Language Notes*, 44/2 (February 1929), 69–77.

Parsons, John Carmi (ed.), *Medieval Queenship* (Stroud, 1993).

Pemberton, Caroline (ed.), *Queen Elizabeth's Englishings*, Early English Text Society, os 113 (1899).

Perry, Ruth, *The Celebrated Mary Astell* (Chicago, 1986).

Pfeiffer, Rudolf, *A History of Classical Scholarship, 1300–1850* (Oxford, 1976). [The standard treatment, to be supplemented by more recent work in the field.]

Purkiss, Diane (ed.), *Three Tragedies by Renaissance Women* (Harmondsworth, 1998).

Reynolds, L. D. (ed.), *Texts and Transmission: A Survey of the Latin Classics* (Oxford, 1983). [A study of the manuscript transmission of each major classical Latin author.]

Robbins-Herring, Kittye Delle, 'Hélisienne de Crenne: Champion of Women's Rights', in Wilson (1987), 177–218.

Rowe, Elizabeth, *Poems on Several Occasions, Written by Philomela* (1696).

Saunders, J. W., 'From Manuscript to Print', *Transactions of the Leeds Philological Society*, 6 (1951), 507–28.

Savage, J. E. (ed.), *The Conceited News of Thomas Overbury* (1609; New York, 1968).

Spence, Richard T., *Lady Anne Clifford* (Stroud, 1997).

Spentzou, Effrosini, and Fowler, Don (eds), *Cultivating the Muse: Struggles for Power and Inspiration in Classical Literature* (Oxford, 2002).

Stafford, Pauline, *Queen Emma and Queen Edith: Queenship and Women's Power in Eleventh-Century England* (Oxford, 1997).

Stevenson, Jane, 'Johanna Otho (Othonia) and Women's Latin Poetry in Reformed Europe', in Laurie Churchill, Phyllis R. Brown, and Jane E. Jeffrey (eds), *Women Writing Latin from Roman Antiquity to Early Modern Europe*, 3 vols (New York, 2002), 3. 189–216.

Stevenson, Jane, *Women Latin Poets* (Oxford, 2005). [An important study, by a leader in the field.]

Stevenson, Jane, and Davidson, Peter (eds), *Early Modern Women Poets: An Anthology* (Oxford, 2001).

Summit, Jennifer, *Lost Property* (Chicago, 2000).

Tanner, Thomas, *Bibliotheca Britanno-Hibernica, sive de scriptoribus qui in Anglia, Scotia et Hibernia ad saeculi xvii initium floruerunt* (1748).

Timmermans, Linda, *L'Accès des femmes á la culture (1578–1715): Un debat d'idées de Saint François de Sales à la Marquise de Lambert* (Paris, 1993).

Tyler, Margaret, *The Mirrour of Princely Deedes and Vertues*, trans. Diego Ortuñez de Calahorra (1578).

Verducci, Florence, *Ovid's Toyshop of the Heart: Epistulae Heroidum* (Princeton, 1985).

von Klarwill, Victor (ed.), *Queen Elizabeth and Some Foreigners, Being a Series of Hitherto Unpublished Letters from the Archive of the Hapsburg Family* (New York, 1928).

Weston, Elizabeth Jane, *Collected Writings*, ed. and trans. Donald Cheney and Brenda M. Hosington (Toronto, 2000).

Wilson, Katharina M. (ed.), *Women Writers of the Renaissance and Reformation* (Athens, GA, 1987).

Wright, Louis B., *Middle-Class Culture in Elizabethan England* (Chapel Hill, NC, 1935).

1.4.B. Sexuality and Desire

Andreadis, Harriette, *Sappho in Early Modern England: Female Same-Sex Literary Erotics, 1550–1714* (Chicago, 2001). [The definitive treatment.]

Barkan, Leonard, *The Gods Made Flesh: Metamorphosis and the Pursuit of Paganism* (New Haven, 1990). [An important, frequently cited book, ranging widely through various aspects of Renaissance culture.]

Barkan, Leonard, *Transhuming Passion: Ganymede and the Erotics of Humanism* (Stanford, 1991).

Boyd, Barbara Weiden, and Fox, Cora (eds), *Approaches to Teaching the Works of Ovid and the Ovidian Tradition* (New York, 2010).

Bray, Alan, *Homosexuality in Renaissance England* (New York, 1995).

Bromley, James, '"Let it Suffise": Sexual and Narrative Structure in *Hero and Leander*', in Stephen Guy-Bray, Vin Nardizzi, and Will Stockton (eds), *Queer Renaissance Historiography: The Backward Gaze* (Burlington, 2009), 67–84.

Brown, Georgia, *Redefining Elizabethan Literature* (Cambridge, 2004).

Carroll, William, *The Metamorphoses of Shakespearean Comedy* (Princeton, 1985).

Carter, Sarah, *Ovidian Myth and Sexual Deviance in Early Modern English Literature* (New York, 2011). [Shows how Ovidian mythology could be recast into a radical challenge to received ideas about gender and sexuality.]

Durling, Robert, 'Ovid as *Praeceptor Amoris*', *Classical Journal*, 34 (1958), 157–67.

Enterline, Lynn, *The Rhetoric of the Body from Ovid to Shakespeare* (Cambridge, 2006). [A wide-ranging comparative study.]

Foucault, Michel, *The History of Sexuality*, vol. 1: *An Introduction*, trans. Robert Hurley (New York, 1978). [The standard study, enormously influential as background for many later books and articles.]

Gil, Daniel Juan, *Before Intimacy: Asocial Sexuality in Early Modern England* (Minneapolis, 2006).

Goldberg, Jonathan, *The Seeds of Things: Theorizing Sexuality and Materiality in Renaissance Representations* (New York, 2009).

Goldberg, Jonathan, *Sodometries: Renaissance Texts, Modern Sexualities* (New York, 2010). [An important book by a leader in the field.]

Guy-Bray, Stephen, *Homoerotic Space: The Poetics of Loss in Renaissance Literature* (Toronto, 2002).

Habinek, Thomas, 'The Invention of Sexuality in the World-City of Rome', in Thomas Habinek and Alessandro Schiesaro (eds), *The Roman Cultural Revolution* (Cambridge, 1996), 23–43.

Hardie, Philip, *Ovid's Poetics of Illusion* (Cambridge, 2002).

Hyde, Thomas, *The Poetic Theology of Love: Cupid in Renaissance Literature* (Newark, DE, 1986).

Kingsley-Smith, Jane, *Cupid in Early Modern Literature and Culture* (Cambridge, 2010).

Moulton, Ian, *Before Pornography: Erotic Writing in Early Modern England* (Oxford, 2000).

Smith, Bruce, *Homosexual Desire in Shakespeare's England: A Cultural Poetics* (Chicago, 1995).

Stanivukovic, Goran, 'Teaching Ovidian Sexualities in English Renaissance Literature', in Boyd and Fox (2010), 189–96.

Traub, Valerie, *The Renaissance of Lesbianism in Early Modern England* (Cambridge, 2002).

Watkins, John, *The Specter of Dido: Spenser and Virgilian Epic* (New Haven, 1995). [The standard treatment of its subject.]

Wilson-Okamura, David Scott, *Virgil in the Renaissance* (Cambridge, 2010). [A broad overview, aimed at recovering what Renaissance readers commonly believed about Virgil.]

1.5. Translation and Imitation

Altman, Joel B., *The Tudor Play of Mind: Rhetorical Inquiry and the Development of Elizabethan Drama* (Berkeley and Los Angeles, 1978). [A valuable study of the role of rhetoric in Renaissance drama.]

Baker, Howard, 'Ghosts and Guides: Kyd's "Spanish Tragedy" and the Medieval Tragedy', *Modern Philology*, 33 (1935), 27–35.

Baldwin (1944): see 1.2.

Baldwin (1947): see 1.2.

Binns, J. W., 'Latin Translations from Greek in Renaissance England, 1550–1640', *Humanistica Lovaniensia*, 27 (1978), 128–59.

Birrell, T. A., 'John Dryden's Purchases at Two Books Auctions, 1680 and 1682', *English Studies*, 42 (1961), 193–217.

The Bodleian Library in the Seventeenth Century (Oxford, 1951).

Bolgar, R. R. *The Classical Heritage and its Beneficiaries* (Cambridge, 1954). [A classic study, still worth consulting.]

Bottkol, J. McG., 'Dryden's Latin Scholarship', *Modern Philology*, 40 (1942–3), 241–54.

Braden, Gordon, 'An Overview', in Braden, Cummings, and Gillespie (2010), 3–11.

Braden, Gordon, Cummings, Robert, and Gillespie, Stuart (eds), *The Oxford History of Literary Translation in English*, vol. 2: *1550–1660* (Oxford, 2010). [The definitive treatment of its subject.]

Briggs, John Channing, 'Chapman's *Seaven Bookes of the Iliades*: Mirror for Essex', *Studies in English Literature 1500–1900*, 21 (1981), 59–73.

Brooks, Harold F., '"Richard III": Unhistorical Amplifications: The Women's Scenes and Seneca', *Modern Language Review*, 75 (1980), 721–37.

Burke, Peter, 'A Survey of the Popularity of Ancient Historians, 1450–1700', *History and Theory*, 5 (1966), 135–52. [An interesting, data-driven analysis of a difficult subject.]

Costa, C. D. N. (ed.), *Seneca* (Boston, 1974).

Culhane, Peter, 'Livy in Early Jacobean Drama', *Translation and Literature*, 14 (2005), 21–44.

Cummings, Robert, and Gillespie, Stuart, 'Translations from Greek and Latin Classics 1550–1700: A Revised Bibliography', *Translation and Literature*, 18 (2009), 1–42. [An important bibliography of primary sources.]

Ebel, Julia G., 'A Numerical Survey of Elizabethan Translations', *Library*, 22 (1967), 105–27.

Gillespie, Stuart, 'Translation and Canon-Formation', in Stuart Gillespie and David Hopkins (eds), *The Oxford History of Literary Translation in English*, vol. 3: *1660–1790* (Oxford, 2005), 7–20.

Gillespie, Stuart, *English Translation and Classical Reception* (Malden, MA, 2011). [An important book, already widely cited.]

Grafton, A. T., 'The Renaissance', in Richard Jenkyns (ed.), *The Legacy of Rome: A New Appraisal* (Oxford, 1992), 97–123.

Greene, Thomas M., *The Light in Troy: Imitation and Discovery in Renaissance Poetry* (New Haven, 1982). [A classic study, with implications for the classical tradition.]

Hammond, Paul, 'Dryden and Trinity', *Review of English Studies*, 141 (1985), 35–57.

Haynes (2007): see 1.1.

Herrick, Marvin T., *Comic Theory in the Sixteenth Century* (Urbana, IL, 1950). [Discusses the Terentian framework for sixteenth-century comedy.]

Hosington, Brenda M., 'Commerce, Printing, and Patronage', in Braden, Cummings, and Gillespie (2010), 47–57.

Hunter, G. K., 'Seneca and Elizabethan Tragedy', in Costa (1974), 166–204.

Hunter, G. K., 'Seneca and the Elizabethans', in Costa (1974), 17–26.

Jayne and Johnston (1956): see 1.4.A.

Kiessling, Nicolas K., *The Library of Robert Burton* (Oxford, 1988).

Lathrop (1933): see 1.4.A.

MacDonald, Robert H. (ed.), *The Library of Drummond of Hawthornden* (Edinburgh, 1971).

McPherson, David, *Ben Jonson's Library and Marginalia: An Annotated Catalogue* (= *Studies in Philology*, 71/5 (1974), 1–106). [A valuable resource for recovering Jonson's responses to the classical texts he reworked in his own poetry.]

Miola, Robert S., *Shakespeare and Classical Tragedy: The Influence of Seneca* (Oxford, 1992). [The definitive treatment.]

Miola, Robert S., *Shakespeare and Classical Comedy* (Oxford, 1994).

Morini, Massimiliano, *Tudor Translation in Theory and Practice* (Aldershot, 2006).

Mossmann, Judith, '*Henry V* and Plutarch's Alexander', *Shakespeare Quarterly*, 45 (1994), 57–73.

Muir, Kenneth, 'Menenius' Fable', *Notes & Queries*, 198 (1953), 240–2.

Muir, Kenneth, *The Sources of Shakespeare's Plays* (1977).

Nørgaard, Holger, 'Translations of the Classics into English before 1600', *Review of English Studies*, 9 (1958), 164–72.

Robbins, Edwin W., *Dramatic Characterization in Printed Comedies on Terence 1473–1600* (Urbana, IL, 1951).

Smith, Bruce R., 'Toward the Rediscovery of Tragedy: Productions of Seneca's Plays on the English Renaissance Stage', *Renaissance Drama*, 9 (1978), 3–37.

Smith, Bruce R., *Ancient Scripts and Modern Experience on the English Stage, 1500–1700* (Princeton, 1988).

Smith, G. Gregory (ed.), *Elizabethan Critical Essays*, 2 vols (Oxford, 1904).

Trevelyan, G. M., 'Undergraduate Life under the Protectorate', *Cambridge Review*, 22 May 1943.

Tuck, J. P., 'The Use of English in Latin Teaching in the Sixteenth Century', *Durham Research Review*, 1 (1950), 22–30.

Winn, James Anderson, *John Dryden and his World* (New Haven, 1987).

1.6. Christianity and the Classics in English Renaissance Culture

Backus, Irena, *Historical Method and Confessional Identity in the Era of the Reformation (1378–1615)* (Leiden, 2003).

Baldwin (1944): see 1.2.

Barker, William W., 'Erasmus, Desiderius', in A. C. Hamilton et al. (eds), *The Spenser Encyclopedia* (Toronto, 1990), 251–2.

Bejczy, István, *Erasmus and the Middle Ages: The Historical Consciousness of a Christian Humanist* (Leiden, 2001).

Binns (1990): see 1.2.

Boyle, Marjorie O'Rourke, *Erasmus on Language and Method in Theology* (Toronto, 1977).

Boyle, Marjorie O'Rourke, *Christening Pagan Mysteries: Erasmus in Pursuit of Wisdom* (Toronto, 1981).

Bray, Gerald (ed.), *Documents of the English Reformation* (Cambridge, 1994).

Bullard, M. R. A., 'Talking Heads: The Bodleian Frieze, Its Inspiration, Sources, Designer and Significance', *Bodleian Library Record*, 19 (1994), 461–500.

Cave, Terence, *The Cornucopian Text: Problems of Writing in the French Renaissance* (Oxford, 1979). [An important, widely cited book whose observations on Renaissance rhetoric are helpful in an English context as well.]

Chartier, Roger, *The Order of Books: Readers, Authors, and Libraries in Europe between the Fourteenth and Eighteenth Centuries*, trans. Lydia G. Cochrane (Stanford, 1994). [A seminal volume in book history.]

Cheney and de Armas (2002): see 1.3.A.

Clausi, Benedetto, *Ridar voce all'antico padre: L'edizione erasmiana delle lettere di Gerolamo* (Soveria Mannelli, 2000).

Coetzee, J. M., *Elizabeth Costello* (New York, 2003).

Colie, Rosalie L., *The Resources of Kind: Genre-Theory in the Renaissance* (Berkeley and Los Angeles, 1973). [A classic study.]

Cummings, Brian, *The Literary Culture of the Reformation: Grammar and Grace* (Oxford, 2002).

Cummings, Brian, and Simpson, James (eds), *Cultural Reformations: Medieval and Renaissance in Literary History* (Oxford, 2010).

Derrida, Jacques, 'Before the Law', in Jacques Derrida and Derek Attridge, *Acts of Literature* (New York, 1982), 183–220.

Dodds, Gregory D., *Exploiting Erasmus: The Erasmian Legacy and Religious Change in Early Modern England* (Toronto, 2009).

Doherty, Mary Jane, '*Flores Solitudinis*: The "Two Ways" and Vaughan's Patristic Hagiography', *George Herbert Journal*, 7 (1983–84), 25–50.

Eden, Kathy, *Friends Hold All Things in Common: Tradition, Intellectual Property, and the Adages of Erasmus* (New Haven, 2001). [An interesting analysis of commonplaces within the literary culture of the republic of letters.]

Ettenhuber, Katrin, *Donne's Augustine: Renaissance Cultures of Interpretation* (Oxford, 2011).

Ferguson, Arthur B., *Clio Unbound: Perception of the Social and Cultural Past in Renaissance England* (Durham, NC, 1979).

Fowler, Alastair, *Kinds of Literature: An Introduction to the Theory of Genres and Modes* (Cambridge, MA, 1982). [A classic study on the Renaissance understanding of literary genre.]

Fulton, Thomas, *Historical Milton: Manuscript, Print, and Political Culture in Revolutionary England* (Amherst, MA, 2010).

Gillespie, Alexandra, *Print Culture and the Medieval Author: Chaucer, Lydgate, and their Books, 1473–1557* (Oxford, 2006).

Gillespie, Stuart, *Shakespeare's Books: A Dictionary of Shakespeare Sources* (London and New York, 2004). [A valuable updating of Geoffrey Bullough's *Narrative and Dramatic Sources of Shakespeare*.]

Grafton, Anthony, *Worlds Made by Words: Scholarship and Community in the Modern West* (Cambridge, MA, 2009). [A collection of essays by a major scholar in Renaissance studies.]

Grafton and Jardine (1986): see 1.2.

Greene (1982): see 1.5.

Hardie and Moore (2010): see 1.3.A.

Haugard, William P., 'Renaissance Patristic Scholarship and Theology in Sixteenth-Century England', *Sixteenth Century Journal*, 10 (1979), 37–60.

Hayum, Andrée, 'Dürer's Portrait of Erasmus and the *Ars Typographorum*', *Renaissance Quarterly*, 38 (1985), 650–87.

Helgerson, Richard, *The Elizabethan Prodigals* (Berkeley and Los Angeles, 1976).

Helgerson (1983): see 1.3.A.

Helgerson, Richard, *Forms of Nationhood: The Elizabethan Writing of England* (Chicago, 1992).

Jardine, Lisa, *Erasmus, Man of Letters: The Construction of Charisma in Print* (Princeton, 1993). [An important intellectual biography, controversial in parts but always stimulating.]

Kearney, James, *The Incarnate Text: Imagining the Book in Reformation England* (Philadelphia, 2009).

Kernan, Alvin B., *The Imaginary Library: An Essay on Literature and Society* (Princeton, 1982).

King, John N., *English Reformation Literature: The Tudor Origins of the Protestant Tradition* (Princeton, 1982).

Lake, Peter, *Anglicans and Puritans? Presbyterianism and English Conformist Thought from Whitgift to Hooker* (1988).

Lambert, Michael, *The Classics and South African Identities* (Bristol, 2011).

Lerer, Seth, *Chaucer and his Readers: Imagining the Author in Late-Medieval England* (Princeton, 1993).

Lerer, Seth, 'Literary Histories', in Cummings and Simpson (2010), 75–91.

Lewalski, Barbara Kiefer, *The Life of John Milton: A Critical Biography*, rev. edn (Malden, MA, 2003).

Ligota, C. R., and Quantin, J.-L. (eds), *History of Scholarship: A Selection of Papers from the Seminar on the History of Scholarship Held Annually at the Warburg Institute* (Oxford, 2006).

Lossky, Nicholas, *Lancelot Andrewes the Preacher: The Origins of the Mystical Theology of the Church of England*, trans. Andrew Louth (Oxford, 1991).

Lyell, James P. R., 'King James I and the Bodleian Catalogue of 1620', *Bodleian Quarterly Record*, 7 (1923), 261–83.

McCullough, Peter (ed.), *Lancelot Andrewes: Selected Sermons and Lectures* (Oxford, 2005).

Maltby, Judith, 'Suffering and Surviving: The Civil Wars, the Commonwealth and the Formation of "Anglicanism", 1642–60', in Christopher Durston and Judith Maltby (eds), *Religion in Revolutionary England* (Manchester, 2006), 158–80.

Martin, Jessica, *Walton's 'Lives': Conformist Commemorations and the Rise of Biography* (Oxford, 2001).

Masson, André, *The Pictorial Catalogue: Mural Decoration in Libraries*, trans. David Gerard (Oxford, 1981).

Milton, Anthony, *Catholic and Reformed: The Roman and Protestant Churches in English Protestant Thought 1600–1640* (Cambridge, 1995).

Moore, Helen, and Reid, Julian (eds), *Manifold Greatness: The Making of the King James Bible* (Oxford, 2011).

Moss, Ann, *Renaissance Truth and the Latin Language Turn* (Oxford, 2003). [An influential study of language use in the Renaissance.]

Murray, Molly, *The Poetics of Conversion in Early Modern Literature: Verse and Change from Donne to Dryden* (Cambridge, 2009).

Myres, J. N. L., 'Thomas James and the Painted Frieze', *Bodleian Library Record*, 4 (1952–3), 30–51.

Nauman, Jonathan, 'Alternative Saints: Eucherius, Paulinus of Nola, and Henry Vaughan's *Silex Scintillans*', *Seventeenth Century*, 26 (2011), 264–78.

Nelles, Paul, 'The Uses of Orthodoxy and Jacobean Erudition: Thomas James and the Bodleian Library', *History of Universities*, 22 (2007), 21–70.

Norton, David, *A History of the Bible as Literature*, vol. 1: *From Antiquity to 1700* (Cambridge, 1993).

Novarr, David, *The Making of Walton's 'Lives'* (Ithaca, NY, 1958).

Olin, John C. (ed.), *Christian Humanism and the Renaissance: Selected Writings of Erasmus* (New York, 1987).

Ovenden, Richard, 'The Libraries of the Antiquaries (*c.*1580–1640) and the Idea of a National Collection', in Elisabeth Leedham-Green and Teresa Webber (eds), *The Cambridge History of Libraries in Britain and Ireland*, vol. 1: *To 1640* (Cambridge, 2006), 527–61.

Pabel, Hilmar M., *Herculean Labours: Erasmus and the Editing of St Jerome's Letters in the Renaissance* (Leiden, 2008).

Pask, Kevin, *The Emergence of the English Author: Scripting the Life of the Poet in Early Modern England* (Cambridge, 1996).

Philip, Ian, *The Bodleian Library in the Seventeenth and Eighteenth Centuries* (Oxford, 1983).

Post, Jonathan F. S., *Henry Vaughan: The Unfolding Vision* (Princeton, 1982).

Prickett, Stephen, *Modernity and the Reinvention of Tradition: Backing into the Future* (Cambridge, 2009).

Quantin, Jean-Louis, 'Du Chryostome latin au Chrysostome grec: Un histoire européenne (1588–1613)', in Martin Wallraff and Rudolf Brändle (eds), *Chrysostomosbilder in 1600 Jahren: Facetten der Wirkungsgeschichte eines Kirchenvaters* (Berlin, 2008), 267–346.

Quantin, Jean-Louis, *The Church of England and Christian Antiquity: The Construction of a Confessional Identity in the 17th Century* (Oxford, 2009).

Rice, Eugene F., *Saint Jerome in the Renaissance* (Baltimore, 1985). [A wide-ranging overview of a figure whose importance in Renaissance culture is often overlooked.]

Ross, Trevor, *The Making of the English Literary Canon* (Montreal and Kingston, ON, 1998).

Rouse, Mary A., and Rouse, Richard H., *Authentic Witnesses: Approaches to Medieval Texts and Manuscripts* (Notre Dame, IN, 1991). [The basic introduction to the medieval book.]

Rummel, Erika, *Erasmus' Annotations on the New Testament: From Philologist to Theologian* (Toronto, 1986). [An excellent book on Erasmus' scholarship.]

Saenger, Paul, 'Silent Reading: Its Impact on Late Medieval Script and Society', *Viator*, 13 (1982), 367–414. [A widely cited, influential article in scholarship on the history of reading.]

Schaff, Philip, and Wace, Henry (eds), *A Select Library of Nicene and Post-Nicene Fathers of the Christian Church*, 2nd ser., vol. 3 (Edinburgh, 1989).

Schwyzer, Philip, *Literature, Nationalism and Memory in Early Modern England and Wales* (Cambridge, 2004).

Sharpe, Richard, *Titulus: Identifying Medieval Latin Texts: An Evidence-Based Approach* (Turnhout, 2003).

Sharpe, Richard, 'The English Bibliographical Tradition from Kirkestede to Tanner', in Charles Burnett and Nicholas Mann (eds), *Britannia Latina: Latin in the Culture of Great Britain from the Middle Ages to the Twentieth Century* (2005), 86–128.

Simpson, James, *The Oxford English Literary History*, vol. 2: *1350–1547: Reform and Cultural Revolution* (Oxford, 2002).

Summit, Jennifer, *Memory's Library: Medieval Books in Early Modern Britain* (Chicago, 2008).

Tadmor, Naomi, *The Social Universe of the English Bible: Scripture, Society, and Culture in Early Modern England* (Cambridge, 2010).

Teskey, Gordon, 'Literature', in Cummings and Simpson (2010), 379–95.

Vessey, Mark, 'John Donne (1572–1631) in the Company of Augustine: Patristic Culture and Literary Profession in the English Renaissance', *Revue des études augustiniennes*, 39 (1993), 173–201.

Vessey, Mark, 'English Translations of the Latin Fathers, 1517–1611', in Irena Backus (ed.), *The Reception of the Church Fathers in the West: From the Carolingians to the Maurists*, 2 vols (Leiden, 1997), i. 775–835.

Vessey, Mark, 'Erasmus' Lucubrations and the Renaissance Life of Texts', *Erasmus of Rotterdam Society Yearbook*, 24 (2004), 23–51.

Vessey, Mark, '*Vera et aeterna monumenta*: Jerome's Catalogue of Early Christian Writers and the Premises of Erasmian Humanism', in Gunther Frank, Thomas Leinkauf, and Markus Wriedt (eds), *Die Patristik in der Frühen Neuzeit: Die Relektüre der Kirchenväter in den Wissenschaften des 15. bis 18. Jahrhunderts* (Stuttgart, 2006), 351–75.

Vickers, Brian (ed.), *English Renaissance Literary Criticism* (Oxford, 1999).

Visser, Arnoud S. Q., *Reading Augustine in the Reformation: The Flexibility of Intellectual Authority in Europe, 1500–1620* (Oxford, 2011).

von Maltzahn, Nicholas, *Milton's History of Britain: Republican Historiography in the English Revolution* (Oxford, 1991).

Warner, J. Christopher, *Augustinian Epic, Petrarch to Milton* (Ann Arbor, 2005). [A nice study of the influence of Augustine on Renaissance epic.]

Waswo, Richard, *Language and Meaning in the Renaissance* (Princeton, 1987). [A controversial book, arguing that several Renaissance intellectuals adumbrated a social constructionist theory of language.]

Wellek, René, *The Rise of English Literary History* (Chapel Hill, NC, 1941).

Witt (2000): see 1.2.

1.7. The Political Context

Achinstein, Sharon, *Milton and the Revolutionary Reader* (Princeton, 1994).

Alford, Stephen, *The Early Elizabethan Polity: William Cecil and the British Succession Crisis, 1558–1569* (Cambridge, 1998).

Alford, Stephen, 'The Political Creed of William Cecil', in John F. McDiarmid (ed.), *The Monarchical Republic of Early Modern England: Essays in Response to Patrick Collinson* (Aldershot, 2007), 75–90.

Blanchard, Alastair J. R., and Sowerby, Tracey A., 'Thomas Wilson's Demosthenes and the Politics of Tudor Translation', *International Journal of the Classical Tradition*, 12 (2005), 46–80. [An interesting article that suggests how a seemingly innocuous activity like translating a Greek text can have profound political implications.]

Braden, Cummings, and Gillespie (2010): see 1.5.

Cheney, Patrick, *Marlowe's Republican Authorship: Lucan, Liberty, and the Sublime* (Houndmills, 2009). [Predicates Lucan as the source for Marlowe's sustained interest in republicanism.]

Collinson, Patrick, 'The Monarchical Republic of Queen Elizabeth I', *Bulletin of the John Rylands University Library of Manchester*, 69 (1987), 394–424 (repr. in Collinson, *Elizabethan Essays* (London and Rio Grande, 1994), 31–57).

Conley, C. H., *The First English Translators of the Classics* (New Haven, 1927).

Gibson, Jonathan, 'Civil War in 1614: Lucan, Gorges, and Prince Henry', in Stephen Clucas and Rosalind Davies (eds), *The Crisis of 1614 and the Addled Parliament: Literary and Historical Perspectives* (Aldershot, 2003), 161–76.

Guy, John (ed.), *The Reign of Elizabeth I: Court and Culture in the Last Decade* (Cambridge, 1995).

Hadfield, Andrew, *Shakespeare and Republicanism* (Cambridge, 2005).

Jardine, Lisa, and Grafton, Anthony, '"Studied for Action": How Gabriel Harvey Read his Livy', *Past and Present*, 129 (1990), 30–78. [An often-cited article, stressing that, for Harvey, reading the classics was more than just a scholarly activity that was carried on in isolation.]

Jones, William R., 'The Bishops' Ban of 1599 and the Ideology of English Satire', *Literature Compass*, 7 (2010), 332–46.

Kewes, Paulina, 'Henry Savile's Tacitus and the Politics of Roman History in Late Elizabethan England', *Huntington Library Quarterly*, 74 (2011), 515–51.

Lake, Peter, 'The Politics of "Popularity" and the Public Sphere: The "Monarchical Republic" of Elizabeth I Defends Itself', in Peter Lake and Steven Pincus (eds), *The Politics of the Public Sphere in Early Modern England* (Manchester, 2007), 59–94.

Levy, F. J., 'Francis Bacon and the Style of Politics', *English Literary Renaissance*, 16 (1986), 101–22.

Mack (2002a): see 1.2.

Moul (2010): see 1.3.B.

Nelson, Eric, *The Greek Tradition in Republican Thought* (Cambridge, 2004).

Norbrook, David, *Poetry and Politics in the English Renaissance* (1984).

Norbrook, David, *Writing the English Republic: Poetry, Rhetoric and Politics, 1627–1660* (Cambridge, 1999). [An important study linking English Renaissance poetry to its political context.]

Paleit, Edward, 'Lucan in the Renaissance, Pre-1625: An Introduction', *Literature Compass*, 1 (2004), 1–5.

Parry, Graham, *The Golden Age Restor'd: The Culture of the Stuart Court, 1603–1642* (Manchester, 1981).

Patterson, Annabel, *Pastoral and Ideology: Virgil to Valéry* (Berkeley and California, 1988). [An influential early effort to clarify the ideological work that literature has done, with several chapters on Renaissance authors.]

Peltonen, Markku, *Classical Humanism and Republicanism in English Political Thought, 1570–1640* (Cambridge, 1995).

Perry, Curtis, *Literature and Favoritism in Early Modern England* (Cambridge, 2006).

Perry, Curtis, 'The Uneasy Republicanism of Thomas Kyd's *Cornelia*', *Criticism*, 48 (2007), 535–55.

Perry, Curtis, 'British Empire of the Eve of the Armada: Revising *The Misfortunes of Arthur*', *Studies in Philology*, 108 (2011), 508–35.

Pritchard, Alan (ed.), *Abraham Cowley: The Civil War* (Toronto, 1973).

Pugh, Syrithe, *Herrick, Fanshawe and the Politics of Intertextuality: Classical Literature and Seventeenth-Century Royalism* (Farnham, 2010).

Sackville, Thomas, and Norton, Thomas, *Gorboduc or Ferrex and Porrex*, ed. Irby B. Cauthen, Jr (Lincoln, NE, 1970).

Salmon, J. H. M., 'Seneca and Tacitus in Jacobean England', in Linda Levy Peck (ed.), *The Mental World of the Jacobean Court* (Cambridge, 1991), 169–88.

Sanders, Julie, *Ben Jonson's Theatrical Republics* (Basingstoke, 1998).

Schwyzer, Philip, *Literature, Nationalism and Memory in Early Modern England and Wales* (Cambridge, 2004).

Scott, Jonathan, *Commonwealth Principles: Republican Writing of the English Revolution* (Cambridge, 2004).

Sharpe, Kevin, and Lake, Peter (eds), *Culture and Politics in Early Stuart England* (Stanford, 1993).

Skinner, Quentin, *Reason and Rhetoric in the Philosophy of Hobbes* (Cambridge, 1996).

Smith, Nigel, *Literature and Revolution in England, 1640–1660* (New Haven, 1994). [An important study of the connection between literature and politics during a key twenty years.]

Smuts, Malcolm, 'Court-Centred Politics and the Uses of Roman Historians, *c.*1590–1630', in Sharpe and Lake (1993), 21–43.

Stacey, Peter, *Roman Monarchy and the Renaissance Prince* (Cambridge, 2007).

Todd, Margo, *Christian Humanism and the Puritan Social Order* (Cambridge, 1987).

Tuck, Richard, *Philosophy and Government, 1572–1651* (Cambridge, 1993).

Walker, Greg, *The Politics of Performance in Early Renaissance Drama* (Cambridge, 1998).

Winston, Jessica, 'Expanding the Political Nation: *Gorboduc* at the Inns of Court and Succession Revisited', *Early Theatre*, 8 (2005), 11–34.

Winston, Jessica, 'Seneca in Early Elizabethan England', *Renaissance Quarterly*, 59 (2006), 29–58.

Worden, Blair, 'Ben Jonson among the Historians', in Sharpe and Lake (1993), 67–89.

2. FORMS AND GENRES (IN ALPHABETICAL ORDER)

2.1. Comedy

Aristotle, *Poetics*, trans. Gerald F. Else (Ann Arbor, 1966).

Baldwin (1944): see 1.2.

Barish, Jonas A., *The Anti-Theatrical Prejudice* (Berkeley and Los Angeles, 1981).

Barnes, Jonathan (ed.), *The Complete Works of Aristotle* (Princeton, 1984).

Bentley, Christopher, '*The Anatomy of Melancholy* and Richard Whitlock's *Zootomia*', *Renaissance & Modern Studies*, 13 (1969), 88–105.

Bentley, Christopher, 'The Life of Richard Whitlock', *English Language Notes*, 10 (1972), 111–15.

Bentley, G. E., *The Jacobean and Caroline Stage*, 7 vols (Oxford, 1941–68).

Bergson, Henri, 'The Comic in General—The Comic Element in Forms and Movements—Expansive Force of the Comic', in *Laughter: An Essay on the Meaning of the Comic*, trans. Cloudesley Brereton and Fred Rothwell (New York, 1911), 1–66. [A classic treatment of comedy, as background for studies in the Renaissance.]

Boas, Frederick S., *University Drama in the Tudor Age* (Oxford, 1914).

Bruster, Douglas, 'Comedy and Control: Shakespeare and the Plautine *Poeta*', *Comparative Drama*, 24/3 (1990), 217–31.

Civardi, Jean-Marc, 'La Dissertation de Heinsius sur le jugement d'Horace au sujet de Plaute et de Térence', *Litteratures classiques*, 27 (1996), 67–116.

Clarke, M. L., *Classical Education in Britain, 1500–1900* (Cambridge, 1959). [A good overview of precisely what an English student would know about the classics during this period.]

Craik, Katharine A., 'Warner, William (1558/9–1609)', *Oxford Dictionary of National Biography* (Oxford, 2004; online edn, 2006) <http://dx.doi.org/10.1093/ref:odnb/28770> (accessed 20 March 2015).

Cressy, David, *Education in Tudor and Stuart England* (New York, 1975).

Day, Cyrus L., 'Thomas Randolph's Part in the Authorship of *Hey for Honesty*', *PMLA*, 46 (1926), 325–34.

Feingold, Mordechai, 'Rainolds, John (1549–1607)', *Oxford Dictionary of National Biography* (Oxford, 2004; online edn, 2006) <http://www.oxforddnb.com.lib-ezproxy.tamu.edu:2048/view/article/23029> (accessed 20 March 2015).

Firth, C. H., and Rait, R. S. (eds), *Acts and Ordinances of the Interregnum, 1642–1660*, 3 vols (1911).

Foakes, R. A., 'Introduction', in William Shakespeare, *The Comedy of Errors*, ed. Foakes, Arden Two (1962), pp. xi–lv.

Green, Ian, *Humanism and Protestantism in Early Modern English Education* (Farnham, 2009).

Hardin, Richard F., 'Encountering Plautus in the Renaissance: A Humanist Debate on Comedy', *Renaissance Quarterly*, 60/3 (2007), 789–818.

Heller-Roazen, Daniel, *The Inner Touch: Archaeology of a Sensation* (New York, 2007).

Herrick, Martin T., *The Poetics of Aristotle in England* (New Haven, 1930). [To be used with Weinberg (1961).]

Herrick (1950): see 1.5.

Hosley, Richard, 'The Formal Influence of Plautus and Terence', in John Russell Brown (ed.), *Elizabethan Theatre* (1966), 131–45.

Kenney, Arthur F., *Markets of Bawdrie: The Dramatic Criticism of Stephen Gosson* (Salzburg, 1974).

Levine, Joseph M., *Between the Ancients and the Moderns: Baroque Culture in Restoration England* (New Haven, 1999).

Lyne, Raphael, 'Shakespeare, Plautus, and the Discovery of New Comic Space', in Martindale and Taylor (2004), 122–40.

McPherson (1974): see 1.5.

Marshall, C. W., *The Stagecraft and Performance of Roman Comedy* (Cambridge, 2006).

Martindale, Charles, and Martindale, Michelle, *Shakespeare and the Uses of Antiquity* (Cambridge, 1998). [An important study.]

Martindale, Charles, and Taylor, A. B. (eds), *Shakespeare and the Classics* (Cambridge, 2004).

Miola (1994): see 1.5.

Moss, Joseph William, *A Manual of Classical Bibliography*, 2nd edn (1837).

Muir, Kenneth, 'Didacticism in Shakespearean Comedy: Renaissance Theory and Practice', *Review of National Literatures*, 3/2 (1972), 39–53.

Mulryan, John, 'Tradition and the Individual Talent: Shakespeare's and Jonson's Appropriation of the Classics', *Ben Jonson Journal*, 10 (2003), 117–37.

Norland, Howard, 'The Role of Drama in Erasmus' Literary Thought', *Medieval & Renaissance Texts & Studies*, 37 (1985), 549–57.

Parker, Robert, 'Terentian Structure and Sidney's Original *Arcadia*', *English Literary Renaissance*, 2/2 (1972), 61–78.

Riehle, Wolfgang, *Shakespeare, Plautus, and the Humanist Tradition* (Cambridge, 1990).

Riehle, Wolfgang, 'Shakespeare's Reception of Plautus Reconsidered', in Martindale and Taylor (2004), 109–21.

Robertson, Jean, 'General Introduction', in Sir Philip Sidney, *The Countess of Pembroke's Arcadia (The Old Arcadia)*, ed. Robertson (Oxford, 1973).

Segal, Erich, 'Introduction', in Segal (ed.), *Oxford Readings in Menander, Plautus, and Terence* (Oxford, 2000).

Sharrock, Alison, *Reading Roman Comedy: Poetics and Playfulness in Plautus and Terence* (Cambridge, 2009).

Smith, Bruce R., *Ancient Scripts and Modern Experience on the English Stage 1500–1700* (Princeton, 1988).

Smith, Bruce R., *Phenomenal Shakespeare* (Oxford, 2010).

Tanner, Lawrence E., *Westminster School: A History* (1934).

Waith, Eugene M., 'Aristophanes, Plautus, Terence, and the Refinement of English Comedy', *Studies in the Literary Imagination*, 10/1 (1977), 91–108.

Weinberg, Bernard, *A History of Literary Criticism in the Italian Renaissance*, 2 vols (Chicago, 1961). [Focused on Italy, but offering an overview that can be transferred in part to England.]

Williamson, George. 'Richard Whitlock, Learning's Apologist', *Philological Quarterly*, 25 (1936), 254–72.

2.2. Complaint, Epigram, Satire

Bates, Catherine, '"A Mild Admonisher": Sir Thomas Wyatt and Sixteenth-Century Satire', *Huntington Library Quarterly*, 56 (1993), 243–58.

Bramble, J. C., *Persius and the Programmatic Satire* (Cambridge, 1974).

Braund, Susanna Morton, '*Libertas* or *licentia*? Freedom and Criticism in Roman Satire', in Ineke Sluiter and Ralph Rosen (eds), *Free Speech in Classical Antiquity* (Leiden, 2004), 409–28.

Braund, Susanna Morton, 'The Metempsychosis of Horace: The Reception of the Satires and Epistles', in Gregson Davis (ed.), *A Companion to Horace* (Malden, MA, 2010), 367–90.

Braund, Susanna Morton, and Osgood, J. (eds), *A Companion to Persius and Juvenal* (Malden, 2012). [A valuable handbook with several articles on reception.]

Burrow, Colin, 'Horace at Home and Abroad: Wyatt and Sixteenth-Century Horatianism', in Martindale and Hopkins (1993), 27–49.

Corns, Thomas (ed.), *A Cambridge Companion to English Poetry: Donne to Marvell* (Cambridge, 1993).

Craik, Katharine A., 'Spenser's *Complaints* and the New Poets', *Huntington Library Quarterly*, 64 (2001), 63–79.

Dessen, C. S., *The Satires of Persius: 'Iunctura Callidus Acri'*, 2nd edn (1996).

Donaldson, Ian, 'Jonson's Poetry', in Harp and Stewart (2000), 119–39.

Dubrow, Heather, '"No Man Is an Island": Donne's Satires and Satiric Traditions', *Studies in English Literature 1500–1900*, 19 (1979), 71–83.

Dutton, Richard, 'Jonson's Satiric Styles', in Harp and Stewart (2000), 58–70.

Fitzgerald, William, *Martial: The World of the Epigram* (Chicago, 2007).

Forshaw, Cliff, '"Cease Cease to Bawle, Thou Wasp-Stung Satyrist": Writers, Printers and the Bishops' Ban of 1599', *EnterText*, 3/1 (2003), 101–31.

Fowler, Alastair, 'Genre and Tradition', in Corns (1993), 80–100.

Gillespie, Stuart, 'Imperial Satire in the English Renaissance', in Braund and Osgood (2012), 386–408.

Guibbory, Achsah, 'John Donne', in Claude Rawson (ed.), *The Cambridge Companion to English Poets* (Cambridge, 2011), 104–21.

Harp, Richard, and Stewart, Stanley (eds), *The Cambridge Companion to Ben Jonson* (Cambridge, 2000).

Helgerson, Richard, 'Ben Jonson', in Corns (1993), 148–70.

Hester, M. Thomas, *Kinde Pitty and Brave Scorn: John Donne's Satyres* (Durham, NC, 1982).

Hooley, Dan, 'Imperial Satire Reiterated: Late Antiquity through the Twentieth Century', in Braund and Osgood (2012), 337–62.

Lewis, C. S., *English Literature in the Sixteenth Century: Excluding Drama,* Oxford History of English Literature Series (Oxford, 1954). [A classic study, sometimes idiosyncratic but worth consulting.]

McCabe, Richard A., 'Elizabethan Satire and the Bishops' Ban of 1599', *Yearbook of English Studies*, 11 (1981), 188–93.

McRae, Andrew, '"On the Famous Voyage": Ben Jonson and Civic Space', *Early Modern Literary Studies*, Special Issue 3 (1998), 8. 1–31 <http://purl.oclc.org/emls/04-2/mcraonth.htm> (accessed 20 March 2015).

Martindale, Charles, and Hopkins, David (eds), *Horace Made New: Horatian Influences on British Writing from the Renaissance to the Twentieth Century* (Cambridge, 1993). [An important collection of essays.]

Martindale, Joanna, 'The Horace of Ben Jonson and his Heirs', in Charles Martindale and Hopkins (1993), 50–85.

Maus, Katharine Eisaman, *Ben Jonson and the Roman Frame of Mind* (Princeton, 1984). [A good treatment of classical influences on Jonson.]

Moul (2010): see 1.3.B.

Nixon, Paul, *Martial and the Modern Epigram* (New York, 1927).

Peter, John, *Complaint and Satire in Early English Literature* (Oxford, 1956).

Piper, W. B., *The Heroic Couplet* (Cleveland, 1969).

Randolph, M. C., 'The Medical Concept in English Renaissance Satiric Theory', *Studies in Philology,* 38 (1941), 121–57.

Rasmussen, Mark David, '*Complaints* and *Daphnaïda* (1591)', in Richard A. McCabe (ed.), *The Oxford Handbook of Edmund Spenser* (Oxford, 2010), 218–36.

Robinson, Christopher, *Lucian and his Influence in Europe* (Chapel Hill, NC, 1979).

Smet, I. De, 'Giants on the Shoulders of Dwarfs? Considerations on the Value of Renaissance and Early Modern Scholarship for Today's Classicists', in S. Harrison (ed.), *Texts, Ideas, and the Classics: Scholarship, Theory, and Classical Literature* (Oxford, 2001), 252–64.

Spisak, Art L., *Martial: A Social Guide* (2007).

Sullivan, J. P., 'Martial's Life and Works', in J. P. Sullivan and Peter Whigham (eds), *Epigrams of Martial Englished by Divers Hands* (Berkeley and Los Angeles, 1987), 1–21.

Sullivan, J. P., 'Martial and English Poetry', *Classical Antiquity*, 9 (1990), 149–74. [A valuable study.]

Sullivan, J. P., *Martial, The Unexpected Classic: A Literary and Historical Study* (Cambridge, 1991).

Wharton, T. F., *The Critical Fall and Rise of John Marston* (Columbia, SC, 1994).

Young, R. V., 'Jonson and Learning', in Harp and Stewart (2000), 43–57.

2.3. Discursive and Philosophical Prose and Poetry

Allen, Don Cameron, 'The Rehabilitation of Epicurus and his Theory of Pleasure in the Early Renaissance', *Studies in Philology*, 41 (1944), 1–15.

Allen, Don Cameron (ed.), *Essayes by Sir William Cornwallis* (Baltimore, 1946).

Armisen-Marchetti, Mireille, 'Imagination and Meditation in Seneca: The Example of *Praemeditatio*', in Fitch (2008), 102–13.

Barbour, Reid, *English Epicures and Stoics: Ancient Legacies in Early Stuart Culture* (Amherst, MA, 1998). [A valuable influence study, precisely focused.]

Barbour, Reid, *Literature and Religious Culture in Seventeenth-Century England* (Cambridge, 2003).

Barbour, Reid, and Preston, Claire (eds), *Sir Thomas Browne: The World Proposed* (Oxford, 2008).

Blackstone, B. (ed.), *The Ferrar Papers* (Cambridge, 1938).

Braden, Gordon, *Renaissance Tragedy and the Senecan Tradition: Anger's Privilege* (New Haven, 1985). [An important book that explains how a group of plays that are uncongenial to many modern readers could have influenced Renaissance tragedy so significantly.]

Burchell, David, '"A Plain Blunt Man": Hobbes, Science, and Rhetoric Revisited', in Juliet Cummins and David Burchell (eds), *Science, Literature and Rhetoric in Early Modern England* (Aldershot, 2007), 53–74.

Burton, Robert, *The Anatomy of Melancholy*, ed. Thomas C. Faulkner et al., 6 vols (Oxford, 1989–94). [A standard edition of an important example of English Renaissance prose writing.]

Carlson, David R., 'Morley's Translations from Roman Philosophers and English Courtier Literature', in Marie Axton and James P. Carley (eds), intro. David Starkey, *Triumphs of English: Henry Parker, Lord Morley, Translator to the Tudor Court: New Essays in Interpretation* (2000), 131–51.

Chalker, John, *The English Georgic: A Study of the Development of a Form* (Baltimore, 1969). [An important early study.]

Chambers, Douglas, *Planters of the English Landscape: Botany, Trees, and the Georgics* (New Haven, 1993).

Cohen, Ralph, 'Innovation and Variation: Literary Change and Georgic Poetry', in *Literature and History. Papers Read at a Clark Library Seminar March 3, 1973* (Los Angeles, 1973), 3–42.

Costa (1974): see 1.5.

Crawford, Rachel, *Poetry, Enclosure, and the Vernacular English Landscape, 1700–1880* (Cambridge, 2002).

Darley, Gillian, *John Evelyn: Living for Ingenuity* (New Haven, 2006).

De ira ad novatum in L. Annæi Senecæ philosophi opera quæ exstant omnia, ed. Justus Lipsius (Antwerp, 1652). [An influential Renaissance reading of Seneca.]

de la Bédoyère, Guy (ed.), *Particular Friends: The Correspondence of Samuel Pepys and John Evelyn* (Woodbridge, 1997).

Dear, Peter, 'Narratives, Anecdotes, and Experiments: Turning Experiments into Science in the Seventeenth Century' (Philadelphia, 1991a), in Dear (1991b), 135–63.

Dear, Peter (ed.), *The Literary Structure of Scientific Argument* (Philadelphia, 1991b).

Edwards, Karen, 'Engaging with Pygmies: Thomas Browne and John Milton', in Barbour and Preston (2008), 100–17.

Evelyn, John, *Acetaria, or A Discourse of Sallets* (1699).

Felltham, Owen, 'Of the Worship of Admiration', in *Resolves: A Duple Century*, 3rd edn (1628).

Fitch, John G. (ed.), *Oxford Readings in Classical Studies: Seneca* (Oxford, 2008).

Fowler, Alastair, 'The Beginnings of English Georgic', in Lewalski (1986), 105–25: see 1.3.B.

Grimald, Nicholas, *Marcus Tullius Ciceroes Thre Bokes of Duties* (1556), ed. Gerald O'Gorman (Washington, 1990).

Hall, Joseph, *Epistles, Containing Two Decades* (1611).

Hall, Michael, 'The Emergence of the Essay and the Idea of Discovery', in Alexander J. Butrym (ed.), *Essays on the Essay: Redefining the Genre* (Athens, GA, 1989), 73–91.

Harvey, Gabriel, *Gabriel Harvey's Ciceronianus* (1577), intro. Harold S. Wilson, trans. Clarence A. Forbes (Lincoln, NE, 1945). [An edition of a work that was important for the understanding of prose style in the Renaissance.]

Holmes, Frederic, 'Argument and Narrative in Scientific Writing', in Dear (1991b), 164–81.

Ingamells, John, *Later Stuart Portraits, 1685–1714* (2009).

Jones, Howard, *Master Tully: Cicero in Tudor England* (Nieuwkoop, 1998).

Lamberton, Robert, *Plutarch* (New Haven, 2001).

Leslie, Michael, and Raylor, Timothy (eds), *Culture and Cultivation in Early Modern England: Writing and the Land* (Leicester, 1992).

l'Estrange, Roger, *Senecas Morals Abstracted* (1679).

Levine, Joseph M., 'John Evelyn: Between the Ancients and the Moderns', in Therese O'Malley and Joachim Wolschke-Bulmahn (eds), *John Evelyn's Elysium Britannicum and European Gardening* (Washington, 1998), 57–78.

Lewalski (1986): see 1.3.B.

Lievsay, John L. (ed.), *The Seventeenth-Century Resolve: A Historical Anthology of a Literary Form* (Lexington, KY, 1980).

Lipsius, Justus, *Two Bookes of Constancie, Written in Latine by Justus Lipsius, Englished by Sir John Stradling*, ed. and intro. Rudolf Kirk (New Brunswick, NJ, 1939).

Lodge, Thomas (trans.), *The Workes of Lucius Annæus Seneca* (1620).

Low, Anthony, *The Georgic Revolution* (Princeton, 1985). [Shows that the georgic provided a counter to the prevailing courtly or aristocratic ideal in Renaissance England.]

McRae, Andrew, *God Speed the Plough: The Representation of Agrarian England, 1500–1660* (Cambridge, 1996).

Motto, Anna Lydia, *Seneca* (New York, 1973).

Murphy, Kathryn, '"A Likely Story": Plato's *Timaeus* in the *Garden of Cyrus*', in Barbour and Preston (2008), 242–57.

Patterson, Annabel, 'Pastoral versus Georgic: The Politics of Virgilian Quotation', in Lewalski (1986), 241–67: see 1.3.B.

Preston, Claire, 'English Scientific Prose: Bacon, Browne, Boyle', in Andrew Hadfield (ed.), *The Oxford Handbook of English Prose 1500–1640* (Oxford, 2013), 268–91.

Reynolds, L. D., 'The Medieval Tradition of Seneca's Dialogues', *Classical Quarterly*, NS 18 (1968), 355–72.

Ross, G. M., 'Seneca's Philosophical Influence', in Costa (1974), 116–65: see 1.5.

Schmitt, Charles, *Cicero Skepticus: A Study of the Influence of the Academia in the Renaissance* (The Hague, 1972). [An important study that has not received the attention it deserves.]

Schuler, Robert M., 'Francis Bacon and Scientific Poetry', *Transactions of the American Philosophical Society*, NS 82/2 (1992), 1–65.

Schurink, Fred, 'Print, Patronage, and Occasion: Translations of Plutarch's *Moralia* in Tudor England', *Yearbook of English Studies*, 38 (2008), 86–101.

Shapin, Steven, and Schaffer, Simon, *Leviathan and the Air-Pump: Hobbes, Boyle, and the Experimental Life* (Princeton, 1985).

Sharland, E. Cruwys (ed.), *The Story Books of Little Gidding* (1899).

Skinner, Quentin, *Visions of Politics*, vol. 2: *Renaissance Virtues*, 3 vols (Cambridge 2002).

Small, Carola, and Small, Alastair, 'John Evelyn and the Garden of Epicurus', *Journal of the Warburg and Courtauld Institutes*, 60 (1997), 194–214.

Stubbs, Mayling, 'John Beale, Philosophical Gardener of Herefordshire', *Annals of Science*, 394 (1982), 463–89.

Williams, A. M. (ed.), *Conversations at Little Gidding* (Cambridge, 1970).

Williamson, George, *The Senecan Amble: A Study in the Prose Form from Bacon to Collier* (Chicago, 1932). [A classic treatment of Senecan style in the Renaissance.]

Wilson, K. J., *Incomplete Fictions: The Formation of English Renaissance Dialogue* (Washington, 1985).

Wright, J. R. G., 'Form and Content in the Moral Essays', in Costa (1974), 39–65: see 1.5.

2.4. Epic

Aguzzi, Danilo L., *Allegory in the Heroic Poetry of the Renaissance* (Ann Arbor, 1971).

Backhaus, B., *Das Supplementum Lucani von Thomas May: Einleitung, Edition, Übersetzung, Kommentar* (Trier, 2005). [An edition and analysis of May's supplement to Lucan, from which much can be learned about how the epic was understood in the Renaissance.]

Baldwin (1944): see 1.2.

Bate (1993): see 1.3.B.

Binns (1990): see 1.2.

Birley, R., *Sunk without Trace: Some Forgotten Masterpieces Reconsidered* (1962).

Borris, Kenneth, *Allegory and Epic in English Renaissance Literature: Heroic Form in Sidney, Spenser, and Milton* (Cambridge, 2009).

Braden, Gordon, 'Epic Kinds', in Braden, Cummings, and Gillespie (2010), 167–93.

Braden, Cummings, and Gillespie (2010): see 1.5.

Bruère, R. T., 'The Latin and English Versions of Thomas May's *Supplementum Lucani*', *Classical Philology*, 44 (1949), 145–63.

Burrow, Colin, 'Original Fictions: Metamorphoses in *The Faerie Queene*', in Martindale (1988), 99–119.

Burrow, Colin, 'Virgil in English Translation', in Martindale (1997b), 21–37: see 1.3.A.

Burrow, Colin, '"Full of the Maker's Guile": Ovid on Imitating and on the Imitation of Ovid', in P. Hardie, A. Barchiesi, and S. Hinds (eds), *Ovidian Transformations* (Cambridge, 1999), 271–87.

Cain (1978): see 1.3.B.

Cheney (1993): see 1.3.A.

Cheney (2009): see 1.7.

Cliff, C. C., 'Thomas May. The Changing Mind of Lucan's Translator', unpublished Ph.D. thesis, Yale, 1999.

Cummings, Robert, and Martindale, Charles, 'Jonson's Virgil: Surrey and Phaer', *Translation & Literature*, 16 (2007), 66–75.

Demetriou, Tania, '"Essentially Circe": Spenser, Homer, and the Homeric Tradition', *Translation and Literature*, 15 (2006), 151–76.

Dixon, W. MacNeile, *English Epic and Heroic Poetry* (1912).

Erskine-Hill, Howard, *The Augustan Idea in English Literature* (1983). [A classic study.]

Esolen, Anthony, 'Spenserian Chaos: Lucretius in *The Faerie Queene*', *Spenser Studies*, 11 (1994), 31–51.

Ewell, Barbara C., 'Drayton's *Poly-Olbion*: England's Body Immortalized', *Studies in Philology*, 75 (1978), 297–315.

Fichter, Andrew, *Poets Historical: Dynastic Epic in the Renaissance* (New Haven, 1982).

Ford, Philip, *De Troie à Ithaque: Réception des épopées homériques à la Renaissance* (Geneva, 2007). [An important study of the reception of Homer in the Renaissance.]

Garrison, James D., *Dryden and the Tradition of Panegyric* (Berkeley and Los Angeles, 1975), index *s.v.* 'Claudian'.

Gentili, V., 'Spenser', in F. della Corte (ed.), *Enciclopedia Virgiliana*, 5 vols (Rome, 1988), 2. 983–90.

Gildenhard, Ingo, 'Virgil vs Ennius, or: The Undoing of the Annalist', in William Fitzgerald and Emily Gowers (eds), *Ennius Perennis: The Annals and Beyond* (Cambridge, 2007), 73–102.

Gillespie, Stuart (2004): see 1.6.

Gillespie, Stuart, 'Literary Afterlives: Metempsychosis from Ennius to Jorge Luis Borges', in Hardie and Moore (2010), 209–25: see 1.3.A.

Grafton, Anthony, 'Renaissance Readers of Homer's Ancient Readers', in R. Lamberton and J. J. Keaney (eds), *Homer's Ancient Readers: The Hermeneutics of Greek Epic's Earliest Exegetes* (Princeton, 1992), 149–74.

Green, Mandy, *Milton's Ovidian Eve* (Farnham and Burlington, VT, 2009).

Haan, Estelle, 'Milton's *In Quintum Novembris* and the Anglo-Latin Gunpowder Epic', *Humanistica Lovaniensia*, 41 (1992), 221–95; 42 (1993), 368–402.

Hadfield (2005): see 1.7.

Hamilton, A. C. (ed.), *The Spenser Encyclopedia* (Toronto, 1990).

Hammond, Mason, '*Concilia Deorum* from Homer through Milton', *Studies in Philology*, 30 (1933), 1–16.

Hardie (1993): see 1.3.A.

Hardie, Philip, 'Spenser's Vergil: *The Faerie Queene* and the *Aeneid*', in Joseph Farrell and Michael C. J. Putnam (eds), *A Companion to Vergil's Aeneid and its Tradition* (Malden, MA and Oxford, 2010), 173–85.

Hardie (2011): see 1.3.B.

Hardie, Philip, 'Lucan in the English Renaissance', in Paolo Asso (ed.), *Brill's Companion to Lucan* (Leiden, 2011b), 491–506.

Hardie, Philip, *The Last Trojan Hero. A Cultural History of Virgil's Aeneid* (2014).

Hardie and Moore (2010): see 1.3.A.

Hardison (1962): see 1.3.B.

Helgerson, Richard, *Forms of Nationhood: The Elizabethan Writing of England* (Chicago, 1992).

Hinman, R., *Abraham Cowley's World of Order* (Cambridge, MA, 1960).

Holaday, A., 'Thomas Heywood's *Troia Britannica* and the Ages', *Journal of English and Germanic Philology*, 45 (1946), 430–9.

Holahan, Michael, '*Iamque opus exegi*: Ovid's Changes and Spenser's Brief Epic of Mutability', *English Literary Renaissance*, 6 (1976), 244–70.

Hughes, M. Y., *Virgil and Spenser* (New York, 1929). [An older work, to be used with Watkins (1995), in 1.4.B.]

Ingledew, J. E., 'Chapman's Use of Lucan in *Caesar and Pompey*', *Review of English Studies*, 13 (1962), 283–8.

Kallendorf, Craig, *In Praise of Aeneas: Virgil and Epideictic Rhetoric in the Early Italian Renaissance* (Hanover, NH, 1989). [Builds on Hardison (1962), in 1.3.B.]

Kennedy, Ross A., 'The *Franciad* of Joshua Barnes: A Previously Unstudied Anglo-Latin Epic', unpublished Ph.D. thesis, Cambridge, 2005.

Leidig, H. D., *Das Historiengedicht in der englischen Literaturtheorie: Die Rezeption von Lucan's Pharsalia von der Renaissance bis zum Ausgang der achtzehnten Jahrhunderts* (Frankfurt, 1975). [A somewhat neglected study, to supplement Quint (1993).]

Levin, Harry, *The Overreacher: A Study of Christopher Marlowe* (Cambridge, MA, 1952).

Lewalski, Barbara K. (1966): see 1.3.A.

Lewalski, Barbara K., *Paradise Lost and the Rhetoric of Literary Forms* (Princeton, 1985).

Logan, G. M., 'Lucan in England: The Influence of the "Pharsalia" on English Letters from the Beginnings through the Sixteenth Century', unpublished Ph.D. thesis, Harvard, 1967.

Lord, George deForest, *Homeric Renaissance: The Odyssey of George Chapman* (1956).

Lyne, Raphael, *Ovid's Changing Worlds: English Metamorphoses 1567–1632* (Cambridge, 2001). [A valuable study of a poem often considered a sort of epic in Renaissance England.]

Lyne, Raphael, 'Ovid in English Translation', in Hardie (2002b), 249–63: see 1.3.A.

Maclean, Gerald M., *Time's Witness: Historical Representation in English Poetry, 1603–1660* (Madison, WI, 1990).

Mahon, J. W., 'A Study of William Warner's Albion's England', unpublished Ph.D. thesis, Columbia, 1980.

Martindale, Charles, *John Milton and the Transformation of Ancient Epic* (Totowa, NJ, 1986). [Studies how Milton used each classical epic, with detailed analysis of verbal influence.]

Martindale, Charles (ed.), *Ovid Renewed: Ovidian Influences on Literature and Art from the Middle Ages to the Twentieth Century* (Cambridge, 1988).

Martindale, Charles, 'Introduction', in *Lucan, The Civil War, Translated as Lucan's Pharsalia by Nicholas Rowe*, ed. Sarah A. Brown and Charles Martindale (1998), pp. i–lxxix.

Moore, O. H., 'The Infernal Council', *Modern Philology*, 16 (1918), 169–93.

Norbrook (1999): see 1.7.

Paleit (2004): see 1.7.

Peacock, J., 2006, 'The Image of Charles I as a Roman Emperor', in I. Atherton and J. Sanders (eds), *The 1630s: Interdisciplinary Essays on Culture and Politics in the Caroline Eras* (Manchester, 2006), 50–73.

Perry, Curtis, 'The Uneasy Republicanism of Thomas Kyd's *Cornelia*', *Criticism*, 48 (2006), 535–55.

Power, Henry, '"Teares Breake Off My Verse": The Virgilian Incompleteness of Abraham Cowley's *The Civil War*', *Translation and Literature*, 16/2 (2007), 141–59.

Proudfoot, Leslie, *Dryden's 'Aeneid' and its Seventeenth Century Predecessors* (Manchester, 1960). [An older study of Dryden's *Aeneid* in relation to other seventeenth-century translations.]

Pugh, Syrithe, *Spenser and Ovid* (Aldershot, 2005).

Quint, David, 'Milton, Fletcher and the Gunpowder Plot', *Journal of the Warburg and Courtauld Institutes*, 54 (1991), 261–8.

Quint, David, *Epic and Empire: Politics and Generic Form from Virgil to Milton* (Princeton, 1993). [An influential book, arguing that Lucan was appropriated by republicans and the vanquished, in opposition to the *Aeneid*, the poem of the imperialist victors.]

Quint, David, 'The Anatomy of Epic in Book 2 of *The Faerie Queene*', *Spenser Review*, 34 (2003), 28–45.

Sanford, E. M., 'The Manuscripts of Lucan: *Accessus* and *Marginalia*', *Speculum*, 9 (1934), 278–95.

Sowerby, Robin, *The Augustan Art of Poetry: Augustan Translation of the Classics* (Oxford, 2006). [A valuable study, extending past the end of the Renaissance.]

Stapleton, M. L., *Spenser's Ovidian Poetics* (Newark, DE, 2009).

Swedenberg, H. T., *The Theory of the Epic in England 1650–1800* (New York, 1944).

Treip, Mindele A., *Allegorical Poetics and the Epic: The Renaissance Tradition to Paradise Lost* (Lexington, KY, 1994).

Vickers, Brian, 'Epideictic and Epic in the Renaissance', *New Literary History*, 14 (1982/3), 497–537. [An often-cited article.]

Watkins (1995): see 1.4.B.

Whitaker, V. K., 'Du Bartas' Use of Lucretius', *Studies in Philology*, 33 (1936), 134–46.

Wilson-Okamura (2010): see 1.4.B.

Yates (1975): see 1.3.B.

2.5. Epistle

Baldwin (1944): see 1.2.

Benner, A., and F. Fobes (eds), *Alciphron, Aelian and Philostratus: The Letters* (Cambridge, MA, 1949).

Brown (2004): see 1.4.B.

Brown, Georgia, *Redefining Elizabethan Literature* (Cambridge, 2004).

Burrow, Colin, 'Wyatt and Sixteenth-Century Horatianism', in Martindale and Hopkins (1993), 27–49: see 2.2.

Carey, John, 'John Donne's Newsless Letters', *Essay and Studies*, 34 (1981), 46–65.

Clough, Cecil, 'The Cult of Antiquity: Letters and Letter Collections', in C. Clough (ed.), *Cultural Aspects of the Italian Renaissance: Essays in Honour of Paul Kristeller* (Manchester, 1976), 33–87. [A key study of an important phenomenon in Renaissance cultural life.]

Day, Robert, *Told in Letters: Epistolary Fiction before Richardson* (Ann Arbor, 1966).

Eden, Kathy, 'Petrarchan Hermeneutics and the Rediscovery of Intimacy', in T. Barolini and H. Wayne Storey (eds), *Petrarch and the Textual Origins of Interpretation* (Leiden, 2007), 231–44.

Eden, Kathy, 'The Renaissance Rediscovery of Intimacy', unpublished essay.

Ewell, Barbara, 'Unity and the Transformation of Drayton's Poetics in *England's Heroicall Epistles*: From Mirrored Ideals to "The Chaos in the Mind" ', *Modern Language Quarterly*, 44 (1983), 231–50.

Grund, Gary, 'From Formulary to Fiction: The Epistle and the English Anti-Ciceronian Movement', *Texas Studies in Language and Literature*, 17/2 (1975), 379–95.

Guillen, Claudio, 'Notes toward the Study of the Renaissance Letter', in Lewalski (1986), 70–110: see 1.3.B.

Henderson, Judith Rice, 'Erasmus on the Art of Letter-Writing', in Murphy (1983), 331–55.

Hutton, Sarah (ed.), *The Conway Letters: Correspondence of Anne, Viscountess Conway, Henry More and their Friends* (Oxford, 1992).

Jacobs, Joseph, *Epistolae Ho-Elianae, The Familiar Letters of James Howell* (1892).

Kerrigan, John, *Motives of Woe: Shakespeare and 'Female Complaint': A Critical Anthology* (Oxford, 1991).

McCabe, Richard, *Joseph Hall: A Study in Satire and Meditation* (Oxford, 1982), 189–96.

Moul, Victoria, 'Donne's Horatian Means: Horatian Hexameter Verse in Donne's Satires and Verse Epistles', *John Donne Journal*, 27 (2008), 21–48.

Moul, Victoria (2010): see 1.3.B.

Mueller, Wolfgang, 'Der Brief als Spiegel der Seele', *Antike und Abendland*, 26 (1980), 138–57.

Murphy, James J. (ed.), *Renaissance Eloquence: Studies in the Theory and Practice of Renaissance Rhetoric* (Berkeley and Los Angeles, 1983). [An important collection of essays with much information that includes letter writing in the Renaissance.]

Patterson, Annabel, *Censorship and Interpretation: The Conditions of Writing and Reading in Early Modern England* (Madison, 1984). [An important study, with ramifications in a surprising number of areas.]

Raine, James (ed.), *The Correspondence of Dr Matthew Hutton* (1843).

Renaissance Studies, 22/3 (2008). [Special topics issue titled *The Rhetoric of Complaint: Ovid's Heroides in the Renaissance and Restoration*; see esp. Danielle Clark, 'Ovid's *Heroides*, Drayton and the Articulation of the Feminine in the English Renaissance', 385–400; Stephen Guy-Bray, 'Rosamond's Complaint: Daniel, Ovid, and the Purpose of Poetry', 338–50; and Alison Thorne, '"Large Complaints in Little Papers": Negotiating Ovidian Genealogies of Complaint in Drayton's *Englands Heroicall Epistles*', 368–84.]

Reynolds, L., and Wilson, N., *Scribes and Scholars: A Guide to the Transmission of Greek and Latin Literature*, 3rd edn (Oxford, 1990). [The standard treatment, engaging and accessible.]

Robinson, Hastings, *Original Letters Relative to the English Reformation* (Cambridge, 1846).

Schneider, Gary, *The Culture of Epistolarity: Vernacular Letters and Letter Writing in Early Modern England, 1500–1700* (Newark, DE, 2005).

Trapp, Michael, *Greek and Latin Letters: An Anthology with Translations* (Cambridge, 2003).

Trimpi, Wesley, *Ben Jonson's Poems: A Study of the Plain Style* (Stanford, 1962). [A classic study, helpful in understanding stylistic currents in the later Renaissance.]

Williamson, George, 'Senecan Style in the Seventeenth Century', in Stanley Fish (ed.), *Seventeenth Century Prose: Modern Essays in Criticism* (Oxford 1971), 112–46.

2.6. Epyllion

Altman (1978): see 1.5.

Baldwin (1944): see 1.2.

Belsey, Catherine, 'Love as Trompe-L'oeil: Taxonomies of Desire in *Venus and Adonis*', *Shakespeare Quarterly*, 46 (1995), 257–76.

Bromley, James, '"Let It Suffise": Sexual Acts and Narrative Structure in *Hero and Leander*', in Stephen Guy-Bray and Stephen Nardizzi (eds), *Queer Renaissance Historiography: Backward Gaze* (Farnham, 2009), 67–84.

Brown (2004): see 1.4.B.

Burrow, Colin, 'Shakespeare and Humanistic Culture', in Martindale and Taylor (2004), 9–27: see 2.1.

Donno, Elizabeth Story (ed.), *Elizabethan Minor Epics* (New York, 1963).

Ellis, James, *Sexuality and Citizenship: Metamorphosis in English Erotic Verse* (Toronto, 2004).

Enterline, Lynn (2005): see 1.4.B.

Enterline, Lynn, *Shakespeare's Schoolroom: Rhetoric, Discipline, Emotion* (Philadelphia, 2012). [An important study of Renaissance education that extends outward to other cultural practices.]

Haber, Judith, *Desire and Dramatic Form in Early Modern England* (Cambridge, 2009).

Halpern, Richard, *The Poetics of Primitive Accumulation: English Renaissance Culture and the Genealogy of Capital* (Ithaca, NY, 1991).

Halpern, Richard, '"Pining their Maws": Female Readers and the Erotic Ontology of the Text in Shakespeare's *Venus and Adonis*', in Philip C. Kolin (ed.), *Shakespeare's Venus and Adonis: Critical Essays* (New York, 1997), 377–88.

Hulse, Clark, *Metamorphic Verse: The Elizabethan Minor Epic* (Princeton, 1981). [The classic study, to be supplemented now by Weaver (2012).]

Jones, Emrys, *The Origins of Shakespeare* (Oxford, 1977).

Kerrigan, John (ed.), *The Motives of Woe: Shakespeare and 'Female Complaint': A Critical Anthology* (Oxford, 1991).

Nelson, William, *A Fifteenth Century Schoolbook* (Oxford, 1956).

Riggs, David, *The World of Christopher Marlowe* (2004).

Sullivan, Paul, 'Playing the Lord: Tudor *Vulgaria* and the Rehearsal of Ambition', *English Literary History*, 75 (2008), 179–96.

Wallace, Andrew, *Virgil's Schoolboys: The Poetics of Pedagogy in Renaissance England* (Oxford, 2011). [Anchors Virgilian interpretation into schoolroom practices.]

Weaver, William, '"O teach me how to make mine own excuse": Forensic Performance in *Lucrece*', *Shakespeare Quarterly*, 59 (2008), 421–49.

Weaver, William, *Untutored Lines: The Making of the English Epyllion* (Edinburgh, 2012). [An important study, interpreting the English epyllion in the light of Renaissance educational practices.]

2.7. Historiography and Biography

Ayres, Philip J., 'The Nature of Jonson's Roman History', *English Literary Renaissance*, 16 (1986), 166–81.

Barton, Anne, 'Livy, Machiavelli, and Shakespeare's *Coriolanus*', in Catherine M. S. Alexander (ed.), *Shakespeare and Politics* (Cambridge, 2004), 67–90.

Cheney (2009): see 1.7.

Culhane (2005): see 1.5.

Honigmann, E. A. J., 'Shakespeare's Plutarch', *Shakespeare Quarterly*, 10 (1959), 25–33.

Jardine and Grafton (1990): see 1.7.

Kewes, Paulina, 'Roman History and the Early Stuart Drama: Thomas Heywood's *The Rape of Lucrece*', *English Literary Renaissance*, 32 (2002), 239–67.

Levy, F. J., 'Hayward, Daniel, and the Beginnings of Politic History in England', *Huntington Library Quarterly*, 50 (1987), 1–34.

Momigliano, Arnaldo, 'Ancient History and the Antiquarian', in *Studies in Historiography* (New York, 1966), 1–39. [A broad study that provides background for the English Renaissance.]

Norbrook (1984); see 1.7.

Norbrook (1999): see 1.7.

Orgel, Stephen, 'The Renaissance Artist as Plagiarist', *English Literary History*, 48 (1981), 476–95.

Osmond, Patricia J., 'Edmund Bolton's Vindication of Tiberius Caesar: A "Lost" Manuscript Comes to Light', *International Journal of the Classical Tradition*, 11 (2005), 329–43.

Pigman, G. W., III, 'Versions of Imitation in the Renaissance', *Renaissance Quarterly*, 33 (1980), 1–32. [An often-cited article, on a key topic.]

Salmon (1991): see 1.7.
Salmon, J. H., 'Precept, Example, and Truth: Degory Wheare and the *Ars historica*', in Donald R. Kelley and David Harris Sacks (eds), *The Historical Imagination in Early Modern Britain: History, Rhetoric, and Fiction, 1500–1800* (Cambridge, 1997), 11–36.
Shuger, Debora, 'Castigating Livy: The Rape of Lucretia and *The Old Arcadia*', *Renaissance Quarterly*, 51 (1998), 526–48. [A stimulating influence study.]
Skinner, Quentin, 'Classical Liberty, Renaissance Translation and the English Civil War', in *Visions of Politics*, vol. 2: *Renaissance Virtues* (Cambridge, 2002), 308–43.
van Es, Bart, *Spenser's Forms of History* (Oxford, 2002).
Whitfield, J. H., 'Livy > Tacitus', in Bolgar (1976), 281–94: see 1.2.
Wright, Alice P., 'A Study of Ben Jonson's *Catiline* with Special Reference to its Sources', unpublished Ph.D. thesis, Yale, 1907.

2.8. Lyric and Other Shorter Poetry

Abrams, M. H., 'Structure and Style in the Greater Romantic Lyric', in Frederick W. Hilles and Harold Bloom (eds), *From Sensibility to Romanticism: Essays Presented to Frederick A. Pottle* (New York, 1965), 527–60.
Bloomfield, Morton W., 'The Elegy and the Elegiac Mode: Praise and Alienation', in Lewalski (1986), 147–57: see 1.3.B.
Braden, Gordon, 'Herrick's Classical Quotations', in Roger B. Rollin and J. Max Patrick (eds), *'Trust to Good Verses': Herrick Tercentenary Essays* (Pittsburgh, 1978a), 127–47.
Braden, Gordon, 'Robert Herrick and Classical Lyric Poetry' (New Haven, 1978b), in Braden (1978c), 154–254. [Examines Herrick's use of classical authors, both as sources of short quotations and as models for a self-contained poetic world.]
Braden, Gordon, *The Classics and English Renaissance Poetry: Three Case Studies* (New Haven, 1978c).
Campion, Thomas, *Works*, ed. Walter R. Davis (New York, 1970).
Donne, John, *Poems*, ed. Herbert J. C. Grierson, 2 vols (Oxford, 1912).
Dubrow, Heather, *A Happier Eden: The Politics of Marriage in the Stuart Epithalamium* (Ithaca, NY, 1990). [An important study of the epithalamium in general.]
Fogle, Stephen F., and Fry, Paul H., 'Ode', in Roland Greene and Stephen Cushman (eds), *Princeton Encyclopedia of Poetry and Poetics* (Princeton, 2012), 855–7.
Fry, Paul H., *The Poet's Calling in the English Ode* (New Haven, 1980).
Greene, Thomas M., 'Spenser and the Epithalamic Convention', *Comparative Literature*, 9 (1957), 215–28. [A classic article.]
Greene, Thomas M., 'The Balance of Power in Marvell's "Horatian Ode"', *English Literary History*, 60 (1993), 379–96.
Hardie, Philip, *Virgil*, New Surveys in the Classics 28 (Oxford, 1998). [An excellent introduction to an author who exerted significant influence on the shorter poem in the Renaissance.]
Hardie, Philip (ed.), *Virgil: Critical Assessments of Classical Authors*, 4 vols (1999).

Jonson, Ben, *Ben Jonson*, ed. C. H. Herford, and Percy and Evelyn Simpson, 11 vols (Oxford, 1925–52).

Lezra, Jacques, *Unspeakable Subjects: The Genealogy of the Event in Early Modern Europe* (Stanford, 1997).

Luck, Georg, *The Latin Love Elegy*, 2nd edn (1969).

Marvell, Andrew, *Poems*, ed. Nigel Smith (2003).

Montrose, Louis A., 'Spenser's Domestic Domain: Poetry, Property, and the Early Modern Subject', in Margreta de Grazia, Maureen Quilligan, and Peter Stallybrass (eds), *Subject and Object in Renaissance Culture* (Cambridge, 1996). [An early effort to open up the study of Renaissance lyric to newer critical methods.]

Philips, Katherine, *Collected Works*, ed. Patrick Thomas, 2 vols (Stump Cross, 1990).

Puttenham, George, *The Art of English Poesy*, ed. Frank Whigham and Wayne A. Rebhorn (Ithaca, NY, 2007). [A new edition of an important treatise in Renaissance poetics.]

Ramazani, Jahan, *Poetry of Mourning: The Modern Elegy from Hardy to Heaney* (Chicago, 1994).

Sacks, Peter M., *The English Elegy: Studies in the Genre from Spenser to Yeats* (Baltimore, 1985).

Sidney, Sir Philip, *The Countess of Pembroke's Arcadia (Old Arcadia)*, ed. Katherine Duncan-Jones (Oxford, 1985).

Sidney, Sir Philip, *An Apology for Poetry or the Defence of Poesy*, ed. Geoffrey Shepherd and R. W. Maslen, 3rd edn (Manchester, 2002).

Skelton, John, *Complete English Poems*, ed. John Scattergood (New Haven, 1983).

Spenser, Edmund, *Works: A Variorum Edition*, ed. Edwin Greenlaw et al., 10 vols (Baltimore, 1932–49). [Contains an enormous amount of information that is still useful even after more than a half century.]

Veyne, Paul, *Roman Erotic Elegy: Love, Poetry, and the West*, trans. David Pellauer (Chicago, 1988).

Richard Will[e]s, *De Re Poetica*, ed. and trans. A. D. S. Fowler (Oxford, 1953).

2.9. Pastoral and Georgic

Bradner, Leicester, 'The Latin Translations of Spenser's *Shepheardes Calender*', *Modern Philology*, 33 (1935), 21–6.

Bradner, Leicester, *Musae Anglicanae* (New York, 1940).

Chaudhuri, Sukanta, *Renaissance Pastoral and its English Developments* (Oxford, 1989).

Cheney (1993): see 1.3.A.

Cooper, Helen, *Pastoral: Mediaeval into Renaissance* (Ipswich, 1977).

Empson, William, *Some Versions of Pastoral* (1935; repr. Harmondsworth, 1966). [A classic study, to which many modern treatments still respond.]

Fowler, Alastair, 'Didactic Kinds', in Braden, Cummings, and Gillespie (2010), 194–200: see 1.5.

Hibbard, G. R., 'The Country House Poem of the Seventeenth Century', *Journal of the Warburg and Courtauld Institutes*, 19 (1956), 159–74.

Laing, Rosemary, 'The Disintegration of Pastoral: Studies in Seventeenth-Century Theory and Practice', unpublished Ph.D. thesis, Oxford, 1982.

Low (1985): see 2.3.

McClung, William A., *The Country House in English Renaissance Poetry* (Berkeley and Los Angeles, 1977). [An interesting study of an important subgenre.]

Patterson (1988): see 1.7.

Pigman, G. W., III, 'Pastoral and Idyll', in Braden, Cummings, and Gillespie (2010), 248–61: see 1.5.

Tuckett, Tabitha, 'Character, Moral Evaluation and Action in Virgilian and Elizabethan Pastoral', unpublished Ph.D. thesis, Oxford, 1996.

Tudeau-Clayton, Margaret, *Jonson, Shakespeare and Early Modern Virgil* (Cambridge, 1998).

Tylus, Jane, 'Spenser, Virgil, and the Politics of Poetic Labor', *English Literary History*, 55 (1988), 53–77.

Walsham, Alexandra, *The Reformation of the Landscape: Religion, Identity, and Memory in Early Modern Britain and Ireland* (Oxford, 2011).

Watson, Robert N., *Back to Nature: The Green and the Real in the Late Renaissance* (Philadelphia, 2006).

Watterson, William C., 'Nation and History: The Emergence of the English Pastoral Elegy', in Karen Weisman (ed.), *The Oxford Handbook of the Elegy* (Oxford, 2010), 135–52.

Williams, Raymond, *The Country and the City* (1973). [An important book that offers a political reading of pastoral.]

2.10. Prose Romance

Barish, Jonas, 'The Prose Style of John Lyly', *Journal of English Literary History*, 23 (1956), 14–35. [A classic analysis of one of the most flamboyant prose styles in English literary history.]

Bate (1993): see 1.3.B.

Bentley, Gerald Eades, *The Jacobean and Caroline Stage*, 7 vols (Oxford, 1941–68).

Burrow, Colin, *Epic Romance: Homer to Milton* (Oxford, 1993). [An often-cited comparative study.]

Carey, John, 'Sixteenth- and Seventeenth-Century Prose', in Christopher Ricks (ed.), *English Poetry and Prose, 1540–1674* (1970), 339–431.

Carver, Robert H. F., *The Protean Ass: The Metamorphoses of Apuleius from Antiquity to the Renaissance* (Oxford, 2007).

Cazauran, Nicole, and Bideaux, Michel (eds), *Les Amadis en France au XVIe siècle* (Paris, 2000).

Chalifour, Clark L., 'Sir Philip Sidney's *Old Arcadia* as Terentian Comedy', *Studies in English Literature 1500–1900*, 16 (1976), 51–63.

Cooper (1977): see 2.9.

Davis, Walter, *Idea and Act in Elizabethan Fiction* (Princeton, 1969).

Doody, Margaret Anne, *The True Story of the Novel* (New Brunswick, NJ, 1996).

Enterline (2012): see 2.6.

Fusillo, Masimo, 'The Conflict of Emotions: A *Topos* in the Greek Erotic Novel', in Swain (1999), 60–82.

Gesner, Carol, *Shakespeare and the Greek Romance: A Study of Origins* (Lexington, KY, 1970). [A valuable synthesis.]

Gillespie, Stuart, 'Shakespeare and Greek Romance: "Like an old tale still"', in Martindale and Taylor (2004), 225–37: see 2.1.

Goldhill, Simon, *Foucault's Virginity: Ancient Erotic Fiction and the History of Sexuality* (Cambridge, 1995).

Goldhill, Simon, 'Genre', in Tim Whitmarsh (ed.), *The Cambridge Companion to the Greek and Roman Novel* (Cambridge, 2008), 185–200.

Greenblatt, Stephen, 'Murdering Peasants: Status, Genre and the Representation of Rebellion', *Representations*, 1 (1983), 1–29.

Greenhalgh, Darlene C., 'Love, Chastity and Women's Erotic Power: Greek Romance in Elizabethan and Jacobean Contexts', in Constance C. Relihan and Goran Stanivukovic (eds), *Prose Fiction and Early Modern Sexualities in England, 1570–1640* (New York, 2004), 15–42.

Hackett, Helen, *Women and Romance Fiction in the English Renaissance* (Cambridge, 2000).

Hannay (2010): see 1.3.A.

Haynes, Katharine, *Fashioning the Feminine in the Greek Novel* (London and New York, 2003).

Henderson, Judith Rice, 'Euphues and his Erasmus', *English Literary Renaissance*, 12 (1982), 135–61.

Kinney, Arthur F., 'Rhetoric and Fiction in Elizabethan England', in Murphy (1983), 385–93: see 2.5.

Kinney, Arthur F., *Humanist Poetics: Thought, Rhetoric and Fiction in Sixteenth-Century England* (Amherst, MA, 1986). [An important, often-cited study.]

Konstan, David, *Sexual Symmetry: Love in the Ancient Novel and Related Genres* (Princeton, 1994).

Maguire, Laurie (ed.), *How to Do Things with Shakespeare: New Approaches, New Essays* (Oxford, 2008).

Martindale (1988), 1–20: see 2.4.

Maslen, R. W., 'Greene and the Uses of Time', in Kirk Melnikoff and Edward Gieskes (eds), *Writing Robert Greene: Essays on England's First Notorious Professional Writer* (Aldershot, 2008), 157–88.

Mentz, Steve, *Romance for Sale in Early Modern England: The Rise of Prose Fiction* (Aldershot, 2006).

Montrose, Louis, 'Spenser and the Elizabethan Political Imaginary', *Journal of English Literary History*, 69 (2002), 907–46.

Moore, Helen, 'Elizabethan Fiction and Ovid's *Heroides*', *Translation and Literature*, 9 (2000), 40–64.

Newcomb, Lori Humphrey, *Reading Popular Romance in Early Modern England* (New York, 2002).

Nuttall, A. D., 'Action at a Distance: Shakespeare and the Greeks', in Martindale and Taylor (2004), 209–22: see 2.1.

O'Connor, John J., *'Amadis de Gaule' and its Influence on Elizabethan Literature* (New Brunswick, NJ, 1970), 183–201.

Parry, Robert, *Moderatus*, ed. John Simons (Aldershot, 2002).

Perkins, Judith, 'Representation in Greek Saints' Lives', in J. R. Morgan and Richard Stoneman (eds), *Greek Fiction: The Greek Novel in Context* (1994), 255–71.

Plazenet, Laurence, *L'Ébahissement et la délectation: Réception comparée et poétiques du roman grec en France et en Angleterre aux XVIe et XVIIe siècles* (Paris, 1997).

Plazenet, Laurence, 'Jacques Amyot and the Greek Novel: The Invention of the French Novel', in Gerald Sandy (ed.), *The Classical Heritage in France* (Leiden, 2002), 237–80.

Pollard, Tanya, 'Romancing the Greeks: *Cymbeline*'s Genres and Models', in Maguire (2008), 34–53.

Saïd, Suzanne, 'Rural Society in the Greek Novel, or the Country Seen from the Town', in Swain (1999), 83–107.

Shelford, April, *Transforming the Republic of Letters: Pierre-Daniel Huet and European Intellectual Life, 1650–1720* (Rochester, NY, 2007).

Skretkowicz, Viktor, *European Erotic Romance: Philhellene Protestantism, Renaissance Translation and English Literary Politics* (Manchester, 2010). [A reception study that extends outward to broader cultural questions.]

Stanivukovic, Goran, 'Introduction', in Emanuel Ford, *The Most Pleasant History of Ornatus and Artesia*, ed. Stanivukovic (Ottawa, 2003), 11–105.

Swain, Simon (ed.), *Oxford Readings in the Greek Novel* (Oxford, 1999).

Travel and Prose Fiction in Early Modern England, *Yearbook of English Studies*, 41 (2011).

Whitmarsh, Tim, 'The Greek Novel: Titles and Genre', *American Journal of Philology*, 126 (2005a), 587–611.

Whitmarsh, Tim, *The Second Sophistic* (Oxford, 2005b).

Whitmarsh, Tim, 'Introduction' (Cambridge, 2011a), in Whitmarsh (2011b), 1–14.

Whitmarsh, Tim, *Narrative and Identity in the Ancient Greek Novel: Returning Romance* (Cambridge, 2011b).

Wolff, Samuel Lee, *The Greek Romances in Elizabethan Prose Fiction* (New York, 1912).

2.11. Tragedy

Baker, Howard, *Induction to Tragedy* (Baton Rouge, LA, 1939).

Binns, J. W., 'William Gager's Additions to Seneca's *Hippolytus*', *Studies in the Renaissance*, 17 (1970), 153–91.

Braden (1985): see 2.3.

Braden, Gordon, 'Herakles and Hercules: Survival in Greek and Roman Tragedy (with a Coda on *King Lear*)', in Ruth Scodel (ed.), *Theater and Society in the Classical World* (Ann Arbor, 1993), 245–64.

Braden, Gordon, 'Tragedy', in Braden, Cummings, and Gillespie (2010), 262–72: see 1.5.

Bullough, Geoffrey, *Narrative and Dramatic Sources of Shakespeare*, 8 vols (New York, 1957–75). [The classic compendium of Shakespearean sources.]

Butterworth, Charles E., *Averroes' Middle Commentary on Aristotle's Poetics* (Princeton, 1986). [An interesting study of an important medieval misinterpretation of Aristotle's *Poetics*.]

Castelvetro, Lodovico, *Castelvetro on the Art of Poetry*, ed. and trans. Andrew Bongiorno (Binghamton, NY, 1984). [An accessible edition of an important Renaissance treatise on poetics.]

Critchley, Simon, 'I Want to Die, I Hate My Life—Phaedra's Malaise', in Felski (2008), 170–97.

Cunliffe, John W., *The Influence of Seneca on Elizabethan Tragedy* (1893). [An older study, to be supplemented by Braden (1985): see 2.3.]

Felski, Rita (ed.), *Rethinking Tragedy* (Baltimore, 2008).

Florby, Gunilla, *Echoing Texts: George Chapman's Conspiracy and Tragedy of Charles Duke of Byron* (Lund, 2004).

Gazzard, Hugh, '"Those Graue Presentments of Antiquitie": Samuel Daniel's *Philotas* and the Earl of Essex', *Review of English Studies*, NS 51 (2000), 423–50.

Greene, John, *A Refutation of the Apology for Actors* (1615).

Helms, Lorraine, *Seneca by Candlelight and Other Stories of Renaissance Drama* (Philadelphia, 1997).

Hunter, G. K., 'Seneca and the Elizabethans: A Case Study in "Influence"', in *Dramatic Identities and Cultural Tradition: Studies in Shakespeare and his Contemporaries: Critical Essays* (Liverpool, 1978), 159–73.

Johnson, Christopher D., *Hyperboles: The Rhetoric of Excess in Baroque Literature and Thought* (Cambridge, MA, 2010).

Jones, Emrys, *The Origins of Shakespeare* (Oxford, 1977).

Kelly, Henry Ansgar, *Ideas and Forms of Tragedy from Aristotle to the Middle Ages* (Cambridge, 1993).

Lamb, Mary Ellen, 'The Myth of the Countess of Pembroke: The Dramatic Circle', *Yearbook of English Studies*, 11 (1981), 194–202.

Michel, Laurence (ed.), *The Tragedy of Philotas by Samuel Daniel*, 2nd edn (Hamden, CT, 1970), 36–66.

Miola (1992): see 1.5.

Pelling, C. B. R., 'Seeing a Roman Tragedy through Greek Eyes: Shakespeare's *Julius Caesar*', in Simon Goldhill and Edith Hall (eds), *Sophocles and the Greek Tragic Tradition* (Cambridge, 2009), 264–88.

Richmond-Garza, Elizabeth M., *Forgotten Cites/Sites: Interpretation and the Power of Classical Citation in Renaissance English Tragedy* (New York, 1994).

Schleiner, Louise, 'Latinized Greek Drama in Shakespeare's Writing of *Hamlet*', *Shakespeare Quarterly*, 41 (1990), 29–48. [Stresses the importance of Renaissance intermediaries in the influence of Greek drama on Shakespeare.]

Silk, Michael, 'Shakespeare and Greek Tragedy: Strange Relationship', in Martindale and Taylor (2004), 241–57: see 2.1.

Soellner, Rolf, 'The Madness of Hercules and the Elizabethans', *Comparative Literature*, 10 (1958), 309–24.

Steiner, George, 'Tragedy, Pure and Simple', in Michael Silk (ed.), *Tragedy and the Tragic: Greek Theatre and Beyond* (Oxford, 1996), 534–45.

Steiner, George, '"Tragedy," Reconsidered', in Felski (2008), 29–44.

Straznicky, Marta, '"Profane Stoical Paradoxes": *The Tragedie of Mariam* and Sidneian Closet Drama', *English Literary Renaissance*, 24 (1994), 104–34.

Taylor, A. B., 'Two Notes on Shakespeare and the Translators', *Review of English Studies*, NS 38 (1987), 522–4.

Thomson, J. A. K., *Shakespeare and the Classics* (1952). [An older study, still worth consulting.]

Walker, Greg, *The Politics of Performance in Early Renaissance Drama* (Cambridge, 1998).

Witherspoon, Alexander Maclaren, *The Influence of Robert Garnier on Elizabethan Drama* (New Haven, 1924).

2.12. Tragicomedy

Archive of Performance of Greek and Roman Drama (APGRD) Database, University of Oxford <http://www.apgrd.ox.ac.uk/database> (accessed 20 March 2015).

Bolgar (1954): see 1.5.

Cartwright, Kent, *Theatre and Humanism: English Drama in the Sixteenth Century* (Cambridge, 1999).

Castelvetro (1984): see 2.11.

Cronk, Nicholas, 'Aristotle, Horace, and Longinus: The Conception of Reader Response', in Norton (1999), 199–204.

Dewar-Watson, Sarah, 'Shakespeare's Dramatic Odysseys: Homer as a Tragicomic Model in *Pericles* and *The Tempest*', *Classical and Modern Literature*, 25/1 (2005), 23–40.

Dewar-Watson, Sarah, 'Aristotle and Tragicomedy', in Mukherji and Lyne (2007), 15–27.

Dixon, Mimi Still, 'Tragicomic Recognitions: Medieval Miracles and Shakespearean Romance', in Maguire (1987), 56–79.

Edwards, Richard, *Damon and Pythias*, in *The Works of Richard Edwards*, ed. Ros King (Manchester, 2001).

Forcione, Alban K., *Cervantes, Aristotle, and the Persiles* (Princeton, 1970). [An influential study, with implications for English literature as well.]

Forman, Valerie, *Tragicomic Redemptions: Global Economics and the Early Modern English Stage* (Philadelphia, 2008).

Gillsepie, Stuart, 'Shakespeare and Greek Romance: "Like an Old Tale Still"', in Martindale and Taylor (2004), 225–37: see 2.1.

Giraldi Cinthio, Giambattista, *On the Composition of Comedies and Tragedies* (1543), in Allan Gilbert (ed. and trans.), *Literary Criticism: Plato to Dryden* (New York, 1940). [An important theoretical treatise from the Renaissance.]

Hall, Joseph, *The Honour of the Married Clergy* (1620).

Haugen, Kristine Louise, 'The Birth of Tragedy in the Cinquecento: Humanism and Literary History', *Journal of the History of Ideas*, 72/3 (2011), 351–70.

Henderson, Jeffrey, 'Introduction', in *Plautus*, Loeb Classical Library, 5 vols (Cambridge, MA, 2011–2012), 1, pp. xi–xvii.

Henke, Robert, *Pastoral Transformations: Italian Tragicomedy and Shakespeare's Late Plays* (Newark, DE, 1997).

Herrick, Marvin T., *Tragicomedy: Its Origin and Development in Italy, France, and England* (Urbana, IL, 1955). [An older study, but valuable both for its scholarship and its comparative context.]

Hirsch, Rudolf, 'The Printing Tradition of Aeschylus, Euripides, Sophocles and Aristophanes', *Gutenberg Jahrbuch* (1964), 138–46.

Hunter, G. K., 'Italian Tragicomedy on the English Stage', *Renaissance Drama*, 6 (1973), 123–48.

Javitch, Daniel, 'The Emergence of Poetic Genre Theory in the Sixteenth Century', *Modern Language Quarterly*, 59/2 (1998), 139–69.

Lefteratou, Anna, 'Myth and Narrative in the Greek Novel', unpublished Ph.D. thesis, Oxford, 2000.

Lesser, Zachary, 'Mixed Government and Mixed Marriage in *A King and No King*: Sir Henry Neville Reads Beaumont and Fletcher', *English Literary History*, 69 (2002), 947–77.

Maguire, Nancy Klein (ed.), *Renaissance Tragicomedy: Explorations in Genre and Politics* (New York, 1987).

Martindale, Charles, 'Thinking through Reception', in Charles Martindale and Richard F. Thomas (eds), *Classics and the Uses of Reception* (Oxford, 2006), 1–13. [An important theoretical statement, with implications for many different areas.]

Mentz, Steven, *Romance for Sale in Early Modern England: The Rise of Prose Fiction* (Aldershot, 2006).

Moore, Timothy J., 'Tragicomedy as a Running Joke: Plautus' *Amphitruo* in Performance', *Didaskalia*, suppl. 1 (1995) <http://www.didaskalia.net/issues/supplement1/moore.html> (accessed 20 March 2015).

Mukherji, Subha, and Lyne, Raphael (eds), *Early Modern Tragicomedy* (Cambridge, 2007).

Munro, Lucy, *Children of the Queen's Revels: A Jacobean Theatre Repertory* (Cambridge, 2005).

Norton, Glyn (ed.), *The Cambridge History of Literary Criticism*, vol. 3: *The Renaissance* (Cambridge, 1999). [A valuable reference work.]

Orgel, Stephen, 'Shakespeare and the Kinds of Drama', *Critical Inquiry*, 6/1 (1979), 107–23.

Pletcher, J., 'Euripides in Heliodorus' *Aethiopiaka* 7–8', in H. Hofmann and M. Zimmerman (eds), *Groningen Colloquia on the Novel*, vol. 9 (Groningen, 1998), 17–27.

Pollard, Tanya, '"A Thing Like Death": Poisons and Sleeping Potions in *Romeo and Juliet* and *Antony and Cleopatra*', *Renaissance Drama*, 32 (2003), 95–121.

Pollard, Tanya, 'Romancing the Greeks: *Cymbeline*'s Genres and Models', in Maguire (2008), 34–53: see 2.10.

Reiss, Timothy J., 'Renaissance Theatre and the Theory of Tragedy', in Norton (1999), 229–47.

Ristine, Frank, *English Tragicomedy: Its Origin and History* (New York, 1963).

Saladin, Jean Christophe, 'Euripide Luthérien?', *Mélanges de l'Ecole française de Rome*, 108/1 (1996), 155–70.

Smith (1988): see 2.1.

Stern, Tiffany, 'Actors and Audience on the Stage at Blackfriars', in Paul Menzer (ed.), *Inside Shakespeare: Essays on the Blackfriars Stage* (Selinsgrove, 2006), 35–53.

Treherne, Matthew, 'The Difficult Emergence of Pastoral Tragicomedy: Guarini's *Il Pastor Fido* and its Critical Reception in Italy, 1586–1601', in Mukherji and Lyne (2007), 28–42.

Underdowne, Thomas, *An Aethiopian History of Heliodorus* (1587).

Walden, J. W. H., 'Stage-Terms in Heliodorus's *Aethiopica*', *Harvard Studies in Classical Philology*, 5 (1894), 1–43.

Yoch, James J., 'The Renaissance Dramatization of Temperance: The Italian Revival of Tragicomedy and *The Faithful Shepherdess*', in Maguire (1987), 115–38.

3. THE RECEPTION OF PARTICULAR CLASSICAL AUTHORS

3.1. Aeschylus

Jepsen, Linda, *Ethical Aspects of Tragedy: A Comparison of Certain Tragedies by Aeschylus, Sophocles, Euripides, Seneca and Shakespeare* (Gainesville, FL, 1953).

Kott, Jan, 'Hamlet and Orestes', *PMLA*, 82 (1967), 303–13.

Roth, Marty, '"The Blood That Fury Breathed": The Shape of Justice in Aeschylus and Shakespeare', *Comparative Literature Studies*, 29 (1992), 141–56.

Schleiner (1990): see 2.11.

Showerman, Earl, 'Orestes and Hamlet: From Myth to Masterpiece, Part I', *Oxfordian: The Annual Journal of the Oxford Shakespeare Society*, 7 (2004), 89–114.

Silk, Michael, 'Shakespeare and Greek Tragedy: Strange Relationship', in Martindale and Taylor (2004), 241–57: see 2.1.

Streufort, Paul D., 'Spectral Others: Theatrical Ghosts as the Negotiation of Alterity in Aeschylus and Shakespeare', *Intertexts*, 8 (2004), 77–93.

3.2. Anacreon and the *Anacreontea*

Achilleos, Stella, 'The *Anacreontea* and a Tradition of Refined Male Sociability', in Adam Smyth (ed.), *A Pleasing Sinne: Drink and Conviviality in Seventeenth-Century England* (Woodbridge, 2004), 21–36.

Hutton, J., *The Greek Anthology in France and in the Latin Writers of the Netherlands to the Year 1800* (Ithaca, NY, 1946). [A classic, providing background to the reception of Anacreon in England.]

Levarie, Janet, 'Renaissance Anacreontics', *Comparative Literature*, 25 (1973), 221–39.

Mason, Tom, 'Abraham Cowley and the Wisdom of Anacreon: Re-Evaluations of Cowley's Anacreontiques', *Cambridge Quarterly*, 19 (1990), 103–37.

O'Brien, John, *Anacreon Redivivus: A Study of Anacreonic Tradition in Mid-Sixteenth-Century France* (Ann Arbor, 1995). [A good update to Hutton (1946), providing additional context for the literary scene in England.]

Revard, Stella P., 'Cowley's *Anacreontiques* and the Translation of the Greek *Anacreontea*', in Alexander Dalzell, Charles Fantazzi, and R. J. Schoeck (eds), *Acta Conventus Neo-Latini Torontonensis: Proceedings of the Seventh International Congress of Neo-Latin Studies, Toronto 8 August to 13 August 1988*, Medieval & Renaissance Texts & Studies 86 (Binghamton, NY, 1991), 595–608.

Rosenmeyer, Patricia A., *The Poetics of Imitation: Anacreon and the Anacreontic Tradition* (Cambridge, 1992). [A valuable study, including information on reception.]

3.3. Aristophanes

Boughner, Daniel C., *The Braggart in Renaissance Comedy: A Study in Comparative Drama from Aristophanes to Shakespeare* (Minneapolis, 1954).

Gruber, William E., 'Heroic Comedy and *The Tempest*', *Classical and Modern Literature*, 1 (1981), 189–204.

Ostovich, Helen M., '"So Sudden and Strange a Cure": A Rudimentary Masque in *Every Man out of his Humour*', *English Literary Renaissance*, 22 (1992), 315–32.

Waith, Eugene M., 'Aristophanes, Plautus, Terence, and the Refinement of English Comedy', *Studies in the Literary Imagination*, 10 (1977), 91–108.

3.4. Aristotle

Alvis, John, '*Coriolanus* and Aristotle's Magnanimous Man Reconsidered', *Interpretation: Journal of Political Philosophy*, 7 (1978), 4–28.

Beauregard, David N., 'Sidney, Aristotle, and *The Merchant of Venice*: Shakespeare's Triadic Images of Liberality and Justice', *Shakespeare Studies*, 20 (1987), 33–51.

Black, Matthew W., 'Aristotle's *Mythos* and the Tragedies of Shakespeare', *Shakespeare Jahrbuch* (1968), 43–55.

Boitani, Piero, '*Anagnoresis* and Reasoning: *Electra* and *Hamlet*', *REAL: The Yearbook of Research in English and American Literature*, 7 (1990), 99–136.

Coogan, Robert R., 'The Triumph of Reason: Sidney's *Defense* and Aristotle's *Rhetoric*', *Papers on Language and Literature*, 17 (1981), 255–70.

Cronk (1999): see 2.12.

Crosbie, Christopher, 'Fixing Moderation: *Titus Andronicus* and the Aristotelian Determination of Value', *Shakespeare Quarterly*, 58 (2007), 147–73.

Curtright, Travis, 'Sidney's *Defense of Poetry*: *Ethos* and the Ideas', *Ben Jonson Journal*, 10 (2003), 101–15.

D'Agostino, Nemi, 'Shakespeare e Aristotele', *Belfagor*, 42 (1987), 369–88.

DeMoss, William F., 'Spenser's Twelve Moral Virtues "According to Aristotle"', *Modern Philology*, 16 (1918), 23–38, 245–70.

Dewar-Watson (2005): see 2.12.

Elton, W. R., 'Aristotle's *Nicomachean Ethics* and Shakespeare's *Troilus and Cressida*', *Journal of the History of Ideas*, 58 (1997), 331–7.

Golden, Leon, 'Othello, Hamlet, and Aristotelian Tragedy', *Shakespeare Quarterly*, 35 (1984), 142–56. [A thoughtful analysis of two of Shakespeare's key tragedies from an Aristotelian perspective.]

Green (1986): see 1.2.

Green, L. D. 'The Reception of Aristotle's *Rhetoric* in the Renaissance', in William Fortenbaugh and David C. Mirhady (eds), *Peripatetic Rhetoric after Aristotle* (New Brunswick, NJ, 1994), 320–48. [A valuable overview.]

Griffiths, Jane, 'Contradiction in Terms: Skelton's "Effecte Energiall" in *A Replycacion*', *Renaissance Studies*, 17 (2003), 55–68.

Haugen (2011): see 2.12.

Heninger, S. K., 'Metaphor and Sidney's "Defence of Poesie"', *John Donne Journal*, 1 (1982), 117–49.

Herrick (1930): see 2.1.

Herrick, Martin T., *The Fusion of Horatian and Aristotelian Criticism, 1531–1555* (Urbana, IL, 1946). [An older study, showing how literary criticism became a hybrid of classical concepts at mid-century.]

Hosley (1966): see 2.1.

Javitch, Daniel, 'The Emergence of Poetic Genre Theory in the Sixteenth Century', *Modern Language Quarterly*, 59 (1958), 139–69. [Examines the role of Aristotle's *Poetics* in the formation of early modern genre theory.]

Jusserand, J. J., 'Spenser's "Twelve Private Morall Vertues as Aristotle Hath Devised"', *Modern Philology*, 3 (1906), 373–83. [Examines the Aristotelian ethical structure of *The Faerie Queene*.]

Kristeller, Paul O., 'Renaissance Aristotelianism', *Greek, Roman and Byzantine Studies*, 6 (1965), 157–74. [A valuable brief overview, confirming that Aristotelianism continued to flourish in the Renaissance.]

Lees, F. N., 'Coriolanus, Aristotle, and Bacon', *Review of English Studies*, 1 (1950), 114–25.

McCanles, Michael, 'The Rhetoric of Character Portrayal in Sidney's *New Arcadia*', *Criticism*, 25 (1983), 123–39.

Payne, Paula, 'Aristotle's *Rhetoric* in Sidney's Eighth Song', *Explorations in Renaissance Culture*, 16 (1990a), 57–65.

Payne, Paula, 'Tracing Aristotle's *Rhetoric* in Sir Philip Sidney's Poetry and Prose', *Rhetoric Society Quarterly*, 20 (1990b), 241–50.

Poisson, Rodney, 'Coriolanus as Aristotle's Magnanimous Man', in Waldo F. McNeir and Thelma Greenfield (eds), *Pacific Coast Studies in Shakespeare* (Eugene, OR, 1966), 210–24.

Reisner, Noam, 'The Paradox of *Mimesis* in Sidney's *Defence of Poesie* and Marlowe's *Doctor Faustus*', *Cambridge Quarterly*, 39 (2010), 331–49.

Rozett, Martha, 'Aristotle, the Revenger, and the Elizabethan Audience', *Studies in Philology*, 76 (1979), 239–61.

Schmitt, Charles B., *Aristotle and the Renaissance* (Cambridge, MA, and London, 1983a). [The standard overview of the subject.]

Schmitt, Charles B., *John Case and Aristotelianism in Renaissance England* (Montreal, 1983b). [A valuable individual study, focused on an important scholar of Aristotle in Renaissance England.]

Sirluck, Ernest, '*The Faerie Queene*, Book II, and the *Nicomachean Ethics*', *Modern Philology*, 49 (1951), 73–100.

Soellner, Rolf, 'Shakespeare, Aristotle, Plato, and the Soul', *Shakespeare Jahrbuch* (1968), 56–71.

Spencer, Eric, 'Taking Excess, Exceeding Account: Aristotle Meets *The Merchant of Venice*', in Linda Woodbridge (ed.), *Money and the Age of Shakespeare: Essays in New Economic Criticism* (New York, 2003), 143–58.

Tigerstedt, E. N., 'Observations on the Reception of the Aristotelian *Poetics* in the Latin West', *Studies in the Renaissance*, 15 (1968), 7–24. [A classic study, brief but valuable as an overview.]

Wheater, Isabella, 'Aristotelian Wealth and the Sea of Love: Shakespeare's Synthesis of Greek Philosophy and Roman Poetry in *The Merchant of Venice*', *Review of English Studies*, 44 (1993), 16–36.

White, Thomas I., 'Aristotle and Utopia', *Renaissance Quarterly*, 29 (1976), 635–75.

3.5. Catullus

Bagg, Robert, 'Some Versions of Lyric Impasse in Shakespeare and Catullus', *Arion*, 4 (1965), 64–95.

Blevins, Jacob, 'The Catullan Lyric and Anti-Petrarchism in Sir Thomas Wyatt', *Classical and Modern Literature*, 19 (1999), 279–85.

Blevins, Jacob, *Catullan Consciousness and the Early Modern Lyric in England: From Wyatt to Donne* (Aldershot, 2004).

Boehrer, Bruce, 'Ben Jonson and the *Traditio basiorum*: Catullan Imitation in *The Forrest* 5 and 6', *Papers on Language and Literature*, 32 (1996), 63–84.

Braden, Gordon, '*Vivamus mea Lesbia* in the English Renaissance', *English Literary Renaissance*, 9 (1979), 199–224. [A fascinating study of how a Latin poem was broken apart and disseminated in Renaissance England.]

Gaisser, Julia Haig, *Catullus and his Renaissance Readers* (Oxford, 1993). [The definitive treatment of the subject, providing background for Catullus' reception in England.]

Hester, M. Thomas, 'Reading "More Wit" in Donne and Catullus', *Ben Jonson Journal*, 16 (2009), 33–56.

McPeek, James A. S., *Catullus in Strange and Distant Britain* (New York, 1972). [Largely a collection of parallel passages.]

Mulryan, John, 'The Function of Ritual in the Marriage Songs of Catullus, Spenser, and Ronsard', *Illinois Quarterly*, 35 (1972), 50–64.

Pearcy, Lee, 'A Case of Allusion: Stanza 18 of Spenser's "Epithalamion" and Catullus 5', *Classical and Modern Literature*, 1 (1981), 243–54.

Warner, J. Christopher, '*Talking Back to Catullus: Lady Mary Wroth's* Pamphilia to Amphilanthus 13', *Explorations in Renaissance Culture,* 23 (1997), 95–110.

3.6. Cicero

Armstrong, E., *A Ciceronian Sunburn: A Tudor Dialogue on Humanistic Rhetoric and Civic Poetics* (Columbia, SC, 2006).

Blackwell, C. W. T., 'Humanism and Politics in English Royal Biography: The Use of Cicero, Plutarch, and Sallust in the *Vita Henrici Quinti* (1438) by Titus Livius de Frulovisi and the *Vita Henrici Septimi* (1500–1503) by Bernard André', in I. D. McFarlane (ed.), *Acta Conventus Neo-Latini Sanctandreani: Proceedings of the Fifth International Congress of Neo-Latin Studies* (Binghamton, NY, 1986), 431–40.

Carlson (2000): see 2.3.

Coronato, Rocco, '"Set Murderous Cicero to School": Ben Jonson e la prima *Catilinaria*', *Merope,* 9 (1997), 43–57.

Cox, John D., 'Shakespeare and the Ethics of Friendship', *Religion and Literature,* 49 (2008), 1–29.

Crider, Scott F., 'The Human Bond, Loosened and Tightened: Ciceronian Sin and Redemption in *King Lear*', in Blake Hobby (ed.), *Sin and Redemption* (New York, 2010), 135–45.

Dzelzainis, Martin, 'The Ciceronian Theory of Tyrannicide from Buchanan to Milton', *Etudes epistémè',* 15 (2009), 59–70.

Finkelstein, Richard, 'Ben Jonson's Ciceronian Rhetoric of Friendship', *Journal of Medieval and Renaissance Studies,* 16 (1986), 103–24.

Harvey (1577): see 2.3.

Grimald (1556): see 2.3.

Grund (1975): see 2.5.

Helfer, Rebeca, 'The Death of the "New Poete": Virgilian Ruin and Ciceronian Recollection in Spenser's *The Shepheardes Calender*', *Renaissance Quarterly,* 56 (2003), 723–56.

Helfer, Rebeca, 'Remembering Sidney, Remembering Spenser: The Art of Memory and *The Ruines of Time*', *Spenser Studies,* 22 (2007), 127–51.

Henderson, Judith R., '"Vain Affectations": Bacon on Ciceronianism in *The Advancement of Learning*', *English Literary Renaissance,* 25 (1995), 209–34. [A valuable study of Ciceronian influence in a key text in English Renaissance literature.]

Jones (1998): see 2.3.

McCutcheon, Elizabeth, 'More's *Utopia* and Cicero's *Paradoxa stoicorum*', *Moreana,* 86 (1985), 3–22.

Marsh, David, *The Quattrocento Dialogue: Classical Tradition and Humanist Innovation* (Cambridge, MA, 1980). [An influential study of the impact of the Ciceronian dialogue on several Renaissance writers.]

Martin, Janet M., 'Cicero's Jokes at the Court of Henry II of England: Roman Humor and the Princely Ideal', *Modern Language Quarterly,* 51 (1990), 185–207.

Murphy, James J. (ed.), and Newlands, Carole (trans.), *Peter Ramus's Attack on Cicero: Text and Translation of Ramus's Brutinae quaestiones* (Davis, CA, 1992). [An edition and English translation of a famous attack on the rhetorical theories of Cicero.]

Schmitt (1972): see 2.3.

Scott, I., *Controversies over the Imitation of Cicero in the Renaissance* (Davis, CA, 1991). [A study of the Renaissance debate over imitating Cicero, with some of the primary texts translated into English.]

Stretter, Robert, 'Cicero on Stage: Damon and Pithias and the Fate of Classical Friendship in English Renaissance Drama', *Texas Studies in Language and Literature,* 47 (2005), 345–65.

Takada, Yasunari, 'Shakespeare's Cicero', *Poetica,* 48 (1997), 157–65.

Vos, Alvin, '"Good Matter and Good Utterance": The Character of English Ciceronianism', *Studies in English Literature, 1500–1900,* 19 (1979), 3–18.

Ward, John, 'Renaissance Commentators on Ciceronian Rhetoric', in Murphy (1983), 126–73: see 2.5. [Shows that Renaissance scholars expanded the number of Ciceronian texts commonly studied and the uses to which these texts could be put.]

Wegemer, Gerard, 'Ciceronian Humanism in More's *Utopia*', *Moreana,* 27 (1990), 5–26.

West, Michael, 'The Controversial Eloquence of Shakespeare's *Coriolanus*—An Anti-Ciceronian Orator?' *Modern Philology,* 102 (2005), 307–31.

Wilson, Kenneth, *Incomplete Fictions: The Formation of English Renaissance Dialogue* (Washington, 1985).

Zielinski, Tadeusz, *Cicero im Wandel der Jahrhunderte,* 3rd edn (Leipzig and Berlin, 1912). [The classic study, with seventy pages on the Renaissance.]

3.7. Epicurus

Allen (1944): see 2.3.

Barbour (1998): see 2.3.

Harrison, C. T., 'The Ancient Atomists and English Literature in the Seventeenth Century', *Harvard Studies in Classical Philology,* 45 (1934), 1–79.

Hopkins, David, 'Cowley's Horatian Mice', in Martindale and Hopkins (1993), 103–26: see 2.2.

Jones, Howard, *The Epicurean Tradition* (London and New York, 1989). [Includes a solid section on Epicurus' influence on English Renaissance culture.]

Kargon, Robert H., *Atomism in England from Hariot to Newton* (Oxford, 1966). [A study of the reception of the atomic theories of Epicurus and Lucretius in late-sixteenth-century and seventeenth-century England.]

Small and Small (1997): see 2.3.

Surtz, Edward L., 'Epicurus in Utopia', *English Literary History,* 16 (1949), 89–103.

Wilson, Catherine, *Epicureanism at the Origins of Modernity* (Oxford and New York, 2008). [A study of Epicurus and Lucretius in the seventeenth century.]

3.8. Euripides

Arnold, Margaret J., '"Monsters in Love's Train": Euripides and Shakespeare's *Troilus and Cressida*', *Comparative Drama,* 18 (1984), 38–53.

Bryant, J. A., Jr, '*Julius Caesar* from a Euripidean Perspective', in Davidson, Johnson, and Stroupe (1993), 144–58.

Davidson, Clifford, Johnson, Rand, and Stroupe, David H. (eds), *Drama and the Classical Heritage: Comparative and Critical Studies* (New York, 1993).

Demers, Patricia, 'On First Looking into Lumley's Euripides', *Renaissance and Reformation/ Renaissance et Réforme*, 23 (1999), 25–42. [Examines Lady Jane Lumley's Tudor translation of *Iphigeneia at Aulis*.]

Dewar-Watson, Sarah, 'The *Alcestis* and the Statue Scene in *The Winter's Tale*', *Shakespeare Quarterly*, 60 (2009), 73–80.

Faas, Ekbert, *Tragedy and After: Euripides, Shakespeare, Goethe* (Kingston, 1984). [A more substantive treatment of Shakespeare's use of Euripides, a subject of several articles in the 1980s and 1990s.]

Jepsen (1953): see 3.1.

Ketterer, Robert C., 'Machines for the Suppression of Time: Statues in Suor Angelica, *The Winter's Tale*, and *Alcestis*', *Comparative Drama*, 24 (1990), 3–23.

Kott (1967): see 3.1.

MacKenzie, Donald, 'Borderlands of Tragedy: *The Bacchae* and *Othello*', *Literature and Theology*, 7 (1993), 1–12.

Purkiss, Diane, 'Medea in the English Renaissance', in Edith Hall, Fiona Macintosh, and Oliver Taplin (eds), *Medea in Performance 1500–2000* (Oxford, 2000), 32–48.

Schleiner (1990): see 2.11.

3.9. Greek Rhetoricians

Beardsley, Theodore S., 'Isocrates, Shakespeare, and Calderón: Advice to a Young Man', *Hispanic Review*, 42 (1974), 185–98.

Blanchard and Sowerby (2005): see 1.7.

Hunter, G. K., 'Isocrates' Precepts and Polonius' Character', *Shakespeare Quarterly*, 8 (1957), 501–6.

Patterson, Annabel, *Hermogenes and the Renaissance: Seven Ideas of Style* (Princeton, 1970). [Demonstrates the wisespread influence of Hermogenes' *Concerning Ideas*.]

Ronan, Clifford J., 'Daniel, Rainolde, Demosthenes, and the Degree Speech of Shakespeare's Ulysses', *Renaissance and Reformation/Rénaissance et Réforme*, 9 (1985), 111–18.

Tangri, Daniel, 'Demosthenes in the Renaissance: A Case Study on the Origins and Development of Scholarship on Greek Oratory', *Viator*, 37 (2006), 545–82.

3.10. Greek Romances

Adams, Martha L., 'The Greek Romance and William Shakespeare', *Studies in English*, 8 (1967), 43–52.

Aiman, Henry C., 'Spenser's Debt to Heliodorus in *The Faerie Queene*', *Emporia State Research Studies*, 22 (1974), 5–18.

Davis, Walter R., 'Robert Greene and Greek Romance', in Kirk Melnikoff (ed.), *Robert Greene* (Surrey, 2011), 201–51.

Gesner, Carol, '*The Tempest* as Pastoral Romance', *Shakespeare Quarterly,* 10 (1959), 531–9. [Proposes Longus' novel as an intertext.]
Gesner, Carol, '*Cymbeline* and the Greek Romance: A Study in Genre', in Waldo F. McNeir (ed.), *Studies in English Renaissance Literature* (Baton Rouge, LA, 1962), 105–31.
Gesner (1970): see 2.10.
Gillespie, Stuart, 'Shakespeare and Greek Romance: "Like an old tale still"', in Martindale and Taylor (2004), 225–37: see 2.1.
Greenhalgh (2004): see 2.10.
Heffernan, Carol, 'Heliodorus's *Æthiopica* and Sidney's *Arcadia*: A Reconsideration', *English Language Notes,* 42 (2004), 12–20.
Houlahan, Mark, '"Like to th'Egyptian Thief": Shakespeare Sampling Heliodorus in *Twelfth Night*', in Neill, Chalk, and Johnson (2010), 305–15.
Hughes, Merritt Y., 'Spenser's Debt to the Greek Romances', *Modern Philology,* 23 (1925), 67–76. [An older study, but still valuable.]
Neill, Michael, Chalk, Darryl, and Johnson, Laurie (eds), *'Rapt in Secret Studies': Emerging Shakespeares* (Newcastle upon Tyne, 2010).
Pollard (2008), 34–53: see 2.10.
Reynolds, Simon, 'Pregnancy and Imagination in *The Winter's Tale* and Heliodorus' *Aithiopika*', *English Studies,* 84 (2003), 433–47.
Reynolds, Simon, '*Cymbeline* and Heliodorus' *Aithiopika:* The Loss and Recovery of Form', *Translation and Literature,* 13 (2004), 24–48.
Silberman, Lauren, '"Perfect Hole": Spenser and Greek Romance', *Spenser Studies,* 23 (2008), 283–91.
Skretkowicz (2010): see 2.10.
Wolff, S. L., *Greek Romances in Elizabethan Prose Fiction* (New York, 1912). [An older study, but still valuable.]

3.11. Homer

Acheson, Arthur, *Shakespeare and the Rival Poet* (London and New York, 1903).
Allen, Don Cameron, *Mysteriously Meant: The Rediscovery of Pagan Symbolism and Allegorical Interpretation in the Renaissance* (Baltimore, 1970). [A classic study, beginning with Homer but extending to broader issues of allegorization in the Renaissance.]
Bednarz, James P., *Shakespeare and the Poets' War* (New York, 2001).
Binns (1990): see 1.2.
Borot, Luc, 'The Poetics of Thomas Hobbes by Himself: An Edition of his Preface to his Translations of Homer', *Cahiers élisabéthains,* 60 (2001), 67–82.
Briggs, John Channing, 'Chapman's *Seaven Bookes of the Iliades*: Mirror for Essex', *Studies in English Literature, 1500–1900,* 21 (1981), 59–73.
Brisson, Luc, *How Philosophers Saved Myths: Allegorical Interpretation and Classical Mythology* (Chicago, 2004). [A good update to Allen (1970).]
Bull, Malcolm, *The Mirror of the Gods* (Oxford, 2005). [An important update of Seznec (1953).]
Bullough (1957–75): see 2.11.

Burrow (1993): see 2.10.

Dawson, David, *Allegorical Readers and Cultural Revision in Ancient Alexandria* (Berkeley and Los Angeles, 1992).

Demetriou (2006): see 2.4.

Dewar-Watson (2005): see 2.12.

Elton, W. R., *Shakespeare's Troilus and Cressida and the Inns of Court Revels* (Aldershot, 2000).

Fay, H. C., 'Chapman's Materials for his Translation of Homer', *Review of English Studies*, NS 2/6 (1951), 121–8.

Fehrenbach, R. J., and Leedham-Green, E. S., *Private Libraries in Renaissance England*, 5 vols (Binghamton, NY, 1992–8).

Ferrucci, Franco, *The Poetics of Disguise: The Autobiography of the Work in Homer, Dante, and Shakespeare* (Ithaca, NY, 1980).

Ford (2007): see 2.4.

Gillespie (2001): see 1.6.

González, Eduardo, 'Odysseus' Bed and Cleopatra's Mattress (69)', *MLN*, 119 (2004), 930–48.

Grafton (1992): see 2.4.

Hale, David G., 'Virgil and Homer in the Early Tudor Period', in Pellegrini (1985), 121–9.

Hammond (1933): see 2.4.

Hardie, Philip, 'Imago Mundi: Cosmographical and Ideological Aspects of the Shield of Achilles', *Journal of Hellenic Studies*, 105 (1985), 11–31.

Hardie, Philip, *Virgil's Aeneid: Cosmos and Imperium* (Oxford, 1986).

Heninger, S. K., *Touches of Sweet Harmony* (Pasadena, CA, 1974).

Hunter, G. K., 'Troilus and Cressida: A Tragic Satire', *Shakespeare Studies* (Tokyo), 13 (1974–5), 1–23.

Ide, Richard S., 'Exemplary Heroism in Chapman's *Odysses*', *Studies in English Literature, 1500–1900*, 22 (1982), 121–36.

James, Heather, *Shakespeare's Troy: Drama, Politics, and the Translation of Empire* (Cambridge, 1997). [A thoughtful analysis of Shakespeare's use of classical epic.]

James, Thomas, *Catalogus Librorum Bibliothecae Publicae Quam Vir Ornatissimus Thomas Bodleius*... (Oxford, 1605).

Justman, Stewart, '*Hamlet* and the *Odyssey*', *Literary Imagination*, 4 (1992), 389–410.

Kallendorf, Craig, *The Other Virgil: 'Pessimistic' Readings of the 'Aeneid' in Early Modern Culture* (Oxford, 2007).

Ker, N. R., 'Oxford College Libraries in the Sixteenth Century', *Bodleian Library Record*, 6/3 (1959), 459–515.

Lord (1956): see 2.4.

Lord, George deForest, *Heroic Mockery: Variations on Epic Themes from Homer to Joyce* (Newark, DE, 1977).

Machacek, Gregory, 'Royalist Homer', *Transactions of the Cambridge Bibliographical Society*, 12 (2002), 331–2.

McPherson (1974): see 1.5.

Mallette, Richard, *Spenser and the Discourses of Reformation England* (Lincoln, NE, 1997).

Martindale (2006): see 2.12.

Miola, Robert S., 'On Death and Dying in Chapman's *Iliad*: Translation as Forgery', *International Journal of the Classical Tradition*, 3 (1996), 48–64. [Focuses on scenes of death as a point of dissonance between original and translation.]

Morgan, Llewellyn, *Patterns of Redemption in Virgil's Georgics* (Cambridge, 1999).

Murrin, Michael, *The Allegorical Epic: Essays in its Rise and Decline* (Chicago, 1980). [Contains much material on Homer, but also on other aspects of allegorization in the Renaissance.]

Olmsted, Wendy, 'On the Margins of Otherness: Metamorphosis and Identity in Homer, Ovid, Spenser, and Milton', *New Literary History*, 27 (1996), 167–84.

Passannante, Gerard, 'Homer Atomized: Francis Bacon and the Matter of Tradition', *English Literary History*, 76 (2009), 1015–47.

Pellegrini, Anthony L. (ed.), The *Early Renaissance: Virgil and the Classical Tradition* (Binghamton, NY, 1985).

Peyré, Yves, 'Shakespeare's Odyssey', in Tom Clayton, Susan Brock, Vincente Forès, and Jill Levinson (eds), *Shakespeare and the Mediterranean* (Newark, DE, 2004), 230–42.

Phinney, Edward, Jr, 'Continental Humanists and Chapman's *Iliads*', *Studies in the Renaissance*, 12 (1965), 218–26.

Presson, Robert, *Troilus and Cressida and the Legends of Troy* (Madison, 1953).

Quint (1993): see 2.4.

Schoell, Franck L., *Etudes sur l'humanisme continental en Angleterre à la fin de la Renaissance* (Paris, 1926).

Seznec, Jean, *The Survival of the Pagan Gods: The Mythological Tradition and Its Place in Renaissance Humanism and Art*, trans. Barbara Sessions (New York, 1953). [The classic study of Renaissance mythology.]

Snare, Gerald, *The Mystification of George Chapman* (Durham, NC, 1989).

Sowerby, Robin, 'Early Humanist Failure with Homer', *International Journal of the Classical Tradition*, 4 (1995), 37–63, 165–94. [Discusses comparisons of Homer to Virgil, with the former found wanting.]

Spingarn (1908): see 1.3.B.

Stoll, Elmer E., 'Art and Artifice in the *Iliad*; or the Poetical Treatment of Character in Homer and Shakespeare', *English Literary History*, 2 (1935), 294–321.

Suzuki, Mihoko, *Metamorphoses of Helen: Authority, Difference, and the Epic* (Ithaca, NY, 1989). [Includes discussions of Homer and Spenser.]

Waddington, Raymond, *The Mind's Empire: Myth and Form in George Chapman's Narrative Poems* (Baltimore, 1974).

Wind, Edgar, *Pagan Mysteries in the Renaissance*, 2nd edn (1967). [An often-cited study of Renaissance mythology.]

Wolfe, Jessica, 'Spenser, Homer, and the Mythography of Strife', *Renaissance Quarterly*, 58 (2005), 1220–88.

Zerba, Michelle L., 'Modalities of Tragic Doubt in Homer's *Iliad*, Sophocles' *Philoctetes*, and Shakespeare's *Othello*', *Comparative Literature*, 61 (2009), 1–25.

3.12. Horace

Baines, Paul, 'Pope's First Horatian Imitation? Ben Jonson's Crispinus and the Poisoning of Edmund Curll', *Review of English Studies*, 20 (2009), 78–95.

Bates, Catherine, '"A Mild Admonisher": Sir Thomas Wyatt and Sixteenth-Century Satire', *Huntington Library Quarterly*, 56 (1993), 243–58.

Boehrer, Bruce, 'Horatian Satire in Jonson's "On the Famous Voyage"', *Criticism*, 44 (2002), 9–26.

Braund (2010): see 2.2.

Burrow (1993): see 2.10.

Civardi (1996): see 2.1.

Coolidge, John S., 'Marvell and Horace', *Modern Philology*, 63 (1965), 111–20.

Cronk (1999): see 2.12.

Edden, Valerie, 'The Best of Lyric Poets', in C. D. N. Costa (ed.), *Horace* (London and Boston, 1973), 135–59. [Surveys the changes in Horace's reputation in Renaissance England.]

Erskine-Hill, Howard, 'Courtiers of Horace: Donne's *Saytre* IV and Pope's *Fourth Satire of Dr John Donne, Dean of St Paul's Versifyed*', in. A. J. Smith (ed.), *John Donne: Essays in Celebration* (New York, 1973), 273–307.

Gregory, E. R., 'Marvell's "Horatian Ode": A Reconsideration', *Forum*, 10 (1972), 11–18.

Guillén, Claudio, 'Notes toward the Study of the Renaissance Letter', in Lewalski (1986), 70–101: see 1.3.B.

Herrick (1946): see 3.4.

Hooley, D. M., '"But above All He Excelleth in a Translation": Ben Jonson's Horace', in Linda Anderson, Janis Lull, and David Haley (eds), *'A Certain Text': Close Readings and Textual Studies on Shakespeare and Others* (Newark, DE, and London, 2002), 150–72.

Hunt, Clay, 'The Elizabethan Background of Neo-Classic Polite Verse', *English Literary History*, 8 (1941), 263–304.

Kupersmith, William, *Roman Satirists in Seventeenth-Century England* (Lincoln, NE, 1985). [An important reception study of Horace, Juvenal, and Persius.]

Levine, Jay Arnold, 'The Status of the Verse Epistle before Pope', *Studies in Philology*, 59 (1962), 659–82.

Martindale and Hopkins (1993): see 2.2.

Moss, Ann, 'Horace in the Sixteenth Century: Commentators into Critics', in Norton (1999), 66–76: see 2.12. [A useful synopsis of the reception of Horatian concepts of literary criticism.]

Moul, Victoria, 'Ben Jonson's *Poetaster*: Classical Translation and the Location of Cultural Authority', *Translation and Literature*, 15 (2006), 21–46.

Moul, Victoria, 'Translation as Commentary? The Case of Ben Jonson's *Ars Poetica*', *Palimpsestes*, 20 (2007), 59–71.

Moul (2010): see 1.3.B.

Mukherjee, Neel, 'Thomas Drant's Rewriting of Horace', *Studies in English Literature, 1500–1900*, 40 (2000), 1–20.

Palmer, D. J., 'The Verse Epistle', in M. Bradbury and D. Palmer (eds), *Metaphysical Poetry* (New York, 1970), 73–99.

Pierce, Robert B., 'Ben Jonson's Horace and Horace's Ben Jonson', *Studies in Philology*, 78 (1981), 20–31.

Regenos, Graydon W., 'The Influence of Horace on Robert Herrick', *Philological Quarterly*, 26 (1947), 268–84.

Ribeiro, Alvaro, 'Sir John Roe: Ben Jonson's Friend', *Review of English Studies*, 24 (1973), 153–64.

Røstvig, Maren-Sofie, *The Happy Man: Studies in the Metamorphoses of a Classical Ideal, 1600–1700* (Oslo, 1954). [Traces the motif of Horace's *beatus ille* in seventeenth-century English poetry.]

Ruggles, Melville L., 'Horace and Herrick', *Classical Journal*, 31 (1936), 223–34.

Salman, Phillips, 'Instruction and Delight in Medieval and Renaissance Criticism', *Renaissance Quarterly*, 32 (1979), 303–32. [Traces the reception of a key *topos* in Horatian criticism.]

Scodel, Joshua, 'Lyric', in Braden, Cummings and Gillespie (2010), 212–47: see 1.5.

Shae, David, 'The First English Editions of Horace, Juvenal, and Persius', *Library*, 25 (1970), 219–25.

Stapleton, M. L., ' "He Nothing Common Did or Mean": Marvell's Charles I and Horace's *Non humilis mulier*', *English Language Notes*, 30 (1993), 31–40.

Steggle, Matthew, '*Valeat res ludicra*: An Imitation of Horace in Jonson's "Ode to Himself" ', *Ben Jonson Journal*, 5 (1998), 101–13.

Syfret, R. H., 'Marvell's "Horatian Ode" ', *Review of English Studies*, 12 (1961), 160–72.

Westbrook, Perry D., 'Horace's Influence on Shakespeare's *Antony and Cleopatra*', *PMLA*, 62 (1947), 392–8.

3.13. Juvenal and Persius

Baumlin, James S., 'Donne's Christian Diatribes: Persius and the Rhetorical Persona of "Satyre III" and "Satyre V" ', in Claude J. Sommers and Ted-Larry Pebworth (eds), *The Eagle and the Dove: Reassessing John Donne* (Columbia, MO, 1986), 92–105.

Bramble (1974): see 2.2.

Corballis, Richard, *George Chapman's Minor Translations: A Critical Edition of his Renderings of Musaeus, Hesiod and Juvenal* (Salzburg, 1984).

Eddy, Y. Shikany, 'Donne's "Satyre I": The Influence of Persius's "Satire III" ', *Studies in English Literature, 1500–1900*, 21 (1981), 111–22.

Hooley (2012): see 2.2.

McEuen, Katherine A., 'Jonson and Juvenal', *Review of English Studies*, 82 (1945), 92–104.

Stein, Arnold, 'Joseph Hall's Imitation of Juvenal', *Modern Language Review*, 43 (1948), 315–22.

Waddington, Raymond B., 'Chapman and Persius: The Epitaph to *Ovid's Banquet of Sence*', *Review of English Studies*, 19 (1968), 158–62.

3.14. Livy

Barton (2004): see 2.7.

Billanovich, Giuseppe, 'Petrarch and the Textual Tradition of Livy', *Journal of the Warburg and Courtauld Institutes*, 14 (1951), 137–208. [A classic study showing that Petrarch refined his scholarly methodology with Livy and used this work as a base for his poetic composition.]

Culhane, Peter, 'Philemon Holland's Livy: Peritexts and Contexts', *Translation and Literature*, 13 (2004), 268–86.

Culhane (2005): see 1.5.

Jardine and Grafton (1990): see 1.7.

Shuger (1998): see 2.7.

Smuts (1993): see 1.7.

Whitfield, J. H., 'Livy > Tacitus', in Bolgar (1976), 281–94: see 1.2.

3.15. Longinus

Cheney (2009): see 1.7.

Cronk (1999): see 2.12.

Elledge, Scott, 'Cowley's "Ode of Wit" and Longinus on the Sublime: A Study of One Definition of the Word "Wit"', *Modern Language Quarterly*, 9 (1948), 185–98.

Hopkins, David, 'The English Homer: Shakespeare, Longinus, and English "Neo-Classicism"', in Martindale and Taylor (2004), 261–76: see 2.1.

Spencer, T. J. B., 'Longinus in English Criticism: Influences before Milton', *Review of English Studies*, 8 (1957), 137–43.

Weinberg, Bernard, 'Translations and Commentaries of Longinus, *On the Sublime*, to 1600: A Bibliography', *Modern Philology*, 47 (1950), 145–51. [Offers valuable primary-source data.]

3.16. Lucan

Backhaus (2005): see 2.4.

Blissett, William, 'Lucan's Caesar and the Elizabethan Villain', *Studies in Philology*, 53 (1956), 553–75. [An interesting study of how one of Lucan's characters became a stereotype in Renaissance literature.]

Bruère (1949): see 2.4.

Cheney, Patrick, 'Milton, Marlowe, and Lucan: The English Authorship of Republican Liberty', *Milton Studies*, 49 (2008), 1–19.

Cheney (2009): see 1.7.

Cliff (1999): see 2.4.

Dörrie, H., 'Lucan in der Kritik des 16. und 17. Jahrhunderts', in Bolgar (1976), 163–9: see 1.2. [A study of Lucan's reputation in the Renaissance.]

Gibson (2003): see 1.7.

Gill, Roma, 'Marlowe, Lucan, and Sulpitius', *Review of English Studies*, 96 (1973), 401–13.

Hardie (2011b): see 2.4.

Hooley, Dan, 'Raising the Dead: Marlowe's Lucan', in Alexandra Lianeri and Vanda Zajko (eds), *Translation and the Classic: Identity as Change in the History of Culture* (Oxford, 2008), 243–60.

Ingledew (1962): see 2.4.

Leidig (1975): see 2.4. [Contains a lengthy section on Lucan in the English Renaissance, with a consideration of whether the work should be considered history or poetry.]

Logan, George M. (1967): see 2.4.

Logan, George M., 'Daniel's *Civil Wars* and Lucan's *Pharsalia*', *Studies in English Literature, 1500–1900*, 11 (1971), 53–68.

Logan, George M., 'Lucan–Daniel–Shakespeare: New Light on the Relation between *The Civil Wars* and *Richard II*', *Shakespeare Studies*, 9 (1976), 121–40.

Martindale (1986): see 2.4.

Martindale (1998): see 2.4.

Paleit, E., 'Lucan in the Renaissance, Pre-1625: An Introduction', *Literature Compass*, 1/1 (2003–4) <doi: 10.1111/j.1741-4113.2004.00123.x> (accessed 20 March 2015). [A valuable overview.]

Paleit, E., 'The "Caesarist" Reader and Lucan's *Bellum Ciuile, ca.* 1590 to 1610', *Review of English Studies*, 62 (2011), 212–40.

Quint (1993): see 2.4.

Ronan, Clifford, 'Lucan and the Self-Incised Voids of *Julius Caesar*', in Davidson, Johnson, and Stroupe (1993), 132–43: see 3.8.

Shapiro, James, '"Metre Meete to Furnish Lucans Style": Reconsidering Marlowe's *Lucan*', in Kenneth Friedenreich, Roma Gill, and Constance B. Kuriyama (eds), *'A Poet and a Filthy Play-maker': New Essays on Christopher Marlowe* (New York, 1988), 315–25.

Shifflett, Andrew, '"By Lucan Driv'n About": A Jonsonian Marvell's Lucanic Milton', *Renaissance Quarterly*, 49 (1996), 803–23.

Wright, Gillian, 'What Daniel Really Did with the *Pharsalia*: The Civil Wars, Lucan, and King James', *Review of English Studies*, 55 (2004), 210–32.

3.17. Lucian

Ashworth, Ann, 'Hamlet's Epic Descent into Lucian's Hades: An Alchemical and Christian Transformation', *Journal of Evolutionary Psychology*, 12 (1991), 165–73.

Branham, R. Bracht, 'Utopian Laughter: Lucian and Thomas More', *Moreana*, 86 (1985), 23–43.

Dorsch, T. S., 'Sir Thomas More and Lucian: An Interpretation of *Utopia*', *Archiv für das Studium der neueren Sprachen und Literaturen*, 203 (1966), 345–63.

Marsh, David, *Lucian and the Latins: Humor and Humanism in the Early Renaissance* (Ann Arbor, 1998). [Describes how Renaissance authors rediscovered the comic writings of Lucian.]

Robinson, Christopher, *Lucian and his Influence in Europe* (Chapel Hill, NC, 1979). [A lively survey of Lucian's influence, heavily grounded in Renaissance writers.]

Thompson, C. R., *The Translations of Lucian by Erasmus and St Thomas More* (Ithaca, NY, 1940).

Wooden, Warren W., 'Thomas More and Lucian: A Study of Satiric Influence and Technique', *Studies in English*, 13 (1972), 43–57.

3.18. Lucretius

Barber, Reid, 'Between Atoms and the Spirit: Lucy Hutchinson's Translation of Lucretius', in Suzuki (2009), 333–48.

de Quehen, Hugh, 'Ease and Flow in Lucy Hutchinson's Lucretius', *Studies in Philology*, 93 (1996), 288–303.

Esolen (1994): see 2.4.

Gillespie, Stuart, 'Lucretius in the English Renaissance', in *The Cambridge Companion to Lucretius*, ed. Stuart Gillespie and Philip Hardie (Cambridge, 2007), pp. 242–53. [A valuable overview.]

Goldberg, Jonathan, 'Lucy Hutchinson Writing Matter', in Suzuki (2009a), 349–76.

Goldberg, Jonathan, *The Seeds of Things: Theorizing Sexuality and Materiality in Renaissance Representations* (New York, 2009b). [Includes chapters on Spenser, Milton, Margaret Cavendish, and Lucy Hutchinson, in their relation to Lucretian atomism.]

Greenblatt, Stephen, *The Swerve: How the World Became Modern* (New York, 2011). [An influential book, aimed at the educated general reader but generally accurate and engaging.]

Hadzits, George Depue, *Lucretius and his Influence* (New York, 1935). [Contains seventy pages on the Renaissance.]

Martin, L. C., 'Shakespeare, Lucretius, and the Commonplaces', *Review of English Studies*, 83 (1945), 174–82.

Palmer, Ada, 'Reading Lucretius in the Renaissance', *Journal of the History of Ideas*, 73 (2012), 395–416. [A thoughtful analysis of what Renaissance readers actually responded to in Lucretius' text.]

Passannante, Gerard, 'The Art of Reading Earthquakes: On Harvey's Wit, Ramus's Method, and the Renaissance of Lucretius', *Renaissance Quarterly*, 61 (2008), 792–832.

Passannante, Gerard, *The Lucretian Renaissance: Philology and the Afterlife of Tradition* (Chicago, 2011). [Traces the survival of Lucretius, showing how the philosophy of atoms and the void re-emerged in the Renaissance as a story about reading and letters before it took on a more purely scientific significance.]

Pollock, Jonathan, '*King Lear* in the Light of Lucretius: *Nullam rem e nihilo*', in François Laroque, Pierre Iselin, and Sophie Alatorre (eds), *'And That's True Too': New Essays on King Lear* (Newcastle upon Tyne, 2009), 165–77.

Ramachandran, Ayesha, 'Edmund Spenser, Lucretian Neoplatonist: Cosmology in the *Fowre Hymnes*', *Spenser Studies*, 24 (2009), 373–411.

Ramachandran, Ayesha, 'Mutabilitie's Lucretian Metaphysics: Scepticism and Cosmic Process in Spenser's Cantos', in Jane Grogan (ed.), *Celebrating Mutabilitie: Essays on Edmund Spenser's Mutabilitie Cantos* (Manchester, 2010), 220–45.
Suzuki, Mihoko (ed.), *Anne Clifford and Lucy Hutchinson* (Surrey, 2009).
Whitaker (1936): see 2.4.

3.19. Martial

Austin, Warren B., 'Thomas Watson's Adaptation of an Epigram by Martial', *Renaissance News*, 13 (1960), 134–40.
Loewenstein, Joseph, 'Martial, Jonson, and the Assertion of Plagiarism', in Sharpe and Zwicker (2003), 275–94.
McPherson, David C., 'Ben Jonson, Martial, and the Bawdy Epigram', *Res Publica Litterarum*, 2 (1979), 217–28.
Nixon (1927): see 2.2.
Sharpe, Kevin, and Zwicker, Steven (eds), *Reading, Society, and Politics in Early Modern England* (Cambridge, 2003).
Simmons, Joyce Monroe, 'Martial and Seneca: A Renaissance Perspective', *Medievalia et Humanistica*, 17 (1991), 27–40.
Stapleton, Paul J., 'A Priest and a "Queen": Donne's Epigram "Martial" ', *John Donne Journal*, 28 (2009), 93–118.
Sullivan (1990): see 2.2.
Sullivan, J. P., *Martial: The Classical Heritage* (New York and London, 1993). [Includes criticism of Martial by Renaissance writers.]
Whipple, T. K., *Martial and the English Epigram from Sir Thomas Wyatt to Ben Jonson* (New York, 1970). [A valuable overview.]

3.20. Other Greek Authors

Barbour, Reid, 'Remarkable Ingratitude: Bacon, Prometheus, Democritus', *Studies in English Literature, 1500–1900*, 32 (1992), 79–90.
Braden, Gordon, ' "The Divine Poem of Muaseus" ', in Braden (1978c), 55–153: see 2.8. [A detailed analysis of Marlowe's adaptation of *Hero and Leander*.]
Heninger (1974): see 3.11. [Explores *inter alia* the kind of poetry created under Pythagorean influence.]
Kroll, Norma, 'The Democritean Universe in Webster's *The White Devil*', *Comparative Drama*, 7 (1973), 3–21.
Revard, Stella P., 'Pindar and Jonson's Cary-Morison Ode', in Claude J. Summers and Ted-Larry Pebworth (eds), *Classic and Cavalier: Essays on Jonson and the Sons of Ben* (Pittsburgh, 1982), 17–29.
Revard, Stella P., *Pindar and the Renaissance Hymn-Ode: 1450–1700* (Tempe, AZ, 2001). [The standard treatment of the subject.]
Rosenmeyer, Thomas, *The Green Cabinet: Theocritus and the European Pastoral Lyric* (Berkeley and Los Angeles, 1969). [An often-cited comparative study.]

Woodward, A. M., 'Greek History at the Renaissance', *Journal of Hellenic Studies*, 63 (1943), 1–14. [Follows the rediscovery of the Greek historians from Italy through the rest of Europe.]

3.21. Other Latin Authors

Carver (2007): see 2.10. [On Apuleius.]

Chevallier, J. R. (ed.), *Présence de César: Hommage au Doyen M. Rambaud* (Paris, 1985). [A large essay collection, half of which is devoted to Caesar in the Renaissance.]

Gaisser, Julia, *The Fortunes of Apuleius and the Golden Ass: A Study in Transmission and Reception* (Princeton, 2008). [The definitive study of the Renaissance reception of the only complete Latin novel to have come down from antiquity.]

Harding, Harold F., 'Quintilian's Witnesses', in Raymond F. Howes (ed.), *Historical Studies of Rhetoric and Rhetoricians* (Ithaca, NY, 1969), 90–106. [Surveys Quintilian's influence in England, stressing the importance of the Renaissance.]

Johnson, R., 'Quintilian's Place in European Education', in M. Kelly (ed.), *For Service to Classical Studies: Essays in Honour of Francis Letters* (Melbourne, 1966), 79–101. ['The history of European education since the Renaissance has been the story, first, of Quintilian's domination and then of reaction against it.']

Kewes, P., 'Julius Caesar in Jacobean England', *Seventeenth Century*, 17 (2002), 155–86. [Explores the representations of Caesar in the context of Jacobean politics and political thought.]

Miller, Anthony, 'The Proem to *The Faerie Queene*, Book II: Spenser, Pliny, and Undiscovered Worlds', *Classical and Modern Literature*, 25 (2005), 1–7.

Nauert, Charles, Jr, 'Humanists, Scientists, and Pliny: Changing Approaches to a Classical Author', *American Historical Review*, 84 (1979), 72–85. [Documents a change in the use of Pliny's work, from a text to be elucidated to a potential source for truth.]

Newlands, Carole E., 'Statius' Villa Poems and Jonson's *To Penshurst*: The Shaping of a Tradition', *Classical and Modern Literature*, 8 (1988), 291–300.

Smuts (1993): see 1.7. [On the Roman historians.]

Stuckey, Johanna, 'Petronius the "Ancient": His Reputation and Influence in Seventeenth-Century England', *Rivista di studi classici*, 20 (1972), 145–53.

Zissos, Andrew, 'Reception of Valerius Flaccus' *Argonautica*', *International Journal of the Classical Tradition*, 13 (2006), 165–85. [Shows how this minor epic became a fashionable subject for artists and writers in the Renaissance.]

3.22. Ovid

Armstrong, Alan, 'The Apprenticeship of John Donne: Ovid and the Elegies', *50 English Literary History*, 44 (1977), 419–42.

Barkan, Leonard, '"Living Sculptures": Ovid, Michelangelo, and *The Winter's Tale*', *English Literary History*, 48 (1981), 639–67. [An interesting interdisciplinary study.]

Baruzzo, Barbara, '"Ten Little *Fabulae*": Ovidian Tales of Love and Metamorphosis in *A Midsummer Night's Dream*', *Cahiers élisabéthains*, 45 (1994), 21–31.

Bate, Jonathan, 'Ovid and the Mature Tragedies: Metamorphosis in *Othello* and *King Lear*', *Shakespeare Survey*, 41 (1989), 133–44.

Bate, Jonathan, 'Ovid and the Sonnets: Or, Did Shakespeare Feel the Anxiety of Influence?' *Shakespeare Survey*, 42 (1990), 65–76.

Bate (1993): see 1.3.B.

Bedford, R. D., 'Ovid Metamorphosed: Donne's "Elegy XVI"', *Essays in Criticism*, 32 (1982), 219–36.

Boehrer, Bruce, 'Ovid and the Dilemma of the Cuckold in English Renaissance Drama', in Stanivukovic (2001), 171–88.

Braden, Gordon, 'Golding's Ovid', in Braden (1978c), 1–54: see 2.8.

Braden (2000): see 1.3.B.

Brown, Sarah Annes, 'Ovid, Golding, and *The Tempest*', *Translation and Literature*, 3 (1994), 3–29. [Shows the importance of a translation as a mediation between a text and its classical model.]

Burrow (1988): see 2.4.

Burrow, Colin, 'Re-Embodying Ovid: Renaissance Afterlives', in Hardie (2002), 301–19: see 1.3.A.

Calabrese (1994): see 1.3.A.

Callaghan, Dympna, 'The Book of Changes in a Time of Change: Ovid's *Metamorphoses* in Post-Reformation England and *Venus and Adonis*', in Richard Dutton and Jean E. Howard (eds), *A Companion to Shakespeare's Works*, vol. 4: *The Poems, Problem Comedies, Late Plays* (Malden, MA, 2006), 27–45.

Carter (2011): see 1.4.B.

Cheney (1997): see 1.3.A.

Cheney, Patrick, 'Career Rivalry and the Writing of Counter-Nationhood: Ovid, Spenser, and Philomela in Marlowe's "The Passionate Shepherd to His Love"', *English Literary History*, 65 (1998), 523–55.

Cheney, Patrick, '"Deep-Brained Sonnets" and "Tragic Shows": Shakespeare's Late Ovidian Art in *A Lover's Complaint*', in Shirley Sharon-Zisser and Stephen Whitworth (eds), *Critical Essays on Shakespeare's A Lover's Complaint* (Aldershot, 2006), 55–77.

Clarke, Danielle, 'The Myth of Philomela and the Origins of English Renaissance Poetry', in Anna-Julia Zwierlein (ed.), *Gender and Creation: Surveying Gendered Myths of Creativity, Authority, and Authorship* (Heidelberg, 2010), 43–63.

Crockett, Bryan, '"The Wittiest Partition": Pyramus and Thisbe in Ovid and Shakespeare', *Classical and Modern Literature*, 12 (1991), 49–58.

Dane, Joseph A., 'The Ovids of Ben Jonson in *Poetaster* and in *Epicoene*', in Davidson, Gianakaris, and Stroupe (1986), 103–15.

Davidson, Clifford, Gianakaris, C. J., and Stroupe, John H. (eds), *Drama in the Renaissance: Comparative and Critical Essays* (New York, 1986).

Davis, Joel, 'Paulina's Paint and the Dialectic of Masculine Desire in the *Metamorphoses*, *Pandosto*, and *The Winter's Tale*', *Papers on Language and Literature*, 39 (2003), 115–43.

Deitch, Judith, 'The Girl He Left Behind: Ovidian *Imitatio* and the Body of Echo in Spenser's "Epithalamion"', in Stanivukovic (2001), 224–38.

Di Biase, Carmine, 'Ovid, Pettie, and the Mythic Foundation of *Cymbeline*', *Cahiers élisabéthains*, 46 (1994), 59–70.

Dooley, Mark, 'Inversion, Metamorphosis, and Sexual Difference', in Stanivukovic (2001), 59–76.

Dorangeon, Simone, 'Réception d'Ovide dans la Renaissance anglaise', in Georges Forestier and Jean-Pierre Néraudau (eds), *Un classicisme ou des classicismes?* (Pau, 1995), 191–7.

DuRocher, Richard J., *Milton and Ovid* (Ithaca, NY, 1985). [An important book, to be used with Kilgour (2012).]

Enterline (2006): see 1.4.B.

Forey, Madeleine, '"Bless Thee, Bottom, Bless Thee! Thou Art Translated!": Ovid, Golding, and *A Midsummer Night's Dream*', *Modern Language Review*, 93 (1998), 321–9.

Fox, Cora, 'Spenser's Grieving Adicia and the Gender Politics of Renaissance Ovidianism', *English Literary History*, 69 (2002), 385–412.

Fox, Cora, *Ovid and the Politics of Emotion in Elizabethan England* (New York, 2009). [Shows how the retellings of Ovidian stories helped redefine emotions and the political efficacy of emotional expression in sixteenth-century England.]

Friedmann, Anthony E., 'The Diana–Actaeon Episode in Ovid's *Metamorphoses* and *The Faerie Queene*', *Comparative Literature*, 18 (1966), 289–99.

Getty, Laura J., 'Circumventing Petrarch: Subreading Ovid's *Tristia* in Spenser's *Amoretti*', *Philological Quarterly*, 79 (2000), 293–314.

Gibbs, Gary G., 'Arthur Golding's *Metamorphoses*: Myth in an Elizabethan Political Context', *Renaissance Studies*, 22 (2008), 557–75.

Gless, Darryl J., 'Chapman's Ironic Ovid', *English Literary Renaissance*, 9 (1979), 21–41.

Gransden, K. W., '*Lente currite, noctis equi*: Chaucer, *Troilus and Criseyde* 3.1422–70, Donne, "The Sun Rising" and Ovid, *Amores* 1.13', in West and Woodman (1979), 157–71.

Green (2009): see 2.4.

Greenburg, Bradley, '"The Double Variacioun of Worldly Blisse and Transmutacioun": Shakespeare's Return to Ovid in *Troilus and Cressida*', *Studies in Medieval and Renaissance History*, 20 (2008), 293–312.

Guy-Bray, Stephen, 'Rosamond's Complaint: Daniel, Ovid, and the Purpose of Poetry', *Renaissance Studies*, 22/3 (2008) [special topics issue titled *The Rhetoric of Complaint: Ovid's Heroides in the Renaissance and Restoration*], 338–50.

Harmer, James, 'Spenser's "Goodly Thought": *Heroides* 15 and *The Teares of the Muses*', *Renaissance Studies*, 22 (2008), 324–37.

Harvey, Elizabeth, 'Ventriloquizing Sappho: Ovid, Donne, and the Erotics of the Feminine Voice', *Criticism*, 31 (1989), 115–38. [An interesting influence study from a feminist perspective.]

Himuro, Misako, 'Donne and Ovid: Two Valedictory Poems in Relation to *Metamorphoses* 11.410–748', *Review of English Studies*, 59 (2008), 677–700.

Holohan (1976): see 1.3.B.

Hulse (1981): see 2.6.

James, Heather, 'Shakespeare's Learned Heroines in Ovid's Schoolroom', in Martindale and Taylor (2004), 66–85: see 2.1.

James, Heather, 'Ovid and the Question of Politics in Early Modern England', in Yvonne Bruce (ed.), *Images of Matter: Essays on British Literature of the Middle Ages and Renaissance* (Newark, DE, 2005), 92–122.

James, Heather, 'Ovid in Renaissance English Literature', in Peter E. Knox (ed.), *A Companion to Ovid* (Oxford, 2009), 423–41. [A useful overview.]

Jameson (1973): see 1.4.A.

Kambasković-Sawers, Danijela, '"Never Was I the Golden Cloud": Ovidian Myth, Ambiguous Speaker and the Narrative in the Sonnet Sequences by Petrarch, Sidney and Spenser', *Renaissance Studies,* 21 (2007), 637–61.

Kambasković-Sawers, Danijela, '"A Satire to Decay": Ovidian Myth and the Secret Rhetoric of Shakespeare's Sonnets', in Neill, Chalk, and Johnson (2010), 231–45: see 3.10.

Keach, William, *Elizabethan Erotic Narratives: Irony and Pathos in the Ovidian Poetry of Shakespeare, Marlowe, and their Contemporaries* (Hassocks, 1977). [An unusually thoughtful, widely ranging influence study.]

Keith, Alison, and Rupp, Stephen, *Metamorphosis: The Changing Face of Ovid in Medieval and Early Modern Europe* (Toronto, 2007). [A valuable volume, not limited to England.]

Kilgour (2010): see 1.3.A.

Kilgour, Maggie, *Milton and the Metamorphosis of Ovid* (Oxford, 2012). [An important new study that analyses Milton's appropriation of Ovid in relation to his predecessors and contemporaries.]

Kitch, Aaron, 'The Golden Muse: Protestantism, Mercantilism, and the Uses of Ovid in Marlowe's *Hero and Leander*', *Religion and Literature,* 38 (2006), 157–76.

Klose, Dietrich, 'Shakespeare und Ovid', *Shakespeare-Jahrbuch* (1968), 72–93.

Koppenfels, Werner, '"Lust in Action": Uber einige Metamorphosen Ovids in der elisabethanischen Literatur', *Deutsche Shakespeare-Gesellschaft West: Jahrbuch* (1989), 242–65.

Lamb, M. E., 'Ovid's *Metamorphoses* and Shakespeare's *Twelfth Night*', *New York Literary Forum,* 5–6 (1980), 63–77.

Lamb, M. E., 'Ovid and *The Winter's Tale*: Conflicting Views toward Art', in W. R. Elton and William B. Long (eds), *Shakespeare and Dramatic Tradition* (Newark, DE, 1989), 69–87.

Laroque, François, 'Ovidian Transformations and Folk Festivities in *A Midsummer Night's Dream, The Merry Wives of Windsor,* and *As You Like It*', *Cahiers élisabéthains,* 25 (1984), 23–36.

Laroque, François, 'Ovidian V(o)ices in Marlowe and Shakespeare: The Actaeon Variations', in A. B. Taylor (ed.), *Shakespeare's Ovid: The Metamorphoses in the Plays and Poems* (Cambridge, 2000), 165–77.

Lugo, Jessica, 'Blood, Barbarism, and Belly Laughs: Shakespeare's Titus and Ovid's Philomela', *English Studies,* 88 (2007), 401–17.

Lyne, Raphael, 'Ovid, Golding, and the "Rough Magic" of *The Tempest*', in Taylor (2000), 150–64.

Lyne (2001): see 2.4.

Lyne (2002): see 2.4.

Lyne, Raphael, 'Intertextuality and the Female Voice after the *Heroides*', *Renaissance Studies*, 22 (2008), 307–23.

MacDonald, Joyce Green, 'Ovid and Women's Pastoral in Lady Mary Wroth's *Love's Victory*', *Studies in English Literature, 1500–1900*, 51 (2011), 447–63.

Macfie, Pamela Royston, 'The Ovidian Underworld in *Othello* 3.3', *Renaissance Papers* (1997), 45–60.

Macfie, Pamela Royston, 'Ghostly Metamorphoses: Chapman, Marlowe, and Ovid's Philomela', *John Donne Journal*, 18 (1999), 177–93.

Macfie, Pamela Royston, 'Marlowe's Ghost-Writing of Ovid's *Heroides*', *Renaissance Papers* (2001), 57–72.

Maisano, Scott, 'Reforming Metamorphoses: The Epic in Translation as a "Major Work" of the English Renaissance', in Boyd and Fox (2010), 142–50: see 1.4.B.

Martin, Christopher, *Policy in Love: Lyric and Public in Ovid, Petrarch, and Shakespeare* (Pittsburgh, 1994). [Attempts to develop a new understanding of private lyric poetry that accounts for its interaction with multiple public audiences.]

Martindale (1986): see 2.4.

Merrix, Robert P., 'The Phaëton Allusion in *Richard II*: The Search for Identity', *English Literary Renaissance*, 17 (1987), 277–87.

Miller, Paul Allen, 'Sidney, Petrarch, and Ovid: or, Imitation as Subversion', *English Literary History*, 58 (1991), 499–522.

Milowicki, Edward J., 'Ovid through Shakespeare: The Divided Self', *Poetics Today*, 16 (1995), 217–52.

Moore (2000): see 2.10.

Moss (1982): see 1.2.

Mueller, Martin, 'Hermione's Wrinkles, or Ovid Transformed: An Essay on *The Winter's Tale*', *Comparative Drama*, 5 (1971), 226–39.

Mulvihill, James D., 'Jonson's *The Poetaster* and the Ovidian Debate', *Studies in English Literature, 1500–1900*, 22 (1982), 239–55.

Newcomb, Lori Humphrey, '"If That Which Is Lost Be Not Found": Monumental Bodies, Spectacular Bodies in *The Winter's Tale*', in Stanivukovic (2001), 239–59.

Nuttall, A. D., 'Ovid's Narcissus and Shakespeare's *Richard II*: The Reflected Self', in Charles Martindale (ed.), *Ovid Renewed: Ovidian Influences on Literature and Art from the Middle Ages to the Twentieth Century* (Cambridge, 1988), 137–50.

Oakley-Brown, Liz, '*Titus Andronicus* and the Cultural Politics of Translation in Early Modern England', *Renaissance Studies*, 19 (2005), 325–47.

Olmsted (1996): see 3.11.

Pearcy, Lee T., *The Mediated Muse: English Translations of Ovid, 1560–1700* (Hamden, CT, 1984). [A useful survey, focused on Dryden.]

Perng, Huizung, 'Genre Study and Intertextuality: The Case of Ovid and Spenser', *Studies in Language and Literature*, 7 (1996), 135–53.

Phillippy, Patricia, '"Loytering in Love": Ovid's *Heroides*, Hospitality, and Humanist Education in *The Taming of the Shrew*', *Criticism*, 40 (1998), 27–53. [An interesting study that uses Ovid's role in a key Shakespearean play to interrogate gender issues in the Renaissance.]

Pincombe, Michael, 'The Ovidian Hermaphrodite: Moralizations by Peend and Spenser', in Stanivukovic (2001), 155–70.

Poole, Kristin, 'The Devil's in the Archive: Doctor Faustus and Ovidian Physics', *Renaissance Drama*, 35 (2006), 191–219.

Pugh (2005): see 2.4.

Reid, Lindsay Ann, '*Certamen*, Interpretation, and Ovidian Narration in *The Faerie Queene* III.ix–xii', *Spenser Studies*, 22 (2007), 171–84.

Roberts, Jeanne Addison, 'Anxiety and Influence: Milton, Ovid, and Shakespeare', *South Atlantic Review*, 53 (1988), 59–75.

Roe, John, 'Ovid "Renascent" in *Venus and Adonis* and *Hero and Leander*', in Taylor (2000), 31–46.

Rudd, Niall, 'Pyramus and Thisbe in Shakespeare and Ovid: *A Midsummer Night's Dream* and *Metamorphoses* 4.1–166', in West and Woodman (1979), 173–93.

Sandvoss, Ernst, '"Pyramus und Thisbe" bei Ovid und Shakespeare: Ein motivgeschichtlicher Vergleich', in Rüdiger Ahrens (ed.), *William Shakespeare: Didaktisches Handbuch* (Munich, 1982), 1. 79–99.

Schulman, Jeff, 'At the Crossroads of Myth: The Hermeneutics of Hercules from Ovid to Shakespeare', *English Literary History*, 50 (1983), 83–105.

Scott, Sarah K., and Stapleton, M. L. (eds), *Christopher Marlowe the Craftsman: Lives, Stage, and Page* (Burlington, VT, 2010).

Scragg, Leah, 'Shakespeare, Lyly, and Ovid: The Influence of *Gallathea* on *A Midsummer Night's Dream*', *Shakespeare Survey*, 30 (1977), 125–34.

Semler, L. E., 'Marlovian Therapy: The Chastisement of Ovid in *Hero and Leander*', *English Literary Renaissance*, 35 (2005), 159–86.

Simpson, James, 'Breaking the Vacuum: Ricardian and Henrician Ovidianism', *Journal of Medieval and Early Modern Studies*, 29 (1999), 325–55.

Stanivukovic, G. (ed.), *Ovid and the Renaissance Body* (Toronto, 2001). [Examines Renaissance reworkings of Ovid as guides to early modern epistemologies and discourses of gender, sexuality, spectatorship, and print culture.]

Stapleton, M. L., *Harmful Eloquence: Ovid's Amores from Antiquity to Shakespeare* (Ann Arbor, 1996). [A valuable comparative study.]

Stapleton, M. L., 'Venus as Praeceptor: The *Ars amatoria* in *Venus and Adonis*', in Philip C. Kolin (ed.), *Venus and Adonis: Critical Essays* (New York, 1997), 309–21.

Stapleton, M. L., 'Devoid of Guilty Shame: Ovidian Tendencies in Spenser's Erotic Poetry', *Modern Philology*, 105 (2007), 271–99.

Stapleton, M. L., 'Edmund Spenser, George Turberville, and Isabella Whitney Read Ovid's *Heroides*', *Studies in Philology*, 105 (2008), 487–519.

Stapleton (2009): see 2.4.

Stapleton, M. L., 'Marlowe's First Ovid: *Certaine of Ovids Elegies*', in Scott and Stapleton (2010), 137–48.

Suzuki, Mihoko, '"Unfitly Yokt Together in One Teeme": Vergil and Ovid in *Faerie Queene*, III.ix', *English Literary Renaissance*, 17 (1987), 172–85.

Taylor, A. B., 'Golding's Ovid, Shakespeare's "Small Latin", and the Real Object of Mockery in "Pyramus and Thisbe"', *Shakespeare Survey*, 42 (1990), 53–64.

Taylor, A. B., 'Melting Earth and Leaping Bulls: Shakespeare's Ovid and Arthur Golding', *Connotations*, 4 (1994–1995), 192–206.

Taylor, A. B., 'Shakespeare Rewriting Ovid: Olivia's Interview with Viola and the Narcissus Myth', *Shakespeare Survey*, 50 (1997), 81–9.

Taylor, A. B. (ed.), *Shakespeare's Ovid: The Metamorphoses in the Plays and Poems* (Cambridge, 2000). [A valuable collection of essays.]

Thomsen, Kerri Lynne, 'Melting Vows: *A Midsummer Night's Dream* and Ovid's *Heroycall Epistles*', *English Language Notes*, 40 (2003), 25–33.

Thorne, Alison, '"Large Complaints in Little Papers": Negotiating Ovidian Genealogies of Complaint in Drayton's *Englands Heroicall Epistles*', *Renaissance Studies*, 22/3 (2008). [Special topics issue titled *The Rhetoric of Complaint: Ovid's Heroides in the Renaissance and Restoration*], 368–84.

Velz, John W., 'The Ovidian Soliloquy in Shakespeare', *Shakespeare Studies*, 18 (1986), 1–24.

West, David, and Woodman, Tony (eds), *Creative Imitation in Latin Literature* (Cambridge, 1979).

Wilkinson, L. P., 'The Renaissance—Sweet Witty Soul', in *Ovid Recalled* (Cambridge, 1955), 399–438. [The classic overview.]

Wilson-Okamura, David, 'Errors about Ovid and Romance', *Spenser Studies*, 23 (2008), 215–34.

Wiseman, Susan, 'The Rhetoric of Complaint: Ovid's *Heroides* in the Renaissance and Restoration', *Renaissance Studies*, 22 (2008), 295–432.

3.23. Plato

Allen, Michael J. B., 'Tamburlaine and Plato: A Colon, a Crux', *Research Opportunities in Renaissance Drama*, 23 (1980), 21–31. [A detailed explanation of a key document in Renaissance Platonism.]

Allen, Michael J. B., *The Platonism of Marsilio Ficino: A Study of his 'Phaedrus' Commentary, its Sources and Genesis* (Berkeley and Los Angeles, 1984).

Arthos, John, 'Milton, Ficino, and the *Charmides*', *Studies in the Renaissance*, 6 (1959), 261–74.

Baker-Smith, Dominic, 'Escape from the Cave: Thomas More and the Vision of Utopia', *Dutch Quarterly Review of Anglo-American Letters*, 15 (1985), 148–61.

Barroll, Leeds, 'Some Versions of Plato in the English Renaissance', *Shakespeare Studies*, 2 (1966), 228–95.

Bennett, J. W., *The Evolution of 'The Faerie Queene'* (New York, 1960).

Bieman, Elizabeth, *Plato Baptized: Towards the Interpretation of Spenser's Mimetic Fictions* (Toronto, 1988).

Birrell, Erica, 'A Midsummer Night's Symposium: Translating Platonic Love in *A Midsummer Night's Dream*', in Liz Oakley-Brown and Ton Hoenselaars (eds), *Shakespeare and the Translation of Identity in Early Modern England* (New York, 2011), 46–73.

Borris (2009): see 2.4.

Burchmore, David W., 'Triamond, Agape, and the Fates: Neoplatonic Cosmology in Spenser's Legend of Friendship', *Spenser Studies*, 5 (1985), 45–64.

Cassirer, Ernst, *The Platonic Renaissance in England*, trans. James P. Pettegrove (Austin, TX, 1953). [A classic study, focused on Cambridge scholars.]

Cheney, Patrick, 'Jonson's *The New Inn* and Plato's Myth of the Hermaphrodite', *Renaissance Drama*, 14 (1983), 173–94.

Cheney, Patrick, '*Colin Clouts Come Home Againe*, *Astrophel*, and *The Doleful Lay of Clorinda* (1595)', in Richard McCabe (ed.), *The Oxford Handbook of Edmund Spenser* (Oxford, 2009), 241–6.

Cody, Richard, *The Landscape of the Mind: Pastoralism and Platonic Theory in Tasso's Aminta and Shakespeare's Early Comedies* (Oxford, 1969).

Comito, T., 'A Dialectic of Images in Spenser's *Fowre Hymnes*', *Studies in Philology*, 4 (1977), 301–21.

Conley (1927): see 1.7.

Cragg, Gerald R. (ed.), *The Cambridge Platonists* (New York, 1968).

Danson, Lawrence, *The Harmonies of 'The Merchant of Venice'* (New Haven, 1978).

Ellrodt, Robert, *Neoplatonism in the Poetry of Spenser* (Norwood, PA, 1960).

Emden, A. B., *Bibliographical Register of the University of Oxford, 1501–40* (Oxford, 1974).

Fogel, French, *William Drummond* (New York, 1952).

Fuzier, Jean, 'Le Banquet de Shakespeare: Les Sonnets et le Platonisme authentique', *Études anglaises*, 34 (1991), 1–15.

Gleason, John B., 'Opening Spenser's Wedding Present: The "Marriage Number" of Plato in the "Epithalamion"', *English Literary Renaissance*, 24 (1994), 620–37.

Gordon, D. J., 'The Imagery of Jonson's *The Masque of Blacknesse* and *The Masque of Beautie*', *Journal of the Warburg and Courtauld Institutes*, 6 (1943), 122–41.

Gray, Ronald, *Shakespeare on Love: The Sonnets and Plays in Relation to Plato's Symposium, Alchemy, Christianity and Renaissance Neo-Platonism* (Newcastle upon Tyne, 2011).

Hankins, James, *Plato in the Italian Renaissance*, 2 vols (Leiden and New York, 1990). [The definitive survey, a necessary background for appreciating Renaissance Platonism in England.]

Harrison, J. S., *Platonism in English Poetry of the Sixteenth and Seventeenth Centuries* (New York, 1903).

Hawkins, Harriett, 'The Morality of Elizabethan Drama: Some Footnotes to Plato', in John Carey and Helen Peters (eds), *English Renaissance Studies Presented to Dame Helen Gardner in Honour of her Seventieth Birthday* (Oxford, 1980), 12–32.

Heninger, S. K., 'Sidney and Serranus' *Plato*', *English Literary Renaissance*, 13 (1983), 146–61.

Hughes, Merritt Y., 'Some of Donne's "Ecstasies"', *PMLA*, 75 (1960), 509–18.

Hutton, Sarah, 'Platonism in Some Metaphysical Poets', in Anna Baldwin and Sarah Hutton (eds), *Platonism and the English Imagination* (Cambridge, 1994), 163–77.

Ker, N. R., *Oxford College Libraries in 1556* (Oxford, 1956).

Kerr, W. A. R., 'The Pléiade and Platonism', *Modern Philology*, 5 (1908), 407–21.

Kristeller, Paul O., 'Renaissance Platonism', in Kristeller (1979), 50–65: see 1.2. [A valuable introduction.]

Krouse, M. F., 'Plato and Sidney's *Defence of Poesie*', *Comparative Literature*, 6 (1954), 138–47.

McCabe, Richard A., 'Spenser, Plato, and the Poetics of State', *Spenser Studies*, 24 (2009), 433–52.

Marks, Carol L., 'Thomas Traherne and Hermes Trismegistus', *Renaissance News*, 19/2 (1966), 118–31.

Martz, Louis, *The Paradise within: Studies in Vaughan, Traherne, and Milton* (New Haven, 1964).

Murphy (2008): see 2.3.

Nelson, John Charles, *Renaissance Theory of Love: The Context of Giordano Bruno's 'Eroici furori'* (New York, 1955).

Neuse, Richard T., 'Planting Words in the Soul: Spenser's Socratic Garden of Adonis', *Spenser Studies*, 8 (1987), 79–100.

Panofsky, Erwin, *Studies in Iconology: Humanist Themes in the Art of the Renaissance* (New York, 1962).

Parker, Barbara L., '"A Thing Unfirm": Plato's *Republic* and Shakespeare's *Julius Caesar*', *Shakespeare Quarterly*, 44 (1993), 30–43.

Partee, Morriss H., 'Sir Philip Sidney and the Renaissance Knowledge of Plato', *English Studies*, 51 (1971), 411–24.

Praz, Mario, *Studies in Seventeenth Century Imagery* (Rome, 1939).

Quitslund, Jon, *Spenser's Supreme Fiction: Platonic Natural Philosophy and The Faerie Queene* (Toronto, 2001).

Samuel (1947): see 1.3.B.

Sears, Jayne, 'Ficino and the Platonism of the English Renaissance', *Comparative Literature*, 4 (1952), 214–38.

Sears, Jayne, *Plato in Renaissance England* (Dordrecht, 1995).

Sensabaugh, G. F. 'Love Ethics in Platonic Court Drama, 1625–1642', *Huntington Library Quarterly*, 1 (1938), 277–304.

Smith, A. J., 'Donne: A Reading in his Time of "The Extasie"', *Rivista di letterature moderne e comparate*, 10 (1957), 260–75.

Soellner (1968): see 3.4.

Spingarn, J. E., *A History of Literary Criticism in the Renaissance* (New York, 1924). [A classic study, one strand of which involves Plato's role in Renaissance literary criticism.]

Tovey, Barbara, 'Shakespeare's Apology for Imitative Poetry: *The Tempest* and *The Republic*', *Interpretation*, 11 (1983), 275–316.

Upham, Alfred, *French Influence in English Literature from the Accession of Elizabeth to the Restoration* (New York, 1965).

Walker, D. P., *The Ancient Theology: Studies in Christian Platonism from the Fifteenth to the Eighteenth Century* (Ithaca, NY, 1972). [An interesting study of the Christian–Platonic synthesis that was so influential in the Renaissance.]

Willey, Basil, *The English Moralists* (New York, 1964).

Wilson, Timothy H., 'The Aesthetics of the Good Physician as Traveller: Plato's Philosopher–Ruler, More's Hythloday, and Spenser's Immeritô', *English Studies in Canada,* 28 (2002), 7–30.

Wind (1967): see 3.11.

Yates, Frances A., *Giordano Bruno and the Hermetic Tradition* (Chicago, 1964). [An important, often-cited study.]

3.24. Plautus and Terence

Arthos, John, 'Shakespeare's Transformation of Plautus', *Comparative Drama,* 1 (1967), 239–53.

Beck, Ervin, 'Terence Improved: The Paradigm of the Prodigal Son in English Renaissance Comedy', *Renaissance Drama,* 6 (1973), 107–22.

Bruster, Douglas (1990): see 2.1.

Bruster, Douglas, 'Comedy and Control: Shakespeare and the Plautine *Poeta*', in Davidson, Johnson, and Stroupe (1993), 117–31: see 3.8.

Chalifour (1976): see 2.10.

Cioni, Fernando, 'A Shrew and the Shrew: Shakespeare, Plautus, and the "Bad" Quarto', *Textus,* 11 (1998), 235–60.

Civardi (1996): see 2.1.

Draper, John W., 'Falstaff and the Plautine Parasite', *Classical Journal,* 33 (1938), 390–401.

Duckworth, George E., 'The Influence of Plautus and Terence', in *The Nature of Roman Comedy* (Princeton, 1952), 396–433. [Focuses on England.]

Forsythe, R. S., 'A Plautine Source of *The Merry Wives of Windsor*', *Modern Philology,* 18 (1920), 401–21.

Girard, René, 'Comedies of Errors: Plautus–Shakespeare–Molière', in Ira Konigsberg (ed.), *American Criticism in the Poststructuralist Age* (Ann Arbor, 1981), 66–86.

Hardin, Richard F., 'The Renaissance of Plautine Comedy and the Varieties of Luck in Shakespeare and Other Plotters', *Mediterranean Studies,* 16 (2007a), 143–56.

Hardin (2007b): see 2.1.

Herrick (1950): see 1.5.

Louden, Bruce, '*The Tempest*, Plautus, and the *Rudens*', *Comparative Drama,* 33 (1999), 199–233.

Lyne (2004): see 2.1.

Miola (1994): see 1.5.

Parker, Robert W., 'Terentian Structure and Sidney's Original *Arcadia*', *English Literary Renaissance,* 2 (1972), 61–78.

Paster, Gail K., 'The City in Plautus and Middleton', *Renaissance Drama,* 6 (1973), 29–44.

Riehle (1990): see 2.1.

Robbins (1951): see 1.3.

Rudd, Niall, *The Classical Tradition in Operation: Chaucer/Virgil—Shakespeare/Plautus—Pope/Horace—Tennyson/Lucretius—Pound/Propertius* (Toronto, 1994). [An interesting study that pairs a key classical author with a later writer on whom he exercised significant influence.]

Smith, Bruce R., 'Sir Amorous Knight and the Indecorous Romans; or, Plautus and Terence Play Court in the Renaissance', *Renaissance Drama,* 6 (1973), 3–27.

Smith (1988): see 1.5.

Svendsen, James T., 'The Fusion of Comedy and Romance: Plautus' *Rudens* and Shakespeare's *The Tempest*', in Karelisa V. Hartigan (ed.), *From Pen to Performance: Drama as Conceived and Performed* (Lanham, MD, 1983), 121–34.

Waith (1977): see 3.3.

3.25. Plutarch

Blackwell (1986): see 3.6.

Clary, Frank N., 'Hamlet's Mousetrap and the Play-within-the-Anecdote of Plutarch', in Joanna Gondris (ed.), *Reading Readings: Essays on Shakespeare Editing in the Eighteenth Century* (Madison, WI, 1998), 164–87.

Cook, Albert, 'The Transmutation of Heroic Complexity: Plutarch and Shakespeare', *Classical and Modern Literature,* 17 (1996), 31–43.

Corti, Claudia, '"As if a Man Were Author of Himself": The (Re-)Fashioning of the Oedipal Hero from Plutarch's *Martius* to Shakespeare's *Coriolanus*', in Michelle Marrapodi (ed.), *Culture in the Drama of Shakespeare and his Contemporaries: Rewriting, Remaking, Refashioning* (Aldershot, 2007), 187–95.

Denton, John, 'Plutarch, Shakespeare, Roman Politics, and Renaissance Translation', *Poetica,* 48 (1997), 187–209.

Dillon, Janette, '"Solitariness": Shakespeare and Plutarch', *Journal of English and Germanic Philology,* 78 (1979), 325–44.

Evans, Robert C., 'Flattery in Shakespeare's *Othello*: The Relevance of Plutarch and Sir Thomas Elyot', *Comparative Drama,* 35 (2001), 1–41.

Fleming, Rudd, *Plutarch in the English Renaissance* (Ithaca, NY, 1935). [An older study, still worth consulting.]

George, David, 'Plutarch, Insurrection, and Dearth in *Coriolanus*', in Catherine M. S. Alexander (ed.), *Shakespeare and Politics* (Cambridge, 2004), 110–29.

Graves, Wallace, 'Plutarch's Life of Cato Utican as a Major Source of *Othello*', *Shakespeare Quarterly,* 24 (1973), 181–7.

Green, David C., *Plutarch Revisited: A Study of Shakespeare's Last Roman Tragedies and their Source* (Salzburg, 1979).

Hearsey, Marguerite, 'Sidney's *Defense of Poesy* and Amyot's Preface in North's Plutarch: A Relationship', *Studies in Philology,* 30 (1933), 535–50.

Heuer, Hermann, 'From Plutarch to Shakespeare: A Study of *Coriolanus*', *Shakespeare Survey*, 10 (1957), 50–9.

Homan, Sidney, 'Dion, Alexander, and Demetrius—Plutarch's Forgotten Parallel Lives—as Mirrors for Shakespeare's *Julius Caesar*', *Shakespeare Studies*, 8 (1976), 195–210.

Honigmann (1959): see 2.7.

Lyne, Raphael, 'Grille's Moral Dialogue: Spenser and Plutarch', *Spenser Studies*, 19 (2004), 159–76.

McGrail, Mary Ann (ed.), 'Shakespeare's Plutarch', *Poetica*, 48 (1997), 1–227. [A special issue of the journal that contains a large group of essays on an important topic.]

Maguin, Jean-Marie, 'Preface to a Critical Edition to *Julius Caesar*, with a Chronological Catalogue of Shakespeare's Borrowing from North's Plutarch', *Cahiers élisabethains*, 4 (1973), 15–49.

Miller, Anthony, 'Sidney's *Apology for Poetry* and Plutarch's *Moralia*', *English Literary Renaissance*, 17 (1987), 259–76.

Mossmann (1994): see 1.5.

Mueller, Martin, 'Plutarch's "Life of Brutus" and the Play of its Repetitions in Shakespearean Drama', *Renaissance Drama*, 22 (1991), 47–93.

Pade, Marianne, *The Reception of Plutarch's Lives in Fifteenth-Century Italy*, 2 vols (Copenhagen, 2007). [Discusses the Latin translations of the *Lives* and the environment in which they were produced.]

Rothschild, Herbert B., 'The Oblique Encounter: Shakespeare's Confrontation of Plutarch with Special Reference to *Antony and Cleopatra*', *English Literary Renaissance*, 6 (1976), 404–29.

Schurink (2008): see 2.3.

Serpieri, Alessandro, 'Shakespeare and Plutarch: Intertextuality in Action', in Michele Marrapodi (ed.), *Shakespeare, Italy, and Intertextuality* (Manchester, 2004), 45–58.

Shackford, Martha H., *Plutarch in Renaissance England, with Special Reference to Shakespeare* (1929; repr. Norwood, PA, 1977).

Shawcross, John, 'The Book Index: Plutarch's *Moralia* and John Donne', *Journal of the Rocky Mountain Medieval and Renaissance Association*, 1 (1980), 53–62.

Stirling, Brents, 'Cleopatra's Scene with Seleucus: Plutarch, Daniel, and Shakespeare', *Shakespeare Quarterly*, 15 (1964), 299–311.

Velz, John W., '"Nothing Undervalued to Cato's Daughter": Plutarch's Porcia in the Shakespeare Canon', in Davidson, Gianakaris, and Stroupe (1986), 150–62: see 3.22.

Westerweel, Bart, 'Plutarch's *Lives* and *Coriolanus*: Shakespeare's View of Roman History', in Karl Enenkel, Han L. DeJong, and Jeanine de Landtsheer (eds), *Recreating Ancient History: Episodes from the Greek and Roman Past in the Arts and Literature of the Early Modern Period* (Leiden, 2001), 187–211.

3.26. Sappho

Aercke (1987): see 1.4.A.

Andreadis, Harriette, 'Sappho in Early Modern England: A Study in Sexual Reputation', in Greene (1996), 105–21.

Andreadis, Harriette (2001): see 1.4.B.

Blank, Paula, 'Comparing Sappho to Philaenis: John Donne's "Homopoetics"', *PMLA*, 110 (1995), 358–68.

DeJean (1989): see 1.4.A.

Greene, Ellen (ed.), *Re-Reading Sappho: Reception and Transmission* (Berkeley and Los Angeles, and London, 1996). [An important collection of essays.]

Harvey (1989): see 3.22.

Harvey, Elizabeth, 'Ventriloquizing Sappho, or the Lesbian Muse', in Greene (1996), 79–104. [Traces the reception of Sappho through Ovid, *Heroides* 15, into Donne's 'Sappho to Philaenis'.]

Losocco, Paula, 'Inventing the English Sappho: Katherine Philips' Donnean Poetry', *Journal of English and Germanic Philology*, 102 (2003), 59–87.

Mueller, Janel, 'Troping Utopia: Donne's Brief for Lesbianism in "Sappho to Philaenis"', in James Grantham Turner (ed.), *Sexuality and Gender in Early Modern Europe: Institutions, Texts, Images* (Cambridge, 1993), 182–207.

Revard, Stella P., 'The Sapphic Voice in Donne's "Sappho to Philaenis"', in Claude J. Sommers and Ted-Larry Pebworth (eds), *Renaissance Discourses of Desire* (Columbia, 1993), 63–76.

West, William, 'Thinking with the Body: Sappho's "Sappho to Philaenis," Donne's "Sappho to Philaenis"', *Renaissance Papers* (1994), 67–83.

3.27. Seneca

Binns (1970): see 2.11.

Braden (1985): see 2.3.

Brooks, Harold F., '"Richard III", Unhistorical Amplifications: The Women's Scenes and Seneca', *Modern Language Review*, 75 (1980), 721–37.

Bull, Malcolm, 'Spenser, Seneca, and the Sibyl: Book V of *The Faerie Queene*', *Review of English Studies*, 49 (1998), 416–23.

Charlton, H. B., *The Senecan Tradition in Renaissance Tragedy* (Manchester, 1946). [Contrasts English Senecan tragedy with Italian and French examples.]

Cunliffe (1893): see 2.11.

Evans, Robert O., 'Jonson's Copy of Seneca', in Davidson, Johnson, and Stroupe (1973), 177–212: see 3.8.

Ewbank, Inga-Stina, 'The Fiend-Like Queen: A Note on *Macbeth* and Seneca's *Medea*', *Shakespeare Survey*, 19 (1966), 82–94.

Helms (1997): see 2.11.

Hill, Eugene D., 'Senecan and Virgilian Perspectives in *The Spanish Tragedy*', *English Literary Renaissance*, 15 (1985), 143–65.

Hunter, G. K., 'Seneca and the Elizabethans: A Case-Study in "Influence"', *Shakespeare Studies*, 20 (1967), 17–26).

Hunter, G. K., 'Seneca and Elizabethan Tragedy', in Costa (1974), 166–204: see 1.5.

Hunter, G. K., 'Senecan and English Tragedy', in Costa (1974), 166–204: see 1.5. [A skilled influence study, noting alternative sources and the scholarly filters through which Seneca passed on his way to English tragedy.]

Jacquot, Jean (ed.), *Les Tragédies de Sénèque et le théâtre de la Renaissance* (Paris, 1964). [An essay collection with several pieces on England.]

Joseph, B. L., '*The Spanish Tragedy* and *Hamlet*: Two Exercises in English Seneca', in M. J. Anderson (ed.), *Classical Drama and its Influence: Essays Presented to H. D. F. Kitto*... (1965), 121–34.

Kaufmann, R. J., 'The Senecan Perspective and the Shakespearean Poetic', *Comparative Drama*, 1 (1967), 182–98.

Kiefer, Frederick, 'Seneca's Influence on Renaissance Tragedy: An Annotated Bibliography', *Research Opportunities in Renaissance Drama*, 21 (1978), 17–34.

Kiefer, Frederick, 'Senecan Influence: A Bibliographic Supplement', *Research Opportunities in Renaissance Drama*, 28 (1985), 129–42.

Langford, Larry, 'The Story Shall Be Changed: The Senecan Sources of *A Midsummer Night's Dream*', *Cahiers élisabethains*, 25 (1984), 37–51.

l'Estrange (1679): see 2.3.

Lodge (1620): see 2.3.

Lucas, F. L., *Seneca and Elizabethan Tragedy* (Cambridge, 1922). [An older study, to be read with Braden (1985), in 2.3.]

McMillin, Scott, 'The Book of Seneca in *The Spanish Tragedy*', *Studies in English Literature, 1500–1900*, 14 (1974), 201–8.

Martin, Richard A., 'Fate, Seneca, and Marlowe's *Dido, Queen of Carthage*', *Renaissance Drama*, 11 (1980), 45–66.

Miola (1992): see 1.5.

Ross (1974): see 2.3.

Salmon (1991): see 1.7.

Small, Samuel A., 'The Influence of Seneca', *Shakespeare Association Bulletin*, 10 (1935), 137–50.

Smith (1978): see 1.5.

Stapleton, M. L., '"Shine it like a Comet of Revenge": Seneca, John Studley, and Shakespeare's Joan la Pucelle', *Comparative Literature Studies*, 31 (1994), 229–50.

Wallace, John M., '*Timon of Athens* and the Three Graces: Shakespeare's Senecan Study', *Modern Philology*, 83 (1986), 349–63.

Wallace, John M., 'The Senecan Context of *Coriolanus*', *Modern Philology*, 90 (1993), 465–78.

Welch, Robert, 'Seneca and the English Renaissance: The Old World and the New', in Robert Welch and Suheil Bushrui (eds), *Literature and the Art of Creation* (Totowa, NJ, 1988), 204–18.

Williamson (1932): see 2.3.

Williamson (1971): see 2.5.

Winston (2006): see 1.7.

Woodbridge, Linda, 'Resistance Theory Meets Drama: Tudor Seneca', *Renaissance Drama*, 38 (2010), 155–39.

3.28. Sophocles

Bushnell, Rebecca Weld, 'Oracular Silence in *Oedipus the King* and *Macbeth*', *Classical and Modern Literature*, 2 (1982), 195–204.

Bushnell, Rebecca Weld, 'Stage Tyrants: The Case of Creon and Caesar', *Classical and Modern Literature*, 7 (1987), 71–85.

Harvey, John, 'A Note on Shakespeare and Sophocles', *Essays in Criticism*, 27 (1977), 259–70.

Jepsen (1953): see 3.1.

Knight, Sarah, '"Goodlie Anticke Apparrell"? Sophocles's *Ajax* at Early Modern Oxford and Cambridge', *Shakespeare Studies*, 37 (2010), 25–42.

Lorant, André, 'Hamlet et Oedipe', *Revue de littérature comparée*, 56 (1982), 40–61.

Lorant, André, 'Oedipus, Hamlet, and Don Carlos: Fathers and Sons in Dramatic Literature', *Neohelicon*, 12 (1985), 115–48.

Pratt, Norman, 'From Oedipus to Lear', *Classical Journal*, 61 (1965), 49–57.

Sansom, Dennis L., 'Ethics and the Experience of Death: Some Lessons from Sophocles, Shakespeare, and Donne', *Journal of Aesthetic Education*, 44 (2010), 18–32.

Searle, Leroy F., 'The Conscience of the King: Oedipus, Hamlet, and the Problem of Reading', *Comparative Literature*, 49 (1997), 316–43.

Shackford, Martha Hale, *Shakespeare, Sophocles: Dramatic Notes* (Natick, MA, 1957).

Stoll, Elmer E., 'Reconciliation in Tragedy: Shakespeare and Sophocles', *University of Toronto Quarterly*, 4 (1934), 11–33.

Zerba (2009): see 3.11.

3.29. Tacitus

Burke, P., 'Tacitism', in T. A. Dorey (ed.), *Tacitus* (1969), 149–71. [Considers Tacitus in style, historical method, morality, and politics from 1580 to 1680.]

Kewes (2011): 1.7.

Mellor, Ronald (ed.), *Tacitus: The Classical Heritage* (New York and London, 1995). [Extracts from thirty-six Renaissance authors who wrote about Tacitus, along with a lengthy introduction.]

Salmon (1991): see 1.7.

Schellhase, Kenneth C., *Tacitus in Renaissance Political Thought* (Chicago and London, 1976). [An important book, not focused specifically on literature but still containing much useful material.]

Smuts (1993): see 1.7.

Whitfield, J. H., 'Livy > Tacitus', in Bolgar (1976), 281–94: see 1.2.

3.30. Virgil

Biow, Douglas, *Mirabile Dictu: Representations of the Marvelous in Medieval and Renaissance Epic* (Ann Arbor, 1996). [Connects a key motif from the *Aeneid* with *The Faerie Queene*.]

Black, James, 'Hamlet Hears Marlowe, Shakespeare Reads Virgil', *Renaissance and Reformation/Renaissance et Réforme*, 18 (1994), 17–28.

Bono, Barbara, *Literary Transvaluation: From Vergilian Epic to Shakespearean Tragicomedy* (Berkeley and Los Angeles). [Traces the epic line from antiquity into the early modern period through the figure of the abandoned woman.]

Burrow, Colin, 'Virgil in English Translation', in Martindale (1997b), 21–37: see 1.3.A.

Burrow, Colin, 'English Renaissance Readers and the *Appendix Vergiliana*', *Proceedings of the Virgil Society*, 26 (2008), 1–16. [A rare, and therefore valuable, study of the influence of the *Appendix Vergiliana*.]

Butler, George F., 'Frozen with Fear: Virgil's *Aeneid* and Act 4, Scene 1 of Shakespeare's *The Second Part of King Henry IV*', *Philological Quarterly*, 79 (2000), 145–52.

Canitz, A. E. C., 'From *Aeneid* to *Eneados:* Theory and Practice of Gavin Douglas's Translation', *Medievalia et Humanistica*, 17 (1991), 81–99.

Chalker (1969): see 2.3.

Chambers (1993): see 2.3.

Cheney, Patrick, '"Novells of his Devise": Chaucerian and Virgilian Career Paths in Spenser's *Februarie* Eclogue', in Cheney and de Armas (2002), 231–67: see 1.3.A.

Crowley, Timothy D., 'Arms and the Boy: Marlowe's Aeneas and the Parody of Imitation in *Dido, Queen of Carthage*', *English Literary Renaissance*, 38 (2008), 408–38.

Cummings, Robert, 'Jonson's Virgil: Surrey and Phaer', *Translation and Literature*, 16 (2007), 66–75.

Cummings and Martindale (2007): see 2.4.

Dearing, Bruce, 'Gavin Douglas' *Eneados*: A Reinterpretation', *PMLA*, 67 (1952), 845–62.

DeNeef, A. Leigh, 'Ploughing Virgilian Furrows: The Genres of *Faerie Queene* VI', *John Donne Journal*, 1 (1982), 151–68.

Donnelly, M. L., 'The Life of Virgil and the Aspiration of the "New Poet"', *Spenser Studies*, 17 (2003), 1–35.

Ettin, Andrew V., 'The *Georgics* in *The Faerie Queene*', *Spenser Studies*, 3 (1982), 57–71.

Fagiolo, Marcello (ed.), *Virgilio nell'arte e nella cultura europea* (Rome, 1981). [An extensive exhibit catalogue with much material on England and the Renaissance.]

Fichter, Andrew, *Poets Historical: Dynastic Epic in the Renaissance* (New Haven, 1982). [Contains a chapter on Spenser in a larger study of dynastic epics that go back to Virgil.]

Fowler, Alastair, 'The Beginnings of English Georgic', in Lewalski (1986), 105–25: see 1.3.B.

Frost, William, 'Translating Virgil, Douglas to Dryden: Some General Considerations', in Maynard Mack and George deForest Lord (eds), *Poetic Traditions of the English Renaissance* (New Haven, 1982), 271–86. [A classic study of English translations of Virgil.]

Gentili (1988): see 2.4.
Gill, Roma, 'Marlowe's Virgil: *Dido Queene of Carthage*', *Review of English Studies*, 28 (1977), 141–55.
Goins, Scott E., 'Pain and Authority in the *Aeneid* and *Henry V*', *Classical and Modern Literature*, 15 (1995), 367–74.
Gregerson, Linda, 'Spenser's Georgic: Violence and the Gift of Place', *Spenser Studies*, 22 (2007), 185–201.
Guy-Bray, Stephen, 'Virgil at Appleton House', *English Language Notes*, 42 (2004), 26–39.
Hager, Alan, 'British Virgil: Four Renaissance Disguises of the Laocoön Passage of Book 2 of the *Aeneid*', *Studies in English Literature, 1500–1900*, 22 (1982), 21–38.
Hale (1985): see 3.11.
Hall, Lewis Brewer, 'An Aspect of the Renaissance in Gavin Douglas' *Eneados*', *Studies in the Renaissance*, 7 (1960), 184–92.
Hamilton, Donna B., *Virgil and the Tempest: The Politics of Imitation* (Columbus, OH, 1990).
Hamilton, Donna B., 'Re-Engineering Virgil: *The Tempest* and the Printed English *Aeneid*', in Peter Hulme and William H. Sherman (ed.), *The Tempest and its Travels* (Philadelphia, 2000), 114–20.
Hardie (1998): see 2.8.
Hardie (1999): see 2.8.
Hardie (2010): see 2.4.
Hardie (2011): see 1.3.B.
Hardie (2014): see 2.4.
Helfer (2003): see 3.6.
Hill (1985): see 3.27.
Hodgkins, Christopher, 'The Nubile Savage: Pocahontas as Heathen Convert and Virgilian Bride', *Renaissance Papers* (1998), 81–90.
Hughes (1929): see 2.4.
James (1997): see 3.11.
James (2009): see 3.22.
Kallendorf (2007): see 3.11.
Keach (1977): see 3.22.
Kennedy, William J., 'The Virgilian Legacies of Petrarch's *Bucolicum Carmen* and Spenser's *Shepheardes Calender*', in Pellegrini (1985), 79–106: see 3.11.
Kilgour, Maggie, 'Heroic Contradictions: Samson and the Death of Turnus', *Texas Studies in Language and Literature*, 50/2 (2008a), 201–34.
Kilgour, Maggie, 'Satan and the Wrath of Juno', *English Literary History*, 75 (2008b), 653–71.
Kilgour (2010): 1.3.A.
Lindheim, Nancy, 'Spenser's Virgilian Pastoral: The Case for *September*', *Spenser Studies*, 11 (1994), 1–16.
Lindheim, Nancy, 'The Virgilian Design of *The Shepheardes Calender*', *Spenser Studies*, 13 (1999), 1–21.

Lotspeich, H. G., 'Spenser's *Virgil's Gnat* and its Latin Original', *English Literary History,* 2 (1935), 235–41.

Low (1985); see 2.3.

Lupton, Julia Reinhard, 'Home-Making in Ireland: Virgil's Eclogue I and Book VI of *The Faerie Queene*', *Spenser Studies,* 8 (1987), 119–45.

Lyne (2001): see 2.4.

Mack, Michael, 'The Consolation of Art in the *Aeneid* and *The Tempest*', in Marc Berley (ed.), *Reading the Renaissance: Ideas and Idioms from Shakesepeare to Milton* (Pittsburgh, 2003), 57–77.

Martindale (1986): see 2.4.

Martindale, Charles, 'Shakespeare and Virgil', in Charles Martindale and A. B. Taylor (eds), *Shakespeare and the Classics* (Cambridge, 2004), 89–106.

Miola, Robert S., 'Vergil in Shakespeare', in John D. Bernard (ed.), *Vergil at 2000: Commemorative Essays on the Poet and his Influence* (New York, 1986), 241–58.

Miola, Robert S., 'Aeneas and Hamlet', *Classical and Modern Literature,* 8 (1988), 275–90.

Neuse (1978): see 1.3.A.

Nicholson, Catherine, 'Pastoral in Exile: Spenser and the Poetics of English Alienation', *Spenser Studies,* 23 (2008), 41–71. [Draws from the *Eclogues.*]

Parker, Michael P, 'Carew's Politic Pastoral: Virgilian Pretexts in the "Answer to Aurelian Townsend"', *John Donne Journal,* 1 (1982), 101–16.

Patterson, Annabel, 'Pastoral versus Georgic: The Politics of Virgilian Quotation', in Lewalski (1986), 241–76: see 1.3.B.

Patterson (1988): see 1.7.

Pellegrini (1985): see 3.11.

Pigman, G. W., III, 'Pastoral and Idyll', in Braden, Cummings, and Gillespie (2010), 248–61: see 1.5.

Pitcher, John, 'A Theatre of the Future: The *Aeneid* and *The Tempest*', *Essays in Criticism,* 34 (1984), 193–215.

Power (2007): see 2.4.

Proudfoot (1960): see 2.4.

Quint (1993): see 2.4.

Rosenberg, Donald M., *Oaten Reeds and Trumpets: Pastoral and Epic in Virgil, Spenser, and Milton* (Lewisburg, PA, 1981).

Rudat, Wolfgang E. H., 'Spenser's "Angry Iove": Virgilian Allusion in the First Canto of *The Faerie Queene*', *Classical and Modern Literature,* 3 (1983), 89–98.

Sowerby (1995): see 3.11.

Stocker, Margarita, 'Remodelling Virgil: Marvell's New Astraea', *Studies in Philology,* 84 (1987), 159–79.

Stump, Donald, 'Marlowe's Travesty of Virgil: Dido and Elizabethan Dreams of Empire', *Comparative Drama,* 34 (2000), 79–107.

Suzuki (1987): see 3.22.

Tuckett (1996): see 2.9.

Tudeau-Clayton (1998): see 2.9.

Tylus (1988): see 2.9.

Venuti, Lawrence, 'The Destruction of Troy: Translation and Royalist Cultural Politics in the Interregnum', *Journal of Medieval and Renaissance Studies*, 23 (1993), 197–219. [An important article that stresses the political work that Virgilian translation did in Renaissance England.]

Wallace, Andrew, 'Placement, Gender, Pedagogy: Virgil's Fourth Georgic in Print', *Renaissance Quarterly*, 56 (2003), 37–407.

Wallace (2011): see 2.6.

Watkins, John, '"Neither of Idle Shewes, nor of False Charmes Aghast": Transformations of Virgilian Ekphrasis in Chaucer and Spenser', *Journal of Medieval and Renaissance Studies*, 23 (1993), 345–63.

Watkins (1995): see 1.4.B.

Webb, William Stanford, 'Vergil in Spenser's Epic Theory', *English Literary History*, 4 (1937), 62–82.

Wells, Marion A., '"To Find a Face Where All Distress Is Stell'd": *Enargeia*, *Ekphrasis*, and Mourning in *The Rape of Lucrece* and the *Aeneid*', *Comparative Literature*, 54 (2002), 97–126.

Wilson-Okamura, David, 'Virgilian Models of Colonization in Shakespeare's *Tempest*', *English Literary History*, 70 (2003), 709–37.

Wilson-Okamura (2010): see 1.4.B.

Wiltenburg, Robert, 'The *Aeneid* in *The Tempest*', *Shakespeare Survey*, 39 (1987), 159–68.

4. CLASSICAL RECEPTION IN SEVERAL KEY ENGLISH AUTHORS

4.1. Donne

Lebans, W. M., 'The Influence of the Classics in Donne's *Epicedes* and *Obsequies*', *Review of English Studies*, 23 (1972), 127–37.

Lein, Clayton D., 'Donne's "The Storme": The Poem and the Tradition', *English Literary Renaissance*, 4 (1974), 137–63.

Stapleton, M. L., '"Why Should They Not Alike in All Parts Touch?": Donne and the Elegiac Tradition', *John Donne Journal*, 15 (1996), 1–22.

See also Dubrow (1979): 2.2; Donne (1912): 2.8; Blevins (1999): 3.5; Hester (2009): 3.5; Erskine-Hill (1973): 3.12; Baumlin (1986): 3.13; Eddy (1981): 3.13; Stapleton (2009): 3.19; Armstrong (1977): 3.22; Bedford (1982): 3.22; Gransden (1979): 3.22; Harvey (1989): 3.22; Himuro (2008): 3.22; Shawcross (1980): 3.25; Blank (1995): 3.26; Harvey (1996): 3.26; Losocco (2003): 3.26; Mueller (1993): 3.26; Revard (1993): 3.26; West (1994): 3.26; Sansom (2010): 3.28.

4.2. Jonson

Baines, Barbara J., 'The Contemporary and Classical Anti-Feminist Tradition in Jonson's *Epicoene*', *Renaissance Papers* (1977), 43–58.

Boehrer, Bruce, 'The Classical Context of Ben Jonson's "Other Youth"', *Studies in English Literature, 1500–1900*, 43 (2003), 439–58.

Burrow, Colin, 'Ben Jonson', in Claude Rawson (ed.), *Cambridge Companion to English Poets* (Cambridge, 2011), 122–38.

Carr, Joan, 'Jonson and the Classics: The Ovid-Plot in *Poetaster*', *English Literary Renaissance*, 8 (1978), 296–311.

Eliot, T. S., 'Ben Jonson', in *The Sacred Wood: Essays on Poetry and Criticism* (1920), 104.

Evans, Robert C., 'Jonson, Lipsius, and the Latin Classics', in James Hirsch (ed.), *New Perspectives on Ben Jonson* (Madison, NJ, 1997), 55–76. [Links Jonson to the classical tradition via an important humanist scholar of his day.]

Helgerson, Richard, 'Ben Jonson', in Thomas Corns (ed.), *The Cambridge Companion to English Poetry* (Cambridge, 1993), 148–70.

Hunter, G. K., *English Drama, 1586–1642: The Age of Shakespeare* (Oxford, 1997).

Jonsonus Virbius; or The Memory of Ben Jonson (1638).

Lyne, Raphael, 'Volpone and the Classics', in Garrett A. Sullivan, Patrick Cheney, and Andrew Hadfield (eds), *Early Modern English Drama: A Critical Companion* (New York, 2006), 177–88.

Parfitt, George, *Ben Jonson: Public Poet and Private Man* (1976).

Riddell, James A., 'Seventeenth-Century Identifications of Jonson's Sources in the Classics', *Renaissance Quarterly*, 28 (1975), 204–18. [An interesting effort to identify the contemporary evidence for Jonson's classicism.]

Schelling, Felix E., 'Ben Jonson and the Classical School', *PMLA*, 13 (1898), 221–49.

Smith, G. Gregory, *Ben Jonson* (1919).

Swinburne, Charles Algernon, *A Study of Ben Jonson* (1889).

Talbert, Ernest William, 'The Classical Mythology and the Structure of *Cynthia's Revels*', *Philological Quarterly*, 22 (1943), 193–210.

Tudeau-Clayton, Margaret, 'Scenes of Translation in Jonson and Shakespeare: *Poetaster*, *Hamlet*, and *A Midsummer Night's Dream*', *Translation and Literature*, 11 (2002), 1–23.

Wheeler, Charles F., *Classical Mythology in the Plays, Masques, and Poems of Ben Jonson* (Princeton, 1938). [An older study, still of value.]

Young, R. V., 'Ben Jonson and Learning', in Richard Harp and Stanley Stewart (eds), *Cambridge Companion to Ben Jonson* (Cambridge, 2000), 43–57.

See also: Helgerson (1983): 1.3.A; Meskell (2009): 1.3.B; Moul (2010): 1.3.B; McPherson (1974): 1.5; Sanders (1998): 1.7; McPherson (1974): 2.1; Mulryan (2003): 2.1; Martindale (1993): 2.2.; Maus (1984): 2.2; Cummings (2007): 2.4; Trimpi (1962): 2.5; Ayres (1986): 2.7; Herford and Simpson (1925–52): 2.8; Tudeau-Clayton (1998): 2.9; Boehrer (1996): 3.5; Coronato (1997): 3.6; Finkelstein (1986): 3.6; Baines (2009): 3.12; Boehrer (2002): 3.12; Hooley (2002): 3.12; Martindale (1993): 3.12; Moul (2006): 3.12; Moul (2007): 3.12; Pierce (1981): 3.12; Ribeiro (1973): 3.12; Steggle (1998): 3.12; McEuen (1945): 3.13; Shifflett (1996): 3.16; Loewenstein (2003): 3.19; McPherson (1979): 3.19; Simmons (1981): 3.19; Whipple (1970): 3.19; Revard (1982): 3.20; Newlands (1988): 3.21; Dane (1986): 3.22; Mulvihill (1982): 3.22; Cheney (1983): 3.23; Evans (1973): 3.27; Cummings (2007): 3.30.

4.3. Marlowe

Blissett, William, 'Caesar and Satan', *Journal of the History of Ideas*, 18 (1957), 221–32.

Braden, Gordon, '"The Divine Poem of Muaseus"', in Braden (1978c), 55–153: see 2.8.

Brooke, Tucker, 'The Marlowe Canon', *PMLA* 37 (1922), 367–417.

Brown, Georgia E., 'Gender and Voice in *Hero and Leander*', in J. A. Downie and J. T. Parnell (eds), *Constructing Christopher Marlowe* (Cambridge, 2000), 148–63.

Brown, Georgia E., *Redefining Elizabethan Literature* (Cambridge, 2004a).

Brown, Georgia E., 'Marlowe's Poems and Classicism' (Cambridge, 2004), in Cheney (2004b), 106–26.

Callaghan, Dympna, 'Marlowe's Last Poem: Elegiac Aesthetics and the Epitaph on Sir Roger Manwood', in Scott and Stapleton (2010), 159–76: see 3.22.

Campbell, Marion, '"*Desunt nonnulla*": The Construction of Marlowe's *Hero and Leander* as an Unfinished Poem', *English Literary History*, 51 (1984), 241–68.

Cheney, Patrick (ed.), *The Cambridge Companion to Christopher Marlowe* (Cambridge, 2004).

Cheney, Patrick, 'Milton, Marlowe and Lucan: The English Authorship of Republican Liberty', *Milton Studies*, 49 (2009), 1–19. [An important article that links Marlowe to a key classical author who influenced significantly the political discourse of the day.]

Cheney, Patrick, and Striar, Brian J. (eds), *The Collected Poems of Christopher Marlowe* (New York and Oxford, 2006).

Clark, James G., Coulson, Frank T., and McKinley, Kathryn L. (eds), *Ovid in the Middle Ages* (Cambridge, 2011). [Contains valuable background material.]

Deats, Sara Munson, '*Dido, Queen of Carthage* and *The Massacre of Paris*', in Cheney (2004), 193–206.

Downie, J. A., 'Reviewing What We Think We Know about Christopher Marlowe, Again', in Scott and Stapleton (2010), 343–6: see 3.22.

Erne, Lukas, 'Biography, Mythography, and Criticism: The Life and Works of Christopher Marlowe', *Modern Philology*, 103 (2005), 28–50.

Gill, Roma, 'Snakes Leape by Verse', in Brian Morris (ed.), *Christopher Marlowe: Mermaid Critical Commentaries* (1968), 135–50.

Healy, Thomas, *Christopher Marlowe*, Writers and their Work (Plymouth, 1994).

Jacobsen, Eric, *Translation, a Traditional Craft: An Introductory Sketch with a Study of Marlowe's Elegies* (Copenhagen, 1958).

James, Heather, 'The Poet's Toys: Christopher Marlowe and the Liberties of Erotic Elegy', *Modern Language Quarterly*, 67 (2006), 103–27.

Kendall, Roy, 'Richard Baines and Christopher Marlowe's Milieu', *English Literary Renaissance*, 24 (1994), 507–52.

Lewis, C. S., 'Hero and Leander', *Proceedings of the British Academy*, 38 (1952), 23–37.

Logan, Robert A., *Shakespeare's Marlowe: The Influence of Christopher Marlowe on Shakespeare's Artistry* (Aldershot, 2007).

McDonald, Russ, 'Marlowe and Style' in Cheney (2004), 55–69.

MacLure, Millar (ed.), *Marlowe: The Critical Heritage 1588–1896* (1979).

Maguire, Laurie E., 'Marlovian Texts and Authorship', in Cheney (2004), 41–54.

Marlowe, Christopher, *The Complete Works of Christopher Marlowe: Vol. 1*, ed. Roma Gill (Oxford, 1987).

Martindale, Charles, *Redeeming the Text: Latin Poetry and the Hermeneutics of Reception* (Cambridge, 1993). [An important theoretical statement, with implications for classical reception throughout the Renaissance.]

Masters, Jamie, *Poetry and Civil War in Lucan's Bellum Civile* (Cambridge, 1992).

Pater, Walter, 'Sandro Botticelli', in *The Renaissance: Studies in Art and Poetry: The 1893 Text*, ed. Donald L. Hill (Berkeley and Los Angeles, 1980).

Rhodes, Neil, *The Power of Eloquence and English Renaissance Literature* (New York, 1992).

Riggs, David, *The World of Christopher Marlowe* (2004).

Summers, Claude J., '*Hero and Leander*: The Arbitrariness of Desire', in J. A. Downie and J. T. Parnell (eds), *Constructing Christopher Marlowe* (Cambridge, 2000), 133–47.

Vickers, Brian (ed.), *English Renaissance Literary Criticism* (Oxford, 1999).

Waddell, Helen, *The Wandering Scholars* (New York, 1934).

See also Sowerby (1994): 1.1; Cheney (1997): 1.3.A; Parrott (1929): 1.4; Greene (1982): 1.5; Cheney (2009): 1.7; Lewis (1954): 2.2; Levin (1952): 2.4; Hulse (1981): 2.6; Reisner (2010): 3.4; Blissett (1956): 3.16; Gill (1973): 3.16; Hooley (2008): 3.16; Shapiro (1988): 3.16; Cheney (1998): 3.22; Keach (1977): 3.22; Kitch (2006): 3.22; Pearcy (1984): 3.22; Roe (2000): 3.22; Stapleton (1996): 3.22; Stapleton (2010): 3.22; Burrow (2008): 3.30.

4.4. Milton (early)

The Blue Letter Bible online <www.blueletterbible.org/Bible.cfm?b=1Cr&c=7&t=KJV#conc/9> (accessed 20 March 2015).

Geertz, Clifford, *The Interpretation of Cultures* (New York, 1973).

Hale, John K., *Milton's Cambridge Latin: Performing in the Genres 1625–1632* (Tempe, AZ, 2005), 1–31. [The definitive study of Milton's Latin work.]

Lewalski, Barbara K., *The Life of John Milton* (Oxford, 2000).

Milton, John, *Of Education*, in *The John Milton Reading Room*, ed. Thomas H. Luxon <www.dartmouth.edu/~milton/reading_room/of_education/index.shtml> (accessed 20 March 2015).

See also Clark (1948): 1.2; Fletcher (1956–61): 1.2; Coiro (1998): 1.3.A; Helgerson (1983): 1.3.A; Johnson (1973): 1.3.A; Kilgour (2010): 1.3.A; Lewalski (1966): 1.3.A; Neuse (1978): 1.3.A; Samuel (1947): 1.3.B; Achinstein (1994): 1.7; Edwards (2008): 2.3; Borris (2009): 2.4; Green (2009): 2.4; Haan (1992-1993): 2.4; Hammond (1933): 2.4; Quint (1991): 2.4; Quint (1993): 2.4; Dzelzainis (2009): 3.6; Olmsted (1996): 3.11; DuRocher (1985): 3.22; Kilgour (2012): 3.22; Laroque (2000): 3.22; Kilgour (2008a): 3.30; Kilgour (2008b): 3.30.

4.5. Shakespeare

Altman, Joel, *The Improbability of Othello: Rhetorical Anthropology and Shakespearean Selfhood* (Chicago, 2010).

Arber, E. (ed.), *A Transcript of the Registers of the Company of Stationers of London*, 5 vols (London and Birmingham, 1875–94).

Barkan (1986): see I.4.B.

Bate, Jonathan, *The Genius of Shakespeare* (1997).

Boas, F. S., *University Drama in the Tudor Age* (Oxford, 1914).

Boyce, Benjamin, 'The Stoic *Consolatio* and Shakespeare', *PMLA*, 64 (1979), 771–80.

Burrow, Colin, 'Shakespeare and Humanistic Culture', in Martindale and Taylor (2004), 9–27: see 2.1.

Burrow, Colin, *Shakespeare and Classical Antiquity* (Oxford, 2013). [An important book.]

Cheney, Patrick, *Shakespeare, National Poet-Playwright* (Cambridge, 2004).

Chernaik, Warren L., *The Myth of Rome in Shakespeare and his Contemporaries* (Cambridge, 2011).

Eccles, Mark, *Shakespeare in Warwickshire* (Madison, WI, 1961).

Hammond, Paul, 'Shakespeare as Collaborator: The Case of *Titus Andronicus*', in Paul Scott (ed.), *Collaboration and Interdisciplinarity in the Republic of Letters: Essays in Honour of Richard G. Maber* (Manchester, 2010), 193–208.

Hanna, Sara, 'Voices against Tyranny: Greek Sources of *The Winter's Tale*', *Classical and Modern Literature*, 14 (1994), 335–44.

Helmes, Henry, *Gesta Grayorum, or, the History of the High and Mighty Prince Henry, Prince of Purpoole, Anno Domini 1594*, ed. Desmond Bland (Liverpool, 1968).

Henslowe, Philip, *Henslowe's Diary*, ed. R. A. Foakes (Cambridge, 2002).

Hoole, Charles, *A New Discovery of the Old Art of Teaching Schoole* (1659).

Hutson, Lorna, *The Usurer's Daughter: Male Friendship and Fictions of Women in Sixteenth-Century England* (London and New York, 1994).

Hutson, Lorna, *The Invention of Suspicion: Law and Mimesis in Shakespeare and Renaissance Drama* (Oxford, 2007).

Jackson, MacDonald P., 'Francis Meres and the Cultural Contexts of Shakespeare's Rival Poet Sonnets', *Review of English Studies*, 56 (2005), 224–46.

James, Heather, 'Dido's Ear: Tragedy and the Politics of Response', *Shakespeare Quarterly*, 52 (2001), 360–82.

Jones, Emrys, *The Origins of Shakespeare* (Oxford, 1977).

Manningham, John, *The Diary of John Manningham of the Middle Temple, 1602–1603*, ed. Robert Parker Sorlien (Hanover, NH, 1976).

Milowicki, Edward J., 'A Measure for Menippean Discourse: The Example of Shakespeare', *Poetics Today*, 23 (2002), 291–306.

Miola, Robert S., '*The Merry Wives of Windsor*: Classical and Italian Intertexts', *Comparative Drama*, 27 (1993), 364–76.

Miola, Robert S., *Shakespeare's Reading* (Oxford, 2000). [An important book, to be used with Stuart Gillespie (2004): see 1.6.]

Norbrook, David, '*Macbeth* and the Politics of Historiography', in Sharpe and Zwicker (2003), 78–166: see 3.19.

Nuttall, A. D., *Shakespeare the Thinker* (New Haven, 2007).

Parker, Patricia, 'Romance and Empire: Anachronistic *Cymbeline*', in George M. Logan and Gordon Teskey (eds), *Unfolded Tales: Essays on Renaissance Romance* (Ithaca, NY, 1989), 189–207.

Plutarch, *Plutarch's Lives of the Noble Grecians and Romans*, ed. George Wyndham (1895).

Poole, Adrian, 'Confundering the Past' [review of Martindale and Taylor (eds), *Shakespeare and the Classics*], *TLS*, 29 July 2005, 10–11.

Roberts, Katherine, 'The Wandering Womb: Classical Medical Theory and the Formation of Female Characters in *Hamlet*', *Classical and Modern Literature*, 15 (1995), 223–32.

Roberts, Sasha, *Reading Shakespeare's Poems in Early Modern England* (Basingstoke and New York, 2003).

Rudd, Niall, '*Titus Andronicus*: The Classical Presence', *Shakespeare Survey*, 55 (2002), 199–208.

Simonds, Peggy Muñoz. 'The Marriage Topos in *Cymbeline*: Shakespeare's Variations on a Classical Theme', *English Literary Renaissance*, 19 (1989), 94–117.

Smith, Bruce R., *Homosexual Desire in Shakespeare's England: A Cultural Poetics* (Chicago, 1991).

Smith, G. C. Moore (ed.), *Gabriel Harvey's Marginalia* (Stratford-upon-Avon, 1913).

Spencer, T. J. B., 'The Great Rival: Shakespeare and the Classical Dramatists', in Edward A. Bloom (ed.), *Shakespeare 1564–1964: A Collection of Modern Essays by Various Hands* (Providence, RI, 1964), 177–93.

Stagman, Myron, *Shakespeare's Greek Drama Secret* (Newcastle upon Tyne, 2010).

Stewart, Alan, '*Edward II* and Male Same-Sex Desire', in Garrett A. Sullivan, Jr, Patrick Cheney, and Andrew Hadfield (eds), *Early Modern English Drama: A Critical Companion* (Oxford and New York, 2006), 82–95.

Sturm, Johannes, *A Ritch Storehouse or Treasure for Nobilitye and Gentlemen* (1570).

Velz, John, *Shakespeare and the Classical Tradition: A Critical Guide to Commentary, 1660–1960*. (Minneapolis, 1968). [An important guide to earlier secondary sources.]

Vickers, Brian, *Shakespeare, Co-Author: A Historical Study of Five Collaborative Plays* (Oxford, 2002).

West, Grace Starry, 'Going by the Book: Classical Allusions in Shakespeare's *Titus Andronicus*', *Studies in Philology*, 79 (1982), 62–77.

See also Baldwin (1944): 1.2; Baldwin (1947): 1.2; Ong (1976): 1.2; Cheney and de Armas (2002): 1.3.A.; Bate (1993): 1.3.B.; Braden (2000): 1.3.B.; Dubrow (1986): 1.3.B.; Gordon (1975): 1.3.B.; Moul (2010): 1.3.B; Magnusson (1999): 1.3.C.; Pennacchia (2009): 1.3.C.; Enterline (2000): 1.4.B; Enterline (2006): 1.4.B; Wilson-Okamura (2010): 1.4.B.; Altman (1978): 1.5; Miola (1992): 1.5; Miola (1994): 1.5; Mossmann (1994): 1.5; Muir (1977): 1.5; Gillespie (2004): 1.6; Conley (1927): 1.7; Hadfield (2005): 1.7; Bruster (1990): 2.1; Foakes (1962): 2.1; Lyne (2004): 2.1; Martindale (1998): 2.1; Martindale and Martindale (1998): 2.1; Martindale and Taylor (2004): 2.1; Muir (1972): 2.1; Mulryan (2003): 2.1; Riehle (1990): 2.1; Riehle (2004): 2.1; Smith (2010): 2.1; Braden (1985): 2.3; Gillespie (2001): 2.4; Kerrigan (1991): 2.5; Belsey (1995): 2.6; Burrow (2004): 2.6; Enterline (2012): 2.6; Weaver (2008): 2.6; Weaver (2012): 2.6; Barton (2004): 2.7; Honigman (1959): 2.7; Pigman (1980):

2.7; Tudeau-Clayton (1998): 2.9; Burrow (1993): 2.10; Gesner (1970): 2.10; Pollard (2008): 2.10; Bullough (1957–75): 2.11; Cunliffe (1893): 2.11; Hunter (1978): 2.11; Jones (1977): 2.11; Pelling (2009): 2.11; Schleiner (1990): 2.11; Silk (2004): 2.11; Taylor (1987): 2.11; Thomson (1952): 2.11; Dewar-Watson (2005): 2.12; Dixon (1987): 2.12; Gillespie (2004): 2.12; Henke (1997): 2.12; Orgel (1979): 2.12; Pollard (2007): 2.12; Pollard (2008): 2.12; Stern (2006): 2.12; Jepsen (1953): 3.1; Roth (1992): 3.1; Showerman (2004): 3.1; Streufort (2004): 3.1; Boughner (1954): 3.3; Beauregard (1987): 3.4; Black (1968): 3.4; Crosbie (2007): 3.4; D'Agostino (1987): 3.4; Elton (1997): 3.4; Golden (1984): 3.4; Poisson (1966): 3.4; Soellner (1968): 3.4; Spencer (2003): 3.4; Wheater (1993): 3.4; Bagg (1965): 3.5; Cox (2008): 3.6; Takada (1997): 3.6; West (2005): 3.6; Arnold (1984): 3.8; Dewar-Watson (2009): 3.8; Faas (1984): 3.8; Beardsley (1974): 3.9; Hunter (1957): 3.9; Ronan (1985): 3.9; Adams (1967): 3.10; Gesner (1959): 3.10; Houlahan (2010): 3.10; Acheson (1903): 3.11; Bednarz (2001): 3.11; Elton (2000): 3.11; Ferrucci (1980): 3.11; Hunter (1974–5): 3.11; James (1997): 3.11; Justman (1992): 3.11; Kallendorf (2007): 3.11; Peyré (2004): 3.11; Stoll (1935): 3.11; Zerba (2009): 3.11; Westbrook (1947): 3.12; Hopkins (2004): 3.15; Logan (1976): 3.16; Paleit (2011): 3.16; Ronan (1993): 3.16; Martin (1945): 3.18; Bate (1989): 3.22; Bate (1990): 3.22; Brown (1994): 3.22; Cheney (2006): 3.22; Crockett (1991): 3.22; Forey (1998): 3.22; Greenburg (2008): 3.22; James (2004): 3.22; Kambasković-Sawers (2010): 3.22; Keach (1977): 3.22; Klose (1968): 3.22; Lamb (1980): 3.22; Lamb (1989): 3.22; Lugo (2007): 3.22; Lyne (2000): 3.22; Martin (n.d.): 3.22; Milowicki (1995): 3.22; Nuttall (1988): 3.22; Roberts (1988): 3.22; Rudd (1979): 3.22; Sandvoss (1982): 3.22; Schulman (1983): 3.22; Scragg (1977): 3.22; Taylor (1990): 3.22; Taylor (1994–5): 3.22; Taylor (1997): 3.22; Taylor (2000): 3.22; Thomsen (2003): 3.22; Velz (1986): 3.22; Birrell (2011): 3.23; Fuzier (1991): 3.23; Gray (2011): 3.23; Parker (1993): 3.23; Tovey (1983): 3.23; Arthos (1967): 3.24; Bruster (1993): 3.24; Cioni (1998): 3.24; Draper (1938): 3.24; Girard (1981): 3.24; Hardin (2007a): 3.24; Rudd (1994): 3.24; Svendsen (1983): 3.24; Clary (1998): 3.25; Cook (1996): 3.25; Corti (2007): 3.25; Denton (1997): 3.25; Dillon (1979): 3.25; Evans (2001): 3.25; George (2004): 3.25; Graves (1973): 3.25; Green (1979): 3.25; Heuer (1957): 3.25; Homan (1976): 3.25; McGrail (1997): 3.25; Maguin (1973): 3.25; Mueller (1991): 3.25; Rothschild (1976): 3.25; Serpieri (2004): 3.25; Shackford (1977): 3.25; Stirling (1964): 3.25; Velz (1986): 3.25; Westerweel (2001): 3.25; Brooks (1980): 3.27; Ewbank (1966): 3.27; Kaufmann (1967): 3.27; Lucas (1922): 3.27; Small (1935): 3.27; Stapleton (1994): 3.27; Wallace (1986): 3.27; Harvey (1977): 3.28; Pratt (1965): 3.28; Shackford (1957): 3.28; Stoll (1934): 3.28; Black (1994): 3.30; Bono (1984): 3.30; Butler (2000): 3.30; Hamilton (1990): 3.30; Mack (2003): 3.30; Martindale (2004): 3.30; Miola (1986): 3.30; Miola (1988): 3.30; Pitcher (1984): 3.30; Wilson-Okamura (2003): 3.30; Wiltenburg (1987): 3.30; Tudeau-Clayton (2002): 4.2.

4.6. Sidney

Coogan, Robert, 'More Dais than Dock: Greek Rhetoric and Sidney's Encomium on Poetry', *Studies in the Literary Imagination*, 15 (1982), 99–113.

See also Payne (1988): 1.3.C; Parker (1972): 2.1; Borris (2009): 2.4; Sidney (1985): 2.8; Sidney (2002): 2.8; Chalifour (1976): 2.10; Beauregard (1987): 3.4; Coogan (1981): 3.4; Curtright

(2003): 3.4; Heninger (1982): 3.4; McCanles (1983): 3.4; Payne (1990a): 3.4; Payne (1990b): 3.4; Helfer (2007): 3.6; Heffernan (2004): 3.10; Olmsted (1996): 3.11; Kambasković-Sawers (2007): 3.22; Miller (1991): 3.22; Heninger (1983): 3.23; Partee (1971): 3.23; Parker (1972): 3.24; Hearsey (1933): 3.25; Homan (1976): 3.25; Miller (1987): 3.25.

4.7. Spenser

Arthos, John, *On the Poetry of Spenser and the Form of Romances* (1956).

Berger, Harry, Jr, 'The Structure of Merlin's Chronicle in *The Faerie Queene* III (iii)', *Studies in English Literature*, 9 (1969), 39–51.

Brand, C. P., *Torquato Tasso: A Study of the Poet and his Contribution to English Literature* (Cambridge, 1965).

Burrow, Colin. 'Spenser and Classical Traditions', in Andrew Hadfield (ed.), *The Cambridge Companion to Spenser* (Cambridge, 2001), 217–36.

DiMatteo, A., 'Spenser's Venus-Virgo: The Poetics and Interpretative History of a Dissembling Figure', *Spenser Stuidies*, 10 (1992), 37–70.

Dorsten, J. A. Van, *The Radical Arts: The First Decade of the Elizabethan Renaissance* (Leiden, 1970).

Draper, John W., 'Classical Coinage in *The Faerie Queene*', *PMLA*, 47 (1932), 97–108.

Dryden, John, *Of Dramatic Poesy and Other Critical Essays*, ed. George Watson, 2 vols (1962).

Dubrow, Heather, 'The Arraignment of Paridell: Tudor Historiography in *The Faerie Queene*, III, ix', *Studies in Philology*, 87 (1990), 312–27.

Durling, R. M., *The Figure of the Poet in Renaissance Epic* (Cambridge, MA, 1965). [A older comparative study, following an important *topos* in epic from antiquity to the Renaissance.]

Ferguson, M. W., '"The Afflatus of Ruin": Meditations on Rome by Du Bellay, Spenser, and Stevens', in A. Patterson (ed.), *Roman Images*, Selected Papers from the English Institute 8 (Baltimore, 1982), 23–50.

Fichter, A., '"And Nought of *Rome* in *Rome* Perceiu'st at All": Spenser's *Ruines of Rome*', *Spenser Studies*, 2 (1981), 183–92.

Giraldi Cinthio, Giovanni Battista, *On Romances*, trans. Henry L. Snuggs (Lexington, KY, 1968).

Girard, René, *Things Hidden since the Foundation of the World*, trans. Stephen Bann and Michael Metteer (Stanford, 2003).

Heninger, S. K., 'The Tudor Myth of Troy-novant', *South Atlantic Quarterly*, 61 (1962), 378–87.

Kelsey, L., and Peterson, R. S., 'Rereading Colin's Broken Pipe: Spenser and the Problem of Patronage', *Spenser Studies*, 14 (2000), 233–72.

Kennedy, W. J., *Authorizing Petrarch* (Ithaca, NY, 1995).

Krier, Teresa, *Gazing on Secret Sighs: Spenser, Classical Imitation, and the Decorums of Vision* (Ithaca, NY, 1990).

Lamberton, Robert, *Homer, The Theologian* (Berkeley and Los Angeles, 1989). [A study of early allegorical interpretations of Homer.]

Lewis, C. S., *Spenser's Images of Life*, ed. Alastair Fowler (Cambridge, 1967).

Lotspeich, H. G., *Classical Mythology in the Poetry of Edmund Spenser* (Princeton, 1932). [An older study, helpful as a beginning place for further research.]

McCabe, Richard A., 'Edmund Spenser: Poet of Exile', *Proceedings of the British Academy*, 80 (1993), 73–103.

McCabe, Richard A., '"Little Booke, Thy Selfe Present": The Politics of Presentation in *The Shepheardes Calender*', in H. Erskine-Hill and R. A. McCabe (eds), *Presenting Poetry: Composition, Publication, Reception* (Cambridge, 1995), 15–40.

McCabe, Richard A., 'Annotating Anonymity, or Putting a Gloss on *The Shepheardes Calender*', in Joe Bray, Miriam Handley, and Anne C. Henry (eds), *Ma[r]king the Text: The Presentation of Meaning on the Literary Page* (Aldershot, 2000), 35–54.

McCabe, Richard A., *Spenser's Monstrous Regiment: Elizabethan Ireland and the Poetics of Difference* (Oxford, 2002).

McCabe, Richard A., 'Parody, Sympathy and Self: A Response to Donald Cheney', *Connotations*, 13/1–2 (2003–4), 5–22.

MacFaul, Tom, '*A Theatre for Worldlings* (1569)', in Richard A. McCabe (ed.), *The Oxford Handbook of Edmund Spenser* (Oxford, 2010), 149–59.

McGowan, Margaret M., *The Vision of Rome in Late Renaissance France* (New Haven, 2000). [A widely cited study, good for comparison to England.]

Miller, David Lee, *The Poem's Two Bodies: The Poetics of the 1590 'Faerie Queene'* (Princeton, 1988).

Patterson, Annabel, 'Re-opening the Green Cabinet: Clément Marot and Edmund Spenser', *English Literary Renaissance*, 16 (1986), 44–70.

Peterson, R. S., 'Laurel Crown and Ape's Tail: New Light on Spenser's Career from Sir Thomas Tresham', *Spenser Studies*, 12 (1998 for 1991), 1–35.

Rasmussen, Carl J., '"Quietnesse of Minde": *A Theatre for Worldlings* as a Protestant Poetics', *Spenser Studies*, 1 (1980), 3–27.

The Remains of Edmund Grindal, ed. William Nicholson (Cambridge, 1843).

Richardson, David A. *Spenser: Classical, Medieval, Renaissance, and Modern* (Cleveland, OH, 1977).

Roche, T. P., Jr, *The Kindly Flame: A Study of the Third and Fourth Books of Spenser's 'Faerie Queene'* (Princeton, 1964). [A classic study of *The Faerie Queene*.]

Rollinson, P., 'The Renaissance of the Literary Hymn', *Renaissance Papers* (1968), 11–20.

Rollinson, P., 'A Generic View of Spenser's *Four Hymns*', *Studies in Philology*, 68 (1971), 292–304.

Scott, S. C., 'From Polydorus to Fraudubio: The History of a Topos', *Spenser Studies*, 7 (1986), 27–57.

Servii Grammatici Qui Feruntur in Virgilii Carmina Commentarii, ed. G. Thilo and H. Hagen, 3 vols (Leipzig, 1881–1902).

Starke, Sue Petitt, 'Briton Knight or Irish Bard? Spenser's Pastoral Persona and the Epic Project in *A View of the Present State of Ireland* and *Colin Clouts Come Home Againe*', *Spenser Studies*, 12 (1998 for 1991), 133–50.

Starnes, D. T., 'E.K's Classical Allusions Reconsidered', *Studies in Philology*, 39 (1942), 143–59.

Stewart, Stanley, 'Spenser and the Judgment of Paris', *Spenser Studies*, 9 (1988), 161–209.

Tucker, George Hugo, *The Poet's Odyssey: Joachim Du Bellay and the 'Antiquitez de Rome'* (Oxford, 1990).

Wells, William (ed.), *Spenser Allusions in the Sixteenth and Seventeenth Centuries*, 2 pts, *Studies in Philology*, Texts and Studies 68, 69 (Chapel Hill, NC, 1971–2).

West, Michael, 'Spenser and the Renaissance Ideal of Christian Heroism', *PMLA*, 88 (1973), 1013–32.

Zitner, S. P. 'Spenser's Diction and Classical Precedent', *Philological Quarterly*, 45 (1966), 360–71.

See also Cheney (1993): 1.3.A; Cheney (1997): 1.3.A; Helgerson (1983): 1.3.A; Loewenstein (1986): 1.3.A; Miller (1983): 1.3.A; Neuse (1978): 1.3.A; Rambuss (1993): 1.3.A; Rambuss (1996): 1.3.A; Holohan (1976): 1.3.B; McCabe (1989): 1.3.B; Yates (1975) 1.3.B; Watkins (1995): 1.4.B; Greene (1982): 1.5; Craik (2001): 2.2; Borris (2009): 2.4; Demetriou (2006): 2.4; Esolen (1994): 2.4; Gentili (1988): 2.4; Greene (1957): 2.8; Hamilton (1990): 2.4; Hardie (2010): 2.4; Hughes (1929): 2.4; Pugh (2005): 2.4; Quint (2003): 2.4; Stapleton (2009): 2.4; Montrose (1996): 2.8; Spenser (1932–49): 2.8; Bradner (1935): 2.9; Cooper (1997): 2.9; Tylus (1988): 2.9; Burrow (1993): 2.10; DeMoss (1918): 3.4; Jusserand (1906): 3.4; Ferguson (1982): 3.5; Mulryan (1972): 3.5; Pearcy (1981): 3.5; Helfer (2003): 3.6; Helfer (2007): 3.6; Aiman (1974): 3.10; Hughes (1925): 3.10; Silberman (2008): 3.10; Allen (1970): 3.11; Bull (2005): 3.11; Mallette (1997): 3.11; Murrin (1980): 3.11; Olmsted (1996): 3.11; Seznec (1953): 3.11; Suzuki (1989): 3.11; Wind (1967): 3.11; Wolfe (2005): 3.11; Ramachandran (2009): 3.18; Ramachandran (2010): 3.18; Miller (2005): 3.21; Cheney (1998): 3.22; Deitch (2001): 3.22; Fox (2002): 3.22; Friedmann (1966): 3.22; Harmer (2008): 3.22; Kambasković-Sawers (2007): 3.22; Keach (1977): 3.22; Laroque (2000): 3.22; Perng (1996): 3.22; Pincombe (2001): 3.22; Reid (2007): 3.22; Stapleton (2008): 3.22; Wilson-Okamura (2008): 3.22; Burchmore (1985): 3.23; Gleason (1994): 3.23; McCabe (2009): 3.23; Neuse (1987): 3.23; Wilson (2002): 3.23; Lyne (2004): 3.25; Bull (1998): 3.27; Burrow (2008): 3.30; Cheney (2002): 3.30; Donnelly (2003): 3.30; Ettin (1982): 3.30; Fichter (1982): 3.30; Gregerson (2007): 3.30; Kennedy (1985): 3.30; Lindheim (1994): 3.30; Lindheim (1999): 3.30; Lotspeich (1935): 3.30; Lupton (1987): 3.30; Nicholson (2008): 3.30; Rosenberg (1981): 3.30; Rudat (1983): 3.30; Watkins (1993): 3.30; Webb (1937): 3.30.

Index

Notes

Page numbers in **bold** denote detailed analysis.

Works receiving frequent or detailed mention are indexed by title (cross-referenced from the author). Works mentioned only briefly appear as sub-headings under the author's name.

Works of unknown or doubtful authorship are indexed by title.

n. = endnote. *t* = table/diagram.

Ablancourt, Nicolas Perrot d' 146 n.55
Académie Française 375
Achilles Tatius 61, 302
  Leucippe and Klitophon 291–2, 293, 298, 303–4, 309 n.36
Act of Union 1707 474
actors
  attitudes towards 405, 407
  social status 408
Addison, Joseph 474, 475
'Addled Parliament' 154
Adlington, William 292
Aeneid (Virgil) 13, 17, 18, 248 n.48, 372 n.80, 373, 520–1, 582
  Book 13 228, 234
  as career move 172–3, 175–6
  contrasted with Lucan 238–9, 242
  contrasted with *Metamorphoses* 518
  Dido episode 162–3, 192, 234, 235
  English editions 49*t*, 61, 62
  English translations 66, 135, 145 n.48, 150, 173–4, **226–7**, 228, 248–9 n.61
  as model for Spenser 11–12, 20, 174, 205, 229, 233, 235, 525–7, 567–8
  as model for other Renaissance writers **232–6**, 242, 244–5, 522–3, 583–5, 605–7
  opening lines (in Renaissance editions) 172–3, 236, 564–5
  praise, as goal of 228
  Renaissance interpretations/reworkings 229, 230–1, 233, 238, 528–9, 530–1, 533, 536–7 nn.36–7, 557–8
  reworking of Homer 14, 229, 232
  as source for Ovid 521–2
  studied in schools/universities 33, 34, 36, 45*t*, 225, 254, 520
  treatment of fame 188, 193, 194
  treatment of Julian bloodline 234–5
Aeschylus 48, 88
  Oresteia 376
Aesop, *Fables* 33, 34, 35, 45*t*, 63, 262–3
Aethiopica (Heliodorus) 291, 292, 295–6, 425
  generic characteristics 421–2, 428
  popularity 422
Agricola, Rudolph 39, 75, 603
  De Inventione Dialectica 41, 42–3, 80
Alabaster, William, *Elisaeis* 231
Alciati, Andrea, *Emblemata* 492
Alciphron 276
Alençon, Duke of (later Duke of Anjou) 148, 222–3 n.28, 560
Alexander, Sir William
  The Alexandrian Tragedy 379
  Croesus 379
  Darius 379
  Julius Caesar 379
Alexander the Great 381, 438

Aleyn, Charles
'The Battailes of Crescey and Poictiers' 243, 244, 251 n.98
'The Historie of Henry the Seventh' 243
allegory 93–4, 557–9
epic read as 229–30, 232–3, 489–92, 499–500 n.18, 557–8
Amadís de Gaula (author uncertain) 294–5, 296, 302
Ambrose, St 113, 321, 562
Ames, William, *De Conscientia* 79
Ammianus Marcellinus 137
Amores (Ovid) 176, 178–9, 188, 315, 335, 370 n.34, 518, 522, 523, 527, 553–4 n.10, 588–9, 594 n.14
influence on Marlowe 582, 583, 592
Amphitruo/Amphitryon (Plautus) 384, 421–2, 423, 425
generic characteristics 420, 421–2, 424
popularity 421, 424
Renaissance performances 424, 430 n.13
as source for Shakespeare 69, 403, 613–14
Amyot, Jacques 66–7, 291, 294, 599
Les Amours pastorales de Daphnis and Chloe 292, 296–7
anachronism 456, 459 n.49
Anacreon 61, 313
Anacreontea (anon.) 346
Andrewes, Lancelot 118–19, 120, 127 n.62, 127 n.64
XCVI Sermons 119, 127 n.64
Andria (Terence) 39, 70, 397, 399, 413 n.7
English translations 400, 402–3
staging 400–1
Anjou, Duke of *see* Alençon
Anne of Denmark, Queen (wife of James I) 194, 509, 510
Anselm, St 129
anthologies 60
of epigrams 346–7
Aphthonius of Antioch 35, 42, 53 n.51, 258, 260
English editions 49t
Progymnasmata 33, 37, **39–40**, 53 n.55, 53 n.58, 75, 77, 603
Apollonius of Tyre (anon.) 296, 301, 309 n.41
Apollonius Rhodius 61
Appian of Alexandria 64, 65, 138
Apuleius (L. Apuleius Madaurensis) 61, 62, 64
'Cupid and Psyche' 293, 295–6
Metamorphoses 292, 303
Arabic, teaching of 37, 58
Aratus 462
Arcadia (Sidney) 82, 95, 208, 209, 211, **301–4**, 306, 322, 425, 495
differences between versions 303–4
political content **442–4**, 446
relationship with Greek sources 302, 303–4
treatments of love/sexuality 302–4
The Countess of Pembroke's Arcadia 301
New Arcadia 294, 295, 301, 303–4
Old Arcadia 294, 301, 303–4, 305
Archias, A. Licinius 91, 407
Archilochus 312, 314
Ariosto, Ludovico 236, 329, 494, 523, 558, 565
Orlando Furioso 18, 20, 93, 229, 230, 233, 294–5, 416 n.40, 536–7 n.37
Aristophanes 30, 60, 355, 396, 413
Renaissance productions/translations 69, **410–12**, 417 n.51
Clouds 411, 412
Eirene (Peace) 410
Knights 399
Plutus 69, 410–11
Aristotle 30, 37, 51, 61, 110, 111, 608
criticisms 462, 511
English editions 49t

influence on Renaissance literary criticism 88, 89, 90, 91, 92, 94, 95–6, 97
literary prescriptions 95–6, 244–5, 395–6, 420–1, 422–3, 427–8, 430 n.10, 489, 573
Categories 41
De Anima 45*t*, 395
De Caelo 45*t*
De Interpretatione 41
Economics 42
Ethics 42, 43, 45*t*, 49*t*
Meteorologia 45*t*
Organon 42, 45*t*, 47
Parts of Animals 395
Physics 42, 45*t*, 49*t*
Poetics 49*t*, 90, 95, 373, 374–5, 376, 406, 408, 416 n.38, 420–1, 565
Politics 42, 147
Rhetoric 42, 43, 49*t*, 75, 77, 78
Sophistical Refutations 41
Topica 41
Arrian of Nicomedia 59
ars dictaminis 274, 287 n.4
Ars Poetica (Horace) 64, 181, 314, 502 n.70, 623
influence on Renaissance literary criticism 88, 89–90, 91, 93, 94, 539–40
Arundel, Thomas Fitzalan, 12th Earl of 135–6
Arundel, Thomas Howard, 21st Earl of 478, 483 n.91
'As a friend, friendlike...' (manuscript poem, anon.) 541–2, 544, 553–4 n.10
Ascham, Roger 14, 89, 90
The Scholemaster **31–3**, 34, 66, 88, 108, 149, 298
Atticus, T. Pomponius 273, 275, 285
Augustine of Hippo, St 11, 110, 113, 187, 574
City of God 125 n.29, 442
Confessions 111, 115, 120, 180, 471
De Genesi Ad Litteram 508
Opera Omnia 113
Augustus, Emperor 15–16, 43, 90, 187, 239, 244, 370 n.36, 379
analogies with later statesmen 209, 220, 550–1
interactions with poets 518–19, 550–1, 560, 563, 582
literary depictions/addresses 152, 153, 193–4, 202, 210, 227, 228, 233, 363, 556 n.32, 633–4
sexual culture under 159
Aulus Gellius 30, 45*t*, 462
Ausonius, D. Magnus 61, 64, 120, 121
Austen, Ralph 463, 475, 479, 482 n.72
Austin, J.L. 256, 260
authorship, evolving notions of 4–5, 13–14
autobiography 471
Averroës (Ibn Rushd) 373, 374, 391 n.1
Ayres, Philip 451

Bacon, Francis 15, 24 n.60, 103, 106, 117, 479, 628
comments on Cicero/Seneca 467–9, 470
comments on Homer 490, 491–2, 495
influence of classical discursive writing on 462, 465, 466
letters 283
The Advancement of Learning 104–5, **112–14**, 115, 125–6 n.41, 217, 473
De Sapientia Veterum 491–2
Essays 281
The History of the Reign of King Henry VII 438, 449
The New Atlantis 461
'Of Adversity' 469
'Of Anger' 471
'Of Fame, a Fragment' 196

Badius Ascensius, Jodocus (Josse Bade) 398–9

Baines, Richard 580
Baker, Howard 74 n.61
Baldwin, T.W. 70, 263–4, 537 n.42, 610
Bale, John 111
Bancroft, Richard, Bishop 348
Barberini, Maffeo, Cardinal 48
Barchiesi, Alessandro 18
Barclay, Alexander 5, 204, 205, 210, 346
Barclay, John, *Argenis* 305–6, 310 n.54
Barkan, Leonard 5–7, 10, 22–3 n.22, 162, 168, 170 n.5
Barker, Robert 115
Barnes, Barnabe 180, 181, 505
Barnes, Joseph 497
Barnett, Lodowick 180
Barnfield, Richard, *The Affectionate Shepherd* 206
Barrow, Isaac 479
Barthes, Roland 2–4, 9, 21 n.3
Barton, John, *The Art of Rhetorick Concisely and Compleatly Handled* 79
Basse, William 219–20
Bastard, Thomas, Rev. 350–1, 357
  'Ad Lectorem' 350–1
  'De Naeuo in Facie Faustinae' 350
  'De Poeta Martiali' 350
Bate, Jonathan 12
Bathe, William, *Janua Linguarum* 52 n.25
Bathurst, Theodore 208, 209, 222 n.20
Batrachomyomachia (Battle of Frogs and Mice, author unknown) **496–7**
  attribution to Homer 181, 496
Baxter, Richard, *The Reformed Pastor* 79
Beale, John 475, 477, 479, 482 n.72
Beaumont, Francis 136
  King and No King (with Fletcher) 427
  Philaster (with Fletcher) 427
  Salmacis and Hermaphroditus 61, 256, 265
Bede, the Venerable 114
bees, imagery of 16, 17, 218, 457 n.7, 536 n.29
Beilin, Elaine 181–2
Bellum Civile (Pharsalia) (Lucan) 152, 153–4, 225, **238–44**, 437, 445, 451, 549, 589–90, 609
  contrasted with *Aeneid* 238–9, 242
  English translations 239, 240–1
  reworkings in English context 239–40, 241–3
Benjamin, Edward 192
Bennett, J.W. 508
Berger, Harry, Jr. 10–11
Bergson, Henri 413
Bernard, Richard
  The Faithful Shepherd 79
  Terence in English 402, 415 n.28
Beroaldus (Matthieu Brouard) 62
Berthelet, Thomas 110–11
Bible 141
  Authorised Version *see* King James Bible
  echoed in Renaissance poetry 363, 644
  Homer compared with 492
  translations 63
  see also New Testament
Biddle, John 204
Bijns, Anna 130
bilingual writers 19, 231, 483 n.90, 550
biography **451–6**
Bion 5, 204, 207, 211, 213
Bishop, George 487
Bishops' Ban (1599) 152, 348–9, 354–5, 357, 369 n.20
Blake, William 174, 627
blank verse *see* iambic pentameter
Blith, Walter 475
bloodlines, as theme of epic 234–5
Bloom, Harold 9, 18, 459 n.49
Bloomfield, Morton 317
Blount, Thomas, *The Academie of Eloquence* 78, 83
Boccaccio, Giovanni 5, 18, 244, 379, 560
  Concerning Famous Women 131
  De Casibus Virorum Illustrium (Examples of Famous Men) 74 n.62
  Il Filostrato 498

Bodley, Sir Thomas 113, 116, 117, 120
Boethius, Anicius Manlius Severinus 61, 62, 120, 135, 137, 187, 373, 465
Consolation of Philosophy 136, 191
Bogan, Zachary, *Homerus Hebraizon* 492
Boileau, Nicolas 90
Bolton, Edmund 448
Averunci, or The Skowrers 450
Hypercritica 196
Nero Caesar or Monarchy Depraved 450
Bonaventure, St 110
Bond, John 48–50, 49*t*
Borges, Jorge Luis 391 n.1
Bower, Richard, *The New Tragical Comedy of Appius and Virginia* 425
Boyle, Roger, *Parthenissa* 292
Boyle, Sir Robert 462, 465, 474, 476, 477, 479, 483 n.86
Accidents of an Ague 471
The Sceptical Chymist 467
Bracciolini, Poggio 12
Braden, Gordon 9, 10, 23 n.36, 66
Bradley, A.C. 588, 592
Bradstreet, Anne **139–42**, 143
Dialogue between Old England and New 141–2
The Four Ages 146 n.64
The Four Elements 141
The Four Empires 146 n.64
The Four Monarchies 141
The Tenth Muse 140–1, 142, 146 n.64, 182–3
Bradstreet, Simon 139, 140
Brandon, Samuel, *The Tragi-Comoedi of the Virtuous Octavia* 277, 379
Brant, Sebastian, *The Ship of Fools* 346
Breton, Nicholas 467
Characters upon Essays 281
Fantastics 218
No Whippinge 357
Poste with a Madde Packet of Letters 276
Bridgewater, John Egerton, 1st Earl of 533, 649
Brierwood, Edward 45*t*, 47
Briet, Margaret 145 n.48
Brink, C.O. 47–8
Brinsley, John 204, 399
Ludus Literarius 32, 35, 38–9, 40, 52 n.42, 53 n.46, 517
The Preachers Charge 79
Bristol, Michael D. 22 n.9
Brome, Richard
Antipodes 500 n.30
Five New Plays 407
Bromley, James 169, 271 n.19, 271 n.21
Brooks, Cleanth 548
Brooks, Harold 71
Brown, Georgia E. 170 n.5, 263, 341–2 n.18, 581–2, 596 n.44
Browne, John, *Marchant's Avizo* 78
Browne, Sir Thomas 462, 463, 465, 466, 475, 477
The Garden of Cyrus 474
Pseudodoxia Epidemica 409–10
Religio Medici 469, 473
Browne, William
Britannia's Pastorals 215
The Inner Temple Masque 491
Bruni, Leonardo 440
Bruno, Giordano 505
Cantus Circaeus 500 n.29
Brutus, L. Junius 443
Brutus, M. Junius 453
Buchanan, George 329, 613
De Prosodia 90
Buckeridge, John 127 n.64
Buckingham, George Villiers, 1st Duke of 153, 154, 450
assassination 154
Bull, Malcolm, *The Mirror of the Gods* 501 n.42
Bulstrode, Cecelia 132–3

Bulwer, John, *Chironomia or The Art of Manuall Rhetorique* 77
Burckhardt, Jacob 5–8, 9, 23 n.28 and 36
Burghley, Mildred Cecil, Lady 130
Burghley, William Cecil, Lord 563
Burrow, Colin 18, 235, 258–9, 343 n.44, 444, 535 n.12, 536 n.36, 540
Burton, Robert 61, 462, 465
  Anatomy of Melancholy 409–10, 469, 472, 473, 512
Burton, William 292
Busby, Richard 58
Bush, Douglas 9
Butler, Charles, *Rhetorica* 34
Butler, Lady Mary 331
Butler, Samuel 479
Butts, Henry, *Dyets Dry Dinner* 461
Bynneman, Henry 48, 55 n.105

Caesar, C. Julius 30, 33, 34, 59, 61, 114, 202, 241, 275, 437, 441–2
  English editions/translations 49*t*, 64
  literary/stage depictions 434, 436–7, 457 n.6, 590
  analogies with later leaders 551, 560
  political/military activities 192, 238–9, 379
  Commentaries 32, 35, 441
  Gallic Wars 43, 440, 454
Caesarius, Johann 43
  Dialectica 42
Caesars Revenge (anon.) 241
Calenus (husband of Sulpicia) 131
Callimachus 322, 550, 581–2
  Aetia 177
  Hymns 321
Callinus 312
Cambridge University 595 n.29
  Chair of History 450–1
  Milton's time at **644–7**, 652
  Neoplatonism 512, 515 n.40
  new colleges 142–3
  reading lists 42, 54 n.75, 59
  stage performances 67–8, 399–400, 410, 415 n.17, 600, 612
  syllabus 41, 43–7, 54 n.69
Camden, William 58, 64, 136, 439, 626, 631
  Annals 458 n.35
  Britannia 454, 457 n.9, 458 n.35
  Remains, Concerning Britain 597 n.58
Camerarius, Joachim 488
Camões, Luis de, *Os Lusíadas* 230
Campbell, Gordon 24 n.42
Campion, Thomas 65, 342 n.25
  Ad Thamesin 231
  Elegiarum Liber 317
  Observations in the Art of English Poesie 108
careers, literary **172–83**
  classical conceptions 172–5, 177–9, 185 n.31
  defined 175–7
  Renaissance 179–83
  single-genre 172–5, 178, 179
  specific classical models 179, 183, 185 n.39, 186 n.46, 186 n.49
  types of progression 174
Carew, Richard 592, 597 n.58
Carew, Thomas 97–8, 510, 523, 554 n.11
  'To My Mistress in Absence' 510
Carey, John 285, 298
Carneades 409
Carnsew brothers 43
Cartwright, William 58, 510
  'No Platonic Love' 510
Carver, Robert 295, 302
Cary, Elizabeth, *Mariam* 379, 393 n.27
Cary, Lucius 336, 338, 635–6
Casaubon, Isaac 47, 496, 513, 582
  De Satyrica Poesi 361, 427
Casaubon, Meric 488
Case, John 43
Castalio, Sebastian 33, 35

Castelvetro, Lodovico 95–6, 374, 376, 422, 431–2 n.29
Castiglione, Baldassare, *Book of the Courtier* 32, 313, 324, 463, 504
catharsis, theories of 95, 395
Catherine of Aragon 129
Catherine of Valois, Queen (wife of Henry V) 235–6
Catilina, L. Sergius (historical character) 433, 436
Catiline (Jonson) 241, **433–8**, 439
  characterization 436–7, 452
  performances 433
  relationship with source material 379, 433–7, 451–2, 623
  verse style 379, 435, 452
Cato, M. Porcius 352, 364, 409, 437, 443, 475
  De Agricultura 477
Catullus, C. Valerius 61, 571, 600
  influence on English satire / epigram / ode 312, 322, 329, 345, 353
  'poem 61' 329–30, 343 n.44
  'poem 62' 343 n.44
  'On the Death of a Pet Sparrow' (Catullus 3) 315, 522
Caussin, Jean, *Eloquentiae Sacrae et Humanae Parallela* 45t
Cave, Terence 16, 17
Cavendish, Lord (later Duke of Devonshire) 331
Cavendish, Margaret
  A Blazing World 461
  Poems and Fancies 461
Caxton, William 135, 146 n.57, 234, 497–8
Cecil, Sir William (later Lord Cranborne) 149
Cerda, Juan Luis de la 36, 52 n.33
Cervantes, Miguel de 215
  Los Trabajos de Persiles y Sigismunda 432 n.43
Chapman, George 4, 389, 585, 593 n.2, 597 n.54
  comments on Homer 20, 90, 93–4, 181, 226, 487, 488–9, 490, 491, 494, 495, 496
  dedication of works 232–3
  literary career 175, 179, 181
  translations of Homer 12, 19, 63, 65, 73 n.37, 181, 226, 227–8, 229–30, 232, 487–8, 495, 496, 498, 498 n.2, 599, 608
  translations of other Greek writers 203, 217
  Achilles' Shield 490, 500 n.25
  All Fools 181, 404–5, 408
  The Blind Beggar of Alexandria 426
  Caesar and Pompey 241, 445, 500 n.30
  The Conspiracy of Charles, Duke of Byron 388
  Epigrams 181
  The Gentleman Usher 69, 400
  Homeric Hymns 181
  The Shadow of Night 322
Chapone, Hester 143
Chappell, William, *The Preacher* 79
Chariton 293
Charles I 41, 141, 153, 220, 275, 337, 343 n.53, 470
  court culture 510
  execution 493, 544, 549
  ill-feeling / hostilities against 154–5, 239, 446
  letters 284
  poetic depictions 549, 551, 554–5 n.21
Charles II 1, 15, 412, 488, 493, 519, 551
Charles V, (Holy Roman) Emperor 440
Charleton, Walter 464
chastity, as feminine virtue 191–2
Chaucer, Geoffrey 5, 6, 111–12, 117, 148, 180–1, 207, 208, 495, 539
  collected works, publication of 110–11

Chaucer, Geoffrey (*cont.*)
The Assembly of Fools (*Parlement of Foules*) 110
The Canterbury Tales 110, 203
The House of Fame 188–9, 194, 195
'The Miller's Tale' 396, 398
'The Squire's Tale' 16–17
'The Tale of Sir Thopas' 567
Troilus and Criseyde 373, 396, 398, 497–8, 608
'The Wife of Bath's Tale' 133–4, 138
Cheney, Patrick 169, 445, 581, 593–4 n.3, 594 n.12
Chettle, Henry 394 n.36
Agamemnon (with Dekker) 376
Orestes' Furies (with Dekker) 376
Chilmead, Edmund 48
Cholmondely, Ralph 42–3
chorus, use of
in tragedy 378–9, 382–3, 384, 386
in tragicomedy 427
Chrestien, Florent 424, 427
Christianity **103–23**
classical epics interpreted in line with 490–1, 492, 497
compatibility of fame with 194–5
and complaint 345–6
epics of 19, 98, 140–1, 174, 195, 225–6, 229, 231, 558–9, 565–6
hymns' exploration of 321–8, 340 n.7
incompatibility with classical epic values 558
and love 323–4, 326–7
merging with classicism in Renaissance thought 8–9, 15, 18–19, 190, 202–3, 558–9
and Neoplatonism 323–5, 327–8
odes celebrating 334–5
in pastoral poetry 202–3
in women's poetry 140–1
see also epic poetry
Church, Rooke 475
An Old Thrift Newly Reviv'd 461
Cicero, M. Tullius 14, 47, 68, 77, 91, 92, 96, 129, 136, 268, 396, 408, 409, 480 n.14, 609
comments on actors 407
comments on letter-writing 281–6
comments on Terence 397
death 473
discovery/publication of letters **273–6**
English editions 48, 49*t*
influence on Renaissance discursive writing 462, **464–5**, 467, 468–9, 470, 476
objections to 274, 285, 468–9
as stage character 151, 436–7
Ad Familiares 39, 273–4, 275, 281–2, 284–5, 287 n.7
Catilinarian orations 379, 436
De Amicitia 32, 33, 43, 45*t*, 139, 397, 399, 628, 638 n.22
De Elocutione 284
De Finibus 45*t*
De Inventione 49*t*, 75, 80
De Officiis 13, 33, 34, 45*t*, 49*t*, 51, 80, 147, **464–5**, 471, 476
De Oratore 42, 49*t*, 75, 80, 91, 196, 600
De Senectute 33, 45*t*
The Dream of Scipio 191
Epistles 31–2, 33, 34, 35, 37, 42, 45*t*, 46, 49*t*, 51
Orations 34, 35, 42, 45*t*, 49*t*
Partitiones Oratoriae 75
Second Philippic 284
Topica 41
Tusculan Disputations 45*t*, 49*t*, 91
Cicero, Q. Tullius 32
Cinthio, Giraldi 422–3, 565
Altile 424
Arrenopia 424
Epitia 424, 425
Hecatommithi 424, 425, 432 n.43
Ciris (anon., attrib. Virgil) 520, 526, 583

Civil War (1642–9) 154–5, 470
foreshadowings 239, 241, 445, 449, 450–1
literary interpretations relating to 493
poetic treatments 241–2
The Civil War (Lucan) *see Bellum Civile*
Clarendon, Henry Hyde, 1st Earl of 473
History of the Rebellion 449, 451, 458 n.35
Clark, D.L. 33
Claudian (Claudius Claudianus) 45*t*, 225, 228, 329, 571
In Rufinum 231
The Rape of Proserpine 230
Cleopatra (historical character) 379
Clerke, Bartholomew 32, 52 n.15
'clerks,' as literary figures 108–12
Clifford, Lady Anne 137
Cloelius, Sextus 284
Cluverius (Philipp Clüver) 45*t*
Coetzee, J.M., *Elizabeth Costello* **103–5**, 107
Coleridge, Samuel Taylor 226
Colet, John 30, 58, 141
Collop, John 492
Colse, Peter, *Penelopes Complaint* 489
Columella, L. Junius Moderatus 463, 473, 475, 477
comedy **395–413**
adapted from classical originals 403–5
debates on moral worth 396–7, 399, 405–6, 409–10
definitions 396
etymology 396
impact of Restoration 412
impact of theatre closures 408–12
performances 399–401
staging 400–1, 403–4
stock characters/plot devices 407–8
terminology 373, 384, 396
theories of 395–8, 406, 408, 413
translations of classical works **402–3**
Comenius, J.A. 52 n.25
commentaries 47, 50–1
commonplace, exercise of 53 n.57
competition (between writers) 349, 369 n.23, 523, 616
on same play 537 n.48, 601–2
complaint, genre of 345–6
female 277–8, 278–9, 288 n.18
composition, exercises in 39–40, 53 n.55, 58
compound epithets 65, 72 n.33
Comus (A Maske Presented at Ludlow Castle, Milton) 491, 511–12, 533–4, 538 n.59, 647–8, 649–50, 655 n.13
Constable, Henry 505
Constantine I 'The Great,' Emperor 114
Cooper, Thomas, *Thesaurus Linguae Romanae et Britannicae* 62, 592
Cope, Antony, *Anniball and Scipio* 440–1, 442
Copeland, William 135
Corderius (Mathurin Cordier), *Dialogues (Colloquia Scholastica)* 35, 36, 398, 399, 414 n.13
Corneille, Pierre 95, 375
Le Cid 375
Horace 138
La Mort de Pompée 138, 241, 375
Cornelia Metella 379
Cornelia Scipionis Africana 131
Cornelius Nepos 59, 275
Cornwallis, Sir William 281, 467, 470
Cotton, Charles 474
Cotton, Richard 218
Cowley, Abraham 19, 58, 98, 251 n.108, 334, 463, 476, 483 nn.89–90, 504, 510, 523
'Answer to the Platonicks' 510
The Civil War (unfinished) 155, 231, 241–2, 244
Davideis (unfinished) 21, 232, 244–5, 520
'Friendship in Absence' 510
'The Garden' 478

Cowley, Abraham (*cont.*)
  'The Motto' 191
  'Of Agriculture' 477
  Pindaric Odes 21, 65
  Plantarum 477–8
  'Quid Relinquendos, Moriture, Nummos' 553 n.4
  Sex Libri Plantarum 461
  'To the Royal Society' 478, 483 n.92
  'Viola' 551–2, 556 nn.31–2
Cowper, Dame Sarah 137
Craik, Katherine 403
Crane, Mary Thomas 26 n.87
Cranmer, Thomas 117, 204–5
Crashaw, Richard 204
  'Hymn of the Nativity' 322
  'In the Glorious Epiphany of our Lord God' 503
Creiznach, Wilhelm 73 n.46
Cremutius Cordus, A. 196
Critolaus 409
Cromwell, Oliver 155, 220, 335–8, 343 n.53, 520, 543–4, 548–9, 551, 552, 554–5 n.21, 555–6 n.28
Crowley, Robert (ed.), *One and Thyrtye Epigrammes* 346
Cudworth, Ralph 490, 492
  The True Intellectual System of the Universe 512
Cuff, Henry 448
Culex (anon., attrib. Virgil) 520, 536 n.29, 567, 583
  see also Spenser, *Virgil's Gnat*
Culmann, Leonhard, *Sententiae Pueriles* 33, 34, 35, 52 n.20
cultural materialism 3
Cumberland, George Clifford, 3rd Earl of 137
Cumberland, Margaret Clifford, Countess of (née Russell) 135, 137
Cummings, Brian 12
Cummings, Robert 72 n.33
Cunliffe, John W. 392 n.14
Cunningham, J.V. 95
Cupids Messanger (anon.) 78
Curtius, Ernst Robert 10, 381
Cutwode, Thomas, *Caltha Poetarum* 369 n.20
Cynic philosophy 359–60

Daniel, Roger 487, 493
Daniel, Samuel 137, 186 n.46, 447, 505, 644
  The Civil Wars between the Two Houses of Lancaster and York 152, 239–40, 243, 451
  Cleopatra 379, 393 n.22
  The Complaint of Rosamond 277, 445
  A Defence of Ryme 15, 97
  'A Letter from Octavia to Marcus Antonius' 277
  Philotas 379, **381–3**, 438, 449–50
  The Queen's Arcadia 426
  Small Poems 449
Dante (Alighieri) 10, 18, 174, 373, 374, 508, 523, 648
  Divine Comedy 373, 396, 561
  Inferno 534, 536–7 n.37
Dares Phrygius, *De Excidio Trojae Historia* 497
Dati, Carlo 645
Davenant, Sir William 93, 94, 98, 243, 412
  Discourse Upon Gondibert 91–2, 97, 98, 244
  Gondibert 244
  Salmacida Spolia 500 n.30
  The Temple of Love 510
Davies, Sir John 348, **352–4**, 369 n.20, 370 n.30, 582
  'In Castorem' 353
  'In Gellam' 353
  'In Priscum' 353
  'Of a Gull' 352
  'Of Tobacco' 353–4
  Orchestra 489

Davis, Walter 300
Davison, Francis 186 n.46
Day, Angel 214, 292, 305
The English Secretorie 77, **81–2**, 275, 276
Day, John, *Law Tricks* 428
Dee, John 410, 509–10
The Defence of Poesy (Sidney) **94–6**, 108, 112, 229, 320, 376, 378–9, 384, 406, 416 n.38
comments on Homer 490, 491
Platonic content 96, 506, 507, 514 n.17
de Grazia, Margreta 7–8, 10, 23 n.24
Dekker, Thomas 363, 628–9
Agamemnon (with Chettle) 376
Match Me in London 428
Orestes' Furies (with Chettle) 376
Satiromastix (with Marston) 363–4, 629, 634–5
de la Rue, Charles 59
Demetrius of Phaleron 89
De Elocutione (On Style) 276, 284
Demosthenes 14, 30, 42, 149, 436
English translations 64, 137, 149
Olynthiacs 149
Orations 45*t*
Philippics 149
Denham, Sir John 227, 474
Derrida, Jacques 103
Descartes, René 513
D'Este family 233
devils, council of (as feature of epics) 231
Devonshire, William Cavendish, 3rd Earl of 78
Dickenson, John, *The Shepheardes Complaint* 222 n.23
Dicta Sapientum (anon.) 64
Dictys Cretensis, *Ephemeris de Historia Belli Trojani* 497
Dido, Queene of Carthage (Marlowe) 181, 227, 528, 580
performances 595 n.24
referenced by Shakespeare 606
relationship with *Aeneid* **583–5**, 590
Digges, Leonard 230
Dio Cassius 138
Diodati, Charles 647, 649, 650
Diogenes Laertius 462
Diogenes of Babylon 409
Diomedes Grammaticus 90, 396
Dionysius of Halicarnassus 65, 90, 444, 456 n.3
Dioscorides 462
discursive writing **461–79**
classical models **461–8**
diversity 461–2
pejorative use of term 462
Renaissance responses to classical models 461, 462–3, **468–71**, **473–9**
scientific 462
terminology 479 n.3
in verse 461, 472–3, 479
disputations, role in school/university education 45*t*, 46–7, 254
Distichs of Cato (anon.) 33, 34, 35, 49*t*
bilingual edition 63–4
Divus, Andreas 228
Dolce, Lodovico, *Jocasta* 377
Domitian, Emperor 349, 355
Donatus, Aelius 90, 173, 397, 400, 413, 415 n.26, 518
Excerpt on Comedy 396, 398, 413 n.6, 414 n.12
Donne, John 1, 62, 69, 97–8, 118, 119–20, 121, 365, 462, 465, 542
elegies **317–21**
influence of Horace 540, 546–7, 552
influence of Ovid 164, 166, 278, 519, 523
letters 285–6
as Platonist 508–9, 513
verse epistles 278, 279–80, 289 n.29, 547
Anniversaries 177
'The Bracelet' 318

Donne, John (*cont.*)
Devotions upon Emergent Occasions 471
'Elegy 19: To His Mistress Going to Bed' 166, 318
'Epithalamion, or Marriage Song on the Lady Elizabeth, and Count Palatine' 313
'The Extasie' 509
'His Picture' 318
Holy Sonnets 120, 320
'Litany' 120
'To Mr Roland Woodward' 279, 289 n.29, 547
'A Nocturnal upon S. Lucie's Day' 164
'On his Mistress' 314, **318–20**
'Sappho to Philaenis' 278
Satyres 320, **362–3**, 367–8 n.2, 371 n.62, 540, 546–7
'To Sir Henry Wotton' 547
Songs and Sonnets 318, 320, 509
'A Valediction: Forbidding Mourning' 509
Dorislaus, Isaac 450–1
double allusion, practice of 18, 19–20, 521–2
Douglas, Gavin 61, 62, 135, 227, 228
Dove, John 208, 209, 222 n.20
drama
'five-act formula' 70, 378
format of printed editions 401–2
generic divisions 384
opposition to 98, 401, 405–6
productions of classics 67–71, 399–401
romance elements 295–6
see also actors; comedy; stage performances; tragedy; tragicomedy
Drant, Thomas 89, 368 n.7
A Medicinable Morall 346, 361, 540
Drayton, Michael 93, 209, 210, 288 n.18, 475, 523, 585, 595 n.26
The Barons' Wars 92, 239–40, 243
Englands Heroicall Epistles 277, 282–3
'The Epistle of Mistress Shore, to King Edward the Fourth' 277
Idea's Mirrour 505
'The Lady Geraldine to Henry Howard, Earle of Surrey' 277
Mortimeriados 239, 240, 371 n.54
Pastorals: Containing Eclogues 209
Poems 92
Poly-Olbion 203, 234, 237, 474
'To . . . Henry Reynolds' 240
Drummond of Hawthornden, William 60–1, 71 n.15, 181, 211, 225, 509, 636–7
Dryden, John 19, 58–9, 71 n.6, 91, 95, 354, 424, 429, 472, 558, 587, 622
Absolom and Achitophel 644
Discourse Concerning the Original and Progress of Satire 367–8 n.2
Of Dramatic Poesie, An Essay 412, 622
translation of Virgil 226, 227, 474, 475, 599
Du Bartas, Guillaume de Salluste
Divine Weeks and Works 141, 218, 230–1
La Muse chrestiene 180
La Semaine ou création du monde 180, 231
Du Bellay, Joachim 329, 523, 567
Les Antiquitez de Rome 566
see also Spenser, *Ruines of Rome*
Dubrow, Heather 362
DuGard, William 408
Dugdale, Sir William, *History of Imbanking and Drayning* 474
Duport, James 59, 71 n.5, 487
Homeri Gnomologia 492
Durand, P., *Le Stile et maniere de composer, dicter et scrire toute sorte d'epistres* 78, 81

Dürer, Albrecht 106
DuRocher, Richard J. 654 n.3

Ebel, Julia G. 72 n.24
eclogues (genre) 5, **201–16**
 Christian elements 202–3, 210, 211–12
 classical models 201–2, 522–3
 departure from classical models 202–3, 206–7, 214–15
 English translations of classics 203–4
 etymology 202
 fantasy elements 214–16
 political content/implications 148, 203, 210, 221
 popularity 201
 post-Restoration developments 221
 sub-genres 210–14
 treatments of women/sexuality 168, 215–16
 use of song 210
 verse forms 208–9
 see also Eclogues (Virgil); *The Shepheardes Calender*
Eclogues (Virgil) 5, 20, 173, 194, 242, 521, 581, 605
 allegorical interpretations 202
 English editions 61
 English translations 203–4
 generic classification 312
 as model for Renaissance pastoral 179–80, 201–2, 204, 205–7, 209, 210–11, 213, 214, 235, 522, 532, 559–61
 studied in schools/universities 33, 34, 36, 45*t*, 203, 517
 'Eclogue 1' 207
 'Eclogue 4' 13, 206, 209, 334, 648
 'Eclogue 5' 206–7, 210–11
 'Eclogue 6' 652
 'Eclogue 8' 330
 'Eclogue 10' 213
Eden, Kathy 285
education *see* grammar schools; universities
education, purpose of 641–2
Edward, Prince of Wales (The Black Prince) 283
Edward II 239, 240
Edwards, Richard, *Damon and Pythias* 425
Edwards, Thomas, *Cephalus and Procris* 265
Edward VI 203
Egerton, John *see* Bridgewater, Earl of
elegy (genre) **314–21**, 339 n.1
 classical understandings 312, 314–15
 distinguished from similar forms 311–12, 315–16
 examples 314, 315–16, 317–21
 love *vs.* funeral 339–40 n.4
 problems of definition 314, 315, 316–17
 Renaissance understandings 312, 315, 316–17
 studies 339–40 n.4
 versification 314–15
 see also pastoral elegy
Eliot, T.S. 181, 549, 621–2, 636, 639 n30
 'Marina' 394 n.39
Elizabeth I 1, 5, 30, 41, 68, 109, 192, 216, 233, 239, 348, 401, 505, 519
 classical learning 149
 poetic depictions/addresses 139–40, 190, 209, 211, 231, 232, 234, 235, 236, 239–40, 351, 526, 560–2, 564, 567–8
 proposed marriage 148, 222–3 n.28, 560–2
 translations from Latin/Greek/French 89, 135–6, 145 nn.37–8, 504
 works dedicated to 448
 Precationes Privatae Regiae E.R. 149
Ellis, James 271 n.31
Ellrodt, Robert 508
Elyot, Sir Thomas 32, 228
 The Governor 66, 582
 Of the Knowledge whiche maketh a wise man 463
Empedocles 461, 490

Empson, William 221 n.3
English (language), choice over Latin 245
Ennius, Quintus 16, 187, 248 n.48
Enterline, Lynn 162, 170 n.5
epic poetry **225–45**, 373, **564–73**
  allegorical readings 229–30, 232–3
  Christian 19, 98, 140–1, 195, 225–6, 229, 231, 558–9, 565–6
  differences between classical models 232, 238–9, 242, 248 n.48, 518
  drama seen as 225
  epideictic reading 228–9
  Homeric tradition 232
  incompatibility of values with Christianity 557–8
  Italian/French 230–1
  literary status 225
  Lucanian tradition 238–44
  mediation with classical models 228, 229–31, 241
  'mock' 567–8
  narrative themes 233–5, 238–9
  national 14, 98, 123, 225, 233–4
  neoclassical 244–5
  Ovidian tradition 236–8
  place in career trajectories 172–4, 175–6, 177–81, 183, 205
  political relevance 225–6
  praise, as aim of 190, 228–9
  in translation 226–7
  versification 226–7, 482 n.58, 495, 518, 587–8
  Virgilian tradition 232–6
  see also minor epic
Epictetus 64, 136, 137, 467
Epicurean philosophy 472, 476, 477
  objections to 466, 470–1
Epicurus 464
epigrams **345–7**, **349–54**, 364–6
  anthologies 346–7
  burning 348–9
  Roman model 346
  violent/scatological imagery 349–50
epistles
  heroic 277–8, 288 n.18
  moral 280–1
  verse 278–80, 545–7
  see also letters
epitaph, distinguished from elegy 315–16
epithalamium **329–33**, 571–2
  distinguished from similar forms 311–12
  examples 314
  range of classical models 329, 332–3
  Renaissance understandings 313, 329–30
  studies 340–1 nn.9–10, 342–3 n.38
epyllion ('little epic'), genre of 162, **253–69**, 522, 533–4
  female characters 265–9
  reflection of writers' educational experiences 254–8, 266–9
  sexual elements 254–5, 257–8, 259–63
  staged versions 268–9
  studies 269–70 n.2
Erasmus, Desiderius 17, 49*t*, 63, 64, 82, 97, **104–12**, 113, 119, 123, 124 n.14, 285, 402, 407, 504, 575
  banning of works 115
  commentaries on Christian texts 106
  impact on education 33, 35, 38, 46, 266
  literary/artistic depictions 106, 107–12, 116, 125 n.29
  New Testament revisions 105, 115
  Adagia 298, 492, 501 n.39
  Apophthegmata 146 n.61
  Ciceronians 104–5
  Colloquia 34, 45*t*
  Convivium Religiosum 467
  De Conscribendis Epistolis 39, 42, 78, 274
  De Copia (De Duplici Copia Verborum ac Rerum) 33, 37, 39, 42, 80, **105–7**, 258, 270 n.17
  De Pueris Statim ac Liberaliter Educandis 582

De Ratione Studii 30–1, 397, 399
Ecclesiastes 42, 80
Enchiridion Militis Christiani 110, 558
Encomium Moriae (In Praise of Folly) 106, 107, 108
Epigrammata 111
Lucubrationes 125 n.29
Paracelsis 119
Similia 298
Erinna 131
Erne, Lukas 4
essay, as genre 281, 462, 466, 470
Essex, Robert Devereux, 2nd Earl of 151, 189, 447, 448
analogies with classical/fictional characters 152, 381, 388
elegies on 192, 211, 223 n.30
literary works dedicated to 73 n.37, 232–3, 448, 488, 493
trial/execution 283, 381–2, 383, 449, 493
Estienne, Henri 292, 506
ethics, teaching in universities 44, 45*t*, 47
Eton College 117
Eucherius of Lyon 121
Euclid 64
Euripides 30, 34, 60, 88, 303, 599
Renaissance productions 431 n.24
as tragicomic writer 421, 429
Alcestis 183, 421–2, 424, 428, 431 n.24
Andromache 183
Bacchae 183
Cyclops 421, 423, 424, 426, 427, 431 n.24
Hecuba 431 n.24
Helen 183, 421
Ion 421
Iphigeneia in Aulis 136, 376–7, 431 n.24
Iphigeneia in Tauris 421
Medea 183, 431 n.24
Orestes 392 n.11
The Phoenician Women 377, 425
Eusebius of Caesarea 110
Eustathius, *Commentaries* 47, 487
Evanthius Grammaticus 90, 413 n.6
Evelyn, John 142, 463, 470, 472
gardens 475–6, 477, 478, 483 n.86, 483 n.91
portrait 476, 483 n.78
Elysium Britannicum 474
Kalendarium Hortense 474
Evelyn, Mary 142
Everard, John 512

Fabri, Pierre, *Le Grant et vray art de pleine rhétorique* 78, 81
Fabricius Luscinus, C. 90
The Faerie Queene (Spenser) 13, 23 n.32, 88, 174, 229, 248 n.47, 563, **564–71**
as allegory 93, 229, 490–1, 567, 572–3
Christian elements 190, 490–1, 557–9, 565–6
construct of British Renaissance 8–9, 11–12, 233–4
continuation of Chaucer 16–17
criticisms 93, 569
departures from Virgil 565–6, 568
echoes in later writers 533–4
as epic 179, 225, 229, 233–6, 558–9
imperialist message 569–70
influence of Homer 232, 248 n.45, 490–1, 494
influence of Lucretius 231, 574
influence of Ovid 20, 238, 525–7, 568–9, 591
influence of Virgil 11–12, 13, 20, 174, 179, 205, 235, 523–4, **525–7**, 531, 566, 567–8
linked with other Spenser poems 325, 572–3
medieval influences 20
narrative structure 228
pastoral elements 564
personification of attributes 190, 229

The Faerie Queene (Spenser) (*cont.*)
  Platonic content 325, **507–8**
  range of sources 229, 536 n.32
  as romance 295, 306, 564–5
  sexual/romantic content 161–2, 234–5, 571
  treatment of British history 233–4, 533–4
  treatment of fame 190
Fairfax, Thomas, General 220–1, 335
Falstaff, Sir John (fictional character) 412
fame **187–96**
  classical treatments 187–9, 195–6
  historiography 195–6
  personifications 188, 190, 196
  range of meanings 188–9
  Renaissance treatments 189–95
'famous clerks' *see* 'clerks'
Fanshawe, Sir Richard 153, 204, 215, 221 n.9, 540–2, 549
  The Lusiad 230
  'My quench't and discontinu'd Muse' 541
  'Ode upon the Occasion of His Majesty's Proclamation in the year 1630' 220
  Selected Poems of Horace, Prince of Lyrics 541
Farnaby, Thomas 50, 408
Feingold, Mordechai 41, 43, 48, 54 n.81
Feltham, Owen 467, 470, 554 n.11
Felton, John 154
Fenne, Thomas, *Hecubaes Mishaps* 489
Fenner, Dudley, *The Artes of Logike and Rhethorike* 79
Ferrar, Nicholas 463–4
Ficino, Marsilio 9, 463, 505, 507, 508, 509, 510, 511–12
  De Amore 503–4, 506
  De Vita 512
Field, Richard 203
Finch, Anne 282
Fineman, Joel 9
Fish, Stanley 365
Fitzalan, Lady Mary (later Duchess of Norfolk) 136
'five-act formula' 70, 378
Flasket, John (ed.), *Englands Helicon* 201, 552 n.1
Flecknoe, Richard 288 n.13
Fleming, Abraham 203–4, 205
  A Panoplie of Epistles 78
Fletcher, Giles 205
Fletcher, John 424, 616
  The Custom of the Country (with Massinger) 429, 432 n.43
  The Faithful Shepherdess 384, **426–7**
  King and No King (with Beaumont) 427
  Philaster (with Beaumont) 427
Fletcher, Phineas 214
  Apollyonists 231
Florus, L. Annaeus 42, 45*t*, 47, 450
  English editions 49*t*
  Epitome 43, 450
Ford, Emanuel, *Ornatus and Artesia* 295
Ford, John 471
  The Golden Meane 469
Forey, Madeleine 66
Forshaw, Cliff 348
Foucault, Michel 2–4, 9, 21 n.3
  The History of Sexuality 170 n.2
'fourteeners', poetry written in 226, 495
Fowldes, William 496
Fowler, Alastair 354, 474
Fowre Hymnes (Spenser) 180, 314, **323–8**, 463, **573–5**
  Platonic content **323–5**, 507, 508
  An Hymne in Honour of Love 323–4, 507
  An Hymne in Honour of Beautie 324–6
  An Hymne of Heavenly Love 326–7
  An Hymne of Heavenly Beautie 326, 327–8, 507, 508, 568
Foxe, John 43
France
  classical drama 375–6

popularity of Plato 504–5, 506–7
Protestantism 506–7
Francini, Antonio 646
Francklin, R., *Orthotonia seu Tractatus de Tonis in Lingua Graecanica* 50
Fraunce, Abraham 61, 208–9, 425, 490
Arcadian Rhetorike 79, 495
Lawiers Logike 204
French (language)
rhetoric manuals 78
translations from 135, 137–8, 141, 214, 230–1
translations into 59, 63, 137, 139, 214, 294
women's reading in 137–9
friendship, as poetic theme 626–8, 638 n.15
Frizer, Ingram 579, 585
Fulbecke, William 139
Fulgentius, Fabius Planciades 522, 557
Fuller, Thomas, *History of the Worthies of England* 281
Fulwood, William, *The Enemie of Idlenesse* 77, 80–1, 275, 276, 285

Gager, William 496, 502 n.67, 502 n.70
Hippolytus (after Seneca) **390–1**, 612
Meleager 390
Ulysses Redux 497
Gainsford, Thomas, *The Secretaries Study* 78
Galba, S. Supicius, Emperor 447–8, 449
Galen of Pergamon 462
Garland, John of 173
Garnier, Robert 375, 393 n.21
Cornélie 241, 379
Marc Antoine 138, 379
Gascoigne, George 90, 377
The Glass of Government 425
Gassendi, Pierre 464
Gataker, Thomas 47–8, 469
Gelli, Giovanni Battista, *Circe* 500 n.29
genre, theories of 15–16, 373–4, 419–20
see also comedy; tragedy
Geoffrey of Monmouth, *History of the Kings of Britain* 150, 153
georgics (genre) **216–21**, 462–3, **472–8**
classical models 216–17
departure from classical models 217–19
diversity 474–5
Edenic imagery 475–6, 478
English translations of classics 203–4
following of classical models 475–8
linked with retreat from public life 476–8
political content 520
post-Restoration developments 221, 223 n.36
practicality 217–18, 474–5
unpopularity 201, 203, 216
see also Georgics (Virgil)
Georgics (Virgil) 173, 187, 191, 201, 203, 461, 605
English translations 203–4, 474, 475
as model for later writers 216–17, 218–19, 475, 477–8, 519, 520, 532–3, 536 n.29
practical basis 216, 218
Renaissance commentary on 473–4
studied in schools/universities 33, 36, 45*t*, 517
Gil, Alexander 643–5, 646, 649
Gillespie, Stuart 26 n.82, 61
Girard, René 18–19, 557, 575
Gismond of Salerne (anon.) 379
Glareanus, Henricus 441
Goldberg, Jonathan 162
Goldhill, Simon 296, 303–4
Golding, Arthur, translation of Ovid 19, 61, 62, 66, 135, 170 n.5, 226, 228, 389, 522, 523, 603
dedicatory Epistle 160–1, 229–30, 238
Goodwin, Thomas, *Roman Antiquities* 35, 45*t*, 46
Goodyer, Sir Francis 286

Googe, Barnabe 5, 204–5, 218
Gorboduc (Norton/Sackville) **150–1**, 239, 241, **378–9**, 380–1, 393 n.24
Gorges, Sir Arthur 153–4, 250 n.81
Gorgias 91
Gosson, Stephen 93, 295–6, 405–6
  The Schoole of Abuse 406
Gough, John, *The Strange Discovery* 295–6
Goulart, Simon 480 n.19
Goulston, Theodore 78, 95
Gower, John 6
Grafton, Anthony 58, 441–2, 444
grammar schools 29–30, **33–40**
  curricula 33–7, 51, 57–8, 75, 225, 254–6, 257–9, 599–600, 610
  (desired) end product 268, 269
  impact on former pupils' careers/writing 254–9, 266–9, 308–9 n.28
  role of drama 268–9, 271 n.36
  subsidiary reading 36
  teaching methods 35–6, 266–7, 520
  teaching of Latin composition 33, 39–40
  teaching of Latin literature 33, 37–9
  teaching of rhetoric 75, 76, 88–9, 254, 256, 258–9, 266–7, 299
  treatises on 88–9
Grantham, Thomas 488
Greek
  teaching in schools 6, 22 n.20, 30–1, 33–5, 37, 51, 57
  tragedy in 62–3, 376–7, 385
  translations into Latin from 62–3, 292, 397, 463
Greenblatt, Stephen 7, 9, 12
Greene, John 374, 385
Greene, Robert 201, 294, 300, 416 n.43
  The Carde of Fancie 309 n.36
  Euphues his Censure to Philautus 494
  Francesco's Fortunes 407
  Greene's Groatsworth of Wit (attrib.) 407, 603
  The Honourable History of Friar Bacon and Friar Bungay 426
  Menaphon 305, 392 n.18
  Pandosto: The Triumph of Time 293, **300–1**, 306
  Penelope's Web 489
  The Pleasant Conceited Comedy of George A Greene 426
Greene, Thomas M. 329, 638 n.13
  The Light in Troy 17–18
Greenway (Greneway/Grenewey), Richard 61, 139, 448, 456
Gregory of Nazianzus, St 117
Gregory the Great, St (Pope Gregory I) 110
Greville, Fulke 379, 380, 451, 505
  Alaham 379
  Antony and Cleopatra 379, 381
  Mustapha 379
Grimald, Nicholas 465, 587
  Christus Redivivus 425
Grindal, Edmund, Archbishop 562
Grymeston, Elizabeth 138
Gualter, Rodolph 282
Guarini, Giambattista 423, 425
  Il compendio della poesia tragicomica 384
  Compendium 423
  Il Pastor Fido 215, 300, 424, 425–6, 431 n.27, 432 n.34
Guazzo, Stefano, *Civile Conversations* 463
Guicciardini, Francesco 312
Guilpin, Edward 354, 362
  Skialethia, or a Shadowe of Truth 348, 352, 357
  The Whipper of the Satyre His Penance 357
Gunpowder Plot (1605) 231, 645
Guy-Bray, Stephen 168

Haber, Judith 259–60, 271 n.19
Habinek, Thomas 159
Habington, William 510

Hadfield, Andrew 250 n.78, 445, 580
hagiography 121
Hale, John K. 646–7
Hall, Arthur, *Ten Bookes of Homers Iliades* 487
Hall, Edward 239
Hall, John 98
Hall, Joseph 354, **355–8**, 360–1, 362, 367, 422, 469–70
  Epistles 281, 288 n.13
  Meditations 281
  Virgidemiae 181, 348, 355, 356–7, 358, 360
Hall, Thomas, *Rhetorica Sacra* 79
Hamilton, A.C. 23 n.32
Hamlet (pre-Shakespeare, author uncertain) 379, 392 n.18
Hamlet (Shakespeare) 67, 70, 95, 258, 374, 378, 384, 392 n.11, 392 n.17, 396, 600
  influence of Seneca 610–11, 612
  reworking of *Aeneid* 528–9, 530, 606
Hammond, Henry 492
Hammond, Paul 71 n6, 458 n.25
Hannay, Margaret P. 181–2
Hardie, Philip 10, 162, 163
Harington, Sir John 90, 91, 316–17, 354, 409, 644
  translation of Ariosto 93, 229
  translation of Cicero 397
  A New Discourse of a Stale Subject, Called the Metamorphosis of Ajax 496–7
Harrington, James 204
  The Commonwealth of Oceana 155
Harrison, Stephen 178
Harrison, William 298
Hartlib, Samuel 475
Harvey, Gabriel 90, 348, 416 n.40, **441–2**, 446, 495, 565, 607
Harvey, William 473
Haynes, Kenneth 72 n.33
Hayward, Sir John, *First Part of the Raigne of King Henry the IIII* 438, 448, 449
Hazlitt, William 580
Hebrew, teaching of
  in grammar schools 34, 35, 37
  in universities 42
Hecuba (fictional character), education/literature themed on 529, 606
Hegel, Georg Wilhelm Friedrich 7–8
Heinsius, Daniel 96, 130, 408, 412, 417 n.47
Helgerson, Richard 3–4, 13–14, 122
  Self-Crowned Laureates 174–5, 176
Heliodorus 64, 294, 305, 429
  see also Aethiopica
Helvidius Priscus 195
Hemmingsen, Niels, *The Preacher* 79
Heninger, S.K. 514 n.17
Henrietta Maria, Queen (wife of Charles I) 284, 510
Henri IV of France 136
Henry I 129
Henry II 277
Henry V 235
Henry VII 1
Henry VIII 68, 111, 204, 440, 441, 567
Henry, Prince of Wales (son of James I) 154, 211, 488
Henryson, Robert 608
Henslowe, Philip 600
Heraclitus 316, 488, 490
Herberay, Nicolas de 294
Herbert, Edward, Lord 510
Herbert, George 35, 58, 62, 120–1, 463–4
  A Priest to the Temple 79
Heresbach, Conrad, *Four Books of Husbandry* 204, 218
Hermogenes 42, 75, 77, 90
  On Types 89
Hero and Leander (Marlowe) 60–1, **168–9**, 181, 256, **259–63**, 296, 581, 582
  competition with *The Rape of Lucrece* 602
  completion 593 n.2, 597 n.54

Hero and Leander (Marlowe) (*cont.*)
influence of Ovid 168–9, 264–5, 579, **590–2**
studies 596 n.48
vocabulary 586
Herodian 60, 64, 445
Herodotus 30, 59, 298, 439
heroic couplets *see* iambic pentameter
Heroides (Ovid) 34, 45*t*, 49*t*, 130–1, 182, 266, 277–8, 288 n.18, 309 n.36, 517, 521, 522, 531, 546
referenced in Renaissance works 601
Heron, Haly, *A Newe Discourse of Morall Philosophie* 470
Herrick, Marvin 94
Herrick, Robert 432 n.30, 474, 544, 554 n.11
(claimed) models 345
'The Apparition of his Mistress Calling Him to Elysium' 345
'Epithalamie to Sir Thomas Southwell and his Ladie' 313
'Panegyric to Sir Lewis Pemberton' 219–20
'Pastoral on the Birth of Prince Charles' 210
'To the King, upon his Welcome to Hampton-Court' 155
'To Virgins' 166–7, 287
'Upon Cupid' 164–5
Hesiod 10, 130, 462, 463, 473, 474, 475
English translations 203, 217
studied in schools/universities 34, 35, 45*t*, 46, 51
Theogony 177
Works and Days 62, 173, 177, 203
Hessus, Eobanus 487
hexameters, attempts to find English equivalent 208–9, 226–7, 495, 587–8
Heywood, John, *An hundred Epigrammes* 346
Heywood, Thomas 277
The Ages 248 n.53
Apology for Actors 405, 407
Appius and Virginia (with Webster) 65, 446
The Captives, or The Lost Recovered 403, 405
The English Traveller 403, 405, 412
Love's Mistress 295
Oenone and Paris 256, 264–6, 269
The Rape of Lucrece 65, 446
Troia Britannica 234
Heyworth, Stephen 178
'H.H.B.' (translator of Aristophanes) 411–12, 417 n.58
Hibbard, G.R. 223 n.47
Higden, Ranulf, *Polychronicon* 109
Hinds, Stephen 18
Historia Ecclesiae Christi (muti-author) 113
historiography **433–56**
history, university courses in 42
Hobbes, Thomas 49*t*, 61, 94, 449, 450
'Answer to Sir William Davenant's Preface' 244
Behemoth 155, 451
A Briefe of the Art of Rhetorique 77, 78
De Cive 154
Leviathan 155
Hoby, Sir Thomas 32, 52 n.15, 505
Holbein, Hans 111
Holdsworth, Richard, *Directions for a Student in the Universitie* **43–7**, 45*t*, 48
Holinshed, Raphael 239, 298, 453
Holland, Hugh, *Pancharis* 235–6
Holland, Philemon 64–5, 447, 458 n.28, 465–6, 480 n.19, 503
Homer 1, 2, 4, 10–11, 14, 16, 20, 60, 93–4, 116, 130, 173, 308 n.11, **487–98**
availability in original 225
as career model 179, 181
commentaries 488 *see also* Chapman, George
dramatic adaptations 497

English translations 12, 19, 63, 64, 65, 90, 143, 487–8, 502 n.67 *see also* Chapman, George
generic features 496–8
'mock-epics' 567–8
as model for later epics 229, 232
moral/allegorical interpretations 488–92
political philosophy 493–4
Renaissance editions 487, 488
self-presentation 177
studied in grammar schools 30, 34, 35, 51
studied in universities 42, 47, 488
(supposed) religious beliefs 490–1, 492, 497
use of epithets 65
verse style 494–5
see also Batrachomyomachia; *Iliad*; *Odyssey*
Homeric Hymns 321
homosexuality
in classical mythology 168
poetic treatments 168–9, 206, 587
see also lesbianism; sodomy
Honigmann, Ernst 453
Hooker, Richard 127 n.56
Hoole, Charles, *A New Discovery of the Old Art of Teaching Schoole* 32, **34–7**, 39, 40, 48, 53 n.47
Horace (Q. Horatius Flaccus) 2, 5, 13–14, 89, 112, 147, 322, 345, 371 n.62, 471, 476, **539–52**
contributions to development of ode 313, 333, 335–6
English editions 48–50, 49*t*, 62, 89–90
English translations/imitations 64, 65, 89–90, **540–52**, 554 n.16, 555–6 n.28, 623
influence on Renaissance satire 346, 357, 362, 367–8 n.2, 368 n.7, 370 n.36
literary career 175, 177, 178, 179, 181
as model for Jonson 13, 92, 152, 179, 181, 186 n.49, **363–7**, 370 n.36, 520, 540, 545–6, 625
reworking by Ovid 188
as stage character 193–4, 227, 363–4, 520, 546, 633–4
studied in grammar schools 30, 33, 34, 35
studied in universities 45*t*, 46, 47
treatments of fame 187–8, 189, 191, 194
'Cleopatra Ode' 549–50
Epistles 278–80, 365–6, 545–7, 623, 638 n.10, 638 n.20
'Epode 2' 219, 223 n.47
'Iccius Ode' 549
Satires 279, 346, 357, 359, 360, 362, 363, 365–6, 370 n.30, 540, 554 n.18
Sermones 59, 64, 278
see also Ars Poetica; *Odes*
Horapollo, *Hieroglyphica* 62, 509
'An Horatian Ode upon Cromwell's Return from Ireland' (Marvell) 155, 242–3, 314, **335–8**, 343 n.53, **548–51**, 555–6 n.28
differing political readings 548–9, 554–5 n.21
Horne, Thomas, *Rhetoricae Compendium Latino-Anglice* 79
Hoskins, John, *Directions for Speech and Style* 78, **82–3**, 86 n.27
Howard, Lady Douglas 211
Howard, Sir Robert 412
Howell, James, *Epistolae Ho-Elianae* **275–6**, 288 n.13
Huet, Daniel 294
Traité de l'origine des romans 291
Hughes, Ted 587
Hughes, Thomas, *The Misfortunes of Arthur* 152, 241, 379, 393 n.20, 612
Huguenots 506–7

humanism **29–33**
blacklisting of texts of 115
and Christianity 104–5, 111–12, 115, 567
drawbacks 258–9
and education 30–3, 51, 58, 104–5, 149, 254–5, 299, 397, 530
and historiography 438–9, 441–2, 456 n.1
and homoeroticism 168
impact on drama 68, 270 n.6, 401–2, 412
letter-writing 274, 287 n.4
origins 29
and philosophy 151
preferred genres 254–5, 263–4
Humphrey, Lawrence 487
Hunter, G.K. 74 n.61, 432 n.34, 610
Hutchinson, Lucy 142, 146 n.69, 472–3
Hutton, Matthew, Archbishop 282
Hutton, Timothy 282
hymn (genre) **321–8, 573–5**
Christianization 321–3, 340 n.7
classical understandings 321
contained within other forms 328
defining characteristics 312–13
distinguished from similar forms 311–12
examples 314, 323–8
studies 340 nn.5–7
in vernacular 322, 342 n.34
Hyperius, Andreas, *The Practis of Preaching* 79
Hyrd, Richard 110

iambic pentameter, use of
rhymed 227, 495, 518, 587–8
unrhymed 65, 226–7, 379, 386, 518, 587–8
Iccius (friend of Horace) 549
ideas, theory of 96
Iliad (Homer) 173, 181, 420, 608
allegorical interpretations 489–92
compared with *Odyssey* 496
denigrations/parodies 497–8
English translations 12, 19, 90, 226, 227, 487, 493
ethical implications 489
narratorial voice 177
political implications 493–4
Renaissance editions 49*t*, 487
rhetorical devices 494–5
studied in schools/universities 36, 45*t*
imitation, theory/practice of 16–19, 58, 457 n.7, 608–9
distancing involved in 18–19
studies 17–18
Innes, James 144 n.18
Inns of Court 82, 254, 600
performances of classical drama 68, 150–1, 152, 403–4
translators trained in 617–18 n.6
Interregnum (1649–60) 377, 520
state of theatre/comedy 408–12
intertextuality 3, 17–18
Ipswich Grammar School 38
Ireland
English rule in 442, 457 n.13, 569–70
role in Spenser's poetry 563–4, 571–2
Irigaray, Luce 271 n.31
Isidore, St 110
Isocrates 34, 35, 51, 64, 91, 136
Italian literature, influence in England 230–1, 293, 294–5

Jack Juggler (anon.) 69, 403
Jacob, Henry (the younger) 48
Jacques, Francis 411, 417 n.56
James VI/I 47, 112, 113, 114, 115–16, 117, 228, 365, 382, 448, 450, 503, 519, 607, 613
court culture 152–3, 509
ill-feeling towards 153–4, 239
public pronouncements 239
James, Heather 4

James, Thomas 113, 116
Treatise of the Corruption of Scripture 117
Jardine, Lisa 441–2, 444
Javitch, Daniel 18
Jeremiah, St, *Lamentations* 346
Jerome, St 106, 108, 109, 110, 111, 114, 115, 125 n.38, 409
De Viris Illustribus 110, 114, 126 n.48
Jewel, John 117
Apologia Ecclesiae Anglicanae 117
Jodelle, Étienne, *Cléopâtre captive* 375
John Chrysostom, St 50, 117, 118, 119
Johnson, Christopher 40, 393 n.33, 496, 502 n.67
Johnson, Elizabeth 143 n.1
Johnson, Ralph 40
Johnson, Richard 295
Johnson, Robert 281
Johnson, Samuel, Dr 384, 589
Life of Milton 221
Jones, Inigo 194
Jones, Richard 50
Jonson, Ben 1, 2, 18, 201, 225, 241, 357, **363–7**, 407, 424, 468, 549, 550, **621–37**, 625
attacks on women writers 132–3
authorial status 4–5, 13
(claimed) moral purpose 629
as classicist **623–8**, 630–1
commentary on poetry 92, 96, 97
comments on contemporaries 132–3, 487, 599, 616–17
comparisons/competition with Shakespeare 616–17, 621–2, 637
contemporary attacks on 607–8, 629
as court poet 152–3, 228
depictions in others' works 243
education 135, 621
ideal character **625–8**
influence of classical drama 21, 376, 389, 616
library 60, 63, 433, 451, 456 n.1, 498 n.3
literary career 175, 177, 179, 181, 186 n.49, **628–34**
modelling on Horace 13, 92, 152, 179, 181, 186 n.49, **363–7**, 370 n.36, 520, 540, 545–6, 552
modern responses to 637
odes/epistles addressed to 545, 554 n.11, 554 n.15
personality 627
political content of drama 152
posthumous reputation 622–3
reading/scholarship 22 n.20, 58, 360, 431–2 n.29, 437–8, 586, 600, **622–5**
relationship with audience 624–5, 629
self-presentation 627–8, 629, 634–5
as tragedian 21, 379–80, 447
as translator 89, 181
treatments of fame 193–4
verse epistles 278–9, 545–6
The Alchemist 405, 408, 412, 509–10
Bartholomew Fair 410, 626
'Cary and Morison' 338
The Case Is Altered 403, 404
Cynthia's Revels 363, 629, 632–3, 635
Discoveries 83, 97, 581, 623–4, 626–7
'An Elegy' 638 n.16
'To Elizabeth, Countess of Rutland' 635
Epicoene, or The Silent Woman 466, 481 n.41, 494
'Epigram 101' ('Inviting a Friend to Supper') 279, 365–6, 367, 628
Epigrammes 279, 354, **364–6**, 623
'Epistle: To Elizabeth Countess of Rutland' 193
'An Epistle Answering One that Asked to be Sealed in the Tribe of Ben' 279, 626
'An Epistle to a Friend' (*Ungathered Verse* 49) 545–6, 628

Jonson, Ben (*cont.*)
'Epistle to Katharine, Lady Aubigny' 625–6
'Epithalamion' 314, 332
Every Man in his Humour 404
Every Man out of his Humour 363, **629–33**, 635
The Forest 635
'The Haddington Masque' 314, 331–2, 343 n.43
'The Induction' 626
Jonsonus Virbius 636, 639 n.30
The Masque of Beautie 509
The Masque of Blacknesse 509
The Masque of Queenes 194, 241, 491
'The Minde of the Front' 196
The New Inn 510
Oberon 427
'On Bacon' 15
'On My First Son' 636, 639 n.28
'A Speech According to Horace' 546
The Staple of News 408–9
'To a Friend and Son' 627
'To Celia' 287
'To Gut' 364
'To Himself' 634
'To My Chosen Friend, the Learned Translator of Lucan, Thomas May, Esquire' 243
'To Penshurst' 218–19
'To Sir Robert Wroth' 218–19
'To Sir Thomas Roe' 625
'To the Memory of my Beloved, The Author Master William Shakespeare' 15, 404, 622
'To William Camden' 626
The Underwoods 635
Volpone 408, 426, 636–7, 639 n.24
'The Voyage It Selfe' 366–7, 372 n.80
Works (1616 Folio) 181
see also Catiline; Poetaster; Sejanus His Fall
Josephus, Flavius 138, 139, 379
Jewish History 43
Julia (daughter of Augustus) 193, 519
Julius Vindex 448, 449
Junius, Franciscus (the elder) 130, 144 n.9
Junius, Franciscus (the younger) 97
The Painting of the Ancients 97
Junius, Hadrianus (Adriaen de Jonghe)
Copiae Cornu Sive Oceanus Enarrationum Homericarum 487
Emblemata 189–90
Justinian, Emperor 114
Justinus, M. Junianus 34
History 35, 45*t*, 46
Juvenal (D. Iunius Juvenalis) 34, 35, 45*t*, 175, 219, 345, 354–5, 367, 437, 600
English editions 49*t*, 60, 62
popularity/influence in Renaissance England 152, 221, 356, 357–8, 361, 362–3, 365, 367–8 n.2
'Satire 1' 346, 356, 357–8
'Satire 5' 356
'Satire 10' 120, 138

Kafka, Franz 103
Kalendrier des Bergers (anon.) 5, 217–18
Kallendorf, Craig 537 n.51
Kant, Immanuel 585
Kastan, David Scott 4, 22 n.12
Keller, Stefan 76
Kempe, William 39
Kendall, Timothy (ed.), *Flowers of Epigrams* 347, 552 n.1
Kerrigan, William 9, 23 n.36
Kewes, Paulina 446
Kilgour, Maggie 646, 649, 655 n.13
King, Edward 652
King James Bible 117, 122, 126 n.46
Preface 114–15, 126 n.50
King Lear (Shakespeare) 302, 377, 381, 387, 388–9
links with classical tragedy 610, 612
Kinney, Clare R. 222 n.13

Kinwelmersh, Francis 377, 379, 425
Knyvett, Sir John 62
Knyvett, Sir Thomas (b. 1539) 61–2
Knyvett, Sir Thomas (b. 1595) 62
Kristeller, Paul Oskar 23 n.34, 513
Kristeva, Julia 3
Kyd, Thomas 585, 600, 607
  Cornelia (translated from Garnier) 151, 241, 250 n.95, 379
  The Spanish Tragedy 70–1, 241, 379, 384, 385, 386, 537 n.44
Kyffin, Maurice 400, 402

la Boderie, Guy Lefèvre de 504
Landino, Cristoforo 70, 557
Lane, John, *Tritons Trumpet* 218
Langland, William, *Piers Plowman* 203
Languet, Hubert 506
Lanyer, Aemilia 135, 474
Laocoön (sculpture) 10
la Planche, Étienne de 146 n.55
la Primaudaye, Pierre de 86 n.27, 463
Latimer, Hugh, Bishop 204–5
Latin
  composition in 39–40, 53 n.55, 58, 274–5
  domination of Renaissance culture 19, 29, 33, 51, 59–61, 64, 131, 142–3
  English writers' poems in 19, 111, 532, 550, 589, 600, 645
  in grammar schools 6, 19, 30–2, **33–40**, 51, 57, 399
  letter-writing in 274–5
  literature, study of 37–9, 44–6, 47, 51, 59
  translations from Greek 62–3, 292
  verse forms 208–9, 226
  women literate in 129, 138, 140, 142–3, 145 n.48
Latomus, Jacobus 43, 49*t*
Laud, William, Archbishop 41, 44–6, 119, 127 n.56
Leach, Edmund 129
Lefèvre, Raoul, *Recuyell of the Historyes of Troye* 135, 234, 497–8
Lefèvre d'Étaples, Jacques 115
Leicester, Robert Dudley, 1st Earl of 160, 229–30, 442, 507
Leland, John 111
Leo The Great, St (Pope Leo I) 110
lesbianism
  sympathetic evocations 278
  women writers attacked for 130–1, 132–3, 138, 288 n.23
L'Estrange, Roger 478–9
letters **273–87**
  ancient, discovery / publication 273–4, 287
  collections 275–6
  Greek 287
  literary forms *see* epistles
  manuals on writing 81–3, 275, 276
  with nothing to say 284–7
  preferred language / style 274–5
  private, publication of 283–4
  school editions 275
  stylistic devices 281–7, 289 n.34
  'unblushing' character 281–4
Lewalski, Barbara 643–4
Lewis, C.S. 351, 585, 589, 591, 592
Libanius, *On Letter Form* 276
libraries (personal) **59–62**, 136
Liceti, Fortunio, *Ulysses Apud Circem* 500 n.29
Licinius Murena, L. 542
Lily, William 297
  Brief Introduction to Latin Grammar 38, 255, 263, 264, 297–8, 600
  Carmen de Moribus 34
Linacre, Thomas 504
  Rudiments of Latin Grammar 47
Lincoln, Thomas Clinton, 3rd Earl of 139
Lindley, David 343 n.43
Lipking, Lawrence, *Life of the Poet* 174–5, 176

Lipsius, Justus 151
 commentary on Seneca 280–1, 467, 469
 historiographical commentary 437, 438, 439, 450, 452
 Epistolica Institutio 82
Lisle, Sir George 139
Lisle, William 204
 The Fair Ethiopian 296
literary criticism **87–98**
 classical models 88–91
 key themes 87–8
 vernacular 91–4
literature, university courses in 44–6, 47, 59
Livy (T. Livius)
 English editions/translations 64–5, 136, 447
 influence on Renaissance political thought/historiography **439–47**, 454–5
 as source for English writers 64–5
 studied in schools/universities 32, 37, 45*t*, 47
 History of Rome **439–47**, 452, 454
Lloyd, Richard, *Artis Poeticae* 90
Locrine (authorship uncertain) 491
Lodge, Thomas 93, 281, 479, 505, 533
 A Fig to Momus 370 n.43, 546
 Glaucus and Scylla 522
 The Wounds of Civil War 445
 see also Scillaes Metamorphosis
logic, teaching in universities 43–4, 45*t*, 46, 47
Lollius Paulinus, M. 545
'Longinus,' *On the Sublime* 89, 90, 97, 98, 99 n.20
'Long Parliament' 154
Longus 64
 Daphnis and Chloe 214, 291–2, 293, 296–7, 303, 304–5, 426
Lorich(ius), Reinhard 39, 75, 270 n.15
'Lothian, Lady' 133
Lovelace, Richard 552
 'Advice to my Best Brother' 542–3
love poetry 13, **162–7**
 see also romance
Lowell, James Russell 585
Lucan (M. Annaeus Lucanus) 4, 35, 45*t*, 59, 136, 226, 249 n.75, 550–1, 554–5 n.21, 567
 English translations 60–1, 152, 153–4, 227, 451, 579, 585, **589–90**
 influence on Marlowe 241, 250 n.91, 579–80, 581–2
 political stance 580, 593–4 n.3, 609
 popularity in Renaissance England 152, 153–4, 157 n.24, 157 n.32
 see also Bellum Civile
Lucas, Sir Charles 139
Lucceius, L. 281–2
Lucian of Samosata 30, 35, 59
 Dialogues of the Gods 343 n.43
 The Double Indictment 359–60
 Icaromenippus 366–7
 Lexiphanes 363
 A True Story 366–7
Lucilius, C. Ennius 280, 281, 359, 370 n.44, 461
Lucretia (historical character) 443, 444, 446
Lucretius Carus, T. 162, 470
 English translations 472–3
 influence on Renaissance discursive writing 461, 462–3, **472–3**, 476
 De Rerum Natura 12, 44, 45*t*, 142, 230–1, 472, 482 n.58, 574
Lumley, Jane, Lady (née Fitzalan) 60
 translation of Euripides 136, 376–7
Lumley, John, Lord 59–60
Luther, Martin 7, 104, 108, 113, 312
Lycidas (Milton) 183, 194–5, 202, **212–14**, 221, 532, 648, 650, **651–3**, 655 n.26
Lycophron 35, 582
Lydgate, John 6, 244
 Troy Book (History of Troy) 109, 497–8, 608

Lyly, John 294, **297–9**
  Euphues: The Anatomy of Wit 297–9
  Euphues and His England 297–8
  Galathea 253, 425
  Midas 426
  Woman in the Moon 500 n.30
Lyne, Raphael 524

Macbeth (Shakespeare) 67, 385–6, 387, 394 n.36
  classical influences 607, 612–13
Machiavelli, Niccolò 312, 439, 452, 554–5 n.21
  The Art of War 442
  Discourses on the First Ten Books of Titus Livy 447
  The Prince 313
Macrobius Ambrosius Theodosius 16, 30, 96
  Saturnalia 45t, 146 n.61, 494
Maecenas, C. Cilnius 279
Magdalen College School, Oxford 257
'Magdeburg, Centuries of' 113
Maier, Michael, *Arcana Arcanissima* 491
Maitland, Marie 138, 139
  'To Your Self' 145–6 n.52
Mallineux, Sir Richard 352
Malpaghini, Giovanni 17
Mancini, Dominici 33, 52 n.21
Manilius, M. 462
  Astronomica 138
Manningham, John 613
Mantuan, Baptista 33, 34, 52 n.21, 203, 335, 523, 560
  as model for English pastoral 204, 207, 209, 210
  Adolescentia 202, 205
Manutius, Aldus Pius (Aldo Manuzio) 49t
Manwood, Sir Roger 589
Marcus Aurelius, Emperor 136, 275, 445, 467, 471
Margaret of Scotland, St 143 n.5
Marino, Giambattista 329, 523
Mark Antony (M. Antonius) 283–4, 377, 379
Markham, Gervase 475
Markham, Joseph 288 n.13
Marlowe, Christopher 2, 74 n.62, 151, 407, **579–93**
  authorial status 4–5
  classicism 585–7, 592–3, 593 n.1
  comparison/competition with Shakespeare 592–3, 602, 606
  contemporaries' comments on 93
  death 4, 579, 585, 607
  education 135, 271 n.23, 585, 586, 594 n.10, 600, 621
  flaws in translations 588, 589–90
  influence of Lucan 241, 250 n.91
  influence of Ovid 168–9, 179, 181, 581, **582–4**
  influence of Virgil **583–5**
  lack of biographical information 580, 594 n.10, 594 n.12
  literary career 175, 177, 179, 181, 186 n.46, 594 n.12
  posthumous reputation 585
  rebellious/dissolute image 519, 580, 581–2, 585, 596 n.44
  as translator 152, 181, 227, 241, 370 n.34, 518, 523, 579, 582, 583, 585, **587–93**, 594–5 n.17, 596 n.41, 599
  verse forms 226–7, 585, 587–8, 589, 596 n.41
  writings in Latin 589, 600
  Doctor Faustus 4, 181, 580, 582, 583, 621
  Edward II 445, 583, 587
  The Jew of Malta 428, 580–1, 587
  Lucan's First Book 181
  Ovid's Elegies 181
  'The Passionate Shepherd to His Love' 26 n.84, 181, 201, 581
  Tamburlaine 386, 503, 580, 582–3, 585–7
  see also Dido, Queene of Carthage; *Hero and Leander*

Marot, Clément 5, 205, 211
  Eglogue sur le trépas de ma Dame Loyse de Savoye 560
marriage
  in grammatical/legal exercises 255
  poetic celebrations of
    see epithalamium
  as social model 159–60, 167–8
Marsh, Thomas 402, 415 n.26
Marston, John 69, 152, 354, **356–61**, 362, 363, 367, 370 n.50, 607–8, 628–9
  Certaine Satyres 348, 356, 359, 360
  The Dutch Courtezan 426
  The Insatiate Countess 387
  The Malcontent 385, 426
  The Metamorphosis of Pigmalions Image 254–5
  Satiromastix (with Dekker) 363–4, 629, 634–5
  The Scourge of Villainy 348, 356, 357, 358, 359, 360, 361
  Sophonisba 65, 438
Marsus, Paulus 444
Martial (M. Valerius Martialis) 34, 45*t*, 46, 130, 131, 195, 345, 367, 369 n.24, 476, 600
  English editions/translations 49*t*, 64, 347, 369 n.25, 623, 626
  English imitations 350–4, 364–5
  epigrams 346–7, **349–54**, 364–5, 623, 626, 633
  stylistic features 349–50
Martin, Gregory 126 n.50
Martin, Henri-Jean 137
Martindale, Charles 528, 605, 618–19 n.21, 649
Martz, Louis 532
Marullo, Michele 322
Marvell, Andrew 1, 26 n.84, 139, 474, 522–3, 574
  adaptations of Horace 540, 543–4, **547–51**, 553 n.4, 555–6 n.28
  Latin poems 19, 550
  wordplay 550
  'Damon the Mower' 20, 221, 224 n.52, 522, 550
  'The Garden' 11, 550, 553 n.4
  'On a Drop of Dew' 550
  'The First Anniversary of the Government under His Highness the Lord Protector, 1655' 543–4, 547–8, 549, 555–6 n.28
  'The Nymph Complaining for the Death of her Fawn' 522
  'To his Coy Mistress' 550
  'Tom May's Death' 243, 549
  'Upon Appleton House' 220–1
  'Upon the Hill and Grove at Bilbrough' 335
  see also 'An Horatian Ode ...'
Marx, Karl 7–8
Mary I 204–5
Mary of Modena, Queen (wife of James II) 144 n.18
A Maske Presented at Ludlow Castle
    see Comus
Massinger, Philip
  The Custom of the Country (with Fletcher) 429, 432 n.43
  The Guardian 510
  The Roman Actor 153
Masters, Richard 282
Matilda, Queen (wife of Henry I) 129, 143 n.5
May, Thomas 240–4
  criticisms 243
  political stance 241
  translations from Latin 60–1, 204, 231–2, 239, 240–1, 243, 451
  Antigone 241
  Continuation (of Lucan) 240–1, 451
  Julia Agrippina 153
  'The Reigne of King Henry the Second' 243, 244

'The Victorious Reigne of King Edward the Third' 243, 244
McCabe, Richard 348
McClung, William A. 223 n.47
McConica, James 41, 43
McRae, Andrew 367, 475, 482 n.65
Melanchthon, Philipp 42, 43, 80, 496
  Institutiones rhetoricae 78
Menander 397, 403, 409
Menippus of Gadara 359–60
Meres, Francis 17, 90, 118, 238, 495, 528, 603, 608, 615
Metamorphoses (Ovid) 13, 18, 19, 20, 137, 178, 201, 389, 390
  allegorical readings 229–30
  contrasted with *Aeneid* 518
  English editions 49*t*, 61
  English translations 62, 66, 160–1, 170 n.5, 226, 227, 228, 229–30, 238
  influence on minor epic 256–8, 261, 263, 264–5, 266
  method of study 38, 39
  as model for later poets **236–8**, 522–3, 526–7, 528–31, 534–5, 550, 563, 568, 592, 601–2, 603–5, 652
  referenced in Renaissance works 601, 603
  retelling of *Aeneid* 521
  sexual content 160–1, 163–4, 165, 166, 257–8, 518
  studied in schools/universities 33, 34, 35, 45*t*, 225, 254, 520
  translation exercises 35–6
  treatment of fame 188–9, 191, 193
metaphysics, teaching in universities 45*t*
metempsychosis (transmigration of souls) 16–17, 187–8, 197 n.3, 568
metres, debate on 246 n.7
  in eclogues 208–9
  in the epic 226
Michael, Ian 53 n.59
Michelet, Jules 6
Micro-cynicon, Six Snarling Satyres (author uncertain) 348, 357
Micyllus, Jakob 488
Middleton, Thomas 348, 357, 432 n.42
  A Mad World My Masters 597 n.50
  The Witch 428–9
A Midsummer Night's Dream (Shakespeare) 164, 296, 378, 387, 505
  classical models 603–4, 612, 614
Milton, Elizabeth 251 n.108
Milton, John 2, 9, 10, 88, 98, 112, **121–3**, 201, 334, 377, 473, 479, 489, 550, 574, 622, **641–53**
  Continental tour (1638-9) 645–6, 647, 648
  education **643–7**
  elegies **212–14**, 532–3, 645, 649
  favourite poets 251 n.108
  influence of Virgil/Ovid 517, 518, **531–5**, 646, 648–9, 652
  Latin poems 19, 532, 645
  literary career 17, 172–3, 174, 175, 177, 178, 183, 186 n.58, 212, 532, 647
  Neoplatonism 511–12, 513, 650–1
  political stance 493
  responses to detractors 642–3
  treatments of fame 194–5
  verse forms 227
  views on education **641–3**
  'Ad Ioannem Rousium' 122, 532
  Apology for a Pamphlet 649
  An Apology for Smectymnuus 511, 642, 643
  Arcades 533, 647–8
  Areopagitica 409, 653
  'At a Solemn Music' 648
  Colasterion 642
  De Idea Platonica 511, 645
  The Doctrine and Discipline of Divorce 492, 511, 650, 654 n.6

Milton, John (*cont.*)
Of Education 32–3, 88–9
'Elegia 1' 532
'Elegia 4' 532, 646
'Elegia 5' 532–3
'Elegia 6' 532, 649
Epitaphium Damonis 212–13, 245, 251 n.109, 532, 650
History of Britain 196
Il Penseroso 322, 511, 648
In Quintum Novembris 195, 226, 231, 645
L'Allegro 322, 648
Naturam non Pati Senium 645
'On Shakespeare' 645
'On the Death of a Fair Infant Dying of a Cough' 532, 645, 655 n.13
'On the late Massacre in Piedmont' 551
'On the Morning of Christ's Nativity' 328, 334–5, 532, 647, **648–9**, 655 n.15
'On Time' 648
Paradise Regained 172–3, 183, 195
Poems (1645) 122, 532
Poems (1673) 643
Prolusions 511, 645
Pro Se Defensio 511
The Ready and Easy Way 155, 511
The Reason of Church-Government 122, 642
Of Reformation 123
Samson Agonistes 172, 186 n.58, 195, 373, 375, 379
'Sonnet 7' 648
Tetrachordon 511
Treatise on Christian Doctrine 511
'Upon the Circumcision' 648
see also Comus; *Lycidas*; *Paradise Lost*
mimesis, theories of 18, 90, 93, 94–5, 96, 557–9, 575 n.1
minor epic *see epyllion*
Minturno, Antonio 95, 431–2 n.29
Miola, Robert 57, 397
A Mirror for Magistrates (multi-author) 244
Momigliano, Arnaldo 444
Montaigne, Michel de 17, 466, 469–70, 473, 481 n.37
Essais 281, 468
Montemayor, Jorge de, *Diana* 214–15, 294–5, 302
Montrose, Louis 3–4, 305
Moore, Helen 175
More, Henry 282, 464, 510
Conjectura Cabbalistica 513
The Immortality of the Soul 512
'Pyschozoia' 512
More, Sir Thomas 107–8, 440
Latin epigrams 111
The History of Richard III 449, **454–6**
Utopia 107, 111
Morel, Jean 130
Morison, Henry 336, 338, 635–6
Mortimer, Roger 239
Moschus 5, 204, 211, 213, 314
'The Runaway Love' 343 n.43
Mosellanus, *Tabulae de Schematibus et Tropis* 78
Moss, Ann 105
Moul, Victoria 365
Moulsworth, Martha 132
Moulton, Ian 168
Munday, Anthony 394 n.36
Munro, Lucy 427
Muret, Marc-Antoine 415 n.26
Murrin, Michael 567
Musaeus Grammaticus 169, 579, 581–2
Hero and Leander 582, 590–1
Muses 132–3
Mussato, Albertino, *Ecerinis* 374, 380

Naevius, Cn. 409
Nashe, Thomas 70, 98, 378, 384, 392 n.18, 407, 580, 610
burning of writings 348

comments on Homer 489, 495
Lenten Stuffe 496–7
'Life of Jack Wilton' 109
The Unfortunate Traveller **107–9**
nationhood, poet as spokesperson for 13–14
Navarre, Marguerite de 504
Mirror of the Sinful Souls 504
neoclassicism 21, 97–8
in epic 244–5
in tragedy 375–6, 378–9, 447
Neoplatonism 215, 463–4, **503–13**
Christian 9, 512
Continental 505–7, 508, 509, 511–12, 513
as courtly cult 509, 510
decline 512–13
Milton and 511–12
Sidney and 96
Spenser and 238, **323–5**, 327–8, 342 n.36, 507–8
Nero, Emperor 239–40, 359, 380, 447, 449, 497, 579
Neville, Alexander, *Oedipus* 70
Newdigate, Dame Alice 136
Newdigate, John 136, 139
New Historicism 3, 7
New Testament
editions/revisions 105, 115
study in schools/universities 35–6, 45*t*, 47, 51
Newton, Sir Isaac 479
Newton, Thomas 378, 385, 403
Nicander 462, 473
Nicholls, Thomas 62
Nicolas of Lyra 110
Norbrook, David 241, 437, 458 n.23
Norris, John 510
North, Dudley 92, 98
North, Sir Thomas 66–7, 135, 136, 138, 389, 451, 599
Norton, Thomas *see* *Gorboduc*
'novel', use of term 307 n.1
Nowell, Alexander 415 n.18
Nuce, Thomas, *Octavia* 378
Numa Pompilius 131, 132, 440
nuts, imagery of 329–30
Nuttall, A.D. 296
'nymphs' *see* women, as characters

Ocland, Christopher, *Anglorum Proelia* 232, 243
Octavian *see* Augustus
ode (genre) **333–8**
defining characteristics 313–14
distinguished from similar forms 311–12
English/Latin versions 553 n.4
examples 314, 334–8
range of classical models 313, 333
Renaissance understandings 334
studies 341 nn.11–12
versification 544, 549
Odes (Horace) 187–8, 189, 191, 389, 563, 600, 623
ambiguity of authorial intent 549–50
English translations/imitations **540–5**, **547–52**, 553 n.4, 554 n.13
Odyssey (Homer) 90, 173, 181, 234, 248 n.45, 533
allegorical interpretations 489–92, 493
compared with *Iliad* 496
English translations 19, 226, 227, 487
as ethical model 488–9
narratorial voice 177
political implications 493–4
Renaissance editions 487
rhetorical devices 494–5
as source for Spenser 568
studies in schools/universities 36, 45*t*
as tragicomic model 420–1, 428
Ogilby, John 62, 204, 227, 488, 493
Ogle, Sir John, *The Lamentation of Troy for the Death of Hector* 489

Ong, Walter 129, 135
Oppian 462, 473
Origen 110
Orphic Hymns (anon.) 321
Osborne, Francis 153
Othello (Shakespeare) 91, 393 n.27
  shifts in dramatic idiom **614–15**
Oughtred, William 478
Overbury, Thomas, *Remedia Amoris* 61
Ovid (P. Ovidius Naso) 2, 4, 5, 13–14, 18, 59, 110, 111–12, 147, 226, 312, 347, **517–35**
  amoral/rebellious image 152, 518–20, 582
  appeal to young 256–7
  contrasted with Virgil 518–20, 563, 583
  English translations 19, 64, 66, 120, 135, 182, 253, 277, 585, **588–9**, 594–5 n.17
  exile 152, 193, 518–19, 520, 523, 536 n.24, 562, 563–4, 582
  humanist reservations concerning 263–4
  imitations 253
  influence, in combination with Virgil 520–3, 528–31, 532–3
  influence on/comparison with Shakespeare 17, 19, 164, 191, 238, 389, 390, 523, **527–31**, **601–5**, 616
  influence on Milton 531–5, 646, 649, 652, 655 n.13
  influence on Renaissance love poetry 163–4, 165, 166, 293, 294, 295, 298, 523, 579
  influence on Spenser 523–7, 568–9, 571, 573
  literary career 175, 176, 177, 178–9, 181, 182, 186 n.46, 518–19
  as model for Marlowe 179, 181, **581–4**, **590–2**
  as model for young poets 517–18
  popularity at Court 520
  Renaissance editions 49*t*, 61, 62, 130–1
  reworkings of Horace/Virgil 188, **521–2**, 529, 532–3
  as stage character 152, 193–4, 519, 520, 523, 582, 633–4
  studied in schools/universities 30, 46, 47, 51, 517–18, 594 n.14, 599
  treatments of fame 187, 188–9, 190, 191, 192–3
  treatments of sexuality 159, 160–1, 162, 163–4, 165, 166, 168–9, 170 n.5, 171 n.19, 536 n.24, 582
  Ars Amatoria 519, 526
  'Amores 1.1' 180
  Epistolae ex Ponto 138, 178, 517, 562, 563–4
  Fasti 49*t*, 444, 524, 527, 529, 532–3, 562
  Medea 179, 531, 581
  Tristia 33, 34, 35, 49*t*, 144 n.9, 178–9, 517, 519, 520, 523, 562, 573, 646 *see also Amores*; *Heroides*; *Metamorphoses*; 'Sappho to Phaon'
Owen, John 354
Oxenden, Henry 589
Oxford University 257
  Chair of History 450–1
  new colleges 142–3
  poetry set in 257–8
  productions of classical drama 399–400, 497
  reading lists 54 n.75
  social class of students 41
  statutes 41, 42, 44–6
  syllabus 42–3, 488
  University Library 113, 116–17, 120

Painter, William 65
  The Palace of Pleasure 446
Paleit, Edward 241, 249 n.75
Palladius, Rutilius Taurus Aemilianus 475
Panofsky, Erwin 10, 22–3 n.22, 504

Paradise Lost (Milton) 1, 21, 123, 172, 213, 244, 249 n.74, 373, 558, 651, 653
choice of language 245
classical models 231, 232, 236, 245, 492, 534–5
generic characteristics 225–6, 238
narrative structure 238
versification 588
Parker, Matthew, Archbishop 55 n.105
Parry, Robert 295
Moderatus 295
pastoral elegy / ies **210–14**
classical models 210–11
favoured subjects 211
on women 211
pastoral poetry *see* eclogues; pastoral elegy; romance
Pater, Walter 513 n.4, 592–3
Paulinus, Bishop of Nola 121
Pazzi, Alessandro 416 n.38
Peacham, Henry
The Complete Gentleman 59
The Garden of Eloquence 78
Pearson, John 48
pedagogy 255–8
Peele, George 231, 407, 600, 607
co-authorship of *Titus Andronicus* 445, 458 n.25, 530, 537 n.48, 601–2
The Arraignment of Paris 425, 491
The Tale of Troy 494
Pembroke, Mary Herbert (née Sidney), Countess of 137–8, 240, 301, 393 n.21, 589
Antonius 137–8, 379
Pembroke, William Herbert, 3rd Earl of 306
'Perilla' (?Caecilia Metella) 144 n.9
Perkins, William, *Prophetica* 79
Persius (A. Persius Flaccus) 34, 35, 45*t*, 345, 354–5
English editions 49*t*, 62
influence on Renaissance satire 356, 357, 361
Satires 346, 355
'Satire 1' 357, 359
'Satire 3' 58
Peter, John 345, 346
Petowe, Henry 593 n2
Petrarch (Francesco Petrarca) 5, 6, 14, 15, 104, 110, 111, 112, 180, 285, 439, 560, 572
discovery of Cicero's letters 273–4
influence on English pastoral 204, 216
influence on Renaissance love / elegiac poetry **163–7**, 216, 265, 323, 339–40 n.4, 339 n.4, 508, 523
Bucolicum Carmen 17
Rime Sparse 163, 165, 346, 571
'Song 23' 163
Trionfi 191
Pettie, George, *A Petite Palace of Pettie his Pleasure* 299
Phaer, Thomas 66, 226, 227, 248–9 n.61
Pharsalia see Bellum Civile
Philips, Katherine 131–2, 138, 139, 331
Pompey 241, 375
Phillips, John, *Cyder* 479
Philo of Alexandria 116
'Philo-Philippa' 131–2, 133
Philostratus, *Love Letters* 287
The Phoenix Nest (anon., ed.) 552 n.1
physics, teaching in universities 44, 45*t*, 47
Pigman, G.W. 16, 17, 339–40 n.4
Pindar 34, 35, 187, 189, 313, 333, 548, 553 n.4, 554–5 n.21, 582
Planudes, Maximus, *Anthology* 346, 368 n.13
Plat, Hugh, *Floures of Philosophy* 182
Plato 2, 10–11, 30, 90, 96, 298, 342 n.36, 406, 408, 466, 467, **503–13**, 609
English / French translations 63, 464, 504–5
influence on Renaissance discursive writing 461, **463–4**
Latin translations 463, 506–7

Plato (*cont.*)
popularity in France 504–5, 506–7
themes of love/beauty 503–4, 507
unpopularity in England 504–5, 508, 511
Charmides 511–12
Ion 90, 91, 95
Laws 507, 511, 512
Phaedo 511
Phaedrus 503–4, 507, 512
Republic 90, 92, 93, 95
Symposium 162, 503–4, 650–1
Timaeus 503, 512
Plautus, T. Maccius 30, 32, 45*t*, 60, 389, 413, 429, 599, 609
adaptations of Greek originals 397
English plays based on **403–5**
English translations 402–3, 406
influence on Renaissance comedy 396, 613–14
objections to 409
Renaissance productions/adaptations 68, 397, 412, 421, 430 n.13
Aulularia 400, 403, 404, 405, 421, 430 n.13
Captivi 403, 404
Menaechmi 68, 402–4, 405, 421, 430 n.13, 613
Miles Gloriosus 400, 421, 430 n.13, 614
Mostellaria 403, 405
Rudens 370 n.41, 403, 405
see also Amphitruo
Pléiade (French writers) 505–6
Pliny 'the Elder' (C. Plinius Secundus) 30, 60, 136, 298, 462
Natural History 37
Panegyrics 35
Pliny 'the Younger' (C. Plinius Caecilius Secundus) 194–5
letters 274, 276, 286–7
Plotinus 95, 96
Enneads 509, 512
Plumptre, Huntingdon 496, 502 n.67
Plutarch (L. Mestrius Plutarchus) 4, 43, 59, 91, 131, 136, 137, 381, 436, 455, 488
English translations 66–7, 129, 135, 138, 139, 503, 599
influence on Renaissance discursive writing 462, **465–6**, 468–9, 481 n.37
influence on Renaissance historiography 439, 441
influence on Renaissance literary criticism 92, 93, 94–5
as source for Shakespeare 61, 76, 135, 377, 389, 394 n.40, 451, **452–4**, 599
De Audiendis Poetis 89
Moralia 465–6, 503
Gryllus 568
Parallel Lives 66–7, 389, 453, 599
Poetaster (Jonson) 152, 193–4, 227, 363–4, 519, 520, 523, 546, 582, 594–5 n.17, 609, 629, **633–4**
social context 607–8
poetics
classical models 89–91
distinguished from rhetoric 88
English commentaries on **94–6**
key themes 87
poetry
definition/functions 87, 94, 405–6
educative qualities 639 n.24
'poets' quarrel' *see* 'War of the Theatres'
politics **147–55**, 241, **433–56**
in Homer 493–4
Poliziano, Angelo 487, 495
Polwhele, John 540, 544, 552, 553 n.6
'The Scope of the Allegory' 544
Polybius 59, 60, 64, 450
Pompey (Gn. Pompeius Magnus) 238–9, 379
Pomponius Laetus 67–8, 73 n.44
Pontano, Giovanni 322, 329
Poole, Adrian 586
Pope, Alexander 226, 354, 587

Eloisa to Abelard 277
Porphyry 62, 488
De Antro Nympharum 491
Isagoge 41–2
Pound, Ezra 587
Prideaux, John, *Sacred Eloquence* 79
Priscian (Priscianus Caesariensis) 42, 90
Proba, Faltonia Betitia 131
compared with Anne Bradstreet 140–2
Cento 140–1, 146 n.63
Proclus 64
Propertius, Sextus 312, 342 n.27
literary career 174, 175, 177–8, 179, 185 n.31
'Elegy 1.2' 314–15
'Elegy 2.34' 176
A Proposition for Advancement of Morality (anon.) 98
Protagoras 490
Prudentius Clemens, A. 19, 120, 321, 340 n.7
Prynne, William, *Histriomastix* 410
psalms, translation of 342 n.34
pseudo-Dionysius the Areopagite 116
Ptolemy, Claudius 62
Publilius Syrus 64
Pugh, Syrithe 526
Pulter, Hester 139, 143
'Upon the Death of my deare and lovely Daughter' 139
puritanism 98, 390, 401
hostility towards 437
Puttenham, George 316–17, 321–2, 330–1, 424, 473, 560
The Arte of English Poesie 78, 94, 206
Pygmalion (mythical character) 104–5, 531
Pynson, Richard 398–9, 402
Pythagoras 129, 188, 191, 237–8, 521, 528

Quarles, Francis 35, 203
Shepheards Oracles 210
'quarrel of the ancients and the moderns' 412, 417 n.59
queens, education of 129
Quevedo, Francisco de 329
Quint, David 231, 238–9, 248 n.45, 655 n.18
Quintilian (M. Fabius Quintilianus) 14, 16, 42–3, 47, 68, 77, 270 n.17, 408, 480 n.25, 600
English editions 49*t*
Declamations 35, 45*t*
Institutio Oratoria 42, 75, 78, 80, 82, 91, 624
Quintus Curtius (Q. Curtius Rufus) 45*t*, 61

Racine, Jean 375, 391 n.7
Rain(h)olde, Richard, *The Foundacion of Rhetorike* 77, 529
Rainolds, John 43, 116, 390, 401, 403
Raleigh, Sir Walter 201, 229, 449, 563, 568
History of the World 141, 196
Ramazani, Jahan 315
Ramus, Petrus (Pierre de la Ramée) 42, 79
Randolph, M.C. 359
Randolph, Thomas 58, 467–8, 523
death 211, 212
translation of Aristophanes **410–11**, 417 n.56
'Eclogue Occasioned by Two Doctors Disputing upon Predestination' 211–12
'To Master Feltham on his Book of Resolves' 280–1
Rankins, William, *Seaven Satyres* 89
The Rape of Lucrece (Shakespeare) 64, 191–2, 256, 265, 444–5
cultural context 602–3
relationship with classical sources 527, 529–30, 602–3, 605–6

Rawlyns, Roger, *Nestor his Antilochus* 494
recognition scenes 428
recusatio, examples/traditions of 140–2, 177–8, 182–3
Renaissance
  classical models 11–12, 15–21
  defined 1, 6–7, 24 n.42
  distancing from classical models 18–20
  early uses of term 6–7, 22–3 n.22
  'linguistic turn' 105
  as literary construct 8–9, 11–12
  merging of classicism and Christianity 8–9, 15, 18–19
  'Renaissance imagination' 10–12
  studies 7–8, 9–11
republicanism
  concerns over rise of 241
  literary interpretations in line with 493–4, 548–9, 609
  writings advocating/influenced by 151–2, 153, 155, 250 n.91, 445–7, 448–51, 580, 593–4 n.3
Restoration (1660) 412, 519
  poetic celebrations 551–2
Reuchlin, Johannes 109, 496
Revard, Stella 223 n.33, 655 n.13
Reynolds, Henry 491
rhetoric **75–84**
  classical texts 42, 75
  and dramatic performance style 69–70, 76
  in the epic 494–5, 502 n.63
  manuals in English 77–9
  and poetics 88–9, 92, 94–5
  in romance 296, 297–8, 301, 308 n.24
  teaching in grammar schools 75, 76, 88–9, 254, 256, 258–9, 266–7, 299, 599–600
  techniques 75–6
  university studies in 41–3, 46, 47
  use in drama **386–9**
Rhetorica ad Herennium (anon.) 42, 43, 49*t*, 75, 78, 80, 82, 600
Ricci, Bartolomeo, *De Imitatione Libri Tres* 457 n.7
Richard III (Shakespeare) 71, 76, 152, 385, **453–6**
  links with classical tragedy 612
  sources 455–6
Richardson, Alexander, *The Logicians School-Master* 79
Ridley, Nicholas, Bishop 204–5
Rilke, Rainer Maria 174
Robortello, Francesco 416 n.38
Roe, Sir John 545–6, 552, 554 nn.15–16
Roe, Thomas 625
romance (genre) 95, 135, **291–307**
  blending of tragedy and comedy 293–4, 300, 302–3
  chastity, as theme of 292, 303–4, 308 n.27
  disruption, as theme of 304–7
  dramatisations 295–6
  female characters, focus on 300–4
  Greek models 291–2, 293–4, 296–7, 302, 309 n.36
  intertextuality 296–7
  narrative structure 293
  narrative themes 292–3, 294, 296–307
  pastoral settings 203, 214–15, 304–5
  sexual awakening, as theme of 292, 296–9
  Spanish/Italian sources 293, 294–5, 302
  terminology 307 n.1
Rome (Ancient)
  honouring of military success 192
  influence of Greece 14–16, 19
  as setting for political drama 151–2
  sexual culture 159
Ronsard, Pierre de 329, 334, 540
  Franciade 248 n.51
Roscius Gallus, Q. 407
Rosenmeyer, Thomas G. 94

Ross, Alexander 490, 493
  Mystagogus Poeticus 45*t*
Rossetti, Dante Gabriel 587
Røstvig, Maren-Sofie 476, 483 n.74
Rosweyd, Heribert 121
Rotherham Grammar School 34–5
Rous, John 116, 122
Rowe, Elizabeth, *Poems on Several Occasions* 129, 143 n.1
Rowe, Nicholas 589
Rufinus, Tyrannius 114
Russell, Donald 88

Sabie, Francis, *Pans Pipes* 209
Sacks, Peter M. 315, 339–40 n.4
Sackville, Sir Thomas 402
  see also Gorboduc
Sackville, William 402
Saïd, Suzanne 304–5
Sainte-Maure, Benoît de, *Roman de Troie* 497
Salel, Hugh 487
Sallust (L. Sallustius Crispus) 30, 33, 34, 45*t*, 47, 147, 441, 449, 455
  English editions/translations 49*t*, 64, 136, 451
  as source for Jonson **433–7**, 451–2
  Bellum Catilinae **433–7**, 439, 452, 455
  Bellum Jugurthinum 43, 436, 455
  Histories 436
Salmasius, Claude 283
Salsilli, Giovanni 646
Saltonstall, Wye 277
Salutati, Coluccio 273–4
Sanderson, Robert 43
Sandwich Grammar School 53 n.51
Sandys, George 35, 61, 62, 227, 230, 522
Sannazaro, Jacopo 5, 214–15, 523, 560
  Arcadia 294–5, 302
Sappho **129–31**, 138, 168, 329
  fictionalised depictions 130–1, 278
  later poets compared to 131, 143–4 n.6, 145–6 n.52
'Sappho to Phaon' (attrib. Ovid) 130–1, 144 n.12, 278, 280
satire(s) 68–9, 221, 345–6, **354–63**, 367–8 n.2, 546–8
  animal imagery 357, 359–60
  etymology 361
  imagery of physical violence 356–9
  obscurity 360–1
  rivalry between writers 357, 369 n.23
  scatological imagery 360, 362–3, 365–6, 366–7
  suppression 348–9, 354
Savile, Sir Henry 50, 61, 117, 118, 139, 447–8, 459 n.47
  'The End of Nero and Beginning of Galba' 447–8, 449
Scaliger, Julius Caesar 96, 226, 343 n.40, 355, 367–8 n.2, 374, 377, 431–2 n.29, 482 n.58, 582
  De Subtilitate 45*t*
  Poetices Libri Septem 94, 329–30, 506
Scapula, John 228
Scève, Maurice, *Délie* 505
Schleiner, Louise 392 n11
scholarship/editing 47–51
Scillaes Metamorphosis (Lodge) 253, 257–8, 263–4, **265–9**
Scipio Africanus, P. Cornelius 192
Scott, William 96, 97
Scrope, Jane 315–16
Scudéry, Georges de 131
Scudéry, Madeleine de 143–4 n.6
  Les Femmes Illustres (with brother George) 131, 144 n.18
Second Shepherds' Play (anon.) 396, 398
Segal, Erich 397
Sejanus, L. Aelius (historical character) 153
Sejanus His Fall (Jonson) 152, 153, 196, 241, 376, 379, 449, 450, 451–2
  relationship with source material 623

Selden, John 50
De Diis Syriis 51
Marmora Arundelliana 50–1
self, formation/performance of 175, 292–3, 465, 471
Selvaggi (Italian Renaissance poet) 646
Seneca, L. Annaeus 59, 60, 73 n.55, 88, 136, 190, 457 n.7, 609
English translations 64, 65, 66, 135, 137, 281, 378, 385, 585
impact on Renaissance drama 69–71, 150–1, 377–8, 380, **384–91**, 437
influence on Renaissance discursive writing 462–3, 466, **467–71**, 473, 476
influence on Shakespeare 389–91, **610–13**, 614–15
letters 273–4, 275–6, 280–1, 285–6, 461, 625
political context 380
Renaissance commentary on 467–70, 472, 478–9, 481 n.37
Renaissance editions 62
Renaissance performances 67–8, 69, 73 n.50, 390–1, 612
studied in schools/universities 34, 35, 43, 45*t*, 599, 610
Agamemnon 385
Consolatio ad Marciam 469
De Clementia 147
Epistle 30 483 n.78
Hercules Furens 71, 387–8
Medea 66, 385
Moral Epistles 16, 274, 285, 462, 468, 623, 624, 638 n.15, 638 n.21
Natural Questions 44, 45*t*
Oedipus 70
Phaedra (Hippolytus) 67–8, 71, 73 n44, 610, 612–13, 387, 390–1, 394 n.36
Thyestes 380, 384, 385, 386, 389, 601, 610–11
Troades (The Trojan Women) 71, 138, 377
Seneca, M. Annaeus (Seneca the Elder) 15, 73 n.55
Sententiæ Ciceronis, Demosthenis, ac Terentii (anon.) 414–15 n.16, 415 n.26
sermon manuals 79, 83
Serres, Jean de 463, 506–7, 513, 514 n.17
Servius Honoratus, M. 36, 62, 173, 202, 522, 559–60, 567
Seton, John 42, 43
Sextus Empiricus 462
sexuality **159–69**
alternate models 167–9
Augustan-era 159–60
in educational establishments 255–8
education in, as theme of romance 292, 296–9
marriage, as model of 159–60, 167–8
poetic treatments 160–7
in tragicomedy 424
Shakespeare, William 1, 2, 9, 74 n.62, 175, 201, 225, 243, 250 n.78, 251 n.108, 308–9 n.28, 505, **599–617**
attacks on 407, 603, 610
authorial status 4–5
characterization 453
comparisons/competition with contemporaries 592–3, **601–3**, 602, 606, 616–17, 622–3, 637
contemporaries' comments on 15, 17, 238, 407, 528, 599, 603, 609, 616–17, 622
eclipsing of earlier writers 585, 587
education/linguistic skills 135, 586, 589, 599–600, 601, 604, 609–10, 621–2
generic classification of works 384
humanism 459 n.49
influence of classical drama 389–91, **609–17**
influence of Ovid 12, 19, 389, 390, 523, **527–31**, 582, **601–5**
influence of Plutarch 61, 76, 135, 377, 389, 394 n.40, 451, **452–4**, 599

influence of Virgil **527–31**, **605–9**, 618–19 n.21
interaction with classical sources 21, **389–91**, 403–4, 451, **601–17**
literary career 389–91
poetic tributes to 15, 352, 404, 616–17
reading matter 61
sources 67
treatments of fame 191–3, 196
use of classical settings 151–2
use of rhetoric 76
use of romance 296, 301, 306, 604
varied nature of classicism 616
All's Well That Ends Well 426
Antony and Cleopatra 67, 451, 606
As You Like It 11, 215, 404, 581
The Comedy of Errors 69, 389, 403–4, 405, 408, 412, 416 n.32, 601
Coriolanus 64, 67, 192, 451
Cymbeline 296, 427, 428, 604, 607, 609
1 Henry IV 67, 192–3
2 Henry IV 192
Henry V 67, 192–3, 384
Henry VI (Parts I–III) 152, 250 n.78, 580
Julius Caesar 67, 151, 152, 192, 451
Love's Labour's Lost 202, 258, 505
Measure for Measure 426
The Merchant of Venice 384, 405, 505, 514 n.9
Much Ado About Nothing 428
Richard II 76
Romeo and Juliet 428, 523
'Sonnet 60' 191
'Sonnet 100' 191
Sonnets 164, 176, 527–8, 571
The Taming of the Shrew 278, 601, 609
Timon of Athens 451
Twelfth Night 296, 405, 408, 613, 614
Two Gentlemen of Verona 164
The Winter's Tale 293, 301, 427, 428, 531, 604
see also Hamlet; *King Lear*; *Macbeth*; *A Midsummer Night's Dream*; *Othello*; *The Rape of Lucrece*; *Richard III*; *The Tempest*; *Titus Andronicus*; *Venus and Adonis*
Sharpham, Edward, *The Fleire* 428
Sharrock, Alison 407–8
Sharrock, John 232
Sharrock, Robert, *The History of Propagation* 474
Shaver, Anne 181–2
Shelley, Percy Bysshe 587
Shelton, Thomas 223 n.35
The Shepheardes Calender (Spenser) 5, 13, 108, 112, 148, 202, **205–8**, 474, **558–64**, 575
allegorical interpretations 558–9
dedication 560
divergences from Virgil 206–8, 562–3, 564
illustrations 207–8
influence of Ovid 524, 562–4
influence of Virgil 179–80, 205–7, 235, 524, 559–60
as model for later writers 209, 210, 213, 220
originality 575
place in Spenser's career path 174, 179–80, 559
Platonic content 507
political implications 559–61
sequel 563–4
translated into Latin 208
'April' 235, 561–2, 568, 573
'June' 207
'October' 179–80, 225, 507, 524
'November' 210–11, 507, 560–1
Sherburne, Sir Edward 204, 472
Sherry, Richard, *Treatise of Schemes and Tropes* 78, 80
Shirley, James, *Narcissus* 256, 265, 266–7
Shrewsbury School 268–9
Shuger, Debora 443, 444
Sibthorpe, Henry 137

Sidney, Mary *see* Pembroke, Countess of
Sidney, Sir Philip 1, 22 n.20, 64, 90, 91, 93, 97, 116, 117, 121, 151, 177, 201, 292, 294, 306, 431–2 n.29, 504, 513, 644
  comments on elegy 316–17, 320, 321
  comments on pastoral/georgic 205, 206, 475
  comments on tragedy/comedy 378–9, 384, 405–6, 416 n.38, 419, 424, 438
  posthumous tributes 140, 189–90, 210, 211, 214
  translation of Horace 542
  works dedicated to 560
  Astrophil and Stella 14, 384, 505–6, 507, 571
  'Come, Dorus, Come' 210
  'Ye Goat-Herd Gods' 322
  see also Arcadia; *The Defence of Poesy*
Sidney family 441, 442
Silius Italicus 195
Silva, Bartholo, *Giardino Cosmografico* 130
Silvestris, Bernardus 557
Simonides 312
Simpson, James 12
Sivvert, François 130
Skelton, John 1, 148, 205, 317, 341 n.17
  Philip Sparrow 134, 315–16
Skinner, Quentin 445, 458 n.21
Skretkowicz, Viktor 302
Slatyer, William, *Palae-Albion* 232, 234, 237
slaves, as characters in comedy 399, 404–5, 407–8, 413 n.7
Smith, Bruce 419
Smith, G. Gregory 622–3
Smith, John
  The Excellency and Nobleness of True Religion 512
  The Mysterie of Rhetorique Unvail'd 78, 83
Smith, Miles, Bishop 114–15
Smith, Nigel 224 n.52
Smith, Sir Thomas 442
  De Republica Anglorum 147–8, 442
  A Letter Sent by I. B. Gentleman unto His Very Friend Master R. C. 442, 457 n.13
Socrates 129, 411, 412, 511, 650
'sodomy', use of term 168, 171 n.20
sonnet(s)
  differentiated from epigram 347
  sequences 505–6, 507, 513, 571
Sophocles 88, 599
  Antigone 376
  Electra 377
  Oedipus at Colonus 377
  Oedipus Tyrannus 377
Southampton, Henry Wriothesley, 3rd Earl of 61, 108, 527
Southwell, Lady Anne 136–7
Sowerby, Robin 26 n.82, 596 n.41
Spanish literature, influence in England 294–5
speculative writing 462
Speght, Rachel 131
Spenser, Edmund 1, 2, 9, 10, 18, 112, 121, 182, 201, 251 n.108, 352, 438, 489, 505, **557–75**, 644
  authorial status 4–5
  contemporaries' comments 416 n.40, 495
  epigrams/short poems 346–7
  influence of Virgil/Ovid **523–7**, 571, 573, 581
  literary career 174, 175, 177, **179–81**, 183, 185 n.39, 581
  Neoplatonism **323–5**, 327–8, 342 n.36, **507–8**
  as translator 536 n.29, 566, 567
  treatments of fame 189–90
  as writer of epic 557–9, 564–73
  as writer of pastoral 559–64
  Amoretti 180, 325–6, 329, 507, 571–2
  Astrophel 210, 211, 214

Colin Clouts Come Home Againe 563–4, 571, 572
Complaints 180–1, 347, 566–7
Daphnaida 211
Epithalamion 326, 329, **571–2**
Letter to Sir Walter Raleigh 229, 568, 571
Muiopotmos 347, **524–5**
The Ruines of Time 191, 566–7
'Sonnet 33' 180
'Sonnet 80' 180
Two Cantoes of Mutability 568, 571, **572–3**, 574
A View of the Present State of Ireland 442, 569
Virgil's Gnat 347
The Visions of Petrarch 347
see also The Faerie Queene; *Fowre Hymnes*; *The Shepheardes Calender*
Spondanus, Johannes 228, 487, 488
stage performances **67–71**
of comedy 399–401, 400–1, 415 nn.17–18
cross-gender casting 268–9
in schools 68, 268–9, 399–400, 403, 412, 415 n.18, 600
see also Cambridge University; Inns of Court
Stanivukovic, Goran 162, 170 n.5
Stanley, Thomas 204, 411
History of Philosophy 464
Stanyhurst, Richard 61, 173–4, 226
Stapleton, Francellina 139
statehood **439–47**
Statius P. Papinius 14, 18, 45*t*, 174, 225, 329, 571
stichomythia 384, 385
Stobaeus, Johannes 462
Stoic philosophy 73, 151, 280–1, 465, 468, 470–1, 476
objections to 466, 469, 470, 471
St Paul's School 33–4, 58, 141, 297, **643–5**
performances of classical drama 399–400, 403
Strabo 91, 92
Strada, Famiano, *Prolusiones* 45*t*
Stradling, John 638 n.10
Strebaeus, Jacobus Ludovicus 43
Studely, John 58, 66
Sturm, Johannes 31, 34, 43, 51–2 n.13, 263–4
Nobilitas Literata 608–9
Suckling, Sir John 510, 523
Suetonius Tranquillus, C. 45*t*, 47, 173, 455
English editions 49*t*, 60
Suidas 462
Sullivan, J.P. 354
Sulpicia (Roman poet) 131, 134
Sulpitius, Johannes 239
Surrey, Henry Howard, Earl of 1, 190, 277
translation of Virgil 65, 150, 226, 227, 518, 587
'Praise of Mean and Constant Estate' 540
Susenbrotus, Joannes, *Epitome troporum ac schematum* 78, 80
Swift, Jonathan 479
Gulliver's Travels 367
Swinburne, Algernon Charles 585, 589, 592, 622, 627
Sylvester, Joshua 141, 218, 230–1
Symmachus, Q. Aurelius 120

Tacitus, P. Cornelius 37, 49*t*, 195, 551, 623
association with revolutionary politics 448–9
commentaries on 458 n.34
criticisms 450
English/French translations 61, 64, 139, 146 n.55, 447, 448, 456
influence on English political thought/historiography 151–2, 153, 438–9, 440, 445, **447–51**, 454–6

Tacitus, P. Cornelius (*cont.*)
  Agricola 139, 440, 447
  Annals 139, 146 n.55, 196, 439, 447, 448, 454, 456
  Germania 456
  Histories 439, 447, 454
Talon, Omer 42, 43, 79
Tanner, Thomas 143 n.5
Tasso, Bernardo 334
Tasso, Torquato 93, 229, 232, 329, 463, 523, 558
  Aminta 215, 424, 425, 431 n.26, 432 n.34
  Gerusalemme conquistata 558
  Gerusalemme liberata 20, 229, 230, 231, 233, 558
Taverner, Richard 58, 63
Taylor, Jeremy 466, 477, 483 n.86
Teive, Diego de 329
The Tempest (Shakespeare) 11, 12, 162–3, **390–1**, 427, 428
  relationship with classical models **530–1**, 604–5, 606
Temple, William 475, 477
Terence (P. Terentius Afer) 60, 147, 413
  biographical background 407
  dramatic structure 70, 401–2, 408
  English plays based on **403–5**
  English translations 63, 400, **402–3**, 406
  influence on French classical drama 375
  influence on Renaissance comedy 396–7, 615–16
  Renaissance editions 48, 49*t*, 90, 398–9, 401–2, 408, 412, 415 n.26, 415 n.28
  Renaissance productions 67–8, 397, 399–401, 403, 412, 415 nn.17–18
  stock characters 399, 404–5, 407–8
  studied in grammar schools 30, 32, 33, 34, 35, 36, 37, 39, 51, 599
  studied in universities 45*t*, 46
  Adelphoe 403, 404–5, 415 n.18
  Eunuchus 415 n.18
  Heauton Timorumenos 403, 404–5
  see also Andria
Terentianus Maurus 125 n.29
Theagines and Chariclea (anon.) 295
theatres, closure of 98, 405, 408–10, 417 n.49
Theocritus 5, 34, 45*t*, 46, 312, 314, 329, 550, 560
  influence on English pastoral 201, 204, 208, 211
  Idylls 173, 522
Theodosius, Emperor 114, 562
'Theodulus', *Eclogue* 204
Theognis 34, 35, 45*t*, 312, 392 n.15
Theophrastus 133–4, 462
Thomas à Kempis, St 558
Thomas Aquinas, St 110, 111, 508
  Summa of Christian Theology 45*t*
Thomason, George 48
Throckmorton, Nicholas 441
Thucydides 59, 60, 61, 62, 130, 438, 449, 455
  English translations 64, 450
Thynne, William 111
Tiberius, Emperor 196, 279, 450, 452
Tibullus, Albius 312, 314
  literary career 174, 177–8, 179
Tiptoft, John 146 n.57
Titus, Emperor 349
Titus Andronicus (Shakespeare / Peele) 67, 69, 253, 389, 445–6
  competitiveness between authors 537 n.48, 601
  as drama of excess **601–2**, 621
  nature of collaboration 537 n.48
  political context 602–3
  relationship with classical models 529–30, 601–3, 607, 609, 612, 621
Toomer, G.J. 48, 50–1
Tottel, Richard (ed.), *Songes and Sonettes (Tottel's Miscellany)* 346, 347, **539–40**, 587

Townshend, Aurelian 228
Tempe Restor'd 491
tragedy **373–91**
five-act structure 378, 383
Greek, English translations 376–7
impact of classical models 376–8, 383–9
'neoclassical' 378–80
political context 380–3
terminology 373–4, 384
theories of 95, 374–6, 395, 408
use of chorus 378–9, 382–3, 384, 386
use of rhetoric 386–9
verse forms 386
The Tragedy of Claudius Tiberius Nero, Rome's Greatest Tyrant (anon.) 378, 445
tragicomedy **419–29**
audience appeal 421, 422–3
as classical genre 419–20
classical models 420–2, 429
generic characteristics 427–8
justifications for existence **420–3**
objections to 419, 422
recognition scenes 428
terminology 375, 384, 420, 425, 430 n.6
theories of 419, 423–4
Traherne, Thomas 512, 513
translation(s) 60–1, **62–7**, **587–93**
of the epic **226–8**
into French 59, 63
impact on English writers 64–5, 69–70
importance to Renaissance culture 19, 135, 142, 227–8
by major writers 72 n.30
quantity 63, 72 n.24
role in grammar school syllabus 31–2, 35–6, 37, 52 n.42
theories of 65–6
of tragedies 376–8
transplantation to English idiom 62, 66, 226
verse forms 587–8, 589
by women 130, **135–43**, 145 n.48
trattati d'amore (Italian genre) 504
Traub, Valerie 168
Trevelyan, G.M. 71 n.5
Trevisa, John 114
Trissino, Gian Giorgio 95, 558
Trithemius, Johannes 109, 114
Trogus, Gn. Pompeius 46, 441
Troilus and Cressida (Shakespeare) 232, 493, 497–8, 568
relationship with classical models **607–9**, 614
'Troy, Matter of' 497–8, 567
Tuckett, Tabitha 222 n.20
Tudeau-Clayton, Margaret 537 n.41, 537 n.51
Tudor, Owen 235–6
'Tudor myth' 235, 239
Turberville, George 182, 205, 277
Turill, Daniel 281
Turner, Robert, *Orations* 45t
Tusser, Thomas 223 n.42, 475
Five Hundred Points of Good Husbandry 217–18, 461, 474
twins, comic plots involving 403–4, 405, 408, 613–14
Two *Most Unnatural and Bloody Murders* (anon.) 394 n.37
Twyne, Thomas 226, 228
Tyler, Margaret 132
tyranny, attacks on 151–2, 445, 449–50
Tyrtaeus 312

Udall, Nicholas 63, 402
Floures for Latine Speakyng 399, 414–15 n.16, 415 n.26
Underdown(e), Thomas 291, 422
Ibis 61
'unities', dramatic theory of 95–6, 374–6
universities 29–30, **40–7**
centrality to national life 40–1

universities (*cont.*)
 courses of study 41–7, 45*t*, 51, 59
 criticisms 642–3
 playwrights educated at 600
 royal interest in 41
 sixteenth-century expansion 142–3
 see also Cambridge; Oxford
Utenhove, Karel 130

Vaenius (Otto van Veen), *Emblemata* 62
Valeriano, Giovanni Pierio, *Hieroglyphica* 509
Valerius, Cornelius 43
Valerius Maximus 192
Valla, Giorgio 416
Valla, Lorenzo 104, 115, 487
 Elegantiae Linguae Latinae 45*t*
van der Noot, Jan, *Theatre for Voluptuous Worldlings* 346, 566
Varro, M. Terentius 125 n.29, 370 n.41, 439, 463, 473, 475
Vasari, Giorgio 22–3 n.22
Vaughan, Henry 120–1, 475, 511, 513
 Flores Solitudinis 121
 Primitive Holiness Set Forth in the Life of Blessed Paulinus of Nola 121
 'The Retreat' 511
 Silex Scintillans 120–1
 The World Contemned 121
Vegetius, P. Flavius 64
Vegio, Maffeo (Maphaeus Vegetius) 228, 234, 557
Velcurio, Joannes 441
Venus and Adonis (Shakespeare) 203, 255, 259, 266, 268, 269, 271 n.20, 523, 527, 529, 534, 592, 594 n.16
Vergil, Polydore 440
Vickers, Brian 76, 89
victory/defeat, as theme of epic 238–9
Vida, Marco Girolamo 322
 Christiad 231
Vigerius, Marcus 45*t*
Virgil (P. Vergilius Maro) 1, 2, 4, 93–4, 96, 110, 112, 147, 148, 226, 314, 462, **517–35**
 appeal to politically marginalized 519–20
 comparisons with Homer 494
 contrasted with Ovid 518–20, 563, 583
 English editions 48–50, 49*t*, 62
 English translations 65, 143, 204, 205, 585
 female reconceptualisations 140, 142, 146 n.63
 humanist preference for 263–4
 image of upright morality 263–4, 518–20
 influence, in combination with Ovid 520–3, 528–31, 532–3
 influence of earlier classical models 19–20
 influence on Marlowe **583–5**
 influence on Milton 517, 518, 531–5, 648–9
 influence on Shakespeare 517, **528–31**, **605–9**, 616
 insect imagery 536 n.29
 literary career model **172–6**, 177, 178–9, 180–1, 183, 185 n.31, 187, 518, 532, 535 n.12, 559
 'mock-epics' 520, 567–8
 as model for Spenser 10, 11–12, 13–14, 20, 517, 518, **523–7**, 559, 573
 as model for young poets 517–18
 rejection by *epyllion* writers 264–5
 relationship with Augustus 159, 518, 560
 as stage character 152, 193–4, 227, 519, 520, 582
 studied in grammar schools 30, 35, 51, 517, 599
 studied in universities 42, 46, 47
 (supposed) magical/prophetic powers 202, 209, 217, 537 n.51, 561

treatments of fame 187, 190, 192–3, 194, 196
Bucolics see Eclogues
see also Aeneid; Ciris; Culex; Eclogues; Georgics
Vives, Juan Luis 97, 111, 115, 442
De Conscribendis Epistolis 274
Instruction of a Christen Woman 110

Waddell, Helen 584
Walker, John, *Clavis Homerica* 488
Walker, Obadiah, *Some Instructions concerning the Art of Oratory* 78, **83–4**
Walker, Robert 483 n.78
Walsingham, Sir Francis 211, 223 n.30
Walton, Izaak 119, 120, 121, 463, 474, 475
The Compleat Angler 461, 463–4
Warner, William
Albion's England 234, 235, 237
Pan His Syrinx 295
'War of the Theatres' 371 n.69, 498, 607–8, 609, 628–9, 634–5
Wars of the Roses 235, 239, 451
Warton, Thomas 231
Wase, Christopher 377
Waswo, Richard 105
Watkins, John 558
Watson, Thomas 376
Lamentations of Amyntas 208–9, 589
Weaver, William 270 n.8, 270 n.12
Webbe, William 206, 217, 493
translations of Terence/Plautus 402–3
A Discourse of English Poetrie 89–90, 92, 93, 204
Webster, John 294, 616
Appius and Virginia (with Heywood) 65, 446
The Duchess of Malfi 385
The White Devil 391–2 n.9
wedding songs *see* epithalamium
Weever, John 357, 369 n.23, 533
wordplay 352
Epigrammes in the Oldest Cut and Newest Fashion 349, 351–2
Faunus and Melliflora 18, 522, 523
'In Cacum' 352
'In Nigellum' 351
'In Rufum' 351–2
Weinberg, Bernard 91
Weldon, Anthony 153
Wellek, René 106
Wendelin of Trier, St 45*t*
Wenman, Richard 219–20
Westminster School 22 n.20, 37, 58–9, 600, 626
productions of classical drama 68, 399–400, 409, 415 n.18
Weston, Elizabeth Jane 132
Wharton, T.F. 357
Wheare, Diagory 459 n.39
De Ratione et Methodo Legendi Historias Dissertatio 450–1
Whetstone, George 419
Promos and Cassandra 425
Whipper Pamphlets (anon.) 348, 357
The Whipping of the Satyre (anon.) 357, 358–9
The White Ethiopian (anon.) 295
Whitelocke, Bulstrode 98
Whitfield, J.H. 439–40
Whitgift, John, Archbishop 348
Whitlock, Richard, *Zootomia* 409–10, 417 n.50
Whitmarsh, Tim 294
Whitney, Geoffrey, *A Choice of Emblemes* 189–90, 218
Whitney, Isabella 134–5, 138
literary career 175, **182–3**
The Copy of a Letter 182, 278
The Maner of her Wyll 182
A Short Nosegay 182
Wilkins, John 483 n.86
Ecclesiastes 78, 79, 83
Willes, Richard, *De Re Poetica* 321, 338
William of Malmesbury 143 n.5

Williams, Raymond 223 n.48
Willich, Jodocus 70
Wilson, Arthur, *History of Great Britain, Being the Life and Reign of King James the First* 153
Wilson, F.P. 73 n.46
Wilson, Thomas 137, 149
  The Arte of Rhetorique 77, 78, **79–80**, 91
Winchester, William Paulet, Marquis of, *The Lord Marques Idlenes* 470
Winchester School 40, 263–4
Wind, Edgar 508, 558
Wither, George 644
Wittig, Monique 271 n.31
Wolff, Samuel 299
Wolsey, Thomas, Cardinal 38
women, as characters
  in eclogues 215–16
  in *epyllia* (minor epics) 265–9
  in heroic epistles 277–8
  in romance 300–4
  voiced by male authors 277–8, 300
women, as readers 597 n.50
women writers **129–43**, 164
  in antiquity 129–30
  attacks on 130–1, 132–3
  career paths 181–3, 186 n.52
  classical models 131–2, 140–2, 519
  Latin-literate 129, 138, 140, 142–3, 145 n.48
  royal 129
  subordinate social/educational position 133–4
  as translators 130, 135–43, 145 n.48
Woods, Susanne 181–2
Woolf, D.R. 450–1
Wray, Sir William 402
Wright, Bridget 285
Wroth, Lady Mary 164, 186 n.52
  The Countess of Montgomery's Urania 306–7
Wyatt, Sir Thomas 1, 18, 73 n.38, 368 n.7, 552
  'Mine Own John Poynz' 540
  'Of the Meane and Sure Estate Written to John Poins' 346, 540
  'A Spending Hand' 540
  'Whoso list to hunt' **165–6**, 171 n.17
Wynkyn de Worde, Jan van 110, 398–9

Xenophon of Athens, *Cyropaedia* 229, 305, 466
Xenophon of Ephesus 293

Yeats, W.B., 'Easter, 1916' 551
Yong, Bartholomew 215
A Yorkshire Tragedy (author uncertain) 394 n.37
Young, Patrick 48, 50
Young, Thomas 532, 643, 646, 649

Printed and bound by CPI Group (UK) Ltd, Croydon, CR0 4YY